WAR IN THE SHADOWS

WAR IN
THE SHADOWS
THE GUERRILLA IN HISTORY

ROBERT B. ASPREY

WILLIAM MORROW AND COMPANY, Inc.

New York

It is the policy of William Morrow and Company, Inc., and its imprints and affiliates, recognizing the importance of preserving what has been written, to print the books we publish on acid-free paper, and we exert our best efforts to that end.

Library of Congress Cataloging-in-Publication Data

Asprey, Robert B.
    War in the shadows : guerrillas past and present / by Robert B.
Asprey.
        p.   cm.
    Originally published: Garden City, N.Y. : Doubleday, 1975.
    ISBN 0-688-12815-7
    1. Guerrilla warfare.   I. Title.
U240.A86   1993
355.02'18—dc20   93-20249
                                                                      CIP

Printed in the United States of America

First Edition

1   2   3   4   5   6   7   8   9   10

BOOK DESIGN BY M M DESIGN 2000, INC. / MICHAEL MENDELSOHN

For Sheila and Gordon Seaver,
dear friends of many years

The World

The Guerrilla strikes and strikes again:
700 B.C. — A.D. 1993

FOREWORD

My original two-volume work, *War in the Shadows,* which was published in 1975, attempted to explain the Vietnam war to American readers in the historical terms of guerrilla warfare. The aim was to give the reader a perspective theretofore denied, yet one essential to an understanding of the conflict that so confused, embittered, and divided intelligent people, civil and military, not only in America but throughout the world. Judging from the work's large sales and from reader feedback, that goal was accomplished—at least in part.

Time and space limitations forced me to close the work at the end of President Richard Nixon's first term in 1972, when all but thirty-nine thousand American troops had departed from Vietnam. Although it was obvious at that time that America had suffered a disastrous defeat in Vietnam, I did not know until too late that Richard Nixon and National Security Adviser Henry Kissinger had authorized the U. S. Air Force to conduct a top-secret B-52 bombing campaign of neighboring Cambodia. What turned out to be a study in deceit commenced in 1969 and, because of an involved system of false and therefore illegal reporting by Air Force personnel, remained secret until a conscience-stricken radar officer blew the operation in 1973. Nor did I learn in time that in defiance of the American Constitution and recently passed U.S. laws, Nixon and Kissinger, enthusiastically supported by the Joint Chiefs of Staff, the Military Advisory Command (MACV) in Saigon, and other civil and military hawks, managed to extend the ground war into Cambodia—a war that, secretly backed by the Nixon and later by the Ford administrations, continued into 1975 when South Vietnam fell to Communist North Vietnam. With that, Cambodia came under the vicious rule of the Communist Khmer Rouge, thus insuring another sixteen years of brutal guerrilla warfare, which, at this writing in late 1993, may or may not be approaching an end (after an estimated ten million Cambodian deaths).

So the first reason for this new and highly abridged work is to reshape some earlier statements and judgments in accordance with the considerable amount of new and reliable information that has since emerged and to complete the story of the Indochina nightmare insofar as this is possible at this time.

The second reason is to bring the reader up to date on the status of the more important guerrilla wars of our day, albeit in an encapsulated form owing to space limitations. At this moment, no less than eighteen countries on planet Earth are hosting guerrilla wars in one form or another; four countries are maintaining a precarious truce between guerrilla actions; and in fourteen countries, including those of the former USSR and the former Yugoslavia, the potential for an expansion of guerrilla war is very real. In 1975, I wrote that

> . . . a historical sampling of guerrilla warfare should claim more than academic interest, for within the context of our day a knowledge of this history, even if sharply abridged, is vital to the understanding and further study of a disturbing fact: For a number of reasons guerrilla warfare has evolved into an ideal instrument for the realization of social-political-economic aspirations of underprivileged peoples. This is so patently true as to allow one to suggest that we may be witnessing a transition to a new era in warfare, an era as radically different as those which followed the writings of Sun Tzu, Machiavelli, Clausewitz, and Mahan.

If we add the current imbroglio created by the aspirations of Islamic fundamentalism, I stick by my earlier statement.

There is a third reason, perhaps more important than the other two, at least for the American people's future. The war was still going on when General William Childs Westmoreland, having returned from Vietnam where for several years he had stubbornly pursued a losing strategy and for his pains had been appointed army chief of staff, set up a consortium of sixteen army officers " . . . to express their views in writing . . . on problems facing the Army then [1968] and in the immediate future." One respondent, Lieutenant Colonel (later Lieutenant General) Robert Schweitzer, won favor with his reply:

> . . . Whether or not Vietnam is regarded as a defeat will depend on the face that is put on it . . . there will be plenty of those who will put the face of defeat on U.S. efforts. Silence on the part of the Army et al. will both collaborate and add numbers to the voices of defeat; the Army must lead the way in conducting a "Psyops [Psychological Operations] campaign" to the end that American Arms accomplished their mission in Vietnam.[1]

The war was scarcely terminated when American civil and military principals began sweeping it under the carpet, a task aided in part as "the nation," in one commentator's words, "experienced a self-conscious, collective amnesia."[2] President Gerald Ford, shortly after succeeding the disgraced Nixon, stressed that the lessons of the past had been learned [!] and that we should focus on the future; Henry Kissinger asked that there be "no recriminations."[3] In 1977, Mike Mansfield, the Senate majority leader who had been privy to some of Nixon and Kissinger's secret machinations, stated: " . . . It seems to me the American people want to forget Vietnam and not even remember that it happened"[4] (a sentiment similar to that felt by the German people, both in 1945 and today, concerning the Holocaust).

But ego being what it is, Lyndon Johnson, Richard Nixon, Henry Kissinger, and other principals hurried to produce self-exculpating memoirs not only justifying but extolling their actions—the first of a revisionist campaign to rewrite the war in a favorable light, just what Lieutenant Colonel (later Lieutenant General) Robert Schweitzer had had in mind. The path ahead was rough. The first to stumble was Westmoreland when Mike Wallace's CBS television program, 60 Minutes, aired a report entitled "The Uncounted Enemy: A Vietnam Deception," which cut the general's professional integrity into bits and pieces of deceit, and caused him to bring an unsuccessful libel suit that led to a disastrous appearance in a court of law. In 1978, William Colby, the retired head of CIA, offered a sugar-coated account of the agency's operations in Vietnam. A retired army colonel, Harry Summers, added his bit with *On Strategy: A Critical Analysis of the Vietnam War* (1982), which, as nearly as I can figure out, suggests that all would have gone well in Vietnam if there had been no guerrillas and Karl von Clausewitz had been in command. President Reagan picked up the banner in 1986 in an attempt, in Larry Bernan's words, " . . . to shift responsibility for losing the war from those who made policy to those who pointed out the contradictions in policy."[5] In 1988, a retired army general, Phillip Davidson, published *Vietnam at War: The History 1946–1975*, which in part parrots Summers' thesis and goes on to deny the validity of "limited war," then ends with the seemingly contradictory statement, " . . . Sad to say, we cannot counter revolutionary war even now—our defeat in Vietnam has taught us nothing."[6] A year later, Westmoreland chugged into print with his memoirs, which are about as interesting as one of Fidel Castro's five-hour monologues. Without doubt, future service historians will repeat the revisionist line—to no avail.

And here is why. In 1976, Gerald Ford declared that " . . . the past should be left to the historians."[7] Aided by a score of earlier critical works, many of which the reader will find cited in my text, it did not take the historians long to open fire on the revisionists by presenting and analyzing a war that changed Southeast Asia, not to mention America and the world, for the worse. The issue might have died there but for the host of other voices that joined those of the historians. Within a decade after America's defeat, scores of books blasted the revisionist school almost to oblivion, its crazy assertions forcefully contradicted by such as Philip Caputo, a marine lieutenant whose *A Rumor of War* depicts the obscenity of the battlefield in the haunting tradition of Stephen Crane's *The Red Badge of Courage* and Erich Maria Remarque's *All Quiet on the Western Front;* or Colonel David Hackworth's recently published best-selling *About Face,* which microscopes the American army's command system and in so doing shakes it to its boots, his revelations of its operation in Vietnam strengthened by his being America's most decorated living veteran; or William Shawcross' *Sideshow: Kissinger, Nixon and the Destruction of Cambodia,* which not only exposes a criminal military-political strategy but nails the principals to a cross of deceit perhaps unparalleled in American history.

Forget Vietnam? No recriminations? Business as usual? Forget fifty-seven thousand Americans dead, the shattered lives of their families, their loss made the greater because among them were the future leaders, black, white, and Hispanic, so desperately needed by their country? Forget 380,000 wounded, limbs missing, eyes gone, minds blown, the amputees so numerous that the government refuses to release the actual figure just as it denies that defoliants are responsible not only for those veterans still hidden away in off-limits sections of veterans hospitals but also for birth defects in some of the veterans' children?[8] Forget the estimated half-million veterans who have suffered or will suffer serious stress syndromes, in many cases leading to loss of jobs and family break-ups—and death from an inordinately high rate of suicide? Forget the millions of Indochinese lives that were lost, the millions of scarred survivors, the hundreds of thousands of acres of defoliated, bomb-cratered countryside? Forget the billions of dollars, many of them never to be accounted for, that could have repaired the disastrous neglect of America's educational system, that could have rebuilt city infrastructures, that could have provided new roads and bridges, that could have furthered vital political goals abroad such as trying to give displaced Arabs a legitimate place in the sun? Forget the morally corrupt civil and military officials who deliberately lied to the American people while defying Congressional laws to set precedents for future administrations?

As it turned out, the American people didn't want to forget. As Frances Fitzgerald wrote over two decades ago, " . . . the United States might leave Vietnam, but the Vietnam War would never leave the United States."[9] How right she was. There was not a collective amnesia so much as what I. F. Stone called a "happy amnesia" of those elected representatives and those civil and military officials responsible for the terrible debacle of American arms. It is to the credit of the American people that this war, far from fading into oblivion, remains of intense interest to many citizens. One writer recently called it "the war that won't go away,"[10] an apt phrase that helps to explain the reception of such best-selling books as Philip Caputo's *A Rumor of War* (1977), Stanley Karnow's *The History of Vietnam* (1983), and numerous other subsequent works. Another writer more recently called it "the war that will not end,"[11] another apt phrase that helps to explain the enthusiastic reception of David Hackworth's best-selling *About Face* (1989) and the fact that in 1985–86 over three hundred courses on aspects of the Vietnam war were taught in American colleges and universities[12]—at the request of students.

There is still much to learn and much to explain. So long as Western governments fail to work with less democratically minded governments in trying to eradicate in whole or in part the basic reasons for regional insurgencies, these will continue to burst forth. So long as conventionally minded military commanders fail to adapt organization, techniques, and tactics to meet the guerrilla challenge instead of trying to convert it to orthodox challenge, these revolutionary campaigns will prosper. Even when properly challenged, however, they do not lend themselves to an exclusive military "solution," which at best is ephemeral. The words "winning" and "victory" diminish in meaning as we face the awesome political-economic challenge that to date many of our leaders, particularly military commanders, seem unable to comprehend—despite manifold lessons of history.

I hope this book will bring home those lessons and will help readers to grasp more fully the ramifications of a complex subject, and thus enable them to question more intelligently the qualifications and attitudes, not to mention personal and professional integrity, of their future elected representatives. The pages that follow emphasize the cost to any country when its civil and military leaders fail to consider yesterday while dealing with today. In this sense, the book is also a warning: America cannot afford another Vietnam.

Many knowledgeable people, some of whom are no longer living, have given generously of talent and time in reading portions of this book in manuscript. They have repaired my work a thousandfold, and I am grateful. The faults remain the author's burden.

In America, I wish particularly to thank: Brigadier General and Mrs. Samuel B. Griffith, Arthur Wittenstein (to whom the original work was dedicated), Professor D. J. A. Harrison, Joseph Buttinger, Professor Lucian Pye, General Matthew B. Ridgway, Colonel David D. Barrett, Dr. George K. Tanham, Professor John A. Armstrong, Professor Theodore Draper, Professor Peter Paret, Colonel George C. Carrington, Professor Roberta Wohlstetter, Ambassador George Kennan, Professor John Beeler, Professor John R. Alden, Professor Russell Weigley, Professor Roger Hilsman, Robert Shaplen, Brigadier General Don Blackburn, Dr. Ellen Hammer, Brian Jenkins, Professor Donald Zagoria, Colonel David Hackworth, Elle Gohl, Professor David Schalk, Professor Leslie Offutt, Dr. Ya'agorziso, Professor Dalila Hannouche, Norma Torney, Professor Nellie Ohr, Colonel Robert Harkins, Colonel Michael Wyly, Lieutenant Colonel David G. Bradford, and John M. Collins. In England: Professor M. R. D. Foot, Professor Hugh Thomas (Lord Thomas of Swynnerton), C. M. Woodhouse, Julian Amery, Philip Ziegler, Colonel F. W. Deakin, Professor Maung Htin Aung, Colonel F. Spencer-Chapman, Brigadier Sir Bernard Fergusson (Lord Ballantrae), Sir Fitzroy Maclean, Colonel and Mrs. David Sutherland, Mrs. Joan Saunders, Sir Alan Urwick, Airey Neave, Eric Christiansen, Major General Richard Clutterbuck, Robert Stephens, Professor Lionel Kochan, General Sir Frank Kitson, Dr. George Boyce, Arthur Koestler, A. R. Burn, Professor A. Andrewes, Sir Nicolas Cheetham, Adam Roberts, Robin Lane Fox, Sir Sidney Ridley, and Teresa Murray-Lyon. In Ireland: Michael Hegarty.

I am further indebted to the staffs of the Vassar College Library; the New York Public Library; the Library of Congress; the Bodleian, Codrington, and New College libraries; the London Library, the British (Museum) Library, and the Ministry of Defence Library.

Finally, I wish to thank my sister, Professor Winifred Asprey, who through the years has provided constant encouragement and support; Dr. and Mrs. Gordon Seaver, to whom this book is dedicated and who for so long have provided so many rich hours of relaxation, my William Morrow editor Andy Dutter for constant encouragement and editorial expertise, and my William Morris agents Robert Gottlieb and Matthew Bialer.

ROBERT B. ASPREY

Foreword

1. Hackworth, *About Face,* 613–15. See also, ibid., 817.
2. Schalk, *War and the Ivory Tower . . . ,* 173.
3. Ibid., 160.
4. Ibid., 173.
5. Bernan, *Lyndon Johnson's War . . . ,* 7.
6. Davidson, *Vietnam at War . . . ,* 811.
7. Schalk, *War and the Ivory Tower . . . ,* 160.
8. Bernan, *Lyndon Johnson's War . . . ,* 5.
9. Frances Fitzgerald, *Fire in the Lake . . . ,* 423–4.
10. Schalk, *War and the Ivory Tower . . . ,* 9.
11. Ibid., 10.
12. Ibid., 9.

CONTENTS

PART ONE

LENIN'S HERITAGE

PART THREE
HO . . . HO . . . HO CHI MINH

worth's extraordinary achievement • The pacification fiasco • American tactics: mobility without purpose and purpose without mobility

PART FOUR

THEN UNTIL NOW: A SURVEY

ernment • *The* jihad *(holy war) declared by mujaheddin guerrillas* • *Collapse of the Afghan army* • *The Soviet army versus the guerrillas* • *Soviet military deficiencies* • *Mujaheddin disunity* • *Pakistan's role* • *U.S. military aid to the mujaheddin* • *Military stalemate* • *The Mohammed Najibullah regime* • *Mikhail Gorbachev pulls out* • *The war continues: Gulbuddin Hakmatyar versus Ahmed Shah Massoud* • *The drug factor* • *United Nations attempts to end the fighting fail* • *The war continues*

LIST OF MAPS

Maps by Mary Potter and Samantha Kirby

PART ONE

LENIN'S HERITAGE

No dictatorship of the proletariat is to be thought of without terror and violence.

VLADIMIR ILICH LENIN

CHAPTER I

Darius bows to Scythian guerrillas • Alexander the Great's tactics against the Asiatic Scythians • Alexander's later guerrilla wars • Hannibal's victory over Alpine guerrillas • Rome's colonial wars • The war of Spartacus • Caesar and Cassivellaunus

ANCIENT CHRONICLES offer countless examples of guerrilla actions, usually of an independent type undertaken in self-defense by nomads and peasant bands, and normally resulting in little more than temporary embarrassment to the incumbent ruler or temporary harassment to the invader.

A splendid exception is related by the Greek historian Herodotus. In 512 B.C., the Persian warrior-king, Darius, wanted to secure his northern flank before reducing Thrace and Macedonia. Marching almost due north through today's Bulgaria, his army accepted tribal submissions, bridged the Danube, and crossed to the land of what were then called the Scythians.[1]

Here was a bloodthirsty race of altogether unpleasant barbarians for whom Herodotus held little brief except

> ... in one respect ... the contrivance whereby they make it impossible for the enemy who invades them to escape destruction, while they themselves are entirely out of his reach, unless it please them to engage with him. Having neither cities nor forts, and carrying their dwellings with them wherever they go; accustomed, moreover, one and all of them, to shoot from horseback; and living not by husbandry but on their cattle, their wagons the only houses they possess, how can they fail of being unconquerable, and unassailable even?[2]

This rhetorical question may explain why Darius chose to invade their lands, although the gold mines of Dacia possibly attracted him more than the thought of enhancing his already formidable reputation. At this time, Darius ruled the largest empire and commanded the best army in the world. Yet, for all its panoply on the march, for all the efficiency of splendidly organized divisions—a tactical advance considered by Professor Breasted to be "... one of the most remarkable achievements in the history of the ancient Orient, if not the world"— the Persians did not subdue the Scythians.[3]

Historians differ as to what happened. Herodotus claimed that the numerically inferior and technically impoverished barbarian army used guerrilla tactics including a scorched-earth policy to force the mighty Darius into retreat: "... and as he did so they attacked his rearguard and captured his baggage train." J. B. Bury judged Darius' adventure a success and pointed out that it led to the eventual submission of Thrace and token submission of Macedonia.[4] A. R. Burn, however, holds that Darius narrowly missed total disaster and at the very least suffered "... some temporary loss of prestige."[5] We also know that Darius withdrew across the Bosporus and did not again contest the Scythians.

Alexander the Great (356–323 B.C.) encountered serious guerrilla opposition when he campaigned against Bessus, the assassin of Darius III, prior to invading India. This two-year campaign in the Persian satrapies of Bactria and Sogdiana (roughly Afghan Turkestan and Bokhara) tested Alexander to the hilt. In J. F. C. Fuller's words:

> ... In this theater the whole mode of fighting was to differ from what it had been. No great battles awaited Alexander; he was to be faced by a people's war, a war of mounted guerrillas who, when he advanced would suddenly appear in his rear, who entrenched themselves on inaccessible crags, and when pursued vanished into the Turkoman steppes. To overrun such a theater of war and subdue such an enemy demanded generalship of the highest order, much higher than needed against an organized army on the plains. ...
>
> Unfortunately Arrian and other historians tell us little about the tactical changes Alexander introduced although we may assume that there was a considerable expansion of light troops, both foot and horse; yet all we hear is the introduction of mounted javelin-men and that Alexander lightened the equipment of part of the phalanx. Whatever the changes, one thing is certain, they were based on mobility and flexibility, coupled with the use of a large number of military posts and military colonies that restricted his enemy's mobility while they added to his own.[6]

In the spring of 329 B.C., Alexander crossed the Hindu Kush in pursuit of the Persian leader Bessus. Bessus had ravaged the countryside, but Alexander's men defied severe cold and slim rations to cross the

600 miles

N

0 100 200 400

Asiatic Scythians

Alexandria

Jaxartes

Maracanda
(Samarkand)

SOGDIANA

Sogdian Rock

Nicaea

Bactra
(Balkh)
(Zariaspa)
BACTRIA

Hindu Kush

Indus

ARABIAN SEA

Aral
Sea

Oxus

Desert

Pura

Persepolis

CASPIAN SEA

Persian Gulf

Babylon

Euphrates

Thapsacus

Jerusalem

Scythians

BLACK SEA

Bosporus

Ancyra

Tyre

RED SEA

Danube

Dacia

THRACE

Nile

MEDITERRANEAN SEA

Alexandria

Memphis

EGYPT

MACEDONIA

Athens

Mt.
Parnassus

Ammonium

Libyan
Desert

Persian Empire

Boundary of
Alexander's dominions

Alexander's route

Darius' march
512 B.C.

M.E.P.

Oxus River, capture (and later execute) Bessus, and begin construction of a garrisoned city (today's Chodjend) on the Jaxartes River. From here he launched a punitive campaign that crushed a rebellion of the Sogdians under Spitamenes.[7]

Alexander still had to reckon with the Massagetae, or "Asiatic Scythians," who lived north of the Jaxartes and harassed the Macedonians from the other side of the river. Alexander mounted catapults on the bank and with the aid of this protective fire crossed the river, his men using skins stuffed with straw. A heavy cavalry attack disrupted the enemy's wheeling tactics; when his formations broke, Alexander exploited the disorder by sending forward infantry and light cavalry, which killed about a thousand and captured one hundred fifty of the Scythians. Although he ordered his cavalry in pursuit, he did not regain contact, and a bad case of diarrhea, caused by foul water, prevented him from going farther. The battle was nonetheless notable: Alexander, who had no experience in "Parthian" tactics, devised a tactic of his own and was completely successful.[8]

The revolt meanwhile had spread to Bactria, where a group of horse archers of the Massagetae, some six hundred men under Spitamenes, laid siege to Maracanda (today's Samarkand). Sent to relieve the garrison, a force under one of Alexander's interpreters, Pharnuches, was teased to pursue into the desert. Suddenly the nomads struck from all sides. Although Pharnuches formed his troops into a square and fought a successful rearguard action back to a river, his troops broke formation in their rush to cross to safety and were virtually annihilated — " . . . the bloodiest, and the only serious, defeat ever suffered by one of Alexander's columns."[9]

Upon learning of the disaster, Alexander marched a mixed force of infantry, archers, and cavalry 135 miles in seventy-two hours to fall on the besiegers of Maracanda, who immediately disappeared in the desert waste. Alexander pursued as far as the desert but made no contact. After burying his dead, he ravaged the villages that had supported Spitamenes and then laid waste the valley to deprive him of future food supply.[10]

After quartering at Zariaspa for the winter, he split his force, leaving a large portion of it in Bactria.[11] With the remainder, he formed five columns, which made a "sweep" against the guerrillas before rejoining at Maracanda. He next sent two of the columns " . . . to raid the independent nomads, among whom Spitamenes was reported, and Hephaistion to unite the villages of Sogdiana into walled towns—i.e., to concentrate the population, so that they could not easily help the guerrillas."[12] Although Alexander captured a number of enemy strongholds, he could not capture Spitamenes, who was raiding behind his lines.

To get Spitamenes, Alexander relied on a strong force which he left to winter in Sogdiana. As he hoped, Spitamenes turned up. But now the guerrilla force, numbering some three thousand horse, found the countryside bare, the food guarded in Hephaistion's walled cities. Forced into a conventional attack, Spitamenes suffered eight hundred killed against only a few Macedonian dead, a disaster that caused him to retreat. Losing some of his savage hordes by desertion, he yielded control of the rest. Their leaders, upon hearing that Alexander was going to pursue, turned on Spitamenes, cut off his head, and sent it to the Macedonian king as token of full submission.

Alexander faced a final challenge from Oxyartes, a Bactrian baron who with a small band had holed up in a mountain fortress. Oxyartes' envoys refused the Macedonian demand to surrender: " . . . They told Alexander with barbaric laughter to look for soldiers with wings to capture the mountain for him, since no other men would give them any concern." By offering special rewards to volunteers with mountain-climbing experience, Alexander recruited three hundred men who made a night ascent of a peak so sheer that it was unguarded. Thirty men fell to their death, but the survivors had gained the drop on the enemy camp by dawn. A herald now informed Oxyartes that he must surrender, for Alexander " . . . had found the men with wings."[13]

Alexander did more than adapt his tactics to counter unorthodox tactics. After subduing various tribes, he invariably tried to win them to his side, a move explained, according to Tarn, by an innate belief in the unity of mankind—the concept of *Homonoia*—but more likely by shrewd political sense.[14] When a nomad chieftain at Chodjend blamed resistance on undisciplined youth, Alexander overlooked contrary evidence and said he believed him, a face-saving move that brought peace and gained him numerous skillful recruits. After capturing Oxyartes, he not only recruited him into his army but married his daughter, the beautiful Roxane.

Guerrillas plagued another great commander, Hannibal, during his epic march from Spain into northern Italy, in 218 B.C. For this surprise invasion, Hannibal gathered an enormous force, recorded by Polybius as ninety thousand infantry, twelve thousand cavalry, and thirty-eight war elephants—but probably less than half this size.[15] After crossing the Pyrenees and traversing the Rhône country, Hannibal outmaneuvered a Roman army under Publius Cornelius Scipio. Although only thirty years old, Hannibal was a proven leader who used his formidable army of veteran campaigners well. He seems to have encountered little trouble with various tribes of southern Gaul, who in any event held no love for the Romans. One authority, Colonel Dodge, noted that he " . . . had a way of propitiating the native tribes which made his march safe and expeditious. Where honeyed words had no effect, gold was used. . . . "[16]

Armed with much needed supply and invaluable guides familiar with the Alpine passes, he now embarked on his famous fifteen-day march. Almost at once, he came up against a warlike branch of the Allobroges, who were guarding an essential pass, but from his Gallic guides Hannibal learned that in accordance with local custom they guarded it only during daylight, since operations at night " . . . were looked on as impossible."[17] Hannibal ostentatiously made camp and lighted numerous fires, then took a hand-picked force and in the darkness occupied the pass without casualties. On the following day, the Gauls attacked and were defeated. Hannibal next encountered the Ceutrones, who were friendly enough but whom he didn't trust. Pretending to ally with them, he accepted some as guides and continued his march, his route probably leading to the Traversette Pass.[18]

Fearful of an ambush in the difficult terrain, Hannibal reversed the order of march, placing " . . . the pack-train and cavalry at the head of the column and the heavy infantry in the rear." He was struck by an attack in force as his vanguard was moving through a particularly close ravine. The barbarians on the heights rolled down boulders and stones on the surprised column. Although causing losses, they erred in delivering the main attack against Hannibal's rear, precisely where he was strongest. Noting where the enemy's weight lay, Hannibal took up an effective defensive position at the mouth of the defile, sent out flanking forces, and held the enemy until his main force completed its night march through the ravine. This limited the enemy to isolated attacks on his vanguard forces the following day. At the summit of the pass,

Hannibal chose another good defensive position and camped for two days while recovering a large number of stragglers and pack animals.[19]

No one can say with certainty how many men Hannibal lost. Whatever his strength upon debouching from the Alps, his army, combined with his brilliant generalship and Roman-army confusions and weaknesses, proved sufficient to put him at the gates of Rome.

Rome followed its victory over the Carthaginians in the Second Punic War with a period of territorial expansion that forced its legions to fight numerous and costly campaigns against such conventionally armed foes as the Macedonians, Sicilians, and Carthaginians, but also against a variety of irregular forces that frequently employed guerrilla tactics. The colonization of northern Italy provoked a general uprising of Celtic tribes, a campaign lasting over twenty years. To subdue this area, the Romans built a series of strong points, which proved only partially successful against continued incursions by the Celts, the Istrians, and the Dalmatians, who were not subdued until 156 B.C.

Sicily also proved a hotbed of insurrection when a rebellion by slaves grew to an island-wide insurgency crushed only by a difficult and costly military campaign. Another major Sicilian outbreak occurred in 109 B.C. under "Salvius the Soothsayer," whose followers, by using guerrilla tactics, held out for nearly five years. In Italy proper, Rome faced a serious uprising of gladiators led by a Thracian, Spartacus, who used guerrilla tactics while forming an army. The war of Spartacus lasted for two years and cost thousands of Roman lives. Spartacus was finally killed in regular battle.

Rome also had to deal with numerous insurrections and guerrilla raids in the east, particularly in the Balkan Peninsula where barbarian tribes continued savage raids until brought to uneasy submission in 73 B.C. Although evidence is scant, the Roman legions undoubtedly encountered guerrilla tactics in the conquest of central Europe and Britain, as is suggested by the frequent use of the word *latrocinium*—brigandage or banditry. Julius Caesar described the ambush of one of his legions shortly after he landed in Britain. Sent to fetch corn, the soldiers discovered that the fields had been gleaned except in one place:

> ... The enemy, anticipating that the Romans would come here, had lain in wait in the woods during the night; then, when the troops had laid aside their weapons and were dispersed and busy reaping, they had suddenly fallen upon them. A few were killed; the rest, whose ranks were not properly formed, were thrown into confusion; and the enemy's horse and war chariots had at the same time encompassed them.[20]

The enemy fought in a way unfamiliar to the Romans, and a relief force led by Caesar executed a fighting withdrawal only with difficulty. The initial success of the Britons made them overconfident, and when they attacked Caesar's camp shortly after, they were defeated.

Upon Caesar's return to Britain a year later, his legions encountered the same tactics employed by a number of tribes that had united under a local leader, Cassivellaunus. By judicious use of cavalry and infantry, Caesar advanced successfully against the Britons until he reached the river Thames. Here he found the enemy deployed in force on the opposite bank:

> ... The bank was fenced by sharp stakes planted along its edge; and similar stakes were fixed under water and concealed by the river.

When Caesar discovered this from prisoners and successfully crossed the river, Cassivellaunus, abandoning "regular" warfare,

> ... disbanded the greater part of his force, retaining only about four thousand charioteers; watched our line of march; and, moving a little away from the track, concealed himself in impenetrable wooded spots, and removed the cattle and inhabitants from the open country into the woods in those districts through which he had learned that we intended to march. Whenever our cavalry made a bold dash into the country to plunder and devastate, he

10

sent his charioteers out of the woods (for he was familiar with every track and path), engaged the cavalry to their great peril, and by the fear which he thus inspired prevented them from moving far afield. Caesar had now no choice but to forbid them to move out of touch with the column of infantry, and, by ravaging the country and burning villages, to injure the enemy as far as the legionaries' power of endurance would allow.[21]

A lack of unity among enemy tribes soon ended resistance. Disloyal chiefs told Caesar the location of Cassivellaunus' headquarters, which he attacked and captured. Shortly thereafter, he forced Cassivellaunus into submission.

CHAPTER ONE

1. Bury, *A History of Greece,* 239. The identity of these tribes is obscure. Professor Bury noted:

   ... North of the Danube, in the lands which are now called Walachia and Moldavia [today's Romania] (between the Danube, the Carpathians, and the Pruth), lived tribes which were allied in many respects to the tribes south of the river. The Greeks included these tribes under the general name of Scythian, which they applied to the whole series of peoples who dwelled between the Carpathians and the Caucasus. While the most easterly of that series approximated in language to the Persian, the most westerly approximated to the Thracian.

   See also, Burn, *Persia and the Greeks.*
2. Herodotus, *The History of Herodotus,* 354–5. Although Herodotus must be read with caution, he can still be read with extreme enjoyment.
3. Fuller, *The Decisive Battles . . .* , I, 16.
4. Bury, 240.
5. Burn, *Persia and the Greeks,* 132.
6. Fuller, *The Generalship of Alexander the Great,* 117.
7. Arrian, *Anabasis Alexandri,* I, 323 ff. See also, Burn, *Alexander the Great . . .* ; Bury; Tarn, I; Wilcken; Fox.
8. Fuller, *The Generalship of Alexander the Great,* 119.
9. Burn, *Alexander the Great . . .* , 190.
10. Arrian, 355, 357.
11. Historians disagree on the identity and location of Zariaspa (Balkh), which some maintain was also Bactria. Our map derives in part from those in Professor Bury's excellent work.
12. Burn, *Alexander the Great . . .* , 197–8.
13. Arrian, 397–403.
14. Fuller, *The Generalship of Alexander the Great,* 277–8:

   ... It was this aspiration which he expressed in his prayer at Opis, and, according to Tarn, it had little to do with his so-called policy of fusion which was 'a material thing,' but with an idea, 'an immaterial thing.' It was firstly, that all men are brothers; and secondly, that he had 'a divine mission to be the harmonizer and reconciler of the world, to bring it to pass that all men, being brothers, should live together in Homonoia, in unity of heart and mind.'

11

   . . . It was and was to remain a dream, but a dream greater than all his conquests. . . .

   See also, Tarn; Badian: Most scholars accept this work as refuting Tarn's thesis.

15. Polybius, II, 83. See also, de Beer, *Alps and Elephants* . . . , and *The Struggle for Power* . . . ; Adcock; Dodge, I. Most contemporary authorities believe these figures excessive. De Beer, *Alps and Elephants,* 27, suggests 38,000 foot soldiers and 8,000 horsemen.
16. Dodge, 176.
17. Ibid., 205. See also, Polybius, 123.
18. Dodge and other older authorities suggest the Little St. Bernard pass, but recent scholarship points to the Traversette. De Beer, *Alps and Elephants,* writes on this in detail.
19. Polybius, 129.
20. Caesar, I, 121–2.
21. Ibid., 139–40.

CHAPTER 2

The Roman pacification of Spain • Reasons for the Roman presence • Scipio's campaign • The first uprisings • Cato's reply to the guerrillas • Guerrilla strength and weakness • Roman atrocities • The Roman investment • Rome's continued political and military failures • The reforms of Gracchus and Marcellus • The shame of Lucullus and Galba • The rise and fall of brave Viriathus • Scipio Aemilianus' reforms • The extraordinary rebellion of Quintus Sertorius • Final Roman "victory"

ROME'S PROBLEMS in pacifying her northern, eastern, and southern ramparts seem slight when compared to the almost two hundred years of guerrilla warfare she encountered in winning control of Spain.

At one time occupied by numerous tribes, some indigenous and some of African stock, Spain had been overrun in the early Iron Age by Celtic tribes from Gaul. Bypassing the ferocious Basques in the Northeast, the Celts slowly melded with the original Iberians to produce a Celtiberian race of hardy and warlike peoples. Such tribes as the Cantabrians and Asturians in the north and west, the Galicians and Lusitanians in the south, and the Carpetanians, Vettones, and Numantians in the center remained virtually untouched by the coastal colonizing efforts of Phoenicians, Greeks, Carthaginians, and Romans, who impressed themselves on the more sophisticated and generally peaceful coastal tribes.[1]

Roman control of Spain stemmed from the Second Punic War, when the Romans landed an army in Spain in order to deprive Hannibal of support from this Carthaginian stronghold. Gnaeus Scipio, who landed with two legions in 218 B.C. at Emporiae (Ampurias) and was joined a year later by his brother, Publius, fought Hasdrubal and the Carthaginians for several years. By 212 B.C., they had pushed well south of the

Roman conquest of Spain 218 B.C.
Naval convoys

M.E.P.

Ebro to occupy an advanced base at Saguntum, from where they had won submission of many of the local tribes. Disaster now struck. Having split his forces, Publius was attacked by a Celtiberian force under the guerrilla leader Indibilis, who destroyed the Roman army and its commander. Gnaeus was betrayed by local tribes, and he and his army were also destroyed. About nine thousand Roman survivors managed to hold the line of the Ebro until late in 211 B.C., when Claudius Nero arrived with reinforcements. The following year, Publius Cornelius Scipio, the twenty-seven-year-old son of the unfortunate Publius, arrived with ten thousand infantry and one thousand cavalry and relieved Claudius Nero. Scipio soon commenced a campaign south of the Ebro that would end Carthaginian rule of this land. Brilliant victories followed one after the other: Cartagena, Baecula, Ilipa—in all, young Scipio defeated four generals in a brilliant campaign.[2]

By 206–205 B.C., Rome had replaced Carthage as the overlord of "civilized" or Nearer Spain, consisting of the coastal areas of Andalusia, Murcia, and Valencia. Her holdings consisted of little more than a series of ports or coastal enclaves with "finger salients" pushing inland, an area occupied both by friendly and by enemy tribes. The Romans ran into trouble almost at once. The major reason was their attitude, which was purely exploitive in the worst sense. The praetors and their legionaries arrived as "civilized" conquerors of "barbarian" peoples. Roman arms had theretofore proved victorious over barbarian rabble and the

Roman senate saw no reason why this would not prove the case in Spain.

Arrogance was not the least of Roman problems. The Roman army was virtually devoid of experience is administering colonial provinces at this time. The efficacy of ensuing military governments waxed and waned in proportion to the individual talents of the praetors, or governors-general, thenceforth sent with bewildering rapidity from Rome.[3] The first Roman commander, Publius Cornelius Scipio, was an excellent general despite his youth. In pacifying and forging treaties with the local tribes, many of whom had been allied with the Carthaginians, he blended force with common sense. His achievement, however, in no way disguised the brutal nature of the military operations or the rapacious quality of the occupation. Scipio frequently slaughtered or sold recalcitrant tribes into slavery and forced others to pay heavy war indemnities. "Scipio sailed for Rome," the historian Appian noted, "with a large fleet magnificently arrayed, and loaded down with captives, money, arms, and all kinds of booty. The city gave him a glorious reception, bestowing noble and unprecedented honors upon him on account of his youth and the rapidity and greatness of his exploits."[4]

Following Scipio's recommendations, the Romans attempted to rule the two provinces, Further and Nearer Spain, by a dual command system (communications being extremely difficult). The administration proved at once corrupt and oppressive, the praetors possessing all of Scipio's personal cupidity but none of his political acumen. Tribal levies continued with the introduction of the hated *stipendium,* a dual tax paid in money and in bodies for service in the Roman army. The praetors were soon systematically plundering the provinces, rich in metals and wheat, olives and wine.

The upshot of the Roman policy was that coastal tribes that had been friendly to Phoenicians, Greeks, and Carthaginians now rebelled. In 197 B.C., the Romans faced a general insurrection in both provinces. In Further Spain this was led by Indibilis, who had defeated Scipio's father and who was finally slain, but fighting continued in Nearer Spain. By 195 B.C., the Roman army controlled only two interior strongholds and the port of Emporiae. A relief army under M. Porcius Cato enticed the insurgents into formal battle and defeated them to win formal submission of the province.

So dissatisfied were the tribes, however, that rumor of Cato's departure prompted a new revolt. Cato answered this insurrection by reducing the dissident communities and selling the people *en masse* into slavery, then by ordering every town in the province to tear down its walls (and thus make itself defenseless against his arms).[5] Following his return to Rome in 194 B.C., however, there was " . . . no cessation of guerrilla warfare . . . with its constant drain upon Roman troops: Livy can write that a new governor lost nearly a half of his army in this manner during his years of office."[6]

Thus began a pattern: a revolt put down, "justice" done, treaties signed, exploitation continued, another revolt. The two decades necessary for Romans to gain control of coastal areas were marked by guerrilla wars involving heavy casualties and what today would be called atrocities. A favorite Roman punishment, short of massacring an entire tribe or selling a tribe into slavery or burning tribal crops for miles around or demolishing all tribal villages, was to cut off the hands of the warriors. The insurgents invariably replied *quid pro quo,* usually by torturing or beheading Roman captives, and then fighting all the harder. Not only did dissident tribes willingly fight for their independence, or even for reasonable survival, but they fought exceptionally well. So long as they avoided set-piece battles in favor of the sudden attack or the ambush, they usually claimed the upper hand, although inevitably their guerrillas tired, tribes fell out with one another, and in the long run Roman force of arms told. But at a tremendous cost to the conquerors, a cost that significantly contributed to the rise of the standing Roman army, to civil strife at home, to civil war, to dictatorship, and finally to the monarchy.

From the beginning, the Spanish experience heavily taxed Roman resources by wiping out as much as one fourth of the burgess population, which furnished the prime recruits. From 206 to 179 B.C., over seventy thousand legionaries and eighty thousand Latin *socii,* or allies, were drafted to the provinces; the two crises of 195 and 187 B.C. account for a proportionately large share of these, " . . . but each province appears to have received fairly regular reinforcements varying from a half-legion, as happened frequently, up to eight or ten thousand men, this incessant drain being caused by the ever-widening area of warfare and partly by the peculiarly wearing and expensive character of guerrilla tactics."[7]

At a time when the Roman army was already spreading thin, the occupation and further conquest of Spain called for four strong legions. This commitment was the more serious, and indeed marks a very significant change in Roman policy: " . . . the old Roman custom of sending troops only where the exigencies of war at the moment required them, and of not keeping the man called to serve, except in very serious and important wars, under arms for more than a year, was found incompatible with the retention of the turbulent and remote Spanish provinces beyond the sea; it was absolutely impossible to withdraw the troops from these, and very dangerous even to relieve them extensively. The Roman burgesses began to perceive that dominion over a foreign people is an annoyance not only to the slave but to the victor, and murmured loudly regarding the odious war-service of Spain."[8]

The troops were also murmuring. By the time provincial riches filtered through praetors, quaestors, and other satraps, both military and civil, precious little remained for the ordinary legionnaire, who found himself in a strange and generally hostile land, his day devoted either to tiresome garrison routine or to extended campaigns "upcountry." Such campaigns called for hard physical labor expended either in hewing elaborately fortified camps out of unfriendly soil or in chasing elusive guerrillas. Conventionally minded commanders insisted on using "mass" tactics that, inappropriate to the terrain, frequently resulted in dreaded and costly ambush by the lurking enemy. Moreover, the ordinary soldier's pay was frequently delayed; so was his relief. Casualties were high and, even worse, the numerous campaigns seemed never-ending in this land " . . . where large armies starved and small armies got beaten."[9]

These difficulties scarcely deterred either the Roman senate or its praetors in Spain from pursuing an expansionist policy designed to win control of the interior of the country. Before the coastal regions were even pacified, expeditionary forces began probing inland to launch a war that would last, with interruptions, for nearly 150 years—a war marked by all the errors of the earlier fighting.

The most striking characteristic of the Roman conquest is not Spanish successes, but rather Roman political and military failures—the seeming inability to adjust sufficiently to meet what in time must have become an obvious challenge. The lessons of the earlier insurrectionary crises must have struck even the most obtuse governor or dim-witted military commander; yet, with the passing of each crisis, the lessons seemingly vanished into the prevailing morass compounded of imperialistic arrogance, personal greed, and professional ineptness.

An enlightened commander appeared only occasionally. Tiberius Sempronius Gracchus was one such. After putting down a severe insurrection in Further Spain in 179 B.C. (with the usual harsh methods), he attempted to exploit his victory by extending Roman friendship to various Celtiberian tribes in the form of equitable treaties: in return for annual tribute, he offered tribes certain economic and administrative advantages. Gracchus followed his conquest of Cantabria by giving " . . . a place in the community to the poorer classes, and apportioned land to them, and made carefully defined treaties binding them to be the friends of Rome, and giving and receiving oaths to that effect. These tactics were often longed for in the subsequent wars."[10] Another moderate and farsighted ruler, Claudius Marcellus, echoed Gracchus' reforms. Marcellus even persuaded major tribes of the interior to send a peace embassy to Rome—an excellent plan voided by the catastrophic refusal of the Roman senate to receive the barbarians.

17

The progressive reforms of these two rulers soon fell victim to re-action. A series of particularly rapacious praetors abrogated the treaties to start new wars. Seriously alarmed, Rome now took the unusual step of sending out a consul, Lucius Lucullus, but, by the time he arrived, peace had been declared.* Unwilling to forsake either fame or booty, Lucullus distinguished himself by attacking and slaughtering some twenty thousand members of a friendly Celtiberian tribe; he followed this with a highlands campaign but, plagued by Pallantian guerrillas, soon retreated south to join forces with the praetor Servius Galba. Soon thereafter, Galba further extended Roman honor by inviting three Lu-sitanian tribes to the treaty table, then loosing general tribal massacres.[11]

In 148 B.C., the wheel of Roman treachery turned full circle. A new governor, Gaius Vetilius, had surrounded a force of some ten thousand Lusitanian rebels. These were about ready to surrender when Viriathus, a minor guerrilla leader who had escaped the earlier Galba massacre, rose in assembly to remind the Lusitanians of Roman promises and Roman deeds—and then led them to a successful retreat during which he set up an ambush in a dense thicket. When these irregulars fell on the pursuing Romans, Viriathus doubled his main force back to the attack: "Vetilius himself was taken prisoner; and the man who captured him not knowing who he was, but seeing that he was old and fat, and considering him worthless, killed him. Of the 10,000 Romans, 6,000 with difficulty made their way to the city of Carpessus on the seashore. . . . "[12] Although casualty figures offered by the ancients are always suspect, there seems little doubt that Viriathus and his guerrillas accounted for thousands of Roman lives in the following virulent decade of what he called "fiery war."

In desperation, Rome sent its best generals, but although these inflicted an occasional setback on Viriathus, he continued to give far more than he received. The Romans now managed to have him stabbed to death while he slept. His death severely weakened the insurrection and led to uneasy peace in 137 B.C., which soon gave way to renewed war. Nor was there peace in the north, where for twelve years guerrilla bands had held two strongholds and on one occasion had forced the surrender of an entire Roman army. Furious in humiliation, the Roman senate turned to P. Cornelius Scipio Aemilianus Africanus Minor, famed conqueror of Carthage, who reached Spain in 134 B.C. to find the army a shocking mixture of " . . . dissoluteness, insubordination and cowardice."[13]

---

* To hasten Lucullus' arrival, the senate shifted the normal date of his taking office from March 15 to January 1, which thenceforth marked the beginning of the new calendar year.

18

Scipio immediately " . . . expelled all traders and harlots; also the soothsayers and diviners, whom the soldiers were continually consulting because they were demoralized by defeat. . . . " After this breath of fresh air, he " . . . ordered all wagons and their superfluous contents to be sold, and all pack animals, except such as he himself permitted to remain. For cooking utensils it was only permitted to have a spit, a brass kettle, and one cup. Their food was limited to plain boiled and roasted meats. They were forbidden to have beds, and Scipio was the first to sleep on straw. He forbade them to ride on mules when on the march; 'for what can you expect in a war,' said he, 'from a man who is not even able to walk?' They had to bathe and anoint themselves without assistance, Scipio saying sarcastically that only mules, having no hands, needed others to rub them. Thus in a short time he brought them back to good order."[14] He then went on to "win" a war against the Numantians, his final "victory" significantly enough involving sixty thousand troops (including forty thousand native auxiliaries) against four thousand enemy.[15] Nonetheless, Scipio ended a black era and in conjunction with a senatorial commission from Rome brought a better day to the peninsula. These reforms helped open the Castiles to the conquerors, who colonized as far north as the Douro River and as far west as the Tagus.

A relatively quiet period was now broken by civil strife at home which led to a rebellion by one Quintus Sertorius. A remarkable man, Sertorius. Veteran of Cimbrian, Spanish, and Italian campaigns (he had lost an eye), he had become a democratic revolutionary, a supporter of Marius and Lepidus. Banished to Spain by Sulla, he soon won a considerable following of dissident officers and soldiers, but was forced to go to Africa, where he led " . . . a restless life of adventure along the Spanish and African coasts, sometimes in league, sometimes at war, with the Cilician pirates who haunted these seas, and with the chieftains of the roving tribes of Libya."[16]

In 81 B.C., the Lusitanians persuaded him to lead them in a revolt against Roman rule, and he returned to Spain, where he commanded a small legion of mostly Roman deserters and Africans. A brilliant commander and organizer, Sertorius organized and trained this nucleus along formal Roman lines. Supported by guerrilla bands, also under his command, he raised the standard of revolt in the interior, where his small army easily evaded the legions of Quintus Caecilius Metellus. Like Viriathus before him, Sertorius used Spain's vast spaces to lure legions from coastal enclaves and then attack lines of communication and harass at will. Clever Sertorius even made common cause with coastal privateers, who intercepted Roman supply ships. But his real key to success lay in building a strong political base from diverse Celtiberian tribes. In contrast to the average Roman governor, Sertorius

... exercised a just and gentle rule. His troops, at least so far as his eye and his arm reached, had to maintain the strictest discipline ... he reduced the tribute, and directed the soldiers to construct winter barracks for themselves, so that the oppressive burden of quartering the troops was done away and thus a source of unspeakable mischief and annoyance was stopped. For the children of Spaniards of quality an academy was erected at Osca (Huesca) in which they received the higher instruction usual in Rome. ... It was the first attempt to accomplish their Romanization not by extirpating the old inhabitants and filling their places with Italian emigrants, but by Romanizing the provincials themselves. ...

By the end of 77 B.C., the whole of Nearer Spain had become " ... by treaty or force dependent on Sertorius, and the district on the upper and middle Ebro thenceforth continued the mainstay of his power."[17]

Pompey arrived with reinforcements the following year. A more skillful tactician than Metellus, Pompey invaded the highlands and slowly forced Sertorius to fragment his forces. Although Sertorius held his own for another few years, Roman weight slowly told, as it had in the case of Viriathus. Loss of his better officers hurt him, as did the defection of various tribes. But Pompey had still not won a "decisive" battle against him when a rival, Perperna, murdered Sertorius, in 72 B.C.

Pompey could scarcely claim victory. Sertorius' legion probably never exceeded five thousand troops, but in trying to capture it and subdue the supporting guerrillas, in all, the Romans employed 120,000 infantry, 2,000 archers and slingers, and 6,000 horse. Mommsen summed up the tragic record:

> ... The [Roman] state suffered from it beyond description. The flower of the Italian youth perished amid the exhausting fatigues of these campaigns. The public treasury was not only deprived of the Spanish revenues, but had annually to send to Spain for the pay and maintenance of the Spanish armies very considerable sums, which the government hardly knew how to raise. Spain was devastated and impoverished, and the Roman civilization, which unfolded so fair a promise there, received a severe shock; as was naturally to be expected in the case of an insurrectionary war waged with so much bitterness, and but too often occasioning the destruction of whole communities. ... The generals had encountered an opponent far superior in talent, a tough and protracted resistance, a warfare of very serious perils and of successes difficult to be attained and far from brilliant.[18]

The final territorial expansion began under Julius Caesar's governorship of Further Spain when, in 61–60 B.C., he extended Roman frontiers to the mouth of the Douro. After the interim of the Caesar-Pompey wars, Augustus continued the task in a series of bloody campaigns that won Rome control of the northwestern corner in the vicinity of the Cantabrian Mountains. With this conquest, completed in 19 B.C., nearly all of Spain lay subject to Roman control. Sporadic uprisings, however, continued to mar the scene, and Augustus was forced to garrison the newly won areas with three legions—a heavy commitment, considering their material value.

Some authorities suggest that, even with various reforms, the essential ruthlessness of the Roman policy had not really changed at the beginning of the fifth century A.D., when Eastern barbarians crossed the Rhine and flooded Gaul and Spain. According to Salvian, local peoples even preferred barbarians to imperial tax collectors, and big landowners had as much to fear from agrarian insurgents, the Bagandae, as from the barbarians.

CHAPTER TWO

1. Bouchier, 1–15.
2. Scullard, 39–107. See also, Parker, for the origin and development of the Roman army; Adcock.
3. Sutherland, 45 ff.
4. Appian, I, 197. See also, Scullard, 108: Upon Scipio's return to Rome, " . . . he deposited in the Treasury 14,324 lbs. of silver (over a million *denarii*) in addition to coined silver."; Schulten.
5. Appian, I, 203.
6. Sutherland, 67.
7. Ibid., 70.
8. Mommsen, II, 389.
9. Sutherland, 71.
10. Appian, I, 207.
11. Mommsen, III, 19. Mommsen concluded, III, 220:

    > . . . War has hardly ever been waged with so much perfidy, cruelty, and avarice as by these two generals; yet by means of their criminally acquired treasures the one escaped condemnation and the other escaped even impeachment. The veteran Cato, in his eighty-fifth year, a few months before his death, attempted to bring Galba to account before the burgesses; but the weeping children of the general, and the gold which he had brought home with him, demonstrated to the Roman people his innocence.

12. Appian, I, 257.
13. Mommsen, III, 228.
14. Appian, I, 273.
15. Sutherland, 86.
16. Mommsen, IV, 281–3.
17. Ibid., 20.
18. Ibid., 29–30.

CHAPTER 3

Hannibal's cunning • Fabian strategy and tactics • Warfare in early China • The amazing Sun Tzu: The Art of War *• Quasi-guerrilla tactics of Goths and Huns • Fridigern and the battle of Adrianople • Political weaknesses of the barbarians • Rise of the Franks • Attila and the Huns Justinian's campaigns • Belisarius: brain versus brawn • Emperor Maurice's defense against guerrilla tactics • Emperor Leo's great work:* Tactics *• Emperor Nikephoros Phokas:* On Shadowing Warfare *• The growing difference in warfare between East and West*

NEITHER EASTERN TRIBES nor Celtiberians monopolized guerrilla tactics. Persian, Greek, and Roman commanders who assembled forces secretly, marched rapidly, and struck unexpectedly often proved victorious. Nor did early guerrillas monopolize cunning and deception. Orthodox generals of antiquity on occasion produced victory, sometimes against great odds, by introducing unorthodox tactics to the battlefield.

Hannibal's early victories in Italy owe considerable to his having acted unexpectedly, for example by taking an "impossible" route of march to ambush a Roman army. " . . . His ruses were so numerous and his stratagems so subtle that the Romans felt constantly insecure. He became the embodiment of what the Romans called 'Punic faith,' by which they meant treacherousness. When they did the same thing, it was of course no longer treachery. . . ."[1]

Hannibal was stymied, on the other hand, by Quintus Fabius Maximus, who turned the Roman army into virtually a guerrilla force. For months, Fabius shadowed Hannibal's marches, " . . . harassing his foragers, cutting off stragglers, nipping off a stray patrol, but never permitting himself to be drawn into full-scale battle."[2] Impatient Romans derisively called him "the Laggard"; history has treated him more kindly by acknowledging him as the inventor of Fabian tactics.

Such tactical adaptation was rare in the West, and almost always was forced by the enemy rather than produced voluntarily by a commander trained to think in terms of either the unexpected or the indirect approach based on cunning.

This was also true in the East for some centuries before the birth of Christ. But in the mid-fifth century B.C., as specific states grew in size and strength and in turn began nibbling at less powerful neighbors, China entered a period known as the Warring States. Feudalism declined sharply and warfare became what one ancient Chinese nobleman termed "a fundamental occupation."[3] Powerful rulers now formed standing armies commanded by professional officers who conducted important campaigns far from their home states. Technological advances such as the invention of the crossbow (which did not appear in the West until the fifth century A.D.) and the introduction of iron weapons spelled the decline of primitive chariot warfare. Armies grew increasingly sophisticated, generals employed staff officers, and highly trained, elite units practiced march security and scouting techniques.

One of the most interesting treatises ever written on warfare dates from this period: Sun Tzu's *The Art of War,* written probably around the mid-fourth century B.C. In thirteen relatively short chapters, this brilliant philosopher-general displayed a strategic and tactical insight as unorthodox as it was astute, and the work undoubtedly caused neighboring rulers much uneasiness. Often standing at odds with Greco-Roman military doctrines (as we believe we know them), it is essentially a demand for an indirect approach to war at political, strategic, and tactical levels.

By Sun Tzu's time, war had become " . . . a matter of vital importance to the State; the province of life or death, the road to survival or ruin." Such are disadvantages of war to the state that it should be avoided whenever possible by clever diplomacy (which should utilize high-level espionage). Able statesmanship, by isolating and demoralizing the potential enemy, should defeat him before the combat stage is reached. In Sun Tzu's mind, " . . . to win one hundred victories in one hundred battles is not the acme of skill. To subdue the enemy without fighting is the acme of skill." Sun Tzu recommended that a state go to war only if the diplomatic offensive failed. But a state should do this only after making a careful estimate of the situation to determine if human, physical, and doctrinal factors favored rapid victory, " . . . for there has never been a protracted war from which a country has benefited."[4]

If a state decided on battle, the able general must pay closest attention to such factors as terrain, weather, and enemy plans, " . . . for the crux of military operations lies in the pretence of accommodating one's self to the designs of the enemy." Therefore: " . . . Know the enemy, know yourself; your victory will never be endangered. Know the ground, know the weather; your victory will then be total."[5]

Sun Tzu insisted that both strategy and tactics be fashioned with the knowledge that " . . . all warfare is based on deception": " . . . Therefore, when capable, feign incapacity; when active, inactivity. When near, make it appear that you are far away; when far away, that you are near." The able general must maneuver his army in such a way as " . . . to make the devious route the most direct and to turn misfortune to advantage." The commander who understands the strategy of the indirect approach "will be victorious."[6]

Having "shaped" his enemy by his own foresight, by control of his forces, by extreme mobility (aided by native scouts) and by careful terrain appreciation, the general next deployed two tactical elements: the *cheng,* or orthodox force, normally used to hold the enemy, and the *ch'i,* or unorthodox force, normally used to attack the enemy's flanks and rear. These two forces " . . . are mutually reproductive; their interaction as endless as that of interlocked rings. Who can determine where one ends and the other begins?" The one complements the other, and if the tactical commander correctly employs them, " . . . his potential is that of a fully drawn crossbow; his timing, the release of the trigger."[7]

Just what currency Sun Tzu's work gained outside China is a moot question. Considering the literacy level of the barbarian tribes that invaded the Roman Empire, a tempting answer is, None at all. But this is to disallow that songs, legends, stories, and teachings have always survived primarily by word of mouth. Commercial intercourse by boat also existed among China, Egypt, and Africa; students may have passed on his teachings, probably in mutilated form, to various incursive tribes such as the Hiong Nu, " . . . who attacked the empire of China in the second and first centuries B.C." before turning west.[8]

These tribes practiced a quasi-guerrilla form of warfare remarkably oriental, but part of the reason was the nomadic quality of the central Asian environment—the necessity for tribal mobility and great stealth in hunting and a marked preference for plunder, not conquest.

Supreme among such tribes in the West were the Goths and the Huns, who in the fourth and fifth centuries overran large parts of both the Eastern and the Western Roman empires. No one is certain of their origins. The Goths, originally a Teutonic people, probably migrated from southern Russia, where they had become expert horsemen, to the middle and lower Danube; by A.D. 236, they had penetrated imperial borders. In the next fifteen years, they crossed over the Danube and into the Balkans, overrunning Moesia and Thrace, a campaign culminating in A.D. 251 in the battle of Forum-Trebonii, where they killed Emperor

Decius and decimated his army. For some twenty years, they virtually controlled the middle provinces, but, about A.D. 270, the Romans stopped fighting each other long enough to force them from the Balkans and, under Diocletian, even to rule them, a task aided by Gothic fear of the Huns.[9]

The Huns may have stemmed from the previously mentioned Hiong Nu. Whatever their antecedents, about A.D. 375 " . . . a combination of overpopulation, the effect of climatic changes on an essentially pastoral existence, and the endless struggle for power among the nomadic tribes north of the Himalaya mountains" combined to drive them west.[10] They apparently arrived in considerable numbers; ancient historians speak of seven hundred thousand, but this is doubtlessly exaggerated. According to the Roman historian Priscus, a chronicler of these dark decades, they " . . . were skilled in hunting but in no other task except this. After they had grown into a nation they disturbed the peace of the neighboring races by thefts and plundering."[11] Another historian, Ammianus, noted that "they are faithless in truces" and "burn with an infinite greed for gold."[12]

Once on the Danube, the Huns subdued neighboring tribes not so much by superior numbers, we are told, as " . . . by the terror of their looks, inspiring them with no little horror by their awful aspect and by their horribly swarthy appearance." Priscus continues to look down his patrician nose at these unwonted intruders: " . . . They have a sort of shapeless lump, if I may say so, not a face, and pinholes rather than eyes. . . . Somewhat short in stature, they are trained to quick bodily movement and are very alert in horsemanship and ready with bow and arrow; they have broad shoulders, thick-set necks, and are always erect and proud. These men, in short, live in the form of humans but with the savagery of beasts."[13]

These men, also in short, were fine warriors. Mounted on light, fast ponies, they traveled in small groups which rapidly concentrated to attack, then quickly dispersed to meet again by prearranged plan. Unlike the Goths, their major weapon was the horn bow, which shot a noiseless, bone-tipped arrow; their skill was such as to literally shower the enemy with these deadly arrows if they did not wish to close with him. According to Ammianus, if they chose to close they used the sword " . . . regardless of their own lives; and while the enemy are guarding against wounds from the sabre-thrusts, they throw strips of cloth pleated into nooses (lassos) over their opponents and so entangle them that they fetter their limbs and take from them the power of riding or walking."[14]

Hun warriors lived on their horses and off the land, their foraging diet supplemented by meat, blood, and milk from extra horses and mares led by each man. The warrior bands preceded women, children,

Goths
Huns
Western Roman Empire
Eastern Roman Empire

N

North
Sea

ATLANTIC
OCEAN

BRITAIN

Rhine

GAUL

Danube

Chalons-
sur-Marne

Attila's Capital
?

SPAIN

MEDITERRANEAN SEA

ITALY

Rome

Sea of
Azov

Black Sea

Danube

DACIA

MOESIA

MOESIA

THRACE

Adrianople

Constantinople

MACEDONIA

375 A.D.?

236 A.D.?

0   100 200   400   600 miles

M.E.P.

and older warriors, who traveled in wagons. In times of danger, they formed these into a defensive laager, or "wagon-city."

Although the Goths feared the Huns, they nonetheless copied their quasi-guerrilla tactics. Under their great chief Fridigern, the Ostrogoths soon rebelled against restrictive Roman rule in favor of plundering raids through Bulgaria and Macedonia. A major weakness, lack of siege trains, prevented Fridigern from capturing Adrianople in A.D. 378 (as it had prevented Hannibal from capturing Roman cities). Having withdrawn a few miles from this walled bastion, Fridigern was attacked by a large Roman force under command of the eastern emperor, Valens. Hastily summoning his cavalry from a raid, the barbarian leader cunningly gained time first by parley with the enemy, then by firing fields ripe with August harvest in order to delay and confuse deployment of the ponderous Roman legions. When these began to close on him, he held them back by volleys of missiles fired from within the protected laager. And now his cavalry returned to charge and rout the Roman horse and then fall on the exposed Roman flank, in Ammianus' words, " . . . like a thunderbolt which strikes on a mountain top, and dashes away all that stands in its path."[15] The Roman ranks, already confused by heavy missile fire, pressed one onto the other, a chaotic mass so compressed that " . . . men could not raise their arms to strike a blow." At this point, Fridigern loosed his carefully hoarded infantry to deliver the *coup de grâce*. Only a few thousand enemy escaped the slaughter. Ammianus Marcellinus estimated a loss of some forty thousand Roman-allied lives—a disaster to Roman arms comparable only to that of Cannae (216 B.C.).[16]

Although Fridigern's quasi-guerrilla tactics are interesting, his victory did not topple the Roman Empire. Along with other barbarians the Goths wanted booty more than "victory," and were content to pillage variously in Greece and neighboring provinces. A new emperor, the Spanish general Theodosius, made peace with the Goths, reorganized the Roman army, raised cavalry units, and " . . . began to enlist wholesale every Teutonic chief whom he could bribe to enter his service."[17] Six years after the Roman defeat, he had brought forty thousand Goths and other Teutons into his army of the east; these became the Teutonic *foederati,* whose dubious loyalty went to the emperor's person rather than to the empire, and which, more than any other influence, explained the eventual disintegration of Roman rule in the West.

The willingness of some barbarian tribes to assimilate with the Romans and fight other barbarian tribes was a major weakness, only slowly overcome by tribal amalgamations and growth culminating in the rise of the Franks. It was not fully repaired until Charlemagne introduced political purpose into tribal conquest to revive the Western

Roman Empire. Earlier tribes, loyal to a single chief, interested only in plunder and not territorial conquest and settlement, refused to unite. At a time when the Roman army was overextended and the empire torn with civil war, a tribe would strike here, another there, spaced onslaughts usually contained by the hard-pressed legions. Had the tribes struck simultaneously, they would have probably overrun the Roman Empire as early as the fourth century.

A large part of this weakness stemmed from the *comitatus* concept, wherein particularly able warriors formed a bodyguard to a chief or supreme warrior: When tribes came together in earlier centuries, intense jealousy invariably ensued, with constant bickering and jockeying for favor by the chief lieutenants. Internecine feuds obliterated whole tribes. Leaders could never feel secure. Attila the Hun acceded to power only by murdering his coregent, his brother Bleda. Attila, who forged a number of tribes into a Danubian kingdom of sorts, undoubtedly recognized the tenuous quality of his political structure. He certainly did not shirk from the violence of his environment. His brutal raids up to the gates of Constantinople and later in the West killed and maimed thousands of hapless victims. Attila rather cleverly advertised himself as "the scourge of God"—meaning, as Professor Hoyt has pointed out, " . . . the punishment visited by God's wrath upon a sinful people. The terror struck into the hearts of his intended victims by this sort of propaganda was a potent 'secret weapon.' "[18]

Attila evidently possessed considerable charisma, as evidenced by his lengthy reign and by accounts left by various Roman ambassadors. A later source described him as " . . . short of stature with a broad chest, massive head and small eyes. His beard was thin and sprinkled with grey, his nose flat, and his complexion swarthy, showing thus the signs of his origins." Haughty in carriage, he cast " . . . his eyes about him on all sides so that the proud man's power was to be seen in the very movements of his body." But although he was a lover of war, " . . . he was personally restrained in action, most impressive in counsel, gracious to suppliants, and generous to those to whom he had once given his trust." He was also something of a politician, for if on occasion he led devastating military raids deep into the empire, he was also content to sit quietly by in his Danubian kingdom receiving tribute from the terrified Romans. (Professor Gordon estimated that, between A.D. 443 and 450, he was paid twenty-two thousand pounds of gold!)[19]

Materially profitable, yes; politically constructive, no. Attila's numerous conquests were no more permanent than those of Fridigern or of Alaric, who, in A.D. 407, led his Goths to the virtual conquest of Italy, including the sacking of Rome. And then? Two years later, on his own volition, he returned to the Rhineland. This was political naïveté in its extreme form and brings to mind the lament of the cavalry general

Maharbal after the Carthaginian victory at Cannae: "You know how to gain a victory, Hannibal; you know not how to use one."

Political naïveté helps to explain the military shortcomings of the barbarians. Their daring and skill and cunning were largely neutralized by a lack of staying power, which in their own minds they did not need. They wanted to eat, plunder, and move on. They invariably followed the line of least resistance, as noted by Amédée Thierry: " . . . The nomads, unlike ourselves, do not consider flight a dishonor. Considering booty of more worth than glory, they fight only when they are certain of success. When they find their enemy in force, they evade him to return when the occasion is more opportune." Although, on occasion, Attila used siege engines and was not above learning from the Romans, for example by replacing his ponies with horses, he generally avoided attacking defended towns and cities: " . . . operations took the form of whirlwind advances and retirements. Whole districts were laid waste and entire populations annihilated, not only in order to establish a heat of terror which would evaporate opposition, but also to leave the rear clear of all hostile manpower and so to facilitate withdrawals. The tactics may be defined as 'ferocity under authority.' Fury, surprise, elusiveness, cunning and mobility, and not planning, method, drill, and discipline were its elements."[20]

When these guerrilla characteristics were not allowed to assert themselves, the result was usually disastrous. Attila was fought to a standstill by Aëtius at Chalons-sur-Marne in A.D. 451, a victory that depended largely on his Teutonic *foederati* buttressed by Theodoric's heavy Visigothic cavalry—barbarians brought under Roman discipline. Attila did manage, however, to extricate his surviving force and continue plundering tactics until his premature death, possibly the result of a hemorrhage on the night of his wedding to the young and beautiful Kriemhild.

We have seen how Theodosius adapted his military machine to repair the disaster of the Byzantine defeat at Adrianople in A.D. 378. While the Western Empire, torn by internal dissension, dissolved into a sea of invading Germanic tribes, the Eastern Empire managed to survive by a judicious blending of city fortifications, native armies, privately controlled mercenary cavalry hosts, and outright bribes to deflect such potential predators as the Huns and the Ostrogoths.

The heavy-cavalry units formed by Theodosius more than justified themselves. By Justinian's reign (527–65), the mainstay of the army was the horse archer supported by light cavalry and heavy infantry.

By building small, mobile armies around such disciplined barbarians, Belisarius and Narses recovered numerous Roman provinces from the Vandals in Africa and from the Goths in Italy, achievements more remarkable considering Justinian's parsimony in supporting these expeditionary forces. Perhaps because of limited means, Belisarius relied on brain rather than brawn. He saw no dishonor in avoiding battle when he could, a lesson driven home early in his career. At twenty-six years of age he commanded a force that was screening a Persian withdrawal. Opposite Callinicum, his officers and troops urged him to take this last opportunity to strike the enemy. In a public harangue, Belisarius replied: " . . . Whither would you urge me? The most complete and most happy victory is to baffle the force of an enemy without impairing our own, and in this favorable situation we are already placed. Is it not wiser to enjoy the advantages thus easily acquired, than to hazard them in the pursuit of more?" Failing to convince his men, he grudgingly agreed to battle, only to suffer a near disastrous defeat. He did not so err again, and in campaigns in Africa, Sicily, and Italy he also displayed political shrewdness, forbidding theft and avoiding "insult or injury" to local inhabitants.[21]

Belisarius' successful campaign in Italy proved a mixed blessing in that by causing the Goths to withdraw troops from the east, it opened Justinian's borders to fresh barbarian incursions. To hold these in check, Justinian relied on a large and expensive fortified complex stretching from Belgrade along the south bank of the Danube to the Black Sea—some sixty fortresses theoretically linked by five hundred intervening towers, probably used to shelter local peasantry until the barbarians passed by on their way to richer loot. In addition to this line, Justinian defended the pass at Thermopylae and, farther south, fortified the isthmus of Corinth; grander by far, he repaired the *Makron Teichos*, or Long Wall, built by Emperor Anastasius: forty miles north of Constantinople, its ramparts stretched sixty miles from the Propontis east to the Black Sea.

So long as troops existed in sufficient numbers to man these defenses, they helped keep barbarians in check. But Justinian overextended both economically and militarily, and the abilities neither of Belisarius nor Narses, once again fighting in Italy, could repair a paucity of military means. Lacking sufficient troops, his border defenses became virtually useless, an unprotected sheepfold according to Agathias, where the prowling wolf, far from encountering a bite, is not even threatened by a bark; and in 559 Zabergan led his Bulgarians into Thrace seemingly without difficulty.[22]

When Justinian died, Constantinople faced the threat of the Avars and Slavs in the north and the Persians in the south. Under Maurice (582–602), " . . . the empire entered a defensive phase which was to be its military outlook for the next 500 years."[23]

Maurice and his successors differed radically from Western tradi-

PERSIA

Red Sea

Black Sea

AVARS

Long Wall

Constantinople

EGYPT

Nile

SLAVS

Danube

Belgrade

Athens

LOMBARDS

Adriatic Sea

MEDITERRANEAN SEA

AFRICA

Rome

BURGUNDIANS

FRANKS

VISIGOTHS

N

▨ Justinian's Empire 527–565 A.D.

xxxxx Northern line of forts

0   200   400   600 miles

M.E.P.

tion in their approach to warfare. Though Hellenistic in outlook in many respects, they seem to have reverted to the oriental thought of Sun Tzu. They definitely preferred diplomacy and deception (including bribery) to battle. Because of limited human resources, war was to be fought only as a last resort. But since almost constant incursions of Slavs, Avars, Bulgarians, Persians, Saracens, Franks, Russians, and Turks meant a good many last resorts, the Eastern Empire attached greatest importance to its armed forces, many details concerning which have been preserved in two treatises, Maurice's *Artis Militaris* and Leo VI's *Tactics*.

To deal with barbarian hordes, Maurice reduced the standing army in size and restored it to control of the central government. He fortified his frontiers in depth and defended them in part with local militia. This system evolved by the end of the seventh century into decentralized defense, with the empire ultimately divided into military districts, or themes, each containing " . . . a permanent army corps, bolstered by local militia and commanded by a *strategos* who was also the head of the area's civil government." The hub of empire, Constantinople " . . . was surrounded by a sixty-foot moat, guarding a triple ring of immense walls, each wall studded with towers at frequent intervals, and the innermost wall reaching a height of thirty feet," a formidable defense, further strengthened by a powerful fleet and by the secret and devastating weapon of "Greek fire," which was poured on ships or on scaling parties.[24]

The relatively small professional army was well ahead of its time. Although continuing to rely primarily on mounted bowmen, it also included infantry and artillery units, the whole supported by engineers and quartermasters, even a medical corps. Other innovations included sectionalized boats, which, transported by mules, could be put together for fording purposes, and a series of military textbooks to instruct officers on diverse strategies and tactics " . . . based on the principle that the methods to be employed must be varied according to the people to be fought."[25]

Maurice wrote knowingly of the battle characteristics of the Persian, Lombard, Avar, and Slav enemy, describing tactics that should be used against each. No detail escaped his attention. He noted of the Slavs that " . . . they have abundance of cattle and grain, chiefly millet and rye, but rulers they cannot bear and they live side by side in disunion." But he was also impressed with their guerrilla tactics and their habit, when pursued, of disappearing under water and breathing through a reed until the danger passed.[26]

Sensing the danger of fighting against greatly superior numbers, yet wishing to avoid overdependence on unreliable mercenaries, Maurice favored a nation-in-arms concept: " . . . We wish that every young Roman of free condition should learn the use of the bow, and be constantly provided with that weapon and with two javelins." This ambition apparently came to nothing during the Persian and Saracen onslaughts of the seventh and eighth centuries, which brought the Eastern Empire continuing crisis and cost it Egypt and Syria.

Maurice's thinking was elaborated three hundred years later by Emperor Leo VI (886–912), whose *Tactics* borrowed freely from Maurice's work. For centuries, the Eastern Empire had been pursuing a "no-win" policy in order to survive against hordes of powerful enemies. At Leo's accession, it stood on the permanent defensive. Faced with fighting Franks, Saracens, Slavs, and Turks, Leo decided that his best defense against Eastern predators was a nation-in-arms, once called for by Maurice, but a lack of internal homogeneity apparently extinguished this scheme.

The tenth century also added to Byzantine military literature. Emperor Nikephoros Phokas, around 965, ordered a handbook of defensive warfare prepared to help counter the incursive raids made by a great Moslem general, Sayf al-Dawla. The work, *On Shadowing Warfare*, reflects many of the earlier teachings of Maurice and Leo; according to its author, it was a method " . . . whereby a small army, too weak to engage the enemy in battle, could nevertheless preserve unharmed both itself and the territory of the state." Dr. Howard-Johnston, the translator of this work, concluded that

> . . . the particular elements of the method resembled those of modern guerrilla warfare, in that they relied heavily upon the natural advantages offered by terrain, on the willing cooperation of the civilian population, on good intelligence, on interrupting the enemy's line of communication, and finally on the demoralizing effect of an endless sequence of small, surprise, "carefully planned tactical attacks in a war of strategical defensive."[27]

On Shadowing Warfare evidences sophisticated military thinking produced by almost continuous offensive and defensive wars. Like Sun Tzu's *Art of War,* and like Maurice's and Leo's writings, it forms an interesting contrast to Western thinking of the time. Oman underlines the vast difference in Eastern and Western military philosophy at this stage:

> . . . Of the spirit of chivalry there was not a spark in the Byzantine . . . but he was equally remote from the haughty contempt for sleights and tricks which had inspired the ancient Romans, and from the chivalrous ideals which grew to be at once the strength and the weakness of the Teutonic West. Courage was considered at Constantinople as one of the requisites necessary for obtaining

success, not as the sole and paramount virtue of the warrior. The generals of the East considered a campaign brought to a successful issue without a great battle as the cheapest and most satisfactory consummation in war. They considered it absurd to expend stores, money, and the valuable lives of veteran soldiers in achieving by force an end that could equally well be obtained by skill. . . . They had a strong predilection for stratagems, ambushes, and simulated retreats. For the officer who fought without having first secured all the advantages for his own side they had the greatest contempt.[28]

The traditional criticism levied on the Byzantines is that, by accepting the strategic defensive, they forfeited initiative and eventually lost the empire. This criticism fails to respect the fact that a defensive strategy demands as competent leadership as an offensive strategy. Byzantine leadership was unfortunately spotty; thus, when the army mutinied and killed Maurice in 602, power went to an imbecile emperor, Phocas, under whom empire fortunes plunged, only to be retrieved by Heraclius' reforms and leadership. Had firm leadership continued, had the nation-in-arms concept worked, the Eastern Empire might have avoided a constant internal weakening by overreliance on quasi-assimilated military mercenaries. Even with these weaknesses, the military disasters against the Seljuk Turks of Arp Arslan, particularly the decisive battle of Manzikert, in 1071, might have been avoided had Romanus respected Leo's and Nikephoros Phokas' tactical instructions instead of yielding to his own rashness.[29] The critic should also remember that, despite its final fall, the Eastern Empire lasted longer than any in history, nor did its eclipse in any way diminish the tactical brilliance of some of its emperor-generals.

CHAPTER THREE

1. De Beer (Alps), 84.
2. Hargreaves, 58–9.
3. Griffith, Sun Tzu . . . , 24.
4. Ibid., 63, 77, 73.
5. Ibid., 139, 129.
6. Ibid., 66, 102, 106.
7. Ibid., 92.
8. Gordon, 57.
9. Oman, A History of the Art of War . . . , I, 5–7.
10. Hoyt, Europe in the Middle Ages . . . , 31.
11. Gordon, 57.
12. Ibid.
13. Ibid., 58.
14. Fuller, The Decisive Battles . . . , I, 288–9.
15. Oman, I, 15. See also, Hoyt.
16. Older historians, such as Oman and Fuller, have held that Fridigern's victory foreshadowed a new epoch in the history of war: cavalry would replace infantry as the decisive arm (which it did in the Middle Ages); but see, Lynn

White, 7, who argues that, during the battle of Adrianople, an impetuous advance had already confused the Roman army and had made it particularly vulnerable to cavalry action, " . . . not because of superior strength [of Ostrogoth cavalry], but rather by effecting a surprise attack which amounted almost to ambush."

17. Oman, I, 15.
18. Hoyt, *Europe in the Middle Ages* . . . , 36.
19. Gordon, 61.
20. Fuller, *The Decisive Battles* . . . , I, 288.
21. Mahon, 95, 107–8.
22. Ibid., 422 ff. See also, 431 ff.: Even Belisarius could not escape the dissension of Justinian's last years. In 564, the emperor accused the general of trying to assassinate him, stripped him of all honors and holdings, and had him blinded. As a beggar, the victim of Justinian's wrath stood before the gates of the convent of Laurus and pleaded, "Give a penny to Belisarius the General."
23. Preston, 52.
24. Ibid., 52–6. See also, Toy, *A History of Fortification*, 52, 61.
25. Ibid.
26. Schevill, 73–4.
27. Howard-Johnston.
28. Oman, I, 201–2
29. Ibid., 219–22. Oman points out that command confusion, specifically alleged treachery of the cavalry commander, Andronicus, undoubtedly played a major role in the Byzantine defeat.

CHAPTER 4

Warfare in the West • The great Mongol invasion of Europe • Vietnam's savior: Marshal Tran Hung Dao • Edward I's pacification of Wales • The English experience in Scotland: William Wallace and Robert Bruce • The guerrilla leader Bertrand du Guesclin •

STRATEGY AND TACTICS of the Middle Ages, particularly of feudal warfare in Europe, remain obscure. Modern historians tend to argue that combat was not as stylized as we normally think, but rather that it differed from country to country and from commander to commander—in other words, that warfare continued to develop as it had since the birth of time. If the mounted knight enjoyed his place in the sun, his role slowly diminished as mercenaries and citizen soldiers augmented feudal hosts and as armies grew in strength and staying power essential for longer campaigns. If the mounted knight outlasted feudal warfare, he eventually succumbed to weapon development, first the longbow, which shredded French cavalry formations at Crécy and Agincourt, then gunpowder.

While Western knights continued to depend on weight to give their armies shock power, Eastern armies continued to stress mobility. Like the Franks and Normans, Eastern peoples were also on the move. By the twelfth century, successive migratory waves (which started around 12,000 B.C.) had populated Vietnam, Malaya, the Philippines, Java, Indonesia, and Australia. The dominant power in Southeast Asia was China, which held suzerainty over what are today's Tibet, Korea, and most of Vietnam.

Toward the end of the twelfth century, the Mongols sharply challenged the Chinese position. Genghis Khan (1162–1227) succeeded in consolidating a group of Mongolian tribes, nomads living between Lakes Baikah and Baikal in Asia, and in forming and training an army which in 1214 penetrated the Great Wall of China and captured Peking, capital of the Kin dynasty.

A few years later, while one army remained to fight in China, Gen-

36

Mongol invasions

0 400 800 1200 miles

M.E.P.

ghis led another force west, conquered the Khwarazm Empire (northern India-Turkestan-Persia), and marched north to defeat a Russian army on the Dnieper. This empire did not collapse with the Khan's death, in 1227; his son Ogdai, aided by such civil counselors as the brilliant Yeliu Chutsai and by such outstanding generals as Subutai, defeated the Hin Chinese to win northern China before invading the lands of the Sung dynasty, to the south. Ogdai then led his army across Asia to invade Russia, sack Kiev, conquer most of Poland, and, early in 1241, occupy Hungary.[1] Ogdai's sudden death caused the Mongols to return to Asia, where, after considerable delay, Mangu Khan was elected Great Khan in 1251. Under his rule and that of Kublai, who succeeded him in 1260, the main empire moved east, leaving subordinate empires in Russia and Persia. Although the Mongolian Empire would prove short-lived, the Yuan dynasty, which Kublai established in China, lasted until 1368.

The Mongol conquests represent a tremendous military achievement. Basil Liddell Hart wrote that "...in scale and in quality, in surprise and in mobility, in the strategic and in the tactical indirect approach, their campaigns rival if they do not surpass any in history."[2]

The Mongol armies consisted primarily of horse archers who, in the Eastern tradition, literally lived on horseback. Armed with bow, lance and scimitar, the hardy, well-trained warriors used two varieties of bows and three "calibers" of arrows for various tactical situations. Some authorities believe that, as early as 1218, Genghis Khan used guns and gunpowder for siege work in the conquest of Turkestan. According to Marco Polo, who visited Kublai Khan's empire, each warrior marched with eighteen horses and mares in order to supply himself with

37

milk, blood, meat and remounts. Subutai's armies marched in widely separated columns, the flanks ahead of the center; such was the mobility of the cavalry that the columns could converge upon plan, after which they were tactically controlled in the Chinese fashion by a variety of signals.

Tactically, Subutai's armies were not suitable for fighting in hilly, wooded country, nor did they carry siege machines. The most effective defense occurred in Bohemia, where Václav I " . . . saw to it that Prague, Olomouc, Brno, and other towns in Bohemia and Moravia were adequately fortified; he also ordered the monasteries to be turned into strongholds so that the civilian population could take refuge there, while the monks, who were provided with weapons, received instructions to store up food."[3] How effective the Bohemian defense would have proved had the Mongols remained is another matter, but perhaps Václav was aware of their political shortcomings. As it turned out, he was correct: Ogdai's sudden death brought a succession problem and caused the Mongols to return to Asia.

A few years later, the Mongols turned south to Vietnam, an invasion of the Red River Valley with a force, according to ancient annals, doubtlessly exaggerated, of two hundred thousand. " . . . The Vietnamese, as they would so often do later, abandoned their cities and headed for the hills, leaving their capital to be burned by the invaders. But the Mongols, still unused to the tropics and tropical diseases, were defeated by the environment; after a fruitless pursuit of the Vietnamese, they withdrew."[4] About 1268, Kublai Khan led another invasion aimed at conquering the Champa kingdom on the Gulf of Tonkin, an inconclusive campaign described by Marco Polo.

Once fleet of foot, the Mongol armies were growing heavier with the addition of infantry and even war elephants. In 1284, such a host descended for the third time on Vietnam. And now appeared a remarkable man: Marshal Tran Hung Dao, " . . . who withdrew to the mountains, wrote his *Essential Summary of Military Arts*, and began to train his troops for protracted guerrilla warfare! 'The enemy must fight his battles far from his home base for a long time. . . . We must further weaken him by drawing him into protracted campaigns. Once his initial dash is broken, it will be easier to destroy him.' "[5]

Three years passed before Kublai's "initial dash was broken," but he nonetheless had to withdraw. Dao now had his guerrillas plant " . . . thousands of iron-spiked stakes in the Bach-Dang river north of Haiphong through which the Mongol fleet had to pass. The ships arrived at high tide, when the stakes were submerged. A small Vietnamese naval force cleverly decoyed the enemy into a fight which looked like an easy victory until the Mongol ships found themselves stranded or gored on the stakes by the momentum of the out-flowing tides. That was the moment Marshal Dao's infantry chose to attack and defeat the invaders."[6]

Marshal Dao knew how to use a victory. Bowing to the inevitable, he voluntarily began paying tribute to the Mongols ruling in Peking.

One of the most interesting pacification campaigns of these turbulent years was Edward I's conquest of Wales. In the preceding two hundred years, Anglo-Norman expeditions had only partially subjugated these rude peoples who enjoyed making war against each other almost as much as against the English.

Edward, who came to the throne in 1272 and reigned until 1307, did not return to England until 1274. To his annoyance, the powerful northern Welsh ruler, Llewellyn ap Gruffydd, otherwise the Prince of Wales, refused to do homage. Edward decided to force the issue and invade the country, but wisely took his time in organizing the expedition. In this interim period, he came on a remarkable analysis of earlier campaigns in Wales written by a highly educated and widely traveled cleric who was half Welsh, Giraldus Cambrensis, otherwise called Gerald de Barri. Giraldus had served in Wales and had advised Henry II on his pacification campaigns.[7] He had written a history of the Norman conquest of Ireland; two other works, *Itinerarium Kambriae* and *Descriptio Kambriae,* not only offered generous and generally accurate information on Welsh guerrilla tactics but possibly gave Edward a rough plan of campaign.[8]

Giraldus emphasized the totally hostile environment of this mountainous and wooded target area: dreadful weather, few roads, mostly barren land whose entire settlements disappeared into remote mountain valleys to leave an invading army to fend for itself.

Although Welsh princes preferred to let land and weather defeat an invader, Giraldus left no doubt of their willingness to fight under favorable conditions. A tradition of universal military service existed: " ... when the trumpet sounds the alarm, the husbandman rushes as eagerly from the plow as the courtier from his court." Wearing light armor to retain mobility and armed with bows and spears, the Welsh bands fought in broken country, where they " ... relied on a single charge accompanied by wild shouts and the noise of trumpets, calculated to demoralize the enemy." If an attack failed, they disappeared into the woods. But Giraldus warned pursuers to look sharply for ambushes. He also warned that " ... the Welsh were as easy to defeat in a single battle as they were difficult to overcome in a protracted campaign."[9]

Was it possible to subdue them? It was, if the prince developed a strategy based on enemy weaknesses. Sounding remarkably like Sun Tzu fifteen centuries earlier, Giraldus wrote:

> ... The prince who would wish to subdue this nation, and govern it peaceably, must use this method. He must be determined to apply a diligent and constant attention to this purpose for a year at least; for a people who with a collected force will not openly attack the enemy, nor wait to be besieged in castles, is not to be overcome at the first onset, but to be worn down by prudent delay and patience. Let him divide their strength, and by bribes and promises endeavor to stir up one against the other, knowing the spirit of hatred and envy which generally prevails among them; and in the autumn let not only the marches [the border country], but also the interior part of the country be strongly fortified with castles, provisions, and trusted families.[10]

The clever prince would place an embargo on food and cloth coming into the country from England and a naval blockade to stop supply from Ireland. Let the harsh winter run out, and when the guerrillas were hungry and the land barren and unfriendly to ambush,

> . . . let a body of light-armed infantry penetrate into their woods and mountainous retreats, and let these troops be supported and relieved by others; and thus by frequent changes, and replacing the men who are either fatigued or slain in battle, this nation may be ultimately subdued. Nor can it be overcome without the above precautions, nor without great danger and loss of men. Though many of the English hired troops may perish in a day of battle, money will procure as many more on the morrow for the same service; but to the Welsh, who have neither foreign nor stipendiary troops, the loss is for the time irreparable.[11]

Supported by Lords Marchers, or English border barons, Edward invaded Wales in 1277, with a force of several thousand cavalry, infantry and the medieval equivalent of engineers, the whole supported by a secure home base and a small fleet sailing from the Cinque Ports.

Edward intended to advance along the coast " . . . and then to strike up the river valleys, fortifying posts provisionally during the campaign, where he could construct permanent castles afterwards when Wales was annexed." His first concern centered on the danger of ambushes in densely wooded border country. Having surmounted this obstacle by building and suitably defending "a very broad road," the king built his first forward base at Flint, the timber being brought around by sea. Here he also received considerable troop reinforcements, so that by the end of August he counted over fifteen thousand infantry, a force that included some nine thousand Welsh allies. He used Welsh labor for road and base construction, and, from extant documents, we know that he paid and fed them well.

Pushing on to Rhuddlan by a newly cut road, he again received supply from his fleet. He now marched to Conway and captured the island of Anglesey, described by Giraldus as "the granary of Wales," in time for the harvest.

Edward's carefully conducted campaign had thrown Llewellyn off balance. Deprived of support from tribes which had submitted to the king, short of food with winter approaching, and unable to attract the invaders to the interior, where he wanted to fight, Llewellyn accepted the inevitable and signed a treaty that extended English rule and administration deep into Wales. Edward had won a magnificent campaign with a minimum expenditure of life, but to maintain his sovereignty he was forced to build a series of expensive castles and to meet heavy administrative costs.[12]

Peace lasted less than five years. Although King Edward apparently

41

did not intend to absorb Wales into England, he and his lieutenants left no doubts of its subordination to his overlordship:

> . . . his officers were nowhere harsher than in Wales, where the people, unaccustomed to a minute legality, complained that they were worse treated than Saracens or Jews. . . . David [Llewellyn's brother] was alienated from the English cause by petty quarrels with Reginald Grey, justice of Chester, who insisted on making him answer before the English courts, hanged some of his vassals, and carried a military road through his woods.

Judging the time ripe for rebellion, in early 1282 Llewellyn and David captured and burned a few fortresses " . . . and the Welsh spread over the marches, waging a war of singular ferocity, slaying, and even burning, young and old women and sick people in the villages." But most strong points held out while Edward, who was unprepared for the rebellion, hastily mobilized an army by summoning troops from all over England and even Gascony. By June, he had collected around seven thousand infantry. Divided into two armies, supported by cavalry and supplied by a small fleet, this expedition marched on Anglesey, which Edward considered "the noblest feather in Llewellyn's wing," and which the navy also attacked.[13]

While the fleet carried out a blockade and soldiers cut down sanctuary forests in the border country, skirmishing continued into early winter, when Llewellyn agreed to negotiate and " . . . presented his list of grievances as justifying the war." Edward refused to discuss them, declaring that Llewellyn's action " . . . was inexcusable, because he had revolted first without appealing to the crown, being himself always ready to hear and investigate."[14]

During a battle in the rugged interior a month after this exchange, Llewellyn, possibly lured by treachery to a meeting of local chieftains, was caught without his armor and run through. Edward sent his head to London, where, garlanded with silver ivy leaves and mounted on a lance, it was carried through the streets and exhibited on the Tower. The campaign continued until David and other chiefs surrendered, in late April.

To judge David, Edward summoned a parliament " . . . of barons, judges, knights and burgesses":

> . . . The sentence, which excited no horror at the time, was probably passed without a dissentient voice. David was sentenced, as a traitor, to be drawn slowly to the gallows; as a murderer, to be hanged; as one who had shed blood during Passiontide, to be disembowelled after death; and, for plotting the King's death, his

dismembered limbs were to be sent to Winchester, York, Northampton, and Bristol. . . . [15]

This short war cost Edward some ninety-eight thousand pounds, an immense sum even though it included about twenty-three thousand pounds for repair of castles. Supplementing an already large income with taxes on his subjects and with loans from Italian bankers, he had continually to borrow more money to fight further guerrilla wars before he controlled the area.[16]

Edward encountered a different set of operational factors in his later pacification of Scotland, where rebel forces enjoyed generous space for temporary sanctuary.

The trouble started in 1295. John Balliol, whom Edward had helped to the throne, had incurred baronial ire by paying homage to Edward's overlordship. Under baronial pressure, he renounced allegiance to England and formed an alliance with France. The following year, Edward invaded the lowlands and captured Berwick, where his army indulged in a general slaughter of Scots, men and women, an estimated eight thousand to sixty thousand lives, who fell "like the leaves in autumn," as one chronicler put it. After capturing other fortresses and towns and subduing the lowlands, Edward displayed a certain clemency, but tried " . . . to introduce the English system of government, for example the Lowlands were divided into shires, sheriffs were elected, and justices appointed. . . . "[17] As he erred in Wales, so in Scotland did he fail to respect the people's temper:

> . . . he tried to tax Scotland on the English scale; to repress the disorders of a rude country, the cattle-lifting and feuds that were almost part of its domestic economy, as rigorously as could be done in the heart of England; and to introduce English monks, and invest English clergymen of Scotch benefices. . . . [18]

Edward's treasurer, Cressingham, was said to have done everything " . . . that could irritate or aggrieve an impatient people," while his lord lieutenant, the Earl of Warrene, resided out of the country " . . . to escape its climate."

> . . . In his absence the soldiery were at once unemployed and uncontrolled, and they behaved with the license of conquerors; while the constant reductions in their number, made by Cressingham's economy, weakened their efficiency, and filled the country with disbanded mercenaries. The people were ready to rise in arms, and only wanted a leader. . . . [19]

Most of the barons were in France fighting for Edward. But now a young gentleman, William Wallace, son of a country laird, took vengeance against some grievance, attacked Lanark garrison and killed a judge. Hunted as an outlaw, he slowly built up a band and acquired a reputation for skill and cunning in attacking English garrisons, that attracted other dissidents such as William Douglas and later young Robert Bruce to what soon became full-blown rebellion. Although Scots nobles came to terms with the English, Wallace continued to fight and in September 1297 won the battle of Stirling, " . . . the turning-point in the fortunes of Scotch independence."[20] After putting John on the throne—he himself became guardian—he raided deep into northern

44

English counties and when pursued scorched the earth in order to defeat the king's hungry soldiers.

Little is known of either Wallace or his tactics. He apparently fought a rigorous guerrilla war; he was later indicted for murders, robberies, and sacrilege in churches. His methods undoubtedly stemmed in part from English severity, and he seems to have won and retained a considerable popular following in these precarious years when he was attempting to move a nation. His over-all strategy backfired in 1298, when Edward cornered and badly beat his army at Falkirk. Relying primarily on the missile (the long bow) as opposed to cavalry charges, the English were said to have taken ten thousand Scots lives.[21] However, as a later historian pointed out: " . . . Edward's victory was decisive, but it was almost profitless. The Scotch left him nothing but the possession of so much desolated land as his army could camp upon."[22]

Wallace escaped to the continent, where he attempted without success to enlist aid from France and from the pope. His best weapon remained the Scots people, especially the lowlanders, who for several years suffered the ravages of the English while still fighting back. The uneven war continued until 1303, when Edward, strengthened at home and at peace with France, led an invasion in such strength as to cause Scots nobles to lose heart and come to terms. William Wallace also petitioned for the king's amnesty—without success. Edward sent him to London, where " . . . he was taken through the streets in a mock procession . . . with a crown of laurel on his head, and tried by a special commission, consisting of three judges." The temper of the day probably explains the severity of sentence. William Wallace was dragged through London streets to the gallows and hanged—but was cut down while still alive and disemboweled.[23]

Robert Bruce, son of a gentleman who had fought on the king's side at Falkirk: as King Robert of Scotland, thirty-two years old, he picked up the standard of revolt and for nearly a quarter of a century waged intermittent warfare against the English. His army was never strong: he never once mustered a thousand cavalry. In the early battle of Methven, he ordered his men to cover themselves with linen smocks to conceal a lack of defensive armor; Pembroke countered this ruse by agreeing to fight on Monday, then marching on Sunday evening to catch Bruce by surprise and destroy his army.

Bruce escaped with a few followers, and it is doubtful that he would have survived except for space and spirit. Although fear caused many Scots to withhold support of the rebels, the dying Edward's harsh policy turned others to Bruce. Edward's temper toward the end is best expressed by his reply to pleas for the life of a captured Scottish baron.

"His only privilege," Edward said, "shall be, to be hanged on a higher gallows than the rest, as his treasons have been more flagrant and numerous."[24]

Bruce saved his cause by disappearing "into the landscape" of the highlands where he slowly gained recruits. Escaping capture or destruction a dozen times, he fought small engagements and his strength continued to grow. Edward died and John of Brittany replaced Pembroke. By the end of 1308, Bruce controlled most of Scotland north of the Tay. A year later he held his first parliament, at St. Andrews; he also gained rapprochement with Philip of France, a diplomatic move that caused Pope Clement once again to excommunicate him for " . . . damnable perseverance in iniquity."[25] For five years, Bruce continued retreating before superior English forces while his army sporadically raided northern English counties, which on occasion bought off the invaders for hefty sums. Guerrilla attacks on English-held castles reduced them one by one. In time, Bruce grew strong enough to meet the enemy in pitched battle at Bannockburn, which he won.

Although the Hundred Years' War holds certain orthodox tactical interest, we are mainly concerned with the figure of Bertrand du Guesclin, a guerrilla leader who eventually became High Constable of France, a Breton, a small man with flashing green eyes over a flat nose, " . . . uncouth, querulous, almost illiterate, without fortune. . . . " But with force, with imagination and with a fine disregard for the artificial niceties of knightly warfare.

At eighteen, he headed a small band of fellow Bretons in a war of ambush against the English who occupied Brittany. At thirty, he achieved sudden fame by disguising his small band as woodcutters and capturing the castle of Fougeray.[26]

Appointed to the king's service for this feat, Du Guesclin next opened a guerrilla campaign against an English army besieging the fortress of Rennes. By a series of hit-and-run raids, he slowly drew the bulk of English forces away from the starving fortress, then captured an English food convoy, which he delivered, along with troop reinforcements, to the hard-pressed defenders. Continuing to lead guerrilla campaigns, he became increasingly famous for his rapid movements, night and day, and for the detailed preparation and suddenness of his attacks against enemy flanks and rear.

During a temporary lull in the war, Charles V gave the fiery Breton the task of freeing the French countryside from the barbaric pillaging of the "Grand Companies"—groups of mercenaries formerly in English and French pay and now little better than outlaw groups, whose leaders bore such picturesque names as "Smashing Bars" and "Arm of Iron."

These *routiers* had " . . . pillaged and plundered the realm to such an extent," says a chronicler, "that not even a cock was heard to crow in it."[27] Du Guesclin bribed the bulk of these to follow him to Spain. In the battle of Navarrete, against the Black Prince, most of them were killed and Du Guesclin was captured, but later ransomed.

When fighting with England started again, Charles V made Du Guesclin the High Constable, or commander in chief, of France. Du Guesclin used Fabian tactics to push the English from the country. With the regular army defending towns and castles in strength too great for English armies to overcome, Du Guesclin used *routiers* to wage almost purely guerrilla warfare. In Basil Liddell Hart's words, " . . . within less than five years he had reduced the vast English possessions in France to a slender strip of territory between Bordeaux and Bayonne. He had done it without fighting a battle."[28]

CHAPTER FOUR

1. Cheshire.
2. Liddell Hart, *The Decisive Wars of History,* 55.
3. Cheshire.
4. Fall, "Two Thousand Years of War in Vietnam."
5. Ibid.
6. Ibid.
7. Giraldus Cambrensis, *The Autobiography of Giraldus Cambrensis.*
8. Beeler, *Warfare in England 1066–1189,* 197.
9. Ibid.
10. Ibid., 198.
11. Ibid.
12. Morris, 81. Edward built ten castles between 1277 and 1295; several of the castles are extant; Pearson, II.
13. Pearson, II, 323–4, 326–7. See also, Davies and Worts.
14. Morris, 179.
15. Pearson, II, 329–30.
16. Morris, 197. Amazingly complete records including military and civil payrolls are extant.
17. Davies and Worts, 211–12.
18. Pearson, II, 404.
19. Ibid., 405.
20. Ibid., 409. See also, Mackenzie, 105: The despised Cressingham fell in this battle. The Scots flayed his body and " . . . distributed the hide as souvenirs."
21. Mackenzie, 111–16, offers an excellent analysis of Edward's tactics.
22. Pearson, II, 415.
23. Ibid., 426–8.
24. Ibid., 444.
25. Mackenzie, 169, 209 ff.
26. Editions G. P.
27. Lacroix, 53.
28. Liddell Hart, *The Decisive Wars of History,* 52.

CHAPTER 5

THE INTRODUCTION and successful application of gunpowder to warfare placed guerrilla operations into general eclipse both in Europe and abroad. A series of peculiar environments unfavorable either to guerrilla or quasi-guerrilla tactics resulted from a technological-tactical competition between emergent European dynastic states. These were sufficiently wealthy to wage almost incessant war in bids for religious-dynastic supremacy at home and imperial supremacy abroad. Although often prolonged and sometimes fought with a ferocity defying even contemporary imagination, these wars were "limited" in the sense of their being fought for specific political objectives usually by professional armies—a state of affairs that in the West was not going to change until the end of the eighteenth century.

In the West, the entire *direction* of war was changing. By the end of the fifteenth century, it was becoming a serious profession, a matter of state interest. One of the first persons to respect this trend was Machiavelli (1469–1527), who, in 1499, witnessed the French invasion of the Italian city-states. In his subsequent, often profound and generally disturbing works, he advised that " . . . the foundation of states is a good military organization"; accordingly, " . . . a Prince should therefore have no other aim or thought, nor take up any other thing for study, but war and its organization and discipline"[1] (which is precisely what Sun Tzu counseled eighteen hundred or so years earlier).

His words gained reinforcement by almost constant weapon development. The appearance of the arquebus, whose primitive and unreliable matchlock ignition was eventually replaced first by the wheel-lock, then the flintlock, systems, the reluctance of some commanders to employ the new weapons without diluting the ranks of pikemen, the discovery of better casting methods for artillery made more mobile and accurate by the development of the limber and trunnion, the invention of the wheel-lock pistol, the evolution of castles into fortifications capable of withstanding prolonged artillery sieges—each made war more expensive, each moved it increasingly into the hands of the state, which relied more and more on professional armies commanded by great captains who changed tactical values of war without altering its ferocity.

Technology ruled the battlefield. The escalation of violence that it wrought was halted not by choice of rulers and commanders but only because the ghastly wars of religion, the plague, and the excesses of the Thirty Years' War, by ravaging large areas of Europe and sharply limiting the supply of manpower, exercised a moderating influence on the battlefield. With soldiers in short supply, difficult to recruit and expensive to train, commanders became increasingly reluctant to expend them in battle. The French general Turenne (1611–75), who, along with Condé, bridged the interim years between the end of the Thirty Years' War and the reign of Louis XIV (1643–1715), " . . . regarded battle as a last resort, to be accepted with caution and then only when conditions seemed favorable."[2]

This made increasingly good sense in the light of tactical changes. Vauban's socket bayonet fitted to the flintlock musket (the *fusil*—thus, the fusilier) had forever eliminated the pikeman and had caused the old infantry formation in depth (*en profondeur*) to yield to an embryonic line formation. During the last half of the seventeenth century, General Jean Martinet (from whom we take our common noun martinet) trained his French troops to deploy from column into line and advance in three ranks, pausing to fire platoon volleys on command, and finally to attack with the bayonet. The "line" was a geometrical formation—it was a prelude to the famed "square" of lines, which provided ideal defense against cavalry charges—and the troops were trained to advance in unison, keeping step at a stately cadence of eighty paces per minute. Naturally enemy artillery fire exacted a tremendous toll from these shoulder-to-shoulder ranks, as did volleys of musket fire delivered at no more than fifty paces (because of technological limitations).

Few commanders could afford the loss wrought by confrontation battles, which were not difficult to avoid. Since the new formations required open and level terrain, a commander not wishing to fight could retire to hilly, wooded country or to a defended strong point or city in order to spend the winter rebuilding forces for a fresh campaign. From this tactical prudence grew the sophisticated tactics of siegecraft and fortification, which further "slowed" battlefield action.

Nature, technology and economics combined to alter this situation, albeit slowly. Man's proclivity to procreation soon repaired former ravages. No less interested an observer than Frederick the Great pointed out that Emperor Ferdinand I had barely supported an army of 30,000, yet, in 1733, Charles VI effortlessly fielded 170,000; Louis XIII supported 60,000 soldiers, but, in the War of Succession, Louis XIV kept between 220,000 and 360,000 men in the field.[3] Technological improvements, for example the ring bayonet and the iron ramrod, started giving an edge to offensive warfare, while riches pouring in from overseas colonies provided rulers with the means to extend the battlefield.

As usual, great captains played a significant role. The efforts of Maurice of Nassau and Gustavus Adolphus to free formations from rigidness and restrictive weight were continued by Marlborough and Frederick the Great. Despite their efforts, war remained very restricted and sharply limited in political purpose, while possessing little tactical subtlety. Charles XII relied primarily on mobile-shock tactics pursued with a reckless charisma to defeat the Russians, Danes, Saxons and Poles in a series of battles, the Great Northern War, fought from 1700 to 1709; his impetuous nature and contempt for Peter the Great and the Russian army brought him defeat in detail at Poltava in 1709 and eliminated Sweden as a major power.

Marlborough's string of victories from 1704 to 1713 hinged on similar tactics, in which surprise played an important role, for example at Blenheim. By discarding care and caution common to the day, he gained complete strategic and tactical surprise, from which the French, fighting well, never recovered; at Oudenarde, he fought and won an "encounter" battle, a decidedly unorthodox practice at the time. Without question Marlborough's victories raised England to great-power status and forced France to sign the Treaty of Utrecht, but all this at a great cost in lives and treasure to gain a peace so fragile as to be chimerical.

Frederick the Great also displayed a tactical dualism. He maneuvered a lot, but he also fought a lot. In the *Instructions to His Generals,* he wrote: "In war the skin of a fox is at times as necessary as that of a lion, for cunning may succeed when force fails."[4] But he also advised: "War is decided only by battles and it is not decided except by them."[5]

If warfare in this transition period was not particularly subtle, neither did it as a rule involve the general population. Yet, here and there, we find suggestions of what was to come. Tyrone's rebellion in Ireland, at the end of the sixteenth century, was in many ways a guerrilla war, with villagers and farmers frequently involved. When the Earl of Essex failed to stamp out the rebellion, Elizabeth turned to Charles Blount, who utilized tactics that would become all too familiar in the colonial period: he burned crops, razed villages and held hostages. He also introduced light and very mobile cavalry units that operated from fortified towns to scour surrounding areas—altogether a tactical adaptation that in time brought an Irish defeat (though not for long).

Frederick the Great was nearly captured by irregular mounted bands of Hungarians and Serbs in his first Silesian campaign, in 1741. So effective were these guerrillas that they screened the Austrian advance and almost cost Frederick a defeat. He was so impressed with their tactics that he organized special light-cavalry units to counter them. In early 1742, he again encountered Moravian irregulars and retaliated by devastating the land and besieging Brünn, neither action very effective. The Hungarians and Moravians provide early examples of guerrilla forces complementing orthodox army operations, in this case those of Austrian and French armies in Silesia, Bohemia and Bavaria.[6]

Frederick encountered another ugly guerrilla situation in the second Silesian war. Leading his army south from Prague in 1744, he found himself in a barren, mountainous land whose peasants had buried their grain and hidden themselves and oxen in the forests. Some ten thousand Hungarian and Croatian hussars buzzed around his line of march, harassing foraging parties, striking columns in short, vicious attacks and cutting lines of communication until couriers failed to get through. Frederick's later, plaintive words describe a kind of warfare that in time would become only too familiar:

> . . . It might appear strange that an army as strong as the Prussian army could not hold this area in awe; force it to necessary deliveries [of supply]; to provide food; and to furnish numerous spies to keep it informed of the enemy's least movement. But one should understand that in Bohemia the nobility, priests and bailiffs are very attached to the house of Austria; that the religious difference furnishes an overwhelming obstacle to those people who are as stupid as they are superstitious, and that the [Vienna] court had ordered the peasants, all of whom were serfs, to abandon their hamlets at the Prussian approach, to bury their corn and hide in the neighboring forests—the court further promised to pay for all damage suffered from Prussian arms.

This was a particularly ugly situation for an army that depended largely on local provisions. Frederick continued:

> . . . The Prussian army thus found only deserted villages and wilderness: no one approached the camp to sell food; and the peas-

ants, who feared rigorous Austrian retribution, could not be won over despite the sum offered. These difficulties were compounded by a corps of 10,000 hussars which the Austrians had sent from Hungary and which cut army communications in terrain composed only of marshes, woods, boulders, and every possible type of defile. Because of his superiority in light troops, the enemy had the advantage of knowing all that transpired in the king's camp [that is, because of intercepted communications]; nor did the Prussians dare send out scouting parties, at least without sacrificing them, due to the superior enemy parties: thus the king's army, entrenched in the Roman style, was confined to its camp.[7]

The net result forced the king's retreat. So traumatic had been the experience, however, that during this hasty maneuver over seventeen thousand troops deserted. One important official, after describing general discontent, added, " . . . More than half the land has grievances against us." The experience exercised lasting influence on the soldier-king. A few months later, he won the battle of Hohenfriedberg, but declined to pursue the retreating columns deep into Bohemia.[8] The Austrians continued to use irregulars—the term guerrilla had not yet come into use—with great skill in the Silesian and Seven Years' wars (in which General Laudon among others emerged as a brilliant guerrilla commander). Almost every action in every campaign of these wars had irregular aspects, usually important and in several cases probably decisive. French and Prussian attempts to counter irregular operations greatly varied in result, but, even when successful, involved heavy investments of men and time. *Freikorps,* or voluntary units of irregulars established by the French and Prussians, notably Colonel Mayer's Prussian units, played a considerable role in the Seven Years' War.

While Frederick was so engaged, Corsican guerrillas were contesting Genoese rule of the island. This was scarcely unique. The Corsicans had been resisting someone from the third century B.C.; in those rare periods when they lacked an enemy, they delighted in fighting each other. The most recent trouble started with a revolt against Genoese rule in 1729. When the Genoese introduced German mercenaries, Corsican volunteers began guerrilla warfare. In 1732, the Germans suffered a bad defeat at Calenzana, the guerrillas being aided by villagers who threw beehives into German ranks.[9]

In 1738, the Genoese persuaded France to intervene. The first battalions, under Count de Boissieux, suffered a series of setbacks, but, in 1739, the Marquis de Maillebois took over, broke guerrilla resistance with a series of flying-column operations, and offered the people a reasonably fair peace. The French departed in 1741 and the Corsicans again rebelled.

After several years of intermittent fighting, Corsican guerrillas were up against it. But, in 1755, the twenty-nine-year-old Pasquale Paoli emerged as a national leader. The ubiquitous James Boswell, who later visited General Paoli, wrote of his accession: " . . . There was no subordination, no discipline, no money, hardly any arms and ammunition; and, what was worse than all, little union among the people."[10] Largely by personal persuasion, the tall, young and forceful general eliminated disruptive vendettas and brought the people to concerted action against the Genoese. Increased autonomy allowed Paoli to introduce reforms " . . . in agriculture, in education, in democratic government, in commerce and in public education."[11]

A legitimate republic might have emerged from Paoli's efforts, but, in 1764, the Genoese persuaded France to occupy the island for four years as payment of a debt, a cynical arrangement causing Rousseau to remark that if the French " . . . heard of a free man at the other end of the world, they would go thither for the pleasure of exterminating him."[12] Paoli's guerrillas forced the small French force into several garrison towns, where they seemed content to wait out their time. But, in 1768, the Genoese sold their interest in the island to France. The following year, in Napoleon's words, " . . . thirty thousand French vomited upon our coasts in drowning the throne of Liberty."[13] Although Paoli's guerrillas fought well, the odds could only have been redressed by foreign intervention. Boswell carried on a vigorous campaign to bring about English intervention and did raise a considerable sum of money to buy arms for Paoli. The English Government was not as impressed as the public with "Corsica Boswell," whose lobbying prompted Lord Holland to the remark, " . . . foolish as we are, we cannot be so foolish as to go to war because Mr. Boswell has been in Corsica."[14]

The French victory at Ponte-Nuovo forced Paoli to flee and practically ended Corsican resistance. The 1769 campaign cost the French, according to the *Annual Register of World Events,* some four thousand killed, and six thousand dead from either wounds or sickness.[15] Figures are lacking for Corsican deaths, but they must have been high.

Paoli's achievement is the more interesting because he wasn't a very good general. But he did foresee the strength inherent in nationalism. When the French objected that the Corsican nation had no regular troops, he replied: " . . . We would not have them. We should then have the bravery of this and the other regiment. At present every single man is as a regiment himself."[16] On another occasion, he said, " . . . all Corsicans should be soldiers and members of the militia with the heart to defend the motherland." He also persuaded priests to preach " . . . that a martyr's crown awaited a Corsican who died for his country."[17] Paoli was not too interested in the philosophy of revolution. He told Boswell, " . . . If a man would preserve the generous glow of patriotism, he must not reason too much. . . . I act from sentiment, not from reasonings." Nonetheless, he remained realistic. When discussing his war against the French, he told Boswell, " . . . Sir, if the event prove happy, we shall be called great defenders of liberty. If the event shall prove unhappy, we shall be called unfortunate rebels."[18]

A paucity of guerrilla warfare also existed in the early-colonial period, when Western explorers sailing east and west found a wide variety of ancient cultures, such as those encountered by Columbus in the Caribbean. Though most of the island tribes were armed with bows and arrows and palm-tree cudgels, some exhibiting a more bellicose attitude than others, the majority greeted the Spaniards in a friendly if cautious manner. The Europeans, in turn, treated them with a sort of genial contempt, not hestitating to impress them as guides or hostages for their interisland voyages, or even as slaves to take back to Spain. Some ugly incidents did occur, but whether in the New World or in Africa and later in Asia and the Pacific, the natives, though greater in number and well armed according to their standards, could not stand for long against trained soldiers protected by body armor and armed with muskets and cannon.[19]

Against such disproportionate odds, the native chose from three courses of action: he came to terms with the white man and attempted to profit thereby, as was the case with many coastal and some inland chieftains; or he retreated into jungle depths, moving when danger threatened either from the white man or from native tribes armed with Western weapons and indulging in the profitable slave trade reinstituted into Africa by the Portuguese and extended to the New World by the Spanish, French, English, Dutch and later the Americans; or, as happened mainly in continental areas, he physically contested the occupation of what he deemed his land.

Leaving location and chronology aside, the process of conversion (theft, if you will) remained generally the same: discovery followed by a coastal settlement, protection (ships' guns, a fort, a small garrison), consolidation (winning the tribes), initial exploitation, further discovery by penetration inland, protection (a fort and a garrison), consolidation, further expansion and further exploitation by the Catholic Church and/ or the throne, later by private but royally chartered commercial "companies"—the Virginia Company, the Dutch East India Company, the (British) East India Company—an inexorable process that gained the riches to support innumerable dynastic-religious wars in Europe while laying the groundwork for later, hemispheric wars.

The colonizing process differed in proportion to motives of the home country, strength devoted to the particular effort, and environment, both human and natural, of the target area. The first settlers in America arrived with a minimum of professional military support. In 1607, Jamestown settlers, heeding Captain John Smith's advice, formed " . . . immediately into three groups: one to erect fortifications for defense, one to serve as a guard and to plant a crop, the third to explore."[20]

In Virginia and New England, settlers encountered hostile Indians almost immediately, and for many decades had to rely for survival on ready militia forces. The effectiveness of these varied considerably. In general, the newcomers tried to assimilate the best features of Indian tactics, which stressed many of the features of guerrilla warfare: small-unit operations, loose formations, informal dress, swift movement, fire discipline, terror, ambush, and surprise attack. They were aided by concentration of numbers, and they also became adept at marksmanship, which grew more accurate as weapons improved.

As frontiers expanded to remove the immediate Indian challenge to rear areas, settled colonists began to adopt European methods of warfare. Professor Weigley has noted that by the time of King Philip's War (1675–76) colonial militia tactics had become too formal and European to fight successful Indian-style warfare. Unable to counter "murderous" ambushes, the colonists began relying on Indian mercenaries. Orthodoxy advanced to such an extent that, by the mid-eighteenth century, militia commanders, upon Colonel George Washington's advice, were studying Humphrey Bland's *Treatise on Military Discipline*, " . . . the leading English tactical manual of the day." In 1754, when the French and Indian War started, Washington wrote that " . . . Indians are the only match for Indians; and without these we shall ever fight upon unequal Terms."[21]

The arrival of regular British regiments under General Braddock to fight the French and Indians encouraged the colonial trend toward orthodoxy. These units, splendidly equipped and perfectly drilled in the formal, Continental school made famous by Frederick the Great, were impressive enough and with better leadership and considerable adaptation might have coped satisfactorily with the new tactical environment. Braddock, however, suffered defeat in detail when he encountered an irregular force of French colonials and Indians in the forests of the Monongahela Valley. His force of fourteen hundred regulars and provincials was shredded by some nine hundred enemy using guerrilla tactics—he lost well over half his men and he himself died from wounds.[22]

The British reacted by slowing down operations and by making specific tactical changes. In 1755, a Swiss mercenary, Colonel Henri Bouquet, assumed command of a new light-infantry regiment and set

56

MONONGAHELA, JULY 8, 1755

- British
□ Wagons
⊢ Cattle, Packhorses
= French, Indians

Hollow Way

Turtle Creek

R. MONONGAHELA

M.E.P.

about teaching it to fight Indians properly. Bouquet was altogether a remarkable man. A skilled veteran of European fighting, he quickly adapted to the American scene, and we are fortunate to have a lengthy work which, though describing his successful campaigns of 1763, offers an insight into his earlier thinking. A paragraph in the introduction of this work bears quoting:

> . . . Those who have only experienced the severities and dangers of a campaign in Europe, can scarcely form an idea of what is to be done and endured in an American war. But in an American campaign every thing is terrible; the face of the country, the climate, the enemy. There is no refreshment for the healthy, nor relief for the sick. A vast unhospitable desert [sic], unsafe and treacherous, surrounds them, where victories are not decisive, but defeats are ruinous; and simple death is the least misfortune which can happen to them. This forms a service truly critical, in which all the firmness of the body and mind is put to the severest trial; and all the exertions of courage and address are called out. If the actions of these rude campaigns are of less dignity, the adventures in them are more interesting to the heart, and more amusing to the imagination, than the events of a regular war.[23]

To this appreciation he added one of the enemy, for whom he held the greatest respect. In the new tactical environment, the Indian, not the white man, was the real professional:

... Let us suppose a person, who is entirely unacquainted with the nature of this service, to be put at the head of an expedition in America. We will further suppose that he has made the dispositions usual in Europe for a march, or to receive an enemy; and that he is then attacked by the savages. He cannot discover them, tho' from every tree, log or bush, he receives an incessant fire, and observes that few of their shot are lost. He will not hesitate to charge those invisible enemies, but he will charge in vain. ... notwithstanding all his endeavours, he will still find himself surrounded by a circle of fire, which, like an artificial horizon, follows him every where.

Unable to rid himself of an enemy who never stands his attacks, and flies when pressed, only to return upon him again with equal agility and vigour; he will see the courage of his heavy troops droop, and their strength at last fail them by repeated and ineffectual efforts.

He must therefore think of a retreat, unless he can force his way thro' the enemy. But how is this to be effected? his baggage and provisions are unloaded and scattered, part of his horses and drivers killed, others dispersed by fear, and his wounded to be carried by soldiers already fainting under the fatigue of a long action. The enemy, encouraged by his distress, will not fail to encrease the disorder, by pressing upon him on every side, with redoubled fury and savage howlings.

He will probably form a circle or a square, to keep off so daring an enemy, ready at the least opening to fall upon him with the destructive tomahawk: but these dispositions, tho' a tolerable shift for defence, are neither proper for an attack, nor a march thro' the woods.

Bouquet was an educated man who could remind his readers that " ... neither is there any thing new or extraordinary in this way of fighting, which seems to have been common to most Barbarians." He offered numerous examples not only from antiquity, but from his own century, pointing to light-infantry formations such as those raised by Marshal de Saxe and Frederick the Great. From his own extensive experience, he knew that as a "general maxim" the Indians " ... surround their enemy. The second, that they fight scattered, and never in a compact body. The third, that they never stand their ground when attacked, but immediately give way, to return to the charge." It followed, then:

1st. That the troops destined to engage Indians, must be lightly cloathed, armed, and accoutred.
2d. That having no resistance to encounter in the attack or defence, they are not to be drawn up in close order, which would only expose them without necessity to a greater loss.
And, lastly, that all their evolutions must be performed with great

rapidity; and the men enabled by exercise to pursue the enemy closely, when put to flight, and not give them time to rally.

He followed these general recommendations with specific advice in considerable detail on such items as clothing, arms, training, construction of camps and settlements, logistics, and various tactical formations—one is reminded of Caesar's work on Gaul. Under his tutelage, the company replaced the battalion as the unit of maneuver; troops learned to fire from kneeling and prone positions, and to march through woods in single file with scouts in front and on the flanks. Such alterations would not work miracles. It was not

> . . . to be expected that this method will remove all obstacles, or that those light troops can equal the savages in patience, and activity; but, with discipline and practice, they may in a great measure supply the want of these advantages, and by keeping the enemy at a distance afford great relief and security to the main body.[24]

The British also used Indian scouts whenever possible and tried, unsuccessfully, to form an Indian regiment. Lord Howe, who arrived in 1757, retained a famous Indian fighter, Robert Rogers, to instruct him and his men in the fine art of guerrilla warfare. Rogers and other scouts later formed independent companies of frontiersmen who were to carry out scouting missions as well as use Indian tactics to protect lines of communication.[25] The British commander in chief in the colonies, Lord Loudoun, attached British officers to these units, and some of them later formed officer cadres for Gage's new regiment formed in 1758—the first light-infantry regiment in the British Army.[26]

Another British general, Brigadier James Wolfe, faced the tactical problems posed by Indians in the Quebec expedition from May to September 1759. His "General Orders" called for constant "care and precaution." But Wolfe introduced a Cromwellian note, not so much from prudery but from sound tactical instinct. He forbade swearing and scalping " . . . except when the enemy are Indians, or Canads [Canadians] dressed like Indians . . . no churches, houses, or buildings of any kind are to be burned or destroy'd without orders . . . the peasants who yet remain in their habitations, their women and children are to be treated with humanity; if any violence is offer'd to a woman, the offender shall be punish'd with death."[27]

Such temporary accommodations to a peculiar tactical environment did not immediately alter an ingrained rigid and inflexible nature of British regiments. Enthusiasm for light infantry did not claim many orthodox commanders, even though, by 1770, each battalion possessed a company of light infantry—but, too often, this unit served more a disciplinary than a tactical purpose, containing the most troublesome soldiers.[28]

American colonists, on the other hand, continued to be influenced militarily by terrain and temperament. Despite the best efforts of Washington and other militia commanders to instill formal British discipline, American formations remained fairly informal.

This was understandable. American settlers possessed a much more individual outlook than their European brethen, and they were better marksmen. The farmers and woodsmen who in 1775 voluntarily took up muskets and rifles to defy British rule were accustomed to hunting small game at a time when laws against poaching and possession of firearms prevailed in Europe. The greenest American recruit aimed instinctively at a target, while his European opposite was trained only to point the piece at the enemy and fire volleys on command.

The potential of this type of warfare, particularly when fought by men infected with the emotional virus of revolution, was not wasted on the British commander in chief, General Gage. Contrary to most British officials and officers, who deemed the colonial soldier inferior to the British regular, Gage warned at outbreak of hostilities that he would need considerably larger forces and a year or two to subdue the New Englanders. Since other colonies would undoubtedly come to the aid of the North, " . . . he urged that the Ministry estimate the number of men and the sums of money needed, and then double their figures."[29]

Although early colonial militias and the 1st Continental Regiment (authorized by the Continental Congress in 1775) soon gave way to a regular army commanded by General George Washington, light-infantry tactics flourished throughout the revolution, which even in the North displayed guerrilla overtones.

One was the American soldier's use of terrain with which he was only too familiar. General Burgoyne, who himself would surrender to rebel wrath, early warned:

> . . . It is not to be expected that the rebel Americans will risk a general combat or a pitched battle, or even stand at all, except behind intrenchments as at Boston. Accustomed to felling of timber and to grubbing up trees, they are very ready at earthworks and palisading, and will cover and intrench themselves wherever they are for a short time left unmolested with surprising alacrity. . . . Composed as the American army is, together with the strength of the country, full of woods, swamps, stone walls, and other inclosures and hiding-places, it may be said of it that every private man will in action be his own general, who will turn every tree and bush into a kind of temporary fortress, from whence, when he hath fired his shot with all the deliberation, coolness, and uncertainty which hidden safety inspires, he will skip as it were to the next,

and so on for a long time till dislodged either by cannon or by a resolute attack of light infantry.[30]

Another tactic was the voluntary co-operation sometimes offered by the civil population to the revolutionary army: Burgoyne, in his Saratoga campaign of 1777, faced something akin to a scorched-earth policy as he marched from Montreal to the Hudson. By the time he reached Saratoga, the Continentals, together with New York and New England militias, had concentrated in strength sufficient to force his surrender.

Another was the individual's role, particularly the marksman armed with the long-barreled Pennsylvania rifle. The Prussian General von Steuben, who arrived at Valley Forge in 1778 to teach Washington's soldiers linear tactics, recognized the difference in individual outlook and marksmanship ability between the farmer-woodsman and the European peasant and dispensed with traditional precision deployment in order to exploit more accurate American firepower.

But, generally speaking, Washington's tactics remained orthodox, nor did he, in Professor Weigley's words, " . . . essay any tactical innovations so unconventional as to approach what later generations would call guerrilla war."[31] Guerrilla warfare, however, did come into its own in the South, where, as we shall see, Lord Cornwallis faced many problems of a modern insurgency.

CHAPTER FIVE

1. Gilbert, 3.
2. Preston, 141.
3. Frédéric II, *Oeuvres* . . . , II, 46.
4. Ibid., XXVIII, 48.
5. Preston, 144.
6. Asprey, *Frederick the Great* . . . , 188–90, 239–45.
7. Frédéric II, III, 67–8.
8. Asprey, *Frederick the Great* . . . , 305, 325.
9. Caird, 85.
10. Boswell, 20.
11. McLaren, 89 ff.
12. Caird, 149.
13. McLaren, 146.
14. Boswell, 34.
15. Caird, 176.
16. Boswell, 72.
17. Caird, 140.
18. Boswell, 91, 71–2.
19. Morison and Obregón, 18 ff.
20. Weigley, 4.
21. Ibid., 11. See also, Fuller, *British Light Infantry* . . .
22. Weigley, 23–4, who suggests that had Lieutenant Colonel Thomas Gage, commanding Braddock's vanguard, reacted correctly, " . . . the superior numbers and discipline of the British would probably have effected the rout of the

enemy. . . . " See also, Fuller, *British Light Infantry* . . . , 85, who stresses Braddock's tactical ineptness. After citing British losses as 63 out of 86 officers and 914 of 1,373 men, he concludes: " . . . A French force of nine hundred irregulars, using Indian tactics, had beaten an English column fourteen hundred and fifty strong, using the tactics of Frederick the Great."

23. Anon., ix.
24. Ibid., 44–6. See also, Fuller, *British Light Infantry* . . . , 110:

> . . . First, by means of his [Bouquet's] advanced posts, he held the enemy at a distance; secondly, he collected his force together; thirdly, by four simultaneous charges, covered by fire, he broke the circle into four segments, that is, forced it to offer eight flanks to his attack; fourthly, he demoralized it by his fire, and, fifthly, pursued and annihilated it by means of his light troops, foot and horse. This formation against a savage foe is probably the most ingenious and effective that the history of irregular warfare has to record.

25. Weigley, 25–6, whose discussion on deeds claimed versus deeds achieved by Rogers is most interesting. See also, Hackworth, 492, 835–6: Rogers' nineteen-point "Standing Orders" was routine issue to American army units fighting in Vietnam in 1965.
26. Weigley, 25–6 See also, Preston, op. cit.; Paret, *Yorck and the Era of Prussian Reform:* in an introductory chapter, Professor Paret argues convincingly against the generally accepted influence of the American wars on European armies and tactics.
27. Fuller, *The Decisive Battles* . . . , II, 247–8.
28. Fuller, *British Light Infantry* . . . , 124–5.
29. Alden, *The South in the Revolution* . . . , 186–7.
30. Lloyd, *A Review of the History of Infantry,* 125–6.
31. Weigley, 67.

CHAPTER 6

Guerrilla warfare in the southern colonies • The background • Clinton's shift in strategy • Capture of Charleston • "Tarleton's Quarters" • Clinton's occupation policy • Conflict with Cornwallis' • Cornwallis takes command • The political situation • Colonial guerrilla resistance • Horatio Gates and the Continentals • Cornwallis' victory at Camden • Guerrilla leaders: Marion, Sumter, Pickens • Cornwallis' punitive policy • His decision to invade North Carolina • British defeat at King's Mountain, and Cornwallis' retreat • Marion's guerrilla tactics • Battles of Cowpens and Guilford Courthouse • Cornwallis marches for Virginia • Greene's offensive: final guerrilla operations

GUERRILLA ACTIVITY in the South occurred as early as July 1775 in Georgia, where Joseph Habersham organized a local group of "Liberty Boys." In addition to stealing gunpowder from a British ship, this group " . . . frightened neutrals and friends of Britain into quiet" during that crucial period when the patriots were rallying their forces. Patriot leaders raised similar groups in other southern colonies—no simple task since in many areas loyalists and neutrals outnumbered patriots. Some of these hastily organized bands contented themselves with chasing colonial governors and other officials aboard British warships and with burning loyalist homes and plantations and driving off the owners after subjecting them to an unpleasant application of tar and feathers. Other groups fought semiorthodox actions such as that at Moore's Creek Bridge, a patriot victory that virtually ended local Tory resistance.[1]

Such activity helped close the southern theater to regular British military operations until late 1778. At this time, General Sir Henry Clinton, British commander in chief, sent a force from New York to join with one raised by General Augustine Prevost from the St. Augustine garrison.[2] Clinton hoped to further an attrition strategy by seizing a series of coastal towns, thus forcing Washington to disperse his armies and lessen pressure against the British in the North. Both Clinton and his superior in London, Colonial Secretary Lord George Germain, also hoped the Tories in the deep South would rise in impressive numbers.[3]

In December, a small British force captured Savannah before seizing Augusta, a noteworthy victory that attracted Tories from as far away as North Carolina to the British colors. These reinforcements sometimes encountered hostile patriot militia forces such as that under Andrew Pickens, who met and defeated seven hundred Tories in South Carolina and " . . . hanged five prisoners as traitors," an example of prevailing sentiment.[4]

The failure of a patriot force supported by a French fleet to recapture Savannah and the withdrawal of this expedition to the West Indies caused Clinton to descend on the South Carolina coast with a large expeditionary force and place Charleston under siege. Cut off from the countryside by an army under General Lord Charles Cornwallis, Clinton's second-in-command, the Charleston garrison surrendered in May 1780.

Clinton now sent two corps into the colony's interior where loyalists came forth " . . . by the hundreds [to] take oaths of allegiance to the crown, and many took up arms in behalf of the King."[5] Cornwallis simultaneously marched against Colonel Buford's remaining rebels. Lieutenant Colonel Banastre Tarleton, commanding a dragoon regiment, caught up with a detachment of rebel infantry close to the North Carolina border. When the detachment commander surrendered, the British troops shot or stabbed 113 of the defenseless men to death and left another 150 bleeding to death before marching off with 53 prisoners—a despicable act indignantly described by the great British historian George Trevelyan.[6] To Carolina backwoodsmen, the senseless act became known as "Tarleton's Quarters"—a phrase we shall hear again.

Clinton's provost marshals meanwhile were rounding up diehard rebels and evacuating them along with prisoners of war to coastal islands. Clinton announced a parole system for those persons who promised not to take up arms against the British, and he also promised royal protection to men who took a special oath of allegiance to the Crown—but woe to any who joined the rebel bands. This carrot-and-stick policy seemed to have ended organized rebel resistance in Georgia and South Carolina by June. Important garrisons had been established in the interior and along the border and, with loyalists stirring in North Carolina, the area seemed under British control. " . . . I am clear in opinion," Clinton wrote to a friend, "that the Carolinas have been conquered in Charleston."[7] Clinton now turned over command to Cornwallis and

British Force 1780
Cornwallis' route
Outposts

0   50   100   200   300 miles

M.E.P.

sailed for New York. His orders to Cornwallis were to become a subject of controversy among historians. Apparently Clinton foresaw Cornwallis working slowly up the Carolina coast in conjunction with the British fleet, developing loyalist bases, then moving inland, building as he went—a methodical but progressive pacification campaign to attract loyalists and consolidate politically and militarily a new theater of war before moving north to take Virginia. The hitch was that Cornwallis lacked food, horses, wagons and money to carry out these orders and, just as important, he was not politically secure.

Cornwallis at first continued Clinton's velvet glove policy, at least to a degree. Although confiscating estates of absentee rebels, he returned stolen and confiscated property to royalists and he continued to carry out Clinton's generous parole system. His attitude, however, began to change in June, when submissive Americans in the Charleston area learned that substantial American reinforcements were on their way from the North and began to jump their paroles. One "good citizen," the second in command of a militia battalion, waited until his men were supplied with arms and ammunition, then hustled them off to join patriot forces in the interior.

Off came the velvet glove. But neither did the naked fist provide an answer. Rebel forces continued to plague the British. A newly arrived British general was soon complaining that " . . . the violence and the passions of these people are beyond every curb of religion, and Humanity, they are unbounded and every hour exhibits dreadful wanton mischiefs, murders, and violence of every kind, unheard of before. We find the country in great measure abandoned, and the few who venture to remain at home in hourly expectation of being murdered, or stripped of all their property."[8]

By mid-July, Cornwallis was complaining to Clinton of Sumter's new militia army of fifteen hundred men, as well as of lack of discipline and confidence in the loyalist militia. General George Washington added to the British burden by sending down a force of Continentals under General Horatio Gates, hero of the battle of Saratoga and, against Washington's wishes, newly appointed by Congress to be commander in chief of the South.

Gates was a good patriot, a poor general. A former British officer turned Virginia squire, he was fifty-two years old, an unhappy-looking man, as well he might have been considering his mixed bag of generally tired, hungry and sick troops. His appearance in the Carolinas in late July exercised a psychological effect that greatly exceeded his combat potential. Tarleton later wrote that " . . . his name and former good fortune re-animated the exertions of the country: Provisions were more amply supplied by the inhabitants, and the continental troops soon reached the frontier of South Carolina."[9] In August, Cornwallis wrote Clinton that " . . . the whole country" between the Pedee and the Santee was " . . . in an absolute state of rebellion, every friend of government has been carried off, and his plantation destroyed."[10]

Gates wisely attempted to exploit the revolutionary air. On the banks of the river Pedee, he issued a proclamation similar in intent to that released by Clinton a few months earlier in Charleston. Gates offered immediate amnesty to all those who had accepted British paroles on grounds that they had acted under duress. He excepted those persons who had either attacked or had seized the property of their fellow citizens, and he warned against further disaffection. Having so pontificated, Gates continued his march south through barren country, which further wore down his relatively meager force.

At this time, a strange assemblage suddenly appeared in his camp. Its leader was another militia officer, Colonel Francis Marion, soon to become famous as the "Swamp Fox." Marion was a small, wiry, and handsome South Carolinian farmer of no great formal education. In 1759, he had enlisted and fought the Cherokees for two years. At the outbreak of revolution, he was commissioned a cavalry captain in the Second South Carolina Regiment. In the back country, Marion organized a ragtag force of locals equipped with home-made weapons and riding stolen horses. A colonel noted that when Marion and his men reported, ". . . their numbers did not exceed twenty men and boys, some white, some black . . . distinguished by small leather caps, and the wretchedness of their attire."[11] The Continentals took one look and laughed until fit to bust. Gates was not amused, nor was he impressed with Marion's theories of Indian warfare; to get rid of them, Gates sent them on some slight errand.

Five days after Gates had dismissed Marion, the American army was dead, dying, wounded, prisoner or, like its commander, on the run. ". . . In less than an hour Earl Cornwallis had shattered the only American army in the south . . . the most crushing victory that British arms ever achieved over the Americans in the Revolutionary War."[12] Marion meanwhile seemed to have disappeared. In reality, he was lying low waiting for an opportunity to strike. It came in the form of some hundred and fifty American prisoners being escorted to Charleston. Marion and his guerrillas swooped on the long column, dispatched guards, and freed the captured soldiers, a daring act that made him famous throughout the South.

Other militia-cum-guerrilla leaders began active operations during the dangerous hiatus created by Gates's defeat. Conspicuous besides Marion were Thomas Sumter and Andrew Pickens. Veterans of earlier fighting, they were natural leaders, at home in the tactical environment. Sumter was forty-six, tall, vigorous, and bold, and known as the "Carolina Game Cock." Pickens, five years younger, lean and rugged, an elder of the Presbyterian Church, seldom smiled and never laughed.[13]

These men attracted some followers, but their real popularity stemmed from British pacification methods. In Professor Alden's words, ". . . the plundering, ravaging, and abuse of civilians by Hessians [mercenaries fighting for the British] and loyalists, and the brutalities of Tarleton, who refused quarter to patriots in the field, drove them to desperation and to bitter resistance."[14]

Cornwallis' failure to compute accurately the extent, real or potential, either of royalist sympathy or of rebel support next led him to a fateful decision: the invasion of North Carolina, which he regarded as a sanctuary that supported the insurrection in South Carolina and Georgia. By his own admission, his southern base was scarcely secure, nor was his military posture particularly prosperous, despite material captured at Camden. But his Camden victory had eliminated the threat of imminent invasion by orthodox Continental forces, and he also believed that Tories by the thousands would rise to greet and support him. Though displeased with the new plan, Clinton now decided to send an expedition to Chesapeake Bay in order to create a "powerful diversion" and strike at the supply depots which would support Continental units opposing Cornwallis.[15]

In early September, Cornwallis reached Charlotte, his left screened by a force of militia under Major Patrick Ferguson. The British were still digging in at Charlotte when a patriot militia force fell on Ferguson at King's Mountain. Ferguson was killed, and some three hundred of his force killed or wounded, and the rest captured. The Americans hanged nine of the prisoners, partly in revenge for British atrocities—"Tarleton's Quarters" come home—and probably also as a warning to other turncoats. Cornwallis was now viturally isolated. In Tarleton's words, " . . . the town and environs abound with inveterate enemies . . . [who] totally destroyed all communication between the King's troops and the loyalists in the other parts of the province. No British commander could obtain any information in that position, which would facilitate his designs, or guide his future conduct."[16] There was nothing for it but to retreat slowly and ponderously over muddy roads and swollen streams. Cornwallis succumbed to fever. Incorrect information from locals constantly frustrated efforts to locate a suitable area for winter quarters. The force finally ended in Winnsboro to suffer an uneasy period compounded by Marion's guerrilla operations. With Gates removed from the picture, the forty-seven-year-old guerrilla leader kept striking at Cornwallis' lines of communication, both to other outposts and to the rear, to keep him off balance until Washington could send reinforcements from the North. Cornwallis had disdained the coast and use of sea power, and henceforth he would pay.

Cornwallis' report to Clinton in early December 1780 suggests the extent of Marion's operations:

> . . . Colonel Marion had so wrought on the minds of the people, partly by the terror of his threats and cruelty of his punishments, and partly by the promise of plunder, that there was scarcely an inhabitant between the Santee and Pedee [rivers], that was not in arms against us. Some [guerrilla] parties had even crossed the Santee, and carried terror to the gates of Charlestown. My first object was to reinstate matters in that quarter, without which Camden could receive no supplies. I therefore sent Tarleton, who pursued Marion for several days, obliged his corps to take to the swamps, and by convincing the inhabitants that there was a power superior to Marion, who could likewise reward and punish, so far checked

the insurrection, that the greatest part of them have not dared to appear in arms against us since his expedition.[17]

This was momentary relief. A report to Clinton concluded ominously:

> I will not hurt your Excellency's feelings by attempting to describe the shocking tortures and inhuman murders which are every day committed by the enemy, not only on those who have taken part with us, but on many who refuse to join them. I cannot flatter myself that your representations will have any effect, but I am very sure that unless some steps are taken to check it, the war in this quarter will become truly savage.[18]

Although Cornwallis, as he explained to Clinton, had " . . . always endeavored to soften the horrors of war," he fully condoned Tarleton's punitive operations, and, after Ferguson's defeat at King's Mountain, he also ordered Lieutenant Colonel Thomas Browne to encourage the Indians to attack outlying American settlements.[19] Moreover, the British army had to eat. Lacking a supply service from Camden or Charleston, this meant virtually living off the land. Since food was short, requisitions (usually paid in promissory notes if paid for at all) further alienated the locals to make many active patriot supporters.[20] Not only did patriot forces benefit from increased support, but Cornwallis increasingly found himself deprived of the key ingredient to counterinsurgency warfare: intelligence.

The final phase of the war in the South began in January 1781. Reinforced by a corps from the North, Cornwallis decided on a second invasion of North Carolina, a plan heartily endorsed by Tarleton. But patriot forces had also been strengthened, and one Nathanael Greene, at Washington's urging, had been placed in command of the southern theater.

Greene was a common-sense general. Son of a Rhode Island Quaker preacher, he had been an ironmaster until the war, in which he had fought hard and well in rising to his present command. At thirty-eight years, he was fit, a big man, hard as nails. But he also was bright enough to respect a formidable enemy. Greene now chose to emulate Quintus Fabius Maximus, and even had boats collected so that if necessary his army could retreat across the numerous rivers![21]

Greene refused to risk his inferior force except on his own terms. He rightly discerned that Cornwallis was operating blind. If guerrillas could cut British communications, either to detachments operating in peripheral areas or to rear garrisons, Cornwallis eventually would have to retire.

And that is just what happened, but only after Tarleton lost some nine hundred men by precipitately attacking a patriot force at Cowpens while Cornwallis fought another expensive battle (some five hundred casualties which he could ill afford) at Guilford Courthouse before retiring on Wilmington to lick his wounds. His claim to victory was disputed not only by a torn, bleeding, almost starving army, but by General Phillips in Virginia as " . . . that sort of victory which ruins an army."[22] Nor was Cornwallis' claim respected in London, the Annual Register of World Events acerbly noting that the battle was " . . . productive of all the consequences of defeat"; Horace Walpole sarcastically wrote, " . . . Lord Cornwallis has conquered his troops out of shoes and provisions, and himself out of troops";[23] Charles James Fox bluntly remarked " . . . that another such victory would ruin the British army."[24]

Clinton later accused Cornwallis of direct disobedience of orders by undertaking the march on North Carolina. By losing more than three thousand men " . . . he accomplished no other purpose but the having exposed, by an unnecessary retreat to Wilmington, the two valuable colonies behind him to be overrun and conquered by that very army which he boasts to have completely routed but a week or two before."[25]

Cornwallis next chose to march north to the Chesapeake Bay area in Virginia. Defense of the South fell to young Lieutenant Colonel Lord Rawdon, at twenty-six years of age a combat veteran of the war. Rawdon commanded about eight thousand troops based in Savannah and Charleston, which he protected by a ring of outposts—isolated garrisons of one hundred to six hundred men[26]—a complex that brings to mind ancient Rome's bastions against the barbarians.

Seeing a God-given opportunity, Greene pushed his irregular forces against these outposts. Within three months after Cornwallis' departure, Rawdon held only Wilmington, Charleston and Savannah—royal enclaves that without reinforcement would prove useless until finally evacuated after the fall of Yorktown—and total British defeat.

CHAPTER SIX

1. Alden, *The South in the Revolution* . . . , 192. See also, Ward, II, 664; Alden, *The American Revolution*.
2. Willcox, *The American Rebellion* . . . , 106. See also, Willcox, *Portrait of a General* . . .
3. Alden, *A History of the American Revolution* . . . , 401, 404 ff. Sir William Howe had warned against this eventuality, but Germain and Clinton, as Professor Alden put it, preferred "hope to information." See also, Willcox, "Sir Henry Clinton . . . "
4. Alden, *The South in the Revolution*, 235.

5. Ibid., 241–2.
6. Trevelyan, I, 293–5. See also, Fuller, *British Light Infantry* . . . , who registers neither surprise nor indignation; Tarleton, *A History of the Campaigns of 1780 and 1781* . . .
7. Wickwire, *Cornwallis* . . . , 134–6.
8. Ibid., 170–1.
9. Tarleton, 97.
10. Wickwire, 171.
11. Trevelyan, II, 116. See also, Bass; Bryant later treated his exploits in the poem "Song of Marion's Men."
12. Wickwire, 162.
13. Ward, II, 662.
14. Alden, *The South in the Revolution* . . . , 242.
15. Willcox, *The American Rebellion* . . . , 209–10, 235.
16. Tarleton, 159–60.
17. Charles, 71.
18. Ibid., 72–3.
19. Ibid., 76.
20. Wickwire, 236–7.
21. Ibid., 250–1.
22. Willcox, *The American Rebellion* . . . , 384.
23. Ibid., 382.
24. Wickwire, 311.
25. Willcox, *The American Rebellion*, 270–1.
26. Ward, II, 798.

CHAPTER 7

England's colonial wars • Indian guerrilla leaders: Sivaji and Tippu • Wellesley's tactical changes • The Vendée rebellion • Hoche's counterguerrilla tactics: "overawing" versus "exasperating" • Napoleon invades Spain • Spanish army disasters • The rise of guerrilla bands • Wellington's early battles and use of guerrillas • French excesses • Guerrilla offensives • French countertactics • Marshal Bessières' testament

AMERICA was not the only place where England had to fight irregular wars. Early in the seventeenth century, she had established her first trading post in India, whose northern area formed part of the vast Mogul Empire. For a century, the Moguls continued to expand into India, but early in the eighteenth century, the dynasty dissolved, not the least of its problems having been the rise of a new Hindu military power, the Marathas, who fought brilliant guerrilla warfare under the famous leader Sivaji.

In the early eighteenth century, control of the country rested in the hands of warring viceroys who fell victim one after another to territorial ambitions of England, France, and Holland. In a series of more or less orthodox military campaigns fought before and during the Seven Years' War, the British General Robert Clive largely eliminated French and Dutch threats to British influence: by 1759, England "was the only European race which counted in India."[1]

England's position was somewhat tenuous. It roughly resembled that of the Romans occupying the coastal fringe of Spain in 206 B.C. In this case, England was reasonably well established in the East, but, in expanding to the South, West, and North, its forces collided with numerous tribes, some equipped with European weapons and trained by the French. To neutralize these people would require nearly sixty years of intermittent warfare punctuated by innumerable campaigns against the Hindus and Moslems in Mysore, the Marathas in the West,

72

INDIA
18th CENTURY
• Towns and Cities

Hindu Kush
Khyber Pass
Kabul
AFGHANISTAN
KASHMIR
Peshawar
Amritsar
PUNJAB
Sobraon
R. Sutlej
R. Indus
BALUCHISTAN
Delhi
R. Jumna
RAJPUTANA
NEPAL
R. Brahmaputra
SIND
Karachi
CENTRAL PROVINCES
Cawnpore R. GANGES
BEHAR
BENGAL
Calcutta
R. Tapti
R. Mahanadi
ORISSA
Bombay
WESTERN GHATS
R. Godavari
ARABIAN
SEA
Goa
R. Kistna
MYSORE
MADRAS
BAY
OF
BENGAL
Seringapatam
MALABAR
Madras
R. Cauvery
N
0   200   400 miles

M.E.P.

and their outlaw offshoot, the Pindaris in central India.

Although the British army displayed admirable perseverance, unquestioned courage and even, on occasion, political acumen, it showed remarkably slight tactical ingenuity throughout the pacification process. It remained deficient in cavalry, an enormous disadvantage, and, to fight guerrilla and quasi-guerrilla formations, commanders stubbornly retained heavy formations noticeably at odds with terrain, weather, and enemy. Had the Indians stuck to Sivaji's guerrilla tactics, the British conquest would have proved far more difficult. But pride and French influence persuaded most native leaders to copy European tactics and to accept set-piece battles made generally fatal by superior English discipline and firepower.

The Indians nonetheless often profited from excessive British weight and tactical rigidity. In the third Mysore war, for example, Tippu's cavalry scorched Cornwallis' route to prevent him from reaching the Mysore capital of Seringapatam. In the fourth Mysore war, the British managed to reach the capital, where Tippu, foolishly giving battle, was defeated and killed.[2]

This particular campaign is the more interesting because of the presence of Colonel Arthur Wellesley, later Duke of Wellington. Wellesley was appalled at the snail-like progress of the British army, and when he gained an independent command in the South, he made some radical changes in order to fight the Marathas. He first speeded up his transport by using the trotting bullocks of Mysore and by devising a pontoon train to give him passage over the numerous rivers. He then defied standard practice by launching a campaign during the monsoon, when neither Europeans nor Indians were supposed to fight. Finally, he used whatever force he commanded in a prompt, rigorous and decisive manner, both to win battles and to avoid battles.

At one point in pursuing a rebellious rajah, he found himself in difficult semijungle country where " . . . every village is a strong fortification," and with a minimum of information concerning his enemy. His force was small, his time limited. Plainly determined to attack, he told villagers he would kill them unless they tore down defenses and co-operated with him. They chose to do so, and with their help he soon captured the rajah and six other rebels, whom he summarily hanged.[3]

Wellesley's subsequent campaigns in India added a great deal to his knowledge of irregular warfare. This was just as well, for in a few years he would be allied with some of its most able practitioners, Portuguese and Spanish guerrillas.

The French, too, would become involved in guerrilla warfare, as a hurtful by-product of the Revolution. In 1793, before Carnot's famous decree called the French nation to arms, republican armies faced a fierce counterrevolution by priest-dominated peasants of Vendée. Finding leaders in local nobles and gentlemen such as Jacques Cathelineau, a linen merchant, these countryfolk picked up scythes, pitchforks, and fowling muskets to win a number of towns from surprised and generally weak republican garrisons. Reinforced with captured arms and fresh volunteers, the inspired irregulars attempted to take Nantes, a defeat in which Cathelineau was killed.

Determined to put down the rebellion, the Convention committed some one hundred thousand troops to the Vendée. Command went to Rossignol, "who was not only a tipsy and dissolute scoundrel, but a stupid and ignorant coward to boot."[4] Generals such as Westermann,

M.E.P.

l'Échelle, and Kléber carried out a scorched-earth policy until the rebels looked out only on "heaps of ashes, death and famine."[5] Weakened further by trying to fight set-piece battles and by dissension among leaders, the force splintered, with some peasants returning to their farms. Some fifty thousand with their wives and children retreated across the Loire into Brittany. Their new commander, the twenty-one-year-old Count Henri de La Rochejacquelein, dramatically told them, "If I retreat, kill me; if I advance, follow me; if I fall, avenge me."[6]

The task of pacifying the Vendée base fell to a young and able general, Lazare Hoche. As Thiers later described his campaign:

> . . . He devised an ingenious mode of reducing the country without laying it waste, by depriving it of its arms and taking part of its produce for the supply of the Republican army. In the first place he persisted in the establishment of entrenched camps. He then formed a circular line which was supported by the Sèvre and Loire and tended to envelop progressively the whole country. This line

75

was composed of very strong detachments, connected by patrols so as to leave no free space by which an enemy who was at all numerous could pass. These posts were directed to occupy every hamlet and village and to disarm them. To accomplish this they were to seize the cattle which usually grazed together, and the corn stowed away in the barns; they were also to secure the principal inhabitants; they were not to restore the cattle or the corn, not to release the persons taken as hostages, till the peasants should have voluntarily delivered up their arms.

By such measures, what Callwell described as "overawing" rather than "exasperating" the enemy, Hoche effectively eliminated the home base of the revolt.[7]

La Rochejacquelein wanted to remain in Brittany until strong enough to return to the Vendée, but older leaders persuaded the force to march north. After failing to capture the seaport town of Granville, the new leaders recommended withdrawal into Normandy. The peasants wished to go home, however, and marched to the Loire. Kléber and Marceau caught them up at Le Mans and Savenay, where probably fifteen thousand of them perished.

This did not end the rebellion. La Rochejacquelein remained in Brittany with a group of followers allied with Breton rebels who called themselves the *Chouans*—literally "long-eared owls." The republican campaign against the main force had exposed the Vendée to further revolt, which defied even the "infernal columns" of General Turreau.

Royalist leaders made a final attempt to save the Chouan survivors in Brittany by landing reinforcements from England. Poor leadership, combined with intraforce rivalries, doomed this to failure, while a vigorous campaign on the part of Hoche destroyed remaining Chouan forces in detail. By the time fighting ended, the once-rich province had become "a desolate and blackened wilderness."

All told, Hoche estimated one hundred thousand insurgent deaths—about one fifth of the Vendean population.[8]

In spring of 1807, the Emperor Napoleon was casting covetous glances at the Iberian Peninsula. He wanted this area in order to exploit "latent Spanish resources, naval and economic," of which he held an exaggerated notion; more important, he wanted to further his "continental system" by which he hoped to force Britain from the war by disrupting its trade with Europe.[9]

Napoleon anticipated little difficulty in occupying the peninsula. Strong militarily, he was also supremely confident. He held only contempt for his Spanish ally and for the decadent Bourbon court: King Charles IV; Queen María Luisa; her favorite, the young, powerful, and greedy Prince Manuel de Godoy; and finally the stupid heir apparent, Prince Ferdinand. Napoleon had long enjoyed Godoy's connivance— among the rewards, he was promised a piece of Portugal—and he was also being courted by Prince Ferdinand and his cabal.[10]

In July 1807, Napoleon sent Junot's army, some fifty thousand troops, across Spain to seize Lisbon and close it to British merchant shipping. As anticipated, Junot crossed Spain without opposition and even managed to insert French troops in the northern garrisons. Napoleon hastened to consolidate his presence by appointing Murat "Lieutenant of the Emperor in Spain." But as Murat led his columns toward Madrid in March 1808, serious riots broke out in Aranjuez. These were the work of Ferdinand's agents, and they caused the fall of hated Godoy and abdication of panic-stricken Charles. But Ferdinand's ambition was checked when Napoleon summoned the royal family to Bayonne, forced Ferdinand to abdicate, and placed his own brother, Joseph Bonaparte, on the throne.

This proved an egregious political error. The people of Spain did not love their monarch, but they did love their country and certainly had no desire to become a French vassal state. The *Madrileños* already had contested Murat's presence. In May, when Ferdinand and his entourage left Madrid, the populace revolted. This was an action of ordinary people, not constituted authority. In Madrid, the Spanish garrison " . . . remained inert or gave that assistance to the French authorities for which Murat publicly thanked them . . . "[11] When the revolt spread to the provinces, in mid-May, " . . . the captains-general and governors, most of them nominees of Godoy, succumbed to a kind of moral paralysis. . . . They appealed for tranquillity and were ignored, but neither would, nor could use the army against the mobs. . . . "[12] The mobs used extreme violence including murder to force " . . . captains-general and local authorities to arm the people and to accept self-constituted local Juntas . . . [which] all over Spain represented the acceptance of the revolution by the local notables."[13] Initially, almost no army officers joined rebel ranks: " . . . it was the men, and groups of junior officers, particularly [artillery] gunners, in liaison with civilian *meneurs* [ringleaders] who made the decisions which brought the army over to the national cause. . . . "[14]

Despite this confusion, the revolt greatly surprised the French. Murat's soldiers were soon driven across the Ebro River. The news caused great rejoicing in London, where the government decided to send an expeditionary force to Portugal.

Although the French recovered and hastily occupied Portugal with sixty-five thousand troops and Spain with eighty thousand, forces sufficiently strong to neutralize local armies, the occupation from the beginning was uneasy, with " . . . murders, assassinations, wholesale butcheries . . . [occurring] in every city."[15] To this opposition, the French reacted promptly and rigorously. Cavalry columns swept down on disordered peasant bands, sabers flashed in the Spanish sun, people died. By torturing and executing civilians, by burning houses and farms, the French did restore order in some areas. But never for long.

The opening phase would have taken a bystander back twenty centuries to the war between Romans and Celtiberians. Spanish armies attempting to fight pitched battles were generally beaten. Those units which took to the hills in small guerrilla bands generally prospered. The French soon claimed the important cities and towns, but this was precarious ownership maintained by shaky communications. Owing to the disorganized state of the defenders, the war undoubtedly would have ended in France's favor—but for British intervention.

News of the Spanish revolt had caused great rejoicing in London with the result that the government, advised by Wellesley (now a lieutenant general), decided to send an expeditionary force to Portugal. Wellesley and a small force arrived in spring of 1808, their landing screened by local guerrillas. Needing time to rebuild the shattered Portuguese army, Wellesley moved cautiously, a crucial period in which his security depended on accurate intelligence from a friendly population. The French interpreted caution as weakness. Junot attacked in August and was beaten at Vimeiro, an important military victory soon converted to a major political defeat by the outrageous Convention of Cintra, which foolishly authorized the French to return to France in British vessels, " . . . incidentally taking with them the loot of Lisbon under the guise of 'private baggage.' "[16] A disgusted Wellesley returned to England.

Meanwhile Sir John Moore landed a small army in Northwest Spain. Napoleon reacted by personally leading in 150,000 troops, which soon shattered the remaining Spanish armies. To give them time to reorganize, Moore struck at a corps of Soult's army, but with Napoleon threatening his right he was forced to retreat to Corunna where he was killed, his army escaping by ship. French arms now reigned supreme—except for the guerrillas.

Explosive nationalism meanwhile had blown a variety of guerrilla bands into existence. These bands were entirely regional. To lead them, " . . . the priest girded up his black robe, and stuck a pistol in his belt; the student threw aside his books, and grasped the sword; the shepherd forsook his flock; the husbandman his home." One of the first leaders was Juan Martín Díaz. In 1809, he was thirty-four, a former private of dragoons, illiterate, married, a father, a farmer in Castile. He gathered together a half dozen trusted neighbors, a rude lot badly equipped, a deficiency repaired by the ambush of a few dozen French couriers. In Navarra, a young student, Francisco Javier Mina, collected a small band

and armed it similarly. In La Mancha, a doctor emerged as leader: Juan Paladea, soon called El Médico; in Soria, the friar Sapia turned leader; in Catalonia, another doctor, Rovera; in Salamanca, the famous Julián Sánchez arose. These and others generally confined early operations to interrupting French communications. But small successes bred expansion. Bands multiplied and began attacking convoys and seizing arms and food and also treasure, for the enemy plundered whenever and wherever possible.[17]

The enemy answered by furnishing larger escorts for couriers, by sending out innumerable armed patrols, and by showing virtually no mercy to anyone remotely suspected of aiding the guerrilla effort. Harsh measures only helped the effort. Cruelty was met by cruelty; terror escalated. The French at Ucles tortured the civil populace in order to learn the location of hidden treasures; they burnt the men, then " . . . tore the nun from the altar, the wife from her husband's corpse, the virgin from her mother's arms, and they abused those victims of the foulest brutality in a way to which death was much to be preferred." The Spanish authorities publicized this treatment " . . . as the most certain means of establishing an eternal and fixed aversion in the heart of every Spaniard, for the name of France."[18]

Wellesley, now Viscount Wellington, returned to Portugal in 1809 with another army. Once again he found the people eminently sympathetic and helpful, and this was important since he had to be careful while playing for time. But he also had to push the French from Portugal which he did by beating Soult on the Douro, then beating Victor at Talavera before retiring on Lisbon.

Wellington knew that he could not rely on Spanish armies. ". . . The Spanish troops will not fight," he wrote, "they are undisciplined, they have no officers, no provisions, no magazines, no means of any description."[19] He knew, however, that Portuguese *ordenanzas* and Spanish guerrillas would give the French little peace, and he cunningly exploited this knowledge in his plans. It is not going too far to say that he envisaged his army as a piece of cheese to attract the rodent enemy into a guerrilla trap.

Wellington needed nearly a year to secure his Lisbon base by constructing the elaborate fortifications of Torres Vedras, three lines in depth that stretched from the sea to the Tagus River north of Lisbon. General Beresford simultaneously reorganized and trained the Portuguese army while Wellington anticipated future operations by building a large transport of mules, vital to supply in a nearly roadless country.[20] *Such was the control of the Spanish and Portuguese countryside by the guerrillas that the French obtained no information as to his activities.* They knew only that guerrilla operations were constantly expanding, a frustrating situation that Napoleon sought to remedy by sending reinforcements and by ordering Masséna's splendid new Army of Portugal to the attack.

Masséna's campaign is a striking example of the arrogance of ignorance. Denied any intercourse with the land, living in a vacuum as it were, he moved to meet an enemy of whom he was totally ignorant. He found Wellington's army in a defensive position outside Bussaco. He learned of Wellington's Portuguese contingent, but, having no notion of Beresford's training program, he dismissed the indigenous troops as so much rabble. He attacked with less than half his force, an effort defeated by about a third of Wellington's army. Wellington was still careful. Why risk his single army attempting to exploit this favorable result, he reasoned, when time could provide a painless victory? Wellington now *retired behind the Torres Vedras defenses.* Masséna, having no idea of their existence, followed him. And while Wellington's army disappeared behind rows and rows of elaborate fortifications to live easily on supplies brought by ship, Masséna's army sat uneasily in a country bereft of provision, with hungry guerrillas constantly nibbling at his communications. The result was inevitable: In March 1810, the starving French army fell back into Spain.

Much of Wellington's tactical success stemmed from this insulating process. Time and again, a French army commander remained in the dark regarding not only Wellington's plans and movements, but also those of other French commanders. Time and again, guerrillas furnished Wellington with important and sometimes vital information. As the bands gained strength and confidence, their missions increased. So effectively did they interdict French communications that couriers were soon being escorted by "units 300 strong."[21] In some instances, detachment commanders retained replacement drafts with the excuse that the roads were not safe. French commanders soon realized that they owned no more than the ground they occupied, an unsettling, indeed humiliating, thought that the more active guerrilla leaders never let them forget.

The guerrillas soon progressed to striking troop formations. These attacks increased as bands grew in strength; in autumn of 1810, they were largely responsible for containing three armies of thirty-eight thousand men that Masséna badly needed. Although their total number probably never exceeded twenty thousand, of which only a portion was operational at any one time, they continued to harass and often tie down French forces many times their own size.[22] By controlling the countryside, guerrillas exercised another important function: they deprived military governors of taxes and food. King Joseph, in Madrid, " . . . could not command a quarter of the sum which he required to pay the ordinary expenses of government. His courtiers and ministers, French and Spanish, failed to receive their salaries, and the Spanish army, which he was busily striving to form, could not be clothed or armed, much less paid."[23] Joseph's natural incompetence already had caused Napoleon to create four autonomous military commands in northern Spain, a decentralization of authority that played into guerrilla hands, besides causing internal army jealousies.

The French fought back in a number of ways, primarily by employing outright repression. In retreating from Portugal, Masséna's commanders impressed peasants as guides and porters, then summarily tortured and shot them; they impaled priests by the throat on sharpened branches of trees and mutilated luckless *ordenanzas*, Portuguese and Spanish recruits, beyond recognition.[24] Sir Thomas Picton, the eccentric British general who, as former governor of Trinidad, was no stranger to torture, witnessed this retreat and wrote a friend, " . . . nothing can exceed the devastation and cruelties committed by the enemy during the whole course of his retreat; setting fire to all the villages, and murdering all the peasantry, for leagues on each flank of his columns. Their atrocities have been such and so numerous, that the name of a Frenchman must be execrated here for ages."[25]

Coercion was integral to the second obvious method of attempting to catch the guerrillas. The usual tactic was the "sweep," which invariably returned empty-handed. Repeated failure naturally proved frustrating. The tactic also wore out men and horses, and, since it involved harsh interrogative methods, it simply widened the gulf between conqueror and peasant.

Even when the French succeeded in capturing a leader and breaking up a band, they accomplished very little. In 1810, the young student Mina was taken prisoner, but his uncle, Francisco Espoz y Mina, soon rallied the remnants of his band and in time extended operations as far afield as Álava and Aragon to contribute enormously to Wellington's operations in Portugal. As Oman points out, French army archives list dozens of officers killed or wounded "in a reconnaissance in Navarre" or "in a skirmish with Mina's bands." At one point, Mina was being hunted by troops from no less than six major commands, " . . . yet none of the six generals, though they had 18,000 men marching through his special district, succeeded in catching him, or destroying any appreciable fraction of his band." Mina's survival depended on mercurial operations: " . . . sometimes he was lurking, with seven companions only, in a cave or gorge; at another he would be found with 3,000 men, attacking large convoys, or even surprising one of the blockhouses with which the French tried to cover his whole sphere of activity." Supported by peasants, at times unwillingly, Mina financed his extensive operations by taking stolen treasures from the French, by collecting rents from national and church properties, by fining "bad Spaniards" [those who had co-operated with the French], and by collecting tribute from French customhouses in return for allowing safe passage of imported goods! Mina's operations worked terrible hardships on the land, which the French often scorched in retaliation. But, again, this only strengthened resistance. When the French summarily shot guerrilla prisoners, Mina responded by shooting more French prisoners, an escalation of horror "put to an end by mutual agreement in 1812."[26]

A third method of neutralizing guerrilla operations proved even less effective. This was King Joseph's attempt to raise a counterforce of guerrillas, which he called "Miquelets" after the famed Pyrenean bandits; at the same time, he attempted to form new regiments from Spanish deserters and prisoners, but neither plan worked. The Spanish recruits soon drifted away to rejoin their armies or to fight with the guerrillas.

In desperation Napoleon finally intervened. Sick of squabbling generals and duplicated efforts (for which he was largely responsible), he reorganized his army, eliminating the separate "military governments" in favor of more-centralized command. In 1811, he created the Army of the North, under Marshal Bessières, who enjoyed no better success in counterguerrilla operations than his fellows.

Bessières' later lament paid unwitting homage both to Wellington's strategy and to Spanish guerrillas. Careful study might well have profited commanders of later generations:

... If I concentrate twenty thousand men all communications are lost, and the insurgents will make enormous progress. The coast would be lost as far as Bilbao. We are without resources, because it is only with the greatest pains that the troops can be fed from day to day. The spirit of the population is abominably bad: the retreat of the Army of Portugal had turned their heads. The bands of insurgents grow larger, and recruit themselves actively on every side. . . . The Emperor is deceived about Spain: the pacification of Spain does not depend on a battle with the English, who will accept it or refuse it as they please, and who have Portugal behind them for retreat. Every one knows the vicious system of our operations. Every one allows that we are too widely scattered. We occupy too much territory, we used up our resources without profit and without necessity: we are clinging on to dreams. . . . [27]

CHAPTER SEVEN

1. Cole, 82.
2. Ibid., 100. See also, Wright, I.
3. Fortescue, 40–1. See also, Longford; Brett-James.
4. MacDonald. See also, Taylor.
5. Ibid.
6. Standing, 20.
7. Callwell, *Small Wars* . . . , 42, 147. See also, 41: Callwell called Hoche's campaign "a model of operations of this kind."
8. Standing, 39.
9. Markham, 151. See also, Lloyd, "The Third Coalition."
10. Carr, Raymond.
11. Christiansen, 10.
12. Ibid., 11. See also, Oman, *A History of the Peninsular War.*
13. Carr, Raymond.
14. Christiansen, 11.
15. Wright, I, 153
16. Two British generals, Burrard and Dalrymple, arrived ahead of the titular commander, Sir John Moore, to negotiate the treaty, which caused a public outcry in England. A court of inquiry subsequently exonerated Wellesley, who had signed the document under orders. The damage remained, as did army intrigues; the cabals of the Horse Guards continued to plague Wellesley throughout the campaign.
17. Wright, II, 243 ff.
18. Ibid., I, 414.
19. Markham, 154.
20. Cole, 132–3.
21. Blair, 5.
22. Oman, III, 490–1.
23. Ibid., 116.
24. Wright, I, 95–8.
25. Ibid., 97.
26. Oman, III, 488–90.
27. Ibid., IV, 208–9.

CHAPTER 8

Hofer's Tyrolean guerrillas fight the French • The Pugachev rebellion • Napoleon's invasion of Russia • The "conquest" of Vitebsk • Kutuzov's strategy • Peasant guerrillas • Denis Davydov and the partisans • The French retreat • The final disaster • Prussia's levée en masse

"THE SPANISH ULCER," as Napoleon called it, was not his single excursion in guerrilla warfare. In 1809, he had been forced to leave the peninsular campaign in Soult's hands and return to Paris to face a fresh war with Austria. This centered on Tyrol, traditionally a Habsburg possession, but ceded by Napoleon, in 1806, to the Bavarians.

Tyrolean mountaineers loathed their new masters and, in the spring of 1809, rose in mass against them. This was pure guerrilla warfare, under such capable if flamboyant leaders as Andreas Hofer, an innkeeper; Joseph Speckbacher, a peasant; and Joachim "Redbeard" Haspinger, a Capuchin priest. To fight the Bavarian army in the Tyrol, Hofer called several thousand peasants together and, after invoking patriotism, God and presumably motherhood, he directed: "Up then, and at these Bavarians! Tear your foes, aye, with your teeth, so long as they stand up; but when they kneel pardon them!" First blood was drawn against a party of Bavarian engineers attempting to destroy bridges that the Austrian army planned to use. When concealed sharpshooters dispersed this group, the Bavarian commander, General von Wrede, advanced from Innsbruck with a Franco-Bavarian army corps. A young innkeeper, Peter Kemnater, ambushed this force so successfully that it abandoned its guns, which the peasants destroyed. Apparently still not impressed, Von Wrede led a new force toward Brixen, but this was ambushed in a mountain defile where falling rocks and tree trunks merged with accurate fire to decimate the intruders. Simultaneously, Hofer cleared the Passeyr area while Speckbacher won the important

84

town of Innsbruck, a combined effort finally resulting in the capture of the entire Franco-Bavarian force: " . . . all the guns, horses and material of war, the two leading general officers, ten staff-officers, upwards of a hundred lesser officers, 6,000 infantry with seven guns and 800 horses and 1,000 cavalry."[1]

This astounding victory was only temporary. The Austrian army, to which Tyrolean fortunes were tied, was soon beaten by Napoleon. Although the Tyroleans continued to fight magnificently, they met political defeat by the Treaty of Schönbrunn, which re-ceded their country to the Bavarians. Hofer continued to lead a resistance force, but, in December 1809, he was betrayed, captured and, a few months later, shot.

Neither "the Spanish ulcer" nor the Tyrolean uprising furnished a warning to Napoleon when it came to invading Russia. Trouble had been brewing between Napoleon and Alexander since 1808, when Alexander expressed his desire to possess Constantinople. The two emperors subsequently clashed over the Polish question and Alexander's trade with England; and the empress dowager of Russia did not help matters by sabotaging Napoleon's marriage to Alexander's sister. Napoleon's temper is evident from a conversation he had with his ambassador to Russia, Armand de Caulaincourt, in the spring of 1811. To Caulaincourt's warning " . . . of the difficulties of the climate, the obstinacy of the Russians and their plan of luring him into the interior by a defensive strategy," Napoleon replied: "Bah! A battle will dispose of the fine resolutions of your friend Alexander and his fortifications of sand. He is false and feeble."[2]

Napoleon nevertheless prepared quite carefully for the pending campaign, which he held to be " . . . the greatest and most difficult enterprise that I have so far attempted." Including allied troops, he collected an army of well over 600,000. Although his strength in Russia never amounted to more than 420,000 to 450,000, his army nevertheless greatly outnumbered the Russian armies.[3]

The Grand Army of 1812, however, was not the polished instrument of earlier campaigns. French soldiers constituted less than half of it; neither allied nor French corps had received enough training, march discipline was poor, the supply system tended to break down, and inadequate facilities existed for sick and wounded. Napoleon also misjudged the attitude of Polish and Russian peasants, who, despite forced requisitions, were supposed to rise in support of the French. Some of these deficiencies might have been corrected, but, by 1812, Napoleon was not in the best physical health and he was totally enslaved by his ego. If all else failed, the Grand Army would march to the beat of his own mystical ambition: " . . . I feel myself driven towards an end that I do not know. As soon as I shall have reached it, as soon as I shall become unnecessary, an atom will suffice to shatter me. Till then, not all the forces of mankind can do anything against me."[4]

Troubles began to plague the Grand Army almost as soon as its vanguard crossed the Niemen, on June 25, 1812. The unusually fast pace soon told, and the roads filled with sick and stragglers. This was partly the result of a late spring and very bad weather, partly a supply failure and poor march discipline.

Napoleon's ambassador and counselor, Caulaincourt, later wrote:

> . . . This rapid movement [to Vilna], without stores, exhausted and destroyed all the resources and houses which lay on the way. The advance guard lived quite well, but the rest of the army was dying of hunger. Exhaustion, added to want and the piercingly cold rains at night, caused the death of 10,000 horses. Many of the young Guard died on the road of fatigue, cold and hunger.[5]

General Carl von Clausewitz, who fought on the Russian side in this campaign, wrote that a general, returning from Napoleon's headquarters on a political errand, was astonished " . . . at the state of the route of the French Army, which he found strewn with the carcases of horses, and swarming with sick and stragglers. All prisoners were carefully questioned as to the matter of subsistence; and it was ascertained that already, in the neighborhood of Vitebsk, the horses were obtaining only green forage, and the men, instead of bread, only flour, which they were obliged to cook into soup. . . . "[6]

Caulaincourt noted that " . . . the pillage and disorders of all kinds in which the army had indulged had put the whole countryside to flight." Outside of Vitebsk, " . . . we were in the heart of inhabited Russia . . . we were like a vessel without a compass in the midst of a vast ocean."[7] Napoleon's aide, Ségur, later wrote that when the Emperor's immediate entourage rejoiced at the "conquest" of Vitebsk, he turned sharply on them and cried, "Do you think I have come all this way just to conquer these huts?"[8]

A different policy toward the peasants still might have saved French fortunes. Although Russian landowners " . . . grew much milder in 1812, and tried to appease the peasants," the latter probably would have supported the French. But Napoleon, " . . . rather than abetting peasant separatist movements, crushed them ruthlessly on behalf of the nobility."[9] The peasants replied with a scorched-earth policy that cost the French dearly.

A hot and dry summer complicated matters. In mid-July, a German mercenary, Captain Franz Roeder, noted in his journal, " . . . if the Russians want to send half our army to the dogs by the winter, all they have to do is to make us march hither and thither with the individual units kept continually under arms. Then if they give us a few battles we shall be in a tough situation, so long as they have plenty of light troops."[10] Such was the isolation of the Grand Army, such its dislocation, that toward the end of July the astute Captain Roeder wrote a book of wisdom in a single sentence: "Every victory is a loss to us."[11]

Alexander had outlined Russian strategy as early as the spring of

1811, when he wrote the King of Prussia: " . . . The system which has made Wellington victorious in Spain, and exhausted the French armies, is what I intend to follow—avoid pitched battles and organize long lines of communication for retreat, leading to entrenched camps. . . ."[12]

Alexander's own ineptness, a divided high command, and the clamor of nobles for action began to jeopardize this strategy in July. Alexander relinquished supreme command in favor of Barclay de Tolly, who continued to retire until forced to fight a holding action at Smolensk in mid-August. This indecisive battle forced Alexander to replace Tolly with a native son, the sixty-seven-year-old Kutuzov, a veteran campaigner who had fought Napoleon at Austerlitz and greatly respected his abilities.

Kutuzov was old and tired and physically a wreck, but he realized more clearly than the other commanders that time was serving Russia's cause. His own preference was to *avoid* battle but he also realized that he had been appointed to the supreme command to *give* battle. For this purpose he retired on Borodino where the two armies met on September 7. In the brief engagement, each side suffered enormous losses; on the following day, Kutuzov began a retreat that would take his armies past Moscow.

Kutuzov was right. Far better to let time and space wear down French regiments, let hunger and sickness do the work of bullets. Fear already was infesting French divisions to compound barbaric behavior of the columns: " . . . the wholesale pillaging by the conquering army, by countless marauders, and sometimes by criminal bands of French deserters, caused the peasants' hatred of the enemy to grow from day to day."[13]

This hatred soon inspired the growth of guerrilla bands. Tarlé has given us the genesis of a partisan detachment. At the end of August, a private in the dragoons, an illiterate named Ermolai Chetvertakov, was taken prisoner, escaped, met a friend, killed two French stragglers, took their uniforms, then killed two French cavalrymen and acquired their horses. These successes helped them recruit forty-seven peasants, an ill-armed band that nonetheless killed twelve French cuirassiers, then a group of fifty-nine French. In time, Chetvertakov's band swelled to over three hundred volunteers operating in the large area around Gzhatsk. Later in the campaign, he led over four thousand peasants against a French battalion supported by artillery and forced it to retreat.[14]

Similar bands sprang up across the land. An infantry private, Stepan Eremenko, taken prisoner at Smolensk, escaped and organized a peasant band of three hundred. A peasant named Ermolai Vasilyev recruited a peasant force of about six hundred armed with rifles taken from the French.

Although Alexander and his generals, most of whom were landowning noblemen, did not want to arm the peasants, the potential of this new force struck a young lieutenant colonel, Denis Davydov, aide to an army commander, Prince Bagration. A few days before the battle of Borodino, Davydov asked Bagration to help him form small cavalry detachments to work with peasant guerrillas in cutting Napoleon's exposed lines of communication. Bagration persuaded Kutuzov to give Davydov fifty hussars and eighty Cossacks. This was the humble beginning of the Cossack-partisan campaign led by such as Figner, Seslavin, Vadbolsky, and Kudashev, many of whose outstanding exploits were later recorded by Davydov in his pioneer work *The Journal of Partisan Actions.*[15]

Captain Roeder graphically described the reaction of his regiment to a partisan attack in October: " . . . this afternoon the news went round that a few hundred armed peasants and Cossacks, who had their base of operations five leagues [10–15 miles] from here [Viazma] had seized the baggage of the Westphalian regiment and murdered the escort. This threw us into a state of unrest and vigilance." One Major Strecker was sent forth on a punitive expedition, his orders being to scour the countryside by shooting any peasants he encountered and burning all dwellings. Roeder sardonically wrote, " . . . I only hope that he omits at least the final measure for our sakes, in order that we may occasionally find somewhere to spend the night!"[16]

Neither Major Strecker nor other commanders assigned to deal with the harassing problem omitted "the final measure," a shortsighted policy that Napoleon probably approved. Certainly his temper was growing short. He should have reached Moscow with two hundred thousand troops; instead, ninety thousand arrived. According to Caulaincourt, the emperor " . . . attributed all his difficulties simply to the trouble caused by the Cossacks . . . he said he had means of obviating this annoyance by placing detachments of infantry in blockhouses linked in a line of defense, and added that, after giving battle to Kutuzov and driving him further back, he would see to the reorganization of all this."[17]

This countermeasure never appeared. For Napoleon, time was running out. Having gained the nothing of Moscow, he learned too late that the Grand Army, what was left of it, owned exactly what it physically occupied—and this was not enough to even feed it. An unidentified Russian officer described the French presence just prior to the retreat: " . . . Every day the soldiers streamed in thousands from the camps to plunder the city, and many thousand others were scattered throughout the countryside foraging and seeking for bread. Peasants armed with staves lay concealed in the woods and marshes and slew hundreds of these marauders every day, and those who escaped the peasants fell into the hands of the Cossacks."[18]

Napoleon's army retreated through land that earlier it had helped scorch. Partisan bands allied with Cossack patrols infested the area to harass columns slowed by hunger and frost and by ponderous baggage trains carrying loot stolen from Moscow. As early as November 6, Ségur wrote:

> . . . great numbers of men could be seen wandering over the countryside, either alone or in small groups. These were not cowardly deserters: cold and starvation had detached them from their columns. . . . Now they met only armed civilians or Cossacks who fell upon them with ferocious laughter, wounded them, stripped them of everything they had, and left them to perish naked in the snow. These guerrillas . . . kept abreast of the army on both sides of the road, under cover of the trees. They threw back on the deadly highway the soldiers whom they did not finish off with their spears and axes.[19]

Not far from Moscow, a group of partisans captured one unit of nearly two thousand men. Near Smolensk, Napoleon's vital supply depot, Cossacks and partisans drove off fifteen hundred oxen. Finding no forage in Smolensk, Napoleon had one commissary officer after another put on trial until he learned from Jomini " . . . that a woman Praskovya led a small guerrilla group that attacked and destroyed French foragers."[20]

Kutuzov watched these developments from the south. Pressed to attack by his superiors, he refused. Instead, he shadowed the French army, a "parallel pursuit" that covered 120 miles in fifty days. His own army suffered, but not to the extent of the French—the horses improperly shod for ice-covered roads,[21] soldiers frequently reduced to cannibalism, foragers frustrated by frozen fields, and behind those fields and lurking in woods the whole panoply of impassioned peasants and fierce Cossacks—here was a people's war, as Tolstoy put it, " . . . in all its menacing and majestic power; and troubling itself about no question of anyone's tastes or rules, about no fine distinctions, with stupid simplicity, with perfect consistency, it rose and fell and belabored the French until the whole invading army had been driven out."[22]

No one knows the exact toll. Clausewitz later wrote that of the original force, 552,000 remained in Russia dead or prisoner, along with 167,000 dead horses and some 1,300 captured cannon.[23]

It was a defeat of such proportion that French veterans could not encompass it when sitting in the village tavern, eyes filled with tears not from smoke alone. The lesson was not altogether ignored when Prussia declared war against Napoleon the following year and proclaimed a *levée en masse*:

... Every man not acting in the regular army or *Landwehr* was to support the army by acting against the enemy's communications and rear. The people were to fight to the death and with every means in their power. The enemy was to be harassed, his supplies cut off and his stragglers massacred. No uniforms were to be worn, and on the enemy's approach, after all food stocks had been destroyed, and mills, bridges, and boats burnt, the villages were to be abandoned and refuge sought in the woods and hills.[24]

CHAPTER EIGHT

1. Standing, 55–6.
2. Markham, 176.
3. Ibid. See also, Stschepkin; Ségur. The figures vary considerably, from Stschepkin's 680,000 (including 500,000 infantry and 100,000 cavalry) to Ségur's 617,000 to Markham's 600,000.
4. Fuller, *The Conduct of War* ... , 43.
5. Caulaincourt, I, 166.
6. Clausewitz, *The Campaign of 1812* ... , 110–11.
7. Caulaincourt, I, 185.
8. Ségur, 30.
9. Tarlé, 185–6.
10. Roeder, 125.
11. Ibid., 129.
12. Markham, 176.
13. Tarlé, 186.
14. Ibid., 247–9.
15. Ibid., 247.
16. Roeder, 155.
17. Caulaincourt, I, 320–1.
18. Roeder, 169.
19. Ségur, 169.
20. Tarlé, 192–3.
21. Markham, 182–3.
22. Tolstoy, 1115.
23. Clausewitz, *The Campaign of 1812* ... , 94.
24. Fuller, *The Conduct of War* ... , 58.

CHAPTER 9

Clausewitz and Jomini on guerrilla war • The French land in Algeria • Abd-el-Kader leads the resistance • Clauzel's strategy and defeat • Valée's Great Wall • Bugeaud's tactics • Shamyl and the Caucasus • Guerrilla warfare in Burma • The Seminole war in Florida • Effects of Industrial Revolution on guerrilla warfare • The American Civil War • Forrest, Morgan and Mosby • Sheridan's countertactics • Pope's policy

LESSONS offered by Napoleon's tragic experiences with guerrilla warfare went largely unheeded by later military commanders. After 1815, warfare in Europe went into partial eclipse. Worn by twenty years of battles, European states welcomed a political status quo as determined at the Congress of Vienna and maintained by regular standing armies whose autocratic leadership stultified any attempt to expand the organizational and tactical reforms suggested either by the Napoleonic wars or by the technological progress inherent in the Industrial Revolution. Aside from maintaining internal order and fighting occasional conventional campaigns such as Field Marshal Radetzky's victory over the Piedmontese at Novara, in 1849, the great powers, particularly England, confined themselves to waging colonial wars. From 1815 to 1854, no British army even saw service on the Continent.

In this tactically dormant period, the lessons of Bonaparte's campaigns in Spain and Russia were all but ignored. Neither victorious nor defeated generals wanted to credit rabble action, nor did governments wish to give peasants any notion of exalted status. Napoleon later blamed his difficulties in Russia on the Cossacks, not the partisans. Most guerrilla leaders of the period faded to an illiterate obscurity, unhonored and unsung except in peasant folklore.

Although a paucity of qualified military analysts existed, two principal theorists did emerge in the wake of Napoleonic destruction. Clausewitz, in his famous unfinished treatise *On War (Vom Kriege),* only touched lightly on partisan warfare, in a short chapter called "Arming the Nation." A "Prussianized Pole," Clausewitz served extensively in the Napoleonic wars but experienced minimum contact with the battlefield—to the extent that the British war historian Sir James Edmonds later wrote that he " . . . seems to have been a courtier rather than a professional soldier."[1] Although recognizing the "new power" of a "people's war," he saw this in terms of a *levée en masse* that favored the defense. Such a war could only be fought under suitable tactical and psychological conditions; moreover, " . . . we must imagine a people-War in combination with a War carried on by a regular Army, and both carried on according to a plan embracing the operations of the whole."[2]

Partisan operations were to be sharply circumscribed. Neither national levies nor armed peasantry were to attack an enemy army:

> . . . "They must not attempt to crack the nut, they must only gnaw on the surface and the borders. . . . " Although their potential was definitely limited, " . . . still we must admit that armed peasants are not to be driven before us in the same way as a body of soldiers who keep together like a herd of cattle, and usually follow their noses. Armed peasants, on the contrary, when broken, disperse in all directions, for which no formal plan is required; through this circumstance, the march of every small body of troops in a mountainous, thickly wooded, or even broken country, becomes a service of a very dangerous character, for at any moment a combat may arise on the march; if in point of fact no armed bodies have even been seen for some time, yet the same peasants already driven off by the head of a column, may at any hour make their appearance in its rear.[3]

Clausewitz pictured partisans as "a kind of nebulous vapory essence." They should

> . . . never condense into a solid body; otherwise the enemy sends an adequate force against this core, crushes it, and makes a great many prisoners; their courage sinks; every one thinks the main question is decided, any further effort useless, and the arms fall from the hands of the people . . . on the other hand, it is necessary that this mist should collect at some points into denser masses, and form threatening clouds from which now and again a formidable flash of lightning may burst forth. . . .

The enemy can only guard against small partisan actions by " . . . detaching numerous parties to furnish escorts for convoys, to occupy military stations, defiles, bridges, etc." His larger garrisons in the rear will remain subject to partisan attack; his force as a whole will suffer "a feeling of uneasiness and dread."[4]

One cannot fault this confirmation of the auxiliary-partisan role, and it is a pity that Clausewitz did not expand his thinking. His own experience in partisan warfare was extremely limited, and apparently so was his historical appreciation of the subject. He found partisan warfare " . . . as yet of rare occurrence generally, and . . . but imperfectly treated of by those who have had actual experience for any length of time. . . . "[5] Neither Clausewitz's treatment nor his turgid presentation of the subject was apt to arouse much interest in its potential. His incomplete and highly abstruse work was published posthumously in German in 1831. Colonel Graham's English translation did not appear until 1873.[6]

The other leading analyst of the day, General Baron de Jomini, a Swiss officer with considerable battlefield experience in Napoleonic warfare, did not publish his principal study, *A Treatise on the Art of War (Précis de l'art de la guerre)*, until 1838.[7] As opposed to Clausewitz, who dwelt in Kantian clouds of theory, Jomini realistically (and professionally) analyzed strategy, tactics, and logistics (the word was in current use) from the standpoint of both ancient and contemporary campaigns in an attempt to establish basic principles of war. His work won almost immediate popularity in the West; Edmonds wrote that it "was studied everywhere" until placed into eclipse by German victories in 1870–71, which signaled the rise of Clausewitzian influence.

Jomini's personal experience in guerrilla warfare, as opposed to Clausewitz, was considerable, but he still treated the subject cautiously, as though he were Pandora well aware of the disruptive force of winds. "National wars," he thought, "are the most formidable of all."

> . . . This name can only be applied to such as are waged against a united people, or a great majority of them, filled with a noble ardor and determined to sustain their independence: then every step is disputed, the army holds only its camp-ground, its supplies can only be obtained at the point of the sword, and its convoys are everywhere threatened or captured.
>
> The spectacle of a spontaneous uprising of a nation is rarely seen; and, though there be in it something grand and noble which commands our admiration, the consequences are so terrible that, for the sake of humanity, we ought to hope never to see it. . . .
>
> This uprising may be produced by the most opposite causes. The serfs may rise in a body at the call of the government, and their masters, affected by a noble love of their sovereign and country, may set them the example and take the command of them; and, similarly, a fanatical people may arm under the appeal of its priests; or a people enthusiastic in its political opinions, or ani-

mated by a sacred love of its institutions, may rush to meet the enemy in defense of all it holds most dear.

After discussing the advantages of forests and mountains to national wars, and offering examples, many already familiar to us, Jomini, with the French disaster in Spain in mind, wrote:

> . . . The difficulties are particularly great when the people are supported by a considerable nucleus of disciplined troops. The invader has only an army: his adversaries have an army, and a people wholly or almost wholly in arms, and making means of resistance out of every thing, each individual of whom conspires against the common enemy; even the noncombatants have an interest in his ruin and accelerate it by every means in their power. He holds scarcely any ground but that upon which he encamps; outside the limits of his camp every thing is hostile and multiplies a thousand-fold the difficulties he meets at every step.
>
> These obstacles become almost insurmountable when the country is difficult. Each armed inhabitant knows the smallest paths and their connections; he finds everywhere a relative or friend who aids him; the commanders also know the country, and, learning immediately the slightest movement on the part of the invader, can adopt the best measures to defeat his projects; while the latter, without information of their movements, and not in a condition to send out detachments to gain it, having no resource but in his bayonets, and certain safety only in the concentration of his columns, is like a blind man: his combinations are failures; and when, after the most carefully-concerted movements and the most rapid and fatiguing marches, he thinks he is about to accomplish his aim and deal a terrible blow, he finds no sign of the enemy but his campfires: so that while, like Don Quixote, he is attacking windmills, his adversary is on his line of communications, destroys the detachments left to guard it, surprises his convoys, his depots, and carries on a war so disastrous for the invader that he must inevitably yield after a time.[8]

Jomini was closer to the mark of guerrilla warfare than Clausewitz, but neither treatise satisfied the immediate military needs of colonial warfare. Neither spoke of changing objectives or of tactics suitable to defeat thousands of mounted natives with a few hundred regular cavalry, or the proper method of controlling hundreds of square miles with under-strength forces. Nowhere in Clausewitz or Jomini is the tactical adaptation suggested that made the "thin red line," the infantry square, the cavalry squadron, or the gunboat as familiar to professional soldiers as the conventional maneuvers of Napoleonic warfare were to another generation. And yet, a year before Clausewitz died and while Jomini was hard at work on the *Précis,* warfare was already pursuing a tan-

gential course that often mocked mere conventional thought and practice.

Before either Clausewitz or Jomini appeared in print, the French became
involved in a major colonial campaign in North Africa.

In the early nineteenth century, Turkey held Algeria in loose hegemony, ruling through a dey of Algiers, whose army frequently had to
fight inland Arab-Berber tribes. The dey's relationship with Europe was
none too healthy, since his ports traditionally sheltered pirates who
preyed on Western shipping. In 1827, the dey insulted the French consul
over a commercial matter, and added injury by allegedly striking him
with a peacock-feather fly whisk. Three years later, Charles X, needing
a diversion for his unhappy regime (soon to end), dispatched an expeditionary force of thirty-five thousand troops, which easily captured
Algiers. Marshal Louis de Bourmont announced: " . . . the whole kingdom of Algeria will probably surrender within fifteen days, without our
having to fire another shot."[9] With that, he pushed inland to subdue
the tribes.

From the beginning, French military behavior left considerable to
be desired. A British admiral and student of the period, C. V. Usborne,
later wrote:

> . . . To obtain wood for their fires soldiers tore down the doors of
> houses or cut down fruit trees; they smashed beautiful marble
> fountains for the pleasure of destruction. They even destroyed aq-
> ueducts, which resulted in their own army being short of water.
> At Blida, taken without resistance on 19 November, 1830, every-
> one found armed over a large area was shot out of hand. The
> punitive destruction of crops resulted in scarcity for the army in
> the following year.[10]

The French expedition caused a famous marabout or holy man,
Mahi ed Dine, to proclaim a *jihad*, or holy war, under the military
command of his son, Abd-el-Kader.

Sidi-el-Hadji-Abd-el-Kader-Uled-Mahiddin had only a few more
years than names. Twenty-four years old, he was a small man
" . . . with a long, deadly-pale face, and languishing eyes, an aquiline
nose, small, delicate mouth, thin, dark chestnut beard, and slight mustache. He had exquisitely formed hands and feet, which he was continually washing and trimming with a small knife."[11] Nobly descended
from the caliphs of Fatima, the young Mohammedan was generalissimo
of several Berber tribes. Upon the outbreak of war, he collected his
people in a *smala*, a mobile headquarters of wives, booty, horses, "and

a whole army of women and retainers" that at one point numbered sixty thousand, and took to the land.

Abd-el-Kader at first ran rings around ponderous French columns, and might well have driven the French from the land but for one major failing: he could not persuade heterogeneous tribes to join in organized, central government, whose weight he needed to beat the French. The tribes nevertheless fought hard, their motivation being clear in an official report made by the newly appointed Commission on Africa to King Louis Philippe in 1833:

> ... We [France] have seized private properties with no compensation; we have even forced expropriated proprietors to pay for the demolition of their houses. We have profaned mosques and graves. We have sent to their death, on mere hearsay and without trial, people whose guilt is extremely doubtful. We have murdered people carrying safe-conducts; killed off, on a mere suspicion, whole populations who have since been found innocent; we have put on their trial men regarded as holy in their countryside, because they have had the courage to speak up for their unhappy compatriots. ... We have surpassed in barbarity the barbarians we came to civilize—and we complain of having no success with them.[12]

When the 1834 peace treaty broke down, the king sent a dashing general, Count Bernard Clauzel, to deal with the stubborn tribesmen. Clauzel had fought in Spain under Marmont, but nothing of the experience with Spanish guerrillas brushed off. Recruiting several regiments of Zouave mercenaries, he undertook a series of expeditions that posed but slight threat to highly mobile Algerian forces. Clauzel exaggerated his reports of success and continued to demand more troops. A major defeat while marching on Constantine cost him his job.[13]

French strategy changed in 1836, when General Bugeaud arrived in western Algeria with some reinforcements. Bugeaud, also a veteran of the Spanish wars, had learned something about guerrilla warfare. After intensively training his troops, he outfitted flying columns and dispensed with ponderous baggage trains in favor of mules and camels. A month later, he beat the emir at Sikkah.[14]

General Valée now assumed supreme command and managed to forge a shaky treaty that let France get on with the colonization effort in the occupied area. Two years later, Abd-el-Kader reopened hostilities. Valée, who commanded a total force of about fifty thousand, hit on a new strategy. As he wrote the Minister of War in Paris:

> ... in Africa war must be defensive. The Arab will flee constantly before our columns, allowing them to advance as far as the necessity for revictualling them will permit, and he will then return,

French Colonization
of Algeria 1830–1881

M.E.P.

giving to their withdrawal the appearance of a reverse. Clever tactics in Africa consist of drawing on the Arabs to fight. With this object one must make permanent works. . . . They will certainly attack them. Our success in a battle on a position chosen beforehand will be certain, and the terror which will follow a defeat will bring about the submission of neighboring tribes.[15]

Before anyone in Paris could object, Valée manned a number of posts, " . . . all of which were invested and their communications cut. Strong columns were required to revictual them, and terrible losses resulted. . . . Disaster followed disaster." Valée also started to construct " . . . a continuous obstacle round the occupied zone, irreverently called the Great Wall of China." This was to be 120 miles long, an "impassable" ditch supported by 160 blockhouses.[16]

At this point, General Bugeaud replaced Valée. The fiery Bugeaud took instant exception to the Great Wall theory. He reported to his superiors in Paris: " . . . I estimate that in summer four regiments will not be enough to guard the obstacle which will yield seven or eight hundred casualties through sickness in five months. From the moment it is finished war will be impossible outside it. We must withdraw the garrisons of Médéa and Miliana and shut ourselves up in a pestilential area. The army will thus have dug its own grave."[17]

Bugeaud insisted instead on expanding the flying-column tactic. "Père," or "Father," Bugeaud, as his troops called him, had come from the ranks, which was rare enough in that day, but, even more rare, he understood the value of "the ruse, the raid, and the ambush." To accomplish these, he formed and trained small, fast-moving task forces, " . . . a few battalions of infantry, a couple of squadrons of cavalry, two

98

mountain howitzers, a small transport train on mule and camel back."[18] By increased mobility, he gained contact with the emir's troops, then beat them with disciplined firepower. One of his officers, the dashing Saint-Arnaud, who later commanded the French army in the Crimea, wrote: " . . . He fights when he wishes, he searches, he pursues the enemy, worries him, and makes him afraid."[19]

Bugeaud's flying columns won a number of important tribal submissions, which the general hastened to exploit with constructive occupation: "The sword only prepared the way for the plough." A mere punitive column advancing into the desert " . . . left no more lasting effect than the wake of a ship in the sea." Bugeaud nonetheless depended more on fear than on persuasion. To bring nomads to heel, he relied chiefly on the *razzia,* or scorched-earth policy, which he " . . . turned into a doctrine of war." Saint-Arnaud wrote: " . . . We have burned everything, destroyed everything. How many women and children have died of cold and fatigue!"[20]

Tribesmen replied in kind, torturing and mutilating captured French soldiers. At times, the French army practiced genocide, as when Colonel Pélissier

> . . . lighted fires at the mouth of a cave in which five hundred men, women and children had taken refuge, and all but ten were asphyxiated. *L'affaire des grottes* reached Paris, and became a scandal, denounced in the French Senate as "the calculated, cold-blooded murder of a defenseless enemy. . . . "[21]

The resultant outcry did not prevent the practice from continuing—the government merely imposed stricter censorship.

Realizing that the emir had to be defeated, Bugeaud continued to aim at the *smala,* the emir's floating political-military headquarters. This was eventually smashed by an attack in the best G. A. Henty tradition. King Louis Philippe's son, the Duc d'Aumale, led a cavalry charge of six hundred tired troopers into the teeth of five thousand surprised Berbers. The natives broke and ran, and the young prince captured four thousand prisoners including the emir's mother, his favorite wife, and vast treasure.[22]

As Bugeaud anticipated, this broke organized resistance. The emir now sought sanctuary in Morocco, where Emperor Abd-er-Rahman began helping him rebuild his force. Without gaining permission from Paris, Bugeaud immediately violated this border sanctuary to meet the Moorish army, some 45,000 horsemen, concentrated at the Isly. Bugeaud's force amounted to 6,500 infantry and 1,500 cavalry. He at once attacked, and in August 1844, decisively beat them. The subsequent

Treaty of Tangier, signed with the Moroccan sultan, provided a wedge for later French expansion into that country.[23]

Bugeaud now claimed most of Algeria and set about administering it through an Arab Bureau, whose officers " . . . had extensive powers, dealt with military and legal matters, collected taxes and engaged in military intelligence activities." Bugeaud's success brought a new horde of European colonists, and, from 1844 onward, the Europeans grew in power while claiming the best farmlands and other concessions at the expense of the tribes.[24]

Abd-el-Kader survived three more years as a fugitive. Finally surrendering, he received a handsome pension from the French, who sent him to Damascus, where he died at the age of seventy-six.[25] His capture did not end resistance, particularly in the Kabylie, where uprisings continued until 1881 and even later.

When Abd-el-Kader began fighting the French, a Mohammedan priest or mullah, the Tartar Shamyl, evoked a holy war against the Russians. The czar's army was determined to subdue the rugged Caucasus, some three hundred thousand square miles " . . . of mountains, table-lands, rapid and shallow rivers," the home of Lezghians, Georgians, and Chechens, the land of Daghestan.[26]

The best modern treatment of this fascinating campaign, in the author's opinion, is found in Lesley Blanch's entertaining book *The Sabres of Paradise.*[27] To defy the Russian intruder, Shamyl led his people to the mountains. There he easily repulsed the first forces to come after him. Not least of his advantages was superior firepower, gained from smuggled rifles, the Russian troops being armed only with smoothbore weapons. The enemy also suffered from overconfidence. In 1837, the visiting Czar Nicholas asked some assembled chiefs, "Do you know that I have powder enough to blow up all your mountains?" On another occasion, General Veliamonif told the natives that " . . . if the sky were to fall the soldiers of Russia were numerous enough to prop it up on their bayonets."[28]

This surfeit of manpower and powder was just as well. Expedition after expedition returned from the mountains to report heavy losses against the achievement of a few burned villages. Occasionally, concentrated forces supported by artillery surprised the guerrillas, and Shamyl was surrounded and twice just barely escaped.

He soon collected another force, however. To insure replacements, he had divided Daghestan into twenty provinces, " . . . placing each under a *naib,* who was bound to provide two hundred horsemen at his bidding. The male population from fifteen to fifty were armed and drilled, and a postal service and foundry for ordnance estab-

THE CAUCASUS
MID-19th CENTURY
0   50   100   200 miles

M.E.P.

lished. Shamyl's personal command consisted of a thousand superb cavalry. . . ."[29]

Shamyl was also greatly assisted by France and England prior to the outbreak of the Crimean War, in 1854. In one sense, this aid backfired: armaments included artillery pieces which, in untrained hands of the Tartars, proved of little more than nuisance value. Yet Shamyl's insistence on using and protecting his precious guns led him to use more conventional tactics and resulted in set-piece battles in which he was defeated. This error, combined with an increase in Russian strength at the end of the Crimean War, eventually caused him to surrender. As with Abd-el-Kader, he received a generous pension. He died while on pilgrimage to Mecca.

Not all colonial peoples fought with the tenacity of Algerians and Tartars, and not all leaned so completely on guerrilla tactics. In the nineteenth century, native leaders came increasingly under Western influence. Competition among European powers in the colonies had led to their aggrandizement by money and arms and to initiation of numerous natives into rites of Western warfare. These developments worked on the pride of the more important princes, many of whose native levies had been scattered by disciplined forces a fraction of the size. With this, came the dawning realization that guerrilla warfare could impede the colonizing process, but could not stop it.

101

To fight guerrilla warfare successfully demanded superb leadership and enormous patience, but, even when these were exercised, the necessity of eventually destroying the intruding force remained, and this meant a set-piece battle. Since fighting a battle is infinitely easier than waging a prolonged guerrilla campaign, most native leaders perhaps unconsciously yielded to such contact, generally to their detriment.

An example is the British conquest of Burma. In 1824, Sir Archibald Campbell, commanding a British-Indian force of eleven thousand, captured Rangoon and turned north in pursuit of the Burman leader Bundoola, whose headquarters were at Ava, on the Irrawaddy.

Campbell's columns immediately struck a series of fortified stockades, which forced British columns to deploy and attack. The Burmese would then float away; the British would have to re-form and finally resume their march. By such methods, Bundoola more than held his own, but in 1825 he foolishly accepted battle and was killed. At this time, Campbell's once-splendid force *numbered thirteen hundred men fit for duty.*[30] With Bundoola out of the way, however, much of the starch disappeared from Burmese resistance. Once reinforcements arrived, Campbell pushed four hundred miles up the Irrawaddy and, in a final set-piece battle, ended the war in his favor.

Native willingness to stand and fight and even to charge invading forces resulted in hundreds of colonial battles in which firepower and disciplined tactics generally proved superior. The colonizing process continued difficult, however. In Burma, Campbell's original regiments had been practically wiped out, with " . . . six out of every seven men engaged becoming casualties, mainly through sickness."[31] In subjugating Madagascar, the French suffered forty-two hundred deaths in only ten months, the result of trying to construct a road through pestilential terrain rather than resistance offered by the Hovas.

Commanders had to remain constantly alert for tactical tricks, invariably some form of ambush that had to be matched by tactical modifications. Until the enemy could be brought to fight, this type of campaign called for extreme patience and tactical imagination. Sometimes the combination of terrain, disease, and enemy cunning proved too formidable even for regular forces, particularly if they were inexperienced and limited in number. In North America, in 1835, a Seminole Indian ambush of Captain Dade's army column in Florida opened a six-year guerrilla campaign that heavily taxed slim army-navy-marine resources. As Professor Weigley has pointed out, the Army at the time

. . . was not much better prepared for guerrilla warfare against the Seminoles in Florida than Napoleon's soldiers had been for the guerrillas of Spain. This was true despite experience in fighting forest Indians and the irregular campaigns that Americans themselves had sometimes waged during the Revolution. A historical pattern was beginning to work itself out: occasionally the American Army has had to wage a guerrilla war, but guerrilla warfare is so incongruous to the natural methods and habits of a stable and well-to-do society that the American Army has tended to regard it as abnormal and to forget about it whenever possible.

At first, various generals tried unsuccessfully to bring the Seminoles to battle. Quartermaster General Thomas Jesup grew so frustrated that he resorted to an ugly expedient used two thousand years earlier by the Romans in Spain: He brought Seminole chieftain Osceola to council under a flag of truce and then imprisoned him, an act which " . . . outraged public opinion and Congress, and the effect on the Seminoles seems to have been mainly to infuriate them and stimulate their resistance." Colonel Zachary Taylor fared better. After beating the Indians in a pitched battle, he began a pacification program that was interrupted by his relief. His successor, Colonel William J. Worth, indulged in a punitive campaign, burning crops and dwellings, which he sustained straight through 1841:

> . . . The cost to Worth's own men in fever and dysentery was high, but the method succeeded. The Indians were broken into small bands that barely subsisted, and concerted resistance to United States authority came to an end.[32]

Even where force of arms told and treaties were signed, the pacification process continued. Throughout the century, dissident tribes and nations continued to revolt in Africa, India, and Burma, just as Indian tribes continued to rise in the western part of North America. Such isolated efforts were increasingly doomed, for, where the native found it difficult if not impossible to repair losses in men and material while maintaining tribal cohesion sufficient to wage war, the Industrial Revolution was constantly increasing the capability of colonizing powers to fight prolonged campaigns. Not only did growing populations furnish manpower necessary to sustain colonial wars, particularly when nations refrained from fighting each other at home, but such technological improvements as the percussion cap and more accurate artillery greatly enhanced the striking power of expeditionary forces against native irregulars.

These new weapons intimidated but did not eliminate the guerrilla. Ironically, by adding weight to war already heavy, they eventually were going to ease his task. If the percussion cap reduced rifle misfires from 40 per cent to 4 per cent, and if the breech-loading rifled artillery piece increased rate and accuracy of fire, they also demanded far more ammunition, which meant increasingly large and vulnerable logistic

Civil War Theaters
1861 — 1865

• Towns and Cities

0 100 200 300 miles

"tails." If improved agricultural and industrial production could support larger armies fighting in diverse theaters of war, these still had to be moved, controlled and supplied by the railroad and telegraph, which were particularly vulnerable to enemy action.

The American Civil War displayed to the world the awesome influence of technology on war, particularly the killing power of rifle and cannon in defense, but it also produced some lively examples of army vulnerability to partisan warfare.

From the beginning, the war featured definite guerrilla overtones—not unnaturally, since the South was numerically inferior and since the war quickly spread to diverse areas, some highly favorable to guerrilla tactics. Moreover, by environment and temperament, the Southerner naturally inclined to irregular war.

This showed even on the battlefield, where the Confederate soldier's highly individualistic comportment contrasted strongly to formal Union ranks. The Confederate, undisciplined but intensely enthusiastic, fought more as an independent skirmisher. As Fuller noted, " . . . the Federal soldier was semi-regular and the Confederate semi-guerrilla."[33] The South wisely exploited this capability by allowing such capable if flamboyant leaders as Forrest, Morgan and Mosby to raise bands of cavalry that operated on the flanks and in the rear of enemy armies—operations invariably aided by local sympathizers.

Morgan and Forrest fought the early part of the war as irregulars attached to General Bragg's army. John Morgan had organized the first band. He was a Confederate officer, a Kentuckian " . . . with a beautiful suit of hair" and an imagination too extensive even for the extensive fields of guerrilla war. Nathan Bedford Forrest, a volunteer who had raised and equipped his own cavalry troop, was a particularly romantic figure, well over six feet tall but very fit, handsome, with penetrating blue eyes and sweeping cavalry mustaches, always incisive, generally impulsive, and occasionally ruthless. His manners at times were charming, but by the end of the war he was said to have killed thirty-two enemy with his own hands; northern generals certainly wanted to kill him, but they nonetheless respected him, and, in the South, Johnston called him the greatest general of the war. Asked the secret of his tactical wizardry, Forrest replied, "I git there fustest with the mostest." What he lacked in grammar, he made up for with charisma. In 1862, when his brigade was trapped in Fort Donelson by Grant's infantry, he snorted at the post commander's suggestion of surrender and instead led his people in a night escape across a freezing river. That spring with perhaps fifteen hundred troopers, he was ready along with Morgan's twenty-five hundred to do Bragg's bidding.

After defeat at Shiloh, Bragg was falling back slowly before Halleck's heavy Army of the Mississippi and Buell's neighboring Army of the Cumberland. Bragg was trying to hold Halleck with the shell of his army while moving its body to Mobile and thence to Chattanooga, from where he could strike into Kentucky. Halleck already was moving slowly—to supply the bulky armies, he was building his own railroad from Columbus. To hinder him further, Bragg now sent Morgan and Forrest on end runs around the northern flanks.

These hard-riding bands fanned across Kentucky and Tennessee. This was the rebel West of the war, and the very ground seethed with hatred of intruding Federals. Earlier, Sherman had been asked to command the Army of the Cumberland, but he was also asked how many men he would require to pacify the area. William Tecumseh Sherman was a realist: "Two hundred thousand," he replied—he not only failed to get the job, but his pessimism caused him to be suspected of treason![34]

And now Morgan and Forrest came to plow the ground of discontent. They found local partisans galore—partisans ready to join their bands, partisans to scout and report enemy dispositions, partisans to help them fall on isolated garrisons, burn ammunition and stores, capture prisoners, cut railroad and telegraph lines—in general, make life a festering hell for the confused Northerners. Forrest's raid culminated in a splendid *coup de guerre,* the capture of Crittenden's reinforced brigade at Murfreesboro, a gigantic bluff in view of Forrest's meager force, but one that worked and allowed him to destroy half a million dollars' worth of Federal supplies as well.

Morgan also prospered. In turning Union defenses upside down, he suffered a hundred casualties but took over a thousand prisoners and, by brisk recruiting among partisans, enlarged his band from nine hundred to two thousand. Grant, who had replaced Halleck, had to pull infantry from his line to serve as railroad guards. Such was the manpower drain that he asked to abandon the railroad, but Halleck, now in Washington, disapproved this. His progress became snail-like; Bragg beat him and Buell to Chattanooga, and the war went on.

Forrest continued screening Bragg's flanks and striking at opportune targets. In December, he bailed Bragg out again by hitting Grant's lines of communication between Jackson and Columbus. After knocking out seven hundred Union cavalry,

> . . . he started along the railroad, eating up the line and the small posts that protected it as a robin eats a worm. His flank-guards roamed fearlessly through the countryside, the telegraph wires went down everywhere and Union regiments wandered helplessly in a land of no information, searching for him while he made his way back to the Tennessee [River], the flatboat and eventually to the flanks of Bragg's command. Grant's supply line was ruined, it would take months to rebuild it and for more than a week he had not even telegraphic communication with the north.[35]

In the spring of 1863, Bragg sent Morgan on another raid to throw the Army of the Cumberland off balance. Morgan performed brilliantly, burning, destroying, capturing prisoners, tapping telegraph wires to send false orders to Union commanders, tearing down wires, eluding regiments and divisions sent to get him. So successful were his operations that he disobeyed orders and crossed the Ohio River to fight in Indiana and Ohio. His was a fantastic effort, altogether covering over a thousand miles in twenty-four days. But, as Federal forces and local militias turned out, his casualties grew heavy, his men and mounts tired, and finally he surrendered with the remnants of his band.*

A third Confederate officer, a small and wiry man named John Mosby, was more fortunate. Serving under Jeb Stuart as a captain, Mosby took twenty-nine volunteer troopers through enemy lines to General Stoughton's headquarters, north of Fairfax. With incredible audacity, he personally penetrated the general's headquarters, reached his bedroom, awakened him, and told him he was prisoner. To eliminate argument, he added, "Stuart's cavalry are in possession of the place [which in a sense was true] and Stonewall Jackson holds Centreville [not true]." The ensuing dialogue remains an all-time classic in the department of captured West Pointers:

STOUGHTON: "Is [General] Fitzhugh Lee here?"
MOSBY: "Yes."
STOUGHTON: "Then take me to him. We were classmates."
(This order may explain President Lincoln's remark upon being told of the capture of Stoughton and a number of horses: "Well, there won't be any difficulty in making another general, but how am I to replace those horses?")[36]

Based in the Shenandoah Valley and supported by partisans, Mosby continued his whirlwind raids to increasing Federal fury. As opposed to Forrest and Morgan, he kept his band small, but still inflicted enormous damage. In 1864, when Early burned Chambersburg, Pennsylvania, Grant found his excuse to scorch Mosby from the valley; after gaining Lincoln's approval, he ordered two corps to the task, and he told Sheridan: " . . . If you can possibly spare a division of cavalry, send them through Loudoun County to destroy and carry off the crops, animals, negroes, and all men under fifty years of age capable of bearing arms. In this way you will get rid of many of Mosby's men. . . . Give the enemy no rest. Do all the damage to railroads and crops you can. Carry off stock of all descriptions, and negroes, so as to prevent further planting. If the war is to last another year, we want the Shenandoah Valley to remain a barren waste." Although Sheridan promised to " . . . leave them nothing but their eyes to weep with," he still did not capture Mosby, now a colonel with a considerable price on his head.[37]

Passions ran high in this war, the inevitable result of total war encompassing a considerable portion of a great nation. But guerrilla warfare evoked a special and deadly kind of anger. G. F. R. Henderson

---

* He later escaped from a prison camp but was killed leading a cavalry charge at Knoxville.

wrote in his splendid work *Stonewall Jackson* that as early as 1862 Pope ordered that in Virginia " . . . the troops should subsist upon the country, and that the people should be held responsible for all damage done to roads, railways, and telegraphs by guerrillas."[38] When later pillaging and rape brought increased resistance, Pope ordered that every Virginian in Union-held areas must take an oath of allegiance. One of his generals, the German Von Steinwehr, arrested five prominent citizens as hostages " . . . to suffer death in the event of any soldiers being shot by bushwackers." The Confederate Government replied " . . . by declaring that Pope and his officers were not entitled to be considered as soldiers. If captured they were to be imprisoned so long as their orders remained unrepealed; and in the event of any unarmed Confederate citizens being tried and shot, an equal number of Federal prisoners were to be hanged. . . . "[39]

Sherman later wrote in a report to Washington, " . . . Forrest is the devil. There will never be peace in Tennessee until Forrest is dead."[40] Morgan and his band, when captured, in the spring of 1863 were treated harshly, " . . . like felons rather than prisoners of war."[41] At war's end, northern officials talked of arresting Forrest as a war criminal. Sherman's march through Georgia was as much an act of passion as one of necessity: a giant "search-and-destroy" operation that insured the hatred of those searched and destroyed.

Union treatment of guerrillas seems to have been based on Old Testament thinking. Guerrilla prisoners were summarily executed in Grant's command, and probably no Union commander was entirely guiltless in this respect. One of them, General Paine, at wits' end in western Kentucky, actually published this proclamation: "I shall shoot every guerrilla taken in my district, and if your southern brethren retaliate by shooting a Federal soldier, I will walk out five of your rich bankers, and cotton men, and make you kneel down and shoot them. I will do it, so help me God."[42]

CHAPTER NINE

1. Edmonds. See also, Leonard; Rapoport; Howard.
2. Clausewitz, *On War*, 343.
3. Ibid., 345.
4. Ibid., 345–6.
5. Ibid., 348.
6. Edmonds.
7. Jomini.
8. Ibid., 129–31.
9. Behr, 17.
10. Usborne, 37–8.
11. Standing, 115. See also, Ponteil, 460–6.
12. Matthews, Tanya, 10, 11.

13. Behr, 19–20.
14. Ponteil, 462.
15. Usborne, 40.
16. Ibid., 40–1.
17. Ibid., 41. See also, Azan.
18. Standing, 111, 114.
19. Ibid., 111.
20. Behr, 22–3.
21. Ibid., 23.
22. Callwell, 82–3.
23. Bernard, 3–5.
24. Gillespie, 21.
25. Standing, 122.
26. Ibid., 126–7. See also, Platonov.
27. Blanch, 27.
28. Standing, 128.
29. Ibid., 130.
30. Cole, 172.
31. Ibid., 172.
32. Weigley, 162.
33. Fuller, *The Decisive Battles* . . . , III, 19.
34. Pratt, 136.
35. Ibid., 138–40.
36. Standing, 177–8.
37. Ibid., 178–9.
38. Henderson, 400–1.
39. Ibid., 401.
40. Standing, 207.
41. Ibid., 193.
42. Bennett, 101.

CHAPTER 10

The American army's preference for orthodox warfare • Brussels conference of 1874 • Indian wars in America • General Custer's disaster • Upton's mission to Europe • Influence of Prussian militarism on the American army • Alfred Mahan and American expansionism • Guerrilla wars in Cuba • General Wyler's tactics • McKinley and American intervention

GUERRILLA OPERATIONS in the American Civil War, though striking, were also limited. Raids by irregular bands of horsemen tearing up railroad tracks and cutting telegraph wires did not decide the war. The decision derived from elaborate strategies, from naval blockades and mass movement of large armies, from conventional if changing battlefield tactics, from big battles and enormous casualties.

A professional officer, John Bigelow, may have treated Sherman's Civil War tactics in his textbook *Principles of Strategy*,[1] but military students continued to concentrate on the battles of Shiloh and Gettysburg and Spotsylvania and Fredericksburg in preference to the spectacular raids of Morgan and Forrest and Mosby, which the orthodox officer held as freakish manifestations in a side show of war.

Had the North lost the war, its conventional outlook might have altered; but, since it won, its principals regarded the irregular aspects as unseemly if not obscene. Other powers understood and agreed. In 1874, an international conference in Brussels, solemn in its stupidity and sounding awesomely like Alice's friend the Queen, announced to the wonderland world that guerrillas in order to be recognized as lawful belligerents must answer to a specific commander, wear a distinctive badge, carry arms openly and conform in operations to the laws and customs of war.[2]

While dark-suited diplomats, paunches suitably adorned with heavy gold watch chains, so pondered and decreed, a portion of the American army was fighting rudely clothed Indians who neither could, nor had

110

any wish to, understand diplomatic proceedings in Brussels. These tribes, diverse in location, numbers and combat capability, knew only that their way of life was yielding with each army stockade raised, with each spike pounded into the Union Pacific railroad track, with each white homestead built and ground broken. They protested by force of arms whenever and wherever possible. From 1865 to 1898, the army fought the amazing number of 943 actions against Indians. This military record should have produced a splendid breed of professionals adept in irregular warfare.

And it did. But on a very small scale and in a sharply circumscribed tactical specialty. The Civil War army, of over a million men, soon fell to some forty thousand, rose briefly to fifty-seven thousand during Reconstruction, then sank to around twenty-seven thousand, where it remained until the Spanish-American War.[3] Three major territorial areas administering 255 military posts claimed this small force. One of them, the Department of the Missouri, consisted of an expanding line of rude stockades supporting a cavalry troop or two in addition to small infantry garrisons. The Midwest and West still resound with their names: Fort Dodge, Fort Kearney, Fort Carson, Fort Reno—these and others a cumulative glove covering the fist of continental expansion.

But an awkward glove for a very big fist. The tactical problems for these troops in some ways paralleled those faced by other colonizing powers. Protesting Indian tribes rarely acted in concert, and tended to avoid set-piece battles except on their own terms. They preferred guerrilla tactics, an ambush or a hit-and-run raid, usually hideous affairs in which bow and arrow vied with repeating rifle (supplied along with whiskey by traders and renegades) to produce carnage cruelly topped by tomahawk and scalping knife giving vent to primitive frustrations.

Small in numbers, these war bands moved fast, struck hard, and disappeared. Little pattern existed in either their strategy or their tactics. Successful countertactics hinged on intelligence and mobility. To supply the former, the army used friendly Indians; to provide mobility, it depended on horses. Troopers enjoyed the advantage of disciplined fire and movement. They suffered from lack of numbers; from the rugged terrain and vast spaces, which usually precluded an artillery train; and from communication difficulties with other posts, which prevented coordinated action.

As Marshal Bugeaud had discovered in Algeria, the lighter the column the better—but this could be abused, particularly where the commander lacked valid intelligence. The classic example of how not to fight the Indians occurred in the spring of 1876 during Sheridan's campaign against the Sioux and Northern Cheyennes. Sitting Bull's force was thought to be in the Little Missouri area, and Crazy Horse was somewhere in the Powder River area in Wyoming. General Terry was

111

U.S. troops
Custer's route
Reno's route
Indians

Custer's fight

Custer last seen here

Custer's Advance

Little Big Horn R.

Reno's 1st fight

Reno & Benteen here surrounded

Reno's Retreat Road

N

0   ½   1 mile

M.E.P.

sent to smoke them out and defeat them. His cavalry consisted of two columns, one commanded by General Crook, one by General Custer. These commanders were to operate in extremely rugged terrain familiar neither to themselves nor to their troopers.

The first warning came in March, when Crazy Horse jumped and badly hurt Crook's force. In June, scouts reported Sitting Bull in the Yellowstone country, somewhere in the valley of the Little Big Horn. Terry now sent Custer's 7th United States Cavalry, a regiment of some seven hundred troopers, into this virtually unknown country against an enemy of unknown strength. Upon approaching Sitting Bull's home grounds, Custer compounded Terry's error by splitting his regiment into a strong advance guard under Major Reno, who was to "charge the village" while Custer's force worked through the hills. Reno ran into an ambush and was badly hurt but managed to survive until Terry's main force arrived. Custer's command, 265 men, was surrounded and slaughtered. The relief force saw their scalped comrades, charged forth in fury—and found space.[4]

Such defeats were rare. The press of civilization, of people and the railroad, increasingly pushed the Indian into barren country, which he would finally forsake for the reservation. Technology might not have given the army superior firepower, but it did offer the means to campaign the year around. As Weigley notes, " . . . thus supported, the Army again and again won its most decisive victories in the winter. Then George Custer won the battle of the Washita; then George Crook and Nelson Miles crushed Sitting Bull and Crazy Horse; then Chief Joseph [of the Nez Percé] vowed to Howard and Miles to fight no more forever."[5] Unlike the European process, which involved military superiority, commercial exploitation and ultimately political failure, the American process depended on military superiority and tribal genocide. In short, the Europeans milched the conquered, the Americans tried to eliminate them.

The Indian wars form a fascinating chapter in American history. They also provide splendid examples of minor tactics. If these primarily were *cavalry* tactics, they nonetheless could have been codified and expanded into a significant doctrine that might have altered the growing American preference for European-style warfare.

This may have been in Sherman's mind. The top army commander, at that time called the Commanding General, William Tecumseh Sherman, reigned from 1869 to 1883. Formerly in command of the Division of Missouri, Sherman retained interest in western fighting and, in the mid-seventies, sent a three-man commission to study British colonial campaigns. The prime mover of this body, which traveled first to Asia and India, then to Europe, was a Sherman protégé, a much decorated Civil War veteran named Emory Upton.

A humorless pedant, General Upton already had wrestled with the challenge to orthodoxy posed by technology, specifically the repeating rifle and breech-loading artillery: " . . . a systematic search for means to escape tactical impasse."[6] His new tactics, adopted by the army in 1867, called for a build-up of the skirmish line by fire and movement. This tactical trend had begun a century earlier with the development of Jäger battalions in Europe and light-infantry regiments in the American Revolution. It had advanced in the Napoleonic wars—Clausewitz and Jomini both concentrated on the problem—and in the American Civil War. Today's tactics are still based on this notion, which has never totally answered the ascendancy of the defense.

Colonial warfare in Asia did not much impress the orthodox, infantry-oriented Upton, who infinitely preferred European warfare. This was the day of emergent Prussian militarism. Prussia's dramatic victories of 1864, 1866 and 1870–71 signaled a battlefield of breech-loading rifles and artillery, large and carefully organized conscript armies, meticulously planned railway nets and mobilization schedules—all arranged by an omnipotent general staff. Upton's report, "The Armies of Asia and Europe," recommended " . . . that the United States adopt a modified form of the German cadre army."[7]

Some of Upton's contemporaries already were influenced by Clausewitz, whose massive *On War* was published in English in 1873. Prussian militarism seemed a logical and even enviable extension to Clausewitzian doctrine, a thought pursued by Upton in another work, *The Military Policy of the United States*. This posthumously published work called for war by superior numbers and armament, or weight rather than mobility and its natural corollary, deception. To Upton and his followers, and they were many and impressive, the military road ahead was plain to behold.

It was not so plain to either the American people or their Congressional representatives, who held the purse strings. Army budgets remained as penurious after Upton's death as before. When purse strings finally loosened, it was for a reason remote from Upton's thinking, and one he probably would not have welcomed.

The conquest of the American continent was still continuing when a navy captain fatefully influenced a small but powerful group of Americans already inclined toward expansionist thinking. This was Alfred T. Mahan, who in 1890 published a work called *The Influence of Sea Power upon History, 1660–1783*.[8] In this and subsequent works, Mahan argued that Britain's world-power status rested on naval supremacy, by which it controlled the balance of power on the land mass of Eurasia. To complement this strategy, America must continue its present construction of a powerful and modern battle fleet capable of controlling North American waters. Such a fleet would need forward bases, coaling stations, and a supply fleet, all of which called for the cooperation and possible acquisition of certain foreign territories. The effort, besides assuring America its due place among the world's great powers, would pay moral, religious, and economic dividends. A spate of magazine articles written by Mahan during the next seven years attempted to convince the reading public that it could not sleep easily until the country had forged Cuba, the Isthmus of Panama (soon to be pierced by a canal), and Hawaii " . . . in a single system vital to American security."[9]

These strategic arguments for limited imperialism impressed a number of important officers, such as George Dewey, and civil officials and politicians, such as Benjamin Tracy, Henry Cabot Lodge and Theodore Roosevelt, who each accepted Mahan's theories and influenced, in turn, other important government voices. But Mahan's arguments also impressed other influential circles: American businessmen who did not object to the idea of new foreign markets and of competing in Asia and Africa with European powers, though most of them wanted nothing to do with American colonies as such. Men of good works, ministers and missionaries, spoke of the moral and religious responsibility of the strong toward the weak—the old "white man's burden" argument. A favorable emotional climate also existed. The glory of nation building had worn thin. Men were bored, frustrated by the economic depression of 1893; they wanted activity, and a foreign excursion did not seem repugnant.

None of these factors alone would have pushed America into an imperialist phase, anyway beyond the acquisition of Caribbean and Hawaiian bases. But, in 1895, the Cuban insurrection began to form a powerful catalyst. When the insurrection broke out, the Cleveland administration was having difficulties with England in Venezuela, and Cleveland favored a hands-off policy. But as fighting continued and was dramatically reported by a sensationalist press, public opinion began to swing in favor of the rebels.

The newly elected McKinley at first ignored increasing pressure for intervention. " . . . We want no wars of conquest; we must avoid the temptation of territorial aggression," he told the nation in his inaugural address.[10] Then and later, McKinley's words rarely impressed the nation's policy makers (the historian S. E. Morison later described McKinley as "a kindly soul in a spineless body").[11] His attempts to cool the situation made little progress. The insurgents, if not winning, were at least holding their own; convinced of eventual American intervention, they were demanding total independence, which the Spanish refused to consider.

The Spanish had only themselves to blame for the contretemps. From time to time, powerful American voices had stressed Cuba's proximity to the United States and called for annexation. Simultaneously, dissident groups backed by wealthy exiles in New York had formed in Cuba to protest against continued Spanish rule. Finally, Madrid should have been warned by the war of 1868, a ten-year insurrection led by a plantation owner, Carlos Manuel de Céspedes, that resulted in a Pyrrhic victory for Spain. The prolonged campaign fought by an army that grew to about seventy thousand men drained countless troop reinforcements from the mother country at a politically awkward time. Spanish deaths amounted to an estimated two hundred and eight thousand, Cuban deaths perhaps fifty thousand. The war cost $300 million, an immense sum, which the Spanish added to the Cuban debt, thus deepening resentment.[12]

The war won Spain only postponement. Perhaps her rule could have survived had she put through reforms leading toward autonomy. But political anarchy at home prevented viable policy abroad. And the war had helped form forces of nationalism that were to explode within a few years. If it claimed the lives of many leaders, it also trained other leaders and gave the people heroes: Carlos Manuel de Céspedes, Antonio and José Maceo, Calixto García, José Gómez, Eduardo Machado, Tomás Estrada Palma—names perhaps unfamiliar to North American readers, but names no less glorious for that, and glorious not only to Cubans but to many other Latin Americans, names that thenceforth tripped frequently from persuasive nationalist tongues.

One of the most persuasive belonged to José Martí, founder, in 1892, of the Cuban Revolutionary Party. Scholar and romanticist, lawyer and poet, Martí worked hard to bring on the 1895 insurrection. Killed a few weeks after its outbreak—he was forty-two years old—he in turn became a legendary hero to the next two generations.

The war of 1895 began in spring of that year with rebel landings from Costa Rica and Santo Domingo. The Spanish doubled their forces to thirty-two thousand, commanded by the hero of Morocco, General Martínez Campos. By June, the Spanish build-up had reached over fifty thousand, a force opposed by six to eight thousand rebels operating mainly in Oriente province, where " . . . all classes openly or secretly backed the rebellion—even sometimes members of the Civil Guard."[13]

Martínez Campos accurately defined the problem to his prime minister in the same month: Spain was faced with a rebellion of major proportions. Ruthless measures were called for; he himself did not feel able to implement them and recommended General Weyler for the job. He warned, however: " . . . Even if we win in the field and suppress the rebels, since the country wishes to have neither an amnesty for our enemies nor an extermination of them, my loyal and sincere opinion is that, with reforms or without reforms, before twelve years we shall have another war."[14]

Martínez Campos retained command until early in 1896. The rebels meanwhile consolidated control of much of Oriente province. As in the earlier rebellion, the Spanish continued to govern important towns; unlike in the earlier rebellion, forceful guerrilla leaders, Máximo Gómez and José Maceo, carried war to the western provinces. By the end of the year, Maceo was approaching the Havana area while other guerrilla commanders controlled significant portions of the middle provinces.

Cuban Revolution 1868 and 1895

- – – → Céspedes 1868-1869
- → Martí 1895
- → Guerrilla operations 1896-1898

0   50   100   200 miles

PINAR DEL RÍO
Havana
HAVANA
MATANZAS
LAS VILLAS
Morón
Júcaro
CAMAGÜEY
ORIENTE
Bayamo

Isle of Pines

C A R I B B E A N   S E A

N

CUBA in relation to WEST INDIES

Gulf of Mexico
FLORIDA
JAMAICA
HAITI
SANTO DOMINGO
Caribbean Sea
SOUTH AMERICA
0   50 miles

M.E.P.

Martínez Campos resigned in favor of the more ruthless General Weyler, a military ascetic who arrived when Maceo's guerrillas were tearing up the westernmost province while Gómez was holding Havana in virtual siege.

An able general, Weyler quickly faced up to the deteriorating situation. After dividing the island into operational spheres, he attempted to regain tactical mobility by reorganizing cavalry and infantry and by eliminating remote outposts. He also recruited militias for town defense and organized units of Cuban counterguerrillas, " . . . these being often much more feared than the Spaniards by the rebels." To deny rebels support and allow his columns unfettered maneuver, he herded thousands of Cubans into "fortified towns" and "military areas," which often proved little more than concentration camps. He ordered all the people of the eastern provinces to register, and he gave his area commanders emergency powers including that of summary execution.[15]

These measures, invoked during 1896 and 1897, worked variously, but definitely helped to check guerrilla operations, particularly in the West. That they did not give Weyler "victory" is explained by several factors. Weyler's army, though well armed and fairly well organized, was not the best: its officers, in part, were venal and corrupt, its men illiterate and often uncaring. A British observer in Cuba at the time, Lieutenant Barnes of the 4th Hussars, later made a comprehensive and penetrating analysis of the Spanish failure. The main problem, Barnes noted, was

> . . . the intense hostility of the inhabitants. They could get no good information of the rebel movements, while the rebels were never in doubt about theirs. An insurgent was distinguished from the peaceful cultivator only by his badge which could be speedily removed, and by his rifle which was easily hidden. Hence the Government forces, whether in garrison or operating in the country, were closely surrounded by an impalpable circle of fierce enemies who murdered stragglers, intercepted messages, burned stores, and maintained a continual observation.

In addition, poor roads hindered Spanish mobility, while smallpox, malaria and yellow fever " . . . filled the hospitals and drained the fighting units." But, as Barnes pointed out to his superiors,

> . . . all these are obstacles to success rather than causes of failure— these latter must be looked for in the tactics and conduct of the Spanish forces. There was a complete absence of any general plan. Columns moved about haphazard in the woods, fighting the enemy where they found them and returning with their wounded to the

towns when they were weary of wandering. Their method of warfare was essentially defensive. They held great numbers of towns and villages with strong garrisons. They defended, or tried to defend, long lines of communication with a multitude of small blockhouses. They tried to treat the rebels as though they were merely agrarian rioters and to subdue the revolt by quartering troops all over the country. The movement was on a scale far exceeding the scope of such remedies; it was a war, and this the Spanish Government would never recognize. Over all the petty incidents of guerrilla skirmishing, the frequent executions and the stern reprisals threw a darker shade.[16]

Spanish excesses disturbed the American public as much as rebel successes thrilled it. Such was the exaggerated and bellicose tone of the day's yellow press—mainly the Hearst, Dana, and Pulitzer papers—that McKinley increasingly found it difficult to steer a neutral course. Hope of a Spanish-Cuban solution meanwhile was growing increasingly dim. By early 1897, Weyler was reporting the western provinces pacified and rebels on the run in Las Villas. Although his *trochas* had impeded and in some cases broken rebel communications and although considerable quarrels were rending the rebel camp, the guerrillas were far from defeated, particularly in Oriente province. Spain had sent an estimated two hundred thousand soldiers to Cuba (of whom tens of thousands died, most from disease), the Philippine troubles were draining more troops and money, and the climate of America was turning increasingly in favor of intervention. In the spring of 1897, a new government in Madrid tried to mollify Cuba's powerful neighbor by promising the Cubans autonomy (but not independence) and by recalling Weyler, now notorious as *El Carnicero*—"the Butcher"—because of the high mortality rate among the four hundred thousand hapless natives penned in concentration camps.[17]

These steps proved too little and too late. In fairness to more lurid press accounts, Spanish promises of reform were halfhearted, nor did the Madrid government respond favorably to McKinley's offer to purchase Cuba for $300 million. A case also existed for intervention on humanitarian grounds, and, by 1898, the humanitarian appeal had broadened in America. By 1898, the strategic, economic, moral, religious and emotional influences of a young and in some respects greedy nation had fused to form a powerful interventionist voice whose cry caused President McKinley to send a battleship, USS *Maine,* to Havana. The dispatch of the *Maine* was not a bellicose act. When its sinking under circumstances still obscure led to war with Spain, General Upton's professional military Utopia was not even around the corner. The American army numbered around twenty-five thousand, its infantry and cavalry were reasonably well trained in minor tactics, it had adopted the excellent Krag-Jörgensen rifle; but its organization was appallingly bad, its artillery deficient, many of its senior officers Civil War veterans.

In April 1898, Congress authorized an increase in regular-army strength to nearly sixty-five thousand and also authorized calling up volunteer and state-militia units. By the end of the war, in August, army strength topped 270,000, twice the number desired by harassed army planners, who lacked camps, uniforms, weapons, and machinery to provide them.[18] Confusion prevailed at all levels, severe epidemics broke out, and the press did not help matters by pointing out raucously and consistently manifold errors that in some instances reached scandalous proportions. Despite such hindrances, General Shafter's expeditionary force finally landed in Cuba, Teddy Roosevelt scampered up San Juan Hill, the enormous but demoralized Spanish garrison surrendered, and the army settled down to a relatively quiet occupation.

Meanwhile, however, acting on secret instructions, Commodore Dewey had sailed his squadron of six warships from Hong Kong. Early on May 1, he slipped into Manila Bay, sank the Spanish fleet, and besieged the city. To exploit his gains, he requested a landing force of five thousand men. President McKinley ordered the War Department to furnish an expeditionary force that would complete " . . . the reduction of Spanish power in that quarter" and give " . . . order and security to the islands while in the possession of the United States. . . . "[19]

These orders were to open a new chapter in American arms—one undreamed of by General Emory Upton and his army disciples of the orthodox battlefield.

CHAPTER TEN

1. Bigelow, 92–103.
2. Asprey, "Guerrilla Warfare."
3. Weigley, 267.
4. Callwell, 179, cites this campaign in his chapter on division of force. Although he held that such division was often necessary in small wars, and practically essential in guerrilla wars, he nonetheless cautioned the commander to be careful when operating independently with limited force and with inadequate knowledge of enemy and terrain.
5. Weigley, 269.
6. Ibid., 275.
7. Ibid., 276–7.
8. Mahan, *The Influence of Sea Power upon History* . . . See also, *The Influence of Sea Power upon the French Revolution* . . . ; *Sea Power in Its Relations to the War of 1812.*
9. Leopold, 120–3.
10. Ibid., 170.
11. Morison, *The Oxford History of the United States* . . . , II, 409.
12. Thomas, *Cuba or The Pursuit of Freedom*, 269.
13. Ibid., 319.

14. Ibid., 321.
15. Ibid., 329.
16. Callwell, 131–3.
17. Leopold, 170–1.
18. Morison, II, 413–14.
19. Kennan, *American Diplomacy, 1900–1950*, 12.

CHAPTER 11

THE PHILIPPINE ISLANDS offered a slightly more complicated situation than Cuba. Toward the end of the century, this enormous archipelago supported a population of nearly 7 million. Spanish rule, particularly the "paternal authority" of Roman Catholic friars, had enslaved natives for nearly four hundred years. The warlike Moros had challenged this dismal state of affairs since the beginning of the eighteenth century—sporadic revolts put down with almost unbelievable harshness. Resistance spread in the nineteenth century, and, in 1896, a major revolt broke out, largely the work of Dr. José Rizal backed by a terrorist society, the Katipunan, or Patriots' League.

Rizal was almost unique in the islands: at thirty-five, he was traveled and educated, " . . . a poet, philosopher, surgeon, and an artist," also the author of a popular protest novel, *Noli Me Tangere* (Touch Me Not).[1] Rizal's revolt triggered a reign of terror under a new governor, General Polavieja, described by an English observer as " . . . an amazing personage, who has never won a battle and never failed to lose one."[2]

Polavieja's troops summarily executed Rizal and hundreds of his

122

followers, but the Katipunan remained intact and revolt spread throughout Luzon. It was not pretty, but hatred never is. The Catholic Church, responsible for much of the misery, proved a particular target. In the village of Imus, " . . . thirteen friars fell into their [native] hands. One was killed by being gradually cut to pieces. Another was set afire, after being saturated with petroleum; still another was pierced through the length of his body by a bamboo split then doused in oil while alive and turned over a moderate fire."[3]

Isolated bestiality does not make a successful revolution. Polavieja's successor, General Primo de Rivera, soon exploited the rebels' willingness to fight pitched battles, which they invariably lost. The revolution could well have been doomed had not a natural leader come to the fore.

Don Emilio Aguinaldo was a Filipino Trotsky. The son of landowning parents in Cavite province, the twenty-nine-year-old rebel was a mixture of Chinese and Tagalog blood. He had studied law in Manila without gaining a degree; in a predominantly Catholic country, he was a Mason; he was said to have been mild and soft-spoken, yet with a charisma that placed him among the young leaders of the revolution.

In August 1896, he personally led a successful assault against the garrison in his home town. By October, " . . . he had become the accepted military commander of the revolution." Showing exceptional administrative ability, he organized a Central Revolutionary Committee and a Filipino Congress, which established a shadow government. In 1897, Aguinaldo was elected president and generalissimo. When a disgruntled associate began a splinter movement, Aguinaldo had him arrested, court-martialed, and shot.[4]

During the next year, the movement survived a series of vicissitudes that demonstrated de Rivera's perfidy to Aguinaldo and the revolutionary junta. Rolling with the punches, Aguinaldo and his principal lieutenants fled to Hong Kong, where they received limited aid from the U. S. Navy (through Commodore Dewey) and also from the U. S. State Department (through Consul Wildman).

After Dewey's victory at Manila Bay, in early May, the revolutionary junta returned to Luzon. By late spring of 1898, Aguinaldo and his military commander, General Luna, boasted an army of nearly thirty thousand. With the bulk of Spanish forces contained in Manila, and with Dewey's fleet in control of harbors and sea, the rebels proclaimed the Visayan Republic and published a declaration of independence.

Aguinaldo's words no doubt flowed from the heart, but his mind also was at work. He was already disturbed by what appeared to be America's contradictory attitude. Only the previous December, in a warm-up speech for war with Spain, President McKinley had said of Cuba: " . . . I speak not of forcible annexation, for that cannot be thought of. That, by our code of morality, would be criminal aggression." In Aguinaldo's mind, this principle would apply to the Philippines. But neither Dewey nor Wildman had seemed wildly enthusiastic about supporting the rebel movement, and they all but ignored the Filipino declaration of independence.

Aguinaldo was a realist, however. He needed American help: Dewey's fleet, troops for the assault of Manila, loans to get his government organized. Knowing that he was going to receive American help, whether or not solicited, he chose to describe the Americans to his people as "our redeemers."[5]

Redeemers or conquerors?

A large portion of the American populace no doubt regarded themselves as redeemers who would establish organized government, as in Cuba—and get out. These were not the sentiments, however, of a strong and influential expansionist group who employed Mahan's doctrines to fit the new situation—with Mahan's full concurrence. With the annexation of Hawaii assured, they raised their sights to the Philippines, arguing that Filipinos could not govern themselves. If America were not to assume the task, then the inevitable anarchic vacuum would be filled either by Japan, particularly dangerous in view of recent victory over China, or by England, Germany, Russia, or France. America, too, needed overseas trade, and here was a splendid opportunity to anchor in new territory—a base from which to nibble at the crumbling Chinese pie.

To some Americans, it seemed as if God were extending America's lease on manifest destiny; to others, a mystic element entered. Shortly before the outbreak of war, the *Washington Post* told its readers:

> . . . A new consciousness seems to have come upon us—the consciousness of strength—and with it a new appetite, the yearning to show our strength . . . ambition, interest, land hunger, pride, the mere joy of fighting, whatever it may be, we are animated by a new sensation. We are face to face with a strange destiny. The taste of Empire is in the mouth of the people even as the taste of blood in the jungle. It means an Imperial policy, the Republic, renascent, taking her place with the armed nations.[6]

The executive instrument essential to planting the American flag in the Philippines, the American army's expeditionary force, was not the sharpest ever forged. Command went to Major General Wesley Merritt, a sixty-two-year-old seasoned campaigner: he had served as a young general with enormous distinction in the Civil War, a reputation enhanced by service in the Indian wars. Now heavy, with white, wavy hair and hard gray eyes, he was also something of a realist. Looking at his two regiments of regulars, the 14th and the 23rd Infantry, supported by a few artillery batteries, he complained in mid-May to President McKinley that such a force would prove insufficient "... when the work to be done consists of conquering a territory 7,000 miles from our base, defended by a regularly trained and acclimated army of from 10,000 to 25,000 men [the Spanish] and inhabited by 14 millions [sic] of people, the majority of whom will regard us with the intense hatred both of race and religion."[7]

Although Merritt's force eventually was fleshed out to eighty-five hundred with National Guard and volunteer units, these reinforcements had to be armed with the old Springfield .45-caliber rifle, a single-shot monster whose black powder puffed like a locomotive over the firer's head. Other essentials remained in short supply, nor were matters remedied upon arrival in the Philippines at Camp Dewey, a former peanut farm:

> ... The heat was oppressive and rain kept falling. At times the trenches were filled with two feet of water, and soon the men's shoes were ruined. Their heavy khaki uniforms were a nuisance; they perspired constantly, the loss of body salts induced chronic fatigue. Prickly heat broke out, inflamed by scratching and rubbing. Within a week the first cases of dysentery, malaria, cholera and dengue fever showed up at sick call.[8]

Merritt and his generals slowly overcame these initial difficulties. In August, Major General Elwell Otis arrived with reinforcements that nearly doubled American strength. Merritt meanwhile was moving his army alongside Filipino units for the cardboard assault of Manila, which fell in August.

This victory failed to repair deteriorating American-Filipino relations. Considering the state of the 1898 world, and particularly the Great Power concept, perhaps an amicable relationship was impossible. Strategic and economic arguments for outright annexation were strong, and Spanish efforts to send a relief force taken with the rude behavior of a German task force in Manila Bay reinforced them.

Overriding these arguments was a paternalism that must have brought bile to Aguinaldo's throat. Nowhere is this better expressed than in an early report of the Philippine Commission, a presidentially appointed body headed by Jacob Schurman, which concluded:

> ... lack of [Filipino] education and political experience, combined with their racial and linguistic diversities, disqualify them, in spite of their mental gifts and domestic virtues, to undertake the task of governing the archipelago at the present time. The most that can be expected of them is to cooperate with the Americans in the administration of general affairs ... and to undertake, subject to

American control or guidance (as may be found necessary), the administration of provincial and municipal affairs. . . .

Should our power by any fatality be withdrawn, the commission believe that the government of the Philippines would speedily lapse into anarchy, which would excuse, if it did not necessitate, the intervention of other powers and the eventual division of the islands among them. Only through American occupation, therefore, is the idea of a free, self-governing, and united Philippines Commonwealth at all conceivable. And the indispensable need from the Filipino point of view of maintaining American sovereignty over the archipelago is recognized by all intelligent Filipinos and even by those insurgents who desire an American protectorate. The latter, it is true, would take the revenues and leave us the responsibilities. . . .

The Commission's arguments had certain merits. Spanish rule had deprived most people of formal education. The Commission reported that Spanish regulations provided one male and one female teacher for each five thousand inhabitants—" . . . this wretchedly inadequate provision was never carried out."[9]

But the Commission, peering from Olympian heights of Western political behavior, failed to recognize either the volatility or the pride of these "backward" peoples, a volatility and pride dangerously compressed by four centuries of misrule. Spanish excesses had filled Filipino hearts with hatred, a nebulous emotion inextricably related to pride. In the eyes of most Westerners, pride and poverty are poles apart; and, all too often, we assume that a poor man *ipso facto* lacks pride, particularly if his skin is not white. The American soldier of 1898 proved true to this philosophy. An army major in an official report noted, " . . . almost without exception, soldiers and also many officers refer to the natives in their presence as 'niggers' and natives are beginning to understand what the word 'nigger' means."[10]

Top American officials, Dewey, Merritt and Otis, added to mounting antagonism by cavalier treatment of Aguinaldo and his officials, whose protests over the continuing arrival of American reinforcements were insolently brushed aside. As the American presence mounted and American intentions became clear, tentacles of native ill feeling began to leave the Spanish corpse to quiver about the newcomers. Aguinaldo meanwhile emphasized Filipino intentions by convening a congress that wrote a constitution for the new republic.

American officials remained unimpressed and successfully communicated their negative attitude to Washington and to influential portions of the American public. Imperialist feeling was now running high despite fulminations of the Anti-Imperialist League, whose members included some of the most respected men in the nation. To suggested

126

alternatives, for example a protectorate role similar to that proclaimed for Cuba, or limited acquisition, say the island of Luzon alone, the expansionists turned a deaf ear.

In October, the American Government opened negotiations with Spain in Paris. Neither Aguinaldo nor his representatives were invited to participate. In November, they learned that the Treaty of Paris granted the United States control of the Philippines, the Sulus, and Guam in return for a payment of $20 million to Spain. Considerable soul-searching accompanied the ratification process, but the necessary Senate majority was won. President McKinley, who before Dewey's victory allegedly confessed he " . . . could not have told where those darned islands were within two thousand miles," bowed to the inevitable.[11]

The treaty, which struck Aguinaldo like a thunderbolt, only intensified Filipino aspirations to independence. To the leaders, it was now clear that war was imminent, war of a kind suggested by preliminary native operations: by rifles smuggled from Manila in coffins supposedly carrying the dead; by orders for secret attacks against American installations in Manila.

That winter, the cloud of ill feeling continued to swell. Soon it enveloped Manila and hung over the two armies, the one now facing the other. On February 4, 1899, an American sentry fired on and killed a Filipino soldier. Firing opened along the line. The Philippine Insurrection was on.

The insurrection should have ended quickly. The Americans incontestably won the first battle, a two-day orthodox infantry attack supported by naval gunfire. This action cost 59 American lives and 278 wounded; the insurgents lost from two thousand to five thousand dead, their army fleeing to the north. Aguinaldo's guerrilla plans for Manila came to nought thanks to American army precautions.[12] Otis cabled Washington, " . . . His [Aguinaldo's] influence throughout this section destroyed. Now applies for cessation of hostilities and conference. Have declined to answer."[13] Or, rather, he answered by conventional military tactics, which he felt certain would result in the capture of Luna's army and the end of the insurrection. These involved sending out task forces to find, fix and destroy. On an island the size of Ohio, they found little, fixed virtually nothing, but destroyed numerous villages. That spring, MacArthur's brigade captured the rebel capital of Malolos at a cost of nearly 550 casualties, but one capital was as good as another to the rebels. Luna's army dispersed, drifted north, and re-formed.

By spring, the war was going badly for the Americans. Otis increasingly resembled Job facing one disaster after another. His restless soldiers liked nothing about the Philippines—not the weather, the people, the tinned-salmon rations—nothing. He had already lost a large number of volunteers whose terms had expired, sick bays and hospitals overflowed with patients, impatient generals were carping at his halting tactics and, even worse, American correspondents were beginning to fathom insurgency warfare.

In June, the American journal *Harper's Weekly* published a dispatch that its respected correspondent, Mr. Bass, had smuggled to Hong Kong. Influential American readers learned that

> . . . since the fourth of February various expeditions have taken place, principally in the island of Luzon. These expeditions resulted in our taking from the insurgent government certain territory. Some of this territory we have occupied; the rest we have returned to the insurgents in a more or less mutilated condition, depending on whether the policy of the hour was to carry on a bitter war against a barbarous enemy, or to bring enlightenment to an ignorant people, deceived as to our motives.

After stating that the American outlook " . . . is blacker now than it has been since the beginning of the war," Mr. Bass offered some reasons: " . . . First, the whole population of the islands sympathizes with the insurgents; only those natives whose immediate self-interest requires it are friendly to us. . . . " The in-again-out-again policy was ridiculous:

> . . . The insurgents came back to Pasig, and their first act was to hang the *presidente* for treason in surrendering to the Americans. Presidents do not surrender towns to us any more. When we returned to Pasig we found the place well fortified, and we suffered some loss in retaking it. This process might go on indefinitely. . . . These expeditions, lacking the purpose of holding the land conquered, alienate the population already hostile, encourage insurgents, teach them true methods of fighting, and exhaust our men.

As for Otis' tactics:

> . . . To chase barefooted insurgents with water-buffalo carts as a wagon-train may be simply ridiculous; but to load volunteers down with two hundred rounds of ammunition and one day's rations, and to put on their heads felt hats used by no other army in the world in the tropics, in order to trot these same soldiers in the broiling sun over a country without roads, is positively criminal. Out of as strong and robust an army as ever wore shoe leather, there are five thousand men in the general hospital. . . . [14]

The press soon suffered a surfeit of copy. In June, a rebel force ambushed four thousand Americans and cut them to ribbons. That summer, the rebels began discarding uniforms, the better to pursue guerrilla tactics. Ambushes became common. American soldiers were murdered, their bodies mutilated. The Americans retaliated by using the "water cure" on natives reluctant to talk: four or five gallons of water were forced down a man's throat, then squeezed out by kneeling on his stomach.[15] If he lived, he usually talked. The guerrillas retaliated by more torturing and mutilating. Americans responded by burning villages and killing indiscriminately. The sick figure rose; morale declined. Otis initiated heavy censorship of news dispatches and was heard to say it was " . . . as though the AP were in the pay of the Filipino junta in Hong Kong."[16]

Otis now resolved to end the war. He had over forty-five thousand troops, with more en route, and, in September, he ordered a three-division operation designed to clear northern Luzon and capture Aguinaldo. Of the three columns, Lawton's fared the worst. Such was terrain and rain that cavalry often averaged only a mile a day! Supply wagons became hopelessly mired. Lawton's cavalry finally broke loose by abandoning wagons and living off the land. This column fell on Aguinaldo's rear guard near San Pedro and captured his mother and son. Aguinaldo and his guerrillas escaped—not surprising, since in six weeks Lawton's task force had covered only 120 miles.

With the rebels underground, the war lost any semblance of orthodoxy—excepting Otis' tactics. These consisted in fanning a series of outposts out from Manila, a serious drain on his forces, which now numbered around sixty thousand. Incredibly he seemed to think that he was winning. In a popular magazine of the day, *Leslie's Weekly,* he stated, " . . . You asked me to say when the war in the Philippines will be over. . . . The war in the Philippines is already over . . . all we have to do now is protect Filipinos against themselves. . . . There will be no more real fighting . . . little skirmishes which amount to nothing." In December 1899, he cabled Washington no less than four times that the war was over![17]

His commanders, or some of them, were growing more realistic. General Lawton described the insurgents as " . . . the bravest men I have ever seen." General Arthur MacArthur noted, " . . . wherever throughout the archipelago there is a group of the insurgent army, it is a fact beyond dispute that all the contiguous towns contribute to the maintenance thereof. . . . Intimidation has undoubtedly accomplished much to this end; but fear as the only motive is hardly sufficient to account for the united and apparently spontaneous action of several millions of people."[18] As Otis pushed outposts farther and farther from the capital, and as punitive expeditions began seeking out neighboring islands, resistance increased. Supply lines became favorite targets. Sometimes guerrillas simply blocked paths and trails by interwoven vines, sometimes they "mined" them by burying sharp bamboo sticks. Rebels constantly cut telegraph lines; villagers stole rifles and ammunition; small bands fell on garrisons or ambushed supply parties. In the first thirteen months, the army reported 1,026 engagements, with 245 Americans killed, 490 wounded and 118 captured, versus 3,854 rebels killed, 1,193 wounded, 6,572 captured.[19]

In an election year, pacification was moving much too slowly for McKinley's pleasure. Otis was replaced by MacArthur, who continued the old and tried something of the new. At first, nothing worked. An amnesty program brought in only some five thousand people to swear allegiance to the American flag; a rifle-recovery program, thirty pesos per weapon, produced an insulting 140 pieces. He continued sending punitive expeditions to other islands, which he blockaded with gunboats; he bribed island chiefs, who took the money but could not stop the fighting.

MacArthur wanted to impose much stricter measures, but his hands were tied by the bitter autumn elections in America. Imperialism was a major theme. Aguinaldo, seeing a Democratic victory as his only hope, called for general escalation of resistance in order to keep the issue in American headlines. The Republican victory came as a terrible blow to the insurgent cause: MacArthur received another seventy-five thousand soldiers and, at the end of the year, placed the islands under martial law. Mass arrests and imprisonment followed. For the first time, the insurgent cause faltered. A native Federal Party, pledged to accept American sovereignty, began to grow in popularity. A few dissident tribes already had come over to the American side, and, for some time, troop commanders had been using native irregulars. In February 1901, Congress authorized MacArthur to recruit " . . . a body of native troops, not exceeding 12,000, called 'Scouts' "—these to consist initially of thirty to fifty companies of one hundred men each, commanded by American officers.[20]

The scouts played an integral role in the first real break in the war. Among dispatches taken from a captured courier was one from Aguinaldo ordering a distant guerrilla chief to send him four hundred troops at once. According to the courier, Aguinaldo was operating in northeastern Luzon, in the mountains of Isabela province. The man who learned this information was Frederick Funston, a thirty-six-year-old brigadier of volunteers, a rugged, brave and intelligent redhead. Funston at once exploited this valuable intelligence by an imaginative, courageous and deceptive plan that hopefully would allow him to attack enemy political-military leadership. With some difficulty, he persuaded seniors to allow him to disguise eighty-one Maccabebe scouts as *insur-*

recto replacements responding to Aguinaldo's orders. Funston and four volunteer officers disguised as prisoners accompanied the draft. After a hazardous march of over a hundred miles, this extraordinary party penetrated Aguinaldo's inner sanctum, took him prisoner, and returned to American territory—one of the most successful *ruses de guerre* of all times. Aguinaldo subsequently swore allegiance to the American flag and issued a proclamation of surrender.

The second break in the war came soon after Aguinaldo's capture. In July 1901, President McKinley appointed William Howard Taft to be chairman of the second Philippines Commission and also civilian governor of the islands. When the portly judge told McKinley that he did not approve of American policy and did not want the Philippines, the President is said to have replied, "Neither do I, but that isn't the question. We've got them."[21]

McKinley furnished his new governor some powerful arms and armor. MacArthur's replacement, General Adna Chaffee, became subordinate to Taft's civil control. To insure Taft's authority, he was given control of every penny of American money spent in the Philippines, including that paid to officers and men of the army, navy, and marines. So armed, Taft set about the immense task of establishing viable civil government.

Neither Aguinaldo's capture nor Taft's appointment ended the fighting, but rebel operations soon began to resemble writhing ganglia of a headless body. Increasingly desperate, the southern rebels turned to outright bestiality such as the massacre of an army infantry company on the island of Samar. Although this massacre succeeded primarily because of the company's lax security precautions, the army commander exacted swift retribution, choosing as his instrument a combat-experienced and very tough marine, Major L. W. T. Waller, of Boxer Rebellion fame. Waller reported with his punitive force to an army officer, Brigadier General "Roaring Jake" Smith, who told him, " . . . I want no prisoners, I want you to burn and kill; the more you burn and kill, the better it will please me."[22] Waller sensibly confined operations to seeking out the guerrilla camp and destroying it along with some insurgents.

Another army general, Brigadier General Bell, personally led a campaign that resulted in breaking up a guerrilla force on a neighboring island and capturing its leader. Bell later codified the experience into a universal that undoubtedly influenced his fellows: " . . . To combat such a population," Bell wrote, "it is necessary to make the state of war as insupportable as possible . . . by keeping the minds of the people in such a state of anxiety and apprehension that living under such conditions will soon become unbearable. Little should be said. The less said the better. Let acts, not words, convey the intention."[23]

Bell's conclusions by no means stood at odds with the opinion of a good many Western colonizers. He forgot to state, however, that inept relocation methods resulted in mass epidemics, which claimed over fifty thousand native lives. How many innocent natives were shot is not known. A witness of Bell's methods, a young lieutenant and later judge, James Blount, wrote, " . . . The American soldier in officially sanctioned wrath is a thing so ugly and dangerous that it would take a Kipling to describe him."[24]

Fortunately for the American cause, Taft already was insisting on a humane approach; indeed, he forced Chaffee to court-martial Waller

132

for executing some native guides whom Waller had found treacherous, and when the court-martial revealed General Smith's punitive instructions to the marine major, he forced the court-martial of Smith.[25]

Taft had at once recognized the need to win native support. Using forceful diplomacy, he persuaded the Vatican to sell America 410,000 acres of prime farmland for over $7 million, then sold land parcels to the natives on easy terms. He also laid the groundwork for a vast civil-affairs program, which was to continue for many years. To start the necessary educational program, he caused one thousand American teachers to be recruited and brought over to the islands. Taft also de-emphasized, as rapidly as possible, the military role in suppressing the insurrection. He relied instead on civil government buttressed by a constabulary police force and the growing Philippine Scouts. After Aguinaldo's renunciation of revolt, Taft treated remaining resistance groups as *ladrones,* or outlaws, which some of them were. Although they were offered full amnesty if they surrendered, the "bandolerismo statute," of late 1902, promised either death or imprisonment for not less than twenty years " . . . for any person proved to be a member of a *ladrone* band (of three or more) . . . and any person aiding a member of such a band. . . . "[26]

By 1903, Taft had given at least some native populations an incentive to protect either what they had or what they believed the future was to offer them. By such methods, Taft slowly won over the bulk of the population. Although sporadic revolts would continue until 1916, by mid-1902 the major insurrection was over.

The final figures were grim: more than four thousand Americans dead (thousands would later die from tropical diseases), thousands wounded; the insurrectos lost about twenty thousand killed; civilian deaths were estimated at two hundred thousand.

The end of the affair came as a great relief to the American people, but it left numerous citizens disturbed. Senator George Frisbee Hoar of Massachusetts, an outspoken opponent of imperialism, addressed his colleagues:

> . . . What has been the practical statesmanship which comes from your ideals and sentimentalities? You have wasted six hundred millions of treasure. You have sacrificed nearly ten thousand American lives, the flower of our youth. You have devastated provinces. You have slain uncounted thousands of the people you desire to benefit. You have established re-concentration camps. Your generals are coming home from their harvest, bringing their sheaves with them, in the shape of other thousands of sick and wounded and insane. . . . Your practical statesmanship has succeeded in converting a [grateful] people . . . into sullen and irreconcilable enemies, possessed of a hatred which centuries cannot eradicate.[27]

CHAPTER ELEVEN

1. Wolff, 23. I have relied on this lively, detailed, and very well written book in the following brief account.
2. Clarke, 459.
3. Wolff, 25.
4. Ibid., 29–30.
5. Ibid., 52.
6. Morison and Commager, II, 324.
7. Wolff, 83.
8. Ibid., 104.
9. *Report of the Philippine Commission* . . . , I, 183.
10. Wolff, 100.
11. Morison and Commager, 338–9. Senator Lodge called it " . . . the hardest fight I have ever known." The victory raised a storm of protest from liberal elements. Mark Twain's letter "To the Person Sitting in Darkness" charged " . . . McKinley with 'playing the European game' of imperialism, and suggested that Old Glory should now have 'the white stripes painted black and the stars replaced by the skull and cross bones.' "
12. Wolff, 227.
13. Ibid., 233.
14. Ibid., 242–3.
15. *Hearings Before the Commission on the Philippines* . . . , II, 1529 ff., 1726 ff.
16. Wolff, 262.
17. Ibid.
18. Ibid., 289.
19. Ibid., 317–18.
20. *Fifth Annual Report of the Philippine Commission—1904*, I, 14.
21. Wolff, 308.
22. Asprey, "Waller of Samar."
23. Wolff, 349.
24. Ibid., 359.
25. Asprey, "Waller of Samar."
26. *Report of the Philippine Commission (1900–1903)*, 492–3.
27. Wolff, 362.

CHAPTER 12

Small-war characteristics • Importance of leadership • Technology and increased weight • British, Russian and French failures • Charles Callwell's classic work: Small Wars *• British operations in Burma • Thibaw's guerrillas • General White's tactics • Sir Charles Crosthwaite's police • The first Boer war • The second Boer war • Conventional opening battles • Buller's errors • Roberts and Kitchener take over • Pretoria falls • Guerrilla war begins • De La Rey and Jan Smuts's commandos • Kitchener's new tactics • British victory • The cost*

THE LESSONS derived from American experience in the Philippines made no great impact on military thinking of the day. In consolidating and expanding overseas empires, European powers had fought scores of campaigns, literally hundreds of battles, that in part or whole foreshadowed the American campaign. The army of each of these countries had faced similar situations, had made the same errors, had suffered but finally survived. Not only had this process happened to these armies, but it continued to happen—each military generation seemed determined to repeat past errors.

Nor was this altogether obtuseness. One small war rarely resembled another: each generally produced specific challenges that had to be met with specific challenges that had to be met with specific and sometimes highly unorthodox tactical modifications. The colonizing giants of the time, Britain, France, Spain, and the Netherlands, supported armies that were too diversified in make-up and interest, too independent in operational responsibility, and too widely separated geographically in an age of limited communications for a healthy exchange of information. Most colonial forces had begun as "company" armies, and only slowly reverted to crown control, but even they tended to remain closed shops, with their own standards and traditions, and showing very little interest

135

in operations elsewhere—an insularity displayed simultaneously by American frontier forces and still displayed by remote garrisons today. In India, two armies existed side by side: the Indian army and the British army, the latter looking down on the former as decidedly inferior and able to teach it nothing. The combined experience of the two forces offered rich lessons in irregular warfare, but these were comfortably ignored by British forces elsewhere. Colonial powers were spoiled: Military successes had far outweighed disasters, and it is a seeming axiom in war that only losers want to know why. Major reasons for this military prosperity have been mentioned earlier: In brief, science and wisdom ruled over superstition and ignorance. The tendency of native forces to indulge charges and set-piece battles against smaller but well-armed and disciplined forces grew as the century waned. Time after time, small colonial armies smashed native hordes ten and twenty times their size. Good leadership continued to play a vital role in the process. Despite certain civil failures, British military reverses must be laid in essence to poor generals. Conversely, successes stemmed in part from leaders such as "Fagin" Napier, Hugh Rose and Horatio Kitchener, each of whom fought and beat vast native armies; in the case of the French, Gallieni and Lyautey each conducted extremely successful pacification campaigns, which we shall examine shortly. At the same time, a lack of native leadership often aided the Europeans. Technology also continued to be important, with the edge going to European powers but scarcely to the exclusion of natives, whose weapons increasingly improved and frequently included artillery. Tactical employment of weapons was something else again, and here technology favored the disciplined force, particularly in the defense. With each progression in the rifle—the Minié to the Enfield to the Snider to the Martini-Henry to the magazine rifle adopted in 1889, the Lee-Metford—speed, range, accuracy, and impact improved, just as it did with embryonic automatic weapons, the Gardner and the Gatling, and with artillery, first the breechloader in 1886, then the quick-firing gun in 1891.

These improvements, as was earlier the case, proved a mixed blessing because again they added weight to columns already heavy. Sir William Lockhart's 1897 expedition south of the Khyber numbered " . . . 35,000 troops with 20,000 more on their lines of communication."[1] Natives were now armed, at least in part, with breech-loading rifles, and the wormlike columns provided first-rate targets. European tactics of halting, dismounting, off-loading mountain guns, and deploying, usually to find nothing, was tiring, time-consuming, and frustrating.*

* Nor were more suitable tactics ever devised. The latter-day Indian campaigns so well described in Robert Henriques' splendid novel *No Arms, No Armour* and in John Masters' exciting novels must have closely resembled the Victorian campaigns.

Other factors joined with tribesmen and terrain to complicate the problem, to tarnish, as it were, the sterling series of tactical successes. Some very serious reverses—for example, the opening phase of the first Afghan war, of 1839–42, the Indian Mutiny of 1857, the opening disasters of the Zulu war at Isandlhwana and Rorke's Drift, the Russian setbacks against the Turkomans, the costly and inconclusive first Boer war of 1881, the French disasters in Algeria and on Madagascar, Gordon's demise at Khartoum—dotted these decades of colonial campaigns.

In general, the lessons of these and other setbacks (as well as those of most victories) seemed to make but fleeting impression on senior military minds. Details of each campaign were recorded (some inaccurately), and a few commentators appeared in print from time to time. General Skobeleff wrote at length of his 1880 campaign; the French officers later wrote of their campaigns.[2] We also find mention in contemporary military literature of the occasional work such as Captain Peach's *Handbook of Tactics—Savage Warfare*.[3]

Until 1896, however, little codification of either strategy or tactics existed for this complicated period of irregular warfare. In that year, in London, appeared the work of a young major: Charles Callwell's *Small Wars—Their Principles and Practice*. Callwell wrote from considerable experience. A regular British officer of the Royal Field Artillery, he was also a scholar and linguist. He had fought in the second Afghan war, in India, and in 1881 had participated in the final operations against the Transvaal Boers, in Africa. Transferred to the Staff College in 1885, the twenty-six-year-old captain submitted an essay, "Small Wars," which won a gold medal from the Royal United Service Institution and caused so much comment that he expanded it into what became the official textbook on the subject.[4]

In the opening pages of *Small Wars*, Callwell took pains to pacify the orthodox military reader. He did not wish to quarrel with " . . . the system of regular warfare of today. Certain rules of conduct exist which are universally accepted. Strategy and tactics alike are in great campaigns governed, in most respects, by a code from which it is perilous to depart." But contiguous to orthodox wars are small wars. A small war " . . . may be said to include all campaigns other than those where both the opposing sides consist of regular troops. It comprises the expeditions against savages and semi-civilized races by disciplined soldiers, campaigns undertaken to suppress rebellions and guerrilla warfare in all parts of the world where organized armies are struggling against opponents who will not meet them in the open field. . . . "[5]

. . . Why are the European nations involved in small wars? Small wars are a heritage of extended empire, a certain epilogue to encroachments into lands beyond the confines of existing civilization, and this has been so from early ages to the present time. Conquerors of old, penetrating into the unknown, encountered races with strange and unconventional military methods and trod them down, seizing their territory; revolts and insurrections followed, disputes and quarrels with tribes on the borders of the districts overcome supervened, out of the original campaign of conquest sprang further wars, and all were vexatious, desultory, and harassing. And the history of these operations repeats itself in the small wars of today.

The great nation which seeks expansion in remote quarters of the globe must accept the consequences. Small wars dog the footsteps of the pioneer of civilization in regions afar off. The trader heralds almost as a matter of course the coming of the soldier, and commercial enterprise in the end generally leads to conquest. Foreign possessions bring military responsibilities in their train which lead to petty warfare. Spain and Portugal in the age of maritime discovery found that it was so, and Great Britain, France and Russia experience it now.[6]

Callwell at times sounded like a latter-day combination of Sun Tzu, the emperors Maurice and Leo, and Marshal de Saxe. In establishing what a small war is and why it came about, he continued:

> . . . The conditions of small wars are so diversified, the enemy's mode of fighting is often so peculiar, the theaters of operations present such singular features, that irregular warfare must generally be carried out on a method totally different from the stereotyped system. The art of war, as generally understood, must be modified to suit the circumstances of each particular case. The conduct of small wars is in fact in certain respects an art by itself, diverging widely from what is adapted to the conditions of regular warfare, but not so widely that there are not in all its branches points which permit comparisons to be established.[7]

The young officer offered three broad classes of small wars: campaigns of conquest or annexation; campaigns for the suppression of insurrections or lawlessness, or for the settlement of conquered or annexed territory; campaigns undertaken to wipe out an insult, to avenge a wrong, or to overthrow a dangerous enemy. Callwell examined major differences from strategic and tactical viewpoints, expounding at length on problems of staff and command, intelligence, communications, supply, and general operations in a host of small-war environments. He followed this with detailed chapters on offensive and defensive tactics in a variety of terrain, pursuits and retreats, feints, surprises-raids-ambushes, night attacks, fighting in hill and bush country, guerrilla warfare. He illustrated critical analyses with campaign episodes, some of which I have cited previously in this book. Throughout this pioneering work, he often demanded extreme tactical modifications, citing verse, chapter, and text of British and European military failures as proof of his conclusions.

Callwell differentiated between small wars and guerrilla wars, but pointed out that they share many common characteristics. In introducing his section on tactics, he presciently wrote:

> ... The military forces of today are complicated organisms which the stress of combat tends to disturb, the more elaborate the machinery the more liable it is to be thrown out of gear by rough handling or by sudden shock; it is owing to this indeed that the art of war has assumed so definite a shape. But irregular warriors have not so highly sensitive a tactical system, they are prepared to disperse should the fates prove unpropitious, and each fighting man enjoys individual independence. In these small wars, in fact, the enemy does not offer an intricate organization as an object for the commander of the regular troops to direct his energies against.[8]

Rather than despising the savage, Callwell continued, his words echoing Bouquet's sage advice of a previous century (see Chapter 5), the orthodox must remember that

> ... irregular warriors are generally warriors not by training but by nature. The fighting instincts of the regular soldier are, in spite of his training and his military calling, dormant till he goes on active service. He lives in a land with a settled social system, where life is secure and where the rights of property are protected by laws which are obeyed ... [the savage] acquires a military sagacity and skill in the use of such weapons as he has at his command which the trained soldier never can aspire to. The one trusts to his own wits in the hour of danger, the other looks to his superior for guidance. And so it comes about that, leaving actual courage and also of course arms out of account, the regular troops are individually inferior to their opponents in these wars. They do not possess the same fertility of military resource, they have not the same instinctive capacity for contriving ambushes and for carrying out surprises, they are amateurs while their adversaries are professional fighting men.[9]

Of the entire *genre* of small wars, from the orthodox commander's viewpoint guerrilla war is the worst *species*:

> ... Guerrilla warfare is what the regular armies always have to dread, and when this is directed by a leader with a genius for war, an effective campaign becomes well-nigh impossible. ... [10]

After proving this disturbing point with historical examples, Callwell offered some hope for the resolute and energetic orthodox commander, but he warned that

> ... The guerrilla mode of war must in fact be met by an abnormal system of strategy and tactics. The great principle which forms the basis of the art of war remains—the combination of initiative with energy; but this is applied in a special form. The utmost vigor and decision must be displayed in harassing the enemy and in giving him no rest; the hostile bands may elude the regular detachments, but their villages and flocks remain. The theater of war must be sub-divided into sections, each to be dealt with by a given force or by a given aggregate of separate detachments. Defensive posts must be established where supplies can be collected, whither raided cattle can be brought, and which form independent bases. To each such base must be attached one or more mobile, self-contained columns, organized to be ready to move out at a moment's notice, and equipped so as to penetrate to any part of the district told off to it and to return, certain of supplies for the task.[11]

Despite the gold medal and official recognition, Callwell's work did not cause a *volte-face* in British military thinking. The time was not ripe for a young man to hold school on his elders—has it ever been?—and indeed Callwell's professional career suffered because of his disturbing and generally accurate conclusions. Although his work failed by omission in that he insufficiently stressed the political task of pacification campaigns, it nonetheless should have been studied and respected by military commanders throughout the empire.

Instead, his teachings apparently failed to reach home, at least in such quarters as British garrisons in Burma and South Africa. The pacification of Upper Burma (1885–90) demonstrated the validity of many of Callwell's teachings. So did the second Boer war, which started in 1899, a turbulent three years in which various British generals managed to commit just about every past error pointed out by Callwell. Ironically, the young author himself served with distinction in this unhappy war—in 1903 he published a revised edition of his work that incorporated the newest lessons.

The first Burma war (1820) established the British presence in three important provinces; the second war (1852) extended British control and placed a co-operative ruler, Mindon Min, on the throne of Upper Burma. Mindon's death, in 1878, ended a relatively quiescent period that witnessed extensive commercial exploitation of the country by British companies.

Mindon's son, Thibaw, was not a strong ruler. Controlled by a reactionary palace group working through Queen Supayalat (who endures as "Thibaw's queen"), Thibaw terminated most of Mindon's reforms and also began quarreling with British commercial interests. When the king opened negotiations with France in 1883, the British Government grew thoroughly alarmed; the quarrel continuing, in 1885 a British military expedition occupied Mandalay and deported Thibaw and his queen. A few months later, Britain annexed Upper Burma and its tributary states and made the entire country a province of the Indian Empire.

The British expedition under General Prendergast had overcome organized resistance with little difficulty. But the British did not capture Thibaw's army, which dispersed with many of the soldiers forming guerrilla bands to carry on the war. The ease with which the larger of these groups gave way to a further British military effort at first caused the interlopers to underestimate the pacification task. They did not realize the extent of the rebellion or its deep-seated nature. Preferring to blame brigands, or dacoits, they failed to understand that spontaneous risings were not alone " . . . led by officers of various grades of the disbanded royal armies" but also by " . . . village headmen, former officials in the service of the king, princes of the blood, and even Buddhist monks. . . ."[12]

To pacify and administer its newest acquisition, the British divided the vast area of some 160,000 square miles into fourteen (later seventeen) districts, each headed by a deputy commissioner " . . . with a British police officer to assist him and such armed force of police, as could be assigned to him. . . . " In the early months, the onus of pacification fell on a Burma Field Force of about fourteen thousand troops commanded by Major General George White.[13] Only six months after formal annexation, White outlined the military problem in a report to superiors in India:

> . . . These bands are freebooters, pillaging wherever they go, but usually reserving the refinement of their cruelty for those who have taken office under us or part with us. Flying columns arrive too late to save the village. The villagers, having cause to recognize that we were too far off to protect them, lose confidence in our power and throw in their lot with the insurgents. They make terms with the leaders and baffle pursuit of those leaders by roundabout guidance or systematic silence. In a country itself one vast military obstacle, the seizure of the leaders of the rebellion, though of paramount importance, thus becomes a source of greatest difficulty.[14]

White attempted to solve the problem by establishing a network of 141 military posts, the weakest consisting of forty riflemen. Patrols of not less than ten men theoretically maintained the peace; if a post could not suppress a local rising, strategically placed garrisons supplied reinforcements. Difficult terrain necessarily limited reaction time as well as operational radius of patrols; where possible, troops traveled by a light-draft river boat.

Although the post system hurt guerrilla operations, it did not stop them. The chief commissioner of Burma from 1887 to 1890, Sir Charles Crosthwaite, later wrote that " . . . when the soldiers passed on, the power of the British Government went with them, and the villagers fell back under the rule of the guerrilla leaders and their gangs." Moreover, troops often remained ignorant of conditions in their immediate areas; districts reported to be "quite peaceful" or "comparatively settled," Crosthwaite wrote, " . . . were often altogether in the hands of hostile bands. They were reported quiet because we could hear no noise. We were outsiders. . . . " The posts also bred an unhealthy reliance on fixed force:

> . . . It was found necessary from the first to restrain firmly the tendency of the local officials to fritter away the strength of the force in small posts. The moment anything occurred they wanted to clap down a post on the disturbed spot; and if this had been allowed to go on unchecked there would not have been a man left to form a movable column or even to send out a patrol of sufficient strength.[15]

Although the military phase proved necessary, Crosthwaite concluded:

> . . . The people might be held down in this way, but not governed. Something more was necessary. The difficulties were to be overcome rather by the vigorous administration of civil government than by the employment of military detachments scattered over the country. A sufficient force of armed police at the disposal of the civil officers was therefore a necessity.[16]

Crosthwaite's answer was to recruit what eventually amounted to fifteen thousand military police from India. Replacing military posts as rapidly as possible with police protection, he relied on troops for special operations against particularly troublesome areas and also to carry out an extensive village resettlement program—a shifting in some cases of entire villages in order to deprive guerrillas of support. Although he reported a greatly improved situation by mid-1888, he had come under some fire for harsh methods of pacification. A modern Burmese historian, Professor Maung Htin Aung, has written that Crosthwaite was a ruthless administrator responsible for thousands of civil deaths. By singling out for persecution families " . . . who had supplied the headmen of villages for several generations," Crosthwaite hoped to destroy any threat from natural leaders. The iron fist failed. Sporadic resistance continued for years and so did Burmese desire for independence. People suffered and died, but the survivors, as Htin Aung wrote, " . . . quietly built little pagodas on the sites of the executions and kept alive the spirit of nationalism. . . . "[17]

The second Boer war had been brewing for nearly twenty years. The failure of the 1899 Bloemfontein conference, followed by Jameson's ill-prompted raid, merely heightened existing tensions to bring war in October.

That the Boers could fight and fight well was already proved by the first Boer war of 1881, when mounted settlers had run rings around Sir George Colley's small British army. The colonizing process, and particularly the Kaffir wars, had produced a nation in arms with a commando system that insured almost instant deployment of every able-bodied man. Few would dispute the Boer's mastery of rifle or horse. His fighting spirit was obvious. President Kruger left no doubt of his determination to fight, and he emphasized his attitude by importing modern arms including large cannon from Germany.

In October 1899, Kruger mustered a total force of about fifty thousand, mostly mounted men thoroughly at home in the vast land. Against this impressive force, Sir Redvers Buller commanded a dispersed British army of about twenty thousand supported by some ten thousand ancillaries—colonials, volunteers, and police.

Although Buller would soon gain substantial reinforcements, Kruger held the initiative. Instead of invading Cape Colony, which was perfectly possible, and which might have resulted in a speedy Boer victory, Kruger attacked British forces immediately at hand. In short order, his commandos invested British garrisons at Ladysmith, in the Northeast, and Mafeking and Kimberley, in the Northwest. These moves, Kruger reasoned, would bring the British north, where he could fight them on his own terms.

Buller reacted predictably: One column, under Sir William Gatacre, moved up the center railway toward Bloemfontein; another column, under Lord Methuen, marched along the western railway toward Kimberley; a final column, under his own command, headed for the Tugela River toward Ladysmith. In addition, Sir John French's first-rate cavalry force was operating in the Northwest, but, by now, both troopers and mounts were tiring.

Buller's greatest enemy was space. His base ports, Cape Town and Durban, lay hundreds of miles apart; Pretoria, capital of the Transvaal, was eight hundred miles from Cape Town. Buller's columns had to cross an area the size of France and Germany. Lack of animal transport and almost no roads tied infantry to single-line railroads. Lack of communications and distance between railways caused Buller to forfeit tactical control. Lack of training and dubious command procedures caused columns to proceed without flank or frontal security. Lack of maps caused commanders to use guides, who generally proved unreliable.

By mid-December, each of the columns was badly mauled and had stopped short of its goal. The press lumped these initial reverses together in the eye-catching term "Black Week"—it was, but it stemmed from the neglect of years.

Early in 1900, however, a remarkable command team arrived to repair matters: Field Marshal Lord Roberts, veteran of forty-one years of Indian fighting, a man who respected his enemy before beating him; his chief of staff, Major General Lord Kitchener, hero of Omdurman, until recently Sirdar of the Egypt Army, not yet fifty years old, a cold, blue-eyed taskmaster who trampled on tradition when necessary to get things done, a hard man who slaughtered the Dervishes in the Sudan, then contemplated having the Mahdi's skull made into a drinking cup.

Roberts, at sixty-eight years of age, was a small, one-eyed, peppery, and able soldier who, just as important, was familiar with war in large theaters and with the particular military problem on hand. Upon disembarking in Africa, he learned that his son had just been killed in the Tugela fighting. With his one good eye, he wept briefly, then turned to the military problem: he would bring the war to Kruger, no doubting that, but scarcely on Kruger's terms. Roberts would use the supply umbilical of the western railway as far as the Modder River, but here he would wean his army in favor of animal transport and turn to advance on Bloemfontein, his interim base for a final advance to Pretoria.

To organize enough transport and to mount colonials into a semblance of a cavalry division required a month of hard and frustrating work, as Kitchener wrote to a friend:

> ...We are getting along a little bit, but we have not a single saddle for love or money; all our water-bottles are so small as to be useless. It was exactly the same in the Sudan, when I had to fit out the whole of the British troops with water-bottles which they had to pay for. Not a single emergency ration, so the men have to fight all day on empty stomachs. I could go on, but what is the use? I am afraid I rather disgust the old red-tape heads of departments. They are very polite, but after a bit present me with a volume of their printed regulations generally dated about 1870 and intended for Aldershot maneuvers, and are quite hurt when I do not agree to their printed rot.[18]

Roberts pushed north in early February, an approach march undetected by Cronjé at Magersfontein. Cronjé paid dearly for ignorance. With Roberts temporarily indisposed, Kitchener took over and lightning struck. Cronjé, surprised and outflanked by French's cavalry, ran due east, his retreat impeded by a train of heavy supply wagons that he stubbornly refused to abandon. Once French had entered Kimberley and cleared the British flank, Kitchener sent him after Cronjé, who was struggling to cross the Modder River at Paardeberg. Still refusing to sacrifice his train—De Wet's commando was supposed to be rushing to his aid—he was caught and forced to surrender.

Despite this happy turn of events, Kitchener and Roberts still had problems: enteric fever, caused by bad water, was sweeping through the ranks; French had lost hundreds of horses; supply was short; and De Wet's considerable commando was somewhere in the area. Roberts nonetheless pushed east toward Bloemfontein. De Wet delayed him but was not strong enough to stop him, and in mid-March the British force reached the important capital.

Roberts was extremely short of supply by now; he lacked cavalry and had no fit horses to pull artillery trains. Enteric fever continued its violent course and he had to clear Boer partisans from his right flank. He took seven weeks to put matters to his satisfaction before advancing north along the railway toward Pretoria.

His campaign soon resembled Halleck's and Grant's march through Tennessee with Forrest and Morgan tearing at their lines of communication. As fast as Roberts' soldiers repaired the tracks, Boer guerrillas tore them up. Out of seventy-five thousand troops, Roberts was forced to use nearly half guarding his single line of communications. And these were none too many. Upon reaching Johannesburg, he cabled the War Office that his troops " . . . were living from hand to mouth," the result of short supply. But now his strategic goal, Pretoria, was in sight. After a brief halt, he continued his push on this capital and, after a final battle, entered it in early June.

In Roberts' mind, his march, by ending organized Boer government, should have ended the war. President Kruger was on the run—indeed he soon sailed for Europe in a futile attempt to find helpful allies. What Roberts failed to realize was a slow but certain change in Boer leadership that had been going on since Cronjé's disaster at Paardeberg. Younger commanders such as Christian de Wet and Louis Botha had long since realized the futility of trying to fight European-style war against heavy British columns. Turning increasingly to guerrilla warfare, they had been joined by such natural leaders as De La Rey and Jan Smuts. These and other leaders were now based, albeit tenuously, east of Pretoria, in the Delagoa Bay area. To them, Kruger's departure mattered but little—his command already was fragmented, the commandos

SOUTH AFRICA 1899
● Towns and Cities
+++ Railways

having fought more or less separately for months. Their commandos were not only intact, but could still tap human and material resources to keep on fighting until the British tired and offered a fair peace. Some of the more fanatic held to a never-surrender policy, but it is probably fair to say that the majority were pragmatists in this sense. In any event, theirs was the decision to keep fighting, and to it De Wet added a powerful spice by very nearly capturing Lord Kitchener.

Considering the situation, the Boers acted boldly. Once in Pretoria, Roberts quickly made good his losses. Reinforcements, both human and material, began to pour in. While Kitchener and French flailed flying columns about the countryside in mostly useless attempts against the guerrillas, Roberts consolidated his command over the towns and, in September 1900, formally annexed the Transvaal. In November, after stating that in his opinion the war was virtually over, he left for London to become commander-in-chief of the British army.

Roberts was unduly optimistic. Far from being over, the war was heating up. Living off the land, the Boer commandos, sometimes separately and sometimes in harmony, continued to strike throughout the Transvaal and the Free State, blowing bridges, pulling up railway tracks and derailing trains, falling on isolated garrisons, burning stores, destroying convoys—all in mocking denial of the British claim to victory.

Kitchener reacted vigorously, first by jury-rigging a mounted force built around French's cavalry, then by starting to turn the entire vast

146

territory into an armed British camp. Kitchener knew that ultimately he would win, and so, probably, did the Boers. As early as February 1901, Louis Botha approached him through an intermediary, which led to a meeting in late February. Both men were realists. Botha wanted Boer independence in return for peace, a hopeless demand which Kitchener rejected out of hand, as Botha knew he would. Botha then named less severe demands and the two soon reached a healthy general agreement. Kitchener subsequently notified the Secretary of State: " . . . It seems a pity that the war should go on for the points raised by Botha, which appear to me all capable of adjustment." Arrogant in its ignorance and in its power, the British Government in the form of Sir Arthur Milner caviled over giving amnesty to the Cape Colony rebels, a debatable refusal to one of Botha's major demands. Stalemate ensued, and, toward the end of March, Botha dropped further negotiations.[19]

Kitchener's hopes for an early peace thus dashed, he turned again to the military problem. Lacking necessary intelligence and essential mobility, his approach tended toward the defensive, his lines of communication now becoming his paramount concern. To guard these, he divided the territory into specific military areas. To each he assigned large numbers of his ever-increasing army to build a series of rude blockhouses, at first along the railway and on vital bridges. Each housed one non-commissioned officer and seven men; it was supported by its neighbor, generally a thousand yards removed, to which in time it became linked by barbed wire. During 1901, the area of operations grew into a labyrinth of such blockhouses. At the end of 1901, Kitchener's new chief of staff, Ian Hamilton, wrote to Lord Roberts:

> . . . Although I had read much of blockhouses, I never could have imagined such a gigantic system of fortifications, barriers, traps and garrisons as actually exists. This forms the principal characteristic of the present operations, supplying them with a solid backbone and involving permanent loss of territory to the enemy, which former operations did not.[20]

Kitchener supported this system with a force of about 240,000, an illusory figure greatly reduced by sickness: in June 1901, the net fighting strength stood " . . . at under 164,000 men."[21] Passive defense—blockhouse garrisons, base garrisons, railway guards, depot cadre and the like—required 100,000 men. Active defense in the form of mounted "flying columns" used the rest. Kitchener sent these columns on "drives" of the increasingly segregated areas. Such drives sometimes involved a single column or less, sometimes five or six columns that could number five thousand men. Kitchener did not expect great bags of prisoners. He had had enormous experience in this type of warfare both in Egypt and Africa: in July 1901, he wrote the Secretary of State, " . . . these flying columns, on extended operations in this vast country, only in great measure beat the air, as the mobile Boers clear off the moment they hear of the columns being sometimes twenty miles away."[22]

Kitchener wanted to keep the commandos off balance and out of touch with each other. To deprive them of hearing of the columns, he began to clear key areas of people, moving women and children into concentration camps, where he kept them despite a fearful outcry from home. To deprive commandos of livelihood, food, and mounts, Kitchener burned farms in the best Sherman tradition. He also deported Boer prisoners—some twenty-four thousand—to overseas camps.[23]

Kitchener suffered any number of setbacks. He was not at all pleased with his army. He thought its discipline was dreadful, and he could not understand the insouciance of younger officers who showed a near camaraderie to the enemy instead of treating them like dervishes. The difficulty stemmed in large part from an essentially defensive army composed largely of non-professionals with little patience for the frustrations inherent in attrition warfare.

At this stage, Kitchener was becoming increasingly pessimistic and even unsure of himself, writing to Lord Roberts on one occasion that " . . . the dark days are on us again."[24]

The dark days were about to lighten. The Boers, reduced to some twenty thousand men, lacked food, mounts, medicine. Continual hardship, desertions, and pursuit had flagged once-ebullient spirits. Peace seemed inevitable and, considering various amnesty statements of the enemy, even enviable. They quit in the spring of 1902.

From 1899 to 1902, the Boers had put 90,000 men in the field. Of these, they lost an estimated 4,000 killed, thousands more wounded and taken prisoner; poor sanitary conditions in the concentration camps accounted for perhaps 20,000 civilian deaths. The British army, which altogether mustered 450,000 men, lost 6,000 killed in action, over 20,000 wounded, and about 16,000 dead from wounds and disease. The war cost England over £200 million, not to mention the investment necessary to rebuild the ravaged country.[25]

CHAPTER TWELVE

1. Cole and Priestley, 248–9.
2. Skobeff; Gallieni; Lyautey. The extensive correspondence of the French officers, much of it concerning professional matters, has been largely preserved and published. See, for example, Deschamps and Chauvet; Gheusi; Lyautey, *Lettres du Tonkin*; Lyautey, *Lettres du Tonkin et de Madagascar (1894–1899)*; Lyautey, *Lettres du Sud de Madagascar (1900–1902)*; Lyautey, *Lyautey L'Africain* . . .

3. Callwell (1906), 498, 525.
4. Callwell (1896). He followed this with revised editions in 1899 and 1906. See also, *Dictionary of National Biography 1922–30:* After distinguished service in the Boer war, Callwell continued to publish military work, sometimes of a critical, sometimes of a frivolous nature, which earned him service enemies. Passed over for promotion to general, he retired in 1909. He was recalled to duty in 1914 and served with distinction, winning promotion to major general and a knighthood. He retired after the war and died in 1928, shortly after editing Field Marshal Sir Henry Wilson's diaries.
5. Callwell (1896), 19–21.
6. Ibid., 22.
7. Ibid., 21.
8. Ibid. (1899), 124–5.
9. Ibid., 125.
10. Ibid (1906), 126.
11. Ibid. (1896), 111.
12. Maung Htin Aung, *A History of Burma,* 266. See also, Maung Htin Aung, *The Stricken Peacock . . .*
13. Crosthwaite, *The Pacification of Burma,* 9, 11, 16.
14. Ibid., 14.
15. Ibid., 14, 29, 57.
16. Ibid., 15.
17. Maung Htin Aung, *A History of Burma,* 267.
18. Arthur, I, 270–1.
19. Watteville, 82.
20. Arthur, II, 8.
21. Ibid., 2.
22. Watteville, 76.
23. Cole and Priestley, 279–81.
24. Arthur, II, 67.
25. Cole and Priestley, 282.

CHAPTER 13

Hubert Lyautey • His background • Gallieni's tactics against Indochinese "pirates" • Origin of the tache d'huile *concept • Gallieni's influence on Lyautey • Pacification of Madagascar • Tache* d'huile *tactics in Algeria • Pacification of Morocco • Lyautey: success or failure?*

MAJOR CALLWELL laid far more stress on military problems of colonization than on political problems, a priority natural for a professional soldier. He did not seem to realize that a solution of the political problem, either in whole or in part, could have diminished or eliminated the military problem—an interesting fact uncovered by the more successful commanders of the colonial era.

The French general Hubert Lyautey ranks as one of these. Born and bred a royalist, Lyautey was a devout Roman Catholic who became interested in social reform while a student at St. Cyr. His continued interest in social welfare, including the mental welfare of his troops, brought him into contact with some of the leading French intellectuals, and he soon began to publish controversial articles in the better journals.[1] Writing in 1889–91, Lyautey thought he saw in the French officer corps of some twenty thousand a potential social force that could bring about necessary reforms. Internal changes in the corps were first necessary: He argued, for example, that an officer must know his men better than his horses, which was not usually the case. Provided the officer acquired a social conscience, however, he could indoctrinate conscripts with essential principles of patriotism and nationalism necessary for a renascence that ultimately would repair the humiliating 1870 defeat by the Prussians.[2] Although the thirty-seven-year-old major conceived this activity within the traditional monarchist-church framework, his ideas created a mild sensation and marked him in some quarters as a socialist and revolutionary. To save his career, sympathetic seniors posted him to Indochina.[3] (See map, Chapter 31.)

150

Lyautey arrived in Saigon in 1894. The French already had staked claim to most of Indochina: Cochin China had been a colony since 1862, and Annam a protectorate since 1885. The governor-general, De Lanessan, ruled these areas with a philosophy that he explained to Lyautey on a train trip to Hanoi:

> ... In every country there are existing frameworks. The great mistake for European people coming there as conquerors is to destroy these frameworks. Bereft of its armature, the country falls into anarchy. One must govern *with* the mandarin and not *against* the mandarin. The European cannot substitute himself numerically; but he can control. Therefore, don't disturb any tradition, don't change any custom. In every society there exists a ruling class, born to rule, without which nothing can be done. Enlist that class in our interests.[4]

Although the French had managed to pacify the southern areas and most of the Tonkin Delta by this time, De Lanessan's rule did not cover the northern provinces of Tonkin, ceded by China to France by the treaty of Tientsin and " ... declared Military Territories, administered by superior French officers, who had to deal with the pirates infesting these regions."[5]

As Joseph Buttinger has pointed out in his comprehensive two-volume work *Vietnam: A Dragon Embattled,* the pirates were often nationalists fighting for independence, a fact overlooked, perhaps intentionally, by most French officials:

> ... the French, totally mistaken about the nature of their enemy and the difficulties of pacifying a nation as old as the Vietnamese, relied exclusively on brute force. "We had at this time no idea," wrote a witness of conquest and pacification, "of the importance and quality of these Vietnamese bands; our first columns merely traversed the country without occupying it; they were putting, a little too indifferently, steel and fire into every village where they met the slightest trace of resistance." The commanders of these columns, who equated spreading terror with creating order, turned more peasants into partisans than the mandarins who agitated for armed resistance. ...
>
> ... [The French] subscribed to the principle of "collective responsibility," which meant summary executions of noncombatants, "the last expedient in all wars against partisans by regular troops that cannot touch their opponents." De Lanessan and others described what this principle meant in practice: "Every village that has given refuge to a band of guerrillas or not reported their passage is declared responsible and guilty. Consequently, the chief of the village and two or three principal inhabitants are beheaded, and the village itself is set on fire and razed to the ground." Pris-

151

oners, of course, as Captain Gosselin reports in his revealing book, were always shot, "on orders from above." Severe repression worked the inevitable result: . . . even the meek among the people, and certainly the terror-stricken, hated the French, and no man of honor among the leaders cooperated with them as long as the partisans continued their fight. "Those who collaborated with us," says a historian of this and later periods of trouble, "succumb to the lure of money, or even worse to unrestrained and unscrupulous ambition. Nobility of soul, disinterestedness, and courage are to be found in the opposition. Against this coalition of moral forces nothing can be done."

The tactical result was equally inevitable:

> . . . The official military history of Indochina again and again tells how the troops engaged in hunting down the guerrillas, although numerically strong, well equipped, and often well led, missed their objective wherever the French had no friends. . . . "A column is helpless against these brigands, who, at the approach of our troops, disperse in the villages, where, thanks to the complicity of the population and probably the indigenous officials, they cannot be found. . . . Moreover, our troops are paralyzed by an absolute lack of information. The commanders of our posts do not have the money to buy informants." The enemy, on the other hand, got all the information he needed without having to pay. "As soon as a patrol starts out, the pirates are warned, while we," wrote one official historian, "walk in a hostile country as though blind."

A few outstanding and experienced French officers had questioned first, and then begun changing, this policy. Colonels such as Gallieni had recognized the political element of the problem:

> . . . These men combined military with psychological action, apart from being the first to take advantage of the country's peculiar geographical circumstances. This they did by the application of measures valid to this day as a condition of success against guerrilla warfare: They counteracted the support, or even merely the sympathy, of the people toward the guerrillas through social, economic, and political measures designed to elicit equal if not greater support.[6]

As temporary chief of staff in Hanoi, Commandant Lyautey was soon conferring with the commander of the effort, the forty-four-year-old Colonel Gallieni, who had made his colonizing reputation in the Senegal and Sudan. Gallieni at once impressed the new arrival, both with the scope of the pacification problem and his solution in pacifying or at least neutralizing pirate camps in "the most hidden places of the

152

great thickets of the forest." Gallieni relied on surprise and mobility—a system of converging mobile columns—to attack these various strongholds, but this was only part of the answer. As he explained to Lyautey: " . . . Piracy is not a necessary historical fact. It is the result of an economic condition. It can be fought by prosperity." Although superior discipline, firepower and mobile tactics could in time subdue the pirates, military success meant " . . . *nothing* unless combined with a simultaneous work of organization—roads, telegraphs, markets, crops—so that with the pacification there flowed forward, like a pool of oil, a great belt of civilization."[7]

Gallieni's radical approach appealed enormously to the socially aware Lyautey. The two hit it off so well that Gallieni arranged for the young major to become his chief of staff. In subsequently submitting a plan of campaign to the governor-general, Lyautey showed the extent of Gallieni's influence on his thinking:

> . . . It should not be overlooked that the pirate is a plant which will grow only in certain soils, and that the surest method is to make the soil uncongenial to him. . . . Similarly with regard to territory given over to brigandage: armed occupation, with or without fighting, is as the ploughshare; the establishment of a military cordon fences it and isolates it definitely, if an internal frontier is in question; and finally the organization and reconstitution of the population, its arming, the setting-up of markets and various cultivations, the driving of roads, are all as the sowing of the good grain, and render the conquered region impervious to brigandage.[8]

A year later, Lyautey continued this policy in Madagascar, where he was summoned by Gallieni, the new resident-general. Having decided to govern *against* the mandarin, Gallieni had stirred up the Hovas and now had a revolt on his hands. He assigned Lyautey to the command of an area ruled by a Hova rebel, a former royal governor, Rabezavana. Lyautey reverted to the methods of Tonkin: he used mobile converging columns to deprive the rebel force of herds and food supply; simultaneously he pinched off bits of territory while showing the people the advantages of coming over to his side, where they would be protected and allowed to earn a good living. Deprived of support, Rabezavana surrendered within a month. Lyautey not only treated him with utmost courtesy, but to the astonishment of all, placed him in charge of the region which he had formerly ruled—where he served loyally and well.[9]

This experience confirmed much of Lyautey's earlier thinking. In an article published during this period, "The Colonial Rule of the Army," he described the pacifying process as " . . . an organization on the march." He continued:

... Military command and territorial command ought to be joined in the same hands. When the high military officer is also the territorial administrator, his thoughts, when he captures a brigand's den, are of the trading-post he will set up after his success—and his capture will be on different lines.[10]

In other words, he will not search and destroy—he will dominate, preserve, and build.

After playing a major role in pacifying Madagascar, Lyautey returned to France to command a hussar regiment prior to retiring from the army. At this point, he happened to meet the new Governor-General of Algeria, Jonnart, who complained about the army's failure to stop guerrilla raids of rebels based in eastern Morocco. Impressed with Lyautey's comments, Jonnart persuaded the minister of war to send the colonel to take command of the turbulent southern Oran area. (See first map in Chapter 9 and map, Chapter 22.) The job carried promotion to brigadier general, but Lyautey found a cool reception by his superior at Oran, who did not relish an "outsider" challenging his theretofore supreme control. The fifty-nine-year-old Lyautey, in turn, found little to admire. The tactical villain remained bulk and weight. At Lyautey's request, a light column paraded before him. Noting the men's high laced boots, haversacks laden as if for a campaign of six months, vast convoys for men who could feed on a handful of dates, the tall general turned to the local commander and asked: "What do you call a *heavy* column?"[11]

Lyautey reported back to Jonnart in Algiers and told him he would take the job only under certain conditions:

> ... I want to have my territory as a whole. I want to have under my orders not only all the military services, but also all the political services, the intelligence officers, everything. ... And then, in case of urgency, I want to be able to have direct telegraphic communication with the Minister of War, without having to do so by way of the Oran division ... if you desire the pacification of southern Oran, this is essential.[12]

Jonnart agreed, undoubtedly to his Oran commander's fury. He made a wise decision, however, for Lyautey was one of the few senior officers in the French army who was temperamentally and professionally suited for the task.

Lyautey's immediate problem centered on the old Algerian rebel Bou-Amama, who was allied with a young Moroccan, Bou-Hamara, a conjurer turned pretender to the sultan and called the Rogui. They operated from a Moroccan sanctuary, the Tafilelt, which they kept under submission while their bands swept across the border to raid French outposts and Algerian tribal settlements. Although the French army was authorized to pursue the guerrillas inside Morocco, their slow columns rarely ran down the fast-moving bands, and they were forbidden to build permanent outposts on the other side of the border.

Lyautey was not as anxious as his predecessors to mount punitive expeditions, and he scornfully rejected the string of small border outposts that failed to prevent rebel incursions. Instead he began to apply his *tache d'huile* or oil-spot technique: winning separate tribes by offering them protection under the French flag, then providing social services ranging from medical clinics to markets—a " . . . military-political pacification and occupation . . . the gradual advance on a wide front instead of a single deep (column) penetration."[13] He used light columns to break up enemy concentrations and to meet subsequent threats, " . . . but the emphasis lay on the *tache d'huile* technique—a methodical, necessarily slow expansion of French control" that used the army not as an instrument of repression but as a positive social force, "the organization on the march."[14] This was an extremely clever concept, a sort of imperialist infiltration in that his showplaces of civilization, by attracting other tribes to the fold, undermined the solidarity and authority of rebel chieftains.

Lyautey's success came at a good time for his career. France was about to expand into Morocco, the result of a deal with England that gave the latter a free hand in Egypt. Morocco in 1904 was a heterogeneous collection of Arabic tribes tied into a loose federation linguistically by Arabic language, spiritually by Islamic religion. This vast area fell under titular rule of a sultan whose practical control extended as far as his troops, or about 20 per cent of the country. Scores of fierce Berber tribes held the rugged mountainous country in semianarchy manifested by frequent intertribal blood feuds and massive revolts against the sultan's government.

Lyautey already had neutralized some of these dissident tribes when he was promoted to the Oran command, in 1906, and charged with the protection of the entire Algerian-Moroccan border. In 1907, he extended operations into eastern Morocco by occupying Oujda. Three years later, he had created a buffer state deep into Morocco composed of diverse tribes who were beginning to favor a more orderly way of life as less costly and far more satisfactory than anarchy.[15]

In 1910, General Lyautey, married now to a colonel's widow, returned to France to command an army corps at Rennes. But the treaty of Fez caused serious revolts in French Morocco, and in 1911 Lyautey was sent to Rabat as resident-general. Lyautey was now nearly seventy, but advancing years seemed only to give him added energy. After putting down the revolts, he turned to administering French Morocco. As was his wont, he upheld the authority of tribal leaders, preserving "all local customs and religious practices." The natives were taught how to improve crops and better market them. Lyautey built hospitals, roads, railroads, and schools besides founding the important cities of Casablanca and Port Lyautey.[16]

Although Lyautey did not hesitate to employ military force when necessary, he believed in applying it in limited amounts. When Mangin exceeded himself in the 1913 fighting in the Middle Atlas massif, Lyautey relieved him of command. And when expansionists in Paris urged him to invade "independent" Morocco, he wrote:

> . . . This country ought not to be handled with force alone. The rational method—the only one, the proper one, and also the one for which I myself was chosen rather than anyone else—is the constant interplay of force with politics. I should be very careful about attacking regions which are "asleep," which are lying still, which are waiting and questioning, which would burst into flames if I entered them, at the cost of many men and much trouble, whereas, once all the neighboring regions are dealt with, these others will find themselves isolated and will fall into our hands by themselves. . . . [17]

Lyautey's pacification formula produced short-term gains for long-term losses. Among its numerous built-in booby traps, it represented one man's idea rather than a national ideal. Essentially a totalitarian concept, it could be and subsequently was subverted by the dictates of other colonial administrators materially far more greedy and politically far more myopic than Lyautey.

Lyautey himself was a one-man show, a prima donna in the Gordon tradition. Dramatic and flamboyant, something of a mystic, he was married to ideals that the majority of his countrymen had long since divorced. He was convinced that he knew better than his government, and in some instances he probably did. At times, the Third Republic seemed like no government, and Lyautey was not alone among prominent officials in refusing obeisance to its oft-changing and oft-contradictory ministerial decrees.

This attitude can be defended if not carried too far. The fractious nature of French politics, particularly in the first decade of this century, increased the responsibility of French officials. To carry on sometimes required intelligent disobedience of orders. Most successful leaders in history at some point have risked their careers by intelligent disobedience. When disobedience, intelligent or otherwise, becomes habit, however, it turns to mutiny, and anarchy is the result.

Lyautey was by no means alone in exploiting the turbulent political scene to gain immense operational freedom. From Gallieni and Jonnart he learned not to respect the state but to outwit it. By the time he rose to prominence, a lack of control already had spelled a loss of discipline sufficient to allow the growth of unhealthy autonomy in the French colonial empire—France already was becoming a prisoner of her empire.

Lyautey aided this pernicious trend. Although he preached a careful admixture of civil and military effort in administering colonial areas, in practice the military officer absorbed civil responsibility, thus giving rise to the unhappy system of the *officier-administrateur,* which called for "... 'special' officers trained and interested in political, social and economic affairs." As Peter Paret has pointed out, this concept was fundamental to a philosophy that we shall come to later, that of the *guerre révolutionnaire,* familiar to Indochina, Algeria, Morocco, and Tunisia, and one that contained the seeds of its own destruction.[18]

This perhaps was the inevitable result of refusing the notion of political growth. Lyautey did not believe that colonies would ultimately emerge as independent, self-governing nations. In Morocco he allowed numerous *colons* to purchase large and choice land tracts at low prices and to work them with minimum-wage labor. His administration made little attempt to train Moroccan administrators or even to develop a stabilizing middle class. By allowing tribal chiefs to retain authority, he insured continued misery of millions, and by supporting a weak and inefficient sultan, he laid the groundwork for the catastrophic Rif rebellion in neighboring Spanish Morocco.

In the main, these were also his country's errors, and they were not confined to France. Lyautey's success in keeping the peace merely compounded rather than solved them. Although he paid lip service to political necessities, he never forgot that the rifle, the French rifle, ruled. Along with most of his fellow humans, he was a slave to the policy of the now. Lyautey refused the past, he blessed the present, he denied the future.

He wrote his own epitaph unknowingly many years before he died. This was in Algeria, after he had ridden around his neat bivouacs wishing his splendid legionaries, his spahis, Zouaves, his Chasseurs d'Afrique, and his *tirailleurs* a happy year. Flushed from his tour of power, he returned to his desk to write a friend. After an almost orgiastic description of troop esprit in the neatly formed camps, he added: "... I don't give a damn for the morrow—the present is enough for me."[19]

CHAPTER THIRTEEN

1. Maurois, 32–7.
2. Paret, *French Revolutionary Warfare . . .* , 107–8.
3. Maurois, 46.
4. Ibid., 48.
5. Howe, 63.

6. Buttinger, I, 134–6.
7. Maurois, 57, 53.
8. Ibid., 61.
9. Ibid., 68–9.
10. Ibid., 73.
11. Ibid., 92.
12. Ibid., 92.
13. Paret, *French Revolutionary Warfare* . . . , 104.
14. Ibid., 104–6.
15. Maurois, 141.
16. Woolman, 168–9.
17. Maurois, 180–1.
18. Paret, *French Revolutionary Warfare* . . . , 105–6.
19. Maurois, 137.

CHAPTER 14

GUERRILLA WARFARE played a spotty but important role in the Mexican revolution from 1910 to 1920. This complex upheaval started as a political revolution but so intense was a need for sweeping social and economic changes that the fighting developed into a series of bloody civil wars. The conflict should prove of particular interest to the North American since it helps to explain a Mexican xenophobia only slowly disappearing and one founded in part on North American territorial acquisition and commercial exploitation, in part on diplomatic and military intervention during the fighting. Washington intervened forcibly on several occasions. Lacking accurate information and not understanding the dynamic forces at work in the impoverished country, the Wilson administration greatly embarrassed itself and extricated its military forces only with difficulty. Wilson's confusion is not difficult to understand. The Mexican revolution seemed to pale in comparison with the dramatic events in Europe. Wilson and his advisers did not and perhaps could not understand that World War I would end a phase of history, while the Mexican revolution would foreshadow a new and as yet incomplete phase.

Although the outbreak of the Mexican revolution surprised everyone, including the revolutionaries, it did not suddenly explode. Rather, it seethed from a centuries-old fermentation familiar to many other areas of the world, a powerful concoction that created and nurtured the host of elements that exploded in 1910. In Victor Alba's words:

... Everything the future was to bring was already foreshadowed: a frustrated middle class, indignant at the arrogance of foreign capital; an urban youth longing for freedom of thought and expression; a proletariat in constant protest; a stultified and downtrodden peasantry, which sent off occasional sparks of rebellion; a certain number of theorists of change, which all the other groups confusedly hungered for; and a few organized and militant groups with programs for action.[1]

160

Guerrilla warfare was not the sine qua non of warfare either during the Spanish conquest of Mexico or even during the intermittent civil wars of the nineteenth century. Guerrilla bands did exist along with "people's generals" such as Miguel Hidalgo and his successor José María Morelos, a particularly able guerrilla leader who was captured and executed in 1815.[2] The Mexican army failed to use guerrilla tactics in its war with the United States (possibly from pride) and was severely beaten, a defeat that cost almost a third of its territory. The man who finally toppled the disastrous Santa Anna dictatorship, Juan Álvarez, depended only in part on guerrilla tactics—the Santa Anna regime was so rotten and the army so demoralized that the rebels won a relatively easy victory. In the civil war that followed—the War of the Reforms— guerrillas operated behind the opposing armies, but, too often, these were little more than bandit groups exploiting an already confused and ravaged countryside.

Guerrilla warfare came into its own during the abortive effort of Emperor Napoleon III to restore a Mexican monarchy and put the Habsburg Archduke Ferdinand Maximilian on the throne. The Monroe Doctrine had theretofore prevented direct foreign intervention, but in 1862 the United States had its hands full with its own civil war. An allied army, mostly French but with Spanish and British contingents, landed at Vera Cruz and began to fight inland. By spring, the French were fighting alone; after a setback at the battle of Puebla, Napoleon sent reinforcements, and the army ably commanded by Marshal Bazaine entered Mexico City. The liberal government of Benito Juárez now moved north to Paso del Norte (Ciudad Juárez), which it defended while waiting for American intervention. By the spring of 1864, organized resistance to French arms had virtually ended, but, throughout the occupied areas, guerrilla actions flared.

None of these actions was particularly important by itself, but together they constituted a challenge to authority. The challenge gained strength because that authority itself was divided: Napoleon was not pleased with what had become an expensive campaign—he had fielded some thirty thousand troops; Maximilian's supporters, the clergy and landowners, were not pleased at his refusal to reinstate various privileges; Bazaine was not pleased, because his army knew no rest and he was spending a great deal of money in fruitless pursuit of these wretched guerrilla bands.

For some time, Bazaine had been arguing for solution by force: he wanted to treat the guerrillas as outlaws, with summary execution of those captured. Maximilian eventually agreed. An overzealous Mexican officer fighting for the French summarily executed two captured generals. The guerrillas retaliated. With each French reprisal, the guerrillas gained new recruits—and the war continued.

But Napoleon was in trouble: at home, a strong and arrogant Prussia was threatening him, and abroad, the United States government was demanding his army's recall. Early in 1867, he bowed to these pressures and withdrew his army. Unable to stand alone, Maximilian surrendered and was court-martialed and shot.

Maximilian's death put Juárez and the liberals back in power. Juárez soon died and the party split into three factions, each devoted to self-aggrandizement. For forty years, leaders such as Manuel González and particularly Porfirio Díaz sold Mexico to anyone who would buy it. Their peculations included the sale of huge tracts of public land, including mineral rights, to a chosen few—either Mexican or foreign speculators—along with railways and mining and later oil concessions. Grand larceny became a way of life: Porfirio and his henchmen disposed of 50 million hectares (one hectare equals nearly two and one half acres) of land, much of it going to foreign ownership and management—about $3.5 billion poured into the dictator's coffers from 1880 to 1910. The Catholic Church once again became a large landowner, as did Porfirio's regional bosses, the hated *jefes políticos*. One Mexican rancher owned 2.5 million hectares in Chihuahua; the Cedros *hacienda* in Zacatecas comprised 750,000 hectares; thirty-two persons owned the sugar-growing state of Morelos; three thousand families owned *half of Mexico*. Landowners frequently forced peasants from common land (the *ejidos*) and dispossessed tribes that had occupied territory for generations. Of 10 million peasants working the land, 9.5 million owned nothing;[3] the *haciendas* offered conditions familiar to the feudal ages:

> . . . Wages were sometimes as low as twenty-five centavos a day; corporal punishment was a normal practice and most peasants fell hopelessly into debt with the *hacienda* store. The diet was insufficient and their housing primitive in the extreme; disease was rife and a school was rarely available for their children. . . . Lands lay fallow, the Indians struggled on the brink of starvation and Mexico was obliged to import foodstuffs for its townspeople.[4]

As one historian wrote, Díaz did " . . . much to develop his country. But he did nothing to develop his people."[5]

His people sometimes protested. A disciple of the French socialist Charles Fourier, one Rhodakanaty, started a small labor movement in 1866. One of his disciples, Julio Chávez, led a short-lived peasant rebellion in 1869—he was captured and shot. The movement continued during the 1870s and was fed by the writings of Marx and Bakunin. Significantly, these doctrines held little appeal to the peons, who were far more attracted by the promise of immediate reforms,[6] but in 1885 the Yaqui tribes of Sonora rose against the government and, for fifteen years, under such capable leaders as Cajeme and Tetabiate, fought a guerrilla war. When government weight finally told, the army rounded up some eight thousand tribesmen and deported them to Yucatán to work on the plantations virtually as slaves. Other revolts occurred, but either the army or a gendarme force, the despised *rurales,* put them down rapidly and cruelly.[7]

Down but not out. The countryside was never completely safe during the Porfiriate, and even if the *rurales* suppressed active opposition, peasant hatred continued to grow.[8] Serious uprisings variously occurred and a revolutionary movement also existed. In 1906, two anarchists, the Flores Magón brothers, well known for their revolutionary newspaper *Regeneración,* formed a Liberal Party whose slogan was "Land and Liberty." These and other labor leaders also incited a series of provincial strikes in mines and factories. A frightened government overreacted—troops put down one strike by killing some two hundred workers.[9]

But a more dangerous situation was developing in Porfiriate ranks. Porfirio and his ancient henchmen had grown increasingly isolated and intransigent. Had they been intelligent, they would have read the increasing demonstrations and uprisings as proper warning of vast social unrest—like Horatio seeing the king's ghost, they would have said, "This bodes some strange eruption to our state." A few of the younger Porfiristas recognized the danger and demanded reforms. When the dictator, soon to turn eighty, refused to name a successor, a party member named Francisco Madero broke away and organized a group called the Anti-Re-electionists. Madero was in his thirties, a small, restless man, rich and well educated, a teetotaler and vegetarian. Arrested during the 1910 presidential elections, Madero upon release fled to Texas, denounced Díaz's re-election as fraudulent, named himself provisional president, and issued a reform program called the Plan of San Luis Potosí.[10]

No mass uprisings followed, but Madero's lieutenants in Chihuahua, Abraham González and Pascual Orozco, raised a number of mounted bands which, using guerrilla tactics, effectively harassed immobile army garrisons. One subordinate leader, typical in some ways, was named Doroteo Arango. A mestizo with a touch of negro blood, at sixteen years of age he had killed the *hacendado's* son, who had raped his sister, and fled to the hills to become a cattle thief. The thirty-year-old Arango knew little of Mexican politics, but, hating government and landowners, he came down from the hills, rounded up fifteen horsemen, and joined Madero. Soon feared by the federals for fantastic mobility and surprise attacks, he became famous as Francisco "Pancho" Villa and shortly commanded a force of some five hundred horses.[11]

Although the army was disorganized and riddled with corruption, it withstood rebel attacks in a war that was cruel from the beginning. Porfirio's generals, deeming the rebels to be bandits, ordered all prisoners shot. The rebels retaliated by executing government officials and all officers (but allowing soldiers to join rebel ranks). Subordinate guerrilla leaders also paid off old scores: on one occasion, Pancho Villa ordered two hundred Chinese killed in one town simply because he hated Chinese.[12]

In relatively short order, rebel forces controlled enough of Chihuahua for Madero to transfer his revolutionary government from Texas. Meanwhile, revolts continued to break out in the North, and also in the South, in the sugar provinces. Those readers who remember Wallace Beery's superb portrayal of Pancho Villa will inevitably connect the Mexican revolution with Villa, but a guerrilla leader named Emiliano Zapata played an even more significant role. Zapata was a tenant farmer in the southern province of Morelos. Incensed at feudal conditions, he became outspokenly critical and was banished to the army. Discharged in 1910, he returned to Morelos, already restive with a few small guerrilla bands operating from the hills. Recognizing the futility of this meager effort, Zapata set out to organize a peasant uprising.[13]

Zapata was neither a Marxist nor a Communist. He was a simple, uneducated and bold man bent on returning land to the people, a small, slender man with a sensuous Asiatic face, mandarin mustache and eyes as black and hard as obsidian. Unlike the rough, rude Villa, Zapata was a dandy. He always wore symbolic, theatrical black—a fitted jacket and tight trousers with silver trimming down the seams. He wore enormous, silver-laden sombreros and his taste extended to fine horses and beautiful women."[14] Deadly earnest in social-economic protest, he rallied peasants by the thousands with the cry: "Men of the South, it is better to die on your feet than live on your knees!" Give us land and liberty, he thundered—and his cry reverberated throughout the province.

Within nine months, Zapata had raised an army of three thousand peasants, a spontaneous and self-supporting uprising: " . . . We have begged from the outside not one bullet," Zapata boasted, "not one rifle, not one peso; we have taken it all from the enemy." The uprising spread quickly, and, in general, regional leaders such as José Trinidad Ruíz, Salazar, Neri, and a man with the unlikely name of De la O proved highly effective guerrilla fighters who soon had government forces in Morelos—some thousand troops and five thousand *rurales*—contained in garrison towns.[15]

In 1911, guerrilla victories in north and south toppled the Díaz government and Madero won the presidency. He was already in trouble with his own party. More like a boy on a pony than a man on horseback, Madero proved far too weak for the enormous task he faced, one he did not even understand. Madero insisted that the people wanted a political revolution, whereas they were vigorously demanding fundamental social and economic changes. But Madero failed to offer even a political revolution. A poor administrator, he quickly lost control to conservative ministers, and, instead of pushing through vital and promised reforms, he followed a vacillating policy that merely bred new discontent. A wary Zapata meanwhile had withdrawn his guerrillas to the mountains, and when Madero failed to push through promised land reforms, Zapata announced his own reform program. In November 1911, "... standing on a table in a mountain hut ... while the Mexican flag was raised and a band played the National Anthem," Zapata read out the Plan of Ayala, a program that markedly resembled Marxist teachings: "... immediate seizure of all foreign-owned lands and of all properties which had been taken away from villages, the confiscation of one-third of the land held by hacendados friendly to the Revolution and full confiscation against owners who 'directly or indirectly' opposed the Plan. ... "[16] Once again, peasants by the thousands flocked to fight under Zapata's banner, a grim death's-head.

After announcing his new program, Zapata resumed fighting in the South. In January 1912, Madero sent a new governor to Morelos, Francisco Naranjo, Jr., a fairly liberal man who carefully studied the situation. "... I found that Morelos lacked three things," he said later, "first plows, second books, and third equity. And it had more than enough latifundios, taverns and bosses."[17] Naranjo had put his finger on the problem, but was unable to effect necessary reforms. Meanwhile, federal troops under Brigadier General Juvencio Robles were marching through the state, burning towns, relocating peasants, shooting guerrillas. When these punitive measures failed and the guerrilla force continued to grow, Madero relieved Robles with General Felipe Ángeles. Ángeles took an altogether new tack and attempted to bring peace to the torn country by general amnesty and good sense. His measures soon began to deprive the guerrillas of recruits and of support from the towns and, had the provincial administration acted forcefully and intelligently, it could probably have stopped the fighting altogether. As it was, it refused to enact the proposed reforms. Zapata, in turn, had changed tactics by ordering his guerrillas to burn cane fields in order to deprive peons of work and thus create recruits. His forces shortly swelled until subordinate leaders were fielding units with as many as eight to twelve hundred guerrillas.[18]

In the North, Pascual Orozco felt himself slighted by the new government and, early in 1912, resumed fighting, though scarcely for a revolutionary cause. His new patron was a millionaire cattle baron who wanted to embarrass Madero's government and cause it to fall. In the event, Orozco was soon challenged by Pancho Villa and then defeated by a federal army under command of General Huerta, an able if drunken and dishonest soldier incongruously known to his admirers as "the Mexican Cromwell." As if Madero did not have enough problems, he now ran afoul of the United States Government.

Public opinion in America originally had favored the revolutionary cause, at least sufficiently to cause President Taft to recognize and even assist the Madero government while officially holding to a neutral policy. But American commercial interests in the country were strong: American companies owned three quarters of the mines, half the oil fields (England owned the other half), and vast cattle ranches in the North—all together, by 1910, an investment of some $2 billion.[19] The tragic exploitation of people and property was in keeping with North America's curious little imperialistic fling that had begun with the Spanish-American War. An American fleet patrolled the Gulf Coast, its purpose according to Philander Knox, Taft's Secretary of State, to keep Mexicans " . . . in a salutary equilibrium, between a dangerous and exaggerated apprehension and a proper degree of wholesome fear."[20]

The American ambassador to Mexico, Henry Lane Wilson, a fifty-five-year-old archconservative, was firmly wedded to American commercial interests. This group, which formed a powerful colonial lobby called The Committee of the American Colony, deplored the notion of a reform government and, through Wilson, did what they could to defeat Madero. Whether through intention or ignorance, Wilson, who admired Porfirio Díaz, misreported the actual situation from the beginning of the revolution. The Mexican Government had interpreted the lull that followed the original outbreaks as a sign of weakness, whereas it was a period of rebel reorganization and recruitment. This was a fundamental error—we have encountered it earlier and shall encounter it again and again—and Wilson went along with it: " . . . The conspiracy lacks coherence and the government will easily suppress it," he reported, also commenting on " . . . the lack of intelligent leadership" among the rebels.[21] Ambassador Wilson's misrepresentations caused Washington to adopt an anti-Madero policy and moved troops to the border. The ambassador's machinations also helped anti-Madero forces to overthrow, indeed to murder the president and the vice-president in early 1913 and install General Huerta in power. Huerta was a dreadful man—an alcoholic, dope addict, thief, and despot—and neither Taft nor his successor, Woodrow Wilson, recognized his government, nor did three northern Mexican states, where revolution again broke out.

The governor of Coahuila, Venustiano Carranza, challenged the Huerta government by announcing still another reform program, the Plan of Guadalupe. Huerta's army at first forced the rebels north but did not

166

destroy Carranza's army. Based at Nogales, on the Sonora-Arizona border, the rebel force was commanded by Álvaro Obregón, thirty-three years old, a former schoolteacher and factory worker who, along with his associates, Adolfo de la Huerta and Plutarco Elías Calles, would soon become important revolutionary characters (and eventually presidents).

Another rebel leader was about to come into his own in neighboring Chihuahua. This was Pancho Villa, who had returned from Texas to organize a new force of mounted irregulars. Such was his charisma that he had little trouble in attracting men to his banner. When federal troops captured and executed his titular commander, General Abraham González, Pancho Villa became military commander of the state.

Villa was not as good a guerrilla fighter as Zapata, but he was as picturesque. A teetotaler and non-smoker, he was a crack pistol shot; as Ronald Atkin wrote, he loved women, ice cream, and war. As long as he commanded a small band, he prospered, but as his force increased, he began to encounter problems that he failed to solve and that eventually brought him to heel.

The opposing forces spent most of the summer of 1913 in strengthening themselves. Huerta's strategy was to defend the towns along the railway, leaving the countryside to the rebels. This was a holding action while he maneuvered to gain American recognition of his government. Woodrow Wilson despised Huerta and what he stood for and steadily refused to recognize him. In spring of 1913 the British Government offered to recognize Huerta in return for a promise of "free elections" as soon as possible. Germany, France, Spain, and Japan played along, but Wilson relieved his ambassador and refused to name a new one. Wilson instead sent a personal emissary to the war-torn country. John Lind, former governor of Minnesota, proposed a cease-fire with "free elections" to follow, with Huerta abstaining from candidacy. Carranza refused the plan and announced that the Constitutionalists would execute anyone recognizing a president elected under it. In the event, the elections proved a farce and Huerta continued as dictator.

But an uneasy dictator. Carranza's armies had been steadily growing. Pancho Villa now commanded some eight thousand men, a force armed and equipped in part by captured government weapons, in part by arms smuggled from the United States and paid for by "contributions" and "loans" exacted from towns in the best medieval tradition. Villa's army even included a modern hospital train staffed with sixty American and Mexican doctors.[22]

In bold contrast, his disparate force included lieutenants as unorthodox as they were cruel: Tomás Urbina, the Lion of the Sierras, an illiterate whose signature was a heart; Fausto Borunda, called the Matador because he always killed prisoners; Rodolfo Fierro, another brute, who on one occasion killed three hundred federal prisoners on the spot.[23] Such men were called "finger generals"—" . . . their nickname coming from the practice of appointing officers by pointing a finger . . . and saying, 'You, be colonel; you, general; you, governor.' "[24] Along with other leaders, they turned up in small bands that included wives, children, and animals; the resultant army strongly resembled the Algerian *smala*, an awkward mob that perforce traveled by rail. Villa exercised unquestioned authority over most of these bands. His personal following was high at this time. Although not understanding the goals of the revolution (nor did the other leaders, with the exception of Obregón and Calles), Villa did understand the peon's desire for land, and, like Zapata, distributed it liberally. He used his guerrilla army in civic works—repairing streets and building schools. Villa also had gained two important aides: General Felipe Ángeles, a professional and capable soldier, and Martín Luis Guzmán, his secretary (who later wrote novels based on his experience).

Villa's army fought well in the early battles. In September, he and Obregón began to push southward. The tactical problem consisted of attacking towns defended by government troops. In the early attacks, Villa developed what became a favorite tactic, *un golpe terrífico* (a terrible blow) delivered by a flank attack of cavalry (a tactic repeatedly used by Frederick the Great). Villa was so impressed with its success that he organized an elite and independent unit, the *Dorados*, three squadrons of one hundred horse each. Both Obregón and Villa scored impressive victories in the autumn fighting. The rebel cause prospered further when President Wilson, early in 1914, changed his policy of "watchful waiting" and allowed the rebels to buy arms in America.

Nothing was pleasant about the war. The rebel attacks were costly, and interspersed with this confused campaign were small bands looting, raping and killing—a terrible period reminiscent of the Thirty Years' War. Neither side gave nor expected quarter. The ghastly war continued through the winter with intense rivalries developing between Carranza, the "First Chief" of the Constitutionalists, and his military commanders, and also between Obregón and Pancho Villa as the rebel armies nonetheless continued to advance toward Mexico City. Although Huerta's cause was virtually lost, he received a temporary boost in popularity in April 1914, when Washington intervened by seizing a ship loaded with munitions, an action that led to the famous Tampico incident and an American force landing at Vera Cruz, killing two hundred defenders and occupying the port. But even this incredibly inept move could not save him—in July he abdicated, and, a month later, the federal army left Mexico City.

Matters were scarcely pacific in the rebel camp. Frightened of Villa's growing power and truculent attitude, Carranza steered him away from the capital. When Villa protested, Carranza stopped coal deliveries to his camp. Villa, who depended on trains to move his *smala,* was stymied—and Obregón's army beat him to Mexico City. Villa did not long remain stymied. At the end of September, when he was again marching south, he issued a manifesto that defied Carranza's authority. Carranza's rule also faced a threat from the South: Emiliano Zapata was pushing toward the capital as well. Like Villa, Zapata had held to a rigorous social-economic interpretation of the revolution. In taking over the countryside of Morelos, Puebla, and Guerrero, he ruthlessly eliminated landowning opposition, killing plantation managers, and burning haciendas. To retain control of the land, he summarily distributed it to peons, who farmed it while carrying rifles. Zapata thus strengthened his power base, and in some ways proved a more formidable enemy than the northern forces. But the states under his control paid a terrible price: whole villages destroyed; thousands of men conscripted and deported north as laborers by government forces; plantations razed and burned; crops destroyed.

Zapata remained strong, however, and, combined with Villa, proved too powerful for Carranza, who moved his government to Vera Cruz, leaving Mexico City to Villa and Zapata. This proved only a temporary setback. Neither rebel leader knew what to do with his power, and soon evacuated the capital. Obregón had used the breathing space to reorganize his army and again take to the field. Fighting seesawed until April 1915, when Obregón tempted Villa to attack his army entrenched at Celaya, west of Mexico City. Villa's military adviser, General Felipe Ángeles, was away, and Villa had failed to learn the lessons of the Russo-Japanese War: horses were useless against trenches defended by barbed wire and soldiers firing rifles and machine guns. A series of abortive attacks cost him perhaps ten thousand killed and broke his army.[25] Retreating north, he halted now and again to fight losing battles. His close friend Tomás Urbina deserted with the treasury; other leaders and their guerrilla followers faded away.

Villa reached his northern sanctuary of Chihuahua with a greatly decimated army. A few months later, another blow fell when Washington, which had recognized Carranza's government, stopped arms from reaching Villa. Partly in retaliation, in January 1916, Villa's troopers held up a train in Sonora and cold-bloodedly murdered sixteen American engineers; in March, his band raided Columbus, New Mexico, and killed eight American soldiers and ten civilians. In response to the public outcry, President Wilson gained Carranza's permission to send a punitive expedition under General John Pershing into the northern provinces. Pershing's expedition failed for two reasons: his troops were neither trained nor equipped for guerrilla warfare, and his operations were constantly hampered by Carranza, who was only too aware of the prevailing Mexican hatred for Yankee intervention. On the one occasion that Pershing's cavalry found Villa, it could not pursue because its horses were worn out. The Americans were operating in hostile country, and soon learned that even federal troops resented their presence. They scored a few successes: on one occasion, a cavalry column surprised a group of rebels and killed forty-four of them; on another occasion, a young lieutenant, George Patton, surprised and killed the commander of Villa's famed *Dorados*. But these were slight when compared to the investment in and embarrassment brought by the expedition. Although Pershing's operations were increasingly restricted—as of July, his patrols could operate only 150 miles into Mexico—the campaign lasted into early 1917.

Pancho Villa continued to operate in the North, though with only sporadic success. In summer of 1919, another American force brought his small army to bay and defeated it. Small bands of Villistas survived, Villa himself outlasting his enemy, Carranza, whose rule had brought continued disaster to Mexico and who was murdered while trying to escape the country. Obregón made peace with Villa and kept him quiet by giving him a large hacienda, which he ruled in the best overlord tradition until he was ambushed and killed in 1923.

Emiliano Zapata also suffered a violent end. Unlike Pancho Villa, Zapata continued to fight guerrilla warfare against the Carranza government. General Pablo González commanded the campaign in Morelos against what he called "the Zapata rabble." González answered Zapata's guerrilla tactics with wholesale spoliation: " . . . Whole villages were burned; crops were destroyed; women and children were herded into detention camps and every man González could lay his hands on was hanged." Zapata replied with wholesale terrorism against landowners and army officers:

> . . . Some victims were crucified on telegraph poles or on giant cactus trees; others were staked out over ants' nests and smeared with honey, or sewn up inside wet hides and left to suffocate as the hides dried in the sun. One of Zapata's favorite execution methods was to stake out a man on a rough framework of branches over the top of a fast-growing maguey cactus. During the night the thorn-tipped blossom stalk of the plant would grow a foot or more, driving itself inch by inch through the staked-out victim.[26]

Although the Carranza government had introduced a new constitution in 1917, Zapata refused to submit to what he believed was reactionary government. Fighting continued into 1919, when Zapata fell victim to an elaborate ruse: an army colonel sent word that he wished to desert along with his regiment. To prove his good intention, he attacked a government force and killed fifty-nine soldiers! Duly impressed, Zapata met him at a rendezvous and was instantly shot dead. The colonel received fifty thousand pesos and a promotion.[27] Following Zapata's death, resistance in Morelos diminished and finally settled into uneasy peace.

The Mexican revolution was expensive. In addition to millions of dollars spent by each side on arms, armies, and ammunition, it cost an estimated three million lives. It left the country virtually bankrupt, with industries and mines at a standstill and virulent hatreds among the populace that would persist for decades. Nor did it accomplish all basic revolutionary aims. But it did clear the way for a system of government that, despite many faults, has without question improved the lives of its peoples—a task of reconstruction not yet completed.

CHAPTER FOURTEEN

1. Alba, 107.
2. Cheetham, 188–90. See also, Prescott; Madariaga; Herring.
3. Alba, 91. See also, Atkin; Cumberland.
4. Cheetham, 198.
5. Atkin, 22. See also, O'Hea, who was a plantation manager before and during the revolution.
6. Alba, 85 ff.
7. Atkin, 31–33. See also, Tannenbaum.
8. Alba, 99.
9. Cheetham, 209 ff.
10. Ibid., 211–13. See also, Alba; Ross.
11. Atkin, 51–3. See also, O'Hea, who writes from a personal acquaintance with Villa.
12. Atkin, 62.
13. Womack, 63–6.
14. Atkin, 54–5.
15. Womack, 67–96.
16. Atkin, 89–90.
17. Womack, 136.
18. Ibid., 157–8.
19. Alba, 106.
20. Atkin, 188. See also, Calvert, for a detailed and excellent political-diplomatic analysis.
21. Atkin, 52.
22. Ibid., 147.
23. Ibid., 144. See also, O'Hea, who knew many of these subordinates.
24. Alba, 119. See also, Harris and Sadler.
25. Alba, 129.
26. Atkin, 303.
27. Alba, 129.

CHAPTER 15

Guerrillas in World War I • Lettow-Vorbeck in German East Africa • The background • A guerrilla army forms • Lettow-Vorbeck's problems • The Boer campaign against him • His incredible retreat • The cost • Lettow-Vorbeck's secret • British weaknesses • Meinertzhagen's prediction

THE STATIC NATURE of World War I prevented major guerrilla operations on the eastern and western fronts but not in subsidiary theaters. Brilliant campaigns were fought in East Africa and Jerusalem—campaigns that bore primarily a military hallmark in that each contributed to the fortune of its parent army, although in totally different fashion.

At the outbreak of World War I, a forty-five-year-old German army officer, Lieutenant Colonel Paul von Lettow-Vorbeck, commanded German East Africa's (later Tanganyika, today's Tanzania) garrison force, a *Schutztruppe* that, together with the police force, numbered about 260 white officers and 4,600 *askaris*, or natives. Though virtually surrounded and cut off from overseas supply by British blockade, Lettow-Vorbeck refused to consider his civilian superior's plea for neutrality. Instead, he insisted on military action in order to pin down "as many troops as possible" and thereby cause England to provide reinforcements otherwise destined for France.

Lettow-Vorbeck told his own story after the war; it was later presented in Leonard Mosley's splendid book *Duel for Kilimanjaro*, on which I have in part based the following brief account.

Shortly after outbreak of war, the British decided to occupy the coastal towns of German East Africa. In early November, two reinforced brigades from India landed near Tanga, in the North, an effort that was supposed to have been supported by another brigade coming overland. This help never arrived, and so inept was the amphibious operation that Lettow-Vorbeck's guerrillas, aided by swarms of local

172

and furious bees, soon caused the enemy to re-embark. This disaster cost the British eight hundred dead, five hundred wounded, and several hundred taken prisoner; it cost Lettow-Vorbeck fifteen European and fifty-four *askari* lives, it brought him recruits by the hundreds, and it also supplied " . . . twelve machine guns, hundreds of rifles, 600,000 rounds of ammunition, coats and blankets enough to last for the rest of the war."[1]

Lettow-Vorbeck was after much bigger game. He wanted to entice a large British expeditionary force into German East Africa, an immense country whose 650,000 square miles of jungle, forests, bushlands, heat, rain, and disease would not gladly suffer large armies. He reasoned that if guerrillas continued to cut the all-important Uganda railway, the British would be stung into the desired reaction—each soldier lured south would be one less available to be sent to Europe.

Throughout 1915, his small guerrilla bands, usually two Europeans and eight *askaris,* operated from Mount Kilimanjaro's wooded slopes, destroying bridges, blowing up trains, ambushing convoys, and capturing arms, ammunition, horses, and mules. At the same time, Lettow-Vorbeck was recruiting and training a guerrilla-type army, which, by late 1915, reached a peak strength of three thousand whites and eleven thousand *askaris.*

Lettow-Vorbeck was supremely suited to carry out this ambitious program. A large, physically tough man, he was a professional soldier who had fought in China in the Boxer Rebellion. In 1904, he had campaigned against the Hottentots in Southwest Africa, had been wounded, but had learned a great deal about guerrilla warfare from these superb bush fighters, who, as the British had earlier experienced with the Zulus, moved faster on foot than the European on horse!

In trying to mobilize German East Africa's resources, Lettow-Vorbeck often fought an uphill battle. His nemesis was the governor, Heinrich Schnee, a vapid little man who wished to keep the area neutral. Reasoning that neutrality would preserve nothing if Germany suffered defeat, Lettow-Vorbeck argued that, in time of war, military authority must rule. Schnee did not agree—a stormy and prolonged relationship that forever hindered Lettow-Vorbeck's operations, as did a perpetual shortage of arms, ammunition, and supply. The British disaster at Tanga and guerrilla forays in the North helped to provide him with needed arms. The British also helped by bombarding coastal towns and turning the apathetic European population into active participants willing to donate goods and services to the army. In spring of 1915, a German freighter evaded the British blockade and crash-landed on the coast to disgorge eighteen hundred rifles, two six-centimeter guns, four machine guns, shells, explosives, tents, and communication materials.[2]

The Royal Navy prevented another such windfall, and Lettow-

Vorbeck's diversely located units were never entirely free from ammunition shortages. They soon became dependent on home-made or ersatz items such as candles, soap, quinine, medicines, cigars, cigarettes, beer, whiskey, boots made from antelope skin (the soles cut from captured British saddles). Later in the war, as the British occupied the towns and pushed inland, most of these items disappeared, with resultant hardship to the guerrillas.

Hardship, however, meant that Lettow-Vorbeck was accomplishing his basic mission. Early British failures and concomitant guerrilla successes had deeply offended British *amour-propre* to decide London on a campaign designed to eliminate the troublesome Lettow-Vorbeck. In early 1916, a mounted brigade of Boers arrived in Nairobi, the vanguard of an impressive force commanded by Major General Jan Smuts, once a hunted guerrilla himself. Smuts commanded a two-year offensive that ended in stalemate, with Lettow-Vorbeck's force, though weakened, still very operational.

General van Deventer next took over the chase, and in late 1917 forced Lettow-Vorbeck to begin a long retreat south into Portuguese East Africa, *a three-thousand-mile trek* that ended back in the German colony in autumn of 1918. Here he rebuilt his shattered force and by November was again wondering where to strike. At this point, the European armistice ended his war.

At a cost of some 2,000 killed, 9,000 wounded, and 7,000 prisoners or missing, besides six or seven thousand native carriers dead (mostly from disease), he had contained 160,000 British troops besides various Portuguese and Belgian expeditions from south and west. In hunting him, the British lost an estimated 10,000 killed, 7,800 wounded, and about a thousand missing or captured in addition to nearly 50,000 native carriers dead. Belgian and Portuguese casualties amounted to 4,700.[3]

How to explain this fantastic record?

Lettow-Vorbeck and his *Schutztruppe* must take most of the credit. He adopted and retained a simple and clear-cut mission, one which his subordinates fully understood and one for which they were trained. He knew his natives, allowed them their customs, offered them understanding, compassion, and success. He knew his country, and consistently paced operations to terrain and weather. He constantly improvised, never ceased experimenting with field expedients. Above all, he remained an indomitable commander who recognized but was not deterred by his own weaknesses, who gained strength when the enemy demanded surrender. Once, when he was fever-ridden and nearly blind, he led his exhausted horse into camp. His adjutant noted, " . . . I am not sure which one more resembled a skeleton. One thing is certain. The horse will not last the next twenty-four hours, but the colonel will."[4]

He did not go into this war lightly. He knew that he was a very small cog on the wheel of total war. He did not know that the British refused to use black soldiers on the western front; he could not have dreamed of the tactical stupidity of a battle such as the Somme, which in one day cost the British fifty thousand dead—so he did not realize that the white soldiers he and his people were retaining by their own agony would not greatly have influenced the European war.

These facts do not shrink the dimensions of his unique accomplishment. Britain had to supply and pay an enormous army, a total bill of £72 million, and she also had to withstand the severe buffeting of German psychological warfare, which constantly harped on the British failure to run down Lettow-Vorbeck.

Nor do facts lessen the import of his decision. He knew that he was inviting wrath to his country, that people would suffer and die, that he himself would have to surmount an endless stream of personal and organizational problems in order to survive. Anyone doubting the ghastly seriousness of his approach need read only his own words concerning organization and training of the first guerrilla groups:

> . . . I had to teach the Europeans that it was possible, in these waterless wastes, to drink their own urine to quench their thirst. It was a bad business when anyone fell ill or was wounded, with the best will in the world it was impossible to bring him along. To carry a severely wounded man from the Uganda Railway to the German camps, as was occasionally done, was a tremendous performance.

So tremendous, Mosley adds, that " . . . he gave orders that it was to stop. A wounded man was relieved of his gun and ammunition, shot through the head, and left to the lions, hyenas or the vultures."[5]

Lettow-Vorbeck was as ruthless with his own body. By early 1917, he was enduring his fourth bout of malaria; sand flies and jiggers lived in his skin, at times he could scarcely walk on a scabbed and festered left foot, his teeth were infected, and he had scratched his one good eye on long elephant grass. By autumn of that year, enemy columns were closing from all directions while enemy aircraft droned relentlessly overhead. His once splendid force numbered only about two thousand rifles, including two hundred Europeans, and some three thousand bearers, who were now frequently deserting. But Lettow-Vorbeck was not ready to quit, at least without trying to wring some profit from disaster:

. . . All I knew was that henceforth we would at least have this over the enemy—we could withdraw quickly anywhere we wished, for we had no more dumps to protect, no more hospitals to worry about. The enemy would have to involve increasing numbers of men in his search for us and would progressively exhaust his strength.[6]

In addition to Lettow-Vorbeck's natural and acquired attributes, he derived considerable strength from his enemy's weaknesses. In 1914, the British high command both in Africa and India epitomized the arrogance of ignorance. Major General Aitken, who commanded the task force of eight thousand that sailed from India to Tanga, informed his intelligence officer, who had given the German enemy a high evaluation, "that the German is worse than we are, his troops are ill-trained, ours are magnificent and bush or no bush he means to thrash the German before Xmas."[7] The record does not offer Aitken's comments after the disaster (which cost him his job and relegated him to the status of colonel on half pay).

The British East African command erred in the opposite direction. The governor, Sir Charles Belfield, did not want a war and " . . . refused to co-operate with his military commanders."[8] The senior military commander, Major General Wapshare, was later described by his intelligence officer, Captain Meinertzhagen, as " . . . a kindly old gentleman, nervous, physically unfit and devoid of military knowledge."[9] Brigadier General Tighe was pleasant but useless, drink having given him gout and a bad liver. Neither general was qualified to divine the military problem, which called for a strategic defensive with strong, mobile patrols to neutralize guerrilla depredations along the Uganda railway. Instead, aided by the wisdom of the supreme command in London, they thought in terms of "expeditions"—vast "sweeps" to envelop and destroy the enemy, a conventional approach that merely helped Lettow-Vorbeck. Had the British not landed at Tanga, had they not bombarded coastal towns, he would have had the devil's own time raising any sort of an effective force. He could never have raised an army large enough to invade neighboring countries, and if he had tried, the British and Portuguese disposed of ample forces to stop him. He should have been allowed to wither on the vine. He knew this, and this is why he set about making himself an excrescence, an insulting, disgusting presence that the British, in their own minds, had to eliminate.

As he hoped, they chose to wipe him out not by a qualitative approach that would have neutralized his operations, but rather by a quantitative approach that represented the summit of Lettow-Vorbeck's dreams. Wapshare's first effort, an overland expedition of eighteen hundred troops and fifty-five hundred bearers ended in the little coastal

Inset labels:
AFRICA
German East Africa

Map labels:
Lake Victoria
Nairobi
BRITISH EAST AFRICA
Mt. Kilimanjaro
Moshi
GERMAN EAST AFRICA
Tabora
Jasin
Tanga
Zanzibar
Dar-es-Salaam
INDIAN OCEAN
Lake Tanganyika
L. Mweru
Abercorn
Fife
Rovuma
Lake Nyasa
R. Zambezi
PORTUGUESE EAST AFRICA
Mozambique

March of
Lettow-Vorbeck's Forces
1916 – 1918
--> Main column
---> Subcolumns
+-+- Railways

N

0   100   200   300 miles

M.E.P.

town of Jasin just south of the border, where, after four companies were lost to an enemy attack, it withered "away from sickness and heat." The highly vaunted Boers did not fare much better. Meinertzhagen found Van Deventer contemptuous in his ignorance of this war "... between coolies and kaffirs":

> ... I tried to explain to them that they had not the slightest idea of climate and health conditions, neither had any of them any experience of fighting in thick bush. I told them I thought that perhaps two years might finish the campaign. They smiled and told me I did not understand the Boer.[10]

Meinertzhagen was correct. In the spring of 1916, Smuts sent Van Deventer south in command of 1,200 mounted troops and 8,600 infan-

177

try and artillery. Lettow-Vorbeck wisely stayed out of sight, letting rain and the tsetse fly fight for him. On April 6, Van Deventer counted 1,150 mounted strength, April 12, 800, and on April 16, 650. By the end of the month, he had a fighting strength of 3,000 left out of 10,000.[11]

Other expeditions fared equally ill. By autumn of 1916, " . . . out of 54,000 horses, mules, donkeys and oxen which had been fed into the supply lines south of the Central Railway . . . all but 600 had died."[12] This appalling expenditure of men, animals and effort would have been difficult to defend even if "victory" had resulted. But "victory" was nowhere in sight. And yet, continued adversity only increased Smuts's tenacity—precisely as Lettow-Vorbeck hoped. The capture of Lettow-Vorbeck became an obsession to Smuts. Van Deventer, in turn, never saw the forest for the trees, never totally modified his conventional thinking to fit the task at hand. Only late in the campaign did the British approach the obvious target of the natives—and then with excellent success, but by then it was too late to matter.

Anyone can be wise after the event, but in the case of this campaign the facts were on hand by summer of 1916. Only one officer in the British camp looked at them objectively. This was Captain Meinertzhagen who during that summer wrote:

> . . . Von Lettow . . . is not going to be caught by maneuver. He knows the country better than we do, his troops understand the last word in bush warfare and can live on the country. I think we are in for an expensive hide-and-seek, and von Lettow will still be cuckooing somewhere in Africa when the cease-fire goes.[13]

CHAPTER FIFTEEN

1. Mosley, 75. See also, Gardner; Lettow-Vorbeck, who claimed that the British suffered closer to 2,000 deaths.
2. Mosley, 88. See also, Lettow-Vorbeck; Hordern.
3. Lettow-Vorbeck, 325–6. See also, Mosley, Gardner.
4. Mosley, 150.
5. Ibid., 96–7.
6. Ibid. 176–7.
7. Meinertzhagen, 84.
8. Ibid. 85 ff., 146.
9. Ibid., 109.
10. Ibid., 163–4.
11. Mosley, 132.
12. Ibid., 153.
13. Meinertzhagen, 195–6.

CHAPTER 16

Thomas Edward Lawrence • His background • The original Arab revolt • Lawrence's first impressions and estimate of the situation • He joins the rebellion • Arab reverses • Lawrence recovers the initiative • His illness • Moment of truth: a new tactical doctrine • His tactics analyzed • The Arab contribution

WHILE LETTOW-VORBECK was training black guerrillas in remote Kilimanjaro hills, a young British intelligence officer in Cairo was tinkering with a different type of war. This was Thomas Edward Lawrence, who was to become famous to the world as "Lawrence of Arabia."

T. E. Lawrence was an illegitimate Welshman, a twenty-six-year-old reserve lieutenant, a short man, slightly built, his boyishly fair countenance belying either an Oxford honors degree or an extensive knowledge of the Near East gained from several years of archaeological digging in northern Syria, a vocation actively encouraged by British Intelligence.

Scholar, linguist, historian, writer, artist, and poet, Lawrence had not proved a quiescent staff officer in GHQ, Cairo. " . . . A subaltern on the staff, without a Sam Browne belt, and always wearing slacks, scorching about between Cairo and Bulaq on a Triumph motor-cycle, he was an offense to the eyes of his senior officers."[1] His ready criticism of the way the Near East war was being fought against the Turks infuriated most of his seniors. The British surrender of Kut-el-Amara, in Mesopotamia, where he served as negotiator, only heightened his disgust.

Lawrence did not believe in empty criticism. He not only told his superiors what was wrong, but he insisted that an Arab revolt was the best way to beat the Turks. In talking this up, he appeared at times brilliant, at times frivolous, generally impudent, often rude. He probably would not have endured in any but the British army, which tolerated eccentrics on the grounds that the genius of a few amply repaid the sacrifice.

Not too many officers listened to Lawrence, fewer still agreed. But one who did agree was Kitchener Pasha, now Lord Kitchener, Secretary of State for War, who offered encouragement to the Arabs. The chief of British Intelligence in Cairo, Major General Clayton, also recognized the possibilities of a revolt and encouraged Lawrence to investigate further. A handful of other high-ranking diplomats and officers agreed, and they helped pave the way for Lawrence to exercise what most held to be perverted military thought, others a whimsical imagination, a few genius.

Lawrence's hoped-for revolt broke out in the Hejaz—the skinny Arabian province flanking the Red Sea—in the summer of 1916. Husein, the sherif of Mecca, succeeded in capturing that holy town from the Turks. But his force as well as those commanded by his sons, Feisal, Ali and Abdullah, were badly organized and lacked arms and equipment. By September, Feisal's and Ali's armies were marking time southwest of Medina; Abdullah, having won Taif (and the surrender of the Turkish governor-general), hovered northeast of Medina with his warriors. In the minds of many ranking British staff officers in Cairo, the Arab revolt had failed.

Lawrence disagreed, believing instead that lack of leadership explained the present dormant state. Arab nationalism, he thought, could become an ideal sufficient to unite all tribes in a war against the Turks—but a leader was needed to translate this into action. At this crucial point, GHQ dispatched a ranking and eminently qualified British diplomat, Ronald Storrs, to Jidda to help Abdullah and his father, Husein, through still another crisis. Lawrence meanwhile had been using influential friends to wangle his transfer to the Arab Bureau; he now *took leave* to accompany his good friend Storrs. On the trip down the Red Sea, Lawrence became close friends with Husein's chief of staff, an Arab-Circassian ex-colonel in the Turkish army, Aziz el Masri, whose advice, albeit cynical at times, greatly helped Lawrence in the difficult months ahead.

The three men landed at Jidda on October 16, a scene Lawrence later used to open his first major work, *Revolt in the Desert*,[2] a short version of his subsequent classic *Seven Pillars of Wisdom*.[3] Emir Abdullah did not overly impress the young intelligence officer. Lawrence found him too clever, his sincerity discouraged by personal ambition; he was " . . . too balanced, too cool, too humorous" to be *the* leader of the revolt, too discouraged to be the armed prophet who " . . . would set the desert on fire."[4]

Storrs now persuaded Husein to allow Lawrence to visit Ali and Feisal. Lawrence met Ali and his nineteen-year-old half brother Zeid at

Rabigh. Ali, too, proved disappointing. Though possessing a " . . . dignified and admirable manner," the thirty-seven-year-old sherif, weakened by tuberculosis, lacked any " . . . great force of character," was " . . . nervous and rather tired," and was not possibly up to the task ahead. Zeid possessed a certain fire, but was too young for the task.[5]

From Rabigh, Lawrence traveled cross-country, a long and dangerous trip by camel, to Feisal's camp at Hamra. This tall, slender, black-bearded prince at once impressed Lawrence as a natural leader. Ensuing talks in which he found the thirty-one-year-old ruler to be " . . . hot-tempered, proud and impatient" confirmed his first impression. Although Feisal was tired and discouraged, he was willing to fight. As he explained to Lawrence, the Arabs, after initial successes, had lost the initiative to the Turks. In his opinion, the enemy would now try to advance on Rabigh and recapture Mecca. To void this plan, Feisal proposed to fall back and then move against the Hejaz railway while his brothers, Abdullah and Ali, struck the Turkish base at Medina. But Feisal needed arms, ammunition and other aid if he was to keep going.

Lawrence welcomed Feisal's aggressiveness as well as the fighting spirit he discerned in numerous tribes. As he visited various tribal levies and talked to individual fighters, he began to form his own idea of the best tactical contribution the Arabs could make. He concluded that Feisal's tribesmen, if supplied with light guns, " . . . might be capable of holding their hills and serving as an efficient screen behind which we could build up, perhaps at Rabigh, an Arab regular mobile column, capable of meeting a Turkish force (distracted by guerrilla warfare) on terms, and of defeating it piecemeal. . . . "[6]

At this stage of his thinking, Lawrence envisioned a Hejaz war

> . . . of dervishes against regular troops. It was the fight of a rocky, mountainous, barren country (reinforced by a wild horde of mountaineers) against an enemy so enriched in equipment by the Germans as almost to have lost virtue for rough-and-tumble war. The hill-belt was a paradise for snipers; and Arabs were artists in sniping. Two or three hundred determined men knowing the ranges should hold any section of them; because the slopes were too steep for escalade. . . .

Similarly, the valleys lent themselves to easy ambush that should frustrate and probably prevent Turkish transit. " . . . Without treachery on the part of the mountain tribes," Lawrence decided, it seemed impossible that " . . . the Turks could dare to break their way through." But,

> . . . even with treachery as an ally, to pass the hills would be dangerous. The enemy would never be sure that the fickle population might not turn again; and to have such a labyrinth of defiles in the

rear, across the communications, would be worse than having it in front. Without the friendship of the tribes, the Turks would own only the ground on which their soldiers stood; and lines so long and complex would soak up thousands of men in a fortnight, and leave none in the battlefront.[7]

After promising Feisal as much help as possible, Lawrence returned to the coast convinced of the possibilities of an effective rebellion. On the return voyage, he found unexpected allies in two important Englishmen. One was Admiral Sir Rosslyn Wemyss, commanding the Royal Navy in the Red Sea, a close friend of the sherif of Mecca; the other was Sir Reginald Wingate, soon to become High Commissioner of Egypt. These officers read Lawrence's reports—and agreed with his conclusions.[8] Thanks to Wemyss and Wingate, Lawrence wafted into Cairo on a lofty cloud of importance. Pleasantly surprised at being closeted with top commanders, he even momentarily forgave their myopic incompetence in order to plead his case—the Arab need for immediate arms and supply as well as for British-officer instructor-advisers. Again to his surprise, his recommendations turned quickly into formal orders. Then, to his consternation, he himself was ordered to report to Feisal as adviser and liaison officer.

Lawrence's protests at his new assignment were genuine. He had never fancied himself a troop leader and certainly not a leader of Arab irregulars. So ill-prepared was he in practical military matters that at Yenbo, on the way to Feisal's headquarters, he took a crash course in demolitions from a British expert. His friend Aziz was still there, desperately trying to whip the native army into some semblance of military organization. Although four British planes had arrived, Cairo had not sent much other aid and no officer-instructors. News from the various rebel forces was favorable, however.

This changed in short order. The hill tribes that formed Feisal's barrier forces gave way to the first major Turkish assault. A Turk cavalry column had pushed on, nearly captured young Prince Zeid's force and now was looking hungrily at the Yenbo base. This unexpected success brought Feisal with his five-thousand-strong camel corps to screen Yenbo, but he in turn was attacked and driven back into the town, where he was protected by the guns of hastily concentrated British warships. These proved too much for the Turks, who backed off to sit like a hungry dog, one eye on Yenbo, one eye on Rabigh.

Lawrence now pulled a master coup by persuading Feisal to march two hundred miles up the coast to the small port of Wejh, from where he could more easily interdict the Hejaz railway. This was a shrewd psychological move that more than neutralized recent Turk successes. Feisal's army on the march, some ten thousand mounted and foot warriors, emphasized the extent of the rebellion and brought dozens of tribes into the fold. From Wejh, taken easily thanks to British warships and slight Turkish resistance, Feisal's agents continued north and east to plead the cause of Arab nationalism and pave the way for further moves by the rebel army.

An equally important result showed in the Turkish camp. The Turks could not pursue Feisal. Sickness already was tearing at their columns, and hostile tribes were slicing their thin lines of communication. They lacked both transport and will to pursue Feisal north. They could probably have captured Yenbo, but Lawrence made that effort unattractive by sea evacuation of stores. They could have marched on Rabigh, but the Arabs there could retreat on Mecca; meanwhile, so the Turks reasoned, Feisal could wheel about and strike Medina. So, instead of pursuit, the Turks chose to fall back on Medina, where half the force guarded the city, half the railway that supplied the city.

Lawrence did not yet know it, but he had hit upon a successful formula for war in the desert. At the moment, other thoughts occupied his mind. Returning to Cairo, he learned of a French plan to land a British-French force at Akaba, and hurriedly returned to Wejh to persuade Feisal against it. Instead, Lawrence sold him on a plan for a land assault of Akaba by *Arab* forces once Feisal had won necessary tribal submissions.

But now Lawrence learned from Cairo that the Turks were planning to evacuate Medina. Although this move would have suited the Arabs, the transfer of some twenty-five thousand Turkish soldiers would threaten British operations in the Beersheba area. Accordingly Cairo wanted to disrupt the move at all costs. This would involve cutting the all-important Hejaz railway—the umbilical cord to Turkish supply from Syria to Medina—and attempting to disrupt any march made by the Turks, preferably by an Arab attack against Medina. Feisal agreed to help. To win Abdullah's co-operation, Lawrence left on another long and dangerous trip, some two hundred miles across the sands to Ais, northwest of Medina.

Readers of Lawrence's books will remember this journey as the one that forced him to kill one of his guides in order to prevent a blood-rift in the ranks—a soul-searing episode that added to personal ravage caused by back boils, dysentery, and enteric fever. Arriving at Ais more dead than alive, he briefed Abdullah and collapsed.[9]

Lawrence nearly died in Abdullah's camp. High fever brought delirium and visions, and these slowly changed to intense pain from a renewed plague of boils as he returned to reality. Lying in a sun-baked tent, a latter-day Job in a military wilderness, he asked himself the why of war against the Turks.

Nothing about it fitted conventional theories of warfare:

> . . . the textbooks gave the aim in war as "the destruction of the organized forces of the enemy" by "the one process battle." Victory could only be purchased by blood. This was a hard saying, as the Arabs had no organized forces, and so a Turkish Foch would have no aim: and the Arabs would not endure casualties, so that an Arab Clausewitz could not buy his victory.[10]

Were the textbooks correct?

Only if one accepted the theory of "absolute" war. The Arab war, however, could not be called absolute: The destruction of the Turkish army by armed confrontation lay hopelessly beyond Arab means. Was it possible that war did not have to be absolute? Clausewitz, whom Lawrence greatly admired, admitted a number of reasons for fighting a war; two eighteenth-century commentators, De Saxe and Guibert, had preached the virtues of "limited" wars, which should be fought (and won) with as few battles as possible.

If one looked on the Arab war as a rebellion, the picture changed. The Arab aim " . . . was geographical, to extrude the Turk from all Arabic-speaking lands in Asia."[11] In gaining the domination of territory,

> . . . Turks might be killed, yet "killing Turks" would never be an excuse or aim. If they would go quietly, the war would end. If not, they must be driven out: but at the cheapest possible price, since the Arabs were fighting for freedom, a pleasure only to be tasted by a man alive.[12]

Lawrence's strategic and tactical analysis hinged on three elements, " . . . one algebraical, one biological, a third psychological." The algebraical element meant "measuring" invariables of the war to arrive at specific conclusions. The Arabs wanted about 140,000 square miles of territory. If they built a regular army and attempted to occupy this area, the Turks would entrench, and, at best, a stalemate would develop. Suppose, however, that Arabs instead formed " . . . an influence, a thing invulnerable, intangible, without front or back, drifting about like a gas? Armies were like plants, immobile as a whole, firm-rooted, nourished through long stems to the head. The Arabs might be a vapor, blowing where they listed."[13]

To meet a vapor attack, an attack in depth with " . . . sedition putting up her head in every unoccupied one of these 100,000 square miles," the Turks would need a fortified post every four square miles:

... 600,000 men to meet the combined ill wills of all the local Arab people. They had 100,000 men available. It seemed that the assets in this sphere were with the Arabs, and climate, railways, deserts, technical weapons could also be attached to their interests. The Turk was stupid and would believe that rebellion was absolute, like war, and deal with it on the analogy of absolute warfare.

The biological factor, what Lawrence called bionomics, respected relations between the organism and its environment. In war, this is the relation of man to battle, the giving and taking of blood until a decision is reached. This could not help the present situation: The Arabs were irregulars, limited in number, " . . . not units, but individuals, and an individual casualty is like a pebble dropped in water: each may make only a brief hole, but rings of sorrow widen out from them. The Arab army could not afford casualties." The Turkish army could afford casualties, but only in men. Materials in the Turkish army were at a premium; therefore " . . . the death of a Turkish bridge or rail, machine or gun, or high explosive" would be more profitable than the death of a Turk.[14]

Lawrence's final factor was the psychological, "the ethical in war"—what Xenophon had called the diathetic. The *will* of the Arab had to repair numerical and material weaknesses. His mind had to be influenced, and not alone his mind, but those of his enemy and his enemy's allies. The French theory of war combined moral and physical factors. Years before, Foch had written that the moral is to the physical as three to one, and on this comforting axiom the French built the disastrous opening strategy of World War I: the *offensive à outrance*, or all-out offensive, that sent hundreds of thousands of French soldiers to unnecessary death. Lawrence separated the factors: " . . . the contest was not physical, but moral, and so battles were a mistake." He was not interested in regimental traditions and elite corps, but rather in men's minds: " . . . the printing press is the greatest weapon in the armory of the modern commander."[15]

The sum of these three factors dictated an indirect approach to war:

> . . . the Turkish army was an accident, not a target. Our true strategic aim was to seek its weakest link, and bear only on that till time made the mass of it fall. The Arab army must impose the longest possible passive defense on the Turks (this being the most materially expensive form of war) by extending its own front to the maximum.

To accomplish this, the Arabs needed " . . . a highly mobile, highly equipped type of force, of the smallest size," which would variously strike at Turkish line of communications. Size was not important, since

" . . . the ratio between number and area determined the character of the war, and by having five times the mobility of the Turks the Arabs could be on terms with them with one-fifth their number."[16]

This was a latter-day approach to De Saxe's eighteenth-century philosophy. To the incredulity of professional British and French officers raised in Napoleonic tradition, Lawrence argued that battles are unnecessary, that they " . . . are impositions on the side which believes itself weaker, made unavoidable either by lack of land-room, or by the need to defend a material property dearer than the lives of the soldiers." The Arabs had plenty of land-room and nothing of material value to lose,

> . . . so they were to defend nothing and to shoot nothing. Their cards were speed and time, not hitting power, and these gave strategical rather than tactical strength. Range is more to strategy than force. The invention of bully-beef had modified land-war more profoundly than the invention of gunpowder.[17]

Conversely, the Arabs had no need to take Medina either by expensive assault or tiresome siege. Let the enemy stay there, or anywhere else, in the largest possible numbers, then destroy him by "killing" his line of communications.

Toward this end, the Arabs added to the sea bases of Yenbo and Wejh by taking Akaba. From these bases, they developed "ladders of tribes" to their advanced bases, from where they seized " . . . Tafileh and the Dead Sea; then Azrak and Deraa, and finally Damascus." With this, the Turks in Arabia were virtually at the mercy of their enemies. In Lawrence's opinion, the Arabs were on the verge of proving Marshal de Saxe's dictum " . . . that a war might be won without fighting battles." In gaining incontestable control of some one hundred thousand square miles, the Arabs had killed, wounded, or captured about thirty-five thousand Turks at little loss to themselves. The Turkish garrisons were totally on edge, morale stood at rock bottom, and undoubtedly the whole army would have collapsed had not General Allenby's immense victory in Palestine summarily driven Turkey from the war.[18]

The enormity of war on the western front, the precipitate fall of the Turks, and the Arab failure to obtain their political aim in the Near East have tended not so much to dim as to confuse the extent of Lawrence's accomplishment. Postwar commentators concentrated on war in the West at the expense of such secondary theaters as Palestine. Most writers treated the Arab war as a guerrilla side show, interesting enough, probably some help to old Allenby, who won the affair in

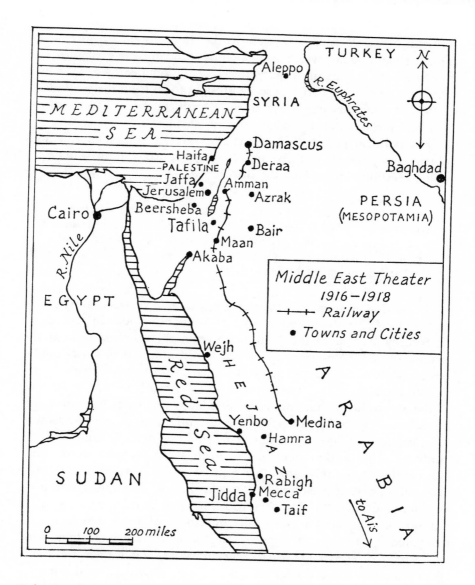

Middle East Theater
1916–1918
—+—+— Railway
• Towns and Cities

Palestine, but not having much to do with "real" war.

This judgment ignores two essential points. One is that Lawrence and his Arabs were fighting a separate war, a carefully defined war of insurrection that, although dependent on British arms and finances, helped Allenby enormously. Lawrence was not afraid of more Turks; indeed, he wanted more Turks, since enemy quantity enhanced friendly quality.

The second point is the "personalized" nature of Lawrence's war. He did not insist on grafting his own and his country's military standards on a body incapable of reception. Instead, and thanks to linguistic ability, imagination, perception, intellectual and moral honesty, and, not least, immense energy, he went to the tribes, found a leader, determined a viable goal, weighed capabilities, and hit on a type of war compatible to leadership, capabilities, and the political goal. The estimate of the situation that Lawrence brought forth from the sand dunes in 1917 is a military equivalent of the British constitution—one of the most interesting unwritten documents of all time.

His political preparation of the area greatly simplified Allenby's subsequent operations, which stood in strong contrast to those in neighboring Mesopotamia, where the British

> . . . remained substantially an alien force invading enemy territory, with the local people passively neutral or sullenly against them, and in consequence had not the freedom of movement and elasticity of Allenby in Syria, who entered the country as a friend, with the local people actively on his side.[19]

In fighting his own war, Lawrence displayed a versatile strategy and tactics at odds with orthodox military thinking. Under his aegis, the Arab army " . . . used the smallest force in the quickest time at the farthest place."[20] Raiding parties struck and ran, and this was fundamental, since it denied the enemy a target. In turn, Arab casualties remained minimum: " . . . many Turks on the Arab front had no chance all the war to fire a shot, and correspondingly the Arabs were never on the defense, except by rare accident." Essential to such operations was " . . . perfect intelligence, so that plans could be made in complete certainty. . . . The headquarters of the Arab army probably took more pains in this service than any other staff." Simple armament was equally essential. Lawrence preferred light machine guns, which the Arabs used as automatic rifles, " . . . snipers' tools, by men kept deliberately in ignorance of their mechanism, so that the speed of action would not be hampered by attempts at repair." Demolitions were important, with each irregular receiving at least rudimentary training in their use. Camels provided standard transport. On occasion, Lawrence used armored cars manned by Englishmen with gasoline either carried by camels or brought in by air. Although they performed well under certain conditions, " . . . the tactical employments of cars and camel-corps are so different that their use in joint operations is difficult. It was found demoralizing to both to use armored and unarmored cavalry together."[21]

Lawrence's tactics might have been countered, at least in part, by intelligent Turkish adaptation. In 1923, Lawrence wrote Colonel A. P. Wavell:

> . . . If the Turks had put machine guns on three or four of their touring cars, and driven them on weekly patrol over the admirable

188

going of the desert E. [east] of Amman and Maan they would have put an absolute stop to our camel-parties, and so to our rebellion. It wouldn't have cost them 20 men or £20,000 . . . *rightly applied.* They scraped up cavalry and armored trains and camel corps and block-houses against us: because they didn't think hard enough.

Lawrence dismissed several other possible Turkish countertactics: well-destruction would not have helped, nor did airplanes, which they used:

> . . . Bombing tribes is ineffective. I fancy that air-power may be effective against elaborate armies: but against irregulars it has no more than moral value. The Turks had plenty machines, and used them freely against us—and never hurt us till the last phase, when we had brought 1,000 of our regulars on the raid against Deraa. Guerrilla tactics are a complete muffing of air-force. . . .

The Turks did miss

> . . . one other thing of which every rebellion is mortally afraid—treachery. If instead of counter-propaganda (never effective on the conservative side) the money had been put into buying the few venal men always to be found in a big movement, then they would have crippled us. We could only dare these intricate raids because we felt sure and safe. One well-informed traitor will spoil a national rising.[22]

Lawrence's most amazing feat was assimilating himself to his environment, or, put another way, the ability to respect the Arabs as individuals leading their own way of life. Many of Lawrence's achievements stemmed from this relatively simple outlook. He refused to impose Western standards on people he regarded as civilized. Since lines of communication and supply troops did not exist, every soldier was a front-line soldier. But he could not be committed in strength; rather, by relay, by individual action, which levied severe strain and exacted from the soldier " . . . special initiative, endurance and enthusiasm." To maintain this, demanded charismatic leadership. English officer-advisers were purposely few in number, not more than one per thousand troops, and " . . . those who were present controlled by influence and advice, by their superior knowledge, not by an extraneous authority."[23]

The sum of the experience was enormous, suggesting to Lawrence that:

> . . . irregular warfare or rebellion could be proved to be an exact science, and an inevitable success, granted certain factors and if pursued along certain lines. Here is the thesis: Rebellion must have

an unassailable base, something guarded not merely from attack, but from the fear of it: such a base as the Arab revolt had in the Red Sea ports, the desert, or in the minds of men converted to its creed. It must have a sophisticated alien enemy, in the form of a disciplined army of occupation too small to fulfil the doctrine of acreage: too few to adjust number to space, in order to dominate the whole area effectively from fortified posts. It must have a friendly population, not actively friendly, but sympathetic to the point of not betraying rebel movements to the enemy. Rebellions can be made by two percent active in a striking force, and ninety-eight percent passively sympathetic. The few active rebels must have the qualities of speed and endurance, ubiquity and independence of arteries to supply. They must have the technical equipment to destroy or paralyze the enemy's organized communication, for irregular war is fairly Willisen's definition of strategy, "the study of communication," in its extreme degree, of attack where the enemy is not. In fifty words: Granted mobility, security (in the form of denying targets to the enemy), time, and doctrine (the idea to convert every subject to friendliness), victory will rest with the insurgents, for the algebraical factors are in the end decisive, and against them perfections of means and spirit struggle quite in vain.[24]

This was not an accidental theory, neither was it applied hit and miss. In 1933, Lawrence wrote a most revealing letter to Basil Liddell Hart, who was about to publish a major work:

> ... You talk of a summing up to come. Will you (if you agree with my feeling) in it strike a blow for hard work and thinking? I was not an instinctive soldier, automatic with intuitions and happy ideas. When I took a decision, or adopted an alternative, it was after studying every relevant—and many an irrelevant—factor. Geography, tribal structure, religion, social customs, language, appetites, standards—all were at my finger-ends. The enemy I knew almost like my own side. I risked myself among them a hundred times, to *learn*.
>
> The same with tactics. If I used a weapon well, it was because I could handle it. . . . To use aircraft, I learned to fly. To use armored cars, I learned to drive and fight them. I became a gunner at need, and could doctor and judge a camel.
>
> The same with strategy. I have written only a few pages on the art of war—but in these I levy contribution from my predecessors of five languages. You are one of the few living Englishmen who can see the allusions and quotations, the conscious analogies, in all I say and do, militarily.
>
> Do make it clear that generalship, at least in my case, came of understanding, of hard study and brain-work and concentration. Had it come easy to me I should not have done it so well. If your

book could persuade some of our new soldiers to read and mark and learn things outside drill manuals and tactical diagrams, it would do a good work. I feel a fundamental crippling incuriousness about our officers. Too much body and too little head. The perfect general would know everything in heaven and earth.

So please, if you see me that way and agree with me, do use me as a text to preach for more study of books and history, a greater seriousness in military art. With 2,000 years of examples behind us we have no excuse, when fighting, for not fighting well. . . . [25]

CHAPTER SIXTEEN

1. Garnett, 182. See also, Graves; Liddell Hart; Nutting; Payne; Brown; Wilson.
2. Lawrence, *Revolt in the Desert,* 1–2.
3. Lawrence, *Seven Pillars of Wisdom.* See also, Wingate, for an excellent background study of the revolt.
4. Lawrence, *Seven Pillars of Wisdom,* 68.
5. Ibid., 76–7.
6. Ibid., 106.
7. Ibid., 107.
8. Payne, *Lawrence of Arabia* 92–4. See also, MacMunn and Falls.
9. Lawrence, *Seven Pillars of Wisdom,* 187–92.
10. Lawrence, "Guerrilla Warfare."
11. Lawrence, *Seven Pillars of Wisdom,* 196.
12. Lawrence, "Guerrilla Warfare."
13. Ibid.
14. Ibid.
15. Ibid.
16. Ibid.
17. Ibid.
18. Ibid.
19. Lawrence, *Seven Pillars of Wisdom,* 60.
20. Lawrence, "Guerrilla Warfare."
21. Ibid.
22. Garnett, 422–3.
23. Lawrence, "Guerrilla Warfare." See also, Liddell Hart, *T. E. Lawrence,* 142–7, who cites Lawrence's "Twenty-Seven Articles"—"a theory of the art of handling Arabs . . . written as a confidential guide to newcomers from the British Army." These can be studied with profit by today's Western advisers to all foreign armies.
24. Lawrence, "Guerrilla Warfare."
25. Garnett, 768–9.

CHAPTER 17

The Irish Revolution • Asquith reacts • Rise of Sinn Fein • Michael Collins and the Irish Republican Army • The IRA and terrorist tactics • The Royal Irish Constabulary • The Black and Tans • The Auxies • Sir Nevil Macready's iron fist • Sinn Fein replies • The war escalates • Partition and British departure • The cost • Question of terrorist tactics • Definition of terror • Rule by terror • Paradox of terror: the double standard • Terror in the East

HAVING BREWED for several centuries, the Irish revolution came to a boil in Dublin on Easter Monday 1916. Padhraic H. Pearse, at thirty-seven years of age a veteran member of the Irish Republican Brotherhood, voiced the insurrectionary words from the wide steps of the general post office. His brogue heavy in lazy, warm air, Pearse proclaimed the end of English rule in favor of a free republic; as his oratory washed by a few startled citizens, fellow conspirators set up a series of fortified strong points in and around the city. By the time authorities awakened, rebels held city center and seemed hopeful of general uprising.

No general uprising.

Although many Irishmen resented English rule, they found nothing attractive about the militant IRB, with its organizational appendages the Sinn Fein (Ourselves Alone) and the Irish Volunteers. For sixty years, power had resided in the Irish Nationalist Party, whose eighty members vigorously and often cacophonously represented their country in the House of Commons. At the outbreak of World War I, John Redmond, speaking for country and party, had pledged Ireland to the war effort. In spring of 1916, some sixty thousand of her sons were serving in France. Heavy casualties, harsh taxation and other wartime measures, many of a niggling nature so dear to bureaucratic hearts, had somewhat soured the glorious opening notes, but martial displeasure was a long way from open rebellion.

And, on that Easter Sunday, most citizens watched apathetically and perhaps even apprehensively, and not a few secretly rejoiced when government recovered to proclaim martial law, arrest ringleaders and several hundred followers, and end the revolt. A popular nationalist paper, *The Freeman's Journal*, judged the abortive effort to have been " . . . an armed assault against the will and decision of the Irish nation itself constitutionally ascertained through its proper representatives."[1]

The attempted *putsch* may have affronted public opinion by challenging legal authority, but it was not entirely sinister. Irish leaders had been demanding home rule for a long time; indeed, such a bill was languishing in the Statute Book in London, deferred until the end of the war.[2] The IRB action should have been construed as an exaggerated demand for political autonomy, the indiscretion of ringleaders punished by mild prison sentences and fines, other "troublemakers" released—life presumably then continuing in its pleasant if turbulent fashion.

But now the English Government erred egregiously. Preoccupied with reverses on the western front, Prime Minister Herbert Henry Asquith foolishly let the Dublin military command court-martial and execute the ringleaders (including Pearse). In the first two weeks of May, fifteen Irishmen were shot, a process that George Bernard Shaw warned was " . . . canonizing the prisoners." Asquith belatedly stopped the executions and hurried to Dublin. He was too late. As Beckett has pointed out, " . . . Ireland was quickly passing under the most dangerous of all tyrannies—the tyranny of the dead."[3]

The IRB efficiently exploited widespread resentment, which continued to spread despite the government's conciliatory efforts. Prompted by England's new ally, America, whose Irish population commanded a large vote, the newly elected Prime Minister, David Lloyd George, in spring of 1917 declared a general amnesty of political detainees and prisoners; in July, he convened an Irish Convention, which unfortunately settled nothing. Former prisoners scurried back to subversive tasks, prison (as usual) having only sharpened revolutionary zeal. A real cause existed now—" . . . the grass soon grows over a battlefield but never over a scaffold."[4]

That scaffold had taken more than rebel lives. It had choked the legitimate party virtually out of existence. In its place rose Sinn Fein, under such able if diverse leaders as De Valera, Arthur Griffith, and Michael Collins. The militants would scarcely lack ammunition. In 1918, the government announced its intention to introduce conscription. The Irish people rose in protest, the English Government backed down, thousands of young volunteers flocked to the now not-so-covert IRB colors. To combat growing subversion, Lloyd George's government seized Sinn Fein leaders, another mistake, in that the arrest of De Valera and Griffith left the future of the movement to fire-eating Michael Collins, who wanted outright insurrection.

In 1919, Collins reorganized the Irish Volunteers into the Irish Republican Army (IRA) and commenced limited war. The government answered by declaring Sinn Fein and its elected assembly, the Dail, illegal. Incidents mounted, and, by 1920, a virtual state of war existed. Collins had no intention of repeating the mistakes of 1916. His was a ragtag army of high-spirited volunteers with little military training, no uniforms and a wild assortment of weapons—Hotchkiss machine guns, Lewis guns, German Mausers, Mannlichers, Winchester repeaters, British army Lee-Enfields, sporting rifles and shotguns, hand grenades and mines—mostly stolen from legal authority. The IRA probably never exceeded fifteen thousand members; according to Collins, its effective strength was " . . . not more than three thousand fighting men." He divided these into brigades, battalions, and companies, but, despite this military veneer, his real strength consisted of small "flying columns" of fifteen to thirty men who trained in guerrilla warfare, particularly the hit-and-run raid and the ambush—terrorist tactics that included assassination.[5] By creating a reign of terror, Collins hoped to make effective government impossible and thus force the British to withdraw. His primary targets were the police and the military, but he soon included prominent government officials and progovernment Unionists. In 1920, his terrorists killed 176 policemen and wounded 251; they also killed 54 soldiers and wounded 118, besides killing and intimidating numerous civilians. They blew up police and military barracks, burned courthouses and tax collectors' offices, destroyed coast-guard stations, robbed the mails, and even sheared girls' heads " . . . because they had been seen talking to soldiers or constables."[6] On the evening before Easter, they destroyed 315 barracks of the Royal Irish Constabulary (R.I.C.) in a single night. Such was the extent of their activities that the English viceroy, Lord French, reported the Sinn Fein as " . . . an army numbering 100,000 . . . properly organized in regiments and brigades, led by disciplined officers. . . . They are a formidable army."[7]

The Royal Irish Constabulary numbered about ten thousand men neither organized nor trained to combat insurgency. Unlike England's unarmed police, the Constabulary was " . . . a para-military force, armed with carbines, bayonets, revolvers and grenades." When countersubversion became a principal activity, their plainclothesmen were loathed by the IRA, who regarded them as spies. In addition to armed attacks, the IRA conducted effective psychological warfare against the Constabulary:

> . . . De Valera stigmatized the R.I.C. as "England's janissaries," and called upon his compatriots to ostracize them. "These men

must not be tolerated socially," he ordered, "as if they were clean, healthy members of our social life. They must be shown and made to feel how base are the functions they perform, and how vile is the position they occupy." Policemen, he emphasized, must be made "to understand how utterly the people of Ireland loathe both themselves and their calling," so as to "prevent young Irishmen from dishonouring both themselves and their country by entering that calling."

Dublin walls sometimes carried the chalked words: "Join the R.A.F. and See the World. Join the R.I.C. and See the Next."[8]

By now, a significant minority of the population actively sympathized with the movement—one authority estimates over one hundred thousand offering *active* support; a large percentage remained apathetic, frightened by Collins' terror. Police morale fell, resignations increased, recruitment fell off. Worse yet, the police had begun to abrogate constituted authority: " . . . Barracks and court houses were abandoned in the remoter parts of the south and west of the country . . . [where] *Sinn Fein* police, young men with green armlets, kept what order there was, and the *Sinn Fein* courts administered their own rough justice with variable, and sometimes impressive success."[9]

"The Irish Question" was progressively dividing the home government. A substantial group of parliamentarians and other officials wanted to deal gently with the rebels; a more substantial group opposed them. The punitive attitude prevailed and resulted in two police forces being recruited in England. One was a large unit of British ex-soldiers who served as constables. Wearing khaki tunics, breeches, and puttees, large tam-o'-shanter bonnets, and belts, bandoliers, and holsters of black leather, the members of this unit, eventually numbering twelve thousand, earned the colloquial name of Black and Tans, derisory in that this was a well-known pack of fox hounds in County Limerick. The other unit was the "Auxiliary Division" of the Royal Irish Constabulary. Known as "Auxies," this unit eventually numbered about fifteen hundred, mostly British ex-officers who wore their old uniforms (minus rank) and Glengarry caps; they later wore dark green and khaki uniforms and fought in one-hundred-man "shock companies" under their own officers.

The government further strengthened Macready's hand by emergency legislation enacted in July 1920, a bill that

   . . . gave wide powers to the military command, including authority to arrest and imprison without charge or trial anyone suspected of *Sinn Fein* associations, to try prisoners by court-martial, to hold witnesses in custody and imprison or fine them for failing to produce evidence, and to substitute military courts of inquiry for coroners' inquests.[10]

Macready pleaded for authority to declare martial law throughout the country, and in January 1921, had declared it in eight southern counties.[11]

The results of this repressive policy were disastrous. Police-state methods turned Ireland into a hostile land, with British forces occupying tiny enclaves and those not entirely secure. Neither the Auxiliaries nor the Black and Tans were trained in counterinsurgency warfare. From the beginning, they presented easy targets to Irish terrorists. In attempting to ferret out miscreants, their heavy hands often fell on innocent civilians, thus further alienating an already hostile population. Each repressive measure worsened matters. No one citizen trusted the other. The old man in the worn trenchcoat standing quietly in a crowd might whip out a pistol and shoot a policeman; the young blade with the pretty girl might throw a hand grenade at a military post. Then the Crossley tenders—awkward lorries holding eight to ten police—would race to the scene, the Black and Tans arresting without caution, interrogating without discretion, on occasion employing torture.[12]

Puffs of hatred rose from the green land, a cloud floated over the island. In early 1921, the vicious exchange was heartily condemned by no less than the Archbishop of Canterbury, who, speaking in the House of Lords, condemned IRA violence, but also British reprisals. " . . . You cannot justifiably punish wrong-doing by lawlessly doing the like. Not by calling in the Devil will you cast out devilry." A few months later, Lloyd George voiced the dilemma: " . . . I recognize that force is itself no remedy, and that reason and goodwill alone can lead us to the final goal. But to abandon the use of force today would be to surrender alike to violence, crime and separatism, and that I am not prepared to do."[13] Privately he told colleagues that he refused " . . . to shake hands with murder."[14]

The war would have continued but for the good reason that both sides were getting tired. Collins' two-fold strategy had failed: Murderous raids and ambushes had, without question, disrupted normal government, but had not driven the English from the country, nor did the English seem on the point of leaving. The general public, always mercurial, was tiring of semianarchy—as Yeats had it: " . . . now days are dragon-ridden, the nightmare / rides upon sleep." Compromise now seemed the only way to end agony.

In July 1921, the British Government proposed what could have become law in 1914: a partition, with an Irish Free State in the South— a self-governing dominion similar in status to Canada. A treaty to this effect was signed in December, and British forces were quickly withdrawn. Peace lasted only a short time. In spring of 1922, civil war erupted between pro- and anti-treaty factions. But this was Irish fighting Irish, so only Irish could win (or lose). This time, the rebel-rebels lost. A year later, the country settled into disturbed peace appropriate to its historical tradition of lilting turmoil.

The Irish revolution raised moral questions scarcely justified by number of casualties. A ranking British official, the Chief Secretary for Ireland, estimated British army losses at 566 killed. General Macready counted 750 rebel-army losses. A contemporary authority believes that fewer than 2,000 civilians lost their lives.[15] Compared with the blood bath of World War I, these figures represent a mild shower.

Yet the use of terror as a major rebel weapon genuinely shocked many English people. In discussing its use by insurgents, even Winston Churchill's normally silky pen jerked a convulsive protest that relied more on contradiction of terms than on rational consideration of traditional and moral aspects.[16]

This naïve reaction was perhaps inevitable in a land still hypnotized by its own majesty and power, a land that was outgrowing the use of force at home but still relied on it to rule an empire, thus a land that had become accustomed to a double standard of application while refusing to admit the paradox of definition.

These good people would probably have agreed with a modern definition of terror as "extreme fear" and "an object of dread."[17] Not only can terror be employed as a weapon, but any weapon can become a weapon of terror: terror is a weapon, a weapon is terror, and no one agency monopolizes it. The point is made with artistic brilliance by Goya, whose *Los Desastres de la Guerra* depict the "excesses" of the Spanish guerrilla war against France; the paradox is emphasized by the corpse-strewn battlefields of World War I caught in the camera's cold eye. Terror is the kissing cousin of force and, real or implied, is never far removed from the pages of history. To define (and condemn) terror from a peculiar social, economic, political, and emotional plane is to display a self-righteous attitude that, totally unrealistic, is doomed to be disappointed by harsh facts.

The paradox of terror, so conveniently ignored by English public opinion, particularly middle- and upper-middle-class opinion during the Irish rebellion, is ages old. Celtiberian slaves working New Carthage silver mines must have regarded Roman legionaries as objects "of dread" inducing "extreme fear." To enslaved minds, the legionaries were weapons of terror designed to keep the slaves in the mines—and apparently they worked very efficiently toward this end. From time to time, these and other slaves secretly rose to attack the Romans, who, upon seeing a sentry assassinated or a detachment ambushed and annihilated, no doubt spoke feelingly about the use of terrorist tactics.

But who had introduced this particular terror to this particular environment? The Romans. Had they other options? Certainly: they could have kept their hands off the Iberian Peninsula, or they could have governed it justly and wisely (as a few officials tried to do). Instead, they came as conquerors ruled by greed, and, in turn, they ruled by oppression maintained by terror. What options did the natives hold either to rid themselves of the Roman presence or to convert it to a more salutary form? Only one: force. What kind of force? That which was limited to what their minds could evoke. Lacking arms, training, and organization, they had to rely on wits, on surprise raids, ambushes, massacres. Was this *terror* or was it *counterterror?*

The paradox survived the Roman Empire. The king's soldiers frequently became weapons of terror, just as did the rack and the gibbet. Feudal government of the Middle Ages rested on force (as opposed to the people's consent), often on terror exercised through the man-made will of God reinforced by hangman's noose or executioner's ax. No student of the period can seriously condemn the protesting peasant as a terrorist, for here, as in the case of Romans in Spain and indeed of most governments, European monarchs and ruling nobility held options of rule ranging from the most benevolent to the most despotic. Their subjects, however, held limited options: submit or rebel. If they chose rebellion, the options were again limited, the main reliance being placed on native wit. But since native wit was often sharply circumscribed, most rebellions were doomed to expensive failure. Whatever the effort, whether a single peasant who in the fury of frustration picked up a scythe and severed the tax-collecting bailiff's head from his body, or the group of peasants who grabbed pitchforks to stand against the king's soldiers—the effort, more often than not, was not *terror* but, rather, *counterterror.*

The paradox survived the Middle Ages and is implicit in many instances cited in preceding pages. But as bourgeois rule began to replace feudalism in Western nations, the paradox of terror donned a camouflage convenient to Christian conscience. As the people's will slowly asserted itself, as dynasties fell or became sharply altered in character, the pattern of rule slowly began to change. As nations came into being, as rule by law began to replace rule by whim, as the concept of democratic government began to claim men's minds, parliamentary processes visibly diminished the role of force and thus of a particular type of terror in civilized government.

The process greatly varied. In England, the bourgeois revolution of 1689, finally consolidated in 1832, established a climate in which rule by law and stable government grew to proud tradition. In France, the bourgeois revolution gave way to reaction unsuccessfully challenged by the proletariat in 1848, an enduring conflict, a climate that barely tolerated rule by law, with the inevitable result of semianarchic government. Each European nation treated the transition from feudalism to bourgeois rule in a different way and at a different time, and each in turn has faced the challenge of the proletariat in a variety of ways and with greatly differing results in which terror has never been far removed.

The paradox of terror remained very much alive in the imperialist philosophy of even the most advanced Western nations. By devious mental exercises conducted in the spiritual gymnasium of Christianity, colonizing powers defended the double standard: force used by themselves became benevolence; counterforce used by natives became terror. The conceit is clearly expressed in Cornwallis' denunciation of Marion and his guerrillas during the American Revolution.

The conceit appeared in both subtle and blunt ways. Most of us do not think of a well-meaning missionary as a terror weapon. But he was just that to political functionaries of some tribes, in that he represented a distinct threat to the existing social-political-economic-religious structure, besides serving as harbinger of white armies that would take tribal lands and place the tribe in perpetual bondage. The missionary was a threat. The missionary was as much a threat to the savage's way of life as, to choose a military analogy, the musket was to the knight's way of life. Some readers will remember the touching scene in *Orlando Furioso* when the knight rowed out to sea and tossed the captured firearm overboard while cursing its invention and hoping it was the only one of its kind, because it would mean the end of knightly warfare. The thought process of the savage was similar when he tossed the first missionary into the cooking pot.

A more blatant example of Western hypocrisy occurred at the end of the nineteenth century, at the Hague conference on the rules of land warfare. One resolution proposed to abolish dumdum bullets. This was a splendid idea: a dumdum bullet is an ordinary cartridge with an X cut on the end, the improvised surgery insuring that the ball, when striking an object, preferably human, will expand and, upon leaving the object, tear away a great portion of flesh. If ever a weapon is terrible, it is a dumdum bullet, and it is not difficult to imagine the effect on an ignorant native's mind, for here terror was heightened by a seemingly magic quality of the white man's military art. Yet, at this conference, the British refused to abandon the use of the dumdum, because of its proven efficiency in breaking up native charges!

The hypocrisy of Western governments also displayed itself in home rule, but in a more subtle form than either a missionary or a dumdum bullet. Neither the rise of democratic government nor technical innovations wrought by the Industrial Revolution resulted in Utopia. Industrialization benefited many people, but it also brought grave social inequities to threaten seriously and frequently the fabric of social government in the most enlightened nations. The overt terror of the king's soldiers, the lord's bailiffs, the rack, and the gibbet was replaced with the covert terror of industrial slavery: in England, the Lancashire cotton mills, the industrial centers of the Midlands, the Ebbw Vale coal pits, the doss houses; in America, the New England railways, the Chicago meat plants, the Allegheny coal mines, the Colorado copper mines— these and other by-products of *laissez faire* economics spelled miserable wages, torturous hours, dangerous and unhealthful working environments, accidents with no compensation, minimum if any retirement benefits, massive layoffs, widespread unemployment, slums, child labor, inadequate schools: altogether a portrait of hopelessness, the dignity of human beings cast like some sort of industrial refuse into gigantic slag heaps to form a social state in which death often became preferable to survival, a state mocking the cultural pretensions of Western civilization.

The deadening process of this social disease was accompanied by a hatred difficult for our affluent society to understand or even to comprehend. But it did exist, and it did assert itself. For then, as now, where man is deprived of dignity and hope, hatred sets in, and a corollary of hatred is a desire for vengeance. And if death is made to appear as good or even preferable to life, then an act of terror against an object of hatred is a simple and even rewarding matter, for the bite of the rifle's bark is momentary, and, as Socrates put it, the sleep is long and can be no less comfortable than life and may be more so.

And yet, to rational man, terror and counterterror are abhorrent and, except for isolated cases, they did not become favored weapons of the discontent in western Eurasia or in America. Men used terror on occasion, and at times the history of labor and, in some instances, agrarian movements in the respective countries is bloody and ugly, and the history of all countries is spotted with political assassinations. But this falls far short of a terror-ridden environment, of systematic repression on the one hand and systematic assassination on the other, far short of outright insurrection. In general, the working classes in western Eurasia and America avoided using terrorist methods primarily because of the lurking knowledge reaching to the depths of the labor movement that legislative processes inspired by the principle of one man-one vote were trying to eradicate social horrors evoked by industrialization and unmitigated greed of some landlords and factory owners. In short, the labor movement chose the ballot, not the bullet, evolution by selective trade unionism, not revolution by the mass proletariat. Particularly in England, a peculiar and in some ways unhealthy calm accompanied the process. In despair, Karl Marx wrote to a friend in 1870: " . . . England possesses all the necessary conditions of social revolution; what she lacks is a universal outlook and revolutionary passion."

If social malaise of such intensity gripped enlightened nations, we can imagine its extent in the autocracies and colonies, where the major labor force remained strapped to the feudal concept of land ownership. In fulminating against social abuses in nineteenth-century France or England or twentieth-century America, neither Zola nor Dickens, neither Dreiser, Sinclair nor London, equaled Tolstoy's or Turgenev's narrative power, simply because of the much more orderly canvas of the West, where man was not yet divorced from his government, where hope for improvement still survived.

British and American workers may have been ill-paid and ill-treated and themselves and families host to a wide variety of social indignities, for any one of which society, industry, and government should have been ashamed, but they were not quelled by the knout under the least possible pretext, their demonstrations were not usually fired upon by troops, they were not subject to mass arrest and detention, they were not executed in wholesale lots when their whispered protests brushed authoritarian ears. Violence was not their chosen way of life, and this is the main reason that English public opinion was so shocked by the "Irish outrages."

That English public opinion was shocked does not alter the fact of terror that reigned in numerous countries throughout the nineteenth and into the twentieth centuries. In 1914, an act of terror began the events that led to the first world war in history. In 1917, a reign of terror culminated in a revolution that changed the political face of the world.

CHAPTER SEVENTEEN

1. Beckett, 441.
2. Churchill, *The World Crisis*, V, 280.
3. Beckett, 441.
4. Churchill, *The World Crisis*, V, 281.
5. Bennett, 29. See also, Costigan, "The Anglo-Irish Conflict, 1919–1922." Flying columns on occasion were larger—in 1921 Tom Barry commanded 104 men in an ambush of British forces.
6. Holt, 210.
7. Costigan.
8. Ibid.
9. Bennett, 31.
10. Holt, 212.
11. Costigan.
12. Ibid.
13. Holt, 237.
14. Costigan.
15. Ibid.
16. Churchill, *The World Crisis*, V, 282 ff.
17. *Chambers Twentieth Century Dictionary.*

CHAPTER 18

THE FALLOUT of radical thought produced by the explosion of the French Revolution filtered only slowly into the reactionary air of czarist Russia. Falling gently and slowly, it penetrated not the minds of peasants and serfs, those unfortunates whose isolated protests marked the decades with the patterned emphasis of tombstones, but, rather, it infected the palace hierarchy, made particularly receptive by the oppressive air of Nicholas I's reign. " . . . By virtually proscribing all forms of political, social and philosophical speculation," E. H. Carr noted, Nicholas "threw the whole intellectual movement of three generations into a revolutionary mould."[1]

The Decembrist uprising of 1825 was the result: " . . . a palace revolution," in Bernard Pares's words, "that did not succeed," but " . . . almost the first that had anything like a political program." Pares, along with most modern historians, marks this revolt " . . . as the first act in the Russian Revolution."[2]

As might be expected, the Decembrist uprising elicited harsh penalties from young and autocratic Czar Nicholas I. Although Nicholas continued to work for peasant reforms, oppression of the intelligentsia continued throughout his long reign (1825–55). But thought has always survived oppression, and if Pushkin and Lermontov were forced to premature deaths because of liberal views, others survived. The provocative thinking of the German philosophers Kant, Fichte, Schelling, Hegel, and Feuerbach, the radical writings of the socialist theorists Saint-Simon, Fourier, and Louis Blanc—all reached Russia and were embraced by the Belinsky-Stankevitch school, which produced such important political theorists as Michael Bakunin and Alexander Herzen.

The intellectual movement gained impetus during the opening years of Alexander II's more liberal reign. Two important revolutionary movements appeared in these years. The young Pisarev opted for " . . . an insurrectionary freedom from all authority and convention," a movement described by Ivan Turgenev in his novel *Fathers and Children* and one that he termed the Nihilists. Another appeared under the aegis of Chernyshevsky, who, influenced by the utilitarian philosophy of Bentham and Mill, broke with the liberal Herzen to demand radical reforms in his *Unaddressed Letters:*

> . . . Fly-sheets began to appear, calling for terrorist acts against the government—such as that addressed *To Young Russia* in 1862, in which even the murder of the Emperor was advocated. . . . Chernyshevsky was tried and, on loose evidence, sent for twenty-four years to Siberia; Pisarev was sentenced to two years' imprisonment. Both their magazines were suspended.[3]

The attempt on Alexander's life in 1866 virtually ended the liberal aspects of his reign. But repression could not stem various liberal movements that for a short time had been allowed to develop and were now nurtured from the West. Where some new movements preached nonviolent methods, notably Lavrov's, who picked up the shreds of Pisarev's nihilist movement, others, such as Michael Bakunin's, called for all-out violence to achieve revolution: " . . . the State, he said, had to be destroyed . . . [by] an armed rising."[4] Bakunin's theories collided squarely with those expressed by Karl Marx who urged that revolution should be achieved within the framework of the state, but asserting that on occasion force was necessary.

In 1872, a group of propagandists attempted to spread the revolutionary word to the peasants. Several thousand men and women—the forerunners of the Narodniks—discovered to their dismay that peasant ignorance, drunkenness, apathy, and misplaced faith in the czar, not to mention the size of Russia, poor communications, and powerful secret police and army made revolution by persuasion a difficult task. Disappointed members of this group soon began returning to the cities, where " . . . they lived without passports and waged a systematic war on the police." Here they frequently joined revolutionary movements of the intelligentsia, who had continued to spread thoughts by the printing press and by word of mouth, the punctuation marks acts of terror. The first revolutionary society, Land and Liberty, formed in St. Petersburg was dedicated "to bring about an economic revolution from below by militant methods. It had a closely systematized staff, which was to produce strikes and riots wherever possible and was also to conduct propaganda. Its 'heavenly chancellery' manufactured false passports, and its 'disorganization department' planned acts of terrorism."[5] Professor Mazour has pointed out that although the new party recognized terroristic acts, "terror could be directed only against individuals who served as instruments of oppression; it had no place in a society where political institutions allow the citizen freedom and justice.[6]

The government's answer to terrorist tactics, repression rather than reform, was exactly what hard-core revolutionists needed to keep themselves in business. Not all revolutionaries embraced a philosophy of terror. Notably G. V. Plekhanov, the father of Russian Marxism, pleaded with his fellows to forgo terrorist methods, which he regarded as a waste of time. His stand split the party into Populists and Terrorists. Other liberal groups abhorred the idea of terror. The government could quite easily have isolated and neutralized the minority extremists had it respected the demands of the public and prevented constant police violation of individual liberties. Proposed liberal reforms of General Melikov, the important first step toward constitutional government, had they been put into effect, would have terminated the reason for terrorist activities. The czar already had signed the first of these when two nihilists assassinated him in 1881.

A reform government or even a government interested in reform might still have succeeded in providing a suitable constitution, but Alexander III, " . . . big, strong and stupid," gave way to the most reactionary of his advisers. Although the revolutionary movement was virtually paralyzed by governmental repression, individual acts continued to plague authorities throughout Alexander's reign (1881–94): in the country, isolated peasant protests; in the cities, student strikes and riots; and, from 1880 onward, increasing industrial unrest and open strikes.

The government replied in kind with "the *okhrana* procedure," which vitiated the few rights given to subjects. Officials were allowed to search without warrants, imprison at will, exile without trial, suppress meetings, and commit other repressive acts. In 1894, the weak Nicholas II insured continuation of this dreadful state of affairs by promising his advisers " . . . an unswerving adherence to the principle of autocracy,"[7] an injudicious statement that elicited a sinister warning by pamphlets distributed in St. Petersburg: "You have begun the struggle, and the battle will not be long delayed."[8]

Revolutionary parties were beginning to look to the worker for support. Plekhanov, who had broken with the anarchists and fled to Switzerland, published a Russian translation of the *Communist Manifesto* in 1882. A year later, he and others founded " . . . the first Russian Marxist group and planted the roots of Marxism in the new industrial proletariat of Russia." This movement spawned "reading circles" in the larger Russian cities and it was in one of these in St. Petersburg that in 1893 the twenty-three-year-old Lenin became convinced that the newly created working proletariat " . . . would provide the driving force and the ideological justification of the Russian revolution."[9]

The rise of industrial strife contributed greatly to the revolutionary cause. In 1896, 118 strikes occurred, 145 in 1897, and 215 in 1898.[10] These and other demonstrations were ruthlessly suppressed, at first by police, both official and company-hired, but increasingly by troops. Where the army intervened in industrial disputes 19 times in 1893, it intervened 271 times in 1901 and 522 times in 1902.[11] Here was a dangerous condition, for where the worker originally began demonstrating and striking for economic betterment, slowly he was moving toward divorce from the harridan monarchy to marry the floozily attractive blonde of radical political change.

A few, a very few government officials recognized what was happening. In 1898, General Trepov, head of the police, presciently wrote that if the government supplied the "minor needs and demands of the workers" the revolutionaries would have nothing to exploit.[12] Colonel Zubatov, head of the Moscow security police and himself a considerable man of mystery, enlarged this idea by attempting to separate " . . . the workers' economic action from the revolutionary political struggle," encouraging unions to air and study workers' problems by appropriate courses and discussion groups. Zubatov succeeded so well that he quickly lost control of the movement, whose solidarity alarmed industry, government, and foreign investors. With his summary dismissal, in 1903, the movement lost momentum, but was revived by a peasant-priest-double agent, Georgi Gapon, who organized St. Petersburg workers into " . . . a cross between a trade union, a mutual aid society and even an underground revolutionary organization."[13]

Prompt and radical industrial and agrarian reforms undoubtedly could still have channeled the organizational trend into an evolutionary direction heartily desired by upper- and middle-class liberals and moderates including professional classes and an increasing number of university students. The new revolutionary parties lacked organization, they represented a minority, and they disagreed as to how revolution should be achieved. Must revolution come from the peasants as the Socialist Party, which inherited the Populist movement, held? Or must it come from the working proletariat of the cities as Marx and the Social Democrats insisted? But here another serious split developed: the Mensheviks, dominated by Plekhanov, believing that the movement must be as broad-based as possible, essentially a trade-union concept; the Bolsheviks holding for the thirty-three-year-old Lenin's " . . . conception of a small dedicated body of professional revolutionaries" to steer the masses—in Max Weber's words, the "principle of the small number," with the Marxian result of the dictatorship of the proletariat—and this is what prevailed in 1917.

Each movement relied on propaganda, masses of it, and also on terror—terror to disorganize the government, terror to draw reprisals and thus involve the whole population and widen the gulf between people and government, terror to protect the movement from spies, *agents provocateurs,* and traitors. Revolutionary parties already had suffered a high casualty rate—Lenin's brother, for example, was hanged in 1891—that necessitated cellular internal structure with emphasis on secrecy to cloak the cunning, tough, brave, and fanatical survivors.

The Socialist Revolutionaries carried out terror missions by a small, secret, and entirely voluntary group whose members were unknown even to the party's central committee. This committee " . . . designated the targets but only the combat organization determined and put into practice the mode of execution."[14]

The bravery, skill, and determination of party agents was dramatically emphasized by the assassination of the universally loathed Minister of Interior, Von Plehve, in 1904. Here was a clear warning, but Czar Nicholas II refused to budge from autocratic absolutism; his ministers of state remained nearly as hidebound in frightened intensity increased by the unmitigated series of military disasters in the 1904–5 war with Japan. The official answer to the relatively modest demands of the people was, once again, repression by army and police.

In January 1905, peasant-priest-double agent Gapon caused near crisis by leading a general strike in St. Petersburg. On a cold Sunday, the tall, bearded Orthodox priest, purple robes flapping in the Neva breeze, gold cross glittering on his chest in the winter's sun, led perhaps two hundred thousand workers and their wives and children to the Winter Palace in St. Petersburg, there to present a people's petition of grievances to the czar. The unarmed, hymn-singing multitude reached the Narva Gate, where it halted before infantry bayonets. Then, without warning, hidden Cossack cavalry units charged the columns of demonstrators while infantrymen fired point-blank into the massed throngs.

Thus Bloody Sunday, a thousand or more people killed, thousands wounded. Bloody Sunday caused the Russian worker and the peasant to question the omniscience theretofore enjoyed by the paternalistic figure of the czar. Bloody Sunday cut the first chunk from the broad-base support enjoyed by Nicholas. In many people's minds, the need not for political reforms but for *radical* political reforms became dominant for the first time. In Lenin's words: " . . . The revolutionary education of the proletariat made more progress in one day than it could have made in months and years of drab, humdrum, wretched existence." The fully charged air of the cities now exploded into a continuous series of protest acts including isolated mutinies in army and navy.

The crisis resulted in the famous October Manifesto, of 1905, seemingly an official surrender. This document guaranteed fundamental civil liberties including freedom of the press, extended the sorely limited franchise, and reformed the Duma, or parliament, into a legislative body. A general amnesty followed, the peasants were tossed some overdue land reforms, and trouble began to decrease.[15]

People reacted variously to this document. The Octobrists, a new, conservative party, embraced it; so did the right-wing Kadets. The manifesto caused violent disagreements among the Social Democrats and other revolutionary parties. The Mensheviks and some of the Socialist Revolutionaries wanted to believe in it. Genuinely inspired, the manifesto could have made history with minimum bloodshed. But it was not genuine. Its intention was as thin as its paper, and Trotsky was right to denounce it as " . . . a cossack's whip wrapped in the parchment of a constitution."

The manifesto was a brake that gained time for government to regroup its forces. When renewed violence broke out in December with a workers' uprising in Moscow, the government put it down swiftly and continued to repress a new wave of demonstrations, student riots, strikes, and peasant uprisings that lasted well into 1906.[16]

Despite the return of troops from the Far East in early 1906, the government held little reason to feel secure. By the end of October 1906, 3,611 government officials of all ranks, from governor-generals to village gendarmes, had been killed or wounded."[17] The new repression could not stop agitation or propaganda, and each function expanded as the impotency of the Duma became increasingly obvious.

The 1905 revolution introduced a new and most important organizational factor, the soviet of workers' deputies. A soviet was a group of elected representatives—one representative per thousand workers—who became a sort of mature strike committee to further workers' demands. The factory soviet, however, soon broadened its base of support by representing more than one factory and by transcending any one political party. The St. Petersburg soviet, which came to life in autumn of 1905, soon grew to 226 members representing 96 factories, and also representatives of five trade unions.[18] This organizational concept quickly spread to other cities and even resulted in soviets of peasants and soldiers. The St. Petersburg soviet led the October 1905 uprising, the Moscow soviet led the December uprising. The idea was to attain a unity of action far superior to that rendered possible by the emasculated trade unions now permitted.

Lenin did not recognize the true potential of the supposedly apolitical soviets, but Leon Trotsky did. In his visionary mind, they fitted nicely into revolution by the "principle of the small number." They would remain outside party jurisdiction but would be regarded as " . . . the embryo of a provisional revolutionary government," the gun of the political party. Having direct and virtually instant contact with the masses, they became prime targets, along with the trade unions, for Bolshevik propaganda.

The forces that exploded into the 1917 revolution were now in play, except for World War I. From 1906 on, a repressive and unyielding government pitted itself against a declamatory if divided people. The infamous White Terror following the 1905 revolt soon smothered the pathetic aspirations of moderate liberals, primarily the Kadets, to legislative reforms through the Duma; the militancy continued, but outlawed parties operated underground in sporadic and often unco-ordinated jabs and thrusts, the casualty rate high with exiles and executions the order of the day as Stolypin's police and soldiers moved ruthlessly across the face of Russia. From 1905 to 1910, the government carried out nearly five thousand executions. Nor did repression end with Stolypin's assassination, in 1911. In 1912, troops put down a strike in the Lena gold fields in Siberia by firing on unarmed men, killing 170 and wounding nearly four hundred. Important strikes followed, to culminate in the massive St. Petersburg general strike of July 1914, which fizzled only in the wash of war's outbreak.

When cannons sounded and cause called, land-hungry peasants and underprivileged workers swallowed grievances to fight for country and czar. Country proved a better cause than czar, who failed with his army as with his people. Russia's disastrous war with Japan might never have been fought, so little were its lessons respected. With a few exceptions, uniformed fools, mostly aristocrats, commanded the army. The army lacked artillery, airplanes, communications, transport, medical services. Its weapons were obsolete and in short supply: millions of mobilized men lacked rifles and even boots.

The emergency of war changed nothing of this hapless picture. Mismanagement, incompetence, corruption, cupidity, nepotism—each bloomed following mobilization. Food supplies quickly grew short, both in the army and at home. Industrial production slowed. Well-meaning officials submitted corrective plans only to see them shelved by Czarina Alexandra, now totally under the demoniac influence of the "Mad Monk," Grigori Rasputin; and when Nicholas II declared himself commander in chief of the army, with headquarters at Tsarskoe Selo, Alexandra became virtually the ruler of Russia.

A palace revolution might have salvaged something from the growing ruin of government. No palace revolution occurred. Instead, the czar and his generals ordered new and voracious offensives that devoured hundreds of thousands of men. At the end of June 1915, Russian losses numbered an estimated 3.8 million and had to be replaced with men taken from factories, mines, and fields. In all, 15 million were mobilized; about half were listed as killed, wounded, or missing. Survivors faced ever-growing shortages in arms, food, and equipment; at home, people faced near-starvation. Production slowed, almost ceased. Riots and strikes in cities proclaimed the growing temper and were ruthlessly suppressed.

Abysmal conduct of the war had gnawed away final and frail supports of government and czar. Finally, even the troops rebelled: in February 1917, the St. Petersburg garrison, ordered to break up a massive hunger demonstration, refused its orders. Demonstrations and riots increased in intensity in early March, and still the garrison, some 160,000 troops, refused to act. A general strike brought three hundred thousand workers into the streets, and now mobs began running amok, attacking police stations, storming law courts, breaking open jails. Police either were killed or fled—or joined the revolution. While ministers paled and the Duma fretted, the troops, with a few exceptions, still refused to act. On March 12, regiments began to mutiny, and that was the end of monarchy. The czar abdicated; the vacillating Duma finally established a provisional government in the form of an Emergency Committee. Frantic revolutionaries meanwhile had been trying to assess events, then harness the revolutionary force. The result was a Soviet of Workers' and Soldiers' Deputies, an organization not unlike that which had emerged in 1905; its Executive Committee soon challenged the Duma's Emergency Committee, and eventually, using armed Red Guards, seized power from it.

The St. Petersburg soviet consisted of about twenty-five hundred deputies including most Socialist Revolutionary and Social Democratic leaders. These formed a Central Executive Committee to carry out policy determined by a small and elite Praesidium. Bolsheviks were not strongly represented in this early body, but nonetheless the differences between it and the provisional government were fundamental.

Russia's attitude toward the war provided the major issue. The Lvov-Kerensky government, strongly influenced by the allied powers France, England, and America, pledged Russia to continue fighting. Unaware of the real situation, the American ambassador urged recognition of the new government, which was given on March 22, 1917; Britain,

France, and Italy quickly followed suit and even sent labor delegations " . . . to reconcile the differences between the Provisional Government and the Socialists." They were going to take some reconciling: on March 27, the Petrograd soviet issued a proclamation to the people of the world calling for " . . . concerted and decisive action in favor of peace,"[19] welcome words to an exhausted, hungry population. The allied powers, by demanding continued Russian participation—as Elihu Root succinctly put it, "no fight, no loans"—helped to widen the already dangerous gulf between the Kerensky government and the Russian people.

To this turbulent, divisive climate, the little, bald-headed, sharp-eyed Lenin returned in 1917 (under German auspices from Geneva by means of the famous sealed railroad car across Germany). He was shortly joined by the tall, imperious Trotsky, an intellectual revolutionary in the Menshevik mold, who had sailed from America. The revolution had surprised both of them, but, they realized that, if properly controlled, it could result in a smashing socialist victory.

In Lenin's mind, the Petersburg soviet formed " . . . the germ cell of a workers' government." With its quasi-military Red Guards, its affinity to workers (the mainstay of the revolution), its contacts in other cities and in the armed forces, the soviet should be able to usurp the function of the badly disorganized and divided provisional government. Once this happened, the small but well-organized Bolsheviks, in turn, should be able to wrest control of the soviet from the majority but divided Mensheviks and Socialist Revolutionaries.

Lenin carefully tailored his appeals to these general objectives. In contrast to the muddled program offered by the Lvov-Kerensky government, Lenin offered a simple three-point program: immediate peace; immediate distribution of land to peasants and seizure of factories by workers; all power to the soviets.[20] In contrast to Mensheviks and most Socialist Revolutionaries, who did not believe the time propitious, Lenin demanded an immediate socialist revolution; in addition, the Bolsheviks, by every means possible, urged extension of soviets into cities and villages to undertake " . . . the task of organizing insurrection and of serving as organs of revolutionary state power."[21]

Lenin was fighting an uphill battle. In June 1917, the Bolsheviks held only 105 seats in the All-Russian Soviet Congress, the Socialist Revolutionaries holding 285, the Mensheviks 248. This called for a great deal of razzle-dazzle to keep the Bolsheviks alive, and in this respect Lenin was a past master. "Loot the looters," he screamed to hysterical masses. "Peace to the village huts," he cried, "war against the palaces." Rubbish slogans, certainly—but flaring as effective matches in that highly tindered air.

Other parties performed a great deal of Lenin's work for him. The

Bolshevik presence should have caused the provisional government to forget its differences, at least temporarily, and govern, but right-wing and moderate liberals and numerous Social Democrats and Socialist Revolutionaries refused to take either Lenin or his group seriously. Lenin and his lieutenants realized what the provisional government and the allied powers failed to realize: the Russian people, particularly workers and peasants, were demanding an end of war and immediate and fundamental changes in their ghastly existence. Kerensky undoubtedly sensed the feeling, but failed to control it. He respected it with the "Declaration of Soldiers' Rights," in May 1917, and he appointed political commissars in the army " . . . and charged them with the responsibility of political leadership."[22]

The declaration proved fatal to army discipline, and Lenin quickly exploited the new political commissars through army soviets. Kerensky's provincial civil commissars, taken from the old zemstvo committees, " . . . had almost as little contact with the people as the authorities whom they displaced," and this greatly simplified the work of the village soviets.[23] Finally, Kerensky erred fatally by ordering an offensive against the Austrians in July 1917.

This effort collapsed within a few days, with entire regiments marching to the rear. The extent of the catastrophe caused Lenin to call on soldiers and sailors in St. Petersburg to seize the government. Lenin was premature; the Party paid the price: Trotsky arrested, Lenin fleeing to Finland, the Bolsheviks momentarily shattered. Instead of exploiting this development, Kerensky refused to break with the St. Petersburg soviet, thus further alienating upper, middle, and officer classes. Moreover, by turning the disorganized and demoralized army over to General Kornilov, a strong man to whom he gave virtually dictatorial powers, he created a dangerous rival.

In September, Kornilov attempted his own putsch. This failed not because of Kerensky's leadership, but, rather, because workers and soldiers refused to countenance it. As Professor Vernadsky pointed out, it left Kerensky " . . . a prisoner of political and economic anarchy," unable to prevent radical socialists from taking the initiative. In September, an increasingly demoralized Kerensky was forced to release Trotsky from prison and overlook Lenin's secret visits from Finland.

In October, Trotsky became president of the St. Petersburg soviet, and Bolsheviks won control of the all-important Military Committee of this body. In November, the Bolsheviks arrested Kerensky's cabinet members and stampeded the Second All-Russian Congress of Soviets into adopting the Bolshevik program, to be carried out by the new government of Russia: the Council of People's Commissars; president: Lenin; Commissar for Foreign Affairs: Trotsky; other key billets: Rykov, Stalin, Lunacharsky. Kerensky fled, the Bolsheviks put down a liberal-student uprising in Moscow and opened secret negotiations with Germany to end the war. Moving swiftly to consolidate his coup, Lenin directed Dzerjinsky to organize a powerful secret police, the Cheka, which immediately invoked a reign of terror designed to eliminate all bourgeois (non-socialist) opposition and to cow lesser adversaries into obedience.

A major stumbling block remained: the Constituent Assembly, whose 703 deputies, elected in late November, included only 168 Bolsheviks. Prior to its first meeting, in January 1918, Lenin's police arrested all non-socialist deputies, murdering two in the process. When socialist deputies, mainly Socialist Revolutionaries and Mensheviks, refused to accept Lenin's self-proclaimed government, the Bolsheviks withdrew from the assembly. On January 20, the Central Executive Committee of the Soviets disbanded the assembly by decree, forcibly removing the deputies.

In less than three months, the work of over thirty years had brought a new government to Russia. Whether it could effectively rule remained to be seen.

CHAPTER EIGHTEEN

1. Carr, E.H., *Studies in Revolution*, 89.
2. Pares, 318. See also, Moorehead, *The Russian Revolution*.
3. Pares, 358.
4. Ibid.
5. Ibid., 374.
6. Mazour, 287.
7. Pares, 404.
8. Masaryk, I, 170.
9. Carr, *Studies in Revolution*, 106–7. See also, Carr, E.H., *Karl Marx* . . .
10. Walsh, 323.
11. Kochan, 33.
12. Ibid., 34.
13. Ibid.
14. Ibid., 58. See also, Masaryk; Walsh.
15. Vernadsky, 188.
16. Pares, 436–7.
17. Kochan, 114.
18. Ibid., 99.
19. Vernadsky, 241. See also, Kennan, *Russia Leaves the War*.
20. Vernadsky, 244.
21. Kochan, 208.
22. Vernadsky, 242.
23. Ibid., 239.

CHAPTER 19

Lenin's problems • The Red Terror • Treaty of Brest-Litovsk • Trotsky builds the Red army • Lenin on guerrilla warfare • Allied intervention • President Wilson's ambiguity • Whites versus Reds • The guerrilla aspects of civil war • Lenin's tactics • Reason for allied failures • Kolchak and Denikin's shortcomings • Cost of allied intervention • Lenin's victory • The Communist International: short-term losses, long-term plans

LENIN faced massive internal and external problems in consolidating his theft of the Russian Revolution: a rapidly demobilizing imperial army, the German enemy pressing against the southern provinces, the Ukraine in revolt, grave shortages of food and materials, minimum agricultural and industrial production, lack of foreign credits and supply, rampant inflation.

The upper, middle, and professional classes and a large portion of bureaucracy and peasantry loathed the Bolsheviks and refused to cooperate with the new government. Deposed military commanders such as Kolchak in Siberia and Alexeiev, Kornilov, and Denikin in the South were organizing former imperial officers into nucleus "White" armies that were attracting regional guerrilla dissidents such as Cossacks, Georgians, and Ukrainians, a growing movement supported by the allied powers, who were muttering thinly veiled threats of open intervention should Russia sign a separate peace with Germany.

The challenge of survival brought forth an intensified display of leadership, discipline, organization, fanaticism, guile, and ruthlessness that already had served Lenin so well. In speaking of political-social change, Bismarck once remarked, " . . . you can't make an omelet without breaking eggs." Lenin put it rather more forcefully: " . . . No dictatorship of the proletariat is to be thought of without terror and violence." Dzerjinsky's Cheka abridged these words to the "Red Terror," a hideous period characterized by torture and summary execution

213

in wholesale lots, summary imprisonment and deportation to Siberia, and, finally, slow starvation of "unproductive elements" by refusal of food-ration cards.

Nor did the peasants escape. To "deepen the revolution," the government sent teams of agitators and Red Guards to organize village soviets and start the all-important flow of food to the cities. When peasants refused to yield hoarded grain supplies, special "food battalions" of Red Guards and secret police relentlessly seized them.[1] To break up united peasant opposition and discredit the Socialist Revolutionaries, Lenin used divide-and-conquer tactics, in this case turning the poorest peasants into "Committees of the Poor," which he pitted against rich and middle-class peasants with the slogan "Loot the Looters"—words used rather differently but a few months earlier.

To rid himself of the German incubus, Lenin signed the treaty of Brest-Litovsk in early March 1918. By this, he ceded vast amounts of Russia: eastern Poland, Lithuania, Estonia, and Latvia to Germany; the Ukraine to be independent; part of Transcaucasia to Turkey—altogether a whopping 26 per cent of the Russian population, 27 per cent of her arable land, 75 per cent of her coal industries.[2] The treaty also brought down the wrath of the allied powers and virtually insured allied intervention. Lenin accepted these consequences as the cost for precious time needed to reorganize his forces to face imminent civil war.

Bolshevik military fortunes in early 1918 rested on a heterogeneous collection of Red Guards plus various imperial units such as those under Muraviev, a former czarist colonel, which had defected to the revolutionaries. The Red Guards consisted of armed bands of former workers and soldiers. They varied greatly in size, allegiance, and effectiveness. The St. Petersburg contingent, ten to fifteen thousand strong, was commanded by a former mechanic, Clement Voroshilov, who marched his force of irregulars to the southeast to fight and beat the counterrevolutionary Volunteer Army, a successful campaign which gained him the support of a number of independent guerrilla bands and swelled his force to some thirty thousand. Other Red Guard units served the party in Moscow and the lesser cities and towns, but Lenin was well aware that this force could not long shelter Communist existence from the dark and rapidly forming clouds of counterrevolution.

In February 1918, Lenin appointed Trotsky chief of the Military Revolutionary Committee, with orders to build a "Workers' and Peasants' Army." Acting swiftly and imperiously, Trotsky started to fashion a Red army suspiciously at odds with revolutionary ideals. Abolishing the Soldiers' Committees created by Kerensky, he replaced them with Communist political commissars, who organized secret Communist cells in each unit. He caused the government to reintroduce conscription, which brought him four hundred thousand men by spring—conscripts armed and equipped from imperial army stocks. Bowing to the inevitable, Trotsky now turned over army organization and training to former czarist officers, most of whom were starving and welcomed any work, but some of whom were coerced into service by the Cheka in order to avoid harm to their loved ones.[3] Trotsky also set up a special Central Operations Department, to control the numerous guerrilla bands scouring the countryside.[4]

That these steps were not popular, and that the Bolshevik hierarchy did not like independent guerrilla bands, was made abundantly clear by a letter from Lenin to party organizations:

> . . . Hundreds and hundreds of military experts are betraying us and will betray us . . . but the guerrilla spirit, its vestiges, remnants and survivals have been the cause of immeasurably greater misfortune, disintegration, defeats, disasters and losses in men and military equipment in our army and in the Ukrainian army than all the betrayals of the military experts.[5]

In April, the British landed troops at Murmansk, Archangel, and Vladivostok; American, French, and Italian landings followed, and the Japanese moved into eastern Siberia in considerable strength.[6] The allied pretext was protection, from the Germans in Finland, of ammunition stores already delivered to imperial Russia. The real motive was to help Kolchak's counterrevolutionary army of Whites forming in the East. Pressed by his allies, and also thinking to neutralize Japanese aspirations on the Asia mainland, President Wilson only grudgingly authorized American forces to land. He instructed the force commander, Major General W. S. Graves, to remain neutral but to support neighboring Czech forces.* Since the Czechs were counterrevolutionary, this, in effect, showed the American hand; in short order, American forces were fighting with the British against the Reds. Nothing so well illustrates the confusion and downright ignorance that influenced the President at this critical juncture—the perhaps inevitable result of inept diplomatic reporting, primarily the failure of sixty-seven-year-old Ambassador David Francis, combined with the inaccurate and often conflicting reports submitted by a host of the President's personal and quasi-personal representatives.[7]

The two-year war that ensued was as unlike war on the western

---

* About 40,000 Czech prisoners had formed brigades to fight on the Russian side against the Central Powers. After the treaty of Brest-Litovsk, they asked for transfer to the western front, which could only be accomplished, due to enemy battle lines, by their sailing from Siberian ports. When, in marching to these ports, their columns were strung from the Volga to Vladivostok, Trotsky, apparently acting under German orders, attempted to disarm and intern them. They successfully rebelled against the Bolsheviks and became an integral if dubious quantity in the counterrevolution.

Russia 1918–1919

front as Lawrence's campaign in Arabia. None of the armies was well organized, armed or equipped, or even well commanded, yet each won impressive local successes that, properly exploited, probably could have proved decisive. Battle plans were either non-existent or meaningless. The White armies spent months in "winning" hundreds of square miles and in reality controlled no more than the ground occupied by the feet of their horses. When their always insufficient numbers stretched thinly enough across the vast Russian steppes, a Red army would strike a weak point of the line to send the entire army hurtling back on its supply depots. One day, a White cavalry unit would liberate a village from Bolshevik control; the next day, a Red partisan unit would liberate it from the Whites—the village being the major loser.

Armies formed and melted away. Irregular, partisan bands roamed the countryside in rapacious fury reminiscent of the Hundred Years' War. Readers familiar with the film *Dr. Zhivago* will remember the guerrilla leader in the black silk mask: this was Vasily Blücher, and his guerrillas fought the Whites east of the Urals throughout the war. Readers will also remember the armored trains that were genuine enough and quite useless. They steamed raucously through the vast countryside carrying Bolshevik leaders to often meaningless rendezvous. Occasionally they fired on an enemy band, usually without effect. A few troops traveled by train, a few by truck. Most of the "Whites" rode horses. In general, the "wheels" of the Red army were human feet.

A dozen times at least, Lenin seemed on the verge of defeat, but in the end he remained master of Russia's fate. In the end, the bumptious allied armies folded their figurative tents and quietly slipped away, the White armies either capitulating or fleeing to leave the torn, bleeding, and famine-stricken country to the Bolsheviks.

The reasons for the Bolshevik success are varied and complex but of immense importance to any study of revolutionary warfare.

On the Bolshevik side, the single overriding key to victory was Lenin's superb leadership, which in time gave the Bolshevik effort the inestimable advantage of unity and fixity of purpose. The hallmark of this leadership was flexibility both of conception and execution.

Retreat was not an ugly word so long as it spelled tactical sense. Space existed solely to trade for time: time for the allied powers to quarrel, time for socialist pressures in England and France to exert themselves, time to exploit enemy political and military errors, time for Russian guerrillas to cut Kolchak's and Denikin's lines of communication; time for loyal Russian peasants to scorch the earth; time for Red armies to form and march from north to south and from east to west to stem off still another enemy incursion.

A number of factors influenced the play. The Red army could not have existed without the supply and ammunition depots taken over from imperial forces. The essentially defensive military task (including the final successful counterattacks against the White armies) was immensely aided by operations on interior lines.* Lenin's lieutenants and most of the Bolshevik hierarchy, recognizing the literal "do or die" situation, shared his fixity of purpose.

Patriotic motivation also helped. The Bolsheviks may have stolen the revolution, but that scarcely made the idea of revolution less popular. The Red army may have been a dubious proposition from the standpoint of capability, as a generation of Western critics have tenaciously and often tediously pointed out, but it was in every sense a people's army and as such it formed a growing organism in which self-sacrifice often vied with refusal to accept defeat. Tables of organization and equipment vital to Western military structures, may have been non-existent, but Voroshilov nonetheless transformed his ragtag collection of Red Guards and guerrillas into the Red Fifth Army, and his soldiers, in being beaten by Denikin and in finally beating Denikin, died just as splendidly as those of more properly organized units on the western front. The Red army may have been battered and close to defeat, it may have lacked proper organization, modern weapons, artillery, commu-

---

* This military term may become clearer by analogy to a beehive: the more territory the Bolsheviks lost, the more compressed became their lines of communication, until they could strike with concentrated forces at any intruder from any direction.

nications, airplanes, medical services—but it did not disintegrate under stress, as did the imperial armies, and, by the end of 1920, it numbered over five million, admittedly an inefficient force that supported only sixteen field armies of varying effectiveness, but nonetheless a force that insured Bolshevik control of what was left of Russia.

A great deal of Lenin's success hinged on his capability of exploiting enemy errors. He did this so constantly and so swiftly and efficiently as to cause the student of the period to suggest that neither the Russian revolution nor the Russian civil war was won so much by the Bolsheviks as the one was lost by the provisional government, the other by the egregious errors of the counterrevolutionary Whites in loose concert with the Western powers.

Intervention in another country's affairs is a delicate matter at best. Whatever happens, the intervening agent is apt to reap the lion's share of the blame if things go wrong and none of the resultant credit if they go right. Primarily for this reason, the objective of the intervening party must be sufficiently important to warrant the risk to prestige. Its importance can be defined only by a careful spelling out of one or more specific aims, as opposed to a conglomerate ambition made the more meaningless by the frippery of legalistic and moralistic window dressing. As an operating rule of thumb: the more vague the stated objective, the less the validity and, in natural corollary, the less the chance of attainment.

But that is only the beginning. Assuming the specific objective is judged sufficiently important, it must be realistically attainable; that is, if disaster is to be avoided. First-rate minds using first-rate intelligence must weigh the effect of the intervening agent on the balance of the struggle, a process that involves consideration of national forces available for the act of intervention. If the amount of available force is clearly insufficient for the task, either at the inception or as it develops, then the importance of the objective must be reassessed in view of the obvious disadvantages including potential catastrophe.*

The allied intervention in the spring of 1918 failed on each count. No single interallied objective existed, but, rather, a nebulous ambition to re-create an eastern front against the Germans, either by persuading the Bolshevik government to this action or by replacing this government with another that would embrace allied interests. A lack of specific objectives prevented allied powers from determining a combined course of action, a deficiency the more glaring in view of the pinchpenny forces committed.

Several reasons explain this failure. The German offensive in France

---

* In rare instances, the action will still be approved, a handy example being the British sacrificial commitment to Greece in 1940.

in the spring of 1918 automatically precluded a major allied diversionary effort, at least in northern Russia. Added to this were Anglo-French suspicions of each other's foreign policy, and Wilson's reluctance to intervene openly in Russian affairs, a natural reluctance reinforced by not wanting to give Japan a pretext to secure a permanent foothold in Siberia. Finally, allied representatives in St. Petersburg failed to determine either the depth of the revolution or Bolshevik ability to retain control of it.[8]

This was a catastrophic failure, but an understandable one. The diplomats and generals on hand were engrossed with the world war. They had switched support almost instantly from the imperial government to the provisional government, and they had been prepared to support the Bolshevik government had it agreed to keep Russia in the war. The chief of the American military mission in St. Petersburg had believed that he could persuade Trotsky to this course; the French and the British had even furnished officer adviser-instructors to the embryo Red army, an extraordinary move sharply terminated when Lenin opened peace negotiations with the Germans.[9] Britain and France already were aiding the White movement when Lenin abrogated Bolshevik responsibility for imperial Russian war debts and other obligations, in February 1918.

The erroneous estimate of allied observers hinged in large part on ignorance of conditions inside Russia. The majority of allied representatives did not speak the language, nor did this seem necessary, since the czar and czarina always corresponded in English, and since the court and diplomatic language was French. In those years an enormous gulf existed in all countries between the educated and the working and peasant classes, and the diplomatic corps saw no reason to bridge it, an attitude explicit in the vapid and saccharine writings of the British ambassador's daughter, Meriel Buchanan.

This attitude, natural perhaps, but nonetheless disastrous, meant that in 1918 allied representatives, with few exceptions, were linguistic prisoners of upper, middle, and professional classes who, desperately longing for active intervention, painted a canvas of falsely bright colors. It meant that they had no idea of the turmoil existing deep inside the country; knew nothing of working-class and peasant attitudes; could not talk or listen to Socialist Revolutionaries or Social Democrats or many other persons except through interpreters; lacked accurate information concerning strength, plans, or even progress of White armies, except what they were told by generally dubious sources.

Taken together, this led to an illusory belief, in allied circles, that Bolshevik control was transitory, and this arrogance of ignorance was expanded into a completely unwarranted assumption that a display of allied flags would cause counterrevolutionary Whites to rally into a cohesive force capable of defeating the upstart Reds. When this did not happen, the allied forces found themselves increasingly paralyzed, their influence sharply curtailed. The November 1918 armistice greatly complicated matters. Although the French and British governments wanted to take more positive action in Russia, their leaders were wary of political repercussions—understandably so, in view of their immense losses in the war, not to mention their teetering on the edge of bankruptcy. Instead of reinforcing northern sectors, the British had to satisfy themselves by occupying the Transcaucasian oil fields, from where they fed increasing amounts of arms and supplies to General Denikin. The French did send troops into the Odessa area, a halfhearted effort neutralized by the Reds, whose propaganda caused some French soldiers to defect!

The allies acted more decisively in the spring of 1919, when the Supreme Council, in Paris, offered the Kolchak Whites "munitions, supplies and food to establish themselves as the government of all Russia" in return for specific political guarantees.[10] In June 1919, the British stepped up deliveries to Denikin, sending him " . . . a quarter of a million rifles, two hundred guns, thirty tanks and large masses of munitions and equipment" as well as two hundred military adviser-instructors.[11] Had Paris promises materialized, they might have reversed the failing situation. But Paris promises vanished in the smoke of the conference table. Churchill later wrote of allied statesmen: " . . . Some were in favor of peace and some were in favor of war. In the result they made neither peace nor war."[12] In the end, they evacuated, a perhaps inevitable decision but one that, first discussed publicly, proved catastrophic. To save their lives, thousands of Russians now left allied and White army ranks to go to the Red camp.

The numerous and serious allied shortcomings paled in comparison with those of the White armies. Here dissension ruled, both internally and externally. Although a joint plan of attack and eventually a jointure of forces might have defeated the Red army, neither was achieved, even regionally. Not only did southern armies pursue separate campaigns, but General Denikin, who had replaced General Kornilov after his suicide in early 1918, constantly alienated the peoples vital to his operational success. Unlike Lenin, he did not understand compromise: He broke with the powerful Don Cossacks, whose chief, or *ataman*, Krasnov, was willing to use German arms and equipment; he held but slight sympathy for land reforms, none for autonomous provincial government. In his numerous and sometimes extensive incursions, Denikin alienated the peasants, not alone by letting his armies live off the land and by commandeering grain and forage as ruthlessly as the Bolsheviks, but also by attempting to give the estates back to private owners. He treated provincial groups such as the Cossacks, the Georgians, and the

Ukrainians not as allies but as subject peoples of the government he was going to re-establish, thereby forfeiting an immense amount of potential strength. Instead of exploiting the loyalty of peasants already disillusioned by Bolshevik rule, he often caused them to fight as a third force, the Greens; in the Ukraine, for example, " . . . the peasant anarchist Nestor Makhno led partisans against, successively, Denikin's Whites, Trotsky's Reds, Wrangel's Whites, and finally everybody, until he fled to Rumania in 1921."[13]

A similar failure in leadership infected the Siberian command, where, after the 1918 armistice, Admiral Kolchak established a dictatorship. Almost at once, he alienated Socialist Revolutionary forces in the area and thus lost peasant support; halfhearted and contradictory measures began losing him support of potentially powerful Czech forces.

When counterrevolutionary fortunes looked up, in spring of 1919, Kolchak foolishly attempted a jointure with the allied-Russian force at Murmansk instead of a straight drive to join Denikin in the South. This abortive lateral movement presented a long exposed flank, which the Reds struck to send the White army spinning back in confusion.

In summer of 1919, the British military representative, General Knox, reported that in Kolchak's armies " . . . the men are listless and slack, and there is no sign of their officers taking them in hand. The men do not want rest, but hard work and discipline. . . . The enemy boasts he is going to Omsk, and at the moment I see nothing to stop him. As it retires the army melts, the men desert to their villages or to convey their families to safety. . . . "[14]

While this deterioration was in progress, General Denikin was enjoying unprecedented success in the South. Between April and October 1919, his forces took " . . . 250,000 prisoners, 700 guns, 1,700 machine guns and 35 armored trains; and at the beginning of October he reached Tula, within 220 [sic] miles of Moscow, with forces approximately equal to those of his opponents, namely, about 230,000 men." Winston Churchill told the British Cabinet: " . . . General Denikin has under the control of his troops regions which cannot contain less than thirty millions of European Russians, and which include the third, fourth and fifth great cities of Russia. . . . "[15] But Denikin lacked " . . . the resources—moral, political or material—needed to restore prosperity and contentment. . . . "[16] Worse than that, however, he refused to come to political terms either with General Yudenich, advancing from Estonia on Petersburg, or with the Poles or with the Baltic States, or with Petlura, the Ukrainian leader. At the apogee of his autumnal advance, Denikin stopped to fight Petlura, a fatal error that opened his twelve-hundred-mile front to successful Red counterattacks. Thus the end of Denikin. The heir to his bankruptcy, General Wrangel, did attempt to introduce social and political reforms, at least verbally, but the movement never recovered its former momentum.

The collapse of the White armies did not surprise everyone in allied councils. During one of the Paris conferences, Marshal Foch is said to have remarked, "These armies of Kolchak and Denikin cannot last long because they have no civil government behind them."[17] An astute participant could have taken this a step further and asked what a military "victory" would have accomplished? Considering the prevalent political anarchy, the demonstrated inability of conservative-moderate-liberal-socialist elements to come to terms, an inability made the greater by the loss of their leaders from the Red Terror, the peasant demands for land reform, and the nebulous but nonetheless autocratic designs of Denikin and Kolchak, the answer would have been political disaster: a divided Russia with the great powers occupying spheres of influence, which would inevitably have led to German-Japanese dominance.

Had these possibilities been respected, then intervention might not have been taken so casually and so aimlessly. Churchill, in *The World Crisis,* plaintively asks, " . . . Could they [the statesmen at Paris] not have said to Kolchak and Denikin: 'Not another cartridge unless you make terms with the Border States, recognizing their independence or autonomy as may be decided.'" Yes, they could have—and *before,* not after, the landings. And if the replies had not been eminently suitable, the landings need never have occurred and the allied powers would have profited immensely thereby. The allied intervention solved nothing and cost a great deal, a cost extending far beyond the cruelty of false hopes raised in the breasts of people far too small to escape the web of events, or beyond the thousands of Russians who did flock to allied colors only to be sacrificed ultimately to Red vengeance. Very probably, the intervention better served Reds than Whites, and one cannot help wondering if Lenin otherwise could have achieved his "backs to the wall" fusion.

Allied intervention, more than any one factor, insured Communist hatred of the Western world. Taken with subsequent Western moves, it formed a convenient international bogeyman on whom to blame the disastrous effects of the postcivil-war famine, Lenin's further and ruthless consolidation of Communist power, the inefficiencies and errors of the regime during the post-Lenin power struggles, and the repressive cruelties of the Stalin and post-Stalin regimes.

Withdrawal of allied forces from Russian soil, defeat of the White armies, and lifting of the naval blockade in January 1920 yielded Lenin a somewhat Pyrrhic victory. Russia was plainly exhausted, her industry at a halt, finances ravaged by hopeless inflation, agricultural production at an all-time low. Serious peasant revolts in 1920–21 further clouded the picture, as did droughts that brought widespread famine in 1921–22. In less than two years, Russia lost perhaps five million people from starvation, a figure that probably would have doubled but for the humanitarian and now scarcely remembered efforts of the American Relief Administration.

Lenin answered this internal crisis by launching his famous New Economic Policy. The NEP, by recognizing the value of incentives to agricultural and industrial production, clearly abrogated basic Marxist principles and was welcomed in the West as an admission of Communist failure. This judgment was premature. The NEP represented a step backward, a temporary mollification of social-economic forces, in military terms the reduction of an awkward salient—but not a reversal of strategy. For, while Lenin was juggling with economic factors, his mind remained intent on achieving world revolution.

Lenin never regarded the Russian Revolution as an isolated phenomenon. As a Marxist, he had to adjust chronologically, in that revolution was supposed to have occurred first in Germany, then spread throughout Europe and the world. This slight anachronism in no way invalidated his belief in world revolution or in the Communist Party as its major organizational force. In spring of 1919, at the height of his country's internal doubt and confusion, he presided over the First Congress of the Communist International—what would become dreaded throughout the world as the Comintern.

Little doubt or confusion reigned at this congress, where Lenin and Trotsky ran the elections and wrote the governing manifesto, a tedious document hopefully calling on the workers of the world to unite and revolt. The Second Congress of the Comintern, called in July 1920, decided on a more indirect approach, of preparing the "world revolution" through "a systematic program of propaganda."

Henceforth the Comintern resembled an angry octopus whose head remained in Moscow while innumerable ganglia slithered into every corner of the globe. The ganglia suffered a high casualty rate: Béla Kun's Communist government in Hungary lasted less than six months. The proletariat of western Eurasia and England responded flaccidly: these states were confused and exhausted, and, despite spurts of Communist enthusiasm in England and the new Czechoslovakia, by 1920 the less militant socialist parties controlled the workers. In America, the national temper and postwar prosperity made the task of selling rebellion tantamount to peddling whiskey to a prohibitionist. Bolshevik agitators received nearly as cool a reception in the Near and Middle East, where only a small proletariat existed and where the reasoned atheism of communism repelled rather than attracted: religion indeed was the opium of the masses, nor did they desire to quit smoking. The Far East offered more fertile grounds, and, in 1920, Lenin called the first "congress of the Peoples of the East" for " . . . the purpose of stirring up and using Asiatic nationalism."[18] Two years later, Comintern agents were active in China, where again the situation permitted no dramatic inroads.

Several factors softened these various rebuffs. By working through the Comintern, Lenin minimized damage to his foreign policy, including the business of the market place: " . . . an Anglo-Soviet Trade Pact was concluded in 1921, and during the years 1921–22 nineteen treaties of peace or of friendship were concluded between the new Soviet state and its neighbors."[19] Nor did the professional revolutionary, long inured to failure, expect to accomplish miracles overnight. If an encircling ganglion were crushed or cut off, the party relied on the biological principle of *l'autotomie*—the virtually automatic regeneration of the hapless limb. If the party's long arms failed to crush postwar political structures of Germany, Italy, France, Spain, and England, they nonetheless began to weaken foundations by establishing local Communist parties and serving as the lines of communication necessary to feed these units with money and propaganda while honeycombing the area with secret party cells.

Widespread unrest greatly aided the process of fomenting revolution from within. The cumulative effects of the Industrial Revolution, the preliminary backlash of colonialism, the social-economic disruption of World War I—each played a contributory role in the social ferment of the day. From this ferment arose a variety of political genies, of democratic states whose weak and uncertain leadership bred reluctance to accept social challenges imposed by international communism, of fascist states dedicated to eliminating challenge imposed by fear with the blunt instrument of force, of nationalist states spurred by challenge but remaining aloof from the ideology—a political potpourri, a confused, frightened, and often brutal world in which revolution and its kissing cousin, guerrilla warfare, were to play significant roles.

CHAPTER NINETEEN

1. Vernadsky, 261.
2. Ibid., 265. See also, Pares.
3. Mazour, 610–11.
4. O'Ballance, *The Red Army*, 50.
5. Lenin, III, 270–1.
6. Vernadsky, 270–1. By September 1919, troop strengths numbered: Japanese (eastern Siberia), 60,000; U.S.A., 8,500; British, 1,500; Italian, 1,400; French, 1,096.
7. Kennan, *The Decision to Intervene*. This work and its accompanying volume, *Russia Leaves the War*, are vital for an understanding of this period, particularly the American participation. As Ambassador Kennan pointed out, Vice Consul Felix Cole had sent a lengthy appreciation from Archangel on June 1. This report, in Kennan's words "what has subsequently proved to be the most penetrating and prophetic of all statements by western observers on the

prospects for allied intervention in Russia," concluded by recommending delay. Ambassador Francis did not approve and did not cable any of it to Washington; it traveled by courier mail and arrived on July 19, too late to influence the President's decision.

8. Kennan, *The Decision to Intervene,* 381 ff.
9. O'Ballance, *The Red Army,* 35. See also, Kennan, *The Decision to Intervene:* the U.S. assistant military attaché briefly participated in this effort.
10. Vernadsky, 281.
11. Churchill, *The World Crisis,* V, 250.
12. Ibid., 256.
13. Schuman, 118.
14. Churchill, *The World Crisis,* V, 245.
15. Ibid., 250–1.
16. Ibid., 253.
17. Ibid., 273–4.
18. Walsh, 409.
19. Ibid., 408.

PART TWO

MAO AND REVOLUTIONARY WARFARE

A revolution is not a dinner party, or writing an essay, or painting a picture, or doing embroidery; it cannot be so refined, so leisurely and gentle, so temperate, kind, courteous, restrained and magnanimous. A revolution is an insurrection, an act of violence by which one class overthrows another. . . .

MAO TSE-TUNG

CHAPTER 20

UNLIKE RIP VAN WINKLE, the "sleeping giant" of China did not suddenly awaken to a new world. Instead, it emerged in a series of internal fits and external starts familiar to a somniloquist reluctant to face a day of gloom and drizzle. The awakening began in the eighteenth century—a labored and sometimes perverted renascence that continues today.

Nor is Napoleon's term essentially correct. Although China shut itself from the West about the time Shih Huang Ti ("the First Emperor") built the Great Wall (200 B.C.), rather than a "sleeping giant" it resembled a fragmented colossus sheltering behind a spiritual-physical screen. In the minds of its rulers, China occupied " . . . the center of the universe; the outer galaxies, except when they bothered China, were of no concern to her."[1] To keep them at safe distance, Chinese rulers relied on a protective ring of tribute-paying states: Japan, Korea, Manchuria, Turkestan, Tibet, Burma, and Annam.

Internal rule derived from a Confucianist-Taoist-Buddhist religious philosophy in which Confucianist teachings remained dominant. Chi-

nese scholars taught the Tao (the Way) as the key to human behavior:
as long as everyone subscribed to the Tao, peaceful harmony would
result. The Tao divided society into "gentlemen" and "small men."
" . . . It was the gentleman's duty to exercise benevolent rule over the
small men: emperor over his subjects, magistrate over the people, husband over wife and children." This would yield a "flat," or peaceful,
existence: " . . . No disturbances in the realm, the village, or the home,
no passion in the life of man, serenity in old age where death calmly
supplanted life."[2]

The "flat" concept of existence was not exactly exciting. Like Plato's *Republic,* it formed a philosophic rationale for an involved type of benevolent despotism (the two words are incompatible). Although in earlier centuries China produced some remarkable discoveries in the sciences and some original and exquisite work in humanities and arts, enforced isolation from the rest of the world and the gulf between the ruler-scholars and its vast millions led at first to tarnishing and then erosion of its political-economic-social structure.

As is invariably the case, benevolent despotism trampled promiscuously on basic human rights, in this case yielding the Chinese peasant an existence that in the nineteenth century would become subhuman. Harsh provincial rulers and rapacious landlords played evil roles in plenty, but to their work must be added frequent and catastrophic floods, droughts, and epidemics. Pearl Buck's novels in no way exaggerate the human degradation and despair suffered by hundreds of millions of human beings.

This perpetual semistarvation status of millions instantly condemns the efficacy of the "flat" theory of government. In any event, the concept proved largely illusory, for under its ostensibly placid surface, human emotions spilled over into countless protests and riots that failed to spread only because of harsh repression and lack of communications.

The basic Chinese conflict between ruler and peasant was traditional. Suggested in the ancient *Book of Songs,*[3] it is manifest in later regional peasant societies. The most famous of these secret organizations, the White Lotus, stemmed from the late fourth century. Originally a religious society, it slowly evolved into a revolutionary order that helped overthrow first the Sung dynasty (960–1279), then the Mongols (1280–1368).[4]

A peasant-monk, Chu Yüan-chang, led the revolt against Mongol rule. Chu had begun leading guerrilla raids on villages when he was twenty-five. Winning an immense following by his policy of forbidding guerrillas to exploit or steal from common people, Chu captured Nanking in 1356 and extended his control south of the Yangtze River. Later, his army toppled the ruling Mongols, and he became the first Ming emperor, Hung Wu. The Ming dynasty lasted until 1644, when the Manchus replaced it. Provincial uprisings continued to plague Manchu authority, but lack of cohesion and communications generally isolated these attempts sufficiently for the emperor's soldiers to "flatten" them.

Economics formed the nub of the difficulty. According to the *Veritable Records* of the Ch'ing dynasty, China's population from 1750 to 1850 increased from 143 million to 430 million.[5] Simultaneously, land under cultivation decreased, a process already familiar to western Eurasia but partially offset there by the Industrial Revolution. No such revolution occurred in China to ameliorate the misery and starvation that increased from year to year.

Nor did the Peking government help matters. Caught in a political web, it struggled only fitfully to escape. Its fatigue increasingly told in the provincial bureaucracy, which found itself hamstrung by overcontrol from Peking's authoritative and increasingly corrupt government. The ruling air was not merely tainted with corruption, it exuded it: " . . . forced crop payments, the pocketing of bribes, fraudulent land registrations (productive land registered as waste land), illegal imposts, the unjust allocation of assessments, the juggling of rates of exchange, and the increasing immunities of the landlords."[6]

These ingredients were ample for trouble, but now a new one was added. This was the great catalyst of modern-day revolution: the foreign state.

More precisely, foreign states. Portuguese and Spanish traders started nudging the southern periphery in the early sixteenth century. By 1715, the Dutch and the English were trading out of Canton, but only with increasing difficulties. The remote Peking government—the throne that ruled through an omnipotent Grand Council—regarded Westerners as tributary guests forced to pay for the privilege of trading with China. A host of intermediary officials, provincial viceroys and governors, extended the emperor's hand, as did port and customs officials and Chinese merchants, who added their own "squeeze."

Why, then, did foreigners stay in Canton? Mainly because of immensely profitable trade. The British East India Company brought in raw cotton, metals, and woolens, and carried away cotton cloth, tea, and silk.[7] Added to this legitimate effort was contraband smuggling of opium, a pernicious trade from which a number of British aristocratic fortunes derived. The company administered Bengal, where most of the opium was grown and prepared, and in time came to depend on the exorbitant profits to pay for its operations in India. But the profits were shared by a great many persons, including Chinese merchants and officials, who generally received the death penalty if caught. In Canton in 1828, " . . . it was estimated that about 90 percent of the total foreign import trade was in opium."[8] A few years later, the company lost its trade monopoly with China: other English merchants moved in and so did Americans, many of them unscrupulous traders.

Peking's attempts to halt the illicit trade were suspicious by their ineffectiveness, but such was the nature of China's monolithic government, so tenuous the chain of command, that orders issued at the top rarely led to compatible action at the bottom.

In 1839, the throne sent an Imperial Commissioner, Lin Tsê-hsü, to Canton to end the trade once and for all. Lin seized all opium stores and, in reply to English intransigence, closed Canton to British ships. The Governor-General of India declared war on China, the famous "Opium War" of 1841–42, which clearly exposed Chinese military weakness to British arms. British occupation of Canton and the coastal cities of Amoy and Ningpo led to lopsided treaties which gave England the almost uninhabited island of Hong Kong, opened Shanghai and major southern ports to Western trade under foreign-imposed "fair and regular" tariffs, established the extraterritorial principle governing land for foreign homes and businesses, and made England a "most favored nation."

As John Harrison has pointed out, the last clause established a disastrous precedent, for all subsequent treaties with other nations, such as that signed with America in 1844, contained a similar clause: " . . . internationally, China became a legal pauper, living on the good will of the treaty nations. The war of 1841–42 contained the seeds of a kind of cultural, economic, and political destruction unknown in any previous war in Chinese history."[9]

The treaties provided only surface solutions to profound problems. Opium smuggling continued, the ghastly "pig trade" in Chinese emigrants sprung up, Chinese pirates and Portuguese mercenary incursions in the South China Sea led to increased presence of Western navies, and as Western merchants exploited extraterritorial privileges in the ports, unpleasant incidents repeatedly occurred with local Chinese.

A competent government would have had its hands full coping with this awkward transitional period. The rigid Peking government could not possibly meet the challenge, and its lesser officials merely exacerbated existing problems. Simultaneously, Peking was faced with a worsening internal situation. Sporadic revolts, which had marked early decades of the century, were steadily increasing. In 1850, by far the most serious of these occurred: the Taiping peasant-based rebellion, which began in the remote southern province of Kwangsi, the work of a peasant-student named Hung Hsiu-ch'üan. Hung was born into a poor peasant family of Hakkas in Kwangtung in 1814.* As a struggling student, he suffered a nervous breakdown manifested by a vivid religious vision. He had been exposed briefly to missionary Christianity, and he " . . . now saw himself as the son of God and the younger brother of Jesus Christ, chosen at God's command for a special mission: to destroy the demons on earth and establish the Kingdom of God."[10]

In principle, the demons on earth were the Manchus at Peking; in

---

* The Hakkas, or "guest settlers," emigrated from northern China in the fourth century to settle in Kwangtung and Southeast Asia, where they eventually numbered some twenty millions. They assimilated slowly: after fourteen centuries, the Hakkas still spoke a different dialect and practiced different customs and habits, which kept them at odds with the local inhabitants, a condition undoubtedly existing today.

practice, they were provincial tax collectors who, supported by despised soldiers, covered the southern provinces like locusts. The peasants of eastern Kwangsi, where Hung launched his revolt understandably flocked to his banner. Here again was guerrilla warfare in its purest form: a few thousand peasants armed with pitchforks and calling themselves the "God-Worshipers." Based in the Thistle Mountains, a remote area safe from imperial infantry and cavalry incursions, these dissidents began striking out at the demon tax collectors, at first by raids on villages to gain support and recruits. Hung's early successes attracted such a variety of anti-Manchu secret societies that the God-Worshipers became a blending of religious, nationalist, and social elements, which, as Professor Franke has written, " . . . constituted the Taiping Rebellion's point of departure."[11] In 1850, Hung's followers, now many thousands, proclaimed him the *T'ien-wang,* or Heavenly King, of the *T'ai P'ing T'ien-kuo,* or Heavenly Kingdom of the Great Peace. The Heavenly King ordained a number of plain Kings, whose followers continued to spread the word to draw in additional strength. Hung used a number of devices to tie these heterodox groups of peasants, coolies, country intellectuals, pirates, miners, and even businessmen into a common band. The Manchus had introduced the queue, or pigtail—the Taipings cut it off; the Manchus shaved the forehead—the Taipings let their hair grow, thus earning the official name "the Long-Hair Rebels." Most of all, however, Hung relied on the appeal of a social-political-economic manifesto that bore a remarkable resemblance to Karl Marx's work of 1848, but was conceived independently of it and was based ideologically on elements of Christianity and structurally on the pre-Christian Chou dynasty.[12]

Hung's manifesto is often termed primitive communism, just as Christ has been called the first Communist. In the Kingdom of Heaven, the state owned and controlled every activity. It assigned land equitably, it paid for tools and seed, for weddings, births, and funerals. Women were fully equal to men, but had to marry, though theoretically someone of their own choice. The state abolished prostitution and footbinding and forbade opium, tobacco, and alcohol. The God-Worshipers could only practice their own brand of Christianity.

The new state would deal with Western nations, but only on an equal basis, thus ending extraterritorial privileges. Hung's manifesto, which also called for immediate calendrical and linguistic reforms, is altogether a remarkable document, and in 1851 it represented the most sweeping demand for change in China's long history.

Equally remarkable was Hung's army. Oriented religiously from inception, soldiers were taught to respect peasant rights. They could neither requisition food without payment nor enter dwellings without permission. They received intense religious instruction, could neither drink, gamble, nor smoke, and stood subject to execution for either rape or desertion. This surely must have been one of the purest armies in history, and since the phrase is contradictory, we must conclude that modern scholarship errs on the romantic side. Hung's army nonetheless differed radically from the utterly dissolute government forces which plundered and raped at will. His early and impressive victories stemmed from guerrilla tactics used in striking the enemy at his weakest points and bypassing major garrisons, which eventually became "islands" in a hostile sea. In 1852, he marched his fifty-thousand-man army into Hunan. After converting the guerrilla formations at least in part to orthodox units armed with captured weapons, he fell on Hankow, Wuchang, and Hanyang, then sailed down the Yangtze to seize the rich prize of Nanking. In late 1853, one of his armies reached Tientsin and marched on Peking, but was turned back by a strong force of imperial cavalry.

Alas!—"moral decay" now set in: " . . . shortly after the capture of Nanking the Heavenly King and other leaders, against all commandments of the revolutionary movement, began a life of excesses—high living, luxury, many concubines. Decay at the top naturally was contagious to those in the lower echelons.[13]

Internecine quarrels played a major role: a power struggle in Nanking in 1856 allegedly took some twenty thousand lives, including those of a great many of the early Taiping leaders. Professor Harrison marked 1856 as the apogee of the rebellion. From then on, " . . . corruption, nepotism, the attrition of leadership, the failure to carry out promised reforms, the loss of zeal by the masses, and simple war weariness all took their toll."[14] Hung's early successes stemmed in part from Peking's failure to recognize the true nature of events. The emperor and his advisers probably interpreted Hung's early raids as the work of bandits, and they may have misread other uprisings, such as the Nien Fei rebellion in Anhui and neighboring provinces, an extensive guerrilla movement led by the White Lotus society, and the Triad movement, which came to control much of Shanghai from 1853–56.

Even had the Peking government earlier recognized the threat, military weakness would have prevented effective action. So grim was the situation from Peking's point of view, that, in 1854, the emperor authorized regional armies of defense, a move previously avoided because of the potential threat to central authority. Viceroys and governors either organized militias or built up existing illegal ones. Some of these in time performed excellent work, the outstanding example being Tsêng Kuo-fan's army in Hunan province. Backed by landed gentry, Tsêng recruited from villages and based training on Confucianist principles as strong as, if not stronger than, Hung's Christian principles. Stressing leadership and discipline, he fed and paid the troops regularly, forbidding them to live off the land. Although a scholar and bureaucrat, Tsêng seems to have had excellent strategic sense and, in a relatively short time, began claiming the initiative from the insurgents.

England, France, and the United States played a complex, confusing, and sinister role in the internal affairs of China at this time. Continuing quarrels with Chinese port officials and merchants led to England's second war with China, an on-again-off-again affair involving France, Russia, and the United States, and finally terminated by Lord Elgin's Anglo-French force burning the complex of buildings known as the Summer Palace, an invaluable architectural masterpiece north of Peking—an "unnecessary act never forgotten or forgiven by the Chinese."[15] The resultant treaties, again very unequal documents that favored the Western powers, increased foreign jurisdiction over Chinese waters, inland and seaboard ports, and trade; extended the foreign presence to the North, including Peking, and in the South inland to the larger cities of the Yangtze Valley; and legalized the opium trade.

Hung's announced reforms did not now look nearly so attractive to the Western nations, which began supplying arms to the Manchus and helping the emperor build the Ever Victorious army composed of Chinese, European, and American mercenaries. Commanded by Li Hung-chang, the new army, working in conjunction with regional armies, slowly pushed the Long-Hairs back to Nanking. Hung's heavenly kingdom fell in the summer of 1864. With his suicide and execution of his principal lieutenants, the movement quickly disintegrated. The regional armies next put down neighboring rebellions. By 1866, the Manchu government could claim the end of the rebellion.

Suppression of the Taiping rebellion offered Peking rulers scant cause for rejoicing. Central China was bled white—some authorities believe that *the rebellion claimed forty million lives*! Internal chaos had helped Western powers to increase their grip on China's economy, and they now began shamelessly dividing the country into spheres of interest for further commercial exploitation. Virtually bankrupt, Peking was forced to borrow large sums from Western bankers in order to fight a costly campaign against Moslem rebels in northwestern provinces. Simultaneously, foreign states began chipping away at China's traditional "buffer" states: England in Burma, France in Vietnam, Russia in Manchuria, and Japan in Korea.

China's continuing decline naturally increased the already wretched plight of the Chinese people, who could only seek survival from the worn and precious earth, and in so doing remained unwilling slaves to the "flat" Confucianist concept of government. A lesser group, known contemptuously to their fellows as "rice-bowl Christians," came to accept the foreign presence: to adopt the new religion, to serve humbly in mines, factories, railroads, warehouses, and private homes of foreign masters. Because foreigners lived in insulated enclaves remote from real China, most of them accepted the comfortable premise of a placid people while failing to recognize the existence of underlying currents caused by a revolutionary minority, which in the best Chinese tradition was widening old channels and creating new.

Dissident groups of militant rebels, although scattered and disorganized, continued to exist in post-Taiping decades. Their activities took two forms: uprisings against the dynasty, which, although invariably quelled, continued to occur, for example the preliminary Boxer risings in 1898–1900; and uprisings against foreigners, usually terrorist displays such as the dreadful Tientsin massacre of 1870, which spelled hatred with missionary blood.

The Boxer movement, in addition to the I Ho Ch'üan societies, included small regional bodies, the outgrowth of provincial militias established to fight the Taiping Long-Hairs. Some authorities say that the name stemmed from the ancient sport of Chinese boxing; others hold that the prebattle ritual dance caused Westerners to think of boxing. For the most part, the Boxers were ignorant peasants who practiced sorcery and superstition, actually believing that they were immune to bullets. In early 1900, they broke loose in northern China, attacking missionary settlements and slaughtering missionaries and thousands of Chinese Christians. Although some provincial leaders put down the risings, others turned a blind eye, as did the throne, which in June sent government units to join rebels in besieging foreign legations in Peking. An international expedition, when finally formed, made short work of the besiegers, the war ending abruptly in August. Harsh peace terms exacted an indemnity of six to seven hundred million dollars, including a principal payment of nearly $331 million in gold.[16]

The Boxer calamity did not spell the end of rebellion. Throughout the 1890s, leading members of the Chinese intelligentsia had been calling for necessary reforms. The outlook of these men varied greatly, and their failure to present a united front to the throne was the major reason for the continuing series of disasters. Chang Chihtung, one of the most able, saw the major need as military reform, a thought abhorrent to the throne as a public confession of " . . . the corruption, incompetence and nepotism of the officer corps of the various armed forces, as well as the failures of the arsenals."[17] Two outstanding scholars, K'ang Yu-wei and Liang Ch'i-ch'ao, pressed for political, economic, and social reforms on what they called progressive Confucianist lines under dynastic supervision. In 1898, they persuaded the emperor, Kuang Hsu, to defy the dowager empress and the ultraconservative elements around him and issue the necessary proclamations. This, a sort of palace revolution in reverse, failed, because the emperor lacked a proper army to back him. The dowager empress, in league with Yüan Shih-k'ai, the powerful viceroy of Chihli forced the emperor to abdicate and took over as regent. She executed six of the Reformers, and the others fled abroad. Here they found other dissidents, true revolutionaries such as Dr. Sun Yatsen, who for years had been arguing for a fundamental change in favor of Western democracy.

In 1898, Sun Yat-sen was thirty-two years old. The son of a poor farmer in Kwangtung province, he spent his childhood in China. At age eleven, he went to Hawaii, where a brother sent him to an Anglican church school. At seventeen, he returned to China, but soon left in favor of medical school in Hong Kong, where he practiced for two years as a doctor before becoming a full-time revolutionist. Returning to Hawaii, he established the Hsing Chung Hui (Revive China Society), a movement of " . . . twenty small Chinese shopkeepers" pledged " . . . to expel the Manchus, recover China, and establish a republic." After several futile attempts at revolution and some narrow escapes, Sun joined another revolutionary, Huang Hsing. In Japan they established the T'ung Meng Hui (United League), a small but militant group that called for a social and economic revolution. This brought them in conflict with expatriate Confucianist reformers who wanted a carefully conducted political revolution with economic and social reforms to follow eventually. The United League wanted action: " . . . between 1907 and 1911 the *T'ung Meng Hui,* despite its lack of a real organization in China, attempted eight armed revolts in Southeast China in an effort to capture the provinces of Kwangtung, Kwangsi, or Yunnan for a base of operations,"[18] efforts that failed for want of a true revolutionary force.

But revolt was in the air. The throne's arbitrary and unfair attitude in the matter of a provincial railroad question brought the people of Szechwan province to arms in autumn of 1911. The revolt quickly spread through the Yangtze Valley, where even army regiments mutinied. A thoroughly alarmed dynasty now called the former viceroystrong man of Chihli province, Yüan Shih-k'ai, from retirement and gave him command of the Northern Army, with orders to put down the revolt. This proved impossible: by mid-November, all but four provinces had seceded in favor of a provisional republic with headquarters at Nanking. Republican leadership consisted of provincial officials and army commanders with revolutionaries present as poor relations. Sun Yat-sen, who was in America when the trouble began, did not appear until the end of December. These disparate groups eventually hammered out a republican form of government that promised a constitution, a cabinet answering to a bicameral parliament, and a president, Yüan Shih-k'ai. The Manchus abdicated in February 1912, a virtually bloodless end to three centuries of bloody rule.

Unfortunately the new rulers answered none of China's problems. Despite republican trappings, Yüan headed a reactionary government supported by the foreign powers, the Northern Army, and a political bloc of conservatives called the Progressive Party. He was opposed principally by the T'ung Meng Hui, which, in 1912, became the Kuomintang, the dominant political party whose leaders preached a muddled blend of social-economic reforms. The party comprised divisive elements, none holding the real support of the people or even much power. Yüan, with his Northern Army, shared real power with provincial military governors, each with his own army, and none held the people's interests at heart.

The people, in short, were left with reactionary and corrupt government at both national and provincial levels, yet general ignorance, lack of organization, and apathy prevented them from seeking another change—they failed, for instance, to support Sun Yat-sen's two attempts at revolt in spring of 1913.

Sun and his followers already had recognized their early mistake in thinking that a constitution and parliament would hold Yüan in hand. Thoroughly alarmed at his steadily increasing reactionary rule, they now tried to check him by parliamentary authority. The showdown came in autumn of 1913. The growth of provincial powers had reduced the central government's income to a trickle, and Yüan could get money only by ruinous loans from foreign powers. That spring, Yüan had negotiated such a loan in the immense sum of £25 million. The governing conditions were so restrictive and humiliating that President Woodrow Wilson forbade American participation. When Yüan sought approval of this measure, the Kuomintang caused parliament to disapprove. In reply, Yüan dissolved the Kuomintang, whose key members fled to Japan.

This cleared the way for Yüan's dictatorship. But even a dictatorship could scarcely thrive when subject either to threat of regional competitors, each backed by arms, or to continuing encroachments of foreign powers, particularly Japan, who used World War I to replace the German presence in Shantung province, a sinister prelude to the famous "Twenty-one Demands"—compliance with which would have reduced China to a vassal state. In 1915, probably with Japan's backing, Yüan stupidly tried to establish a new monarchy (with himself as emperor), an idea quickly abandoned because of widespread protest which split China, the southern half becoming a hotbed of revolution.

Yüan died in 1916, to leave China in the hands of provincial military governors, powerful war lords who ruled with scant heed of Peking. Between 1916 and 1926, the impotent central government was run by " . . . six Presidents . . . [who] had a total of nineteen Prime Ministers, none with a tenure of more than a year."[19] Whoever the presi-

239

dent, he ruled only through the grace of local war lords, and a more squabbling bunch of dissembling chieftains probably never existed.

Anarchy spawned two other national forces. In 1917, Sun Yat-sen and his Kuomintang followers took advantage of the South's open break with Peking and returned to Canton to establish "the Military Government of the Republic of China."[20] Unable to gain a popular base of government, Sun depended in large part on the local military governor's support, his fortunes and those of his followers fluctuating accordingly. During this period, Sun wrote the *San Min Chu I* (Three Principles of the People), a wooly but nonetheless influential dissertation calling for nationalism, democracy, and the people's welfare as goals for his party, now renamed the Chinese Revolutionary Party. As Professor Harold Isaacs has pointed out, up to mid-1919 " . . . his hope was to bring about the peaceful and benevolent transformation of Chinese society after first securing power for himself and his followers by purely military means. This was the aim of his long series of invariably fruitless military adventures and alliances."[21]

Considerable revolutionary activity meanwhile had been building in the North. The immediate motivation was the disastrous Versailles decision that approved Japan's dominating presence in Shantung province, the outcome of one of those wretched secret agreements that England and France were forever signing. In May 1919, students at Peking University rioted against the Peking government, burning the houses of pro-Japanese ministers. Governmental suppression of this and other demonstrations gave birth to a revolutionary May Fourth Movement, " . . . a catalyst that united large-scale organizations—students, labor, merchants, and guilds . . . " in an almost total rejection of the West and a reappraisal of traditional values.[22]

Having rejected the West and seeing the inability of political leaders to come to terms with reality, segments of this movement eyed the triumph of the Russian revolution and began moving toward communism. In 1920, the Socialist Youth Party emerged from the ferment in the Shanghai area, and in 1921 a Comintern agent, Voitinsky, helped them establish the Chinese Communist Party. But another Comintern agent, Maring, already had recognized a more viable revolutionary force in Sun Yat-sen's Chinese Revolutionary Party. The May Fourth Movement had caused Sun to broaden his party's base by flirting with student and trade-union movements, in which he played increasingly influential roles. Maring's reports induced Lenin's government to send a top diplomat, Adolf Joffe, for lengthy talks with Sun. Joffe offered to help reorganize and arm the Kuomintang so that it could lead a revolution; this was not to be a Communist revolution, since communism was " . . . unsuitable to Chinese conditions."[23] Surrounded by mostly hostile war lords, looking at a hostile Peking government and hostile foreign powers, recognizing the Kuomintang as still disorganized and virtually bankrupt, Sun accepted Joffe's offer. Joffe planned to use the Kuomintang only as a stepping stone to an eventual Communist takeover, and almost immediately began arguing for a marriage of convenience between the Kuomintang and the Chinese Communist Party.

Enter Chiang Kai-shek: thirty-four years old, a small, thin soldier whose varied and, at times, seamy career stood at odds with the Confucianist asceticism he so ostentatiously professed. Born in Chekiang province, Chiang had grown up in great poverty, his father, a small farmer, having died when he was nine. At age eighteen, he entered China's first military academy. An honor student, he was sent to Japan for further training. Here he fell under the revolutionary influence of Sun Yat-sen's teachings, and in 1911 participated in the overthrow of the Manchus; in the dismal aftermath of that effort, he " . . . disappeared somewhere into Shanghai's murky underworld." For nearly a decade, he lived a quasi-covert life, apparently under protection of the notorious Green Gang, a highly organized group of cutthroats that would make the Mafia look like a boy-scout troop. After a brief stint of service with a "Fukienese warlord," Chiang came to the attention of Sun Yat-sen, with whom he quickly rose in favor.[24]

In 1922, Chiang headed a military mission to Moscow while two Russian Communists, Mikhail Borodin and Vasily Blücher (alias General Ga-lin), worked with Sun to reform the Kuomintang along Leninist, or pyramidal-command, lines. Still another shift of regional power allowed Sun's return to Canton, where, strongly supported by the Comintern, he reorganized the Kuomintang into an independent political force with its own police and army elements.

A year later, Chiang Kai-shek, somewhat disillusioned with Soviet rule, returned from Moscow to set up the famous Whampoa military academy. Provided with arms, money, and advisers from the Comintern, he began training cadre officers for the new Kuomintang army. Also in 1924 Sun decided, against the wishes of many of his Chinese advisers, to admit Chinese Communists into the Kuomintang, thus beginning a twenty-five-year power struggle.

Man's ego plays an enormous role in the affairs of man. Like many statesmen before and since, Sun refused to accept the possibility of his own death. He believed that he could control the Communists, and he probably planned to squash them once revolution became a fact—his death in 1925 precludes a positive answer.

Sun's error was Faustian; in fostering revolution, he contracted with the devil. He had asked the Kuomintang to be too much to too many people. The major codicil in his will was a promotion of party factionalism, not only among conservatives, moderates, leftists, and Communists, but in each of the splinter groups. Chiang Kai-shek's retention of power depended as much on rejection of extreme conservatism as on retention of communism, and from 1925 until his break with the Communists in 1927 he constantly juggled the power factors, his success stemming far more from control of the army than from his ability to reconcile dissident groups. The only cohesive element at work during this period was negative: the inability of any group to carry out the revolution alone.

The revolution moved north in spring of 1926, but a more disparate revolutionary force never marched. The vanguard consisted of the People's National Revolutionary Army—three corps that totaled less than one hundred thousand soldiers, under the over-all command of Chiang Kai-shek. Two of these corps marched north to the Wuchang-Hankow area on the Yangtze; the third, under Chiang's personal command, moved north up the coast toward Shanghai. Nationalist-Communist agents, such as the young Mao Tse-tung, had spent years preparing the Yangtze Valley by organizing sympathetic trade unions in the cities and peasant associations in the countryside. The Nationalists had also come to terms with the major war lord in the area, the famous "Christian General," Fêng Yü-hsiang, who baptized his troops en masse with a fire hose.[25] The two corps on the left advanced with little difficulty and, in October, occupied Wuchang and began consolidation of the entire target area. On the right, Chiang ran into trouble with some local war lords and did not reach Shanghai until March 1927. Although the city was his for the taking—the work of local Communist agents—Chiang now paused.

For some time, Chiang had been receiving disquieting reports from the West. In January, the Kuomintang government had moved from Canton to Hankow, where, under the aegis of its forceful Russian adviser, Mikhail Borodin, it began consolidating power in the Yangtze Valley area. The new government allowed its Communist elements full sway: prodded by professional agitators, labor unions and peasant associations seized and distributed private property—a violent period accompanied by a flow of both Chinese and foreign blood. In short, the revolution was assuming Bolshevik dimensions totally anathematic both to Chiang and to the middle-conservative elements of the Kuomintang.

Chiang hesitated for several weeks. But when it became clear to him that the moment of truth was at hand, he acted quickly, decisively, and brutally. Leagued with conservative business elements of Shanghai, including foreigners and the notorious bandit gangs, he launched a surprise attack against the area's Communists. This, the beginning of the infamous White Terror, quickly spread to other power centers; he followed it by setting up a Nationalist government at Nanking. Chiang's army undoubtedly would have fought the Hankow forces but for the war lord Fêng Yü-hsiang, whose army stood between them.[26] Before either side could bribe Fêng, the Communists overplayed their hand. Joseph Stalin, fresh from his triumph over Trotsky, ordered the Chinese Communist Party (which was subordinate to the Comintern) to take over the revolution. This extraordinary order, naïve in the extreme, caused an immediate and terrible resentment throughout the Kuomintang. It virtually shattered the Communist movement. Borodin and other Soviet agents escaped to Russia; their Chinese opposites, those who survived the White Terror, went into hiding. Chiang Kai-shek exploited this development by hammering the remaining elements of the Kuomintang into an embryonic Nationalist government, which by 1928 claimed control of China.

A brave claim. Internally, the Kuomintang remained greatly divided: war lords showing fangs too sharp to be ignored yapped in defense of sectional interests and foreign powers representing vast financial empires. Chiang was too strong to abdicate, too weak to protest. So he compromised: the highly vaunted revolution had stirred up the forces of power without removing the evils of their burden from the people. Chiang merely replaced Manchuism and warlordism with a dictatorship. His suppression of the Autumn Uprising of 1927—a peasant movement—was as thorough and heartless as any of the numerous Taiping suppressions.

Ironically, Chiang was too weak to forge even an effective dictatorship. The slave of Confucianist thinking and the pawn of commercial interests, domestic and foreign, Chiang found himself blocked from reform on almost every side. The bulk of Chinese people remained miserable. Here and there, they continued to protest their misery. Here and there, small groups, led by Communists, waged guerrilla war. Here and there, the idea of social revolution lived on. Here and there, a few forceful leaders had survived to fight.

One of them was Mao Tse-tung.

CHAPTER TWENTY

1. Schurmann and Schell, I, xviii. The reader will find this three-volume work essential to further study of ancient and modern China.
2. Ibid.
3. Waley.
4. Dun-jen Li, 269–70.
5. J. A. Harrison, 31. I have relied heavily on this splendid and immensely readable work.
6. Ibid., 33. See also, Goodrich.
7. J. A. Harrison, 15. See also, Tsiang Ting-fu. Some Western apologists, for example Cole and Priestley, have argued ingeniously (if speciously) that the relatively low profits from legitimate trade " . . . forced the west, primarily England, into the opium trade."
8. J. A. Harrison, 16. See also, Schurmann and Schell.
9. J. A. Harrison, 21. See also, Schurmann and Schell, 125: " . . . the Nanking

Treaty (1842) signed at the conclusion of the war represented China's point of no return. Hereafter, the tide of foreign penetration could not be reversed."

10. Franke.
11. Ibid.
12. Ibid.
13. Ibid.
14. J. A. Harrison, 39.
15. Ibid., 29.
16. Ibid., 91.
17. Ibid., 79.
18. Ibid., 94–6.
19. Ibid., 106–7.
20. Ibid., 109.
21. Isaacs, 57.
22. J. A. Harrison, 122.
23. Schurmann and Schell, II, 88.
24. White and Jacoby, 118–19.
25. Vandegrift and Asprey, 74.
26. Malraux, *Man's Estate,* for a striking narrative of this turbulent scene.

CHAPTER 21

MAO TSE-TUNG (or Zedong, according to the revised Romanization system) was born in 1893, the son of hard-working peasants in Hunan province, in central China. As a "middle peasant," Mao's father, a harsh taskmaster and disciplinarian whom Mao loathed, was able to give his son the almost unheard-of luxury of a provincial education through high school level. Mao responded by reading whatever he laid his hands on, an eclectic assortment ranging from traditional Confucianist classics to the great Chinese historical novels and to translations of Western works in economics, political theory, and history.[1]

In these formative years, Mao learned more away from the classroom, where life was a constant fight for survival. In addition to normal stresses, the recurring plagues, famines, and floods, the tax collectors, landlords, and bandits, Mao witnessed something of the revolutionary turmoil surrounding the fall of the Manchus. As a keen student, he also realized the new government's inadequacy to solve old problems, particularly those affecting hundreds of millions of Chinese peasants. Mao soon became a socially aware and resentful young man; service as a private soldier, as servant to officers in an army ridden with nepotism, corruption, and inefficiency, only increased his resentment. When he went to work in the Peking University library, in 1917, he was, at twenty-four years, the Chinese version of an angry young man.

Angry young men are prone to swallow morphia-ridden political panaceas in much the same way that country people take to cure-all elixirs. Mao found his nostrum at Peking. Under tutelage of hard-line Marxists, Mao soon became a convinced Communist, who in 1921 helped organize the Chinese Communist Party in Shanghai. Thenceforth he served as an activist in the revolutionary movement, which was still a joint Kuomintang-Communist affair.

In keeping with fundamental principles of Marxism-Leninism, the new Communist Party concentrated on organizing the Chinese proletariat into trade unions. It found a fertile field. The war had swollen the labor population to some two million persons, a miserably paid and ill-treated force particularly receptive to Communist propaganda. Party newspapers, youth movements, schools, clandestine meetings, strikes, and demonstrations—each prospered in the factories and along the wharves and in the mines. As a political agent, Mao Tse-tung found himself in the middle of this activity, eventually becoming chairman of the Hunan branch of the Trade Union Secretariat, a front organization in which capacity he led three major strikes.[2] Some Chinese Communists meanwhile had turned to organizing peasants of the central provinces. In Kwangtung province, membership rose in five years from a few thousand to 665,000, with other significant increases in Honan and Hunan provinces. Probably because of Mao's rural background, he was early assigned to agitation-propaganda activities in his home province, Hunan. He excelled in this work and, in 1926, was elected chairman of the All-China Association of Peasant Associations.[3] But even Mao was surprised at the outbreak of peasant violence in support of the Kuomintang army's northern march. Early in 1927, he spent a month touring Hunan province. In a prescient report to the Central Committee, he emphasized the need for party reorientation, with concentration on peasant forces:

> . . . For the present upsurge of the peasant movement is a colossal event. In a very short time, in China's central, southern and northern provinces, several hundred million peasants will rise like a mighty storm, like a hurricane, a force so swift and violent that no power, however great, will be able to hold it back.[4]

In but months, Mao reported, membership of Hunan peasant associations had jumped from a few hundred thousand " . . . to two million and the masses directly under their leadership increased to ten million." Showing no sympathy for the victims of revolution to date, " . . . the local tyrants, the evil gentry and the lawless landlords," he mocked protests of conservative Kuomintang elements. If peasants on occasion were going too far, their excesses still did not match those of earlier governments. Besides,

> . . . a revolution is not a dinner party, or writing an essay, or painting a picture, or doing embroidery; it cannot be so refined, so leisurely and gentle, so temperate, kind, courteous, restrained and magnanimous. A revolution is an insurrection, an act of violence by which one class overthrows another. A rural revolution is a revolution by which the peasantry overthrows the power of the feudal landlord class.[5]

The break between Chiang Kai-shek and the Hankow government, followed by Chiang's general purge of all Communists, may have removed luster from Mao's enthusiasm, but it in no way dimmed his basic convictions. At great danger to his own life, he willingly participated in the Autumn Harvest Uprising, of September 1927. This abortive effort, which centered in Hunan province, caused him to question one of the Chinese Communist Party's basic tenets: that unarmed and untrained peasants could bring about revolution. In the event, he commanded four "auxiliary" regiments, but these were scarcely strong enough to stand against the Nationalist army. Disobeying party orders, he broke off the action to seek sanctuary with remnant followers in the Chingkang Mountains of southern Hunan-Kiangsi-Fukien provinces.

Late in 1927, Chiang announced the end of the Communist threat. He was wrong: The Communists were down, but not yet out. Early in 1928, the capable Chu Teh joined Mao, as did other fugitive survivors. The two Communists organized fellow fugitives, local bandit groups and peasant volunteers into a small, rudely equipped guerrilla army to keep alive the almost defunct revolution. Respecting the need for a political base, they turned local peasant associations into *su-wei-ai,* or soviets, of " . . . soldiers, peasants, and workers which assumed administrative control over the Red areas."[6] They also established local militia forces which Mao called " . . . the Red guards and the workers' and peasants' insurrection corps." The work moved slowly: in the winter of 1928, according to Mao, the Red Guards possessed a mere 683 rifles of assorted calibers. Moreover, Communist methods of land sequestration and redistribution had antagonized a good many "rich" and "middle" peasants in the area.

The movement not only survived, it grew stronger. Using the plow of propaganda to till fertile "poor" peasant soil into acquiescence if not wholesale support, Mao and his fellows relied on coercion, including terrorist methods, to gain financial support from local merchants and landlords. Intelligence provided by peasants enabled guerrillas to fight local provincial forces on their own terms, utilizing mobility and surprise—short, sharp actions that avoided pitched battles.

In these early, crucial months, Mao's guerrillas profited from Chiang's concentration on more immediate problems besetting the Kuomintang as well as from his patronizing attitude, which led him consistently to underrate his enemy, whom he contemptuously dismissed as "communist-bandits." Mao and Chu, on the other hand, paid closest attention to Kuomintang power struggles, which so obviously influenced the amount of Nationalist army strength that would be used against them. Mao regarded the instability of national rule as a prerequisite for setting up " . . . an armed independent regime," but success, in his opinion, also depended on:

> . . . 1) a sound mass base [i.e., a willing peasant population]; 2) a sound Party organization [i.e., completely disciplined to pursue basic objectives]; 3) a fairly strong Red army [as Mao later wrote, "Political power grows out of the barrel of a gun."]; 4) terrain favorable to military operations [including a sanctuary area]; and 5) economic resources sufficient for sustenance [i.e., to come from local sources such as landlords or merchants, from the people themselves, and from outside agencies such as the Comintern].[7]

While Mao was so theorizing, Communist success remained very limited. The ragged force euphemistically called the Red army suffered severe shortages of arms and equipment. Recruits reported literally with pitchforks, spears, and fowling pieces, weapons later replaced with captured rifles. Officers and soldiers alike received a ration of rice and five cents a day for " . . . cooking oil, salt, firewood, and vegetables"—a monthly payroll of more than " . . . ten thousand dollars, which are obtained exclusively through expropriating the local bullies [landlords and merchants]," and was not always met.[8]

In the freezing mountain sanctuary, soldiers shivered in light cotton clothing; over eight hundred lay ill from cold, malnutrition, and wounds but the army lacked doctors and medicine. To hold the ranks together, leaders relied on discipline engendered and maintained through ideology. A party political representative supervised each soldiers' council at each command level down to and including the company; political indoctrination surpassed practical training in frequency and intensity, as is evident from Mao's 1928 report. This proved the more important because, in the relatively barren border areas, the White Terror had frequently cooled revolutionary fervor: "Wherever the Red Army goes,"

Mao wrote in 1928, "it finds the masses cold and reserved; only after propaganda and agitation do they slowly rouse themselves"—and Mao held no intention of letting such apathy infect his army. His was scarcely an easy task, and his words reflect a winter of discontent: "We have an acute sense of our isolation which we keep hoping will end."[9]

Still, the Red flag flew and the ragtag army continued to elude government forces. In mid-1929, Mao and Chu moved from the remote Chingkang Mountains to a new base in southwestern Kiangsi province. A more realistic land policy gained them considerably wider support here, and, with an influx of recruits, they reshaped their army to win a number of significant local victories.

Li Li-san, Chou En-lai, and other members of the Central Committee of the Chinese Communist Party, long since operating underground in Shanghai, misread the limited success of their agrarian counterparts. Still under Russian influence and convinced that revolution must come from the proletariat, Li and his associates, in 1930, ordered Mao and Chu to begin a series of attacks against southern cities, which would be "prepared" internally by labor strikes and uprisings. This called for a complete reversal of Communist tactics to carry out a campaign for which the Red army was neither trained, organized, nor equipped. The first attacks succeeded, although at a cost in lives that they could ill afford. Then came the nearly disastrous defeat at Changsha, which caused a costly retreat to the hills of Kiangsi and a refusal to undertake further urban operations. Mao and Chu were now convinced that victory must come from peasant and countryside, not worker and city, " . . . the single most vital decision in the history of the Chinese Communist Party."[10] A refutation of Marxism-Leninism, it was also a demonstration of where real Communist leadership lay in China, and it helps to explain a great deal of the subsequent Chinese relationship with the Soviet Union.

Taking heart from the Nationalist victory at Changsha in the autumn of 1930, Chiang Kai-shek announced a "bandit-suppression campaign." Commencing in November, this looked better on paper than it proved in fact. Mao and Chu refused the Nationalist invitation to battle (except on their own terms), preferring a Fabian strategy designed, in Mao's later words, to lure the enemy deep and, with the aid of intelligence provided by peasants, destroy him piecemeal. This was particularly appropriate in view of Chiang's forces, which already were displaying deficiencies that he never could repair: riddled with inefficient and corrupt leadership, his divisions flailed over the land like locusts, further alienating peasants, the ill-treated, illiterate soldiers frequently deserting to the Communists.

Chiang followed the abortive first campaign by a second, equally unsuccessful effort in spring of 1931. Chiang himself commanded an army of some three hundred thousand in a third campaign, but made little progress before having to march north to meet Japanese military incursions in Manchuria. As Kuomintang fortunes plunged, Communist fortunes soared. Shortly after Chiang's precipitate departure in summer of 1931, the Comintern persuaded the Chinese Communist Party to proclaim existence of the Chinese Soviet Republic. On November 7, the Chinese Red army raised this flag at Juichin, in southwest Kiangsi, and Mao Tse-tung became the new republic's president. At this time, his area of operations covered a large part of Kiangsi and extended into Fukien, Hunan, and Hupeh—an area containing around 25 million Chinese. Mao's army had grown to an impressive sixty thousand, with recruits continuing to come in.

In 1932, Chiang returned to the attack in the South. His fourth "encirclement and annihilation" campaign succeeded only in capturing some small Communist bases in Hupeh province. Impressed by Communist resistance and somewhat humbled by the poor performance of the Nationalist armies, he prepared carefully for the fifth campaign, opened in October 1933 under direction of German officers headed by able General von Falkenhausen. Drawing on the lessons of the Boer War, Falkenhausen advanced a force of over half a million men, supported by artillery and aircraft, slowly and methodically, evacuating peasants from villages and consolidating gains by building a massive series of mutually supporting blockhouses.

Although Mao's army numbered perhaps 250,000, continuing pressure soon began thinning the ranks. Deprived of peasant support, and thus of information and food, Mao's people slowly withdrew into the hills. Communist bases fell one by one until by 1934 Mao held only three small areas, each encircled by Chiang's divisions. Unless leaders of the new Soviet Republic acted quickly, they and their army would be exterminated. They finally decided to seek sanctuary in the remote northern province of Shensi, whose hills already sheltered a small Communist group. Their actual destination, the loess caves of Pao An, lay twelve hundred miles away "as the crow flies." Since Nationalist divisions and war lords friendly to Chiang interdicted virtually the whole route, the Communists would have to escape around Robin Hood's barn: southwest deep into Yünnan, then north through the tortuous mountains of Szechwan, all together some six thousand miles of difficult terrain, much of it contested by war lords, Chiang's armies, and by hostile tribes.

In October 1934, like Xenophon's Greeks twenty-three centuries earlier, the Communists burned granaries, backpacked meager possessions, fought through Chiang's encircling army, and began one of the most extraordinary marches in man's history.

The Long March, which lasted over a year,

... led across eleven provinces, over remote regions inhabited by suspicious peoples, through murderous marshy lands overgrown by grass, and in face of continuous danger from local and governmental forces. It is claimed that the three Communist armies who participated in the march crossed eighteen mountain chains and twenty-four large rivers, broke through the armies of ten war lords, defeated dozens of Kuomintang regiments, and took temporarily sixty-two cities.[11]

Of an estimated 130,000 persons who left Kiangsi, no more than thirty thousand arrived in Shensi—Mao Tse-tung's wife numbered among the dead.

The Communist ledger of hardship and sacrifice nonetheless held a profit column. The Long March established the Chinese Soviet Republic in a new, temporarily safe sanctuary. In remote loess caves of Pao An (Protracted Peace), Mao reorganized battered ranks of party and army. Losses had been heavy but the hard core of survivors breathed the zeal of ideologically devoted men.

Stories of their epic retreat circulated throughout China to belie Kuomintang claims of total victory over the Reds. The Long March brought Mao into contact with other Communist groups and a variety of peasant and nationalist groups, whose civil and military leaders had to be propagandized into accepting his authority.[12] As his armies struggled over mountains and through rivers, he assigned small agitation-propaganda cadres to remain in likely areas to talk up the revolution. In time, he would send trained teams to reinforce these cadres, and he left secret caches of arms and ammunition for their later use.

The Communists resumed operations in surprisingly short time. As his initial target, Mao chose neighboring *Shansi* province. In February 1936, three Red army columns, numbering some thirty-four thousand men, crossed the Yellow River, brushed aside provincial forces of the governor, and occupied large areas, where they " . . . collected grain and money, shot rich landlords and tax collectors, recruited thousands of peasants for their armies, and began organizing the rural masses." By their own account, they returned to Shansi with some eight thousand volunteer recruits, not only peasants, but students, bureaucrats, shopkeepers, workers, and soldiers.[13]

Mao's incursions into Shansi decided Chiang Kai-shek to complete the extermination campaign begun in Kiangsi. To carry this out, he deployed the Northeastern and Northwestern Defense Armies, a heterogeneous collection of some 150,000 troops, along the Yellow River

251

under command of "Young Marshal" Chang Hsueh-liang, who established "Bandit-Suppression Headquarters" at Sian.[14]

Chiang's fear of the Communists as the real threat to China was not shared by all members of the Kuomintang. A considerable faction disagreed outright, and for good reason: not only did the Japanese virtually control Hopei province, in the North, but they were slowly pushing into Kiangsu and Honan provinces, farther south. Chiang's failure to stem these incursions became Mao's gain. By taking up the cause of resistance to the Japanese invader, and in the process villainizing Chiang Kai-shek and the Kuomintang, Mao gained a fantastic psychological advantage. As John Harrison put it, the Communists " . . . appropriated nationalism from the Nationalists and made it a powerful Communist weapon."[15]

The denouement of this internal drama had already begun, the *deus ex machina* being the external force of the Soviet Union. Aware of Japanese aspirations on the Asian continent, Stalin had never broken with the Kuomintang, whose power he regarded as essential to checking Japan's invasion of China. Now, threatened by the rising prominence of Hitler in the West, he ordered Mao Tse-tung to make common cause with Chiang Kai-shek through a United Front.

Although such an alliance upset Mao's revolutionary timetable, this was in any event flexible and Mao stood to profit in other ways. Since 1932, he had been calling for war against Japan, and much of the Communists' popular appeal derived from this position. He had even found an ally of sorts in the Young Marshal Chang Hsueh-liang* on whom Chiang Kai-shek was depending to hold Mao in check and eventually destroy him. The security derived from Mao's improved relationship with Chang in Sian probably explains why Mao was able to move his headquarters to the town of Yenan, which, in December 1936, became the capital of the Chinese Soviet Republic.

Chiang Kai-shek refused the notion of a United Front, despite considerable pressures from within the Kuomintang. In mid-1936, he ordered Marshal Chang to attack the Communist bases in Shansi, an order refused not only by Chang but by subordinate war lords. In December a furious Chiang Kai-shek traveled to Sian to order Chang " . . . to mount a full attack against the Communist bases in Shansi."[16]

Chang not only refused, but literally kidnapped the president of China and issued a manifesto calling for an end to civil war in favor of united action against Japan. Mao undoubtedly was involved in this move, although to what extent is not known. Professor Harrison be-

* Harrison E. Salisbury, "The Kidnapper's Dream," *International Herald Tribune*, June 15–16, 1991: The "Young Marshal," aged ninety, "[is presently attempting] to bring Beijing and Taiwan into a unified China."

252

lieves that Chiang probably would have been executed but for Stalin's intercession on his behalf which caused Chang to release Chiang Kai-shek toward the end of December.

Although Mao hated to let Chiang go—Edgar Snow wrote that Mao " . . . flew into a rage when the order came from Moscow to release Chiang"[17]—he hastened to make political capital from Chiang's release. In a much publicized letter to the Generalissimo, Mao reminded him that he owed his freedom to the Communists, who had intervened solely in order for China to get on with the war against the Japanese invader; if Chiang would cease fighting the Communists, Mao offered to call off revolutionary activities in return for a joint war effort against the Japanese.

Formal agreement between Nationalists and Communists emerged in September 1937, shortly after the Japanese captured Peking and Shanghai and began to fight toward Chiang's new capital at Nanking. But only for the moment was the very real threat of the foreign invader to overshadow severe internal antagonisms.

The years in the south that culminated in the Long March made Mao Tse-tung undisputed leader of the Chinese Communist Party. And now, in the loess caves of Pao An, the forty-three-year-old Communist leader began to frame the theory and doctrine of "people's war"—a thesis that would influence his world to an immeasurable degree.

Mao did not arrive easily at this doctrine. Prior to the Long March, however, he had concluded that revolution in China depended ultimately on " . . . three essential principles . . . the central role of the army, the importance of rural base areas, and the protracted character of the struggle," and he also had tested and improved many of its strategic and tactical aspects.[18] Fundamental to the process was guerrilla warfare, and, in 1937, he defined its revolutionary role in a definitive work called *Yu Chi Chan*, or *Guerrilla Warfare*.[19] Mao followed this with a book titled *All the Problems of the Anti-Japanese Guerrilla War*. In the same year, he delivered a series of complementary lectures on guerrilla tactics, subsequently published under the title of *Basic Tactics*, to a group of young officer cadets.[20]

Mao looked on a country

> . . . half colonial and half feudal . . . a vast country with great resources and tremendous population, a country in which the terrain is complicated and the facilities for communication are poor. All these factors favor a protracted war; they all favor the application of mobile [that is, orthodox] warfare and guerrilla operations.[21]

Mao carefully elaborated on this statement:

... The concept that guerrilla warfare is an end in itself and that guerrilla activities can be divorced from those of the regular forces is incorrect ... in sum, while we must promote guerrilla warfare as a necessary strategical auxiliary to orthodox operations, we must neither assign it the primary position in our war strategy nor substitute it for mobile and positional warfare as conducted by orthodox forces.[22]

With regard to the whole war,

" ... there can be no doubt that our regular forces are of primary importance because it is they who are alone capable of producing this favorable decision. Guerrilla warfare assists them ... mobile warfare is primary and guerrilla warfare supplementary; with regard to each part, guerrilla warfare is primary and mobile warfare supplementary.[23]

Since Mao's force, known as the Eighth Route Army, was fighting "a part," he called for a basic strategy of "guerrilla warfare." But, he warned, " ... lose no chance for mobile warfare [operations of regular armies] under favorable conditions."[24]

Whether fighting the Japanese or later the Kuomintang armies, Mao demanded a three-phase war. Phase One

... is devoted to organization, consolidation, and preservation of regional base areas situated in isolated and difficult terrain. Here volunteers are trained and indoctrinated, and from here, agitators and propagandists set forth, individually or in groups of two or three, to "persuade" and "convince" the inhabitants of the surrounding countryside and to enlist their support. In effect, there is thus woven about each base a protective belt of sympathizers willing to supply food, recruits, and information. The pattern of the process is conspiratorial, clandestine, methodical, and progressive.

Phase Two steps up the action:

... Acts of sabotage and terrorism multiply; collaborationists and "reactionary elements" are liquidated. Attacks are made on vulnerable military and police outposts; weak columns are ambushed. The primary purpose of these operations is to procure arms, ammunition, and other essential material, particularly medical supplies and radios. As the growing guerrilla force becomes better equipped and its capabilities improve, political agents proceed with indoctrination of the inhabitants of peripheral districts soon to be absorbed into the expanding "liberated" area.

Phase Three is decisive: the enemy's destruction by orthodox military operations which do not necessarily deny guerrilla operations but place them in a subsidiary role.[25]

The hallmark of this blueprint is flexibility. The phases are coactive: Phase Two and even Phase Three may concern one theater of operations, Phase One another. While the process normally proceeds upward, Phase Three may retrogress into Phase Two and even Phase One. Timelessness, or protraction, also plays an important part—a single phase may last two, ten, or twenty years.

Echoing Clausewitz, whom he had studied, Mao insisted on subordinating combat to an over-all political strategy:

> . . . Because ours is the resistance of a semicolonial country against an imperialism, our hostilities must have a clearly defined political goal and firmly established political responsibilities. Our basic policy is the creation of a national united anti-Japanese front. This policy we pursue in order to gain our political goal, which is the complete emancipation of the Chinese people.

Guerrilla warfare cannot be separated from national policy:

> . . . What is the relationship of guerrilla warfare to the people? Without a political goal, guerrilla warfare must fail, as it must if its political objectives do not coincide with the aspirations of the people and their sympathy, co-operation, and assistance cannot be gained. The essence of guerrilla warfare is thus revolutionary in character. . . . Because guerrilla warfare basically derives from the masses and is supported by them, it can neither exist nor flourish if it separates itself from their sympathies and co-operation.[26]

Mao returned to the political priority in a later chapter of *Yu Chi Chan,* a chapter that many Western military commanders subsequently seemed unable to understand. Some of Mao's generals seemed equally obtuse:

> . . . There are some militarists who say: "We are not interested in politics but only in the profession of arms." It is vital that these simple-minded militarists be made to realize the relationship that exists between politics and military affairs. Military action is a method used to attain a political goal. While military affairs and political affairs are not identical, it is impossible to isolate one from the other.

Mao's insistence on the overriding importance of the political factor resulted in his concept of the "three unities":

... These are political activities, first, as applied to the troops; second, as applied to the people; and, third, as applied to the enemy. The fundamental problems are: first, spiritual unification of officers and men within the army; second, spiritual unification of the army and the people; and, last, destruction of the unity of the enemy.[27]

The first of the unities represented a radical departure from oriental military tradition. Although admitting need for obedience in any army, Mao held that " . . . the basis for guerrilla discipline must be the individual conscience." Mao wanted only "pure and clean" volunteers "willing to fight." His soldiers were to be just, honest, and courteous when dealing with civilians. They were to return anything borrowed and replace anything broken—and they were not to bathe in the presence of women.[28]

... Many people think it impossible for guerrillas to exist for long in the enemy's rear. Such a belief reveals lack of comprehension of the relationship that should exist between the people and the troops. The former may be likened to water and the latter to the fish who inhabit it. How may it be said that these two cannot exist together? It is only undisciplined troops who make the people their enemies and who, like the fish out of its native element, cannot live.

The enemy's unity would be destroyed by "propagandizing his troops, by treating his captured soldiers with consideration, and by caring for those of his wounded who fall into our hands."[29]

Mao lists seven ways in which guerrilla units are originally formed. The "fundamental type" is formed from people automatically springing to arms to oppose the invader, the "pure" type of guerrilla warfare earlier illustrated in this book. In addition to spontaneous resistance, guerrilla warfare may be fought by units assigned from the regular army, by a combination of regular army soldiers and peasant-guerrillas, by units of local militia, by enemy deserters, and by former bandits and bandit groups. Each category poses special problems in recruiting and organizing, but the catalytic agent is political and the effort worthwhile, since " . . . it is possible to unite them to form a vast sea of guerrillas. The ancients said, 'Tai Shan is a great mountain because it does not scorn the merest handful of dirt; the rivers and seas are deep because they absorb the waters of small streams.' "[30]

Mao's basic guerrilla unit, the squad, comprised nine to eleven men who did not require sophisticated arms. Two to five Western-style rifles were sufficient for a squad, " . . . with the remaining men armed with rifles of local manufacture, bird guns, spears, or big swords." Members of militia and self-defense units ". . . must have a weapon even if . . . only a knife, a pistol, a lance, or a spear." Each guerrilla district commander should establish an armory to make and repair rifles and produce cartridges, hand grenades, and bayonets. However, ". . . guerrillas must not depend too much on an armory. The enemy is the principal source of their supply."[31]

Each guerrilla carried a minimum of clothing and equipment. Clothing must be procured by higher echelons, since it is an error to take clothes from prisoners. In general, equipment becomes more sophisticated as unit size increases. Larger units will carry telephone and radio equipment as well as propaganda materials, which ". . . are very important. Every large guerrilla unit should have a printing press and a mimeograph stone. They must also have paper on which to print propaganda leaflets and notices. They must be supplied with chalk and large brushes."[32] Medical services are also most important, and if Western medicines cannot be procured from "contributions," then local medicines must be used. The logistics requirement at all times is held to a minimum: . . . The equipment of guerrillas cannot be based on what the guerrillas want, or even what they need, but must be based on what is available for their use.[33]

In discussing strategy and tactics essential to accomplishing such missions, Mao borrowed freely from Sun Tzu's thesis of the indirect approach:

> . . . Guerrilla strategy must be based primarily on alertness, mobility, and attack. It must be adjusted to the enemy situation, the terrain, the existing lines of communication, the relative strengths, the weather, and the situation of the people.
>
> In guerrilla warfare, select the tactic of seeming to come from the east and attacking from the west; avoid the solid, attack the hollow; attack; withdraw; deliver a lightning blow, seek a lightning decision. When guerrillas engage a stronger enemy, they withdraw when he advances; harass him when he stops; strike him when he is weary; pursue him when he withdraws. In guerrilla strategy, the enemy's rear, flanks, and other vulnerable spots are his vital points, and there he must be harassed, attacked, dispersed, exhausted and annihilated.[34]

Surprise and deception are the hallmark of guerrilla tactics: ". . . Cause an uproar in the east, strike in the west." Of all offensive tactics, Mao favored ambush, ". . . the sole habitual tactic of a guerrilla unit."[35]

As opposed to orthodox warfare, which is frequently static, Mao wanted

> . . . constant activity and movement. There is in guerrilla warfare no such thing as a decisive battle; there is nothing comparable to

the fixed, passive defense that characterizes orthodox war. In guerrilla warfare, the transformation of a moving situation into a positional defensive situation never arises. The general features of reconnaissance, partial deployment, general deployment, and development of the attack that are usual in mobile warfare are not common in guerrilla war.

Instead of fixed defense, Mao calls for

> . . . alert shifting . . . when the enemy feels the danger of guerrillas, he will generally send troops out to attack them. The guerrillas must consider the situation and decide at what time and at what place they wish to fight. If they find that they cannot fight, they must immediately shift.

Although the guerrilla will defend his own operational bases, these must be abandoned when necessary. " . . . We must observe the principle, 'To gain territory is no cause for joy, and to lose territory is no cause for sorrow.' " Nevertheless, " . . . the operations of a guerrilla unit should consist in offensive warfare." Offensive tactics, he was careful to stress, demand " . . . careful planning . . . those who fight without method do not understand the nature of guerrilla action. A plan is necessary regardless of the size of the unit involved; a prudent plan is as necessary in the case of the squad as in the case of the regiment." Good planning depends on superior intelligence, and this can be gained only from the people, who, in turn, must withhold such from the enemy. In the end, it is peasants who give the guerrilla liberty of action essential to maintaining the initiative: " . . . When an army loses the initiative, it loses its liberty; its role becomes passive; it faces the danger of defeat and destruction."[36]

The validity of functional theory lies in practice. We have seen already that much of the Red army's success in occupying, consolidating and enlarging base areas lay in almost magical appeals of basic Communist social and economic reforms. In working with peasants of northern China, Communist agents undoubtedly exaggerated the quality of their wares by offering Barnum-style promises to people who had never seen a circus. But this scarcely lessened the impact of immediate reforms, which resembled an elixir that may not have cured the disease but at least alleviated considerable pain.

Communist magic rested on refutation: refutation of everything evil in traditional rule. Although the United Front temporarily tied Mao's hands in so far as seizure and redistribution of land were concerned, the Communists continued to abolish usury, reduce rents, and lighten taxes; the Red army no longer seized and executed landlords (at least not *en masse*), but it did grade them carefully as to productivity under the credo originally and ironically voiced by Dr. Sun Yat-sen: "Land to those who till it."[37] By refuting if not necessarily replacing evil, the Communists restored to the common peasant two emotional ingredients that make the difference between existing and living: dignity and hope. To the long-suffering peasant, the price tag of discipline, of unquestioned loyalty and obedience to the Party, seemed reasonable.

Discipline formed the foundation of the meticulous organization imposed on peasant communities and based on the village soviet, proceeding upward to district, county, provincial, and central levels. As Edgar Snow wrote in his classic work *Red Star over China*:

> . . . Under the district soviet, and appointed by it, were committees for education, cooperatives, military training, political training, land, public health, partisan training, revolutionary defense, enlargement of the Red Army, agrarian mutual aid, Red Army land tilling, and others. Such committees were found in every branch organ of the soviets, right up to the Central Government, where policies were coordinated and state decisions made.[38]

The Japanese war also favored the Communists. John Harrison goes so far as to call this invasion " . . . the real revolutionary force in China," and there is no doubt that Japanese occupation and fighting played a horribly destructive and divisive role that in the end favored Mao Tse-tung more than Chiang Kai-shek.

Nationalist armies, in retreating from Peking, Shanghai and Nanking in 1937, suffered enormous losses. Alone and increasingly isolated from foreign military aid (the Russians alone providing pilots, planes and money), Chiang Kai-shek was desperately trying to rebuild his army and could risk no part of it in a new campaign against the Japanese. In the north and north-central provinces, this left the field open to the Communists.

Under the terms of the United Front, the Red army became the Eighth Route Army, of three divisions comprising about forty-five thousand troops, under command of Mao's old Kiangsi comrade, the able Chu Teh. This army, by partially filling the military hiatus, served as an organized rallying point for national resistance. Mao also controlled perhaps another forty-five thousand troops, whose standards, though not blatantly unfurled, attracted numerous followers.

Adding to Mao's military largess, the Japanese army behaved in a manner to insure the popularity of Communist armies. Such bestiality as displayed in the infamous "Rape of Nanking," which shocked the world in 1937, hallmarked the earlier Japanese invasion and occupation of Hopei province. Any organized force wanting to fight against such treatment found immediate and widespread popularity among the people, particularly among those peasants already impressed with Communist land and tax reforms.

The Japanese also erred tactically. In the 1932 invasion of Manchuria and subsequently, their armies showed well—strong, splendidly equipped, tactically well disciplined, flexible, capable of long marches and devastating night attacks. With continuing prosperity, their military commanders, never self-deprecating, grew increasingly arrogant. In September 1937, Lieutenant General Itagaki Seishiro marched his division into an ambush cunningly laid by Lin Piao, commanding the 115th Division of the Eighth Route Army. In a brief but furious action, Itagaki suffered perhaps five thousand casualties besides losing most of his arms and supply trains, including the paymaster's money chests—the first major Japanese defeat and one trumpeted to the world by jubilant Chinese Communists.[39]

Mao was much too smart to try for a repeat victory of this nature. Instead, he concentrated on occupying and consolidating three major "base areas" in Shansi province. From here, his units fanned out to establish "guerrilla areas," which supported what Mao called "mobile-striking war"—guerrilla tactics which " . . . harassed and irritated the Japanese and tied thousands of troops, who might otherwise have been employed to better advantage, to static guard duties."[40]

The war continued in this fashion until 1940: Chiang and the Nationalists on the defensive outside of Chungking; Mao and the Communists, securely based in Shansi, on the limited tactical offensive with successes in the countryside but unable to contest Japanese control of the cities.

While Chiang's military fortunes waned, Mao's fortunes waxed—to the extent that, in 1940, he organized the New Fourth Army to fight south of the Yangtze, in Chekiang province. Already seriously alarmed at the growth of Communist power, Chiang reacted vigorously by ambushing the Communist force as it was crossing the Yangtze. Chiang then placed an economic embargo on Communist-held areas and followed this with troop operations against the Communists.

Mao, meanwhile, was facing another threat—from the Japanese general Tada Hayao, who took command of the North China Area Army in late 1939. As Kitchener had done in South Africa and Chiang in Kiangsi, Tada began systematic construction of forts, in this case by thousands of impressed coolies. This, his "cage policy," was described in an American military intelligence report:

 . . . Deep and wide ditches or moats were dug and high walls built along the sides of the railways and highways in Central and Southern Hopeh in order to protect them from attacks and, more important, to blockade and to break up the Communist base areas. At the same time, hundreds of miles of new roads with protecting ditches were built with the object of cutting up the guerrilla bases into small pieces which would then be destroyed one by one. The number of blockhouses along the railways and roads, manned by Japanese soldiers, was greatly increased. . . . [41]

Mao responded by a massive guerrilla operation, the "Hundred Regiments Offensive," launched in August 1940: this co-ordinated operation continued

> . . . with several interludes, for three months. In its overt aspects, the campaign was a success. Guerrillas made hundreds of cuts in rail lines; derailed trains, blew up small bridges and viaducts, attacked and burned stations; destroyed switches, water towers, and signal-control equipment, and otherwise seriously damaged and temporarily disarranged the railway system in North China. As a substantial dividend, Japanese garrison forces, necessarily concentrating on counterguerrilla operations and major restoration projects, were unable to get into the countryside to confiscate the autumn harvest. The Communists . . . reported more than 20,000 Japanese killed; 5,000 puppet troops killed and wounded; 281 Japanese officers captured, and 18,000 puppet prisoners. They claimed that almost 3,000 forts and blockhouses had been destroyed and large quantities of arms and ammunition taken.

Although these figures were undoubtedly exaggerated the Communist offensive nonetheless hurt the Japanese. Tada's successor, General Okamura Yasuji, attempted to repair the damage, in the summer of 1941, with what he called a "three-all policy"—"Kill all, burn all, destroy all." As the year closed, Okamura's powerful mobile columns began pushing back Communist guerrillas in numerous areas. Simultaneously, Mao's relations with Chiang Kai-shek were worsening. By the end of 1941, China's chances for survival seemed remote, even if a rapprochement should occur between Nationalists and Communists.

Then, suddenly, the entire situation changed. On December 7, 1941, the Japanese bombed Pearl Harbor, which brought America into the war. China no longer stood alone against the Japanese enemy. This radical shift in the power position was going to bring significant and indeed fatal consequences to the torn and bleeding country.

But this introduces another phase in the Eastern struggle. We must now return to the West and to revolutions of another sort, in which guerrilla warfare, unaided by Marxist motivation, also played a major role.

CHAPTER TWENTY-ONE

1. Schram, *Mao Tse-tung*, 15 ff.
2. Ibid., 120.
3. Schurmann and Schell, II, 123.
4. Mao Tse-tung, *Selected Works*, I, 23.
5. Ibid., 28. See also, Payne, *Mao Tse-tung*, who points out that his words gain an added bite when the adjectives are identified with the Confucianist *Analects*.
6. Schurmann and Schell, II, 195.
7. Ibid., 73.
8. Ibid., 82, 84–5.
9. Ibid., 97–8.
10. Mao Tse-tung, *On Guerrilla Warfare*, 16–17.
11. Mende, 110–11.
12. Ibid., 111–12.
13. Griffith, *The Chinese People's Liberation Army*, 58.
14. Ibid.
15. J. A. Harrison, 168.
16. Ibid., 169–70.
17. Snow, *Random Notes on China . . .*, 2.
18. Mao Tse-tung, *Basic Tactics*, 25.
19. Mao Tse-tung, *On Guerrilla Warfare*. This work was translated into English in 1939 by S. B. Griffith, at the time a young marine officer and Chinese-language student in Peking, and was published in the *Marine Corps Gazette* in 1940 (and largely ignored by America's professional military body).
20. Mao Tse-tung, *Basic Tactics*.
21. Mao Tse-tung, *On Guerrilla Warfare*, 68.
22. Ibid., 55–7.
23. Ibid., 56. See also, Griffith, *The Chinese People's Liberation Army*, 72 ff.
24. Mao Tse-tung, *Selected Works*, 239–44.
25. Mao Tse-tung, *On Guerrilla Warfare*, 20–2.
26. Ibid., 42–4.
27. Ibid., 89–90.
28. Ibid., 92.
29. Ibid., 92–3.
30. Ibid., 73, 76.
31. Ibid., 79–81, 83.
32. Ibid., 85. See also, Lawrence, *The Seven Pillars of Wisdom*: " . . . The printing press is the greatest weapon in the armory of the modern commander."
33. Mao Tse-tung, *On Guerrilla Warfare*, 82.
34. Ibid. See also, Griffith, *Sun Tzu . . .*: Dr. Griffith has made an excellent comparative study in his Introduction, 46.
35. Schram, *Mao Tse-tung*, 60, 102.
36. Mao Tse-tung, *On Guerrilla Warfare*, 52, 103–4, 98.
37. Snow, *Red Star over China*, 220.
38. Ibid., 221.
39. Griffith, *The Chinese People's Liberation Army*, 62–3.
40. Ibid., 67–8.
41. Ibid. 70.

CHAPTER 22

The Rif rebellion • Spain and Morocco • Condition of the Spanish army • The Regulares and the Tercio • Spanish pacification policy • Early operations • Guerrilla resistance • Abd-el-Krim • Spanish defeat • The war continues • Africanistas versus Abandonistas • Primo de Rivera's "line" • Abd-el-Krim and the great powers • French intervention • Rebel strength • The Rif offensive • Escalation • Abd-el-Krim's fall • Spain's "victory"

THE 1904 TREATY that turned England and France loose in Egypt and Africa also opened northern Morocco to Spanish influence. In 1912, France formally placed this area under a Spanish protectorate.

It was not a great prize. Consisting of some eighteen thousand square miles, it supported no less than sixty-six tribes (subdivided into numerous clans and subclans), many of them tucked away into formidable mountain areas where they lived a way of life established long before the birth of Christ and where they spoke dialects often unintelligible to other tribes. Illiterate and poor, these peoples were nonetheless proud. Many tribes were also bellicose (bloody intertribal feuds were common), and they were also resentful of any foreign incursion into what they regarded as their lands.

Spanish proponents of an aggressive colonial policy in Morocco, particularly members of army and Church, argued that a successful conquest would help repair Spain's status as a world power after its disastrous defeat by America, and would also provide new markets and enormous mining profits and would secure the southern approach to the Spanish mainland.

Not everyone agreed: From 1904 on, Spain itself was divided: the Africanistas holding for conquest; " . . . the Spanish masses . . . either apathetic or apprehensive about engaging in further military action."[1] The latter were particularly wise. In trying to develop mining areas in the Rif, the Spanish stirred up local tribes and had to fight a brief but bloody war in the Melilla area in 1909, a Spanish "victory" of Pyrrhic proportions: Besides costing the Spanish some four thousand casualties, it aroused severe internal protest in Spain and also displayed to friend and foe alike the army's general ineptitude. Two years later, the army again clashed with western tribes.

Spain thus acquired a restive protectorate. World War I, which brought German influence into the country, created more friction points in the five major tribal areas. In the main, these existed in the West, or Jibala area, ruled by the powerful chieftain Ahmed er Raisuli, and in the East, or Rif area, ruled by Abd-el-Krim. Theoretically subordinate to the sultan's deputy at Tetuan, the khalifa, these rulers in practice all but ignored him, nor did they prove willing onlookers to Spanish invasion. Not that they ruled supreme: internecine tribal wars in the respective enclaves as well as traditional enmity between Jibilans and Rifians sharply circumscribed their powers. Nonetheless, they remained important forces, to be reckoned with by the wise, ignored by the foolish.

To bring peaceful unity to northern Morocco would have taxed the talents of ten Lyauteys. Spain lacked even one such. In 1919, Major General Dámaso Berenguer assumed the post of high commissioner, with headquarters in Ceuta. Berenguer came from an army family. A heavy man—some said fat—with a pleasant if brooding face, a sensitive mouth hidden by pointed mustachios, Berenguer, at forty-six years, was a man of considerable experience in Morocco, where he had campaigned for years and in the process had organized and trained a native constabulary: a paramilitary organization called the Regulares. He knew and admired Lyautey and tried to emulate his colonial policy:

> ... he was convinced that the most prudent course lay in presenting a peaceful show of force. He neither expected nor wished to use this power against the Moroccans in the fashion of a conqueror. He did expect to establish an indigenous administration in Spanish Morocco and to achieve Spain's ends through it. Berenguer viewed the pacific occupation of the Spanish Protectorate as a political rather than a military problem.[2]

In attempting to carry out a sane policy, Berenguer faced innumerable disadvantages. The state of his army was dreadful. Most officers were venal martinets, the obese generals often unable to read a map. Factionalism riddled junior-officer and non-commissioned-officer ranks; many units supported *juntas de defensa,* or military defense councils, which very nearly approached seditious intent. The troops were ill-trained, generally illiterate, peasants. Most of their pay was siphoned off by superiors. Poorly disciplined, they lacked equipment, proper arms, essential services, even proper food. Replacements and supply arrived in irregular driblets from the mainland. The War Ministry, in Madrid, sent vacillating, often contradictory, orders, and both civil and military appointments frequently went to King Alfonso's favorites.[3]

One of these became Berenguer's military commander at Melilla in the Northeast. Manuel Silvestre was a fire-eating colonel, a dashing cavalry officer whose body was said to hold the marks and scars of sixty wounds. Silvestre's adjutant stated command policy: " . . . The only way to succeed in Morocco is to cut the heads off of all the Moors."[4] Despite Silvestre's brutal and bellicose attitude, his troops were no better trained than Berenguer's, in the West.

To repair some of these military deficiencies, Madrid authorities organized an entirely new command, the Tercio—the Spanish version of the French Foreign Legion. Command went to Major José Millán Astray, a forty-year-old combat tiger. " . . . Death in combat is the greatest honor," he wrote. "One dies only once. Death arrives without pain, and is not so terrible as it seems. The most horrible thing is to live as a coward." Known in Spanish history as the "glorious mutilated one," Millán Astray would leave an eye, an arm, and a leg in Morocco.[5]

One of Astray's commanders would leave a different sort of personal imprint. This was a young major, also holding a formidable combat record in Morocco: Francisco Franco-Bahamonde, twenty-eight years old, a little man, five feet three inches tall, uninterested in women or drink—" . . . a first-class organizer, a harsh disciplinarian, and a fearless fighter." He once declared vigorously in his high-pitched voice: "I don't want medals. I want promotion."[6]

The Tercio was still forming in 1920, when Berenguer commenced military operations designed to extend Spanish hegemony into the hinterland of Morocco. His plan was simple: a western force, in all some forty-five thousand troops based on Ceuta, to march some fifty miles south to occupy the town of Chaouen in order to splinter Jibilan power; Silvestre's eastern force, some twenty-five thousand, based on Melilla, to march west to Alhucemas Bay in order to split the Rifian movement.

Berenguer's column moved out in September. Before the expedition reached Chaouen, one General Girona, disguised as a charcoal burner, entered the citadel and persuaded the chiefs by threat and bribery to surrender. Two circumstances marred this neat piece of work: a surprise attack by local tribesmen, countered only with considerable casualties; and the execrable behavior of Spanish troops, the officers (by bringing in their own whores) vying with the men (who defiled mosques and otherwise insulted locals). Still, Berenguer had achieved his primary mission—a new base to support operations that in time would lead to

Raisuli's capture. Neither he nor his staff seemed unduly concerned about a line of communications stretching some fifty miles over difficult terrain occupied by generally hostile tribes.

Silvestre's march west from Melilla also proceeded quite smoothly. Ignoring Berenguer's injunction of caution, the fiery Silvestre moved rapidly through country made more barren by a series of poor harvests. Spanish columns dealt quickly and ruthlessly with any opposition, burning houses and crops, collecting whatever cattle they could find—altogether a punitive display that quickly alienated the local populace. By spring of 1921, Silvestre's vanguard stood on Sidi Driss, not far from its objective of Alhucemas Bay, its front extending south some thirty-five miles to Zoco el Telata, smack in the Rif hinterland. To garrison nearly a hundred fifty outposts including larger forts that required eight hundred or more soldiers, Silvestre spread his army of about twenty thousand Spanish and five thousand Moroccan Regulares rather thinly across the face of conquest, a minor blemish but one compounded by poor morale, lack of combat readiness, and by tenuous supply lines between often isolated posts. The relative ease of the advance had powdered over these imperfections, which Silvestre, in his ardent desire to kiss victory, chose to ignore. Not only did he plan to push on to Alhucemas Bay but, according to an intimate, he relished the thought of battle: " . . . We need a victory so overwhelming that it will convince the Moors that they cannot afford the price of resistance to Spanish domination."[7]

Unknown to Silvestre, a coterie of spies was keenly observing the progress of his columns and the state of his local defenses, their reports (often delivered verbally, since illiteracy ruled) going to a twain of remarkable nationalists, the brothers Abd-el-Krim.

Mohamed and Mhamed Abd-el-Krim were the sons of a Rifian nobleman, a judge (some say schoolteacher) both anti-Spanish and anti-French, a not unnatural attitude for an educated Moroccan, and one undoubtedly accentuated by German propaganda during World War I. The elder Abd-el-Krim gave each of his sons a university education that resulted in a successful career in journalism for Mohamed and graduate study in engineering for Mhamed, ten years younger.

As a journalist in Melilla, Mohamed grew increasingly disillusioned with Spanish colonial policy, particularly its blatant intent to exploit Morocco's mineral wealth. Imprisoned by the Spanish in 1917, he escaped and returned to journalism, but in 1919 threw over his job, joined his father in the mountains ringing Ajdir, and summoned Mhamed from Madrid. Although his father was poisoned to death in a tribal feud a year later, the three already had decided to raise a rebellion designed to oust the Spanish and create a Moroccan or at least a Rifian state, and now the surviving brothers turned to this task.

Neither brother was particularly imposing. Mohamed, traditionally known as Abd-el-Krim, at thirty-nine years of age was what London tailors describe as S&P—short and portly. Mhamed was taller and slimmer. Both were dark and both wore the standard Rifian dress, a dark-brown homespun wool *jellaba* with loose-fitting sleeves and a cowl, bagged trousers, grass sandals, and white cotton turban.

Abd-el-Krim affected a black beard and sweeping mustache. Small dark eyes flicked from an otherwise benign face to suggest a contradictory character: Abd-el-Krim would lovingly pat children on the head; but he would also stand by approvingly while Rifian guerrillas slit a Spanish officer's throat. Denied a hereditary charisma, Abd-el-Krim seems to have relied on superior education and knowledge of Spanish ways to impress various tribal chiefs. In no way ostentatious, he used remoteness to impress the ordinary native, who in time willingly proffered him demigod status.[8] Mhamed cheerfully played a subordinate (but key) role and remained not only loyal but of enormous help to his older brother.

The brothers needed all such strength to accomplish their self-appointed task. The territory called the Rif, an area about the size of Massachusetts, contained eighteen major tribes, divided and subdivided into several dozen, a bewildering complex whose jealous chieftains, some of whom covertly dealt with the Spanish, had to be alternately threatened and cosseted for support. In the formative days, money and arms constituted perennial problems. Building a regular army was out of the question. Instead, the tribes slowly accumulated rifles and bullets, either by barter from Spanish soldiers (such was the demoralized state of the Spanish army) or smuggled in from Algeria or French Morocco. This painstaking effort finally resulted in several thousand armed but widely dispersed warriors. According to one authority, Abd-el-Krim's original cadre, or *harka*, numbered only 125 men, but this number quickly increased.[9]

Silvestre at first heard only rumors of this guerrilla force. His attitude is best judged by his response at that time to Abd-el-Krim's warning for him to remain east of the Amerkan River. Silvestre told a friend: " . . . This man Abd el Krim is crazy. I'm not going to take seriously the threats of a little Berber *Caid* whom I had at my mercy a short while ago. His insolence merits a new punishment."[10] To Berenguer's word of caution, Silvestre replied, "I shall drink tea in Abd el Krim's house at Ajdir whether he wills it or not."[11]

In May 1921, Silvestre pushed a detachment across the Amerkan with orders to establish an outpost on the hill of Abarran. But now native auxiliaries, the Regulares, mutinied, and, together with local

MOROCCO
1919-1926
• Towns and Cities

M.E.P.

tribesmen, fell on the Spanish force, killing 179 out of 250. Other Rifian guerrillas attacked the Spanish base at Sidi Driss, inflicted about a hundred casualties, and disappeared.

These opening strikes caused fierce argument between Silvestre and the high commissioner, Berenguer, who wanted his military commander to backtrack. Silvestre instead continued to expand by building a new outpost three miles south of a small fort at Anual. When the enemy failed to contest this work, Berenguer's immediate panic subsided, but Abd-el-Krim's guerrillas soon struck again, this time an attack in force against the new outpost at Ighriben followed by attacks two days later against Anual. Ighriben quickly fell, as much from a water shortage as enemy fire. An alarmed Silvestre meanwhile hurried to the Anual base. Several factors, including an ammunition shortage, caused him to order a retreat on the following day. With this, all discipline vanished, the retreat becoming a rout with few survivors. Hatred of the past caused shame of the present: guerrillas fell on small groups of Spanish soldiers, jabbed and slashed bodies with knives and bayonets, gouged out eyes, cut off genitals and jammed them in the victim's mouth, ran stakes through helpless bodies. Silvestre disappeared, presumably tortured and killed.

The initial victories brought whole tribes to the Rifian banner. Guerrillas continued to strike luckless garrisons, sending survivors panic-stricken to Melilla. Here and there, senior officers corralled these hordes to make last-ditch stands, but the poor location of most of the posts, usually remote from adequate water supply and lacking ammu-

268

nition and medical services, turned these makeshift positions into scenes of carnage that would have taxed the experienced talent of Goya to portray. In less than a month, guerrillas were fighting in the outskirts of Melilla.

But now Abd-el-Krim called off the attack. Authorities differ as to the reason. Furneaux argued that Abd-el-Krim wanted to avoid a bloody orgy of townspeople, which he realized would cost him international sympathy; Woolman argued that other factors such as lack of cannon and demands of the imminent harvest influenced the decision, " . . . one of Abd el Krim's very few major errors, for with its [Melilla] possession or destruction he might have gained the time to create a Rifian state strong enough to defy Spain—and if he had, the course of history would have been very different."[12]

Abd-el-Krim could still claim a fantastic victory. In a few weeks, his guerrillas had eliminated Spanish presence in the Rif in " . . . the greatest military disaster suffered by a colonial power for twenty-five years, since the Abyssinians had destroyed an Italian army at Adowa."[13] The Spanish army admitted to over thirteen thousand battle deaths; the true figure probably approached nineteen thousand. The Spanish lost nineteen thousand rifles, several hundred machine guns and cannon, and over one thousand prisoners who were later ransomed for fat prices.[14]

Berenguer reacted by recalling his own expeditionary force and sending massive reinforcements to Melilla, an effort spearheaded by the recently formed Tercio. Though badly shaken, the Spanish Government sent Berenguer new troop levies, reinforced with armored cars and airplanes. By 1922, the high commissioner disposed of some 150,000 troops, but as Woolman has pointed out, Spanish policy perforce had changed " . . . from one of outright conquest to the far less ambitious one of limited occupation and political control through bribery of certain caids and chiefs."[15]

Increased numbers allowed Berenguer to occupy major towns and to encircle once again the wily Raisuli. Berenguer's successor, General Ricardo Burguete, who took over in mid-1922, chose to make a deal with this powerful leader by buying his "retirement" (at a monthly subsidy of twelve thousand dollars) in order to free troops from the Jibala area.

In the East, the army reoccupied much of the territory evacuated after the Anual disaster, but as they moved into mountain country, progress slowed and then stopped. Spanish troop reinforcements proved virtually useless in fighting guerrillas, which left the lion's share to the Tercio and Regulares, both outfits suffering a high proportion of casualties. Moreover, the Rifians were growing sophisticated. One group used a captured cannon to sink a Spanish warship in Alhucemas Bay;

another band attacked and destroyed a force of armored cars. When Burguete pushed forward to Tizzi Azar as a preliminary move to an all-out offensive, Abd-el-Krim's guerrillas fell on the outpost, a bloody action costing the Spanish about two thousand casualties and decisively ending their offensive plans.

Burguete instead decided on a blockade punctuated by naval bombardment. This punitive action failed, because villagers moved inland, nor did the blockade prevent money and arms reaching guerrillas from Tangier—Vincent Sheean has described the relative ease of traveling back and forth either by sea or land.[16]

This series of military failures widened the internal political rift that had long been developing in Spain between Africanistas, who demanded Spanish conquest of Morocco, and Abandonistas, an increasingly powerful group which wanted total withdrawal from the colony. The Abandonistas now won an important round by forcing Burguete's recall in favor of a civilian high commissioner but neither this man nor another civilian successor could solve the "Moroccan question."

Spanish ineptitude and dissension contributed to the growth of Abd-el-Krim's ambitions. Early in 1923, he took the title of emir, or prince, of the Rif, and in June attacked the key position of Tizzi Azar—again held by the enemy—a failure that cost him heavy casualties and, incidentally, led to Franco's taking command of the Tercio.

The ensuing stalemate brought the Rifian Government to the conference table, in the bowels of a Spanish ship off the coast of Morocco. Since Abd-el-Krim wanted total Spanish withdrawal, and since the Spanish offered " . . . a kind of independence—economic and administrative—to the Rifian tribes," the talks came to nought.[17] Instead, the Spanish began to fortify the "Silvestre Line" in depth. Abd-el-Krim responded by attacking a Spanish convoy, another costly tactical failure. This seesaw state of affairs was working in Abd-el-Krim's favor. The war was costing Spain some £20 million a year and was causing virtual anarchy on the mainland where at Barcelona a regiment destined for Morocco mutinied in protest. And now, in late summer of 1923, Primo de Rivera, an army general and politician of extensive experience at home and abroad, brought off a bloodless coup to establish himself as dictator of Spain.

A large man of keen wit and robust physical appetites—he was to die in Paris, " . . . his last hours divided between brothel and confessional,"[18]—Primo de Rivera at fifty-three years held a charismatic appeal that made him many things to many people. Reputedly an Abandonista regarding Morocco, he had been brought to power by a group of royalist generals. Soon after taking over, he announced withdrawal plans, which caused Marshal Lyautey, nervously looking on from French Morocco, to exclaim: "My God! An army retreats when it must but it does not announce the fact to the enemy in advance."[19]

Once in office, however, Rivera fell under army influence: " . . . his military policy changed from one of outright disengagement in Morocco to one of aggression. . . . The new dictator promised "a quick, dignified, and sensible" solution to the Moroccan problem."[20]

Hollow words, these: Raisuli, in the Jibala, was becoming increasingly demanding in his "retirement," while, in the East, Abd-el-Krim continued to ride a wave of local and international popularity. As underdog biting the heel of Spanish colonialism, he attracted world-wide sympathy, particularly from nationalist leaders in other colonial countries, but also from French Communists; he probably received financial aid from British and German mining interests as well.

His power easily allowed him to retain initiative in the Rif and to extend operations into Jibala territory, his brother Mhamed being increasingly active in this area. The Spanish also helped him win new tribes by an inane policy of bombing villages populated mostly by women and children.[21] To the Spanish claim that airmen dropped preliminary warning leaflets in Arabic and Thamazighth, Woolman has evidenced the telling point that most tribesmen were illiterate!

So successful were the guerrilla operations, that Abd-el-Krim continued attacking throughout the summer, his total impact such that several Spanish outposts owned no more than the ground enclosed by wire. The entire picture so distressed Rivera that after an inspection tour in 1924 he declared, " . . . Spain cannot continue to maintain her soldiers on isolated crags."[22] Coming full circle in thought, he announced withdrawal to a fortified line, telling an American correspondent:

> . . . Abd el Krim has defeated us. He has the immense advantages of the terrain and a fanatical following. Our troops are sick of war, and they have been for years. They don't see why they should fight and die for a strip of worthless territory. I am withdrawing to this line, and will hold only the tip of this territory. I personally am in favor of withdrawing entirely from Africa and letting Abd el Krim have it. We have spent untold millions of pesetas in this enterprise, and never made a *céntimo* from it. We have had tens of thousands of men killed for territory which is not worth having. But we cannot entirely withdraw, because England will not let us. . . . England fears that if we withdraw, the territory will be taken by France. . . . They don't want a strong power like France here![23]

Contrary to the Spanish dictator's belief, England presented less of an obstacle to withdrawal than his own army, particularly fanatic Africanistas spearheaded by the Tercio. Only when Franco threatened to resign command of the foreign legion did Rivera modify his plans: a compromise that in the West placed the one-hundred-thousand-man army behind a fortified "Primo Line," the idea being to strengthen and reorganize units into a new striking force. Grudgingly accepted by the army, various withdrawals of outer posts began in September and were carried out under almost constant harassment by guerrillas. This effort culminated in evacuation of the important base of Chaouen, a forty-mile anabasis beginning in November and ending a month later at Tetuan, *the Rifians having pursued the rear guard, Franco's Tercio, to the city gates.* Rifian casualties were never published. Spanish dead numbered an estimated eight hundred officers and seventeen thousand men—some authorities say more.[24] The words of a Spanish officer survivor form a fitting epitaph: " . . . We made war against shadows, and we lost thirty men to their one!"[25]

For the time being, the Spanish army in the West was safe behind the "Primo Line": " . . . a series of typical blockhouses about a quarter of a mile apart, each built on dominating ground wherever possible and equipped with strong searchlights. The spaces between the blockhouses, particularly around Tangier, were usually mined."[26] All this did not much impress the American correspondent Vincent Sheean: After a lengthy stay with rebel hosts, he was ushered quite easily through the line at night.

Abd-el-Krim's primary problem was not the Spanish army; it was those European powers that did not want an independent Moroccan state. His several overtures to the British to help him remove the Spanish presence were brushed aside; the British, after all, governed an enormous colonial empire and frowned on any trend toward self-government. Spain would not acquiesce, not only because Primo de Rivera was staking his political reputation on favorable settlement of the Moroccan question, but also because the government thought that Spain's international prestige rested on a favorable settlement.

Far more important, however, was the attitude of France, to whom the thought of an independent Moroccan state was particularly abhorrent. France had been having her own troubles with rebellious tribes in French Morocco. In 1924, France did not wish to test her strength in the rest of Morocco and in Tunis and Algeria. An independent Moroccan state would automatically void the sultan's over-all authority—and that, in colonial administrative minds, would begin the end. Thus a political paradox emerged: Although Abd-el-Krim remained respectful of French military power and did not wish to antagonize France, his success in the North automatically brought him into conflict with his powerful colonial neighbor. When his expansion sloshed over into French Morocco, the French began to build a *casus belli*.

Already in 1924, Lyautey had crossed the Wergha River to create a northern front under the able General Chambrun, a line of intersupporting posts, backed by aircraft, that constituted a direct challenge to Rifian control of the disputed area. If Lyautey displayed some concern over the strength of the "Wergha Line," higher echelons refused to accept his pessimism, even denying his request for additional troops.[27] The French Minister of Foreign Affairs, Aristide Briand, expressed comfortable arrogance to an American correspondent: " . . . You have seen the great Abd el Krim. These native chiefs . . . we know them well. They are really simple fellows. Properly handled, they respond to kindness. There is, of course, not the slightest chance that this one will ever attack us."[28]

Lack of military strength formed Abd-el-Krim's second major problem. His army was strong enough to contain the Spanish in two coastal enclaves, but not to drive them out of Spanish Morocco and certainly not to fight the French at the same time. He would never command a stronger army than that of 1925, but, out of a total force estimated variously at 80–120,000, he commanded perhaps a maximum 10,000 riflemen augmented by a pathetically small artillery unit of some 350 gunners. Although his combat areas featured strategically located supply dumps and were connected by a primitive telephone system, his army remained primitive in the extreme.

Neither did his political organization represent any great achievement. Despite a political "cabinet" of mostly young and keen revolutionaries, Abd-el-Krim remained a dictator whose respect for republican institutions he claimed to admire diminished as his responsibilities increased. His command of the diverse northern tribes was never too secure, and it is problematical that he ever could have forged the cohesive state he talked about—any more than Feisal could have melded Syrian tribes into a viable political entity in 1918.

His conflict with France centered on control of a border tribe, the Beni Zerwal. When this tribe opted for war against France, the Rifians were forced to a decision. Woolman marks this in the early months of 1925:

> . . . Provoked by French depredations, worried about his food supply, goaded by questions of honor and prestige, and lured on by his own over-confident advisers, Abd el Krim was drawn into the fatal decision to attack the French. . . . Fear and desperation must have been the deciding factors.[29]

The rebels attacked in April, their goal the major French base at Fez. Its capture, they believed, would force France to a reasonable settlement in the North. Abd-el-Krim's brother, Mhamed, commanded the operation, which involved an estimated four thousand tribesmen, with another four thousand in reserve. The dispersed attacks caught the French by surprise. Rebel units tore through Chambrun's careful defenses and, in a few days, advanced to a line some twenty miles north of Fez. Supported by certain border tribes the French had expected to remain loyal, the rebels within a month wiped out northern French garrisons. Many fought literally to the last man:

> ... By the end of June, the Rifians had taken forty-three of sixty-six French posts. They had captured an estimated 51 cannon, 200 machine guns, 5,000 rifles, millions of cartridges, 16,000 shells for cannon, 60,000 grenades, and 35 mortars with 10,000 shells. They had carried off at least seventy Frenchmen and 2,000 mercenaries as prisoners, and no one cared to report publicly how many French troops had been killed and wounded.[30]

On the surface, this represented a fantastic victory. In reality, it amounted to a painful sting, though of sufficient dimensions to bring a combined Franco-Spanish peace offer: a guarantee of Rifian autonomy, but no Rifian state. Abd-el-Krim turned it down.

He probably erred. Lack of army organization and supply difficulties, not to mention tenacious resistance of the enemy, already were robbing him of momentum. He suffered a political setback from refusal of important tribes north of Fez to come over to him. And now French strength began to tell. Lyautey was relieved as military commander in favor of the able General Naulin. Marshal Pétain, the hero of World War I, inspected the entire front, his report causing Paris to dispatch one hundred thousand more troops. Meanwhile, French military commanders conferred with Spanish opposites to come up with a combined quasi-pincer operation: the French to drive north into the Rif, the Spanish to pull off a large-scale amphibious landing at Alhucemas Bay and drive in to Abd-el-Krim's headquarters at Ajdir.

The Spanish landing began on September 7. The following day, the first assault waves, men of the Tercio under Franco, set up a beachhead rapidly expanded to eight thousand troops including artillery, a force soon raised to twelve thousand. Despite Spanish air bombing and strafing, artillery fire and use of poison gas, the Rifians continued to resist the Spanish advance practically yard by yard. Rifian determination, coupled with the terrain, held the Spanish to small gains—an average four hundred yards per day at heavy cost in lives, but nonetheless the invaders pushed through to Ajdir, the Rifians retiring south. Farther east, another Spanish force pushed inland and, in October, joined a French column coming from the south.

Although the campaigns cost the Spanish and French heavily, by November French numbers had risen to over 300,000, Spanish numbers to 140,000 with reinforcements constantly arriving. The Rifians also had suffered heavy casualties—losses compounded by poor harvests and large areas of scorched earth. Typhus now scourged the sad, hungry tribes. Desultory winter operations further weakened Abd-el-Krim's army, for if guerrilla bands struck successfully here and there, he could not prevent the Franco-Spanish build-up from continuing, nor could he alleviate constantly increasing tribulations of diverse tribes. Wanting also to take advantage of favorable public opinion in France and Spain (and other Western nations) to his cause, he bowed to the inevitable and asked for peace talks. Grudgingly the Spanish and French governments agreed to a conference at Ujda in April.

Abd-el-Krim's hopes for a reasonable peace were almost immediately dashed by increased European arrogance, not unnaturally, since the powers were negotiating from a military strength of about forty to one. While talks dragged on, French and Spanish army commanders shuffled troops for a final offensive. When the talks halted in early May, the temporary allies struck, their armies within the month overrunning most organized resistance in the central Rif. In late May 1926, Abd-el-Krim surrendered to the French. To the fury of the Spanish, he was exiled to the island of Réunion, in the Indian Ocean, given a comfortable estate and a generous annual subsidy—altogether a fortunate end, since capture by the Spanish undoubtedly would have meant execution.

Abd-el-Krim's exile did not end the campaign, which continued into 1927, with sporadic resistance up to 1934. But these were relatively minor actions, and Spain, by the end of 1926, could claim "victory."

"Victory" left Spain exhausted, sick in mind and spirit, a giant, disjointed body increasingly prone to disastrous factionalism and internal strife. Rivera's attempts to repair political and economic deficiencies proved fruitless. With dissolution of his dictatorship, in January 1930, a power vacuum developed. King Alfonso's failure to fill it led to his self-imposed exile in 1931 and to the ill-fated Second Republic, with its equally ill-fated liberal constitution.

This was part of the price of "victory" in Morocco. It would result in catastrophic civil war in less than five years.

CHAPTER TWENTY-TWO

1. Woolman, 36. See also, Bertrand and Petrie.
2. Woolman, 64–5.
3. Barea. Corporal Barea was undoubtedly prejudiced against the regular army, but his criticism in general is variously confirmed in other contemporary accounts and by later, serious commentators. See also, Furneaux, 50, who noted, for example, that " . . . in 1920 the [Spanish] army's strength stood at 100,000 men and 12,000 officers, a disproportionate number whose ranks were headed by 690 generals and 2,000 colonels."

4. Woolman, 72.
5. Ibid., 67–8.
6. Ibid., 68.
7. Ibid., 86.
8. Sheean, for this background. See also, Sheean, 97: At great personal risk, this American newspaper correspondent twice visited Rif country. On the first occasion, he was impressed by a group of tribal chiefs " . . . who spoke of the glory of Abd el-Krim, the splendor of his victories over the Spaniards, the certainty with which those who fought for Abd el-Krim would go to heaven and all others to hell . . . "; Ibid., 140: On the second occasion, when the Rifian bloom of victory was wearing off, Sheean wrote in his notebook of Abd-el-Krim: " . . . his courage is magnificent. His ideas have not changed, have even been reinforced by the present danger. From what I saw of him today I knew that I had no idea of him before. He has a grandeur, added to by the circumstances of horror and great danger. But in spite of this he is humorous, funny . . . "
9. Furneaux, 58.
10. Woolman, 88.
11. Furneaux, 67.
12. Woolman, 95.
13. Furneaux, 76.
14. Ibid., 74: Abd-el-Krim used the ransom money to buy more arms.
15. Woolman, 104–5.
16. Sheean, 83–164.
17. Woolman, 115–18. The Spanish delegates called Abd-el-Krim's representative, Mohamed Azerkan, "Punto," because "as a boy he had cadged 'puntos'— cigarette butts—from the Spanish officers."
18. Thomas, *The Spanish Civil War*, 17.
19. Furneaux, 96.
20. Woolman, 124.
21. Furneaux, 116.
22. Ibid., 124–5.
23. Woolman, 131–2.
24. Furneaux, 132.
25. Woolman, 140.
26. Ibid., 141.
27. Usborne, 261–2.
28. Woolman, 175.
29. Ibid., 172. See also, Furneaux, 24, who points out that Abd-el-Krim attained unity " . . . by the employment of the powerful shame compulsion, the *aar*," which caused tribes to forgo feuds in favor of a common cause. The protective alliance, or *liff*, spread throughout the Rif and finally reached the southern tribes whose call for help against the French could not be ignored—thus, Furneaux implies, Abd-el-Krim was hoist with his own political petard.
30. Woolman, 135.

CHAPTER 23

SPAIN AND FRANCE were not the only great powers that had to fight guerrilla actions in the years following World War I. Uprisings and rebellions broke out in most colonial areas—even the United States became embroiled with guerrillas in the New World.

In occupying and policing mandated portions of the old Ottoman Empire, the British began to rely on air power. World War I had brought birth of the Royal Air Force (RAF), whose leader, Hugh "Boom" Trenchard, was a man of imagination, force and political shrewdness. Part of Trenchard's postwar task, a large part, was to justify RAF existence, not an easy job in view of innate hostility forcibly expressed (and often demonstrated) by army and navy, and in view of still unproven virtues of the relatively new weapon.[1]

Trenchard used any occasion to demonstrate air power's versatility. Of twenty-five operational squadrons, he based nineteen overseas, where they performed a wide variety of both peace-keeping and house-keeping tasks. In early 1920, he scored a significant success when RAF planes intimidated the Mad Mullah and helped end his rebellion in Somaliland. The RAF's main chance came a few months later, when a small uprising in Mesopotamia (today's Iraq) caught fire and spread despite suppression efforts by some sixty thousand British troops. (See map, Chapter 16.) Worried by political implications of the widening conflict, Britain's new Secretary of State for Colonies, Winston Churchill, sought Trenchard's help. The Chief of the Air Staff turned to with a will: Once again, the bomber worked magical effect against recalcitrant tribes and helped bring peace, though only after British forces had suffered some two thousand casualties and Whitehall had spent about £100 million.[2]

The total experience led Trenchard to argue for a new RAF mission, that of substituting air for ground power in keeping the king's peace in vast Middle Eastern reaches. Trenchard and his fellows contended that, in suitable operational areas, what they called Air Control would prove more effective than Ground Control. One of air power's most effective voices, Marshal of the RAF Sir John Slessor (who was very active as a young flier in those early days and whose arguments gained great strength from an innate charm and intelligence evident to all fortunate enough to have known him), later wrote in his excellent book *The Central Blue:*

> ... The Ground Method ... involves invasion by a column on the ground, sometimes permanent but more often temporary, of his territory.... The trouble was that the areas of undeveloped tribal territory within the Empire or on the fringes of British-administered territory were in those days so vast that occupation could not be complete. So the Ground Method really boiled down to one of temporary and partial occupation, with the establishment of garrisons at suitable places whence more or less mobile columns could be despatched into the tribal areas when necessity arose.
>
> The job of these columns was to occupy temporarily the country of the offending tribe; if possible to inflict a sharp lesson in the form of casualties to their fighting men; to exact the necessary retribution in the form of fines or rifles surrendered or by destroying property or crops, and then withdraw. It was fatal to leave small detachments of troops unsupported in potentially hostile territory—for instance the overrunning of the little garrison of Rumaitha in the Iraq rebellion of 1919 increased the number of insurgents against us from 85,000 to over 130,000 in one night. That meant that even when we had garrisons right in the heart of tribal territory they had to live in one central strongly fortified cantonment—as at Razmak. When there was some tribal affair which had to be dealt with then, having dealt with it, the column still had to withdraw behind the wire into cantonments. It was always the Air Staff contention that this method, known unkindly by its critics as "Burn and Scuttle" or "Butcher and Bolt" was very expensive and did not in fact achieve the object of maintaining order in these remote and inhospitable lands.[3]

Trenchard and his staff argued that air power by its mobility and fire potential could not only reach remote tribal areas immediately but that it could coerce far more humanely and at much less cost than ground power, though control of more developed areas such as Palestine would require ground operations. Their general idea was to conduct gunboat diplomacy from the air. Lawless tribes would be warned and, if failing to come to heel, would be punished—their villages bombed and herds dispersed—until they changed their minds. By reacting selectively to tribal disturbances, Air Control would reduce the expense and unfavorable publicity attendant upon raising a punitive ground expedition. Slessor saw it as a sort of "inverted blockade" that kept the enemy from his country in order to win his submission without inflicting human casualties and with minimum material damage. In the words of the old RAF manual, it was to interrupt " . . . the normal life of the enemy people to such an extent that a continuance of hostilities becomes intolerable."[4]

These arguments greatly impressed Winston Churchill. Mesopotamia's fragile peace depended in part on Emir Feisal, who became king in late 1921. Wanting to prop up a weak throne at minimum expense, Churchill embraced the concept of Air Control which did not immediately leave the ground. The army did its best to sabotage the operation—when it refused to furnish troops, Trenchard organized his own ground forces, including armored-car units. The effort encountered other delays and some operational difficulties, not to mention an early misunderstanding as to punishment of recalcitrant tribes.

Shortly after operations had commenced, Trenchard instructed his Middle East commander, Geoffrey Salmond:

> . . . The air force is a preventative against risings more than a means of putting them down. Concentration is the first essential. Continuous demonstration is the second essential. And when punishment is intended, the punishment must be severe, continuous and even prolonged.

Trenchard insisted on numerous humane precautions, including leaflet warnings at least twenty-four hours before a raid. His biographer concluded that often a "demonstration" flight was enough to quell an uprising. One of Trenchard's and Churchill's principal arguments centered on RAF ability to mete out selective punishment. Trenchard's attitude was clear in an early letter written to a squadron commander in India who complained " . . . about the hazards of operational flying against turbulent tribesmen in the Himalayan foothills":

> . . . You state that it is impossible to see snipers. Nobody ever expected to see them and I should have thought this idea of looking for them ought to have been long since dead in India. . . . Indis-

criminate bombing should never be allowed. Surely this was dead five years ago.[5]

What the commander wants and what he gets are often different. Early in the Air Control experiment, some young political officers, wanting to make " . . . a special example . . . of an exceptionally unruly tribe," brought down winged wrath to the extent that the RAF report read:

> . . . The eight machines . . . broke formation and attacked at different points of the encampment simultaneously, causing a stampede among the animals. The tribesmen and their families were put to confusion, many of whom ran into the lake, making good targets for the machine-guns.[6]

The report brought a sizzling rocket from Churchill to Trenchard:

> . . . I am extremely shocked. . . . If it were to be published it would be regarded as most dishonoring to the air force and prejudicial to our work and use of them. To fire wilfully on women and children is a disgraceful act, and I am surprised you do not order the officers responsible for it to be tried by court-martial. . . . By doing such things we put ourselves on the lowest level.[7]

This early aberration aside, subsequent results more than pleased most concerned persons. The deterrent effect generally sufficed to keep the peace. Where eighty battalions initially kept the peace in Mesopotamia and Palestine, three battalions eventually remained in Mesopotamia, a tremendous financial saving.

Other benefits resulted. We should remember that air power was in its infancy—Charles Lindbergh did not fly the Atlantic until 1927. Flying over trackless deserts and daily contact with frontier defense forces and political officers proved invaluable experience to future commanders. More than this, however, the need to patrol desert areas meant charting air routes, a time-consuming and frequently hazardous prelude that was nonetheless essential to British interests in the air age. The day's primitive machines, courageously flown in the most appalling extremes of weather with minimum navigational aids, foretold many future possibilities. The RAF carried mail, passengers, and supply; the planes helped centralize administration and they delivered civil officers to remote areas when necessary; they evacuated sick and wounded; in 1928, they flew over the Hindu Kush (familiar to Alexander the Great twenty-three centuries earlier) to evacuate the beleaguered British colony at Kabul. (See map 1, Chapter 7.)

A cost-conscious British Government judged Air Control operations so successful that it extended the plan to cover the Northwest Frontier of India, Trans-Jordan, the Aden protectorate, and, in a modified form, Palestine.

The concept of Air Control suffered from two major difficulties: it inherited the onus of enforcing a colonial policy that was becoming increasingly less acceptable to world (including British) opinion; and it proved of limited application.

More liberal minds of the period held that the sole justification for British control of Mesopotamia and ancillary territories—indeed, for British and great-power control of *any* area—was to bring more benefit than harm to the peoples concerned. Here as elsewhere in the British Empire, the overlords unquestionably improved the lot of some of these peoples. Introducing law and order of sorts in place of constant raids and small tribal wars was a major contribution, as was introduction in some areas of schools, hospitals and reasonably efficient administration.

This was fine—as far as it went. It could even have been noble, had Britain been prepared to invest time, effort, and money essential to preparing these peoples for eventual self-government. No such intention existed. Rather, it was colonialism on the cheap. All great powers practiced it, America included. It was exploitive in the worst sense—it was maintaining a primitive status quo in order to ease commercial exploitation of natural commodities, in this case primarily oil.

Within this framework, neither Air Control nor Ground Control could serve other than a holding, or deterrent, function. British rule was by force and coercion rather than consent, and when that force found physical expression, either by punitive columns or air-delivered bullets and bombs, it was rule by terror—more selective terror than employed by ground columns, as Sir John Slessor argued, but nonetheless terror, as anyone knows who has had his house or town or city or fox-hole bombed. The British were ruling, in short, without the consent of the governed, and so long as this was the case, the instrument of rule did not much matter in the end: coercive rule builds and expands antagonisms into forces of rebellion which eventually explode. Like Ground Control before it, Air Control inhibited but did not stop native political ambitions. It helped produce short-term gains for long-term losses.

The second point is the limited application of Air Control. The psychological effect of air power—remember that the natives had never seen an airplane—played a major role in the new concept. When demonstration failed to keep the peace, we have noted that the RAF stepped up pressure by political or diplomatic warning, and if that failed, by overt punishment " . . . severe, continuous and even prolonged." We are told that in practice this meant bombing a village (after due warning) and dispersing a flock—economic pressure, in other words, which usually did the job.

Two observations follow: such pressure could be applied only in compatible environment, preferably desert, and such pressure proved effective only against fragmented tribal society, either nomadic or primitive agrarian. Air Control could not work in more developed countries, such as Palestine, a limitation readily admitted by Slessor.

But what Sir John and other proponents failed to consider is the rationale behind the concept of Air Control. Deterrence all too often is a euphemism for blackmail by force. What if a person or tribe or country refuses to be blackmailed? In the case of the Middle East, what would have happened had deterrence, warning, and physical punishment failed to bring around a tribe? Logically, the RAF would have had to continue punishment until the tribe no longer was capable of resistance. But this contradicts the principle of selective, or "humane," application of punishment, forwarded by air-power proponents, for if bombing one village and dispersing one herd do not work, then presumably punishment must embrace two villages and two herds and so on. This is the genesis of escalation, a subject we shall come to much later in this book. The point is that far from being selective in face of genuine resistance, Air Control would have had to resort to destroying villages and herds and starving people into submission. Carried to its logical conclusion, this is genocide.

British army leaders never accepted the validity of the Air Control concept, in part because it threatened army pre-eminence, in part because application was so limited. Throughout the 1920s and early 1930s, empire forces faced a number of rebellions and small wars, several of which were analyzed in a book published in 1934: *Imperial Policing*, by Major General Sir Charles Gwynn.

An army's police duties, Sir Charles argued, fell into three categories. The first was to fight small wars in order to establish or reestablish civil control (a subject brilliantly treated a half century earlier by another British officer, Charles Callwell—see Chapter 12). The second was to maintain or restore order when normal civil control either does not exist or has temporarily broken down. The third was to assist civil control without assuming governmental responsibility. Such was the advanced state of empire that the second task had now replaced the first in importance:

> . . . The principal police task of the Army is no longer to prepare the way for civil control, but to restore it when it collapses or

shows signs of collapse. Subversive movements take many forms and are of varying intensity; but even when armed rebellion occurs, it presents a very different military problem from that of a deliberate small-war campaign. There is an absence of a definite objective, and conditions are those of guerrilla warfare, in which elusive rebel bands must be hunted down, and protective measures are needed to deprive them of opportunities. The admixture of rebels with a neutral or loyal element of the population adds to the difficulties of the task. Excessive severity may antagonize this element, add to the number of rebels, and leave a lasting feeling of resentment and bitterness. On the other hand, the power and resolution of the Government forces must be displayed. Anything which can be interpreted as weakness encourages those who are sitting on the fence to keep on good terms with the rebels.[8]

The British army was facing three main classes of disorder. One was the revolutionary movement " . . . organized and designed to upset established government." Another was rioting or other lawbreaking " . . . arising from local or widespread grievances." A third was communal disturbances " . . . of a racial, religious or political character not directed against Government, but which Government must suppress." The first category particularly interested Sir Charles, who presciently observed:

> . . . Revolutionary movements, again, may be divided into violent and, professedly, non-violent movements. The former may be on a scale which amounts to fully organized rebellion, necessitating operations in which the Government forces employ all the ordinary methods of warfare. More commonly, however, they imply guerrilla warfare, carried on by armed bands acting possibly under the instructions of a centralized organization, but with little cohesion. Such bands depend for effectiveness on the capacity of individual leaders; they avoid collisions of a decisive character with Government troops. Their aim is to show defiance of Government, to make its machinery unworkable and to prove its impotence; hoping by a process of attrition to wear down its determination. Their actions take the form of sabotage, of ambushes in which they can inflict loss with a minimum of risk, and attacks on small isolated detachments. By terrorizing the loyal or neutral elements of the population, they seek to prove the powerlessness of the Government to give protection, and thus provide for their own security, depriving the Government of sources of information and securing information themselves.
>
> The suppression of such movements, unless nipped in the bud, is a slow business, generally necessitating the employment of numbers out of all proportion to the actual fighting value of the rebels, owing to the unavoidable dispersion of troops and the absence of a definite objective. It becomes a battle of wits in which the de-

velopment of a well-organized intelligence service, great mobility, rapid means of inter-communication and close cooperation between all sections of the Government forces are essential.[9]

Normal military operations did not suffice to meet these challenges. The military police task differed fundamentally from normal, or orthodox, operations in that it had to achieve its object with *minimum* exercise of force. Training for such operations is therefore a difficult task, the author made clear in a series of chapter analyses beginning with the Amritsar riots of 1919 (see map 1, Chapter 7), which resulted from Mahatma Gandhi's arrest, which were ineptly controlled due to overreaction on the part of security forces, and which killed a great number of people. A more intelligent application of force, however, resulted in satisfactory suppression of an ugly riot situation in Egypt in the same year.

The Moplah rebellion of 1921 in the Madras District of India was one of the most instructive from the guerrilla-warfare standpoint. This was a religion-based uprising; almost immediately, a British army force using orthodox tactics " . . . broke the center of the rebellion" and arrested a principal leader, Ali Musaliar. This prompt action " . . . eliminated the chief military objective" without ending the rebellion. But now the Madras government and its security forces stood still. Both civil and military officials interpreted an ensuing lull as rebel weakness. Instead of firm, positive action including rapid trial and sentencing of rebel leaders, authorities adopted a vacillating attitude, the Indian Government forbidding courts-martial of rebels (one result of the Amritsar debacle).

Moplah rebels meanwhile were organizing for further action. They were not well armed, and although they enjoyed protective terrain they lacked outside reinforcement (no Communist element was involved). Their object was to wage guerrilla warfare: not to fight the army, but " . . . rather to prove the impotence of Government" by sabotage and selective terror against Hindus. Incidents soon developed. By October, the situation had deteriorated to the degree that the government was reporting to London that the rebels, numbering eight to ten thousand, were ambushing and sniping at government troops whose movements were reported by "spies everywhere."[10]

London responded by sending more troops. At this point, security forces had been operating by patrols based on various village centers, but now more extensive operations began, including at least one massive "drive" that failed. By early December, security forces had broken up the larger bands. To run smaller groups to ground now became the task of separate battalions assigned to specific areas. Simultaneously, security forces gradually transferred control to police and civil authorities and phased out altogether at the end of February. The tally was impressive: 2,300 rebels killed, 1,650 wounded, and 5,700 captured. Security forces claimed 39,000 "voluntary surrenders." The number of civil deaths caused by rebel terrorist acts was unknown but high. Troop casualties numbered 137![11]

In analyzing the action, Sir Charles noted that the original rebellion had evolved into a small war,

> ... that is to say, that the troops were called on to act with the maximum force they could develop under the conditions imposed by the terrain and the methods adopted by the enemy.
>
> There was, however, no strategic objective the capture of which would decisively affect the enemy's operations, and the will of the Government could be imposed on the enemy only by a process of attrition and exhaustion, the result of a continuous unrelenting pressure.
>
> Although in the nature of a small war, it may be noted that it opened with a purely police operation in aid of which a small detachment only of troops was called in. Similarly, it was left to the police to sweep up the last fragments of resistance when the troops had sufficiently restored order to permit the civil power to resume control. The military intervention, although it involved war-like operations, was in essence, therefore, police work on a large scale.[12]

Sir Charles believed that the government's major error lay in limiting military powers under martial law, which hindered security forces in preventing neutrals from helping the rebels. He also pointed to a language difficulty which made troops dependent on police intelligence. Operations depended primarily on infantry, although on occasion trucks gave extra mobility and armored cars effectively patrolled roads. Artillery played almost no role and air power none.

America meanwhile was involved with guerrilla warfare in attempting to pacify certain Caribbean and Central American countries. Almost perpetual revolution and troublesome banditry plagued most of these tiny places, and, in the first two decades of the century, American marines landed dozens of times, power demonstrations that often restored order either without shooting or with minimum force.

Although marines had brought peace of sorts to Santo Domingo by the end of World War I, trouble continued to break out. In 1919, a marine infantry-air expeditionary force landed to try to suppress local guerrillas, particularly in the eastern part of the area. The bulk of action consisted of small patrols which in 1919 fought " . . . 50 major contacts

M.E.P.

and at least a hundred lesser skirmishes" at a cost of three marines killed and four wounded. Marine aircraft worked closely with these patrols, supplying information, flying in mail and supply, and evacuating sick and wounded. They also co-operated tactically, either strafing or bombing selected guerrilla targets. Marine pacification involved two main efforts. One was to organize and train a native constabulary, the Policía Nacional. Simultaneously the marine commander wanted to break up the most troublesome guerrilla bands. In the eastern district, the marines employed a device we shall encounter again:

> ... After blocking off bandit-infested areas, troops and *Guardias* rounded up virtually every male for a series of mass line-ups in which carefully hidden informers picked out known bandits. After five months of the "cordon system," nine successful roundups had been carried out, and more than 600 courtroom convictions for banditry resulted. Following this crackdown, the cordons were discontinued because of the resentment aroused by such methods among those who were innocent.

The Americans also declared an amnesty period in which guerrillas could surrender without prejudice. They also formed and trained " ... five special anti-bandit groups ... from among Dominicans who had suffered at bandit hands." By spring of 1922, the country was reasonably quiet, and, in 1924, the American Government withdrew the last of its forces.[13]

286

A few years later, another marine infantry-air task force landed in Nicaragua to prevent a revolution. President Calvin Coolidge sent a personal representative, Henry L. Stimson, to mediate between rival political parties. Stimson found a military deadlock and a country tired of civil war. He recommended the " . . . gradual political education of Nicaraguans in self-government through free elections" supervised by United States Marines. Marines would disarm both armies and maintain internal order while training a Nicaraguan constabulary to take over the policing task. Leaders of both parties accepted this solution, which unfortunately involved two unfounded assumptions, both basic: that all Nicaraguans would embrace the principle of free elections as a satisfactory method of choosing leaders; that the presence of American marines would insure peace.[14]

Within two weeks of the Peace of Tipitapa, renegade bands began raiding towns to plague marine detachments posted about the country. The most serious challenge came from a former officer, Augusto César Sandino, who, instead of turning in his arms, vanished with some 150 followers into the remote mountains of his home province, Nueva Segovia.

Brigadier General Logan Feland, commanding the marines, started after Sandino almost at once. He garrisoned such northern towns as Ocotal, Telpaneca, Quilalí, and El Jícaro, which served as bases for aggressive patrolling intended first to disrupt rebel operations, next to defeat them entirely.

Sandino was riding quite high at this point. In July 1927, he attacked the Ocotal garrison of some thirty-seven marines and forty-seven guardias, but an air patrol spotted the fight and summoned help: that afternoon, five De Havillands peeled off smartly to plaster rebel positions with twenty-five-pound bombs and strafe them with machine-gun fire to kill fifty-six and wound an estimated one hundred guerrillas. The garrison lost one dead and five wounded. Two months later, Sandino attacked another garrison but was beaten off, again with heavy casualties.[15]

Despite Sandino's ability and willingness to attack fortified positions in strength, American officials refused to accept him as anything more than another bandit leader. The marines constantly underestimated his military strength and extent of civil following. Instead of reinforcing the marine effort, Washington recalled a regiment; simultaneously, the Nicaraguan Government assigned new Guardia Nacional units to more heavily populated areas.[16]

This was a mistake, because Sandino was much more than a bandit. A native Nicaraguan, he had fought with Pancho Villa in Mexico, where he subsequently worked, and caught the raging revolutionary fever. Along with tens of thousands of Nicaraguans, he deeply resented

American overlordship reflected in Nicaragua's political system, which primarily served local politicians and such North American commercial interests as United Fruit Company. He returned to Nicaragua determined to fight for independence despite American intervention. He had revolutionary connections in Mexico and Honduras (and later the United States), he had virtually an automatic following of disgruntled Nicaraguan peasants, and he held a good grasp of guerrilla tactics. He built a fortified mountain base, Chipote, not far from Honduras.

In locating and trying to eliminate this headquarters, marine patrols found themselves in considerable difficulty. Sandino's guerrillas had grown up in the country. They knew the jungle and the peasants, whom they used in a variety of ways, not hesitating to gain co-operation by selective terrorism when necessary. More than once, marine patrols walked into well-laid ambushes, which they survived, though not without casualties, only through disciplined fighting ability and timely support in some cases from aircraft.

Early reverses brought a fresh build-up in marine strength, and in January 1928, an infantry-air attack captured Sandino's base but netted only a few prisoners. Marine and guardia units now garrisoned more towns and stepped up patrolling, including night work. By mid-1928, Sandino had lost sixteen hundred men, who had turned themselves in under government amnesty (and who received ten dollars for each rifle).[17] But Sandino was patient, determined, wily, and intelligent. Despite shortage of arms, lack of money, generally poor lieutenants, and bad communications, he led marines a merry chase for more than five years.

The marines faced two major difficulties. One was the tactical environment, particularly the eastern area, where Sandino operated in "... swamp, jungle, banana plantations, mahogany forests, and occasional gold mines."[18] Getting Sandino meant sending patrols and expeditions, one after the other, through seemingly impenetrable terrain devoid of communications and any roads but an occasional trail where an ambush could await each turn. " ... In one [cavalry] march which kept us afield 31 days," wrote a veteran captain, "we actually marched 23 days with four night marches besides, and in my last long spell afield, we actually marched 39 out of 45 days from home."[19]

Local commanders lacked sufficient men, horses, mules, rations, and equipment. Intense heat, broken only by torrential downpours, filled jungle country with malaria-bearing mosquitoes and myriad ticks, which soon covered human flesh with festering, very painful sores. After marching for weeks under such conditions and usually falling into at least one ambush, an expedition such as Captain Edson's celebrated four-hundred-mile effort into the interior time and again would reach a reported enemy camp only to find it vacated. Such operations, however, kept Sandino disorganized while a viable Guardia Nacional was being trained and, in so doing, prevented him from disrupting national elections held in 1928, 1930 and 1932 (a brief spurt of democracy that soon yielded to military dictatorship). In 1929, guardia units commanded by marine officers and non-commissioned officers began replacing marine units, and in the following year took over most offensive duties, albeit with marine air support. After a brief time in Honduras, Sandino returned, now backed by left-wing groups in Mexico and the United States. The guardia, though not without faults, countered his new efforts. In early 1934, a year after marines had left Nicaragua, the guardia lured Sandino to Managua (some said the bait was a woman), where he was shot and killed.

Guerrillas played a peripheral but still interesting role in the Spanish civil war. As if in remembrance of things past, the war began with an army revolt in Morocco, at Melilla, where soldiers and members of the Civil Guard arrested all Republicans and Republican sympathizers and summarily executed the leaders. With the Nationalist flag hoisted, the rebellion spread the following day to the mainland. (See maps, Chapters 7 [Map 3] and 22.)

Lines were quite clearly drawn. The bulk of the army, about forty thousand men, sided with rebel officers, but these soldiers for the most part were two-year conscripts of more use for garrison than for combat purposes.[20] About two thirds of the Civil Guard, some twenty-two thousand men, opted with the rebels, as did about one thousand Assault Guards, fourteen thousand Carlist Requetés, fifty thousand Falangist irregulars, and thousands of volunteers. The rebel mainstay consisted of the Army of Africa, of which about sixteen thousand soldiers of the Tercio and Moroccan Regulares stood ready to come to the mainland under Franco's command.

About a third of the army, some twenty thousand scattered and ineffectual, conscript troops, remained loyal to the Republic. About two hundred officers remained loyal, including thirteen generals. Major military strength consisted of trade-union militias, including the paramilitary *Asaltos*, reinforced by bands of untrained and generally unarmed workers and peasants. Most of the navy remained loyal.

The first phase bore a certain resemblance to the 1808 uprisings against Napoleon's armies. In trying to defend legitimate government against regular army, Civil Guard, and paramilitary Falangist units, poorly armed and organized Republican forces relied primarily on guerrilla warfare—almost as if the Nationalists were a foreign invader. Anarchist, socialist, and Communist leaders begged the government to arm the workers; other voices called for a genuine people's war. In invoking the memory of 1808, the Communist leader Dolores Ibarruri, famous as La Pasionaria, broadcast a demand for " . . . resistance throughout the country, urging the women of Spain to fight with knives and burning oil, and ending with the slogan, 'It is better to die on your feet than to live on your knees! *No pasarán!*"*[21]

In these confused days, Spain became a mélange of confused battles. In the cities, regular-army garrisons attempted to overcome Republican forces and in places succeeded. In other cities, the Republicans held, their ragged units reinforced by angry workers or by peasants streaming in from the countryside, their weapons hoes and flails. In smaller cities and villages, hastily organized guerrilla bands of workers and peasants sometimes fell on surprised local garrisons, usually shooting the lot. This early fighting fitted the 1808 pattern and could have inspired a latter-day Goya to another *Dos de Mayo,* which depicts the revolt against Murat's soldiers, or to that other great canvas in the Prado which shows post-rebellion executions, or to any of the famous *Los Desastres* etchings. Extreme cruelty crowned these many executions and battles that in a month of fighting cost perhaps a hundred thousand Spanish lives and hundreds of thousands wounded.

The war quickly veered from the 1808 situation. Readers of Ernest Hemingway's classic novel *For Whom the Bell Tolls* will remember the old crone Pilar describing an initial uprising in her village.[22] After eliminating the army garrison, local guerrillas rounded up middle-class "fascist" citizenry, forced them to run a gauntlet of flails and finally flung them over a cliff to their deaths. Hemingway based this brutally dramatic scene on an uprising in the Andalusian town of Ronda, " . . .where 512 people were murdered in the first month of war."[23] Brutality aside, the significance lies in the temper of the Republicans, who were simultaneously defending Republican government against Fascist rebels while rebelling against middle-class liberal participation in that Republican government. In a more quiet way, Elliott Paul described the same ideological play in his account of the Nationalist conquest in Ibiza, *Life and Death of a Spanish Town,* but probably the best fictional account of the political turbulence, at least on the Republican side, is offered in André Malraux's *L'Espoir (Days of Hope*—an artistic *tour de force*).

Ideology soon spilled over borders. Germany and Italy vied in supplying rebels with arms and men; Republicans received weapons from Mexico and France, planes, tanks, and artillery from the Soviet Union and Comintern-recruited voluntary battalions. In short order, civil war assumed many conventional aspects. Communiqués began to speak of lines, offensives and counteroffensives planned by professional staffs and executed by divisions and brigades supported by aircraft, tanks,

---

* "They shall not pass"—the famous rallying cry of the French at Verdun in 1916.

and artillery. Armies of both sides expanded: the Nationalists to perhaps six hundred thousand, the Republicans slightly less. German pilots tested Douhet's theories of strategic bombing, eliminating the town of Guernica to determine psychological and economic effects of "carpet bombing" techniques. German advisers working with Nationalist armies realized the futility of committing armor in pinchpenny packets, a lesson that shortly would be applied in a bigger war.

Despite such conventional trappings, two factors make the war of interest for our purposes: one is the overtone of guerrilla warfare, the other the role played by Russian communism. Republican armies never did attain full growth, the result of a deficiency in arms and training but also the result of earlier guerrilla orientation. At outbreak of war, union militias lacked formal military training. Volunteers often trained on the way to the front; a fortunate few received an eight-day course in Madrid. The Fifth Regiment, which became famous in the Sierra fighting, started with two hundred survivors from earlier Madrid battles; by the end of August 1936, this regiment had fielded sixteen thousand volunteers.

Individual charisma played an important role in Republican forces, but this bore a definite political tint. El Campesino (Valentín González) was a large, physically strong peasant whose heavy, black-bearded face became a symbol of resistance throughout Republican ranks. When Nationalists first marched on Madrid, El Campesino rounded up " . . . 29 men, two lorries, rifles and one machine gun." A consummate showman, he named his command Group Chapaev, after a popular guerrilla leader of the Russian Revolution. Reinforced by volunteers, he deployed his men in the Somosierra passes against Franco's oncoming columns. In time, Group Chapaev grew to become the 46th Division, but its commander, who remained intensely individualistic and obstructive to the over-all effort, retained two companies of guerrillas for special operations.[24]

The paucity of arms, particularly of artillery, tanks, and aircraft, stamped many Republican units with semiguerrilla characteristics. A Republican veteran of the Basque fighting offered a splendid picture of his army:

> . . . We were a strange army composed of students, mechanics and peasants, led by a handful of regular officers. We wore navy blue coveralls, and we used whatever weapons were handy—French rifles, which were last used during the Franco-German War of 1870, and the most up-to-date rifles from Czechoslovakia. . . . We also had home-made dynamite bombs—three sticks of dynamite in a tomato can with a sixteen-second fuse. We lit the fuse with a cigarette.

Such armies fought for months in the Basque hills:

> . . . We fought best at night. We would dig into the hills, and send out scouting parties to find the weak points of the enemy, and push them back. By night we advanced, but during the day, without supporting artillery, airplanes and tanks, we were often forced back. Yet we could not afford to retreat, because there was so little ground to retreat to. . . . [25]

No army could stand forever against such odds, but the Nationalist task was never easy. After the Republicans fell in the Asturias, " . . .18,000 maintained themselves as guerrilla forces in the Leonese mountains, so delaying new offensives by the Nationalist armies."[26]

Franco's armies in the South did not face the extensive guerrilla action familiar to Napoleon's armies, and for several reasons. Much of the south-central Spanish countryside was barren and sparsely populated, devoid of roads. Nationalists advanced in columns, and effective resistance could only have come from contiguous terrain, particularly mountain passes. Nor did the people living in and around cities, towns, and villages form a homogeneous body defying an invader. To a great many persons on Nationalist lines of march, Franco and his generals appeared as liberators, and these persons, Monarchists, Carlists, and Fascists, did not hesitate to identify Republicans. Similar groups existed in larger cities, where the famous Fifth Columns performed limited acts of sabotage, provided information to Nationalists, and emerged from hiding when their armies moved in. Advancing Nationalists showed virtually no compassion in consolidating gains. Potential cadres of resistance fell to swift, brutal action—Republicans, including prisoners of war, were marched to the nearest bull ring, lined up, and shot.

Some escaped. Hemingway based his guerrilla band in *For Whom the Bell Tolls* on a realistic situation. His assortment of Republican fugitives chose a cave high in the " . . . forested slopes of the Sierra de Guadarramas 60 miles north-west of besieged Madrid and behind the Fascist lines."[27] Similar small bands existed in the same area, but a number of difficulties prevented these guerrillas from realizing their full potential.

One was lack of training and supply: Robert Jordan, the idealistically motivated American who joined them, backpacking in his own dynamite in order to blow a vital bridge, was a forerunner of allied teams who brought skills and arms to World War II guerrilla bands.

Another problem was Nationalist use of airplanes to find and attack guerrillas forced into the open—readers may remember the gripping scene of El Sordo's band trapped on a hilltop.

A third problem was lack of communication and control: the Republican general, Golz, ordered Jordan to blow the bridge on a certain hour of a certain day; in the event, the main attack aborted, but no method existed to cancel Jordan's orders, which meant a needless waste of lives, including his own.[28]

Jordan's own failure and Golz's failure and the Republic's failure were foreshadowed when Karkov, the *Pravda* correspondent, told Jordan in Madrid that although things were better and that reliable units were emerging in the army, the basic problem remained:

> ... "But an army," Karkov went on, "that is made up of good and bad elements cannot win a war. All must be brought to a certain level of political development; all must know why they are fighting, and its importance. All must believe in the fight they are to make and all must accept discipline. We are making a huge conscript army without the time to implant the discipline that a conscript army must have, to behave properly under fire. We call it a people's army but it will not have the assets of a true people's army and it will not have the iron discipline that a conscript army needs. You will see. It is a very dangerous procedure."[29]

It was a very dangerous procedure in another sense. The Communist attempt to capture the Republican cause and subvert it to the Soviet Union's political convenience presaged the future as much as dive-bombing or armor warfare, though in a far more subtle, in a political, way. Nowhere was the dualism of communism better illustrated than in Spain, nowhere the intricacy of Soviet thought better displayed.

Far from appealing to Stalin, the Spanish civil war came at a most inconvenient time. Since 1934, he had been moving toward an alliance with Britain and France against the threat of Hitler and Mussolini: The Soviet Union had joined the League of Nations, had signed a defense pact with France, and had ordered the Comintern to push a policy of the Popular Front, whereby local Communists allied with left-wing and liberal-middle-class parties against Fascism. A Nationalist or Fascist victory in Spain naturally held little appeal to the Kremlin. But a Socialist-Communist victory, as Thomas has pointed out, would have antagonized the U.S.S.R.'s important potential allies Britain and France, and might even have led to war. Still consolidating his internal rule (the massive purges were to resume in 1937), Stalin was not ready for war.

All this explains why Stalin did not exactly leap into the Spanish fray. Although he sent food, raw materials, and money, he at first refused to send arms. Under extreme pressure, he dispatched professional Comintern agents into Spain besides authorizing an international Comintern movement to provide "humanitarian" aid to Republicans. Only when Italo-German military aid to Nationalists became widely reported, did Stalin change his mind and dare to circumvent Franco-British non-intervention policy, and then only under further pressure from non-Russian Communists.

Military supplies did not begin trickling into Spain until late September 1936. Soviet aid eventually reached respectable proportions, including several hundred aircraft with pilots and ground crews, tanks, artillery, trucks, and military advisers and instructors, but it was given grudgingly and paid for, in advance, with Spanish gold.

Stalin's opportunistic attitude contrasted with that of non-Russian Communist members of the Comintern. This amazing organization exerted an influence both inside and outside Spain far beyond anything suggested by its limited numbers. Through a maze of "front" organizations, which fooled a great many non-Communist liberals, the Comintern recruited, trained, armed, and equipped perhaps forty thousand foreigners who served at one time or another in one of seven international brigades. No matter the slapdash character of these units, particularly in early days, their formation bespoke a determined and disciplined effort, which, allied with the small but disciplined Communist Party in Spain, very nearly captured the Republican cause. This was a classic example of exploiting liberal idealism, and it was not lost on Hemingway, whose American protagonist, Robert Jordan,

> ... fought now in this war because it had started in a country that he loved and he believed in the Republic and that if it were destroyed life would be unbearable for all those people who believed in it.

Jordan was not a Communist, but he willingly had placed himself

> ... under Communist discipline for the duration of the war. He accepted their discipline for the duration of the war because, in the conduct of the war, they were the only party whose program and whose discipline he could respect.[30]

No matter that the effort failed, that Jordan and many others of his kind died, that the Republicans suffered ultimate defeat. As German and Italian air and ground officers returned to their respective countries rich in battle experience, Communist survivors also returned rich in another kind of battle experience. They were still too weak to launch revolutions in their own countries. They would need another war for that. But they were prepared to wait, and as it turned out, they hadn't to wait for long. Less than six months after the close of the Spanish civil war, World War II began.

CHAPTER TWENTY-THREE

1. Boyle, 317 ff. See also, Slessor, 45–75.
2. Slessor, 52. See also, Boyle, 365, 369.
3. Slessor, 59–60.
4. Ibid., 63, 54.
5. Boyle, 389–90.
6. Ibid.
7. Ibid., 389.
8. Gwynn, 4–5. See also, Skeen.
9. Gwynn, 10–12.
10. Ibid., 98.
11. Ibid., 109.
12. Ibid., 110.
13. Heinl, 250–1.
14. Wood, 24, 41–5. See also, Vandegrift and Asprey.
15. Asprey, "Small Wars—1925–1962."
16. Heinl, 266 ff.
17. Ibid., 277–9.
18. Ibid., 281.
19. Asprey, "Small Wars—1925–1962."
20. Thomas, *The Spanish Civil War*, 205.
21. Ibid. See also, Ibarruri.
22. Hemingway, 97–127.
23. Thomas, *The Spanish Civil War*, 176. See also, Baker.
24. Payne, *The Civil War in Spain*, 55, 59.
25. Ibid., 227.
26. Thomas, *The Spanish Civil War*, 480. Sporadic guerrilla resistance lasted in the Cantabrian Mountains until 1939. Remnants of Republican bands made a serious effort at a comeback in the Pyrenees in 1945–47.
27. Baker, 257.
28. Thomas, *The Civil War in Spain*, 299. Hemingway based the character of General Goltz on one General "Walter," who was the Polish Communist General Karol Swierczewski. He based the tactical situation on an actual Republican offensive planned along the Segovia front. Although Colonel Dumont's 14th International Brigade broke through Nationalist lines at San Ildefonso, the attack ran out of steam at La Granja, owing in part to jealousy between Walter and Dumont, and possibly also to betrayal, as Hemingway suggested.
29. Hemingway, 236.
30. Ibid., 158.

CHAPTER 24

*World War II • German and Japanese victories • Guerrilla warfare
begins • Allied support of resistance movements • Special Operations
Executive (SOE) • Office of Strategic Services (OSS) • The British-
American policy analyzed • The Communist element • Reasons for a
quantitative approach • Churchill and Roosevelt • European
resistance analyzed • The complex political element • German
occupation policy • German errors • Growth of underground
movements • Resistance in Czechoslovakia, Poland, Italy, and Norway*

ON SEPTEMBER 1, 1939, Hitler loosed the full force of Germany's infantry-armor-air power against Poland, whose army was so obsolete that Polish cavalrymen *armed with lances* charged German tanks. In less than a month, the Wehrmacht overran this tragic country in violent demonstration of a new type of warfare, the *Blitzkrieg,* or lightning war, which Western military leaders failed to comprehend.

After a winter of uneasy quiet, Hitler moved again, this time occupying Norway in order to gain naval and air bases. On May 10, 1940, he struck. Denmark quickly capitulated, Holland fell to aerial bombing and paratroopers, German armored columns pushed through the supposedly impassable Ardennes in a giant sweep into France.

In fourteen days, German armored columns encircled allied armies in northern France, forcing the British to evacuate nearly a third of a million men from Dunkerque. Meeting only scattered resistance, the Germans continued south across the Aisne and the Seine. On June 16, Marshal Pétain surrendered the French army.

Hitler followed this victory with an air offensive against England. By breaking the back of the Royal Air Force, he hoped to soften the island's defenses for an across-the-channel invasion. His plan buckled before a determined aerial defense—the famous Battle of Britain—from which the Spitfire fighter emerged superior to the Messerschmitt; in early October 1940, the Luftwaffe conceded its first defeat, a crucial one in that heavy German losses of aircraft and pilots could not readily be replaced.

Hitler's ally Mussolini next launched two offensives: one against Greece, the other against the British in North Africa. By early 1941, the Italian dictator was in severe trouble in each theater. To rescue him, Hitler sent an armored force under General-leutnant Erwin Rommel to Africa; in early April 1941, a German army invaded Yugoslavia, pushed through in five days and, with forces based in Hungary, Bulgaria, and Romania, went on to conquer Greece and seize Crete by a daring, if costly, airborne assault.

With this flank protected, Hitler turned east: in late June 1941, three powerful German armies invaded the Soviet Union. By early November, vanguard divisions had pushed seven hundred miles, to within fifteen miles of Moscow. But now cold weather and a Russian counteroffensive forced them on the defensive along the entire front.

On December 7, 1941, Japanese bombers flying from a secretly concentrated task force of aircraft carriers attacked Pearl Harbor, America's major Pacific naval base. Within hours, the bulk of the American battleship fleet had been sunk. In ensuing weeks and months, Japanese ground, air, and sea forces seized allied bases throughout the Pacific and Southeast Asia. French Indochina, Siam, and Malaya at once capitulated; Singapore fell, then Burma, the Dutch East Indies, the Philippines, Guam, Wake. By spring of 1942, the enemy was threatening Australia from nearby New Guinea and from bases in the neighboring Solomon Islands.

By spring of 1942, then, battles lines east and west were drawn. For the next three years and more, mighty armies, giant naval fleets, and vast air armadas clashed again and again in a global war without precedent.

And a global war that spawned an immense variety of irregular-warfare operations. For, whatever the conquest, whoever the conqueror, the clash of fundamental ideologies combined with brutal occupation policies resulted in resistance that varied from the lone saboteur to entire guerrilla armies. Wherever possible, hard-pressed allied powers eagerly embraced such movements, their general policy being to help anyone willing to fight the enemy. Technological advances, particularly the airplane, the portable radio transmitter, the parachute, and the submarine, enabled them in time to support almost any group anywhere.

No real precedent existed for the over-all situation—massive global war: massive global resistance. To exploit the potential, England established "an independent British secret service" known as Special Operations Executive (SOE). America followed suit with the Office of Strategic Services (OSS). Russian support of guerrillas either inside or outside the country became the Red army's responsibility, but with numerous political ramifications. In China, Chiang Kai-shek similarly controlled his guerrillas, though much less effectively; Mao Tse-tung continued to use guerrilla forces as the keystone of political-military operations earlier described.

As might be expected, guerrilla operations world-wide varied considerably in size, composition, motivation, mission, and effectiveness. Such were differences in enemy strength and counteractions, in political environments, in guerrilla leadership, and in allied assistance and supervision, that one resistance action often bore only generic resemblance to another. This lack of cohesive operation lessens neither the single nor the collective value of the experience and its contribution to guerrilla warfare. Neither does it eliminate some "constant" factors that can be retrieved from various operational theaters, which we shall get to in a moment. But since we are still living with some results of allied support of various resistance groups, we should examine first not only its genesis and extent but the reasons for it.

The immense task of supporting resistance movements and of trying to form them into a cohesive weapon that would fire at allied will fell to an organization not heretofore seen in warfare. This was a British group, Special Operations Executive (SOE), which functioned under the Ministry of Economic Warfare, itself activated only in 1939 and later directed by a prominent laborite and socialist, Dr. Hugh Dalton. The interested reader will find detailed information on this mysterious and complex organization in two serious works: M. R. D. Foot's *SOE in France*, an official but nonetheless lively and at times controversial work; and E. H. Cookridge's *Inside SOE*, which offers a more dramatic and wider survey of SOE operations. Literally dozens of works complement these two, and many are listed in the respective bibliographies.

SOE traced from a small research section of the British General Staff, the GS-R, which in 1938–39 prepared two anticipatory pamphlets, *The Art of Guerrilla Warfare* and *Partisan Leader's Handbook*. At this time, only a few British officers realized the potential of guerrilla warfare—a surprising fact in view of British military history. One who did was a forty-five-year-old lieutenant colonel, Colin McVean Gubbins, a regular soldier decorated for bravery in World War I who subsequently served in the Irish rebellion and in India during the riots. In the 1930s, he made personal reconnaissances in Poland and the Baltic States, where he envisaged the possibility of guerrilla actions, and in 1939 he headed the intelligence section of a British mission to Warsaw and narrowly missed capture by the Germans. He next organized, trained, and commanded the first Striking Companies, which fought in Norway and later became the Commandos. Gubbins and a few men with similar backgrounds were called to SOE, where most of them subsequently served with great distinction—as did many civilians with non-military backgrounds.

But, for every Gubbins, a thousand regular officers existed who, wedded to orthodox military tradition, disdained irregular warfare. Cookridge later described early confrontations of regulars with "the others":

> . . . The horrified generals, brigadiers, admirals and air marshals were confronted by men some of whom had never heard a shot fired in anger, and who talked about politics, ideologies, psychology and subversion. Employing saboteurs and guerrilla leaders was alien to the traditions of Sandhurst men. Many of them were still fighting the last war but one, and dreamed of the Charge of the Light Brigade. . . . [1]

And not alone Sandhurst men! At a time when German bombers were battering Britain, Air Marshal Portal objected to an SOE operation designed to ambush and kill German pathfinder bomber pilots. Portal wrote to a responsible official: " . . . I think you will agree that there is a vast difference, in ethics, between the time honored operation of the dropping of a spy from the air and this entirely new scheme for dropping what one can only call assassins."[2]

Such service delicacy in part prompted Winston Churchill to place SOE under the Ministry of Economic Warfare rather than either the War Office or the Foreign Office. In approving the formation of SOE, Prime Minister Winston Churchill exhorted the new minister of economic warfare, Hugh Dalton, " . . . to set Europe ablaze."[3] In more prosaic language SOE was " . . . to create and foster the spirit of resistance in Nazi-occupied countries," and "once a suitable climate of opinion had been set up . . . to establish a nucleus of trained men who would be able to assist 'as a fifth column' in the liberation of the country concerned whenever the British were able to invade it."[4] From the beginning, SOE proved politically promiscuous, " . . . ready to work with any man or institution, Roman Catholic or masonic, trotskyist or liberal, syndicalist or capitalist, nationalist or chauvinist, radical or conservative, Stalinist or anarchist, gentile or Jew, that would help it beat the Nazis down."[5]

The American equivalent to SOE, the Office of Strategic Services (OSS), was the brainchild of a World War I hero and civilian attorney, William J. "Wild Bill" Donovan.[6] OSS began life as the Office of Coordinator of Information. Personnel experienced in irregular warfare were virtually non-existent. Although marines saw considerable action in Nicaragua and Haiti in the 1920s, this was limited to a handful of officers and men (see Chapter 23). As one result, the organization was slow in getting organized; as another, it recruited numerous officers who later proved unsatisfactory.

Transformed into the OSS by a presidential order in 1942, it became a federal agency responsible for covert operations in enemy-occupied areas. As such, it naturally came together with SOE in London, with whom it would enjoy numerous successes and suffer numerous failures. A good many persons, including most professional military officers, have held subsequently that failures overshadowed successes, that the greatest error, according to later critics, lay in indiscriminately arming various resistance groups, some of which were politically antagonistic to the West.

Winston Churchill set the Anglo-American pace in this respect by demanding British support of anyone willing to kill Germans. As he once said, " . . . If Hitler invaded Hell, I would make at least a favorable reference to the Devil in the House of Commons." In retrospect, in view of complicated and greatly varying local political situations, it seems far too simple a policy, altogether unworthy of the British, who were scarcely naïve in international politics. Its chief disadvantage centered on the dissidents themselves. Although many of these were patriots willing to die for love of country, most of them wanted fundamental political changes in that country once the war ended. In many countries—not all—the most determined opponents of Fascist conquerors were Communists, who wanted postwar control.

Two decades of attempted suppression had inured local Communist parties to an underground existence ideal for the present situation. Where advantageous terrain existed, such as in Yugoslavia, the raised standard, hastily painted over in nationalist colors, attracted thousands of well-meaning citizens, of whom many, in the end, became converts. In countries less suitable for guerrilla warfare, Communists operated more covertly. Their infiltration and organizational ability, in almost all cases, paid immense dividends by insinuating party members into responsible resistance roles while superb propaganda techniques won new adherents to the cause: in virtually all cases, they ended the war in a far stronger position than they began it—as witness Communist attempts to take over France and Italy in immediate postwar years. Similarly in the Far East, SOE armed dissident groups, in some cases nationalist, in some cases Communist, in Burma and Malaya. OSS furnished arms and equipment to Mao Tse-tung in China and even to Ho Chi Minh in Vietnam, and in supplying guerrillas in the Philippines, they inadvertently supported the Communist movement there.

Why were Churchill and Roosevelt willing to play games with the devil?

Britain's initial position, established and maintained by Winston Churchill and graced by Cabinet and government, is not difficult to understand. After the fall of France, the island kingdom literally stood alone, resources of empire as yet unharnessed, the Soviet Union allied with Germany, the United States just beginning to awaken from a long isolationist sleep. A desperate Churchill stared at a doomed England. Unlike Dr. Faustus, who wanted mere knowledge, Churchill demanded survival.

But after light entered these dark days, after the U.S.S.R. was fighting Germany and after the U.S.A. had come into the war, why did the game continue? Although mystery still shrouds the issue, the key reason—and one all too often overlooked—centered on the possibility of developing an atomic bomb. Background development of this weapon is complex—the reader can study it in such works as Leslie Groves's *Now It Can Be Told* and Lewis Strauss's *Men and Decisions*. According to Strauss, the term "atomic bomb" first occurred in a letter to him from the brilliant Hungarian immigrant Leo Szilard. By spring of 1939,

> . . . Szilard was gravely worried by the possibility of an early German success in producing a new weapon based on nuclear fission. The liberation of vast energy from a quite small amount of material had suggested to him the feasibility of making a weapon which would utterly dwarf any chemical bomb and with which, should Hitler be the first to achieve it, the conquest of Europe would be quickly accomplished. . . . [7]

This led to the famous "Einstein letter" to President Roosevelt, in autumn of 1939. After reviewing atomic research to date, Einstein stated the probability of achieving " . . . a nuclear chain reaction in a large mass of uranium," a new scientific phenomenon which " . . . would also lead to the construction of bombs, and it is conceivable—though much less certain—that extremely powerful bombs of a new type may thus be constructed. . . . " Einstein left little doubt of German interest in this possibility:[8]

> . . . I understand that Germany has actually stopped the sale of uranium from the Czechoslovakian mines which she has taken over. . . .

The incubus of the Germans developing an atomic weapon grew after the invasion of Norway, in spring of 1940. By midsummer,

. . . the eagerness shown by the Germans to capture a Norwegian plant producing heavy water gave color to the apprehension that *the German military establishment was vigorously engaged in some kind of atomic weapon project.* We knew that several kilograms of heavy water were produced daily at Trondheim. . . . [9]

Enough progress in atomic physics had been made on the continent and in England for everyone to know the value of heavy water, deuterium oxide, for experiments in atomic energy. When Germany invaded France, French scientists managed to spirit away their supply of the precious stuff to England. British intelligence soon learned that German scientists in the Norsk Hydro Elektrisk plant near Vemork had ordered Norwegian engineers to increase heavy-water output to three thousand pounds a year, a figure soon raised to ten thousand pounds. This uncomfortable fact led to a British Combined Operations plan to blow up the hydroelectric plant. In late November 1942, two gliders attempted to land special teams in the area, a disastrous failure in which most participants were either killed in crash landings or executed by the Germans. A later effort by a very brave Norwegian team partially closed down operations, and later RAF raids continued to damage the plant. In early 1944, a Norwegian agent, Knut Haukelid, who had participated in the earlier raid, learned that the Germans were shipping a half year's production of heavy water to Germany. Haukelid and two companions managed to plant explosives that blew up the ferry and destroyed fifteen thousand liters of heavy water. [10]

The allies did not know that in 1943 Albert Speer, Hitler's armaments chief, already had drastically limited nuclear research. A shortage of heavy water further hindered German scientists, whose researchers in any case were lagging far behind their Western counterparts. Strauss does not state when the veil began to part, but does remark that ". . . as the war with Germany drew to a close, it became more and more clear that the apprehensions as to what the Germans were doing in atomic energy had been exaggerated." [11] By this time, England and the United States long since had embarked on quantitative support of dissident peoples.

Juxtaposed to this overriding and eminently justified fear of Germany producing an atomic weapon were the dominant personalities of Roosevelt and Churchill. Each was convinced of his ability to control the world's destiny: a splendid egotism reinforced by a host of erroneous information furnished by outstanding specialists of both countries; by cunning Communist strategy which downplayed Communist preeminence in certain areas; and, in Roosevelt's case, by an anti-colonial attitude distinctly at odds with Churchill's imperial desires. Above all, an egotism that completely ignored the possibility of death—either natural or political—of either leader.

302

In view of these quixotic personalities and the momentous issues at stake, the initial decision to support whoever would kill Germans (or Japanese) is perhaps defensible if only on grounds of survival. Once the danger passed—Strauss marks this in 1944 at the latest—a re-evaluation by Western powers was in order. In view of the momentous forces of war then swirling over the world, it was perhaps expecting too much for concerned governments to have stopped for a moment to cast critical eyes on resistance movements and to ask themselves: where are we going and why? Such were the day's operational confusions, such the political naïveté of the allied powers, that intelligent examination might not have changed allied resistance policies for the better. This we shall never know, because these policies were not re-examined. Like Topsy, the resistance effort continued to grow.

During most of World War II, resistance forces in Poland, Czechoslovakia, Norway, Denmark, Holland, Belgium, France, and Italy concerned themselves with a more subtle type of guerrilla warfare than practiced, for example, in the Soviet Union and Yugoslavia. In the former countries, a variety of factors hindered attempts to build operational guerrilla armies. Lack of suitable terrain for sanctuary purposes, inadequate internal communications, conflicting national temperaments and political attitudes—each sharply influenced resistance efforts. While attempting to build secret guerrilla "armies" that would emerge at the appropriate time to fight in conjunction with allied land armies, these partisans operated either as individuals or in small groups to carry out tasks of terror, subversion and sabotage. Equally important missions included securing and transmitting intelligence on enemy strength, activity, and movements, and in helping allied soldiers, principally downed airmen, to evade capture while escaping to neutral countries.

In performing these manifold missions, resistance members in all countries constantly risked imprisonment, torture, deportation, and death. Although many participants died and, in many instances, records were lost or destroyed (or not kept), sufficient sources survived to give us a good insight into operational aspects of this type of warfare and the numerous factors that created and sustained it.

The indigenous populations of occupied countries formed the most important factor. Each of the above-named countries contained citizens who either overtly or covertly embraced the Fascist cause—the quisling, or outright traitor, element who argued primarily that fascism was necessary to defeat communism or socialism, the collaborator who came to terms with the enemy for other reasons. These groups often differed radically within themselves. Some quislings and collaborators, motivated by a pathological fear of communism, desired German control;

303

others wanted more local autonomy under some sort of protectorate arrangement; some regarded the occupation as a *fait accompli* and decided to profit from it.[12]

For every citizen so inclined, thousands regarded fascism as the antithesis of civilization. But this group, too, differed within: some anti-Fascists—the *attentistes*, or fence-sitters—refused to take a stand; some preferred mild accommodation to the enemy to avoid reprisals; others, under no circumstances, would permit the conqueror an easy occupation. Of the latter group, some fought solely for unselfish motives; a good many, including most Communists, used the effort to strengthen the party's position in postwar years. Hundreds of thousands, indeed millions, of people found themselves in the middle, perhaps loathing the conqueror but rationalizing that the conquest was an accomplished fact and that one had a duty to support one's dependents. This middle group comprised a wide range of attitudes: citizens who accommodated the enemy for profit, or from fear, or because, in their minds, no reasonable alternative existed, or for an ulterior motive of serving him with one hand and stabbing him with the other, or for gaining time in order to plan escape to an allied country or to a guerrilla refuge.

Despite a confused and divided citizenry, the German conqueror everywhere faced a certain amount of *natural* resistance—fanatical patriots of every political party who would prostrate themselves to the enemy only in death. In overcoming such resistance and in consolidating occupation, German conquerors naturally tapped pro-Fascist sections of the population. These generally included important industrialists and prominent businessmen who either inclined toward or embraced a Fascist form of government, but it also included a less desirable element—quasi-Nazi groups containing the scum of society. In utilizing the bullying tactics of this element, the Germans at once offended a considerable portion of citizenry otherwise prepared to remain acquiescent.

The Germans also offended by their almost unbelievable display of the arrogance of power. The true Nazi doubted not that Germany shortly would rule the world. Military and civil governors quickly began turning their newest acquisitions into German satrapies. Regarding all foreigners as inferior, they practiced patronizing attitudes that endeared them to no one, nor did they hesitate to invoke severe occupation policies: inconvenient curfews and travel restrictions; confiscation of houses and buildings; strict rationing; hurtful taxes; impossible production norms; plundering of private and public property; arrest and deportation or outright elimination of Aryans and non-Aryans, with emphasis on Jews and Communists. While these actions did not necessarily create resistance movements, they did aid incipient movements to survive by enlisting sympathies of otherwise apathetic citizens.

As resistance survived and developed, the conquerors replied with most-brutal reprisals: mass arrests, imprisonment, torture, deportation to forced-labor and concentration camps, and summary executions, including those of hostages and innocent persons. The Germans complemented this effort by introducing wholesale conscription for service either in armed forces or for labor in factories at home and abroad. Besides further alienating the general population, this drove thousands of young men to mountain and forest sanctuaries, where some of them in time formed effective guerrilla bands such as the French *maquis*.

Perhaps the outstanding lesson of this period of European resistance should be the innate booby trap contained in reprisal philosophy. Reduced to its simplest terms, reprisal illustrates the fallacy of answering lawless behavior with lawless behavior—and this seems to be a universal *bête noir* of the military mind. One story of Czechoslovakian resistance, possibly apocryphal but offered as truth by a former British intelligence officer who related it to the writer, illustrates this point. Contrary to general belief, the Germans were not badly received when they took over most of Czechoslovakia. Perhaps for this reason, occupation authorities did not rule as harshly as elsewhere, and thus did not face as much of a resistance problem. Although members of the intelligentsia and a large number of the middle class suffered under occupation, workers and peasants, in general, fared reasonably well—or well enough so that they did not indulge in spontaneous resistance.

Lack of resistance is said to have greatly annoyed the exiled president, Eduard Beneš. Beneš allegedly was responsible for a plan to assassinate the German governor, Reinhard Heydrich, the theory being that this act would cause widespread reprisals, which would turn the citizenry against the occupying enemy. With Winston Churchill's alleged cognizance and co-operation, Beneš arranged for SOE to drop a team of specially trained Czech volunteers into the occupied country. Whatever the details, Heydrich *was* assassinated, in the spring of 1942, by an SOE-supported operation, and this did cause widespread reprisals, such as the destruction of Lidice, a mining village, all of whose inhabitants were either executed or deported. The German storm eventually passed but it embittered a large part of the population, which in part supported a resistance movement lasting until the war's end, though not to the intensity desired by Beneš![13]

The political factor even more strongly influenced the Polish resistance movement. A substantial portion of the population, particularly peasants and urban socialists, while remaining opposed to communism, nonetheless wanted a new postwar political order. This forced reactionary leaders, mainly army officers at home and abroad, into an uneasy alliance that, coupled with Communist diversions, frequently dissipated the total resistance effort.

As in other occupied countries, Germany did her best to generate maximum resistance. In that part of western Poland annexed to the German Reich,

> ... all available industrial and agricultural resources were to be fully exploited and expanded for the benefit of the Reich. At the same time the population was to be germanised. Jews and the most intractable Poles, especially members of the intelligentsia, were deported to the General Government [the rest of Poland]. Large numbers of able-bodied male Poles were deported to other parts of the Reich to work in factories or fields.... The Polish language was not permitted in administration or schools within the annexed territories. ...

What was left of Poland, the area called General Government, was to be stripped. Governor-General Hans Frank at the Nuremberg trials voiced German policy: " ... Poland shall be treated as a colony; the Poles shall be the slaves of the Greater German World Empire."[14] Jews could not be tolerated. By spring of 1943, over three hundred thousand had been deported from Warsaw alone; in April, the German army attacked the remaining one hundred thousand unarmed Jews living in the Warsaw ghetto and eliminated them. The Germans established special concentration camps where Jews from Poland, central Europe, and western Russia were murdered—one estimate places the figure at four million.[15]

The ruthless German policy almost immediately generated widespread Polish resistance. Sikorski's government in exile in London remained in reasonably close contact with indigenous resistance forces, which it directed " ... to build up a secret government, administration, army, press and even law courts and schools."[16] Resistance in general became the responsibility of the Home Army and of special groups, including guerrilla detachments, formed by various political parties.

Although the Home Army and other units performed some effective guerrilla actions, the long distance from England hindered supply by air. Nor was terrain particularly suited to guerrilla operations: the forests, where some guerrilla groups existed, were generally remote from major German installations and lines of communication. Poor internal communications also tended to prevent co-ordinated actions. But these deficiencies could in part have been overcome had Soviet Russia played a true allied role.

Soviet Russia did nothing of the sort. Stalin's attitude became clear as early as 1940, when he siphoned off a portion of General Anders' army-in-exile, placed it under command of a Polish Communist, and affixed it to a puppet exile group called the Union of Polish Patriots. Russia also made common cause with the indigenous Communist movement, which supported a People's Army and which, joined with the Union of Polish Patriots, formed the Lublin Committee, in 1944. Meanwhile Russia had been dropping Polish and Russian saboteurs inside Poland, an effort that frequently brought German reprisals. In turn, local peasants, on occasion, fought these saboteurs—to German advantage.

Mainly for these reasons, Polish resistance consisted of sporadic, small-scale actions while local patriots built an underground army supplied with weapons either flown in from England or manufactured in underground factories or captured or stolen from the Germans. General Anders later estimated the size of this force at 380,000, of whom 40,000 were in Warsaw.[17]

When Russian armies approached the Vistula, in early August 1944, the Home Army rose in Warsaw, a premature action, the result either of poor communications or a Communist trap designed to eliminate organized resistance to a postwar Communist take-over.[18] Whatever the reason, the Home Army, supported by most Warsaw civilians, fought off joint attacks of five German divisions for sixty-three days before surrendering. Although Polish resistance continued in the western provinces, the Warsaw disaster took the heart from it.

Terrain played an important role in shaping European resistance, as we have seen in the cases of Czechoslovakia and Poland. The mountains of northern Italy proved more hospitable, and here large guerrilla groups eventually did form. But here also an ugly political factor existed. In 1944, when allies began supporting Italian resistance in the North, it rested in a Committee of National Liberation of Northern Italy, with operations run by a Corps of Volunteers of Liberty, both organizations containing strong Communist elements. Such was the day's feeling, such the overwhelming priority awarded to purely military considerations, that the allies never hesitated in supplying quantitative aid even though one of the two resistance chiefs of staff was Luigi Longo, the Communist who had served with distinction in Spain.[19]

This resistance movement grew to perhaps ninety thousand members, who could not have survived without allied support delivered through SOE and OSS missions, which operated in separate areas. Whether the return on this considerable investment was adequate is debatable. Although the resistance hindered Kesselring's operations and final withdrawal, Communist guerrilla groups used a large portion of arms and money in consolidating their own positions. As one result, the Italian Communist Party became the most powerful in postwar Europe.

Norwegian sanctuaries offered a different problem, in that mountain retreats actually proved hostile to guerrillas. As C. N. M. Blair has pointed out, food to feed guerrillas had to come either from thinly populated valleys easily controlled by small German garrisons or from air drops made difficult by distance and adverse weather conditions.[20] Until the end of the war, guerrilla operations in Norway consisted of small groups sometimes buttressed by teams parachuted in for special operations. Meanwhile, SOE was arming a secret force, the Milorg, which, by early 1944, was administered in eleven districts " . . . with an effective strength of 33,000 well-disciplined and armed men."[21] At war's end, this organization threw off its wraps, accepted German surrender, and maintained order until the government-in-exile returned.

Without arms, equipment, or food, and without organization, communications, or training, early resistance groups created little more than nuisance value—but a value greatly enhanced by German overreaction, as explained above. It was up to SOE, and later OSS, to exploit the potential of these groups, an effort that encountered numerous difficulties, frustrations, and failures, but one that also paid handsome dividends.

CHAPTER TWENTY-FOUR

1. Cookridge, 19.
2. Foot, *SOE in France*, 153.
3. Dalton, 366, 368.
4. Foot, *SOE in France*, 11–12. See also, Foot, *Resistance*.
5. Foot, *SOE in France*, 13–14.
6. Alsop and Braden, 12–13.
7. Strauss, 176.
8. Ibid., 179.
9. Ibid., 176–7. My italics. See also, Clark.
10. Clark, 142–3, 147.
11. Strauss, 183.
12. Seton-Watson, *The East European Revolution*, 106–7. The writer has differentiated among no less than five major types of quislings and collaborators. See also, Woodhouse, *Apple of Discord*.
13. Private information in the writer's files. See also, Seton-Watson, *The East European Revolution*, 72, who notes that German repression in Czechoslovakia became more severe in autumn of 1941. After sabotage of a munitions plant and power station, Himmler appointed Heydrich as Protector, or governor: " . . . For eight months Heydrich conducted a regime of terror, with firing squads, concentration camps and deportations to forced labor." See also, Wighton.
14. Seton-Watson, *The East European Revolution*, 73–5.
15. Ibid., 77–113. This figure was taken from Wilhelm Höttl's later testimony.

Although Höttl is notoriously unreliable, no doubt exists as to the huge number of victims. See also, Krausnick.

16. Seton-Watson, *The East European Revolution,* 111.
17. Anders, 200.
18. Ibid., 200–4, 218–26. According to the writer, he and his military colleagues in London advised against the rising, but the civil government, generally at odds with the military (and themselves), disagreed and authorized it. See also, Foot, *SOE in France,* 24. For a long period, SOE was the "sole liaison" between the Polish ministries of interior and national defense, "an impossible but typical Polish situation"; Seton-Watson, *The East European Revolution,* 115–17, suggests a Russian dilemma that could explain the Soviet failure to advance, and even to refuse the use of Soviet airfields to allied supply planes.
19. Blair, 102.
20. Ibid., 117–18.
21. Cookridge, 539. An interesting "non-violent" resistance also developed and played an important role in over-all resistance. See also, Skodvin.

CHAPTER 25

French resistance in World War II • The political caldron • De Gaulle and the BCRA • Conflict with SOE • SOE's early difficulties • The German occupation policy • Growth of resistance • German errors • Rise of the maquis • Guerrilla warfare increases • SOE/OSS special units • Guerrilla support of allied landings • The cost

FRANCE was SOE's most important target in Europe, and SOE almost at once found difficulty in trying to work effectively in that country. After the fall of France in 1940, a considerable body of French soldiers managed to escape either to England or to Algeria. In London, this group formed the nucleus of the Free French under a dynamic officer, Charles de Gaulle, who was not then known outside the French Army. In Algeria, a similar group formed somewhat later under General Giraud, De Gaulle's rival. In France itself, Nazis or no Nazis, the political caldron never stopped bubbling, and this was even more the case when Germany split the country into Occupied and Unoccupied France, with Marshal Pétain heading the *État français*, or what the allies called Vichy France.

Just how responsible SOE officials overlooked this political turbulence is difficult to imagine, particularly in view of unsettled French politics of the 1930s. But overlooked it was. As Professor Foot wrote,

> . . . at first SOE's staff was ingenuous enough to imagine that all anti-German Frenchmen would work happily together; this was at once discovered to be wrong. Strong anti-Nazi elements in Vichy France refused to have any dealings with General de Gaulle, who in turn rejected anything and anybody that savored of co-operation with Pétain's regime.[1]

General de Gaulle had his own ideas for developing French resistance, a subject on which he was particularly touchy. As he later wrote,

FRANCE 1940-1945
● Towns and Cities

NETHERLANDS
ENGLAND
LONDON
GERMANY
Dunkerque
Calais
Boulogne
BELGIUM
R. Somme
Mézières
Dieppe
Verdun
Caen
NORMANDY
PARIS
Nancy
Strasbourg
CÔTES DU NORD
Alençon
Le Mans
R. Loire
Nantes
Châteauroux
Bay of Biscay
Vichy
Lyons
Angoulême
UNOCCUPIED
FRANCE
Bordeaux
R. Garonne
Vercors Plateau
Montauban
Montpellier
Avignon
Nice
Biarritz
Marseille
Bilbao
San Sebastián
Toulon
SPAIN
Perpignan
English Channel
R. Thames
R. Seine
R. Rhône
BRITTANY
SWITZERLAND
ITALY

0   50   100   150 miles

M.E.P.

... The most urgent thing was to install an embryo organization within the national territory. The British, for their part, would have liked to see us simply send over agents with instructions to gather, in isolation, information about the enemy with reference to defined objectives. Such was the method used for espionage. But we meant to do better. Since the action in France would be carried on in the midst of a population which would, we thought, be teeming with well-wishers, we meant to set up networks. By binding together hand-picked elements and communicating with us through centralized means these would give the best return.[2]

De Gaulle assigned the function to an amateur, the brilliant Major André Dewavrin, who, under the alias of Colonel Passy, headed the Bureau Central de Renseignements et d'Action, or BCRA which conflicted with

311

SOE almost immediately. SOE had established Section F to build resistance groups inside France. It now established another section, Section RF, to work with BCRA, and only too soon discovered highly restrictive aspects of French policy:

> ... to the Gaullists, the question of who was to be in power in France after the Germans had been driven out was always *the* question; and they necessarily mistrusted bodies of armed men at large in France of whose allegiance they were uncertain.[3]

The British Government and SOE did not view the situation through the same politically colored glasses. Section DF, for example, which was trying to establish escape routes in France for downed airmen, did not give a hoot about the politics of those Frenchmen willing to risk their lives for this vital effort. And, while SOE attempted to appease De Gaulle with Section RF, it nonetheless retained Section F, whose agents worked secretly with other politically aligned resistance groups. The bulk of these agents were non-French and, according to Foot,

> ... knew little of French politics and cared less; and when they had a political aim at all, beyond helping in the overthrow of Hitler and Pétain, it was simply that of the British War Cabinet: to give the French every chance of a quite unfettered choice of their own system of government once the war was won.[4]

Free French discovery of Section F's separate existence created a furor. In De Gaulle's words,

> ... A regular competition therefore started immediately, with us appealing to the moral and legal obligation of Frenchmen not to join a foreign service, and the British using the means at their disposal to try and gain for themselves agents, and then networks, of their own.[5]

Hard feeling continued—but so did Section F. At this time, SOE held the most important cards: It got first crack at arriving French refugees, who, if suitable for resistance work, were often recruited without BCRA knowledge. It also owned the few arms and delivery systems available, all training centers, and, not least, the money. Later, when the United States entered the picture, Roosevelt's antipathy to De Gaulle further strengthened SOE's hand. In time, Section F " ... built up almost a hundred independent circuits—networks of subversive agents on French soil; it armed several scores of thousands of resisters, who fought well."[6] Communists numbered among those armed, but, seeing which way political winds blew, quickly came to terms and remained in uneasy alliance with the Free French. Similarly, BCRA and SOE eventually worked quite well together. The one needed the other, they both needed Communists, and Communists needed them.

SOE faced other difficult problems. A year after the organization's inauguration, one of its members, veteran diplomat Bruce Lockhart, commented in a letter to Anthony Eden on "inter-departmental strife and jealousies." The disruptive tendency was probably inevitable, considering the nature of the organization, the prima-donna temperament of many of its members and the complexity and secrecy of its functions. Duplication also existed, mainly the result of the private battle between Giraud and De Gaulle in Algiers for control of the Free French.

SOE personnel usually encountered a frosty reception from the Foreign Office. Nor was the covert organization always popular with the armed forces, which ran their own intelligence-collection operations and even their own escape routes, a conflict well brought out in Airey Neave's recent book *Saturday at MI-9*. The armed forces also organized special operational forces such as Commandos, which sometimes operated independently, sometimes in conjunction with SOE, and on occasion operational conflicts resulted.

A final complication occurred in the form of America's equivalent to SOE, the OSS. As was the case with SOE, OSS grew too rapidly and recruited too many persons, some of whose qualifications were more suited to drawing-room soirées. Its fundamental and continuing enmities with other American organizations—the armed forces, the Federal Bureau of Investigation, and the Department of State—often resulted in wasteful duplication of facilities and operations.

OSS at first did not collide with SOE, at least not in western Europe. In autumn of 1942 American and British chiefs of staff fused special operations of each organization in north-western Europe into a section called SOE/SO, an arrangement reflected in Algiers by a combined Special Forces Headquarters (SFHQ). In time, OSS won its operational spurs to indulge in operations sharply at variance with SOE, though not so much in France as in Italy and the Far East. A ranking SOE official later wrote: " . . . By the end of the war their [OSS] bitterest detractors would be forced to admit that they had become quite as good as the British at getting secret intelligence and at carrying out special operations, and I personally thought they were doing better."[7]

SOE would have suffered major problems even under ideal circumstances if only because of the state of the art at the time: political naïveté, operational inexperience, communications difficulties, limited delivery means, top-heavy organization. But the quantitative approach it insisted on resulted in a duplication of covert operations, which sometimes severely complicated basic SOE missions, generally resulting in reduced efficiency and sometimes in operational catastrophes. Considering the extent of the German effort, the thousands of agents and secret police and scores of military units involved, allied catastrophes were remarkably few. One of the most valuable lessons offered by French resistance is the relative ease with which resistance members operated in occupied areas, where by no means all of the civil population was friendly to the allied cause. A large number of postwar memoirs underlined this lesson, my own favorites being George Millar's *Horned Pigeon* and *Maquis*, Peter Churchill's *Of Their Own Choice,* and Bruce Marshall's *The White Rabbit.*

Although concerned allied organizations and incredibly brave agents can take some credit, much of it must go to the enemy, whose inept occupation procedures for the most part not only failed to exploit the divisive environment but caused many Frenchmen to take a stand, if only of inert sympathy, in favor of the resistance. As early as August 1940, the Germans responded to acts of sabotage by ordering a curfew and seizure of hostages. This solved very little, and continuing repressive measures served to expand isolated and unco-ordinated resistance nuclei. Anti-German posters appeared, underground newspapers multiplied, sabotage continued. The German invasion of Russia brought French Communists to life. Peculiarly prepared for resistance work ". . . by their organization in cells, the anonymity of their hierarchy and the devotion of their cadres," they believed in striking whenever and wherever possible, violence that brought savage reprisals and enlarged the resistance. In August 1941, Pétain admitted the growing problem in a radio address:

> . . . From several regions of France I can feel an evil wind blowing. Unrest is taking hold of people's minds. Doubt is seizing their souls. The authority of the Government is being called in question. Orders are being carried out badly. A real uneasiness is striking at the French people.[8]

A month later, resistance fighters killed the colonel commanding Nantes garrison, an officer in Bordeaux, and two German soldiers in Paris. The Germans shot forty-eight French citizens in Nantes and fifty in Bordeaux. To prevent further escalation, De Gaulle ordered a temporary halt:

> . . . It is absolutely natural and absolutely right that Germans should be killed by Frenchmen. If the Germans did not wish to receive death at our hands, they had only to stay at home. . . . But there are tactics in war. War must be conducted by those entrusted with the task. . . . For the moment, my orders to those in occupied territory are not to kill Germans there openly. This for one reason

314

only: that it is, at present, too easy for the enemy to retaliate by massacring our fighters, now, for the time being, disarmed. On the other hand, as soon as we are in a position to move to the attack, the orders for which you are waiting will be given.[9]

Resistance elements controlled by Gaullist officers generally conformed to these orders. Other units, including most Communist maquis, did not. Continued reprisals and German behavior in general helped resistance to grow, as did inept enemy propaganda and German refusal to release over a million French prisoners of war being used as a labor force in Germany. The creation of and reliance on special French police forces such as Joseph Darnand's Service d'Ordre de la Légion—which in 1943 would become the brutal and hated Milice—also did much to antagonize an increasingly restless population.[10]

In mid-1942, the Germans erred seriously by introducing a forced-labor scheme, the dreaded STO, or Service du Travail Obligatoire, under which men of military age were taken to Germany. Although the Germans shipped twenty thousand men a week from Paris, thousands more fled to the hills and mountains, there to form the famed maquis.[11] A recruiting leaflet of the time suggests their over-all frame of mind:

> . . . Men who come to the maquis to fight live badly, in precarious fashion, with food hard to find; they will be absolutely cut off from their families for the duration; the enemy does not apply the rules of war to them; they cannot be assured any pay; every effort will be made to help their families, but it is impossible to give any guarantee in this matter; all correspondence is forbidden.
>
> Bring two shirts, two underpants, two pair wool socks, a light sweater, a scarf, a heavy sweater, a wool blanket, an extra pair of shoes, shoe laces, needles, thread, buttons, safety pins, soap, canteen, knife and fork, flashlight, compass, a weapon if possible, and also if possible a sleeping bag. Wear a warm suit, a beret, a raincoat, a good pair of hobnailed shoes.
>
> You will need a complete set of papers, even false, but in order, with a work card to pass you through road-blocks. It is essential to have food ration tickets.[12]

German occupation of Vichy France in response to allied landings in North Africa further extended the meaning of the war to the French nation—in other words, it stirred up what Lyautey would have termed an "asleep" area and forced people to take a position for or against resistance.

German security services, the Abwehr and Gestapo, were not up to the increased task. German countermeasures suffered from competing counterespionage organizations and police forces whose " . . . senior staffs were obsessed by service intrigues, and their junior staffs were often as incompetent as they were cruel." As early as October 1942, the German high command was becoming apprehensive, Hitler himself ordering:

> ... In future, all terror and sabotage troops of the British and their accomplices, who do not act like soldiers but rather like bandits, will be treated as such by the German troops and will be ruthlessly eliminated in battle, wherever they appear.[13]

By the end of 1943, Marshal von Rundstedt noted:

> ... It was already impossible to dispatch single members of the Wehrmacht, ambulances, couriers, or supply columns without armed protection to the First or Nineteenth Army in the south of France.[14]

SOE did not actively promote guerrilla warfare at this time, but instead was trying to build a secret army by furnishing necessary arms and equipment to the newly formed maquis. Owing to a severe shortage of aircraft, these units received only meager arms and supply during 1942. Progress nonetheless resulted. In February 1943, when Commander Yeo-Thomas (the White Rabbit), Colonel Passy, and Pierre Brossolette slipped into France, they found five distinct resistance groups. Of the Gaullist formations, the Organisation Civile et Militaire was the most highly organized and had the best security. The Front National, a Communist organization that supported the Franc-Tireurs et Partisans, or FTP, without question " ... formed the strongest and most effective Resistance group. ... They claimed to carry out roughly 250 attacks and to kill between 500 and 600 Germans every month."[15] In time, the FTP furnished nearly a third of the maquis. Although they refused to relinquish control of their units, they agreed to join the other organizations in establishing a secret army commanded by General Delestraint—a co-operation prompted more by need for recognition, arms, and money than by patriotism.

In June, the Gestapo, which had penetrated the National Committee of Resistance, suddenly struck. General Delestraint (known as General Vidal), was shot: " ... The national organization was shattered and Resistance groups throughout the country suffered heavy losses." Despite this major setback,

> ... the second line of the leadership and the hard core of local and regional groups had survived. Surprisingly, only a small percentage of supplies were lost. Elated by the capture of many prominent Resistance leaders, the Germans had failed to find the hideouts and dumps of arms, ammunition and explosives which

SOE had been delivering on an increasing scale. In many areas, reception committees, reorganized and led by local leaders, continued to welcome new supplies and new SOE instructors, liaison officers and radio operators from Britain.[16]

In October 1943, the German commander in chief in France, von Rundstedt wrote to Hitler, noting " . . . with alarm the rapid increase in rail sabotage." In September, he reported, "534 very serious rail sabotage actions, as compared to a monthly average of only 120 during the first half of the year." Vichy police reported " . . . more than 3,000 separate attempts by Resistance saboteurs to wreck the railway system, of which 427 resulted in very heavy damage while 132 caused derailment with serious loss of German troops." Continuing destruction forced the Germans to import 20,000 German railway workers, and " . . . SS units had to be diverted from the front to guard stations, locomotive sheds, workshops and thousands of miles of track by day and night."[17]

London still did not want a general uprising until the planned allied landings. In January 1944, some maquis chiefs refused to obey De Gaulle's instructions to lie low until D-Day, and guerrilla activity notably increased. In words reminiscent of a French marshal in Spain in 1810, Von Rundstedt later wrote:

> . . . From January, 1944, the state of affairs in Southern France became so dangerous that all [German] commanders reported a general revolt. . . . Cases became numerous where whole formations of troops, and escorting troops of the military commanders were surrounded by bands for many days and, in isolated locations, simply killed off. . . . The life of the German troops in southern France was seriously menaced and became a doubtful proposition.[18]

In the first three months of 1944, guerrillas destroyed 808 locomotives (as opposed to 387 destroyed by allied air action).[19]

French and British planners in London meanwhile incorporated guerrilla warfare into plans for the Normandy landing: Plan Green to sabotage all railway lines; Plan Violet all telephone lines; Plan Tortoise all main roads. Special command teams, the Jedburghs, would help the secret army. Each team consisted of two officers—French, British, or American—and a sergeant radio operator, with each man trained in guerrilla tactics. Special Air Service, or SAS, units, consisting of thirty to sixty " . . . heavily armed, Commando-trained men," complemented this effort. So did Operational Groups, or OGs, " . . . airborne commandos of thirty-two men, who could be split up into two or four independent groups."[20] The Aloés Mission completed the list; this was a complete headquarters that would go into action after the landings. Jedburgh, SAS, and OG units were to parachute into rendezvous areas prearranged with resistance groups.

In March 1944, De Gaulle formally created the French Forces of the Interior (FFI) to which SOE/OSS became subordinated; in the subsequent battle for France, however, FFI remained subordinated to Supreme Headquarters Allied Expeditionary Forces (SHAEF).

A lack of aircraft had continued to hinder the supply effort, but increasing American air force participation greatly helped matters. In the first six months of 1944, in addition to large shipments of explosives and ammunition, SOE dropped into France 45,354 Sten guns, 17,576 pistols, 10,251 rifles, 1,832 Bren guns, 300 bazookas, and 143 mortars. On D-Day, June 6, 1944, about twenty thousand resistance fighters were fully armed; another fifty thousand were armed " . . . in some degree."[21] Prearranged signals from the SOE, broadcast by BBC, called for a general insurrection.[22]

Commencing in June, in one week guerrillas cut or blew up over one thousand railroad lines to prevent eight enemy divisions from immediately entering the battle of the beaches. On June 6, the German high command, for example, ordered the Second SS Panzer Division to march from Montauban to the Normandy beachhead, normally a three-day effort. Confined to roads because of railway sabotage and constantly attacked by maquis, the division did not arrive at Alençon until June 18. The Eleventh Panzer Division, hastily summoned from Russia, reached the French border in eight days but required another twenty-four days " . . . to cross France from Strasbourg to Caen."[23]

Not all maquis units prospered. Some small groups, such as a fifteen-man unit in Caen, were captured and executed to a man the day after D-Day. On D-Day, a Corcieux maquis of thirty-four men, attacked a German garrison of several hundred soldiers at Taintrux, in the Vosges area, a failure costing most of them their lives and bringing severe reprisals on the civilian population.[24] In other areas, notably near Saint Marcel, in Brittany, pitched battles developed between large maquis forces reinforced by SAS and OG units. On June 18, a powerful German force attacked and drove the maquis from its redoubt area, but at a cost of over five hundred German dead. On June 24, maquis on Vercors Plateau fought off a large-scale German attack but suffered severe casualties before withdrawing.

In general, the maquis served brilliantly, not only on and immediately after D-Day but throughout crucial summer months. In July a pro-Nazi French official complained by letter to Ambassador Otto Abetz:

> . . . It is no longer possible today for private persons or for Wehrmacht vehicles to travel along the roads of France. It is impossible

to go freely from Paris to Lyons, from Lyons to Bordeaux, from Paris to Châteauroux from Châteauroux to Angoulême. . . . The roads of Brittany are impractical. Behind the Normandy front, the Chief of Staff of the Army, whose headquarters are at Le Mans, has told me that German convoys are far from safe owing to particularly active maquisards. The roads from Paris to Nancy and Verdun, and from Paris to Mézières, have been cut by the Maquis. . . . The Maquis forces are so numerous that one is forced to the conclusion that, since the month of May, a veritable mobilization has taken place in the towns and villages of central France, as well as in the south and southeast.[25]

According to the historian Robert Aron, between July 10 and August 4 in the department of Côtes-du-Nord, the maquis put 2,500 Germans out of action, cut 300 telephone and high-tension lines, effectively sabotaged railways, derailed 40 trains, ambushed 50 convoys and captured 200 vehicles, burned 10,000 gallons of German gasoline, and captured a prison and liberated 32 Frenchmen condemned to death.[26]

None of this came easy. French resistance agents paid a premium price for each operational success whether a piece of vital intelligence, an escaped pilot, or a blown-up train. The clandestine organizations lost over five hundred agents, generally ghastly deaths. French civilians suspected of being resistance workers were arrested by the tens of thousands. General de Gaulle later wrote that:

> . . . with the co-operation of a considerable number of officials and a mass of informers, 60,000 persons had been executed and more than 200,000 deported of whom a bare 50,000 survived. Further, 35,000 men and women had been condemned by Vichy tribunals; 70,000 "suspects" interned; 35,000 officials cashiered; 15,000 officers degraded under suspicion of being in the resistance.[27]

According to Robert Aron, some twenty-four thousand maquisards were killed—a high percentage in view of their total strength of two hundred thousand. French headquarters in London distributed over 15 billion francs to resistance forces; the cost to SOE and OSS must have been astronomical. SOE and OSS dropped more than half a million small arms and four thousand larger weapons, many of which fell into enemy hands.[28]

France paid another internal price—that of revenge. Maquis units summarily executed an estimated 6,675 collaborators before the liberation, another 4,000 after. Tribunals subsequently condemned 2,071 persons to death (De Gaulle commuted 1,303 of the sentences); the courts also passed 39,900 prison sentences.[29]

Resistance is not an easy task.

CHAPTER TWENTY-FIVE

1. Foot, *SOE in France,* Introduction, xx.
2. De Gaulle, I, 157.
3. Foot, *SOE in France,* Introduction, xx. See also, Sweet-Escott; Piquet-Wicks.
4. Foot, *SOE in France,* Introduction, xx.
5. De Gaulle, I, 157.
6. Foot, *SOE in France,* Introduction, xx.
7. Sweet-Escott, 126. See also, R.H. Smith.
8. De Gaulle, I, 265.
9. Ibid., 266.
10. Ehrlich, 35, 130. Darnand's original organization was a fascist group composed of loyal gentlemen but in reality mainly brutal jailbirds. According to the writer, each member swore " . . . to fight against democracy, against Gaullist dissidence and against the Jewish leprosy." Darnand became head of Vichy police " . . . with power over all law enforcement agencies under French control." In 1943, his "legion" became the Milice, described by the writer as "a fully equipped little army of young Frenchmen, with special spy services to uncover resistance and to infiltrate resistance movements. They were noted for their joyous viciousness."
11. Ibid., 149. *Maquis* " . . . is a Corsican word for the dense brush of the hill country, to which Corsicans historically repair when they are in trouble."
12. Ibid., 156.
13. Foot, *SOE in France,* 187. In North Africa, Rommel refused to pass on this order to his subordinates.
14. Ibid., 233, 285.
15. Marshall, 26–7.
16. Cookridge, 25.
17. Ibid, 313.
18. Foot, *SOE in France,* 356.
19. Cookridge, 313.
20. Aron, 179–80.
21. Cookridge, 312.
22. Aron, 133–4. Professor Foot has informed me that " . . . those BBC messages calling out resistance all over France were sent on Eisenhower's direct order, against the advice of his technical advisers of several levels and nationalities." Private letter in the writer's files.
23. De Gaulle, II, 285–6.
24. Aron, 134.
25. Ibid., 209–10.
26. Ibid., 178.
27. De Gaulle, III, 108.
28. Aron, 283. See also, Miksche, 148: " . . . During the war the following arms supplies were parachuted into France: 198,000 Sten guns, 128,000 rifles, 20,000 Bren guns, 10,000 carbines; 58,000 pistols, 595,000 kilograms of explosives, 723,000 hand grenades, 9,000 mines, 2,700 bazookas, 285 mortars."
29. De Gaulle, 42–3, 108–9.

CHAPTER 26

German invasion of Russia • Ukrainian apathy • The Red army and guerrilla warfare • Stalin calls for guerrilla resistance • Early guerrilla operations • Guerrilla problems • Germany's extermination policy • German counterguerrilla tactics • Kaminski and Vlasov • German intransigence • Stalin's reorganization of partisan units • Guerrilla hardships • Early guerrilla tactics • Long-range guerrilla operations • Over-all effectiveness of guerrilla warfare

FEW INVADING ARMIES in history have received the spontaneous welcome accorded to Hitler's powerful legions in some areas of the Ukraine in 1941. Instead of sniper fire or Molotov cocktails, Panzer commanders received floral bouquets from cheering civilians who greeted the Teutonic host as "liberators" from Soviet rule. Ukrainian nationalists in eastern Galicia actually rose against their Soviet masters, " . . . a revolt savagely repressed by the retreating Red Army and NKVD [secret police]. . . . "[1] If local reception was less enthusiastic in other areas, in general it was at first pacific, the population showing every desire to accommodate itself to the new masters.

This halcyon state of affairs sprang from a variety of reasons: general hostility of border peoples to the Soviet regime; Kremlin failure to plan effectively for partisan resistance; the surprise, speed, and weight of the German advance, which in many areas temporarily neutralized small guerrilla groups that managed to form.

The touchy international political situation helped explain the Kremlin's reluctance to plan extensive guerrilla resistance. Red army planners obviously respected the potential. Shortly after the 1917 revolution, the father of the Red army, Frunze, demanded " . . . the spirit of offensive maneuver" but stressed need for " . . . preparation for conducting partisan warfare in the territories of possible theatres of military activities."[2] Subsequent Red army planners stressed regular army operations, but did not exclude guerrilla warfare. Although the government organized and partially equipped small guerrilla bands in some border areas, lack of organization and official fears greatly restricted the project. The Kremlin had no wish to create a Frankenstein monster of armed peasants, any more than the Spanish Republican Government had wanted to arm workers in 1936. Civilian morale also entered: to prepare for partisan warfare bespoke retreat of regular forces, an admission of weakness which did not square with Kremlin infallibility.[3]

In the event, the Kremlin tried to make up for lost time. Five days after the German invasion, the head of the Ukrainian Communist Party, Nikita Khrushchev, " . . . gave fairly detailed instructions on partisan organization to a provincial Party secretary. . . . "[4] In early July 1941, in a backs-to-the-wall broadcast to the Russian people, Joseph Stalin ordered:

> . . . In areas occupied by the enemy, guerrilla units, mounted and on foot, must be formed; diversionist groups must be organized to combat the enemy troops, to foment guerrilla war everywhere, to blow up bridges and roads, damage telephone and telegraph lines, set fire to forests, stores, transports. In the occupied regions conditions must be made unbearable for the enemy and all his accomplices. They must be hounded and annihilated at every step and all their measures frustrated.[5]

A new army command charged with partisan warfare ordered political leaders in combat areas to organize guerrilla units:

> . . . Generally they were to operate only at night and from ambush. Their mission was to attack troop columns and assemblies, motorized infantry, camps, transports of fuel and ammunition, headquarters, air bases, and railroad trains previously halted by rail demolitions.[6]

Special diversionary units were to carry out sabotage, " . . . cutting telephone lines, firing fuel and ammunition dumps, railroad demolition, and attacks on individual or small groups of enemy vehicles."[7]

The army also began setting up guerrilla training camps to furnish small teams that would parachute behind German armies. Army Group South encountered these in late July and learned from interrogation that they had been charged with intelligence collection, sabotage and terror missions. Later, the camps trained persons to organize resistance and carry out various technical aspects of guerrilla activities.

The first guerrilla groups consisted mostly of NKVD officials and party members from towns and cities.[8] But Red army fugitives, at first officers and political commissars, followed civilians into forests and swamps, where ordinary soldiers and civilian refugees began joining them:

> ... before the first of July [1941] infantry units of *Army Group North* were harassed from all sides by bypassed Red elements. Numbers of Soviet troops were still roaming the swamps and forests, von Leeb reported to OKH [army high command], many in peasant clothes, and effective counter-measures were frustrated by the expanse and difficulty of the country and by manpower limitations. . . . [9]

Nowhere was this resistance serious. German weight had severely dislocated embryo partisan activity. The few guerrilla bands that managed to form became greatly segmented and devoid of central control. Although one German division operating in northeast Belorussia in late July 1941 spoke of "partisan regions" and reported " . . . that roads were mined daily,"[10] this was the exception.

Most partisans were having too much difficulty keeping alive to worry about resistance. In the south, flat and treeless steppes broken only by isolated forests and swamps provided unsuitable sanctuary, and the bands here were early eliminated. In general, a hostile population hindered the guerrilla effort. Peasants and townspeople in numerous areas refused to give guerrillas food or information and did not hesitate to report their presence to the enemy. Primarily for this reason, partisan movements in the mountain areas of the Caucasus, the Crimea, and western Ukraine never developed into a serious threat.

Guerrillas in the center and north found far more suitable terrain in wide belts of swamps, forests, and lakes encircling the Pripet Marshes. Not only did the land provide sanctuary, but, by channeling enemy communications to a few roads and railroads, it provided suitable targets for guerrillas. However, peasants and townspeople here and especially in Baltic areas, to the north, also proved hostile, and survival was not easy.

The first winter, of 1941–42, hurt the movement everywhere: forays to collect food and fuel meant tracks in the snow, and naked trees often meant naked guerrillas. In order to survive, various bands amalgamated into good-sized camps, and some of these became vulnerable to German attacks. As in Poland, the more secure the camp, the farther it lay from profitable targets, thus complicating operations. Three factors, however, saved incipient guerrilla groups at this crucial time, and even allowed them to expand: German occupation policy, German counterguerrilla methods, and Soviet organization and support of the guerrilla effort.

* * *

323

By far the most important of the three was the overriding German attitude toward the Russian population. From Hitler down, the Nazi high command regarded Russians as *Untermenschen,* or subhuman beings, an attitude succinctly noted by Goebbels in his diary: the Russians ". . . are not people, but a conglomeration of animals. . . . Bolshevism has merely accentuated this racial propensity of the Russian people."[11] Before the Wehrmacht marched, Hitler had decided that Russia must cease to exist as a nation. Expecting to accomplish her military destruction within four months, he foresaw a civil occupation and ultimate partition that would eliminate Bolshevism, the Russian nation, and most Soviet states, to provide a vast and rich area for German colonization and exploitation. Hitler decreed a civil occupation just as soon as possible and created a Ministry for the Occupied Eastern Territories (the Ostministerium), under Alfred Rosenberg, to accomplish it. Each of three army groups held responsibility for a Zone of Operations, which was divided into a Combat Zone and Army Rear Areas. The area behind this became the bailiwick of Rosenberg's civil commissars, who followed closely the army groups to take over territory as fast as the military forged ahead.

So far, so good. But, sandwiched between army groups and civil functionaries and lapping over into each sphere, came Himmler's SS organization, ". . . charged with preparation for political administration in the military zone of operations."[12] To confuse matters further, Hitler turned over economic exploitation of occupied areas to Goering, which could not but lead to conflict with Rosenberg and even with Himmler and army group commanders.

Himmler's mission spelled evil. His was a murder function authorized by Hitler's Commissar Order, which called for elimination of all Communist Party officials and Red army commissars at " . . . not later than the transit prisoner of war camps."[13] To eliminate the Jewish-Bolshevik enemy, Himmler set up special action teams (*Einsatzgruppen*) composed of SS, SD, and Gestapo troops and agents who " . . . would move in behind the conquering army, comb the newly-won lands, and mercilessly exterminate ideological and racial enemies. . . ."[14] The teams were not only operationally independent from army group commands, but their activities often spilled over into rear civil areas, which in any event eventually reacted adversely to their bestial activities.

The fragile and confused bodies of this organization would have had a difficult time instilling order even in victory. When the Wehrmacht failed to destroy the Red army, Hitler's jerry-built administrative house found itself in charge of an area of about four hundred thousand square miles holding some 65 million heterogeneous peoples. Within a few months, Hitler's basic premise had vanished, but the mission remained: exterminate and exploit.

This incredible policy immediately affected prisoners of war and people of occupied Soviet areas. Within six months of invasion, German armies had captured some 3 million Soviet soldiers, with hundreds of thousands of additional prisoners coming in each month. No particular arrangements existed to care for these unfortunates; very little food existed to feed them and very little humanity to serve them. Murder resulted:

> . . . Testimony is eloquent and prolific on the abandonment of entire divisions under the open sky. Epidemics and endemic diseases decimated the camps. Beatings and abuse by the guards were commonplace. Millions spent weeks without food or shelter. Carloads of prisoners were dead when they arrived at their destination. Casualty figures varied considerably, but almost nowhere amounted to less than 30 per cent in the winter of 1941–42, and sometimes went as high as 95 per cent.

The shocking conditions even filtered back to Berlin. Goering complained to Count Ciano that Soviet prisoners were not only eating their own boots but " . . . they have begun to eat each other, and what is more serious, have also eaten a German sentry."[15]

Inadequate security forces, particularly in forward prison camps, allowed thousands of Soviet prisoners to escape. Others, cut off by the German advance and learning of German treatment of their fellows, refused to surrender. Throughout autumn and winter, some of these fugitives reached woods and swamps to bring badly needed military skills to hard-pressed guerrilla bands. By spring of 1942, three or four hundred thousand soldiers were roaming free, and many of these, from sheer necessity, drifted into the forest and joined the guerrillas.[16]

Meanwhile the first bloom on the German rose of occupation had vanished. Most senior army commanders had welcomed the relatively pacific reception that promised secure lines of communication—particularly important in view of voracious appetites of tanks, trucks, and aircraft for fuel and oil. But as their progress continued, initial victories seemed to validate Hitler's notion of a short war in the east. Nazi arrogance, never far below the surface, at once asserted itself, and the *Untermensch* philosophy captured many minds. As war continued into autumn and winter and no victory resulted, as casualties continued to soar and Hitler's strategic incompetence became obvious, arrogance began turning to fear.[17] In partisan areas, " . . . military considerations and often a sense of physical danger, isolation, and self-defense on occupied soil, caused commanders to attempt to eliminate the partisans 'at all costs' "—to insist on "prophylaxis by terror." "Collective measures of force" were to be applied promptly in any instance of even

325

"passive resistance" in which the perpetrator could not be immediately identified. Soviet soldiers behind the lines who refused to turn themselves over to the Germans were to be considered insurgents " . . . and treated accordingly." In rear army areas, Himmler's special teams caused additional terror:

> . . . One of the four *Einsatzgruppen* commanders, Otto Ohlendorf, stated [at the Nuremberg trials] that during the first year of the campaign, the group under his command liquidated about 90,000 men, women and children. The activities of these teams were dictated not by military necessity but purely by ideological considerations.[18]

The general policy of terror carried over into Reich Commissariat Ostland and Reich Commissariat Ukraine, vast areas that fell to German civil administration. Gauleiter Erich Koch who ruled the Ukraine, believed that his subjects " . . . stood [sic] far below us and should be grateful to God that we allow them to stay alive. We have liberated them; in return, they must know no other goal except to work for us. There can be no human companionship. . . . " Koch's colleague Lohse ruled the center and north with the same philosophy.[19]

Part of their task was to siphon off agricultural production for relief of the homeland, just as Goering's people were attempting to exploit various industrial complexes. But part also was to siphon off skilled workers. By early spring of 1942, the *Ostarbeiter* program had sent fifty thousand persons to Germany, by that summer 1 million, and a year later 2 million.[20]

Meanwhile Himmler's people were happily conducting the extermination task: One *Einsatzgruppe,* in the spring of 1942, complained that only 42,000 out of 170,000 political undesirables (Bolsheviks and Jews) had been exterminated. The general commissar there, Wilhelm Kuhe, soon put matters right, announcing in July that " . . . in the past ten weeks we have liquidated about 50,000 Jews in Belorussia. In the rural areas of Minsk, Jewry has been eradicated without jeopardizing the labor situation."[21]

Exploitation and extermination could only create local hatreds. As the over-all German policy of genocide, direct or indirect, became clear, numerous peasants and workers preferred to risk life under the partisans. German failure to capture Moscow in late winter of 1941–42 also exercised a major psychological effect and tended to make the civil population more co-operative in supporting guerrilla units with recruits, food, and intelligence. As these grew stronger and their activities increased, German authorities had to expand security measures, which in turn added to the general climate of terror.

Each of the three German army group commanders depended on a rear-area headquarters and three "security divisions" to safeguard his immediate rear while " . . . maintaining the supply of the field armies and guaranteeing the exploitation of the land for the immediate use of the military."[22] A security division only remotely resembled its combat brother. It consisted of two regiments, one of regular combat infantry whose three battalions would furnish "alert units" for mobile operations, and one of *Landesschützen,* or second-line battalions, to carry out static guard duties. Support units such as motorized military police, engineers, and signal troops fleshed out these jury-rigged divisions.

Although the regular infantry and motorized police were well trained, with many combat veterans, *Landesschützen* units consisted of older, often unfit men. Supply officers were "inadequately trained," and intelligence officers were " . . . admittedly inept in intelligence matters and generally had no knowledge of counter-intelligence methodology." Transport was short, arms and equipment second rate, morale and discipline generally poor.[23]

The primary task of security divisions centered on protecting supply depots, railheads, and airfields, and keeping open lines of communication to the front. Since the war would be over in four months, the problem of pacification and thus counterguerrilla warfare had not been studied: The German army did not even possess a standard operating procedure for counterguerrilla warfare, and only in October 1941 did the high command issue a *Directive for Anti-Partisan Warfare*—a rather innocuous work.[24]

When guerrilla attacks began, security divisions working with Himmler's SS security and police units replied with severe punitive measures that more often hurt the general population than the guerrillas:

> . . . Because of the expanse of country which had to be covered, they took positive measures against the partisans only when the supply lines and installations were openly threatened. Even then they stuck closely to the roads and rail lines and the urban areas, and avoided the more difficult terrain and back-country regions . . . victorious in a few insignificant incidents over small insurgent groups, the security units gained in confidence. . . . They felt they were winning their war and that their areas of responsibility would be completely under control in a matter of weeks or days.[25]

When guerrilla attacks continued and mounted in intensity, rear-area commanders responded by "logical" measures—by trying to tighten unit security, by offering bribes of money and food for accurate information on guerrilla activities, by weapons collection, by setting up intelligence nets of *Vertrauensleute,* or collaborators, by trying to streamline intelligence procedures—carrots that never totally replaced sticks of severe reprisals. More imaginative commanders formed "counter" or "dummy" bands,

> ...made up of units from the security police and the security service and of the *Ordnungspolizei,* with a number of reliable natives, and committed in partisan-dominated areas in the manner of a genuine partisan unit. In this manner they would be able to keep a constant check on the sentiments of the population, make contact with irregular units, and often quietly eliminate partisan leaders.[26]

Commanders also strengthened strong points, added guards to bridges and railway lines, and developed small, mobile pursuit units (the *Jagdkommando*). As matters worsened for the Germans, measures became more extreme. In the Bryansk area, the local commander insisted on escorted motor convoys traveling by daylight and on armored trains; troops built special security zones up to nine miles wide on each side of major railroad lines: " . . . Brushwork and forests were cleared, all civilian residents registered, and movements of the people controlled day and night."[27]

In the center and north, harassed commanders began early to conduct counterguerrilla "sweeps," the intention being to uncover and destroy the bands. These operations normally utilized combat units temporarily transferred from the front. The basic technique involved locating the general guerrilla area, surrounding it, and then "combing" through it with additional units. One of the earliest counterguerrilla operations occurred in spring of 1942 north of Smolensk, where guerrillas controlled an impressive area of some two to three thousand square miles. For about a month, " . . . all or parts of nine German divisions mounted an attack which shattered the partisan movement." The German forces reported that out of fifteen to twenty thousand enemy, about two thousand broke out and another two to three thousand went into hiding, but that the remainder were killed or captured.[28]

The Germans may well have exaggerated their success. Certainly other "combing" operations did not similarly prosper. Also in spring of 1942, in the Bryansk area, Operation *Vogelsang* employed local troops reinforced by one armored and two infantry regiments. At small cost to the Germans, 58 dead and 138 wounded, the operation allegedly killed 1,193 guerrillas, wounded an estimated 1,400, and captured 498. Security forces arrested 2,249 men and evacuated 12,531 persons from the area. These impressive figures did not impress the Second Panzer Army, which reported:

> . . . The success did not measure up to expectations. The partisans continued their old tactics of evading [contact], withdrawing into the forests, or moving in larger groups into the areas south and south-west of the Roslavl-Bryansk highways and into the Kletnya area. Although no attacks were noted in the pacified section, mines continued to be planted and . . . several vehicles were damaged. . . .

Two authorities who studied this operation, DeWitt and Moll, concluded that " . . . the later reappearance of these partisans suggests that a large proportion of the casualties reported by the Germans consisted in fact of non-partisan members of the local population." Subsequent counterguerrilla "sweeps" in the same area tended to confirm this significant conclusion.[29] So did Operation *Kottbus,* a year later in northeastern Belorussia, which involved a prolonged attack by sixteen thousand German troops:

> . . . Reporting to Rosenberg [Minister of Eastern Territories] on the first phase of this operation, the German Commissar General . . . for Belorussia pointed out that among the 5,000 people shot for suspicion of collaborating with the partisans, there were many women and children. He also argued that if for 4,500 enemy dead only 492 rifles were captured, the implication clearly was that the dead included many peasants who were not necessarily partisans. The effect of these operations on the partisans was negligible. Within a few weeks they reappeared as strong as ever. . . . [30]

Few military or political commanders at first protested, since extreme repression fitted Nazi political policy. Professor Armstrong concluded:

> . . . Most of the time . . . the German counter-guerrillas took the position that the civilians, since they had supplied the partisans with food and information, ought to be punished. The Germans also imagined that by destroying agricultural production they would starve the partisans. Consequently, horrible atrocities were committed against the civilian population, including the elderly, women and children. Village-burning was the main feature of the combing operations. In addition, the Germans rounded up all able-bodied younger men and women for the *Ostarbeiter* program of [forced] labor in Germany. The combined effect of these measures was to turn neutral elements of the population toward the partisans, and particularly to send them a constant flow of new recruits seeking to escape the *Ostarbeiter* program. . . .

As Armstrong pointed out, theoretically the Germans might have isolated guerrilla units by evacuating specific areas, but the size of areas, the vast population, and partisan strength prevented this.[31]

Even where combing operations broke up guerrilla activities, the effect was only temporary. They did break up some bands, however, and eliminated the immediate threat to communications by keeping them off balance. The Germans continued to employ the tactic almost to the end and would have used it more often had enough soldiers been available.

Security divisions suffered constantly from manpower shortages. Once Soviet counteroffensives began, German army commanders did not hesitate to transfer regular infantry regiments away from security divisions to front-line duty. Conversely, only occasionally could security divisions obtain services of front-line units for counterguerrilla operations. At one point in 1942, in the north, thirty of thirty-four security battalions had been ordered to the front. Rear-area commanders attempted to solve the manpower problem in several ways. In addition to front-line troops, they used satellite security divisions, generally unreliable units. Sometimes they suborned German replacement units still in training, definitely an unsatisfactory arrangement. They also formed indigenous battalions called *Osttruppen,* but Hitler's political policy and the sharp eyes of Nazi purists made this a disjointed, generally surreptitious effort (although eventually it recruited some five hundred thousand locals). Later, when German losses and Soviet battle successes caused Nazis to have second thoughts, theretofore-willing recruits changed their minds and if impressed into duty often deserted in droves to the partisans. Similar programs to enlist local peoples in various types of militias, village defense forces, and youth movements (to deprive partisans of recruits) encountered the same political obstruction.

Even when these measures materialized, most came too late and in too slight quantity to radically influence the counterguerrilla campaign. Had the Germans mobilized the generally anti-Soviet border populations in 1941 and early 1942, the whole tenor of the campaign would undoubtedly have changed. Even after this error, opportunity still remained. As one example, south of Bryansk German officials quietly supported an irregular group of anti-Soviet Russians, the Kaminski band, which eventually numbered some nine thousand irregulars and performed valuable counterguerrilla services.[32] On a bigger scale, more imaginative German officials sponsored an anti-Soviet army recruited from prisoners of war and commanded by a prisoner, an anti-Soviet General, Vlasov. Although Vlasov could easily have raised an army of from ten to twenty divisions, he understandably demanded some postwar political guarantees, which ranking Nazis refused to give him. The program died, only to be revived at too late a date.

Some German overlords early recognized the stupidity of official policy. After ten weeks of battle, Field Marshal von Kluge

> . . . issued an order sharply condemning plundering and wanton requisitions by German troops, and demanding the prompt and complete cessation of all abuse under threat of summary punishment.[33]

As early as December 1941, Goebbels expressed concern " . . . about the extent to which the occupation authorities were antagonizing the population."[34] That winter, a host of occupation authorities, civil and military, warned officials in Berlin of the disastrous policy. In August 1942, an OKW (Army High Command) report reflected the feelings of many occupation officials in the Soviet Union:

> . . . Time after time the population of the Ukraine shows itself grateful for every instance when it is dealt with humanely on the basis of equality, and reacts strongly against contemptuous treatment.[35]

At a conference of military and civil occupation officials in October 1942,

> . . . Colonel Claus von Stauffenberg, Hitler's would-be assassin, took the floor to flail German policy in an impassioned half-hour impromptu speech. The Reich, he exclaimed, was sowing a hatred that the next generation would reap; the key to victory was winning the sympathy and support of the people who lived in the East![36]

But dissenters already had lost their case. In late 1942, Hitler, while making counterguerrilla operations in combat areas a General Staff responsibility, gave over rear army areas to the SS, which was charged with total extermination of the partisans.

German failure to pacify, let alone mobilize, occupation areas immeasurably aided the Soviet high command's effort to harness diverse guerrilla forces, both to cause damage to the enemy and to prevent anti-Soviet forces from arising.

In spring of 1941, Stalin replaced makeshift partisan staff arrangements with the Central Staff of the Partisan Movement, headed by Marshal Voroshilov, soon replaced by a high-ranking party official, P. K. Ponomarenko, and operating directly under the Supreme Defense Council. The NKVD also formed a partisan section, as did army groups and armies a few months later.

Liaison teams trained and sent to the guerrilla units by these various headquarters did not fare well to start with, but, by summer of 1942, German brutality and Red army gains were causing passive acceptance by peasants and townspeople, and they were beginning to give direction to the guerrilla movement. Simultaneously, the Soviets began to win local air superiority, which greatly eased delivery of more teams, arms, and equipment, increased liaison between guerrillas and operational headquarters, and provided evacuation for badly wounded fighters. *The Partisan's Handbook* appeared in quantity from Moscow to offer ". . . guides on partisan tactics, Soviet and enemy weapons and explosives, German anti-partisan tactics, first aid," and other pertinent subjects.[37] By mid-1942, fifteen guerrilla training centers existed *behind* German lines around Voronezh alone; one of them taught a six-week course to classes ranging from 170 to 250 guerrillas.[38] Larger units, in the north, claimed a doctor and several nurses, also the ubiquitous political commissars. Arms began arriving in some quantity, and in addition to rifles included light mortars, machine guns, automatic rifles, bazookas, grenades, mines, and explosives. More airfields appeared in guerrilla country. As early as August 1942, leading guerrilla officials flew to Moscow to receive Stalin's direct orders and return to their units![39]

Progress remained slow, however, and setbacks frequent. German counteroperations kept many units on the run. By July 1942, Central Headquarters " . . . was in radio contact with only ten per cent of the partisan groups," and nowhere along the great battle line were guerrillas really hindering the German military effort. Hunger and sickness plagued many units. Guerrillas suffered from rheumatism, scurvy, pellagra, boils, toothaches, stomach and intestinal disorders—one "regiment," of 737 men, recorded 261 casualties from sickness, 52 from combat and 20 from desertion.[40]

Matters slowly improved. By mid-November, central headquarters was in radio contact with 20 per cent of the guerrilla units, more and more of which were receiving radio transmitters. Recruits continued to flow in: from thirty thousand in early 1942, the movement had grown to some two hundred thousand in mid-1943.

In the center and north, large partisan areas existed, some numbering between twelve thousand and twenty thousand. These comprised operational "brigades" of from three hundred fifty to two thousand guerrillas. Each brigade consisted of battalions, companies, and platoons which " . . . might be dispersed over ten or twenty square miles. Groups of brigades occasionally occupied areas of several hundred square miles."[41]

WESTERN U.S.S.R.
1940
• Towns and Cities
o–o–o German line
       November 1942
x–x–x German line
       October 1943

Units devoted a great deal of effort, particularly in early stages, to security and survival. In populated areas, this meant almost constant involvement with the civil population. Although partisan commanders forbade indiscriminate looting, in order to gain food and supply and to deny it to the enemy and also to assert the government's presence, they did not hesitate to burn collective farms and destroy farm machinery. Under direction of political commissars, units barraged the people with propaganda, often using boards, glass, and cloth in place of almost non-existent paper.

The propaganda effort eventually became much more sophisticated and gained greatly because of enemy atrocities. Partisans also used selective terrorism, frequently killing German officials and Russian collaborators.

Small guerrilla units tried to become as self-sufficient as possible. Although air drops supplied essentials such as sugar, salt, and coffee, bands relied on the land and on raids of German dumps for food. A few isolated units tilled their own fields and kept herds of cattle.[42] One forest base of the time.

> . . . included a log encampment, with flour mills, vats for soap-making, forges and home-made lathes for the repair and alteration of weapons. In addition to a wireless transmitting and receiving station, there was the inevitable printing works for the production of propaganda material and news sheets.[43]

In addition to "natural" defense provided by distance, terrain, and civil co-operation, the partisans depended on fortified permanent camps. One German lieutenant later described the defenses he encountered:

> . . . The bunker was solidly built. The walls were made of five to six inch logs, extending only about a foot above the level of the ground. The dugout was covered with earth, with only the entrance and window left uncovered. The roof was supported by two log beams and covered with a foot of ground. . . . The bunker on the inside measured about twenty-six feet in length, sixteen feet in width, and six feet in height. Nearby we found a supply of firewood, a kitchen dugout, and a well. The small stock of food was worthy of note.[44]

Partisan combat operations varied enormously. Some units worked out of base areas, returning after a specific operation. Others operated independently in German rear areas. One unit leader led a "roving band" on an eight-thousand-mile patrol over a twenty-six-month period. Moving mainly at night, the guerrillas concentrated on attacking enemy lines of communication and isolated enemy detachments. Ironically the unit was nearly destroyed when it sought sanctuary in the northern Carpathians, where the people refused to support it.[45] In the center and north, guerrilla units concentrated on destroying railroads and roads and on ambushing German detachments. At first, guerrillas struck targets of opportunity, but as units grew stronger and communications improved, they sometimes co-ordinated operations with the Red army. In the case of larger targets, for instance an enemy headquarters or an airfield,

> . . . in general, three echelons formed a raiding party: a "combat group," a "demolition group," and a "reserve" (which often ambushed pursuers). All raids and ambushes were prepared in advance with meticulous care, which comprised detailed reconnaissance observation (often performed by girls), detailed planning and the allotment beforehand of specific individual tasks, and cautious execution.[46]

The Soviet high command constantly called for maximum performance in striking priority targets:

> . . . At the top of the list were roads, rail lines, bridges, and enemy vehicles and rolling stock. Secondary targets comprised telephone and telegraph lines and supply depots. The bands were to take offensive action against German guard posts, patrols, and other small units only when they had a definite superiority in numbers.[47]

Authorities differ as to how much damage guerrillas inflicted. Central Staff claims of three hundred thousand Germans killed and thousands of tanks, armored cars, airplanes, and trucks destroyed are almost certainly exaggerated. John Armstrong has argued that total German military casualties inflicted by partisans probably did not exceed thirty-five thousand and that no more than half of these were German soldiers. Other authorities have pointed out that nowhere did guerrillas prevent the supply of German front-line troops and that in general they did not cause the high command to divert front-line troops to anti-partisan warfare.

> . . . Certainly the bands hurt the *Wehrmacht*. Every rail break, every piece of rolling stock damaged or destroyed, every German soldier killed, wounded, or diverted from other duties to guard against the bands hurt. But the damage was never decisive.[48]

This seems a reasonable conclusion, although it is based primarily on German reports by professional officers probably unwilling to give the guerrilla his complete due. The immense battle action also hindered objective measurement. A few trains or convoys blown up could not overly impress German commanders who in five days of Operation *Zitadelle*, for instance, lost 2,268 armored vehicles and suffered thousands of casualties.[49]

The guerrillas nonetheless plagued the enemy in a hundred ways and often caused him to commit troops that could better have used rest. They slowed and sometimes stopped important road and rail movements. During later offensives, they often operated effectively with regular army units. They supplied valuable intelligence from the beginning. They also played a passive role of a force in being—an effective psychological presence attested to by numerous German and Austrian survivors who, years later, shuddered when speaking to this writer of the dreaded *Partisanen*. As a force in being, they also formed a strong political influence in many areas and played a major role in preventing Germans from exploiting the civil population to maximum effectiveness.

Finally, many deficiencies that plagued the guerrilla movement were being repaired when the Red army began its vast series of offensives that eventually recovered Soviet territory and ended the guerrilla movement. Because of internal difficulties and German suppression, it had attained neither full growth nor full striking power. Had it been needed in case of battle reverses, its role might indeed have proved decisive. In the event, the Kremlin was delighted to pat it on the back and end its existence as soon as possible.

CHAPTER TWENTY-SIX

1. Dallin, 119.
2. Garthoff, 391–2.
3. Armstrong and DeWitt.
4. Armstrong, 14.
5. Armstrong and DeWitt, 76.
6. Howell, 48.
7. Ibid.
8. Garthoff, 396.
9. Howell, 43.
10. Mavrogordato and Ziemke, 528.
11. Dallin, 68.
12. Ibid., 27.
13. Howell, 16 ff.
14. Dallin, 29.
15. Ibid., 414–15.
16. Ziemke, 144.
17. Dallin, 74. See also, Dallin, 80: ". . . By the end of the year [1941] about one out of every four German soldiers in the East had been killed or wounded, and the Wehrmacht needed 2.5 million troops as replacements."
18. Ibid., 73–5.

19. Ibid., 148.
20. Ibid., 431.
21. Ibid., 208. Kuhe was killed by a bomb placed in his bed by a "trusted" chambermaid.
22. Howell, 12–13.
23. Ibid., 13.
24. Ibid., 71.
25. Ibid., 54.
26. Ibid., 119
27. DeWitt and Moll, 502.
28. Weinberg, 397.
29. DeWitt and Moll, 505.
30. Mavrogordato and Ziemke, 538.
31. Armstrong, 30.
32. Howell, 89.
33. Dallin, 515.
34. Ibid., 146.
35. Ibid., 500.
36. Ibid., 358.
37. Garthoff, 398.
38. Ziemke, 156–7.
39. Garthoff, 401.
40. Ziemke, 164.
41. Ibid., 156, 151.
42. Howell, 84–5.
43. Blair, 126.
44. Ziemke, 161.
45. Blair, 124. See also, Armstrong.
46. Garthoff, 407.
47. Howell, 141.
48. Ibid., 210.
49. Ibid., 128–9.

CHAPTER 27

The Germans occupy Yugoslavia • Guerrilla units form • The Balkan guerrilla tradition • Scanderbeg • Heyduks and klefts • Kosta Pečanac • World War II: Chetniks versus Partisans • Tito and the Yugoslav Communist Party • Early operations • SOE intervenes • German counterguerrilla offensives • Tito's growing strength • New German offensives • Fitzroy Maclean reports • Tito grows stronger • His near capture • Final guerrilla actions • German and Yugoslav losses • German strength in Yugoslavia • German operational problems • Tito and Yugoslav nationalism • The Hauspartisanen • Tito's guerrilla tactics • Kosta's operations • SOE's liaison problems • The Russian attitude

ELEVEN DAYS after Germany invaded Yugoslavia in March 1941, King Peter and his government fled to England, and the Yugoslav army, not yet fully mobilized, surrendered. To eliminate what Hitler regarded as a threat to his southern flank, he divided Slovenia between Germany and Italy, fed chunks of border areas to his satellite hounds—Hungary, Albania, Bulgaria—and established an independent Croatia under titular rule of Ante Pavelić, boss of an extremist Croat party called the Ustasi. What was left of Serbia went to the quisling rule of General Nedić. German minions, following hard on the heels of the fast-moving Wehrmacht, soon introduced wholesale conscription of men for forced labor in Germany and exploitation of food and economic resources.

Numerous Yugoslavs already had escaped the Nazi juggernaut by fleeing to traditional refuge in the mountains, and now thousands more left villages to escape forced labor or deportation to Germany. By midsummer 1941, scores of guerrilla bands were roaming broad mountain ranges that stretch 450 miles through Slovenia and Montenegro—rugged terrain which continues inland from the coast and runs southeast to the Yugoslav-Greek border.

Had Adolf Hilter paid attention to history, he would have braced for trouble. Greek, Roman, and Byzantine armies at one time or another received bloody noses in the Balkans. Although the Slavs were dominated first by Avars and then by Greeks, their military reputation early became formidable. Passing centuries of conflict that saw the emergence of ethnic groups, of Slovenes, Croats, Serbs, and Bulgars, enhanced this reputation. Almost constant war between Arabs and Greeks frequently lapped over the Balkan Peninsula and nearly always proved cruel in the extreme.[1] The rise of the Ottoman Empire brought no surcease to the Balkans. Defeat at Kosovo in 1389 cost Serbia her independence for more than four centuries. But Turkish rule was never secure. Montenegrins under George Balsha shut themselves up in the Black Mountains to wage guerrilla warfare against both Turks and Venetians. In Albania a natural leader arose to challenge the splendid Turkish presence. This was a tribal chief, George Castriotes whom the Turks named Scanderbeg and who fought guerrilla warfare so successfully that Mohammed II finally came to terms with him: " . . . The fame of Scanderbeg . . . went like wild-fire throughout Balkania and the West. Great states like Hungary and Venice sought his alliance; the pope hailed him in quaint and picturesque phrase as 'the athlete of Christendom.' "[2] Scanderbeg died in 1467. The tribes he had welded together by his own charisma soon fell apart and submitted to Turkish rule. The Montenegrins continued to hold out. In 1484, they burned their capital and withdrew to the mountain village of Cetinje, which they held for another 150 years, their attitude best expressed by the words spoken over male infants at the baptismal font: "God save him from dying in his bed."[3] Their guerrilla tactics infuriated Napoleon, who swore to turn Monte Negro into Monte Rosso. Even their Austrian allies shied away:

> . . . the Emperor of Austria desired to employ their assistance as little as possible, "as from their savage characters and the lawless ferocity of their manners they must spread terror among the peaceable inhabitants, and produce ill-will and hatred towards the troops of His Imperial Majesty."[4]

The rest of the Balkans continued to suffer under the Ottoman yoke. The Turks considered the peoples as "rayahs," or "conquered infidels," who held " . . . no rights or privileges, who paid to the Sultan 'haratch,' and a tenth of the product of their labor, and who were at the mercy of their Turkish landlords, Turkish officials and warriors." Beginning about 1750, Turkish oppression brought guerrilla bands into being. Called *heyduks* by the Serbs and *klefts* by the Greeks, these bands

... moved through the Servian mountains and forests, hurrying from one point to another, where a specially brutal misdeed of Turks against the Christian men and women was to be avenged. The Hydooks were a sort of irregular national force, insurgents who were permanently leading a guerrilla war against the Turks. They were the original model of the Committadjis of our days, only without a central leadership and without committees. Fear of the Hydooks was the only consideration which restrained the Turkish lawlessness, rapacity and violence. The Turks called them "brigands," and whoever of them fell into their hands was mercilessly impaled alive.[5]

The crimes continued despite the heyduks, but the Serbs had just about had enough. In 1804, four Turkish captains known as the *Dahees* murdered the ruling Vizier Mustapha and formed

... a peculiar political, military and commercial partnership, proclaimed themselves masters of the entire Pashalik of Belgrade. They covered the country with a net of wooden blockhouses (*Hans*), which were occupied by their armed agents, who lived there at the expense of the neighboring villages, and collected the increased taxes and new imposts introduced by the Dahees.[6]

Frightened by rising restlessness of the people, they reacted by repression—by trying to kill every native leader or potential leader in the country. One of these intended victims was a heyduk chief, George Petrovich, who escaped to organize guerrilla war against the Janissaries. Successful in this, he led a revolt against the Turks and became famous as Black George. In 1813, however, he panicked and fled. Serbia returned to Moslem rule but, two years later, Milosh Obrenovich led a new and successful revolt. Obrenovich is believed to have arranged for Black George's murder, which started a dynastic feud that lasted over a century.[7]

Interminable quarrels that made the Balkans famous as "the cockpit of Europe" invariably involved border guerrilla actions and terrorist raids. World War I brought more conventional battle to Serbia, whose small but courageous army eventually succumbed to the weight of German, Austro-Hungarian, and Bulgarian forces. The shattered army escaped to the Albanian coast and allied ships only with the greatest difficulty and enormous losses. The peasants who remained refused to submit to Austrian rule. In 1916, the allies flew in a famous guerrilla leader, Kosta Pečanac, who started irregular warfare against the enemy.

... Although this rising, like all the others, was suppressed with the utmost ferocity and cruelty, reprisals being taken against old men, women and children if the rebels themselves could not be caught, Kosta himself remained at liberty and fighting right to the end of the war.[8]

In summer of 1941, numerous guerrilla bands struggling to survive in Yugoslav mountains served one of two flags: Chetnik or Partisan. Division between the two was deep, for little unity had existed in this Balkan country since its optimistic creation at the Paris Peace Conference.

Kosta Pečanac, hero of Serbian resistance in World War I, headed the Chetniks, a Serbian nationalist organization.[9] In theory, Chetniks formed the guerrilla arm of the Royal Yugoslav Army and were organized on a country-wide basis. In fact, no such organization existed. Pečanac, obsessed by reprisals that followed the Partisan rising in 1916, preferred to accommodate the enemy and took a number of Chetniks over to General Nedić's puppet government. This left the main body of Chetniks in the hands of a regular officer, Colonel Draža Mihailović, who set up guerrilla headquarters in the mountains near Valjevo, in western Serbia.

Cored by the Yugoslav Communist Party, the Partisans formed a much more homogeneous force than the Chetniks. Forced underground in 1921 because of terrorist activities, party members had led a clandestine life, depending on wits, courage, and discipline to survive a series of police states. Originally sixty thousand strong, the party succumbed to feuding factionalism until, by 1928, membership numbered only three thousand. Government repression further hurt it until, in 1934, it was falling apart at the seams.[10]

Meanwhile a young Croat metalworker, Josip Brozovich, had been rising in party ranks. Born in 1892, the seventh of fifteen children in an impoverished home in a small village, Josip completed elementary school before leaving home to work as a locksmith and mechanic. Enlisting in a Croat regiment to fight for Austria in World War I, he rose to warrant-officer rank, was badly wounded and captured by the Russians, learned the language, and, in 1917, joined the Bolsheviks. He married a Russian, fought with the Kirghiz nomads, who were Mongol horsemen, and in 1920 returned to what had become Yugoslavia, a state of 12 million persons. Josip Broz, as he had become, worked as party organizer and agitator, slowly rising in the party while fathering a family and spending a good many years in jail. In 1935, he worked for the Comintern, then returned to Yugoslavia to set up a "rat-line" which fed some fifteen hundred volunteers to the fighting in Spain; many of his future generals fought with international brigades. In 1937, the Kremlin liquidated his boss and made him secretary-general of the Yugoslav party. Tito, as he was now known, reorganized the party, raising its membership to twelve thousand, a small but disciplined group dedicated to the Communist ideal.[11]

In 1941, the German invasion caught Yugoslav Communists off balance, mainly because of the existing German-Russian non-aggression pact. When Hitler's legions broke that by invading Russia, the Comintern cabled Tito to "take all measures to support and alleviate the struggle of the Soviet people."[12] Out went word to take to the hills. Tito set up Partisan headquarters near Užice, in western Serbia, not far from Mihailović's camp.

The German invasion of Russia brought Partisan recruits to each camp. Tito at once exploited the prevailing mood, insisting on offensive action against the enemy in order to disrupt its forces, hinder operations, and provide his own guerrilla bands with arms, equipment, food, and clothing. Mihailović, who considered himself the legitimate representative of the government-in-exile, wanted to avoid enemy reprisals by taking no overt action but instead building a resistance movement for later co-operation with the allies and also for postwar political purposes.

Although Chetniks joined Communists in clearing the Užice area of enemy garrisons, the truce quickly disintegrated. The first British liaison officer smuggled into the country, Captain Hudson, found some Chetnik and Communist units in open battle.[13] Hudson managed to bring the leaders together—a strange meeting: the slightly built eminently proper professional officer Mihailović, steel-rimmed spectacles, his beard trimmed, his words demanding cautious tactics; the *nouveau* Tito, the rebel, guest of royalist jails, big and tough, Slav features passive, blue eyes cold in rejection of all Mihailović stood for. The meeting accomplished nothing except to expose to Hudson the opposite, intransigent attitudes.

Hudson represented the main headquarters of the British organization devoted to covert operations, the Special Operations Executive (SOE). At this stage, late 1941, SOE suffered a terrible ignorance of the true situation in most world battle areas. Lacking organization and communications, SOE could not repair its deficiencies overnight, nor did it yet own either supplies or delivery means to aid dissident groups. In the case of Yugoslavia, Hudson reported to the best of his ability. Poor communications and his own limitations—he was a young mining engineer—severely hindered his attempts to unravel the tangled skein of Yugoslav politics to his London superiors, and shortly after his arrival in the country he was forced off the air for nearly six months. SOE attempts to infiltrate other agents during this crucial period failed, primarily from want of satisfactory means. Meanwhile, Mihailović's optimistic reports to London of Chetnik resistance resulted in the Yugoslav government-in-exile promoting him to general and minister of war. SOE(London) also declared for the Chetniks, an understandable error in view of their ignorance of the true situation, and in any event an academic error, considering SOE's lack of resources.

During this confused period, the German army, in mid-November 1941, launched its first offensive against the guerrillas. In two weeks, the Wehrmacht gained control of the Užice area. Tito's Partisans bore the brunt of this fighting, which ended with retreat to mountains in the Northwest. Some Chetnik units, disillusioned by Mihailović's refusal to fight, joined the Partisans, who also found new allies hiding in Bosnian mountains. Mihailović's fear of reprisals had proved correct: "Thousands of Serbs were shot or hanged, and thousands more were arrested, maltreated and imprisoned or deported to forced labor . . . "[14]

Tito had just established new headquarters northeast of Sarajevo when a second German offensive forced him to retreat south to the formidable mountains of the Drina headwaters—a defeat caused in part by refusal of Chetnik units to fight. Hard on the heels of this disaster came another Communist defeat, in Montenegro, one partially brought on by savage reprisals of Communist guerrillas against anyone co-operating with Italian occupation forces. With Mihailović's blessing, Chetniks openly co-operated in an Italian offensive that drove Communist bands back into Herzegovina and Bosnia.

By mid-1942, an irreparable rift existed between Chetniks and Partisans. Chetnik groups in Herzegovina, Montenegro, and Dalmatia collaborated openly with Italians. In Serbia, Mihailović commanded about ten thousand Chetniks who, based on the countryside, maintained an armed truce with the Nedić quisling and German troop units. Ustasi militia in Croatia formed pro-Axis shock-troop units whose members, as with Darnand's *milice* in Vichy France, provided invaluable local knowledge to German commanders.

Tito, on the other hand, despite severe setbacks, never stopped fighting. Nor did he ever forget that he was fighting for a purpose, a political purpose. He early began building a political base by creating local administrations in liberated areas which he called OBDORs. In November 1942, at Bihać, in southern Bosnia, he and his followers unfurled the flag of the Anti-Fascist Council of National Liberation, or AVNOJ. AVNOJ at once publicized its dedication to freeing the country and forming a state along democratic and federal lines, welcome words that brought fresh recruits flocking in.

Simultaneously, Tito was developing a regular army. He began this effort during the retreat after the First German Offensive by creating the First Proletarian Brigade. By mid-1942, he claimed two "divisions"—unorthodox formations each about twenty-five hundred strong, but sufficient when combined with other Partisan units to regain the area vacated in the Second Offensive and to push on into Bosnia and

Croatia. This led to the "People's Army of Liberation," or JANL, created in late 1942 and composed of seven "shock divisions." In addition he developed an ever-growing guerrilla army, and he also relied on part-time Partisans, who lived and worked among the enemy—gentle farmers and civil folk by day, cutthroat assassins and saboteurs by night.

During mid-1942, SOE officers in London and Cairo began forming a more accurate picture of Yugoslav resistance. Hudson again was transmitting, as was Radio Free Yugoslavia, a Russian-sponsored operation that supported Tito. Mihailović continued to flood London with reports, claims, demands, and protests—each increasingly scrutinized and questioned by SOE officers in view of Mihailović's inaction.

Toward the end of the year, SOE(London) sent in a new mission, under one Colonel Bailey. Shortly after his arrival, SOE(Cairo) infiltrated several liaison teams to Mihailović's units. Independent reports from Bailey and these new teams confirmed not only Mihailović's inaction but his collaboration with the enemy. SOE(London) now began to look more favorably on Tito's Partisans.

Tito's Partisans had their hands full. In January 1943, the Germans opened a Fourth Offensive: a two-prong thrust from the north intended to drive Tito's forces south to the river Neretva, strongly defended by Italian and Chetnik units. Learning of the German plan, Tito sent three divisions south to break through before the defenses hardened.[15] They were still attacking when the Germans struck from the north. Fighting hard, the Partisans slowly withdrew to the south, but suffered heavy casualties before punching through the Italo-Croat-Chetnik defense. On the credit side, the Partisans blasted Mihailović's Chetnik force, some twelve thousand irregulars, whom the Partisans, despite their own serious losses, chased into Montenegro.

At the end of May 1943, the enemy struck again. This, the Fifth Offensive, involved German, Ustasi, Bulgar, and Italian troops, an immense force of over one hundred thousand supported by tanks, artillery, and aircraft while encircling and closing on the Partisan stronghold. A captured German order revealed high hopes: " . . . Now that the ring is completely closed, the Communists will try to break through. You will ensure that no able-bodied man leaves the ring alive."[16] In an almost superhuman effort the Partisans finally broke out to the northwest. General von Löhr later wrote that " . . . the Germans were too exhausted to stop them and there were no reserves."[17] The effort nonetheless cost Tito about ten thousand dead or missing.[18] Survivors found respite in the mountains north of Sarajevo. Joined by fresh guerrilla forces, Tito rested briefly before expanding his area of operations. Meanwhile the British had dropped a liaison officer, an Oxford historian, F. W. Deakin, who reached Tito at the height of the Fifth Offensive (and was wounded along with Tito). His favorable report prompted SOE(London) to send

Tito an aid mission. Still hoping for maximum resistance, SOE(London) also reiterated willingness to aid Mihailović, but only if he ceased collaboration with the enemy and came to operational agreement with the Partisans.

Tito exploited Italy's collapse, in September, by establishing contact with Partisan units in Slovenia and by occupying a large portion of the Dalmatian coast and offshore islands. Although the Germans soon expelled the guerrillas from the coast, Tito retained the islands, his forces growing stronger in the process—tactical gains shortly to pale in comparison with a political victory.

For, also in September, a powerful SOE mission under Brigadier Fitzroy Maclean reached Tito's headquarters. Maclean was not a career officer. A testy Scot, at thirty-two years of age he had served eight years in diplomacy, felt at home in difficult political situations, and was a sufficient realist to appreciate the dimensions of Tito's past work and future potential. More important, he belonged to the British Establishment—a member of Parliament, he was a personal friend of Winston Churchill, who appointed him his personal representative much to the annoyance of SOE and the Cairo military command. Maclean did not take long to make up his mind: Tito must be supported to the maximum of SOE's ability.

In sorry contrast to Maclean's optimistic reports stood those from a regular British officer, Brigadier Armstrong, who headed a new mission to Mihailović. Colonel Bailey and Mihailović had long since fallen out, and Armstrong quickly suffered a similar disillusionment. He found Mihailović " . . . dominated by the single thought of how to overcome the Partisans, to whom he was bitterly and irreconcilably hostile. He appeared completely disinterested in attacks on communications. . . . "[19] Armstrong's blunt reports brought forth a series of SOE demands blithely ignored by Mihailović. After repeated warnings, SOE suspended further aid, in December 1943; with departure of the last liaison team, in spring of 1944, allied contact ceased.

While Mihailović's star declined in the allied sky, Tito's was rising, mainly due to the exuberant Maclean, who presented the Partisan case in most vigorous terms to his own government. In November, the Partisan government, the AVNOJ, met to proclaim " . . . a new federal Yugoslavia, having denounced the exiled King and Government, and promoted Tito to the rank of Marshal." Almost simultaneously, Maclean's representations caused allied heads of state at Tehran to agree that " . . . the Partisans in Yugoslavia should be supported by supplies and equipment to the greatest possible extent. . . . "[20]

Maclean himself suffered no illusions concerning Tito's political bent. He reported that " . . . in any event, [allied] help or not, the partisans were going to be a decisive post-war influence in Jugoslavia."

He went on: "Much will depend on Tito, and whether he sees himself in his former role of Comintern agent or as the potential ruler of an independent Jugoslav State." In Cairo he explained this to Mr. Churchill, and stressed the probability of Yugoslavia becoming a Communist state. Churchill's reaction underscored his priority concern for winning the war:

> "Do you intend," he asked, "to make Yugoslavia your home after the war?"
> "No, Sir," I replied.
> "Neither do I," he said. "And, that being so, the less you and I worry about the form of Government they set up, the better. That is for them to decide. What interests me is, which of them [Partisans or Chetniks] is doing most harm to the Germans?"[21]

The allied decision to support Tito at first held but slight material value. In summer of 1943, SOE had been talking grandly of supplying 500 tons a month to the Partisans; they actually delivered a meager 230 tons for *all* of 1943. And in December of that year, Tito once again was fighting for his life, in the Sixth Offensive, Operation *Kugelblitz* (Thunderbolt), a massive effort undertaken by over fourteen German divisions and five non-German divisions. Lasting several weeks, this effort forced Partisans out of all offshore islands except Vis, a major Partisan base, and it also penetrated into the mountains of Slovenia, Bosnia, and western Serbia before running out of steam. It left the Germans generally in command of towns and most communication centers, but it left Partisan forces relatively intact throughout the country.

With increased allied aid, the Partisan movement began to take off. In September 1943, Maclean estimated a total Partisan force of one hundred thousand. By spring of 1944, this had grown to over two hundred thousand and Tito was demanding tanks, artillery, and aircraft. Allied planes were also flying out wounded Partisans: " . . . During 1944 more than 10,000 military and 2,000 civilian casualties were thus evacuated."[22] Meanwhile, at allied request, Tito raised Partisan units in Serbia to interdict German communications through the Morava Valley, a successful effort that attracted thousands of Serbs to the Partisan banner. Again at allied request, Tito ordered units in Slovenia to prepare for Operation Bearskin: by cutting roads and railroads in the north, allied planners hoped to prevent German troop reinforcement either to northern Italy or to Normandy, where the allies would soon land.

At this point, Tito was riding high and perhaps grew complacent. Neither he nor his staff officers at the cave command post in Drvar seemed suspicious of a German airplane that " . . . spent half an hour or more flying slowly up and down at a height of about two thousand

YUGOSLAVIA 1941
- Towns and Cities
-|- Railways
✕ Major operational areas
0   50   100   150 miles

feet."[23] The British mission did not like it and moved off into surrounding hills. Four days later, at the end of May, with no warning, bombers plastered the area, then six JU-52s dropped paratroopers, who were followed by troops crash-landing in gliders while a three-column ground attack pressed in overland. While Tito's "palace guard" held off German paratroopers, the Partisan leader escaped through a rear exit. After a furious pursuit, Tito, his principal staff officers, the British and Russian missions, and 118 wounded guerrillas were evacuated by a series of hastily improvised airlifts. Tito subsequently established himself on Vis, where his headquarters remained until war's end.

This interruption upset planning for Operation Bearskin, as did increased enemy security in target areas and poor weather, which hindered airdrops of vital demolitions. For all these reasons, Bearskin only partially succeeded. But, in September, Partisans brought off Operation Ratweek, by cutting roads and railroads from one end of the country to the other. In restricting German troop movements, this guerrilla effort primarily assisted the British-U.S. offensive in northern Italy; secondarily it assisted the Russians moving into Bulgaria.

The final major Partisan offensive concentrated on interdicting the German XXI Mountain Corps during withdrawal north. Although guerrillas, heavily supported by the allies, caused the enemy to abandon transport and heavy equipment, they did not prevent his main body from reaching the northern border. Maclean has pointed out, however, that in the last two months of the fighting, the Germans lost close to one hundred thousand killed and over two hundred thousand captured.[24] Captured German figures reported twenty-four thousand Germans killed and twelve thousand missing. According to the Yugoslav Government, the Yugoslavian people lost over 10 per cent of its population and over 60 per cent of its national wealth: " . . . 1,685,000 people, of whom over 75 per cent were shot or lost their lives in Fascist camps or death chambers. We lost over 90,000 skilled industrial workers and miners and 40,000 intellectuals. There are 425,000 wounded or disabled. . . . "[25]

By January 1945, what was left of Yugoslavia was virtually clear of enemy troops. Most Ustasi and Chetnik leaders had fled. Supported by the Russians, Tito easily expanded his power base, and by the end of the war had emerged incontestably as the new ruler of Yugoslavia.

The German experience in Yugoslavia emphasized the importance of a guerrilla force in being. Without Tito's Partisans, the Germans could have enjoyed an easy occupation with benefits the term implies: total access to the country's manpower and economic resources, a fertile ground for New Order propaganda—all for a minimum investment of occupation forces.

As it was, until autumn of 1943, the guerrilla threat forced Germany to keep nine Wehrmacht divisions in Yugoslavia, a hefty force buttressed by ten Italian divisions and numerous Bulgarian and local quisling units, the value of which was questionable.

Italy's collapse, in late 1943, forced Germany to raise its occupation troops to 14-plus divisions, a force augmented by five satellite divisions: an estimated total of 140,000 German troops and 66,000 satellite troops. In addition, Germany supported 150,000–170,000 Bulgar, Croat, and Chetnik troops. In 1943, establishing a new command in Belgrade, Army Group F, the German high command in effect changed an army of occupation to an operational fighting force. Tito's force at this time numbered around 100,000 soon to climb to some 220,000.[26]

This number ratio helps to validate Partisan operations, as do certain enemy testimonials:

> . . . Field Marshal von Weichs, the German Commander-in-Chief South-east (Balkans), directed his formations to refer in their reports to Tito's partisans not any longer as bands but to brigades, divisions and so on, and expressed himself to the effect that they had to be considered as the equivalent of the regular forces of Germany's other enemies.[27]

Final proof rests in the seven major German attempts to capture Tito and eliminate the Partisans. These were not slapdash affairs, but were carefully planned military operations. They suffered a host of problems but ultimate failure stemmed not from these but from what history already should have taught the German high command: the seemingly uncanny ability of guerrillas to survive in home grounds. The lesson gains in importance when large areas of these home grounds, unlike vast forests of the Ukraine, held considerable hostile forces, in this case Croatian Ustasi, Serbian Chetniks, and Nedić quislings, not to mention German, Italian and Bulgarian occupation troops.

How to explain this?

The first factor was the fertile field of human feeling, a sort of patriotic anarchy best described in the controlled panic of a dispatch sent by a ranking German civil official, Dr. Thurner, from Belgrade, in August 1941:

> . . . All our attempts to canalize these people in a constructive direction and separate them from the Communists have failed and had to be abandoned. We have argued with them, conferred with them, cajoled them and threatened them, but all to no purpose. We do not believe that it is possible to achieve anything in this country on the basis of authority. The people just do not recognize authority . . . They do not believe in anyone any more and they follow the Communist bandits blindly. With their slogans the Communists have succeeded in rallying round them elements who in the past would never have dreamt of co-operating with them. Some go so far as to prefer Bolshevism to occupation by our troops. . . . My impression is that even the news of the capitulation of the Soviet Union would not cause these bandits to capitulate. They are tougher than anything you can imagine. What is more, their organization is excellent. It might serve as the classical example of a perfect secret organization.[28]

Thurner hit on the second factor, which was qualitative. In contrast to leaders of pro-German parties, Tito headed a small and disciplined organization, the Communist Party, whose members never questioned the Partisan mission of fighting the enemy and never forgot the party's political goal of constantly expanding to achieve postwar power. Tito constantly stressed the necessity of retaining support of the general population, a bellicose demand for unity that contrasted violently with the attitude of other national groups such as the Chetniks—a splintered organization with important segments either remaining feckless in pathetic desire to let war wash harmlessly over them or waiting to see the probable result, sometimes secretly aiding Partisans, sometimes even coming over to them.

Tito exploited divisive national feeling in several ways. Partisan propaganda, particularly the promise of "a liberal and democratic" postwar government, appealed to a great many unaligned people who loathed the repressive prewar order represented by the government-in-exile through Mihailović's Chetniks. The harshness of German and Italian occupation policies further influenced the population in favor of the Partisans, who possessed much wider support than either western allied observers or Germans supposed.

Tito always respected the need for this support. When he was on the run after the First German Offensive, his meager supply train still included twelve oxcarts that held a printing press and five thousand newly printed copies of *The Short History of the Communist Party*.[29] He insured discipline by attaching political commissars to Partisan units at all levels. He also harnessed national feeling by establishing local administrative units, or OBDORs, in "liberated" areas. When the enemy "captured" such an area, OBDOR became a "shadow" government and, as such, performed numerous valuable functions, for example acting as a deterrent to would-be collaborators and helping to establish and maintain one of the Partisans' most valuable adjuncts: small groups of volunteers who stayed in their own locality and " . . . lived as civilians among the population, followed their normal occupations and worked as part-time partisans." In addition to furnishing food and intelligence, " . . . they killed sentries, threw hand-grenades into German barracks, burned down garages, mined village streets and house entrances, destroyed railway lines—in one night they blew up the rails of the Agram-Belgrade railway in eighty places—and did all the other jobs which partisans usually perform."[30] The Germans called them *Hauspartisanen,* or Home Partisans, and detested them. Colonel General Rendulic, commanding a German Panzer army, later stated that

> . . . The life and tasks of the German troops would have been much easier if the opponent had only closed formations. The Home Partisans were a much more dangerous enemy because it was from them that all the hostile acts emanated against which the troops could protect themselves only with the greatest difficulty and which caused them large losses. They could seldom, if ever, be caught."

In attempting to catch them, Germans killed and imprisoned thousands of innocent people, thus creating new Partisans. The effect of Home Partisans was beyond all proportion to their limited numbers—an estimated eight thousand in June 1944.[31] Tito was also smart enough to keep his regular military organization simple. JANL, despite regular army trappings, remained essentially a guerrilla organization of small, semi-independent, and lightly armed bands. Tito could boast about "divisions"—but a Partisan division counted only about twenty-five to thirty-five hundred men divided into "brigades" consisting of several groups, or "battalions." These units lacked any sort of artillery or formal communications, but, singly or in unison, they fought extremely well under tough, self-reliant leaders of unquestioned loyalty. Moving often at night, guerrilla bands covered vast areas, often fighting against great odds with no doctors or medicines to treat their wounded. Allied observers remarked feelingly on Partisan resilience and the high state of morale, and this must have been the case in order for them to have survived numerous vicissitudes of war such as the 180-mile retreat with thousands of wounded during the Fourth Offensive.

Tito later offered Brigadier Maclean a remarkable analysis of his operational success, words as pertinent today as then. The Partisan achievement depended in large part on disciplined troops highly motivated by constant political instruction. Rather than suffering adversity in defeat, the guerrillas at once struck back, thus immediately raising morale. Leadership of course played an important role, but so did clever tactics. Tito was always careful to retain mobility. At the time of the Fourth Offensive, he wrote:

> We must avoid fixed fronts. We must not let the enemy force us by clever tactics on to the defensive. On the contrary, the spirit of our troops must be offensive, not only in the attack, but in defense as well. During an enemy offensive the offensive spirit must find expression in vigorous and audacious guerrilla tactics, in operations behind the enemy's lines, in the destruction of his communications, in attacks on his supply centers, and on bases which are temporarily weakened. We must be no more afraid of being surrounded now than when we had fewer troops. We must make up for the loss of an area by the conquest of a larger and more important area.[32]

Brave words these, and only partially carried out. The almost always precarious position greatly restricted offensive operations. Tito was never strong enough to strike where he wished, but he was often strong or daring enough to strike where the enemy least expected. Many sensitive targets such as communication centers lay beyond reach; supply lines did not. Co-ordination of effort at times was very poor, the inevitable result of primitive communications. Partisan operations perforce were often decentralized, which meant that Tito had to rely on subordinate leaders—with varying results.

The guerrilla's lot could have been greatly eased by a more realistic allied aid policy. Tito's accomplishments loom considerably larger when we consider that, up to the end of 1943, he received the barest minimum of arms and equipment. Almost entirely on his own, he had organized an army and government while alternately harassing the enemy and escaping from him. An earlier supply effort would have solved many of his problems, besides saving thousands of lives.

The basic British difficulty stemmed from lack of area intelligence, surprising in view of Britain's political sophistication, and the failure of means to repair that deficiency. A more objective appraisal of the resistance movements was also hindered by natural sympathy for the Royal Yugoslav Government as exemplified by Mihailović and his Chetniks. A serious rift between pro-Mihailović and pro-Tito factions soon developed in SOE(London) and SOE(Cairo) as well as in Yugoslavia, an often vociferous quarrel that continues today. David Martin's recent book, *The Web of Disinformation: Churchill's Yugoslav Blunder,* severely denigrates Tito's Partisan achievements, as does Michael Lees' book, *The Rape of Serbia—the British Role in Tito's Grab for Power 1943–1944.*[33] Properly trained liaison officers possessing adequate communications probably could have cleared the confusion in short order. SOE never overcame the liaison problem, and Blair concludes that, in general, Maclean's liaison officers

> . . . knew nothing of guerrilla warfare and little of the Yugoslav language, history or politics, and their reports were of limited value. Very few actions were ever fought which would not have taken place without the missions, and as one description states, 'half a ton of ammunition and explosives would in most areas have been more effective than half a ton of BLOs [British liaison officers].' Their presence was also a source of suspicion to the Partisans.

An interesting side effect resulted from their reports, which the BBC used: Although broadcasts of world news by this august organization were renowned for accuracy, its Yugoslav coverage drew heavy criticism for inaccuracy, Maclean himself complaining, and the Germans making a propaganda field day out of patent errors.[34]

SOE operations also suffered from tortured command channels. This sometimes led to the ludicrous, as in the case of Bailey's mission to Mihailović. While Bailey at Mihailović's headquarters duly reported to SOE(London), his subordinates, liaison officers in the field with Chetnik units, *reported independently to SOE(Cairo).* On at least one occasion, SOE(Cairo) acted under duress from the military high command and issued orders that had to be countermanded by SOE(London). Maclean wore three hats: SOE commander to Tito, personal representative to Supreme Allied Commander, Middle East, and personal representative to the British Prime Minister. The latter appointment obfuscated the other two and, at best, meant that, should his nominal superiors tread at all, they would tread very lightly.

352

Command confusion grew along with the allied effort. SOE could handle a supply problem of a few hundred tons; it could not support large training programs, supply a small army, and co-ordinate required air, naval, and ground efforts. This difficulty led to drastic command reorganization, in spring of 1944.

Despite these shortcomings, British and American military aid to Tito represented a distinct sacrifice, both in early stages, when arms and supply were measured in single tons and in delivery requirements of one or two aircraft, and later, when this aid measured thousands of tons delivered by squadrons of aircraft and ships. Military critics of the time, including some ranking officers, argued that this considerable investment in men and material could have been used more profitably in more orthodox operations.

This assessment depended on ultimate objectives. If the allied objective had been merely to sustain Tito in harassing the enemy, then a great deal of aid and the concomitant machinery could have been eliminated in favor of "hard" supply of small arms. Allied planners, however, looked far beyond this mundane achievement. Until late 1943, their most distant horizon comprised a joint Chetnik-Partisan resistance, and one can argue that such a contingency either would have reduced the enemy to abject impotence or forced him from Yugoslavia. The Chetnik default dimmed this glorious horizon but briefly, for now Maclean painted a glorious picture of an enormous Partisan army of combined arms, and indeed in some very valid colors. Nor did Tito hesitate to jump on the new bandwagon: early in 1944, he was demanding tanks, artillery, and aircraft.

This was not as stupid as it sounds in retrospect, and for reasons already mentioned. No one knew in early 1944 when the war would end—the atomic-bomb situation was still far from clear. In the event, Tito's army became superfluous, at least, to allied military operations. And hereby hangs a curious irony. Had Tito not built his Partisan army, in part with allied aid, a most uncomfortable vacuum would have existed in postwar Yugoslavia—a geographical entity traditionally in the Russian sphere of influence. Stalin did not wait for cannons to stop firing before asserting his dominance over Tito and the country. But Stalin had showed up badly compared to the West. Tito had begged the Soviets to send him arms beginning in August 1941. Stalin paid no attention either to that or subsequent requests, and a Soviet military mission, which did not even reach Tito until February 1944, accomplished nothing. Tito had never been overly impressed with the Russian Communists, and his war experience did not endear them to him. Although he would have trouble with the West in postwar years, he still had to face the inescapable fact that the West had helped him when the chips were down.

So it was that Tito not only filled the Yugoslav vacuum left by World War II, but, shortly after doing so, proved to the world that communism and Moscow were not synonymous. If his rule left much to be desired, it turned an area once riddled with factionalism into a reasonably stable country whose insistence on independent political status has more than once proved a healthy stabilizing factor in international diplomacy. To accomplish this, his people paid the piper by sacrificing individual liberties in another totalitarian regime.

A final irony exists. Like Churchill and Roosevelt, Tito did not sufficiently respect the fact of his own mortality, and thus build a lasting government. Considering the fiery and divisive elements at work in the Balkan States, he probably could not have done so. Whatever the case, his death removed the center pole of the political tent that covered Yugoslavia. Local conflict bred non-local conflict until the final explosion in 1991 when Serbian troops, spearheaded by guerrillas, invaded Croatia to begin a civil war—the outcome of which, as of late 1993, is still anyone's guess.

CHAPTER TWENTY-SEVEN

1. Schevill.
2. Ibid., 204. See also, Devine.
3. Devine, 7.
4. Ibid., 8.
5. Majatovich, 5–6.
6. Ibid., 8.
7. Temperley, 195.
8. H.D. Harrison, 94. See also, West.
9. Seton-Watson, *The East European Revolution*, 126: " . . . Literally . . . a member of a *Cheta*, which is the Serbian word for an armed band."
10. Maclean, *Disputed Barricade*, 46.
11. Ibid., 1–99.
12. Ibid., 128.
13. Blair, 44–5.
14. Seton-Watson, *The East European Revolution*, 120–1: in one town "8,000 people are believed to have been shot, including several hundred schoolchildren." See also, Maclean, *Eastern Approaches*. The author offers an excellent description of both German and Partisan tactics in this exciting book; Department of the Army, *German Antiguerrilla Operations in the Balkans (1941–1944)*.
15. Blair, 32, suggests that perhaps a ranking German officer who was a secret agent tipped off Tito.
16. Maclean, *Disputed Barricade*, 226. See also, Deakin.
17. Maclean, *Disputed Barricade*, 228.
18. Heilbrunn, 159.
19. Blair, 51.
20. Ibid., 55. See also, Maclean, *Disputed Barricade*, 256. An American OSS officer joined the British Mission in September; American OSS missions later worked with both Tito and Mihailović.
21. Maclean, *Eastern Approaches*, 402–3.
22. Seton-Watson, *The East European Revolution*, 159–60.

23. Maclean, *Eastern Approaches,* 450.
24. Maclean, *Disputed Barricade,* 295.
25. Davidson, 331.
26. Maclean, *Disputed Barricade,* 247–8.
27. Heilbrunn, 203–4.
28. Maclean, *Disputed Barricade,* 137–8.
29. Ibid., 159. See also, Lawrence, "Guerrilla Warfare." " . . . The printing press is the greatest weapon in the armory of the modern commander."
30. Heilbrunn, 157.
31. Ibid.
32. Maclean, *Disputed Barricade,* 204–5.
33. Lees. In attempting to discredit Tito while glorifying Mihailović, Lees seems to overlook the fact that Winston Churchill was bent on supporting guerrilla formations of any hue, so long as they were killing Germans. Proof of Chetnik collaboration with the German/Italian enemy abounds as does proof of vigorous Partisan operations against this enemy. Lest Churchill be condemned for an unwise decision, it should be remembered that in 1943 he and Roosevelt had good reason to believe that Germany was well on the way to developing an atomic bomb.
34. Blair, 54–5.

CHAPTER 28

German occupation of Greece • Political and military background • Initial resistance • Greek passivity to occupation • First SOE mission • Conflict among resistance groups • SOE difficulties, internal and external • Operation Animals • The ELAS guerrillas • German countertactics • The Russian mission • Operation Noah's Ark • Italian occupation of Albania • Albanian resistance • Enver Hoxha and the LNC • First SOE mission • Internal political conflicts • The Germans arrive • The Davies mission • Maclean's new mission • Hoxha's guerrilla operations

IF RESISTANCE became confused in Yugoslavia, it grew positively chaotic in Greece—traditionally the home of violent politics.

In spring of 1941, the German invasion of this Mediterranean country sent King George II and the monarchist government into exile, first in Cairo, then in London. By June, the enemy held the entire country. As in the case of Yugoslavia, Hitler distributed large portions of it to his allies: Thrace and eastern Macedonia to Bulgaria, central and western Greece to Italy. The German army concentrated primarily on protecting main lines of communication running from Montenegro in the north through the Struma and Vardar valleys south to the trading center of Salonika and on to Athens and Piraeus (and across the Mediterranean to North Africa). As elsewhere in the Axis world, occupation proved harsh and brutal, and, in short order, resistance movements appeared.

Those readers who know Greece will remember the strong individualism of her peoples, a national characteristic of great charm but one that has helped to keep her politically splintered through the ages. The monarchy founded after the War of Independence, in 1821, ended in a shaky republic established in 1924. When King George II regained the throne eleven years later, his was a disputed mandate. Besides such non-royalist parties as republicans and socialists, the Communists had grown quite strong, a worker-oriented party founded in 1918 and affiliated to the Comintern in 1920 as the Communist Party of Greece, the KKE.[1]

Political anarchy followed restoration, and, in 1936, the Prime Minister, General Metaxas, established a dictatorship and forced the KKE underground. Metaxas continued to purge the army of republican and Communist officers, and he also treated Italy's occupation of Albania with restraint, quietly strengthening diplomatic ties with Turkey, France, and Britain while trying to strengthen his armed forces. When Mussolini demanded partial occupation of Greece, in October 1940, Metaxas refused and ordered general mobilization. Within weeks, the small but keen Greek army, ably commanded by Lieutenant General Alexander Papagos, reinforced by Royal Air Force squadrons, had smashed Italian attacks in the Pindus Mountains and driven thirty miles inside Albania.

Metaxas died in early 1941. Mussolini's failure meanwhile had caused Hitler to intervene, not so much to save Mussolini's reputation as to secure the Balkan flank prior to his invading Russia. In March, he sent troops into Hungary, Romania, and Bulgaria. The Greek Government now accepted British reinforcements. By April, a British (mainly Australian-New Zealand)-Polish force of some seventy thousand men hastily mobilized in Egypt, had landed and deployed along a line southwest of Salonika. Inadequate liaison between Greek and British high commands exposed the left flank of this force by leaving General Papagos and most of the Greek army isolated on the Albanian front. The Germans struck in early April, soon pushing the shattered British force from the country. Three weeks later, the enemy marched into Athens, went on to capture Crete, and, in June, the Greek Government fled to Cairo.

German occupation authorities working with Prime Minister Tsolakoglou's puppet government cracked down hard on some Communists, arresting and deporting such prominent leaders as Nikos Zakhariadhis, Secretary-General of KKE. Working on the principle of divide and conquer, the Germans released other Communists from prison. Zakhariadhis' replacement, Yioryios Siantos, organized an underground labor movement, the EEAM, and, in September 1941, the Greek Liberation Front, or EAM, which gained some socialist support. In spring of 1942, EAM formed the National Popular Liberation Army, or ELAS, its agents recruiting in Roumeli, Thessaly, and Macedonia.

At about the same time, three republican resistance movements sprang up: EDES, headed by Colonel Zervas; a much smaller group, EKKA, whose military leader was Colonel Psaros; and the AAA, headed by Colonel Saraphis. A royalist organization also appeared, the Six

Colonels, an operationally impotent group, as did a student organization under Professor Kanellopoulos.

Six more disparate groups probably never existed. Their single common trait was a distinct preference to fight anyone but the enemy. By spring of 1942, Italian and German garrisons carried out duties generally unmolested, and since duties included supporting Rommel's armored forces in North Africa, guerrilla inactivity brought increasingly blue language to British military conferences at GHQ, Middle East, Cairo.

Resistance leaders were not altogether to blame. In 1941, the stuff of their armies was a generally inert mass of country people who expressed but slight desire to fight the Germans. Will to resist had to be imposed from without. Resistance had to be generated. As C. M. Woodhouse later wrote,

> ... it was not the easy-going peasant who started the resistance to the Germans in the mountains. That was the last thing they wanted: they had hardly seen a German, or noticed the slightest difference in their way of life, until the talkers from the towns arrived with exhortations to take arms against the invader. For them the resistance movement meant the loss of their livelihood, the burning of their homes, the looting of their property; all of which they endured as long as they believed the cause to be a good one; but none of which they would have inflicted upon themselves without prompting. . . . [2]

Primarily for this reason, Communist leaders of EAM spent a year in developing a clandestine network of cadres

> ... so efficiently woven and deployed that when, in the summer of 1942, the first guerrilla bands under the name of ELAS appeared in the mountains, they multiplied quickly. When they could they swept out of their way or absorbed all rival bands that they came across. . . . [3]

Part of the difficulty also stemmed from ignorance of Greek politics on the part of British Foreign Office officials who supported Prime Minister Tsouderos' promonarchist government-in-exile. The king, who had seriously violated the Greek constitution in 1936 by dissolving parliament and failing to hold a general election within the prescribed period, refused to admit his lack of popularity in Greece; in Cairo and later in London, he insisted that he would restore monarchical rule after the war. Meanwhile he did not want the British to aid other than *royalist* guerrilla groups. In view of the inability of royalist leaders in Greece to

358

raise such groups, this meant guerrilla inactivity at an extremely crucial time. GHQ Middle East found this unacceptable. Wanting support for a planned allied offensive in North Africa, it ordered SOE(Cairo) to contact and support any guerrillas willing to fight the enemy.

SOE's first attempt to contact resistance leaders met almost instant disaster. Landed by submarine on the island of Antiparos, the British party fell into Italian hands, as did " . . . complete lists of men they intended to meet in Athens, all of whom were promptly arrested. Many lost their lives. . . . "[4]

Despite this setback, an SOE mission parachuted into northern Greece in autumn of 1942. Colonel E. C. Myers, a thirty-six-year-old army engineer, commanded this effort, with Captain C. M. Woodhouse, a twenty-five-year-old scholar fluent in Greek, serving as deputy.[5] Myers and Woodhouse found considerable guerrilla, or *andarte*, activity. Strikes and other resistance efforts in cities had caused the Germans to make mass arrests, and in August they began organizing forced-labor transports—repressive measures that resulted in growth of guerrilla groups.

The British officers also found a serious antagonism existing between ELAS and EDES, and only with a great deal of effort did Meyer and Woodhouse persuade them to co-operate in destroying a vital rail viaduct.[6] After this success, which cut rail communications between Salonika and Athens for six weeks and thus helped deprive Rommel of much needed supply, SOE(Cairo) ordered Myers and Woodhouse to Athens, there to contact the organization known as Six Colonels, which Cairo, mistakenly thought would co-ordinate all guerrilla activities in Greece. Myers and Woodhouse pointed out that the moribund Six Colonels organization was incapable of co-ordinating anything, that they could not repair the rift between ELAS and other guerrilla organizations, indeed that EAM/ELAS was Communist controlled. They sensibly concluded " . . . that the practical answer was to limit the guerrilla movement to a few small independent bands who by their very smallness would be able to operate on a hit-and-run basis when and where required in support of Allied strategy."[7]

SOE(Cairo) refused to listen to common sense. A newly infiltrated British liaison officer attached to ELAS headquarters, a man who knew but little Greek " . . . continued to report on ELAS and EAM as a national uprising which must be given British support so that the democratic parties in the movement might be strengthened."[8] ELAS, he insisted, had " . . . no political aims whatsoever" and was " . . . purely a military Resistance Movement."[9] Refusing to abandon dreams of a vast guerrilla army in Greece, SOE(Cairo) now attempted a compromise by organizing independent guerrilla areas, each commanded by a Greek officer working with a British liaison team.

EAM/ELAS quickly scotched this plan by attempting to take over the entire resistance movement. An ELAS unit captured Colonel Saraphis, titular head of Six Colonels, and other units attacked EDES forces under Colonel Zervas. Myers answered this insubordination by requesting SOE(Cairo) to cut off aid to EAM/ELAS, but Cairo, unduly influenced by its liaison officer with ELAS, refused. To add to Myers' temper, Saraphis, whom Myers had saved, now went over to the Communists to become military commander of ELAS!

As a final straw, EAM/ELAS persuaded SOE(Cairo) to establish a joint guerrilla headquarters with representation so rigged as to leave EAM in control.

SOE's continued ignorance and confusion stemmed in part from divided responsibility. SOE(Cairo) not only answered to its parent, the Ministry of Economic Warfare, but to Foreign Office and military representatives, a triple responsibility that could only result in confusion. It also suffered from poor internal organization, a sort of Topsy characteristic whereby in four years it carried eight different names and eight different chiefs: " . . . three of them were civilians who did not entirely trust soldiers, and five were senior officers who did not entirely trust politicians or diplomats."[10] Bickham Sweet-Escott, who served in the Cairo office, later wrote:

> . . . Nobody who did not experience it can possibly imagine the atmosphere of jealousy, suspicion, and intrigue which embittered the relations between the various secret and semi-secret departments in Cairo during that summer of 1941, or for that matter for the next two years. It would be quite beyond my powers to describe it.[11]

Such internal flux hampered relations with the field, as did distance and communication problems. The above authority later noted that " . . . there was no coherent planning . . . all the emphasis in Force 133 had been getting parties with radio transmitters into the field as soon as possible. But no provision had been made to have enough people in Cairo to cipher and decipher the messages which would result."[12]

Poor agent preparation played a destructive role. Most British liaison officers

> . . . entered Greece for the first time with no previous knowledge of the country, the people, or the language. . . . Few of them had political opinions, but their unconscious sympathies were rather to

the left than the right. What formed their prejudices was not how they thought but whom they liked. In most cases, that meant whatever guerrillas they were with.[13]

Allied military pressures also influenced SOE representatives in Cairo and in the field. Foremost was the coming invasion of Sicily. Allied planners wanted guerrilla help in Greece in order to try to fool the Germans into believing that the invasion would occur there and thus tie down as many enemy troops as possible. This project, Operation Animals, required ELAS support, and Myers and Woodhouse gained it only by overlooking EAM/ELAS insolence and continued growth of EAM/ELAS power. In the event, a small British team destroyed the key Asopos viaduct in a model operation.

ELAS and EDES forces in time partially co-operated by ambushing German troops, cutting telephone communications, and making forty-four major cuts in road and rail communications—an effort that indicated their very considerable but never fully realized potential.[14]

Colonel Saraphis had greatly improved the fighting potential of ELAS, which now amounted to over fourteen thousand guerrillas, divided into six territorial commands.[15] A guerrilla "band" varied from thirty to one hundred men, several bands forming a "battalion." These units received Communist political indoctrination, although this was not overly stressed in view of EAM claims to represent a broad front. Saraphis also developed ELAS reserve units in the villages, youth units (to provide couriers) known as EPON, and he even organized a small navy (ELAN).

By autumn of 1943, guerrillas controlled nearly two thirds of Greece, and EAM/ELAS controlled a large portion of that area. Their hold on the new joint guerrilla headquarters resulted in the Communists administering large areas, where they established food depots, communications, schools, courts, and newspapers. Tens of thousands of refugees streamed in from enemy-controlled areas, and, in feeding and caring for these generally illiterate mountain peoples, EAM/ELAS (financed by a British subsidy of about $120,000 per month) mixed a strong ration of Communist propaganda. Woodhouse, who was on hand, later wrote:

> . . . EAM/ELAS set the pace in the creation of something that Governments of Greece had neglected: an organized state in the Greek mountains. All the virtues and vices of such an experiment could be seen; for when the people whom no one has ever helped started helping themselves, their methods are vigorous and not always nice. The words "liberation" and "popular democracy" filled the air with their peculiar connotations. Uneasy stirrings were breaking

the surface everywhere, but only the KKE knew how to give them direction. . . . [16]

Although guerrilla attacks remained minimal, ELAS units did build a landing field and support other covert allied activities such as gathering intelligence and helping downed airmen to escape.[17]

In August, a joint guerrilla deputation flew to Cairo and a confrontation with monarchists that demonstrated the existing gulf between the exiles and the guerrilla forces, with everyone condemning everyone else. Guerrilla leaders returned to Greece " . . . disappointed, angry and with the fixed idea that the British government intended to reimpose the monarchy."[18] Matters rapidly deteriorated to the extent that Woodhouse later wondered if the campaign should not have been terminated in autumn of 1943. Already-strong ELAS forces had gained more arms and supply from Italy's collapse in September. Saraphis now converted his territorial commands into five "divisions" deployed in the most vital areas, and opened attacks against Zervas' EDES groups. But Saraphis had been moving too rapidly, and these attacks generally failed. Moreover, German temper had been growing short and the high command now launched a series of strong offensives against ELAS mountain strongholds. Three months of operations scattered Communists and disintegrated their new "mountain state." The Germans also allowed the Greek puppet government to form anti-Communist "security battalions" of about five hundred men each, an organization eventually numbering about fifteen thousand and active for the most part in the Peloponnese.[19]

Adversity forced EAM/ELAS to a more co-operative attitude, a development welcomed by British officers in Cairo trying to plan Noah's Ark, an operation designed to hinder German withdrawal from Greece. Renewed negotiations with disparate guerrilla units led to the "Plaka Agreement," of late February 1944 which provided only temporary postponement of hostilities. EAM now created the Political Committee of National Liberation, or PEEA, whose strong non-Communist representation was supposed to insure a national bias; in reality, PEEA formed a rival to the government-in-exile.

In April, an ELAS unit attacked the small EKKA group and murdered Colonel Psaros. Tempers again flared into fighting between ELAS and EDES units before the situation quieted, possibly due to the influence of a Russian mission that arrived secretly in EAM/ELAS headquarters. Woodhouse, who meanwhile had taken command of what became known, thanks to the addition of two American OSS officers, as the Allied Military Mission (AMM), later wrote:

> . . . ELAS, who had expected the Soviet Mission to bring manna from heaven, found Colonel Popov unable even to supply his own

362

party with vodka, let alone ELAS with gold, arms and ammunition. On the other hand, the Soviet Mission, which had expected to find an army of at least the same kind, if not the same magnitude, as Tito's partisans, found a rabble thinly veiled by an elaborately centralised command. . . . Neither on the military nor on the political level does it seem likely that a favorable report on EAM/ELAS went to Moscow. . . . Circumstantial evidence suggests that EAM/ELAS suffered an abrupt shock as a result.[20]

Although infighting continued through summer and autumn, plans for Noah's Ark moved slowly forward. EAM/ELAS agreed to participate in phase one—guerrilla strikes scheduled to harass retreating Germans in conjunction with allied air attacks. Phase two called for a British landing in the Athens area, and both Saraphis and Zervas agreed to keep their guerrillas in the country while the Greek Government landed.

Noah's Ark began in September 1944, the guerrilla units concentrating on cutting road and rail networks and attacking ponderous German convoys. Neither ELAS nor EDES fought to maximum capability, but Woodhouse and other observers nonetheless estimated that guerrilla action destroyed a hundred locomotives and five hundred trucks, besides killing some five thousand enemy.

Phase two, the British landing and return of the Greek Government, also occurred on schedule. But that begins another saga, to be narrated in a later chapter.

The forces found in Greece displayed themselves simultaneously in Albania, the tiny mountainous country (eleven thousand square miles) tucked between Greece and Yugoslavia on the Adriatic Sea. In some ways similar to Morocco, this feudal remnant of civilization consisted of a long coastal plain that supported a peasant agricultural economy and was backed by rugged mountains, the home of a welter of tribes whose conflicting traditions, loyalties, and religions frequently flared into serious feuds: Roman Catholics, Moslems, Greek Orthodox—perhaps one million people divided roughly into the Ghegs of the North and the Tosks of the South, but each division ruled by factionalism of centuries.

Long under Italian influence, the country offered but little resistance when Mussolini's divisions landed, in April 1939. King Zog and his government fled, leaving the country at the mercy of some five Italian divisions. These encountered resistance from guerrilla bands, or *chetas,* mainly in the mountains, but it was sporadic and unco-ordinated. Attempting to exploit the situation, in mid-1939 the British infiltrated an agent from Belgrade with orders to work up a guerrilla united front. The fall of Yugoslavia cut short this effort and led to the agent's capture.

Almost no information filtered from the country in the next two years. But as allies began planning for the invasion of Italy, interest revived in Albania. In spring of 1943, Bill Maclean, a young British SOE officer with guerrilla experience in Palestine and Abyssinia, led a small mission into the South. Maclean found a situation akin to those in neighboring countries. Three main groups had developed: the Royalist, or Zogist, movement, led by Abas Kupi, a promonarchist army officer, and confined largely to the North; the Republican, or Balli Kombetar (National Union) movement, which developed along the coast and central foothills and was strongly rightist; the Communist, or LNC, forces, led by Enver Hoxha, in the South.[21]

Hoxha's movement was by far the most active. As Julian Amery explained in his interesting book *Sons of the Eagle*, Italian influence had resulted in some youths being educated abroad. These young men, who neither owned land nor respected tribal tradition,

> . . . could find no outlet for their energies within the narrow limits of independent Albania. . . . They were thus peculiarly susceptible to the influence of revolutionary ideas. In other countries such young men often inclined to Fascism, but in Albania Fascism was the creed of the overlord and, in their search for faith and discipline, they therefore turned to the Communists. It is unlikely that there were ever more than two, or at the most three, thousand of these young men, but they were to be the backbone of the Communist organization and the leaders under whom the landless peasants were organized. The combined discontent of these two classes—the youth of the towns and the landless peasants— produced a social revolutionary movement, which presently won the support of many of the richer peasants as well by its appeal to their patriotism or their land hunger. This, in turn, provoked the most conservative elements to combine for the defense of their own interests; and so the general unrest among the Tosks was increased.
>
> The general poverty of the Albanians, their resentment of foreign rule, the anarchy and mercenary economy of the Ghegs, and a growth of a crisis in social relationships among the Tosks were thus the conditions out of which the Albanian resistance movement grew. . . .[22]

Enver Hoxha stemmed from the bourgeoisie. He was a thirty-two-year-old professor of history who had been educated in France and Belgium, and many of his subordinate leaders came from the same middle-class background. In late 1942, he persuaded the most important royalist-Gheg guerrilla bands to join the partisan movement under the banner of the National Liberation Movement, or LNC. The collaboration proved highly tenuous, with one of the strongest Gheg leaders, Abas Kupi, never a willing participant. Despite the LNC veil, Hoxha remained a hard-line Communist with Comintern connections to KKE in Greece and Tito in Yugoslavia.[23]

Albanian Communists, including some Gheg bands, were fighting the Italian enemy when Maclean's mission arrived. Impressed by their activity, Maclean arranged for delivery of arms and equipment and began training two shock brigades. Other SOE teams parachuted in to join the various groups. But as the Italians showed signs of surrendering, the question of a new government arose, and conflict developed between the partisans and the Republican Balli guerrillas. The Italian surrender heightened tension, since Italian arms equipped more guerrillas, who also recruited Italian deserters.

Subsequent German occupation further hindered the resistance movement. Moving in about two and a half divisions, the Germans soon pressed various guerrilla bands back into the hills: " . . . within a fortnight the insurgents were everywhere on the defensive." The Germans were essentially interested in coastal defense against an allied landing and contented themselves with occupying principal towns and keeping roads open. " . . . The rest of the country they determined to neutralize by policy rather than force." They released political prisoners, announced that they would withdraw from Albania once war ended, and set up a puppet government.[24]

This policy played into Enver Hoxha's hands. If Germans controlled cities and coastal communications, Hoxha would control the rest of Albania, and, in autumn of 1943, he ordered his people to begin attacking and destroying his rivals in the South, the Balli bands. The Ballis soon began falling back toward the coast, where, to survive, they collaborated with the Germans, who willingly fitted them out for counter-guerrilla duties: " . . . The civil war in Southern Albania was thus indefinitely prolonged, to the exhaustion of the Albanians and the repose of the German army."[25]

At this critical point, SOE replaced Maclean with a more senior representative, Brigadier "Trotsky" Davies. A Sandhurst regular and twice-decorated veteran of the Mesopotamia campaign (1920) and the Palestine fighting in 1938, Davies brought in a small staff, which he based at Biza, in the South. He also brought in nearly half a million dollars in gold to help him accomplish his major task of backing those guerrilla organizations which would fight the enemy.[26]

Although he had some good men who subsequently performed well in the field and although he was a man of considerable charm and unquestioned personal courage, Davies erred in trying to implant regular army order in guerrilla warfare disorder. Where Maclean traveled light, Davies dug in and soon had an impressive but useless headquarters of " ... interpreters, Italian cooks, servants, mulemen and others," all requiring food and quarters, and one calculated to attract the attention of even the most myopic enemy.[27]

Thus situated, Davies turned to the immense task of forging peace between Enver Hoxha and the Balli, a task that would have required a skillful diplomat armed with Jobian patience. The old boy simply wasn't up to the challenge. At his first conference with the Communist leader, he refused Hoxha's request to review the present world political situation:

> ... Enver said, very pointedly, "The military situation depends entirely on the political situation, so why will you not first give us your impression of world politics?"
> I replied, "Because I am a soldier and not a politician."[28]

As Davies continued to argue, with both Hoxha and the Balli, the situation continued to deteriorate, the *chetas* merrily shifting sides, while almost no one fought the Germans. Davies himself grew increasingly frustrated, disgusted, and unrealistic:

> ... I felt that we could bring the country to a standstill with two brigades of British troops acting as guerrillas, or with half a dozen *Commandos* [i.e., special operation units]. ... [29]

That such a notion was never tried was just as well. After moving his ponderous headquarters two or three times in response to German pressure, he decided to break off the guerrilla campaign until spring and move his headquarters south in conjunction with Hoxha's forces. Although Hoxha and his guerrillas reached sanctuary, the Davies group never made it. Hotly pursued by Germans and turncoat Albanians, Davies was wounded and captured, his organization broken up. His field missions suffered various fates: Many were captured and their gold stolen; a few survivors escaped north to join Abas Kupi's guerrillas. As though to haunt the mission's failure, gold circulated by Davies caused severe inflation in the mountains, thus exercising an effect precisely opposite to the intention.[30]

In spring of 1944, SOE parachuted a new mission, again under Maclean, into the North, to try to build a resistance movement cored by Abas Kupi's group and even to bring Abas Kupi into joint effort with Enver Hoxha. Maclean and two principal lieutenants, Smiley and Amery, found considerable potential in the northern mountains—Amery estimated a total fifteen thousand rifles with possibility of another ten thousand. But they found the tribes "divided among themselves by ancient feuds, personal

GREECE, ALBANIA 1941
• Towns and Cities
0   50   100   150 miles

×××× Greek defensive line
⟶ German armies

M.E.P.

jealousies, and their varying attachment to the Allied or to the German cause."[31] Although they managed to bring off some small operations, they did not receive support necessary to bring about a general uprising—and very possibly they could not have accomplished this even with prodigal supply.

In contrast, Hoxha and his guerrillas in the South prospered, their numbers growing from an estimated five thousand in January 1944 to over twenty thousand by May. Allied supply, though still in limited quantities, began arriving by air and sea, and LNC units soon were striking German convoys and even garrisons throughout the area with operations expanding north to the other side of Tirana.

In June, the German high command brought in the 1st Mountain Division, a crack outfit which in a month " . . . succeeded in closing the Allied bridgehead north of Saranda, reopening communications with Greece and scattering Partisans into the mountains."[32]

With transfer of this division to Yugoslavia and replacement by a second-rate outfit, LNC quickly reorganized and recommenced harassing activities. Its units now came into open conflict with royalist and republican movements, but, with SOE support, neutralized these organizations while spreading farther north.

Ensuing internecine fighting greatly helped the Germans to evacuate Albania. If Partisans and Zogists harassed the German retreat, they expended their real energy in fighting civil war, a war the Partisans won. With the ignominious retreat of Abas Kupi and SOE advisers, LNC controlled the country, which became and remained Communist until very recent events radically changed the situation.

CHAPTER TWENTY-EIGHT

1. Woodhouse, *The Story of Modern Greece*. A Greek scholar and historian, and an active participant in Greece with SOE(Cairo) during World War II, Mr. Woodhouse has written a splendid short history of this troubled and complicated land. See also, Woodhouse, *Apple of Discord*. This excellent study of the Axis occupation of Greece and the subsequent civil war contains a thoughtful defense of the Metaxas dictatorship, 14–17.
2. Woodhouse, *Apple of Discord*, 55.
3. Ibid., 61.
4. Sweet-Escott, 119.
5. Myers, *Greek Entanglement*.
6. Ibid., 63–87, for an excellent account of this operation.
7. Blair, 75.
8. Ibid.
9. Myers, 127.
10. Woodhouse, *Apple of Discord*, 45.
11. Sweet-Escott, 73.
12. Ibid., 173.
13. Woodhouse, *Apple of Discord*, 99.
14. Myers, 202 ff.
15. O'Ballance, *The Greek Civil War . . .* , 65 ff.
16. Woodhouse, *Apple of Discord*, 147.
17. Blair, 80.
18. Ibid., 82.
19. O'Ballance, 68–9. See also, Woodhouse, *Apple of Discord*, 27–8. Prime Minister Rallis " . . . regarded the force as a bridge across which Greece would pass from German occupation to Allied liberation without an interval of chaos."
20. Woodhouse, *Apple of Discord*, 198–9. See also, O'Ballance, 78. Neither before nor after the visitation did ELAS receive military aid from the Soviet Union, nor, at this time, was Tito furnishing aid to ELAS.
21. Amery, 54 ff.
22. Ibid., 24.

23. Blair, 92.
24. Amery, 64.
25. Ibid., 65–6.
26. Davies, E.F., 71.
27. Blair, 96.
28. Davies, 77.
29. Ibid., 86.
30. Blair, 96.
31. Amery, 172.
32. Blair, 98.

CHAPTER 29

Japanese conquests • Australian coastwatchers • American marines on Guadalcanal • Japanese occupation of Timor • Australian independent companies • Callinan fights guerrilla warfare • Japanese countertactics • The native element • A summing up

SPRING OF 1942: Japanese armies occupied all of Southeast Asia, the Philippines, and the Dutch East Indies—the so-called Co-Prosperity Sphere, whose eastern flank Japan protected by a string of newly occupied bases terminating in New Guinea and the Solomon Islands, the western flank by the conquest of Burma, which isolated China and posed a direct threat to India.

The rapidity of these conquests threw potential resistance movements into considerable confusion. With few exceptions, no real resistance organizations existed, although, as in European countries, local Communist parties converted quite easily into militant organizations. Temporary defeat and immense distances prevented the allies from supplying essential arms and ammunition to, or even communicating with, much less controlling, dissident groups. In some areas, important segments of the population either welcomed Japanese as liberators or suffered them in preference to white colonial rule. Although harsh occupation policies usually changed such halcyon situations, delayed emergence of dissident groups again posed communications and supply problems.

Terrain also influenced the situation: Tiny Pacific islands such as Tarawa and Iwo Jima offered neither natives nor sanctuaries for infiltrated teams, nor did the American navy or marines dispose of specially trained groups for use in more likely target areas such as Guam. An inhibiting political factor also existed, particularly with the British, who did not want the natives of such empire possessions as Burma and Malaya promiscuously supplied with arms in the postwar era.

* * *

Almost alone in the vast area of conquest, the Australian high command had taken certain "stay behind" precautions against war with Japan. The original idea stemmed from 1919, when an Australian naval intelligence officer " . . . put forward a suggestion that Australia's vast coastal areas be policed by a network of 'watchers' to report any suspicious characters and happenings in isolated parts."[1]

Through the years, naval intelligence extended the system to New Guinea, Papua, and the Solomon Islands, an intelligence net supported by government officials, missionaries, pilots, and planters. Alarmed by the worsening international situation, in 1939 Commander Eric Feldt recruited small "stay behind" teams and equipped them with teleradios and codes. When war broke, these incredibly brave men, usually white district officers or plantation managers assisted by a few loyal natives, took to the hills, where, often living like animals, they reported enemy strength and dispositions to Port Moresby. Just such a report first disclosed Japanese presence on Guadalcanal and led to U. S. Marine Corps landings in August 1942.

The coastwatcher who reported this development was named Martin Clemens. About a week after marines landed, he presented himself to Major General Alexander Vandegrift. The marine commander found him " . . . a remarkable chap of medium height, well-built and apparently suffering no ill effects from his self-imposed jungle exile."

> . . . Clemens brought with him a small and loyal group of native scouts including Sergeant Major Vouza, a retired member of the Solomon Islands constabulary. At the outbreak of war Vouza, a black and bandy-legged little fellow, as were all the natives, reported to Clemens and accompanied him into the hills. There they recruited a goodly force of natives who hated the Japanese because of cruelty to the islanders. Clemens and Vouza trained these young men as scouts and when Clemens offered me his and their services I was delighted to accept. Vouza later rendered superb service as did all the scouts—of the entire coastwatcher organization I can say nothing too lavish in praise.[2]

The coastwatchers were neither trained nor equipped to generate native guerrilla movements, but their operations nonetheless profited immensely from Japanese occupation policy, which treated Solomon Islands natives as so much dirt. This was a gross error, for these natives possessed eyes and ears and swift jungle feet and the ability to jabber in pidgin English—and their words frequently sang through the ether to Port Moresby, often a siren song calling down air and naval attacks.

Guadalcanal offers the first tactical paradox in the Pacific war. Despite training that stressed extreme mobility and quasi-guerrilla jungle tactics, Japanese soldiers no more found themselves at home in Guadalcanal jungles than the Americans. Command jealousies, disease, and supply and communication problems combined to frustrate attacks against the marine perimeter guarding Henderson Field. Although supported by clear naval and air superiority, various attacking columns suffered thousands of casualties both from marine fire and from subsequent retreat through jungle rapidly becoming hostile as rations and medicines were consumed and not replaced.

The marines also suffered. At one point, most of Vandegrift's large command was down with dysentery or malaria or both. On several occasions, the jungle slowed, then halted, his limited offensive actions. But marines came to terms with the jungle, not only surviving but fighting and fighting well to invalidate forever the carefully inculcated myth of Japanese tactical invincibility. Part of the reason stemmed from Vandegrift's personal leadership and his refusal to accept defeat, a charismatic performance of enormous importance, considering the long odds against him.

Nor was this sheer bravado. Vandegrift was no stranger to jungle, having campaigned for years in Nicaragua and Haiti. If jungle could hide Japanese, it could also hide marines. In early September, he learned that the American navy could no longer support operations on Guadalcanal—that, literally, he and his marines would have to fight on alone:

> . . . I walked back to the CP [command post] with my operations officer [Lt. Col. G. C. Thomas]. "You know, Jerry," I told him, "when we landed in Tientsin, China, in 1927, old Colonel E. B. Miller ordered me to draw up three plans. Two concerned the accomplishment of our mission, the third a withdrawal from Tientsin in case we got pushed out." We walked a bit farther. "Jerry, we're going to defend this airfield until we no longer can. If that happens, we'll take what's left to the hills and fight guerrilla warfare. . . . "[3]

On the more positive side, Vandegrift used jungle later in the campaign when he sent Carlson's Raiders on a wide sweep intended to intercept a withdrawing Japanese column. Aided by native scouts and porters under Vouza and supplied by airdrop, Carlson extended the patrol far to the west. Although he missed the main body, he ambushed a number of rearguard units and cleaned out bothersome artillery positions—in all, killing some 450 enemy at a cost of seventeen killed and seventeen wounded.[4]

* * *

Another relatively simple action played itself out early in the war on Timor, a large island lying about five hundred miles northwest of Port Darwin, in northern Australia. Timor formed a natural protective flank for Japanese-held Java. Planes flying from its two airfields could neutralize Port Darwin, and it also furnished a staging-support area for operations in the Solomon Islands and New Guinea.

Timor is a large island, about three hundred miles long and an average forty miles wide; a central mountain range has produced terrain varying from scrub-covered slopes to open coastal areas interspersed by dense jungle. Before the war, the Netherlands owned its western half, Portugal its eastern half. In December 1941, a small contingent of Dutch and Australian troops known as Sparrow Force occupied the Dutch portion. When Portugal remained neutral, the Dutch and British persuaded her to allow "a friendly occupation" by Sparrow Force troops, in particular the Australian 2/2 Independent Company.

Britain had started the concept of independent raiding companies—forerunner of her famous Commandos—shortly after the fall of France in June 1940. With help of a small British military mission, Australian and New Zealand armies trained a total of eight such companies for independent harassing operations in the Middle East. A member of the British team, a thirty-three-year-old captain and former explorer and teacher, F. Spencer-Chapman, later described the operational thinking of the day:

> . . . We talked vaguely of guerrilla and irregular warfare, of special and para-military operations, stay-behind parties, resistance movements, sabotage and incendiarism, and, darkly and still more vaguely, of "agents"; but the exact role of the Commandos and Independent Companies had never been made very clear.

Some believed that if the Japanese overran various islands,

> . . . the role of the Companies would then be to stay behind, live off the country or be provisioned by air, and be a thorn in the flesh of the occupying enemy, emerging in true guerrilla style to attack vital points and then disappear again into the jungle.[5]

The Japanese advance caused the high command to commit the newly trained companies to islands closer home. Australian 2/2 Independent Company went to Timor and subsequently to adventures beyond dreams of its hardy back-country-Australian members. The story is well told by the company commander, Major Bernard Callinan, in his book *Independent Company,* which I have relied on in the following brief account.

Variously reinforced, 2/2 Independent Company comprised around 325 men totally unfamiliar with Timor. Sent to the Portuguese area of Dili, on the coast, the company completed what defenses it could before the Japanese onslaught in February 1942. Some fourteen thousand Japanese troops landed at Koepang, in Dutch Timor, and about six thousand at Dili. On Dutch Timor, the bulk of Sparrow Force fell back, only to encounter Japanese paratroopers fighting a guerrilla-style action in their rear. Inadequately trained and equipped, this force soon lost tactical cohesion, the units either surrendering or escaping to Portuguese Timor.

While 2/2 Company also fell back, its commander held no intention of surrendering. His situation was scarcely happy. The company was not supposed to be fighting independently on Timor, and logistically was anything but self-sufficient. It even lacked a radio transmitter capable of raising Port Darwin. It was well armed, however, for guerrilla warfare—its men carried the proportionately high number of sixty submachine guns and were splendidly trained for small-unit operations. Instead of surrendering, as the high command in Australia supposed had been the case, the company commander immediately chose defensive positions and began harassing the newly arrived enemy.

The Australians wisely refrained from complicating the relatively simple tactical problem of containing Japanese in the Dili area. To accomplish this, they set up a fluid defense in surrounding hills, from where small units ambushed roads and paths, besides raiding suitable enemy targets. Wishing to push back the Australians so that their forces in the west could deliver the *coup de grâce*, the Japanese reinforced Dili

374

units and began dispatching strong probing patrols into surrounding hills.

For combat veterans, they seemed surprisingly inept. They almost constantly telegraphed their movements, frequently walking through one ambush position to be attacked by a second; survivors were then struck from the rear. Small ambushes contantly hit enemy motor patrols, an activity that increased when the Japanese set up a base twenty miles inland from Dili. Australian roadblocks " . . . varied from rolling large rocks or felling trees across the roads, to blocking up culverts to cause the road to be washed away, and to blowing embankments away and then diverting creeks to continue the erosion." This facilitated successful ambushes,

> . . . and our tally of enemy killed grew. To reduce the attacks the enemy established strong posts along the road, and from these patrols went out to keep the area clear. This was the culmination of all our efforts; we now had the enemy thoroughly worried, and his troops were being dispersed, and tired out on sentry and patrol duties. This system of posts also suited our capabilities as we were able to provide small parties which sat above these posts and observed them, and when the routine of the post was known a raid would be carried out. . . . One typical raid was carried out by Sergeant James, who with two sappers [engineers] sat less than one hundred yards from a Japanese post for two days. When he knew the routine of the post well, he decided that the best time to strike was just as the enemy were having breakfast. So the following morning there was a sharp burst of fire and twelve Japanese were killed, the raiders disappearing into the scrub.[6]

Two or three such raids per week, each claiming from five to fifteen Japanese lives, worked an "enormous" effect on Japanese morale.

Australian morale meanwhile was none too good. By now, malaria claimed most of the company. Boots were wearing fast, weapons needed repair, ammunition was running low, money was needed to pay natives. So far as the world knew, 2/2 Company languished in some Japanese prison camp.

Imagine the surprise, then, of radio monitors one morning in Port Darwin picking up a faint signal from Timor. This came from a transmitter made by a radioman ingeniously working with two field radios and bits of variously acquired junk. New sets brought in from Darwin eventually replaced this Rube Goldberg contraption, and supply drops naturally increased 2/2 Company's effectiveness, to the degree that the Japanese accepted the tactical status quo and began concentrating on raising natives against the Australians.

Timor natives give still another lie to the pleasant fiction of people everywhere wanting to die for what the West likes to call freedom. Timor natives did not know the meaning of freedom. To them, the white man represented oppression. At one point during the campaign, Callinan watched a two-hundred-man Portuguese force launch a punitive expedition against some rebel natives: " . . . Compared with this, the Japanese efforts at subjecting areas were just child's play. Every village and crop was burnt; every woman, child, and animal was driven off and fell as spoil to the victors. . . . "[7] Was it any wonder that Japanese agents before the war had successfully implanted anti-white propaganda, not alone in Timor but throughout Pacific colonial areas?

After the landings, the Japanese continued to cultivate the native population by simple propaganda reinforced by a strong physical presence. They also put a considerable price on each Australian head, and they worked up active native opposition *behind* the Australians by sometimes threatening to burn villages and crops. None of these measures deprived Australians of the initiative, though enemy caution forced them to drastic action. Patrols armed with three-inch mortars sent from Port Darwin sneaked close to Dili to launch surprise bombardments that caused Japanese patrols to issue forth (and frequently stumble into ambushes). Other brave souls relying on friendly native cover advanced to close range and eliminated enemy groups with submachine-gun fire.

To counter native treachery, Australians employed friendly natives, who proved surprisingly loyal. A native servant, or *criado,* served each Australian, following him into combat and relieving him of gear, then helping him escape over difficult and unfamiliar terrain. Later in the campaign, 2/2 Company trained several native units in marksmanship and partially equipped them with rifles. Recruiting grew easier as occupation continued and Japanese cruelties multiplied. Natives particularly resented Japanese attacks on native women and girls. Australians also gained a psychological advantage over natives from their own air raids (by far the most important accomplishment of these raids). Finally, they relied on active patrol and area security and instant reprisal in case of native attack.

Mobility remained their best ally. Time and again, Japanese columns rushed from Dili only to encounter space. If they rushed too far, they found themselves cut off. If they did happen onto a few guerrillas, the latter quickly disappeared. It was as if guerrillas sprang from ground to disappear in sky. It seemed easy; in fact, it hinged on an extremely cunning organization whose disciplined members constantly utilized security measures.

The operational key was Force Headquarters, tucked away in the hills. This organization supported the active guerrilla groups and also administered a rear-area sanctuary in a mountain village, " . . . a remarkable achievement comprising a hospital, a convalescent depot, and a reinforcement training depot. . . . " Force Headquarters remained extremely mobile.[8] On one occasion the Japanese homed in on transmissions and followed with a raid in force to find nothing, the signal unit having packed up and left within fifteen minutes.

Far from exterminating the Australians, the Japanese seriously threatened their existence on only a few occasions. They could not prevent airdrops from reaching the guerrillas. A few ships also managed to bring in supply, an effort culminating by landing 2/4 Independent Company as much-needed reinforcement. In thirteen months, the Australians killed some fifteen hundred enemy troops at a cost of forty men.

But this was not their real accomplishment. Their supreme moment occurred when the Japanese high command, fearful of an allied landing on Timor, committed the 48th Infantry Division, fifteen thousand veterans of China, Philippines, and Java campaigns. As Nevil Shute pointed out in an introductory chapter to *Independent Company,* " . . . this at a time when their advance in Burma had been halted, when the American Marines were fighting on Guadalcanal, and bitter fighting was in progress in Papua [New Guinea]"—in other words, at a time when the Japanese had a dozen and one other uses for a good infantry division.

Australians on Timor undoubtedly could have insured a successful allied landing by temporarily protecting a beachhead. But, in 1943, the "withering on the vine" strategy, whereby allied forces bypassed island redoubts, leaving them to starve and eventually surrender, made pointless such a landing. Instead the Australians were safely evacuated to leave the Japanese in uneasy occupation of the island.

CHAPTER TWENTY-NINE

1. Murray, 26.
2. Vandegrift and Asprey, 136–7. In later scouting behind the Japanese lines, Vouza was captured, tortured unmercifully, and left for dead. He chewed through his ropes and crawled to a marine outpost to report valuable information. Vandegrift awarded him the Silver Star medal. See also, Griffith, *The Battle for Gaudalcanal.*
3. Vandegrift and Asprey, 153.
4. Mirillat, 217–27.
5. Spencer-Chapman, 7–8.
6. Callinan, 103–4.
7. Ibid., 155.
8. Ibid., 126.

CHAPTER 30

Guerrilla resistance in the Philippines • Area of operations • Kangleon's guerrillas on Leyte • Major missions • Japanese occupation policy • Japanese countertactics • Fertig's guerrillas on Mindanao • Major missions • Failure of Japanese countertactics • Communist resistance • Luis Taruc and the Huks • Volckmann's guerrillas on Luzon • His organization and growth • Major missions • The Japanese attitude • Host to MacArthur's landing

A MUCH LESS COHESIVE but no less instructive guerrilla resistance sprang up in the Philippine Islands after the fall of Corregidor, the island bastion lying off Bataan, in early 1942. Not all of the American-Philippine garrison surrendered to the Japanese. Although MacArthur's command was totally surprised, some commanders sent officers behind Japanese units with orders to raise guerrilla groups. During retreat to the island bastion, a good many soldiers, cut off by the Japanese advance, had escaped to remote areas of Luzon, where willing Filipinos helped hide and feed them while they organized guerrilla units. (See map, Chapter 11.)

Elsewhere in the vast complex of islands, Filipino and American officers often refused to surrender, preferring instead to take to the hills to form resistance nuclei, which attracted fellow citizens, survivors of sunk American ships, and various American civilians who managed to elude the Japanese dragnet. Still another guerrilla movement, and a potent one, centered around the Communist Party of the Philippines, which, like European Communist parties, was small but well organized.

About fifty guerrilla groups emerged in the islands before the Japanese had even consolidated their conquest, and a surprising number of these survived and prospered. In the vast archipelago, 7,100 islands with a land area of 114,830 square miles, they occupied in the main Luzon in the North, the Visayan Islands (particularly Leyte and Samar) in the center, and Mindanao in the South,[1] although small groups ex-

378

isted on many smaller islands, where they eventually lined the beaches to greet returning Americans.

At first, these units were out of touch with allied headquarters in Australia or even with each other. Nor were their aims always harmonious. While killing Japanese was the announced goal, some groups existed more to survive than to fight, some to prey as bandits on relatively helpless native barrios, some, particularly Communists, to fight but also to consolidate in so far as possible their power for postwar purposes, and some to fight as hard as they could until the Americans returned.

Whatever the goal, no one group enjoyed an easy existence, despite a good many natural sanctuaries. Some of the immense problems have been well presented by Ira Wolfert in his book *American Guerrilla in the Philippines,* which is the story of an American naval officer, Cliff Richardson, who joined a guerrilla force organized and commanded by a regular Philippine Army officer, Lieutenant Colonel Ruperto Kangleon.

After escaping from a Japanese prisoner-of-war camp, Kangleon recruited a small guerrilla group in southern Leyte. Some natives wanted to help the guerrillas, their motivation intense nationalism rather than particular ideology. About 70 per cent of the population, however, greatly feared the Japanese and did not hide their relief when guerrillas had vacated barrio or village areas. Initial enthusiasm later waned when a bandit group calling itself guerrillas "requisitioned" anything they could find, including women, with no notion of fighting the Japanese. Bandits provided but one difficulty to Kangleon's embryo army, which suffered from shortages of everything but spirit. The band owned few rifles and little ammunition. To keep rifles in repair and provide fresh ammunition, guerrillas rounded up " . . . a hand-forge, some hacksaws, and a file. That was a small arms factory." Brass curtain rods taken from schoolhouses were cut and filed to make bullets.

> . . . For the primer, we used sulphur mixed with coconut shell carbon. Later we were able to get hold of some antimony and add it to the mixture. . . . Our main source of powder was from Japanese sea mines that we would dismantle. We'd mix in pulverized wood to retard the burning because mine powder is too violent for a rifle bullet.[2]

So laborious was filing down the curtain rods that "our production never got better than an average of 160 bullets a day."

Despite such disadvantages, the guerrilla force rapidly expanded. Almost all raw materials continued to come from the people—general requisitions carried out through local government. Guerrillas made their own ink, essential for news sheets and money; they made fuel for their few vehicles by distilling alcohol from tuba; they constructed 140 kilometers of telegraph lines by using nails made from barbed wire and insulators from old soda-pop bottles.[3]

Kangleon did not contact MacArthur's headquarters in Australia until spring of 1943, when an American naval commander arrived by submarine to talk to guerrilla leaders and set up a chain of coastwatcher stations. MacArthur recognized Kangleon as the official guerrilla commander on Leyte and two American submarines began the hazardous task of bringing in arms and supply.[4]

Kangleon's early survival rested in part on a relatively light Japanese garrison in southern Leyte, but as the Japanese experienced fresh reverses in the Pacific theater, they reinforced Leyte garrisons and attempted to clean out guerrilla bands. By this time, Kangleon had organized a quasi-regular army, whose companies maintained " . . . a guardhouse, barracks, mess hall, officers' quarters" protected by

> . . . a whole network of volunteer guards . . . civilians serving without pay, donating one day out of every four to act as sentinels or relay men for messages or lookouts. When Japanese approached, the civilians were warned, too, and in the hills and many coastal barrios patrols found only empty houses and vacant towns. . . .[5]

Beginning in late 1943, the Japanese increased size and frequency of patrols. Utilizing information supplied through collaborators they captured numerous guerrillas and guerrilla sympathizers, summarily executing each. Guerrillas replied by killing one collaborator for each victim:

> . . . Cinco's [a unit leader] men developed the habit of killing Japan's "good neighbors," leaving their faces untouched so that they might be recognized but mincing up their bodies gruesomely, then floating them downstream to their home barrio where they could serve as an example to the others.[6]

Tactically the Japanese relied on large expeditions, or "sweeps," sometimes supported by aircraft whose bombs and machine-gun bullets proved virtually useless in heavy jungle. Once a patrol had worn itself out in a day of fruitless marching through difficult terrain, guerrillas frequently ambushed it on its way back to barrio.

Failure to eliminate guerrillas infuriated the Japanese, who resorted to harsher and harsher treatment of the civil populace. Suspect guerrillas or sympathizers often received the salt-water torture:

... they tied a man's hands and feet and ran the cord around his neck so that if he struggled he would strangle himself. Then they forced a wedge into his mouth to hold it open, held his nose, and poured sea water into his mouth. He had to swallow to breathe.[7]

If he talked, they stopped the torture; if not, they continued until his death. These and other punishments often caused people to leave villages for the hills, where the Japanese ruthlessly tried to ferret them out, often killing entire hill families and burning hill barrios in the process. To prevent this, guerrillas frequently attacked enemy units close to coastal towns rather than in more favorable ambush areas in the hills.

Hill people also reacted vigorously. The men began carrying a second, and smaller, bolo under the shirt, attacking Japanese soldiers as they closed in to tie their hands. When the Japanese learned this trick and made victims remove their shirt, " . . . the Filipinos took to carrying shards of glass in their mouths, razor blades if they found them and sharpened nails to strike enemy eyes—anything that would do damage and keep a man from feeling he was a dumb beast standing mutely to be killed." Hill natives also planted *suak,* or barbed pieces of tetanus-poisoned bamboo, along trails used by Japanese patrols. When a patrol passed, natives would " . . . fire a shot or . . . shout and the Japs would drop flat against the *suak.*"[8]

The combination of hill natives and guerrillas proved too much for the Japanese, who slowly yielded all but coastal towns, finally not daring even to send patrols to the hills. Nor did the Japanese commander dare to report failure. Instead, he insisted that, from January through August 1944, his troops fought 561 engagements with guerrillas, killing and capturing thousands of Filipinos (and a few Americans) with only slight Japanese casualties. Kangleon, on the other hand, reported minimum guerrilla casualties and significant Japanese losses as his movement grew. Armed with radios and new weapons landed from submarines, he continued to report valuable intelligence, and when American armies returned to the islands a few months later, they were greeted by a potent and helpful force.

On Mindanao, the vast southern island, an American mining engineer and reserve officer, Colonel Wendell Fertig, built an impressive guerrilla organization from a cadre of five officers and about 175 enlisted men.[9] Although Mindanao proved ideal for guerrilla operations—it offered ample food, mountain sanctuary, and easy access to the sea and thus eventual supply by submarine—the movement did not immediately prosper. American defeat had caused important segments of the population to either support or submit to the Japanese presence. Japanese troops, not the guerrillas, soon changed this disadvantageous situation by inflicting their boorish presence on the locals, frequently slapping men and molesting and raping women. As early as September 1942, forty-five uprisings occurred on Mindanao, and Fertig found himself heading a viable guerrilla movement.

The Japanese had intended to rule through the legal Philippine government and native police, an intention voided by the army's stupid behavior. Instead, they organized a constabulary of native quislings brought in from other islands. These became the priority target of Fertig's guerrillas, who harassed them so effectively that they soon ceased patrolling and eventually confined themselves to two general areas.

Although the Japanese maintained about 150,000 troops on Mindanao, they held back in committing them to counterguerrilla actions. When they did so, they proved as inept as on the Visayan Islands, in general relying on "sweeps" that devastated "guerrilla areas" and accomplished little.

The Japanese failed to understand the nature of the target. Believing that they were fighting isolated groups of bandits, their various area headquarters refused to co-ordinate counterguerrilla operations, relying instead on local punitive actions. They did not realize, or anyway would not admit, that they were fighting an entire population. A significant exception occurred in 1944, when one Japanese general chose a conciliatory approach to the people and nearly wrecked the guerrilla movement! More often, however, the enemy fell into the traditional trap: the more countermeasures failed to eliminate guerrilla activity, the more they persecuted the people and the stronger the movement became.

Fertig's substantial growth was recognized in early 1943, when allied headquarters designated Mindanao as the 10th Military District. Some escaped Australian army prisoners of war, including Major Rex Blow, landing in northern Mindanao in June 1943 found a quasi-military organization of impressive proportions—the 105th Regiment of guerrillas commanded by Colonel Hedges.[10]

Although Hedges, who had managed a timber company in the area before the war, commanded about ten thousand guerrillas, he was temporarily lying low as a result of vigorous Japanese punitive measures. Major Blow learned something of prevailing spirit, however, when he asked a young Filipino intelligence officer to type out some reports. "Sir," Lieutenant Villanueva replied, "I do not wish to work in an office, I want to kill Japs." He subsequently did so, only to lose his life while singlehandedly attacking some fifty Japanese soldiers.[11]

Hedges faced another problem in the form of confused religions. About two thousand Christians were fighting as guerrillas in coastal areas; the rest of his command consisted of fierce Mohammedan Moros, who fought under their old sultans. Moros not only battled Japanese and Christians but also each other, and Hedges and Blow spent a great deal of time trying to minimize their extracurricular wars.

The main guerrilla function in the north at this time was to survive while providing allied headquarters with intelligence. Fertig frequently changed "headquarters"—the longest he ever stayed in one place was two months. He also used aggressive measures to throw the enemy off. The favorite was the small patrol to harass the usual two-hundred-man Japanese patrol. Filipinos knew every foot of the area, knew where to strike and where likely ambushes could occur—hill natives could actually *smell* the presence of Japanese. Without the people's help, guerrillas would not have survived. For a long period, Fertig depended for interisland communication largely on a "bamboo telegraph," in which ten-year-olds played an integral role despite the blandishments of enemy, who, although offering candy one day, offered blows the next. Major Blow's fourteen-year-old houseboy and bodyguard, Sabu, had watched Japanese soldiers kill his father and rape his mother and sisters, an experience scarcely unique. As a result, people constantly risked their lives on behalf of guerrillas. Blow later wrote of an offensive that eventually forced the Japanese to evacuate Iligan:

> . . . When out on patrol we never carried anything but a change of clothes, a toothbrush and our arms. Every house we passed would offer us something to eat, whether it was a piece of corn or a fat chicken. The Japs were now offering quite a large reward for my head, dead or alive—the price being 5,000 yards of West Point khaki drill, valued at about twenty pesos a yard then. But there was never the slightest suggestion of earning that prize. . . .

In the Lianga area, Blow continued:

> . . . During these difficult days we were given great assistance by the Assemblyman, Mr. Lluch. He organized a body of young girls who cooked, sewed, and tended our wounds. They were a stout-hearted group and always back in town the day after the Japs had passed through, ready to organize a concert or dance, repair our clothes and feed us. . . . [12]

So effective were guerrillas in this area that, by the time of American landings, most of the considerable area of Lanao, including beaches, was devoid of Japanese. In the Malabang area, Blow's guerrillas seized and held an airstrip from which American marine fliers operated against Japanese for a week prior to troop landings.

* * *

383

Still another movement centered on the Communist Party of the Philippines, which in 1938 had been joined by the Socialist Party. At the outbreak of war, Communists formed the *Hukbo ng Bayan so Hapon* (People's Army to Fight the Japanese), which we have come to know as the Hukbalahap, or Huks. Organized on quasi-military lines and commanded by twenty-nine-year-old Luis Taruc, whom we shall meet again after the war, these units formed regiments, battalions, companies, platoons, and squads. Leaders in time established semiliberated and liberated areas from where they harassed Japanese to a far greater extent than has usually been admitted by anti-Communist postwar commentators. By August 1942, the Huks were regularly attacking Japanese units in order to gain arms and supply. Early successes produced an unhealthy overconfidence, however, and in 1943, Japanese troops attacked and practically destroyed the Mount Arayat stronghold—the only major counterguerrilla success during the occupation.[13]

The Huks soon recovered to become a real menace to the Japanese, particularly in central Luzon but also on other islands. Captured Japanese files bulged with reports such as that of September 24, 1944, to the puppet President Laurel: " . . . about 1,000 Hukbos armed with machine guns, automatic rifles and pistols struck Jaen in Nueva Ecija . . . looting, burning: 1 policeman dead; 2 Hukbos killed, 4 wounded. . . ." Three months later, the unhappy president learned " . . . that the mails coming from the Visayas and Mindanao are practically nil while those from Luzon are extremely limited."[14]

A variety of guerrilla movements took place on the northern island of Luzon. One of the most viable sprang from the efforts of a young West Pointer, thirty-year-old R. W. Volckmann, who began his Philippine experience a captain and ended a colonel—a remarkable saga well told in his book *We Remained.* Promoted to regimental commander during the retreat down Bataan, Volckmann refused the final surrender order and took to the hills, where a number of small bands already had formed, a disjointed effort, under two American army officers, Colonels Moses and Noble.

After a series of incredible adventures and hair-raising escapes, this latter-day Lawrence found himself in northern Luzon, a victorious trek that depended in part on his own incredible stamina and courage, in part on willingness of hundreds of natives to risk their lives and the lives of families and friends to hide, feed, and nurse him. Arriving more dead than alive, in September 1942, he recovered to organize and command one of the most valuable guerrilla nets in the archipelago.

Volckmann started nearly from scratch. He was not familiar with the history or philosophy of rebellion and guerrilla warfare, he probably had not read Lenin and certainly not Mao Tse-tung. Using common sense, he was aware that the first element essential to a resistance movement existed in the Philippines: a cause. Japanese invasion and occupation, he reasoned, " . . . were opposed in varying degrees by the vast majority of the people." A capable leader, he believed, could organize and direct this "underlying potential for resistance." Mountains, forests, and limited roads of northern Luzon favored guerrilla operations as did numerous villages, " . . . a source of food and shelter." The Japanese could be expected to conduct extensive campaigns "against guerrilla forces and their supporting populace" until allied forces landed in strength:

> . . . each Allied victory and the reduction of the time and space between the Allied forces and Luzon would reduce Japanese capabilities and in turn strengthen Filipino morale. I was certain also that reduction of the time and space factor would likewise mean material support, provided, of course, that contact could be established with friendly forces. To me, then, the time and space factor was the key.[15]

Volckmann thought that an earlier attempt to go into action had been a mistake. Lacking external pressure,

> . . . the Japs retaliated in force and rushed thousands of troops into North Luzon. For eight months they conducted relentless mopping-up operations against the guerrilla forces and the loyal civilians supporting the resistance movement. Every town and city was garrisoned, and ten-day patrols which combed the surrounding country were kept out by each garrison. Entire civilian settlements suspected of supporting the "banditos" were destroyed.
> . . . The entire civilian population was organized into "Neighborhood Associations" in which fifteen families were placed under a head, the "Presidente," who in turn was held directly responsible to the mayor of the municipality for the families under him. The mayor was answerable to the local Japanese garrison commander. The Neighborhood Associations were required to post around-the-clock guards on all trails and roads and to report all guerrilla activities.
> As a check on their system the Japs hired spies and informers from among the natives who could be bought. These spies were paid large bonuses, in addition to their normal salaries, for information of particular value. Large rewards were placed on the heads of all Americans and of the better-known Filipino guerrilla leaders. To augment and strengthen their army the Japs organized and armed Filipino constabulary units and stationed them under close Jap supervision.[16]

These various measures severely impeded the guerrilla movement, which, in spring of 1943, numbered fewer than two thousand men dispersed throughout Luzon, a command known grandly as U. S. Army Forces in the Philippines—North Luzon. With the capture of Colonels Moses and Noble, Volckmann took command to carry out MacArthur's "Lay Low Order" which sensibly ordered guerrillas on Luzon to organize combat cadres and intelligence nets but avoid more active operations until arms and ammunition could be sent from Australia.

Volckmann realized from the beginning the importance of civilian co-operation—his escape alone had constantly emphasized this. In this respect, the major enemy was not Japanese " . . . but rather the spies, informers and collaborators operating for them." Volckmann came up with an answer reflected in a simple order: eliminate them. After six months of often brutal countermeasures, the threat greatly diminished and even

> . . . the so-called "fence-sitters" began toppling in the right direction. . . . The civilian support thus brought about was then organized and the civilian was made to feel that he was part of the resistance movement. Once fully committed to such a role, it was very unlikely that people will ever again turn to the enemy. . . . [17]

Despite any number of setbacks, the movement continued to grow. Within a year, Volckmann had established reliable communications with district commands. His combat units had grown from less than two thousand to about eight thousand with a reserve of another seven thousand plus about five thousand men organized into "bolo battalions," or service units. In August 1944, he gained radio contact with Australia, which meant direct transmission of intelligence as opposed to sending it via guerrilla commands to the south. It also meant some long-delayed help, and, in November, the first submarine reached the area.

With the influx of arms, radios, and other essential supply, Volckmann shifted from "lay low" to aggressive operations. Concurrently, he relayed a steady flow of intelligence to MacArthur's headquarters. Documents discovered in a crashed plane disclosed a major change in Japanese plans: General Yamashita had decided to withdraw from the Lingayen area into the northern hinterland. Such was Volckmann's flow of intelligence from the proposed allied landing area that, two days prior to D-Day, he sent a dispatch to MacArthur: " . . . There will be no repeat no opposition on the beaches." Simultaneously, his guerrillas throughout the area struck the Japanese:

> . . . The numerous small enemy garrisons were quickly isolated and destroyed. Extensive demolitions, road-blocks, and continuous

ambushing and destruction of transportation greatly reduced the mobility of large enemy concentrations and seriously aggravated their already difficult supply problems.[18]

When the U. S. Sixth Army landed in January 1945, Volckmann reported for duty as commander of a force numbering nearly twenty thousand with its own service of supply—a force organized and in action *behind* enemy lines.

From January to June 1945, his five guerrilla regiments constantly disrupted Japanese lines of communication, intercepted and destroyed foraging and scouting parties, and ambushed troop units. Although official accounts later minimized the guerrilla contribution, Volckmann estimated that his people accounted for about fifty thousand Japanese casualties. When Sixth Army headquarters questioned casualty reports of one regimental commander, he showed a team of Rangers enemy bodies that his Igorot guerrillas had carefully stacked like cordwood for easier counting!

As Sixth Army units worked north to close with Volckmann's guerrilla strongholds, irregular units joined army divisions to furnish invaluable aid in the severe fighting ahead.

CHAPTER THIRTY

1. Cannon, 10.
2. Wolfert, 64, 144.
3. Ibid., 155–9.
4. Cannon, 16–20. See also, Morison, *Leyte* . . .
5. Wolfert, 161.
6. Ibid., 147.
7. Ibid., 207–8.
8. Ibid., 227–8.
9. Hosmer.
10. Blow.
11. Ibid.
12. Ibid. See also, Morison, *Leyte* . . .
13. Valeriano and Bohannan, 23. See also, Volckmann; Taruc.
14. García.
15. Volckmann, 105–8.
16. Ibid., 108–9.
17. Ibid., 126.
18. Ibid., 181–2. See also, Morison, *Leyte* . . . , 130 ff.

CHAPTER 31

Japanese occupation of Indonesia • Historical background • Dutch overlords • Sporadic Indonesian resistance • Early nationalist movements • Sukarno and the PNI • Japanese exploitation and bestiality • Effects of the occupation • Indonesian independence • Dutch demands • Allied intervention • Japanese occupation of Thailand • Limited OSS operations • The Japanese occupy Indochina • Historical background • The French conquest • Fallacy of "peace and security" argument • The French contribution • Fallacy of the "non-profit" argument • Failure of French colonial policy • Conditions inside Indochina: the double standard • Indochinese resistance • Early guerrilla wars • Rise of nationalism • Bao Dai and Ngo Dinh Diem • The Yen Bay mutiny • Enter Ho Chi Minh • The Vietnamese Communist movement • Ho's peregrinations • Further Vietnamese uprisings • The Cao Dai and the Hoa Hao • The Japanese threaten French Indochina • America's position • French capitulation • Decoux's dictatorship • President Roosevelt's anti-colonialism • Ho Chi Minh and the Viet Minh • Vo Nguyen Giap • OSS support of Giap • Allied postwar policy • British and Chinese occupation of Vietnam • Ho proclaims the Democratic Republic of Vietnam • Communist failure in the South

AS IN THE WEST, so in the East. Not all countries invaded and occupied by Japanese troops proved suitable to guerrilla resistance. The Japanese army, in refreshing contrast to its usual barbarous behavior, exploited the favorable political climate of the Dutch East Indies and, at first anyway, avoided provoking local resistance. So detested were the Dutch overlords that in early 1942, large numbers of

Indonesians greeted the invaders more as liberators than as enemy—not unlike Ukrainians welcoming Germans in the previous year.

Indonesia's anti-European attitude had been building for nearly 350 years, during which the Dutch (and at one point the British) had exploited the natural riches of Java, the Celebes, Sumatra, western New Guinea, and most of Borneo (see map, Chapter 44). From time to time, the native peoples had rebelled: early in the eighteenth century, the Java War, which lasted five years and cost the Dutch some fifteen thousand killed (including eight thousand Europeans) and an estimated 20 million florins, the defeated Javanese perhaps two hundred thousand dead (mostly from cholera), resulted in an even more avaricious colonial policy. Later in the century, the kingdom of Atjeh in northern Sumatra fought a thirty-five-year war that lasted until 1908 and cost the Dutch an estimated 400 million florins.[1]

Despite or perhaps because of refusal to implement long-overdue reforms, such as a decent educational system, a variety of nationalist movements emerged early in the twentieth century. Foremost among these was the Sarekat Islam (Moslem Society), which in 1919 boasted 2.5 million members. Its radical section soon broke away to establish the Partai Komunis Indonesia—the Communist PKI, which instigated a 1927 uprising savagely put down by government forces. From the ashes arose the new Indonesian National Party (PNI), whose chairman was a twenty-five-year-old engineer, Dr. Achmed Sukarno, soon to be jailed and exiled. The small party included most of the students and proved to be increasingly powerful. It wanted " . . . complete economic and political independence for Indonesia, with a government elected by and responsible to all the Indonesian people," a goal that could only be reached " . . . by non-cooperation with the Dutch."[2] Sukarno's leadership was inherited by Dr. Mohammed Hatta and Sutan Sjahrir, who, along with radicals of the Greater Indonesian Party (PIR), had little difficulty in keeping the nationalist movement alive.

And little wonder: in 1939, per-capita annual income of the 70 per cent of the Javanese population dependent upon agriculture for a living was " . . . estimated to be only $8.32."[3] In 1940, 1,786 Indonesians attended high school and only 637 college.[4] Seven per cent of 70 million people were literate at the outbreak of World War II.[5] Europeans held 90 per cent of the high administrative posts and a Dutch governor-general held veto power over any legislation passed by the Volksraad (People's Council).

Welcome *any* invader.

But not for long. Japanese brutality almost immediately asserted itself. It was in part neutralized by Mohammed Hatta, who openly collaborated, and by Sutan Sjahrir, who remained underground in charge of the resistance movement. When the people failed to meet Japanese production requirements, Hatta won important concessions, including the return of Sukarno, the establishment of limited self-government, the promise of eventual independence (within the Co-Prosperity Sphere), and, for a brief period, even an Indonesian army 120,000 strong.

Despite unpleasant aspects of the occupation, the Indonesians gained rather than lost by their refusal to fight a guerrilla war, which would have been difficult at best considering geography, language, religion, and traditions of the various islanders. By war's end, " . . . Indonesia had provisional government, a national army, district administration, a national flag and a national anthem."[6] Sukarno proclaimed national independence in August 1945. The Dutch refused to accept this and moved to restore rule by force of arms. What the former masters failed to realize, as we shall see, was that the Indonesians were equally determined to retain a new-found freedom.

Guerrilla movements in the East suffered from factors similar to those at work in other theaters of war: lack of allied organization, initial inability to overcome weather and distance, enemy countermeasures, and awkward internal political conflicts.

The kingdom of Siam (Thailand) posed a unique problem to British and American planners in India and China. An independent country, it had slipped into the Japanese orbit and had even declared war on America and England, a bellicose posture that seemingly denied a tradition of diplomatic dexterity, the work of Prime Minister Pibul Songgram.

At first glance, the operational climate in Thailand for either SOE or OSS appeared unfavorable, particularly since some fifty thousand Japanese troops occupied the country. But Thailand had not forsaken its tradition of international opportunism. The Thai ambassador in Washington, Seni Pramoj, refused to deliver Pibul's declaration of war. As one result, America did not declare war on Thailand; as another, Seni rounded up various students and officials abroad to establish a "Free Thai" movement bankrolled by OSS.

A secret resistance movement under the regent Pridi Phanomyong was meanwhile growing in Thailand. Early in 1943, OSS learned of Pridi's double role. The OSS effort to exploit the situation has been told in part in Alsop and Braden's book *Sub Rosa*. Although Thailand is a country roughly the size of France, early attempts to infiltrate teams proved unsuccessful. The situation grew more favorable from mid-1944 when Pibul resigned and Pridi became the real power behind the new government. But so unfavorable were operational conditions that not until early 1945 did OSS officers start transmitting valuable information from Bangkok.

The movement blossomed in the following months with OSS and SOE setting up guerrilla camps throughout the country. Such was their success that Pridi, though walking a dangerous tightrope *vis-à-vis* Japan, wanted to start a guerrilla war against the now detested Japanese. American and British officers of South-East Asia Command persuaded him to hold off until allied forces could strike simultaneously—a plan voided by Japan's sudden collapse.

An even more complicated situation influenced the resistance effort in French Indochina, the large land mass of some 285,000 square miles that forms the eastern promontory of Asia and, in 1940, supported perhaps twenty-three million people.[7]

As with Indonesia, the Indochinese peoples suffered under the yoke of colonial exploitation, in this case French, who in the nineteenth century, using a massacre of French missionaries as pretext, intervened militarily. This led to the occupation of Saigon in 1859 and, two years later, to the acquisition of three eastern provinces of Cochin China by a treaty forced on the imperial court at Hué. Continued opposition from western provinces soon justified French authorities, or so they reasoned, in adding this area to their new colony. The insinuating process continued during the next two decades, both to the west, where France gained predominant influence in Cambodia, and to the north, which she explored for commercial possibilities.

In planting the flag ever farther from Saigon, French colonizers played on traditional regional rivalries, a process never far removed from troops and gunboats. By a treaty of 1884, the boy emperor Kien Phuc ceded all of Cochin China and the cities of Tourane, Haiphong, and Hanoi to France, which placed them in a colonial status; the treaty also reduced Annam and Tonkin to protectorate status. China protested, but, after fighting and losing a war with France, agreed to the acquisitions and signed the 1885 treaty of Tientsin. Two years later, France extended her protective presence to the kingdoms of Laos and Cambodia, the whole euphemistically termed the Indochinese Union, a heterogeneous administrative hodgepodge whose three peoples distrusted each other and were distrusted in turn by ethnic minorities such as the Thai of the Tonkinese Mountains and the Montagnards in southern Annam.

The subsequent pattern of development and exploitation in its worse sense is all too familiar. Almost every evil that a colonial power could dream up—the list is long—was practiced by the French in Indochina:

starvation wages, usury, lack of schools, meager health facilities, trampling of basic human rights, instant and brutal eradication of suspected opposition.

Opposition never died. A series of serious guerrilla wars in the late nineteenth century were put down only with the greatest difficulty. In the Tonkin Delta, partisan leaders led French forces a merry chase until they were subdued in 1892:

> ... Here and there, they "transformed villages into fortresses, surrounding them with deep ditches filled with water and protected by bamboo fences as well as enormous walls of earth crowned with battlements in stone." But as a rule, the war in the delta was fought by small and constantly moving groups of twenty to twenty-five guerrillas. These groups usually attacked by night and only when they were certain to take the enemy by surprise. They wasted no ammunition and promptly retreated when they met a superior force. Retreat, to the despair of the pursuing French, always meant that the guerrillas disappeared, either hiding in rice fields or resuming their original role of peaceful peasants, whom no other peasant or mandarin in the village in which they hid would betray. In the delta, says Isoart, these partisans "had the broadest popular support. Indeed, in a land of vast plains, only the support of the population could assure the existence of the rebellion."[8]

Resistance continued in northern Tonkin, where, as we have seen (Chapter 13), Gallieni and Lyautey had their hands full bringing local nationalist-bandit groups to submission. They were not altogether successful: French forces fought wily guerrilla leader De Tham, the "Tiger of Yen Tre," off and on until 1913, when they caught and executed him.[9] These rebels were not fighting "for social or political reform . . . They fought for independence from France as their ancestors had fought to oust the Chinese from Viet Nam since the first century A.D."[10]

Sporadic resistance continued as emperors came and went. In 1932, the young emperor Bao Dai . . . "proclaimed his desire to reign as a constitutional monarch. He also announced his intention of reforming the mandarinate and the administration of justice and reorganizing public education. . . . "[11] As his minister of interior and head of a reform commission, Bao Dai chose a province governor, Ngo Dinh Diem. French and senior court officials frustrated the commission's work by playing regional power factions and individual leaders one against the other, a disruptive game eagerly embraced by the French commercial community, which also refused the notion of widespread reforms. Combined opposition proved too strong. Diem resigned to begin a life of contemplative protest. Bao Dai resigned himself to role of puppet ruler, his material extravagances paid for by the French. They will enter our story again in later chapters.

New groups of dissidents meanwhile contested French administration. In 1927, a young teacher, Nguyen Thai Hoc, founded the Viet Nam Quoc Dan Dang—the VNQDD, or National Party of Vietnam,[12] which grew to about fifteen hundred members in two years:

> ... But the party's activities, which included blackmail, assassination and the manufacture of bombs, soon attracted the attention of the French authorities, and after the arrest and interrogation of some of its members the French Security Service discovered the revolutionary aims and extensive ramifications of the organization.[13]

The VNQDD continued to operate, however, and, in early 1930, took the lead in ordering a general rebellion. In the event, four companies of troops mutinied at Yen Bay and killed their officers; sporadic outbursts occurred elsewhere. The French replied quickly and brutally, and VNQDD leaders who survived fled to Yünnan, in southern China. Nguyen Thai Hoc and twelve comrades died on the guillotine.

Meanwhile, a more vigorous movement was under way. Beginning in 1925, a thirty-five-year-old Vietnamese expatriate and Comintern agent named Nguyen Ai Quoc was training a cadre of young Communists in the Chinese city of Canton. This man, who would one day become famous as Ho Chi Minh, was born in central Vietnam about 1890. Like Mao Tse-tung, his father was a relatively well-off peasant (some authorities describe him as a scholar), an ardent nationalist whose activities in anti-French organizations got him in periodic trouble with authorities. The youngster enjoyed a village education, an experience enlivened by acting as covert courier for his father's seditious letters. After attending the Lycée Quôc-hoc, at Hué, which taught in nationalist rather than French tradition, the student became teacher in a southern Vietnam fishing village.

In 1911, he studied briefly in Saigon, a trade-school course, perhaps in pastry cooking. He then signed on as kitchen boy aboard a French ship which sailed to Africa, Europe, and North America. He spent most of World War I in London working as a school janitor and at night as pastry cook in the Carlton Hotel under the famous chef Escoffier. He also joined an Asian revolutionary organization, the Lao-Dong Hai-Ngoa, or Overseas Workers' Association. From London he sailed for America and may have worked for a time in New York's Harlem district.

In 1918, the young man lived in Paris, working as a photo retoucher and political agitator among Vietnamese expatriates. In the following year, he formed a one-man lobby at the Versailles Peace Conference, demanding " . . . that a stop should be put to the abuses caused by the arbitrary exercise of power in Indochina and that the Vietnamese should be accorded certain basic liberties including protection from arbitrary arrest and imprisonment."[14] His attempt to enlist allied support failed— not surprising, in view of Great Power determination to avoid the awkward colonial question.

Now a member of the French Socialist Party, the twenty-nine-year-old rebel spent considerable time working with a large residue of Vietnamese soldiers waiting return from France to the Far East. When Socialists splintered over the colonial question, he joined the new French Communist Party, where he soon began making his mark as a colonial expert. At this time, he attacked French policy in a book, *French Colonization on Trial,* which, smuggled into Indochina, " . . . became the bible of nationalists."[15]

In 1922, he attended the Fourth Comintern Congress, in Moscow, met Lenin, and probably became a member of the Comintern's newly created Southeast Asia Bureau. Subsequently he became active in the Peasant International, or Krestintern. In 1924, he moved to Moscow for study at the University of the Toilers of the East and there impressed important party members as an intelligent and hardworking activist.

Posted to Canton in late 1924, he quickly and efficiently organized Vietnamese and other Asian nationalists into a League of Oppressed Peoples of Asia, which was nothing less than " . . . the Comintern front organization for the whole Far East and soon became the Nan-yang or South Seas Communist Party—the parent organization of later Communist parties in Korea, Indonesia, Malaya, India, China, and Vietnam."[16] Under Ho's aegis, young Vietnamese students graduated from Whampoa, the military academy established by Chiang Kai-shek; others received advanced political training in Moscow; in two years Ho " . . . formed 200 *can-bo* [political cadres], which were infiltrated back to Indochina."[17]

This beehive of subversion burst into cells with Chiang Kai-shek's sudden crackdown on Communists. When Mao Tse-tung fled south, Ho escaped across the Gobi Desert to the Soviet Union, operated as a Comintern agent in Europe for two years, then returned to the Far East to reorganize the party effort. Working in Hong Kong under the alias Tong Van So, Ho partially succeeded in restoring party unity and, in October 1930, forming an expanded Indochinese Communist Party which began to lead peasant demonstrations and uprisings in northern Annam (where the peasants " . . . sold their starving children for a couple of francs if they could find a buyer, hoping that they would be fed and that the proceeds from the sale of some of their children would enable them to keep the remaining ones alive").[18]

To reclaim control over peasant-administered local "soviets," the French rushed in troops and, in a chaotic few months, restored order at a cost of some ten thousand civilian casualties.[19] Widespread arrests followed, with perhaps fifty thousand persons deported. In the general roundup of the next two years, many of Ho's colleagues in Vietnam, names that one day would become only too familiar in the West—Pham Van Dong, Vo Nguyen Giap, Truong Chinh, Tran Phu—went to jail: " . . . in 1932 the number of political prisoners confined in Indochinese jails, penal settlements, and 'special camps' was estimated at 10,000."[20]

Meanwhile, British police in Hong Kong, acting on information supplied by a French Comintern agent, picked up Ho in June 1931. While serving a six-month sentence, he successfully fought extradition by the French in Vietnam (who had sentenced him to death *in absentia*). Released from jail, he slipped away to remote Amoy, then to Shanghai, and finally back to the Soviet Union, where, allegedly, he attended two senior party schools. He next appeared in Mao Tse-tung's new base, in northwestern China. After performing relatively menial jobs, he accompanied a Chinese Communist mission to Tonkin, where it trained Chinese Nationalist guerrillas.

Ho's Indochinese Communist Party also continued in adversity. In the South, in Cochin China, general repression continued to hinder the movement. In 1940, an important party leader in the South, Tran Van Giau, foolishly led a peasant uprising which the French crushed quickly and effectively; they squelched another insurrection in the Lang Son area, in the North, and executed the veteran revolutionary leader Tran Tung Lap.[21] As a result of these and other repressive measures, the party remained weak and divided at the outbreak of war.

In addition to nationalist and Communist movements, two other potential power groups appeared in these turbulent prewar years. These were the Cao Dai and the Hoa Hao quasi-religious sects. The Cao Dai originated in the Saigon area in 1925 and spread through Cochin China and into Cambodia, numbering some three hundred thousand members by 1940. The Hoa Hao also functioned in Cochin China, particularly in western regions. Although neither group constituted an organized political force, each manifested the divisive nature of Vietnamese politics, and the French feared each sect as a potentially powerful political instrument.[22]

Instead of fostering healthy political growth in Indochina, then, the French spawned only discord: a weak, ineffectual emperor; a squabbling, impotent court; a nationalist party with leaders mostly in exile; a torn and divided but still organized Communist party; two large but politically undeveloped sects—an altogether frustrated, fragmented, underdeveloped, impoverished country of strangely diverse national leaders whose only common ground consisted of an intensely emotional desire for national independence.

Outbreak of war in Europe further diminished the unity of Vietnamese opposition to French rule. The Indochinese Communist Party (ICP), faithful to Moscow, denounced the French war against Germany and in 1939 was outlawed and forced underground.

The French administration in Indochina had far more to worry about than the ICP, either above or underground. Its regular army garrison amounted to some eleven thousand troops, a force backed by fifteen modern aircraft and one light cruiser. Thailand's flanking army was a joke; British garrisons in Malaya and Burma, Dutch garrisons in the East Indies, and American garrisons in the Philippines were as unprepared for war as the French in Indochina. Yet each of these areas held a strong attraction for Japan, already moving south.

The fall of Holland and France drastically changed the power picture in the Far East. Japan, intent on cutting the railroad leading from the Tonkin port of Haiphong to Yünnan, in China, in order to deprive Chiang Kai-shek of a major supply line, already had demanded joint control of the Tonkin border. The Japanese ultimatum placed the French governor general, in a virtually impossible position. Isolated and alone, he yielded to Japanese demands, a move that cost him his job. His replacement, Vice-Admiral Jean Decoux, fared no better. Washington not only refused to intervene, but actually blocked the sale of aircraft and anti-aircraft guns. In August 1940, the American State Department informed Vichy France that " . . . the United States was unable to come to the aid of Indochina but that it "appreciated the difficulties with which the French Government was faced and did not consider that it would be justified in reproaching France if certain military facilities were accorded Japan."[23]

England proved no more venturesome: in mid-August, Japanese threats caused it to close the Burma Road for three months, thus depriving China of much needed supply. Lacking British or American support and strongly sympathetic to axis aims, the Vichy government recognized Japan's "pre-eminent position" in the Far East and instructed Decoux to come to an agreement that would retain French sovereignty over Indochina. When Decoux hesitated, the Japanese attacked French border forts and bombed Hanoi. These actions led to an agreement whereby Japan occupied three airfields in Tonkin, her total occupation force not to exceed six thousand troops; in addition, Tokyo agreed not to send more than twenty-five thousand Japanese through Indochina at a time.[24]

In January 1941, Japan's ally, Thailand, sent an expeditionary force into Cambodia and a naval force to Hanoi. The French blew the Thai navy out of the water; Japan interceded, and in March forced the French to cede rich provinces in Cambodia and Laos to Thailand. A few months later, the Vichy government accepted Japan as a defensive partner in Indochina, removed all restrictions as to the number of troops stationed there, and also made available ports and airfields.[25]

Japan's surprise attack against Pearl Harbor on December 7, 1941, rocked French forces in Indochina. In Fall's words,

> ... On the night of the strike against Pearl Harbor, Japanese troops surrounded all the French garrisons, and Decoux was faced with yet another ultimatum: to stay put and cooperate with the Greater East Asia Co-Prosperity Sphere or face the immediate destruction of his garrisons as well as the loss of even nominal French sovereignty. Decoux yielded, thus saving 40,000 of his countrymen from the immediate ordeal of Japanese concentration camps and saving for France at least the appearance of being in command of the local population.[26]

Fall tried hard to defend this abject surrender, pointing out that no French troops later fought against allied troops, and that leaving the French troops intact "compelled the Japanese to maintain a far larger force 'in being' in Indochina" than otherwise.[27]

With due respect to this writer-scholar who met death in Vietnam, he failed to consider the effects had a guerrilla campaign been waged by this French force. Even a fighting withdrawal across Thailand into Burma would have proved preferable to capitulation. Had the French promised Vietnamese people postwar independence, they undoubtedly would have supported, in time, any resistance effort against the Japanese and would have proved valuable Asian partners in a postwar commonwealth arrangement.

Decoux wanted none of this. After brutally crushing Communist and nationalist peasant uprisings in 1940 and 1941,[28] he established a dictatorship modeled on Marshal Pétain's fascist National Revolution:

> ... Pétainism thrived and Admiral Decoux sounded its keynote. He ruthlessly applied the laws of Vichy against Gaullists, against liberals, against Freemasons, against Jews. And to Vietnamese, whether nationalists or communists, he applied the same policy. Some eight to ten thousand Indochinese political prisoners, most of them Vietnamese were in French jails in Indochina in March 1945.[29]

In attempting to preserve a status quo that did not exist, Decoux was mounting his cannons in sand. The political threat of the Japanese Greater East Asia Co-Prosperity Sphere, which, as in Indonesia, held considerable appeal for already anti-Western peoples, prompted Decoux and his lieutenants to a counteroffensive. In reply to the popular Japanese appeal of "Asia for the Asiatics," the French began talking long and seemingly in earnest of an Indochinese Federation, " . . . a mutually beneficial organization of different peoples, each with their separate traditions, held together and directed by France." Decoux's courtship extended to the people as well. The French opened new schools, encouraged teaching the Vietnamese language, sponsored public works, organized a youth program over a million strong, brought in more Indochinese to run civil services and promoted others, developed industries, and introduced new crops. At the same time, he made it abundantly clear that France would retain control of Indochina. He failed to understand that he had opened Pandora's box. By admitting and even encouraging forces of nationalism, he was yielding what artificial control he still exercised—a slow process that would culminate finally in total French surrender to the Japanese. In a world at war, Decoux was attempting to preserve without fighting. In sacrificing duty for survival, he unwittingly was insuring the eventual end of French hegemony in Indochina.[30]

Not all Frenchmen subscribed to Decoux's accommodation. As early as 1941, intelligence began filtering from the country, and American agents operating in southern China even established a few networks. A Free French mission that reached Kunming in 1943 enlarged the effort. As allied victories became known and as allied naval blockade and aerial bombing made life in Indochina increasingly uncomfortable, a good many Frenchmen swung from the Vichy to the Gaullist camp to provide resistance nuclei which, taken with indigenous guerrilla groups, could have grown to considerable dimensions. Working with SOE Force 136 in Calcutta and later Ceylon, and with OSS officers in China, French dissidents conceived a general resistance plan that included a rising against the Japanese in event of an allied landing in Indochina.

Several factors hampered the plan's growth and execution. The first was President Roosevelt's anti-colonial attitude. Roosevelt regarded the humanitarian principles set forth in the Atlantic Charter more seriously than Winston Churchill, who held no intention of losing the British Empire. Of many crosses that Churchill bore as a poor relation, the colonial issue reigned supreme. Roosevelt frequently infuriated Churchill with his nagging concern for India's future, and he left no doubt in Churchill's mind that he would prevent a French return to Indochina.[31] Roosevelt deplored what he felt was indefensible exploitation of this land by French colonials, and he never forgave the French surrender to Japan, but he did seem willing to recognize special interests of colonial powers so long as they guaranteed colonies eventual independence under separate plans. As early as March 1943, Roosevelt suggested to Anthony Eden, Britain's foreign secretary, a postwar trusteeship for Indochina, an idea later presented to Stalin and also discussed at the November 1943 Cairo Conference. Roosevelt pursued the topic at Tehran, where he found Stalin in general agreement. The trusteeship question again rose at Yalta, but this time Churchill proved obstructive and the matter quietly rested. Roosevelt died before it could be revived. But, at Tehran, the powers had agreed to immediate postwar occupation of the area by British forces up to the 16th parallel, by Chinese forces north of the parallel. The Potsdam Conference confirmed this operational decision that soon reached American command headquarters in China, which thenceforth confined its clandestine effort in Indochina to collecting intelligence and rescuing downed allied airmen.

The British labored under no such anti-colonial policy. Their attitude, taken with growing strength of the Free French and liberation of France in mid-1944, brought new and awkward forces into play. SOE Force 136, operating out of Lord Louis Mountbatten's South-East Asia Command in Ceylon, began setting up resistance groups that were supposed to work with French garrisons in Indochina. Despite various hindrances, the effort grew: " . . . By the beginning of 1945 an Allied ferry service was dropping men and equipment into Indochina on an average of twice a week."[32]

Roosevelt meanwhile refused to support the French. In October 1944, he wrote Hull " . . . that we should do nothing in regard to resistance groups or in any other way in relation to Indochina." Other factors also hurt the effort. Dissension and treachery ruled French garrisons in Indochina. So did military stupidity. Despite pleas of resistance agents such as Paul Mus to arm Vietnamese guerrillas, the army refused to release arms brought in by parachute for this purpose. The principal Vietnamese resistance group, the Viet Minh, repeatedly " . . . called upon the French to work with it against the Japanese. But the French authorities had chosen to regard its members as bandits, of which the Tonkinese countryside had seen many, and had started a clean-up drive against them, bottling them up in the forests."[33] The principal Free French representative in Indochina, General Mordant, was unable to co-ordinate the work of various underground groups from headquarters in Hanoi. Apparently, all French officers were privy to plans for an uprising and were inclined to discuss them openly. As a result, Japanese counterintelligence agents became privy to most details.

In early 1945, the Japanese quietly reinforced Indochinese garrisons. In March, they surrounded principal French garrisons and arrested senior French commanders. Some units managed to hold out and some to escape and fight as guerrillas in mountainous areas of the North. But despite impassioned pleas, Washington refused to reverse its policy and allow Chennault's 14th Air Force to drop vital supplies. By the time he received a green light, French resistance had virtually ended.

The whole affair proved costly. The Japanese action caught perhaps thirteen thousand French troops outright. Another four thousand fell during the fighting and retreat. About fifty-five hundred soldiers, of whom some two thousand were Europeans, survived the eight-hundred-mile exodus to Yünnan.[34]

Adding insult to injury, the Japanese simultaneously bestowed their particular brand of "independence" on Vietnam by a formal radio announcement that " ... the colonial status of French Indochina has ended."[35] Emperor Bao Dai at once affirmed the independence of Vietnam (the Japanese remaining in direct control of Cochin China), his words soon echoed by King Norodom Sihanouk of Cambodia and King Sisavang Vong of Luang Prabang, in Laos.[36] In the Japanese mind, Indochina was to be a viable political entity in the Greater East Asia Co-Prosperity Sphere. This enterprise, however, survived but a few months. Scarcely had Bao Dai appointed a prime minister and necessary ministers and officials, than Japan surrendered.

An indigenous resistance movement had developed simultaneously with the French effort. This was largely the work of Ho Chi Minh, whom we left with a Chinese Communist mission in Tonkin early in the war. When this mission moved North, Ho apparently returned to Comintern activities, probably joining a group of Vietnamese nationalists and Communists at Liuchow, in Kwangsi province. He definitely attended the eighth meeting of the Central Committee of the Indochinese Communist Party, held in northern Vietnam in May 1941. As party charter member and important Comintern agent, he was instrumental in establishing a new front organization, the Viet Minh.[37]

Ho now returned to China, to the camp of a powerful war lord who, with Chiang Kai-shek's blessing, was subsidizing a Vietnamese Special Training Camp outside Liuchow. Although details are contradictory, Ho apparently contested the war lord's own designs on Vietnam and was imprisoned for just over a year, a particularly harsh experience which he captured in haunting verse:

> ... My body has been battered under the changing weather of China,
> My heart is sorely troubled by the misfortunes befallen Viet Nam. . . .[38]

400

CHINA

Red River

TONKIN

BURMA

Yen Bay
Hanoi
Haiphong

HAINAN

Mekong R.

VIETNAM

L A O S

Vientiane

THAILAND

Hué
Tourane

A N N A M

Bangkok

CAMBODIA

VIETNAM

3

Phnom
Penh

Mekong R.

COCHIN CHINA

Saigon

Gulf of Siam

N

THAILAND

THAILAND

SOUTHEAST ASIA 1941
• Towns and Cities

0   100   200   300 miles

M.E.P.

While Ho scratched this and other painful verses in a Chinese jail, the Chinese sponsored a coalition of Vietnamese revolutionary parties which emerged as the Dong Minh Hoi, or Vietnam Revolutionary League. He was now released from jail and made head of the Dong Minh Hoi, whose most valuable member from the resistance standpoint was the Viet Minh. Disorganization and internecine feuding of other Vietnamese nationalist units played into Viet Minh hands. Preaching nationalist gospel, Ho had little trouble in winning Kuomintang and OSS support for active Viet Minh guerrilla operations in Indochina. Nor did he fail to insinuate himself and Communist cohorts into leadership of the Provisional Republican Government of Vietnam, organized in March 1944.

Guerrilla operations in northern Vietnam were in the hands of a young history teacher and militant Communist, Vo Nguyen Giap, who commanded some ten thousand irregulars by 1945. Not only did OSS provide Giap's units with liaison teams, which in turn procured arms and supply, but OSS missions operating in Vietnam came to rely on Vietnamese interpreters, many of whom reported back to Giap and Ho.[39]

The Viet Minh apparently performed various missions to OSS satisfaction. In accordance with Washington policy, these primarily concerned intelligence collection and evacuation of downed allied airmen. In return, the Viet Minh consolidated its ranks and won numerous recruits to the Communist cause. The Japanese take-over of Vietnam, in March 1945, brought further action. The Viet Minh ordered the people to

... Organize demonstrations, processions and strikes; close down all the markets and hinder, through boycott and other means, the enemy's last desperate effort. Destroy all communication and transport facilities; tear down all telegraph wires and destroy their ammunition dumps and foodstores; launch surprise attacks on their isolated outposts and ambush their patrol units in order to prevent them from turning against our population.[40]

In April, Viet Minh leaders proclaimed a liberated zone consisting of seven northern provinces. At war's end, Ho and Giap commanded a powerful and cohesive guerrilla force whose disciplined organization contrasted strongly with the confused and divisive elements that constituted Bao Dai's government.

In August 1945 the Indochinese Communist Party held a national conference. In a remote village in northern hills, the party, according to its secretary-general,

... advocated an extremely clear policy: to lead the masses in insurrection in order to disarm the Japanese before the arrival of the Allied forces in Indo-China; to wrest power from the Japanese and their puppet stooges and finally, as the people's power, to welcome the Allied forces coming to disarm the Japanese troops stationed in Indo-China.[41]

Three days later, the Viet Minh announced creation of the National Liberation Committee of Vietnam. Meanwhile, British forces had landed in the South, but they numbered a mere 1,400; several Chinese armies were inching down from the north, an aggregate 150,000 troops far more interested in what the occupation could do for them (food, women, loot) than in what they could do for the occupation. French forces either were shaking prison lice from clothes or were strung out in defensive mountain enclaves generally out of touch with each other. Bao Dai's officials, in any event ill-prepared to administer the country, were at each other's throats in the struggle for political pre-eminence. A severe famine developed in the ravaged country. Bao Dai's government fell.

Here was a power vacuum, and Ho's people set about to fill it. Ho's main forces occupied Hanoi; a week later, Viet Minh forces moved into Saigon. In early September, Viet Minh leaders (accompanied by OSS officers) stood on the balcony of the Hanoi opera house to proclaim the new Democratic Republic of Vietnam (the DRV).

Ho's hold on this immense country was tenuous in the extreme. But bold action more than paid off. In the North, Viet Minh forces fell heir to large French and Japanese weapon dumps, and also purchased arms from newly arrived Chinese armies—weapons manufactured in America and supplied by America to Nationalist China.

Bold action did not similarly prosper in the South. Major General Gracey, commanding the small British occupation force, refused to acknowledge Viet Minh authority. In contravention of his orders, he allowed skeleton French forces to eject the self-proclaimed Viet Minh government from Saigon. He then released French prisoners from Japanese stockades and allowed them to organize into military units. Fighting soon broke out between occupation forces and the Viet Minh, fighting that would increase with arrival of Free French expeditionary forces in October.

CHAPTER THIRTY-ONE

1. Fischer, 18–20, 44.
2. Palmier, 25.
3. Kahin, 19.
4. Fischer, 53.
5. SORO, 49.
6. Ibid., 56.
7. Hammer, 11.

8. Buttinger, I, 134.
9. Ibid.
10. Hammer, 55, 59.
11. Lancaster, 75.
12. Hammer, 82.
13. Lancaster, 78.
14. Ibid., 14. See also, Fall, *The Two Viet-Nams,* 81 ff.
15. Hammer, 76.
16. Fall, *The Two Viet-Nams,* 93.
17. Ibid.
18. Buttinger, I, 170.
19. Lancaster, 83.
20. Ibid.
21. Hammer, 24.
22. Fitzgerald, 57–9.
23. Fall, 43. *The Two Viet-Nams,*
24. Hammer, 22. See also, Lancaster.
25. Lancaster, 95. The writer points out that Japanese bombers flew from the airfield at Saigon to sink the British battleships HMS *Prince of Wales* and HMS *Repulse* off the Malayan coast.
26. Fall, *The Two Viet-Nams,* 45. See also, Sherwood.
27. Fall, *The Two Viet-Nams,* 45.
28. Buttinger, I, 244.
29. Hammer, 30.
30. Ibid., 30–1. The Japanese jailed Decoux in March 1945. After the war, the Gaullist government arrested him and held him in jail for two years. Finally released because of poor health, he was formally cleared of charges in 1949— a decision that raised considerable protest in France.
31. Sherwood, 511–12, 844.
32. Hammer, 36.
33. Ibid., 41–2.
34. Fall, *The Two Viet-Nams,* 55, 58. The writer has largely blamed American policy, but see, Buttinger, I, 286, who points out that the attempts of the French

> . . . to remain in the country as *maquis* failed, not so much because they did not receive the requested assistance from the American air facility in China, but rather because of lack of support by the local population. They did not seek this support, because they did not want it, for equally unsound political and military reasons.

35. Hammer, 41.
36. Ibid.
37. Ibid., 95. See also, Lancaster.
38. Ho Chi Minh, *Prison Diary,* 80.
39. R.H. Smith, 320–60.
40. Hammer, 99.
41. Fall, *The Two Viet-Nams,* 63.

CHAPTER 32

Japanese conquest of Malaya • Japan's surprise tactics • Prewar British attitude • Japanese army training • The SOE in Malaya • The historical background • British colonization • Origin of the Malayan Communist Party (MCP) • Its alliance with SOE • Early resistance to the Japanese • SOE problems • Japanese counterguerrilla operations • MCP organization, training, and tactics • Communist use of propaganda • SOE reinforcements • MCP strength at war's end

THE JAPANESE CONQUESTS of Malaya and Burma required considerably more planning than those to south and east. To achieve desired surprise against reasonably strong defending forces, the Japanese high command introduced a tactical concept that represented as radical a departure from orthodox tactics as the German *Blitzkrieg*. Paradoxically, the oriental version scorned the technological sophistication of its German ally by employing quasi-guerrilla tactics that enabled its forces to strike where the enemy least expected.

British commanders in Malaya and Burma long since had agreed with the Chinese philosopher-general Sun Tzu that jungle is "difficult ground" and no place to wage war. In Malaya, the British considered jungle country "out of bounds" for training:

> . . . No specialized jungle technique or equipment had been evolved, and of all the troops stationed in Malaya only the 2nd Battalion of Argylls had had any serious training in jungle warfare. Nor had the natives of the country been in any way prepared to expect or resist invasion.[1]

The Singapore fortifications, built at a cost of £60 million, defended this vital base only against sea-borne attack.

A veteran of Burma fighting, Major General (later Field Marshal Viscount) William Slim, wrote:

405

MALAYA 1941

THAILAND

South China Sea

Penang PERAK

Strait of Malacca

PA HANG

SELANGOR

NEGRI SEMBILAN

MALACCA

JOHORE

SUMATRA

Singapore

N

0 50 100 150 miles

.M.E.P.

... to our men, British or Indian, the jungle was a strange, fearsome place; moving and fighting in it was a nightmare. We were too ready to classify jungle as "impenetrable," as indeed it was to us with our motor transport, bulky supplies, and inexperience. To us it appeared only as an obstacle to movement and to vision. . . .[2]

Deciding to exploit this allied weakness, the Japanese in the mid-1930s began training selected divisions for jungle warfare. The experience caused senior commanders to revise tactical and logistic concepts in favor of small and relatively self-sufficient tactical movements. By drastically trimming bulky supply lines and by exploiting jungle terrain, unit commanders soon achieved extraordinary mobility. Once troops learned to live in the jungle, keeping reasonably comfortable while avoiding sickness and disease, units achieved satisfactory staying power.

This was not easily accomplished, nor did the Japanese ever totally master the jungle, but in coming to terms with its traditionally awesome environment, they acquired an invaluable ally which they fully exploited in 1941–42.

A large part of their strength derived from British ignorance. No less an authority than the official British war historian later wrote:

> ... An inadequate staff and neglect of training, partly accounted for the fact that no detailed study of the available information regarding the training and tactics of the Japanese army was made at Command level, despite the fact that Japan was the only possible enemy and that the danger of war in the Far East had greatly increased as a result of the outbreak of war in Europe.

Military attachés in Tokyo had for many years

> ... sent accurate reports to the War Office showing that the Japanese Army was a most efficient force. Yet Malaya Command consistently underrated the efficiency and skill of the Japanese. It may have been the fact that they appeared unable to subdue the poorly-equipped Chinese forces that led to the belief wide-spread throughout the Far East, that their armed forces were inefficient.
>
> That two views of Japanese military prowess existed is seen in the fact that in 1940 Army Headquarters Australia and Malaya Command held almost opposite views on this vital matter. The 8th Australian Division, before it left its homeland, had been issued with training pamphlets which gave warning that the Japanese were ruthless, had a high standard of armament and technical training, great physical endurance, few bodily requirements compared with British troops, a talent for misleading their opponents, a large potential fifth column in Malaya, and ample experience of landing operations. This pamphlet stated that Japanese troops could move across country at great speed and could be self-supporting for several days; that, as the thick country did not favor static defense, offensive action should be taken against the enemy wherever he was met; and that there was a need for training all ranks in moving through jungle. . . . [3]

In the event, a British intelligence officer who observed diverse Japanese units working down the Malay Peninsula was not as impressed with their tactical performance as he was with the simplicity of their logistics:

> ... Their cooking gear was also of the lightest, and they were living off the country by collecting rice, fowls, and vegetables from the roadside villages. We saw several parties cooking their evening

meal. . . . [which] only took a quarter of an hour to prepare and eat.[4]

This courageous observer was F. Spencer-Chapman, whom we met earlier when he was training Australian independent companies. Transferred in September 1941, he joined the staff of Special Operations Executive (SOE), which had set up Number 101 Special Training School in Singapore. Spencer-Chapman later wrote that the school wanted to train " . . . all types of personnel—military and civilian, European and native—in irregular warfare . . . " for special operations throughout Southeast Asia. The concept included training and equipping stay-behind parties, small guerrilla units of Asians commanded by British officers, that would supply intelligence and operate against Japanese lines of communication. The commander in chief, Malaya, turned this down on the grounds that it

> . . . would be too great a drain on European man-power, and that in any case white men would not be able to move freely in occupied territory. Objection was taken to the employment of Asiatics on the grounds that a scheme which admitted the possibility of enemy penetration would have a disastrous psychological effect on the Oriental mind. Nor might any Chinese be armed, since many of them belonged to an illegal organization, the Malayan Communist Party. . . . [5]

The British attitude can best be explained by a brief look at Malayan history. An ancient empire like its neighbors, Malaya at the end of the eighteenth century consisted of a welter of kingdoms or sultanates, some small, some large, all generally feuding.[6] Largely to counter Dutch presence in Indonesia, the English East India Company acquired the island of Penang by lease in 1786; in 1795, the British occupied Malacca, which they returned to the Dutch but gained permanently in 1824. Meanwhile, in 1819, Sir Thomas Stamford Raffles had left Indonesia to develop the island of Singapore, which he acquired from the sultan of Johore. British influence continued to spread, and, in 1867, the government proclaimed the three settlements a crown colony. A few years later, Great Britain, alarmed by an increasing German presence, began pushing inland, a process encouraged by the breakup of the Johore Empire and a series of fratricidal wars among the rajas.

British influence mounted in Perak, Selangor, Pahang, and the Negri Sembilan to the extent that in 1895 the four states accepted a federation status under British aegis. As the colonizing effort prospered, British capital flowed increasingly into the peninsula. In 1909, Britain won a treaty transfer of the northern states from Siam, and in 1914, the sultan of Johore, the last independent ruler, appointed a British "adviser" to administer the sultanate: " . . . All Malay states south of Siam were then under the protection of Great Britain."

By comparison to the French in Indochina and the Dutch in Indonesia, British colonial administration continued to claim positive gains. Apologists point out that, prior to World War II, Malayans enjoyed one of the highest standards of living in the Far East—a statement that would have provided the average rubber or tin worker with scant comfort. Here, as elsewhere, European colonists and indigenous royalty profited immensely, as did sharp Chinese and Indian traders. Rather than train Malayans for self-government, Britain continued to exercise a paternalistic attitude that remained virtually unchallenged by rich and lazy sultans and resulted in fragmented and unhealthy political environment.

In the 1920s, the Malayan Communist Party (MCP) began emerging—the spawn of the Chinese Communist Party, established in 1921. Progress from the Marxist-study-group phase remained slow, the result of party setbacks in Indonesia and China. The MCP itself only emerged in 1930, under aegis of the Nan Yang, or South Seas Communist Party. Professor Lucian Pye, an expert in the field, has described the 1930 child as " . . . an ill-organized movement dedicated to conspiracy. . . . " The party enjoyed no spectacular growth during the 1930s, but it did train a large cadre of professional revolutionaries who fomented some serious strikes in the 1936–37 period. Foreign, rather than internal, developments, however, changed the MCP " . . . from a curious, at times annoying, but never profound movement into one of rising political power."[7]

The Japanese attack on China brought the MCP into collaboration with the Kuomintang in order to raise funds for Chiang Kai-shek. For this purpose, the MCP established a front group, the Anti-Enemy Backing-Up Society, or AEBUS. Japanese landings in the north of Malaya in December 1941 brought the MCP into increased importance. Where the British command once refused to arm Asians, it now urgently sought help. In desperation, SOE officers with command blessing accepted an offer from the AEBUS. Early in 1942, SOE members hastily trained 165 Communists, mostly Chinese, supplied them with arms, demolitions, and food, and sent them north on the peninsula, where each was to raise a small guerrilla unit of ten to fifteen people. SOE officers also established a series of hidden supply dumps to support the guerrillas.

The fall of Singapore and evacuation of SOE headquarters to India vitiated the stay-behind effort. Spencer-Chapman's unit joined Communist groups that had been forming in the jungle. But these units possessed no radio transmitters, and Spencer-Chapman's radio had been stolen. His colleagues had hidden supply dumps so well that most of them were lost; bandits stole other precious supplies. Out of touch with SOE(India) and reduced to minimum supply, Spencer-Chapman could do little more than strike at targets of opportunity while staying alive and trying to keep his organization intact until help arrived.

His isolation continued for two years. At times, he scored dramatic successes against the enemy. Early in this period, in one two-week flurry, he estimated that his small group of guerrillas " . . . derailed seven or eight trains, severely damaged at least fifteen bridges, cut the railway line in about sixty places, damaged or destroyed some forty motor vehicles, and killed or wounded somewhere between five and fifteen hundred Japs. . . . "[8] This effort convinced the Japanese that two hundred Australians were in the vicinity. The local commander detailed two thousand soldiers to hunt them down.

On a later occasion, Spencer-Chapman learned of a pending Japanese raid against a guerrilla camp. After evacuating the guerrillas, he prepared an observation post so that he could " . . . study the Jap methods of attack":

> . . . At earliest dawn, about 5:45 A.M., without a sound to warn us of what was coming, two or possibly more mortars opened up from the rubber [plantation] and plastered the whole area with bombs. . . . Apparently the Japs had nobody spotting for the later shots were no more accurate than the earlier ones but they systematically raked the whole area of the camp, and every hut was hit without actually being destroyed. After this there was silence for some time and then machine-gun fire broke out from the hill above the camp and continued for about ten minutes. Of course, there was no target other than the empty huts, and even if the camp had been occupied at the time of the attack, we should all have disappeared into the jungle after the first mortar bomb, and only the heavy baggage would have been lost. After this about a hundred Japanese soldiers and as many Malays and Indians charged down the hill with loud shouts and fixed bayonets. They then stood in a huddle on the parade-ground, gazing round them like a party of tourists, and I only wished I had a machine-gun with me. After shouting and talking excitedly for some time, they set fire to all the huts and retired hurriedly.
>
> I later learned that at about four o'clock that morning the Japs had surrounded the Chinese *kampong* which lay a mile from the camp and had sent the 160 inhabitants—men, women, and children—away in the lorries which had brought the troops. When they had reached a deserted area of tin-tailing ground on the way to Kuala Lumpur, they had made the men dig a trench and had then stood everybody in a row beside it and had tommy-gunned them to death.[9]

In ensuing months and years, the Japanese did not materially alter counterguerrilla operations. Although they enjoyed co-operation of a

410

great many Malays and Indians, and some Chinese, they scored few successes.

After the British surrender at Singapore, the MCP established headquarters in remote Johore and formed the Anti-Japanese Union and Forces (MPAJUF), which consisted of two main branches, the Anti-Japanese Union (MPAJU), and the Anti-Japanese Army (MPAJA). The party ordered AJU members to remain in villages and towns to endure rigors of occupation while secretly supporting the AJA, the rather grand title for the few guerrilla bands that existed in the jungle under leaders the British SOE had helped to organize and train. Chinese squatters along the jungle fringe acted as liaison between the two factions.[10]

The movement never proved a real threat to the Japanese. In August 1942, the *kempetai,* or secret police, arrested and executed top party leaders in Singapore, and, in the following month, eliminated a good portion of the Central Committee and top guerrilla leaders by a surprise raid in the Batu Caves area of Selangor. The party's secretary-general, Lai Teck, survived (some authorities think he betrayed his comrades), as did his able and industrious assistant, Ch'en P'ing, and, under their leadership, the movement continued. Pye later wrote:

> ... The great effort expended by the MCP in organizing the MPAJA did not mean that the party leaders contemplated engaging in extensive military operations against the Japanese. Rather, it was recognized that the function of the army was to provide an opportunity for individuals to feel that they were contributing something to the defeat of the hated Japanese without forcing them to expose themselves to the risks involved in fighting. . . . The leadership of the MCP had the task of effectively substituting indoctrination, propaganda, and camp life for actual military operations, thus ensuring that all members of the MPAJA felt they had gone through the rigors of combat without at the same time risking the organization in any serious test of battle. . . . The entire Chinese community had to be convinced that the MPAJA was a champion of all loyal Chinese and a powerful force striking against the Japanese enemy.[11]

To accomplish these goals, the Central Committee established eight regional guerrilla "groups." Each group controlled a number of "patrols." A patrol consisted of about one hundred men (and a few women) divided into sections of eight to ten that operated from a series of jungle camps.

Major Spencer-Chapman, who spent nearly a year with a guerrilla patrol operating in Pahang, later wrote that centralized command ruled

411

in the best Marxist-Leninist-Maoist tradition: "Policy, discipline, routine, ethics, and above all political ideology were entirely regulated from above—and as the penalty for disobedience was death, opposition in word or spirit was practically unknown." Lack of arms and equipment constantly hindered the guerrilla effort, as did insufficient training and poor commanders. A vertical administrative concept, which helped central headquarters to retain control, severely limited initiative: " . . . there was no communication between groups except with the express permission of general headquarters. Every detail had to be referred above and the answer, if it came at all, would take several months to receive."[12] Bad planning doomed most operations to failure, particularly if anything went wrong. Only a few guerrillas had been trained, and much of Spencer-Chapman's effort went to teaching them basic fundamentals of guerrilla warfare.

Awkward as was the vertical command concept, it paid off in that defectors could offer only slight information to the Japanese, usually no more than the location of a jungle camp, which could be easily changed. Intense unit discipline and indoctrination resulting in *gung ho* psychology peculiar to the Communists also held down desertions, even though only about 10–15 per cent of the group were Communists. Deterrence and retaliation figured prominently in the Communist code. The Central Committee maintained special "traitor-killing" camps, one of which Spencer-Chapman later visited and whose twenty members claimed to have killed over a thousand informers. Armed with weapons captured from local police stations, they also liberated guerrilla prisoners, destroyed police records, intimidated Japanese work parties, and performed sabotage at will.[13]

Supply shortages greatly restricted operations, but once the British opened the Burma front, the Malayan theater grew in importance, particularly since active guerrilla units could prepare the way for an allied landing. In May 1943, a small SOE liaison team reached the peninsula by submarine. Though other teams buttressed this effort, the distances were so great, supplies in such short quantity, delivery means so stringent, enemy troops so active, and the theater of operations so elongated and difficult to traverse that resistance continued to languish. The area remained out of air range from India and Ceylon until advent of the Liberator bomber, in 1944.

In November 1944, the MPAJA began to receive regular airdrops, and, in 1945, various shortages began to ease. Early in 1945, Spencer-Chapman transmitted his first radio message, and, by July, a number of SOE teams—something over three hundred men—were working with indigenous guerrilla units and had armed an estimated thirty-five hun-

412

dred men. Japanese surrender, in August, summarily terminated this effort. British troops landed in due course, and, within a few months, most guerrillas had turned in arms and been paid off.

This did not end the matter. Malayan Communists may not have fought the Japanese as actively as the allies desired—Pye credits them with killing only a few hundred Japanese—but they ended the war politically well organized: " . . . about 7,000 guerrillas came out of the jungle fully convinced that it was their might which had defeated the enemy, and they were welcomed by large elements of the civil population as heroes."[14] Although a good many AJA members yielded arms (for a considerable sum of money), enough weapons remained hidden to constitute a severe threat to internal security if utilized for improper purposes.

Nor did AJA's official demise, at the end of 1945, dispel threat of subversion. The MCP remained intact, with none of its virility sacrificed by temporary acceptance of British rule. What the British mistook for internal peace unfortunately would prove little more than uneasy truce.

CHAPTER THIRTY-TWO

1. Spencer-Chapman, 14. See also, Smyth.
2. Slim, 117–18. This is one of the liveliest command memoirs ever written, but Viscount Slim was surely one of history's liveliest commanders. Perhaps the ablest tactician of World War II, he accepted resounding and humiliating defeat (through no fault of his own)—but, with minimal means and relying largely on charismatic leadership and professional ability, turned it into ultimate victory.
3. Kirby, 166–7.
4. Spencer-Chapman, 28.
5. Ibid., 11–12, 15.
6. Winstedt. My historical summary is taken from his article in the *Encyclopaedia Britannica*, 1968.
7. Pye, 51–2.
8. Spencer-Chapman, 91.
9. Ibid., 127–8.
10. Pye, 66–9. See also, Blair.
11. Pye, 68.
12. Spencer-Chapman, 157–8.
13. Ibid., 317–18.
14. Pye, 69.

CHAPTER 33

The Japanese invade Burma • Allied defeat • Allied strategy • Stilwell versus British and Chinese • Historical background • British colonial administration • Saya San's rebellion • The Thakin movement • Aung San's collaboration with the Japanese • SOE organizes guerrilla units • A modern major general (I): William Slim • He adapts to the tactical challenge • First Arakan offensive • A modern major general (II): Vinegar Joe Stilwell • His Chinese command and training programs • Orde Wingate and guerrilla warfare: Palestine and Ethiopia • His concept of "Long Range Penetration" operations • The first Chindit operation

WHEN THE DUST of Japanese conquest settled in Southeast Asia, the picture, in spring of 1942, looked something like this: Japanese armies occupied Malaya and Burma as well as Indochina (in alliance with Vichy-French civil and military forces) and Thailand, whose government had declared in favor of the Japanese. Remnants of the Burma army, hastily reinforced by reserve Indian army divisions, were defending some four to five hundred miles of India-Burma frontier. This force belonged to British India Command, under General Wavell, soon to be replaced by General Auchinleck.

Up north, in Assam, about nine thousand Chinese troops who had escaped from Burma were being reorganized by an American officer, Lieutenant General Joseph "Vinegar Joe" Stilwell. Stilwell commanded the China-Burma-India theater; wearing a second hat, he served as chief of staff to Chiang Kai-shek. He had flown into Burma titularly to command the two Chinese armies present; in reality, he accomplished little more than witnessing disorganized and costly retreat, an experience not without lessons. Still another Chinese force that had escaped from Burma was reorganizing in Yünnan province, bordering northeastern Burma. China itself stood on the defensive against strong Japanese armies. Loss of the Burma road irrevocably cut Chinese Nationalist armies from land communication with India, the single remaining supply life line being the hastily organized and still ineffectual American airlift over the Himalayas, the famous "Hump."

Allied reverses elsewhere meant continued supply shortages, with first claim exercised by the airlift to Kunming. India writhed with internal disorder, particularly in Bengal and Sind, where authorities had their hands full defeating local insurgencies.

Dark days, indeed, made darker still by national interests colliding with strategic thunder. Allied strategy, as determined by the Combined Chiefs of Staff, directed British-American-Chinese forces to exert maximum pressure against the Japanese in Burma in order to prevent reinforcements from being shifted to the Pacific theater and also to prepare the way for a future offensive designed to re-establish land communication with China.

Stilwell ultimately envisaged a three-prong attack: the British from the west; his own Chinese-American force from the northwest; the Yünnan Chinese force from the northeast. The plan suffered British and Chinese disapproval. For political reasons, the British wanted to return to Rangoon, in the south, and then only when they held a preponderance of strength. Chiang Kai-shek, convinced that America would ultimately defeat the Japanese, wanted only to build and preserve military strength for the showdown he believed would come with Mao Tsetung's Communists in northwestern China. In short, three major allied commands headed in three different directions, a dispersion of effort that would adversely affect nearly every aspect of operations including those in enemy-held country.

As might be imagined, British exodus from Burma in spring of 1942 left a confused resistance situation, particularly since a late start had prevented Special Operations Executive (SOE) from establishing clandestine resistance groups. Such was the state of the art and apathy of the regular military establishment regarding special operations that the task could never have been simple. Nor, considering the country's internal state and the divisive forces at work, could it ever have prospered.

Burmese nationalist leaders, influenced by relatives and friends who were victims of pacification pogroms of 1885–90 (see Chapter 12), refused to be satisfied with British administration of what they regarded as their country, a country older, by far, than England.

As happened elsewhere in Southeast Asia, blatant exploitation of human and natural resources, coupled with the rise of Japan after 1905 as an international power, provided ample fuel to keep the grumbling pot of nationalism at a boil. In the century's early years, young Burmese students educated in Britain, many of them as lawyers, returned to practice in Rangoon and Mandalay and, almost from the beginning, exhibited an uncomfortable independence in relations with British magistrates and civil servants. A few Burmese newspapers appeared to rally further the forces of nationalism, which even prior to World War I inextricably mingled with Buddhism.[1]

The Great War weakened without destroying Britain's control of Burma. Nationalist opposition now became more vocal and led to boycotts and major strikes. Ill feeling deepened despite British political reforms. The world economic depression in 1930 raised further boils on an already irritated rice-paddy economy. A former monk and native quack, Saya San, felt called upon to cure the disease.

Saya San's remedy, the Tharawaddy rebellion in Lower Burma, proved worse than the disease. It soon spread to central and Upper Burma and involved native-led guerrilla bands. Lacking arms, outside support, and central leadership, the insurgents fought uncoordinated actions and in 1932 succumbed to British arms. Professor Htin Aung claimed that the rebellion cost ten thousand rebel lives with nine thousand rebels captured and 128 ringleaders later hanged. He concluded that this rebellion " . . . was perhaps the nearest Asian counterpart of the peasants' rebellion in medieval England, and it was a rebellion born of sheer desperation."[2]

Neither rebellion nor suppression settled very much. Indigenous political ferment continued, but with a significant addition: an extremist university student movement that began organizing a militant movement undreamed of by British officialdom. Charter members went so far as to take the prefix-name "Thakin"—this because British officials and officers since 1886 had called themselves *thakin,* or "master."

The outbreak of World War II only aggravated matters in Burma. Political arrests by the British drove dissident parties such as the Thakins underground. Their leader, Aung San, escaped to Amoy, where he attempted to contact left-wing Chinese groups; his followers in Rangoon contacted Japanese agents, who offered aid if the Thakins would rebel against the British. These agents had been active in the country for some time, stirring up dissidence and collecting intelligence neccessary to weaken British administration and force the government to close the Burma Road, and to prepare the country for ultimate invasion by Japanese troops.

British weakness in general immensely aided the Japanese task. In July, Britain temporarily closed the road as a "friendly" gesture to Japan, but three months later, when that country failed to sheath its aggressive claws, Britain reopened it. Aung San meanwhile was hustled off to Tokyo for special indoctrination in the Asia for the Asiatics concept. Returning to Rangoon in March 1941, he selected a number of volunteers—known in Burmese history as the "Thirty Comrades"—and, with Japanese connivance, took them to Formosa (at that time a Japanese satrapy) "for intensive military training."[3] There they agreed to work with the Japanese army in the invasion of Burma.

In the event, they did this and, as will be seen, attracted numerous recruits to carry out various fifth-column activities. Not everyone in Rangoon was like-minded, and in the countryside the British retained some good friends. Beginning in late 1941, an SOE mission partially armed some fifteen hundred members of a loyal hill tribe, the Karens, and this irregular force screened the British army's left flank during the initial retreat.

When the British moved north up the Irrawaddy Valley, the Karens buried their arms and returned to their villages to await contact by SOE officers. As retreat continued, the British sent most regular Burmese soldiers home: " . . . Each man was given his rifle, fifty rounds [of ammunition], and three months' pay, told to go to his village, wait for our return, and be ready to join any organization we should start to fight the Japanese in Burma."[4] These men came mostly from traditionally friendly hill tribes, and SOE officers on the way out of the country managed to organize a guerrilla unit from the Shans in the East and several units from the Kachins in the Northeast. Taken with the Nagas and the Chins along the western border, these tribes, each varying in strength from fifty thousand to over a million, represented a potential force of understandable interest to SOE, which spent the rest of the war trying to raise them against the Japanese.

A variety of operational factors frustrated this effort. Shattered remnants of the Burmese army in India consumed all available weapons and supplies, already scarce because of demands levied by Stilwell in the North and by Chiang's insatiable appetite in Kunming and Chungking. A chronic shortage of delivery means also existed. Even when proper planes were available (late in the war), long distances, difficult weather, and rugged and unhealthy terrain made airdrops a costly and discouraging business. SOE also lacked Burmese-speaking officers to head essential liaison teams, and though former planters and civil officials partially repaired this deficiency, the few early teams still had to work in a dangerous political climate. If a liaison party survived local political vicissitudes to contact a friendly tribe, it found little or no resistance organization among tribesmen, nor were radios technically up to sustained transmissions necessary to arrange essential supply drops.

In central and southern Burma, only a few intelligence-collection missions existed by end of 1944, mainly in Arakan. SOE experienced better luck in the Northeast, working with the Kachins. Here the British early had established an outpost at Fort Hertz that supported an or-

417

ganization called the North Kachin Levy, or NKL. Eventually amounting to six "companies" of guerrillas, the NKL provided intelligence essential for orthodox operations and, as will be seen, performed valuable work both on its own and in conjunction with those forces.

With these exceptions, the Burma resistance movement remained fairly stifled, although in later stages it picked up momentum. In the interim, however, other developments were proving of decided interest to guerrilla warfare: allied attempts to build armies suitable for fighting under the unorthodox tactical conditions imposed by the Japanese presence in Burma; and, an offshoot, the creation of special task forces to wage guerrilla warfare behind enemy "lines."

British-Chinese retreat from Burma left remnant survivors in a state of shock reminiscent of Roman legionaries who fell victim to Goth incursions in the third century. Fortunately for the allied cause, two military commanders of exceptional merit picked up fragments and eventually formed them into first-class fighting forces. One of these commanders was British, Major General William Slim, the other American, Major General Joseph Stilwell.

A supremely able and highly imaginative commander, the fifty-year-old Slim exercised that commodity too often lacking in his colleagues: professional objectivity. Wounded at Gallipoli in World War I and again in Mesopotamia, Slim served two extensive postwar tours in the Indian army in addition to normal staff and command assignments. Early in the war, he commanded a brigade in the famed Gazelle Force, which chased Italians out of East Africa. Again wounded, he recovered to command an Indian division in Syria-Persia-Iraq, from where he was rushed to the Far East.

Even while this stocky, jut-jawed Englishman chewed defeat in trying to hold his corps together during the nine-hundred-mile retreat through Burma, he was analyzing reasons for Japanese success. Surprise headed the list, along with its corollary, British unpreparedness. But what impressed him most was Japanese use of the jungle to support quasi-guerrilla tactics:

> . . . The Japanese obviously were able to move for several days at a time through jungle that we had regarded as impenetrable. This was not only because they had local Burmese guides, but they traveled lighter than we did and lived much more off the country. Nearly all our transport was mechanical, and this stretched our columns for miles along a single road through the jungle, vulnerable everywhere from air and ground.[5]

To exploit this supreme weakness, the Japanese employed the basic tactic of the hook, that is holding the British force in front and sending a mobile force around the flank through "impenetrable" jungle to block the single road that "fed" the advancing force. When this happened, "... we had ... to turn about forces from the forward positions to clear the road-block. At this moment the enemy increased his pressure on our weakened front until it crumbled."[6]

Such tactics depended on an efficient intelligence organization, which the Japanese founded in part on British unpopularity in Burma. In contrast, the British intelligence system was practically non-existent. Slim later wrote:

> ... It is no exaggeration to say that we had practically no useful or reliable information of enemy strength, movements, or intentions. Our first intimation of a Japanese move was usually the stream of red tracer bullets and the animal yells that announced their arrival on our flank or rear.

In the early fighting,

> ... our only source of information was identification of enemy units by their dead and by documents found on them. Exploitation of even this source was limited because in the whole corps there was only *one* officer who could speak and read Japanese reasonably well. ...[7]

The Japanese not only depended on Burmese guides, informants, and saboteurs (who cut telephone lines), but did not hesitate to disguise hostile Burmese and Japanese soldiers as peaceful villagers whose bullock carts held machine guns. On occasion, the Japanese wore uniforms taken from dead soldiers of Burma Rifle regiments.[8]

Only the monsoon halted this determined Japanese drive, which, by late spring 1942, had pushed British and Chinese armies from Burma. Several strategic forces thenceforth intervened to keep Japanese divisions poised on China-India borders, a respite used to reorganize defeated armies and begin the long road back.

Slim realized that a successful return would require tactics never taught in a Western staff college. A successful return demanded an abandonment of orthodox thinking in favor of untried and sometimes even unknown tactical procedures. Slim started putting his ideas to test as commander of 4 Corps. His soldiers, most of whom were Indian but who included Gurkhas, Burmese, and British, had to learn to live in jungle before being able to use it " ... for concealment, covered move-

Burma Theater 1942
→ Japanese invasion
×××× Burma road
━━━ Stilwell road
+—+ Railway   • Towns and Cities
0   100   200   300 miles

M.E.P.

ment, and surprise." All units, including medical sections, became responsible for their own security: " . . . there are no non-combatants in
jungle warfare." Unit commanders had to rely on patrols, for
" . . . patrolling is the master key to jungle fighting." Commanders also
had to practice fluid tactics: they had to get used to having Japanese
parties in their rear, and, when this happened, regard not themselves,
but the Japanese, as "surrounded." Officers had to stop thinking in
terms of frontal attacks; instead, " . . . attacks should follow hooks and
come in from flank or rear, while pressure holds the enemy in front."
In defense, " . . . no attempt should be made to hold long continuous

420

lines. Avenues of approach must be covered and enemy penetration between our posts dealt with at once by mobile local reserves who have completely reconnoitred the country." Commanders had to acquire and retain mobility, for " . . . by mobility away from roads, surprise, and offensive action, we must regain and keep the initiative." Commanders also had to start thinking in terms of supply by air—bulky road columns had to go.[9]

Slim and his division commanders were still wrestling with this immense transition problem when they were committed to the first Arakan offensive. Originally envisaged as an allied drive into central and northern Burma, it started 4 Corps into action in mid-December 1942, a series of operations that at first progressed favorably. In early January, however, the effort fell victim to a number of misfortunes, chief among them a well-dug-in and determined enemy who launched powerful counterattacks; but sickness in British ranks also played a major role, as did lack of command co-ordination and insufficient training. At the last minute, Chiang Kai-shek also proved intractable and refused to allow either Stilwell's force or the Yünnan force to participate. The 4 Corps action lingered on until early spring—a tactical failure. Slim regarded the experience as worthwhile, however, in that he learned what deficiencies still had to be overcome in his units and in that it tended to verify his tactical ideas, including resupply of an entire division by airdrop.

While Slim fashioned his force, "Vinegar Joe" Stilwell, also in India, was accomplishing what many Western commanders considered impossible: training Nationalist Chinese divisions to fight modern warfare.

Stilwell was not a newcomer to the China scene. A West Point graduate, the sixty-year-old Stilwell had spent fifteen years in prewar China, where, concentrating on language study, he learned a great deal about Chinese history and culture. As military attaché in Peking, he had been known as a family man, virtually a teetotaler, who appeared only at "command" social functions; as a troop commander, he was known for professional excellence punctuated by profanely picturesque language. Tall and lanky, his eyes deceptively quiet and even morose behind steel-rimmed glasses, always vigorous and on occasion overbearing, he probably suffered an inferiority complex; the reader can gain an excellent insight into his thinking and behavior from his various writings, which T. H. White expertly edited after the war, and also from Barbara Tuchman's biography, *Stilwell and the American Experience in China 1913–1945.*

Stilwell's familiarity with the Chinese army did not prepare him for the scene that greeted him in early 1942, when Chiang Kai-shek ordered him to take command of two Chinese armies fighting in northern Burma. Finding himself more onlooker than commander, due to jealous Chinese generals, he was appalled at the professional ineptitude and personal corruption that claimed commanders on every level. The experience convinced Stilwell that if the Japanese were to be driven from northern Burma, which was essential to reopen land communications between China and India, he would have to train and equip a new Chinese army.

In summer of 1942, the American military mission in Kunming began to train and equip "Yoke Force," designed to strike into northeastern Burma from Yünnan. In India, Stilwell used the nine thousand Chinese survivors of the retreat from Burma as nucleus for a new army to be fleshed out by soldiers flown from Kunming over the Hump. In the event, he received about sixty-six thousand soldiers whom he turned into four divisions. Stilwell was convinced, and Slim agreed with him, that if the Chinese soldier could be removed from control of corrupt and inefficient officers, he could be trained and equipped to perform as well as any other national, including the Japanese. The British co-operated in Stilwell's plan by furnishing an old Italian-prisoner-of-war camp, Ramgarh, in central India. As White later wrote:

> ... What Stilwell proposed to do was this: to take raw troops, divorce them from the possibility of retreat, abandon fixed supply lines as completely as did Sherman in Georgia, make them dependent on air drops alone, drive them two hundred miles through jungle, swamp, and mountain to conquer a skilful, entrenched and desperate enemy.[10]

Stilwell's accomplishment, like Slim's, has never been fully appreciated in Western military circles. Stilwell insisted on "discipline, training and military organization," which he hoped to achieve by giving the Chinese peasant something to fight for—pride in himself. Mao Tsetung already had accomplished what Stilwell was trying to accomplish. This was no easy task when dealing with illiterate conscripts commanded by poorly trained and exceedingly corrupt officers.

Once American teams cleaned up the troops, properly fed, clothed, equipped, and paid them, they offered the simplest possible instruction. Stilwell wished to avoid frontal attacks both because the Chinese proved hopeless when it came to precise timing required for co-ordinated attacks and because they did not have adequate supporting weapons. Stilwell preferred the original Japanese tactic of establishing a roadblock behind the enemy, then engaging his front to hold him for a flank attack from the jungle by swift-moving irregular forces.

By late 1942, the lanky general believed, perhaps optimistically, that

Chinese forces in India and Yünnan could participate effectively in the Slim-Wingate offensive. He had reckoned without Chiang Kai-shek. Wanting to retain his forces intact to fight Communists once allies had won the war against Germany and Japan, Chiang refused to release divisions either in Yünnan or India. Failing to sway the Generalissimo, Stilwell could only swear—and keep on training.

Slim and Stilwell were not the only commanders with imagination and flair in India. If they professed a sort of bent military orthodoxy, Brigadier Orde Wingate preached tactical heterodoxy in the Lawrence tradition. The eldest of seven children, Orde Wingate was the son of an Indian army officer. Raised in a deeply religious English household, he graduated from the Royal Military Academy in 1923 and became a regular-army artillery officer. After routine garrison service and a six-year stint in the eastern Sudan, Wingate was ordered to Palestine as a staff intelligence officer.[11] Here he made a service reputation by introducing counterinsurgency tactics against Arab terrorists who were raiding Jewish settlements and blowing up oil lines. The almost total failure of orthodox tactics caused Wingate to opt for night patrols carried out by "Special Night Squads" composed of Jewish reserve constables commanded by British officers and NCOs—a concept that enjoyed impressive success under Wingate's undeniably charismatic leadership. Badly wounded during one action, Wingate was awarded the DSO and dubbed the Lawrence of Judea. From stubby beard to ancient tropical helmet to grease-stained uniform, he played the part—sometimes fulsomely.

While Wingate's tactics could scarcely be faulted—the reader will find the entire fascinating story in Christopher Sykes's comprehensive biography *Orde Wingate*—his means of achieving tactical success were highly suspect: He indulged in one tantrum after another, even against commanders favorable to his views; if a recruit misbehaved either in training or on patrol, Wingate was apt to strike him; when a *Kibbutz* leader walked on a terrorist mine and was killed, Wingate retaliated with a daylight raid in which innocent villagers were shot. Sykes has explained these actions as those of a highly strung, impulsive man of unquestionable talent.[12] Those readers with extensive military experience will reply that good leaders can obtain success with more acceptable methods.

To further test his superiors' patience, Wingate became an ardent Zionist, convinced that Palestine must become a state with its own national army. At times, his zeal for Zionism brought him uncomfortably close to treasonable disclosure of confidential information to Jewish leaders. Desirable as it might have been for these leaders to have the information, it surely was not the function of a captain, a junior staff officer, to provide it.

Wingate increased his reputation in the brief Ethiopian campaign in 1940–41 when he organized, trained, and commanded Gideon Force, an irregular unit of natives under British officers. Again, his tactical thinking could scarcely be faulted. But he erred operationally in trying to use camels where camels could not be used, and he seriously erred tactically in insisting on an initial and disastrous cross-country march.

In subsequent operations against Italian garrisons, he displayed considerable tactical agility, relying largely on mobility and frequently deception to gain tactical surprise. He preached and wrote a qualitative approach to irregular warfare, for instance calling for small attacks: " . . . twenty men is a good number to work with, but fifteen is better than twenty, and at night ten is better than fifteen." He stressed psychological warfare and he again proved the charismatic leader who displayed unquestionable personal courage. Two other factors entered, however, in assessment of Wingate's contribution to the campaign. The first was enemy weakness. Italian defenders did not provide a true test of arms. The British advanced, the Italians retreated. While Gideon Force was running out of camels and otherwise suffering enormous hardships in cross-country advance, two orthodox British forces were making excellent progress with much less effort. General Cunningham's force of three divisions advanced over a thousand miles in thirty days, a feat not many guerrilla forces could equal.[13]

The second was personal weakness. In Cairo and Khartoum before the campaign, Wingate continued to behave strangely and often abominably:

> . . . he took to wearing a miniature alarm clock strapped to his wrist so that he could time his interviews exactly by the ringing of the bell. He took again to brushing his body instead of bathing and caused much amazement to some people with whom he had business by receiving them naked in his room in the Grand Hotel, brushing himself thoroughly the while. . . . His rudeness now went to grotesque lengths. . . . [14]

Physical cruelty appeared. An interpreter's mistake caused him to knock the man down with blows of a hide whip; he struck an Ethiopian soldier wrongly turned out. He fought almost constantly with colleagues, juniors or seniors. He soon fell out with the able Daniel Sandford, a man of extensive experience in Ethiopia who masterminded the campaign and who served during it as the emperor's political and military adviser. As had happened with Zionism, the emperor's cause became Wingate's cause, and he grew convinced that his own country was defeating the emperor's best interests.

In Cairo, after the campaign, bitter and ill from malaria, he wrote a lengthy and vitriolic report that, according to his friend and protector, General Wavell, " . . . would almost have justified my placing him under arrest for insubordination."[15] After detailing his qualitative theory of guerrilla warfare—which, he argued, contrasted with Lawrence's saturation theory—Wingate tore into authorities who, in his opinion, had sabotaged Gideon Force. Attacked from all sides, Wingate continued to nurse real and imagined grievances, a hideous period that ended with a serious attempt at suicide.[16]

After lengthy recuperation in England, he rewrote his report and expanded his thinking into a proposal for "Long Range Penetration" operations. Friends saw that this material reached Winston Churchill and the new Chief of the Imperial General Staff, Sir Alan Brooke. Their influence, in part, brought orders in early 1942 for Wingate to report to Wavell's staff in Burma " . . . for operational and liaison duty with the Chinese in Burma."[17]

Wingate was thirty-nine years old when he arrived, shortly after the fall of Rangoon. A stocky, powerful-looking man of medium height, he impressed most people with a sort of Old Testament melancholy and a professional intensity that at times bordered on the fanatic. Wavell appears to have backed Wingate's long-range penetration concept. A young major who became intimately associated with Wingate, a regular officer named Bernard Fergusson, later described the plan in his splendid book *Beyond the Chindwin:*

> . . . Briefly, his [Wingate's] point was that the enemy was most vulnerable far beyond his lines, where his troops, if he had any at all, were of inferior quality. Here a small force could wreak havoc out of all proportion to its numbers. If it should be surprised, it could disintegrate into smaller prearranged parties to baffle pursuit, and meet again at a rendezvous fifteen to twenty miles farther on its route. Supply should be by air, communication by wireless: these two weapons had not yet been properly exploited. His proposal was to cut the enemy's supply line, destroy his dumps, tie up troops unprofitably far behind the line in the endeavor to protect these vulnerable areas, and generally to help the army proper on to its objectives.[18]

Wavell gave Wingate, as nucleus of a force, remnants of a guerrilla organization commanded by a brave and resourceful officer, Michael Calvert. Three battalions brought the new command to brigade strength: the 77th Indian Infantry Brigade, a heterogeneous force of about three thousand British, Gurkha, African, and Burmese soldiers that Wingate divided into seven lightly equipped mobile columns. Each column included a specialist guerrilla force, a signal section, and a small RAF section " . . . to direct, organize, and advise on supply by parachute."

Wingate's first operation was scheduled to complement the Arakan offensive earlier described. But when Chiang Kai-shek refused to let either Stilwell's force or the Yünnan force participate, Wavell canceled Wingate's part in the operation. Wingate would not be put off. In vigorous prose, he offered Wavell what both believed were convincing arguments:

> . . . if the expedition were cancelled, "the vast majority of Staff officers who denied the theory of Long Range Penetration would . . . continue to deny it"; the brigade stood in peak condition and could only decline if not committed to action; the British would remain ignorant of Japanese military methods unless Wingate provoked them to action; the Japanese were apt to overrun Fort Hertz in the north as well as to implant themselves on both sides of the Chindwin; without "the serious interruption of enemy plans and confusion in his military economy throughout Burma," such as 77 Brigade would bring about, the Japanese would be "free to develop offensive intentions."[19]

Wavell should have questioned Wingate's logic, which contradicted his tactical concept. The finest brigade in the world could scarcely prove a theory if the major operational ingredient—three attacking armies— was missing. Further, only two months earlier, Wingate had expressed serious doubt as to his brigade's readiness for what in anyone's tactical book was a major operational commitment; Slim and other veterans of the Burma retreat were already sufficiently familiar with the enemy's military methods. Wingate's fears concerning Fort Hertz were more imaginary than real, at least according to Ian Fellowes-Gordon, who commanded a guerrilla company in the target area, which at this time was of secondary importance to the enemy.[20] The Japanese were holding Burma with at least four divisions, battle-tested, dug in. The argument that a small brigade, not yet battle-tested, could divert and defeat major units was a totally unjustified conceit, the more so since the brigade would operate in an area of but slight tactical importance.

Wavell nonetheless accepted Wingate's arguments and the brigade moved out. Of subsequent accounts, my own favorite is Fergusson's, in *Beyond the Chindwin*, but Calvert's account is also worth while, as is Sykes's. The columns crossed Chindwin River in two groups. Complete with bullocks, elephants, mules, horses, and a few messenger dogs, the men pushed through two hundred miles of some of the most difficult jungle terrain in the world. After numerous difficulties, including brushes with the enemy that scattered two columns, the remainder of the Chindits, as they would become known, reached the Mandalay-Myitkyina railroad. Here Calvert's and Fergusson's columns blew some bridges and cut the line in several places.

The columns then crossed the Irrawaddy in an attempt to cut the Mandalay-Lashio railroad. By now, a good many men were nearing the end of their strength; the columns had stirred up the enemy and were on the run, which hindered scheduled airdrops, already made difficult by terrain and weather. The sick and exhausted columns disintegrated into small parties that eventually struggled back across the Chindwin. Some eight hundred troops did not return. Of the 2,182 who reached India, only six hundred were sufficiently fit " . . . for active soldiering again."[21]

From the operational standpoint, Wingate's first raid was a supreme and expensive flop, but Slim, Fergusson, and others were correct in awarding it a psychological value reminiscent of that given Doolittle's expensive air raid on Tokyo in 1942. Blown up by army and press into major victory proportions, it flashed a beacon of hope at a very discouraging time for England, and even Slim concluded that it " . . . was worth all the hardship and sacrifice his men endured."[22] This was not only a debatable conclusion, it was a dangerous conclusion in that men who should have known better, including Alan Brooke, Churchill, and Wingate himself, started believing their own propaganda.

CHAPTER THIRTY-THREE

1. Maung Htin Aung, *A History of Burma*. A professor of history and veteran Burmese diplomat, the author enjoyed advantages derived from personal experience. If the Westerner objects to a nationalist bias in this and similar revisionist works of history, the Easterner for long has been exposed to Western bias in traditional histories. Hopefully a working synthesis for the oft-bewildered student will eventually be provided.
2. Ibid., 292.
3. Ibid., 299.
4. Slim, 113.
5. Ibid., 29.
6. Ibid., 119.
7. Ibid., 28–9.
8. Ibid., 62.
9. Ibid., 142–3.
10. Ibid., 268. See also, Eldridge.
11. Sykes, *Orde Wingate*, Chapters 1–5. See also, Mosley, *Gideon Goes to War*.
12. Sykes, *Orde Wingate*, 104–60.
13. Ibid., 295.
14. Ibid., 249.
15. Rolo (Wavell's *Introduction*).

16. Sykes, *Orde Wingate,* 324–31.
17. Ibid., 354.
18. Fergusson, *Beyond the Chindwin,* 21. See also, Rolo; Calvert.
19. Sykes, *Orde Wingate,* 384–5.
20. Fellowes-Gordon, 15.
21. Sykes, *Orde Wingate,* 432. See also, Fergusson, *Trumpet in the Hall.*
22. Slim, 163.

CHAPTER 34

Wingate's fame • South-East Asia Command • Slim inherits Fourteenth Army • Slim's genius • Wingate's new "stronghold" concept • Slim's second Arakan offensive • Wingate's second offensive • His death • Stilwell's northern command • Merrill's Marauders • The Kachins • Japanese occupation excesses • Aung San deserts the Japanese • The Karen guerrilla offensive • Japanese evacuation • The postwar political situation

THANKS to cooked press reports and tired allies who embraced them, Wingate's failure brought him considerable fame and even influence. He returned to England a hero. Already familiar to important members of the Establishment, he basked in strategic and tactical heterodoxy, a fulsome period capped by Winston Churchill's taking him (and his wife) to the Quebec Conference.

Already winged, Wingate's fortunes soared. As Christopher Sykes has pointed out, he became " . . . a sort of point of agreement" between Churchill and his discordant chiefs of staff, and also between British and American chiefs. On the voyage to Canada, he persuaded Churchill and the British chiefs to favor an offensive in Burma—a plan calling for a second Chindit expedition of six brigades, or some 26,500 men. The British chiefs went so far as to specifically allocate units, including Slim's one jungle-trained division, to Wingate's command and to recommend to New Delhi that Wingate become the army commander in Burma! Although Auchinleck firmly squashed the latter notion, at Quebec President Roosevelt and the Joint Chiefs of Staff embraced Wingate's operational proposals.[1] General Henry Arnold, chief of the U. S. Air Force, personally promised him air support. After ordering special arms and equipment in America and London, Wingate returned to Delhi, an acting major general holding right of direct communication to Churchill whenever necessary—an unfortunate commitment that in effect belied trust in senior commanders.

429

The Quebec Conference also ordered a new South-East Asia Command (SEAC), headed by Admiral Lord Louis Mountbatten, who knew and supported Wingate. In late 1943, Mountbatten took over, with Stilwell as deputy commander (Stilwell remained Chiang Kai-shek's chief of staff as well as commander of American forces), and SEAC became responsible for allied operations in Burma, Ceylon, Malaya, the Dutch East Indies, Siam, and Indochina.[2]

One of Mountbatten's early acts in autumn of 1943 created the Fourteenth Army, with Slim in command. Its units had known only defeat. Composed predominantly of Indian soldiers, most of its neglected divisions stood bewildered and confused, highly unsure of themselves. The army lacked thousands of items needed to live and fight. Malaria, dysentery, and other tropical diseases ravaged entire units.

Here was an army that, in Frederick the Great's words, was " . . . fit only to be shown to the enemy at a distance." In converting it to a viable offensive force, Slim's accomplishment ranks high in military annals.

What was his secret?

In two words, leadership and simplicity. Like Scipio Aemilianus in Spain twenty-one centuries earlier, Slim splintered (and sometimes burned) the dead wood that invariably accumulates in large commands. What was left received massive doses of conditioning already injected into 4 Corps. Every man in Fourteenth Army was put through weapons training. All units, including senior staffs, were conditioned to life in the jungle. Preventive medicine drastically lowered malaria incidence and other jungle diseases. Duck farms, fish saltings, and market gardens "almost in the battle line" provided greatly improved rations.[3]

Slim emphasized patrolling as the key to jungle fighting. In time, training-patrols gave way to reconnaissance patrols, then small combat patrols, and finally unit offensives in such preponderant strength against minor targets as to guarantee victory and thus build a feeling of superiority. Training concentrated on the small unit. Slim made companies, even platoons, the basic units of jungle warfare, marching them off to patrol and fight on their own, sometimes for days. Unit commanders had to reorient their entire thinking in order to survive and fight well. Instead of relying on elaborate bridging units, for example, men were taught to swim and to make rafts from jungle materials; army engineers commandeered old boats and launches and built new ones to support infantry river crossings and to wage guerrilla warfare along waterways; airplanes used parachutes made out of jute to supply columns, and on occasion used such makeshift containers as old inner tubes to drop water. Resupply by air became standard operating procedure, and, in con-

430

sequence, greatly increased ground mobility by drastically reducing supply columns and echelons.

Slim pared staffs to the bone, cut paperwork to a minimum. Applying a carefully thought-out formula of leadership based on spiritual, intellectual, and material factors, and on years of experience, Slim infused his army with unity of purpose, a sort of command osmosis absorbed by the most junior commander, who understood, respected, and acted upon the army commander's *intention:*

> . . . this acting without orders, in anticipation of orders, or without waiting for approval, yet always within the overall intention, must become second nature in any form of warfare where formations do not fight closely *en cadre,* and must go down to the smallest units. It requires in the higher command a corresponding flexibility of mind, confidence in its subordinates, and the power to make its intentions clear right through the force.[4]

Slim was still training his army when the allied chiefs, meeting at Cairo in November 1943, agreed to an expanded Arakan offensive. But at the Tehran Conference immediately following, the grandiose scheme of multipronged invasion fell victim to various shortages. When the Combined Chiefs canceled part of the plan, Chiang Kai-shek immediately withdrew Chinese participation. Instead of the reconquest of Burma, Fourteenth Army, including Wingate's new force, undertook a limited offensive beginning early in 1944.

As with the earlier Arakan offensive, this change of plan pulled the rug out from under Wingate's long-range penetration concept. To save his operational skin, he now came to the surprising conclusion that his group, suitably reinforced, should provide the main effort by operating from a series of "strongholds" established miles behind enemy lines. A "stronghold" would serve two purposes: by defending an airfield, it would provide an administrative-supply base for his columns; by constituting a distinct threat, it would attract the enemy to attack a defended point. In Wingate's words, " . . . the stronghold is a machan [elevated platform] overlooking a kid tied up to entice the Japanese tiger."[5]

Wingate's new concept was expensive in men and material. Primarily for this reason, Slim objected to it; the Combined Chiefs had not improved his temper by allocating his one " . . . completely jungle-trained division" to Wingate's command. Slim also argued that the Japanese were not going to be so easily drawn from their major defensive complex and that even if they were, Wingate's people " . . . were neither trained nor equipped to fight pitched battles, offensive or defensive."[6] The forceful and politically powerful Wingate nonetheless sold the idea to Mountbatten, who authorized " . . . ever-increasing scales of defensive equipment, artillery, anti-aircraft guns, mines, machine-guns, sandbags, and the rest."[7] To transport and supply this miniature army, the U. S. Air Force provided Wingate with Philip Cochran's special unit " . . . containing not only fighters and light bombers for close support, but transport aircraft, gliders, light planes for inter-communication and evacuation of wounded." This caused added hard feeling in SEAC and in Tenth Air Force, which understandably resented committing so much of its strength to one subsidiary operation.

Other responsible officers expressed certain misgivings. Bernard Fergusson logically feared " . . . the threatened repetition of the starvation conditions of the year before [the first Chindwin operation] and of renewed reprisals against our Kachin and other helpers within Burma." Wingate had to argue vigorously with Fergusson to keep him in command of 16th Brigade. Wingate's expansionist theories also alarmed Mountbatten—not surprising, since Wingate argued that if the present operation succeeded, he would need twenty to twenty-five brigades, or some one hundred thousand troops, not only to occupy Indochina but to join hands with the Americans in the Pacific![8]

Despite this infighting, which reached majestic proportions, Slim kicked off the second Arakan offensive with a series of probing efforts. These met only limited success and soon stung the Japanese into a counterinvasion of India. Although this surprised him, units that once had folded and fled now held and fought back. The enemy penetrated as far as Imphal, but paid heavily for its presumption. One major strike force lost almost its total of seven thousand. Slim himself later marked the Arakan battle as " . . . one of the historic successes of British arms. It was the turning-point of the Burma campaign. . . . "[9]

Wingate's force meanwhile had gone into action in early March, two brigades being airlifted and one marching into the interior of northern Burma. For the most part, the columns performed very well in this second offensive. Wingate soon wired an optimistic progress report directly to Churchill and concluded: " . . . Enemy completely surprised. Situation most promising if exploited."[10] In the following days, the brigades continued to consolidate their strongholds. The operation was still in a crucial stage, however, when, on March 23, Wingate took off from Imphal in a Mitchell bomber which crashed with no survivors.

His successor continued the operation, which, lacking the simultaneous advance of a regular army, deteriorated into a series of virtually independent actions. In early May, SEAC ordered the brigades to evacuate.

While Slim and Wingate were committing their forces, Stilwell was buzzing between Delhi, Ramgarh, and Chungking in desperate effort to launch an offensive from the north. Finally gaining Chiang Kai-shek's approbation, Stilwell started his divisions moving southeast from Ledo in April 1944. His Northern Combat Area Command comprised three brigades, each consisting of one American battalion and two Chinese battalions, supported by light tanks and aircraft. Integral to the operation was a U. S. medium-range penetration unit, Merrill's Marauders, trained to fight primarily in jungle. As the entire force moved south, it would also find itself fronted and flanked by friendly Kachin guerrillas.

Merrill's Marauders had started life as the 5307th Composite Unit Provisional, assigned to Orde Wingate's command. With considerable difficulty, Stilwell had brought about its transfer to his command. One veteran later described the unit in terms that belied its code-name "Galahad":

> ... It was 3,000 infantrymen so recruited as to ensure that they would exhibit the extremities of human character, the worst as well as the best, the best as well as the worst. It was a band of men who were unready and ill-prepared for the mission they had and who lived with fear. It was an organization that was never given time to organize, that was caught up in historical currents and crosscurrents far beyond its control or even understanding, that was mismanaged, that was driven until the accumulation of hardships and strain and the seeds of corruption it contained brought about its undoing.[11]

Colonel (later Major General) Frank Merrill, who had been Stilwell's G-3, or operations officer, commanded the unit, which attempted to snake behind the Japanese and strike from the flanks. As with Wingate's columns, American infantrymen soon began to tire and then flounder in difficult terrain and climate. Although they performed good work, the Marauders lasted only about a hundred days—and their lifespan probably would have been shorter but for Kachin guerrillas.

Originally under British command, the Kachins had been operating out of Fort Hertz since early in the war. Known as Northern Kachin Levies, or NKL, the guerrilla companies, of about 125 men, fanned out quite far south, where each carved out a drop area and turned to performing a twofold mission: gathering intelligence and killing as many Japanese as possible. After a slow start, they became skillful practitioners of guerrilla warfare, relying primarily on jungle ambushes, simple grenade booby traps, and concealed sharp bamboo stakes.

In December 1943, a theater reorganization placed NKL under Stilwell's Northern Combat Area Command. As Detachment 101 under OSS command, the companies performed invaluable service during Stilwell's advance in spring of 1944 by harassing enemy units, dislocating communications, and by guiding Merrill's columns through the tortuous terrain. In the final push on Myitkyina, two Kachin groups working with Wingate's columns effectively prevented enemy reinforcement, while still another unit led the strike column almost to the airfield at Myitkyina without arousing the enemy.   •

Detachment 101 continued to grow to a strength " . . . of more than 500 Americans, with organized guerrilla bands of 8,500 native Kachins." In the war's last stages, which saw retreat of the Japanese 56th Division, Kachins fell on enemy columns, killing and wounding thousands. Had Chinese Yoke Force moving down from Yünnan lived up to tactical expectations, the joint effort could have annihilated the Japanese division. In the event, Yoke Force, restrained by Chiang Kaishek, moved like molasses.[12]

The primary secret of OSS success, according to Alsop and Braden, was the difference in attitude between OSS and SOE officers vis-à-vis the Kachins, who " . . . hated the Burmese, the Chinese, and the British, with varying degrees of intensity." Detachment 101 veterans later explained that

> . . . unlike the British, they did not treat them as "natives." The Americans were, they said, quite natural and open with the Kachins, asked their advice, which was frequently badly needed, and even on occasion slapped them affectionately on their bare backs. The Kachins, after their initial amazement, reacted highly favorably to this treatment, and took the Americans to their hearts.[13]

This is much too pat an explanation. British officers had worked with Kachins since mid-1942 and, as related, had built them into a formidable guerrilla force by the time Americans took over. To the OSS, northern Burma was a place to punch a road through—one shudders at what our officers whispered to Kachin chiefs about postwar independence and other political goodies. To the British, Burma was a possession they would continue to govern after the war, so British officers could promise nothing to tribesmen. The British enjoyed considerable success in working with other Burma tribes. Slim relied on intelligence provided by "V" force in Arakan, where British officers led small units of Chin tribesmen. Wingate also used "Dahforce," which consisted of Kachins led by British officers; the independent Lushai Brigade " . . . operated for six months . . . across two hundred miles of jungle mountains, against the enemy flank and rear," operations greatly aided by Shan tribesmen.[14]

But the most important British guerrilla success occurred in the South and not only involved Karens but also the Burmese puppet army, supposedly controlled by the Japanese.

The Japanese quickly disillusioned the Thakins, the Burmese dissidents led by Aung San. Not only did Tokyo refuse to declare Burmese independence, but it disbanded the Burmese Independence Army. In its place, the Japanese established the Burma Defense Army, a force of five to eight thousand, titularly headed by General Aung San but actually controlled by Japanese advisers backed by military forces.[15] Similarly, a puppet government under Dr. Ba Maw exercised no real civil power. This was held by a Japanese military government, which " . . . treated Burma as if it were an occupied enemy territory."[16]

But where Ba Maw and his followers accepted the status quo, Aung San again rebelled. As early as May 1942—shortly after the fall of Mandalay—he sent a lieutenant to India to ask British help in establishing an underground movement. Although this led to nothing except intense criticism from other nationalists, his judgment was vindicated as Japanese occupation continued. Professor Htin Aung, himself scarcely pro-British, wrote that three years of Japanese rule proved " . . . more irksome than some sixty years of British rule."[17]

As in the Philippines and elsewhere, Japanese behavior in Burma became so stupid as to defy credulity. Military police of a Gestapo type controlled major cities. A minor traffic violation by a cyclist earned a slap in the face; if a girl hesitated to show a cholera-inoculation card, a Japanese military policeman would pull up her skirt in full view of the public to search for inoculation marks on her buttocks. Arrests, beatings, tortures, and forced-labor camps became the order of the day. In Professor Htin Aung's words, " . . . the Japanese imposed a reign of terror."[18]

Aung San had soon organized a secret anti-Fascist league comprising most of his old followers but including nationalist and Communist components. In late 1944, he again contacted the British to ask for money and arms. Although SOE was actively at work organizing and arming Karen tribes, its officers wanted to help Aung San as much as possible. But civil-affairs staff officers, influenced by the Burmese government-in-exile, opposed giving aid on grounds that Aung San's organization " . . . especially after the liberation of Burma would be more trouble than use. . . . " Mountbatten and Slim decided in favor of SOE even though Slim did not expect the Burmese National Army "to exert any serious influence on the campaign."[19] Slim later received a great deal of intelligence from this secret force. He also received a great deal of help from the Karens, who, contacted by British liaison teams, had been partially armed and equipped in early 1945. During Fourteenth Army's advance south from Meiktila, this guerrilla force prevented a Japanese division from reinforcing the key town of Toungoo. Once Slim controlled Toungoo, his Dakota planes supplied the guerrillas with over thirteen hundred tons of supplies, a miraculous figure when compared to aid previously furnished. Despite enemy pressures from all sides, Karen force continued to grow to about twelve thousand strong while effectively harassing Japanese who were trying to fall back on Moulmein. Blair estimated that this force killed about 12,500 Japanese while indirectly accounting for many more during final Japanese retreats.[20]

The Japanese left Burma in a terrible mess. Slim later wrote that

> ... insecurity and dacoity [brigandage] were rife. Great acreages had gone out of cultivation, while trade had vanished with the breakdown of communications and the loss of security.... large sections of the population were on the verge of starvation.[21]

Nor was the political situation happy. At the approach of allied forces, Ba Maw and followers fled to the Japanese camp. For all practical purposes, Aung San, commanding general of the Burmese National Army, held real power. Wisely recognizing this, Slim soon sent for the young nationalist leader. At their first interview, Aung San " ... began to take rather a high hand," an attitude eventually dispelled by Slim, who not only held powerful cards but evinced an obvious concern for the war-torn country. The dialogue then and later was not one-sided. In Slim's words:

> ... I was impressed by Aung San. He was not the ambitious, unscrupulous guerrilla leader I had expected. He was certainly ambitious and meant to secure for himself a dominant position in post-war Burma, but I judged him to be a genuine patriot and a well-balanced realist.... I have always felt that, with proper treatment, Aung San would have proved a Burmese Smuts.[22]

With Mountbatten's blessing, Slim attempted to woo this important personality. Professor Htin Aung concluded that the British " ... behaved as true liberators and treated the Burmese with sympathy and consideration. General Aung San and his Burmese troops were even absorbed into the British forces."[23] This arrangement continued under a British military governor, Major General Hubert Rance, who wisely recognized Burmese political aspirations and dealt reasonably with Aung San's new and powerful party, the Anti-Fascist People's Freedom

League (AFPFL), which was rapidly becoming the core of a new national congress.

By the time of Japanese surrender, British and Burmese were working more or less together to put the country right. Htin Aung later wrote that, at this time, Aung San and his party were still aiming at dominion status " . . . rather than full independence."[24] This attitude sharply changed when the policy of moderation and conciliation practiced by the British military gave way to a civil policy of vindictiveness and stubbornness. Although the British managed to avoid bloodshed, they quickly lost control and were soon forced to grant the unhappy country its independence.

CHAPTER THIRTY-FOUR

1. Roosevelt loved the unorthodox, as did Churchill, possibly as one means of deflating pompous admirals and generals, but undoubtedly also from the standpoint of political appeal. Inspired by his son James, a U.S. Marine Corps officer strongly influenced by Evans Carlson (see Chapter 29), President Roosevelt foisted the Raider-battalion concept on the Marine Corps, most of whose senior commanders frowned on it in that this was merely making elite units out of units already elite. Roosevelt won, but when A.A. Vandegrift became commandant, he soon disbanded such ancillary units as the Raiders, Paratroopers, and Beach-Jumpers.
2. Mountbatten.
3. Slim, 128, 191.
4. Ibid., 542.
5. Heilbrunn, 71, 168–9.
6. Slim, 217–18.
7. Ibid., 220.
8. Sykes, *Orde Wingate*, 510–11.
9. Slim, 246.
10. Sykes, *Orde Wingate*, 523.
11. Ogburn, 7.
12. Alsop and Braden, 184–200. See also, R.H. Smith.
13. Alsop and Braden, 193–4.
14. Slim, 147–8, 265, 275, 339.
15. Sweet-Escott, 243–4.
16. Htin Aung, *A History of Burma*, 300–1.
17. Ibid., 301.
18. Ibid.
19. Slim, 485.
20. Blair, 155. See also, Sweet-Escott.
21. Slim, 513–14.
22. Ibid., 519.
23. Htin Aung, *A History of Burma*, 303–4.
24. Ibid., 306.

CHAPTER 35

FROM THE STANDPOINT of guerrilla operations, China also proved disappointing—perhaps the inevitable result of conflicting interests both there and abroad. Western leaders regarded the war as an all-out battle against Germany and Japan, and naturally assumed that Chinese leaders would do everything in their power to defeat the common enemy. Chiang Kai-shek and Mao Tse-tung regarded World War II as but an interlude in civil war. Each believed that America ultimately would defeat Japan. They saw themselves, as Dr. Griffith has observed, " . . . in the situation of those ancient ministers who craftily 'used barbarians to control barbarians.' "[1]

Despite intensive American persuasion, Chiang and Mao devoted far more effort to husbanding men and resources for the postwar showdown than in fighting Japanese. Although a veneer of rapprochement appeared between Nationalist and Communist camps, civil war continued to manifest itself in a variety of divisive ways. Failure of American officials from President Roosevelt on down to grasp this disappointing fact and take appropriate countermeasures led to a disastrous policy which indirectly played a significant role in Chiang's demise on the mainland of China.

* * *

To review briefly, Chiang faced real trouble by December 7, 1941. For two years, Japanese armies had controlled Manchuria, northern China, and important cities in the Southeast; Mao and the Communists controlled a large area in the Northwest. Nationalist strategy, as determined by Chiang and a newly created emergency body, the Supreme National Defense Council, " . . . was one of hoarding strength and waiting, keeping the army intact for one final smashing offensive."[2] This was siege strategy designed to trade space for time—time to enable the army to rest and reorganize. His supply lines to the West remained open while his political piano tinkled louder and louder—tunes calculated to

439

shame Washington and arouse American public opinion in his favor. Roosevelt already had tried to help him financially by purchasing Chinese silver in 1937; in 1941, he authorized Claire Chennault to organize the American Volunteer Group, the famous Flying Tigers, composed of American pilots—regular officers hastily resigned from their respective services—flying the latest pursuit aircraft.

Nonetheless, the situation continued to deteriorate. One by one, supply lines to the West were falling to enemy control. By mid-1941, Japan already dominated the greater part of Indochina, including the important railway from Haiphong to Kunming, and was exerting strong pressure in Thailand, whose government capitulated in December. Within a few months, the Japanese flag flew over Hong Kong, the Malay Peninsula, most of Indochina, and most of Burma. By spring of 1942, China was encircled, her only supply line being by air over the Hump.*

America's entry into the war somewhat altered this dismal picture. A shower of gold, $500 million in 1942 alone (at the time an astronomical sum), filled Chiang's empty coffers, and when his associates and senior officials and generals made off with that, more was forthcoming. The trickle of supply over the Hump also continued to support Chennault's valorous effort. Meanwhile the militarily able Lieutenant General Stilwell and his task force of advisers arrived, vanguard of a small military and diplomatic army ready to help Chiang cure Nationalist China's ills while building strong forces that ultimately would expel the Japanese from China.

The newly arrived Americans found plenty of ills. A corrupt and ineffective government was sucking the country dry. The people daily experienced all the evils that Mao Tse-tung and his Communist agents so effectively exploited. Extortion, usury, police and army coercion, impossibly high taxes and rents, unfair prices for produce—Chinese peasants could have been living two centuries earlier. The army was even worse, a conscript mass commanded by corrupt and, in general, poorly trained and inefficient senior officers. Recruits were so miserably treated that in some areas a training death rate of 80 per cent or more was the norm. Survivors fared badly. Division commanders received pay for their troops, passing on only what they judged fitting; unscrupulous commanders frequently sold unit rations; supplies, including arms and ammunition, disappeared into the vortex of greed to be sold to any buyers, Communists included. Armies lived off the countryside, robbing peasants and raping their women, human locusts as perverted as the

* One land route remained through central Asia. The Russians refused to permit passage here for political reasons, namely fear that Western aid would be used against Communists in the Northwest.

Japanese enemy. In January 1943, Stilwell vented private feelings in his journal:

> . . . Cowardice, rampant, squeeze [bribery] paramount, smuggling above duty, colossal ignorance and stupidity of staff, total inability to control factions and cliques, continued oppression of masses. . . . And we are maneuvered into the position of having to support this rotten regime and glorify its figurehead, the all-wise great patriot and soldier—Peanut [Chiang]. My God.[3]

Stilwell suffered no illusions concerning either mission or boss. To make the Chinese peasant a good fighter, drastic army reforms were necessary to ameliorate the fear and distrust that permeated feckless ranks. Although Stilwell forced Chiang to furnish over sixty thousand men for training at Ramgarh in India, these were a drop in the bucket. Other training programs did not enjoy Ramgarh's success. As supplies continued to arrive over the Hump, Chiang's divisions received American arms, equipment, and training. But without repair of basic and traditional abuses, this was like hanging tinsel on a dead Christmas tree.

The major villain was Chiang Kai-shek. Unable or unwilling to redress Kuomintang evils, he had come to deny existence of these evils. Time insulated him ever further from reality. Sun Yat-sen's ghost long since had fled his conscience; in its place ruled only the vain, cruel, contemptuous, and uncaring spirit of past Peking emperors. While he paraded himself to the West as China's savior, he was in reality a xenophobic dictator without real plan, a weak, not very bright man, a prisoner held in a life cell of vanity and fear. Dominated by his wife and her powerful family, surrounded by venal and disloyal advisers, forced to bribe and otherwise coerce independent war lords and underworld leaders in order to survive, Chiang resembled a feudal ruler being driven mad by forces he could not identify. He therefore chose not to believe in their existence. In July 1942, General Stilwell exploded in a letter to his wife: " . . . This is the most dreary type of maneuvering I've ever done, trying to guide and influence a stubborn, ignorant, prejudiced conceited despot who never hears the truth except from me and finds it hard to believe. . . . "[4]

The situation fairly screamed for a prescient diplomat with a pipeline to the President, a strong ambassador enjoined to present a policy of *quid pro quo*—we'll help you, Chiang, but, at the same time, you must clean your own house. In the context of 1942, this approach perhaps was impossible. Roosevelt's China policy was based as much on romanticism as on reality, what Churchill liked to call "the great American illusion." We don't know the President's real feelings about Chiang—they met only once, in Cairo, briefly—but Roosevelt's admiration cooled considerably as war continued and Chiang remained intransigent regarding necessary internal reforms. Unfortunately, a powerful Nationalist China lobby existed (and still exists) in Washington; Roosevelt, consummate politician that he was, held no intention of antagonizing its members. Perhaps, had the President been fully briefed on Chiang's despotism, he, too, would have been disillusioned, as were so many American officials on the spot. Roosevelt, however, seems to have been fooled, perhaps willingly, by Chiang's flamboyantly advertised personal asceticism and his widely proclaimed and utterly meaningless New Life Movement. By ennobling Chiang as a member of the Big Four, Roosevelt virtually placed him above reproach or, at very least, far from control either of a tired and embittered American ambassador, Clarence Gauss, or a spunky, not always tactful lieutenant general in the U. S. Army, Joseph Stilwell.

Stilwell's mission was primarily military, not political. Considering that he was checkmated before he started, he still played a pretty good game, frequently giving Chiang and his cohorts bad moments. He would have done much better, but for a divided American camp. For Stilwell not only had to fight entrenched Chinese bureaucracy at every turn, but he almost immediately collided with Major General Claire Chennault, and he also had to suffer Commander M. E. Miles, who headed the clandestine U. S. Naval Group, China, and later OSS-Far East.

Claire Chennault, airman, a short, stocky man of rugged features, a flier's piercing eyes, brown, and a stubborn chin, but soft of speech and pleasant enough until the name of Stilwell cropped up.[5] Chennault, legendary boss of Flying Tigers, American champion of the Generalissimo and his clique. As commander of 14th U. S. Air Force he believed, as did many Air Corps brethren, that war could be won only in the air. Chennault's strategic beliefs, vigorously promoted by his aide, politically powerful Joseph Alsop, suited Chiang's position perfectly: use of American air power would preserve the Nationalist army for postwar showdown with the Communists.

On Chennault's recommendation, Chiang obtained Combined Chiefs of Staff approval to construct a series of airfields in eastern China from where, so they argued, planes could interdict Japanese shipping and, in time, bring the air war to Japan proper. Stilwell fought this plan, arguing that the Chinese army could not possibly protect the fields and that the Japanese could move into the area at will. In spring of 1943, Stilwell lost the argument to Chennault, and the fields were built. A year later, the Japanese did open a major offensive and soon overran the airfields, stopping only at Kweilin. Chennault accused Stilwell of

442

deliberately weakening Nationalist defenses to prove himself correct. Chiang Kai-shek echoed the charges and ordered Stilwell to transfer Chinese divisions from the Burma front. Stilwell refused, and the ensuing imbroglio led eventually to his dismissal.

That did not alter the ugly fact of the Japanese offensive. Not only did it cost Chiang a great many material resources, all in short supply, but it sent Nationalist and allied morale plunging. In retreating from Honan, one Nationalist army so ravaged the population that the people " . . . turned on them and destroyed them." By yielding large areas to repressive Japanese occupation forces, the Nationalists only added to peasant disaffection, thereby enriching the ground for the Communist subversive effort.[6]

Stilwell fared no better with the U. S. Navy. For an experienced naval officer, "Mary" Miles was painfully naïve, as is variously disclosed in a posthumously published book, *A Different Kind of War*. An Annapolis graduate, the forty-two-year-old Miles arrived in Chungking in spring of 1942, his primary mission to establish a series of clandestine radio stations along the southern coast in order to transmit weather reports and Japanese shipping movements. In carrying out this mission, Miles contributed satisfactorily to the war effort, but he also paid the piper by attaching himself, and thus the American flag, to one of the most sinister persons in the Far East: Lieutenant General Tai Li, head of Chiang's secret police.

The liaison could have been suffered had Miles remained limited in his operations. Unfortunately he saw himself as an oriental Lawrence, and, in attempting to set up a widespread guerrilla organization, he was soon rubbing elbows with a variety of cutthroats familiar to readers of *Terry and the Pirates*. Of the thousand or so Americans sent to China, only a few spoke Chinese. The rest were totally dependent on interpreters in trying to control some hundred thousand guerrillas. One can suggest that these interpreters were hand-picked by General Tai Li and that the Americans were told precisely what Tai Li wanted them to be told.

Miles' early attempts to establish transmitting stations fell victim to Japanese counteraction. S. E. Morison later wrote:

> . . . By the end of 1942 Miles realized that the weather-reporting network would have to be turned into a secret army to be really useful. Tai Li needed more guerrillas to protect the weather men, and more Americans to train the Chinese. On Commander Miles's recommendation an agreement was signed 15 April 1943, establishing the Sino-American Cooperative Organization (SACO),

commanded by Tai Li with Miles as his deputy. Volunteers were carefully screened by the SACO office in Washington and put through a special training course before being sent out to China. No "old China hands" with preconceived ideas were wanted. . . .

Later attempts to merge Miles' effort with OSS activities by making Miles director of OSS in China proved futile when Tai Li refused to carry out Washington's orders.[7]

SACO rapidly expanded. Miles's and Tai Li's headquarters, Happy Valley, outside of Chungking, supported five separate intelligence efforts as well as a number of guerrilla-training units headed by American officers. Later in the war, Miles commanded some 2,500 Americans, whose logistic appetite never ceased growing. From June to November 1944, American pilots flew in nearly 900 tons of arms, ammunition, and explosives—plus 227 tons of gasoline [!], 51 tons of passenger baggage [!], and 185 tons of miscellaneous items such as trucks, office supplies, clothing, and mail, items hardly compatible with a mobile, hard-hitting guerrilla organization.

Considering SACO's size and impressive logistic support, operational results against the Japanese seem surprisingly mild. Although " . . . comprehensive weather maps were being broadcast daily to the Pacific Fleet" by October 1944, along with information on coastal shipping,[8] this activity scarcely justified SACO's expense. A less pretentious organization could have fielded small and select Chinese teams, much as Australian coastwatchers operated, and precisely as Mao's Communists were doing in Yenan in supplying "an astonishingly large number of useful [weather] reports" to Colonel David Barrett, who commanded an American observer group sent there in 1944.[9]

Regarding damage to the enemy from guerrilla operations, Miles's claims probably err on the side of optimism, particularly the figure of seventy-one thousand Japanese killed. Although guerrillas, variously trained and commanded by American teams, at times scratched the enemy façade, their reports should not have been taken at face value. Chinese face is omnipresent. One Chinese guerrilla leader was not going to be outdone by another, a characteristic also familiar to most non-Chinese guerrillas. One fact is certain: the effort in no way prevented the Japanese army, itself greatly weakened, from carrying out the 1944 offensive against Chennault's exposed airfields.

As Miles developed his mission, he invariably collided with Stilwell, who, on one occasion, "held up all SACO's air shipments for six months."[10] Tai Li's intransigence also caused OSS to undertake an independent effort. As early as 1943, American military and civil officials wanted to arm Mao Tse-tung's guerrillas, a notion successfully fought by Chiang Kai-shek. During the successful Japanese offensive of 1944, the issue again grew dominant, and played a role in Stilwell's dismissal.

Miles and his group were also falling from official favor. When General Albert Wedemeyer replaced Stilwell, in late 1944, he dropped Tai Li in favor of General Chen Kai-ming. Miles later wrote that Wedemeyer apparently did not realize that Chen was Tai Li's number-two man—nor, apparently, did Miles see fit to tell him.[11] Wedemeyer suffered Miles' independent operations until spring of 1945, when Admiral King, Chief of Naval Operations, placed the naval group under Wedemeyer's command.[12]

In Yenan, to the northwest, Mao and his Communists were also dragging heels in the war against Japan. Even had Mao been inclined to wage more vigorous war, he would have found rough going. General Okamura's policy of "Kill all, burn all, destroy all" continued to hurt Mao in 1941 and 1942. Okamura later claimed that his forces killed about a hundred thousand of Mao's guerrillas and that he would have eliminated them altogether except that, in late 1942, the Japanese high command began transferring seven of his best divisions to the Pacific theater.[13]

By late 1942, Japan had assumed the strategic defensive in China and Southeast Asia. In northern and central China, large garrisons defended major cities which were linked by strong points to keep open lines of communication, a static situation accepted by Mao, who, convinced that America would win the war, continued to concentrate on consolidation and expansion of his forces and of territory abandoned by the Japanese.[14]

Had Mao been supplied with arms, American observers reported, he might have constituted a significant threat to the Japanese presence.[15] In spring of 1944, Stilwell favored arming the Communists, though this was probably as much to force Chiang to implement necessary reforms as it was to help Mao build a modern army. The threat did make Chiang more pliant. In June 1944, Chiang told Vice-President Henry Wallace that he " . . . would welcome the assistance of the President in the settlement of the Communist problem, even though it was an internal one"; he also agreed to send a team of American military-civil observers to Mao's headquarters at Yenan, a move previously recommended by Stilwell's headquarters but refused by Chiang.[16]

As enemy action continued through summer and threatened to cut China in two, Roosevelt took increasingly positive action. In July, he promoted Stilwell to four-star rank and told Chiang that he wanted him made commander in chief of the Chinese armies. He also sent two personal representatives to Chungking, Major General Patrick Hurley, to iron out existing problems between Chiang and Stilwell, and Donald Nelson, to work out a more generous aid program. By the time Hurley and Nelson arrived in Delhi, Stilwell had announced the capture of Myitkyina—the first major tactical success enjoyed by the Nationalists since 1937—and had started another offensive from Yünnan. The three traveled to Chungking in early September.

At sixty-one years of age, Patrick J. Hurley featured considerable experience in arbitration. A self-educated Oklahoma lawyer and decorated veteran of World War I, he had served government with the same unflagging zeal that had made him a fortune from representing private oil interests. A cabinet officer in the Hoover administration, he more recently had functioned as Roosevelt's ambassador to New Zealand and to Iran, besides representing the President to Stalin and other foreign figures. Tall and lean, with a neat mustache and tailored uniform heavy with decorations, genial Pat Hurley looked the perfect diplomat. The look deceived. Hurley believed that " . . . contagious friendliness could be made a fundamentally effective part of diplomacy." If his Oklahoma drawl and fund of homespun stories amused President Roosevelt, they bored most people. In negotiations demanding the deepest knowledge and objectivity, Hurley preferred prejudice to fact. Basically an idealist, either unwilling or unable to differentiate between national ambitions and attainable objectives, he was becoming an increasingly embittered man, at odds with anyone who disagreed with him. He was already convinced that Britain and Russia were fighting only for sinister imperialist purposes, as opposed to Atlantic Charter ideals, and in China his suspicions hardened into soul-destroying conviction that the U. S. Department of State consisted of two parts, half pro-British, half pro-Russian—the whole scheming to subvert the foreign policy of the United States, which he, Patrick J. Hurley, alone seemed intent on preserving. When personal diplomacy failed, Hurley sought to blame others, whom he accused of disloyalty and subversion. Pat Hurley came to China to advance the American dream; he helped set the stage for the American nightmare.

Hurley's primary error consisted of oversimplification. His orders were "to promote efficient and harmonious relations" between Chiang and Stilwell (tantamount to bringing together a cat and a dog), which meant resolving the issue of aid to the Communists. Roosevelt refused to arm the Communists "unless and until they acknowledged the National Government of the Republic of China, and the leadership of Generalissimo Chiang Kai-shek." Hurley's mission thus became that of making peace not only between Chiang and Stilwell, but between Nationalists and Communists.[17]

By the time Hurley arrived in Chungking, in September, an American military-civil mission was working with Mao Tse-tung in Yenan. The Dixie Mission, as it was known, had arrived in July under command of an experienced China hand, Colonel David Barrett, American military attaché in Chungking. Mao and his lieutenants welcomed the Barrett mission. In turn the Americans were favorably impressed, although recognizing a political-military situation unfamiliar to Western warfare. As Barrett reported:

> ... The Communists could almost always count on the cooperation and support of a local population which had excellent opportunities to acquire important information about the enemy and were eager to report it whenever they could. Thus their training, unlike ours, laid little stress on scouting, patrolling, air reconnaissance and other means of gathering enemy intelligence.[18]

An important civil member of the team, John Paton Davies, informed State Department seniors that "the Chinese Communists are so strong between the Great Wall and the Yangtze that they can now look forward to the postwar control of at least North China."[19] His colleague, John Service, reported that:

> ... This total [Chinese Communist] mobilization is based upon and has been made possible by what amounts to an economic, political and social revolution. .... I suggest the future conclusion that unless the Kuomintang goes as far as the Communists in political and economic reform, and otherwise proves itself able to contest this leadership of the people (none of which it yet shows signs of being willing or able to do), the Communists will be the dominant force in China within a comparatively few years.[20]

While Barrett, Davies, and Service were so occupied, a storm of monumental proportions had broken in Chungking. A few days after Stilwell's return in September, the continuing Japanese advance had forced him to order demolition of the large American base at Kweilin, an act that earned harsh words both from Chennault and Chiang Kai-shek. Hurley, meanwhile, continued to confer with Chiang, who finally agreed to recognize Stilwell as his new commander in chief, but in return demanded control of lend-lease supply. He also demanded return of Chinese divisions from Burma, which Stilwell refused to consider.

Stilwell at this point was a tired man, his normal irascibility honed razor-sharp. He had recently spent six active months in a jungle campaign that claimed as victim most men half his years. He had heard all Chiang's promises before. Hurley was convinced that he had persuaded Chiang to his way of thinking; Stilwell, from sad experience, pointed out that Chiang forever said yes and always did no.

On September 26, Stilwell informed Marshall:

. . . Chiang Kai-shek has no intention of making further efforts to prosecute the war. Anyone who crowds him toward such action will be blocked or eliminated. . . . Chiang Kai-shek believes he can go on milking the United States for money and munitions by using the old gag about quitting if he is not supported. He believes the war in the Pacific is nearly over, and that by delaying tactics, he can throw the entire burden on us. He has no intention of instituting any real democratic regime or of forming a united front with the communists. He himself is the main obstacle to the unification of China and her cooperation in a real effort against Japan. . . . I am now convinced that, for the reasons stated, the United States will not get any real cooperation from China while Chiang Kai-shek is in power. I believe he will only continue his policy and delay, while grabbing for loans and postwar aid, for the purpose of maintaining his present position, based on one-party government, and reactionary policy, on the suppression of democratic ideas with the active aid of his Gestapo.[21]

The imbroglio soon reached ultimatum proportions with Chiang demanding Stilwell's recall. In October, the American general departed, his job taken over by Major General (soon promoted to Lieutenant General) Albert Wedemeyer.

Wedemeyer might have been in a different army than Stilwell. Also a West Pointer, the forty-eight-year-old general had served in Washington before joining Mountbatten's staff in Ceylon. As he makes clear in his book *Wedemeyer Reports,* he fancied himself a global strategist of no mean talent. Unlike Stilwell (whom he disliked and who held him in genial contempt), the husky Nebraskan sympathized deeply with Chiang Kai-shek and set about to bail him out militarily.

Hurley meanwhile continued trying to bail Chiang out politically. In early November, he flew to Mao's headquarters at Yenan to present a draft agreement from Chiang Kai-shek (probably drawn up by the U.S. Department of State), which would have incorporated Mao's forces into the Nationalist army in return for legalizing the Chinese Communist Party.[22] Despite considerable bonhomie—Hurley's habit of emitting Indian war whoops on the odd occasion appalled both American and Communist camps—the talks did not prosper. Mao believed that he was powerful enough to demand a coalition government—the main feature of his rebuttal to Chiang's draft. Hurley returned to Chungking with Mao's Five-Point Proposal; Mao's chief lieutenant, the young and bright Chou En-lai, accompanied him.

Subsequent talks with Nationalists dragged on inconclusively—not surprising in view either of Chiang's intransigence or of Mao's relatively strong bargaining position. More to the point, neither side made any obvious effort to carry the war to the Japanese—a serious deficiency that was soon to exercise an important and harmful influence on American strategy.

When President Roosevelt flew to Yalta, in February 1945, the European war was approaching climax, but the Pacific war, though progressing well for the allies, was far from won. Although danger now seemed slight of the enemy developing an atomic bomb, Hitler still spoke of new and secret weapons of great power. Question marks still embraced the American-British atomic-bomb effort: scientists could not, in early 1945, promise a bomb that worked, let alone a delivery date.

Roosevelt met with Stalin before American marines landed on Iwo Jima. Chiang seemed no more anxious than ever to fight the Japanese, and Chinese Nationalists and Communists remained at each other's throats, to the enemy's immense profit. Roosevelt and Churchill had been advised by their respective chiefs of staff " . . . that the war in the Pacific would last eighteen months after the end of hostilities in Europe."[23] According to military estimates, the invasion of Japanese home islands would cost perhaps one million American lives. Roosevelt's interpreter at Yalta, Charles Bohlen, later pointed out that, according to American military estimates, it would have " . . . cost about 200,000 more in American casualties to assault the Japanese islands before rather than after Soviet entry into the Pacific war."[24]

The agreements made at Yalta aroused enormous controversy in postwar years. Leaving aside arrangements for Poland and the rest of Europe, Roosevelt was and still is criticized for negotiating Far Eastern questions without China's presence and in controverting certain clauses of the Cairo Declaration. The document in question, the "Far Eastern Agreement"—" . . . negotiated by Roosevelt, Stalin, Harriman, and Molotov without the full knowledge of either the State Department or the Joint Chiefs of Staff and without Churchill's participation until the very end"—granted Stalin four major concessions, abridged by Professor Richard Leopold in his excellent work *The Growth of American Foreign Policy:*

> . . . Stalin obtained four things exactly as he wished: the annexation of the Kuriles, the cession of southern Sakhalin, the naval base at Port Arthur, and the maintenance of the *status quo* in Outer Mongolia. His desire to lease [Port] Dairen and to control the Chinese Eastern and South Manchuria [railroad] lines did not fully materialize, the port being placed under international jurisdiction and the railways under joint operation.[25]

The agreement concerning Outer Mongolia and Manchuria would require concurrence of Generalissimo Chiang Kai-shek. In return for these concessions, Stalin promised to enter the war against Japan, once Germany had surrendered. The final clause of this top-secret agreement read:

> ... For its part the Soviet Union expresses its readiness to conclude with the National Government of China a pact of friendship and alliance between the USSR and China in order to render assistance to China with its armed forces for the purpose of liberating China from the Japanese yoke.[26]

This document was neither as evil as postwar critics have made out, nor as sound as defenders have claimed. Two important considerations governed presidential thinking at Yalta (the claim that Roosevelt was feeble-minded, later advanced by Wedemeyer, Hurley, and others who were not present, and picked up by the right wing, must be discounted in view of overwhelming contrary evidence; ill he was, crazy he was not): One was the human and material cost to the United States of invading Japan, the other his belief that he could handle Stalin after the war, that, in William Bullitt's words, " . . . he could convert Stalin from Soviet imperialism to democratic collaboration."[27] Roosevelt can scarcely be faulted for respecting the first consideration, and only a curious kind of American would suggest that the Joint Chiefs of Staff distorted their discouraging estimates in Stalin's favor. One of America's ablest wartime intelligence officers, Rear Admiral Ellis Zacharias, later wrote a sympathetic epitaph for the JCS report: " . . . It was an unfortunate and altogether wrong estimate, its authors being deceived by a purely military and quantitative evaluation of the enemy, a treacherous trap into which even the greatest military leaders are likely to fall occasionally."[28]

Roosevelt can be and has been heavily criticized for the ego inherent in his assumption of personal supremacy over Stalin. In the final analysis, however, it is what raises him above his predecessors or successors—the insistence on attempting to alter the great-power concept in favor of world government. In his desire for a free, peaceful, and prosperous world, Roosevelt embodied the real spirit of what he believed to be the American ideal. He recognized that the only hope for an ultimately peaceful world lay in a viable United Nations. Critics have condemned him for paying too much attention to military strategy and not enough to postwar politics. But at Yalta and elsewhere in intercourse with Stalin, Roosevelt acted with the very realistic knowledge that the United Nations or a similar organization could not function without Stalin's participation. Finally, such was deployment of forces, that Stalin had immediate access to the controversial areas which he would have occupied in any case. As Ambassador Charles Bohlen concluded:

> ... It cannot be said that Yalta was a success, but, as I wrote earlier, there are no grounds for supposing that it was the folly or the weakness of the Western powers which made this true. The map of Europe would look exactly the same as it does today if there had never been a Yalta Conference.[29]

How many, if any, of the Yalta decisions were passed by Stalin to Mao Tse-tung is not known. Chiang Kai-shek was not consulted, only because his senior councils were so riddled with spies that Tokyo would have learned all.[30] Ambassador Hurley informed Chiang of the agreement in June 1945. Chiang " ... seemed disappointed but not upset" and began planning for appropriate talks with Russia.[31] At this time, Nationalist-Communist talks were still in progress under Hurley's aegis. Whether Mao ever intended to join the Nationalist government is not known; he probably would have, had circumstances warranted this interim measure. But he was in no hurry. In Chungking, his trusted and most able lieutenant, Chou En-lai, at once had recognized and defined divisive influences surrounding Chiang, news welcome to Mao. Stilwell's abrupt departure and Chiang's subsequent failure to cleanse his military stables (much less his house of government) also contrasted with Communist army strength, daily growing more powerful. In April 1945, General Chu Teh, its commander in chief, reported to the Seventh Party Congress a regular army strength of nearly one million, augmented by a militia of well over two million, an organization devoted to bringing " ... Mao's revolution to almost 100 million peasants living in the plains, valleys, and mountains of North China."[32]

CHAPTER THIRTY-FIVE

1. Griffith, *The Chinese People's Liberation Army*, 73.
2. J.A. Harrison, 176.
3. Stilwell, 191. See also, Romanus and Sunderland; White and Jacoby; Tuchman.
4. Stilwell, 126.
5. Wedemeyer, 201–3.
6. J.A. Harrison, 184.
7. Morison, *The Liberation of the Philippines*, XIII, 290–1, 293.
8. Ibid., 292.
9. Barrett, 35.
10. Morison, *The Liberation of the Philippines*, XIII, 293.
11. Miles, 438. A former naval intelligence officer on Admiral Nimitz's staff has informed me that the information passed by Naval Group China was not only useless but tainted because it came from Tai Li and his people. (Letter in the author's private files.)
12. Wedemeyer, 341.

13. Griffith, *The Chinese People's Liberation Army,* 71, 75.
14. Ibid., 73–4.
15. U.S. Department of State, *United States Relations with China* . . . , 86–92. See also, Barrett, 36.
16. U.S. Department of State, *United States Relations with China* . . . , 57.
17. Lohbeck, 233–4.
18. Barrett, 43.
19. U.S. Department of State, *United States Relations with China,* 566.
20. Lohbeck, 328–9.
21. U.S. Department of States, *United States Relations with China* . . . , 68.
22. Barrett, 56–9. The writer gives the draft treaty and also describes in detail the frustrating but always fascinating subsequent conferences and counterdrafts.
23. Bohlen, 34.
24. Ibid., 35.
25. Leopold, 618. See also, Ibid., 615–19, for an excellent critique of the Yalta agreements.
26. Ibid., 615.
27. Bullitt.
28. Lohbeck, 354.
29. Bohlen, 46.
30. U.S. Department of State, *United States Relations with China* . . . , 115.
31. Leopold, 618. See also, Wedemeyer, who was present and who credits Chiang with a more severe reaction.
32. Griffith, *The Chinese People's Liberation Army,* 76.

CHAPTER 36

PRESIDENT ROOSEVELT'S DEATH and the ensuing confusion in Washington played directly into Chinese Communist hands by prolonging and even intensifying the divisive nature of American policy. When Harry Truman became President in April 1945, three distinct schools of thought existed among concerned officials in China.

The first might be called the Stilwell syndrome: the continuing effort, mainly by Department of State representatives, both in the Chungking embassy and in Wedemeyer's headquarters, to make common cause with Mao's Communists. There were two reasons for this: first to more effectively fight the Japanese; second to force Chiang into political, economic, and military reforms by suggesting that the soft rug of American support could be pulled from under him to leave him standing on the cold floor of reality. Some powerful non-Communist Chinese political leaders agreed with this policy, as did many knowledgeable American military officers and most American journalists in the area. Ambassador Hurley did not agree, and succeeded in having leading proponents of military co-operation variously transferred and even persecuted, and he refused to consider furnishing arms and supply to the Communists. Hurley was actively pursuing a conciliation policy that he believed was going to result in amalgamation of Nationalist and Communist forces. He had convinced himself that the Chinese problem was totally internal—this primarily the result of an earlier conference with Molotov, who promised to back Chiang Kai-shek's government— and that he, good fellow, could bring about a working conciliation between the two major power factions. A meeting with Stalin in April 1945 confirmed his belief. The Russian leader, as Hurley reported to Washington,

> . . . wished us to know that we would have his complete support in immediate action for the unification of the armed forces of China with full recognition of the National Government under the leadership of Chiang Kai-shek. In short, Stalin agreed unqualifiedly to America's [Hurley's] policy in China as outlined to him during this conversation.[1]

Hurley's naïveté frightened among others the American chargé d'affaires in Moscow, George Kennan. Kennan had studied the Russians and their language for years and now cabled Ambassador Harriman, who had returned to Washington at President Roosevelt's death:

> . . . There was, of course, nothing in Ambassador Hurley's account of what he told Stalin to which Stalin could not honestly subscribe, it being understood that to the Russians words mean different things than they do to us. Stalin is of course prepared to affirm the principle of unifying the armed forces of China. He knows that unification is feasible in a practical sense only on conditions which are acceptable to the Chinese Communist Party. . . .

After detailing what he believed to be specific Soviet aims, Kennan concluded:

> . . . It would be tragic if our natural anxiety for the support of the Soviet Union at this juncture, coupled with Stalin's use of words which mean all things to all people and his cautious affability, were to lead us into an undue reliance on Soviet aid or even Soviet acquiescence in the achievement of our long-term objectives in China.

Both Harriman and Secretary of State Edward Stettinius took this prescient warning to heart and attempted to impress Hurley with the complexity of the situation, including the peril of arousing "unfounded expectations" in giving Chiang an "over-optimistic account of his conversations with Stalin."[2]

Albert Wedemeyer would have heartily applauded this advice. Unlike Hurley, with whom he had been quarreling for some time, the American general saw the greatest danger in postwar Russian moves and was convinced that the Kremlin " . . . sought from the outset to wreck the Nationalist Government" through its control of Chinese Communists. Primarily for this reason, he agreed with Hurley that America should not furnish arms and supply to the Communists as recommended by such diplomats as John Vincent of the American embassy in Chungking.[3]

A very harassed President Truman bought bits and pieces from each of the three schools. While willing to accept the State Department's expressed long-range goal, " . . . the establishment of a strong and united China as a necessary principal stabilizing factor in the Far East," he also made it clear that if Nationalists wanted American help they would have to carry out overdue reforms, not to mention fighting the Japanese. In essence, Truman merely continued an already unsatisfactory policy, whose pragmatism remained subservient to its poverty. Like Foch in 1918, he should have walked in his garden and asked himself: *De quoi s'agit-il* (Just what is the problem)? The problem obviously was an intractable Chiang Kai-shek, whose external power position derived in part from strategic factors, in part from conflicting American policy with a strong emotional bias.

The end of the war with Japan would solve the strategic conundrum. The policy aspect was the difficult one, and such were the ponderous and complex factors that perhaps a complete solution did not exist. A partial solution could have resulted, however, by twisting loose threads of executive policy into a rope or even a noose with which to confront Chiang Kai-shek. Truman did nothing of the kind. While summer months spun away, one branch of his power maintained diplomatic dalliance with Chinese Communists, whose strength was and remained space-time-will; another paid court to Chiang, who, reassured by the powerful China lobby in Washington, remained confident of continuing American support; a third, in the form of Pat Hurley, kept buzzing from one camp to another like some kind of crazy bee gathering in meaningless political pollen.

The situation screamed for dynamic action; the administration replied by mediocrity, best expressed by one of Wedemeyer's reports in the final days of the war:

455

... Based on [my] limited knowledge, neither the Chinese Communist Party nor the Kuomintang is democratic in spirit, or in intentions. China is not prepared for a democratic form of government with 95 per cent of her people illiterate and for many other cogent reasons. The inarticulate masses of China desire peace and are not particularly interested in or aware of the various ideologies represented. An opportunity to work, to obtain food and clothing for their families and a happy peaceful environment are their primary concern.

Conditions here could best be handled by a benevolent despot or a military dictator, whether such dictator be a Communist or a Kuomintang matters very little. From my observation practically all Chinese officials are interested in their selfish aggrandizement. I retain the impression that the Generalissimo's friendship offers best opportunity at this time for stabilization in the area, political and economic.[4]

If astute American officials were not pleased with Chiang Kai-shek's inept government, very few, if any, thought in the confused summer and autumn of 1945 that China would ever fall under Mao Tse-tung's control. Most observers agreed that the talks engineered and steered by Hurley between Nationalists and Communists would lead eventually to coalition government. When these talks terminated in September and the first military skirmishes developed in northern China and Manchuria, informed persons spoke in terms of temporary suspension, not war.

Nor did the first shooting incidents create panic. In numbers, Chiang held a comfortable military balance. By war's end, the Nationalist army numbered around three million men, and would soon increase. Despite deficiencies noted by Stilwell and others, this army included five divisions equipped and trained by Stilwell's India command. In addition, Chiang's army included some twenty-five divisions trained and equipped by the American military mission at Kunming, some of which were also battle tested.

Chiang's modern divisions contained artillery, armor, transport, and communication units, and, thanks to Stilwell's teachings and Wedemeyer's various reforms, had attained a degree of operational sophistication undreamed by either Nationalist or Communist commanders. Chiang also possessed an air force of about eight groups, with a pool of some five thousand American-trained pilots, and he knew that the Western horn of plenty would continue spewing forth dollars and airplanes and guns and tanks and bullets and food to help him achieve stable postwar government.

Mao Tse-tung, by comparison, was a poor relation. His army may have numbered around a million, but it remained essentially a guerrilla force that lacked small arms and supply in all categories, let alone such supporting arms as armor, artillery, and aircraft. Nor did Mao's prospects for substantial aid seem great. In the treaty signed between Nationalist China and Russia in August, Stalin promised to support Chiang's government, and, at this stage, he did not seem to be going out of his way to help Mao.

On paper, then, the numerical balance strongly favored Chiang. In the minds of Chiang and his closest advisers, elimination of the Japanese threat had brought back the problem of the early thirties: suppression of Communist bandits. That the problem's dimensions had drastically altered, Chiang refused to admit, and he also refused to repair deficiencies in government and army. He fancied himself much stronger than he was, the Communists much weaker than they were. With considerable optimism, even elation, he insisted on occupying not only northern China but all of Manchuria as rapidly as American planes and ships could move his armies.

The Japanese surrender had found Nationalists unprepared to move forces rapidly to major cities in central and northern China, there to reassert governmental authority and to begin the immense task of repatriating nearly four million Japanese soldiers and civilians. After appealing successfully to the Americans for transportation, Chiang forbade Chinese Communists to accept surrender of Japanese arms. In turn, General Douglas MacArthur ordered Japanese units *not* to surrender to Chinese Communists. Simultaneously, an impressive American airlift carried three Nationalist armies to key points in eastern and northern China, including Shanghai, Nanking, and Peiping. Wedemeyer asked the Joint Chiefs of Staff for seven U.S. divisions " . . . in order to create a barrier through North China and Manchuria against Soviet Russia."[5] Not having seven divisions available, the JCS sent a U. S. Marine Corps task force of about fifty thousand troops, which landed in October " . . . and occupied Peiping, Tientsin, the coal mines to the north and essential railroad depots." Ostensibly provided to accept surrender of Japan's North China Army on behalf of Chiang Kai-shek and to start repatriation of Japanese nationals, the marine force in reality attempted to deny the area to Communist influence—an impossible task in view of its limited numbers and of Communist organizational strength in the countryside.

The sad truth was that none of these measures frightened Mao Tsetung, any more than did Chiang's paper strength. While peace talks continued with Nationalists, Mao sent units by forced marches to northern China and Manchuria. Some Japanese units voluntarily surrendered to these on-the-spot forces; others resisted in at least token fashion. In northern China, Communists soon controlled most of the countryside and, from that power position, began claiming control of most railroads. Incidents, including quite serious skirmishes, now began between Communist forces and Nationalist-American forces.

Wedemeyer had vigorously objected to Chiang's occupation of Manchuria until he had consolidated his positions in northern China, both because the problem of maintaining large forces a thousand miles north loomed enormous and because of the possibility of Communist interdiction of vital lines of communication. Chiang greeted Wedemeyer's recommendation of a temporary five-power guardianship over Manchuria with complaisance, not compliance. He insisted on sticking to his overly ambitious plan, and the American administration foolishly acquiesced. After delay caused by procuring cold-weather clothing from Alaska and by inoculating troops, American planes and ships began lifting Chinese armies into Manchuria, an impressive effort that involved nearly half a million men.

Meanwhile, under terms of the Yalta and Potsdam agreements and the Sino-Soviet treaty, Soviet troops had occupied Manchuria and had accepted the surrender there of Japanese forces. The agreement called for the Soviets to remain for three months. But such was the delay in deploying Nationalist armies, that, in November, Chiang asked Stalin to extend his occupation. Stalin gladly agreed—his locustlike minions were stripping Manchuria's industrial plants. Nor did the Soviet dictator object to Chinese Communists rapidly infiltrating the area. Whether the Chinese Communist move accorded with Stalin's wishes is a moot question, despite later assertions by a vociferous American faction who endeavored to paint a black-and-white picture of a scene fraught with nuance and subtlety. Some evidence exists that Mao acted independently and presented Stalin with a *fait accompli* which he may not have welcomed, but which he could not reverse.

The newly arrived Communist Chinese force in Manchuria was commanded by the able Lin Piao, who had two targets: one, the cities and all-important Japanese arms dumps; the other, the countryside and all-important peasants who would bear arms to make a new field army. No question exists as to his acquisition both of Japanese arms and Chinese peasant recruits. As the build-up of Communist and Nationalist troops continued in Manchuria and northern China, serious clashes began to end Western hopes for coalition settlement. The Cassandra tone of Wedemeyer's final reports on Nationalist combat efficiency deepened Washington gloom. Although Hurley had succeeded in forging a Nationalist-Communist agreement that " . . . promised to lead to true peace in China," his own behavior grew increasingly morbid. For months, he had been complaining of slights by State Department officials while impugning the loyalty of certain of his Chungking subordinates. Instead of returning to China, as he promised Truman, he suddenly resigned and in late November delivered a speech at the National Press Club that, in Truman's words, attacked " . . . the administration, the State Department, our foreign policy and me personally."[6]

Truman now appointed a special representative with personal rank of ambassador, the recently retired and extremely able General of the Army George C. Marshall, to try to negotiate a peace. Despite Wedemeyer's gloomy prognostications, Marshall succeeded in bringing both sides to the conference table, where Mao's representative, Chou En-lai, " . . . acknowledged the leadership of Chiang Kai-shek and disavowed any desire to establish a separate government."[7] This favorable beginning unfortunately meant very little. When it came to working out participation in a government, each side remained intransigent. Chiang, his confidence increased by a series of minor military victories in early 1946, demanded full control of Manchuria prior to initiating legislative reforms; Mao Tse-tung, aware that his own power was growing daily in the area, refused to accede. While talks continued, clashes between the two armies grew more frequent and severe. In March, the Russians transferred garrison areas to Nationalists and withdrew their forces. Active fighting set in.

Although Marshall arranged another cease-fire, in spring of 1946, he was holding two tigers by the tail and finally had to let go. His failure did not surprise Wedemeyer, who returned to America in April, critical of administration policy and scornful of Marshall's efforts. In July, Marshall received a rather more helpful associate in the person of Dr. J. Leighton Stuart, the newly appointed American ambassador.

Neither Stuart nor anyone else seemingly could disturb Chiang Kai-shek's complacency. Marshall warned him that he was not winning in Manchuria, that at best Nationalists " . . . were holding their own while draining away those forces needed to hold China proper."[8] Chiang refused to respect Marshall's views and also vigorously rebutted a strong warning by President Truman to settle the problem by negotiation and not force. When Chiang opened an offensive in northern China in the autumn, Truman placed a limited embargo on arms shipments to China. Despite these and other measures, the Communists openly accused Marshall of belonging to Chiang's camp. In November, Chou En-lai returned to Yenan; in December, Marshall returned to America and, shortly after, became secretary of state.

Marshall delivered a final warning to Chiang Kai-shek: the Communists were too powerful to be eliminated by military force alone; in view of current Nationalist military expenditure—about 70 per cent of the total government budget—the country would face economic collapse before eliminating the Communists. Chiang replied that he would exterminate the Communists in from eight to ten months.[9]

For a time, Nationalist armies seemed to give the lie to Marshall's warnings. In winter of 1946–47, they incontestably held major cities of northern China and Manchuria; in March 1947, a Nationalist offensive in northern China captured a number of Communist-held towns, including the capital of Shensi province, Yenan. These gains proved dangerously illusory, as reported by Ambassador Stuart:

> . . . It has long been apparent that the Communists have prepared well for this eventuality and that they never had any real intention of defending Yenan should such action appear to be costly. Rather it is more in keeping with their long developed tactics to evacuate any given point in the face of enemy pressure, draw him into a pocket, and thereafter gradually sap his strength with guerrilla tactics. . . . "

Sadly, Chiang and his principal advisers either would not or could not recognize the true nature of this war. Nationalist armies in Manchuria and northern China behaved like conquerors, looting and raping virtually at will. Local commanders used puppet troops and even Japanese troops in carrying out the occupation. Professor Harrison wrote that

> . . . in the countryside the Kuomintang returned the land titles of the landlords and permitted them to demand impossible back rents and interests for the years they had been absent. In addition, returning officials attempted to collect back taxes for the years of Japanese occupation. No actions could have been more calculated to enrage the peasants and throw them into the waiting arms of the Communists.[11]

Nepotism, corruption, and inefficiency continued to infest top-heavy officer ranks already torn with intense jealousy and internecine feuds. At a time when running the elusive enemy to ground called for carefully co-ordinated operations, the army was disintegrating into a welter of feuding factions, and American advisers could not persuade Chiang to relieve incompetent generals who were friends in favor of competent leaders whom he did not trust. As early as spring of 1946, " . . . entire companies and battalions of provincial troops" had begun to defect to the Communists; in October an entire Nationalist division went over to the enemy. Morale plunged further when Nationalist armies cooped themselves in the cities for winter—what Chiang called "sitting the enemy to death," but what proved to be the death warrant of his own armies.[12]

Contrary to Kuomintang belief, attrition warfare suited the enemy, whose forces had grown remarkably strong in Manchuria, primarily the result of incessant political effort that exploited Nationalist weaknesses. In early 1947, Lin Piao assumed command of a new People's Liberation Army. In April, he began attacking small Nationalist garrisons throughout Manchuria; in May, his Fifth Offensive forced almost all Nationalist garrisons in Manchuria on the defensive. At month's end, the American consul general at Mukden reported that deteriorating Nationalist morale was a "matter of wide public knowledge and talk."[13] By autumn, Communists virtually controlled the area, with exception of isolated Nationalist garrisons in the big cities. Meanwhile, other Communist forces in northern China were striking at Chiang's lines of communication, primarily railways. The deteriorating situation had caused President Truman to send General Wedemeyer as his personal ambassador to make still another survey. The Wedemeyer Mission reached China in July 1947.

Wedemeyer did not like what he found, and he took the unusual step of saying so in an address the following month to Chiang Kai-shek, his ministers, and the State Council. Wedemeyer told his listeners in substance that owing to inefficiency and corruption at all civil and military levels, . . . the National Government could not defeat the Chinese Communists by force and could win the loyal, enthusiastic, and realistic support of the Chinese people only by improving the political and economic situation immediately.[14]

Wedemeyer privately advised Truman to end the fighting by United Nations intervention and work out some sort of international trustee arrangement in Manchuria—as he had recommended to Chiang in 1945. He also recommended " . . . a bold program of military and economic support, lasting at least five years . . . [and] contingent upon Chiang's promise to initiate sweeping political and social reforms."[15]

Scarcely had administration officials in Washington digested Wedemeyer's pessimism than a new crisis exploded in a government already shaken by Greek and European crises. In October 1947, *Life* magazine published a long and explosive article, "A Report to the American People on China," written by its special correspondent William C. Bullitt, former American ambassador to the Soviet Union. A one-time intimate of Roosevelt, he had been dropped from 1940 onward to the extent that in 1944 he became a major in the Free French army under De Gaulle. After the war, he unsuccessfully tried to reinsinuate himself into government. In 1947, the Republican Party and

461

Henry Luce found him a convenient device by which to break the presidential pre-election storm.

Bullitt followed a scare opening with a flattering account of Chiang's political acumen and a highly critical précis of Roosevelt's wartime diplomacy. Writing of the Yalta agreements, Bullitt thundered: " . . . No more unnecessary, disgraceful, and potentially disastrous document has ever been signed by a President of the U.S."; the clauses relating to Manchuria represented a plot by Stalin to gain eventual control not only of Manchuria but of all China. General Marshall's postwar success in gaining a cease-fire, Bullitt went on, played into Soviet hands by giving Chinese Communists time to replace Soviet forces in Manchuria. Truman's embargo on further arms shipments to Chiang " . . . resulted in disarming our friends while the Soviet Union was arming our enemies." Unless America took prompt action, Chiang would lose Manchuria and " . . . a course of events fatal to China would follow."

Bullitt wanted Truman to release vast quantities of non-essential arms and supply, including aircraft, to Chiang and also to grant credits of $450 million a year for a minimum of three years " . . . to break the vicious circle of Chinese inflation. . . . " He then recommended an eighteen-point reform program (which would have warmed Stilwell's heart). Bullitt ended his article with a "domino" prediction as frightening as it was inaccurate: " . . . If China falls into the hands of Stalin [!], all Asia, including Japan, sooner or later will fall into his hands. The manpower and resources of Asia will be mobilized against us. The independence of the U.S. will not live a generation longer than the independence of China."

Bullitt's suggestions for political, economic, and military reforms read sensibly enough, except that they were all old hat. Stilwell had started citing them in 1942, his words repeated and embroidered by Hurley, Wedemeyer, and Marshall, as well as a host of important visiting firemen. All had told Chiang that he must initiate sweeping political, social, and military reforms and had been ceremoniously promised that this would happen. But it never happened—and, in view of Chiang's severe limitations, possibly it never could have happened. President Truman, who has been severely criticized for inaction during this period, was being more realistic than his critics. American observers were reporting that lack of arms and supply was least of Chiang's problems. He was already receiving substantial financial aid—since Japan's surrender, he had received a good portion of what eventually would total two billion dollars, and this did not include another billion dollars' worth of arms.[16]

Although Truman refused to be stampeded, Chiang continued to demand increased aid; Republican voices such as Dewey's echoed

Chiang, and, in December, Congress rebuked the President by voting a specific $338-million appropriation for China as part of the European aid bill.[17] In a new year's address to his country, Chiang promised that the "Communist bandits" would be eliminated within a year. Neither money nor words provided the answer. Nothing short of dynamite could have blasted Nationalist armies from rotting to pieces in their city-islands. While Congress was voting dollars, Lin Piao, commanding an army of about 320,000, struck out in the "Seventh Offensive," designed to eliminate the few remaining connecting points between Nationalist-held cities. In northern China, Communist guerrilla units, though outnumbered three to one, " . . . found ample opportunity to cut communications, attack weak detachments, and otherwise punish isolated Nationalist forces."[18] Farther south, Communist guerrillas were well on their way to dominating railway lines essential to support of northern China and Manchuria garrisons.

Early in the new year, Lin Piao began the siege of Mukden. In March, Chiang's American military adviser, Major General David Barr, sensed disaster and recommended "progressive withdrawal" of Nationalist forces from Manchuria. Chiang refused to consider this, nor would he concentrate forces by evacuating the important northern garrisons into Mukden. Throughout spring and summer, Communists continued encircling tactics and Nationalist morale continued to deteriorate. In final battles that autumn, entire regiments and divisions laid down arms. Chinchow fell in mid-October, Changchun and Mukden soon after. By early November, Communists controlled all of Manchuria. Chiang had lost some thirty-three divisions—over 320,000 men. Eighty-five per cent of these units were equipped with the best American weapons: Rifles, machine guns, mortars, artillery, radios—all went to Lin Piao's guerrillas.[19]

Mao turned now to two tasks: the conquest of northern China and, simultaneously, a push into the Yangtze Valley. Each battle area favored his tactics. In the North, as in Manchuria, static Nationalist city garrisons lent themselves to isolation and attack. Farther south, Chiang insisted on defending along the railway line east and west of Hsuchow, itself defended by an enormous garrison that included Chiang's last major artillery and armor units.

Mao's commanders in the center and South had proved as adept as Lin Piao in applying standard Communist tactics. Beginning in late October, General Liu Po-ch'eng applied pressure to the western force while his columns snaked between army groups and garrisons to interdict communications between defenders as well as between the battle area and the Yangtze. Simultaneously, General Ch'en Yi's army struck the eastern defenders, the Seventh Army Group. By early November, the situation was so serious that General Barr recommended a fighting withdrawal of the Hsuchow garrison to the line of the Hwai. A few days later, Seventh Army Group surrendered to Ch'en Yi—"... almost 90,000 officers and men; 1,000 howitzers, cannon, and mortars; and vast stores of other weapons, ammunition, and assorted matériel."[20] Despite this disaster, the battle of Hwai-Hai, fought by Chiang's last real army and involving over a million troops, lasted sixty-five days before final Nationalist defeat, which cost Chiang sixty-six divisions surrendered or destroyed.

With Nationalist armies shattered and Communists in control of China north of the Yangtze, the end was clearly in sight. General Barr's final reports put one in mind of Kierkegaard's pessimistic thought: "... The individual cannot help his age, he can only express that it is doomed." Barr concluded that only massive U.S. aid would "... enable the Nationalist Government to maintain a foothold in southern China against a determined Communist advance. ... The complete defeat of the Nationalist army ... is inevitable."[21]

Washington correctly translated "massive U.S. aid" to mean direct intervention, which for a variety of reasons President Truman would not consider. Although remnant Nationalist forces held the line of the Yangtze during winter 1948–49, Chiang had almost run out of time. Mao's knowledge of the favorable political situation only added to the tidal crest of victory. In April 1949, when his call for unconditional surrender and the trial of Chiang Kai-shek as a war criminal went unanswered, he ordered Ch'en's and Liu's victorious armies to cross the Yangtze.

By autumn, resistance had virtually vanished. On the first day of October 1949, Mao proclaimed the People's Republic of China. In early December, Chiang and the remnants of government and army slipped away to Formosa.

A number of factors hindered healthy analysis of the China disaster. The emotional and psychological impact of Nationalist China's defeat reverberated throughout the West. Coming on the heels of Soviet explosion of an atomic bomb, in September 1949, it seemed to many good citizens to portend disaster. Convictions of Alger Hiss for perjury and of Klaus Fuchs for atomic espionage, early in 1950, added to general gloom.

Fear began to fill otherwise rational minds.

Instead of objective study of complex issues raised by the administration's White Paper on China, published in August 1949, influential portions of the American public turned to the deceptively simple but politically powerful thesis that a small group of diplomats and army officers was responsible for "the loss of China"—a thesis so successfully developed by that great American shame Senator Joseph McCarthy. Minds that refused fear, cooler and calmer minds, which under normal circumstances would have examined Chiang's defeat analytically, continued to be burdened with domestic and international crises that culminated in the outbreak of the Korean War in June 1950.

Thus it was that the fall of the House of Chiang produced a disastrous rubble of conflicting and generally erroneous conclusions in American political and military circles. Although a few observers bravely insisted on the ingenuity of Mao Tse-tung's revolutionary strategy and tactics, almost no one probed beneath the wreckage to discover precisely what had happened in Mao's camp.

And such was the impact of the crash, such the emotional outbursts and almost panic-stricken air, that only a superficial correlation emerged between the civil war in China and guerrilla actions being fought in Greece, Indonesia, the Philippines, Malaya—and French Indochina.

Failure to study each of these actions in its own right and to identify common and peculiar characteristics, simply added to the general ignorance that traditionally had surrounded guerrilla war.

CHAPTER THIRTY-SIX

1. Lohbeck, 372.
2. Ibid., 373–4. See also, Kennan, *Memoirs*, I.
3. Lohbeck, 382.
4. Truman, *Years of Trial and Hope*, 63–4.
5. Wedemeyer, 348.
6. Truman, *Years of Trial and Hope*, 65–6. See also, Acheson.
7. Leopold, 669.
8. J.A. Harrison, 189.
9. U.S. Department of State, *United States Relations with China . . .*, 211–12. Widespread optimism infested the Chinese military high command. Chiang's chief of staff publicly claimed that the Communists would be defeated in six months; Chiang told Ambassador Stuart that " . . . by the end of August or the beginning of September the Communist forces would either be annihilated or driven into the far hinterland."
10. Ibid.
11. J.A. Harrison, 191.
12. Griffith, *The Chinese People's Liberation Army*, 89.
13. U.S. Department of State, *United States Relations with China . . .*, 315.
14. Ibid., 257.
15. Leopold, 671.
16. Acheson, 147.
17. Leopold, 671.
18. Griffith, *The Chinese People's Liberation Army*, 97.
19. U.S. Department of State, *United States Relations with China . . .*, 325.
20. Griffith, *The Chinese People's Liberation Army*, 101–2.
21. U.S. Department of State, *United States Relations with China . . .*, 336.

PART THREE

HO...HO...HO CHI MINH

...Marx, Engels, Lenin and Stalin are the common teachers for the world revolution. Comrade Mao Tse-tung has skilfully "Sinicized" the ideology of Marx, Engels, Lenin, and Stalin, correctly applied it to the practical situation of China, and has led the Chinese Revolution to complete victory.

Owing to geographical, historical, economic, and cultural conditions, the Chinese Revolution exerted a great influence on the Vietnamese revolution, which had to learn and indeed has learned many experiences from it.

HO CHI MINH

CHAPTER 37

*A disrupted world • Soviet political aims • Western weaknesses •
Communist-inspired insurrections • The Cominform • American
reaction • Allied occupation of Vietnam • Conflict in the South •
The French take over • The Chinese in the North • Ho Chi Minh's
problems • His isolation • The French arrive in strength • Chinese
exit • The French solution • Viet Minh opposition • Guerrilla
warfare in the South • Trouble in the North • Outbreak of insurgency*

NO WAR IN HISTORY solved so much and yet so little as World
War II. No war so suddenly defeated ambitions of either victors or vanquished. No war opened such a Pandora's box, not to release
winds but, rather, hurricanes of political, social, and economic change,
which hurled existing structures into turmoil, confusion, and battle,
what Cyril Falls, a lifelong student of warfare, has aptly called *se-
quelae*—morbid conditions following upon disease.

In retrospect, the subsequent cold war between East and West is
not difficult to understand. In 1945, however, the West held not the
U.S.S.R. but Germany and Japan to be the real villains. Despite Stalin's
increasing dissemblance and duplicity, still slight enough in view of the
manifold problems on hand, at war's end sufficient of the Big Three
spirit survived to kindle Western hopes for a peace to be established
and maintained by the new world body, the United Nations, supported
alike by the Soviet Union and the United States.

Fundamental to these hopes was the conceit that Stalin would behave in the Western definition of a civilized manner—the legacy, in part,
of President Roosevelt but a legacy buttressed by American monopoly
of the atomic bomb. That heritage, temperament, and environment precluded such behavior, was generally overlooked. Voltaire once said,
" . . . When you speak with me, define your terms." Had Stalin and his
treaty makers been so pressed, American statesmen might have discovered a variance in contract law, including pertinent definitions, between

469

East and West. Unfortunately, American statesmen did not so press our stubborn ally. The shock, then, was almost as great as the conceit when, shortly after Axis defeat, the relationship between East and West began deteriorating.

The rot resulted primarily from two major Russian political aims. Stalin wanted to establish a protective insulation of Communist-controlled border areas and states stretching from Finland down the Baltic coast to Germany, then across Europe to the Balkans and east to China. Partly to help free his hand for this task (by keeping the West off balance), partly to pave the way for traditional Russian expansionist ambitions, and partly to exploit the appeal inherent in Marxist-Leninist political destinies, he also wanted to foment the spread of communism in various war-torn countries.

Stalin accomplished his first aim more easily than the second. Unburdened by conscience and in full control of his ravaged country's domestic and foreign policies, he skillfully utilized his own strength in exploiting Western weaknesses. Various allied conferences during the war had conceded Eastern Europe to the Soviet sphere of influence, and Stalin did not hesitate in using preponderant Soviet military presence to reap the harvest carefully sown by Communist guerrilla activity during the war.

A vigorous and unified West might have blunted Stalin's sword in immediate postwar years, but such did not exist. France, Italy, and Holland lay shattered, England exhausted, economically *in extremis,* none able to cope effectively with such severe problem areas as Indonesia and Palestine—areas the result of crumbling colonial empires, areas remote from Communist control yet frictionally convenient to Stalin's Communist cause. Neither President Truman nor other American leaders leaped to accept the challenge of international leadership being inexorably thrust on them, and certainly nothing in Harry Truman's career had prepared him to meet the complexities of the situation. Forced politically into hasty demobilization of the armed forces, the American President thenceforth bargained from the unusable strength of the atomic-bomb monopoly and from the awkward peace-making machinery of the United Nations. When neither served him well, when Stalin virtually ignored the unspoken threat of the atomic bomb to define borders, reparations, elections, and governments in terms foreign to Western understanding, Truman's growls, reluctant at first, lacked the teeth of either sufficient military presence or positive and determined policy, and he could find no effective voice in a temporarily strangled Europe.

Stalin's second goal, though more nebulous, complemented the first. To foment insurrection in various war-torn countries, the Soviet leader relied on local Communist guerrilla organizations. As we have seen, these included determined resistance fighters and those who scarcely fought at all. No matter the combat record, nearly all these indigenous forces ended the war with an effective and disciplined organization and with at least some arms and equipment—an insurrectionary capability strengthened both by chaotic and often anarchic local conditions and usually by carefully calculated and widely broadcast political appeals that subordinated Communist to nationalist aims.

Some readers will have forgotten the enormous threat posed by these forces in Europe alone. Not once, but several times, from 1946 to 1949, Communist movements threatened to capture the governments of France, Italy, and Austria. Their near success in Greece prompted the Truman Doctrine of March 1947, the first of a series of drastic political, economic, and military measures that announced American determination to halt Soviet-inspired aggression, and that led ultimately to NATO and a relatively stabilized Europe.

But this healthful accomplishment did not stop Stalin from hanging the final drapes of the Iron Curtain. Nor did it prevent his pursuing the second aim elsewhere. He resembled, in these years, a skillful improvisator playing a political pipe organ. In Europe, he gave all support possible to local parties, and eventually established a restricted Comintern, the Cominform, for the long-range support task. In Greece, he played a waiting game; not only did he refuse to support the insurrection materially, but he did not hesitate to back away when the odds dramatically turned against it. In Manchuria, he offered partial, almost reluctant support to Chinese Communists. He did not support, at least materially, Communist insurrections in the Philippines, Indonesia, and Malaya, and he was careful with support in Vietnam.

Stalin nonetheless profited enormously from these activities, not least because of their continued demands on Western, and particularly American, resources. The United States was not prepared to cope with subtleties of political warfare. For a long period, it reacted rather than acted, dashing here and there like a delirious fire department confronted by a dozen professional arsonists. Forced to retain strong military forces in Europe while simultaneously reducing overall military strength, it soon found itself overcommitted in trying to police the rest of the world. In time, this led to a serious weakening of so-called bastion areas such as Korea.

An important psychological element also entered. Desperately seeking friends to stem the Communist tide, the United States began to give military and economic aid to almost any declared anti-Communist government, some of which were decidedly reactionary if not totalitarian. Compounding this political anomaly, the U.S.A. was becoming increasingly tied to its European allies and, as one result, was slowly being forced to condone what amounted to colonial regimes in Southeast

Asia. Soviet Communists naturally made capital propaganda from this, but that was to be expected. Far more serious: liberal and influential thinkers around the world began to contrast American foreign policy with its traditionally expressed libertarian ideals. In the U.S.A. itself, a divisive political movement began that would grow to serious rupture and, as a by-product, furnish excellent propaganda for Communist use.

Had basic assumptions of American foreign policy been correct, this would have provided no more than a temporary embarrassment easily absorbed by a country beginning to learn the truth of Admiral Mahan's somewhat cynical dictum: " . . . Defeat cries aloud for explanation; whereas success, like charity, covers a multitude of sins."

But fundamental to American foreign policy was the assumption of a Kuomintang-ruled China. When Chiang Kai-shek's government fell in late 1949, American policy makers envisaged Southeast Asia as lying naked to the threat of Communist expansion. In seeking to clothe the area properly, the U. S. Government unfortunately chose only inferior materials from which to fashion a series of particularly ill-fitting and inappropriate suits.

Under terms of the Potsdam Conference as confirmed at Yalta, Britain and China shared responsibility for occupying Vietnam: British forces moving in south and Chinese forces north of the 16th parallel.

In the South, in Saigon, the British immediately collided with Tran Van Giau's hastily established Viet Minh regime, the Provisional Executive Committee of the South. Cunningly identifying with the allied cause, Giau's committee had assumed leadership of a tenuous local nationalist movement, but Giau already had partially alienated such important local groups as the Trotskyists and the two large and powerful religious sects, the Cao Dai and the Hoa Hao, an error repaired only in part by the time the first British troops arrived.[1]

Gaiu met total rebuff from the British commander, Major General Douglas Gracey. To insure control of the area, Gracey fleshed out his small force not only by rearming some five thousand former French prisoners of war, but by retaining the better part of seventy thousand Japanese soldiers under arms. Gracey answered civil disobedience by severe press censorship, martial law, and a strict curfew. In late September, he widely exceeded his directive by allowing the local French commander, Colonel Jean Cédile, to eject Tran Van Giau's government from Saigon and to replace the republic's flag, a gold star on a red field, with the old and loathed tricolor.

Tran Van Giau unwisely retaliated with mass terror methods, which resulted in large numbers of civil deaths, including those of some of his

472

nationalist opponents, and widened the breach both between indigenous power groups and between those groups and the occupying powers. In late September, shooting started in the city and spread to the country. Gracey managed to bring both sides to the conference table only to learn what he already knew: that the French had no intention of yielding to the Viet Minh demand for independence. The talks soon broke down in favor of renewed fighting. In mid-October, French reinforcements arrived to join British and Japanese troops in clearing Saigon and environs of Viet Minh guerrilla resistance.

By late December, about fifty thousand French troops, commanded by General Leclerc, occupied the South, a good part of them Free French units (including twelve thousand men of the Foreign Legion) from Europe. Well organized, trained, and equipped, many of them combat veterans, their artillery shone and their armor gleamed; their tanks and trucks covered the countryside as their fighters and bombers (along with Royal Air Force planes) filled the skies. Nearly everyone in Saigon agreed that the fast-moving combat columns would quickly pacify the countryside to extend French control throughout Indochina, just as in the old days. Leclerc himself spoke of " . . . a simple 'mopping-up operation' which would take no more than four weeks." The British, beset with empire commitments, left at year's end.[2]

Developments in the North meanwhile moved at a slower tempo. Chiang Kai-shek and the Kuomintang had no intention of rejecting Ho's government in Hanoi as long as the Viet Minh did not interfere with the eating, raping, and looting habits of 180,000 Chinese soldiers worming their way down from Yünnan.[3] Chiang not only recognized Ho's *de facto* government, but his local commander refused to arm the thirty-five hundred French troops in Hanoi, leaving the policing and administration to the Viet Minh authorities.[4]

This was calculated policy on Chiang's part. China had suffered long decades of humiliation by the West, and the French, along with other Western powers, repeatedly had exacted profitable concessions at what amounted to gun point. Although Chiang knew that his presence in Vietnam was only temporary, he intended that the French would pay heavily for his departure (which is what happened). Meanwhile, he happily let the Viet Minh suffer the day's problems.

The Viet Minh faced plenty of problems. The Japanese surrender had left the north country in abysmal condition. Insatiable Japanese demands on the rice crop already had brought numerous deaths from starvation—locals said nearly 2 million deaths the previous year. Widespread floods of the Red River, followed by severe drought, had ruined most of the current rice crop in Tonkin, and the bulk of what survived went to the voracious Chinese. Hundreds of thousands of people were starving; disease swept the land; the 1945–46 death toll would reach perhaps a million; millions more suffered helplessly, and the country looked to the Viet Minh for relief.

The new government not only abolished the opium, alcohol, and salt monopolies but also the head tax, besides eliminating or drastically reducing land taxes and interest on loans. As one result, the new government was broke. It was also decidedly factional, its Communist element a minority that survived mainly because of Ho's charisma, his appeal to non-aligned nationalists, and the disciplined organization of the Communist Party, as opposed to ineffectual leadership, organization, and traditional enmities of varied nationalist elements. Where possible, the Viet Minh brought these elements into its organization, one of the main instruments in the process being selective "physical extermination."

The new government without question appealed to large numbers of peasants, not alone because of tax reforms but also because of a crash program against illiteracy which produced greater results in one year than the French had been able, or rather had cared, to produce in more than sixty years.[5] The government similarly mobilized the people to attack flood and famine. Nonetheless, by the end of 1945 rival parties controlled important provinces bordering the Chinese frontier, while elsewhere peasants found themselves subject to Viet Minh-imposed "voluntary" contributions and "public" subscriptions which " . . . turned out to be at least as heavy as the tax load imposed by the colonial regime."[6]

Outside Vietnam, the Viet Minh government had almost no friends and a great many enemies. Contrary to what many persons in the West have assumed, the Kremlin at this time showed as much interest in helping Ho Chi Minh as it did the Republican Party in the United States. Nor could Mao Tse-tung, isolated in China's northwestern provinces, come to Ho's relief. French Communists and Socialists paid grudging lip service to the movement, but offered no material support. Ironically, Ho's greatest support came from the American command in Kunming, which refused to help De Gaulle's able representative, Major Jean Sainteny, in a grotesque attempt to replant the French flag in Hanoi, and from the small American military command that accompanied Chinese troops to Hanoi and continued OSS policy of supplying arms and equipment to the Viet Minh, a policy approved by Washington. But this honeymoon would be short-lived. The French returned to Saigon with at least tacit approval of Washington, and Ho could not have been pleased when Washington announced the sale of $160 million worth of surplus arms and equipment to the French Government.[7]

A very lonely Ho was also Communist Ho was therefore realist Ho. Having taken two steps forward, he took one step backward. In November, he dissolved the Indochina Communist Party, thus emphasizing the Viet Minh's nationalist character. He also began sending diplomatic flowers to the new French high commissioner, Admiral Thierry d'Argenlieu, a personal friend of De Gaulle—a part-time Carmelite monk who was so reactionary that a member of his staff described him as having " . . . the most brilliant mind of the twelfth century."[8] Ensuing negotiations can best be described as imperative diplomacy: Each side loathed the other, yet the state of confusion demanded some solution.

The Chinese presence posed the first problem. D'Argenlieu and his new deputy, Major Sainteny, rid Vietnam of the Chinese incubus by renouncing French "special rights" in China as well as giving Chiang special railway and port rights in Tonkin. With China out of the way, Sainteny hammered out an agreement with Ho Chi Minh, signed in March 1946. Wanting to split Vietnam, France recognized the Democratic Republic of Vietnam (DRV) as " . . . a free state, having its own government, parliament, army, and treasury, belonging to the Indo-Chinese Federation and to the French Union."[9] In return, Ho allowed fifteen thousand French troops to replace the Chinese garrison. The French were to train and equip the Viet Minh army, which would replace French occupation troops at a rate of three thousand per year for five years. French negotiators also agreed to hold a referendum to determine whether Cochin China " . . . should be reunified with Annam and Tonkin."[10] In mid-March, the first French troops arrived in Hanoi to commence what might have proved a workable solution to the Vietnam problem.

But a viable contract depends a great deal on the spirit of contracting parties. D'Argenlieu, who had been in Paris during the negotiations, openly criticized Sainteny and Leclerc's moderate policy, expressing amazement "that France has such a fine expeditionary corps in Indochina and yet its leaders prefer to negotiate rather than to fight."[11]

Ho Chi Minh also had difficulty in persuading what he called "extremists" to accept the arrangement, which, he argued, was a necessary step toward full independence. As a realist willing to compromise, Ho regarded the accords as an interim agreement, a temporary truce to be broken when he was strong enough to enforce a demand for unity and independence of all Vietnam. But Ho faced serious party opposition: Bellicose voices demanded immediate action, just as, in the South, D'Argenlieu was demanding French control of Indochina.

D'Argenlieu was already feeling quite secure in Saigon. In late February 1946, General Leclerc proclaimed " . . . the total reestablishment of peace and order" throughout Cochin China and southern Annam,[12] without adding that by early March French losses amounted to twelve hundred killed and thirty-five hundred wounded.[13] If Leclerc exaggerated, he could at least point to French columns busily "pacifying" the countryside and to a force pushing into Laos. Saigon also had quieted: Although metal grill cages protected the better outdoor restaurants from grenade-throwing terrorists—the American correspondent Robert Shaplen noted that, in mid-1946, murders averaged fifteen per night!—the Viet Minh seemed increasingly subdued, the colony well on its way to prewar languor.

Scarcely had Ho and other Viet Minh political leaders, Communist and nationalist, sailed for France to work out a final agreement with the home government, when D'Argenlieu, under pressure from conservative colonialists and without authority from Paris, recognized the free state of Cochin China and its puppet president, and also ordered the army to occupy the Moi Plateaux, in the southern Annam central highlands, a provocative act that drew immediate protests from Hanoi. D'Argenlieu's unilateral act contradicted the earlier agreement with the Viet Minh and helped torpedo the Paris talks. Since France had neither a government nor a constitution at this time, these probably would not have resulted in meaningful agreement on basic issues, but they could have laid the groundwork for a later treaty.

D'Argenlieu's action, which he compounded in August by calling a federation conference without inviting the Viet Minh, led to a more serious result. Ho's control of the Viet Minh was by no means assured at this time. The Hanoi government, in some respects, resembled more a coalition than a single-party Communist government, a fact acknowledged by Ho when, at the end of May, he created the Communist-dominated Lien Viet Front. This did not fool major nationalist parties which continued to control important northern provinces and to call for direct action against the French with such vigor that French forces temporarily allied with Viet Minh forces to reclaim control of the Tonkin provinces and to chase dissident leaders into exile in China. In Ho's absence, extremist Viet Minh leaders, particularly the Minister of Interior, Vo Nguyen Giap, opened war on other, non-Communist nationalists and on pro-French Vietnamese. The net result was a greatly strengthened and unified Viet Minh—the core of the larger Lien Viet, or Popular National, Front.[14]

Annoyed by French duplicity and possibly to dampen further criticism from Communist extremists, Ho became increasingly antagonistic in negotiations with the French. Although, according to Jean Sainteny and other observers, he seemed genuinely upset by continuing failure of negotiations, he nonetheless remained a hard-core revolutionary who, together with thirty of his comrades, had shared two hundred and twenty-two years of imprisonment and exile. "If we have to fight, we will fight," Ho realistically observed to Sainteny. "You will kill ten of our men and we will kill one of yours, and in the end it will be you who will tire of it."[15] Shooting incidents already had occurred when

Ho was in France; upon his return they began to multiply.

The French were consistently underreading the southern situation. Despite D'Argenlieu's and Leclerc's early optimism, a nasty guerrilla war continued. If the French controlled towns, Viet Minh-controlled villages and countryside, particularly at night. A writer and historian who accompanied Leclerc's early expeditions, Philippe Devillers, pinpointed the main tactical result:

> ...If we departed, believing a region pacified, they [Viet Minh guerrillas] would arrive on our heels and the terror would start again. There was only one possible defense: to multiply the posts, to fortify them, to arm the villagers, and to train them for a co-ordinated and enlightened self-defense through a thorough job of information and policing. But this required men and weapons. What was needed was not the 35,000 men (of which Leclerc then disposed) but 100,000, and Cochin-China was not the only problem.[16]

Far more than additional troops were needed: Leclerc and his successors in time fielded an expeditionary corps exceeding 150,000 men. The great lack was a political policy to give the Vietnamese people reason to accept the Saigon government and deny Hanoi's attempt to establish a Communist regime.

Leclerc and his successor, Étienne Valluy, were fighting against an extremely capable guerrilla leader, Nguyen Binh, who knew how to exploit French political weaknesses. A master of ambush, Nguyen Binh soon had his frustrated enemy indulging in mass terror methods such as "... the burning of villages from which guerrillas had fired and disappeared" and torture of suspects, "often as not ... innocent people, frequently delivered into French hands by false denunciations." Such acts "... turned thousands of lukewarm nationalists and even people loyal to the French into their bitter enemies ... the French methods of fighting the guerrillas made many more Vietminh fighters than they were able to kill."[17]

Meanwhile, the breach between North and South widened. Just when either side decided to seek a military solution to the impasse is problematical. Such was the rampant mistrust and hatred that a war probably was never far removed from either French or Vietnamese minds. That momentous autumn saw military forces of both sides acting with an unhealthy arrogance that heightened tension everywhere. The explosion did not instantly occur. It began with a skirmish between French soldiers and Viet Minh militia in Haiphong. It continued with stupid and isolated attacks by the Viet Minh that killed twenty-three French soldiers in Haiphong and six more in Lang Son. To teach the

FR. INDOCHINA
1945–1954

- Towns and Cities
— Roads
+++ Railways

miles
0   100   200

Viet Minh a "hard lesson," French raids in Haiphong sent a civilian mob streaming from the town toward the French air base at Cat Bi. The captain of a French cruiser, mistakenly believing that the mob intended to attack the air base, opened fire and killed some six thousand unarmed civilians.

Although the tragedy brought an uneasy truce, Ho, prompted by Giap and other militants, not to mention the belligerent French attitude, decided that the time had come for war. Faced with a French demand to surrender its forces in Hanoi, on December 19 the Viet Minh attacked French garrisons in Hanoi and elsewhere in Vietnam. The Indochina war had begun.

CHAPTER THIRTY-SEVEN

1. Kahin and Lewis, 19.
2. Hammer, *The Struggle for Indochina* . . . , 120.
3. Kahin and Lewis, 24.
4. Isaacs.
5. Buttinger, I, 347–9. See also, Lancaster.
6. Hammer, *The Struggle for Indochina* . . . , 142.
7. Shaplen, *The Lost Revolution*, 6.
8. Fall, *The Two Viet-Nams* . . . , 72.
9. Lancaster, 147.
10. Kahin and Lewis, 26. See also, Lancaster; Buttinger.
11. Buttinger, I, 370–1.
12. Lancaster, 136.
13. Hammer, *The Struggle for Indochina* . . . , 156.
14. Lancaster, 166 ff. See also, Hammer, "Genesis of the First Indochina War: 1946–1950."
15. Shaplen, *The Lost Revolution*, 48.
16. Buttinger, I, 337.
17. Ibid. Nguyen Binh was killed in Cambodia in 1951.

CHAPTER 38

IN DECEMBER 1946, the Viet Minh army numbered about sixty thousand, of whom forty thousand possessed rifles.[1] Paramilitary and militia formations, such as the youth-oriented Tu Ve, numbered perhaps another forty thousand. Although this force had received some training from Japanese and Chinese instructors, it was not an orthodox army capable of launching and sustaining co-ordinated offensives against units equipped with artillery and armor and supported by aircraft. Within a few weeks, French units had beaten off the various attacks and forced Viet Minh units to disperse. Ho and the main body almost immediately went into hiding in their old stamping grounds, the ideally defensive Viet Bac region, in upper Tonkin.

General Valluy and his staff sought to clarify the situation in the best colonial tradition.[2] This meant occupying and defending important cities and towns and protecting lines of communication by a series of strong points. Local commanders began the arduous task of dividing assigned areas into small operational squares (the *quadrillage*) and trying to clear each of insurgents (the *ratissage*). To do this, unit commanders were to establish small operational bases in the disputed areas and commence *tourbillon,* or whirlwind-type, tactics essential to what Colonel John McCuen has called "the territorial offense": " . . . that is, the detachments should keep constantly on the move within their assigned zones, attacking, ambushing, patrolling, searching, establishing an intelligence system and, perhaps most important, contacting and assisting the people. . . . "[3] This was basically Marshal Lyautey's famous *tache-d'huile,* or oil-spot, technique. Civil forces followed the military to clean out the insurgent apparatus and establish or re-establish civil government. Once military and civil forces had fashioned a secure strategic base, the military again moved out to repeat the process.

As we have pointed out (Chapter 13), the tache d'huile is essentially a qualitative approach to the pacification problem. It was necessitated by limited forces operating in vast areas inhabited and defended by heterogeneous tribes. Not least of the reasons for its success were the social, political, and economic attractions offered by the pacified areas to primitive and insurgent tribesmen. In this sense, the tache d'huile was expansion by osmosis. It did not always work, but most of the time it did. At all times, it called for extreme patience and forbearance on the part of colonizers. On occasion, strong and homogeneous tribes occupying naturally defensive terrain spelled a halt to the tache-d'huile process. Lyautey generally preferred to leave these "asleep" areas alone. If an enemy became too annoying and if his own strength justified it, he permitted raids in strength—the traditional *bouclage,* or "sealing-off," operation, which attempted to surround and destroy the enemy force. But he infinitely preferred to convert neighboring areas to his support so as to isolate the difficult areas, which then " . . . will fall into our hands by themselves. . . . "

In 1946 and 1947, General Valluy, from a purely military standpoint, was on the right track in his use of the tache-d'huile technique, but he underrated both political and military strength of the Viet Minh. Prompted by the colonial government and *colons,* he tried to do too much too soon. Neither military forces nor civil administration that followed won control of target areas. Instead, the French flag flew over main cities and towns, and roads remained open at least in daylight— but Viet Minh guerrillas continued to control the countryside. Valluy would have had his hands full in consolidating a strategic base in Cochin China alone. Yet Valluy not only attempted to develop strategic bases in Cochin China, Annam, and Tonkin, but, in the fall of 1947, he decided on an all-out attack—the *bouclage*—against Ho and the main body of insurgents holed up northwest of Hanoi.

Operation Léa began in October. Involving fifteen thousand troops, or over a third of the total French force, it attempted to seal off an immense triangle of jungle and mountains in Tonkin. French commanders spoke excitedly of "encirclement"—just as German commanders had spoken in the Soviet Union and Yugoslavia in World War II. Operation Léa fared no better than any of the German offensives designed to capture Tito: close, but no cigar. Although the French claimed eight thousand enemy dead and the capture of thousands of arms and tons of ammunition and equipment, the effort failed to capture Ho and his lieutenants or even to disperse for very long the Viet Minh com-

481

mand. By year's end, the French main force had returned to the low-lands, having established a string of vulnerable border outposts and forts more appropriate to Gallieni's 1884–85 strategy against insurgents and pirates than to a 1947 campaign against Viet Minh guerrillas.

This combination of area pacification and sporadic attacks continued throughout 1948 and into 1949. Without a political impetus, it was doomed to fail. The French answer to the political problem—the dusting off of Emperor Bao Dai—would have become a meaningful weapon only if Paris had been serious about granting Vietnam independence and only if Bao Dai's followers had been capable of legitimate government. In May 1949, a worried French Government sent out General Revers, Chief of the General Staff, who in a secret report called for evacuation of the newly established garrisons in the North, and a rapid build-up of the Vietnamese army in order to buttress French diplomacy which "must have precedence over military considerations."[4]

French civil and military officials failed to understand new and revolutionary political forces at work. The average Vietnamese peasant did not care about communism. He wanted *doc-lap*—a national independence—which he supposed would bring him and his family a better life (it could not bring a worse one). Japanese conquest and occupation of Southeast Asia had shattered the myth of white supremacy. The peasant may have known little about political forms and parties or even what the future was to hold under Vietnamese rule—but he wanted that rule, or, rather, he wanted an end to French rule.

French authorities would have none of it. In 1948, the French rejected a proposal by the nationalist Ngo Dinh Diem for dominion status of the country. Instead, a Provisional Central Government of Vietnam emerged along with the concept of " . . . associated statehood within the French Union for each of the three states of Indo-China."[5] By the time Bao Dai agreed to lead a Vietnamese Government—June 1949—most important nationalist leaders either had gone into exile or joined Ho's camp in the North; others, such as Diem, who headed the powerful Catholic League, refused to serve on grounds that France had no intention of ever granting Vietnamese independence. On the other hand, whole hosts of nationalists, the *attentistes,* were sitting on the fence, refusing to commit themselves until one government or the other showed itself the probable victor.

America's role in the stand-off was scarcely in keeping with its libertarian ideals. President Roosevelt held positive feelings about the future of Indochina, but after his death and Japan's surrender nothing stood in the way of the French return, which was scarcely surprising within the day's political context. The sad truth was the minimal importance of an artificial political entity called French Indochina (Laos, Cambodia, and Vietnam) in world affairs. Geographically, economically, and politically, the area was a cipher. This unpleasant fact had been somewhat camouflaged by Japan's initial use of the country as a staging area—a strategic convenience in the days of short-range aircraft, but even then not a strategic necessity. Tactically and strategically, Indochina was less than a sideshow; it was a military neutrino—a whirling nothing. American interest in the area was as negative as American knowledge of the area. When General George C. Marshall was in Chungking in 1946, he spent an evening with a group of young Vietnamese nationalists and at one point remarked, " . . . Viet-Nam must be a very interesting country. Tell me, do you have your own language?"[6]

In the hurly-burly of events accompanying the end of the war, Indochina grew from a nothing area to a nuisance area, a threat to allied and particularly American-French relationships. Truman apparently did not share Roosevelt's desire to exclude France from the area. In a meeting with De Gaulle in August 1945, he decorated the French leader, presented him with a new DC-4 airplane, and emphasized that " . . . my government offers no opposition to the return of the French Army and French authority in Indochina."[7] By seeming to support a renewed French presence, the American President found himself dangerously at odds with his purported belief in the principles of the Atlantic Charter. Here was a real dilemma—the frequent result when political idealism collides with political reality. Dexterous diplomacy probably could have resolved it, but unfortunately a number of factors inhibited the practice of dexterous diplomacy in this crucial period.

The first was turbulence within the Department of State itself, an orchestra of feuds and cabals cacophonously conducted first by old Cordell Hull, then by globe-trotting James Byrnes. Small at war's beginning and limited in imaginative policy by the isolation years, the department had swelled inexorably and often with as much purpose as a blowfish out of water. Concurrently, the American military had frequently preempted the State Department's traditional authority in the conduct of foreign affairs—an ugly habit continued into postwar years. Postwar confusion, which often gave rise to divided counsels, helped prevent the department from reasserting its authority, a state of affairs well described in two important books, George Kennan's *Memoirs* and Dean Acheson's *Present at the Creation*. Finally, heavy demands on existing talent, both individual and organizational, meant stringent rationing, which resulted in slim diplomatic pickings for Indochina as well as for many other areas.

International turbulence played a major role. From the moment President Truman assumed office, in spring of 1945, he faced far more urgent challenges that, shortly after war's end, began turning to crises. As these grew in importance and complexity, Vietnam remained a low-priority area. By the time Ho Chi Minh attacked French garrisons, in December 1946, Stalin already had made clear his intentions to go about as far as he could in Europe and the Middle East. Here the United States and the West attempted to stop him. The Truman Doctrine, announced in March 1947, flashed the first red light. George Kennan's realistic statement of need for new principles of selected containment—the famous X article published in the July 1947 *Foreign Affairs*—called for the political containment of Soviet power: " . . . a long-term, patient but firm and vigilant containment of Russian expansive tendencies."[8] Although Kennan was thinking primarily in political terms, the principles when applied necessarily involved military action, and, during the next three years, the deterrents differed considerably: the Truman Doctrine, the Marshall Plan, the Berlin airlift, the North Atlantic Treaty Organization. Crumbs from this table, both of effort and of money, fell to the other side of the world, to China and the Philippines and Indochina; although they sometimes were big crumbs, relatively speaking they were still crumbs.

These two factors helped to explain a third: the Franco-American relationship in Indochina itself. No question existed in the mind of the French Government—when there was one—as to the legality of the French presence. Although De Gaulle had attempted to appease Roosevelt on the subject of eventual self-government for Indochina, his confreres would not hear of compromise. France was the legal government in Indochina, and it was in no mind to yield its hold in order to conform to the quaint American notion of self-determination and eventual independence. France would continue to rule the area as a colony, a policy opposed to that of "assimilation," which ultimately could have yielded Vietnamese independence.[9]

Nor did the United States see fit to force the issue. Ally by tradition, America had felt a genuine sympathy for France's defeat in World War II and for the horrors of German occupation and loathsome Vichy government. The U.S.A. also realized that the French return to Indochina was in part a matter of *amour propre* and that to have contested it would have led to an ugly quarrel with a power whose co-operation was essential to a stable Europe.* Moreover, the French seemed to be working out a viable federation agreement with the Viet Minh. By the time this effort failed and shooting started in earnest, the international situation had changed to such a degree that the French presence, far from proving embarrassing, was beginning to appeal to a United States

---

* Unfortunately, overburdened and, in some cases, frightened American policy makers failed to realize that France needed American aid more than the United States needed French co-operation. France would not have jeopardized her own future position in Europe for the sake of her Indochina holding, particularly since popular French sentiment did not support a costly colonial policy.

hard-pressed to provide economic and particularly military resources necessary to fight a world-wide cold war.

Later critics have suggested that French, and by implication American, diplomacy erred in not attempting to convert Ho Chi Minh into an Asiatic Tito. Several conditions would have had to exist for even a trial run. The first was an imaginative French high commissioner working with a viable home government within the framework of a liberal colonial policy. France possessed none of these. That the idea did not occur to American officials is not surprising. In Western eyes, this was the day of monolithic communism, this the day when some outstanding intellects, driven by fatigue and fear into near panic, envisaged communism as a poisonous black cloud of no molecular structure quite capable of covering the sun of civilization. Although Tito's defection and subsequent expulsion from Cominform, in June 1948, suggested a cloud of factious elements, the worsening China situation tended to obscure this significant development. In 1948, the West was too far gone in worry for immediate reappraisal that could have led to a qualitative rather than quantitative policy in combating the threat by exploiting its essential weakness.

Pride also entered: the French had lost one war before it really started; they were not going to lose another, and certainly not to a bunch of peasants some of whom were not even armed. Fear formed still another factor. If Vietnam gained independence, "the already-restive nationalists in Algeria, Morocco, and Tunisia would be inspired to follow their example."[10] Finally, and very important: In these formative and crucial years, the French army believed, as did American observers, that it was well on the way to defeating the Viet Minh. In May 1947, the French Minister of War, M. Paul Coste-Floret, concluded: " . . . There is no military problem any longer in Indo-China. The success of French arms is complete."[11] Even after the failure of Operation Léa, in late 1947, and increasing evidence that the Viet Minh controlled a large part of the countryside, the French administration in Indochina and particularly the French military command (with some worthy exceptions) refused to reverse Coste-Floret's comforting conclusion. Perhaps French commanders would have admitted some concern had the Viet Minh fielded its own army. Lacking direct confrontation, Valluy and his successors spoke in terms of "mopping-up" operations. They failed to realize either that the Viet Minh were building a regular army behind a screen of guerrilla operations, or that the Viet Minh were simultaneously mobilizing large parts of the population to fight a war beyond limits of their comprehension.

Continuing military stalemate and some setbacks in 1948 prompted President Vincent Auriol's government in Paris to re-examine the political question. Coupled with the deteriorating position of the Nationalist

Chinese, this led to the Élysée Agreements, of March 1949, which formally created the Bao Dai government and made Vietnam an "associated state," along with Cambodia and Laos, in the French Union. The agreements also authorized for Vietnam " . . . its own army for internal security," a role " . . . in foreign and defense policies, and a [national] bank of issue."[12]

Had France been sincere, the agreements might have led to satisfactory political compromise with the Viet Minh. Unfortunately France relinquished precious little control over Vietnamese affairs with the agreements, which the National Assembly did not even ratify until February 1950. The net result of deed versus intent was a political sugar castle bound to deteriorate in fortune's rain:

> The only conclusion Vietnamese patriots could reach was that France, with Bao Dai as its agent, continued to run that part of the country not under the Vietminh. The effective range of political alternatives for these patriots remained quite as narrow as before— the Vietminh or the French—and this polarization grew more pronounced as the French now regularly labeled all those who resisted them or opposed Bao Dai as "communist." For more and more Vietnamese that word came to connote something good—a badge of honor, representing patriotic nationalism and courageous opposition to French rule. Thus did French intransigence in Vietnam further strengthen the ties between nationalism and communism there—a circumstance unique in southeast Asia.[13]

The Élysée Agreements also provoked international moves that widened the breach between East and West to make a political settlement even more remote. During negotiations, the Soviet Union and Communist China recognized Ho Chi Minh's DRV. A week after signing, Britain, the United States, and twenty-eight other governments recognized the three Associated States, but whereas Britain urged France to give greater independence to the new countries, the United States adopted a much more moderate attitude. Privately, the Department of State feared a Viet Minh victory, as Secretary of State Acheson later wrote, " . . . unless France swiftly transferred authority to the Associated States and organized, trained, and equipped, with our aid, substantial indigenous forces to take over the main burden of the fight." Acheson later explained his dilemma:

> . . . Both during this period and after it our conduct was criticized as being a muddled hodgepodge, directed neither toward edging the French out of an effort to re-establish their colonial role, which was beyond their power, nor helping them hard enough to accomplish it or, even better, to defeat Ho and gracefully withdraw. The

description is accurate enough. The criticism, however, fails to recognize the limits on the extent to which one may successfully coerce an ally. Withholding help and exhorting the ally or its opponent can be effective only when the ally can do nothing without help, as was the case in Indonesia. Furthermore, the result of withholding help to France would, at most, have removed the colonial power. It could not have made the resulting situation a beneficial one either for Indochina or for southeast Asia, or in the more important effort of furthering the stability and defense of Europe. So while we may have tried to muddle through and were certainly not successful, I could not think then or later of a better course. . . . [14]

The principal difficulty had appeared earlier: the conflict between American policy in Europe and the situation in Indochina. In January 1949, Walter Lippmann had astutely spelled it out in the New York *Herald Tribune*:

> . . . Our friends in Western Europe should try to understand why we cannot and must not be maneuvered, why we dare not drift, into general opposition to the independence movements in Asia. They should tell their propagandists to stop smearing these movements. They should try to realize how disastrous it would be to them, and to the cause of Western civilization, if ever it could be said that the Western Union for the defense of freedom in Europe was in Asia a syndicate for the preservation of decadent empires.[15]

Unfortunately, the Western Union was leaning toward precisely that. The North Atlantic Treaty, signed in April 1949, made France the most important member of new Europe. The Truman administration believed that the treaty, if it was to serve Western, including American, strategic interests, had to expand into some kind of political-military organization, a growth dependent in part on French co-operation.

Other events were adding to the importance of the Western alliance. Fighting continued in Greece; in 1948, Communist rebels had tripped off emergencies in nearby Malaya, Burma, and Indonesia; the Hukbalahap insurgency in the Philippines was gaining ground. In 1949, Ho Chi Minh put the DRV squarely in the world Communist movement, removing any moderate government officials and replacing them with hard-line Communists. In September of that year, explosion of an atomic weapon by the Soviets ended the security engendered by American monopoly of the weapon. Fears raised by this development gained fantasies from Chiang Kai-shek's fall and subsequent flight to Formosa.

As one result, the French effort in Indochina changed form still further in American administration minds. No longer did it seem such an embarrassing little colonial war. In late 1949 and early 1950, the

United States, encouraged by France, began to paint the war in ideological colors: it started to become part of the free world's effort against communism. The U.S.A. now promised limited military and economic aid. Although she insisted on supplying economic aid directly to the three states—Vietnam, Laos, and Cambodia—she perforce supplied military aid to the French overseers, Vietnam not having an army worthy of the name. The outbreak of the Korean war, in June 1950, hastened the process of the American Government's conversion. In June 1950, President Truman informed a group of legislators that he had " . . . directed acceleration in the furnishing of military assistance to the forces of France and the Associated States in Indo-China and the dispatch of a military mission to provide close working relations with those forces."[16]

The United States was now hooked to help France fight a war the exact nature of which neither country had yet identified.

CHAPTER THIRTY-EIGHT

1. Tanham, *Communist Revolutionary Warfare* . . . , 9.
2. Hammer, *The Struggle for Indochina* . . . , 193. General Leclerc, who left Indochina in spring of 1946 and returned later that year as an official observer, warned his government against trying to seek a military solution to what he believed had become essentially a political problem.
3. McCuen, 207.
4. Buttinger, II, 748: " . . . His [Revers'] recommendations shared the fate of most later ones—being misunderstood or disregarded. In any case, they had no influence on either the military or political conduct of the war."
5. Hammer, *The Struggle for Indochina* . . . , 213.
6. Author's personal files.
7. De Gaulle, *The War Memoirs of* . . . , III, 242.
8. "X" (George F. Kennan), "The Sources of Soviet Conduct." This penetrating article was variously interpreted, as the author makes clear in his *Memoirs*. See also, Lippmann; Leopold.
9. Duncanson, *Government and Revolution in Vietnam*, 86–7. See also, De Gaulle, *The War Memoirs of* . . . , III (Documents), for the complete French declaration made at the March 1945 conference.
10. Kahin and Lewis, 27–8. See also, Buttinger, II, 683: General Leclerc refused the post of commander in chief and high commissioner primarily because he considered the task to be political but—shades of William Tecumseh Sherman (see Chapter 9)—also because the government would not give him 500,000 troops to fight the Vietnam war.
11. Shaplen, 58.
12. Acheson, 671. See also, Buttinger; Lancaster.
13. Kahin and Lewis, 29–30.
14. Acheson, 672–3.
15. Kahin, 404–5.
16. Truman, *Years of Trial and Hope*, 339.

CHAPTER 39

Change in Viet Minh tactics • *Vo Nguyen Giap* • *Mao Tse-tung's influence* • *Communist tactics in the South* • *Viet Minh military organization* • *The political base* • *Special Viet Minh units* • *Guerrilla tactics* • *French countertactics* • *Terror tactics* • *Enter Communist China* • *Viet Minh expansion*

Ho CHI MINH and his military leader Vo Nguyen Giap had seriously erred by attacking French garrisons in December 1946. Forced into precipitate retreat, they narrowly avoided capture in 1947. This was the perigee of their fortunes, and they owed much of their salvation to a realistic appreciation and acceptance of their peculiar situation. In their simple mountain hide-out northwest of Hanoi, they vaguely resembled Mao and his lieutenants hiding in the Ching-kang Mountains in 1927. And like Mao and his lieutenants, they spent the time in considerable soul-searching, which brought a conversion to Mao-style warfare—partly through the influence of the party's secretary-general, Truong Chinh, who in 1947 published a Vietnamese version of Mao's theory of protracted warfare, *The Resistance Will Win*.[1] To what extent Ho Chi Minh favored this and to what extent his hand was forced by more militant Communists, Giap included, has never been satisfactorily determined by Western observers.

Vo Nguyen Giap took the lead in military thinking at this time. Giap was thirty-five years old, a socialist turned Communist, veteran of French jails, history teacher turned soldier. In 1950, he published a book, *La guerre de la libération et l'armée populaire*, which eventually appeared as *People's War, People's Army*.[2]

Admitting to the 1946 errors, Giap argued in favor of a three-phase, Mao-style war. The first phase called for a strategic defense, a passive resistance to wear the enemy down while both regular and irregular Viet Minh units reorganized and built up strength. Giap wrote that this phase ended in 1947 in favor of the second phase, active resistance and

489

preparation for the counteroffensive by extensive guerrilla attacks as well as a continued propaganda-subversion effort. The final phase, Giap wrote, would consist of a general counteroffensive designed to defeat the French army. Timing did not much matter. The war in the South proceeded at a slower pace and in a different fashion from that up North, and even in the North the final phase of what Mao Tse-tung called "mobile," or orthodox, warfare was to be carried out with massive injections of guerrilla tactics.

Tran Van Giau's Committee of the South was waging guerrilla warfare by late 1945. Although Communist-inspired, this was frequently a nationalist effort and Ho Chi Minh rightly recognized the necessity of harnessing it to the Communist effort, not alienating it as Tran Van Giau was doing. Ho instead concentrated on building a political-military organization throughout Vietnam with offshoots, in due course, in Cambodia and Laos. Although this was the main work of the formative years, it was not a phased effort but, rather, organic and continuing. It resulted in an organization of which some understanding is necessary if the reader is to appreciate fully the subsequent fighting and final French defeat, not to mention subsequent American political and military failures.

Basically, the Viet Minh depended on an organization similar to that forged by Chinese Communists, but one that, because of what Ho called " . . . geographic, historical, economic, and cultural conditions," differed in growth and activity.[3] The military machine consisted of three groups: regular army, regional forces, and popular troops. The Viet Minh recruited, organized, and trained regional and popular forces on a territorial basis. The high command divided the country into six interzones, each containing zones, provinces, districts, intervillages, and villages. Where possible, zones, provinces, and districts each raised and maintained provincial forces, while intervillages and villages raised and maintained popular forces. Impetus, however, stemmed from bottom upward, and this is the essential point: neither the regular army nor provincial forces could have existed for long without multifaceted support provided by villages and popular troops.

Accordingly, the Viet Minh made every effort to win control of peasant hamlets and villages. From their mountain sanctuary northwest of Hanoi, Ho and Giap dispatched a steady stream of agitation-propaganda teams. These trained teams either contacted resident Communist cells working covertly or overtly to "develop" popular Viet Minh "bases" or they set about recruiting such cells.

What was their siren song?

The reader perhaps will be surprised to learn that it was not the virtues of communism. The pitch, as signaled by Ho in late December 1946, carefully avoids the word:

On map: CHINA, Viet Tonkin Bac, Red River, Black River, Hanoi, Haiphong, VIET MINH INTERZONES, •Towns and Cities, THAILAND, CAMBODIA, Mekong River, Hue, Saigon, COCHIN CHINA, L A O S, A N N A M, I, II, III, IV, V, VI, N, 0 100 200 miles

M.E.P.

   . . . Compatriots! Rise up!
    Men and women, old and young, regardless of creeds, political parties, or nationalities, all the Vietnamese must stand up to fight the French colonialists to save the Fatherland. Those who have rifles will use their rifles; those who have swords will use their swords; those who have no swords will use spades, hoes, or sticks. Everyone must endeavor to oppose the colonialists and save his country.[4]

Revolutionary teams concentrated on the single issue of *doc-lap,* of independence, a magic word made into a vocal harp on which these agents skillfully played appealing variations on a theme. These teams formed the Communist version of Lyautey's civil-military task forces, but instead of spreading brightly colored wares in the village market place, they spread words of hope and dignity in men's minds. The Viet Minh agents cared. They cared about high rents paid by peasants, usurious interest on loans, the lack of food that plagued the land, epidemics, illiteracy, lack of schools, teachers, hospitals, doctors. They condemned greedy landlords and rapacious tax collectors and corrupt officials who kept men indebted for life, debts that passed as legacy to survivors. They discussed all these things and more, and they told the people that *doc-lap,* by returning the land to the people, would erase such injustices and allow everyone a happy and full life for the first time in anyone's memory.

How was *doc-lap* to be achieved? As Uncle Ho said: by the people. By peasant and worker, by people gathered listening to the song of Viet Minh agents. The Viet Minh was the people's party; it was recruiting to fight the people's war. Everyone had a task in the Viet Minh, young and old, able and infirm, men and women, boys and girls. The Viet Minh needed men to fight as part-time guerrillas, to fight as village militia, to fight in regional forces, to fight in the regular army. The Viet Minh needed support of all the people. As Uncle Ho said: The people would furnish food to the guerrillas, they would shelter them and care for them when wounded, give them information and money, act as messengers. They would spread the word to other people. Some would carry supplies for the regular army. Others would spy. All would lie. Some would kill. Each in his own way would fight. Some would fall; many would die. That was the price of *doc-lap.*

Where people responded, an organization emerged. The "popular forces" of a village or a complex of villages consisted of the Dan Quan,

... essentially a labor force with a tinge of military training. Though occasionally they performed sabotage, their main responsibility was to collect intelligence, serve as guards, make road repairs, build bases, fortify the villages, and—very important—act as porters. They wore no uniforms and had virtually no weapons, except for some sabotage materials.

A smaller group, the Dan Quan Du Kich,

farmers by day—guerrillas by night, ... undertook guerrilla actions on a small scale. They received rudimentary military training and were expected eventually to become line soldiers.

Provincial forces existed at district level, usually in company strength, and at province and zone levels, usually in battalion and, later, regimental strength. Though full-time soldiers, these troops wore a variety of uniforms and lacked heavy weapons and sophisticated equipment. This in no way diminished operational responsibilities:

> ... One of the primary duties of the regional forces was to protect an area and its population. They were the troops that met the French clearing operations, launched small attacks, and generally harassed the enemy; in short, they were the "mature guerrillas," who kept the enemy off balance and ambushed his reinforcements.[5]

Throughout this period, Ho and Giap carefully husbanded regular army units. Men who graduated from regional forces into the regular army received fairly systematic training in more or less orthodox military subjects including use of such heavy weapons as machine guns, mortars, bazookas, recoilless rifles. For a couple of years, the regular army consisted of battalions; in time, these battalions grew to regimental strength, and in 1950, to division strength (far inferior numerically to orthodox Western divisions).

The Viet Minh military organization was never far removed from political influence and control both inside and outside the army. Political officers from company level upward dealt with " . . . proper ideological indoctrination of the soldiers and the integration of military actions with political objectives." The system stressed the soldier's political training as much as if not more than his military training.

As Mao had done in China in the early stages of revolution, Ho also set the regular army to the recruiting task by dispersing companies "to infiltrate different regions and cement their friendly relations with the local populace" in order to establish "popular bases."[6] In working with the people, these Viet Minh soldier-agents were to unconditionally follow Ho's "forbiddances" and "permissibles." They were to avoid upsetting the people in any way. They were to help with "harvesting, fetching firewood, carrying water, sewing" and were "to teach the population the national script and elementary hygiene" while creating "an atmosphere of sympathy first, then gradually to explain to the people to abate their superstitions."[7]

Viet Minh leadership devoted equal care to political organization of the people. Each zone, province, district, and village fell under a separate committee command usually called the Committee of Resistance. At interzone or zone level, this committee " . . . dealt not only with the political, economic, and military aspects of the war but also with local problems of health and culture." Subordinate committees were less elaborate, those at the village level being responsible for " . . . the defense of the village and the day-to-day activities of the guerrillas." Where covert cells existed, as was usual in French-occupied areas, the Viet Minh tried to establish shadow, or "parallel," governments.[8]

This system of what the French called *hiérarchies parallèles* was the key to Viet Minh control at each level of government. Based on Lenin's and Mao's teachings, it operated in two ways, either by utilizing " . . . existing administrative structures through the infiltration of subversive individuals, or the creation of altogether new clandestine structures designed to take over full administrative responsibilities when political and military conditions are ripe."[9]

The Viet Minh accomplished none of this organization overnight. Singers of the *doc-lap* song found a greatly varied reception. They were far more popular in the North, in the Red River Delta, than elsewhere. Mountain tribes surrounding their northern sanctuaries did not trust them (or anything else that was Vietnamese) and were pacified only with greatest difficulty. Various opposition nationalist groups, many in the South, wanted nothing to do with the Communist-dominated Viet Minh, even though rejecting French rule.

The Viet Minh countered a certain amount of this opposition by playing on the people's desire for independence. Once it controlled villages, it extended control by weaving the population together through the activities of Lien Viet, which, according to a French army report,

> . . . included youth groups, groups for mothers, farmers, workers, "resistant" Catholics, war veterans, etc. . . . no one escaped regimentation . . . the [normal] territorial hierarchy was thus complemented by another which watched the former and was in turn watched by it—both of them being watched in turn from the outside and inside by the security services and the Party. The individual caught in the fine mesh of such a net has no chance whatever of preserving his independence.[10]

The Viet Minh enforced discipline and extended control of the population by a civilian secret police force, the Cong An; a special military intelligence force, the Trinh Sat; and a special terrorist organization the Dich-Van; which we will shortly examine more closely.

In these formative years, the Viet Minh suffered a considerable number of internal problems. From time to time, Ho complained of bureaucratic fumbling that resulted in waste and corruption. The armed forces lacked trained officers and specialists. Severe supply shortages also existed. Although weapons and other supplies arrived from Nationalist China, Thailand, and the Philippines, these sources eventually dried up, to leave the Viet Minh mainly dependent on captured weapons or on "cottage production." This varied from factories employing as many as five hundred people and situated in sanctuary areas, to mobile shops of from ten to fifteen workers producing anything from paper to medicines.

Despite difficulties, the Viet Minh continued to grow in size and effectiveness. Although poverty of organization and strength confined operations to the guerrilla level—to raids on French outposts, ambush of patrols and convoys, and interdiction of roads—by 1948, these operations were displaying characteristics that made them increasingly difficult to counter. Viet Minh raids were not slapdash affairs but generally well-thought-out and carefully planned operations in which mobility and surprise dovetailed to produce satisfactory results. They served both a political and a military purpose. Politically, they demonstrated that the Viet Minh intended to "liberate" an area from French control thus adding muscle to Viet Minh propaganda and strengthening further the covert Viet Minh presence in that area. Militarily, they captured weapons and ammunition and also helped units to perfect infiltration and assault tactics while exercising a demoralizing influence on the French.

Usually made at night, attacks were rarely prolonged. If successful, intruders gathered up weapons, perhaps a prisoner or two, and whatever ammunition and equipment they could carry. If a raid failed, attackers generally broke off action and fled, either to designated rendezvous areas or, if cut off, to friendly villages, where they merged with the population.

A successful raid depended in large part on accurate intelligence. Guerrilla teams not only wanted to strike the weakest outposts but the weakest part of a weak outpost. Here is where careful preparation of the population was paying off: French outposts were under almost constant scrutiny both from inside by various Vietnamese lackeys and from outside by peasants.

A sympathetic population also greatly aided Viet Minh construction and security of defensive areas. In the North, these usually consisted of fortified villages. Guerrillas and villagers devoted thousands of man-hours to preparing underground labyrinths cunningly camouflaged and often stocked with food and water in case of prolonged occupation. A security network of innocent-looking peasants guarded these strongholds against surprise, thus allowing guerrilla inhabitants the option of escape or ambush of an intruding French force. If outnumbered, or if other factors were unfavorable, the Viet Minh did not hesitate to abandon the village.

Inept French tactics, for example clearing operations that destroyed huts, damaged crops, and maltreated peasants, greatly aided the Viet Minh in their effort to win the people's co-operation. To counter French progress in the pacification program, notably in the South, the Viet Minh used more militant tactics. This was the task of the special terrorist organization, the Dich-Van, whose members did not hesitate to murder officials who co-operated with the French. In Viet Minh eyes, this was not wanton slaughter. Except in isolated and undisciplined cases, such murders served specific political goals: If the official was corrupt, his murder constituted a popular act; in any case, it served as a bloody warning that the French, despite martial trappings, did *not* control the area and that anyone impeding the fight for Vietnamese independence by trafficking with the French could and would be summarily dealt with.

We see here in these years the gradual appearance of all ingredients of an insurgency situation. Had the battle remained an internal affair confined to limited French and Viet Minh forces, it could perhaps have been resolved by political means—by some sort of standoff agreement similar to that reached in March 1946—before it broadened. Despite the intensity of the Viet Minh effort, their strength would probably not have increased to the point where they could have undertaken the final, or mobile, phase of the war, anyway for many, many years.

But Communist China's victory, in 1949, greatly altered matters. The Viet Minh could now hope to enter the third phase of warfare. In late 1949, Ho Chi Minh's government proclaimed a national mobilization and began conscripting males between the ages of eighteen and forty-five. This guarantee of almost limitless porters, the promise of military aid from China, of sanctuary in case of defeat, and the peculiar vulnerability of French outposts in the North allowed Giap to become more tactically daring than his meager resources warranted. In anticipation of bigger things, in late 1949 he began attacking French outposts in the Black River Valley, northwest of Hanoi.

CHAPTER THIRTY-NINE

1. Buttinger, II, 751.
2. Giap, *People's War, People's Army*. Although written primarily for internal consumption and thus heavily propagandistic, General Giap's work nonetheless provides a wealth of information on Viet Minh organization, strategy, and tactics.
3. Ho Chi Minh, *Ho Chi Minh on Revolution* . . . , 207–8.
4. Ibid., 172. See also, Mao Tse-tung, *Basic Tactics*.
5. Tanham, *Communist Revolutionary Warfare* . . . , 50–1.
6. Ibid., 18.
7. Ho Chi Minh, *Ho Chi Minh on Revolution* . . . , 191–2.
8. Tanham, *Communist Revolutionary Warfare* . . . , 44.
9. Fall, *The Two Viet-Nams* . . . , 133–4.
10. Ibid., 134.

CHAPTER 40

Viet Minh offensives • French disasters • La sale guerre • General de Lattre de Tassigny • Giap's mistakes • Change in Communist tactics • French strategy and tactics • De Lattre's "crusade" • American intervention • American-French conflict • George Kennan's warning to Acheson • Acheson's dilemma (II) • Gullion and Blum dissent • Congressman John Kennedy's position

THE COMBINATION of superb intelligence gained from peasants, meticulous planning, mobility, and surprise, which characterized the Viet Minh's early guerrilla raids, was carried over to Giap's first major offensive. Operation Le-Loi concentrated on destroying a series of small French outposts located in the Black River Valley. By January 1950, fifteen Viet Minh battalions had overrun these small forts to drive a wedge between the Thai Highlands and the Red River Delta.

Giap's success here, taken with the arrival of Chinese Communist forces on the border, caused him to undertake the more ambitious operation of clearing the northern border area. In February 1950, Giap declared that the second phase of the war, guerrilla warfare, was over and that the third phase, mobile warfare, was to begin. Giap now opened Operation Le Hong Phong I. Five Viet Minh regiments struck throughout the region and, after some sharp fighting, occupied major towns to leave French forces in northeastern Tonkin compressed into a string of forts stretching some one hundred and sixty miles along a single-lane highway, Route Coloniale 4, from Cao Bang to the Gulf of Tonkin. These were the forts that, in 1949, the French chief of staff, General Revers, had wanted evacuated.[1]

Giap next turned his attention to these forts. Using fresh troops trained and equipped in China and supported by American artillery pieces that Communist Chinese had captured from the Nationalists, he attacked and briefly held the fort of Dong Khe. Throughout the summer, Viet Minh guerrillas interdicted the long and vulnerable French supply line. Giap meanwhile brought battle-tested regiments through China to the east, where they joined with " . . . ten newly formed Viet-Minh battalions, reinforced by a complete artillery regiment." In September, he opened Operation Le Hong Phong II by again attacking and capturing Dong Khe, which effectively cut communications between Cao Bang, a key garrison eighty-five miles distant from the southern forts.

An alarmed French headquarters in Hanoi ordered the Cao Bang commander to blow up artillery and motor transport and march south; simultaneously, it started a relief force of thirty-five hundred men marching north, where it would take Dong Khe and join the retreating Cao Bang garrison. This plan probably would have salvaged most of the troops, but the Cao Bang commander sabotaged it by refusing to abandon his artillery and transport. Having tied his retreat to the jungle-flanked windings and flimsy bridges of Route Coloniale 4, he immediately struck a series of Viet Minh ambushes so fiercely executed that, " . . . after one day of arduous work, the force had covered *nine* miles." Not until Giap's guerrillas chewed columns to shreds did he abandon transport and guns, but, by then, the relief force marching from the south was under heavy attack.[2]

Remnants of the two forces met outside Dong Khe, where, despite reinforcement by three battalions of paratroopers, they were virtually annihilated. General Carpentier now evacuated the southernmost fort of Lang Son, leaving most of its thirteen hundred tons of supply to the Viet Minh. By the end of October 1950, " . . . almost the whole northern half of North Viet-Nam had become a Viet-Minh redoubt. . . . " Fall summed up the disaster:

> . . . When the smoke cleared, the French had suffered their greatest colonial defeat since Montcalm had died in Quebec. They had lost 6,000 troops, 13 artillery pieces and 125 mortars, 450 trucks and three armored platoons, 940 machine guns, 1,200 submachine guns and more than 8,000 rifles. Their abandoned stocks alone sufficed for the equipment of a whole additional Viet-Minh division.[3]

With the French troops falling back to the Red River Delta, where panic-stricken civilians greeted them with demoralizing rumors, it looked as if the Viet Minh would soon claim all of northern Vietnam. The disaster coincided with General MacArthur's serious reverse in Korea occasioned by Chinese entry into the war. French morale at home plunged. French Communists assumed a new militancy designed to prevent soldiers and weapons being sent to Indochina. Such was the re-

Map labels: CHINA, Black River, Red River, Cao Bang, Dong Khe, Lai Chau, Thai Highlands, Phu Doan, Yen Bai, 4, Na San, Vinh Yen, Dong Trieu, Lang Son, Mao Khe, Gulf of Tonkin, Hanoi, Hoa Binh, Haiphong, Thai Binh, Day R., Plaine des Jarres, NORTHERN VIETNAM 1950–1953, • Towns and Cities, •••• "de Lattre line", — Routes 4 and 1, THAILAND, N, Hué, Da Nang, CAMBODIA, 0 100 200 miles, Interzone V, Nha Trang, M.E.P.

action to what Communists termed *la sale guerre*—the dirty war—that important non-Communist voices began calling for French withdrawal.

One of these belonged to Pierre Mendès-France, a former Gaullist and future premier, who, in November 1950, laid basic issues on the line in the National Assembly:

> . . . It is the overall conception of our action in Indochina that is false, because it relies both on a military effort that is too thin and weak to provide a solution through strength, and on a political effort that is too thin and weak to secure for us the allegiance of the population. . . . There are only two solutions. The first would be to fulfil our objectives in Indochina by force of arms. If we choose it, let us now give up illusions and pious falsehoods. In order to achieve decisive military successes rapidly, we will need three times as many forces on the ground and three times as many funds, and we will need them very quickly. . . .

The effort would demand drastic sacrifices on the home front. The alternative

... is to seek a political agreement, an agreement, obviously, with those who oppose us. ... An agreement means concessions, wide concessions. ... A choice must be made. ... Apart from the military solution, the solution of force, there is only one possibility—negotiation. ... Have we the means of escaping this outcome when we ourselves have made it unavoidable by our failures and mistakes?

Mendès-France told the Assembly that concessions would include Vietnamese independence, negotiated withdrawal of French troops, and free, supervised elections.[4]

In the ensuing debate, Jean Letourneau, Minister for the Associated States, stated " ... that the government of Premier René Pleven intended to carry out the March 8, 1949 [Élysée] agreements with the greatest liberalism. Virtually all of the administrative machinery would be in Vietnamese hands by January 1, 1951, he promised, and the French would hand over power as rapidly as possible to a Vietnamese army." Having won Assembly approval, Pleven's government recalled Carpentier and Léon Pignon and appointed the forceful general Jean de Lattre de Tassigny to the dual civil-military command.[5]

Although a sick man, De Lattre possessed considerable charisma, and his evident enthusiasm and tireless efforts brought a much needed boost to morale and army discipline. A cocky little fellow, called "Le Roi Jean"—King Jean—by some, De Lattre promised his troops no easy road, but he also told them, " ... No matter what, you will be commanded."[6] De Lattre walked into an extremely crucial tactical situation. Giap's autumn victories had ideas made the more grandiose by initial Chinese successes in Korea and by an increasing flow of arms from Communist China. The Democratic Republic of (North) Vietnam was now unquestionably committed to the Communist camp—in early 1951, the government would re-create the Indochinese Communist Party, under the title of Lao Dong, and would begin the transformation of the state to a "people's democracy."[7] By late 1950, the army included heavy weapons, artillery, and even engineer units.

As prelude to a push on Hanoi itself, Giap attacked the outpost of Vinh Yen with two divisions in January 1951. This kicked off with a skillful diversionary effort that enticed a French mobile group into ambush and cost it some two battalions in casualties. But unexpectedly strong defenses at Vinh Yen, including well-directed artillery support and aircraft dropping newly introduced napalm, stopped the main effort. Giap foolishly ordered mass, or "human sea," tactics that sent wave after wave of infantry against determined defenders well dug in and supported by heavy artillery and air. Giap's logistics system was not up to this kind of warfare. Each of his divisions of about twelve thousand men depended on about fifty thousand human porters to support an offensive role. Although he was said to have utilized 180,000 porters during the action, his primitive supply lines were unable to furnish resupply. Continuing intermittently for four days, the Viet Minh attacks suddenly ceased—a major setback which cost the Communists some six thousand killed, several thousand wounded.[8]

Apparently undeterred, Giap shifted his effort to the east, to the hill range around Dong Trieu. A successful attack here would open approaches to the coal-mining area and would cut the delta from the vital port of Haiphong. In late March, three divisions struck at Mao Khe. The small French garrison held out until reinforced by paratroopers; once again the attack failed at considerable cost to the Viet Minh.

Giap struck next from the south, a surprise attack aided by a regiment he had infiltrated behind French lines. In late May, three of his divisions fell on Thai Binh. But their lines of communication ran across the Day River and here were interdicted by French river units and by planes dropping napalm. Thus hindered, assault units could not sustain the attack. In mid-June, having lost about a third of their force, the Viet Minh abruptly broke contact and retreated to the mountains.

This series of battles produced important developments in each camp. As a Viet Minh failure, the actions caused Giap to reverse his thinking and postpone the third, or all-out offensive, phase. Rightly assuming that time was on his side, he spent summer of 1951 in rebuilding shattered divisions. He then turned to the Thai Highlands and Laos and in September began a series of nibbling actions against semi-isolated outposts.

Equally important developments occurred in French and American camps. The winter-spring battles, though far from "victories," removed much of the sting from earlier French defeats. By so doing, they combined with other factors—with De Lattre's conventional military background, with his dangerous belief in superiority of Western-style warfare in a guerrilla-warfare environment, perhaps with his illness—to blind him to the exact nature of the political challenge.

By spring of 1951, the French staff held ample evidence that France was fighting an extremely determined enemy whose operations depended in large part on co-operation of the Vietnamese people. Yet, no more than earlier administrators and military commanders, did De Lattre come up with a plan to steal this support and thus weaken his enemy perhaps irreparably. Instead, De Lattre sought to inject enthusiasm into his forces and into the Vietnamese people, particularly the *attentistes,* or fence sitters, *not* by changing the nature of the political approach, but by changing the nature of the war. As opposed to the French high command, which " . . . recommended a concentration of effort in southern Indochina," De Lattre insisted that " . . . the loss of

Tonkin would lead to the West's loss of Indochina and Southeast Asia."[9] De Lattre vigorously denied that his was a colonial war. He told Robert Shaplen that " . . . he was leading a crusade against Communism . . . that there was no longer an ounce of colonialism left in French intentions."[10] In July 1951, De Lattre stated that the war " . . . no longer concerns France except to the extent of her promises to Vietnam and the part she has to play in the defense of the free world. Not since the Crusades has France undertaken such disinterested action. This war is the war of Vietnam for Vietnam."[11]

Whether De Lattre believed this or whether he realized the appeal that his words would have to conservative members of the American Congress and public, it was palpable nonsense: " . . . [the French] owned all the rubber plantations . . . two-thirds of the rice, all the mines, all the shipping, virtually all the industry, and nearly all the banks."[12]

Prompted by French and American governments, the former furnishing the authority, the latter most of the money, De Lattre also turned to building the authorized Vietnamese army of thirty battalions. Owing to hostility of French officialdom and Vietnamese apathy, a widespread recruiting campaign only partially succeeded—under the circumstances, a major failure. But he did succeed in obtaining some fresh troops from North Africa.[13]

Wanting to deprive the Viet Minh of the Red River Delta rice bowl, he attempted to seal off this vast area, about seventy-five hundred square miles and eight million inhabitants, with a complicated complex of forts, some twelve hundred large and small concrete structures, known as the "De Lattre Line."[14] At the same time, he introduced the tactical innovation of mobile groups, special task forces of his best infantry, armor, and artillery units used " . . . as offensive striking forces to attack key Viet Minh installations and force combat on . . . [De Lattre's] own terms."[15] Together with eight parachute battalions, they constituted his striking force, which was supposed to check and defeat between six and seven Viet Minh divisions. Although De Lattre commanded a force of about half a million men, 350,000 of them " . . .were tied down in static assignments . . . or in noncombatant supply. . . ."[16]

De Lattre continued to rely on his air force and on two other tactical innovations. One consisted of Dinaussauts, or special river units of various-sized landing craft that patrolled numerous waterways. The other was an attempt to outdo the Viet Minh at their own game by sending special teams, consisting in part of "converted" Viet Minh prisoners, into Viet Minh territory to work up guerrilla resistance. The command of these units, called *Groupements de Commandos Mixtes Aéroportés,* or GCMA, went to a young paratroop major, Roger Trinquier, of whom we will hear more in the final chapter of this war. The units, which mostly parachuted into target areas, were supplied by airdrop while working with tribes loyal to the French.[17]

Thus armed, De Lattre set to work to "win" the war.

De Lattre's "victories" in winter and spring of 1951 also influenced American officials, both in Indochina and in Washington. The American attitude toward Indochina, if anything, had grown more ambivalent. Prime Minister Nguyen Phan Long had complicated matters in early 1950 by asking for economic and military aid directly from the United States. The prime minister optimistically argued that a grant of $146 million would allow him to build a national Vietnamese army that would defeat the Viet Minh in six months. This had drawn a sharp retort from the French commander at the time, General Carpentier:

> ... I will never agree to equipment being given directly to the Viet Namese. ... The Viet Namese have no generals, no colonels, no military organization that could effectively utilize the equipment. It would be wasted, and in China the United States has had enough of that.[18]

The pending conflict, never satisfactorily solved, was noted by Walter Lippmann, who in April 1950 pointed out that the "great majority of the people of Indo-China" could only be united by an independent Indochina Government. Then came the catch-22:

> ... if Bao-Dai or anyone else were promised independence, it is equally certain that the French army could not be induced ... to fight a dangerous, dirty, inconclusive war which is to end in the abandonment of the French interests in Asia. ... The French army can be counted on to go on defending Southeast Asia only if the Congress of the United States will pledge itself to subsidize heavily—in terms of several hundred million dollars a year and for many years to come—a French colonial war to subdue not only the Communists but the nationalists as well.[19]

When the United States agreed, in autumn of 1950, to help France raise a Vietnamese army, Secretary of State Acheson was advised by one of his lieutenants that "... Prince Bao Dai should be pushed to assume maximum effective leadership" and "... that although Indochina was an area of French responsibility, in view of French ineffectiveness it would be better for France to pull out if she could not provide sufficient force to hold; that we should strengthen a second line of defense in Thailand, Malaya, Laos, Cambodia, the Philippines, and Indonesia. . . . " Just prior to Chinese intervention in Korea, still another lieutenant presciently warned the Secretary of State

> . . . that the appearance of the Chinese in Korea required us to take a second look at where we were going in Indochina. Not only was there real danger that our efforts would fail in their immediate purpose and waste valuable resources in the process, but we were moving into a position in Indochina in which "our responsibilities tend to supplant rather than complement those of the French." We could, he added, become a scapegoat for the French and be sucked into direct intervention. "These situations have a way of snowballing," he concluded.[20]

American officials in Vietnam thus began to find the going increasingly frustrating. The aid question became a particularly sore point. During the 1950 negotiations, American officials wisely had held out for bilateral aid agreements between the United States and the three Associated States: Vietnam, Laos, and Cambodia. Most economic aid, which, up to July 1951, amounted to $23.5 million, went to Vietnam. But in administering funds, the head of the American aid program, Robert Blum, collided with French officialdom, which accused him of undermining French interests by fomenting Vietnamese nationalism. As one result, the French used obstructive methods to downplay the American effort and, at times, to nullify its most beneficial effects.

A strong diplomatic stand undoubtedly could have rectified this unsavory situation, but external factors previously discussed continued to play a major role by dividing American councils. In Washington, George Kennan, by far the most prescient diplomat in the State Department, had become so alarmed by events in Indochina that in August 1950 he wanted the American Government to inform the French that:

> . . . we cannot honestly agree with them that there is any real hope of their remaining successfully in Indo-China, and we feel that rather than have their weakness demonstrated by a continued costly and unsuccessful effort to assert their will by force of arms, it would be preferable to permit the turbulent political currents of that country to find their own level, unimpeded by foreign troops or pressures, even at the probable cost of an eventual deal between Viet-Nam and Viet-Minh, and the spreading over the whole country of Viet-Minh authority, possibly in a somewhat modified form.[21]

Dean Acheson could not be persuaded to such a course. Committed to forging a defensive pact in Europe, he refused to antagonize the French by withdrawing support for their effort in Indochina. Donald

Heath, American minister (and later ambassador) in Vietnam, " . . . did not believe in rocking the boat, and when De Lattre arrived, he fell completely under the General's spell."[22] Edmund Gullion, Heath's consul general and later minister counselor, opposed such a compliant attitude, as did Robert Blum, the aid chief, but the impact of their worthy efforts was largely absorbed by continuing American support of the French military effort. In December 1950, the American Government agreed that all military aid " . . . would be handed over to the French Command, while direct relations between the Associate States and MAAG were to be expressly precluded."[23] In 1951, the United States furnished French forces in Indochina over half a billion dollars' worth of military aid.

The United States could not satisfactorily identify with both the French and the Vietnamese. Neither De Lattre nor French and American officials who had donned armor and were marching on what they appeared to believe was a God-given anti-Communist crusade could persuade the Vietnamese to enthusiasm, particularly since the Vietnamese were consigned to hold the horses of the French knights. The Vietnamese wanted independence, and, in autumn of 1951, they wanted the United States to help them gain it. Instead, America was obviously backing France. As Robert Blum sadly concluded, " . . . on balance, we came to be looked upon more as a supporter of colonialism than as a friend of the new nation." De Lattre, who called Blum " . . . the most dangerous man in Indo-China," was instrumental in getting him relieved, in late 1951. Soon after his return to the United States, Blum summed up both the French and the American dilemmas:

> . . . The attitude of the French is difficult to define. On the one hand are the repeated official affirmations that France has no selfish interests in Indo-China and desires only to promote the independence of the Associated States and be relieved of the terrible drain of France's resources. On the other hand are the numerous examples of the deliberate continuation of French controls, the interference in major policy matters, the profiteering and the constant bickering and ill-feeling over the transfer of powers and the issues of independence. . . . This distinction is typified by the sharp difference between the attitude toward General de Lattre in Indo-China, where he is heralded as the political genius and military savior . . . and in France, where he is suspected as a person who for personal glory is drawing off France's resources on a perilous adventure. . . .

Blum went on to analyze the dichotomy of American participation in this colonial affair:

... It is difficult to measure what have been the results of almost two years of active American participation in the affairs of Indo-China. Although we embarked upon a course of uneasy association with the "colonialist"-tainted but indispensable French, on the one hand, and the indigenous, weak and divided Vietnamese, on the other hand, we have not been able fully to reconcile these two allies in the interest of a single-minded fight against Communism. Of the purposes which we hoped to serve by our actions in Indo-China, the one that has been most successful has been the strengthening of the French military position. On the other hand, the Vietnamese, many of whom thought that magical solutions to their advantage would result from our appearance on the scene, are chastened but disappointed at the evidence that America is not omnipotent and not prepared to make an undiluted effort to support their point of view.... Our direct influence on political and economic matters has not been great. We have been reluctant to become directly embroiled and, though the degree of our contribution has been steadily increasing, we have been content, if not eager, to have the French continue to have primary responsibility, and to give little, if any, advice.[24]

Blum's and Gullion's dissent was not altogether wasted, for their obvious sincerity in wanting to help the Vietnamese help themselves won the U.S.A. numerous friends in the area. Nor did their dissent go unnoticed at home. In 1951, a young congressman, John F. Kennedy, visited Vietnam, where he listened to Edmund Gullion, among others. Upon his return to the United States, he stated:

... In Indo-China we have allied ourselves to the desperate effort of a French regime to hang on to the remnants of empire.... To check the southern drive of communism makes sense but not only through reliance on the force of arms. The task is rather to build strong native non-Communist sentiment within these areas and rely on that as a spearhead of defense rather than upon the legions of General de Lattre. To do this apart from and in defiance of innately nationalistic aims spells foredoomed failure.[25]

CHAPTER FORTY

1. Fall, *The Two Viet-Nams* ..., 108–11: The Viet Minh code name always carried a psychological connotation; in this case, the operation was named after the first secretary-general of the Indochinese Communist Party.
2. Ibid. See also, Buttinger.
3. Fall, *The Two Viet-Nams* ..., 111.
4. Devillers and Lacouture, 24–5.
5. Hammer, "Genesis of the First Indochina War: 1946–1950."
6. Fall, *The Two Viet-Nams* ..., 115 ff. See also, Buttinger, and Lancaster, for a more critical appraisal.

7. Lancaster, 227.
8. Ibid., 225. See also, O'Ballance, *The Indo-China War . . .* , 123–139.
9. Devillers and Lacouture, 27–8.
10. Shaplen, *The Lost Revolution,* 80.
11. Buttinger, II, 669.
12. Shaplen, *The Lost Revolution,* 80.
13. Devillers and Lacouture, 28–9.
14. Fall, *Street Without Joy,* 173.
15. Tanham, *Communist Revolutionary Warfare . . .* , 102.
16. Devillers and Lacouture, 33.
17. Trinquier, Introduction, XIII.
18. Lancaster, 205.
19. Ibid., 206–7.
20. Acheson, 673–4.
21. Kennan, *Memoirs 1950–1963,* 59.
22. Shaplen, *The Lost Revolution,* 86.
23. Lancaster, 207.
24. Shaplen, *The Lost Revolution,* 90.
25. Schlesinger, *A Thousand Days,* 321.

CHAPTER 41

De Lattre's new tactics • General Salan takes over • Jean Letourneau • French political failure • Acheson's dilemma (III) • Giap's problems • His shift in targets • Salan's countermoves • Orde Wingate's ghost (I) • Continued French failure • Acheson loses patience • Giap fans out • General Henri Navarre arrives

CONGRESSMAN KENNEDY'S expressed pessimism concerning the Indochina scene represented a minority opinion—so often the natural corollary of uncomfortable fact. De Lattre and his fellow crusaders, French and American, clearly won the opening rounds. In spring of 1951, American officials, legislators, and faithful friends of Vietnam, riding the anti-Communist bandwagon, saw to it that De-Lattre was well received in Washington, where press and television interviews " . . . did much to persuade the American public not only that effective national independence had been given to the Associate [sic] States but also that France's role in Indochina was disinterested."[1] He also won the promise of greatly increased military aid.

Flushed with this triumph and with renewed support from his own government, De Lattre, upon his return, embarked on a fresh tactical adventure. Impressed by the obstinacy of Viet Minh attacks at Thai Binh (see map, Chapter 40), he decided to try to woo Giap into another "meat-grinder" situation where superior French firepower could tell. As bait, he chose the town and surrounding area of Hoa Binh, southwest of Hanoi, a key communications point between Viet Minh forces in the Northeast and a Viet Minh division in Annam. In mid-November, three battalions of paratroopers dropped into the area and, within twenty-four hours, secured all objectives—with minimum resistance. This alone was suspicious, but no one at De Lattre's headquarters seemed alarmed, his press officer announcing to foreign correspondents that " . . . the conquest of Hoa-Binh represented a pistol pointed directly at the heart of the enemy."[2]

The conquest? The conquest was occupation uncontested because Giap pulled back his units until he could send in reinforcements and reclaim the initiative; that is, until he could fight on his own terms.

The heart of the enemy? The French task force interdicted a road flanked by dense jungle. Roads mean many things to many people. To armies dependent on motor transport and tanks, they are all-important. Giap's supply traveled on very few trucks; it either rode to Annam on coolie backs or on coolie-pushed bicycles. Within a month, " . . . the Viet-Minh had (in its usual fashion) built a bypass road around Hoa-Binh."[3] In so far as effectively interdicting Viet Minh communications was concerned, the French battalions might as well have remained in Hanoi.

But what of De Lattre's main tactical objective? De Lattre unquestionably brought the Viet Minh to combat, but with unforeseen results. Giap waited until his units had infiltrated the area in strength and then struck at French lines of communications. Although the Viet Minh employed a variety of guerrilla tactics to interdict De Lattre's supply lines, they did not hesitate to use costly assault tactics where necessary to eliminate key outposts. These attacks also took a heavy toll of French defenders. By the time that De Lattre, a sick man, suffering from terminal cancer, was evacuated, in December, he had already begun committing his limited reserves.

His successor, General Salan, found the operation so costly that, in January, he terminated it. By now, the Hoa Binh task force was encircled! In the end, over three reinforced regiments spent eleven days fighting their way down twenty-five miles of road, a rescue effort that cost dearly in men's lives, precious vehicles, and time. In capturing, defending, and evacuating Hoa Binh, De Lattre and Salan had used about a third of their mobile forces, which weakened other areas and opened the delta to extensive infiltration by Viet Minh regulars. According to Fall, " . . . by March, 1952, the French were mounting combined operations involving several mobile groups *behind* their own lines in order to keep their communications open."[4]

Nothing epitomized the French dilemma more clearly than this situation, which directly resulted from refusal to equate forces with mission. De Lattre and Salan were indulging luxury operations in an environment that called for strictest stringency. Ironically, the French command was concurrently supporting a number of *ratissage* operations much more in keeping with the tache-d'huile technique. Colonel John McCuen described one such operation in the Red River area, a subsector assigned to an Algerian rifle battalion supplemented by a Vietnamese company, a force of about one hundred locally recruited Vietnamese guerrillas, and a river patrol of a few landing craft. Dividing his subsector into four parts, as dictated by terrain and enemy activity, the commander opened a vigorous territorial offense consisting of active and aggressive patrols and ambush operations, a six-month effort that virtually cleared the subsector "of regular, regional, and local Vietminh forces." So far, so good. At this advanced point in the pacification process, a civic action team should have entered the play. These teams, Mobile Operational Administrative Groups, or GAMO (*Groupes administratifs mobiles opérationnels*), were supposed to complete the pacification process: screen and clear the area of *all* Viet Minh military and civil agents and generate a viable local administration while temporarily supplying basic needs—food, clothing, shelter, medical treatment, and security (through local militia).[5]

Several factors hindered GAMO operations. The first was scarcity of properly qualified teams—again, a matter of matching resources and mission. The second was lack of political appeal: team members could tell peasants that the Viet Minh were evil, but peasants, from personal experience, knew that the Viet Minh were no more evil than the French. Lacking political inspiration, teams perforce had to rely on superior performance, on setting up and running viable community services and continuing to protect the people until they could protect themselves. This frequently called for the regular military force; where this force had been transferred to a new area, the GAMO stood naked before renewed Viet Minh attacks. In the case cited above, GAMO operations never did take place and "within a few months, much of the Red River Sub-sector was again well on the way to becoming a Vietminh base."[6]

The devastating effect of the French political failure on military operations did not seem to strike the French high command. De Lattre and his successors, Letourneau and Salan, persisted in dragging their feet on the issue of real Vietnamese independence and the building of a viable Vietnamese army and officer corps.

So it was that the French high command continued to fail both politically and militarily. Nor did the Truman administration intervene actively to force the French hand. In February 1952, the United States agreed to provide further military aid (it was already contributing more than a third of the cost of the campaign). In May, prior to Secretary of State Acheson's meeting with the French and British in Bonn, President Truman instructed him " . . . to avoid mentioning any specific amount of further aid and of internal changes in Indochina beyond the development of the forces. It was thought that such an agenda would keep the French to the points of immediate practical importance and avoid irritation on secondary and peripheral matters."[7]

It was these " . . . secondary and peripheral matters" that should have been discussed—and resolved. But factors present since 1946 had come of age to father new factors, all of them continuing to play a blocking role, as the Secretary of State later wrote: French resentment of "United States intervention" and concomitant failure to provide the American Government with accurate military progress reports; Bao Dai's weak performance in pulling Vietnam together; and, the major millstone, the American Government's conclusion that " . . . the struggle in Indochina was a part of the worldwide resistance to 'communist attempts at conquest and subversion,' and [that] France had a 'primary role in Indochina,' such as we had assumed in Korea"—thus "we would increase our aid to building the national armies."[8]

One very good reason for French silence was considerable ignorance. Where General Giap knew virtually every move contemplated by the French army, General Salan literally had no idea of Giap's next move. Typical was the post-Hoa Binh period. Although Giap could claim the upper hand in the Hoa Binh fighting, it was a fairly expensive claim. His casualties of just over a year probably topped twelve thousand dead, with many more thousands wounded. Not only were such losses difficult to replace, but they created a decided morale problem, and they also brought increasing criticism from party leaders beset with major agricultural and economic crises on the home front. The French pacification effort was also beginning to cause Giap difficulty by depriving him of popular support that was essential to his tactics, particularly in predominantly Catholic areas. In September 1952, Giap's first priority was "to reinforce the popular bases" while shifting strike operations from the Red River Delta to a less likely and, from the French standpoint, a more vulnerable area.[9]

The Viet Minh had been allied with the Communist-oriented Pathet Lao movement in nearby Laos since 1950. For some time, four Viet Minh battalions had been training Laotian cadres as well as spreading propaganda among Vietnamese living in Laos. Now, in autumn of 1952, Giap decided to push an army across the Thai Highlands in order to reach the Laos border (see map, Chapter 40).

In October, Giap started three divisions across the Red River. Within a week, they had overrun a series of small French outposts. But, in the interim, Salan organized defensive airheads at Lai Chau and Na San. In late November, the Viet Minh attacked Na San, where they expected little resistance. Instead, they encountered heavy fighting and, significantly, reverted to earlier and costly tactics, suffering an estimated seven thousand casualties in three unsuccessful attempts to overrun the position. Giap now ordered his troops, somewhat belatedly, to bypass Na San. The Viet Minh advance forced Salan to evacuate other, smaller outposts, such as that at Dien Bien Phu (see maps, Chapters 37 and 47). By end of November, the Viet Minh army controlled much of the northwestern area and had reached the Laos border.

As Giap had foreseen, French artillery and armor had proved relatively useless against foot troops traveling in jungle, which also furnished excellent cover from French aircraft. Thus stymied, Salan reacted in two ways.

Despite failure of the Hoa Binh "meat-grinder" strategy, he and his staff were impressed at casualties inflicted on the Viet Minh, and they continued to think in terms of luring the enemy into attacking defended positions. The experience at Na San—Salan had hastily reinforced the garrison by airlift—encouraged the idea and led to establishing a series of *Bases Aéro-Terrestres,* or air-ground strong points, in the Northwest.

The reader will perhaps recognize a *Base Aéro-Terrestre* as the French version of Orde Wingate's "stronghold" concept (see Chapter 34). A strongpoint consisted of a small garrison located in a remote mountain area, generally where local tribes had remained friendly to the French. Largely supplied by air, garrisons theoretically performed a psychological mission by maintaining French presence and a tactical mission by luring Viet Minh units to the attack. They also supported limited offensive actions by such as Roger Trinquier's GCMA units.

At the same time, General Salan thought to check Giap's drive toward Laos by a massive operation against his supply bases at Yen Bai and Phu Doan on either side of the Red River. Involving thirty thousand troops, " . . . by far the largest force ever assembled in a single attack in Viet-Nam," Operation Lorraine kicked off in late October, its first goal a hundred miles distant. Giap did not respond as Salan had hoped. Correctly reasoning that the French counteroperation would soon run out of steam, he kept his divisions on the Laos border while sending two regiments to fight a guerrilla-style delaying action. Although the French force "captured" the Phu Doan supply depots, the hard-pressed Salan called off the operation in mid-November. On the long road home, a Viet Minh regiment successfully ambushed two French mobile groups to cause heavy casualties.[10]

All this tactical activity personified protracted war, which at this stage clearly benefited the Viet Minh. The sad truth was that, while Ho Chi Minh and Giap relentlessly pursued limited and realistic goals, France continued to drag its heels both politically and militarily, the inevitable result of fecklessly pursuing an impractical, if not hopeless, ambition of retaining complete control of Indochina. Not only was increasing failure causing dangerous political explosions in France proper, but it was beginning to rile its most generous supporter—the United States. Despite Letourneau's promises to Acheson, no real information had been provided by the French, although it was obvious that the situation was deteriorating. So was Acheson's temper. At a later meeting, when Letourneau made an impassioned plea for more money, Acheson refused unless he would host an American fact-finding mission.[12]

Jean Letourneau was in no position to have his Indochina books audited. He had installed as premier a rubber stamp named Nguyen

Van Tam, who had failed, as had his predecessors, " . . . to build up any popular support, despite his talk of agrarian and other reforms."[13] Militarily, he had become increasingly insolvent. Although Vietnam forces had increased to sixty battalions comprising some 150,000 men, these were being organized, trained, and employed in the French tradition of conventional warfare, with French officers and (generally) NCOs in command. Yet the Vietnamese were playing an increasingly important combat role: in 1952, 7,730 of them were killed serving either with the Expeditionary Corps or in their own army—about a third more than French casualties.[14] Not unnaturally, the Vietnamese Government and general staff wanted increased autonomy over its units, yet it lacked Vietnamese officers. In early 1953, only twenty-six hundred Vietnamese officers were serving (versus seven thousand French officers) and too many of these were incompetent and often corrupt. This military difficulty, lack of indigenous leadership, paralleled the civil, or political, difficulty, and derived directly from it:

> . . . The best elements of the Vietnamese educated middle class had no desire to serve in an army created to fight, still under French over-all direction, for a regime they despised and against people who, even if led by Communists, were still known to be fighting primarily for national independence. For these political reasons, which the colonial French mind failed to grasp, the Vietnamese National Army never became much of a fighting force.[15]

Failure to create a viable Vietnamese army forced Salan to remain generally on the defensive. The famed "de Lattre Line" (which he privately called " . . . a sort of Maginot Line") had more holes than a Swiss cheese, yet Salan continued to use some eighty thousand troops to man " . . . more than 900 forts . . . using an armament of close to 10,000 weapons, 1,200 mortars and 500 artillery pieces." Viet Minh strength *behind* the line continued to grow until Giap's three regular regiments were working with fourteen regional, or semiregular, battalions and an estimated 140 peasant militia companies—some thirty thousand irregulars. What the French termed the Viet Minh strategy of *pourrissement*—of "rotting away"—was far more effective than that of meeting French forces head on—so long as the French remained blind to the necessity of winning the population to their side.[16]

With the bulk of French forces tied down, Giap continued to probe into Laos while simultaneously expanding his control of central Vietnam. By spring of 1953, his units, working with various mountain tribes, had reduced French control to a few beachhead areas such as Hué, Da Nang and Nha Trang. In April, Giap's main force began infiltrating into Laos. To gain time to build a central defense, Salan withdrew his outposts, two of the garrisons being badly mauled in the process. But, with help of an around-the-clock airlift, he organized a central defensive position on the Plaine des Jarres. Viet Minh attacks against this and against Luang Prabang failed, and in May, at onset of the rainy season, Giap called his divisions back to Vietnam. Important Viet Minh cadres remained behind, however, to continue working with the Pathet Lao.

If all this filled Foggy Bottom with alarm, it created something akin to panic in the Quai d'Orsay. In spring of 1953, a French Parliamentary Mission of Enquiry visited Vietnam and accused Letourneau of maintaining a " . . . veritable dictatorship, without limit or control," and of playing a game of " . . . power and intrigue." Shortly after, a new French Government dismissed Letourneau and Salan, and appointed General Henri Navarre as commander in chief.[17]

Navarre's appointment opened the final chapter in the French saga in Indochina. But before proceeding to those dramatic events, we must turn to equally vital guerrilla actions that were being fought elsewhere in a tragically torn world.

CHAPTER FORTY-ONE

1. Lancaster, 232.
2. Fall, *Street Without Joy*, 48.
3. Fall, *The Two Viet-Nams* . . . , 119.
4. Fall, *Street Without Joy*, 56–8.
5. McCuen, 224, 226.
6. Ibid., 224.
7. Acheson, 675.
8. Ibid., 676.
9. Tanham, *Communist Revolutionary Warfare* . . . , 77.
10. Fall, *Street Without Joy*, 95–100. See also, Lancaster; O'Ballance, *The Indo-China War* . . .
11. Truman, *Years of Trial and Hope*, 519.
12. Acheson, 677.
13. Shaplen, *The Lost Revolution* . . . , 92.
14. Lancaster, 281.
15. Buttinger, II, 762.
16. Fall, *Street Without Joy*, 177.
17. Buttinger, II, 726. See also, Hammer, *The Struggle for Indochina* . . . ; Lancaster.

CHAPTER 42

The Greek civil war • Postwar confusion • Communist organization and strength • Communist defeat • Markos changes tactics • Growth of Communist strength • Government strength and weakness • The balance sheet • Communist guerrilla operations • Communist strength and weakness • Yugoslavia and Albania • The Truman Doctrine • The American army's quantitative approach • Greek army offensives • Communist political errors • Tito's defection • End of the war • The cost • Reasons for Communist defeat • Western "victory"

THE COMMUNIST-LED INSURRECTION in Greece broke out even before World War II ended (see Chapter 28). Following German evacuation, a British force commanded by Lieutenant General Scobie landed in early October 1944; Prime Minister Papandreou and the government followed two weeks later. Scobie commanded a hodgepodge force: two British brigades, British and American commandos, and some Free Greek units. Called III Corps, it numbered about twenty-six thousand men supported by five squadrons of aircraft—a weak army further diluted by erroneous command estimates that credited the Communist organization, EAM/ELAS, with co-operative intentions and with considerably less strength than they had.[1]

Scobie could do little more than occupy principal towns while UNRRA [United Nations Relief and Rehabilitation Administration] units began the immense task of civil rehabilitation. EAM/ELAS used this confusing period to strengthen its ranks for all-out civil war. As Germans moved out, ELAS units filled vacuum areas and, in the North, established liaison with Albanian and Yugoslav Communist guerrillas. EAM already had organized a secret police (OPLA) and a gendarmerie (EP), both of which began to consolidate control of the countryside, major targets being hated Greek security battalions. EAM also used various delaying and obstructive tactics to prevent Papandreou from organizing a national army and a national guard. With the worsening situation apparent, Scobie called for reinforcements and received two Indian brigades.

The KKE Central Committee, the real authority behind EAM/ELAS, now came to a fateful decision that rested in large part on an arrogance derived from ignorance of the enemy's strength. Over the strong objections of Yioryios Siantos, who had led EAM during World War II, it decided to shift " . . . from infiltration and political intrigue to force." According to Major Edgar O'Ballance, whose excellent book *The Greek Civil War* I have largely relied on in this brief account, ELAS strength at the time had risen to above forty thousand, divided into two "armies": Army Southern, commanded by Siantos and Mandakas and comprising "three divisions," or about eighteen thousand; and Army Northern, commanded by Saraphis and Aris and comprising five "divisions," or about twenty-three thousand. The idea was for Army Southern to drive the British from Athens and establish the new Communist government while Army Northern destroyed what was left of EDES resistance group.

Fighting broke out in early December 1944. Army Southern quickly gained the upper hand, separating and besieging British forces in Athens and Piraeus. Scobie, hastily reinforced by a division from Italy, counterattacked in late December. Churchill and Eden also flew in and managed to bring dissident nationalist parties together in a new government under Plastiras, with Archbishop Damaskinos as regent.

Scobie quickly drove Army Southern from its positions, and a ceasefire, in mid-January, forced ELAS units to withdraw one hundred miles from Athens as well as from Salonika and the Peloponnese. ELAS foolishly refused to release civilian hostages, estimated between fifteen and twenty thousand, which greatly reduced its popularity in the country and allowed the Plastiras government to assume control of large areas.

These serious defeats jolted the KKE back to a covert strategy of infiltration. Under terms of the Varkiza Agreement of February 1945, ELAS demobilized and disarmed its units, and released prisoners and hostages. The government reinstated regular army officers who had been serving with ELAS into the new national army, and it also legalized the KKE and promised to hold a plebiscite to determine whether monarchy should be restored and also a general election as soon as possible.

Although a few ELAS units refused to disband and took to the hills, the main body turned in arms and went home. The uneasy peace soon broke down. The KKE accused the government of stalling. Rampant inflation, " . . . largely because of the influx of gold sovereigns through the Allied Military Mission" during the war, helped Communists to foment unrest and demonstrations. The government, accusing ELAS of secretly burying arms and wholesale murder of hostages, instigated a repressive policy that included widespread arrest and detention of Communists, suspected Communists, and sympathizers. This policy helped to revive the Communist movement, as did return from German captivity of the former secretary-general of the KKE, Zakhariadis, in spring. Throughout summer and autumn of 1945, charge and countercharge reverberated through the warm Greek air to intensify passions already inflamed by terrible human suffering. German occupation had left hundreds of thousands homeless and hungry; in the war's last months, only UNRRA relief shipments fended off mass starvation.[2]

The end of World War II brought some relief to Greece, but the reconstruction task demanded a unified effort, with concomitant party and personal sacrifice. Instead, the country remained occupied by British troops whose commander attempted to reason with innumerable squabbling political factions, a boiling caldron of internecine hatred fired by traditional, deep-seated, and often petty feuds fattened from the war years. When the British, virtually frantic in frustration, asked Washington for financial help in autumn of 1945, President Truman gladly promised aid if the Greek Government would "adopt a program of [effective] stabilization."[3] Although some progress resulted, nothing approximating good government appeared. Wanting to exploit the muddled situation, in December 1945 the KKE decided to reorganize scattered insurgent forces into a secret army capable of challenging the legitimate government. These groups now filtered across the border into Yugoslavia and Albania, which furnished training camps and some material aid. Although Stalin approved the decision, the Soviet Union subsequently furnished neither arms nor supply.[4]

Nikos Zakhariadis, who launched this effort, continued to preside over a policy of infiltration and subversion of government. In March 1946, the KKE refused to participate in a general election, which overwhelmingly returned a rightist administration. Communists replied by stepping up disruptive tactics on two levels: in cities, by continued infiltration and obstructionism in government, armed forces, and labor unions; and in the country, by revival of small ELAS raids on villages. In summer of 1946, the newly formed Communist army began sending in small guerrilla units from Yugoslavia and Albania to carry out hit-and-run raids on villages to obtain food and also recruits. In September, Markos Vaphiadis assumed command of the new army. A man of about forty years, Markos had joined the party in his teens, had been imprisoned, and had served with ELAS forces in Macedonia. Markos established small bases inside Greece and, aided by old EAM/ELAS village networks, stepped up guerrilla raids in quantity, depth, and purpose. In October, his groups began killing village policemen and progovernment peasants as well as taking hostages to insure later village co-operation.

Confused government reaction helped the Communist movement more than it hurt it. The initial error already had been made: a much too severe repressive policy, which allowed police, national guard units, and such paramilitary right-wing organizations as Colonel George Grivas' "X" group virtually a free hand in "cleaning up" ELAS remnants. By September, this policy had driven hundreds of people either to ELAS bands in the countryside or to Markos' new army across the border. When a September plebiscite returned a nearly 70 per cent vote to restore the monarchy, the new Tsaldaris government expanded its repressive policy by purging former ELAS officers from army and government service, closing down Communist and left-wing newspapers, and similar measures.

The government should have directed its zeal to the countryside, both to alleviate human suffering and to protect the people from guerrilla depredations. Partially influenced by British advice, the Tsaldaris government continued to think in "bandit" rather than "guerrilla" terms. To suppress "bandits," government relied on security forces totaling about thirty thousand—village gendarmerie, town police, and national guard units. Though not well organized, trained, or equipped, this total force, despite unco-ordinated operations, probably could have coped with bandits. It could not cope with Markos' fast-moving guerrillas, and the government continued to lose control of area after area.

In October, the government persuaded the British to go along with its committing regular army units. The Greek national army numbered only about a hundred thousand at this time and, like the national guard, was neither organized, trained, nor equipped for counterinsurgency operations. It also suffered from political controls: Powerful politicians insisted on guarding their own areas of interest, which meant tying up units in static defense; division commanders literally could not move units without permission from the army general staff in Athens, and the general staff itself was subordinate to a large, unwieldy, and politically divisive National Defense Council. In this respect, the Greek scene resembled that in Nationalist China and, as we shall see, the Philippines.

At this stage, then, winter of 1946–47, considerable red ink appeared in the Greek ledger: a continuing political anarchy that British efforts failed to ameliorate and that continued to hinder a proper attack on economic problems; a paucity of British aid, due to Britain's own severe economic problems; a repressive rather than progressive political policy, which drove some people to join the Communist insurgency; and a disorganized army and other security forces operationally hindered by severe deficiencies in organization, training, and equipment.

But black ink also appeared. In December 1946, in answer to formal complaint by Greece, the United Nations Security Council authorized a commission of inquiry to investigate and report on the allegedly Communist-provoked insurgency. This brought the problems of Greece into world focus. The United States simultaneously sent an economic mission to determine the country's needs. The people themselves remained amazingly resilient—a vast reservoir of strength, if only the government had recognized it. Significantly, a government amnesty policy (in refreshing contrast to over-all policy) had brought in several hundred deserters from Markos' ranks by the end of 1946.

Red ink nevertheless splashed over black, and government pusillanimity, fear, and corruption, prospered the Communist cause. Markos had started serious operations in September with about four thousand guerrillas divided into small, semi-independent units of about one hundred fifty men each. At year's end, his forces numbered perhaps seven thousand. In early 1947, this force (now called the Democratic Army) controlled a large area of northern Greece, including perhaps one hundred villages. He next established general headquarters *inside Greece* at the junction of Albania, Yugoslavia, and Greece, the rugged terrain of the Grámmos and Vítsi mountain ranges. In March, he counted some thirteen thousand armed insurgents. In addition, the KKE in Athens, though operating underground, continued many subversive activities. Its highly secret terrorist organization, the OPLA, continued to intimidate and assassinate effective opponents. Of more importance to Markos was the country-wide organization known as YIAFAKA, which furnished his groups with intelligence, supply, recruits, and money, and sometimes performed propaganda and terrorist missions. Operating clandestinely, this organization probably had one or more "cells" in every town and village in Greece. Major O'Ballance estimated that, in mid-1947, it numbered some fifty thousand active members plus another quarter of a million sympathizers![5]

Red ink also appeared in the KKE ledger. As early as the end of 1946, the insurgency was falling between two stools of internal and external communism. The exile army needed material aid of Balkan countries, but, in exchange, Tito and Enver Hoxha demanded portions of northern Greece once the KKE won control. These guarantees caused a good deal of grumbling from the nationalist element of KKE, many of whom favored the Siantos theory of revolution from the inside. Markos himself saw the danger of removing the revolution from the country, which was one reason he insisted on spreading operations throughout Greece, including the Peloponnese. But this also backfired, in that he needed at least fifty thousand armed rebels for the purpose. In trying to expand his meager force, he began impressing recruits, whom he held by threat of reprisals against village wives and families.

This proved a basic error—and on several counts. When unwilling recruits deserted, and they frequently did, Markos ordered reprisals, which further alienated the people from the insurgency. Unwilling recruits who remained in the mountains formed an abrasive element in a small guerrilla army whose ranks already were becoming disaffected by isolation, meager rations, physical discomforts, and inadequate arms and supply from parsimonious Yugoslavs and Albanians. Markos countered growing disaffection by sterner discipline and by circulating a false rumor that international brigades were on their way to aid the cause. Such palliatives only partially succeeded: By end of 1946, Markos faced a deserter problem.

The attempt to claim national affinity also explained in part transfer of Democratic Army headquarters to Greek territory, a step imposed on Markos not only by a substantial element within the KKE but also by Tito and Hoxha. The move established both an identity for the Athens government to exploit (particularly important from the standpoint of American public opinion) and a specific target for the Greek national army; it also represented the first step in reverting to the earlier and unsuccessful doctrine of revolution by conventional warfare.

This new strategy might have worked had the Greek national army remained dependent on its moribund British military parent. But, in February 1947, the Attlee government suddenly informed Washington that economic circumstances would force British withdrawal from Greece at the end of March. American advisers in Greece simultaneously warned Washington of an imminent Communist takeover. President Truman responded to the crisis with a massive military-economic aid program, announced in mid-March.[6]

The famous "Truman Doctrine" provided a much-needed shot in the arm to the Greek Government. In April, the army managed to round up fifteen thousand troops to launch a surprise offensive in the North. Although it caught Democratic Army units napping and inflicted reasonable casualties, the effort lasted only two weeks. But when Markos, goaded by Balkan allies, launched attacks on such towns as Flórina and Kónitsa, local garrisons held until reinforced by neighboring units. This disappointing result caused the Democratic Army to revert temporarily to guerrilla tactics. The KKE suffered another setback in summer when the Athens government launched a country-wide crackdown on known and suspected Communists. Although this got out of hand—some fifteen thousand persons were deported to the Aegean Islands—and brought down the government, it nonetheless disrupted and in some cases stopped the OPLA and YIAFAKA from supporting Markos.

Markos' strength continued to grow, however. In mid-1947, his forces numbered about twenty-three thousand, with perhaps seven thousand more in training. He now increased operational unit strength to about two hundred fifty men—some sixty-five to seventy "battalions" supported by a special area network, the ETA, whose units delivered supplies and evacuated wounded. His northern neighbors had also provided machine guns, mortars, and light artillery. His bands roamed virtually unimpeded over northern Greece, they were becoming increasingly active in central Greece, and one was even operating in the Peloponnese. According to Greek Government figures, in October 1947 the Democratic Army " . . . attacked and pillaged 83 villages, destroyed 218 buildings, blew 34 bridges and wrecked 11 railway trains."[7] Major towns managed to hold out, however, and Markos lacked strength and the necessary logistic setup for sustained attacks. He also lacked suitable officers and faced constant ammunition shortages. Moreover, he had lost command autonomy to a Yugoslav-dominated Joint Balkan Staff, which increasingly began to call operational signals. Partly at Tito's and probably Stalin's instigation, the KKE announced formation of the "Free Democratic Greek Government" in December. Simultaneously, the Democratic Army attacked the major town of Kónitsa, which was to serve as the new capital. Although Markos supported the attack with mortars, machine guns, and 105-mm. guns, it failed at considerably heavy cost: twelve hundred including deserters; as added mortification, not one ally recognized the new government, nor was it allowed to join the recently established Cominform.

The spirited defense of Kónitsa reflected some healthy changes in the Greek army, which showed both in increased firepower of infantry units and in air support. Massive shipments of military equipment from the United States—$71 million worth—had been arriving since summer. Simultaneously, an American military mission worked with the government in enlarging and reorganizing the Greek armed forces, an effort that eventually resulted in an army of two hundred thousand supported by artillery, armor, and aircraft. To free the army for offensive operations, a reconstituted National Guard numbering about fifty thousand and comprising some hundred battalions became responsible for local security.[8]

The American organization responsible for this new look was a ponderous thing called the Joint United States Military Advisory and Planning Group (JUSMAPG), headed from February 1948 on by General James Van Fleet. JUSMAPG already had decided on a "military" solution of the insurgency problem, and neither Van Fleet nor the Greek National Defense Council objected. A combined Greek-American planning staff worked out a series of offensive operations, a co-ordination extended to the field via American officer advisers attached to Greek units. In theory, the newly organized Greek army should have walked over Markos' twenty-three thousand guerrillas. In fact, nothing of the sort happened. Although local garrison defenses improved, which caused increased guerrilla casualties, large-scale government offensives, or "search-and-clear" operations, met only limited success. In June, for example, forty thousand troops attacked eight thousand guerrillas in the Grámmos Mountains area. Late in August, when the national army was pushing in, Markos broke out. The government admitted to eight hundred killed and five thousand wounded; they claimed three thousand guerrilla dead, 589 captured, and over six thousand wounded. Meanwhile, JUSMAPG had been feverishly training fresh units; the magnitude of their effort was suggested by arrival from the United States of 8,330 trucks and four thousand mules in June 1948. At the end of August, the army again attacked, with about fifty thousand troops, in the neighboring Vítsi Mountain area. Markos, with some thirteen thousand guerrillas, counterattacked and actually pushed the army back, although at the price of heavy casualties.[9]

Considerable political action accompanied military give-and-take. In autumn of 1947, the Greek Government, prodded sharply by American authorities, had cracked down hard on Communist elements. Actions included "total" conscription, with segregated political instruction or permanent detention for left-wing and Communist dissidents. Government police closed Communist newspapers, attempted to purge the civil service of suspects, and abolished the right to strike; repressive measures continued throughout winter: In February the government publicly executed sixty-five Communists. In May, when Communist terrorists murdered the Minister of Justice, in Athens, the government replied with a bloodbath so severe that Britain and the United States finally protested.[10]

All this activity unfortunately furnished excellent propaganda both for the KKE and the Communist cause in general. Had the KKE acted more wisely, it could have been exploited into a powerful weapon. Instead, the KKE acted stupidly, by continuing to misuse the valuable weapon of terror. Markos' units displayed almost no discretion in dealing with villagers. Shortly after the civil war, this writer visited countless villages in Macedonia and Thrace, and the extent of wanton destruction and reported cruelties defied belief. In March, the KKE allowed Markos' units to spirit away nearly thirty thousand children for rearing in Cominform countries, a heinous act that caused widespread protest. The murder of Justice Ladas in Athens was equally pointless, as were other random acts of terror, which only brought wholesale reprisals. The biggest blow of all came in June and was no fault of the KKE: the Cominform suddenly expelled ingrate Yugoslavia.

Although Tito continued to support the insurgency, just how long his aid would last was anyone's guess. By late autumn, Markos' fiction of international brigades had become obvious to all, as had failure of the general population to rise inside Greece. Markos was forced to repair losses in the Grámmos-Vítsi campaigns only by brutal conscription. To add to his woes, Zakhariadis, the powerful secretary-general of the

KKE, forced him to abandon protracted guerrilla strategy in favor of forming conventional units, small brigades of three or four battalions, the whole forming five "divisions." This fundamental split in the insurgent camp occurred in November 1948; it swiftly widened, and, at the end of January 1949, Zakhariadis replaced Markos in command of the Democratic Army.

Meanwhile the national army had grown much stronger. The failure of the Grámmos-Vítsi campaigns had caused a basic change in tactics. Beginning in January 1949, the government lowered sights to concentrate on specific areas. By temporarily removing whole sections of population—a costly and onerous but highly effective process—it began to deprive guerrilla bands of intelligence and material support and led to some important gains. By end of January, the army had cleared four thousand insurgents from the Peloponnese at a cost of fifty-eight killed (versus sixteen hundred insurgent dead). In February, the government appointed a new commander in chief of the army, the able and popular architect of the 1940 triumph over the Italians, General Papagos. Papagos accepted only after being promised that the National Defense Council would not intrude in field operations.

Although some heavy fighting lay ahead, the days of the Democratic Army were numbered. The final blow fell in July, when Tito closed his border to the insurgents. Papagos now attacked in six-division strength and, by end of August, cracked the Vítsi stronghold. In mid-October, Zakhariadis, possibly at Stalin's insistence, asked for a cease-fire.

The physical cost of the Greek civil war was enormous. The Greek Government later claimed that the war had taken nearly twenty-nine thousand Communist lives and that perhaps twice as many were wounded. Greek army losses included almost eleven thousand killed, some twenty-three thousand wounded, and thirty-seven hundred missing. Civilians suffered much more severe losses. Major O'Ballance estimated that, all told, 158,000 Greeks died, about half of whom were militant Communists.[11]

This tragic war also produced other losses, which paradoxically accrued as a result of what the West called "victory." The first such loss was Western failure to analyze the war accurately and learn thereby. American military commanders, primarily army commanders, concluded that a Communist insurgency could be defeated by conventional methods of warfare. In subsequent years, army planners gave far too much credit to the importance of regular armies and increased firepower, and insufficient credit to the success of such methods as temporarily removing the civil population from guerrilla-infested areas and to the importance of a single, forceful commander not unduly restricted by civil control.

Neither did the enemy receive proper attention. If questioned on the cause of Communist defeat, most American officers today would mention Tito's defection and subsequent closing of the border, a misconception also held by the author of this book until he was a member of a U. S. Marine Corps mission to Greece in the early 1950s and discussed the insurgency with numerous senior Greek officers and officials, in addition to traveling extensively in the north.

Tito was not the principal cause of Markos' defeat. Markos was beaten before he started. The KKE had never concentrated on establishing an identity with the people needed to support a protracted insurgency. " . . . Guerrilla warfare must fail," Mao Tse-tung instructed, "if its political objectives do not coincide with the aspirations of the people and their sympathy, cooperation, and assistance cannot be gained."[12] As early as winter of 1941–42 Greek nationalists began to see through the fiction of EAM/ELAS, which, despite its coalitionist pretensions, would brook no minority opposition. British SOE officers operating in Greece in World War II remarked on the cavalier behavior of ELAS leaders toward the civil population. ELAS' disregard increased in the civil war, as evidenced by barbarous treatment of civilian hos-

524

tages, rapacious behavior in villages, and kidnapping children and sending them from the country—stupid actions personally and feelingly described to this author by numerous villagers in Macedonia and Thrace. This major miscalculation stemmed in part from the urban bias of Marxist-Leninist teachings (as opposed to those of Mao Tse-tung), teachings seemingly substantiated by immediate popularity and success of the insurgency, which unduly impressed the Soviet-oriented element of the KKE Central Committee; Zakhariadis was probably in large part responsible for this major error.

The second important Communist mistake also appeared during World War II, the attempt to acquire power by a military putsch. After the failure of EAM/ELAS to take power in 1945, the KKE should have followed Siantos' advice to revert to infiltration and penetration tactics. Failing that, they should later have let Markos continue with guerrilla warfare; whether he could have survived with only Romanian and Bulgarian help is a moot question that probably would have involved the Soviet Union.

The West greatly overestimated the Soviet role in Greece. What Western leaders considered a great "victory" against Russian communism did not bother Stalin nearly as much as Tito's defection. *There* was a victory for the West—and one far removed from influence of Western arms.

Believing that it had won a victory in the conventional sense, the West could only have been disillusioned by subsequent events in Greece. The war did not eliminate Communist influence. Country people may have come to loathe Markos' guerrillas, but that does not mean they came to love their deliverers. Although a healthy political stability followed the end of the war—two prime ministers, or governments, in twelve years—the work of reconstruction proceeded slowly, partly the fault of fiscal demands of a military plant far too large for a small state to support. A plodding and generally feckless reconstruction naturally caused grumbling and, in time, turned some Greeks once again to the Communist cause. As political conditions grew more unsettled, the government again exacerbated matters by invoking the traditional repressive policy that jailed thousands and eventually led to the loathsome dictatorship of the colonels.

CHAPTER FORTY-TWO

1. O'Ballance, *The Greek Civil War . . .* , 42 ff.
2. Woodhouse, *Apple of Discord*, 263 ff., 281.
3. Truman, *Year of Decisions 1945*, 522.
4. O'Ballance, *The Greek Civil War . . .* , 121 ff.
5. Ibid., 142.

6. Truman, *Years of Trial and Hope*, 98–107. See also, Kennan, *Memoirs 1925–1950.*

7. O'Ballance, *The Greek Civil War* . . . , 156.

8. Ibid., 154, 156.

9. Ibid., 174.

10. Ibid., 167 ff.

11. Ibid., 202.

12. Mao Tse-tung, *On Guerrilla Warfare*, 42–3.

CHAPTER 43

The Philippine problem • Postwar situation • The Huks • Basis of Communist popularity • Communist tactics • Government countertactics • American army influence • Success and failure • Magsaysay takes over • Limited progress in land reform • His untimely death • Revival of the Communist Huk movement: the New People's Army (NPA) opens guerrilla warfare • President Ferdinand Marcos • Nur Masouri's Moslem Moro National Liberation Front (MNLF) in Mindanao • The Bangsa Moro Army (BMA) • Marcos declares martial law • Military stalemate • Guerrilla operations expand • Fall of Marcos • Corazon Aquino's ineffectual government • Increasing guerrilla operations • General Fidel Ramos takes over • Ramos' problems • Success and failure • The job ahead

ONE OF PRESIDENT TRUMAN'S earliest official callers in April 1945 was the exiled president of the Philippine Islands, Sergio Osmeña, who expressed concern for the postwar future of his country. Truman hastened to assure him that he would ask Congress to support a reconstruction effort for this American possession that had been promised independence.

The war left these islands in appalling condition: Over a million Filipinos had been killed and hundreds of thousands wounded; disease filled the barrios; millions of people were homeless and hungry; Manila and other important cities lay in ruins; the transport network essential to ship produce in a country predominantly agricultural had been virtually destroyed, along with schools, hospitals, and villages. The political framework essential to proper government had been splintered by Japanese occupation forces and wartime collaborators. The volatile nature of Filipino politicians caused further discord, as did the crying need for legislative reforms, particularly land reforms, a banner immediately

527

hoisted by the Communist Huks, a group that survived the war in very real strength (see Chapter 30).

The Huks did not attempt a putsch during the immediate reconstruction period. One reason was the powerful and popular presence of American military forces. The obvious desire of the United States Government to grant independence also enhanced this popularity, as did human relief soon felt from a generous aid program. Still another, more subtle reason existed. In 1945–46, the Communist Party of the Philippines was not a cohesive political party controlled from either Moscow or Yenan. It contained socialist and Communist components, and each component contained members holding a variety of views generally expressed with nationalist bias. The Communist hierarchy included Mao-oriented Chinese members, but these were in a minority. Party officials had remained out of touch with each other for long periods, and no single voice dominated party councils. Luis Taruc, the *Supremo,* or commander in chief, of the Huks during and after the war, claimed that in autumn of 1945 he wanted a political solution.[1] Taruc won a seat in the new Congress, elected in April 1946. Just what would have happened had Taruc and his fellows been allowed a minority function in the new government is anyone's guess. Disruptive they were, but they were scarcely alone in using strong-arm methods before and during the election. Their subsequent opposition to such legislation as the Bell trade agreement and a military-bases agreement with the United States should have surprised no one, particularly since Filipino and American non-Communist liberals also questioned the terms of these acts.

Although the Communists were disqualified from their congressional seats on grounds of using terrorism during the campaign, the trouble went much deeper. Taruc and his associates represented a distinct challenge to a hegemony exercised by immensely powerful landowners and industrialists spawned during four decades of American overlordship. This group, which included substantial American interests, had usurped the old landowning role of the Church, which had made itself hated by peasants. William Howard Taft's dreams of giving peasants a fair shake (see Chapter 11) had disappeared into a day of real greed: In 1944, peasant farmers still owned only about 10 per cent of the land they tilled. They farmed remaining land on a tenant basis, with the average plot too small to support the farmer once his rent, 50 per cent of the crop, was paid. Nothing was secret about system or figures. They were over four hundred years old. They explained four centuries of poverty punctuated by uprisings, and, in 1946, they explained a Communist popularity that a reactionary government was too greedy and frightened to admit or accept.

Quiet analysis would have shown the fragile nature of this popularity, which derived from protest against perverted democracy, not belief in atheistic communism—abhorrent to good Catholics. It was a Red balloon highly vulnerable to puncture by proper leadership and corrective legislation, but a balloon equally capable of expansion to unpleasant proportions. A genuine land-reform bill in 1946 would have deflated the balloon virtually overnight and would have saved the government a long and costly war that nearly resulted in Huk victory. Instead of absorbing and then neutralizing opposition by healthy legislation, the government challenged the enemy. Charge collided with countercharge, the friction depositing powder that soon exploded into intimidation and murder. When the government unseated Communist members of Congress, the Huks took to the hills and raised the standard of revolt.

This was not as forlorn as it sounds. Many Huks had buried World War II weapons against such a contingency, and, in the back country of central Luzon, had little trouble in finding relatively secure bases. The Politburo in Manila ordered dissidents to revert to wartime organization and establish Regional Commands or, Recos. Each of the half dozen Recos occupied a specific area, where it operated in squadrons of varying size. The party had also kept alive its village network, which was called the Barrio United Defense Corps or BUDC, the "farmers by day, guerrillas by night." BUDC units normally operated " . . . in their own locality, attacking targets of opportunity, assisting or reinforcing forces from the higher strata, or simply maintaining the 'guerrilla presence,' their domination of the local citizens."[2]

In short order, then, the Huks had a cause centered on the age-old cry of "land for the landless," and they had a viable organization that, for the moment, answered such urgent problems as food, clothing, and shelter. There were weaknesses. They would need food, clothing, shelter, and security over a long period. They would need communications between units operating in six thousand square miles of primitive country and between units and the underground Central Committee in Manila. They would need additional weapons and, most of all, information as to government strength and weakness.

The factor common to these needs was the peasant population. Although no figures exist, veteran observers have suggested that the Huks probably found about 10 per cent of the peasants actively favoring them, about 10 per cent actively opposed to them, and about 80 per cent neutral. This middle body, this frightened and apathetic 80 per cent, would have to furnish food, clothing, shelter, security, and information essential to Huk survival. They constituted Mao's famous water in which guerrilla fish were to swim.

How did the guerrilla go about winning peasant support? He used to advantage his physical and armed presence in proclaiming a cause that struck a responsive note among many disgruntled peasants. The

Huks oriented their appeal personally rather than politically. The honeyed words held a strong nationalist bias that associated people virtually devoid of hope and dignity with the freedom fighters of yesterday and today, the whole performance gaining force from contrast of the guerrilla presence with either minimum or no government presence. The guerrilla did not appeal by words alone. By successfully attacking police stations and small military outposts, the Huks encouraged the eager and intimidated the wary, and in the process, gained arms for new recruits. Nor did they hesitate to eliminate known opponents by using selective terrorism, usually torture and murder.

This consolidation process should have been a dangerous time for the Huk movement. Despite advantages gained by seizing the initiative, the Huks could not set up communication networks overnight; neither could they effectively broaden their support base in a short time. Had the government reacted skillfully, it might have ended the insurgency in short order. Unfortunately, its reaction was such as to help, and not hinder, the insurgent cause.

The Philippine Government was ill-equipped to cope with this insurgency. Police forces, along with other public services, were still being reorganized. The government's armed forces consisted only of a constabulary, the Military Police Command (MPC), equipped with small arms and supervised by American army officers. These company-size units lacked training and discipline, and in early raids on suspected Huk hideouts, they used little restraint either in rounding up suspects or in dealing with peasants.

This was partly the government's fault. President Roxas and his advisers failed to understand that the basic mission of democratic government is to represent the people and defend their interests. It follows that, in an insurgency situation, the first mission of government is to protect the people, not alone on humanitarian grounds but also because only the people can furnish information necessary to accomplish the corollary mission of destroying insurgent organization. As two veterans of the Philippine insurgency, Colonels Valeriano and Bohannan, have pointed out in their invaluable book *Counter-Guerrilla Operations— The Philippine Experience,* Roxas confused priorities and ordered the constabulary to eliminate the threat without due heed of either security or rights of peasants. He compounded this error by placing operational restraints on the constabulary. In effect, the government told the constabulary to suppress the rebellion by arresting rebels, but, at the same time, it refused to pass emergency legislation giving the constabulary sufficient powers to accomplish the task. Under the writ of habeas corpus, a suspect could be detained only seventy-two hours, an insufficient time for methodical interrogation. The normal troop solution was to beat a suspect as warning. This, the theory of deterrence, had been exploded a thousand times in all countries, and is particularly dangerous if the suspect happens to be innocent.[3]

The government also erred in ordering the MPC to place garrisons in towns and villages and on large estates of powerful politicians. This tied down units, and such was general behavior of troops that their presence further alienated the peasant population. Huk spies were everywhere, and soldiers could not move without their knowing it.

Deprived of information, the MPC could not begin to accomplish its mission. Initial failure produced frustration. The Huks, on the other hand, were daily gaining support and, with it, ample information on MPC plans and movements. As MPC patrols fell into ambushes and small outposts suffered surprise attacks, fear joined frustration to increase brutality toward people whom the soldiers were supposed to be protecting. Each instance of brutality converted more people to the Communist cause, a vicious circle that could only have been terminated by intelligent and decisive action at top governmental levels.

Roxas not only failed to assuage peasant dissatisfaction with half-baked legislative measures, he positively encouraged it with his executive policy. He answered initial Huk successes by building an imposing (and expensive) national army, a policy encouraged by American military advisers and supported by the American Government. The new battalion combat teams were splendid enough, supported as they were by armor, aircraft, artillery, and even war dogs, but they continued to fight guerrillas as if waging conventional war. Although search operations at times disrupted guerrilla communications and even, on occasion, trapped a few Huks, they more often than not disrupted and antagonized the native population. Unable to obtain accurate information from alienated peasants, the army employed *the zona* technique of sealing off and "screening" one or more hostile villages. The *zona* was stupid psychologically, because the Japanese had used it frequently and people associated it immediately with horrible tortures and executions. If employed at all, it should have been but sparingly and then only by disciplined troops who would go out of their way to regain support of villagers. Instead, it was used frequently, and, all too often, to gratify baser instincts of soldiers. Large-scale search-and-destroy operations also backfired. The army would spend weeks and sometimes months preparing a surprise attack in force against a guerrilla redoubt. Then several battalions suitably reinforced by artillery and air units would throw what communiqués called "a ring of steel" around the target area. These attacks rarely, if ever, achieved surprise. Taruc later wrote:

> . . . If we knew it was going to be a light attack, we took it easy.
> If it might give us more trouble than we could handle, we slipped

M.E.P.

out quietly in the darkest hours of the night, abandoning the area of operation altogether ... it could be both amusing and saddening to watch the Philippine Air Force busily bombing and strafing, or to see thousands of government troops and civil guards cordoning our campsite and saturating, with every type of gunfire, the unfortunate trees and vegetation. Or we would watch them, worn and weary, scaling the whole height and width of a mountain, with not a single Huk in the area.

Taruc claimed that six years of fighter-bomber attacks killed exactly twelve guerrillas![4]

These "ring of steel" operations inevitably involved peasant communities, whose villages sometimes became subject to *zona* treatment or even to outright attack. This merely deepened basic antagonisms, while false claims of success only heightened Huk prestige. The gulf between army (government) and people was so great that, by 1950, army units

... adopted the practice of entering every inhabited area in Huklandia in an exaggerated combat posture.... From their demeanor, it was to be assumed that they felt they were among enemies, that they anticipated momentary attack. The psychological effect of this was deplorable....

Other gimmicks proved harmful to the objective of winning over the population. One was the absurd " . . . reconnaissance by fire—firing into areas where guerrillas might be, without concern for the civilians who might equally well be there." Similarly, the "open area" technique allowed troops in certain areas to shoot at anything that moved. Road checkpoints further antagonized the populace, because, more often than not, the soldiers " . . . were collecting toll while disrupting thoroughly a great deal of commercial traffic." Propaganda posters depicting Huk cruelties were so realistic that they frightened peasants not *away* from but *toward* the Huks.[5]

More sophisticated tactics also boomeranged. In theory, the Nenita unit seemed unbeatable. This was a small detachment that was organized and trained " . . . to seek out and destroy top leaders of the Huk. Openly based in the heart of the strongest Huk area, it sought by disciplined ruthless action to strike terror into the Guerrillas and their supporters." In practice, " . . . the unit did succeed in capturing or killing many Huks, in substantially dampening the fighting spirit of many more, and in reducing the effectiveness of local support organizations." Alas, the operation was a success, but the patient died:

> . . . the overall effect of the Nenita operation . . . was, on the whole, to increase support for the Huk. How could a government claiming concern for the welfare of the people and protection of their interests support a gang of ruthless killers, many of whose victims were not proved traitors? . . . In the end, many Filipinos were convinced that the government, by the use of such a force showed itself to be at least as bad as the Huk, and perhaps less deserving of support than the "agrarian reformers."[6]

Luis Taruc succinctly summed up the lesson: " . . . One thing seems clear: no country—least of all a Christian land—can defeat Communism by the use of un-Christian methods."[7]

During this crucial period neither the Philippine Government nor its American advisers correctly analyzed the nature of the insurgency, which would have caused a rearrangement of priorities. Clouds of confusion continued to cover the action, with a harmful and wasteful proliferation of official agencies. Constabulary, army, national police, and Manila police *each* maintained an intelligence organization. ". . . Nearly a dozen other agencies, ranging from the special agents of the Office of the President to the Customs Secret Service, thought they had a proper role in the collection of intelligence about Communists, or the Huk, or both, and they too engaged in it."[8] The Huks prospered from this needless competition and from misplaced military zeal. While government troops harassed the people by day, " . . . every night the barrios were visited by

Huk units, organizers, and propagandists who held impromptu meetings enlivened by revolutionary songs and short political skits."[9] Such grass-roots propaganda sessions allowed the Huks to disrupt communications between government and people by constantly contrasting official sayings with official doings.

Nocturnal visits also obtained young recruits for guerrilla units in the hills. Here the recruit usually attended school: " . . . a school for cadet officers, another for mass organizers . . . schools for intelligence officers, couriers, and medical workers. . . . The more advanced students attended classes in Philippine and world history, social and civic science, politics and government, mathematics." The Huks used group forums both to disseminate slanted news and for the weekly "production meeting"—" . . . a criticism and self-criticism session of the type common in all Communist parties everywhere."[10]

Such methods resulted in steady growth of Huk strength, which Taruc later reported as ten thousand armed fighters and two thousand active sympathizers in 1948. Valeriano and Bohannan agreed with the figure of twelve thousand guerrillas, but concluded, " . . . perhaps 150,000 of the nearly two million people in the area [of central Luzon] were sympathizers and supporters of the Huk." This did not include an undoubtedly high percentage of the passive population, which the Huks continued to intimidate in their favor.[11]

Despite substantial Huk gains, the insurgency confined itself largely to central Luzon. Although the Central Committee in Manila grandly proclaimed formation of a People's Liberation Army, with " . . . a time-table for expansion and for the seizure of national power,"[12] the socialist and Communist factions already were arguing over long-term goals. Neither the Central Committee in Manila nor the most united and determined Huk leadership in the field could overcome logistic and administrative problems in converting guerrillas to a semiregular force. Units lacked supporting arms and services of all types, and they possessed neither geographical proximity nor logistic means to gain these arms. They lacked safe areas in which to organize and train semiregular forces, and their supply system probably could not have supported the effort. An army would have ended the almost autonomous authority jealously protected by Reco commanders. Necessarily rudimentary communications also hindered disciplined and co-ordinated operations, and the Huks never did eliminate the bandit and criminal element that often hurt the insurgency by exploiting the environment for private gain.

Lack of co-ordinate command and growing dissension in higher ranks tended to panic some units into placing mistaken emphasis on terrorist methods, which culminated in April 1949 with the ambush and murder of a motor party that included the popular widow of President Quezon: " . . . For the first time, widespread popular wrath flared against the Huk." The high command also incensed public opinion by ordering all-out attacks on cities and army garrisons in 1950.[13]

By this time, the insurgency had produced some excellent counter-tactics by the Philippine army and constabulary. By far the best army tactic was the small patrol (as Americans had learned in 1898–1902). Ranging from half-squad to platoon size, patrols extended the government's presence to villages, they sometimes obtained intelligence on guerrilla movements, and they set up mobile checkpoints to disrupt guerrilla communications. Extreme mobility of patrols kept the guerrilla off balance and, not least, they allowed the soldier an active and interesting role, as opposed to the deadening garrison, or passive role, and thereby spawned new and sometimes effective tactical ideas.

The best army commanders practiced a variety of patrol tactics:

> . . . regular patrols which passed through specified areas almost on a schedule, following roads or trails. There were unscheduled, unexpected patrols, sometimes following an expected one by fifteen minutes. There were patrols following eccentric routes, eccentric schedules, moving cross-country at right angles to normal travel patterns, which often unexpectedly intercepted scheduled patrols.[14]

In guerrilla-infested country, one patrol paralleled another so that either could respond to an attack. Some commanders saturated an area with patrols to overload the guerrilla intelligence service—rather like dropping strips of tinfoil to jam a radar screen.

Colonel Valeriano's constabulary company trained a force of four officers and seventy-six men, Force X, as " . . . a realistic pseudo-Huk unit that could, in enemy guise, infiltrate deep into enemy territory." The reader may remember that General Funston employed a similar device to capture the insurgent leader Aguinaldo in 1901 (see Chapter 11). In addition to excellent "kills" of Huks, Force X

> . . . found that most of the town mayors and chiefs of police were in collusion with the enemy. They discovered that there were enlisted men in the PC [constabulary] company on the other side of the swamps who were giving information to the Huks. They learned that supplies were left by women in selected spots along the road to be picked up at sundown by the Huk. . . . [15]

On occasion, Valeriano's regular company would "capture" some of his Huks and turn them over to local police. In jail, they frequently obtained valuable intelligence on collaborators. Valeriano also tested loyalty of local officials by "kidnaping" peaceful farmers: If the local mayor or police chief failed to report the man's absence within five days, he was probably pro-Huk.[16]

Other units used civilian disguises to infiltrate villages and pick up valuable information. One unit acquired small panel trucks and filled the back end with soldiers—an unpleasant surprise for any Huk foraging patrol that stopped the vehicle. A commander well versed in old Moro campaigns remembered an American army habit of "losing" .45-caliber cartridges. Loaded with dynamite, they blew the Moro to bits when he fired them. This particular commander prepared cartridges that would blow up only the rifle, then inserted them into Huk supply channels with reportedly substantial "psychological and physical effects." Some commanders left units behind to surprise guerrillas after a regular army "sweep"; others confused guerrillas into precipitate action by firing hundreds of flares.

Well-trained and -motivated soldiers will usually come up with shrewd and cunning battle practices, but these count for little if basic strategy is in error—and that was the case in the Philippines. Fortunately for the future of that country, a natural leader finally tore himself from Manila's festering political womb to emerge in 1950. This was the famous Ramon Magsaysay, who became Minister of National Defense in the Quirino government. Magsaysay was a peasant with a purpose hammered home by a determined but winning personality, which partially removed the sting from his decisive and sometimes ruthless actions. Believing that the power of his country lay in peasant hands, he insisted that the first mission of government was to represent and protect peasants. In its simplest form, this meant returning government to people or, conversely, convincing the people that representatives of the government existed to serve their needs. To the fury of many politicians, Magsaysay usurped the Communist call of "land for the landless" to make it the rallying cry for his party in the 1950 elections. Though his plans were later sabotaged, these were not empty words, and he went to a great deal of trouble explaining his reform program to the peasants.

Appointed Secretary of National Defense, Magsaysay turned to the immense task of effectively organizing the counterinsurgency for the first time. One of his early successes consisted in arresting the Politburo and Secretariat of the Communist Party in Manila. He then turned to teaching the army to associate itself with the people. He first introduced widespread internal reforms designed to check corruption and improve discipline. At the same time, he tried to explain the government's mission to the military and show commanders how to carry it out. Magsaysay summarily eliminated such flagrant violations of human rights (and common sense) as "free-fire" areas, and he sharply curtailed the "combat-posture" of troops "at the ready" entering villages they theoretically were to protect. He changed the *zona* technique to a civilized interrogation, which insured individual privacy and, just as important, left no doubt in the individual's mind that the purpose of the operation was his own protection. He insisted that the major aim of any military operation was to win civil co-operation—for, without it, the army would lack information and would not catch guerrillas. If a village was short of food because of its contribution, voluntary or forced, to the Huks, Magsaysay ordered the soldiers to replace the food. As peasant hostility disappeared, military commanders began to receive valid and timely intelligence on which they based operations that soon yielded Huks—killed, captured, or surrendered. A generous amnesty program also attracted Huk defectors, particularly when pressure mounted from military operations. Eighteen months after taking office, Magsaysay had brought the insurrection under control.

Magsaysay's political reforms did not work as well. In resigning his cabinet post, in February 1953, he wrote:

> . . . Under your concept of my duties as Secretary of National Defense, my job is just to go on killing Huk. But you must realize that we cannot solve the problem of dissidence simply by military measures. It would be futile to go on killing Huk, while the Administration continues to breed dissidence by neglecting the problems of our masses.
>
> The need of a vigorous assault on these problems I have repeatedly urged upon you, but my pleas have fallen on deaf ears. To cite an instance, some eight months ago I informed you that the military situation was under control, and I offered to leave the Department of National Defense in order to speed up the land-resettlement program of the government. My purpose was to shift our war on Communism to one of its basic causes in our country, land hunger. . . . [17]

A few months later, Ramon Magsaysay was elected president and set about implementing long-overdue reforms. Owing to the opposition of very determined landowners, a very determined Magsaysay had made only limited progress in his land reform program before his untimely death in an airplane crash in 1957.

Any hope of reform died with Magsaysay. The gap between rich and poor remained the widest in Southeast Asia, with 60 per cent of its sixty million people living in poverty, that is with an income of less than $120 a month.[18] No wonder that in the ensuing years the Communist Party revived and with it the former Huk guerrilla movement now in the guise of the New People's Army (NPA), which began life with sixty guerrillas and thirty-five rifles.[19] In the late 1960s, the guerrillas began operations in central Luzon, an unhappy event answered by President Ferdinand Marcos with a major but not very effective counterinsurgency campaign against "the Communist menace." Marcos faced still another menace from Mindanao (see map, Chapter 11), where more than five million Moslem Moros had formed the Moro National Liberation Front (MNLF) headed by Nur Masouri. The Moros had been fighting for survival for as long as they could remember. The most recent threat to their livelihood if not their existence occurred in the early 1950s when the Magsaysay government opened Mindanao to Filipino settlers and to international companies. In opposing this massive land grab, the Moros incurred governmental wrath in the form of the Marcos-sponsored Ilaga group of terrorist mercenaries. Lionel Davis, not an altogether unbiased observer, credits Ilaga and the army with the slaughter of more than one hundred thousand Moslems, including women, children and the elderly, and the destruction of two hundred thousand houses and mosques "together with hundreds of Islamic schools and vast plantations."[20] Having repeatedly been denied autonomous rule, the MNLF was now demanding independence in order to establish an Islamic state,[21] a demand backed by the Bangsa Moro Army (BMA).[22]

Such was the extent of both threats that in 1972 Marcos declared martial law in order to contain the "Communist rebellion." Troops sent to Mindanao only exacerbated a tense situation. The Moro revolt spread to the Sulu archipelago and fighting intensified. By early 1973, " . . . some 3,000 people had been killed and hundreds of villages burned."[23] Marcos now backed off, recalling the troops and promising amnesty and economic aid if the Moros would turn in their arms—a program that died at birth.

For the next fourteen years, Marcos and wife Imelda ruled the islands as if they were a private fiefdom, amassing in the process an immense fortune (still not completely accounted for). As land and economic reforms remained a dead issue, as impoverished farmers abandoned the land to subsist in squalid city barrios, the Communist movement expanded, its political wing the Maoist National Democratic Front, its military wing the New People's Army (NPA). Moro insurgents on Mindanao similarly expanded their war by means of the growing Bangsa Moro Army.

In 1986, a bloodless revolt against the patently fraudulent election of Marcos caused his hurried departure from the country. Heading the interim government was the opposition "people power" candidate, Corazon Aquino, widow of reformist politician Benigno Aquino, Jr., who had been assassinated three years earlier. At this point, the seventeen-year-old communist insurgency " . . . affected the lives of Filipinos in 20 percent of towns and villages throughout the archipelago,"[24] a figure that almost daily was increasing. After declaring a policy of national reconciliation, the new president arranged a sixty-day cease-fire beginning in December 1986.[25] This was to be followed by peace talks with the Communist insurgents and a country-wide program of land reform and economic development designed to create self-sufficient communities, particularly in rural areas from where the NPA drew the bulk of its recruits.

There is little doubt that Corazon Aquino meant well and she did have many things working for her. She was relatively young, intelligent, industrious, and immensely popular. But she was also a scion of a large landowning family and to a certain degree a prisoner of her conservative heritage. Inexperienced in government, she lacked not only the qualifications but the essential toughness necessary to shake down a civil administration and army riddled with political factionalism and widespread corruption. If she enjoyed a popular base, she lacked a political base (the coalition that put her in power soon fell to pieces), and she was faced with an almost superhuman task of repairing decades of damage resulting from inept and dishonest government. The mainstay of her power, the armed forces, consisted of several opposing factions, not all of them loyal to her government, nor did senior commanders hold a close consensus on how best to fight the insurgents. The economy was in deplorable condition. Scores of state-owned enterprises were in bankruptcy, there was a steady outflow of private capital, the external debt stood at about $25 billion.

In addition, there were the insurrections. The fighting in the south, which had taken an estimated sixty thousand lives since 1972,[26] showed no signs of abating. The Moro MNLF's guerrilla army, financed by Iran and Libya, numbered more than thirty thousand regulars divided into four mobile armies and ten provincial armies supported by thousands of armed barrio defense forces.[27] The Communist NPA, now "a well-armed and trained force" estimated by some analysts to number twenty-two thousand,[28] by others thirty thousand,[29] was said to be operating in sixty-nine out of seventy-three provinces.[30] Supported by a reported one hundred thousand sympathizers and financed by $2.6 million a year derived from extorting businessmen,[31] it continued to demand total reform and in the interim a place in a coalition government.

To no one's great surprise, the peace talks with the Communists never got much further than a general disagreement on the agenda before National Democratic Front representatives broke them off at the end of January.[32] Meanwhile, a protest march on the presidential palace by ten thousand farmers demanding land reform ran into police resistance, with some twenty people killed and a hundred injured, an event that Cardinal Jaime Sin, a supporter of Aquino, blamed "in great measure" on the government's failure to launch an effective land reform program.[33]

The rest of the year was all downhill. Talks with the Moro MNLF in January resulted in an agreement soon shredded by Moslem dissidents and by a wave of armed attacks by a second guerrilla group. Fresh talks in February failed to resolve the autonomy issue, as did further talks in July. Government vacillation on reforms alienated more and more of Aquino's earlier supporters, not to mention opposition groups. Negotiations with the Communists and a steadily worsening security situation had widened rifts in the armed forces, segments of which mounted two coup attempts and one assassination attempt on Aquino during the year. In mid-1987, Communist "sparrow units"—commando assassination teams—opened up on police, military officers, and politicians, and would take a hundred victims by year's end.[34] NPA attacks increased in the countryside and expanded to southern Luzon. In October, guerrillas killed three U.S. servicemen—henceforth, the National Democratic Front warned, all U.S. military and civilian personnel, " . . . aid officials and corporate executives linked to the U.S. . . . 'are to be targets for attack by the New People's Army.' "[35]

The Aquino administration, which lasted until spring of 1992, stumbled from one failure to another as the president increasingly lost what little control she had ever exercised over the government. No one could fault her courage—she somehow managed to survive seven attempted military coups,[36] and at least two assassination attempts in five years. It was her performance that did the damage, her failure to ameliorate the conditions that helped to keep the insurgencies alive and well.

In May 1992 her defense secretary and chief of the armed forces, General Fidel Váldez Ramos, was elected president for a six-year term. The Communist and Moro insurgencies were only two of his problems. Corruption in both public and private sectors was strangling the economy, yet a revival of the economy was vital in a country of increasing unemployment and an average per capita income of $740 a year.[37] A major power shortage that had resulted from unbelievably corrupt mismanagement of the National Power Corporation had brought daily brownouts and frequent blackouts in the major cities, a chaotic situation that was said to have cost industry $16 million a day in lost production and canceled orders, not to mention thousands of laid-off workers.[38] A major crime wave, abetted by widespread corruption in the national police, included the kidnapping of wealthy Chinese for huge ransom payments. All this not unnaturally was driving foreign investment away, a disastrous trend which Ramos attempted to stem by wooing major foreign companies to the islands by means of tax breaks and other concessions. His initial priority, however, concerned the insurgencies. Following Aquino's lead in 1986, Ramos at once launched a peace initiative, offering amnesty to all rebels including the Moros " . . . who renounce armed struggle,"[39] and holding out a further olive branch by asking the Filipino Congress to legalize the Philippine Communist Party.

Progress on all these issues was slow during 1992, and not a few skeptics wrote Ramos off. This was a mistake. Ramos is an experienced bureaucratic infighter with a strong following not only in the armed forces but also among Manila's business elite. He also realized that most of his countrymen were tired of the war and desperately wanted a turn-around in government.

In February 1993 Ramos surprised both critics and supporters by pledging "to cut the poverty rate in half" and "raise Filipino income by a third" before the end of his office. Moreover, he promised to have electric power fully restored by September. In April he pushed the Electric Power Crisis Act through Congress, a draconian set of measures that won him World Bank financing to build new power plants. According to information received by this writer in December 1993, the power situation is greatly improved, with more progress to come.[40]

Ramos skillfully handled another thorny issue by forcing Imelda Marcos to bury her husband's corpse in a remote Luzon town, thus turning what could have become a disruptive event into a virtual non-event[41] (followed a few weeks later by Imelda's being sentenced to eighteen to twenty-four years of imprisonment on proven corruption charges).[42] Another major victory followed in November 1993 when talks took place between the government and Nur Masouri's National Liberation Front, the first in more than twenty years. Although the two-week session left a great many problems unresolved regarding Moro autonomy, it did come up with a cease-fire agreement—the results still to be determined. A few weeks later, Ramos capped this breakthrough with the makings of a $2.5 billion investment in the Philippines by a U.S. consortium, the details of which remain to be announced as of this writing (December 1993).

This is not to suggest that the battered old Philippines are out of the woods. A good many thousand Communist guerrillas are said to control several thousand of the country's one hundred thousand villages; exiled Communist Party hardliners are allegedly still calling for stepped-up attacks against villages and government installations.[43]

Obviously a great deal remains to be done if government performance is to turn the wheel full circle. It is just possible, however, that the country has finally been blessed with a leader who eventually can implement the vital reforms once dreamed of by Ramon Magsaysay.

CHAPTER FORTY-THREE

1. Taruc, 24 ff.
2. Valeriano and Bohannan, 62.
3. Ibid., 66–7.
4. Taruc, 42.
5. Valeriano and Bohannan, 124, 96–7.
6. Ibid., 97–8.

7. Taruc, 57.
8. Valeriano and Bohannan, 174–5.
9. Taruc, 43.
10. Taruc, 47.
11. Valeriano and Bohannan, 23.
12. Ibid.
13. Ibid., 117.
14. Ibid., 130.
15. Ibid., 143–8.
16. Hosmer.
17. Valeriano and Bohannan, 107.
18. Burton, 533.
19. Davis, 42–3, 49.
20. Ibid., 45.
21. International Institute for Strategic Studies, *Strategic Survey 1986–87*, 171.
22. Davis, 18.
23. *Columbia Encyclopaedia 1975*, 2132.
24. Burton, 527.
25. Davis, 3.
26. Clutterbuck, *Terrorism and Guerrilla Warfare*, 131.
27. Davis, 46.
28. International Institute for Strategic Studies, *Strategic Survey 1986–87*, 171.
29. Davis, 50, citing an alleged 1987 CIA report.
30. Ibid., 48.
31. Clutterbuck, *Terrorism and Guerrilla Warfare*, 130.
32. Davis, 3.
33. International Institute for Strategic Studies, *Strategic Survey 1987–88*, 173.
34. Clutterbuck, *Terrorism and Guerrilla Warfare*, 130.
35. International Institute for Strategic Studies, *Strategic Survey 1987–88*, 174.
36. *International Herald Tribune*, May 2, 1991.
37. *Newsweek*, February 8, 1993.
38. *International Herald Tribune*, April 6, 1993.
39. *Newsweek*, September 7, 1992.
40. Private information in the author's files.
41. *The Independent* (U.K.), August 30, September 8, 1993.
42. *New York Times*, September 25, 1993.
43. *Newsweek*, September 7, 1992.

CHAPTER 44

Rise of Indonesian nationalism • Allied occupation • Clashes with the British • The Communist element • Negotiations break down • The Dutch take over • A military solution • Guerrilla warfare • Sukarno's problems • The Communist revolt • Dutch intransigence • American intervention • The Dutch yield

So INTENSE the cold war, so mighty the issues, that it became tempting to blame all world problems on this quarrel of ideologies. To do so was to ignore recognized historical forces, particularly that of nationalism, which, decades earlier, had created and subsequently sustained a host of problem areas. In some instances, the Kremlin and local Communist parties attempted to exploit the condition. Other areas, however, held but peripheral connection to the conflict between the Soviet Union and the West, and almost no connection with communism. Such was the case with Indonesia and Palestine, whose peoples now used differing forms of guerrilla warfare to achieve specific political goals.

The Dutch never did regain balance in the East Indies. World War II left the Netherlands bruised and battered, unable to fill the power vacuum created by Japan's surrender. A powerful expeditionary force, acting promptly and effectively, would have had its hands full in reclaiming the islands from the new Sukarno-Hatta government. The Netherlands had no such force. Instead, it had to rely on Admiral Lord Mountbatten's South-East Asia Command, itself stretched thin in this vast area.

Dutch attempts to have the Japanese govern by proxy proved futile. Clashes between Japanese soldiers and Indonesian nationals soon turned to heavy fighting. The first allied officers who reached Djakarta in September 1945 reported that the nationalists " . . . controlled the public utilities of Jakarta and many more cities. The Republican gov-

INDONESIA
• Towns and Cities

0   400   800 miles

M.E.P.

ernment had set up ministries, was operating radio stations and newspapers, and regarded itself as the nation's functioning authority."[1] Professor Kahin noted " . . . throughout most of the area, in Java and Sumatra in particular, civil administration was operating at a level of efficiency that quite amazed the Allied forces."[2]

In mid-September 1945, a military mission arrived with Dutch representation, and toward the end of the month Mountbatten sent in a company of troops. The Dutch wanted this mission to arrest the republican leadership in order to strip the movement of its strength. Refusing the request, Mountbatten advised Dutch officials to open negotiations with Sukarno's government, wise advice in view of Japan's legacy to Indonesia.[3]

However empty Japanese words, the promise of independence during the occupation had claimed millions of minds. The Japanese also left the newly proclaimed republic with a militia-style army, the Peta, which numbered about 120,000. Japanese reliance on Indonesians during the occupation also left a reasonable framework of government. In Dr. Otto Heilbrunn's words, " . . . The Indonesians were provided with a national will to independence, the military means to achieve it, and the administrative ability to sustain it."[4]

The Dutch refused this premise. A build-up in occupation forces, both British and Dutch, caused the newly appointed lieutenant governor to insist on non-appeasement. His hand was strengthened in late October, when the British commander, Lieutenant General Sir Philip Christison, told Sukarno that the British recognized only the Netherlands government of the East Indies. Continuing clashes between Dutch and Indonesian nationals caused Christison, however, to prohibit more Dutch troops from landing in Java.

Christison's recognition of the Netherlands Government infuriated Indonesians. So did his use of Japanese troops in reclaiming cities from republican forces in Java, Sumatra, and Bali. When a British task force attempted to reoccupy the major port of Surabaya, in Java, some twenty thousand republican troops supported by a hundred twenty thousand civilians brandishing krises, clubs, and poisoned spears attacked a British Indian brigade. British troops were actually being torn limb from limb when Sukarno and Hatta flew in and tried to stop the massacre. The British finally had to land another division, supported by air and naval gunfire—a battle that lasted until the end of November, when the Indonesians gave way.[5]

This unfortunate period, in which other serious clashes occurred between Indonesian and British troops, convinced the British more than ever that a solution had to be reached through negotiation.

> . . . As this became clear, the British commenced to stiffen against the refusal of the Dutch to deal with the Republic and put strong pressure on them to negotiate to the end that peaceful compromise might be effected.[6]

Although the Dutch army continued "pacification" operations, sometimes with considerable brutality as in southwestern Celebes, local Dutch officials were inclined to agree to solution by negotiation. If they detected a factional threat to the Sukarno-Hatta government, mainly from Communists led by Tan Malaka, they nonetheless estimated that seventy-five thousand troops would be needed to pacify the archipelago—whatever the ruling party. At the end of 1945, their military force numbered about twenty thousand, with a promise of ten thousand more during 1946.

Sukarno and Hatta also were willing to negotiate. Frightened by extremist elements that brought about the Surabaya rebellion, they attempted to broaden the base of their government, by introducing a prime minister, the able and pro-Western Sutan Sjahrir, who was to answer to a parliament, KNIP. Although this was a far cry from parliamentary democracy, Sjahrir introduced a modifying element both within republican ranks and in the conflict with the Dutch.

The British, cautiously backed by the United States, brought contesting parties to the conference table in February 1946. Although talks began quite favorably, extremist elements of both states soon brought impasse. In the case of Indonesia, the obstruction came from the National Front, a Communist organization dominated by Tan Malaka. In March 1946, Sukarno invited the Front to form a cabinet, and when it failed to do so, he returned Sjahrir as prime minister. He answered the Front's next attempt to overthrow the government by jailing its prominent leaders. The government, however, was walking on eggs and could not afford to be too conciliatory in negotiating with the Dutch.

Despite all this trouble, Sjahrir had still introduced a workable proposal which got as far as a conference in the Netherlands in April. And here the Dutch conferees proved intransigent. Their attitude befitted the seventeenth century, not the mid-twentieth:

> ... a major difficulty was the permeation of Dutch politics by religious ideas. Many Dutchmen believed in the divine right of the Dutch to rule the Indies. " ... all authority derives from God," said Mr. Max van Poll, leader of the big Roman Catholic party, " ... therefore, Dutch authority in the Netherlands East Indies is willed by God." Similarly, Mr. J. Meijerink of the Anti-Revolutionary (Calvinist) party, declared, "To maintain God's authority, the [Dutch] government may consider itself in God's service. . . . It must not hesitate to wield the sword if necessary."[7]

Mainly by threat of withdrawing all troops by November, the British again brought the Dutch to new talks in September. To everyone's surprise, this meeting prospered from the beginning. After agreeing to a cease-fire, the two sides worked out an agreement in line with the Sjahrir proposals. The Netherlands recognized " ... the Republic of Indonesia as exercising *de facto* authority over Java, Sumatra, and Madura." The two governments were to co-operate in forming " ... a sovereign democratic state on a federal basis to be called the United States of Indonesia." Together with the Netherlands, this would form a Netherlands-Indonesian Union. Meanwhile, the republic would resist extending its contacts abroad.[8]

Dutch and Indonesian representatives initialed the agreement in November 1946. Although important political groups in both countries opposed the main provisions, the agreement is one of the might-have-beens of history. The Dutch Government, however, failed to sign the document until the end of March 1947. By that time, goodwill was fast disappearing, and each government was violating one or more clauses. Before the meeting, the Dutch had set up the puppet state of East Indonesia; they now established the states of West Borneo and West Java. When the British evacuated their troops in late 1946, the Dutch extended control to coastal areas on Java and Sumatra that they soon held with ninety-two thousand troops. By late 1946, the Dutch Government was strong enough to undertake a "pacification campaign":

... In the areas where Indonesian resistance was most stubborn, authority was given to the savage Captain "Turk" Westerling to do what was necessary to break it. His most effective method was to have his troops round up village populations in the areas of principal resistance and arbitrarily pull men out of the crowd and shoot them, continuing this process until he was satisfied that the assembled villagers had yielded sufficient information concerning which of their members had been active in the resistance and the whereabouts of resistance forces. Probably between 500 and 1,000 Indonesians were killed in this manner, while probably at least 10,000 others were killed in the course of the whole campaign [that is, the pacification campaign from mid-December 1946 to March 1947]. Most of those associated with the resistance who were not killed were jailed and for the most part remained in jail until after the transfer of Dutch sovereignty at the end of 1949. ... [9]

Understandably, Indonesians reacted violently to this treatment, and incidents mounted. The republican government continued to sabotage the Dutch Government in East Indonesia, and also to extend contacts abroad in search of international support. Nor did the government seem in a hurry to ship rice necessary to feed Dutch-occupied areas of the large islands.[10]

The Dutch seized on this last issue as an excuse to solve the issue by military means. In July 1947, the army launched a "police action"— a euphemism for a large-scale attack supported by aircraft and spearheaded by tanks that soon rolled over hundreds of miles to occupy cities, ports, and other key areas in Java and Sumatra. Although republican forces numbered perhaps five hundred thousand, they included a good many disparate units neither organized, trained, nor equipped for modern warfare. Wisely, the Indonesian high command ordered all units to carry out scorched-earth tactics and retreat to woods and hills, there to wage guerrilla warfare as best they could. By the time the United Nations brought about a cease-fire, the Dutch occupied nearly two thirds of Java and large areas of Sumatra and Madura. Fighting continued in numerous areas; under guise of "mopping-up operations," the Dutch seized large amounts of territory: " . . . Such actions and the refusal of the [UN] Security Council to contest them demonstrated to Indonesians how little in awe of the Security Council the Netherlands stood."[11]

A UN "Committee of Good Offices," consisting of Belgian, Australian, and American representatives, next brought antagonists together to hammer out the Renville agreement. Although this saved the republic, it left the Dutch with its gains until various plebiscites could determine the people's wishes. The agreement favored the Dutch far more than the Indonesians, who signed under considerable pressure from

Western powers; subsequent failure of the Dutch to abide by the agreement and failure of the Western powers to reinforce it caused most Indonesian leaders to suspect Western, particularly American, motives.[12]

Sukarno's republic was now in bad shape. Compressed into one third of Java, the poor one third, its normal population of 23 million swollen by some seven hundred thousand refugees, the republic visibly faltered. Prime Minister Sjarifuddin, who had replaced Sjahrir, resigned in January 1948. Mohammad Hatta replaced him and at once began drastic surgery on economy and army, transferring hundreds of thousands of people to the land. He reduced the army from nearly half a million to a regular force of 160,000 plus some irregular, guerrilla-type units. He hoped eventually to reduce it to fifty-seven thousand regulars, a well-armed and well-trained force that

> ... would be prepared to operate at battalion strength in a mobile, hard-hitting guerrilla war against the Dutch, should they again attack. The old "static defense" would be changed into a "mobile offensive system" of shifting pockets that could not be mopped up. Supplementing this force of highly trained regulars would be a wide network of territorial militias made up of the local peasantry, who would be called upon to devote part of their time to military training.[13]

Hatta could do little, however, to repair material shortages incurred by a Dutch blockade or alleviate severe human hardships and inevitable inflation that arose from a distorted economy.

Hatta's reforms, coupled with the deteriorating domestic situation and the pro-Dutch attitude of the United States, made numerous enemies for Communists to exploit. Sjarifuddin, who was probably a secret Communist while serving as prime minister, openly joined the movement, which gained impetus from those headed by other Communist leaders such as Musso. In September, Communists rose in the city of Madiun and proclaimed a soviet government. Sukarno successfully rallied the rest of the country and managed to keep control of the army, which put down the rebellion. In late October, the last large rebel unit surrendered to republican forces. Musso was killed, Sjarifuddin executed. Such were the intricacies of Indonesian politics that the veteran Communist Tan Malaka had opted for the Sukarno-Hatta government. Released from jail, he was returned to house arrest when the revolt failed; he was later executed by a republican officer.

The Communist revolt further weakened the republican government. UN efforts to solve the impasse between the republic and the Dutch had come to nought. Observers reported frequent truce violations by each side. The Dutch steadily strengthened their economic grip on the islands and seemed particularly unwilling to co-operate and compromise over conflicting interpretations of various aspects of the Renville agreement. But time was serving the republicans. The occupation was costing the Netherlands an immense sum of money—well over a million dollars a day—that she could ill afford. In December, the Dutch broke off UN negotiations and, presumably wanting to exploit Sukarno's immediate weaknesses, started the Second Police Action by a surprise bombing of the capital, Jogjakarta. Dutch troops quickly rounded up Sukarno and his principal officials and banished them to Sumatra.

This crass refutation of the Renville agreement triggered violent world reaction against the Dutch. The UN Security Council called for an immediate cease-fire and a release of republican leaders. When the Netherlands ignored the demand, the United States suspended Marshall Plan aid to the Dutch in the Indies and threatened to stop it to the home country. Governments around the world protested to The Hague, which at first denied responsibility, then attempted to defend the action.[14]

The Netherlands was fighting a losing battle. It could not afford to forfeit American aid, about $400 million in 1948. Nor had her second offensive brought about the republic's collapse: " . . . by late January the 145,000 Netherlands troops in Indonesia were actually more on the defensive than on the offensive."[15]

In anticipation of the Dutch attack, the government had studied the earlier action carefully. As one result, it immediately enlisted its people in the new war. Citizens in Jogjakarta, for example, were ordered " . . . to obstruct and sabotage every effort to consolidate the Dutch government." Civil servants were to be " . . . 100 per cent noncooperative." The people must hinder production of goods in every possible way; nor could they serve the Dutch politically: " . . . better to be jailed than to be a puppet and traitor."[16]

Another result of republican concern was army reorganization pushed through by Hatta, who also placed increased emphasis on guerrilla warfare. The chief of operations, thirty-year-old Abdul Haris Nasution, realized that the army could not stand against modern Dutch forces, but he also knew that " . . . to occupy Java down to the subdistricts, he [the Dutch] would need more than ten divisions, and it is certain that he is unable to form as many."[17] Nasution reckoned that with a limited strength of three to four divisions the enemy could occupy major towns and control communications, but could not destroy the Indonesian forces if they were properly organized and dispersed.[17]

In essence this is what happened in the Second Police Action. As usual, the Dutch high command underestimated staying power of the republicans. In early January the Dutch commander announced " . . . that he would be able to crush the guerrillas within three months."

His optimism soon faltered. As Dutch units moved into the country, occupying cities and towns and protecting lines of communication, they became increasingly immobile resembling nothing so much as Chiang Kai-shek's troop tied to static defense of cities and highways. Guerrilla forces now began to surround enemy garrisons and increasingly to isolate them. If the guerrillas, unlike Mao Tse-tung's forces, were not strong enough to attack, neither was the enemy strong enough to eliminate them.

Here was a military stalemate that could have been solved only by greatly increased Dutch strength. But, for the Dutch, time and money were running out. In April 1949, the Dutch Government agreed to release of prisoners and to new negotiations with the republican government. A series of summer conferences yielded a cease-fire in August. Subsequent conferences at The Hague brought the republic into common cause with Holland and the other federal states to form a Republic of the United States of Indonesia—" . . . a federal government formed of the Republic of Indonesia and the fifteen political units established by the Dutch."[18] On December 27, 1949, the Netherlands transferred full sovereignty to the new nation.

CHAPTER FORTY-FOUR

1. Fischer, 81.
2. Kahin, 142. See also, Ray.
3. Fischer, 81.
4. Nasution, 2.
5. Wehl, 55–6.
6. Kahin, 144–5.
7. Fischer, 93.
8. Ibid., 97. See also, Kahin; Palmier; Westerling.
9. Kahin, 356.
10. Fischer, 98.
11. Kahin, 213–14, 218. See also, Alastair Taylor.
12. Kahin, 224–9.
13. Ibid., 264–5.
14. Ibid., 339–45. Professor Kahin offers a detailed analysis of these complex negotiations, with emphasis on the ambivalent American role. See also, Fischer; Palmier.
15. Kahin, 391.
16. Ibid., 394.
17. Nasution, 109.
18. Kahin, 433.

CHAPTER 45

The Palestine problem • Historical background • The British role • Jews versus Arabs • The Zionist position • Origin of Haganah • World War II and the postwar situation • David Raziel: the militant element • Irgun and terrorism • Stern and the FFI • Menachem Begin • Guerrilla war • British countertactics • UN intervention • The British yield

THE PALESTINE PROBLEM was nearly as old as Jerusalem hills. Orthodox Jews had never yielded spiritual claim to the Holy Land, where some brethren remained after Romans destroyed the Judean state. Through vicissitudes of ages, many Jews continued to look eastward: As early as the fourteenth century, Jewish refugees from Europe began trickling into Palestine. Over the centuries, desire for a "national home" continued to grow, especially in European ghettos burdened with poverty and all too frequent pogroms. In the 1870s, a wave of anti-Semitism started new migration from central Europe. Then, in 1898, Theodor Herzl organized a Zionist international movement, aimed at " . . . establishing in Palestine a home for the Jewish People secured by public law."[1] The trickle of refugees into Palestine increased. At the century's turn, the Jews there numbered perhaps forty thousand; in 1917, the figure reached eighty-five thousand.

Now came the watershed, the Balfour Declaration, which pledged England's support of Zionist aims. Its origins are obscure. According to Lloyd George, it was made " . . . for propagandist reasons"—to win support of international, particularly American, Jewry to the allied side at a crucial time in World War I. In his provocative book *Promise and Fulfilment—Palestine 1917–1949*, Arthur Koestler calls it " . . . one of the most improbable political documents of all time. In this document one nation solemnly promised to a second nation the country of a third."[2] Whatever the case, the Paris Peace Conference and subsequent conferences converted Palestine into a British mandate (later approved by the League of Nations), and this encouraged further Jewish immigration during the 1920s.

As might be expected, Palestine Arabs resented intrusion into what they regarded as their land. In 1920, Arabs attacked Jews in Jerusalem, in 1921 in Jaffa. British administration, which tended to favor the Arab population, and economic improvements brought by Jews somewhat mollified Arab grievances, but did not ameliorate the land question. In selling land to Jews, rich Arab and Turkish absentee landowners deprived some Arab tenants of ancestral homesteads; though they received compensation, this fundamental grievance was ignored by British administration. In 1929, an anti-Semitic nationalist, the British-appointed Mufti of Jerusalem, struck out by inciting a series of violent attacks against Jews.

The British Government faced a major dilemma. It could not defend the Jewish cause without irreparably alienating Arab countries. In view of Western need for Middle Eastern oil, this would have created serious economic difficulties. To avoid a split and yet honor their pledge to Zionism, the British chose a compromise policy that often favored Arabs. But political pragmatism can sometimes become self-defeating: Attempting to walk a middle path softly, the British administration soon bogged down in Palestinian sands of intrigue. By attempting to satisfy everyone, the British satisfied no one.

While British policy maintained precarious peace, forces of discontent gathered strength. Hitler's anti-Semitic policy increased the refugee flow and added to Arab resentment. In 1932, the Jewish population numbered two hundred thousand; in 1935, nearly half a million. The Arab rebellion broke out in 1936 and continued to spread until suppressed two years later by a major British military effort (which, considering the European situation, Britain could ill afford).[3]

Various commissions meanwhile studied the problem, usually to recommend partition—that is, creating a small but separate Jewish state. Arab countries refused this solution, however, and such was their supposed importance to the coming international struggle that the British Government supported them. The famous Chamberlain White Paper of 1939 called for greatly restricted Jewish immigration—fifteen thousand a year at a time when tens of thousands were trying to escape concentration camps and ovens of central Europe—which would end altogether in five years; it also virtually prohibited land purchase by Jews; finally, it called for an Arab state within ten years, a state in which Jews would hold minority status.[4] A grossly unfair solution, the White Paper only added to smoldering Jewish discontent. When war broke out, however, the international Zionist organization and its executive, the Jewish Agency, chose to support Britain, as did the Jews in Palestine, the Yishuv.

Several factors explain the considerable forbearance shown by Jews in dealing with Arabs and the British administration. The Jewish Agency remained fully aware of basic antagonisms to the notion of a Jewish state: not only those of anti-Semitic gentiles, but of Jews themselves, of non-Zionists and anti-Zionists both in Palestine and the world. The two great Zionist leaders, Chaim Weizmann and David Ben-Gurion, were as much concerned with building and preserving as with administering. Money was as short as tempers; splinter movements were forever forming. To Weizmann and Ben-Gurion, only a policy of moderation could hold the movement together while retaining the support of international Jewry and sympathy of British and American governments.

The second factor was Jewish weakness in Palestine. In attempting to keep the peace, the British had never encouraged Jewish resistance. In the very old days, Jewish survival depended on assimilation with Arabs. As immigration continued and Jewish settlements developed, a sort of local militia sprang up. Then, in 1905, pogroms in Russia introduced new immigrants: tough, young men, for the most part socialist revolutionaries, who had experience in European arms and who founded " . . . the first country-wide para-military organization," Hashomer, or the Watchman—" . . . a kind of Hebrew cowboy or Wild West ranger, highly respected among Arabs"—to protect lives and property.[5]

Hashomer slowly evolved into an underground Haganah (Defense Organization), " . . . a voluntary militia, organized in local units primarily for local defense."[6] The Haganah expanded during the 1936–39 Arab rebellion—as we have seen (Chapter 33), Orde Wingate organized "Special Night Squads" from its reserve constabulary—but soon reverted to a protective role.[7] In 1941, the British allowed the Haganah to organize full-time guerrilla shock units, the Palmach, for fighting in Syria, but British policy continued to discourage a separate Jewish military force.

The war nonetheless strengthened the Zionist hand. In 1942, Zionist leaders met in New York's Hotel Biltmore to censure the unpopular White Paper. The Biltmore Program, as it came to be known, called for unlimited immigration of Jews to Palestine, which, after the war, would become a Jewish commonwealth state. The war also strengthened the Haganah's military arm: Some thirty-two thousand Palestine Jews served in British forces and, in 1944, the British authorized a separate Jewish Brigade Group. The group dissolved at war's end, when a large British army occupied the area, but an underground Haganah army continued to exist. Commanded by a professional cadre of some four hundred soldiers, it consisted of Palmach guerrilla units totaling about twenty-one hundred men and women, backed by a small but ready reserve, and of a widespread territorial militia of some thirty thousand with many thousands of covert supporters.

* * *

Over-all weakness had caused the Jewish Agency and the Haganah to follow a defensive policy—the Havlagah—during the Arab rebellion, and a co-operative policy with the British during World War II. A good many Jews deeply resented what they deemed timid policies. In 1925, militant Zionists had formed the Revisionist Party, under Vladimir Jabotinsky, who " . . . declared himself against any co-operation with Arabs until the Jews were their effective masters in Palestine, and he was pressing for the formation of a Jewish Legion to conquer the promised land."[8] In 1935, the Revisionist Party splintered from the World Zionist Organization. Two years later, younger Revisionists formed a militant force, the Irgun Tsvai Leumi, or Etzel (National Military Organization),[9] under a dynamic young leader, David Raziel. A brilliant student, Raziel switched from mathematics to military subjects in preparation for his messianic role:

> . . . He wrote (together with his colleague, Abraham Stern) textbooks on the revolver and on methods of training. He conducted courses in the use of small arms and in the manufacture of homemade explosives. . . . He was convinced that Jewish statehood could be attained only after an armed struggle with the British and he would have preferred to build the Irgun to meet the inevitable clash, rather than concentrate on retaliation against the Arabs.[10]

Under Raziel's inspired leadership, the Irgun concentrated first on smuggling illegal refugees into Palestine. Arab attacks on Jews in 1939 caused Irgun to open a terrorist campaign against the general Arab population. To protests of Zionist leaders, to the Jewish Agency and the Haganah, who pleaded the Sixth Commandment, "Thou Shalt Not Kill," the Irgun answered with Exodus xxi, 23–25: " . . . life for life, eye for eye, tooth for tooth, hand for hand, foot for foot, burning for burning. . . . " The Chamberlain White Paper brought another change, this time to British military targets; when a police inspector tortured some Irgun leaders, Raziel had him murdered. Raziel and his coleader, Abraham Stern, were themselves arrested, soon released and quickly resumed operations, but Stern, also a brilliant student, disagreed with Raziel's policy of wartime truce with the British. In 1940, Stern broke from Irgun to form the Lokhammei Kherut Israel (Fighters for the Freedom of Israel), or FFI. The Stern Gang, as it was generally known, concentrated on fighting the British by eliminating some Jewish moderates as well as gentiles: Anyone who opposed creation of a Jewish state became fair game. Raziel, in turn, agreed to work for the British

554

army during the pro-German revolt in Iraq, and was killed in 1941, on his first mission. Stern fell to police bullets in 1942. A year later, another fanatic believer in the Jewish state, a Polish intellectual named Menachem Begin, took command of the Irgun. Stern's successor, a young scientist named David Friedman-Yellin, continued a policy of "unrestricted and indiscriminate terror"—from 1939 to 1943, Sternists killed eight Jewish, six Arab, and eleven British policemen, not to mention other victims.[11]

Continued British refusal to accept the Biltmore Program caused the Irgun, in 1944, to renounce its truce with the British and to form a loose, sometimes uneasy alliance with the Stern Gang in a new war for a Jewish state. By early autumn, the Stern Gang had murdered fifteen men, mostly moderate Jews, and destroyed several important government installations including four police stations.[12]

Irgun strategy hinged on three considerations, as later clarified by Menachem Begin in his tormented book *The Revolt*. From a study of " . . . the methods used by oppressor administrations in foreign countries," the terrorists concluded that to destroy British prestige in Palestine would destroy British rule:

> . . . The very existence of an underground, which oppression, hangings, tortures and deportations, fail to crush or to weaken must, in the end, undermine the prestige of a colonial regime that lives by the legend of its omnipotence. Every attack which it fails to prevent is a blow at its standing.

Two other considerations strengthened this belief: the international situation and Britain's position therein, as well as Britain's internal strength. The terrorists concluded:

> . . . As a result of World War II the Power which was oppressing us was confronted with a hostile Power in the east and a not very friendly power in the west. And as time went on her difficulties increased.

Begin and his fellows naturally counted on international sympathy and aid, particularly from the Hebrew Committee of National Liberation, in the United States.[13]

A great many Jews, in and out of Palestine, disagreed with Irgun-Stern terrorism both on grounds of humanity and because they felt that evil acts would bring wholesale reprisals. Contrarily, terrorists shrewdly reasoned that a civilized power would find its retaliatory hands increasingly tied so long as the problem area claimed world attention. The Irgun drew a limit to terror, the Stern Gang did not. In November 1944, two Stern Gang terrorists assassinated Lord Moyne, the Minister of State in Cairo. Public indignation, Jewish and gentile, ran high. The terrorist campaign already had alarmed the Jewish Agency and the Haganah, which believed that peaceful settlement could be made with England. Lord Moyne's death brought an open breach, with Agency and Haganah officials working with British authorities in rounding up and deporting nearly three hundred Stern and Irgun activists.[14] Since a good many Palestine Jews who deplored terrorist activities would still not turn in their fellows, the terrorists survived, though with greatly restricted means. Samuel Katz later wrote bitterly:

> . . . The whole machinery of the Jewish Agency's security forces were now organized to wage war against the Irgun. . . . Expulsions from schools, dismissals from places of work, kidnappings, beatings, torture, direct denunciations to the British, became the sole occupation of the action-hungry soldiers of the Haganah and the Palmach.[15]

Zionist co-operation with the British did not reduce Zionist goals. In May 1945, after the German surrender, Dr. Weizmann wrote Prime Minister Churchill,

> . . . demanding on behalf of the Jewish Agency the full and immediate implementation of the Biltmore resolution: the cancellation of the White Paper, the establishment of Palestine as a Jewish State, Jewish immigration to be an Agency responsibility, and reparation to be made by Germany in kind beginning with all German property in Palestine.[16]

Immigration headed the list. The Jewish Agency wanted unrestricted immigration for a hundred thousand Jewish, mostly Polish survivors of German bestiality who languished in displaced-persons camps.[17] British delay, first by the Churchill government, then by Clement Attlee's Labour government, in treating this demand led to an extensive smuggling operation by the Haganah and, far more ominous, to an operational rapprochement between the Haganah, which claimed a country-wide membership of some forty thousand, and the Irgun-Stern groups, themselves steadily growing in strength and claiming thousands of passive sympathizers. Refugee smuggling increased, and, in October, the Haganah's clandestine radio station, Kol Israel, proclaimed the beginning of "The Jewish Resistance Movement":

> . . . On the night of the 31st of October the "single serious incident" took place. Palmach troops sank three small naval craft and wrecked railway lines in fifty different places; Irgun attacked the

railway station at Lydda, and the Sternists attacked the Haifa oil refinery. The attacks were accomplished with great skill and little loss of life, probably none intentionally. The operation had the desired effect of making the British Government think seriously about Palestine, but it also had the effect of solidifying yet further [Ernest] Bevin's resistance.[18]

The British enlisted American aid in form of an Anglo-American committee of inquiry, but domestic politics in both countries slowed formation of this body. Illegal immigration activities continued to increase, as did ugly incidents between Palestinian Jews and British troops (which would soon number eighty thousand). In early 1946, the new high commissioner, Sir Alan Cunningham, " . . . promulgated severe emergency laws which among other provisions ordained death as the maximum penalty not only for taking part in a terrorist raid but for belonging to a terrorist society."[19]

The Anglo-American Committee's report merely exacerbated the situation by recommending immediate admission of a hundred thousand Jewish DPs. In refusing this and other proposals at a time when " . . . the situation was particularly propitious for carrying out Partition in a bloodless operation," Bevin and the Labour government were imprisoned by the old Arab complex that had restricted British policy for so long. The picture of the "Middle East going up in flames" seemed to paralyze realistic thinking, and in so doing, brought a near crisis in British relations with the Truman administration, itself acting far too cautiously as a result of domestic political pressures to solve a problem that the United States had helped create.[20]

Bevin and the Labour government were now on a collision course with disaster. In June, a new wave of sabotage swept over Palestine. In addition to usual attacks, terrorists destroyed twenty-two RAF planes at one airfield. The harassed British " . . . ordered the arrest not only of members of Palmach but of the Agency leaders. Ben Gurion was in Paris, or he would have been taken with the rest."[21] During what Arthur Koestler has termed "Mr. Bevin's 18th Brumaire," the British also occupied the offices of the Jewish Agency, where they found documents that proved the Haganah's complicity in earlier terrorist operations.

Partly to destroy these documents and partly in keeping with its policy of reprisal, the Haganah agreed to an Irgun attack on British headquarters in the King David Hotel in Jerusalem. Although Irgun terrorists later claimed that ample warnings were given, the hotel was not evacuated, and the bombings claimed ninety-one British, Arab, and Jewish dead and forty-five wounded. The deed shocked most of the civilized world, but what should have been a propaganda victory for the British turned sour when the British commander, General Barker, sent his officers a non-fraternization order at once intercepted and published by the Irgun. It reminded some observers of Gauleiter orders only too familiar from World War II:

> ... I am determined that they (the Jews) should be punished and made aware of our feelings of contempt and disgust at their behavior ... if the Jewish community really wanted to put an end to the crimes it could do so by co-operating with us. I have accordingly decided that ... all Jewish places of entertainment, cafes, restaurants, shops and private houses are out of bounds. ... I understand that these measures will create difficulties for the troops, but I am certain that if my reasons are explained to them, they will understand their duty and will punish the Jews in the manner this race dislikes most: by hitting them in the pocket, which will demonstrate our disgust for them.

Uproar over this ill-advised order more than neutralized adverse publicity reaped by the ghastly hotel attack. Each incident, however, served the Irgun goal of focusing world attention on this torn and bleeding country.[22]

In August, the British replied further with a massive raid on Irgun "headquarters" in Tel Aviv, which they sealed off with some twenty thousand troops supported by tanks. Katz later wrote that the British captured only two terrorists. Menachem Begin spent the emergency in a tiny cupboard and was not discovered.[23]

The worsening situation caused the Jewish Agency to lower its sights by requesting a reasonable partition arrangement. Fearful of Arab reaction, the British responded with a trusteeship plan, but the Attlee government also appointed a new Colonial Secretary, who was more sympathetic to Jewish aspirations and who initiated an appeasement policy by freeing Jewish Agency leaders. In return,

> ... Haganah dissociated itself from the terrorists and signalized the end of the alliance by issuing propaganda against them. The Central Executive of the Zionist organization condemned terrorism and called on the Yishuv to take action against the criminals.[24]

Something might have come of these moves but for the intransigence of the Arabs, who refused to countenance any partition plan; for the sympathy of the American Government to the Jewish plan, which infuriated the British; and for continued Irgun-Sternist activity.

By end of 1946, the Irgun-Sternist groups had killed 373 persons. Although the police and army had imprisoned and deported some members, the organization continued to operate with at least tacit support of a large number of ordinary citizens. Considering the size of its full-time staff, never more than fifty persons, the task of running the Irgun to the ground was immense. British security forces could disrupt various groups and even cause operations to be suspended, but they could not eliminate the hard-core top command—at least without receiving far better intelligence. Instead of improving intelligence procedures, which, among other things, required moderation in dealing with the general population, the British high command frequently antagonized the people.[25] Its use of corporal punishment on suspected terrorists was quickly stopped when the Irgun kidnaped two British soldiers and gave them each eighteen lashes before sending them back to their units. The British next organized a counterterror unit, but it soon died an ignominious, if gory, death. In early 1947, the British sentenced a young terrorist, Dov Grüner, to death by hanging, for his part in the murder of a policeman. His execution made him a popular hero and won many converts to the Irgun-Sternist cause both in Palestine and abroad. It was Ireland all over again (see Chapter 17).[26]

Against this sordid background, the British Government continued efforts to effect a political compromise. But time was running out and criticism mounting on the British home front:

> . . . In the House of Commons, at the height of the coal crisis, Winston Churchill warned that Britain could not sustain, morally or materially, a long campaign in Palestine. He pointed to the expenditure of eighty million pounds in two years to maintain 100,000 soldiers there. She had no such interests in Palestine as to justify such an effort. . . . [27]

Ernest Bevin disagreed. Misreading the Jewish Agency's conciliatory attitude as weakness, he still thought he could bring Arab and Jew together under the British flag. To gain time, he turned to the United Nations in mid-February, a move that some interpreted as the first step in abandoning the mandate. The UN appointed a special committee, UNSCOP, to investigate the problem and recommend a new solution.

Meanwhile, terror and counterterror ruled Palestine, a ghastly period that kept the torn country in international headlines. Dov Grüner's execution brought widespread Irgun reprisals. In early March, terrorists attacked British installations and, in one day, killed or wounded some eighty soldiers. The British replied by declaring martial law, which infuriated the civil population without halting Irgun operations. The British also sentenced three captured terrorists to death. In May, Irgun units attacked Acre jail and released forty-one terrorists (and two hundred common criminals). In July, the refugee ship *Exodus 1947* arrived with forty-five hundred Jews aboard, only to be sent back to Europe to disembark its human, generally penniless, cargo on a Hamburg dock—a

PALESTINE

• Towns and Cities

1946–1947

tragic event resulting from Bevin's intransigence, and giving militant Jews an enormous propaganda victory further exploited by Leon Uris' best-selling novel *Exodus*. Also in July, the British hanged the three sentenced terrorists. The Irgun kidnaped two British sergeants and hanged them on a tree outside Tel Aviv.

Undeterred by reciprocal savagery, the UN committee worked throughout summer and autumn, finally to recommend an end of the British mandate in favor of still another partition plan, one reluctantly adopted by the Jewish Agency when the British made it clear that they intended to yield the mandate and withdraw troops in near future. In late November 1947, the UN accepted the plan. The Arab League responded by ordering attacks against Jewish settlements not only in Palestine but throughout the Middle East. In December, the Colonial Secretary announced that Great Britain would terminate its mandate on May 15, 1948.

By then the Haganah had secretly mobilized and Jew was fighting Arab as the beleaguered British garrison stood increasingly to one side. The British would remain for another few months, but their war was over. The Arab-Israeli war had started.

CHAPTER FORTY-FIVE

1. Lorch, 2.
2. Koestler, 4. See also, Sykes, *Cross Roads to Israel;* Marlowe.
3. Sykes, *Cross Roads to Israel,* 130 ff. See also, Sykes, *Orde Wingate.*
4. Marlowe, 165–189.
5. Koestler, 69.
6. Lorch, 27.
7. Koestler, 73–5.
8. Sykes, *Cross Roads to Israel,* 96.
9. Ibid., 216. See also, Katz, 4 ff. Katz places the origin of the Irgun, also called Haganah B, at an earlier year; Koestler, 90–1, offers a particularly interesting account:

    . . . Its rank and file were recruited from the Revisionist Youth Organization *Betar,* and from the "colored Jews"—Yemenites and Sephardis—for whom its flowery, chauvinistic phraseology had a particular appeal. These oriental Jews were eventually to constitute about one-half of Irgun's total strength, while the leaders were almost exclusively young intellectuals who had grown up in the Polish revolutionary tradition. This created the peculiar ideological climate of Irgun—a mixture of that quixotic patriotism and romantic chivalry which characterized the Polish student revolutionaries, with the archaic ferocity of the Bible and the book of the Maccabees.

10. Katz, 17.
11. Koestler, 91–3.
12. Sykes, *Cross Roads to Israel,* 248–9.
13. Begin, 52.
14. Sykes, *Cross Roads to Israel,* 257. See also, Costigan: Eliahu Bet Zouri, one of the assassins of Lord Moyne in 1944, had been taught in Tel Aviv by

Esther Raziel, sister of David Raziel, commander of the Irgun. She had a plentiful supply of IRA literature about the Irgun conflict, and held up as heroes to her youthful Zionist pupils Robert Emmet and Michael Collins, as well as Garibaldi, Mazzini, and Washington.

15. Katz, 85.
16. Sykes, *Cross Roads to Israel*, 270.
17. Koestler, 101: About a million Jews escaped death in German concentration camps. Of these, some 300,000 were living in Western Europe with a "fair chance of rebuilding normal life"; 100,000 of the remaining 700,000 "driftwood" lived in DP camps in the Western occupation zones. The record of the Western countries in absorbing these Jewish remnants is, at best, modest.
18. Sykes, *Cross Roads to Israel*, 283.
19. Ibid. See also, Katz, 75-7, who lists the regulations in detail.
20. Koestler, 114–17. See also, Sykes, *Cross Roads to Israel*; Truman, *Year of Decisions, 1945*; Acheson.
21. Sykes, *Cross Roads to Israel*, 300.
22. Begin, 221–2.
23. Ibid., 228.
24. Sykes, *Cross Roads to Israel*, 305.
25. Ibid., 307–8.
26. Begin, 251–68 for the sordid details.
27. Katz, 122.

CHAPTER 46

Postwar Malaya • Chin Peng's Communist guerrilla army • Communist tactics • Government reaction • Counterinsurgency tactics • Chin Peng's tactical adjustment • British problems • British tactical adaptation • The Briggs Plan • Guerrilla setbacks • Templer takes over: the qualitative approach • The tactical challenge • The cost

SEEDS OF TROUBLE planted in prewar Malaya burst into discomfiting bloom not long after Japan's surrender. Here, as elsewhere in Asia, a variety of elements enriched already fertile soil of dissatisfaction: initial Japanese victories over the white man, the white man's frantic effort to recover initiative by political promises inherent in such documents as the Atlantic Charter, political and economic dislocation caused by Japanese occupation, political awareness among all groups produced as defense against brutal Japanese occupation policies, active opposition by and consequent improved organization of the Communist Party, the political vacuum created by Japanese defeat, the British return with initial political confusion and economic hardship, delay in restoring tin mines and rubber plantations to prewar condition.[1]

Soon after British troops returned to the peninsula, Whitehall announced a new political arrangement known as the Union of Malaya. This was an attempt to juggle the three major ethnic groups (Malays, Chinese, and Indians)—some 5.5 million people—into a viable colonial state by improving the Chinese and Indian political position. It failed mainly because of opposition from powerful Malay sultans and the well-organized Malayan civil service. In December 1946, Whitehall began to consider a federation plan, not announced until 1948.

The political hiatus caused by bumbling bureaucracy suited the Communist Party of Malaya (MCP), which finished the war in a relatively strong position (see Chapter 32). In 1945, it ostensibly disbanded its field army and turned in arms; in reality, it retained a cadre organization in form of an Old Comrades Association and buried a significant number of weapons. Its leader, Lai Teck, judged that he was not strong enough to seize power outright, a decision that some believe was occasioned by his being a British secret agent. The MCP did begin to attack by infiltration and subversion, however. Communist propaganda fell on willing ears, and Lai and his fellows successfully brought off numerous demonstrations and strikes which disrupted but did not prevent postwar recovery.[2] As was and is quite common in Communist parties, a rift now developed: The Central Committee ousted Lai Teck, who disappeared, taking party funds with him.[3] His deputy in World War II, Chin Peng, replaced him as party leader.

Chin Peng was twenty-six years old in 1947. He had joined the MCP in 1940. During the war, he worked closely with the SOE (Force 136), an effort acknowledged by his being chosen to march in the Victory Parade in London and by being decorated with the Order of the British Empire![4] A British veteran of Malaya and expert on counterinsurgency warfare, Major General Richard Clutterbuck, later wrote, " . . . few people who have worked with him . . . deny that he is likable, intelligent and sincere."[5]

In 1947 Chin Peng was sincere only in bringing about a revolution in Malaya. Whether inspired by his own confidence, by an erroneous estimate of party strength, or by such outside influences as the Soviet Union and China is not known; he was never captured. He did send representatives to the Asia Youth Conference held at Calcutta in February 1948—a meeting that some authorities hold responsible for the outbreak of "wars of liberation" all over Southeast Asia.* Probably a combination of the three factors moved him to abandon infiltration strategy in favor of Mao's three-step plan: a limited guerrilla phase to wear down government strength while building MCP strength; an expansion phase with development of "popular bases" in towns and villages; a consolidation phase with conversion of guerrilla forces into an army and subsequent defeat of government forces.

To accomplish this program, Chin Peng reactivated his World War II army of small guerrilla bands based in jungle areas. In 1947, the Malayan People's Anti-British Army consisted of about four thousand guerrillas, 90 per cent of whom were Chinese. Divided into eight regional regiments, they lived in large jungle camps, "normally of company size."[6]

Chin Peng's army could not have functioned effectively without civilian support provided by an organization called the Min Yuen, which

---

* Psychologically a good year in that it was the centenary of the European revolutions that so inspired Marx and Engels.

consisted of perhaps five thousand "formal" members assisted by thousands of Chinese rubber and tin workers living in villages bordering the jungle. In each village, one or more Communist "cells" performed a variety of essential tasks such as furnishing guerrillas with intelligence, recruits, food, medicine, clothing, and money. Armed members of the Min Yuen—plantation workers by day, guerrillas by night—undertook propaganda, sabotage, and terror missions. Administratively, the cells formed shadow governments, what the French in Indochina called "parallel hierarchies," at village, district, and province levels. This machinery enabled the Central Committee of the MCP to control Min Yuen activities as well as provide an instant government for "liberated areas." The Central Committee also organized bands of thugs called "Blood and Steel Corps" for terrorist activities in cities.[7]

This primitive but effective organization unleashed a mounting reign of terror: in cities, strikes, bombings, assassinations (particularly of Chinese Kuomintang leaders), extortion from merchants (particularly Chinese), bank robberies; in carefully selected country areas, theft, arson, murder of policemen and village officials, sabotage of rubber trees and tin mines. Chin's purpose was twofold: By such means he partially financed his movement and broadened his base of support, besides gaining recruits and necessary arms and supply; at the same time, he hoped to induce popular revolts that would give him control of "liberated areas," essential to the next revolutionary phase.[8]

He nearly carried off his plan. The Malayan police force numbered only nine thousand constables, who were neither organized nor equipped to deal with this rash of violence, nor did thinly spread military units at first prove effective. The British Government, beset by problems at home and elsewhere in the Commonwealth, reacted only sluggishly. Encouraged by initial successes, and possibly under orders from Yenan or Moscow, Chin Peng stepped up the tempo in early 1948 in anticipation of establishing the Communist Republic of Malaya in August.[9]

Chin Peng had underestimated both governmental and popular reaction. Despite numerous attacks and murders, many constables and officials proved extremely brave and loyal, and as a result, most villages remained politically viable. People may have been cowed and intimidated, but nowhere were there mass uprisings. Whitehall also pulled itself together to replace the moribund Union of Malaya with a federation scheme that introduced centralized direction of government and a formal recognition of the threat to legitimate government. In June 1948, the high commissioner, Sir Edward Gent (soon after killed in an air crash), declared a state of emergency, and the legislature passed an Emergency Regulations Act, which, without invoking martial law, nonetheless provided security forces with some sharp teeth. Malaya's new laws called for country-wide registration of all citizens over twelve years of age, temporary abandonment of habeas corpus, right of search without warrant, heavy sentences including that of death for illegal possession of weapons, severe sentences for anyone assisting the Communist propaganda effort, right to impose curfews as needed. Later measures gave security forces the right to shoot anyone found in certain prohibited areas (a dubious practice) and also authorized courts to impose heavy sentences on persons supplying guerrillas.

No one can deny the severity of these and other "control" laws, but at that time in Malaya no one could deny the severity of Communist threat to legitimate government. If the laws were harsh and if some defied principles of Western jurisprudence, they nonetheless brought home to the general populace the government's determination to restore and maintain law and order. The government's promise of immediate repeal, once proper government was restored, also caused the average citizen to co-operate in hopes of return to normality. The registration system further stressed the incentive aspect, since, without an identity card, the citizen could not " . . . obtain a food ration, space in a resettled village, a grant to build on it, an extra patch for growing vegetables, and many other things. . . . " He was also assured of being asked blunt questions if he could not produce his card.[10]

Thus armed, the government turned to its primary mission, providing security to the people, with secondary missions of separating the guerrilla from the people and then eliminating him. At first, this required a holding operation. The police could neither adequately protect the populace nor pursue the guerrillas. They had their hands full protecting themselves. Military forces, eleven battalions of British, Gurkha, and Malay troops, necessarily concentrated on providing static guards, mainly in plantation and mine areas. Malaya is a country larger than England, and the army quickly spread itself thin.

By holding or even retreating a little, the government won vital breathing space. One of its first steps was an enormous police-expansion program. Within six months, the police force grew from nine thousand to forty-five thousand; a part-time Home Guard augmented the police effort, and in time grew to about fifty thousand members. Military forces reached forty thousand, including twenty-five thousand troops from Britain and over ten thousand Gurkhas; they would number fifty-five thousand before the Emergency was over.[11]

During the government's build-up of security forces, guerrillas continued to raid almost at will. They struck plantations, police stations and small military posts; they threatened people, burned houses and stole money and supplies. In 1948, guerrillas killed 315 civilians, eighty-nine policemen, and sixty soldiers. Although the MCP was gaining support, Chin Peng and his close associates still saw no signs of a general uprising. He now shifted tactics. Seeing that he faced a protracted war, which would require jungle bases, he reorganized his army (which became the Malayan Races Liberation Army, or MRLA). Pulling perhaps two thirds of his force deep into the jungle, he left the remainder to operate among squatters and in rubber estates and tin mines. This failed to work—the number of terrorist incidents fell to less than half in summer of 1949—so, in late 1949, he again shifted tactics. Bringing his forces from the jungle, he attempted to form "liberated areas" along the jungle fringe. Terrorist activity rose sharply. In 1949, guerrillas killed 723 persons, including 494 civilians. In May 1950, terrorist incidents climbed to 534.[12]

Government reaction still lagged. The police remained in throes of reorganization. Although reinforced by British veterans from the Palestine police, the greatly expanded force lacked sufficient leaders and recruit training was understandably rudimentary. Guerrillas continued to attack local police posts, not alone to kill policemen and steal arms but often to intimidate and sometimes even to recruit them. A favorite tactic was to disarm constables and warn them to keep to their compound at night, thus leaving the village under Communist control—often without authorities realizing it.[13]

The natural ally of the police, the military, was also suffering teething problems. The average operation from 1948 to early 1950 can be described as "too big and too late." This operational difficulty resulted mainly from trying to use conventional tactics in an unconventional situation—from trying to destroy the enemy in one fell swoop instead of breaking up his larger units in order to neutralize and destroy them piecemeal. The World War II veteran usually failed to realize that concentration of force essential to an ordinary battlefield made little sense in a guerrilla environment, that preponderant force was not usually a vital element in this type of war. A handful of guerrillas could not stand against a handful of well-trained and well-armed soldiers. Moreover, guerrillas did not know in what strength soldiers were approaching, and could not afford to stick around to find out. The cumulative effect of this experience caused the military to decentralize control of operational units. General Clutterbuck later wrote:

> . . . As we gained experience, infantry battalions were spread out in company-size camps, each company being responsible for patrolling the rubber estates and the neighboring jungle, and for aiding the village police posts in its area. These camps were not "forts" or "strong points"; they were merely living quarters for the soldiers.[14]

Battalion commanders perforce yielded tactical control of their companies. Similarly, company commanders often yielded control of an action to the platoon leader. The platoon leader, in turn, frequently utilized small patrols—generally self-sufficient, two-to-three day efforts commanded by sergeants and corporals.

Foreign as decentralized control at first seemed to regimental and battalion commanders (and their staffs), it soon paid off. As soldiers established closer contact with local functionaries and police posts, the flow of intelligence increased. Freed from higher staff delays, young officers learned to react quickly and effectively. As a natural corollary, unit commanders began to employ finesse in jungle operations by stressing tracking and listening operations. Instead of companies and battalions crashing through jungle to alert every guerrilla within a hundred miles, small patrols "disappeared" into jungle, where, in time and with the help of Dyak tribesmen from Borneo, they learned to track, observe guerrilla movements, set ambushes, and often locate and raid guerrilla camps.[15]

These and other healthy changes were in the making when the counterinsurgency effort received a real boost. In April 1950, a recently retired general, Sir Henry Briggs, arrived to serve as director of operations. The fifty-five-year-old Briggs introduced an operational concept derived from the Boer War. The Briggs Plan, as it came to be known, recognized that the key to the situation lay in winning support of the civil population or at least in depriving guerrillas of that support. So long as guerrillas controlled large segments of the Chinese "squatter" population, police and troops would be deprived of intelligence concerning Communist village infrastructure and guerrilla movements; conversely, guerrillas would continue to receive intelligence regarding police and military movements.

To turn this about Briggs instituted an imaginative resettlement plan that called for rounding up and moving almost half a million people into four hundred newly constructed villages:

> . . . In his first directive, Briggs put his finger on what this war was really about—a competition in government. He aimed not only to resettle the squatters but to give them a standard of local government and a degree of prosperity that they would not wish to exchange for the barren austerity of life under the Communists' parallel hierarchy; in other words, to give them something to lose.[16]

Briggs also recognized need for a unified command. At federal, or top, level he introduced a War Council of civil, police, and military representatives. This was not a command organization, but a coordinating committee, with each voice heard in formulating plans. The same system operated at state and district levels by War Executive Committees (SWECs and DWECs). By eliminating duplicate operational efforts and by providing more rapid and effective exchange of intelligence, the area committee system also began to produce better operational results.[17]

None of these measures took place overnight. Civil deaths continued to rise, the guerrillas claiming about twelve hundred victims in 1950 and about a thousand in 1951 (including the high commissioner, Sir Henry Gurney, killed in a road ambush). Guerrilla raids had caused about $27.5 million in damage to rubber plantations; general morale was sinking.

The government had scarcely been idle. By autumn of 1951, over a quarter of a million people had been resettled at a cost of $21.5 million; the police numbered nearly eighty-four thousand including auxiliaries and special constables; the Home Guard counted another sixty thousand; troop strength reached fifty-five thousand and comprised over twenty-five battalions supported by several squadrons of aircraft including one of helicopters.[18] The government was also actively promoting an amnesty program for surrendered Communists, and three hundred of these had agreed to return to the jungle in special units to fight their brethren.

As security forces cleared fringe areas, as more police and troops appeared in the field to work with village militia units in providing local security, as troops grew more adept in jungle operations, pressure against Communist communications and logistics slowly began to tell. As early as 1950, the guerrillas had abandoned "regimental" operations; by 1952, "even the platoons were being broken up."[19] With central leadership giving way to state and district leadership, any semblance of a co-ordinated guerrilla campaign vanished. Despite "formal" directives, plans, and orders (often reaching jungle headquarters months late), local guerrilla leaders increasingly turned to terrorism to survive. The MRLA began to suffer distinct supply shortages. At first, guerrillas overcame this difficulty by direct purchase at inflated prices, but increased security measures began to dry up necessary money income from extortion and theft. Recruits no longer flocked willingly to the guerrilla banner.[20]

At this stage, a remarkably able commander appeared on the government scene. General Sir Gerald Templer arrived in early 1952 in the dual role of high commissioner and director of operations. If Briggs had struck the correct operational note, Templer brought with him the correct political tone: " . . . the policy of the British Government is that Malaya should in due course become a fully self-governing nation." This promise of eventual independence, and particularly the optimism inherent in its expression at a critical time, cleared the air to an astonishing degree and virtually allowed Templer a dictatorial policy during the next two vital years in which the guerrillas suffered military defeat.[21]

These years recorded steady gains, a series of contacts and small battles that neutralized guerrilla operations by hindering communications and reducing forces. Although a dynamic and, on occasion, explosive leader, Templer was " . . . a great listener, particularly to the people with ideas, the policemen, platoon commanders, district officers, and rubber planters." He insisted that " . . . the fighting of the war and the civil running of the country 'were completely and utterly interrelated.' " He refused to allow a military takeover of what essentially remained a civil problem. As director of operations, he utilized a staff that *never exceeded nine officers,* its main element being " . . . a team of four officers of lieutenant colonel level—a soldier, an airman, a policeman, and a civil servant."[22]

Field operations followed a low tempo, with village security the primary mission. This is the first of two points to stress, for local security is vital to waging successful counterinsurgency warfare. The decisive tactical element in Malaya was not a troop unit (though troops were vital). It was the village police post, which, as General Clutterbuck has emphasized,

> . . . was the only thing that could provide security against the threat that really mattered in the villages—the man with the knife, who lived in the village and prowled the streets at night seeking out those people who had actively supported the Government or betrayed the guerrillas during the day. They were, I believe, far

more frightened of this man than of any raid coming in from the outside. I believe that the primary function of the army during this period was to operate in such a way that the guerrillas could never attack in such strength that they could destroy the police post before help could arrive, and this, in general, was achieved.[23]

In early 1951, halfway through the resettlement program, construction of new fortified villages moved ahead of police expansion. After one or two ugly experiences, General Templer wisely delayed further occupation of new villages *until a police post was functioning in that village.*

Once local security was achieved, if only partially, real flow of intelligence began. This is the second point to stress, for, without intelligence, the security forces are blind and cannot possibly pursue the selective tactics demanded by this type of warfare. The intelligence flow began in late 1951, only when police posts in general were secure, which meant protection to the population—not necessarily 100 per cent protection, but protection in that the government obviously cared and was doing its best to protect its people. As security forces continued to regain control of large areas while preventing guerrilla raids in any strength, civil administration daily grew stronger, and the population, protected and promised political gains, increasingly furnished information necessary to root out the Min Yuen guerrilla infrastructure. The government could now concentrate on improving flow of intelligence and further hurting Chin Peng's guerrilla bands. Of decisive importance to the intelligence-collection process was Special Branch, which utilized Chinese operatives and, in 1952, began to achieve spectacular results. The police were now sufficiently strong to form jungle squads which, aided by Special Air Service (SAS) units, began manning "forts" deep in the jungle. From these strongholds, patrols interdicted MRLA communications while attempting to win co-operation of primitive Sakai tribes.[24] The government also strengthened the police hand by offering impressive rewards to informers: Capture of a state committee member earned the informant about seven thousand dollars; a district committee member brought four thousand dollars, lesser persons two thousand dollars.[25]

Like the rest of the emergency, the offensive phase was a time-consuming process that demanded enormous patience. Large-scale battalion and regimental "sweeps" had proved useless. Random shelling of open areas or suspected guerrilla areas had produced minimal results, as had Lincoln bombers and Hornet and Vampire fighters plastering various areas of the jungle. Instead, the war reverted to the small infantry unit, often operating entirely on its own. General Clutterbuck concluded:

> . . . our best commanders in Malaya were the ones who set themselves the task of managing the war in such a way that their small

patrols came face to face with the guerrillas on favorable terms; in other words, with good intelligence. This meant long hours of tactful discussions with police officers, administrators, rubber planters, tin miners, and local community leaders, getting them to cooperate with the soldiers and to promote the flow of information to them. Such commanders would regularly accompany their patrols, often placing themselves under the platoon commanders, so that they really understood the war and knew what was needed to win it.[26]

What *was* needed to win it?

Basically, a realignment of tactical thinking—away from conventional terms of "battle" and "victory" to much more sophisticated terms of "pressure" and "gain." Commentators then and later sometimes missed this essential requirement. One top American analyst later wrote that

> ... this failure of the MCP is significant as a demonstration that guerrilla warfare cannot achieve victories over an enemy vastly superior by conventional military standards. Although the Security Forces in Malaya have had a difficult and thankless task in fighting the Communists, they have proved that superior technology and resources provide the same advantages in irregular as in regular warfare.[27]

Nothing could be farther from the mark, yet this belief was to gain and hold considerable currency in U.S. military circles. It completely contradicted lessons offered by China, the Philippines, Indonesia, Greece, French Indochina, and Malaya. In Malaya, superior technology and resources played a shadow second to human performance in a war that blended civil and military factors to an almost inexplicable degree. The airplane, the artillery piece, the psychological warfare program, the jungle "fort"—none approached the importance of the individual working among the people, his determination and brain his best weapons. Superior technology and resources did not "win" the Malayan war; they did help the government to establish an effective pacification program, and they did help the military carry out effective small-unit operations. But it was the pacification effort combined with the small-unit military effort that prevented the guerrilla threat from growing and finally countered it to the extent that guerrillas were unable to fight effectively any longer.

Tactically, patience had to replace impetuosity. At times, guerrillas holed up for weeks and even months. A young British officer, Arthur Campbell, later wrote a book, *Jungle Green,* that brought home the new tactical challenge faced by the Western soldier. One ambush he described, a fifty-hour effort in a filthy, insect-ridden jungle swamp, succeeded in killing one guerrilla. Other ambushes trapped no one; sometimes guerrillas appeared but escaped into the night; sometimes his people scored several kills and broke up guerrilla camps.[28] Similarly, police and soldiers, on occasion, spent months locating an enemy camp which soldiers, after enduring appalling physical hardships, attacked only to discover that the enemy had fled to still another sanctuary. Disappointment caused by such fruitless efforts, each calling for extreme individual sacrifice, was overcome only by outstanding leadership.

Frustrating as these operations were, they eventually paid off. To accomplish his mission, indeed to survive, the guerrilla had to leave his jungle sanctuary sooner or later in order either to mount an attack or to receive food and supply from clandestine supporters. That was his vulnerability, and that was where the tactical force had to outdo him in patience—not an easy requirement, in view of the hurly-burly Western environment.

Patience and persistence, and a combination of small civil and military efforts from one end of the infected areas to the other, slowly cracked the insurgency. As the first, halting movements produced intelligence and machinery to exploit it properly, the effort became a crawl, and, as more intelligence flowed in to co-ordinated commands and as police and military tactics improved, the crawl became a walk. In two years, from 1952 to 1954, " . . . two-thirds of the guerrillas were wiped out," and the terrorist incident and murder rates were cut to 20 per cent of the 1951 peak.[29] Where once guerrilla leaders whistled and new guerrillas appeared, now they whistled in vain. The remainder found themselves increasingly cut from support forces and increasingly under pressure from military units. Time favored security forces, for as strength, organization, and tactical abilities increased, the guerrilla could only suffer proportionally.

The process was painfully slow and very expensive. The government's offensive phase did not end until 1955, and the consolidation phase continued until 1960. The twelve-year war cost the lives of nearly two thousand men of the security forces; guerrillas killed or kidnaped over 3,000 civilians in the same period and also did millions of dollars' worth of damage to mines and plantations.[30] The guerrillas themselves lost nearly six thousand killed, 1,752 surrendered, and 1,173 captured.[31] Chin Peng and four hundred of his fellows escaped to the Malaya-Thailand border area, where, after a short hiatus, they resumed operations.

CHAPTER FORTY-SIX

1. Pye for an excellent background discussion.
2. Paget, 46: the author cites 300 major industrial strikes in 1947.
3. Pye, 85. See also, Special Operations Research Office.
4. Paget, 43. By the time the decoration reached Malaya in 1948, Chin had taken to the jungle and would soon have a price of £30,000 on his head.
5. Clutterbuck, *The Long, Long War* . . . , 17.
6. Ibid., 46. See also, Blair; Pye, who offers organizational and operational details including an interesting camp schedule.
7. Pye, 86–91. A Central Committee member served as secretary of each State Committee, and at least one State Committee member sat on the next-lower District Committee, an overlap system that was supposed to insure continuity of policy. In most cases, regimental commanders belonged to the appropriate State Committee, and important Min Yuen leaders sat on district committees.
8. Ibid., 88 ff. The British at first called the perpetrators "bandits," as had Chiang Kai-shek, Japanese military commanders, the Greeks, and the Filipinos; in Malaya, the authorities wisely changed to the more realistic term of Communist Terrorist, or CTs. See also, Thompson, *Defeating Communist Insurgency,* for an excellent account of the opening of the insurgency.
9. Special Operations Research Office, 76.
10. Clutterbuck, *The Long, Long War* . . . , 36–9.
11. Ibid., 44, 72.
12. Department of Information, Federation of Malaya.
13. Clutterbuck, *The Long, Long War* . . . , 48.
14. Ibid., 49. See also, Robinson.
15. Robinson.
16. Clutterbuck, *The Long, Long War* . . . , 57.
17. Ibid., 57–9.
18. Blair, 170.
19. Pye, 91.
20. Ibid., 95 ff.
21. Clutterbuck, *The Long, Long War* . . . , 80. See also, Thompson, *Defeating Communist Insurgency* . . . ; Thompson, *No Exit from Vietnam.*
22. Clutterbuck, *The Long, Long War* . . . , 83–4.
23. Clutterbuck, private letter to the author.
24. Woodhouse, J.M.
25. Pye, 118.
26. Clutterbuck, *The Long, Long War* . . . , 52.
27. Pye, 95.
28. Campbell, Arthur, 48–57.
29. Clutterbuck, *The Long, Long War* . . . , 187.
30. Thompson, *Defeating Communist Insurgency* . . . , 27.
31. Pye, 109.

CHAPTER 47

The Vietnam War • Navarre's tactics • Chinese aid • The American position • Erroneous estimates of the situation • Genesis of the domino theory • On strategic values • "Strategic keys" versus "strategic conveniences" • Mark Clark's recommendations • General O'Daniel's mission • The Navarre Plan: ". . . light at the end of a tunnel" • Giap's response • Orde Wingate's ghost (II) • Dien Bien Phu • Giap's secret plans • Navarre's problems • Origin of the Geneva Conference • Navarre's continuing errors • American aid

LESSONS LEARNED from insurgencies in the Philippines, Greece, Indonesia, Palestine, and Malaya did not rub off on the French in Indochina. Despite American and British appeals, France refused to push through political reforms that, in spring of 1953, might still have stolen nationalist thunder from Ho Chi Minh and the DRV Government.

Premier Laniel's new government offered only negative direction to its new commander in chief in Vietnam, fifty-five-year-old General Henri-Eugène Navarre, an armor officer, a military intelligence specialist, European-oriented, a reserved, somewhat colorless man, an art collector and cat-lover, of whom a friend said: " . . . There is an eighteenth century fragrance about him."[1]

Navarre was a mortal given an almost superhuman task. He was to expect no further troop replacements from France; his mission was to defend Laos while jockeying for a favorable negotiating position with the Viet Minh, but he was not to risk defeat of his forces. Navarre remained under no illusions as to the military situation, secretly reporting to his government " . . . that the war simply could not be won in the military sense (just as the Korean War could not, without drawing Red China into it) and that all that could be hoped for was a *coup nul*—a draw."[2]

Like De Lattre and Salan before him, Navarre found himself tactically restricted:

> . . . with an organized and better-equipped fighting force, almost twice the size of Giap's regular army, fewer troops were available to them for offensive action than to the Vietminh. Navarre estimated that of the total of 190,000 men in the Expeditionary Corps, at least 100,000 were tied down in static defense duties. Lacouture and Devillers claim that of the 500,000 soldiers of which the French disposed after the build-up of the Vietnamese National Army in 1953, no less than 350,000 were assigned in "static duties." The Vietminh battle corps consisted of six divisions; the French had only the equivalent of three, including their eight parachute battalions. The other 350,000 were assigned to defending cities, holding isolated strongpoints, accompanying convoys, patrolling highways, and conducting punitive actions against villages suspected of hiding and feeding the guerrillas, and of informing them about French moves. Alone sealing off and trying to pacify the [Red River] delta absorbed almost one-third of the Expeditionary Corps, a force obviously still insufficient for the task. When Navarre, in May, 1953, looked over the northern scene, he discovered that of the 7,000 villages in the delta, the French could boast of fully controlling no more than 2,000.[3]

Despite paucity of means, Navarre struck out variously at Viet Minh forces in the delta area. He also evacuated a series of outposts and garrisons, including the expensive airhead at Na San, which had been under siege since late 1952, and those ten battalions proved a welcome addition to his small operational force. By means of letters in the army newspaper, he exhorted troops elsewhere to adopt aggressive tactics:

> ... Your posts and blockhouses are only shelters. ... Your best defense is to seek out the enemy. ... By organizing frequent patrols and ambushes, you will restrict the enemy's freedom of movement and prevent him from undermining your sector, gathering intelligence and massing for surprise attacks. This is the only way by which you can gain the moral ascendancy essential to victory.[4]

These sounds words produced no magic, nor did Navarre's tactical "jabs" result in lasting effect. Attacks on occasion hurt a few of Giap's units, but most of them avoided direct confrontation and continued to interdict French lines of communication. At this crucial period, Giap had five regiments operating in the delta, that is, behind the "De Lattre Line," where an estimated sixty thousand guerrillas, not to mention innumerable Viet Minh sympathizers, supported them.[5]

The Korean cease-fire, signed in late July 1953, allowed the Chinese to provide instructors and quantities of captured American arms and equipment. In mid-1953, the army boasted " ... seven mobile divisions and one full-fledged artillery division, and more [units] were likely to come rapidly from the Chinese divisional training camps near Ching-Hei and Nanning."[6]

Extensive American military aid was also flowing into Saigon and Hanoi in keeping with the new Eisenhower administration's determination to bring about French "victory"—an ambition more hotly pursued by Secretary of State Dulles, prompted in part by his own hatred of communism, in part by pressures from anti-Communist crusaders in government, military, and Congress, than by President Eisenhower himself. Dulles was greatly concerned that a cease-fire in Korea would cause Communist China to turn southward. His was not a layman's opinion entirely, but, rather, the expressed fear of many senior military commanders. The military opinion, which so largely influenced American actions, derived in part from fear produced by the Communist-monolith theory, in part from an exaggerated estimate of Communist China's aggressive intentions, and in part from warning reports submitted by members of the U.S. military aid group in Indochina. In 1953, most military analysts unfortunately were not impressed with developing strains in the Communist bloc: If a rift had not yet occurred between the Soviet Union and China, the rupture between the U.S.S.R. and Yugoslavia proved beyond doubt that communism meant many things to many people. The misreading of Communist China's aggressive intentions stemmed from the Korean War and a refusal to recognize that China's entrance therein resulted directly from General MacArthur's aggressive and incredibly inept strategy. As for reports from American officers in Indochina: not understanding the nature of the war, these observers, with some splendid but unheralded exceptions, failed to realize that Giap neither needed nor wanted Chinese troops to fight the French, so long as the French remained intent on defeating themselves.

The erroneous military estimate of the situation does not excuse the administration's failure to make a more realistic strategic appraisal. But here two villains were at work. We have seen how Indochina, from the standpoint of American national interests, grew from a "nothing area" to a "nuisance area" to a "crucial area"—the result primarily of French intransigence coupled with the fall of Chiang Kai-shek. Having made political capital from Chiang's defeat, the Republicans fell prisoner to their own inflamed oratory. They had not only accused the Democrats of losing China, but had imputed the loss to sinister deeds of American officials. As one result, they could not think of losing even a portion of Indochina to the Communists.

To the villain of political opportunism, however, must be added that which afflicted the administration's military advisers: ignorance. In 1950, Representative Walter Judd had reported on a fact-finding mission to the Far East in part as follows:

> ... The area of Indochina is immensely wealthy in rice, rubber, coal, and iron ore. Its position makes it a strategic key to the rest of Southeast Asia. If Indochina should fall, Thailand and Burma would be in extreme danger, Malaya, Singapore, and even Indonesia would become more vulnerable to the Communist power drive. ... Communism would then be in an exceptional position to complete its perversion of the political and social revolution that is spreading through Asia. ... The Communists must be prevented from achieving their objectives in Indochina.[7]

This appraisal, an extension of William Bullitt's lopsided thinking in 1947 (see Chapter 36), the genesis of the later, famous domino theory, was as impassioned as it was specious. As any interested CIA analyst could have testified, Indochina is not immensely wealthy in natural resources. In 1937, Virginia Thompson published vital and depressing statistics substantiated more recently by Gunnar Myrdal's comprehensive study of the Asian economy.[8] Vietnam's coal traditionally has gone from North to South, its rice from South to North. The French exported

Vietnamese rice only at expense of the Vietnamese people's health. Rubber and coal exports were valuable to owners of French plantations and mines; they were not vital to Western production. Compared to Burma, Malaya, Thailand, and Indonesia, French Indochina is a poor area. Just as inaccurate was Judd's assertion that Indochina forms " . . . a strategic key to the rest of Southeast Asia." In the first place, Vietnam belongs to East Asia, not to Southeast Asia—an intense rivalry has always existed between the Thai and the Vietnamese (see Chapter 31).[9] Nor is Indochina a "strategic key." If it were, it would follow that whoever held Indochina would control Southeast Asia, a falsehood repeatedly demonstrated by history.

The term "strategic key" should be used with great caution. Like "communism," it means many things to many people. A diplomat of the caliber of Ambassador George Kennan saw it in 1947 in terms of

> . . . areas that I thought vital to our security and ones that did not seem to me to fall into this category. . . . There were only five regions of the world—the United States, the United Kingdom, the Rhine valley with adjacent industrial areas, the Soviet Union, and Japan—where the sinews of modern military strength could be produced in quantity. . . . [10]

A military planner concerned with armies and fleets and air armadas tends to demand certain geographical characteristics for a "strategic key." These usually concern control of communications—hence the geographer's terms "control cities" and "control points," for example Istanbul and Gibraltar, the Suez and Panama canals.

A "strategic key" logically should fit a door of national policy. A "strategic key (or necessity)" for one country is not necessarily a "strategic key (or necessity)" for another. Gibraltar, for example, would be a "strategic nothing" for a nation without a navy (unless the nation profited by granting base rights to a nation with a navy). Airfields in Morocco or Spain would scarcely serve the national interest of Lesotho, nor would Polaris-submarine bases in Scotland prove of interest to Ecuador.

Strategic values also change: Where once Gibraltar was a "strategic key" to British naval control of the Mediterranean, with the demise of the British Empire, it has become less important and Britain could comfortably survive without it, just as she survives without possession of the Suez Canal—a "strategic key" so long as national policy supported a Far Eastern empire. To take an example closer to home, the strategic value of the Panama Canal was far greater to the United States in the days of a one-ocean fleet than it is today. It is still important; it is not vital to the continued existence of the United States.

Technology also affects strategic values. Development of synthetic rubber in World War II, for example, almost canceled loss of the world's major rubber-producing areas to Japanese conquest. The development of super oil tankers cut sharply into the strategic importance of the Suez canal. Concentrated exploitation of rich oil fields in Alaska, Mexico, Siberia, and undoubtedly other areas, taken with the concerted development of alternate fuels, will eventually reduce the strategic importance of Middle Eastern oil fields to Western nations, as will development of a practical electric car—surely within the capability of nations that can place humans on the moon.

The majority of so-called "strategic keys" in reality are "strategic conveniences." The difference is immense. Whereas a genuine "strategic key" is vital to a nation's existence, a "strategic convenience" is not vital, and acquisition or retention can be measured in terms of limited investment. Control of Albania, for example, would be a "strategic convenience" for the United States and the West—but invasion and possession essential to control are not worth the world war that they would undoubtedly bring about. In 1956, when Britain yielded control of the Suez Canal, it had become a "strategic convenience" to her and was not worth a threatened atomic holocaust—and recently Britain and the West have survived quite comfortably without it. American air bases in Libya and Morocco were "strategic conveniences" yielded without significant weakening of U.S. defense posture. In 1954, Britain deemed the island of Cyprus a "strategic key" to her Middle East position. When the cost of fighting for its control became too great, its importance was reduced to a "strategic convenience"; accordingly, control was relinquished to the United Nations in return for two base enclaves, which have served its military purposes adequately. U.S. air bases in Spain were "strategic conveniences"; the recent loss of them was a virtual nonevent, strategically speaking. U. S. bases in the Philippines were rather more important "strategic conveniences," but certainly not "strategic necessities," as is evident from the recent (1992) closing of these bases. The eclipse of the Soviet Russian empire and the end of the cold war altered and will continue to alter former definitions of strategic conveniences and necessities as the world approaches the twenty-first century.

French Indochina has never formed a "strategic key." The area became a "strategic convenience" to the French for reasons discussed in Chapter 31. Japan utilized it similarly in World War II. Both countries used the northern region to support incursions into southeastern China, and Japan also used it to support southern, eastern, and western incursions. The ease of its occupation and the abject French surrender only underlined Indochina's awkward geographic position from the standpoint of military defense, as did the subsequent allied blockade that effectively interdicted communications between Indochina and Japan proper. Also significant, Chiang Kai-shek and the Kuomintang government could have made a good case with the allied powers for acquiring control of the northern area; instead, Chiang contented himself with a temporary occupation followed by evacuation with material profit.

No more is French Indochina a "strategic key" for Communist China. The prize of the Southeast Asian littoral is Burma, which borders China for over a thousand miles. A direct Chinese conquest of Burma would not depend on Chinese control of French Indochina, though, again, the area would be a "strategic convenience," as it would also be for a drive to the south. But, in 1953, China was not strong enough to drive either west or south, nor was there good reason for her to do so in view of continuing Viet Minh gains in Indochina and of the success of various subversion efforts elsewhere.

From the American standpoint, the area could scarcely form a "strategic key" unless the United States wished to invade southern China. In 1953, it did form a "strategic convenience" in that the French presence served to "contain" communism, or, put another way, continued to deny the area to the "enemy." Had the Eisenhower administration regarded Indochina as a "strategic convenience" and no more, it might have charted a more realistic course. It might have questioned the psychological sacrifice of the United States identifying itself with a colonial power detested throughout Asia, North Africa, and the Middle East. It might have questioned the validity of the French effort to retain northern and even southern Vietnam (as George Kennan questioned it in 1950), an effort largely subsidized with American dollars. It might even have questioned the retention of southern Vietnam as essential to American interests, reasoning instead that a "strategic presence," an enclave or two similar to Guantánamo Bay, in Cuba, would suffice (and could be secured in return for continuing aid from the "legitimate" French Government). In answer to those who pleaded the cause of humanity—prevention of Communist "enslavement" of millions—the Administration might have answered that it had no intention of going to war to free the satellite millions of Europe, preferring instead to preserve a world while trying to free people by other means; it might have added that the bulk of peasants in Indochina, as in China, were probably as well if not better off than under former regimes; and it might have recommended that the few thousand prominent Vietnamese Catholics, good healthy Asian-Christian stock who would have suffered under Communist rule, could have been shipped to underpopulated Australia under an American-subsidized scheme.

The Rolling Red Horde theory fathered a series of deeds designed to maintain the French "bulwark" against communism. In March 1953,

General Mark Clark, commanding in Korea, visited Vietnam and concluded that " . . . the Vietnamese needed rifles, automatic rifles, machine guns, light mortars and transportation facilities that could carry them over the water-soaked rice paddies in the Delta sector. . . . " General Clark recommended that Washington supply these and other arms and equipment; in an attempt to remedy what he believed was a deficient French troop-training program for the Vietnamese, he also arranged the transfer of some American and Korean advisers to Indochina. In addition, he released transport aircraft, Flying Boxcars, to the French command.[11] In spring of 1953, an American military mission arranged by Acheson and Letourneau surveyed the Indochinese scene, which resulted in *another* aid grant of nearly $400 million a few months later.[12]

Various French officials quickly fell in line with the American desire of saving Indochina. *Time* magazine's cover story of September 25, 1953, on Navarre, quoted him as saying: " . . . A year ago none of us could see victory. There wasn't a prayer. Now we can see it clearly like light at the end of a tunnel."[13] (The French expression in Algeria was *le dernier quart d'heure*—the last fifteen minutes.)[14] Not to be outdone, Secretary Dulles spoke grandly of "the Navarre Plan," which was designed to " . . . break the organized body of Communist aggression by the end of the 1955 fighting season."[15] In late November, Navarre advised his government that he did not believe the time had come to try to start peace negotiations. At month's end, the French high command in Indochina deigned to reply officially to an offer by Ho Chi Minh of a battlefield armistice followed by direct negotiations.[16] At the Bermuda Conference, in December, the French Foreign Minister, M. Bidault, told President Eisenhower that the situation " . . . was better than it had been for a long time . . . for the first time they were thinking of winning eventually."[17]

This verbal enthusiasm seemed to imply that, by some *deus ex machina,* France had suddenly reclaimed the military initiative. Nothing was further from the truth. While Navarre was rushing slim reserves about trying to plug holes in the "De Lattre Line" and prevent further losses in central Vietnam, Giap began striking at what the French were to call *zones excentriques,* that is, " . . . strategic points which were relatively vulnerable." He chose Laos, at first striking central and southern areas in addition to northern Cambodia, then attacking in greater strength in the North. Navarre reacted to this new threat by establishing a series of fortified airheads in the Northwest, "a mediocre solution," but the only favorable way in his mind of preventing direct invasion.[18] He placed the largest of these in Dien Bien Phu, an immense valley of seventy-five square miles surrounded by partially jungle-covered hills. He ordered the French task force, about six thousand troops, to build a series of defenses around the airfield while designated battalions patrolled aggressively as prelude to linking up with French forces in nearby Laos; the base would also support GCMA units—specially trained guerrilla units operating with friendly tribes in this region.

This was precisely the system that Navarre had inherited from Salan and in part discontinued as an unproductive drain on his relatively meager resources. He nonetheless proceeded with what Wingate had attempted in Burma: building a fortified camp "behind" enemy lines to support active operations against the enemy, a camp that was to be held "at all costs."[19]

In so doing, Navarre ignored three extremely valid arguments. The first already had been discreetly forwarded by President Eisenhower, who later wrote:

> ... the occupation of Dien Bien Phu caused little notice at the time, except to soldiers who were well acquainted with the almost invariable fate of troops invested in an isolated fortress. I instructed both the State and Defense Departments to communicate to their French counterparts my concern as to this move.[20]

Navarre's own commander of ground forces in northern Vietnam, General Cogny, presented a second:

> ... It seems that to the general staff (EMIFT), the occupation of Dien Bien Phu will close the road to Luang-Prabang and deprive the Viet-Minh of the rice of the region.
>
> In that kind of country you can't interdict a road. This is a European-type notion without any value here. The Viets can get through anywhere. We can see this right here in the Red River Delta. . . .
>
> I am persuaded that Dien Bien Phu shall become, whether we like it or not, a battalion meat-grinder, with no possibility of large-scale radiating out from it as soon as it will be blocked by a single Viet-Minh regiment (see example of Na-San). . . . [21]

French intelligence reports presented the third: the presence in the area of the 316th Viet Minh Division complete with an artillery battalion firing recoilless rifles and heavy mortars.[22]

As was his wont, Giap did nothing to stop the French from occupying and defending Dien Bien Phu. Only when the French plan became clear did Giap postpone his invasion of northern Laos in favor of an attack in strength against the new French position. His decision drew considerable argument from subordinate commanders, who remembered with distaste the cost of earlier Viet Minh attacks against French defensive positions. Giap answered these arguments by promising slow and methodical preparation that included careful training of assault troops and by secretly bringing up over two hundred heavy artillery pieces as well as anti-aircraft guns and ammunition to feed them.[23]

Giap thought he could achieve strategic and tactical surprise at Dien Bien Phu. Once he decided to attack, he started concentrating three assault divisions plus a new artillery division equipped in part with pieces captured in Korea by the Chinese. Simultaneously, thousands of coolies went to work improving hundreds of miles of a provincial road from the Chinese border to the battle area sufficiently to carry heavy "artillery pieces and the 800 Russian-built Molotova 2½-ton trucks which were to become the backbone of the conventional supply system."[24]

Meanwhile, French patrols, as called for in Navarre's original orders, began probing the periphery of the valley and beyond, operations that took place in the winter months and, due to repeated skirmishes, soon proved costly to the French. By February 1954, several painful facts had validated General Cogny's arguments against the operation. The first was the immensity of the operational task in relation to assigned resources. The attempt to base offensive operations on Dien Bien Phu had failed. Costly probes had disclosed extensive Viet Minh positions, artfully camouflaged and defended in strength. Neither could a few battalions hope to secure a defensive perimeter of some thirty miles nor, lacking construction materials and engineering know-how, could they build adequate internal defenses. To link Dien Bien Phu with garrisons in Laos by road would have taken months of heavy construction through jungle and mountain terrain.[25] Even worse, Paris left little doubt that Navarre would be going it alone. The Laniel government had made no secret of its desire to end the Indochina war, which, at home, was causing an extremely serious political rift. Abroad, the Berlin conference of foreign ministers of Britain, France, the Soviet Union, and the United States, in February 1954, agreed to " . . . a conference [at Geneva] to bring about a peaceful settlement in Korea and Indochina."[26] At long last, it seemed, the big powers were opting for political settlement.

None of these facts seemed to impress General Navarre except to cause him to convert the purpose of Dien Bien Phu from that of supporting offensive operations to that of forming a tactical piece of sugar to attract and finally destroy Viet Minh ants, in other words to the Hoa Binh "meat-grinder" concept of offering the Viet Minh a suitable target and defeating their attacks by superior firepower. Navarre's disastrous decision was the perhaps inevitable result of his predilection for European-style warfare, of his own ignorance of the Viet Minh and of war in northwestern Vietnam, and of believing what he wanted to believe and not what was variously reported by his staff.

According to a later official investigation, Navarre seriously underestimated Viet Minh capabilities. He did not believe that Giap could concentrate more than one division in the area within a month, nor maintain more than a limited siege by two divisions. He discounted the possibility of the Viet Minh bringing up heavy artillery despite indications reported by French intelligence. Navarre believed that French transport aircraft could supply the garrison while French fighter-bombers supported ground troops and effectively interdicted Giap's lines of communication. He also apparently placed considerable stock in Roger Trinquier's GCMA units, which had been causing the Viet Minh increasing concern and which, in the event, were supposed to cut Viet Minh supply lines.[27] Perhaps unconsciously, Navarre believed that the French Government would not allow a defeat at Dien Bien Phu. Possibly he was unduly impressed by the new American doctrine of threatened instant and massive retaliation against an aggressor—for example, China—announced by Dulles in late January 1954; later events suggest that he might have been promised American air support in case of trouble—in February 1954, the United States supplied B-26 bombers to his command along with 250 U. S. Air Force technicians, vanguard of an eventual twelve hundred men who would keep them flying. Finally, an inhibitive psychological factor in form of a "last-chance" philosophy might have been at work, as suggested by a lecture Navarre delivered four years later:

> . . . We had no policy at all [in Indochina]. . . . After seven years of war we were in a complete imbroglio, and no one, from private to commander in chief, knew just why we were fighting.
>
> Was it to maintain French positions? If so, which ones? Was it simply to participate, under the American umbrella, in the "containment" of Communism in Southeast Asia? Then why did we continue to make such an effort when our interest had practically ceased to exist?
>
> This uncertainty about our political aims kept us from having a continuing and coherent military policy in Indochina. . . . This rift between policy and strategy dominated the entire Indochina war.[28]

CHAPTER FORTY-SEVEN

1. *Time*, September 28, 1953. See also, Fall, *Hell in a Very Small Place* . . .
2. Fall, *The Two Viet-Nams* . . . , 122.
3. Buttinger, II, 760. See also, Lancaster, 264–5: . . . whereas the Viet Minh had at their disposal seven regular infantry divisions, which together with their independent regiments were now estimated to constitute an operational force with a strength equivalent to nine divisions, the French Union forces were only able to muster seven mobile groups and eight parachute battalions, or the equivalent of three divisions; Giap, *People's War, People's Army*.
4. McCuen, 266.

5. Fall, *The Two Viet-Nams,* 125.
6. Fall, *Hell in a Very Small Place . . .* , ix.
7. Gurtov, 26.
8. Thompson; Myrdal for the specifics.
9. Myrdal, 882.
10. Kennan, *Memoirs 1925–1950, 359.*
11. Clark, Mark W., 320–1.
12. Acheson, 677.
13. *Time,* September 28, 1953.
14. Schalk, 29.
15. Fall, *The Two Viet-Nams . . .* , 122.
16. Fall, *Hell in a Very Small Place . . .* , 47.
17. Eisenhower, *Mandate for Change . . .* , 246.
18. Navarre, 191.
19. Lancaster, 286.
20. Eisenhower, *Mandate for Change,* 339.
21. Fall, *Hell in a Very Small Place . . .* , 35–6.
22. Ibid.
23. Giap, *People's War, People's Army,* 180 ff.
24. Fall, *Hell in a Very Small Place . . .* , 128.
25. Ibid., 76–7. See also, Lancaster, 286 ff.
26. Acheson, 677.
27. McCuen, 250–1. In late 1953, the designation changed to GMI (*Groupement Mixte d'Intervention*); by the end of the war, the GMI numbered 15,000 troops supported by 300 tons of air-dropped supply monthly. See also, Tanham, *Communist Revolutionary Warfare . . .*
28. Devillers and Lacouture, 4.

CHAPTER 48

Vietnam: French and American estimates • Giap attacks Dien Bien Phu • Viet Minh tactics • The guerrilla effort • Crisis • Question of American military intervention • Dissenting voices • General Ridgway's warning • Eisenhower backs down • The fall of Dien Bien Phu

WHATEVER THE REASONS behind the tactical aberration of Dien Bien Phu, General Navarre was not the only one who erred. Western military conceit not only carried over to numerous members of his staff and to ranking commanders in Hanoi and Dien Bien Phu, but also overflowed area lines. In February 1954, the French Minister of National Defense, René Pleven, and the Chief of the French General Staff, General Paul Ély, visited Vietnam, including Dien Bien Phu. Although Pleven was critical of Navarre's "hedgehog" strategy, which, he feared, created "game preserves" for the Viet Minh,[1] Ély described Dien Bien Phu as an " . . . extremely strong position, which could only be attacked by a very powerful force," and, even then, he believed that the advantage would be with the defenders.[2] Also in February, the head of the American military advisory group, Lieutenant General O'Daniel, visited Dien Bien Phu and reported so favorably to Washington that President Eisenhower cabled Secretary of State Dulles, then attending the foreign ministers' conference in Berlin: " . . . General O'Daniel's most recent report is more encouraging than that given to you through French sources."[3]

By March 1954, the Dien Bien Phu garrison numbered some seventeen thousand troops, who occupied a sector system of defense supported by artillery and aircraft. These troops were still digging in when the Viet Minh opened fire to begin a siege action that would last a little longer than two months. The reader will find a blow-by-blow account of this heart-rending battle in Bernard Fall's book *Hell in a Very Small Place*. We can only note that events swiftly disproved all of Navarre's suppositions, to result in tactical defeat that, despite limited proportions, brought resounding military and political repercussions.

Giap's most important success lay in secretly bringing up artillery and other heavy weapons through jungles and over mountains, a fantastic logistics effort that resulted in bombardment of French jerry-built positions by 75-mm. and 105-mm. howitzers, 75-mm. recoilless rifles, 120-mm. mortars, and, toward the end, Soviet multiple-rocket launchers. Aided by direct artillery fire (frowned on by Western officers as too simple), Viet Minh assault teams from four secretly concentrated divisions pinched off outer defense sectors until artillery interdicted the vital airstrip to render it inoperable. This disaster forced the French to drop ammunition and supply by parachute, but Giap now unleashed his second surprise, a ring of anti-aircraft guns which produced flak so murderous that C-119s flown by American civil pilots under contract to the French resorted to higher altitudes, which meant widely dispersed cargo drops, with much vital supply falling to the Viet Minh.[4]

Guerrilla activity elsewhere behind French lines also took a major toll of French resources. In early March, Viet Minh teams struck three French airfields to destroy thirty airplanes and fifty-three thousand gallons of fuel; at heavily fortified Cat Bi Airfield, raiders crawled through sewers to reach eighteen transport aircraft, six reconnaissance planes, and four B-26 bombers.[5]

French combat air support proved a disappointment. The distance of the target area from French fields gave the B-26s only limited time on target—fighters had only ten minutes!—while uncomfortably accurate flak coupled with extremely effective camouflage discouraged the direct support task. Poor weather and jungle terrain hindered observation. Planes bombed roads and bridges by day, but Vietnamese coolies either repaired them or built bypasses at night. Interdiction, on occasion, halted the several hundred trucks at Giap's disposal; it almost never stopped thousands of coolies laboriously pushing bicycles loaded with ammunition and supply.[6] As with American air power in Korea, French air power impeded, but never halted, the flow of material. Trinquier's GCMA teams also proved disappointing. Despite his later assertions to the contrary, they did not "seal off" the target.[7]

Giap also faced enormous problems. Early assaults on outer hill positions, carried out in a manner reminiscent of American marines attacking Pacific beaches in World War II, but lacking a sophisticated system of artillery and air support, cost so heavily that Giap changed his tactics to a trench warfare reminiscent of World War I. Viet Minh morale sagged, and was revived only with considerable difficulty. Largely untrained replacements were slow in arriving. Medical services were appallingly inadequate. Transcending these problems was strategic and tactical surprise, which Giap had achieved and which caused the panic-stricken French high command to start thinking in terms of American air support.

The confusing and frightening events of this period were later pieced together by veteran Washington journalist Chalmers Roberts in a superb piece of reporting. According to his account, on March 20, the French army's chief of staff, General Paul Ély,

> ... arrived in Washington from the Far East to tell the President, Dulles, Radford [Chairman of the Joint Chiefs of Staff], and others that unless the United States intervened, Indochina would be lost. This was a shock of earthquake proportions to leaders who had been taken in by their own talk of the Navarre Plan to win the war.[8]

Admiral Radford took the lead. A man of forceful action, he insisted that carrier air strikes—presumably using atomic bombs—were necessary to retrieve the situation at Dien Bien Phu. His words caused a decided flurry in the National Security Council. Supported by Vice-President Nixon and Secretary of State Dulles, Radford held " ... that Indochina must not be allowed to fall into Communist hands lest such a fate set in motion a falling row of dominoes." A few days later, President Eisenhower ominously stated in a press conference that Southeast Asia was of the " ... most transcendent importance." In early April, at Eisenhower's behest, Dulles, backed by Radford, told eight Congressional leaders that he wanted

> a joint resolution by Congress to permit the President to use air and naval power in Indochina. . . . If Indochina fell and if its fall led to the loss of all of Southeast Asia, he declared, then the United States might eventually be forced back to Hawaii, as it was before the Second World War.[9]

Congressional leaders, Lyndon Johnson among them, determined by astute questioning that the single proposed air strike from U. S. Navy carriers and land-based bombers from the Philippines would mean war, that if it did not succeed in relieving Dien Bien Phu, further action would have to follow, that none of the three service chiefs constituting the Joint Chiefs of Staff agreed with Radford, that Dulles had not gained allied approval of such a course, and that no one could say whether China or the Soviet Union would also go to war over the issue. Not all questions rang brilliantly; the domestic political factor showed in some. They collectively demonstrated, however, the administration's jerry-built plan that might well have precipitated an atomic war and the end of civilization as we know it: " ... In the end, all eight members of Congress, Republicans and Democrats alike, were agreed that Dulles had better go shopping for allies. . . . "[10]

The Administration was not yet ready to yield. Key figures began to prepare the home front for American intervention. President Eisenhower, at a press conference, parroted Radford by speaking of a "row-of-dominoes" to conjure to the American public a black-and-white picture of the conquest of Southeast Asia by "communists." Having decided that the loss of Indochina would prove a greater calamity than the loss of Korea, Secretary of State Dulles reasoned that " . . . the commitment of American ground forces and the sacrifice of American lives would be fully justified."[11] In mid-April, Admiral Radford publicly stated that loss of Indochina " . . . would be the prelude to the loss of all Southeast Asia and a threat to a far wider area." Vice-President Nixon told a group of newspaper editors: " . . . The United States as a leader of the free world cannot afford further retreat in Asia. It is hoped the United States will not have to send troops there, but if this government cannot avoid it, the Administration must face up to the situation and dispatch forces."[12]

Meanwhile, Secretary of State Dulles was trying to win the allied approval demanded by Congressional leaders for the proposed intervention. Although talks went smoothly with France, Australia, New Zealand, the Philippines, Thailand, and Vietnam, Laos, and Cambodia, he ran into a brick wall when it came to Great Britain. Speaking for Churchill and the British Government, Foreign Minister Anthony Eden voiced three major objections: British military advisers did not believe that air action alone would be effective (it followed that ground troops would have to be committed); direct intervention would torpedo the Geneva Conference, for which Eden held great hopes; in view of the existing Sino-Soviet treaty, direct intervention might well lead to general war.[13]

Despite Dulles' frantic efforts during the next few weeks to overcome British intransigence, Churchill and Eden held firm against direct intervention, preferring instead to attain a political settlement—some form of partition—at Geneva. The British provided only one stumbling block. In early May, Eden notified Churchill that " . . . only Mr. [Walter] Bedell Smith [a retired U. S. Army general now U. S. Under-Secretary of State] seemed to have any real comprehension of the reasons which had led us to take up our present position." In opposition to the Administration's domino theory, so favored by Dulles, Smith thought

> . . . that though it would be quite impossible to attempt to stop a communist advance on the border of Malaya, it was possible to find a position from which Thailand, Burma and Malaya could be

defended. One of the difficulties was that they had never been able to sit down with the French over a map and examine the military possibilities of the situation.[14]

Coming from Eisenhower's chief of staff in World War II and former head of the Central Intelligence Agency, Smith's opinion would certainly have told in Eisenhower's mind. Another important dissident was the U. S. Army's chief of staff, General Matthew B. Ridgway, surely one of the most capable generals in history. Ridgway had never been impressed with the French defense of Dien Bien Phu, a fight, he believed, that "... could end in but one way—in death or capture for the defenders. ... " But, in spring of 1954, the army's chief of staff was more alarmed

> ... to hear individuals of great influence, both in and out of government, raising the cry that now was the time, and here, in Indo-China, was the place to "test the New Look" [i.e., in American air-oriented military forces], for us to intervene, to come to the aid of France with arms. At the same time that same old delusive idea was advanced—that we could do things the cheap and easy way, by going into Indo-China with air and naval forces alone. To me this had an ominous ring. For I felt sure that if we committed air and naval power to that area, we would have to follow them immediately with ground forces in support.

Ridgway had commanded in Korea, where he had extricated UN forces from MacArthur's catastrophic strategy, an experience that left him with few illusions. War in Asia, he knew, was not a pinchpenny business:

> ... I also knew that none of those advocating such a step [intervention at Dien Dien Phu] had any accurate idea what such an operation would cost us in blood and money and national effort. I felt that it was essential therefore that all who had any influence in making the decision on this grave matter should be fully aware of all the factors involved. To provide these facts, I sent out to Indo-China an Army team of experts in every field: engineers, signal and communications specialists, medical officers, and experienced combat leaders who knew how to evaluate terrain in terms of battle tactics. ...
>
> Their report was complete. The area, they found, was practically devoid of those facilities which modern forces such as ours find essential to the waging of war. Its telecommunications, highways, railways—all the things that make possible the operation of a modern combat force on land—were almost non-existent. Its port facilities and airfields were totally inadequate, and to provide

591

the facilities we would need would require a tremendous engineering and logistical effort.

The land was a land of rice paddy and jungle—particularly adapted to the guerrilla-type warfare at which the Chinese soldier is a master. . . .

Neither Ridgway nor his army was afraid of a war in Indochina; his point was the immensity of the effort, for, " . . . if we did go into Indo-China, we would have to win. . . . "

> . . . We could have fought in Indo-China. We could have won, if we had been willing to pay the tremendous cost in men and money that such intervention would have required . . . In Korea, we had learned that air and naval power alone cannot win a war and that inadequate ground forces cannot win one either. It was incredible to me that we had forgotten that bitter lesson so soon—that we were on the verge of making that same tragic error.[15]

The Ridgway report reached President Eisenhower, probably in late May, about the same time General Ridgway personally briefed him.[16] Eisenhower mentioned nothing of it in his memoirs, which are particularly ambiguous for this crucial period. So far as one can gather, the President was not steering a firm course toward intervention but, rather, was allowing his ship of state to be blown into it by Dullesian-Radford war winds. Eisenhower, all along, had objected to tactical aspects of the French stand at Dien Bien Phu; as an old soldier, he must have raised a tired eyebrow when still another airman claimed he could win a war with bombs alone. The Ridgway report presumably made a considerable impact; as General Ridgway later wrote, " . . . to a man of his military experience its implications were immediately clear." It is probably safe to say that the report and its author steered Eisenhower to a more cautious course at an incautious time of government.[17]

While international diplomacy so ran the course, the plight of the Dien Bien Phu defenders grew steadily worse. On May 8, 1954, the beleaguered garrison surrendered to the Viet Minh. Over two thousand defenders had died; the remainder, including some five thousand wounded, marched forlornly into captivity.[18]

Here was a crushing defeat too great for the French to accept and still fight on. The Paris and Saigon governments fell; in June, General Ély replaced General Navarre. Although the French army in Indochina remained a cohesive unit, with 95 per cent of its strength intact, government and country had suffered enough. Despite American pressure, the new prime minister of France, Pierre Mendès-France, hastened to a political settlement that, had it been made in a yesterday, would have solved many problems of the morrow.

CHAPTER FORTY-EIGHT

1. Devillers and Lacouture, 62.
2. Lancaster, 294–5: Pleven later told Premier Laniel " . . . that he viewed the prospect of such an attack with misgivings, describing the Expeditionary Corps as 'exhausted' and the general military situation as essentially 'precarious.' " See also, Devillers and Lacouture, 64: Ély and two of his fellow generals later reported " . . . that no military solution could be achieved," that France " . . . had already reached the limits of its military effort," and that " . . . the most it could now hope to achieve was the optimum military conditions for a political settlement."
3. Eisenhower, *Mandate for Change* . . . , 344.
4. Fall, *Hell in a Very Small Place* . . . , 127, 185, 265.
5. Ibid., 159.
6. Ibid., 452.
7. Trinquier, xiv. See also, Fall, *Hell in a Very Small Place* . . . ; Tanham, *Communist Revolutionary Warfare* . . .
8. Roberts, Chalmers M.
9. Ibid. See also, Frances Fitzgerald, 33.
10. Roberts, Chalmers M.
11. Rovere, 192–3.
12. *New York Times,* April 17, 1954. See also, Eisenhower, *Mandate for Change* . . .
13. Eden, *The Memoirs of Anthony Eden—Full Circle,* 113–17.
14. Ibid., 125–6.
15. Ridgway, *Soldier* . . . , 275–7.
16. Personal letter from General Ridgway to the author.
17. Ridgway, *Soldier* . . . , 277:

> . . . when the day comes for me to face my maker and account for my actions, the thing I would be most humbly proud of was the fact that I fought against, and perhaps contributed to preventing, the carrying out of some hare-brained tactical schemes which would have cost the lives of thousands of men. To that list of tragic accidents that fortunately never happened I would add the Indo-China intervention.

18. Fall, *Hell in a Very Small Place* . . . , 431–2. See also, Lartéguy. The author offers a gripping account in this novel of subsequent treatment of prisoners of war; Giap, *People's War, People's Army.*

CHAPTER 49

*The Geneva Conference • The American position • Dulles' defeat •
The agreements • SEATO • Ngo Dinh Diem • His background
• The refugee problem • American support • Eisenhower's letter •
The Collins mission • Diem takes over*

IN SEPTEMBER 1953, sixty-five-year-old Secretary of State John Foster Dulles told listening representatives at the United Nations that U.S. leaders

> . . . are ready to learn from others. Also we recognize that our views may not always prevail. When that happens, we shall regret it, but we shall not sulk. We shall try to accept the result philosophically. We know that we have no monopoly of wisdom and virtue. Also we know that sometimes time alone proves the final verdict.[1]

Dulles of that speech and Dulles at Geneva seven months later seemed to be different persons. Arriving in the old Swiss city in a state of near funk, his mood darkened when Anthony Eden reported the British Government's final decision against direct intervention at Dien Bien Phu. Dulles' views having prevailed neither with allies nor Eisenhower, he went into a diplomatic sulk far removed from philosophical acceptance of recent events. He could not withdraw the American delegation from the conference, but he could pretend that the conference did not exist, just as he pretended, in refusing to acknowledge the presence of Chou En-lai, the Communist Chinese foreign minister, that Red China did not exist. Even before Vietnam appeared on the agenda, Dulles returned to the United States, leaving Walter Bedell Smith in charge of American representation.

Dullesian boycott of the Geneva Conference changed neither the fact of the conference nor the awkward situation faced there by Western powers. Eisenhower's change of posture did not help matters, in that it

594

seemed to abandon Indochina to the Viet Minh, who, at this stage, were riding high. They controlled over three fourths of Vietnam, and left no doubt in anyone's mind that they believed themselves capable of totally evicting the French from Indochina. So determined were Viet Minh representatives to continue the war, that the Soviet Union and China, each wanting a settlement for its own political purposes, restrained their ally only with considerable difficulty. Ho and his fellows agreed to a settlement mainly because it transferred the situation to the political plane, where they felt equally confident of victory.

The Geneva Conference produced two agreements, the first a bilateral armistice between Ho Chi Minh's DRV and France, the second a "Final Declaration" that established a " . . . provisional military demarcation line," the 17th parallel, "pending the general elections which will bring about the unification of Viet Nam . . . "[2]

The "Final Declaration" evoked two important dissenting voices. The first belonged to Dr. Tran Van Do, who represented the Associated States of Vietnam. Titularly headed by Bao Dai, its premier had become the redoubtable nationalist Ngo Dinh Diem, who instructed Dr. Do " . . . to disassociate South Vietnam from the agreements that were signed, thereby laying the legal groundwork for his subsequent refusal to abide by them . . . "[3] The second voice belonged to the American delegate, Walter Bedell Smith, who, instructed by Dulles, refused to sign. Other participating governments—Great Britain, Communist China, the Soviet Union, Cambodia, Laos, DRV, and France—circumvented this contretemps by awarding the document "oral assent," the United States and Vietnam refusing. Smith "took note" of the Agreements and declared that the United States would " . . . refrain from the threat or the use of force to disturb them" and that it " . . . would view any renewal of the aggression in violation of the aforesaid Agreements with grave concern and as seriously threatening international peace and security"—an attempted face-saving declaration not unlike the "non-injury oath" familiar to the feudal period of history.*[4] What Dulles was up to is anyone's guess. For five years, the Republicans had made political capital out of the fall of Nationalist China. Now, suddenly, a similar disaster loomed on *their* political horizon. As one result, American diplomacy, in Joseph Buttinger's splendid phrase, had become "wildly incoherent."[5] It seems reasonable to suggest that a more determined Dulles practicing first-rate diplomacy could have come closer to

---

* S. Runciman: In the First Crusade, Raymond of St. Gilles, count of Toulouse, refused to take an oath of allegiance to the Byzantine emperor, Alexius. Under pressure from other crusader leaders, Raymond eventually " . . . swore a modified oath promising to respect the life and honor of the emperor and to see that nothing was done, by himself or his men, to the emperor's hurt. Such an oath of non-injury was often taken by vassals to their overlord in southern France; and Alexius was satisfied with it."

a partition arrangement similar to that of Korea, indeed similar to that contained in a seven-point proposal sent to the French during negotiations.[6] Even as drawn, the Agreement and Final Declaration smack of partition, and it is difficult to believe that the representatives of the major powers did not foresee such an eventuality.

Dulles' external answer to the diplomatic defeat at Geneva was the South-east Asia Collective Defense Treaty and Protocol, signed by the United States, Great Britain, France, Australia, New Zealand, the Philippines, Thailand, and Pakistan, in early September 1954. The Southeast Asia Treaty Organization, or SEATO, bound its members to a "security" pact which meant so many things to so many people as almost to vitiate logical meaning. The nub of the document occurs early in Article IV:

> ... Each Party recognizes that aggression by means of armed attack in the treaty area against any of the Parties or against any State or territory which the Parties by unanimous agreement may hereafter designate, would endanger its own peace and safety, and agrees that it will in that event act to meet the common danger in accordance with its constitutional processes. ...

An additional protocol extended the provisions of this article to Cambodia, Laos, and " ... the free territory under the jurisdiction of the State of Vietnam."[7]

In Dulles' mind SEATO existed to halt the spread of communism in Southeast Asia, and particularly in Vietnam, " ... and to build up in that country 'a strong government which commands the loyalty of the people, and which has an effective police and constabulary at its command to detect and run down subversive activities.' "[8]

Even had signatories stood solidly behind SEATO, it would have had difficulty functioning as an effective regional security organization. Unlike NATO, no combined command existed, no country committed military forces to SEATO, and no country had to respond in case another was attacked.[9] The Geneva Agreements, at least for some time, prevented overt military action—but not covert political preparation—by the Viet Minh in Indochina, the area Dulles was most concerned about. As a psychological force, SEATO suffered from failure of major neutralist states, Burma, India, and Indonesia, to join. Still, it represented a common voice of sorts and, judging from the flood of counterpropaganda it loosed from DRV and from China and the Soviet Union, it obviously hit a Communist nerve.

Simultaneously with organizing SEATO, Dulles and the State Department concerned themselves directly with developments inside Vietnam. This meant dealing with the new premier, Ngo Dinh Diem. In 1954, the prime minister of Vietnam, Ngo Dinh Diem, was fifty-three years old. Robert Shaplen, who later knew him, described him as " . . . a short, broadly built man with a round face and a shock of black hair, who walked and moved jerkily, as if on strings. He always dressed in white and looked as if he were made out of ivory. . . . "[10] A bachelor and ascetic, he lived remote from his world. Surrounded by sycophants, he saw few strangers. Those received into his presence generally found themselves subject to a monologue that betrayed extreme egocentricity.

Diem was the third child in an ancient family of Catholic aristocrats. His father had served as court chamberlain to Emperor Thanh Thai at Hué; when the French deposed Thanh Thai, the elder Diem became a reasonably prosperous rice farmer. After elementary schooling, young Diem entered a monastery but later gave up the idea of the priesthood and graduated from the School of Public Administration and Law at Hanoi. He began imperial service as a mandarin, or court official, rose to provincial-governor level, and spent much of his time effectively countering Communist activities in his province. In 1933, the French appointed him Minister of Interior in young Emperor Bao Dai's Annam Government. Unable to persuade French overlords to reforms he felt essential to combating communism, Diem resigned. For ten years he lived quietly, mostly in Hué, " . . . the reflective life of a scholar-revolutionist," but with little contact with the people. In 1942, he tried to interest the Japanese in establishing a free Vietnam, and when that failed, he remained in political limbo along with other nationalists. In September 1945, Viet Minh Communist agents arrested and imprisoned him. At about the same time, the Communists killed his older brother Ngo Dinh Khoi, who was governor of a northern province.

In February 1946, Ho Chi Minh ordered Diem's release and brought him to Hanoi. Trying to corral nationalist figures, Ho offered him an important position in the new government. Diem refused, mainly because of his brother's death. He next tried to organize anti-Communist guerrilla activity but without success. After a short stay in a Hanoi monastery, he disguised himself as a monk and wandered around the country trying to work up anti-Communist activity among his contacts. Finally forced into complete hiding, he eventually went south and lived with his brother Thuc near Saigon.

In spring of 1947, Diem became a founding father of the National Union Front, a nationalist movement quickly and efficiently sabotaged by the French. Diem gained considerable prominence, however, and became go-between with the French in Saigon and Bao Dai in Hong Kong. The French wanted Bao Dai to return to Saigon and head a new government; Diem wanted him to hold out for a promise of Vietnamese independence. When Bao Dai chose to become puppet ruler, Diem dissociated himself from the new regime. Subsequent efforts to enlist him in the government failed because of French refusal to promise what Diem believed were essential reforms. Diem himself was unable to form a genuine nationalist movement to force these reforms. In 1950, the Viet Minh sentenced him to death *in absentia,* the French refused him police protection, and he wisely left on a trip that ended in the United States.

Diem lived for two years at Maryknoll Seminary, in Lakewood, New Jersey. In addition to lecturing at universities and writing articles pleading for an independent Vietnam, he won the ear of a number of influential Americans, including Francis Cardinal Spellman, Supreme Court Justice William Douglas, and various congressmen, among them Mike Mansfield, John F. Kennedy, and Walter Judd.[11] From time to time, Bao Dai tried to persuade him to return to Saigon and participate in his government. In mid-1953, when Diem was living in Europe, Bao Dai promised him full political powers if he would return to Vietnam, but the French would not agree to Diem's demand that " . . . the Vietnamese be allowed to conduct the war." Finally, in early July 1954, toward the final stages of the Geneva Conference, Diem accepted the premiership.

Although Diem had dissociated Vietnam from the Geneva Agreements, he was nonetheless compelled to work with the French in carrying out cease-fire provisions and trying to bring some order into the country south of the 17th parallel. Neither task proved easy:

> . . . The country was in ruins. Most bridges had been blown up. Canals, roads, railways, telephone and telegraph services had been either destroyed or were in disrepair. Dykes, too, were destroyed; vast regions of rice land were uncultivated; countless peasants who had fled the countryside found themselves unemployed in the cities. And Diem's administration, run by an incompetent civil service, politically hostile and disintegrating, had to provide the human and material resources for receiving, feeding, and temporarily settling hundreds of thousands of refugees. . . .[12]

In the months following the Geneva Conference, the armed forces of both sides had to be evacuated. About fifty thousand Viet Minh troops and twenty thousand Communist sympathizers went North. Following French evacuation of the Red River Delta, Vietnamese civilians, mostly Roman Catholics, began flooding South. With the help of American ships and planes, some 860,000 refugees eventually arrived; another four hundred thousand who wanted to come were prevented by the Viet Minh (in contravention of the Geneva Agreements).[13]

This influx of population would have taxed the resources of an efficient government. In Diem's case, it nearly brought ruin. He not only lacked experienced administrators and personal advisers, but he soon found himself in active opposition to Bao Dai, to Bao's army chief, General Nguyen Van Hinh, to many French officials and most French civilians, to powerful political-religious sects in the South, and to Viet Minh cadres that, at Ho Chi Minh's behest, remained in the South. About the only bright note at this critical time was American support. Diem found help both in Saigon and Washington, where President Eisenhower and Secretary of State Dulles had determined on a "security and reform" policy:

> . . . With Diem as a nationalist fulcrum, the Americans wanted to build up a single army that would be trained by American officers and could serve as the instrument for pacification in the country-side, where a land distribution program and other social-economic reforms would be introduced.[14]

Such a policy conflicted with French desire to dump Diem in favor of a ruler more sympathetic to French interests. The French now turned to General Nguyen Van Hinh, who was ready to attempt a military coup. An American counterinsurgency expert from the Philippines, a forty-six-year-old Air Force officer on loan to Central Intelligence Agency, Colonel Edward Lansdale, deftly parried this threat with a counterthreat of having American aid stopped. Diem gained further strength from a U. S. Senate report of mid-October prepared by Senator Mike Mansfield, who praised him and called for total American support of his government. In case anyone still doubted the Administration's intention, President Eisenhower wrote President Diem a cordial letter delivered in late October. This has subsequently become famous as the letter that "morally" committed successive American administrations to Diem's and South Vietnam's support. It did no such thing. It authorized the American ambassador to Vietnam, Donald R. Heath, to work out "an intelligent program of American aid," provided Diem guaranteed satisfactory "standards of performance," which would "contribute effectively toward an independent Vietnam endowed with a strong government . . . responsive to the nationalist aspirations of its people."[15]

These words represented challenge more than commitment. American moral involvement derived from an attempt to convert a political zombie into a rational human being. At no time was the involvement such in the eyes of the world that it could not have been abrogated with impunity. Eisenhower followed his frank statement of American intentions by dispatching General J. Lawton Collins as ambassador. Upon arriving in Saigon, Collins stated: " . . . I have come to Vietnam to bring every possible aid to the government of Diem and to his government alone."[16]

Diem's immediate internal-security problem centered not on the Viet Minh who had remained in the South, but, rather, on the Vietnamese army first, the neo-military Binh Xuyên second, and the political-religious sects third. Diem was relieved of the first problem by Collins' stated policy. The United States would not consider " . . . training or otherwise aiding a Vietnamese army that does not give complete and implicit obedience to its premier."[17] This effectively pulled the power rug from beneath the feet of Diem's main rival, General Van Hinh. There remained Hinh's fall: the American Government persuaded Bao Dai to order him to Paris and dismiss him as army head. Collins, meanwhile, set up a combined American-French training command headed by General O'Daniel, who was also chief of MAAG. O'Daniel undertook the task of organizing and training an indigenous Vietnamese army. One of his four division heads, Colonel Lansdale, commanded the National Security division, " . . . the only one actually advising the Vietnamese on operations."[18]

The second and third problems were not so simple. The Binh Xuyên, a sort of oriental Mafia that controlled the vice and police in Saigon-Cholon, was a well-entrenched organization protected both by Bao Dai and by a private army of some twenty-five hundred thugs. As in any gangster activity, millions of dollars went into local payoffs that benefited numerous officials—French, Vietnamese, and Chinese. The Cao Dai and the Hoa Hao were something else again. Offshoots of the Buddhist religion, they formed virtually separate states, the Cao Dai northwest of Saigon, the Hoa Hao southwest. The Cao Dai supposedly maintained twenty thousand men under arms, the Hoa Hao fifty thousand, but each sect claimed over a million supporters in its particular area.[19]

Diem moved very carefully against the sects, appointing four leaders from each to his Saigon cabinet. He then spent $12 million of American taxpayers' money in bribing these and other leaders to assimilate at least some of their armed forces into the Vietnamese army. Thus prepared, he challenged the Binh Xuyên, in January 1955, by closing down gambling casinos.

This reads more smoothly than it happened. The confusion and intrigue of the day would have furnished Milton Caniff's comic strip, *Terry and the Pirates,* enough plots for fifty years—and should have furnished concerned American officials a caution sign in future rela-

600

tionships in South Vietnam. For, while Diem was attempting to consolidate his power, a great number of people, including Bao Dai and local French and Vietnamese officials, not to mention Viet Minh cadres, were doing their best to sabotage his every effort. Moreover, the important and powerful General Collins was becoming increasingly disillusioned with Diem, as were various sects that felt their powers slipping away. Diem, however, retained Lansdale's support in Saigon and that of the Dulles brothers, important State Department officials, and Congressional leaders in Washington.

The situation exploded in March 1955, when Diem refused to give the sects more power in his government. Hoa Hao and Cao Dai cabinet members resigned, and the two sects joined with the Binh Xuyên to form the United Front of Nationalist Forces. A few days later, Binh Xuyên forces attacked the presidential palace. Although the French arranged an uneasy truce, the new war widened the breach between Diem and Collins. Collins returned to Washington in mid-April determined to dump Diem. Backed by President Eisenhower, he had set the wheels in motion when, to the surprise of all, excepting possibly Colonel Lansdale, important units of Diem's army remained loyal and thrashed the Binh Xuyên. A month later, Diem had driven the Binh Xuyên out of Saigon (they eventually disintegrated) and had the Cao Dai and Hoa Hao forces either on the run or coming over to his side.

Diem's victory deflated Collins' effort to unseat him. Far worse, Diem suddenly appeared to be the strong leader so desired by the American Government. Not only Senator Mansfield now reiterated his belief in Diem, but such as Hubert Humphrey joined the chorus: " . . . Premier Diem is the best hope that we have in South Vietnam. He is the leader of his people. He deserves and must have the wholehearted support of the American Government and our foreign policy. . . . "[20]

In Paris, during a NATO meeting in May,

> . . . the French called Diem an American puppet and threatened that unless Diem was removed they would pull out their troops and cancel other forms of assistance they were still rendering Vietnam. Dulles called their bluff and told them to go ahead, and at one point threatened that if the French did leave, the Americans would get out, too. This upset the French so much that they subsided.[21]

Dulles unknowingly was touching on a solution that perhaps would better have served his own country's and Vietnam's best interests. At this time, Diem already was exhibiting those administrative traits that contrasted so strongly with promises made to President Eisenhower in return for American aid. This was the time for the President's ambassador—Collins or anyone else—to inform Diem that he either would rule as promised or he would rule alone until deposed by a more popular choice. Unfortunately, powerful American voices, absurdly strengthened by a pathological fear of communism, already had elevated Ngo Dinh Diem as savior of Southeast Asia, an incorruptible Christian patriot who alone could guard his country from the Red Menace. Here was a peculiar concept well suited to the black-and-white thinking of that American day: Here was GOOD challenged by EVIL, the hero facing the villain. In mid-May, Eisenhower relieved Collins in favor of Ambassador G. Frederick Reinhardt, who stated upon his arrival in Saigon: " . . . I come here under instructions to carry out United States policy in support of the legal government of Vietnam under Premier Ngo Dinh Diem."[22]

The stage was now set for old-fashioned melodrama. It remained for the United States cavalry, banners flying, bugles blowing, and hoofs thumping, to charge across the plain. Figuratively, this is what happened—and hereby melodrama changed to tragedy.

CHAPTER FORTY-NINE

1. *Time,* September 28, 1953.
2. Kahin and Lewis, 48–54, for details.
3. Shaplen, *The Lost Revolution,* 113. See also, Pike.
4. Kahin and Lewis, 53–4. Smith stated further that United States policy in the case of divided nations was " . . . to seek to achieve unity through free elections, supervised by the United States to ensure that they are conducted fairly"; he also reiterated America's traditional position " . . . that peoples are entitled to determine their own future."
5. Buttinger, II, 827–8.
6. Zagoria, 42. Professor Zagoria points out that " . . . in early 1957, Moscow proposed the admittance to the United Nations of both North and South Vietnam, thus tacitly accepting the position." See also, *The Times* (London), July 28, 1971. Chou En-lai told American students " . . . that inexperience in matters of international diplomacy had allowed him to permit the United States to avoid formally signing the 1954 Geneva agreement ending the war in Indo-China."
7. Kahin and Lewis, 61.
8. Ibid.
9. Rostow, 324–5.
10. Shaplen, *The Lost Revolution,* 104.
11. Buttinger, II, 847.
12. Ibid., 852.
13. Shaplen, *The Lost Revolution,* 114–15.
14. Ibid., 118.
15. U.S. Senate Committee on Foreign Relations, *Background Information Relating to Southeast Asia and Viet-nam.*
16. Buttinger, II, 864.
17. Kahin and Lewis, 68.

18. Shaplen, *The Lost Revolution,* 119.
19. Ibid., 116. See also, Hammer, *The Struggle for Indochina* . . . ; Fall, *The Two Viet-nams* . . .
20. Kahin and Lewis, 23.
21. Shaplen, *The Lost Revolution,* 127.
22. Buttinger, II, 886.

CHAPTER 50

Diem's early government • *The Fishel mission* • *Diem's house of power* • *"Communist"-suppression campaigns* • *The Diem dictatorship* • *Failure of Diem's reforms* • *The Montagnard problem* • *Question of general election* • *The American role* • *ARVN* • *MAAG's influence* • *The result*

WITH THE TROUBLESOME SECT PROBLEM temporarily under control, with the army temporarily loyal and daily being strengthened by American arms and equipment, Prime Minister Ngo Dinh Diem should have turned with a will to the major task of broadening his base of support by instituting greatly needed political, social, and economic reforms, particularly in the countryside. Despite the turbulent events surrounding him, he had made a reasonable start in areas evacuated by the Viet Minh. Early civic-action programs had worked quite well, and by spring of 1955, local Self-Defense Corps and Civil Guards were coming into existence. The viability of these and other measures depended almost entirely on peasant co-operation, and this, in turn, depended on the validity of Diem's promised reforms.

Diem pretended to want these reforms. Shortly after becoming premier, he had named as civil adviser a young assistant professor of political science, Wesley Fishel, of Michigan State University, who had earlier befriended him in Tokyo and helped him in America. At Diem's request, Fishel, supported somewhat grudgingly by the U. S. Operations Mission in Saigon, was collecting a team of specialists to provide the Diem government with " . . . a massive program of technical assistance in four areas: public administration, police administration, public information, and economics and finance."[1]

Here was an ambitious program that, carried out effectively, might have resulted in a viable government. Unfortunately, almost from the outset of operations—Fishel's staff began arriving in spring of 1955— the effort faced major and often insurmountable obstacles. In a sense, the eighty-eight academicians, police experts, administrators (and a sprinkling of CIA types) who descended on Saigon in the first year resembled in miniature the experts who had arrived in Washington twenty years earlier to help Franklin Roosevelt implement the New Deal. Their intentions were honorable and their theories beautiful, but, alas, the theories too often failed to work, or, if they worked, they alienated the people concerned and were quickly sabotaged.

The almost inconceivable operational independence granted to the Fishel mission automatically brought it into conflict with other American civil and military missions. This could have been suffered in view of the importance of its task, but what neither Fishel nor his sponsors seemed to realize was that Diem did not want a democratic government. Diem almost immediately eliminated the public-information mission and sharply curtailed the economics and finance effort. The mission subsequently did some good work in training civil administrators and policemen—with results considerably different from those envisaged. In almost every respect, the group encountered obstructionism, with Diem's entrenched bureaucracy proving more than a match for the newcomers, the majority of whom were unfamiliar with the country, its peoples—and their language.[2]

Similar difficulties plagued other American aid programs. By spring of 1955, Diem was already dragging his feet when it came to devising and implementing economic and agrarian reforms, an attitude that brought him into continuing conflict with American officials in Saigon, particularly with General Collins. The difficulty stemmed first from Diem himself, a mandarin born and raised, a man who had become incapable of recognizing a grass root, much less its importance to the garden of state. But, more than Diem, the problem stemmed from his family. A disgusted American diplomat once told the writer: "Half of our troubles in Vietnam would have vanished if Diem had been an orphan."

Diem's family shared his power. One brother, Monsignor Ngo Dinh Thuc, a Roman Catholic bishop, had long been prominent in central Vietnam and, with Diem's rise, grew increasingly powerful and rich. Another, Ngo Dinh Luyên, a mechanical engineer and the least troublesome, became Diem's ambassador to England. A third brother, Ngo Dinh Can, became virtual ruler of central Vietnam. A fourth, but scarcely runt of the litter, Ngo Dinh Nhu, a trained librarian-archivist, became Diem's "personal adviser." To the discomfiture of all concerned, Nhu's advice included that of his ambitious and venal wife, Tran Le Xuan (Beautiful Spring)—as early as February 1955, Mme. Nhu was accused in a Saigon court of extensive corruption resulting from official connections.[3]

After occupying the choice suites in Diem's house of power, this oligarchy rented remaining rooms to men of their own breed hastily appointed to important key civil and military posts in Saigon and the provinces. A considerable number of appointees were Catholic Northerners whom Diem and Company felt they could "trust"—and who trampled over regional and Buddhist customs to disrupt further an already disrupted country.

Diem's first task was to consolidate his newly won control. His most important target was Viet Minh cadres who had remained in the South—an estimated ten thousand persons, most of whom were militant Communists, albeit with a strong nationalist bias.[4] Non-Communist nationalists, feared by Diem and his cohorts, formed a second target. Professor Scigliano later described the slapdash methods employed by the Department of Information and Youth, whose chief, Tran Chanh Thanh, had learned political propaganda methods from service with the Viet Minh:

> . . . As government troops occupied Viet Minh and sect-controlled areas in the spring and summer of 1955, Information agents swarmed in their wake denouncing the triple evils of Communism, colonisation, and feudalism, and extolling the Ngo Dinh Diem government. Those themes were pounded home in posters, banners, leaflets, radio messages, and rallies. . . . [5]

In mid-1955, Tran Chanh Thanh launched the first Denunciation of Communism campaign:

> . . . In a typical denunciation ceremony, Viet Minh cadres and sympathizers would swear their disavowal of Communism before a large audience; the repentants would recount the atrocities of the Viet Minh and, as a climax to their performance, would rip or trample upon the Viet Minh flag and pledge their loyalty to Ngo Dinh Diem.[6]

In May 1956, Thanh claimed that the campaign had " . . . entirely destroyed the predominant Communist influence of the previous nine years."

> . . . According to Thanh, in this short period 94,041 former Communist cadres had rallied to the government, 5,613 other cadres had surrendered to government forces, 119,954 weapons had been captured, and 75 tons of documents and 707 underground arms caches had been discovered.[7]

Had these figures been accurate, Diem's problems would have been largely solved. They were not accurate, and neither this attempt nor others launched by the National Revolutionary Movement and various youth and group movements could claim notable success.[8]

Ngo Dinh Diem held no intention of rebuilding South Vietnam in the image desired by Washington. In October 1955, Diem, strongly influenced by brother Nhu, proclaimed a referendum between himself and Bao Dai. After a campaign " . . . conducted with such a special disregard for decency and democratic principles that even the Viet Minh professed to be shocked,"[9] a limited electorate returned an improbable 98.2 per cent in favor of Diem, who became the new President of Vietnam. Brother Nhu followed this victory by expanding his personal political party, the Can Lao,

> . . . that served primarily as a political intelligence agency for Nhu; he used it to detect Communists or anyone he suspected of Communist or other oppositionist tendencies, and it was thus a powerful weapon in obtaining and maintaining loyalty to the Ngo family.[10]

This insidious beginning of dynasty rule expanded during 1956. As opposed to decentralized rule practiced both by early emperors and by the French, Diem insisted on centralized rule, creating "forty-one provinces . . . with a chief in each directly responsible to the President. . . ."[11] In spring of 1956, Diem eliminated village elections in favor of appointment by province chiefs—a disastrous error that installed many northern Catholic officials in the South, to alienate the peasant further from the new government.[12] The following October, he completed political carnage by forcing through a constitution in a vain attempt to legalize what already was a dictatorship. Diem meanwhile was filling jails and concentration camps not alone with "communists" but with communist "sympathizers," which meant anyone seriously at odds with the regime. Philippe Devillers estimated that the Diem government was holding fifty thousand political prisoners by the end of 1956. Official figures listed between twenty and thirty thousand former Viet Minh cadres, but a British observer, P. J. Honey, himself no liberal, visited these concentration camps and reported that " . . . the majority of the detainees are neither Communist nor pro-Communist."[13]

In the crucial years 1957–60, the Diem regime followed its earlier pattern with but few variations. By continuing dynasty rule, a cabal within a clique, a totalitarian regime cloaked with brother Nhu's mystique of Personalism,[14] Diem continued to alienate important nationalist elements that should have provided political leaders and administrators essential to stable government. He erred not only in ignoring these voices but by constantly suppressing them, by imprisoning or exiling or otherwise silencing them. He attempted to suppress all criticism by rigorous censorship and by a wide-ranging network of secret police. In spring of 1959, the regime enacted legislation that gave special military courts the right to pass death sentences without right of appeal for a host of political crimes including the spreading of anti-government rumors.[15] The cumulative effects were disastrous, not alone in depriving the new state of both intelligent support and intelligent dissent, but in setting up brooding centers of dissension that eventually would lead to open rebellion, for example among students and Buddhists.

Neither did Diem's alleged reforms mollify the effect of these harsh measures. Particularly wanting were his land-reform laws. When Diem came to power in 1954, " . . . forty per cent of the nation's 2,300,000 hectares of riceland was owned by *a quarter of one per cent of the rural population;* about a fourth of the large landholdings were French, and the rest were owned by wealthy Vietnamese or by the Catholic Church." The peasant farmed land under a short-contract, share-crop system whereby he paid the landlord about 50 per cent of the crop in rent.[16]

Diem's reform laws extended length of contract and brought rent down to a more reasonable 25 per cent of the crop. The most liberal reform laws would have been unpopular in many areas because landlords had abandoned almost a third of the riceland—land sequestered by the Viet Minh and given to peasants rent free. The Diem government now allowed absentee landlords to begin collecting rent, and, if this was reduced to 25 per cent of crop value, it did not make the peasant any happier; neither did taxes freshly imposed from Saigon. In areas under strong Viet Minh influence, if not control, the peasant sometimes found himself paying two sets of taxes, one to the Viet Minh and one to Saigon. Some landlords continued to collect more than 25 per cent of the crop in rent, violations often overlooked by agrarian courts controlled by landowning officials.

In 1956, Diem's government introduced a land-purchase plan whereby the government purchased riceland and sold it to the peasant. Landlords were allowed to retain a hundred hectares, or nearly two hundred fifty acres; " . . . some seven hundred thousand hectares belonging to twenty-five hundred owners were declared subject to transfer." The peasant could buy this land at an average price of two hundred dollars per hectare, an enormous sum to a peasant but one that he could pay off in six annual installments without interest, each installment being the estimated rough equivalent of 25 per cent of the crop value. This program encountered difficulties familiar to the rent-reform laws. Peasants who, in some instances, had already been "given" land by the Viet Minh naturally resented now having to pay for it, but

> . . . perhaps the most disturbing aspect of the land redistribution program was the manner in which influential politicians and mem-

bers of Diem's family obtained huge amounts of land that had been taken over by the government from French or Vietnamese landlords but had not been distributed to the peasants. . . .

When rural cadres of the powerful Confederation of Vietnamese Labor attempted to explain the program to the peasants, they were often arrested and jailed by government agents. Farmers' associations, which were supposed to help the peasant with credit and other aids, too quickly " . . . came to be dominated by local officials and landlords, and consequently were more paternalistic than progressive."[17]

Subsequent government measures did little or nothing to ameliorate these difficulties. In a situation demanding drastic action, the government refused to act—an intentional sabotage of a program the Diem regime never believed in and adopted only as a sop to American officials. Some evidence exists that the Eisenhower administration did not fully sympathize with proposed reforms, in that the American Government " . . . refused to provide the $30,000,000 needed to pay off the landowners. . . . It appears that the United States was unwilling to support the appropriation of private property openly. Similarly, the American government was long opposed to aiding public-controlled industrial development. . . . "[18]

Diem also alienated primitive Montagnard tribes of the central highlands. Unlike the Viet Minh, which had allowed Montagnards considerable autonomy, Diem incorporated their lands into the South Vietnamese state and tried to assimilate what he held to be inferior peoples into the southern culture. In 1957, he worked further hardship on the primitives by transferring over two hundred thousand northern refugees to Montagnard areas, which made eventual conflict with the nomads almost inevitable. By awarding security priority over other factors, he did much to defeat success of the highlands development program. Diem's penchant for security, and the inefficiency of his administrators, similarly ruined the government's later attempts to create fortified hamlets and villages. By mid-1959, Viet Minh attacks forced the government to undertake the "agroville program," an attempt to regroup whole villages into "protected" settlements called *agrovilles,* both to offer the peasant security and to prevent him from supporting the guerrilla effort. Directed by Diem's brother Nhu, the plan called for eighty to a hundred *agrovilles* of two to four thousand persons each, besides several hundred smaller communities. Each peasant was supposed to tear down his present house and carry the materials to the new area, where the government loaned him money to buy an acre and a half of new land.[19] The program scarcely got off the ground. Forsaking village graveyards and thus abandoning one's ancestors struck many peasants as a heinous crime. The government's arbitrary orders and pitiful resettlement allowances infuriated others, nor was the concentration-camp aspect popular. Diem's insistence on siting *agrovilles* along tactically important lines of communications brought immediate and destructive Viet Minh attacks.[20] Finally, corruption and inefficiency ruled from the beginning. Only about a score of *agrovilles* were built in a year and a half, before the government abandoned the effort.

Diem's dictatorial measures not only failed to neutralize the Communist threat, but his diplomatic intransigence opened South Vietnam to reprisals from the North. In mid-1955, as provided for in the Geneva Agreements, the DRV sought to open talks with South Vietnam concerning arrangements for elections slated by July 1956. Diem categorically refused to discuss the matter, telling the South Vietnamese people that his government was not bound by the Agreements, and denying that fair elections could be held in North Vietnam, an objection publicly sustained by Mr. Dulles. The DRV continued to press for talks. Diem, despite prodding by a few far-sighted American and South Vietnamese officials and by the governments of England and the Soviet Union—the cochairmen countries of the Geneva Conference—continued to refuse right through the July 1956 deadline. He did not act unilaterally: " . . . in this stand he continued to receive warm American encouragement and the fullest American diplomatic backing."[21]

This was a very serious action. The ambivalent air that surrounded the Geneva Agreements and the principle of a general election did not hide the fact of the provisions from an interested world. The provisions gave both sides option to insist on an election; perhaps neither side took this seriously, but, nonetheless, each side held the option. If either the DRV or the government in the South refused to hold such an election, the other side could claim that the cease-fire, what was in effect an armistice, was null and void. Although Diem headed a government that had refused to sanction the Geneva Agreements, he was presumably within his rights, but so was the DRV, which *had* sanctioned the agreements, to call for an election. The DRV had broadcast Diem's action to the world as a *casus belli,* meanwhile making capital propaganda from it at home and abroad, including the hamlets of South Vietnam. American officials who encouraged Diem in perversity did him a great disservice. No matter how well-intentioned the advice, it was contrary to common sense, not only because it brought a propaganda defeat and further allied friction, but because it opened the way for renewed Viet Minh activity in the South at a time when the Diem government was particularly vulnerable.

The United States Government originally wanted an autonomous Vietnamese army of about ninety thousand troops, its sole purpose "to preserve public order and suppress any attempts of subversion," leaving SEATO forces to deter aggression from the North.[22] Diem instead turned the army into the major prop of his regime, with his military supporters holding lucrative and powerful positions. The majority of French and American military advisers did not understand the essence of guerrilla warfare and how to train troops to counter the threat. Lieutenant General Samuel Williams, who replaced O'Daniel as head of MAAG at the end of 1955, received several hundred U.S. officer "advisers" who began reorganizing and training Diem's army. Although the Americans managed to reduce its bulk of some 270,000 men, they probably did not trim it to much below 150,000. Influenced by Diem's wishes and by the Korean War, they fashioned an army " . . . organized for conventional warfare in regiments, divisions, and corps. This military force was mechanized, motorized, and road-conscious."[23] Hundreds of young Vietnamese officers attended training courses at American bases in the Philippines, Okinawa, and the United States to learn conventional Western military doctrine. Concurrent with this shift to a more conventional, or "heavy," organization, the Diem government relieved the army of what O'Daniel had believed was its most important mission, that " . . . of spotting Communist guerrillas and Communist efforts at infiltration." Diem turned these functions over to the Civil Guard and the Self-Defense Corps, neither of which could conceivably carry them out.

This fundamental error was in part the fault of American military advisers, who believed that the "commies," or "reds," having attacked overtly in Korea, would attack similarly in Vietnam. Thus Pentagon and Saigon planners deemed the problem that of defense against a conventional army spilling across the 17th parallel. The new Vietnamese army, supported by its proud artillery, armor, and air units would rush forward to hold the breech until SEATO powers, or at least American forces, would land and "win" the war.

This political-strategic-tactical concept stood at odds with the political-strategic-tactical problem. Direct invasion from the North was highly unlikely at this time. Korea had demonstrated to Moscow and Peking alike that the U.S.A. and its allies would respond to any such action with armed force, and Secretary of State Dulles quite recently had warned that this could include atomic weapons. Always a realist, Ho Chi Minh remained well aware of the international situation, but, discounting that, he was facing severe internal problems, problems undoubtedly known to Western intelligence agencies but evidently not appreciated by either Diem or his Western military advisers.

To build large and heavy units in South Vietnam worked a threefold disaster: First, they were useless in that they deterred nothing, because the northern enemy had no intention of direct military invasion. They were also extremely expensive, and to build and maintain them, totally at American cost, necessarily reduced the amount of American funds available for essential civil projects. They were also destructive, in that, wherever based, they took without giving, whereas the original concept had called for them to work alongside civilians in the country's reconstruction. Generally commanded by inept and corrupt officers, they became a drain on the state, a monster exercising "squeeze" in a thousand forms on already disgruntled peasants. Flying the Saigon flag, they turned it in short order into a symbol as repressive as the old French tricolor.

Second, the new army contained the seeds of state destruction, an indirect objection that apparently escaped American civil and military minds. By creating regiments and divisions instead of light, mobile battalions, Diem brought into being an armed force that could either bolster or threaten his regime. To make it an ally meant installing politically safe senior officers in top-command and staff billets, a pernicious practice that reminded some observers of Chiang Kai-shek and the old war-lord concept. Senior commanders perforce demanded and received command autonomy, which too often meant flagrant failure to correct military deficiencies and widespread corruption in the military body itself. Diem thus created and condoned a disaster-prone army not far removed, despite Western window dressing of snappy uniforms, shiny weapons, and American quantitative tactics, from the old mainland armies of Chiang Kai-shek. Worse by far, army power soon spilled over into civil areas. Corps, division, and regimental commanders virtually ruled command areas and, almost without exception, refused to implement necessary civil reforms. Regular army officers had always occupied powerful positions, but with the growth of Viet Minh activity, Diem entrusted civil administration more and more to them. By autumn of 1960, however, regular officers ruled twenty-one of the thirty-six provinces, with younger officers holding numerous interprovince positions, a disturbing trend that by 1962 would result in total military administration.[24]

Third, Diem's military task was essentially pacification: securing the countryside under his control and extending that control to peripheral areas. The first steps in the process were to provide his peoples with security while rooting out Viet Minh cadres, an onerous and difficult task that would have taxed the efforts of a small army trained along lines recommended by O'Daniel. By assigning the all-important functions to the Civil Guard and the Self-Defense Corps, Diem virtually assured their non-fulfillment. Diem's Department of National Defense administered the forty-thousand-man Self-Defense Corps. MAAG paid its members and furnished a few arms, but the Vietnamese regular army provided most of the officers and was responsible for training. In the event, this proved rudimentary, and many of its members were armed with " . . . sticks, clubs and other such makeshifts."[25]

The fifty-thousand-man Civil Guard, administered by Diem's Department of the Interior, became the responsibility of the Michigan State University group, to the extent of training and equipping its units. An operational dichotomy resulted almost at once. Police advisers of the group wanted to halve the Guard's size and equip and train it as a rural police organization, " . . . which should not live apart in military posts but among the villages it would protect." Here was a key concept, ranking in importance only under political reforms. Had it been carried out effectively, as in Malaya and Kenya, had a rural police organization emerged to work in conjunction with national police and army units, many of Diem's security problems would have vanished. Instead, the Diem government and MAAG rejected the group's recommendation, insisting that the Civil Guard become a paramilitary adjunct to the regular army. This led to conflict so bitter that, in 1957, the Michigan group began withholding considerable aid and in mid-1959 the group abandoned this particular mission. MAAG eventually took it over, and, with that, any hope of a rural police force vanished.[26]

By this time, the Michigan group's efforts to organize a viable national police force had also backfired. Instead of the organization envisaged—a country-wide network to aid the rural police force—a variety of police forces existed. Regular police operated under Department of Interior, but the Civic Action, Information, and Defense departments also supported police networks. The key agency was secret. Called the Social and Political Research Service, it was run by Dr. Tran Kim Tuyen, a chum of Nhu's. Tuyen's American-trained agents, rather than ferreting out Viet Minh cadres, concentrated on collecting information " . . . on government officials, military officers, businessmen, intellectuals, students, and others," and preventing them from upsetting Diem's political applecart.[27]

Few, if any, of these failures caused an outcry from concerned officials. Persons who had promoted Diem continued to congratulate themselves on soundness of judgment. Yet, by the end of the decade, the Diem regime, aided by American advisers and vast American expenditures, had laid the groundwork for disaster. It remained for the Communists to exploit the target.

CHAPTER FIFTY

1. Scigliano and Fox, 2.
2. Ibid., 3–4, 50 ff., 57.
3. Fall, *The Two Viet-nams* . . . , 252.
4. Pike, 58–60.
5. Scigliano, 167.

6. Ibid.
7. Ibid., 168. See also, Pike.
8. Scigliano, 168.
9. Lancaster, 398.
10. Shaplen, *The Lost Revolution,* 130.
11. Ibid., 133.
12. Buttinger, II, 945: " . . . Village autonomy was one of the strongest Vietnamese political traditions, dating back to the fifteenth century and sanctioned both by tradition and precolonial law." See also, Frances Fitzgerald.
13. Buttinger, II, 977. See also, Scigliano.
14. Lacouture, 20, 88.
15. Kahin and Lewis, 101. See also, Scigliano.
16. Shaplen, *The Lost Revolution,* 143–4.
17. Ibid., 144–6.
18. Scigliano, 199–200.
19. Shaplen, *The Lost Revolution,* 142–3.
20. Scigliano, 179–80.
21. Kahin and Lewis, 112, 114.
22. Devillers and Lacouture, 373–4.
23. Trager, 163.
24. Scigliano, 166.
25. Ibid., 164.
26. Ibid., 201.
27. Ibid., 187.

CHAPTER 51

Revolution in the South • Ho Chi Minh's problems • His attitude toward the South • Viet Minh tactics in the South • The National Liberation Front (NLF) • Non-Communist opposition to Diem • The 1960 revolt • Diem's refusal to effect reforms • His civil and military weaknesses • The American contribution

IMMENSE DEBATES in the West have centered on the extent of Ho Chi Minh's collusion with the Viet Minh in the South from 1954 onward. The American Government's position was a simple black-and-white insistence that the DRV, aided by China and the Soviet Union, totally controlled the Viet Minh movement in the South and concentrated almost exclusively in this period on fomenting revolution from within. Once subversive tactics succeeded, the official thesis argued, Hanoi called into being the National Liberation Front (NLF) and, later, the People's Revolutionary Party (PRP) to prepare the country for the forces of "external aggression" from the North that would bring about a general "people's uprising."

A number of qualified observers have taken vigorous exception to this position. Prominent are Philippe Devillers and Jean Lacouture, George Kahin and John Lewis, Bernard Fall, Joseph Buttinger, and Donald Zagoria, whose reasoned arguments, buttressed by cited evidence, should not be ignored. These experts have argued that the revolutionary impetus derived from southern elements almost in spite of Ho Chi Minh and the DRV, that, indeed, on occasion, they were embarrassing to the North. Although Ho aided the movement in the South, the argument continued, it retained a distinctly regional independence throughout formative years.

The argument is important mainly because the simplistic position adopted by the American Government was fundamental to official performance. In maintaining its position, the American Government was indulging in deductive thinking in a situation demanding skillful appreciation of complex political factors. It is regrettable that responsible American officials, civil and military, did not attempt to more closely determine the facts instead of basing a position on the convenient but, in part, erroneous accusation of "external aggression."

The end of the war with the French left the DRV in an awkward position. The fighting had destroyed large areas in the North, which always depended on rice imports from the South in return for coal and electricity. Diem's refusal to commence limited trade with the North forced Ho to almost total dependence on Peking and Moscow, which in 1954 supplied economic relief, mostly food. A visit to the two capitals in summer of 1955 yielded Ho $350 million in economic credits—a considerable sum, but one not nearly sufficient to turn the North into an industrial-socialist state.

To further this aim, Ho embarked on "agrarian reforms" based on the Chinese model of collectivization and communal farming. Apparently the work of Truong Chinh, the Communist Party's secretary-general, the radical program caused widespread resentment in the countryside. Government officials summarily executed numerous "middle" and "rich" peasants and dispossessed thousands of hapless farmers of already marginal holdings. So ruthless were the reforms that, in 1956, peasants began organized uprisings. Ho put these down sharply with troops—all together, the regime probably executed between ten thousand and fifteen thousand peasants and deported and imprisoned between fifty thousand and a hundred thousand.[1] But Ho also dismissed concerned officials (including the powerful Truong Chinh), modified the program, and eventually restored order in the countryside. Ho's confidence in his remedial measures showed in late 1956, when he lifted press censorship only to find his regime inundated by complaints. As in China following the "Hundred Flowers Movement," the new freedom quickly gave way to an even more repressive air than existed formerly.

Internal difficulties notwithstanding, Ho began in mid-1955 to press Diem and the South Vietnam Government for a general election in accordance with the Geneva Agreements. Diem's refusal to even discuss elections placed Ho in a difficult position. Neither Moscow nor Peking seemed inclined to push the matter (other than, in the case of the Soviet Union, as one of the cochairmen of the Geneva Conference). Not only militant elements in Ho's government objected to the delay, but thousands of cadres and Viet Minh sympathizers in the South, who daily were losing ground to Diem's government, vociferously clamored for action from the DRV.

Despite the opening given him by Diem's refusal, Ho could not consider overt military action, for a variety of reasons. He was not strong enough, and in 1956 a drought further complicated the restive peasant situation. But, more than this, he was intent on building an industrial-socialist state, a priority he made clear in a letter of mid-June 1956 to southern cadres: " . . . Our policy is: to consolidate the North and to keep in mind the South."[2] Ho's Three Year Plan, from 1958 to 1960, concentrated on agrarian and industrial growth in the North: " . . . even before the Soviet Union in 1960 gave Hanoi a long-term loan for forty-three new industrial plants, North Viet-Nam was well on the road toward becoming the most industrialized country of Southeast Asia."[3]

Several other factors probably influenced Ho into soft-pedaling the situation in the South. Ho was Moscow-trained, and Moscow preferred the technique of self-sustaining revolution, as the Communist efforts in Yugoslavia and Greece so well illustrated. This was common sense. As the Soviets knew from experience in World War II, central direction of guerrilla warfare is always difficult and sometimes impossible (see Chapter 26). Regional revolution, further, brings immense problems in leadership, with only grudging acceptance of outsiders, as, for example, Zapata demonstrated in the Mexican Revolution (see Chapter 14).

Ho Chi Minh also faced a delicate and complex international situation. Chinese and Russian reluctance to stir up trouble overtly in Indochina grew rather than diminished, the inevitable result of basic differences that were emerging in late 1957, but also the result of Dulles' announced intention to intercede in case of enemy invasion of the South.[4]

Another factor was the increasingly turbulent situation in South Vietnam. Despite massive injections of American aid, Diem was failing to build a viable state, a failure that not only opened the way to increased Viet Minh activity but also increased Viet Minh popularity, particularly in the countryside. In this respect, Diem, his imperial court, and his senior American advisers were doing Ho's job for him, rather like the earlier situation in China, in which Chiang Kai-shek and company had so ably prepared the soil for Mao Tse-tung's destructive seeds.

Ho, perforce, concentrated on wringing a great deal of propaganda value from Diem's continued refusals while mollifying the South and continuing to build in the North. Like a good Communist, he encouraged southern dissidence where he could—for example, in the central highlands, where his agents were working actively with the Montagnards, and by allowing some Communist cadres that had returned North to go back South to help organize the revolutionary movement. In time, success of Viet Minh cadres would cause him, or perhaps force him, to lend a more forceful hand. Meanwhile, he seemed content to let Diem go his destructive way.

Diem's repressive measures in both city and countryside, without doubt, severely damaged the organization of Viet Minh cadres that had remained in the South in 1954. Enough of them survived, however, to instigate a campaign of propaganda and subversion that, in places, prospered as the inevitable result of Diem's inept government.

In the early years, the Viet Minh used mainly agitation-propaganda tactics to accomplish their purpose. As their strength grew and after Diem refused to consider elections called for by the Geneva Conference, the hard-core Viet Minh turned to terror tactics that frequently involved the "trial" and execution of village officials, members of the Civil Guard and Self-Defense Corps, and teachers and administrators sent from Saigon.

Viet Minh terrorism was not as haphazard as some commentators have suggested. It was subordinate to the propaganda effort. With few exceptions, the Viet Minh indulged in selective terrorism, that is, killing for a specific political purpose. The picture of a disemboweled body of a village headman or government official aroused deepest feelings in the West, but, all too often, local peasantry welcomed the killing in that it offered relief, if only temporary, from repressive government. At very least, the killing impressed the peasantry with Viet Minh power, and it often frightened other headmen and officials into accommodating to Viet Minh aims. Nothing is pleasant about terror, because man was put on earth to trust, not fear—but, to write it off as indiscriminate killing, as a form of warfare unacceptable to Western quantitative theories, is scarcely conducive to countering it successfully. The Diem government's inability to prevent selective terrorism increased its importance as a weapon in these years. Frank Trager estimated that " . . . by 1959, Viet Cong violence of this type accounted for between fifteen and twenty assassinations of provincial-government officials per month." Terrorism formed only part of a process already familiar from earlier Viet Minh resistance to the French:

> . . . Insurrection took the form of guerrilla action against villages still under government control; it usually led to the surrender or the wiping-out of the local self-defense units and Civil Guards charged with ousting the guerrillas. Organized, indoctrinated, and led by Communist cadres, the Vietcong, as these guerrillas were henceforth called, soon controlled almost the entire countryside by night and about two-thirds of it in daytime. The Vietcong set up their own administration, imposed their own taxes, conscripted the local youth into military service, provided education and medical care, collected food supplies for their fighting units, dug bomb shelters, built defense works along the regions they controlled, and

continuously trained new men for stepped-up military operations. For years, they increased the number of their fighting men (if not their cadres) entirely through local recruiting, and their arms supply more through the capture of arms from government units than through infiltration from the North. . . . From 1960 on, they began to operate in ever-larger groups, and to attack and overrun government outposts held by the army, as well as to ambush and destroy army units sent to relieve outposts under attack. . . . [5]

Neither Communist leadership nor Communist guerrillas, however, monopolized the resistance effort. Diem may have bested the Hoa Hao and Cao Dai sects, but he had not eliminated them. In places, the remnants made common cause with the Viet Minh; indeed, Fall has suggested that the bulk of early opposition came from the sects. Remnants of the Dai Viet party were also working against the government, as was another group, the National Salvation Movement, sponsored by Vietnamese dissidents in Paris.[6]

From this mélange of dissent arose the National Liberation Front, or NLF. Its birthdate is not definitely known in the West but in 1958 the NLF flag was seen in Viet Minh-dominated areas of the South. Probably a Communist-front organization imported from Hanoi, the NLF depended on indigenous and not alone Communist support:

> . . . Members of the original NLF, and its most ardent supporters in the early years, were drawn from the ranks of the Viet Minh Communists; the Cao Dai and Hoa Hao sects; a scattering of minority group members, primarily ethnic Cambodians and montagnards; idealistic youth, recruited from the universities and polytechnic schools; representatives of farmers' organizations from parts of the Mekong delta, where serious land tenure problems existed; leaders of small political parties or groups, or professionals associated with them; intellectuals who had broken with the GVN . . . ; military deserters; refugees of various sorts from the Diem government, such as those singled out by neighbors in the Denunciation of Communism campaign but who fled before arrest.[7]

Opposition to Diem did not end with this heterogeneous bunch. In spring of 1960, before Hanoi had officially admitted NLF's existence, mounting criticism in Saigon civil and military circles found voice in a public protest—the Caravelle Manifesto—to Diem signed by eighteen prominent Vietnamese, ten of them former government ministers who protested against "anti-democratic elections" and "to continuous arrests [that] fill the jails and prisons to the rafters." Diem cracked down hard on this group, arresting all signatories. A few months later, a group of army officers rebelled and three paratrooper battalions surrounded

Diem's palace in Saigon. Leaders of the revolt called on Diem " . . . to rid himself of his family advisers and follow a political course more sensitive to the country's needs." While stalling the rebels, Diem and Nhu called up loyal elements, which broke up the revolt. Once again, the government cracked down hard and arrested many civil and military opposition leaders. Others went underground or fled the country.[8]

Only after these developments did Hanoi officially announce the existence of NLF and a program calling for liberation of the South, departure of the Americans, and final reunification of the country. The sanction came during the Third Congress of the Vietnam Communist Party, in September 1960, but the same Congress stressed the necessity for continued internal development of North Vietnam. Vo Nguyen Giap, DRV Minister of Defense, told the Congress that " . . . today, the economic construction in the North has become the central task of the Party."[9]

The exact extent of Hanoi's participation from 1954 to 1960 is relatively unimportant. Had Diem, with all the millions of dollars and expertise furnished by the United States built even a reasonable government in the South, he would have neutralized the Viet Minh threat and then some. No matter what the American Government, or its particular spokesmen in this matter, would have had us believe, Ho Chi Minh did not bring about the attempted coup of 1960. The villains were and remain Ngo Dinh Diem, his imperial court, his ambitious and venal family members, generals and officials, and his Vietnamese and senior American advisers. By 1960, Diem was a prisoner of forces as strong as those that ever surrounded Chiang Kai-shek. Had his warders ably administered the country, Diem might have survived. They did not. Not only were they inefficient, but they were repressive and corrupt, and they could only keep the government on a collision course with disaster.

The army was symptomatic of the regime. By 1960, its major faults were becoming all too clear to objective observers. Far from being a national force that offered protection and security to peasants, the army served the political purposes of Diem and the ruling oligarchy. As had been the case with Chiang Kai-shek's mainland armies, officer promotion depended on political whim. As had been the case in Greece, location of units more often satisfied private interests than public welfare, the estates of prominent politicians, for example, being guarded while rural areas lay open to Viet Minh depredation. As in the case of all totalitarian countries, "palace guard," or trusted, units never ventured far from the capital's periphery and played little part in combating increasingly serious guerrilla attacks in the countryside.

Operationally, the army had failed to neutralize Viet Cong tactics. Too often, corps commanders either refused to fight or were forbidden to fight or were unable to fight effectively. Politically tainted command relationships often meant confused and lackadaisical operations in situations demanding immediate and forceful response. Almost total lack of identification with peasants meant corresponding lack of information on which to base operations. Fear and frustration entered the picture to cause the army to use increasingly repressive measures and thus further to alienate the peasantry. Morale remained low, desertions high.

The American response to Diem's deteriorating position was mixed. Not only did the two camps, official and unofficial, hold frequently opposing views, but individual opinions in each camp often radically differed. Among other things, this caused uneven reporting, both public and private, at a time when a thoroughly confused and dangerous situation demanded objective coverage in order to be understood either by concerned officials in Washington or by the American public.

The basic villain was ignorance, which prompted fear among officials at all levels. So long as American officials believed in the "domino theory," so long as they insisted that South Vietnam was a "strategic necessity" as opposed to a "strategic convenience," their vision remained myopic, unable to see beyond the day to recognize inherent fallacies in Diem's repressive policies. Part of this failure rested on misconception of enemy capabilities and intentions, part on ignorance of Vietnam—a natural ignorance compounded by an insulated and luxurious life in Saigon, where the true situation in the countryside was not to be learned. Results were disastrous. Typical of misinformation broadcast by Eisenhower administration officials was that contained in an emotive speech by Walter Robertson, Assistant Secretary of State for Far Eastern Affairs, in June 1956, in which he insisted that Vietnam was

> progressing rapidly to the establishment of democratic institutions by elective processes, its people resuming peaceful pursuits, its army growing in effectiveness, sense of mission, and morale, the puppet Vietnamese politicians discredited, the refugees well on the way to permanent settlement, the countryside generally orderly and calm.

William Lederer, an experienced participant in and student of the area and author of *The Ugly American,* quoted the above words in his book *Our Own Worst Enemy* and added:

> . . . There is not one single true statement in this excerpt from Assistant Secretary of State Walter Robertson's address. I do not know of a single living historian or student of Vietnamese affairs, official or otherwise, who would disagree with me.[10]

In summer of 1959, Major General Samuel Myers, deputy chief of MAAG, ingeniously reported that the Viet Minh guerrillas were ". . . gradually nibbled away until they ceased to become a major menace to the government."[11] In July, Ambassador Elbridge Durbrow told a Senate committee: ". . . The [Vietnam] government is becoming more and more effective in curbing these terrorist acts . . . [and] the internal situation has been brought from chaos to basic stability." Wesley Fishel, who headed the Michigan State University-CIA mission to Saigon, wrote in the autumn issue of *Yale Review* for 1959:

> . . . the Communist capability in Vietnam, south of the 17th parallel, has been reduced to one of sheer nuisance activity. . . . It is one Asian area where Communism has been rolled back without war. . . . There is little likelihood of a revolution against the regime.

Other important voices echoed these sentiments, including those of Admiral Arthur Radford and Admiral Felix Stump, who agreed that ". . . President Ngo Dinh Diem was the most brilliant and successful Asian leader of democracy since Chiang Kai-shek."[12]

These incredibly inaccurate statements played directly into Diem's hands. The optimism of American Pollyannas created an ideal blackmail situation ably exploited by experienced mandarins who surrounded Diem. American policy makers had been told for so long that Diem was the only man who could prevent Vietnam from falling to Communists that they believed it, and they did not stop to examine sources: frightened politicians, officials who had staked careers on the Diem regime, militarists who wanted to expand the armed forces, even an American public-relations agency hired by the Diem government to perpetuate throughout the United States the myth of his indispensability!

Ignorance existed in other areas, the MAAG mission typifying one. In 1960, MAAG advisers were only beginning to comprehend Viet Minh techniques, and then only in part. Civil-aid officials erred just as badly by continuing to back expensive projects either without realizing, or realizing but refusing to admit, that success of such projects hinged almost totally on political and social reforms that the Diem government refused to make.

Efforts to inform the American public of burgeoning disaster did not prosper, and for several reasons. At first, the relatively low-priority area from the news standpoint attracted but few reporters. Later, when French defeat and withdrawal brought more extensive coverage, newcomers were impeded both by ignorance of the area and by suspicious and unco-operative American and Vietnamese official spewing out of lies that they wished reported to American taxpayers. Personal and official hindrances sometimes prevented accurate reporting, as did confused issues and failure to identify the type of war being fought. This naturally contributed to American public apathy, but we must remember that, from the news standpoint, Vietnam continued to be a relatively low-priority area—it was difficult for the American public to identify with strange-sounding names in a country of which many had never previously heard and did not even know the exact location.

In 1960 and later, it was far easier to accept official pronouncements than to seek out issues and decide for oneself. In this sense, the Vietnam lobby in Washington had things largely its own way. Large blocs of the American public, if thinking about Vietnam at all, believed that, if South Vietnam fell to the "Communists," all of Southeast Asia would be overrun and Red hordes would shortly appear off the California coast. Preventing this, so they were told time and again, was the Christian savior, Ngo Dinh Diem; therefore the American Government had no option but to support the Diem regime.

This was the general picture when John F. Kennedy became President of the United States. His relatively brief administration would soon suffer the Vietnam problem and would greatly change its dimensions. At this juncture, however, we must interrupt the Vietnam story to look at contemporary insurgencies in Kenya, Cyprus, Algeria, and Cuba.

CHAPTER FIFTY-ONE

1. Buttinger, II, 908–16; see 914: " . . . Many regained their freedom, though perhaps not their former rights and possessions." See also, Lancaster.
2. Ho Chi Minh, *Ho Chi Minh on Revolution*, 302.
3. Buttinger, II, 906, 966: " . . . For each factory built under Diem—there were less than two dozen—the Communist regime in the north built fifty." See also, Zagoria.
4. Lowenthal.
5. Buttinger, II, 983–4.
6. Kahin and Lewis, 110.
7. Pike, 83. See also, Lacouture; Shaplen, *The Lost Revolution*.
8. Kahin and Lewis, 117.
9. Ibid.
10. Lederer, *Our Own Worst Enemy*, 33–4.
11. Hilsman.
12. Lederer, *Our Own Worst Enemy*, 87. See also, Frances Fitzgerald, 86–94, for an excellent analysis of and damage done by the Fishel mission.

CHAPTER 52

WHILE FIGHTING CONTINUED in French Indochina and Malaya, a new insurgency broke out in Kenya, the large British colony in East Africa. Unlike the other areas, communism did not fuel this boiling pot of trouble, which soon became known as the Mau Mau rebellion. Although the Kenyan political leader Jomo Kenyatta had fallen under Marxist influence during his long period of self-imposed exile in England, the instrument of rebellion that he fashioned in Nairobi after World War II bore but slight resemblance to other Communist-inspired and -directed guerrilla movements. For here the mantle of Marx soon slipped away to expose a primitive body of rebellion that fed on a weird admixture of religious-tribal cultism while performing violent deeds particularly abhorrent to the Western world.[1]

Robert Ruark's best-selling novel, *Something of Value*,[2] published in 1955, stressed Mau Mau excesses. The historian cannot justify these, but he can explain them. The explanation begins in the nineteenth century and might be called the story of an insurgency that need never have happened.

* * *

624

Dozens of tribes had occupied eastern Africa over the centuries. These pastoral bodies migrated to lush plains, and when they had killed the game and their cattle and goats had eaten the tender grass, they moved to greener pastures. Some fell prey to other, more warlike tribes, some to natural disasters and epidemics. Some tribes survived and even prospered; some disappeared.

The Bantu-speaking Agikuyu, or Gikuyu tribe, which we know as the Kikuyu, is probably seven or eight hundred years old. Toward the end of the sixteenth century, a population increase caused the tribe to advance into the Kiambu district and north to fertile plains of Nyeri and Mount Kenya. Here the Kikuyu settled to farm the land while protecting it from incursions of the warlike Masai, which, in the nineteenth century, stressed a warrior cult and terrorized such neighboring tribes as the Bantu, Taveta, and Kikuyu. Whether the tribal complex ever would have amalgamated into a peaceful state, we don't know. But anthropologists long since have exploded the popular conception of savage hordes living in an anarchic state. We know that a *modus vivendi* often existed between tribes, and we also know that some tribes possessed a viable political structure as well as moral codes that, in result, often compared favorably with the Christian ethic—belief realized through feathers and blood instead of bread and wine, but belief just as firm and perhaps more so than that in the West.[3]

We also have a good deal of firsthand information about the Kikuyu from Jomo Kenyatta's early book *Facing Mount Kenya*. Those inclined to shrug away his words as obviously prejudiced will find much of what he wrote confirmed by independent scholarship and particularly by the works of Dr. L. S. B. Leakey. A son of missionaries, Leakey grew up among the Kikuyu, where he mastered the difficult language, became a member of a tribal age-group and later a first-grade elder of the tribe. He also became a distinguished archaeologist and historian. His books on Kenya and the Kikuyu should be read in order to understand the underlying grievances that allowed the insurgency to form and caused so many Africans to support it.[4]

"The Kikuyu were a deeply religious people for whom life without religion was unthinkable." They worshiped a god, angry old Murungu, or Ngai—". . . supreme, almighty, unseen but all pervading, having four 'homes' in the four sacred mountains of the Kikuyu." Ngai forever required propitiating by animal sacrifice and a mumbo-jumbo that meant nothing to the Westerner but a great deal to the African. The Kikuyu also practiced ancestor worship and a form of animism in which they recognized spirits in trees, large rocks, waterfalls, and epidemic diseases. Ceremony played a vital role in their religion. So did the related all-important oath, which, varying from the supreme, or *githathi*,

SUDAN   ETHIOPIA

L. Rudolf

K   E   N   Y   A

UGANDA

Rift
Valley   Central Province.

Mt.
Kenya
Naivasha   Nyeri
Lari
Kiambu   Nairobi

Lake
Victoria

SOMALI REP.

L. Natron
Mt. Kilimanjaro ▲

TANGANYIKA   Mombasa

N   INDIAN

ZANZIBAR

OCEAN

KENYA
• Towns and Cities
White Highlands
African Reserve

AFRICA

KENYA

South
Atlantic
Ocean   0   100   200   300 miles

'M.E.P.

oathing ceremony to less severe forms, governed tribal society, economics, marriage, even tribal health. White magic was the province of the *mundu mugo*, or "medicine man," who functioned as doctor, seer, and protector against black-magic practitioners:

> . . . It was this absolute fear of magic powers that was the foundation stone of all Kikuyu ceremonies of oath taking, and in consequence the taking of a solemn oath was an act never lightly undertaken, and once sworn, its effect upon the taker was very great.

Animal sacrifice normally accompanied oath taking—" . . . in the course of the life of an individual Kikuyu there were no less than 108 occasions from birth to death which required the slaughter and sacrifice of a goat or a sheep." The Kikuyu governed themselves by regional, or "ridge," councils of elders—the *athamaki,* whose spokesmen and members had trained for the role since adolescent initiation into an age-group followed by specific *rites de passage,* each of which increased importance and responsibilities. Farming and animal husbandry were the main occupations. People lived in villages fortified for protection against Masai raids. Individuals owned farms and even estates worked by tenants. A strict moral code governed buying and selling of land. Tribal law preserved certain forest areas for purposes of hunting and beekeeping and also for fuel reserves. Early Western explorers, toward the end of the nineteenth century, were in general impressed with Kikuyu territory: " . . . as far as the eye could see . . . was one vast garden."[5]

Toward the end of the nineteenth century a smallpox epidemic tore through the Kikuyu and other eastern African tribes to decimate humans, as a rinderpest epidemic decimated cattle. Severe drought and a locust invasion followed. Leakey has estimated that the combined tragedy took from 20 to 50 per cent of the tribe. It also caused families to evacuate lands in the Kiambu country, where farms reverted to bush country. As if this weren't sufficient, the Kikuyu now faced invasion from the West. Toward the end of the century, Germany and Great Britain carved out respective spheres of commercial influence in eastern Africa through the purchased co-operation of the sultan of Zanzibar. In 1890, the British East Africa Company began moving inland, an effort soon taken over by the British Government, which established a protectorate over Kenya and, at the turn of the century, built a railroad from Mombasa to Uganda, nearly six hundred miles into the interior. To help justify this expensive project, the British began colonizing south-central Kenya, the supply railhead being the village of Nairobi. In this area, the government acquired sixteen thousand square miles of prime land, the White Highlands, for distribution to settlers.[6]

The colonizing task fell to two men: to the high commissioner, Sir Charles Eliot, a thirty-seven-year-old scholar and diplomat, and to an eccentric, adventure-loving nobleman, Lord Delamere. Considering natural hazards and costly discouragements involved in establishing and building farms, both men rate high from the technical standpoint, and in helping to bring numerous benefits to Africans. Tribal wars, in general, vanished. European doctors and veterinarians began to eliminate dreadful epidemic diseases that had wiped out tribes and herds of cattle since time immemorial; Western methods and medicines brought general improvement in health and a lowering of the high infant-mortality rate. European farming methods brought bigger and better crops. European and Asian merchants filled market places with new and exciting wares. Missionaries, mostly Scottish preachers, established schools and spread the Christian gospel, which held considerable appeal to illiterate natives. Had the white man respected the native's identity, his traditions and beliefs, his dignity and natural ambition, he might still be in control of a prosperous Kenya. He did no such thing. Exercising an arrogance of ignorance that would persist in subsequent decades, he interpreted the situation as it fitted his convenience, often riding roughshod over a "simple and yet highly organized system of decentralized control of religious, judicial, and secular affairs."[7]

The European also erred, perhaps intentionally, in land acquisition. Government officials assumed that large areas of "empty" land in the Kiambu district were for the taking. This was not always the case. As we have seen, calamity had forced widespread evacuation of Kiambu lands legitimately owned by individual Africans. In his mind, the African had not relinquished title, nor had the tribe yielded valuable forest reserves. Bushland that officials assumed was not being used was in reality serving as grazing land for the all-important cattle and goats. Governmental payments for land sold to white settlers (". . . a halfpenny an acre plus survey fees")[8] meant one thing to the government, another to the native, who regarded the deal as temporary since sale or transfer of privately owned land involved a host of tribal-religious rites essential to freeing it from evil spirits. Here was the genesis of the later Kikuyu complaint that the land was stolen by the whites—a grievance fundamental to the rebellion.

The white man's attitude, in general, was uncompromising. Our old friend Captain Richard Meinertzhagen (see Chapter 15) was sent to Kenya as a young officer. In 1902, he met Eliot, who

> . . . amazed me with his views on the future of East Africa. He envisaged a thriving colony of thousands of Europeans. . . . He intends to confine the natives to reserves and use them as cheap labor

628

on farms. I suggested that the country belonged to Africans, that their interests must prevail over the interests of strangers. He would not have it; he kept on using the word "paramount" with reference to the claims of Europeans. I said that some day the African would be educated and armed; that would lead to a clash. Eliot thought that that day was so far distant as not to matter . . . but I am convinced that in the end the Africans will win and that Eliot's policy can lead only to trouble and disappointment.[9]

He was no more in harmony with Delamere who, upon their meeting, declared: "I am going to prove to you all that this is a white man's country."[10]

Eliot, Delamere, and most of their subordinates exemplified the concept of the Christian white man's burden. Under their aegis, an entire colony was developing to further this notion. In essence, the Africans existed for the white man's convenience (profit). In essence, the black was not a human being, and few white men in Kenya would have agreed with Meinertzhagen, who noted, upon his departure in 1904:

> . . . I am sorry to leave the Kikuyu, for I like them. They are the most intelligent of the African tribes I have met; therefore they will be the most progressive under European guidance and will be more susceptible to subversive activities. They will be one of the first tribes to demand freedom from European influence and in the end cause a lot of trouble. And if white settlement really takes hold in this country it is bound to do so at the expense of the Kikuyu, who own the best land, and I can foresee much trouble.[11]

As presciently foreseen by Meinertzhagen, Eliot's policy led precisely to trouble, disappointment—and finally rebellion. Under Eliot's administration, the white man not only took land that was not his, but compelled the African to work this land under an arrangement close to slavery. He kept natives in large reserves and denied them identity to other than themselves and their employers. Although Eliot left Kenya in 1904, his legacy continued to rule: In 1915, for example, the Crown Lands Ordinance made all Africans "tenants at the will of the Crown," the government refusing to issue them land title deeds.[12]

The African's service in two world wars, his stumbling attempts, beginning in 1920, to gain a political voice, his efforts to educate himself (encouraged finally by the government, deprecated by white Kenyans), did not alter his status. Those blacks who demanded the return of "stolen lands" might as well have saved their breath; those who demanded a place in government were marked as agitators and carefully watched. Although the British Government made Kenya a colony after World War I and, in 1923, announced that it would respect African rights by a "trusteeship," matters changed but slightly. Education continued in the hands of Scottish missionaries, who too often taught form but not substance of Christianity. In their eagerness to learn to read and write at mission schools, many young Kikuyu embraced Christianity but

> . . . did not accept the Christian doctrine or have any intention of really trying to live up to Christian standards of morality, honesty, and codes of behavior. At the same time, many of these young men—and as time went on young women too—learned enough to make them cease to have real faith in their own Kikuyu religious beliefs and practices, so that a body of people sprang into being who had abandoned one faith without accepting another in its place and who were thus without any real guiding principles in their lives.[13]

Secular education was limited in the extreme, the government failing to live up to its responsibilities by providing needed teachers and schools. The few educated blacks could not find jobs commensurate with ability. They were accepted neither into government nor into white society. The white man, long before, had closed the door to the evolutionary notion, and he was not now going to open it.

The black political movement in Kenya began in 1921, with the Young Kikuyu Association, which a few years later became the Kikuyu Central Association, or KCA. In the twenties and thirties this organization exploited the old grievance of "stolen lands," a sore point which survived even though a Royal Commission in 1932 investigated and awarded "appropriate" compensation. It also exploited new grievances such as the hated *kipande,* or compulsory black worker registration; low wages; a law that prohibited Africans from raising coffee; lack of African representation in the colonial legislature; and the color bar.

The KCA movement did not prosper. White settlers disrupted it whenever possible; older tribal chiefs, appointed by the new government and relatively well off, did not trust young Kikuyu leaders.

But neither did the movement die. Failure of the colonial administration to provide proper education, coupled with the Church of Scotland's insistence on banning such tribal rites as *irua,* or female circumcision, and festival dances, turned the Kikuyu to providing their own schools and religion, which soon became the main instruments of propaganda to serve the KCA's militant identity.[14]

World War II also played a role. The government declared the KCA illegal, which brought its leaders increased prominence among tribesmen. The war transported numerous Africans abroad, in some ways a broadening and awakening experience that made them more receptive

630

to KCA propaganda when they returned. In their absence, Kenya had enjoyed considerable prosperity, and postwar years seemed to promise more. From a social-political-economic standpoint, however, the returning black veteran found but slight improvement. Although the government established a number of industrial training schools, openings for subsequent employment "were very limited." F. D. Corfield, in an official report published in 1960, noted:

> . . . over and above these economic grievances there was a deeper sense of resentment, caused by the various forms of discrimination . . . the restriction on the planting of cash crops, such as coffee; the fact that Africans were not permitted to acquire land in the White Highlands; the different wage scales which applied to Europeans, Asians and Africans by the Government; the restrictive covenants which applied to housing in European areas, some municipalities, and the opposition to entry into some of the larger hotels.[15]

To the returning veteran, the colony seemed as devoid of opportunity for the black man as formerly. But now the black man was finding his voice, and now appeared a formidable leader, Jomo Kenyatta, who, to many, resembled a latter-day Moses intent on leading his people from the wilderness.

Jomo Kenyatta was born on a tribal reserve outside Nairobi around 1893. Educated in a Church of Scotland mission school, he worked as a clerk in Nairobi, edited a newspaper, and, in 1925, joined the KCA, becoming secretary-general in 1928. A year later, the association sent him to London to present a list of grievances to the Colonial Office. Staying on, he joined the Communist Party and toured England and the Soviet Union; after a brief stay in Kenya, he returned to England, where he obtained a degree in anthropology at the London School of Economics, his thesis being published as a book, *Facing Mount Kenya*. He also married an English woman, who bore him a son but remained in England when he returned to Kenya, in 1946.[16]

The first phase of what came to be called the Emergency began shortly after Kenyatta's return to Nairobi. Here he reorganized remnants of the illegal KCA into a militant party that operated under cover of the Kenya African Union, Kenyatta becoming its president in 1947. Inflammatory speeches became the order of the day, as did ugly rumors of special oathing ceremonies along with talk of killing all Europeans. District officers began to report sinister activities of a new organization, the Mau Mau, in 1948, and missionaries, tribal chiefs, police, and civil officials began to confirm the reports. Neither governor nor government seemed unduly alarmed. In 1950, the government recognized the Mau Mau as " . . . an evil and subversive association" and brought a gang to court; found guilty, the nineteen Africans won an appeal on a slim technicality. Although this led to proscription of the Mau Mau and to more prosecutions, the government did not take further remedial action.

Considerable blame must rest on the governor, Sir Philip Mitchell, who felt he knew more about Africans than some of his better-informed subordinates. If ever a man believed in the Christian white man's burden, it was Mitchell. An old Africa hand, he held that natural inferiority of Africans explained their dismal circumstances. An imperialist to the core, he saw England as the Trustee charged with converting African "poverty, sorcery, superstition and ignorance" into "a Christian civilization, tolerant of course of other faiths, with 'equal rights for all civilized men' as its major political principle." "African independence was not to be thought of." The Trustee policy administered by a strong and enlightened colonial power was Kenya's only hope for the future.[17]

Poor old Mitchell. As he was writing these words, the rebellion had broken out to shatter his imperialist dreams. Perhaps colonial bureaucracy was the real villain, as Mitchell suggests in his book, but it is difficult to deny that the function of a governor is to govern. Despite significant theft of arms and ammunition from government depots, security remained lax. Mitchell apparently did not reinforce the police function significantly, the main instrument for intelligence collection and collation. The police section responsible, a small and impoverished Special Branch, operated mainly in Nairobi and Mombasa, which severely limited its activities. Command channels remained muddled: Corfield concluded that most of the intelligence reports forwarded in the "formative" years " . . . just 'disappeared' into the Central Secretariat." As one result, the government lacked clear definition of the Mau Mau, of its origin, organization, methods, and goals; as another result, it failed to impede the spread of Mau Mau propaganda and recruitment.[18]

Official ignorance was startling. The anthropologist Dr. Donald Barnett has suggested that Mau Mau itself is a meaningless term that may have been corrupted by a European policeman from the word *muma*, or oath, or may have derived from a derogatory term for venal tribal elders. Africans did not use the term, any more than the Viet Minh in Indochina used the term Viet Cong. What some Africans called "The Movement" was in reality the work of the KCA, which was far more extensively organized than local authorities imagined. Beginning in 1950, the KCA " . . . underwent a dramatic shift . . . from a highly selective, elite organization to an underground mass movement." From headquarters in Nairobi, organizers traveled the land recruiting new members and setting up cells and units. A ceremonial oath had been essential to membership for years, but the new underground movement

" . . . demanded strict secrecy as well as total commitment and the oath was altered to meet these requirements." Persons who would not voluntarily submit to the oath were forced to submit whenever possible, an unseemly business conducted at night with black-magic overtones.[19]

The program worked for several reasons. The first and, according to Dr. Leakey, the foremost was legitimate grievances, which made Africans receptive to KCA "land and freedom" propaganda. The land grievance topped the list. Another was the government's educational failure, both religious and secular: the one creating a group of confused Christians, the other maintaining a high level of ignorance and illiteracy. A third was the administrative system of government-appointed "chiefs," who often lacked popular following. Another was the peculiar psychology of the oath:

> . . . a Kikuyu who takes a solemn oath is punished by supernatural powers if he breaks that oath, or if he has perjured himself. . . . Having once made such an oath, even under pressure, no ordinary Kikuyu would dare to go and make a report to the police or to his employer, because, were he to do so, he would be breaking the oath and thus calling down upon himself, or upon members of his family, supernatural penalties.

His only recourse was a "cleansing ceremony" to nullify the force of the oath, but

> . . . participation in such a ceremony could not be kept quiet for long, since, to be effective, it must be carried out in public and before many witnesses. The Mau Mau people made it very clear to their victims that if they tried to get out of their obligations under the oath by such means, they would be victimized and even, if necessary, murdered.[20]

Some loyal Christian Kikuyu reported Mau Mau activities, and other Kikuyu, the victims of fear and shock, refused to join the movement. The KCA approach nevertheless contained an inherent appeal, and the government continued to underestimate the movement's growth (an estimated quarter of a million by mid 1952). A Central Committee, in Nairobi, ran the movement by means of seven district committees, each supporting division, location, and sublocation committees.[21]

Although only a fraction of the Mau Mau were armed—Corfield estimates that, in 1952, the movement possessed between four hundred and eight hundred modern weapons, stolen from government arsenals—Mau Mau leaders grew increasingly bold. Early in 1952, terrorist gangs started burning huts of African officials and fields of some white farmers. The Mau Mau oath also continued to change and, by spring, included an ominous promise to kill on order. In June the governor retired. The interregnum proved no more energetic in coping with the deteriorating situation. In August, in response to demands of a legislative group for action, the acting governor stated: " . . . I categorically deny that there is a state of emergency."[22]

Despite Jomo Kenyatta's alleged denunciation of the Mau Mau, reports of large-scale oathing ceremonies continued to reach Government House. In September, police reported the murder of fourteen Africans by Mau Mau gangs, who also burned some white farms and killed or mutilated several hundred cattle and sheep. At the end of the month, the new governor, Sir Evelyn Baring, arrived and inspected disturbed areas. While Baring was so engaged, the Mau Mau brazenly murdered a Kikuyu senior chief in daylight a few miles from Nairobi. Baring notified his government: " . . . It is now abundantly clear that we are facing a planned revolutionary movement. If the movement cannot be stopped, there will be an administrative break-down, followed by bloodshed amounting to civil war."[23]

In late October, a British battalion arrived by air from Egypt and a British cruiser sailed into Mombasa. Early the next morning, police arrested Kenyatta and 182 followers. A short time later, Baring broadcast a state of emergency.

If Sir Evelyn Baring, Kenya's new governor, hoped to disrupt the Mau Mau rebellion by forceful action, he was disappointed. Government had waited too long. Two weeks after the declaration of emergency in October 1952, a Mau Mau gang killed a white farmer and two of his African servants. Ugly incidents continued against Europeans and Africans alike. In late November, a Mau Mau gang killed a white retired naval commander and badly cut up his wife; four days later, terrorists in Nairobi murdered a leading African politician, a moderate. Although official reports noted "increasing lawlessness," the government apparently did not respect the implications of these murders: Arrests of Kenyatta and other Mau Mau leaders had not broken the insurgency.

Lacking positive identification of the organization and of its strength and objectives, the government adopted a defensive strategy, farming out its limited number of troops to support local police units. At the same time, it began to expand police forces; Baring also sent for an intelligence expert, Sir Percy Sillitoe, to reorganize the all-important but theretofore neglected police intelligence service, Special Branch. Finally, government began to organize a Kikuyu Home Guard cored by Tribal Police to protect native villages against Mau Mau depredations.

These measures, valid enough, suffered from several disadvantages. The first was the theater of operations, which comprised, in addition to

Nairobi, " . . . the whole of the Central Province . . . ten Districts in all, about 14,000 square miles or about one-sixteenth of the country."[24] Two large areas of forests and mountains, the Aberdare Range of some six hundred square miles and the Mount Kenya area of about nine hundred square miles, provided natural sanctuary for Mau Mau guerrilla gangs. Since these forests bordered the African Reserve, they greatly eased the Mau Mau task of agitation and recruitment—much as jungle-based terrorists in Malaya gained sustenance from bordering Chinese villages.

Security forces lacked a single commander to provide common plan and purpose. The official responsible for security operations, the Member for Law and Order, was also Attorney General, a latter-day Pooh-Bah who carried out his own orders. The major security instrument was the Kenya Police, a colonial force with mostly white officers. This group included a reserve force, soon mobilized. The Kenya Police Reserve, or KPR, consisted mostly of white settlers who wanted direct action and who were not inclined to respect legal niceties. Still another security force existed: the Tribal Police, which was made up of Africans who operated under white District Officers and looked after security needs of the DOs and various chiefs and headmen. They were not, technically, police and had no official relationship with the Kenya Police (which helps to explain early intelligence failures).

Troops provided a further complication, in that most Europeans did not speak Swahili and were definitely not at home in a forest environment. Time and space were the villains. Some companies were spread over seventy miles of often difficult terrain. As in Malaya, some units perforce operated independently for days and even weeks, their only ally an occasional police detachment.

A political complication also existed. The arrest and deportation of Kenyatta and his lieutenants were neither as intelligent nor as effective as people believed at the time. If this action disrupted the movement's leadership, it also removed what might well have proved a restraining hand, and it removed a leader with whom the government in time might have been able to negotiate. In the event, lesser KCA members immediately took over the movement's leadership, and when these were arrested, still lesser members moved in. The ultimate result was a diluted thing called the Council of Freedom, which from Nairobi maintained liaison with district and locational committees. But, at some point, the Nairobi group, or "passive wing," lost control of terrorist gangs in Nairobi and in the forests, thus yielding to fanatical and ignorant leaders whose excesses horrified the civilized world and badly damaged the movement.

Such was early support enjoyed by the movement, and such its organization, that Kenyatta's arrest did not seriously upset operations.

Early in 1953, the Mau Mau opened a general offensive against Europeans and loyal Africans. Terrorist raids on farms to gain food and cattle and terrorist assaults that involved murder or attempted murder generally occurred at night, usually with the co-operation, willing or unwilling, of African servants. Although, in the first two weeks of the new year, the Mau Mau killed two Europeans and thirty-five Africans, other European farmers, including women, successfully beat off attacks, as did units of the expanding Kikuyu Home Guard. The murders nonetheless drove settlers into frenzy and, as undoubtedly planned by the Mau Mau, brought severe repression on Africans in general.

Continued attacks caused the government to make the administering of the Mau Mau oath a capital offense. At this time, security forces

> . . . concentrated on breaking or at least neutralizing the popular base of the revolt among the peasant masses in the Kikuyu Reserve. In addition to curfews, movement restrictions, new pass requirements, collective fines and punishment, "cleansing" and counter-Mau Mau oathing campaigns and severe methods of interrogation, Government launched a strong anti-Mau Mau propaganda campaign, raised personal taxes and introduced a "communal" or forced labor scheme whereby damaged roads and bridges could be repaired, guard and police posts erected and new agricultural schemes enforced without cost.

Drawing on lessons of Malaya, the government declared the Kikuyu Reserve a Special Area, " . . . wherein a person failing to halt when challenged could be shot"; the Aberdare and Mount Kenya forests became Prohibited Areas—anyone found in them could be shot on sight. The government cleared some European areas of Kikuyu labor; in other areas, African farm workers voluntarily returned to the Reserve. The government also organized three-man committees—civil, police and military—to run operations at district and province levels. Finally, Baring brought in a senior military adviser, Major General W. R. N. Hinde.[25]

Once again, these measures seemed valid enough, but did not immediately produce desired results. The influx of natives to the Reserve proved particularly unfortunate, since they could not be readily absorbed, which meant that the Mau Mau exploited their subsequent discontent. Raids and attacks continued, culminating at the end of March in a two-pronged operation against the native village complex of Lari and the police post at Naivasha. The night attack at Lari, carried out in the most bestial fashion, took eighty-four native lives; terrorists mutilated another thirty-one natives and burned a large number of huts. The Naivasha attack killed one policeman and gained the Mau Mau eighteen automatic weapons and twenty-nine rifles; the attackers also released 173 prisoners.[26]

Although attacks were reasonably well co-ordinated, they succeeded as much from government errors as from Mau Mau skill. In the long run, they proved a serious mistake, because they tipped the Mau Mau hand and caused a good many *attentiste* Kikuyu to turn to the government, providing information or joining the Home Guard. They also brought Kenya into world focus with sympathy automatically given to the victims, and thus weakened the Mau Mau hand. They inspired Hinde to work out the committee system of operations, to start arming the Kikuyu Guard, and to conscript from the colony's 150,000 Asians, a move theretofore opposed by the white community. They also brought military reinforcement, a brigade, from England and caused the War Office to establish a separate military command for East Africa under General Sir George Erskine.

Erskine did not accept prevailing defensive strategy, but instead sought a military solution. Wanting to eliminate or at least diminish contact between forest gangs and supporters in the Reserve, he cleared a one-mile-wide strip along the hundred miles of forest Reserve, a new Prohibitive Area occupied by police posts that were to create a sort of *cordon sanitaire*. Although lacking troops, he managed to form an infantry force to protect the Reserve until the Kikuyu Guard was strong enough for the task. At the same time, he set the RAF to bombing forest areas in hope of trying to keep pressure on the gangs, and he commenced operations in the forest itself. To carry out the new mission, his troops at first tried massive sweep operations, "grouse drives," which generally failed to catch any quarry. By this time, various terrorist gangs had become at home in the forest. Karari later wrote that, unlike the adversary,

> . . . our fighters were very good at spying and detecting the enemy through hearing, a nervous [i.e., intuitive] sense of danger and smelling. The latter sense had grown strong in such a way that our warriors could smell the enemy at more than 200 yards away; notably soap and any form of tobacco.

Animals, which had grown used to the natives and which had a much keener sense of smell, frequently served as sentries alert to any intrusion by foreign bodies. If an operation happened to blunder into a Mau Mau camp, or "hide," the Mau Mau quickly packed up and experienced little difficulty in snaking through "lines" of soldiers struggling awkwardly through heavy forest. Realizing, finally, that the soldiers themselves had to become at home in guerrilla environment, the high command ordered construction of roads leading some five or six miles into the forest. A troop unit moved to each terminal point, set up base, and fanned out patrols.[27]

The forests held a vast number of surprises for troops. The two ranges, Aberdare and Mount Kenya, climbed steadily through belts of woods and bamboo split laterally into ridges and gulleys—cruel territory at best, but, with its strange sounds and hidden dangers, anathema to ordinary troops, no matter how well trained. The vast areas swallowed both Mau Mau gangs and troop units. Erskine called for more and more troops. By late autumn of 1953, forest operations were claiming eleven infantry battalions supported by young officers from Kenya Regiment and by African trackers. A group of young Kenyan pilots flying light aircraft also worked closely with patrols, both in spotting Mau Mau targets and in relaying messages and dropping supply; the RAF continued to bomb forest areas, using both the Harvard trainer and, later, the Liberator bomber (with generally poor results).[28] By end of 1953, the government had deployed over ten thousand troops and expanded the police from seven thousand to fifteen thousand plus six thousand part-time auxiliaries. The Home Guard numbered some twenty thousand. Government forces claimed over three thousand Mau Mau killed and over a thousand captured. Security forces had arrested about 150,000 Kikuyu and brought sixty-four thousand to trial.[29]

Mau Mau gains were not so impressive. Despite wanton killing, which would continue, Mau Mau leaders realized that they had failed to unite the tribe in a general uprising. If gangs remained intact inside forests, communications between gangs and also with supporters in the Reserve and in Nairobi were becoming more difficult. Gang leaders faced increasingly severe morale problems, and leadership quarrels also developed. Early in 1954, the government scored a major victory: the capture of Waruhiu Itote, or General China, the thirty-two-year-old leader of the Mount Kenya gangs—some five thousand Mau Mau who operated independently of the Aberdare gangs. His patient interrogation by a Kenyan police officer, Ian Henderson, not only produced a wealth of intelligence that dealt a blow to the support organization in the Reserve, but also resulted in surrender or capture of other important Mau Mau leaders.[30]

The situation was still unfavorable from the government's standpoint. In January 1954, a parliamentary delegation concluded " . . . that the influence of Mau Mau in the Kikuyu area, except in certain localities, has not declined; it has, on the contrary, increased." So grave had the situation in Nairobi and adjoining Kiambu District grown that General Erskine had ordered the wholesale removal of some hundred thousand Africans from the city and surrounding areas for screening purposes, the theory being that the forest gangs could not survive without this support. For several weeks, twenty-five thousand police and soldiers screened Nairobi's Africans to send thousands of Mau Mau suspects to specially prepared detention camps. Although criticized as unduly harsh, it accomplished its mission: It broke up the Mau Mau support organization in Nairobi and Kiambu, which never recovered. It also eliminated a great deal of crime within the city, and it yielded valuable intelligence.[31]

Erskine further tightened control of the civil population by a more rigorous identity-card system. Follow-up raids, known as "pepper-pots" and conducted by special intelligence teams, kept remaining Mau Mau off balance and continued to provide intelligence. The government also carried out a resettlement scheme that, by end of 1954, had moved about a million natives into villages that could be more easily protected and controlled.[32]

Although Erskine's strategy necessarily interrupted forest operations, a few units continued to press the gangs or at least to impede their contact with the Reserve. By now, some units were becoming quite skillful in forest environment, and new operational techniques also improved efficiency. A young British regular officer named Frank Kitson had already introduced pseudo gangs; that is, small units led by Europeans and consisting of captured Mau Mau and loyal Kikuyu fitted out to resemble real gangs. Pseudo gangs made contact with real gangs either in the Reserve or in the forest in order to get intelligence or to carry out offensive action against them if circumstances were favorable. Kitson had told his story well in his book *Gangs and Counter-gangs*. As he points out, this is an old technique and variants of it were used in the Philippine insurrection and in Malaya, among other places. The disturbing fact is that a young British officer had to introduce it in Kenya, where it should have been standard operating procedure at once invoked by those responsible for the colony's security.

Erskine also improved his *cordon sanitaire* by building a fifty-mile ditch along eastern and southern borders of Mount Kenya forest:

> . . . It was eighteen feet wide and ten feet deep, the most primeval of military obstacles, the fosse. Along its bed bristled thousands of sharpened stakes and these were augmented by miles of barbed wire which had been booby-trapped. At half-mile intervals there were police posts and the half-mile between them was continuously patrolled by night and by day. Massed African labor created this ditch and it proved a highly successful barrier to the barefoot Mau Mau terrorist. . . .

Erskine also enforced a rigorous food-denial policy. Special laws required farmers to lock up cattle after dark and prohibited food crops being planted within three miles of forests.[33]

Despite the success of all these measures, the gangs continued active, stealing or destroying cattle, burning homesteads, murdering natives and even a few Europeans. In January 1955, the military opened Operation Hammer, a sweep of the Aberdares in approximately division strength. What military commanders fondly thought of as a "combing" operation unfortunately lacked teeth. Operation Hammer brought to earth just over a hundred fifty Mau Mau. This disappointing result produced a more sophisticated tactic known as "domination of areas":

> ... The essence of this was that instead of sweeping the forest, units would be given areas of it to dominate. Every unit and sub-unit would therefore have its own bit of forest to take charge of and get to know intimately so that the enemy would have difficulty in entering it without the fact becoming known.[34]

A two-month effort along these lines in the Mount Kenya forests netted 277 Mau Mau killed, captured, or prisoner, a meager result, considering the investment, which included airdrops of over one hundred thousand pounds of supply.

The key to productive counteroperations remained intelligence. Erskine's successor, General Sir Gerald Lathbury, established a separate police section called Special Forces, which enlarged Kitson's pseudo-gang technique and proved probably the most successful of all methods employed. The Administration developed a related technique of considerable interest, from both psychological and operational standpoints. This involved forest sweeps by largely native lines; in one instance, seventeen thousand natives, mostly women, cleared a large area of forest, the Mau Mau either surrendering or being hacked to pieces. Although the army continued operations in certain parts of the forest, from late 1955 Special Forces increasingly took over the task of tracking down the two thousand terrorists who remained in Aberdare forest under command of Dedan Kimathi. This police action, thrilling in the extreme, demanded infinite patience and is well told in Ian Henderson and Philip Goodhart's book *The Hunt for Kimathi*. The hunt ended in October 1956, when the deranged terrorist was wounded and captured; he was later executed.

Kimathi's capture virtually ended Mau Mau resistance. All told, security forces had killed over eleven thousand Mau Mau (presumed) and captured some twenty-five hundred, at a cost of 167 dead (101 Africans) and over fifteen hundred wounded (1,469 Africans). Civilian casualties, including those of the Kikuyu Guard, totaled almost nineteen hundred dead (1,819 Africans) and almost a thousand wounded (916 Africans). By spring of 1959, the counterinsurgency had cost British and Kenya governments £55 million.[35]

At the height of the emergency, security forces detained seventy-seven thousand Africans. This figure shrank to about two thousand by end of 1958. Meanwhile, the government had held elections " . . . on a qualitative franchise for the eight African seats in the legislature." In the next two years, more Africans were brought into government until they formed a majority in the Legislative Council. Kenyatta and his lieutenants meanwhile had been removed from jail and held under house arrest. The government freed Kenyatta altogether in 1961. Just over two years later, Kenya became a republic, with Jomo Kenyatta its first president.

CHAPTER FIFTY-TWO

1. Colonial Office (F.D. Corfield), 219–20. Corfield suggests that Kenyatta learned Soviet Communist agit-prop and organizational techniques on short visits to the Soviet Union, first in 1929–30 and later in 1933, when he attended the Lenin School. This suggestion appears impractical to me in view of Kenyatta's brief stay in the U.S.S.R. and the hiatus of thirteen years between techniques learned and techniques practiced. More logically, Corfield points to the lack of Communist bias in Mau Mau leadership and also that a Communist Party did not exist in Kenya:

   > . . . It can accordingly be concluded that Mau Mau had virtually no connection with Communism, but was developed by Kenyatta as an atavistic tribal rising aimed against Western civilization and technology and in particular against Government and the Europeans as symbols of progress.

   See also, Leakey, *Mau Mau and the Kikuyu*, and *Defeating Mau Mau*. Leakey awards the movement more of a religious-nationalist bias; Barnett and Njama, 199: " . . . My own investigation of Mau Mau ideology," Dr. Barnett wrote,

   > viewed as the unifying set of aims, interests and beliefs of the Movement, has shown it to be a rather complex phenomenon containing at least four major aspects or components; namely secular, moral-religious, African national and Kikuyu tribal.

2. Ruark.
3. Leakey, *Mau Mau and the Kikuyu*, 1–8. See also, Oliver and Mathew, I; Kenyatta.
4. Leakey, *Mau Mau and the Kikuyu*, vii–viii. See also, Barnett and Njama; Corfield; Majdalaney.
5. Leakey, *Mau Mau and the Kikuyu*, 28–46, 7.
6. Ibid., 57 ff. See also, Hemphill.
7. Leakey, *Mau Mau and the Kikuyu*, 36.
8. Meinertzhagen, 80.
9. Ibid., 31.
10. Ibid., 78.
11. Ibid., 152. See also, 132: Meinertzhagen also disapproved of colonial administration. In 1904, he noted in his journal

    > . . . the low class of man who is appointed . . . Few of them have had any education, and many of them do not pretend to be members of the educated class. One can neither read nor write. This is not

surprising when one realizes that no examination is required to enter the local Civil Service.

12. Barnett and Njama, 33.
13. Leakey, *Mau Mau and the Kikuyu*, 60.
14. Ibid., 86 ff. See also, Kenyatta, who explains the importance of female circumcision to tribal tradition and mores.
15. Colonial Office (F.D. Corfield), 25. See also, Barnett and Njama, 27, who offer interesting comparisons between wages received by Africans, Asians, and Whites.
16. Majdalaney, 52–3.
17. Mitchell, 220.
18. Colonial Office (F.D. Corfield), 35.
19. Barnett and Njama, 53, 55.
20. Leakey, *Mau Mau and the Kikuyu*, 36–7, 98–9.
21. Barnett and Njama, 63 ff., for the situation in detail.
22. Majdalaney, 93.
23. Colonial Office (F.D. Corfield), 157, 159.
24. Majdalaney, 132. See also, Slane.
25. Barnett and Njama, 211.
26. Majdalaney, 137–47. See also, Barnett and Njama, 137–8.
27. Barnett and Njama, 29. Karari Njama describes in detail the life of his forest gang.
28. Kitson, *Gangs and Counter-gangs*, 155–6. See also, Slane; Barnett and Njama.
29. Majdalaney, 188.
30. Henderson, Ian, 32 ff. See also, Barnett and Njama, who suggest lesser results than those claimed by security forces.
31. Barnett and Njama, 331–2. The authors cite 50,000 detained, a figure that perhaps included families of the detainees who were sent back to the Reserve. See also, Majdalaney, who states that the operation screened 30,000 Africans, with just over half sent to detention camps; Frank Kitson states that 10,000 Africans were incarcerated.
32. Majdalaney, 203 ff.
33. Ibid., 216–17.
34. Ibid., 213.
35. Colonial Office (F.D. Corfield), 316. See also, Cameron.

CHAPTER 53

The Cyprus rebellion • Historical background • The question of enosis • The 1931 rebellion • The postwar situation • Makarios and Grivas • Grivas' estimate of the situation • Origin of EOKA • Opening attacks • Early guerrilla operations • Harding's negotiations • He deports Makarios • His military solution • Organization and strength of EOKA • British counterguerrilla tactics • Grivas' critical analysis of British tactics • Attempts at a political solution • Fragile peace • The cost • Grivas defends his tactics • The new Republic of Cyprus • Fighting breaks out between Greeks and Turks • Makarios deposed • The Turkish invasion • Cyprus divided • The United Nations arranges a cease-fire • UN peace plan rejected • Trouble in the Turkish Cypriot camp • Breakdown of peace talks

BRITISH TROOPS were still fighting guerrillas in Malaya and Kenya when a serious insurgency broke out in Cyprus, the eastern Mediterranean island that the British had ruled for over seventy-five years and that, in 1954, had become British military headquarters in the Middle East.

The Cyprus rebellion had been a long time forming and was neither Communist-inspired nor Communist-directed. All elements of rebellion were present in 1878, when Disraeli, in furthering his Middle East strategy, wrested Cyprus from Turkish control.[1] Nominally Ottoman territory—it lies only forty miles from the Turkish coast—it held two distinct ethnic groups, which differed in race, religion, and language. The Turkish population, 18–20 percent, accepted British rule amicably, but the Greek portion, 80 percent, at once expressed desire for *enosis*, or union, with Greece. Whitehall refused, holding that, under terms of the Anglo-Turkish Convention, it was governing only by proxy. This argument vanished when Turkey joined the wrong side in 1914; Great

Britain annexed the island and, in the following year, offered it to Greece if she would declare war against the Central Powers. Greece refused and Britain retained possession.

Greek Cypriotes argued after the war that Britain, free of treaty entanglements with Turkey, could grant enosis if she wished. Although Prime Minister Lloyd George seemed favorably disposed, " . . . the War Office opposed on strategic grounds any change in the island's status."[2] In 1925, the island became a crown colony.

In 1931, Greek Cypriotes angered by new taxes spontaneously rebelled against British rule (enforced by police and a garrison of one infantry company—125 men) by setting fire to Government House.[3] Police opened fire, killing one Cypriote and wounding sixteen. Captain Freeman marched his company to the scene and successfully dispersed the crowd. Whitehall dispatched another company of troops from Egypt (by air!) and, two days later, two cruisers and two destroyers arrived to add to government muscle. Within a week, " . . . this badly organized rebellion" was broken:

> . . . six Cypriots were killed, and over thirty wounded. The bishops of Kition and Kyrenia and eight other Greek Cypriot religious and political leaders were banished for life from the island. Two thousand others were sent to prison and fines amounting to £66,000 were imposed on the Greek Cypriots to pay for the damage. Constitutional government was suspended, the Legislative Council and local councils abolished, political parties banned and the press put under censorship. The governor was empowered to rule by decree. The Colonial Office promised to review the constitutional future of the island but no new constitution was put forward until 1948.[4]

World War II somewhat relaxed political tensions on the island. As in 1914, so in 1940, numerous Greek Cypriotes volunteered to fight for the allies. The Anglo-Greek alliance, as opposed to Turkish neutrality and pro-Axis attitude, brought a softening in British attitude, and, in 1941, the administration allowed political parties to form once again. The war also created considerable prosperity for the people. Perhaps more important, Greek Cypriotes reckoned that self-determination of peoples promised by allied declarations would at last result in long-awaited enosis with Greece.

They reckoned without other factors, however. One was continuing antagonism of Turkish Cypriotes to enosis, a feeling strengthened by island Communists, both Turkish and Greek. Another was Greek civil war and cold war in general: Greece was in no position to effectively press either Great Britain or the United States for enosis while depending on them for survival. Once Greece and Turkey, as members of

NATO, formed a strategic flank against the Soviet threat, the United States turned a deaf ear to Greek demands, since to respect them would mean a break with Turkey. Finally, loss of Palestine and unsettled conditions surrounding bases in Egypt and Iraq increased the strategic importance of Cyprus to Britain, though scarcely to the degree the War Office believed.

Mr. Clement Attlee's Labour government nonetheless allowed exiled Cypriote leaders to return to the island and attempted to substitute constitutional reforms for enosis. Had either party faced reality, a working arrangement might have resulted in 1948. But clouds obscured common sense: in the case of Greek Cypriotes, who now numbered some four hundred thousand, a political immaturity and naïveté—the result largely of British refusal to encourage indigenous political growth from 1931 onward—that prevented them from grasping opportunities inherent in the proposed constitution; in the case of the British, failure of the Labour government and particularly of Mr. Ernest Bevin and his advisers to respect the depth of Greek Cypriote feeling regarding this issue. Once negotiations lapsed, the gulf widened; in 1950, a plebiscite showed 96 percent of Greek Cypriotes in favor of enosis. The plebiscite was allegedly inspired by the young and determined bishop of Kition, who, at thirty-seven years, became the new archbishop of Cyprus, Makarios III.[5]

New negotiations might now have commenced but for factors previously mentioned and for the introduction of a new and in some ways sinister character in the Cyprus drama: George Grivas. At fifty-three years of age, Grivas was a good-looking man, short and broadly built, " . . . with a strong, unsmiling face and deep-set eyes under fierce brows; his thin mouth . . . topped by a dark moustache."[6] A Cypriote born and raised, son of a prosperous grocer, Grivas graduated from the Athens Military Academy to become a professional officer in the Greek army, where colleagues found him dour and determined, a Spartan " . . . tireless and demanding, a martinet who required no less of himself than he did of the soldiers under him. . . . "[7] We earlier encountered him briefly in the Greek civil war (see Chapter 42), when, as a colonel, he commanded the irregular *Khi*, or X, organization, an extreme-rightist movement dedicated to killing as many Communists as possible—an experience that left Grivas impressed with the effectiveness of Communist subversive warfare in accomplishing limited goals. Retired because of extreme political views, he studied Communist methods of warfare with the same intensity bestowed on his stamp collection; he also ran for parliament on a promonarchist platform and was defeated. Adrift in the political caldron of Athenian politics, he brushed against Greek nationalists and Cypriote exiles, finally to join the stew of enosis: In 1951, the small but determined group decided that Grivas

" . . . should undertake the leadership of an armed struggle to throw the British out of Cyprus."[8]

Grivas has described the ensuing struggle in two books, *The Memoirs of General Grivas* and the rather more technical but no less Zarathustrian work *General Grivas on Guerrilla Warfare*.[9] Grivas does not emerge as a particularly attractive man in these works, but rather as a man with a mission, a man who faced up to means at hand which he used with great effect for a particular end. His task was extremely difficult. He knew and respected the British and had every reason to believe that they would fight and fight hard to retain sovereignty over Cyprus. A conventional campaign was thus hopeless, but so was a guerrilla campaign: Only the western, mountainous half of the relatively small island (some hundred forty miles long and sixty miles wide) offered natural sanctuary, but good roads meant rapid troop movement; a Royal Navy blockade would make it difficult to receive arms and supply; only a relatively few Greek Cypriotes had had military training, and most were skeptical about his plan, including Archbishop Makarios. These adverse factors meant that priority would be given to continual harassment of the British in order " . . . to draw the attention of international public opinion, especially among the allies of Greece, to the Cyprus question."[10]

Meager resources compelled him to spend the next three years in Athens collecting arms and smuggling them into Cyprus, where volunteers recruited from two Christian Youth movements received and hid them. Progress remained slow: The new Prime Minister of Greece, Marshal Papagos, would not support the movement. Archbishop Makarios feared reprisal effects of violence and ran hot and cold on Grivas' preparations. By late 1954, when Grivas landed secretly on Cyprus, only one arms shipment, with a total value of £600, awaited him. Actual shooting stock amounted to seven revolvers, forty-seven rifles of assorted calibers and manufacture, and ten automatic weapons.

Known now as Dighenis—a mythological Byzantine warrior-hero—Grivas began training saboteurs while organizing small guerrilla groups, distributing and hiding weapons and explosives and establishing intelligence and courier services. Leaning heavily on youthful volunteers, he selected only the most suitable, each of whom swore to obey his orders while preserving utmost secrecy. Thus the origin of *Ethniki Organosis Kyprion Agoniston* (National Organization of Cypriote Fighters) or EOKA; at the start of the rebellion, April 1955, it numbered fewer than a hundred activists. The majority of the Greek Cypriote population, however, sympathized in whole or in part with its professed aims.

* * *

EOKA's greatest ally was the British Government. Continuing to misread the depth of Greek Cypriote feeling, the British military, in spring of 1954, moved Middle East land and air headquarters from Suez to the island. Throughout summer and autumn, various official spokesmen left no doubt that Britain would retain sovereignty over Cyprus, which, so the argument ran, was needed " . . . to fulfil her treaty obligations to the Arab states, NATO, Greece, Turkey and the United Nations." Greek willingness to guarantee her old ally military bases on Cyprus was brushed aside, as was a Greek appeal to the UN to debate the case for the island's self-determination.[11] Having been forced to leave Palestine and Egypt, the British were in no mood for compromise: in July 1954, the Minister of State for the Colonies told the House of Commons that Cyprus could "never" hope to become an independent state.

Such sentiments further charged island air. The colonial government was not popular, to start with. British intransigence now eliminated the moderating forces of Archbishop Makarios on Cyprus and Marshal Papagos in Athens and brought them into Grivas' camp. It also helped Grivas to arrange a series of demonstrations, strikes, and riots that effectively screened his own clandestine preparations. The opening of the rebellion by EOKA attacks on government, police, and military installations in April 1955 caught the government completely by surprise. Confused intelligence agents studied inflammatory leaflets distributed by the thousands and frowned: What was EOKA? Who (or what) was DIGHENIS?

Grivas continued the attacks for a few days before switching to demonstrations, mostly by young students. In June, he opened a prolonged series of attacks that killed one policeman and wounded sixteen others, besides causing considerable property damage and agitation among the British population. Although disappointed in material results, Grivas exulted in international publicity (engendered in large part by Radio Athens, which would continue to report the campaign to the world); Grivas reasoned that this would force the UN to reverse its earlier decision and debate the Cyprus question. He now moved to the mountains to organize guerrilla groups prior to opening a new series of operations intended " . . . to terrorize the police and to paralyze the administration, both in the towns and the countryside."

UN refusal to reopen the Cyprus question, in September, brought a new spurt of EOKA activity in the autumn. While guerrillas began striking primarily military targets in the countryside, selective terror tactics in cities and towns resulted in more police deaths, which, according to Grivas, soon " . . . shattered opposition to EOKA among the Greek police." These tactics succeeded in part because the hostile population refused to co-operate with police and army. Grivas constantly exploited what often was only incipient hostility. He showered the population with leaflets and pamphlets, a propaganda campaign augmented by the technique of the Voice—megaphoned instructions to a village in the dead of night. While EOKA did not hesitate to kill informers and traitors, its members treated the people with great circumspection—for example, always paying for food or goods and maintaining strict sexual morality.[12] The tactics were immensely aided by police inefficiency and, perhaps most important, by continuing Whitehall refusal to abandon or even question the right of British sovereignty.

Despite operational flaws, EOKA clearly held the initiative. In October, a distinguished soldier, Field Marshal Sir John Harding, arrived as the new governor, empowered to negotiate with Makarios and, once reinforced militarily, to quell EOKA.[13] Negotiations with Makarios made some progress over the next few months: Harding yielded on the important question of self-determination—but in the unspecified future. He also dangled a £38-million development scheme before the people, a futile gesture in view of continued British political intransigence. The talks also suffered from disruptive forces already discussed, as well as from concomitant forces: from continuing EOKA successes, which placed uncomfortable pressure on Makarios to refrain from yielding on enosis, pressure increased by civil hostility engendered by British countermeasures; from a new administration in Athens, the Karamanlis government, which did not feel strong enough to intervene forcefully; from Prime Minister Anthony Eden's mistrust of Makarios; from the deteriorating position in Jordan, which, in British minds, increased further the strategic value of Cyprus.

In late February 1956, the British broke off the talks. A few days later, security agents intercepted Makarios on his way to Athens and, shades of 1931, deported him to the Seychelles Islands—thus leaving the field open to Grivas. Since Grivas was not willing to reveal himself, this, in effect, eliminated further negotiations. As Charles Foley later noted: " . . . Harding, by signing the deportation orders, had cut himself off from four-fifths of the population. No Greek Cypriot would enter Government House."[14]

Field Marshal Harding now removed the velvet glove to seek a military solution. At this time, his security forces amounted to some five thousand police and about twenty thousand troops with another five thousand scheduled to arrive. British intelligence did not know it, but Grivas commanded 273 "regulars," who shared about a hundred weapons and who were augmented by some 750 villagers armed with shotguns (from which he formed OKT, or ambush units)—a hard core that the Greek Cypriote population increasingly supported, though sometimes with sorrow and misgiving. By this time, Grivas had divided the island into sectors, which, at his order, undertook specific tasks and enjoyed support of two main groups, ANE, a youth organization, and PEKA, a covert civil organization. Although his later claim that " . . . every Greek Cypriot, from the smallest child to old men and women, belonged to our army . . . " was exaggerated, there is no doubt that he had fashioned an effective organization in a remarkably short time and with remarkably few materials at his disposal.[15]

Harding and his advisers apparently did not have a clue concerning the depth of EOKA. Convinced that he was up against a few terrorists who enjoyed the support of no more than 5 per cent of the population,[16] the field marshal "attacked" in two directions, a quantitative approach designed to eliminate terrorist attacks in the cities and guerrilla activity in the mountains. Continued EOKA raids already had caused him to proclaim a State of Emergency, and, following what Charles Foley, publisher of *The Times of Cyprus,* termed the Templer Bible of Malaya, to invoke stringent regulations governing the civil population. Anyone carrying firearms was subject to a death sentence; persons could be detained or banished without trial. Rewards were offered for information on terrorist activities; Dighenis carried a £10,000 price on his head. As extra measure, Harding proscribed the local Communist Party, AKEL, and locked up 129 of its members—a strange move, since the party *opposed* the rebellion.[17] Other measures involved not only such collective punishments as regional curfews and large community fines, but indiscriminate and often insulting search methods:

> . . . The "security forces" . . . burst into people's homes by day and night, made them stand for hours with their hands up, abused and insulted them. Soldiers would empty sacks of grain on the floor of a farmhouse and pour oil, wine or paraffin over it [sic], thus ruining enough food to keep a family for a year.[18]

In spring of 1956, Harding executed two terrorists, which further antagonized the people (and caused Grivas to execute two captured British soldiers). Grivas, himself, was now on the run. A British patrol almost captured him in May—on May 25, he noted in his diary: " . . . This day is the worst of the struggle for me." In early June, he fled from another patrol in such haste that he left behind personal gear including his diary.[19] British hopes for his capture or surrender soared. In autumn, Harding replied to a cease-fire called by Grivas with an insulting ultimatum to surrender. Grivas answered by renewing his campaign—and by remaining at large:

Harding already had sent sizable task forces into the mountains to break up guerrilla bands, operations later criticized by Grivas:

> . . . Twice from my hiding place in the mountains I watched forces of up to 1,000 troops looking for me, with helicopters flying over-

head. I did not even trouble to move off as they approached, so aimless was their search. Officers, remaining on the road, shouted orders as if on an exercise. In Limassol later the strong patrols which so often passed our house went by as though on a route march. This, then, was the "spider's web" which Harding said he was weaving for us.[20]

Harding tried to repair tactical poverty by a number of devices. One was tracking-dogs, which terrorists sabotaged by liberal use of pepper. Another was "Q patrols"—". . . small mobile units of strong-arm men from the Special Branch [police intelligence], both British and Turkish, which relied on Greek traitors and informers for their leads into the organization."[21] The patrols enjoyed only limited success, due to EOKA's excellent intelligence and courier system. A later tactic of counterambushes produced far better results, but to Grivas' relief the British failed to expand the technique. Still later, the British began using helicopters but in general failed to benefit tactically from them. (In his later work, *Guerrilla Warfare*, Grivas stressed the importance of the helicopter to future guerrilla campaigns, and noted, in passing, " . . . its vulnerability because of its low speed and its proximity to the ground."[22])

Some of Harding's subordinates employed more-radical measures. According to Foley and other observers, British intelligence officers used torture while interrogating captured terrorists. Security forces also seem to have frequently employed indiscriminate detentions. The hostile civil climate, without question, adversely affected some conscript or National Service soldiers, who mistreated not only "suspects" but ordinary citizens—stupid behavior that could only benefit the EOKA.

After early failure, British military tactics grew more sophisticated, but even the most carefully planned and executed operations left escape gaps for the guerrillas, although, on occasion, some were captured or killed and, in time, whole groups were neutralized. Grivas himself remained unimpressed with general British military performance:

> . . . The officers lacked initiative and judgement and the other ranks lacked training, dash and personal courage. This is a harsh verdict, and I think that this seeming indifference to duty, so unlike what I knew of the British Army, was due in part to the fact that many of them felt that they were fighting for an unjust cause; this view is supported by the fact that frequent instances of military disobedience occurred, and sometimes developed into mutinies.[23]

Nor did Harding's performance particularly impress the guerrilla leader. Although British operations became more co-ordinated in 1957, they never grew subtle, at least in Grivas' mind:

650

... Harding disliked changing a decision, once he had made it; if the results were not all he expected he would go on just the same, thus opening the way to a series of mistakes. His soldierly bluntness, which put the whole country against him, was also a valuable index to me of his military intentions. In speeches and broadcasts, and through newspaper interviews which he gave so prodigally, I was kept in constant touch with the way in which his mind was working. No less lavish were his assurances of early victory: did he believe them himself? It seemed that he did, and thus fell into what Napoleon called the biggest mistake a General could make: to paint an imaginary picture and believe it to be true.[24]

Harding's real failure lay in underrating his enemy and overrating his own forces. "The British were hunting field-mice with armored cars" instead of using

> tiny, expertly trained groups, who could work with cunning and patience and strike rapidly when we least expected. . . . the British flooded Cyprus with troops, so that one met a soldier at every step, with the only result that they offered plenty of targets and so sustained casualties."[25]

The abortive Suez Canal operation, at the end of October, greatly facilitated Grivas' campaign by drawing off a large number of troops. EOKA carried out 416 attacks in November alone—"Black November" to embarrassed British authorities, who replied with even more stringent regulations. The conflict now widened into fighting between Greek Cypriotes and Turkish Cypriotes, the latter recruited in considerable quantity by the British for the police force. When EOKA agents killed Turkish policemen, the Turks formed an underground terrorist organization, Volkan, for reprisal purposes.[26]

In December, the British flew in a peace dove in form of the Radcliffe Constitution, which, although suggesting a division in low-level rule between Greeks and Turks, changed little at the top: " . . . Cyprus must remain under British sovereignty; . . . Britain must have the use of the island as a military base; . . . external affairs, defense and internal security were to remain in British hands." The Greek Government rejected the proposals " . . . even before the Cypriots had seen them," and Makarios, a prisoner in the Seychelles, refused to discuss them until he was released.[27]

The rebellion continued in cruel intensity into 1957, with each side recording major gains and losses. The first real breakthrough came in March 1957: A renewed British military effort had cost Grivas the loss of over sixty hard-core fighters since the turn of the year; although plenty of fight remained in EOKA, Grivas now offered another cease-fire in return for Makarios' release. The Suez fiasco had cost Anthony Eden his job, and his replacement, Harold Macmillan, urged on by President Eisenhower, agreed to the archbishop's release but refused to allow his return to Cyprus.

Britain followed a welcome lull in the fighting with two additional moves, one secret and one not. The former consisted of a strategic re-appraisal, the first step in abandoning the theretofore sacrosanct de-mand for continued British sovereignty over all of Cyprus. The Macmillan government next replaced Harding with Sir Hugh Foot, a " . . . colonial civil servant with a liberal reputation." The Greek Gov-ernment, in turn, began to yield on the question of enosis—perhaps, her leaders reasoned, independence would be sufficient for the time be-ing. The UN also came around to supporting, albeit mildly, the right of Cypriote self-determination. The Menderes government, in Turkey, continued to hold for partition.[28]

A good bit of blood would spill before these discordant goals merged into a working plan. Grivas' cease-fire, fragile at best, gave way to renewed fighting in late 1957. In early 1958, Grivas added to guer-rilla-terrorist tactics by launching a Gandhi-like campaign of "passive resistance," which included an island-wide boycott of all British goods. By year's end, British security forces seemed no closer to "winning" the war than they had three years earlier.

But if EOKA resistance had once gained considerable international sympathy, it was beginning to lose it, as the rift between Turkey and Greece widened to NATO's disadvantage and as danger of total civil war developed in Cyprus. The home front was also feeling the pinch: " . . . the economic repercussions of the boycott and the British counter-measures—curfews, mass detentions, dismissal of workers from military establishments—were beginning to be felt by the Greek Cypriot popu-lation."[29] The British were no happier: The boycott proved effective and thus expensive, and so was support of twenty-eight thousand troops (about one to every twenty civilians) plus greatly expanded police forces, all hunting a few hundred terrorists; a civil war would prove even more costly and would produce severe international repercussions. Resumption of emergency measures, including wholesale round-up and detention of Greek Cypriotes, was bringing unfavorable international publicity without seeming to influence the military situation favorably.

The Macmillan government now decided that the whole of Cyprus was not a "strategic necessity" but, rather, a "strategic convenience," not worth the foreseeable cost of retention. Instead, Britain could yield sovereignty in return for base rights (which the Greek Government had suggested four years earlier), a decision aided by the fall of the Iraqi Government and that country's withdrawal from the Baghdad Pact. Turkey also indicated a new willingness to negotiate—the result of international pressure by countries, mainly the United States, on whom she depended for economic and military aid. The effect of these shifting pressures enabled Britain to bring the Greek and the Turkish governments into direct negotiations in late 1958. Makarios recognized the changing situation and approved. With the political rug pulled from under him, Grivas, in early 1959, announced a final cease-fire. Conferences in Zurich and London followed, and Cyprus eventually emerged as a republic with its own constitution and a complicated series of treaties meant to protect British, Greek, and Turkish interests.

Though opposed to the settlement, Grivas disbanded EOKA and left the island. In Athens, he enjoyed a hero's welcome, including promotion to lieutenant general and a life pension[30]—exaggerated tribute, perhaps, considering the muddled fate that awaited Greek Cypriotes, a fate influenced in part by his subsequent mysterious and at times sinister machinations. Grivas had not gained his intended goal of enosis, nor had he forced the British from Cyprus. All things considered, however, he could claim the upper hand in this war that had taken five to six hundred lives, wounded over twelve hundred persons and, according to Charles Foley, cost the British Government an estimated £90 million.[31] Starting from scratch, for four years he not only had fought a greatly superior force to a draw at an estimated financial cost of about £50,000, but, at the end, he was prepared to carry on the battle, as witness the imposing amount of arms and ammunition finally surrendered by EOKA fighters at Grivas' orders.[32]

Most Western observers found it difficult to award more than grudging admiration to Grivas' employment of Byzantine tactics, and many of them spoke in terms of moral abhorrence. Such judgments seem to this writer to lack balance, in that they fail to weigh British culpability in the emergency; first by a myopic prewar policy; second by failing to adopt a mature and rational, as opposed to primarily an emotional, attitude concerning the future government of Cyprus; third by deporting Makarios and thus creating a political vacuum; and fourth by inviting the disputatious and disreputable Menderes government to debate the question and thus inflame already heated island passions. These and other actions were predicated on the assumption that force would rule. They thus invited counterforce (the potential of which the British Government failed to respect) and opened the way for a Grivas, unhappily an astute military professional able to adapt tactical thinking to the tactical problem.

Grivas was not deaf to cries of outrage from Western voices or from objections by Makarios and Papagos, or to distaste of island moderates. Rather, like Marion and his North Carolinians in the American revolution, like Lenin and his fellows before and during the Russian revolution, like Michael Collins and the IRA during the Irish revolution, and like Menachem Begin in Palestine, he was contemptuous. In defending his techniques, he later wrote words that, despite translation, carry a Lawrentian ring:

> ... The British, who arm their commandoes with knives and instruct them to kill in just this way—from the rear—protested vociferously when such tactics were applied to themselves. It may be argued that these things are only permissible in war. This is nonsense. I was fighting a war in Cyprus against the British, and if they did not recognize the fact from the start they were forced to at the end. The truth is that our form of war, in which a few hundred fell in four years, was far more selective than most, and I speak as one who has seen battlefields covered with dead. We did not strike, like the bomber, at random. We shot only British servicemen who would have killed us if they could have fired first, and civilians who were traitors or intelligence agents. To shoot down your enemies in the street may be unprecedented, but I was looking for results, not precedents. ... All war is cruel and the only way to win against superior forces is by ruse and trickery ... [33]

Independence was scarcely the political panacea of Cypriote dreams. Matters went fairly well at first. With Archbishop Makarios as president and Turkish Cypriote Fazil Kücük as vice-president, the Republic of Cyprus gained admission to the United Nations and, in 1961, to the British Commonwealth. Disruptive ties with the home countries, Greece and Turkey, were never broken, however, nor were ancient animosities between Greek Eastern Orthodox Christians and Turkish Sunnite Moslems ever submerged. Quarrels over local administrative problems led to an outbreak of fighting in 1963 between Greek and Turkish factions, and an uneasy cease-fire was maintained only by means of a United Nations military force.

Quarreling continued during the 1960s and came to a head in July 1974 when a group of the Cyprus National Guard, led by Greek officers, attempted to assassinate Makarios and establish the old dream of enosis—union with Greece. Makarios escaped the country. A former EOKA member was summarily installed as president, a move answered by Turkey with an armed invasion of the island, a whirlwind campaign of a few weeks that left Turkish Cypriotes in command of 37 per cent, the northern portion—of Cyprus, and caused some 180,000 Greek Cypriotes to flee to the South.

Another uneasy cease-fire maintained by the United Nations force followed between Greek Cyprus and what Turkish Cypriotes call the Turkish Republic of Northern Cyprus (recognized solely by Turkey).

Reunification talks throughout the 1980s got nowhere. Relations between Greece and Turkey improved somewhat in the early 1990s, the result of a United Nations initiative supported by the United States, to bring more encouraging talks between the opposing Cypriote leaders.

These continued under UN auspices in 1992 and early 1993, but neither the newly elected conservative Greek Cypriote President Glafcos Cerides nor the Turkish Cypriote President Rauf Denktash agreed with the plan.[34] The talks broke down in July when the Turkish Cypriote Prime Minister Dervis Eroglu undercut Denktash by declaring that any form of federation between the two communities "could bring a bloodbath."[35] Denktash subsequently withdrew from the talks which, judging from the general intransigence of both parties, not to mention the innate antagonism between the client countries, Greece and Turkey, would not easily have resulted in an agreement. Should one ever emerge, it would probably establish some sort of bizonal federation—which, ironically, is what the Turkish Cypriotes proposed, and the Greek Cypriotes rejected, in 1975.

CHAPTER FIFTY-THREE

1. Stephens, 14, 62–9.
2. Ibid., 110.
3. Freeman.
4. Stephens, 111–12.

5. Ibid., 129. See also, Foley.
6. Foley, 49. See also, Barker; Byford-Jones.
7. Thayer, 114–15.
8. Grivas, *The Memoirs of General Grivas*, 13. See also, Foley and Scobie.
9. Grivas, *General Grivas on Guerrilla Warfare*.
10. Ibid., 5.
11. Stephens, 136–7.
12. Alastos, 91.
13. Stephens, 143 ff. See also, Durrell, who served as press adviser to the government during the early years of the insurgency.
14. Foley, 69.
15. Grivas, *General Grivas on Guerrilla Warfare*, 101–5. Mines, for example, were made from stolen dynamite or explosive from old shells dumped offshore by the British at the end of World War II and from local materials.
16. Foley, 91. On one occasion Harding told him: " . . . Not five percent of Greek Cypriots are behind this evil organization. Not five percent!"
17. Alastos, 98–9.
18. Grivas, *The Memoirs of General Grivas*, 53.
19. Barker, 126.
20. Grivas, *The Memoirs of General Grivas*, 125. See also, Diacre, who describes a typical raid on a mountain village.
21. Grivas, *The Memoirs of General Grivas*, 105.
22. Grivas, *General Grivas on Guerrilla Warfare*, 75–6.
23. Grivas, *The Memoirs of General Grivas*, 82–3. See also, Foley.
24. Grivas, *The Memoirs of General Grivas*, 125–6.
25. Grivas, *General Grivas on Guerrilla Warfare*, 46.
26. Stephens, 147.
27. Ibid., 148.
28. Ibid., 151.
29. Ibid., 158.
30. Ibid., 166.
31. Foley, 242.
32. Ibid., 235.
33. Grivas, *The Memoirs of General Grivas*, 43.
34. *Facts on File*, Vol. 53, No. 2726, February 25, 1993.
35. *The Independent* (U.K.), July 14, 1993.

CHAPTER 54

The Algerian crisis • Historical background • The French conquest • French colonial policy • Growth of nationalism • The 1945 riots • Ahmed Ben Bella and the OS • Belkacem Krim's guerrillas • The internal situation • FLN emerges • Outbreak of rebellion • Soustelle's pacification strategy • Origin of SAS • French military and political errors • La guerre révolutionnaire

THE INK HAD SCARCELY DRIED on the Geneva Agreements, which extricated France from Indochina, when the Mendès-France government faced another major crisis, in Algeria. As in Indochina, trouble in this principal North African colony as well as in Tunisia and Morocco had been brewing for a long time. The Maghreb otherwise resembled Indochina. Algeria was an older holding, the occupation having begun in 1830 (see Chapter 9), but Tunisia did not become a protectorate until 1881 and Morocco only in 1912. Algeria occupied a colonial status similar to Cochin China, or southern Vietnam; Tunisia and Morocco retained their monarchs and something of their local administration, as did the other French Indochina kingdoms. Tunisia and Morocco claimed more-cohesive cultures than the semi-nomadic Algerians, but some Algerian tribes traced from antiquity, and all were proud: The French did not subjugate them until 1857, and active resistance continued until 1881. Tunisia submitted more readily to French rule; the pacification of Morocco continued until 1934 (see Chapter 22).

In theory, French colonial policy in North Africa called for assimilation—a civilizing mission to convert Arab-Berber peoples into good and loyal Frenchmen. In practice, Paris allowed European colonizers to develop the countries on a double-standard basis, their local powers steadily increased by continuing dissension in the French Government. While the Moslems enjoyed certain benefits brought by the newcomers, most notably in health, trade, and administration, reactionary colonial

657

governments dominated by *colons* soon brought conditions matching those in Indochina (see Chapter 31): extensive land ownership by Europeans and a local Moslem elite who controlled the economic and financial structure while the bulk of the people were landless and hungry, a vast illiterate body suffering a pastoral-agricultural economy with distinct feudal overtones.[1]

With one result: although each North African country was said to be pacified, the French never ruled comfortably, and force was never far removed from government. An Arab Bureau with a strong military arm put down early, spasmodic resistance without much trouble, though often with considerable brutality. But the multiplying germs of nationalism that ultimately infected Indochina and the Far East also settled in North Africa and the Middle East.

The germs attacked variously. In Tunisia, a nationalist political party, the Neo-Destour, emerged in the early 1930s under Habib Bourguiba and, despite a host of vicissitudes, continued to grow and, finally, in 1956, to win a relatively peaceful battle for independence. Morocco reacted more slowly: In the 1940s, nationalists strongly influenced by their Cairo brethren nationalists founded *Istiq-lal,* which won the backing of Sultan Mohammed V and, as in the case of the Neo-Destour, overcame multiple obstacles to wage a successful campaign for independence, again a relatively peaceful transition, occurring in 1956.[2] The process in both cases involved considerable guerrilla-terrorist activity, but, like international liberal pressures, this proved contributory rather than fundamental. Both countries owed an immense debt first to the Indochinese insurgency, which drained France of so much of her strength, including troops from North Africa, and second to the Algerian rebellion, which began in late 1954.

Algeria was a late-comer to the Arab nationalist movement, primarily because of its special relationship with France. Unlike other colonies, Algeria constituted part of metropolitan France. Europeans had begun settling in coastal areas soon after Bugeaud had put down initial resistance in 1836 and in time grew to a heterogeneous colony of over a million Frenchmen, Italians, Spaniards, and Corsicans. French culture affected Algeria more than Tunisia or Morocco; educated Algerian Moslems often regarded themselves as French rather than Algerian. Probably for this reason, no forceful leader such as Habib Bourguiba emerged from the educated classes during the fateful thirties and forties, nor did a monarchical symbol exist as a nationalist rallying point.

Despite wishful thinking of European Algerians who denied Moslems a national tradition, nationalist murmurings before World War I found voice shortly after the war, when Ferhat Abbas, representing a group of French-educated Moslems and former Moslem officers in the French army, unsuccessfully demanded social and political reforms. Returning Algerian soldiers—about one hundred thousand had served in France—and Algerian workers showed more interest in economic reforms, which, together with a demand for independence, became the rallying cry of the ENA (*Étoile Nord-Africaine*) movement, soon led by Messali Hadj, a Communist who subsequently left the party and became strongly pro-Islamic. A small Communist Party also emerged, but was banned in 1929. In the mid-thirties, a religious movement called the Association of Ulemas (religious teachers) added to the cry for reforms and independence. Though alarmed, the administration and the powerful European community turned a deaf ear to all these voices. Shortly after the war, they had neutralized Clemenceau's effort to introduce parity in the French-Moslem relationship, and the next twenty years saw no change in their attitude.[3]

In World War II, the European colony accepted Vichy rule and, in turn, gained a free hand to ban various nationalist movements and imprison such leaders as Messali. Ferhat Abbas and other prominent Moslems nonetheless survived to present the Free French Government with an Algerian Manifesto—a demand for self-determination and specific rural reforms in return for Moslem participation in World War II.[4] While promising nothing specific, De Gaulle seemed sympathetic and, once again, Moslems fought on the side of France. Ferhat Abbas and his intellectual following, now supporting a party called the AML (*Amis du Manifeste et de la Liberté*), continued to press for reforms within the system. The ENA, however, which had become the PPA (*Parti du Peuple Algérien*) " . . . advocated direct action in the countryside as the only way of achieving improvements."[5] On V-E Day, May 8, 1945, the PPA instigated Moslem riots that led to the death of perhaps a hundred Europeans in Algeria.[6] European "militia" forces, supported by police and army units, attacked Moslem settlements throughout Algeria; French authorities admitted to fifteen hundred Moslem deaths, but more realistic estimates varied from twenty thousand, reported by *Time* magazine, to forty-five thousand, claimed by Algerian nationalists.[7]

The slaughter quieted matters—temporarily. Under Governor General Chataigneau's rather liberal aegis, Ferhat Abbas converted his following to a new party, the UDMA (*Union Démocratique du Manifeste Algérien*), and continued to follow a moderate policy. Also in 1946, Messali Hadj converted the remnant PPA organization to a new party, the MTLD (*Mouvement pour le Triomphe de Libertés Démocratiques*). This party, too, seemed to follow a moderate policy despite militants who wanted to use force to fight the government.[8] Decisive action by the French Government might now have steadied matters. Instead, the Algerian Statute of 1947 merely modified the existing system, with real power remaining in hands of a new governor general, a reactionary socialist, Marcel-Edmond Naegelen. Internal administration remained lopsided and corrupt. Rigged elections in 1948 offered flamboyant proof that nothing had really changed: precisely what the European colony intended.[9]

Their error lay in believing same. As happened elsewhere, World War II had caused fundamental changes. The fall of France and the loyalty of Algeria's Europeans to Vichy had discredited the administration. Some Algerians had taken allied promises of self-determination seriously; returning veterans who had fought long and hard in Italy looked forward to overdue reforms. Instead, they found the Algerian people victims of reaction—and a few rebelled. In 1947, a small group, which included a number of war veterans, splintered from the MTLD to launch a secret paramilitary movement, the OS (*Organisation Secrète*), under the titular control of handsome and magnetic Ahmed Ben Bella, a twenty-eight-year-old combat veteran and former sergeant major in the Free French army, where he had been decorated for bravery. Drawing on Mao Tse-tung's writings, lessons of the Sinn Fein movement, and Tito's World War II resistance, in three years Ben Bella and his fellows built the organization to some five hundred trained militants. In addition, the OS won new members from MTLD ranks and, in time, attracted another underground movement, Belkacem Krim's guerrillas already active in Kabylie. The first important overt action by OS occurred in 1949, when Ben Bella, remembering Lenin's teachings, masterminded a robbery of the Oran post office, which yielded party coffers over three million francs. Following this short-lived success, French police closed in, arrested Ben Bella and other leaders, and captured numerous caches of arms. Important lieutenants fled to Cairo, however, where Ben Bella joined them after escaping from jail, in 1952.[10]

The young rebels now formed the League of Nine (*Club des Neufs*), which, early in 1954, became the CRUA (*Comité Révolutionnaire pour l'Unité et l'Action*). Ben Bella and three other members remained in Cairo as an External Delegation to drum up political and material support for the rebellion from sympathetic states. The other leaders returned to Algeria as an Interior Delegation, each to organize and train guerrilla forces in an assigned *wilaya,* or operational district. In October, the six wilaya commanders secretly met and decided to start the shooting. Their decision cannot be justified, but it can be explained. It was a decision of desperation. The majority of Algeria's nine and a half million Moslems were living in abject poverty, devoid of either dignity or hope. A French official investigation in 1954 revealed the travesty of the comforting fiction that Algeria was France:

660

... 90 percent of Algeria's wealth was in the hands of ten percent of its inhabitants; nearly one million Moslems were totally or partially unemployed, and two more millions seriously underemployed. . . . Eighty percent of all Moslem children did not go to school at all. The report stressed French achievements in road building, urban development and public health, but, taking account of the changing value of the franc, it estimated that France was spending on Algeria, in 1953, about the same amount yearly as she had spent in 1913.[11]

The French Government, rather a succession of divergent governments representing the controlled anarchy under which France labored for as long as one could remember, had recognized the unhappy situation and attempted without success to implement overdue reforms. Much of the failure rested on lack of stable government, with accompanying inefficiency, which in turn made it easier for the *colons,* some one million Europeans of whom about half were French, to sabotage reform measures in favor of rule by force, a policy in general approved by local French civil and military authorities. As had happened to the British in Cyprus and Kenya, and to French and Dutch *colons* in Indochina and Indonesia, they refused to recognize the strength of nationalist feeling that contributed to CRUA support. Such was their arrogance derived from ignorance that they failed to recognize and correct a collision course with disaster.

In choosing force, however, the rebels also displayed an arrogance of ignorance:

> . . . They underestimated both the umbilical cord linking Algeria to France in the minds of the great majority of public opinion in metropolitan France, and the diehard courage, tenacity and obstinacy of the European inhabitants of Algeria. They underestimated the military forces against them . . . [and] Algeria's importance as a pawn in the Cold War, and naively failed to realize that France's allies, however disapproving, would neither interfere nor proffer advice until French public opinion had reconciled itself to the eventuality of Algerian independence.[12]

On November 1, 1954, rebel bands—perhaps a total of two to three thousand poorly armed guerrillas—struck more than thirty targets, the majority being gendarmerie posts in the Aurès Mountains of eastern Algeria. Liberally scattered pamphlets announced that the National Liberation Front (*Front de Libération Nationale,* or FLN, the new name for the CRUA) and its army—soon to be called the National Liberation Army, or ALN—would lead Algerians to independence. If France were to grant this, the tract explained, European nationals would retain their rights and presumably France would enjoy a special relationship with the new nation. Here was a basis for negotiation. French rejection automatically meant war.[13]

French military force in Algeria numbered about fifty thousand. While armored columns struck out for the Aurès area to crush the rebels, the Mendès-France government rushed in three paratrooper battalions from France. The military showed no great concern: this was a local uprising, the work of Communist *fellaghas*, or bandits, who would quickly yield to superior power of the French army.

As any veteran of Indochina might have informed the military commander, mechanized columns accomplished little except to provide numerous targets of opportunity for lurking guerrillas. Nor should the reader be surprised to learn that simultaneous police measures only exacerbated the situation: for example, police arrested one hundred and sixty MTLD members, some of whom were moderates wanting to avoid war. Police brutality almost immediately provided another divisive issue: In December, forty-six Moslem members of the Algerian Assembly protested against " . . . illegal searches, arbitrary arrests and inhuman brutalities to which prisoners . . . are subjected." The vicious circle of terror and counterterror soon neutralized moderating forces such as those led by Ferhat Abbas. Revolution spread rapidly, the guerrillas ruthlessly killing or maiming any moderates ("traitors") who stood in the way. The new Governor General, Jacques Soustelle, inspected the Aurès area in early 1955 and found a countryside frozen by fear. Soustelle told the Algerian Assembly that he intended to pacify the country, which would continue to " . . . form an integral part of France, one and indivisible."[14]

Within months, rebellion had spread north to coastal areas and then west. In April, the French Government declared a limited state of emergency and endowed certain local authorities with powers similar to those exercised by British forces in Malaya. Soustelle's pacifying hand was checked by limited resources—in May, the army numbered only one hundred thousand. The European colony also frustrated most of his administrative reforms. He did establish a new administrative corps, the SAS (*Sections Administratives Spécialisées*), which sent young French officers to remote parts of the country to function similarly to British civil district commissioners.

The SAS was still in the formative stage when Moslem uprisings in eastern Algeria brought another wave of terror. The ghastly killings and counterkillings of August 1955 led to three important developments. The first was the effect of Moslem terror on the new Governor General. Soustelle, a young scholar and anthropologist who had served De

Gaulle in an intelligence capacity during the war, arrived in Algeria with a liberal reputation. *Colon* hostility seemed to shake his limited assurance, as did Moslem savagery; in short order, his liberal intentions disappeared like gilt in the acid of reality. The second was the effect outside Algeria: The Afro-Asian bloc introduced the subject of the rebellion into the United Nations, much against France's will. The third was the effect on Algerian Moslem "moderates" such as Ahmed Francis and Ferhat Abbas, who published a manifesto addressed to the French Government and urging "the Algerian national idea," a document that " . . . both encouraged the rebels to continue and had a considerable effect on French public opinion in France."[15]

Inept French countertactics remained the rebellion's best friend. The French military build-up was still under way during 1955, and commanders did not possess sufficient troops to carry out traditional pacification tactics. Once troops occupied important towns and villages (the *quadrillage*), few units remained for the *ratissage* (cleaning out grid areas so that SAS units could proceed with pacification) or for the *bouclage* (sealing off and combing known insurgent areas). The FLN also benefited from Arab League support, particularly from Nasser's Egypt, and from Tunisian and Moroccan sanctuaries, which provided arms and supply.

French political weakness also aided the rebels. In early 1956, the new French premier, socialist Guy Mollet, appointed Soustelle's successor, seventy-nine-year-old General Georges Catroux. In Algiers to install his new minister resident, Mollet faced a hostile European mob, which pelted him with rotten vegetables, while police stood idly by. Bowing to mob authority, Mollet canceled the appointment and named a man acceptable to Algerian *colons,* Robert Lacoste. Mollet's disastrous capitulation provided false strength to Europeans in Algeria and blinded them even further to political realities. In their own eyes, they had become a law unto themselves, an attitude that nullified further conciliatory efforts toward Moslems. Mollet's political insouciance infuriated and frightened Moslem moderates and inevitably drove more of them into supporting and even joining the FLN. Mollet's action, as analyzed by Edward Behr, did not stem from cowardice but, rather, from ignorance derived by listening to the wrong people—a tragedy, since, " . . . on any number of occasions, civilians and officers alike could have gauged the true nature of the situation in Algeria by questioning men of proven experience whose testimony was not likely to be false." Ignorant of " . . . the true nature of the situation," Mollet succumbed to military blandishments and agreed to let the army " . . . use political propaganda weapons" in addition to other pacification measures. With this decision, Mollet tacitly yielded control over the French military at a time when control was vital.[16]

The French army was in a particularly dangerous frame of mind at this time. Its collapse in 1940 and its defeat in Indochina had left it laboring under a gigantic inferiority complex. Although blaming the home front for the Indochinese disaster—the stab-in-the-back thesis so effectively enunciated by Hindenburg and Ludendorff in 1918—the army, in reality, had been greatly impressed by the Viet Minh intermingling of political and military factors to fight revolutionary warfare. Returning prisoners of war also had been indoctrinated in Viet Minh ways, and, in time, a powerful school of revolutionary warfare—*la guerre révolutionnaire*—had developed in the French army.

We are unable here to analyze it in detail; that has been done by Professor Peter Paret in his excellent book *French Revolutionary Warfare from Indochina to Algeria—The Analysis of a Political and Military Doctrine*.[17] In brief, the French school dissected Chinese and Viet Minh revolutionary doctrines and developed a counterrevolutionary doctrine that depended on powerful ideological and moral forces to produce a "dynamic strategy." If communism formed a strong ideology, then hatred of communism would form a stronger one. If Communists could indoctrinate soldiers and civilians with certain beliefs, the French could indoctrinate them with counterbeliefs.

Proponents of the new school recognized that the army would have to change its ways, relying heavily on psychological warfare in reeducating soldiers and target peoples to the glory and grandeur of a new crusade. But the nation, too, would have to change its ways: There would be no shirking, as in the case of Indochina; if government could not lead the people to support counterrevolutionary warfare, then the army would have to educate government and people! The doctrine contained certain strengths. At a time of defeat and doubt, it offered a positive program, a splendid vision of a new France. Militarily, it admitted past errors and sought to correct them, in some cases successfully, as will be seen. Its weaknesses, however, far outweighed strengths. Approaching the subject deductively, its proponents had gathered operational flowers from Mao's and Giap's works while ignoring thorny philosophical stems. The doctrine of *la guerre révolutionnaire* as applied to the Algerian rebellion failed from the beginning, because, as noted by that sound reporter C. L. Sulzberger, it ignored Mao's first lesson: " . . . If the political objectives that one seeks to attain are not the secret and profound aspirations of the masses, all is lost from the beginning."[18]

Nor is genius required to recognize the doctrine's fascist connotations. As Professor Paret asked: Is it accidental that so many of its theorists and supporters " . . . are found among the leaders of the various putsches and rebellions that shook France during the past year [1963]?" Its proponents made no secret of their disgust not alone for the Fourth Republic, which they insisted had let down French arms so badly, but also for the reigning political philosophy: In Colonel Hogard's words of 1958, " . . . it is time to realize that the democratic ideology has become powerless in the world today."[19] In the minds of the new school, democratic ideology could only be replaced by totalitarian ideology, which was and is foreign to political beliefs held by most Frenchmen.

The doctrine contained other weaknesses. In its civil application to Algeria, it was far too ambitious, considering size and training of the French army. It was also too negative: Its ideology pre-supposed a constant state of war with Communists, a war of no compromise, a fight to the finish. This was repugnant to millions of Frenchmen, including hundreds of thousands of conscript soldiers who were tired of war and held little respect for the professional army. At this crucial time, proponents of *la guerre révolutionnaire* badly overestimated the strength of appeal to fellow countrymen. They undoubtedly believed that the bulk of the army subscribed to their new mission—that of preventing a Communist takeover of the world. Despite the Communist threat and the anarchic quality of the home government, the bulk of the army, not to mention that of the citizenry, did not believe in the mission. Civil and military leaders, finding its proponents a bore, shrugged off the new propaganda. This was a mistake: Boring it was, but, as will be seen in the next chapter, it was also dangerous.

CHAPTER FIFTY-FOUR

1. Gillespie, Chapters 1 and 3. See also, Behr.
2. Bernard.
3. Gillespie, 44 ff.
4. Behr, 51. See also, Gillespie.
5. Special Operations Research Office, *Casebook on Insurgency and Revolutionary Warfare.*
6. O'Ballance, *The Algerian Insurrection . . .* , 33.
7. *Time,* February 17, 1958.
8. Behr, 55–9.
9. Ibid., 55–6.
10. Ibid., 59–60.
11. Ibid., 194–5.
12. Ibid., 62–3.
13. Gillespie, 95–6. See also, O'Ballance, *The Algerian Insurrection . . .*
14. Behr, 77.
15. Ibid., 85.
16. Ibid., 97.
17. Paret, *French Revolutionary Warfare . . .*
18. Sulzberger, 182.
19. Paret, *French Revolutionary Warfare . . .* , 112, 28.

CHAPTER 55

REVOLUTIONARY DOCTRINE OR NO, the French army continued to rely on traditional techniques in fighting the Algerian war. In March 1956, shortly after Mollet's abdication to the Algiers mob, the army executed two Moslem terrorists. The FLN replied by killing or wounding a number of Europeans—and the gulf between European and Moslem again widened, to FLN advantage. The FLN also gained when the French granted independence to Morocco and Tunisia, thus easing the flow of arms into Algeria besides providing border sanc-

SPAIN

Mediterranean Sea

TUNISIA
(Eastern Base)

Tunis
Sakiet-Sidi-Yousset
Tébessa
Aurès Mts.
Constantine
Bône
Kabylie Mts.
R. Soummam
Algiers
ATLAS
Djelfa
Oran
Sidi-bel-Abbès
Aïn Sefra
SAHARA
El-Oued
Touggourt

MOROCCO
(Western Base)

N

0   100   200 miles

ALGERIA: 1954–1962

• Towns and Cities
+++ Railways
═══ Roads
→ Rebel supply routes
◗ Wilayas (sectors)

M.E.P.

tuaries and training areas for guerrilla forces. The abortive Anglo-French campaign in Suez, during summer of 1956, further helped rebel operations by drawing off French military units. The army's interception and arrest, a few months later, of Ben Bella and several associates who were flying from Rabat to a conference called by Habib Bourguiba in Tunis was a grave error; since the party was a guest of the Moroccan sultan, the act insulted Moslem hospitality and made Tunisian and Moroccan leaders even more sympathetic to the Algerian rebel cause. The Mollet government acquiesced in the deed, thus compounding damage both by eliminating a powerful Algerian nationalist with whom to conduct negotiations, and by further alienating the most powerful leader in the Maghreb, Bourguiba, who was actively trying to promote a peaceful solution to the Algerian problem.[1] Taken with inept French military tactics, these events helped FLN to increase during 1956 to an estimated eighty-five hundred guerrillas supported by twenty-one thousand auxiliaries, who greatly expanded the rebellion.

The French military, however, enjoyed some important advantages. One was increasing strength: By April 1956, the forces in Algeria numbered 250,000, which, by utilizing conscript soldiers and reservists, would rise to four hundred thousand by autumn. Another was the factious nature of the rebellion. Ferhat Abbas and other UDMA moderates did not leap into FLN arms, but, rather, displayed an independence that, properly exploited, might well have become an important and perhaps even decisive divisive force. Nor did Messali Hadj and the MTLD join FLN ranks. Instead, he reconstituted the party into the Algerian National Movement (*Mouvement National Algérien*), or MNA, which rivaled the FLN both in Algiers and in the countryside, as well as in France proper. Although the Communist PCA joined forces with the FLN in Algiers, neither organization trusted the other, a precarious relationship that ultimately resulted in almost total demise of the Communists. The FLN and its militant arm, the ALN, were also becoming divisive. Conflict would probably have developed between the two branches—the External Delegation in Cairo and the Internal Delegation inside Algeria—even with proper communications. With messages taking up to three months to deliver by courier and with long delays in delivery of arms and supply, misunderstandings frequently occurred and rivalries flourished. Lack of internal cohesion also played a disruptive role. Tribes within one wilaya held little interest in other wilayas (precisely what Lawrence had discovered in Palestine in 1917). Tribal rivalries not only prevented co-ordinated operations, but also hindered equitable distribution of arms and supply. Ambitious and inexperienced guerrilla leaders began outright attacks on French units, a disaster that, according to Major O'Ballance, cost six thousand insurgent lives—about a third of the guerrilla army—in just two months, April and May of 1956; French authorities later claimed fourteen thousand insurgent deaths by year's end. Leadership arrests and fatalities meant the rise of new leaders such as the young Kabyle, Ramdane Abbane, who soon challenged Ben Bella's leadership. In August 1956, Abbane arranged the Soummam conference, which brought together some two hundred and fifty wilaya rebels in a valley shown as "pacified" on French military maps. Members of the External Delegation (Cairo) were delayed and never did arrive, a confusion that some observers traced to Abbane's machinations.[2]

Abbane was a rough but clever and forceful leader who now established a new governing body, the CNRA (*Conseil National de la Révolution Algérienne*) which, together with its executive, the five-member CCE, was to challenge the Cairo group for leadership of the rebellion. Abbane charged the CCE with introducing a coherent administrative system in each wilaya as well as co-ordinating wilaya operations. He also persuaded his fellows that time was ripe for an all-out urban terrorist campaign—" . . . A curfew in Algiers," he argued (in the Lenin tradition), "is worth two hundred dead in the mountains"—a dreadful decision that not only would cost the FLN numerous sympathizers abroad but would nearly cost it its existence. Ironically, Ben Bella, who recognized the error and probably could have prevented the campaign from taking place, was arrested the following month.[3]

Abbane should have moved more cautiously. A new factor, discovery of valuable oil fields in the Sahara, had stiffened French determination to quell the insurrection. The Mollet government had all but abrogated its authority over Algerian affairs when it allowed the army in Algeria to kidnap Ben Bella—and the leadership of that army was determined to eliminate the guerrillas. Optimistic military reports from the field also had favorably impressed the civil representative in Algiers, Robert Lacoste. When Algiers police failed to cope with FLN's new terror campaign, Lacoste turned the suppression problem over to Major General Jacques Massu and the 10th Parachute Division. The battle of Algiers, which began in late January 1957 and lasted until September, left little doubt in Moslem minds of French military determination and strength and little doubt in colonial minds that the French military was in full control of French policy in Algeria.

In killed, wounded, and maimed, and in brutality and terror, the battle of Algiers compares to the 1944 battle of Warsaw (see Chapter 24). The rebels started the battle with about twelve hundred well-organized hard-core terrorists supported by perhaps forty-five hundred members of the FLN, an organization financed by taxation and extortion which yielded perhaps three hundred thousand dollars a month.[4] According to one French officer, Colonel Roger Trinquier, whom we met earlier in Indochina (see Chapters 40 and 48), they faced only about a thousand police, neither trained nor equipped for insurgency warfare. Moslems relied on unrestricted, promiscuous terror that struck at innocent and guilty alike. Based in the notorious casbah, terrorists stole snake-like through the city to bomb and kill and then hide in the sympathetic Moslem quarter—one important rebel leader, Yassef Saadi, later lived within two hundred yards of army headquarters.[5]

When Lacoste turned the problem over to the army, Massu went after them. Massu was not very bright. A big man with enormous ears and a nose that brought to mind Cyrano de Bergerac, "Roughneck" Massu, as he was known, embraced excesses preached by younger proponents of the *guerre-révolutionnaire* school, colonels such as Trinquier, Ducasse, and Thomazo, who believed, like Communist leaders they had studied, that end justifies means—that fire must be fought with fire. Lacking co-operation of the Moslem population, Massu depended on informers for intelligence. He established military "special police" units called DOPs (*Détachements Opérationnels de Protection*), which incorporated Moslem defectors; he used hooded informers to identify terrorists; he formed Moslem militia units, and he

> . . . started the "ilot" system of surveillance and checking personnel, by making one man responsible for a family, and another responsible for a building or house in which there were invariably many families, another for a whole alleyway or street, and so on. In this way they were able to lay their hands on any wanted Muslim in the Casbah within hours.[6]

Counterterrorist organizations also flourished. Consisting of European *ultras,* these employed agent-provocateur techniques: blowing up Moslem and even European dwellings to provoke army reaction. Most of all, Massu's people depended on fear and duress, and their activities soon equaled anything practiced by the Gestapo in France during World War II. In addition to beatings and killings, the paratroopers used torture—the famous *gégène,* by which field-telephone wires were attached to the victim's genitals and current shot through them. Massu and some of his officers openly defended the usage, Massu himself submitting to it.[7] His intelligence officer, Colonel Roger Trinquier, later argued that a terrorist cannot claim the same honors as a soldier if he rejects the same obligations; rather, he is beholden to yield vital information such as the name of his superior. If not, he can be tortured.[8]

Trinquier's philosophy, widely shared by army and police officers, represented a tragic reversion to a medieval thinking abhorrent to many French citizens—particularly those who had suffered German barbarism in World War II. The bulk of French society, including a good portion of the army, had no idea that torture had become standard operating procedure in many army units. Greater was the shock, therefore, when such works as Jean-Jacques Servan-Schreiber's *Lieutenant in Algeria*, Lartéguy's *The Centurions*, and Henri Alleg's *The Question* revealed a military depravity that brought howls of liberal protest and a "crisis of conscience" to the army high command—a military depravity that in time would culminate in unsuccessful rebellion against legitimate government.[9] As Edward Behr later wrote, the French army, along with many other armies, on occasion, had behaved badly; in the Algerian rebellion, however, " . . . police and army brutality became a permanent and quietly efficient instrument, a weapon of war of the same caliber as the grenade or the mortar-bomb."[10] Pierre Vidal-Naquet went further:

> . . . The part played by torture throughout the Algerian war can be summed up in a few words; it started as a police method of interrogation, developed into a military method of operation, and then ultimately turned into a clandestine institution which struck at the very root of the life of the nation.[11]

French policy, which could be described as controlled genocide, seemed to work: By October 1957, the army had destroyed the FLN apparatus in Algiers; its leaders dead, captured, or fled; the city quiet. A massive French effort in the countryside also brought favorable results.

Or so it seemed. The total campaign had not eliminated the FLN. Killings and arrests and tortures that affected thousands of innocent persons had shocked the population, as ice numbs a wound. As shock wore off, as people realized this was a fight to what the army intended to be their finish, they turned increasingly to the FLN. Moderate leaders such as Ferhat Abbas not only joined the organization but became one of its leaders. Tunis and Morocco increased support of the rebellion, as did Arab League countries.

The situation in the countryside resembled a small-scale Vietnam. A rebel colonel commanded each wilaya and was responsible for civil as well as military functions. Each wilaya consisted of operational zones and subzones, and each zone, in theory at least, supported a "regular" battalion of twenty officers and three hundred and fifty men. These were full-time soldiers, the *moujahidines*, who were paid. Part-time irregulars, the *moussebilines*, the equivalent of the Viet Minh "peasants by day—guerrillas by night," assisted them, as did less-trained *fidayines*, many of whom belonged to the civil support system, the OPA, which also included women and probably children.[12]

Although FLN leaders claimed that their guerrillas acquired most arms by raids on French posts, the bulk of arms, ammunition, and supply probably came from neighboring Morocco and Tunisia. In spring of 1957, the FLN's Exterior Delegation had moved from Cairo to Tunis at invitation of Habib Bourguiba, ambitious in his new-found freedom. What became known as the Eastern Base (as opposed to Morocco—the Western Base) would support some thirty thousand rebels by the end of the year. Financed in part by Arab League countries, in part by taxes and extortions collected in Algeria and France, the FLN bought arms wherever possible; Egypt also sent arms captured from British stocks at Suez, and Syria supplied old French weapons. The system may have been rickety, but there was no doubt that it helped FLN forces inside and outside Algeria to grow during 1957.[13]

The French faced a twofold counterinsurgency task: destruction and construction, as General Allard put it.[14] Security forces had to separate the guerrilla from the civil populace and destroy him along with the political-economic infrastructure that supported him. The construction phase involved converting the population to the government's side in order to prevent re-emergence of the rebel organization. To carry out the first phase, the French relied on the traditional concept of the *tache d'huile,* modified to circumstances. The *quadrillage* requirement—setting up garrison networks in specified areas—consumed the bulk of forces. Of three hundred thirty thousand troops assigned to rural pacification during 1957–58, three hundred thousand carried out more or less static duties in occupying towns and villages. Some thirty thousand elite troops—paratroopers, marines, and legionnaires—formed a Réserve Générale, a mobile force complete with helicopters to carry out the *ratissage,* or raking operations, and the *bouclage,* or encircling operations, designed to eliminate guerrillas in each area.

Several factors combined to lessen over-all effect of French tactics. One was the inhibiting influence of the garrison concept, which tended to leave the countryside to the guerrillas, a failing already familiar from Indochina. Another was inexperienced conscripts, who could scarcely be expected to understand intricacies of guerrilla warfare, particularly since few seniors understood those intricacies. A third was the old bugaboo from Indochina: an inadequate force for the mission. A fourth was guerrilla reinforcement from neighboring sanctuaries. A fifth was FLN determination: According to Colonel Antoine Argoud, in one small village, " . . . the OPA reorganized ten times in three years, despite public executions having been carried out in the village square."[15] A sixth was French barbarism: torture, summary executions, a disregard for civilians perhaps best exemplified by Colonel Argoud's order that children should search for mines![16] A seventh was the extent of the "destruction" phase, particularly in the Kabylie, areas of which experienced repression bordering on genocide.

The French defended the garrison concept on grounds that the flag had to fly in order to instill law and confidence and thus gain intelligence essential to fighting guerrillas. The conscript problem persisted to the end: An intense psychological program designed to convert the recruit either to *la mission civilisatrice* or to a "new France," failed almost completely. The French expanded their forces with Moslems who either volunteered or were drafted for auxiliary service, usually in small *harkas* commanded by French officers and non-commissioned officers, and also in village defense forces. Although Moslem soldiers eventually numbered about 150,000, they tended to be unreliable and undoubtedly supplied a great deal of intelligence to the FLN.[17]

To neutralize Moroccan and Tunisian bases, the French navy maintained a patrol blockade that claimed right of intercept and involved the French Government in steady international imbroglio. France did not lack weapons here. As a senior member of NATO, she claimed powerful allies, and her later threat to publish a list of countries that were furnishing FLN support, including Switzerland and West Germany, effectively diminished the blockade-running operation. She could not, however, blockade the Libyan coast, and arms continued to arrive in that country for road shipment to Tunis, and also cross-country from Egypt.

Simultaneously, the French Government carried on a diplomatic offensive designed to prevent other nations from supporting the FLN. It put particular pressure on Moroccan and Tunisian governments, which, due to natural sympathy for the rebels reflected in internal political pressures, were not inclined to co-operate. It was a difficult situation: Increased pressure would further alienate one of the best friends the West had in Africa, Habib Bourguiba. To "seal off" the Tunisian border, the army began building a fortified barrier, a forty-meter-wide complex cored by an electrified fence that stretched two hundred and fifty kilometers (about 150 miles) from Bône to south of Tebessa. Surveyed by radar and human patrols and, in places, covered by searchlights and artillery, its approaches were mined, its avenues patrolled. Like all static defenses the new Morice Line held disadvantages: It cost a great deal to build (one sixth of the total cost of French military operations for a year); it required thousands of troops to patrol the often tortuous terrain; in places, it was as far as fifty miles from the border, a disadvantage corrected in time by two expedients: clearing the natives from the area and burning off brush to make a free-fire zone (*zone interdite*) suitable for ground and air interdiction, and in places building a second parallel fence; finally, it could be outflanked. The Morice Line, however, seriously impeded infiltration, though probably not to the degree claimed by military authorities.[18]

The army also moved operations closer and closer to the border, finally to exercise "the right of pursuit" into Tunisia, killing six Tunisian soldiers in the process. Instead of condemning the action, the Gaillard government defended it, which worsened already bad relations with Bourguiba's government.[19] A few months later, in February 1958, an air force colonel ordered a bombing and strafing mission against a Tunisian border village on the pretext that machine guns located there fired on French aircraft three miles away in Algerian skies! The raid killed eighty and wounded seventy-nine Tunisians, including children.[20] The Gaillard government again defended the action, this time to hostile allies as well. Bourguiba broke off relations with France and protested to the United Nations, thus "internationalizing" the war—which France had tried to prevent. Although a patchy truce emerged, the episode contributed to the fall of the Gaillard government in April.[21]

The army also ran into trouble in its *regroupement* program, which overlapped the constructive phase of *la guerre révolutionnaire*. Moving hundreds of thousands of people is a difficult task at best. The French, for the most part, did it badly. Hastily organized and almost totally inadequate centers caused thousands of Moslem deaths from cold and hunger. Word quickly spread among the people, many of whom resisted removal and turned to the rebels.

Regroupement also had another purpose: to provide security for the people and then educate them to support the government. This task fell largely to two groups: to the psychological warfare staffs of military units, and to SAS units, which, for some time, had been working in remote areas attempting to protect and mobilize the population. Of the two organizations, SAS performed more satisfactorily, yet, in the end, failed in its task. The basic fault lay in attempting to sell an inferior product, French hegemony, to people who had already tried and rejected it. Overcommitment also plagued the effort. At its maximum strength, the program utilized fewer than thirteen hundred officers, administering some six hundred and sixty sections with the help of about six hundred and fifty non-commissioned officers and about three thousand civilians. A confusion of mission also told. Professor Paret concluded:

> ... The SAS officers were less concerned with understanding the Algerians than with turning them into docile collaborators.
> From imposing French bureaucratic control and instructing the population in French principles of public health, it was a short step to advocating French social and cultural values while—implicitly or explicitly—condemning native traditions.
> Far from uniting the two races, such paternalistic tactics were divisive and could easily recoil on their users.[22]

In spring of 1958, political poverty of the Fourth Republic turned to bankruptcy, the catalyst significantly being an uprising of European ultras in Algiers. When Algerian rebels shot three French soldiers in reprisal for execution of three terrorists, the European colony spilled into Algiers' streets. With full military co-operation, angry mobs seized Government House and established a Committee of Public Safety—an insurrection seemingly blessed by thousands of Moslems, some of whom acted spontaneously, some under coercion. Failing to cope with this new crisis, the Fourth Republic fell under the weight of its own weakness. When dust settled, General Charles de Gaulle occupied the chair of power—the beginning of a curious dictatorship that, in repairing what De Gaulle termed "the degradation of the state," would bring numerous surprises to France and the world.

And to his military brethren in Algeria. De Gaulle held no intention of supporting an "integration" policy that he reasoned had come too late. If the Algerian situation was to be salvaged, he warned soon after resuming power in June 1958,

> . . . opportunities must be opened that, for many, have until now been closed. This means that a livelihood must be given to those who have not had it. This means that the dignity of those who have been deprived of it must now be recognized. This means that a country must be given to those who may have thought they had no country.[23]

De Gaulle moved slowly but steadily to re-establish state authority over the military. Dissident officers in Algeria received transfers to home commands. He ordered his new commander, General Salan, to begin replacing military administrators with civilians, and he also curtailed budget allotments for "psychological warfare," SAS, and *regroupement* activities. In September, he ordered Salan to terminate army participation in Committees of Public Safety: " . . . The moment has come," De Gaulle wrote, " . . . for the military to stop taking part in any organization which has a political character."[24] When Salan demurred, De Gaulle relieved him in favor of a civilian, Paul Delouvrier. The new army commander, General Maurice Challe, became subordinate to Delouvrier—at least in theory.

As De Gaulle consolidated his position, he moved more openly, calling for peace in Algeria. At first, he hoped to negotiate with Moslem moderates inside the country, but as he grew more aware of the real political situation, he extended overtures to the FLN, which meanwhile had established a provisional government-in-exile, the GPRA, in Tunis. Although not recognizing the new government, De Gaulle could scarcely ignore names such as Ferhat Abbas, its prime minister; Ben Bella (still in prison), its deputy prime minister; Belkacem Krim, its defense minister; and dozens of other persons representing just about every shade of Algerian nationalism. Moreover, Tunisia, Communist China, Pakistan, Morocco, Egypt, and a number of African nations had recognized it, and some were providing support.

In October 1958, De Gaulle announced a five-year reform program for Algeria, the Constantine Plan.[25] A few weeks later, at a press conference, he emphasized the continuing cost of the war, which, since November 1954, had taken the lives of seventy-two hundred French soldiers, seventy-seven thousand insurgents, fifteen hundred European civilians, and over ten thousand Moslems.[26] Offering rebels an amnesty, he called for a "peace of the brave" and even suggested, albeit cryptically, self-determination (" . . . the political destiny of Algeria is Algeria itself") and a new Algeria, " . . . a vast physical and spiritual transformation," hopefully under French aegis.[27] The FLN refused these overtures even though military pressure was beginning to hurt.

De Gaulle's words were no more welcome to European ultras or military commanders. Each group believed that a military "victory" was at hand—just as "victory" had been achieved in Algiers. The army held reasonable grounds for optimism. Increasing rebel strength had brought change in rebel tactics: Units up to battalion strength had begun attacking French positions, the prelude, according to some, of the third, or "mobile," phase of Mao-style warfare to be undertaken by the "regular" army training in Tunisia. Considering French strength and armament, the rebel action proved premature and ALN units began suffering high casualties. By the time of the frontier battles in 1958, the French claimed thirty thousand insurgent dead and thirteen thousand wounded; in early 1958, they were claiming three thousand insurgent "kills" per month. Allowing for normal military hyperbole—somewhere between 50 and 75 per cent—little doubt existed that the insurgents were being hurt.[28]

French tactics, moreover, were becoming increasingly sophisticated. General Salan and his successor, General Challe, developed a more qualitative approach by organizing *commandos de chasse,* elite units of sixty to a hundred men that disappeared into rebel country for weeks at a time, all-purpose units collecting intelligence, setting up ambushes, and attacking targets of opportunity while impressing the local population with French power. Helicopters had also come into their own; they numbered about two hundred and, although the air force retained operational control, which led to late reaction, they were beginning to provide considerable operational gains. Enemy resistance had caused the French to arm helicopters with machine guns and rockets and to protect pilots with armored seats and flak suits. Vulnerability to guerrilla fire was still high, but improved tactics reduced it: in 1957, enemy fire killed nine crew members, in 1960 none.[29]

The Challe Plan, as it became known, continued to introduce more mobile tactics. Large-scale *bouclage* operations also grew in size and intensity throughout 1959 to produce thousands of insurgent dead—according to French reports. Less-biased observers questioned that many of the dead were insurgents and that Challe's widely publicized plan was as productive as he claimed. De Gaulle himself refused to share military optimism. Challe may have frustrated the final "mobile" phase of the insurgency, but that did not mean he had eliminated the guerrilla threat. Notwithstanding Challe's assertions, urban terrorism was increasing, and guerrilla action continued in the countryside. De Gaulle realized that the French could fight in Algeria for the next hundred years, a war that for some time had been costing France over a billion dollars a year. Military action, he realized, had become of subordinate importance—a necessary prelude to bringing the FLN to the negotiating table. The sooner he could accomplish this, the better, for the GPRA was steadily gaining international sympathy, including substantial Communist support, a fact exploited by French rightists, who forever argued that the rebellion in reality was a Communist putsch.[30]

In September 1959, De Gaulle made his famous "self-determination" speech that, within four years after peace, offered Algeria a choice of three courses: to continue as an integrated part of France; to become a federated member of the French Union; or to secede entirely from French control (in which case, France would retain the Sahara region). Once again, De Gaulle probably did not expect instant action. Astute politician that he was, he probably hoped to clear the air further: to satisfy allies, particularly the United States; to cause militant FLN leaders some soul-searching and to let natural pressures exert themselves on the FLN, for instance the four hundred thousand Moslems working in France; to show European ultras and the army in Algeria his intention either to gain their acquiescence or provoke a showdown. At the time of his speech, he was aware of military recalcitrance, particularly on part of Challe and Massu, who, backed by a number of "activist" groups in Algiers, were increasingly hindering Delouvrier's reform attempts.

The crisis came in January 1960, when Massu openly criticized De Gaulle in a newspaper interview. De Gaulle promptly transferred him. A protest demonstration of European "territorial units" in Algiers exploded into an insurgency that the gendarmerie could not contain and the army refused to put down. "Barricades Week" was an incipient attempt to unseat De Gaulle. Fortunately for him, a good many units remained loyal and the action fizzled—but only after French soldiers had fired on French civilians, increasing the bitterness of the European population. The action left De Gaulle more determined than ever to re-establish state authority; in February, he obtained "special powers" for one year and, virtually in a dictatorial role, continued his peace offensive throughout 1960.

De Gaulle continued to meet obstructionism from the European ultras and his own military leaders. Certain of the latter insisted that the FLN rebellion had failed: they pointed to successful border suppression operations and to a marked decrease in size of guerrilla units and scope of guerrilla actions. They failed to understand that De Gaulle's promise of self-determination had moved rebellion to the political arena, a fact De Gaulle realized and one emphasized both by continuing guerrilla-terrorist actions where necessary to serve FLN political purposes and by massive Moslem pro-FLN demonstrations when De Gaulle again visited the country in December 1960.

To strengthen his hand further, De Gaulle held a referendum, in January 1961, which overwhelmingly approved his Algerian policy. Thus armed, he secretly approached the FLN to arrange talks at Évian. FLN fears of a doublecross had just been assuaged when De Gaulle faced another rebellion, the price of his refusal to take drastic action against dissident military commanders. Men such as Raoul Salan, André Zeller, and Edmond Jouhaud did not suffer retirement gracefully. Instead, with the help of Algerian Europeans and other senior military officers, they organized the OAS (*Organisation de l'Armée Secrète*), whose slogan was "French Algeria or Death." Early in 1960, the OAS had opened a terrorist campaign against the De Gaulle government *inside* France. The movement grew until, at some point, General Maurice Challe, De Gaulle's former military commander in Algeria who subsequently served at NATO headquarters, joined it. In April 1961, Challe and Zeller arrived secretly in Algiers. A few days later, the military junta proclaimed open rebellion and, for a few days, France stood in grave danger of falling under a military dictatorship.

As happened earlier, the bulk of conscripts remained loyal to De Gaulle, as did the commander in chief, General Gambiez, all of the navy, and most of the air force. Major O'Ballance has estimated that perhaps forty thousand troops opted for the junta, whose hard core numbered about eighteen thousand paratroopers and legionnaires. In addition, the army distributed an estimated thirty thousand arms to civilian supporters. But junta leadership seemed vague, and when other military units did not join the rebellion, the leaders lost heart. Within four days, Challe surrendered, Zeller followed suit; Jouhaud and Salan went into hiding. De Gaulle arrested five generals and some two hundred officers, dissolved disloyal units—and carried on negotiations with the FLN.[31]

The rebellion now entered a new and final phase. The FLN and ALN, already on the defensive, responded favorably to conciliatory moves by further reducing guerrilla-terrorist activity while peace talks continued. Unfortunately, this did not stop the shooting. The De Gaulle government had to fight a take-over attempt by the OAS both in Algeria

678

and in France, a seamy period, with Frenchmen killing Frenchmen, that lasted until spring of 1962. Shortly after the OAS collapsed, France agreed to Algerian independence, which, for better or worse, was proclaimed in July.

The rebellion cost both sides heavily. All told, the French army suffered perhaps twelve thousand troops plus twenty-five hundred Moslem auxiliaries killed. About three thousand Europeans lost their lives and thousands more were wounded. Algerian Moslems suffered about 141,000 deaths, according to the French;[32] the FLN estimated six hundred thousand deaths.[33]

Algeria never fully recovered from its long war of liberation. The economy was in ruins, but in view of the natural riches of the country, particularly its vast oil and natural gas deposits, repairs should have been only a matter of a few years before the government could turn to the *raison d'être* of the revolution—the improvement of its people's lives. The trouble was that, as skilled as the FLN leaders were in waging insurgency warfare, that did not make up either for their inexperience in government or for an innate and vicious cupidity that almost at once submerged the proclaimed humanitarian goals of the revolution.

After considerable legislative confusion—as a portent of things to come, a ranking FLN officer departed with most of the party's funds in early 1963[34]—a constituent assembly was formed, a constitution approved, and Ahmed Ben Bella was elected president of a single-party socialist government that would eventually establish the hallmark of Algeria's future: a deteriorating economy and limited social reforms that were the inevitable result of a highly inefficient, quarrelsome, and corrupt government. In 1965, Houari Boumedienne, Algeria's defense minister who controlled the army and who had backed Ben Bella, deposed him in a bloodless coup. Boumedienne at once suspended the constitution in favor of rule by a revolutionary council, which he headed until his death in 1978. Owing to oil and natural gas exports—Boumedienne nationalized the French-owned companies in 1971—the economy revived somewhat during his regime. His successor, Colonel Chadli Bendjedid, was not so fortunate. A drop in oil prices in the early 1980s brought economic chaos only temporarily solved by external borrowing.

That was only one of Bendjedid's problems. By now the gulf between the FLN leaders, who had vowed " . . . to create an egalitarian progressive society with an economy to match its oil wealth,"[35] and the bulk of Algeria's sixteen million people had widened to an extremely dangerous degree, and would continue to do so under the seeming indifference of the immense and corrupt governmental bureaucracy. The sizable income from oil and gas exports had been steadily dissipated in pursuing hundreds of ill-advised, socialist-inspired industrial, business and agricultural adventures. Bendjedid was shortly looking at an external debt of $26 billion, the servicing of which absorbed the bulk of external income. Meanwhile, the economy stagnated. Unemployment stood at over 30 per cent, this in a country where 70 per cent of the population was under twenty-five.[36] Owing to a lack of schools and teachers, over four fifths of the population aged twenty-five and over had not had formal schooling. Less than 50 per cent of the people were literate. Due to a scarcity of hospitals or even rudimentary clinics, endemic diseases such as tuberculosis, trachoma, measles, dysentery, and typhoid fever abounded.[37] All this and more was suffered under a government of repression so myopic as to disallow any outlet for pent-up social and political frustrations built from over two decades of misrule.

The manifold ingredients of social explosion—repression, unemployment, food shortages, and illness—coalesced in autumn of 1988 into widespread riots put down by army troops at a cost of hundreds of civilian lives. A shakened president now began a political turnaround that in 1990 brought a new constitution, an end to socialist government, a promise of free elections under a multiparty system, and the beginnings of a change to a free-market economy and to less individual and press restrictions.[38]

But the riots also brought into prominence a fundamentalist religious organization called the Islamic Salvation Front (FIS) as champion of the poor demanding an "Islamic solution" to the country's myriad problems, specifically a return to fundamentalist ways including veiled women and rule by what most Westerners regard as unduly harsh and inhibitive Islamic law, the *sharia*.[39] As FLN power weakened, as youngsters remained without jobs, as the economy further deteriorated, and as the government persevered in its blindness, the FIS attracted hundreds of thousands of young members. By the time of scheduled parliamentary elections in December 1991, of the forty-nine political parties the FIS formed the largest opposition group, the Socialist Front ranking a distant second.

A government could not have been more greatly condemned than by the result of these elections. Of 430 seats, the FIS won a stunning 189, the Socialists 20, the FLN 16. That left 205 seats up for grabs in the run-off elections slated for mid-January 1992. Of those the FIS needed only 27 to win the parliamentary majority legally necessary to pass new legislation. To win the two-thirds majority necessary to change the constitution, that is to impose a fundamentalist Islamic government on the country, they needed 97 more seats, which most political pundits believed they would win if the FLN and other parties did not get together and bring the estimated 40 per cent of the electorate which had failed to vote—some five million individuals—to the polls.

The run-off elections were never held. **FLN** and army leaders had been extremely apprehensive concerning Bendjedid's political reforms. In mid-1991, the two top FIS leaders, Abessi Madani and Ali Belhadj, had been sentenced to twelve years in jail for " . . . plotting to take charge by force."[40] Now, in early 1992, Chadli Bendjedid suddenly resigned, an ominous move compounded by army units moving into Algiers. FLN parliamentary leaders, pressured by the army and supported by important segments of the citizenry including Algeria's largest trade union syndicate, canceled both the results of the December elections and the run-off elections and appointed an interim government run by a State Council headed by seventy-four-year-old Mohammed Boudiaf, a hero of the war against the French who had chosen to exile himself as manager of a brick factory in Morocco.

The problem was what to do next. The majority of FLN and army leaders wanted to eradicate the fundamentalist menace. Other, perhaps cooler heads questioned the extent either of their evil or their electoral influence, pointing out that the FIS victory stemmed as much from protest as from religious belief. Still others argued that the Algerian Sunni Moslems were not as intensely fanatic as the Iranian Shiite Moslems, that the FIS contained a number of factions, most of them moderate, and that it was the extremists who were causing the trouble. A few brave souls suggested that the fundamentalists should be allowed to govern because they would make such a mess of it that they would soon be voted out of power.[41]

Acting as much from panic as from sense, senior government and army leaders concluded that " . . . the only way to restore order and prosperity [!] is to root out the fundamentalist leadership, isolate the militants, and purge Algeria's mosques of their political role."[42] The mosques were put under close armed surveillance, FIS street gatherings were banned, and the party was outlawed. Violent incidents occurred almost at once and by February had developed into bloody confrontations. By late February, FIS groups were barricading Islamic areas and hurling rocks at police intruders—one group of Islamic extremists killed ten policemen. Meanwhile, the top sixty FIS leaders and over a thousand subordinates had been arrested; by March, thousands of suspected fundamentalists had been moved to internment camps in the southern Sahara.[43]

Boudiaf himself adopted a plague-on-both-your-houses stance, pointing to the pervasive corruption in senior army circles, and going so far as to suggest that "FIS and long-time FLN members" be excluded from a new parliament.[44] In July, the old man who had remained loyal to revolutionary ideals was gunned down while addressing a Moslem group—not by the FIS but by a second lieutenant, a member of his presidential guard (twenty-three members of the guard were eventually implicated in the murder). Boudiaf was replaced by an FLN veteran, Ali Kafi, and the war went on.

Despite the government's increasingly stringent counterinsurgency measures, including the execution of convicted guerrilla terrorists, the militant Islamic movement continued to grow. In spring of 1993 the Algerian government announced that guerrilla activists numbered perhaps eleven hundred, but more reliable sources believe that the movement numbered from ten to fifteen thousand, including at least a thousand Islamic guerrilla veterans of the Afghanistan war (see Chapter 92), a guerrilla "army with an increasingly unified command . . . [and] a dedicated base of support,"[45] including money and arms from Islamic sympathizers in France, Tunisia, Morocco and Egypt.

Whatever the figure, the government has been unable either to break up the insurgent organizations or to stop guerrilla terrorist murders not only of government officials, policemen, and soldiers, but, commencing in June 1993, a number of prominent "professors, writers, journalists and lawyers," who opposed the uprising,[46] a new tactic designed to create a general "climate of fear" and thus further weaken an already shaky government.[47]

As inefficient and corrupt as it is, that government shows no signs of giving in to guerrilla demands, other than President Ali Kafi's vague promises of economic reforms and eventual new elections,[48] which almost nobody believes. A midsummer shakeup in the ruling High State Council resulted in even more extensive counterterrorist measures, which suggests that the government intends to ride out the storm in the hope of returning prosperity.[49]

This may prove to be a forlorn hope. The government is in desperate financial straits. Tourism, a major source of income, is virtually dead. Unemployment is high, morale low. The foreign debt is over $25 billion and steadily increasing. As of this writing (December 1993), the expensive war shows no sign of ebbing. Commencing in September a splinter group of guerrilla terrorists began attacking foreigners, nine of whom have been killed within three months,[50] a campaign that has caused a general exodus, at least of foreign dependents, and shows no signs of easing. Well over two hundred policemen and soldiers have so far been killed, and several thousand guerrillas have been killed, wounded, or jailed, with the number of executions rising almost monthly.

The sides are clearly drawn. On the one hand, a moribund government hanging on to power by means of dictatorial repression—like its French colonial predecessors; on the other hand, a powerful social-religious movement striving to seize power by violent methods—like the FLN in the 1950s and 1960s.

CHAPTER FIFTY-FIVE

1. Eisenhower, *Waging Peace* . . . , 104–5. In late 1956, at President Eisenhower's request, Habib Bourguiba, the new ruler of Tunisia, outlined a plan that called for France to grant independence to Algeria. As with Tunisia, it would be granted in stages—a plan that in the end, he believed, would prove beneficial to France. As for his own position: "The fighting in Algeria," he told the President, "holds back Tunisia and economic and social progress. I want to do everything to promote a happy solution of the Algerian problem."
2. O'Ballance, *The Algerian Insurrection* . . . , 65.
3. Gillespie, 96–100, 105. Ben Bella subsequently condemned the action in letters sent from prison to FLN leaders. Abbane himself did not long remain in power; in June 1958, FLN newspapers announced his death by a French ambush—possibly arranged by the party.
4. Ibid., 145.
5. Trinquier, 13.
6. O'Ballance, *The Algerian Insurrection* . . . , 80.
7. Vidal-Naquet, 50–1. See also, Behr, 240: This grandstand play proved nothing for, as Behr points out, Massu submitted only to limited pain, like going to a dentist, whereas torture derives much of its force from the victim's contemplation of prolonged pain; Alleg, for a vivid description of French army methods; Schalk, 66: Alleg was arrested in June 1957, and subsequently was tortured by French military authorities. Such was the outcry caused by his book that in early 1958 in France the remaining stocks were seized and further publication banned.
8. Trinquier, xv, 20–3.
9. Servan-Schreiber published his work in serial form in *L'Express* with the open support of one of Massu's generals: General de Bollardière commanded the Blida Atlas area and—brave and good man—forbade the use of torture in his command.
10. Behr, 238–9.
11. Vidal-Naquet, 15.
12. O'Ballance, *The Algerian Insurrection* . . . , 73–5. See also, Gillespie; Vidal-Naquet.
13. O'Ballance, *The Algerian Insurrection* . . . , 85 ff.
14. Paret, *French Revolutionary Warfare* . . . , 30–2.
15. Vidal-Naquet, 43.
16. Ibid., 44.
17. Paret, *French Revolutionary Warfare* . . . , 40–1.
18. O'Ballance, *The Algerian Insurrection* . . . , 92, 117–20. See also, *Time*, March 3, 1958.
19. *Time*, September 16, 1957.
20. Ibid., February 17, 1958.
21. Sulzberger, 34.
22. Paret, *French Revolutionary Warfare* . . . , 51.
23. Behr, 152. See also, de Gaulle, *Memoirs of Hope*, I.
24. Sulzberger, 91–2.
25. Tanya Matthews, 93. De Gaulle promised

   . . . that wages in Algeria would be raised to levels comparable with those paid in France, that housing would be provided for a million people, that two-thirds of the Moslem children of school age would be sent to school, that more land would be provided for Moslem farmers and that . . . 400,000 new jobs would be found for Moslems in Algeria in the next five years.

See also, Gillespie; De Gaulle, *Memoirs of Hope.*

26. O'Ballance, *The Algerian Insurrection* . . . , 129.
27. Behr, 154–7.
28. O'Ballance, *The Algerian Insurrection* . . . , 120.
29. Béthouart.
30. O'Ballance, *The Algerian Insurrection,* 160. O'Ballance estimated that by the end of 1960, Communist China was supplying half of FLN's annual $80-million budget, with Moslem countries making up the other half. In addition, terrorists extracted large sums by blackmail and extortion from Moslem workers—perhaps as much as $30 million a year in France. See also, Eisenhower, *Waging Peace* . . . , 429: " . . . De Gaulle's concern over suspected Communist influence in Algeria was strong"—and it was one reason that he shied away, at first, from dealing directly with FLN leaders; Ibid., 417: Chancellor Adenauer of Germany " . . . seemed almost obsessed with the Algerian problem" and the fear that the entire area would fall under Communist control—a fear that Eisenhower claimed he did not share.
31. O'Ballance, *The Algerian Insurrection* . . . , 180. Subsequent trials sent Challe and Zeller to prison for fifteen years; sentenced Salan, Jouhaud, and other fugitives to death *in absentia;* dismissed other officers from the service without pension; and summarily retired still others. See also, De Gaulle, *Memoirs of Hope;* Behr.
32. O'Ballance, The Algerian Insurrection . . . , 200–1. See also, Schalk, 93–4: The FLN claimed 1.5 million deaths; Jean-Paul Sartre one million. Most scholars accept the figure of 600,000 dead, including Algerian and European casualties.
33. Gillespie, 174.
34. *Encyclopaedia Britannica 1991,* Vol. 24, 933.
35. *New York Times,* December 30, 1991. I have relied heavily on this and other articles on the Algerian crisis written by the astute journalist Youssef M. Ibrahim.
36. Ibid., October 17, 1991.
37. *Encyclopaedia Britannica 1991,* Vol. 1, 264.
38. *New York Times,* December 28, 1991.
39. Ibid., December 28, 29, 1991.
40. Ibid., December 28, 1991.
41. *Forbes,* March 2, 1992.
42. *Newsweek,* March 9, 1992.
43. Ibid., February 24, March 9, 1992.
44. Ibid., July 13, 1992.
45. *International Herald Tribune,* May 15–16, 1993.
46. *Daily Telegraph* (U.K.), June 21, 1993.
47. *International Herald Tribune,* June 28, 1993.
48. *Newsweek,* May 31, 1993.
49. *International Herald Tribune,* June 28, 30, July 12, 1993.
50. Ibid., December 7, 1993.

CHAPTER 56

The Cuban Revolution • Special characteristics • Its psychological impact on the United States • Historical background • Early American presence • The Platt Amendment • American military intervention • Gerardo Machado and the strong-man tradition • Internal opposition mounts • Early rebellions • Washington intervenes • The Batista era • His strength and weakness • The political situation • The American position • Enter Fidel Castro • His background • The 26th of July Movement • Trial, imprisonment, release

AN INSURGENCY of particular importance to the United States marked the end of the turbulent 1950s. The first phase of the Cuban revolution, fought from 1953 to 1959, replaced Fulgencio Batista with Fidel Castro as Cuba's ruler—the opening act of a drama that would soon raise a Communist flag over this large island lying only ninety miles from Florida's coast.

The rebellion was peculiarly Cuban. Its outbreak surprised both Cuban and American authorities, who seemed reluctant to admit the threat to government. Its suppression, even when that threat became real, seemed generally apathetic. The insurgency followed no particular precedent, combining, as it did, peasant, proletarian, and middle-class elements which finally fused to produce popular revolution. Castro's leadership proved important, but revolution might have occurred without it. It could not have occurred without Batista's government. It is not an easy revolution to understand: It was fought in a welter of confusion compounded by divisive movements inside and outside Cuba, by American diplomatic and military ambivalence, and by dramatic and frequently erroneous press reports.

In terms of carnage, it did not approach other insurgencies of the day. Castro's first attempt to seize government, in 1953, failed at the cost of perhaps seventy rebel lives. Three years later, when he landed in Oriente province, his force numbered eighty-three men and, in a few days, had been reduced to twelve men struggling to survive in the Sierra Maestra. For months, he commanded a handful of guerrillas. As late as mid-1958, his columns counted no more than three hundred irregulars, some not even armed; at war's end, the rebel army totaled a thousand or two, with perhaps another thousand active supporters. Guerrilla columns fought but few battles and suffered minimum casualties—probably no more than fifty men were killed after reaching the Sierra Maestra sanctuary in early 1957.

Batista's small army expanded to only modest figures—about thirty thousand—despite the increasing urgency of the situation from 1957 onward. Though equipped with American weapons and supported by tanks and aircraft, in only one operation did it aggressively seek out the guerrillas, and this failed. Probably no more than three hundred soldiers lost their lives in the rebellion's last two years. Far more casualties occurred in cities and towns, where a variety of resistance organizations employed selective terrorism answered in kind by Batista's police and soldiers. No one knows how many casualties resulted from urban warfare. The Castro government later claimed that the revolution exacted twenty thousand lives; more realistic appraisals put the figure at around two thousand killed.[1]

Casualties do not necessarily determine residual importance of insurgencies. The sudden consummation of the Cuban rebellion, followed swiftly by Castro's conversion to communism, introduced catastrophic change to Cuban fortunes, besides directly affecting American strategic and commercial interests. Castro's blatant challenge to hemispheric hegemony levied a psychological impact on the United States tantamount to those experienced by France and England during their colonial upheavals, and it led to equally futile reactions. As had happened in Washington following Chiang Kai-shek's fall, charges and countercharges filled the air. A score of biased books appeared to obfuscate further the analysis of events and any lessons to be drawn from them. Subsequent scholarship, fortunately, has done much to unravel the twisted skein of rebellion. An American scholar, Theodore Draper, early attempted to place the Cuban rebellion in honest perspective[2] and a British scholar, Hugh Thomas, opened new vistas with his definitive history, *Cuba, or the Pursuit of Freedom*—a must for any reader interested in the island's past (and future).[3]

As with other insurgencies, the etiology of the Cuban Revolution was old and complex, its roots growing from soil prepared by prolonged Spanish occupation, its early blooms the 1865 and 1895 uprisings, its growth from 1898 directly related to American policy deriving from the

Spanish-American War (see Chapter 10) which cost perhaps three hundred thousand Cuban lives and brought something akin to anarchy to Cuba. The survivors, about a million and a half people living on an island roughly the size of Pennsylvania, were eager for independence but ill-prepared for self-government. Public services had broken down; people were ill and hungry; bands of Spanish counterguerrillas turned outlaws roamed the island in manner reminiscent of French *routiers* in the Hundred Years' War.

Convinced that Cubans could not govern themselves, President McKinley assigned the problem to the U. S. Army, which occupied and administered the war-torn country until 1902. As in the Philippines, most American civil and military officials tended to treat the native with contempt. General Young described García's veteran guerrilla army as " . . . a lot of degenerates, absolutely devoid of honor or gratitude. They are no more capable of self government than the savages."[4] American soldiers treated Negro guerrillas with open disdain, but got on well with Spanish survivors, and many of the latter continued to serve in official capacities. The uneven occupation produced a number of benefits to Cubans, particularly in health and education, and it also resulted in considerable U.S. commercial investment, about $100 million, mostly in tobacco, sugar, and railroads. While this brought welcome prosperity to some, it also introduced a lopsided economy, whose expansion too often depended on bribery and corruption.[5]

But for Congressional legislation (the 1898 Teller Amendment, which renounced American sovereignty over Cuba) and anti-administration pressures arising from the Philippine insurrection, McKinley might have annexed Cuba. Instead, the American Government secured indirect control through the Platt Amendment. This incredible document gave the United States the right to maintain military bases in Cuba and to intervene either to preserve Cuban independence or to maintain stable government. The United States also reserved right to ratify treaties Cuba made with other nations! Theodore Roosevelt's administration extended the legislation by forcing Tomás Estrada Palma's government to incorporate the amendment in the Cuban constitution and in the 1903 treaty between the United States and Cuba.[6]

The Platt Amendment disguised a commercial wolf in the sheep's clothing of strategic necessity. It tried to reap the fruits of colonialism without accepting responsibilities of colonialism. It was the opening chapter in the U.S.A.'s imperialistic fling, and no one quite knew how to interpret it. By the time the American Government and people came to their senses, a great deal of damage had been done.

* * *

Cuban self-government proved disastrous. Although Estrada was honest, his administration was not; a weak man, he failed to check venal officials more interested in amassing personal fortunes than in weaving sound fabric of government. When opposition developed, Estrada turned to the United States for support. McKinley's and Roosevelt's refusal to annex Cuba should have left the island to work out its own political destiny. It possibly could have happened, had the commercial element been absent. American investment soon doubled, to approximately $200 million, and the pot of gold lying beneath the Cuban rainbow seemed scarcely touched. When General Piño Guerra's guerrillas began threatening Estrada's government, Roosevelt found himself under severe pressure to intervene. He refused, but when Estrada resigned, in late 1906, Roosevelt saw no alternative.[7] A few days later, a hastily improvised force of two thousand U.S. marines landed "to restore order," the vanguard of some five thousand U.S. Army occupation troops, which remained for two and a half years. During the interregnum, a provisional governor, Charles Magoon, introduced political, administrative, and military reforms—a program only partially completed when he returned the country to its newly elected president, José Miguel Gómez, in 1908.

The Gómez government and its successor, the Menocal government, virtually legalized what the Estrada administration had practiced: wholesale corruption that made the two presidents and their senior lieutenants millionaires at the country's expense. American investment continued to increase. In 1912, to protect American interests against an uprising of Negro field hands, Secretary of State Philander Knox arranged a "preventive" landing of American marines. In 1917, marines briefly landed in support of Menocal's regime, which was being challenged by a Liberal revolution. At Menocal's request, the Wilson administration stationed twenty-six hundred marines in Cuba, where they remained until 1923, an important instrument in maintaining the fragile "stability" so sought by American commercial interests, particularly during the sugar crisis of 1920 and the election that placed Menocal's candidate, Alfredo Zayas, in the presidency.

Zayas changed nothing of Cuba's political pattern. A rich man by the end of his term, he had insured the growth of forces of discontent. In 1921, rebellious University of Havana students had organized a student federation, the FEU. In 1925, a trade union federation, CNOC, appeared, as did a small Communist Party. Zayas' successor, General Gerardo Machado, turned increasingly to strong-arm methods, as befitted one whose hero was Benito Mussolini. Machado cunningly disguised his methods, at least sufficiently to fool the Coolidge administration. By this time, however, the American Government had become so wedded to the strong-man concept of Cuba government that little fooling was necessary. Even when Machado abrogated the constitution to extend his term of office, American apologists defended the action in interests of "stability"; nor did the Hoover administration seem entirely displeased so long as "peace, order, and 'political cooperation' " would continue.[8]

If Washington turned a blind eye, influential segments of the Cuban population did not. Continued opposition had long since caused Machado to compound wholesale corruption by the unpleasant expedient of imprisoning, torturing, and murdering political opponents. With the constitution defunct and the sugar market at an all-time low, Cuba faced political and economic bankruptcy. Underground opposition spread among students and middle-class citizens. An organization known as ABC undertook " ... by the deliberate creation of terror to cause a break-down in governmental activities, so, they assumed, making action of some sort by Washington inevitable."[9] Machado blamed political assassinations of his *porristas* on "Communist" elements and replied with counterterror. Murder became commonplace: " ... Scarcely a night passed in Havana without some attempt at assassination, or some cruel measure of reprisal by the secret police"[10] Early in 1933, the CNOC called out twenty thousand sugar workers at beginning of harvest. In May, a rebellion broke out in Santa Clara.

The American Government intervened, but not quite in the way imagined by Cuban terrorists. Instead of marines, the newly elected president Franklin Roosevelt sent Sumner Welles as his ambassador to "mediate." After studying the situation and consulting with various opposition groups, Welles attempted to force Machado to step down. Deserted by a graft-ridden army, Machado abdicated in August. A ghastly period followed, in which ABC terrorists killed any *porristas* they could find. The blood bath probably took a thousand lives before the government restored precarious order by help of a U.S. fleet which effectively strengthened Welles's hand.[11]

Cuba's new ruler, Carlos Miguel Céspedes, was Sumner Welles' compromise selection. Too weak for the task, he almost at once succumbed to forces unleashed by the "sergeants' revolt": a small but powerful group of well-organized non-commissioned officers who, incredibly, led a bloodless coup that installed a thirty-two-year-old sergeant-typist, Fulgencio Batista, as army chief of staff! An exceptional man, Batista. Son of a sugar worker, he was of mulatto-Indian extraction. At age eight, he was working in cane fields; orphaned at thirteen, he attended a night school run by American Quakers.[12] He later held a variety of common-labor jobs and finally enlisted in the army, was promoted to sergeant and held a staff job that allowed him to participate in and soon lead the army rebellion.

Batista was young, smart, handsome in a way, charming when he wished to be. He possessed considerable charisma and was also a realist. Recognizing his limited strength and particularly Welles' opposition, he formed a military-student junta that replaced Céspedes with a provisional revolutionary government headed by the dean of the University of Havana's medical school, Dr. Ramón Grau San Martín.

Whether the Grau government would have effected the revolution it proclaimed is a moot question. Its radical intentions frightened Sumner Welles nearly to death, and if he failed in having marines landed to put things right, he succeeded in preventing Washington from recognizing the new government.[13] No Cuban government could long endure without Washington's approval, and no one recognized the fact more than Batista. After cementing his position as army chief—a nasty fracas that eliminated officer opposition—he installed a compromise president, Colonel Carlos Mendieta. He himself remained the real boss.

Thus began the Batista era. As with most dictatorships, a period of consolidation proved necessary to eliminate or at least neutralize active opposition. Batista possessed three allies during this crucial period: the Mendieta government, which he virtually ruled but which offered at least a façade of legitimate government; the army, which he did rule; and the Good Neighbor Policy, which caused the American Congress to abolish the Platt Amendment even while insuring American commercial dominance in Cuba.

Although Batista ruled as dictator, he somewhat mollified the Roosevelt administration (which had numerous other problems) by providing stability and continued protection of American investments. He also introduced a good many social reforms, including labor laws. If rule by army increased rather than decreased, he nonetheless permitted return of opposition groups; he not only allowed Communists a legitimate existence, but, in answer to middle-class and student opposition, he actively allied with them and with labor. Finally, he permitted election of a constituent assembly, which wrote the 1940 constitution: " . . . a real attempt at social democracy. It was, however, rarely read after it was written."[14]

Elected president in 1940, Batista continued a warm alliance with the United States and Great Britain. In the fever of war, no one seemed to notice that the new constitution became as dead as yesterday's newspaper. Bolstered by U.S. loans and huge sugar crops, the economy surged forward. In 1944, Batista stepped down. When his presidential candidate lost to Grau San Martín, head of the rival Auténtico party, Batista retired to his Florida holdings and a personal fortune estimated at about $20 million.

But not for long.

His successors, Grau and, in 1948, another Auténtico leader, Carlos Prío Socarrás, ruled in the Batista mold but without Batista's effectiveness. Corruption appeared in a thousand new forms, and from corruption grew violence until government became a riddled mass of competing forces, legitimate and illegitimate. Batista returned to this political maelstrom in 1948, as a newly elected senator. Three years later, he declared himself a candidate for president and two months before scheduled elections, stole the government in a bloodless coup d'état carried out by a group of army officers. Batista might have emerged a Salazar or a Franco—even a Bolívar or a Martí. He enjoyed considerable personal popularity despite former excesses. In general, the army supported him and, in turn, he cosseted officers and noncommissioned officers with increased pay and other perquisites. The twelve-thousand-man army was becoming reasonably well organized, trained, and equipped—the work, largely, of a U.S. military mission that operated under the terms of a hemispheric Mutual Security Pact. Batista soon installed his own followers in other key departments, particularly in the enlarged police force, and he made considerable progress in neutralizing activities of gangster elements. Promise of stable government appealed to wealthy businessmen and landowners and to the Catholic Church, but a large and reasonably articulate middle class also was tired of corruption and inept government and probably would have supported a progressive administration. The small Communist Party, the PSP, was well disciplined; its main strength lay in trade unions whose leaders Batista had paid off, and it readily assumed a working relationship with Batista.[15]

The American Government almost immediately recognized the new regime—according to some experts, a fatal error—and promised to continue supplying it with arms and military advisers. This was the McCarthy era, and Batista knew how to whisper the magic phrase "Communist threat"—little fear of the neighboring horn of plenty drying up, and almost none after the U.S.S.R. broke diplomatic relations with Cuba. As a boon, in 1953 the new President, Dwight Eisenhower, named Arthur Gardner, " . . . an unabashed admirer and ardent abettor of Batista," to Havana as U.S. ambassador.[16]

Cuba itself was prosperous enough, though with shocking inequities. The sugar market had remained healthy since the early 1940s, and the Korean War had sustained it. Ample labor and American capital existed to expand and diversify the lopsided sugar economy. Despite the financial drain of a half century of venal rule,[17] urban dwellers— 57 per cent of the population—fared reasonably well. In terms of per-capita income, Cuba's six and a half million people ranked fourth in Latin America and also ranked high in percentage ownership of such

692

material possessions as cars and radios. Trade unions were bringing social security and other advantages to the working man. With proper leadership, the country could probably have advanced to a level sufficient to support major social, economic, and political reforms.[18]

Batista nevertheless faced a number of problems that demanded urgent attention. Cuba's five hundred thousand peasants all too often lived in impoverished circumstances. Cuba's illiteracy rate was 11.6 per cent in the cities; in the countryside, it reached a shocking 41.7 per cent.[19] A team of non-Cuban economists later concluded:

> . . . in the countryside social conditions were very bad. About a third of the nation existed in squalor, eating rice, beans, bananas, and root vegetables (with hardly any meat, fish, eggs, or milk), living in huts, usually without electricity or toilet facilities, suffering from parasitic disease and lacking access to health services, denied education (their children received only a first grade education, if that). Particularly distressing was the lot of the *precaristas*—those squatting in makeshift quarters on public land.[20]

According to C. Wright Mills,

> . . . almost two-thirds of the children were *not* in any elementary school and most of those who did start in school soon dropped out. In 1950, for example, 180,000 children began the first grade, but less than 5,000 began the eighth grade. That figure is not for the countryside only; it is for the whole of Cuba, city and country.[21]

The peasants needed not only land, houses, schools, and hospitals, but also crop diversification to allow more than a few months' work each year harvesting the sugar crop. By ignoring their plight, Batista encouraged a rural dissidence that needed only to be harnessed to become a viable revolutionary force; perhaps as important, the peasants constituted the bulk of his army, a venal, corrupt, and factional body that offered the recruit no more pride in country than offered by his earlier, grim rural environment. Cuba also suffered from a high rate of chronic employment and underemployment, with accompanying poverty in the towns:

> . . . squatters living in shacks, and of course . . . slum tenements. In 1953, no less than one-fifth of these families lived in single rooms, and the average size of those families was five, according to the census. Taking the urban and rural population together, 62 per cent of the economically active population had incomes of less than $75 a month.[22]

693

Batista now faced the ugly fact that he, self-pronounced father of constitutional government, violated his own tenets. His pose as savior of democracy by rape possibly could have come off had he restored the 1940 constitution and implemented administrative reforms. Pleading need for time, he promised elections in late 1953. In the interim, he abrogated civil rights and resorted to one-man rule. Although eventually permitting "cooked" elections, he retained authoritarian rule, his power dependent on police and army, each of which harbored dangerous intrigues on the part of officials and officers as corrupt as they were ambitious.[23]

Batista did not solve these various problems, and he accomplished very few reforms. The why of his failure is not clear. Professor Hugh Thomas suggests that years of exile had made him lazy and petty. Economic prosperity probably added to his fecklessness, as did American support of his armed forces and regime. As long as he could offer "stable" government, he would continue to attract American capital and thus insure mounting prosperity. He also seems to have underestimated opposition. Cuba's security problem was not the Communist threat to the American hemisphere posed by the Soviet Union and preached by the Pentagon. It was an internal threat, and, as in the Philippines, Vietnam, and other trouble areas, it called for accurate recognition and intelligent suppression by small, specially trained units, as opposed to shiny battalions supported by armor and air and taught conventional tactics by conventionally minded American officers.

Most of all, however, it called for solution by good government. But Batista, from the beginning, refused the task of democratic government. Instead, like some fat slug, he retired into the official cocoon of the Presidential Palace seemingly secured by martial trappings of police and troops. The trappings would hold for a while. Intimidation and arrest, beatings and torture and murder would mute but not calm breezes of dissidence. When breezes swelled to winds of change, the trappings would waver and begin to snap until a final hurricane swept them away to demolish the cocoon they supported.

Enter Fidel Castro Ruz.

Castro was born in 1927, the illegitimate and eldest son of Ángel Castro, a hard-working and shrewd peasant. Although Ángel became a landowner sufficiently wealthy to leave each of seven children a considerable sum, his house lacked both bathroom and running water, as did nearly all houses in Birán, in Oriente province, an impoverished area dominated by American fruit and mining companies. Fidel attended good Jesuit schools, and, in 1945, went on to study law at the University of Havana. A poor student, he concentrated on politics, associating with campus branches of two gangster groups, the MSR and the UIR, and finally joining the Ortodoxo party; he may have participated in two political assassinations.[24] In 1947, he joined an MSR-sponsored expeditionary force that planned to overthrow the neighboring Trujillo regime, a plot foiled by the government. A year later, he headed a delegation to an anti-imperialist student congress in Bogotá; serious riots broke out—an estimated three thousand deaths resulted—and Castro escaped the country only with difficulty.

Returning to the university, he married and became active in the Ortodoxo Youth Movement. He graduated in 1950, joined a law firm, defended impoverished Cubans, and also entered politics. In 1952—he was twenty-five years old—he ran for Congress as an Ortodoxo. He protested Batista's coup as unconstitutional by filing briefs with two courts, a right granted by the 1940 constitution. After this courageous but futile demonstration of dissent, he became a full-time revolutionary and emerged as leader of various underground organizations. He had flirted with Marxism, but he had flirted with a lot else; his briefs, though powerful indictments of tyranny, do not suggest that he was a Marxist or a Communist.[25]

Castro spent nearly a year organizing and training a heterogeneous armed group with which he hoped to overthrow Batista. On July 26, 1953, his force attacked two military posts in Oriente province: Fort Moncada in Santiago and a smaller one at Bayamo, an ill-advised effort that resulted in his capture along with most of his 150-man army. Only a few on either side fell in the brief actions. Batista's soldiers and police, however, tortured and killed a large number of rebel survivors with Castro barely escaping death. At his trial in October, he defended himself, a spirited effort that concluded with his famous "History Will Absolve Me" speech, which became the hallmark of the 26th of July Movement. Castro's appeal failed to move his judges, who sentenced him to fifteen years' imprisonment on the Isle of Pines; brother Raúl, a Communist at this time, received a thirteen-year sentence.

Batista did not seem to realize that government overreaction swung a considerable number of persons to Castro's cause. In addition to abrogating various civil rights and exercising press censorship, he outlawed the PSP, a curious move in that Blas Roca's Communists had nothing to do with the rebellion and even criticized Castro's tactics. Batista, already riding the anti-Communist bandwagon so popular in Washington, now became one of the drivers. At Ambassador Gardner's urging and with CIA help, he established a special police section, BRAC (Buró de Represión a los Actividades Comunistas), designed particularly to suppress Communist activity.[26] Batista's confidence showed in May 1955 when, in an attempt to gain goodwill from dissident liberal parties, he declared a general amnesty—which freed the brothers Castro.

Prison had diminished none of Fidel's fire. From the Isle of Pines, he had sent a flow of organizational missives to various leaders of the Movement. He read a great deal and, though he quoted Marx, he seemed to prefer José Martí's inspiration. He early concluded that unity was essential. As he wrote to a friend:

> ... I must in the first place organize the men of the 26th of July and unite, into an unbreakable bundle, all the fighters, those in exile, those in prison, those free, who together amount to over eighty men implicated in the same historic day of sacrifice. . . . Conditions indispensable for the integration of a true civil movement are ideology, discipline, leadership. All are desirable, but leadership is essential. . . . [27]

CHAPTER FIFTY-SIX

1. Thomas, *Cuba* . . . , 1044. See also, Goldenberg; Draper, *Castroism* . . .
2. Draper, *Castro's Revolution* . . .
3. Thomas, *Cuba* . . . See also, Chapman; H.A. Herring; Batista.
4. Thomas, *Cuba* . . . , 410.
5. Ibid., 502: The real figure is higher, since land bought in huge parcels by U.S. companies was so cheap; the American Government eventually rented the Guantánamo base area—45 square miles—at a rent of $2,000 a year!
6. Wood, 48–50. See also, Special Operations Research Office, *Casebook on Insurgency and Revolutionary Warfare.*
7. Thomas, *Cuba* . . . , 478. To clarify matters, McKinley sent his Secretary of War, William Howard Taft, to Havana. Taft reported unfavorably on the rebel movement: " . . . It is not a government . . . only an undisciplined horde of men under partisan leaders. The movement is large and formidable and commands the sympathy of a majority of the people of Cuba but they are the poorer classes and uneducated." See also, ibid., 481–2: Roosevelt cabled Taft:

   > . . . If the Palma [Estrada] government had shown any real capacity or self-defense and ability to sustain itself and a sincere purpose to remedy the wrongs of which your telegrams show them to have been guilty, I should have been inclined to stand by them no matter to what extent, including armed intervention. But as things already are we do not have a chance of following any such course . . . [since] they absolutely decline either to endeavor to remedy the wrongs they have done or to so much as lift a hand in their own defense . . . we must simply put ourselves . . . in Palma's place, land a sufficient force to restore order and notify the insurgents that we will carry thru [sic] the program in which you and they agreed. . . .

8. Wood, 51.
9. Thomas, *Cuba* . . . , 595. See also, Phillips: ABC used a cellular organization based on a secret French revolutionary society.
10. Welles, 194. See also, Wood, 59–69, for a detailed analysis of the Welles negotiations; Hull.
11. Phillips. See also, Wood.
12. Chester, 6. This fulsome account must be read with care: Chester was Batista's public-relations adviser. See also, H.L. Matthews, *The Cuban Story;* ibid., *Castro* . . .

13. Wood, 87 ff. Grau called Welles's non-recognition policy " . . . a new type of intervention—intervention by inertia," that "intensifies the very ills it claims to pacify, maintaining a condition of intranquillity in our social and economic structure."
14. Thomas, *Cuba* . . . , 720.
15. Goldenberg, 112–13.
16. Draper, *Castro's Revolution* . . . , 162. See also, ibid., 39: In 1945–1960, U.S. military aid to Cuba totaled "only" $10.6 million; Tannenbaum; Taber.
17. Taber, 304:

> . . . Felipe Pazos, head of the Banco Cubano Continental, Cuba's largest private bank under the Batista administration, said that graft on public works during the seven years of Batista's rule came close to 500 million pesos on a total public-works budget of less than eight hundred millions.

18. Draper, *Castroism* . . . , 79, 94, 98, but per-capita measure of income is often misleading. See also, Seers, Bianchi, Jolly, and Nolff, 18: In 1958, Cuba's per-capita income had risen from the 1952 figure, yet " . . . averaged about $500 or one-fifth as much as the average in the United States (far lower even than in any Southern state there)"; Goldenberg.
19. Draper, *Castroism* . . . , 104.
20. Seers, Bianchi, Jolly, and Nolff, 18.
21. Mills, 45.
22. Seers, Bianchi, Jolly, and Nolff, 18.
23. Taber, 304:

> . . . The officers of the general staff—Tabernilla and the rest—were notoriously Cuba's greatest smuggler of automobiles, refrigerators, cigarettes, whiskey; the police fattened on the brothels and invested their illicit gains in apartment houses; Batista himself received a slice of everything, including the fantastic revenue of the great gambling casinos run by American gangsters.

24. Goldenberg, 147–50.
25. Taber, 29, cites one of the briefs.
26. Thomas, *Cuba* . . . , 855.
27. Ibid., 858.

CHAPTER 57

IN LATE SPRING OF 1955, Fidel Castro traveled to the United States, where he raised several thousand dollars for "the cause." In Mexico City, he rounded up other Cuban exiles, mostly middle-class dissidents belonging to the Movement, and put them on a ranch to train for invasion—the task of one Colonel Alberto Bayo, a former Cuban air force officer, a veteran of the Spanish civil war, and supposedly an expert in guerrilla fighting.[1]

Enter Ernesto Guevara Lynch.

Che Guevara was twenty-six years old when he met Castro in Mexico. Son of a left-wing Argentinian architect, he had extended a medical career to revolutionary politics. He had participated in several unsuccessful attempts to depose Juan Perón, and the previous year had allegedly served in a minor capacity in Arbenz's Guatemalan Communist government. After Arbenz's overthrow, he went to Mexico and was working either in a heart institute or as an itinerant photographer (the record is cloudy) when he met Castro. Politically, he was far left, though

698

not necessarily a Communist. He was well read in Marx and Lenin—he carried their books with him—and he was anti-United States, mainly because of the CIA's role in Guatemala.[2] He enthusiastically joined the Movement and, despite chronic asthma, devoted himself to serious guerrilla training, serving also as the army's doctor.[3]

Castro himself paid little attention to operational matters. Instead, he continued to seek support both inside and outside Cuba. The internal situation was scarcely conducive to his plans. Batista seemed stronger than ever. After rigged elections returned him to the presidency, he received a fulsome Vice-President Nixon and, later, Allen Dulles, head of CIA. In early 1956, he offered an olive branch to opponents and began the short-lived *Diálogo Cívico*. Cuba's economy was expanding and, to the casual observer, Batista's government appeared stable.[4]

Batista's refusal to negotiate in depth with opposition groups and to restore civil rights had created a good deal of dissidence, however, not only outside government but inside and particularly in the army. Serious incidents including assassination of Batista's intelligence chief plagued the government during 1955 and 1956. Splinter opposition groups formed and dissolved; students continued to protest through the FEU's newly formed militant group, the DR (Directorio Revolucionario), which agreed to support Castro, although most of these groups did not recognize Castro and the Movement as the key to Batista's overthrow. Castro did gain other new allies from the remnant MNR, notably Frank País, a Baptist and former teacher in Santiago, whom Castro named as head of all "action groups" in Cuba, and Armando Hart and Faustino Pérez in Havana. Cuban exiles in the United States and Mexico also supported him.

Castro was plagued by Batista's secret police, who arranged raids by Mexican police on his various headquarters and even arrested him. Such were the vicissitudes of Cuban politics that Castro now gained an important backer: Prío Socarrás, Cuba's former President, who was spending millions in trying to overthrow Batista, donated at least fifty thousand dollars to Castro. Castro used fifteen thousand dollars to buy a battered yacht, *Granma*; he also procured arms and supply, and in late 1956, *Granma* sailed for Cuba with Castro and eighty-two guerrillas aboard. Castro planned to land with the help of local guerrillas. The new army would then attack Manzanillo garrison to capture arms and equipment. Simultaneously, urban terrorists would attack various targets, and finally a general strike would bring down the government. In case of a general uprising, Castro's force would arm the peasants and march on Havana; in case of trouble, it would escape to the mountain vastness of the Sierra Maestra to organize and train a volunteer army.[5]

This was an extremely optimistic plan. Frank País, Castro's agent in Santiago, had warned him against it. In the event, no local guerrillas met *Granma*. Badly overloaded, she landed late and off course, disgorging passengers in a swamp where much food and supply were lost. Even before she landed, País' people, some three hundred young rebels, had attacked various targets in Santiago, a fiasco, as it turned out. Most other "action groups" remained inactive.

No general uprising—no local uprising. A Cuban frigate spotted *Granma;* troops and planes rushed to the coast. With help of a turncoat guide, soldiers cornered the guerrillas in a cane field and killed or captured about seventy. Twelve or fifteen survivors, including Castro, his brother Raúl, and Che Guevara, who was wounded, escaped to the Sierra Maestra. For several weeks, they lived precariously, unable to trust most peasants, almost constantly hounded by army patrols.

This was what Che later categorized as "favorable ground" for guerrillas, and though patrols often came close, they never captured the errants. The Sierra Maestra was too big, the terrain too difficult, for troops to plug all exits. Moreover, the peasants, including large numbers of impoverished *precaristas,* or squatters, proved receptive to revolutionary propaganda, notably the old song Land to the Landless. In time, Castro established a "safe" base and set to the task of revolution.[6]

The original plan to overthrow Batista's government having failed, Castro adopted a two-front strategy: warfare in cities and warfare in the country, the one (the *Llano*) to support the other (the *Sierra*)—or vice versa. Urban warfare—strikes, riots, and terrorism—fell to Civic Resistance (*Resistencia Cívica*) movements in Havana and Santiago, which forced the government to keep numerous army units in cities and thus ease pressure on guerrillas in the Sierra Maestra; urban units also sent money, arms, supply, and recruits to the mountain sanctuary. Rural guerrillas began to enlarge the mountain base by enlisting peasant cooperation while training a regular army. Simultaneously, Castro's guerrilla units began to strike small army outposts such as La Plata, which yielded arms and ammunition. This and other attacks goaded the army into ever more repressive measures that ensured revolutionary growth in both cities and countryside.

For a long period the urban effort sustained the rebellion. The "peasant revolution" later claimed by Castro and publicized by Che Guevara, Régis Debray, and C. Wright Mills did not exist—neither at this time nor later. Unlike Mao Tse-tung and Ho Chi Minh, Castro had not prepared the peasantry; he and his lieutenants were intellectuals, and neither class easily identified with the other. Rather than turning peasants of Oriente province into a grand army, Castro had all he could do to prevent peasants from turning him in. Life in the mountains also proved hard: morale plunged. Castro concerned himself more with security and sustenance than with fighting.

At this point, February 1957, the outside world knew little either of Fidel Castro or the rebellion. Taking the government's word, United Press and the *New York Times* had reported Castro's death in early December. Batista, who, in private, referred to the guerrillas as "a bunch of bandits," seemed to control the situation, and the Eisenhower administration continued to bless him. An American military advisory group daily strengthened his army; Batista and his officers received American decorations, and American officers received Cuban decorations.[7] The Cuban economy was booming, with large increases in American investments. Batista's propaganda machine continued to insist that Castro was dead; his security forces added to the illusion by promptly and ruthlessly suppressing local outbreaks. On Christmas Day 1956, a provincial commander rounded up, tortured, and executed twenty-two men and boys, a stupid act exploited by rebels as "Batista's Christmas Present."[8]

To dispel the notion of security and to broadcast his intentions to the world (following Grivas' example in Cyprus), Castro arranged a rendezvous with a senior *New York Times* editor, Herbert Matthews, a fifty-seven-year-old peripatetic reporter nudging the Richard Harding Davis tradition. In mid-February 1957, Castro agents shepherded Matthews to Castro's camp in the mountains. Castro immediately impressed him: " . . . a powerful six-footer, olive-skinned, full-faced, with a shapely beard. He was dressed in an olive grey fatigue uniform and carried a rifle with a telescopic sight of which he was very proud."[9] They spent the night talking, or, rather, whispering, since, according to Matthews' dramatic account, Batista's soldiers were hovering nearby. Castro evidently whispered persuasively: Matthews, who was with him less than a day, became as pro-Castro as Ambassador Gardner was pro-Batista. The first of three articles opened:

> Fidel Castro, the rebel leader of Cuba's youth, is alive and fighting hard and successfully in the rugged, almost impenetrable fastnesses of the Sierra Maestra.

Matthews found Castro's personality " . . . overwhelming. It was easy to see that his men adored him. . . . Here was an educated, dedicated fanatic, a man of ideals, of courage and of remarkable qualities of leadership . . . one got a feeling that he is now invincible." As for his aims:

> . . . His is a political mind rather than a military one. He has strong ideas of liberty, democracy, social justice, the need to restore the Constitution, to hold elections. . . . The program is vague and couched in generalities, but it amounts to a new deal for Cuba, radical, democratic and therefore anti-Communist.

Castro whispered to the reporter:

> ... We have been fighting for seventy-nine days now and are
> stronger than ever. . . . The soldiers are fighting badly; their morale
> is low and ours could not be higher. We are killing many, but when
> we take prisoners they are never shot. We question them, talk
> kindly to them, take their arms and equipment, and then set them
> free. . . . Batista has 3,000 men in the field against us. I will not
> tell you how many we have, for obvious reasons. He works in
> columns of 200; we in groups of ten to forty, and we are winning.
> It is a battle against time and time is on our side.[10]

The articles caused a furor in the United States. Batista had recently
lifted censorship, and they were also published in Cuba where officials
immediately denied that a meeting had taken place. The *New York
Times* replied by publishing a photo of Castro and Matthews in the
mountains. Cuban dissidents reacted enthusiastically to the story, with
many townspeople joining Civic Resistance units. Like the poet Byron,
Castro and the Movement awoke famous. A CBS television documentary filmed in the mountains a few weeks later added to Castro's now
considerable fame in North America.

Matthews had bought a gold brick. No one, probably including
Castro, knew his political loyalties at this time. A complex man, Castro,
" . . . as much demagogue as idealist, as much adventurer as revolutionary, as much anarchist as Communist or anything else"—superfi-
cially a bright man, but an undisciplined man whose brain was not to
cope with the challenge of democratic government, whose quixotic personality was to take refuge in the role of twentieth-century "Leader,"
with the disaster it entailed.[11] But all this lay ahead. At the time of the
Matthews visitation, Castro's background was known. Despite relatively moderate social, economic, and political reforms called for in the
"History Will Absolve Me" speech, he obviously was an angry young
man who stroked and sometimes embraced far-left philosophies. Matthews found Raúl Castro "slight and pleasant" but said nothing of his
known Communist background, nor did he mention Che Guevara,
much less *his* background.

Matthews also falsely reported Castro's strength. What seemed an
endless flow of guerrillas in and out of the Castro camp was the same
group, herded by brother Raúl. This was the force that " . . . had been
fighting for seventy-nine days"—fighting mainly to stay alive. By Castro's later admission, his "army" at this time consisted of eighteen
men![12]

Thus the foundation of a myth: in part, the result of sensational, as
opposed to in-depth, reporting. How to explain this monumental ab-

erration on the part of a senior *New York Times* editor? Matthews helped us when he later wrote: " . . . I knew I had a sensational scoop. I exulted at the fact that at the age of fifty-seven I could still show a younger generation of newspapermen how to get a difficult and dangerous story, and how to write it. And I was moved, deeply moved, by that young man."[13]

Pride first, emotion second. But on what other grounds did Matthews justify his positive assertions? Where was the discipline of objectivity? Matthews later tried to justify his reporting, but it remains cheap and tawdry stuff—a costly episode that should come to the minds of those persons who write words for publication and who are tempted to abnegate the tremendous responsibility involved.

Despite Matthews' publicity, Castro's situation remained precarious. An influx of fifty recruits allowed him to organize his force into platoons, which often lived and fought independently. These units worked hard in attempting to win over local peasants, but their support probably depended as much on repressive army counterguerrilla measures and on landlords seizing land temporarily vacated by precaristas (at army orders) as on Castro's blandishments. This does not detract from the work and accomplishments of the various columns, and Che Guevara's account of life in the mountains is well worth reading as a primer on guerrilla warfare.[14]

Castro and Che claim to have developed guerrilla techniques independent of either Mao's or Giap's teachings.[15] Whatever the truth, they bore a marked resemblance to these teachings. They concentrated on agitation and propaganda techniques to win over peasants and gain their support, both active and passive—what Guevara called " . . . dressing the guerrillas in palm leaves."[16] Small bands raided army outposts and ambushed army columns and convoys to gain arms and supply and prisoners (treated well and released) and to provoke the government to extreme countermeasures. In May, the guerrillas were strong enough to carry out a successful frontal attack in daylight against a defended village.

The main accomplishment was survival during a critical period—what Guevara called the nomadic phase. Whether we like it or not, Castro was (and is) a charismatic figure with tremendous appeal to a large number of his countrymen. By keeping the standard of revolt flying in the Sierra Maestra, he succeeded in polarizing opposition elements that daily became more daring in the cities. Urban guerrilla tactics proved a two-edged weapon, particularly when they were uncoordinated and lacked single political purpose, and various urban movements suffered some serious defeats. Time favored the guerrillas only because Batista failed to cope intelligently with the situation. Political mistakes aside (though here lay the key to his ultimate defeat), his counterguerrilla tactics proved inept. Conventional efforts to "seal" the guerrillas in the mountains and to bomb and starve them into submission were expensive flops. Summary evacuation of precaristas played into landlord hands and increased already wide dissatisfaction to bring more security and recruits to Castro. His strength in 1957 amounted to only about two hundred guerrillas operating in small units that defied the keenest bombardier's eye. The guerrillas daily were growing tougher and, for some time, had existed, when necessary, on one meal a day. As with other guerrilla units throughout history, Castro's people were becoming increasingly self-sufficient. Small workshops appeared, a dispensary, armory, a shoe factory; the guerrillas printed and circulated a mimeographed newspaper and, in time, built a cigar factory! And all in remote mountain valleys approachable only through most difficult and hostile terrain.[17]

By early 1957, press and television coverage was making Cuba a domestic political issue in America with Castro rapidly emerging as Hero against Villain Batista. That spring, Eisenhower removed Ambassador Gardner (no easy task) in favor of a generous Republican backer, Earl Smith, a fifty-four-year-old investment broker with Ivy League background—his first wife was Consuelo Vanderbilt—who lacked diplomatic experience. Eisenhower's choice was unfortunate. The situation demanded a master, not a student, a person trained in professional diplomacy with sufficient local knowledge to unravel the complex political snarl. The Eisenhower administration was veering toward what it called a "neutral" attitude. Smith was instructed to " . . . alter the prevailing notion in Cuba that the American Ambassador was intervening on behalf of the government of Cuba to perpetuate the Batista dictatorship."[18] Considering decades of involvement, American neutrality was as ludicrous as the attempted "neutral" role of the British in Palestine after World War II—a fact that a competent ambassador would have stressed to the Secretary of State. It perhaps would have done no good. The Administration, the State Department, and the military were split into pro- and anti-Batista factions, a split that carried to the Havana embassy, where the CIA was operating virtually independently of the ambassador. The situation called for a united stand on the part of his embassy—and perhaps no one could have achieved this, considering the military-political schisms of the day and the bewildered man in the White House.

Eisenhower apparently did not realize the rotten structure of Batista's government. Batista's crusade against "communism," his expanding economy and so-called stable rule were daily attracting diverse American investments, which only added to the strength of the pro-Batista lobby in Washington. And yet American officials, diplomats, CIA agents, and newspapermen were reporting the sordid and increasingly obvious facts.

Positive action in mid-1957 might not have salvaged anything in the end, but it was the only hope: To let matters continue on a disaster course, to pursue a policy of diplomatic "neutrality" not only solved nothing but caused considerable harm. For "neutrality," as defined by the Administration, meant arms and shipments to Batista and harassment of anti-Batista forces in the United States; it meant continued presence of the American military mission in Havana—and all this, in Cuban minds, spelled support of the regime. This produced two results. So long as Batista felt that he could count on continued American support, he refused to change his ways. Yet his regime was growing so distasteful that theretofore moderate and *attentiste* Cubans were veering toward the opposition. A scholar of the period later concluded:

> . . . It would appear that American policy in this period was so inept and ineffectual that it was pro-Batista to Castro and pro-Castro to Batista. On the whole, however, Batista was favored as long as he was capable of benefiting from favors, and this period constitutes a sorry and sometimes shameful interlude in the history of recent Cuban-United States relations.[19]

Throughout summer of 1957, the threat to Batista's government steadily grew in scope. In July, two opposition leaders from Havana, Raúl Chibás, of the Ortodoxos, and Felipe Pazos, a respected economist, visited Castro to work out an alliance. The Pact of the Sierra called for a united revolutionary front to oust Batista in favor of free elections and democratic government. Significantly, it asked Washington to stop sending arms to Batista and otherwise not to intervene in Cuban affairs.

Meanwhile, terror in the towns continued to do Castro's work for him. Toward the end of July, his chief organizer, Frank País, fell to police bullets in Santiago. The funeral brought a massive and impressive demonstration by Santiago mothers. Ambassador Smith witnessed this sad group, which Batista's police broke up with a violence that caused the new ambassador's public protest (and, in turn, elicited Batista's protest against Smith's statement). A strike followed, which police and troops savagely broke within a week.

By autumn of 1957, civil war existed in Cuba. In September, dissident naval elements working with the 26th of July Movement (and probably the CIA) attempted a mutiny, an abortive effort called off at the last minute. Not getting the word, Cienfuegos rebels rose, captured the base, and seized most of the town. Troops, supported by armor and aircraft, arrived in the afternoon and soon eliminated all opposition, killing perhaps three hundred rebels. The revolt made headlines in the

United States. A small anti-Batista bloc in Congress objected to American arms being used to suppress internal disorders and there was criticism of Batista's strong-arm methods in the press. Some State Department officials began talking about prohibiting further arms shipments to Cuba.[20] Influential voices spoke just as loudly in defense of such shipments, and there the matter rested—for the moment.

Castro's guerrillas meanwhile made several small but successful attacks on outposts, and at least one ambush of a relief column. Castro now controlled about two thousand square miles of Oriente province and was strong enough to send two columns from the mountains: one, seventy men, of whom only twenty-eight were armed, under Juan Almeida, to work slowly toward Santiago; the other, sixty-five partially armed men under brother Raúl, to work north toward the Central Highway.[21] Local columns, one commanded by Che Guevara, continued to expand the Oriente base, striking at army outposts in fringe areas. All was not roses for Castro, however. His people remained desperately short of arms, and supply was also difficult. In early 1958, the American reporter Dickey Chapelle visited Castro: " . . . at one point I lived on raw sugar cane for two days, and at another time I ate only one meal a day for five days in a row."[22] Contrary to sensational reporting by American correspondents, Castro's total force numbered closer to three hundred, than to the several thousand alleged. His army lacked discipline, while a good many peasants refused his blandishments and had to be coerced and (foreshadowing the future) sometimes executed.[23] In December, he ordered widespread burning of the sugar crop which caused considerable resentment and was later canceled. Representatives of various opposition groups meeting in Florida presented him with the Miami Pact, which called for a joint resistance effort under a Council of Liberation, a notion he angrily rejected while criticizing Prío Socarrás' followers for storing arms in Havana, where they most likely would be captured, when they were needed in the countryside.

Batista, on the other hand, counted some positive gains. Despite bombings and murders and the fighting in Oriente, the Cuban economy continued to prosper and more capital to flow in, mostly from the United States.[24] The U.S.A. was also providing weapons including armored vehicles. Security forces in cities kept terrorists splintered and frequently on the run.

Neither CIA nor State Department officials favored Castro so much as they condemned Batista. While he burbled on about spring elections, police and troops continued to operate with such undisguised violence that theretofore-neutral agencies began to swing over to the revolutionary cause. The Communists, whom Batista had been blaming all along, only started to veer toward Castro's support in February 1958. Significantly, prominent church leaders and judges also began protesting. In mid-March, a Havana magistrate ordered indictment of two of Batista's hatchet men (and barely escaped with his life). Batista suspended constitutional guarantees, reimposed censorship, and postponed scheduled elections. The university long had been closed; secondary schools now closed. Urged by resistance leaders in the city, Castro ordered a general strike for early April, to be followed by a massive civil-disobedience campaign throughout the country.

A blow to Batista far worse than these was about to fall. The American public had become increasingly upset by Batista's brutality and by liberal press reports that portrayed Castro as a liberator who "promised genuine representative government."[25] Cuba had become a domestic political issue. Eisenhower could no longer watch, he had to act. Citing the charter of the Organization of American States, he placed an embargo on further arms shipments to Batista.

The arms themselves were not so important as the moral effect of the deed. Batista at once ordered arms from Europe and England. He could not replace the tacit support of the Eisenhower administration, even though, ambiguously enough, the Administration bowed to Pentagon pressures and left the military advisory mission in Havana. Ambassador Smith remained close to Batista, and the U. S. Army tactlessly decorated one of Batista's pet colonels with the Legion of Merit (for prior services on the Inter-American Defense Board). The arms embargo nonetheless proved a welcome shot in the arm to the rebels, who hastened plans for a general strike. They may have moved too rapidly. Some evidence suggests that Castro himself did not really favor the tactic, perhaps because of its organizational difficulties, perhaps because success would have allowed a junta to take over. Whatever the case, the strike, or what Hugh Thomas more accurately calls an urban uprising, failed, and caused Castro to resume guerrilla tactics in both cities and countryside.* Batista answered in two ways, the first being increased counterterror, with emphasis on students who were " . . . blamed as the main troublemakers. . . . It became safer for young men to take to the hills than to walk in the streets."[26]

Next came Operation Summer, the biggest military operation in Cuban history, launched toward end of May and designed to eliminate Castro. Thirteen combat teams of about three hundred fifty men each— some forty-five hundred troops—supported by tanks, artillery, naval gunfire, and aircraft, and supplemented by Rural Guard units, pushed in from two directions toward Castro's headquarters.

The attacks progressed satisfactorily for a few weeks, then petered out. Batista's two senior commanders loathed each other. Like Rennen-

---

* Castro would have been wise to have read Chorley on the efficacy of the general strike in the history of revolutionary warfare.

kampf and Samsonov, who brought the Russian armies to disaster at Tannenberg in 1914, they refused to co-operate either with each other or with the General Staff. Batista's orders tied up about a quarter of the troops in guarding coffee and sugar plantations in Oriente. Army morale, in general, was poor; most units were untrained for guerrilla warfare. Upon leaving the lowlands, they succumbed to fatigue and disease; the rainy season slowed them even more.[27] They pushed on, however, and, by mid-June, had boxed Castro into a four-square-mile area; in his later words: " . . . Our territory was reduced and reduced until we could not reduce any further."[28] But now columns lacked sufficient strength to deliver a *coup de grâce,* nor were reinforcements available to help them.

Nor had the push fragmented the guerrillas. Learning of Batista's plans in ample time, Castro pulled in his outposts and his roving units. As soldiers advanced, he retreated. Knowing literally every move made by the army, he kept one step ahead. When the columns reached the end of their tether, he attacked. One army column, nearly a thousand men, lost two thirds of its strength in killed and wounded, not to mention loss of arms, radios, and code books.[29] Batista's army was soon on the run. The retreat yielded rifles, machine guns, mortars and bazookas, even a 14-ton tank.[30] The entire action cost the guerrillas perhaps twenty-seven killed and fifty wounded.

Batista's army was still extricating itself from the Sierra Maestra when Raúl Castro's guerrillas struck in the north to protest American delivery of rockets to the army by kidnaping a number of American and Canadian mining employees, along with twenty-seven American sailors and marines from Guantánamo and several officials of United Fruit Company. This bold act caused ranking officials in Washington to argue for armed intervention against the guerrillas, but the storm blew over when Raúl released them and they reported that they had been well treated.[31]

Batista's failure in the countryside, graphically described to the Cuban people by Radio Rebelde broadcasting from the Sierra, brought near panic in top government circles. Batista attempted to counter Castro's growing popularity with incessant propaganda and large rewards, such as a hundred thousand dollars offered for the capture of the bearded guerrilla leader. In cities, police rounded up thousands of "suspects" in a desperate attempt to quell growing revolution fed by rebel broadcasts. In July, in Caracas, agents of the Movement brought together representatives of other underground groups (Communists excluded) to form a Junta of Unity (Frente Cívico Revolucionario Democrático), which designated Castro commander in chief of revolutionary forces and issued a revolutionary manifesto. Although Batista prevented publication in Cuba, it was published in the United States and elsewhere in the hemisphere and was broadcast in Cuba both from stations in Caracas and from Radio Rebelde.[32] About this same time, the Communists, who had been edging closer to Castro and the Movement since early in the year, saw the light and sent a representative to the Sierra, much to the delight, no doubt, of Raúl Castro and Che Guevara.

Failure of Operation Summer sounded the knell to Batista's hope of restoring control in southern Oriente. A large part of the area now lay under Castro's direct or indirect command, to the extent that local mills paid him a tribute of fifteen cents per 250-pound bag of sugar shipped to Havana—an income, according to Batista, of millions of dollars used to bribe more soldiers and buy more weapons. In August, Castro established central headquarters in the hills above La Plata. A few weeks later, his units started toward the coastal city of Santiago. Simultaneously, Guevara and another lieutenant, Cienfuegos, led columns west, toward Las Villas province, where Guevara was to establish a new base and take command of Directorio guerrilla groups fighting in the Escambray area. Both Guevara and Cienfuegos have written graphically of the hardships of this forty-day march. Although the enemy shot up one of Guevara's units, the guerrillas received considerable help from local Communists; they may also have bribed Batista's local commander in Camagüey—the suggested figure is one hundred thousand dollars—to let them transit the province. By end of October, Guevara and Cienfuegos had absorbed the Directorio and Communist units and were controlling a large portion of Las Villas, even going so far as to distribute privately owned land to local peasants. Guevara now began working across the island to sever the government's east-west communications.

Castro's columns meanwhile had snaked toward Santiago and other towns and were cutting communications and ambushing increasingly demoralized army units. Castro increasingly resembled an army theater commander more than a provincial guerrilla leader. Political envoys, couriers, and foreign correspondents arrived and left the La Plata headquarters in a steady stream. The guerrillas were on the offensive and would remain so until Batista's fall.

Batista fell with surprising swiftness. A rigged election of a new President in November, a Batista candidate, Rivero Agüero, fooled no one. Although Rivero attracted limited American support, mainly from the pro-Batista lobby, the government's situation was deteriorating beyond salvation. Panic in Havana washed over Washington. Eisenhower's later words unintentionally emphasized the poverty of his Cuba policy:

> . . . During the rush of these last events in the final days of 1958, the Central Intelligence Agency suggested for the first time that a

Castro victory might not be in the best interests of the United States. (Earlier reports which I had received of Castro's possible Communism were suspect because they originated with people who favored Batista.)

"Communists and other extreme radicals appear to have penetrated the Castro movement," Allen Dulles said. "If Castro takes over, they will probably participate in the government." When I heard this estimate, I was provoked that such a conclusion had not been given earlier.

One of my advisers recommended that the United States should now back Batista as the lesser of two evils. I rejected that course. If Castro turned out to be as bad as our intelligence now suggested, our only hope, if any, lay with some kind of non-dictatorial "third force," neither Castroite nor Batistiano.[33]

Eisenhower was about five years too late. Guevara now cut the island in half and continued to receive surrender of principal city garrisons. At year's end, Batista gathered wife and children and, with a personal entourage " . . . of bodyguards, retainers, and erstwhile military and political accomplices" who filled five airplanes, flew into an exile that would end in Florida—no great hardship, in view of a personal fortune estimated as high as $300 million.[34]

Batista's exodus was Castro's victory. In early January 1959, Che Guevara and his ragged band entered Havana and took control of government. Castro triumphantly followed, the Liberator claiming the country for the Movement.

The political revolution was over, the social revolution about to begin—with results disastrous to Cuba and her long-suffering people.

From the standpoint of guerrilla warfare, Che Guevara's expedition to Bolivia constitutes an important postscript to the Cuban revolution. Daniel James, who translated and edited Che's captured diaries, offers an excellent account of this ill-fated expedition in his book *The Complete Bolivian Diaries of Ché Guevara*, on which the following brief account is largely based.[35]

Almost immediately upon assuming power, Castro began to alter facts of the multifaceted revolutionary experience. A combination of arrogance of ignorance and political opportunism caused him and Che to invent a theme that, by means of a peasant uprising, the rebels had established a peculiar "Latin American way" to revolution. Che Guevara developed the theme:

. . . We consider that the Cuban Revolution made three fundamental contributions to the laws of the revolutionary movement in

710

the current situation in America [i.e., Central and South America]. They are: Firstly, people's forces can win a war against the army. Secondly, we need not always wait for all the revolutionary conditions to be present; the insurrection itself can create them. Thirdly, in the underdeveloped parts of America the battleground for armed struggle should in the main be the countryside.[36]

Che foresaw a continental struggle brought on by a series of local insurrections—the famous *foco insurreccional*.[37] Here was a sort of revolutionary *tache d'huile* concept that, in time, Che supposed would result in a large revolutionary base from which to carry on the armed struggle:

> . . . As Fidel said, the Andes will be the Sierra Maestra of America, and all the immense territories that make up this continent will become the scene of a life-and-death struggle against the power of imperialism.[38]

This grandiose dream might have died, except for a peculiar combination of factors. One was Castro's and Che's belief, probably genuine, in historical determinism:

> . . . We cannot tell when this struggle will acquire a continental character nor how long it will last; but we can predict its advent and its triumph, because it is the inevitable result of historical, economic and political conditions and its direction cannot be changed.[39]

Allied to this factor was Castro's determination to retain his own revolutionary personality, particularly as regards Soviet influence. Castro and Che's revolutionary thesis was a synthesis owing much more to Mao Tse-tung and Ho Chi Minh than to the Soviets. This was all right so long as Castro did not have to depend on the U.S.S.R. for survival. When that unhappy state of affairs arose, the unorthodox revolutionary line could scarcely be tolerated, and, indeed, from 1961 onward, Guevara found himself in nasty fights with doctrinaire Communists at home and abroad.

Add to this Che's own performance as president of the Cuban National Bank and as Minister of Industry. Dr. Guevara's treatment of the Cuban economy very nearly killed the patient. His ineptness both in economics and in politics brought him into increasing conflict with Castro, whom he was beginning to criticize, albeit guardedly, and who saw him as a rival in any event.

In late 1964, Che evidently fell from grace, leaving Havana and becoming a sort of revolutionary ambassador without portfolio, in some

BOLIVIA
•Towns and Cities
0   100   200   300 miles

M.E.P.

ways a romantic figure—a Walt Whitman with machine gun. In New
York, he delivered a fiery address to the United Nations attacking both
the United States and the Soviet Union as imperialist powers; he went
on to Africa, made more bellicose speeches, and returned to Havana in
March 1965, apparently impressed with the revolutionary possibilities
offered by Congo troubles. He now went underground, resigning all
official positions and renouncing Cuban citizenship, his goal to carry
revolution abroad.[40]

Backed by Castro, he took 125 Cuban guerrillas to join the Kin-
shasa rebellion in the Congo. This effort totally failed, and he returned
to Havana in autumn of 1965. He next decided to carry revolution to
South America by establishing an insurrectional *foco* in Bolivia—a plan
approved by Castro, who allowed him to recruit and train some twenty
Cuban guerrillas and also supported him financially. At first glance,
Bolivia seemed just the country in which to launch an agrarian revolution. The population was predominantly peasant. Terrain favored
guerrilla warfare. The Barrientos government was authoritarian and
seemed to Che and Castro to resemble Batista's former government.
The army was small and ill-trained. A local Communist Party existed
to carry revolution to the cities.

Disguised as a traveling salesman, Che arrived in Bolivia in November 1966. The young French Communist Régis Debray had arrived ear-

712

lier " . . . to make a geopolitical study of the selected zone."[41] Che now organized a headquarters for his small group, which included twenty-nine Bolivians. After a short training program, he started his force, about fifty, on a training march designed to learn the terrain, to perfect guerrilla tactics, and to recruit local peasants. In late March, the guerrillas successfully ambushed an army patrol, a success repeated in April.

Also in April, an army patrol elsewhere captured Régis Debray and two followers, and the Barrientos government agreed to accept a sixteen-man team of American Special Forces advisers to train a regiment of Rangers in counterinsurgency tactics. By May, considerable steam had gone out of Che's operations. Che was recording frequent quarrels in the ranks; lack of food and general illness were slowing his movements; he had recruited no peasants. Although he remained optimistic and, in July, briefly "captured" a town, he was forced to split his group and, in general, to keep moving. By now, Bolivian army intelligence had closed in on his earlier headquarters and had identified him and most of his lieutenants. By August, he admitted he was in " . . . a difficult situation." Matters steadily worsened. In early October, Ranger units surrounded his small group. He was wounded, captured, and presumably summarily executed.

What went wrong?

Castro's and Che's estimate of the situation was nearly as faulty as that made by Lyndon Johnson, Eugene Staley, Maxwell Taylor, and Walt Rostow in Vietnam in 1961 (see following chapter). The terrain in southeastern Bolivia favored guerrilla warfare only so long as one *knew* the terrain. Neither Che nor his Cubans nor his Bolivians knew the terrain, which meant that they had to depend largely on the peasants.

Che miscalculated badly here. The peasants, in this case Indians, who constituted more than two thirds of Bolivia's 4.25 million people, were not to be stirred. As Daniel James noted,

> . . . The National Revolution had radically transformed the life of the Bolivian Indian . . . and that was probably its greatest single accomplishment. It had done so, first, through an agrarian reform law enacted in 1953, which made landholders of the virtually landless Indian peasantry and gave them pride of ownership, even if it was but a little plot they were given. Second, the whole body of revolutionary legislation had the effect of raising the Indian out of age-old serfdom and enabling him to exert his rights as a citizen.

Guevara's chief selling point of revolution—Land to the Landless—automatically fell flat when pitched to Indians with land. But, more than that, in Che's area of operations, his *foco insurreccional* in southeastern Bolivia, the Indians were a particular sort, parochial and suspicious of any outsiders. Che and his guerrillas had studied the dominant Indian language, Quechua, but, in the Southeast, the Indians spoke Guaraní: " . . . Not one of the guerrillas, including the Bolivians, could speak it. . . . "[42] Lacking a valid sales pitch and easy communication, Che failed not only to win over peasants but to gain even limited co-operation. His monthly analysis for April included the ominous statement: " . . . The peasant base has not yet been developed although it appears that through planned terror we can neutralize some of them; support will come later. Not one enlistment has been obtained."[43] The May analysis included this statement: " . . . Complete lack of peasant recruitment, although they are losing their fear of us and we are beginning to win their admiration. It is a slow and patient task. . . . "[44] In June, he noted: " . . . The lack of peasant recruits continues. It is a vicious circle: to get this enlistment we need to settle in a populated area, and for this we need men."[45] And the last analysis, in September: " . . . the peasants do not give us any help and are turning into informers."[46]

Peasants had been informing all along. Though no great shakes, the Barrientos government and the Bolivian army impressed the peasants far more than did Che's guerrillas. This was partly because of land reforms, partly an "ingrained fear and respect" of the army, and partly because it was a peasant army and its recruits were aware that the government had been trying to help peasants. American army advisers had been on hand since 1958, their influence evident in a Civic Action Program which, by late 1963, had the army spending 20 per cent of its time in civil works, mostly in the countryside. Che's early successes caused peasant organizations throughout Bolivia to denounce "the invaders" and to organize armed peasant detachments to fight them, the prelude to a later formal "alliance of the peasantry with the Armed Forces."[47] For this reason, the army gained intelligence it needed to run down guerrillas; guerrillas lacked intelligence needed to survive, prosper, and grow.

Che fared no better with local revolutionary groups. Two such could have helped: the Communist Party, or PCB, headed by Mario Monje, with primarily an intellectual-student following; and the miners, helped by one Guevara (no relation). Castro and Che alienated Monje with their initial decision to use Bolivia as a revolutionary comfort station, a decision taken without consulting him.

Debray added to conflict by dealing with miners instead of with Monje—a futile gesture that resulted in only a few, undesirable recruits for Che. Che's own insistence on leading a rural revolution with the military struggle predominant over the political struggle completed Monje's alienation. Monje " . . . saw the revolution in more orthodox

714

Leninist terms, as emerging from a mass uprising in the cities"[48] as soon as a national crisis occurred. Monje, moreover, felt that he should lead the effort. When Che refused to consider this, the two fell out—to Guevara's great cost.

Even had Monje remained co-operative, he could have offered only limited help. He could have supplied Bolivian recruits, but whether they would have known terrain and Indians any better than Che is problematical. He also could have kept open a line of communication to Che, but whether Fidel Castro would have filled that line with revolutionary needs—arms, supply, and money—is also problematical: Daniel James suggests that Castro was not sorry to be rid of his old lieutenant.

That his old lieutenant was failing seems to have been the case. From his arrival in Bolivia, he had begun violating his own basic tenets of guerrilla warfare. By June, he was a sick man gradually losing control of himself and his group. It is possible that he wanted to die a martyr. He had seen his economic theories refuted. He might have believed that Castro was compromising Marxism-Leninism by accepting an imperialistic Soviet presence. He had failed in the Congo, and almost daily, despite various euphoric diary entries, he was seeing his theories fail in the Bolivian wilderness. Whether asthma and general debilitation dulled his senses or whether he underestimated the army, he refused to cut out for the border in time to avoid capture. On the basis of diary entries, not to mention his previous behavior and personality in general, we can conclude that Che's ego overcame his common sense. We don't know where his body lies but if ever a plaque is erected it should bear only two words, as fatal to a guerilla as to those who fight guerrillas: VANITAS VANITATUM.

CHAPTER FIFTY-SEVEN

1. Taber, 50 ff., for details of this training.
2. Goldenberg, 154. The author, himself a former Communist, described Che as a Marxist closely linked to international communism. See also, James, *Che Guevara* . . .
3. Guevara, *Reminiscences* . . . , 14, 38 ff.
4. Thomas, *Cuba* . . . , 874.
5. Guevara, *Reminiscences* . . . , 38–41.
6. Ibid., 131 ff., 196 ff.
7. Draper, *Castro's Revolution* . . . , 162.
8. Taber, 84. Rebels later assassinated the responsible officer.
9. H.L. Matthews, *The Cuban Story*, 36. See also, Pflaum, 16. The author found Castro shorter than six feet, pudgy, and with sloping chin.
10. H.L. Matthews, *The Cuban Story*, 27–39.
11. Draper, *Castro's Revolution* . . . , 56.
12. Ibid., 190. See also, Guevara, *Reminiscences* . . . This is scarcely an original *ruse de guerre*. While Castro at this time could have commanded a meaningful force, that was not proof that he *did* command one—and it was a reporter's responsibility to either discover the strength or report it with qualification.

13. H.L. Matthews, *The Cuban Story*. See also, Draper, *Castro's Revolution* . . . 191–2. On March 11, 1966, Draper wrote Matthews:

> . . . I strongly doubt that your articles would have had such an electrifying effect if you had not personally vouched for Castro's large and winning force. You now claim that you "guessed at the time that he had about forty men." Then why did you report at the time, without any hint of skepticism, his boast that he had "groups of ten to forty"? And you gave a different version of this matter in your book.

14. Guevara, *Che Guevara on Guerrilla Warfare*.
15. Debray, 20–1: Castro relied politically on Marx, Martí, Lenin; militarily on Engels and Hemingway's *For Whom the Bell Tolls,*

> . . . not so much as sources as . . . coincidences; Fidel found in them only what he was looking for. Mao Tse-tung's *Problems of Strategy in Guerrilla War Against Japan* [sic] came into Fidel's and Che's hands after the 1958 summer offensive: to their surprise they found in this book what they had been practising under pressure of necessity.

16. Guevara, *Reminiscences* . . . , 197.
17. Ibid., 205.
18. Thomas, *Cuba* . . . , 958. See also, Smith.
19. Draper, *Castro's Revolution* . . . , 162–3.
20. Taber, 204.
21. Ibid., 210.
22. Chapelle.
23. Guevara, *Reminiscences,* see, for example 246–7.
24. H.L. Matthews, *The Cuban Story,* 66, 236–7. See also, ibid., 246: " . . . in 1958, United States interests controlled 80 per cent of Cuban utilities, 90 per cent of the mines, 90 per cent of the cattle ranches, all of the oil refining and distribution (with the Royal Dutch Shell) and 40 per cent of the sugar industry"; Draper, *Castroism* . . . ; Mills; Thomas, *Cuba* . . . , 967.
25. Draper, *Castro's Revolution* . . . , 16.
26. Ibid., 14.
27. Mallin.
28. Thomas, *Cuba* . . . , 997. See also, H.L. Matthews, *Castro* . . .
29. Thomas, *Cuba* . . . , 997.
30. Ibid., 998. See also, Taber.
31. H.L. Matthews, *Castro* . . . , 106. See also, Taber; Mallin. From the guerrilla standpoint, the kidnapings made sense. Raúl's idea was to force the United States to negotiate and thus grant the rebels a sort of diplomatic recognition important for propaganda purposes; the divisive kidnapings also demonstrated widespread guerrilla control of the area.
32. Special Operations Research Office, *Casebook on Insurgency and Revolutionary Warfare,* 186:

> . . . The agreement called for cooperation in the common cause, continued cooperation after victory, the arming of the people, and the cooperation of labor and business in a general strike to be called to aid the military front when needed. The manifesto called on the soldiers to desert, and on everybody else to support the revolution. Above all, it stressed the theme of unity.

33. Eisenhower, *Waging Peace* . . . , 521. See also, H.L. Matthews, *The Cuban Story,* 172: The Deputy Director of CIA, General C.P. Cabell, testified to the Senate Internal Security Committee on November 5, 1959, that his organi-

zation believed that Castro was not a member of the Communist Party, and did not consider himself to be a Communist.

34. Thomas, *Cuba . . .* , 1027. See also, H.L. Matthews, *The Cuban Story.*
35. James, *The Complete Bolivian Diaries . . .* See also, Guevara, *Bolivian Diary.*
36. Lavan, *Che Guevara Speaks . . .* , 75, for his interview with two Chinese Communist journalists in April 1959.
37. James, *The Complete Bolivian Diaries . . .*
38. Lavan, *Che Guevara Speaks . . .* , 86.
39. Ibid.
40. Ibid., 98, 102. See also ibid., 139–41 for his "Farewell Letter to Fidel": ". . . Other nations of this world call for my modest efforts."
41. James, *The Complete Bolivian Diaries . . .* , 11, 32.
42. Ibid., 59–61. See also, Fagg.
43. James, *The Complete Bolivian Diaries . . .* , 151.
44. Ibid., 164.
45. Ibid., 176.
46. Ibid., 219.
47. Ibid., 22, 60.
48. Ibid., 62–4.

CHAPTER 58

John Kennedy inherits a war • General Lansdale's estimate of the situation • Kennedy's strategic appraisal • His early errors • Lyndon Johnson's report • Hawks versus doves • Military versus political strategy • The Staley Plan • The Taylor mission • The military solution • Kennedy's reservations • Roger Hilsman dissents • De Gaulle's warning • Kennedy acts • His relations with Diem • The situation in South Vietnam

SINCE 1951, John Kennedy had interested himself in the Vietnam scene, on several occasions pressing his views on fellow legislators and the nation.[1] For nearly ten years, protests of dissident officials had claimed his ear. He had listened to such Saigon veterans as Robert Blum and Edward Gullion, and he knew and approved of some of Colonel Edward Lansdale's views.

In June 1956, the young senator told a meeting of American Friends of Vietnam: " . . . What we must offer [the Vietnamese people] is a revolution—a political, economic, and social revolution far superior to anything the Communists can offer—far more peaceful, far more democratic, and far more locally controlled."[2]

Kennedy's error, and that of hundreds of influential and well-intentioned Americans, was the assumption that President Ngo Dinh Diem both wished and was able to effect such a revolution—an assumption unfortunately voided by Diem's behavior, which increasingly caused some of his most enthusiastic American supporters to have second thoughts on his performance. Although the Eisenhower administration was preparing to send more advisers and more aid, Ambassador Durbrow " . . . had been required to bear so many messages of disapproval from the United States that he had not been welcome at the presidential palace in Saigon for several months."[3]

Although Vietnam played no prominent role in 1960 U.S. presidential elections, Kennedy entered office displeased with the situation in

Indochina. He was scarcely reassured when, in early February 1961, presidential assistant Walt Rostow handed him a memorandum prepared by the Pentagon's leading expert on guerrilla warfare, Brigadier General Edward Lansdale, who, in Robert Shaplen's words,

> ... felt that the Vietnamese military structure and military methods of operation (which the Americans, in their pale advisory role, were countenancing) were all wrong. He felt that if the bitter conflict stood any chance of being won, we would have to be firm in insisting on a complete reorganization of the government's fighting machine; we would have to make it a force capable of dealing with Communist subversion in a meaningful and imaginative way, much as Magsaysay had done in the Philippines in 1951–52.[4]

Kennedy read the paper through and turned to Rostow: "This is the worst yet," he said. "You know, Ike never briefed me about Vietnam."[5]

Kennedy early concluded that guerrilla warfare—what he termed "internal" or subterranean" war—was the real challenge of the sixties and ordered Secretary of Defense Robert McNamara to begin weaning the United States from dependence on the Eisenhower-Dullesian massive-retaliation strategy of nuclear warfare. The Lansdale report so impressed Kennedy that he decided to send its author back to Vietnam as American ambassador. The threat of Lansdale's disruptive presence to sacrosanct bureaucratic and military empires caused a storm of protest from Washington and Saigon officialdom.[6] Unfortunately, the young President succumbed to these forces (which he would never quite tame), and dispatched Frederick E. Nolting as his new ambassador. A soft-spoken Virginian, Nolting was a fifty-year-old former philosophy professor turned diplomat, a man without experience in Southeast Asia,

> ... a big, soft-spoken man who was so comfortable to be with that almost everyone used his nickname, Fritz. He was ideal for the job of restoring good relations with Diem and attempting to influence him toward concessions that would bring his regime wider support from within Vietnam and make it politically easier for the United States to give him the aid he requested.[7]

Instead of getting off to a good start, then, Kennedy kept the pot of South Vietnam bubbling as it had been for the previous five years. A change of faces and additional American aid meant no fundamental improvement of a worsening situation. Instead, it meant privately compounding past and present errors while publicly defending them as a viable program. A number of reasons exist for Kennedy's disappointing performance in this troubled area, and we shall discuss them in due course. But first we must present in brief the turbulent events of these crucial years of the insurgency.

In spring of 1961, Kennedy and his advisers were still deeply concerned about the American role in Vietnam and particularly in Laos, where the Joint Chiefs of Staff (JCS) had recommended committing American ground troops. General James Gavin, whom Kennedy had appointed ambassador to France, hotly opposed the idea, and bluntly told Kennedy:

> . . . that Laos was a landlocked area in which it would be very difficult to bring U.S. power to bear in any meaningful way, even if it should be in the U.S. interest to do so. I felt Laos would turn into a bottomless pit into which we would pour soldier after soldier. I recounted for the President the history of the debate inside the Pentagon after Dien Bien Phu and said I felt this new situation was similar. There was little to be gained and a great deal to be risked by U.S. military action.[8]

While a special task force of ranking officials studied the problem, Kennedy sent Vice-President Lyndon Johnson on a general tour of Southeast Asia. In Saigon, the lanky Texan talked to Diem and his officials, promised increased aid, and stated the Administration's confidence in the Diem government. Ngo Dinh Diem, he told reporters, was the Winston Churchill of Southeast Asia. Far worse, he told Kennedy that

> . . . the basic decision in Southeast Asia is here. We must decide whether to help these countries to the best of our ability or throw in the towel in the area and pull back our defenses to San Francisco and a "Fortress America" concept.

Johnson "did not consider Southeast Asia lost, 'and it is by no means inevitable that it must be lost.' " Diem was

> . . . a complex figure beset by many problems. "He has admirable qualities, but he is remote from the people, is surrounded by persons less admirable than he. The country can be saved—if we move quickly and wisely."[9]

Johnson's mission produced varied, generally unfortunate results. Perhaps the most harmful was to reinforce the concept of South Vietnam as a "strategic necessity" to the United States, along with the notion of Diem's indispensability—not only in his and his intimates' minds but in those of the Administration and the American public. Johnson made plain his attitude, on the plane flying from Saigon, when a reporter started discussing Diem and his faults. " . . . Don't tell me about Diem," Johnson answered. "He's all we've got out there."[10]

Kennedy simultaneously fell victim to another pernicious influence, his Secretary of State, Dean Rusk, a small man in a big job:

> . . . While the President and a number of his advisers saw the insurgency primarily as a civil war . . . Rusk tended to ignore the highly complex causes and history of the insurgency and developed the theme of "aggression from the North," which was to become increasingly prominent as the American-sponsored efforts of the Saigon regime proved ineffective against the rebellion. As early as 1961, Rusk was speaking of "the determined and ruthless campaign of propaganda, infiltration, and subversion by the Communist regime in north Viet-Nam to destroy the Republic of Viet-Nam."[11]

Rusk's indignation was shared by Secretary of Defense Robert McNamara and, to a lesser degree, by Kennedy's national security adviser, McGeorge Bundy, an "establishment intellectual" who, along with Rusk and McNamara, favored a military strategy. Bundy's deputy, Walt Rostow, was particularly hawkish and epitomized the dubious talent with which Kennedy surrounded himself. Forty-five years old, he was a Yale man, a Rhodes scholar, an economist and historian long associated with government; in World War II, he had served with the OSS in Burma. Rostow shared Rusk's belief in "aggression from the North" (or perhaps Rusk shared Rostow's belief). Rostow made his thinking known publicly at West Point, in spring of 1961, where he argued that emerging nations must be protected against external Communist aggression to the point that it might be necessary to " . . . seek out and engage the ultimate source of aggression."[12] Although Hanoi at this time was helping insurgents in the South, the effort nowhere near approached that claimed by Rusk and Rostow, and they were as much at fault for preaching this as others were for denying its existence.

Still other presidential advisers, most of them close to Kennedy, though admitting the North's unsavory role in the South, wanted to counter it, along with the actual insurgency, with a political strategy that would have sharply subordinated military operations. This group, which would be termed doves, included Robert Kennedy, Averell Harriman, George Ball, Roger Hilsman, and Michael Forrestal.

The hawks—Johnson, Rusk, McNamara, Rostow, and the JCS—formed a formidable pressure group. Although Kennedy, in general, favored a political strategy, he could not ride roughshod over those who favored a military strategy. He was also increasingly incensed, as were many Americans, with Viet Cong terrorist tactics, and he realized that implementation of a political policy would involve military aspects, which posed the problem of preparing the nation to follow him. Heretofore restrained in public utterances on the subject, he now began emphasizing the theme of Communist revolutionary warfare and external aggression, telling a joint session of Congress in late May:

> ... their aggression is more often concealed than open. They have fired no missiles; and their troops are seldom seen. They send arms, agitators, aid, technicians and propaganda to every troubled area. But where fighting is required, it is usually done by others, by guerrillas striking at night, by assassins striking alone, assassins who have taken the lives of 4,000 civil officers in the last 12 months in Vietnam, by subversives and saboteurs and insurrectionists, who in some cases control whole areas inside of independent nations.[13]

Kennedy next dispatched Professor Eugene Staley, who spent summer of 1961 preparing a report on Diem's needs. Although not made public, Staley's recommendations included " ... a number of changes in the administration of aid, as well as certain reforms of a political nature."[14] He also allegedly recommended increasing Vietnamese army strength to 170,000, doubling the Civil Guard to a total 120,000, equipping the Self-Defense Corps with modern small arms and radios, and constructing a network of fortified, or strategic, hamlets.[15] Kennedy was mulling over the Staley Plan when Diem sent an anguished plea for help. Kennedy now dispatched a larger mission, headed by sixty-year-old General Maxwell Taylor, a former army chief of staff whom he had consulted in the Bay of Pigs fiasco, assisted by Walt Rostow. Kennedy wanted to know in particular if the Diem government could be "saved." Taylor (and Rostow) " ... was dismayed by a number of things he thought were wrong with the Diem regime and he recommended a tougher approach." He recommended among many other things

> ... that we stand firm on our demand that Diem and Nhu decentralize their administration, both in its civilian and its military aspects, and that we insist on a revamping of the muddled system of collecting and interpreting intelligence about the Vietcong. Taylor also felt strongly that certain political reforms should be instituted and that bona fide nationalist leaders who were in jail should be freed.[16]

On the positive side:

... their collective answer to Kennedy's question was that South Vietnam had enough vitality to justify a major United States effort ... they recommended increased American intervention—in effect, a shift from arm's length advice to limited partnership. While only the Vietnamese could finally beat the Viet Cong, Americans at all levels, Taylor and Rostow argued, could show them how the job was to be done.[17]

Taylor's recommendations meant openly refuting the manpower ceiling laid down by the Geneva Agreements. The American role would be enlarged, " ... essentially through the penetration of the South Vietnamese army and government by American 'advisers,' attached to Vietnamese military units or government offices and designed to improve the level of local performance";[18] these included American helicopter and air-reconnaissance units for logistics-support purposes. The report also called for committing American ground troops (which the JCS had recommended a few months earlier): an eight-to-ten-thousand-man task force would be provided as "engineers" to help in flood-control work; such a force, in addition to raising Vietnamese morale and demonstrating United States determination to Hanoi, Peking, and Moscow, would be capable of conducting " ... combat operations for self-defense and perimeter security and, if the Vietnamese Army were hard pressed, of providing an emergency reserve." In case this force provoked invasion from the North, additional troops would be required. Moreover—and here was Catch-22—" ... Taylor and Rostow *hoped* that *this* program would suffice to win the civil war—and were sure it would *if only* the infiltration from the north could be stopped. But if it continued, then they could see no end to the war. ... "[19] Finally, " ... the whole program was only an important first step in the direction of the longer-run goal, eventually to contain and eliminate the threat to the independence of South Vietnam ... for final victory the U.S. might have to strike the source of the aggression (though this decision could be deferred)."[20]

Here was a qualitative change in addition to a quantitative change of means to realize the grand ambition: *stop communism*. Taylor and Rostow's rationale was as fascinating as it was dangerous. Instead of appreciating the political nature of an insurgency, he was attempting to change the rules. As Roger Hilsman later noted,

> ... The mission of these American troops—revealing the continued focus in General Taylor's mind on the possibility of a conventional, Korea-type attack—would be to hold the ring against invasion from the north by regular North Vietnamese divisions and to man the northern borders against infiltrators, while the South Vietnamese dealt with the guerrillas in the rear.[21]

Far from being the far-sighted strategist that Kennedy needed, Taylor might as well have donned an air force uniform and stood in the public pulpit to preach the virtues of massive retaliation. Far from approaching the problem with imagination and flexibility (and caution), he was thinking primarily in conventional-force terms.

Apparently, Taylor and his fellows were either ignorant of or oblivious to the estimate of the situation that General Matthew Ridgway had presented in 1954 (see Chapter 48) and that emphasized incompatibility between the American military machine and the tactical environment of Vietnam. In 1961, the highest American military councils unfortunately lacked any semblance of Ridgway's intelligent restraint. Only that spring, General Lyman Lemnitzer, chairman of the JCS, had returned from an inspection trip to Vietnam and, according to newspaper reports,

> . . . felt that the new administration was 'oversold' on the importance of guerrilla warfare and that too much emphasis on counter-guerrilla measures would impair the ability of the South Vietnamese Army to meet a conventional assault like the attack on South Korea by the ten or more regular North Vietnamese divisions.

In early November, speaking at Fordham University, General Earle G. Wheeler, army chief of staff, told his audience

> . . . that what the United States was committed to support in Vietnam was "military action. . . . Despite the fact that the conflict is conducted as guerrilla warfare," Wheeler went on to say, "it is nonetheless a military action. . . . It is fashionable in some quarters to say that the problems in Southeast Asia are primarily political and economic rather than military. I do not agree. The essence of the problem in Vietnam is military."[22]

Taylor now was proposing a course of action consonant with Lemnitzer and Wheeler's antiquated reasoning—a course of action that, if it did provoke the enemy to conventional counteraction, would lead to an escalation projected by the JCS in a report on Laos: If landing American troops in Thailand, South Vietnam, and government-held portions of the Laotian panhandle did not produce a cease-fire, the JCS

> . . . recommended an air attack on Pathet Lao positions and tactical nuclear weapons on the ground. If North Vietnamese or Chinese then moved in, their homelands would be bombed. If massive Red troops were then mobilized, nuclear bombings would be threatened and, if necessary, carried out. If the Soviets then inter-

vened, we should "be prepared to accept the possibility of general war." But the Soviet Union, they assured the President, "can hardly wish to see an uncontrollable situation develop."[23]

Taylor's plan contained no less a number of "x" factors. Rostow was an even more outspoken advocate of escalation, arguing " . . . for a contingency policy of retaliation against the north, graduated to match the intensity of Hanoi's support of the Viet Cong. . . . "[24] Secretary of Defense Robert McNamara also reported to the President a conclusion shared by his deputy secretary Roswell Gilpatric, and by the JCS,

> . . . that the chances were against, probably sharply against, preventing the fall of South Vietnam to Communism by any measures short of the introduction of U.S. forces on a substantial scale . . . though of great help to Diem, even the initial U.S. task force of about 8,000 men, would not convince the other side that we meant business, unless we accompanied the introduction of the initial force with a clear commitment to the full objective of preventing the fall of South Vietnam to Communism and warned Hanoi through some channel that continued support of the VC would lead to punitive retaliation against North Vietnam. . . . If the proposed commitment and force deployment were undertaken, the President was warned of the possibility that Hanoi and Peiping might intervene openly, in which case as many as, but (given logistic difficulties of the other side) not more than six U.S. divisions, or about 205,000 men would be required.[25]

The Taylor-Rostow mission evoked several responses. Not long after the mission's return, Kennedy met with his close friend and adviser Arthur Schlesinger, Jr.:

> " . . . They want a force of American troops," he told me early in November. "They say it's necessary in order to restore confidence and maintain morale. But it will be just like Berlin. The troops will march in; the bands will play; the crowds will cheer; and in four days everyone will have forgotten. Then we will be told we have to send in more troops. It's like taking a drink. The effect wears off, and you have to take another." The war in Vietnam, he added, could be won only so long as it was *their* war. If it were ever converted into a white man's war, we would lose as the French had lost a decade earlier.[26]

Although pressured by the JCS and by some principal advisers to commit a task force of American troops, Kennedy refused. The Bay of Pigs disaster had made him suspicious of experts, especially when other experts disagreed.[27] One important dissenter was Roger Hilsman. A West Pointer ('43) from Texas, forty-one-year-old Hilsman had served with OSS in Burma; after the war, he had earned a Ph.D. from Yale, left the army, and taught international affairs until entering the State Department, in 1961, as director of its intelligence section. Hilsman differed sharply with the Pentagon and with Rusk and Rostow as to Vietnam. He saw the challenge as political—as a war of ideas that demanded essentially a political strategy designed to gain popular support:

> . . . that government existed for the benefit of the people, that a government could really *care,* was as revolutionary in most of Asia as anything the Communists had to offer. . . .

He concluded that a viable strategy " . . . would require an emphasis on political, economic, and social action into which very carefully calibrated military measures were interwoven."[28] Militarily, guerrillas must be fought with guerrilla, rather than conventional, tactics. This opinion, shared by other experts, military and civil, struck a responsive note with the President, who a few months earlier had been warned by Charles de Gaulle that

> . . . to intervene in this region [Indochina] will be to catch yourself in the cogs of a machine. . . . the more you become involved there fighting Communism, the more Communists will appear as champions of national independence. . . . We, the French, have experience of that. You, the Americans, wanted to take our place in Indo-China. Now you want to take over where we left off and restart the war which we ended. I predict that you will sink bit by bit into a bottomless military and political swamp however much you pay in men and money.[29]

Kennedy moved cautiously. He probably hoped that the psychological effect of committing more "advisers" and logistics-support troops such as helicopter units would warn Hanoi that he meant business, would revive South Vietnamese morale, would cause Diem to reform his government, and would satisfy administration hawks. He also ordered his military chiefs " . . . to be prepared for the introduction of combat troops, should they prove to be necessary."[30] In addition, he authorized continued CIA support of agents infiltrated into North Vietnam and Laos to work up covert resistance against the Communists, a program started in the Eisenhower administration.[31]

What he did not do—and this is one of his great failures—was to pursue his doubts. What he did not do was to call for a re-examination of what was passing for political policy and military strategy. He badly needed a devil's advocate with intelligence and courage sufficient to question underlying assumptions held by the majority of his advisers. He turned down recommendations to commit troops in Laos and Vietnam partly because the JCS and the CIA had so terribly misjudged the Cuban situation. What made him think that prevailing notions of policy and strategy in Southeast Asia were any more valid, particularly in view of General Ridgway's earlier dissent? That the domino theory could hold up under intelligent analysis? That the Pentagon would be content to remain in an advisory role? That Diem was indispensable? That Nolting and Harkins could manage Diem? That he himself could foist the Diem regime on the world as free, democratic government? That, had the American people been properly informed, they would not have trusted him and backed him in a "risk" strategy necessary to straighten out the Diem regime? Instead, he remained a prisoner to this regime, to his own bellicose advisers, and to his own unsure self.

The Taylor report had brought explosive response from the Diem government in Saigon and from the Vietnam lobby in the United States, and this alone should have caused doubts to arise in the minds of the military missionaries in the White House and Pentagon. Stung by Taylor's criticisms and prompted by brother Nhu, the Vietnamese President huffed and puffed about his country's sovereignty. In Shaplen's words, " . . . what followed over a period of several weeks was a game of bluff, which the Vietnamese won hands down."[32] Instead of pressing the issue to final conclusions, the Administration yielded and pretended to find solace in Diem's empty promises. This was a vital error. Diem had consistently refused to allow either a political opposition or a coalition government in order to broaden his support. Diem was incapable of understanding representative government, and, by 1962, this fact was obvious. Despite such sops as a National Economic Council and provincial councils, Diem and his ruling oligarchy had refused to relinquish any real powers. Millions of American dollars continued to fall into their hands—$300 million in army credits alone in 1961—and, either in cash or kind, precious little of these funds reached the countryside, where the war was being fought. U.S. protests aroused only further threats from Diem and his advisers. At Ambassador Nolting's urging, the Administration agreed to a "soft" approach in hope that Diem would change his ways.[33]

Instead of political reforms, Diem pushed through his rubber-stamp assembly such restrictive legislation as the Public Meetings Law, " . . . a law that forbade all kinds of meetings unless they were authorized by the government," and the Bill for the Protection of Morality, a piece of legislative nonsense sponsored by Mme. Nhu and one comparable to Chiang Kai-shek's New Life Movement. Total censorship prevailed and Nhu's secret police prowled everywhere to pounce on dissidence:

... by 1962 there were some thirty thousand prisoners in about fifty jails throughout the country, about two-thirds of whom were classified as political prisoners. Many were captured Vietcong insurgents, but there were also a lot of "suspects" who had languished in jails for months or even years. Among the prisoners were some three hundred non-Communist liberals arrested solely for having expressed anti-Diem views or for being suspected of having spoken out in favor of the abortive 1960 coup.[34]

The regime's suspicions extended to the army, which continued to stir restlessly despite Diem's efforts to control it:

> ... Promotion on the basis of personal loyalty rather than ability, the use of informers, the banishment of men of integrity and initiative, and the domination of all strategy had not made the Army more loyal; these methods had merely brought about a tenuous control, and badly compromised and diluted a military force which was in a fight to the death with a tough enemy.[35]

A confused and demoralized army not only could not fight a successful counterinsurgency, but its ranks became increasingly vulnerable to the enemy's proselyting effort, the *binh van* program, which one expert believed was " ... the most deadly weapon" in the Viet Cong arsenal.[36] In emphasizing the Communist and northern-aggression themes that so appealed to American officials and politicians and in steadfastly refusing to recognize his real enemy, the NLF and the emphasis it placed on the "armed struggle," particularly the political struggle, Diem remained bent on polishing the veneer of government at a time when termites were gnawing away its essential supports.

CHAPTER FIFTY-EIGHT

1. Kennedy, *The Strategy of Peace*, 57.
2. Buttinger, II, 936.
3. Hilsman, 419–20.
4. Shaplen, *The Lost Revolution*, 148.
5. Schlesinger, *A Thousand Days*, 320. See also, Sidey, for a slightly different version; Clifford who, as Kennedy's "transition planner," arranged a briefing on Southeast Asia in January 1961. Clifford later wrote:

   > My notes disclose the following comments by the President [Eisenhower] ... [who] said, with considerable emotion, that Laos was the key to the entire area of Southeast Asia. He said that if we permitted Laos to fall, then we would have to write off all the area. He stated we must not permit a Communist takeover.

6. Mecklin, 85. See also, Hilsman, 421–2, 439. The State Department recommended sending Lansdale out on three subsequent occasions without success; in 1965, Lodge finally insisted on his presence.
7. Hilsman, 420.

8. Gavin, *Crisis Now*, 51.
9. Schlesinger, *A Thousand Days*, 542–3. See also, Johnson, *The Vantage Point* . . .
10. Halberstam, *The Making of a Quagmire*, 69.
11. Kahin and Lewis, 127.
12. Rostow, "Guerrilla Warfare . . . "
13. Kennedy, *Public Papers of* . . . , I, 397.
14. Shaplen, *The Lost Revolution*, 153.
15. Fall, *The Two Viet-Nams* . . . , 332. See also, Lacouture.
16. Shaplen, *The Lost Revolution*, 153–4.
17. Schlesinger, *A Thousand Days*, 546. See also, Ellsberg, who points out that the reports called for the short-run goal of "frustrating" the Communists; i.e. " . . . halting or reversing a current downward trend or spiral of deterioration," and the long-run goal of "defeating" them; i.e. the " . . . ultimate goal of eliminating the Communist threat."
18. Schlesinger, *The Bitter Heritage* . . . , 22.
19. Schlesinger, *A Thousand Days*, 546. My italics. See also, Hilsman.
20. Ellsberg:

    > . . . Taylor underlined the urgency by making explicit his recognition of an impressive list of disadvantages of the proposed move, including weakness of the U.S. strategic reserve; increased engagement of U.S. prestige; difficulty of resisting pressure to reinforce the first contingent if it were not enough (with no limit to the possible commitment, unless we attacked the source in Hanoi, if we sought ultimately to clean up the insurgents); and the risk of an escalation into a major war in Asia. It was in the face of all these possible drawbacks that he made his recommendation to introduce a Task Force without delay: made it on the grounds that a U.S. program to save South Vietnam simply would not succeed without it.

    See also, Hilsman.
21. Hilsman, 423.
22. Ibid., 415–16, 426.
23. Sorenson, 644–5.
24. Schlesinger, *A Thousand Days*, 546–7. See also, Halberstam, *The Making of a Quagmire*.
25. Ellsberg.
26. Schlesinger, *A Thousand Days*, 547. See also, Sorensen, 654:

    > . . . He had watched the French, with a courageous well-equipped army numbering hundreds of thousands, suffer a humiliating defeat and more than ninety thousand casualties. Now the choice was his. If the United States took over the conduct of the war on the ground, he asked, would that not make it easier for the Communists to say we were the neo-colonialist successors of the French? Would we be better able to win support of the villagers and farmers so essential to guerrilla warfare—than Vietnamese troops of the same color and culture? No one knew whether the South Vietnamese officers would be encouraged or resentful, or whether massive troop landings would provoke a massive Communist invasion—an invasion inevitably leading either to nuclear war, Western retreat or an endless and exhausting battle on the worst battleground he could choose.

27. Sorensen, 644, 652.
28. Hilsman, 433 ff., 425, 435.
29. *The Sunday Telegraph* (London), November 11, 1970. See also, De Gaulle, *Memoirs of Hope*.
30. Sorensen, 654. See also, Hilsman.

31. *The Times* (London), June 23, 1971.
32. Shaplen, *The Lost Revolution*, 154.
33. Lacouture, 63.
34. Shaplen, *The Lost Revolution*, 156–7.
35. Halberstam, *The Making of a Quagmire*, 59.
36. Pike, 253.

CHAPTER 59

WHAT OF THE ENEMY written off so comfortingly by General Myers and Ambassador Durbrow in 1959? As we have seen, in December 1960 the National Liberation Front (NLF) appeared in the South, published a "Ten-Point Manifesto" that called for a democratic, coalition government, and embarked on an "action program" to achieve this end. A year later, it gained a leader in the person of Nguyen Huu Tho, a fifty-two-year-old Saigon lawyer and Marxist who had escaped after five years of imprisonment for political activities.

The interworkings of NLF leadership in these years are not particularly well documented in the West (despite the capture in 1966 of some six thousand NLF documents). NLF leaders remained underground. They did not reside at a permanent headquarters, they met infrequently, and those of their records later captured are sketchy. By the time Tho joined his comrades, Communists both in the South and in Hanoi apparently were worried about ultimate control of the liberation movement. In January 1962, militant Communist elements of the NLF established a revolutionary front, the People's Revolutionary Party (PRP), which now became the radical branch of the movement, the "vanguard" of the revolution. The PRP, most experts believed, was

" . . . the Southern branch of the Lao Dong [Communist] party which rules Hanoi," its main function being "to insure political control of the military arm of the NLF and to guide the movement's political struggle."[1] This did not mean, as asserted by South Vietnamese and American officials at the time, that Hanoi either absorbed the movement or thenceforth directly controlled it. Professor Donald Zagoria, among other experts, concluded that " . . . the NLF includes very significant political forces that are not Communist and still harbor long-held apprehensions about both Communist domination and domination by Northerners."[2] In other words, the NLF remained a specific political entity and, despite the extent of Hanoi's control, it might have been wiser to recognize it as such if only to influence its non-Communist and even some of its Communist members.

Two months later, in March 1962, the NLF held its first congress, which elected Nguyen Huu Tho president and Nguyen Van Hieu, a mathematics professor believed by many to have been the real driving force of NLF, secretary-general of the Central Committee. The congress also announced a new objective: independence of South Vietnam, an objective extended in July to making " . . . south Viet-Nam, Laos, and Cambodia a neutral zone with all three states enjoying sovereign rights." Simultaneously, the NLF continued appealing to all " . . . parties, sects, and groups representing all political tendencies, social strata, religions, and nationalities of South Vietnam."[3] The Geneva Agreements of 1962, which resulted in a neutralized Laos (in theory), strengthened the NLF (and Hanoi) in demands for a neutral, coalition government in the South.

No matter the ultimate NLF and PRP intention, which Communist leadership cunningly concealed during formative years; at a time when Diem was adamantly refusing representative government, his enemy was stressing its desire for such, a brilliant tactic in the propaganda war. Continued U.S. association with and support of the Diem regime also offered a superb propaganda target for Communists to exploit. In 1962, NLF leaders introduced the term *special war*—" . . . described as a form of neocolonialism in which a colonial power, no longer able to use expeditionary forces to assert its control, worked through a clique of compradors whom it 'advised,' with the rank-and-file military force being supplied by the colonialized nation."[4]

The NLF, or anyway its Communist leadership, sought to gain either direct control of the South Vietnam Government through a general uprising, or to gain indirect control by establishing a coalition government and working on from there. Essential to the process was "the struggle movement," a two-pronged program well described by Douglas Pike:

> ... Within the generic term "struggle," there were two types of struggle movements; The political struggle (*dau tranh chinh tri*) and the armed, or military struggle (*dau tranh vu trang*). To the NLF, as to the Viet Minh and Chinese Communists before it, victory would be achieved through the proper balance of political and military activities or, in Communist terms, by the proper combination of the political struggle and the armed struggle.

The political struggle, which, in accordance with Mao's teachings, gained primary ascendancy, called for a three-pronged program: consolidation of areas already controlled by Viet Cong; the "liberated areas" or base sanctuaries so essential to further revolutionary activity (the *dan van,* or "action among the people"); organization of the countryside under GVN control, the agit-prop task discussed earlier (the *dich van,* or "action among the enemy"); proselyting of ARVN and the GVN civil service (the *binh van,* or "action among the troops"). The military struggle, which at first remained subordinate to the political struggle, consisted " . . . not simply [of] guerrilla military attacks but kidnappings, assassinations, executions, sabotage"—what Pike succinctly calls the "violence program." Military organization strongly resembled that of the Viet Minh earlier discussed (see Chapter 39). Operations remained the responsibility of the "People's Self-Defense Armed Forces Committee." As with other national committees, this extended downward through provincial and district organizations. The Liberation Army consisted of two parts: Main Force regiments, or what might be called regulars; the Guerrilla Popular Army or paramilitary forces— peasants by day, guerrillas by night—organized in small units that varied in function from village militia duty (generally covert) to active combat often in conjunction with Main Force or regional units. The Guerrilla Popular Army formed the reservoir of men that supplied the regular units. It also maintained three-man "special activity cells," which

> . . . would strike anywhere at any time. From the roster of these cells were drawn the assassination teams, the volunteer grenade hurlers, the death or suicide squads. Most of the spectacular acts of sabotage, assassinations of province chiefs, or daring military escapades were the work of a special activity cell, sometimes working with demolition experts or other military specialists supplied by the provincial-level central committee.

Although the importance of the political and military struggles would vary, each complemented the grand design.

. . . Vo Nguyen Giap wrote that if an uprising was an art, the chief characteristic of its leadership was the ability to change the struggle form in accordance with changed events. At the beginning, he said, the political struggle dominated and the armed struggle was secondary. Gradually the two assumed equal roles. Then the armed struggle dominated. In the end came the return to the political struggle. Struggle was *the word*. Its goal, toward which the cadres pledged themselves, toward which each Vietnamese was expected daily to contribute a little, was the General Uprising, the nationwide, simultaneous grand struggle movement.[5]

By 1962, the NLF controlled large areas of South Vietnam, including two rich areas in the Mekong Delta. While they busily converted these into "liberated areas," Viet Cong units continued to ambush ARVN columns and attack ARVN and police outposts. Terrorists struck at government officials, particularly village officials and school teachers. Hideous tactics these, but not often promiscuous and less hideous in final result than quantitative military tactics: mass artillery bombardment or aerial bombings. Above all, tactics with a purpose, tactics that formed part of a relentless propaganda war designed to consolidate and expand a peasant base that Communist leaders realized was essential to future operations.

The song had not changed, and now, after more than twenty years of singing, the voices were good. The communism that Kennedy was endeavoring to stop did not enter the picture. Human misery did. John Mecklin later described the Communist target, a typical Vietnamese hamlet of fewer than a thousand people:

. . . a cluster of straw and bamboo huts with earthen floors and straw sleeping mats. The land between the huts was a quagmire of ankle-deep black mud in the rainy season, choking dust in the dry season. The peasant's wife or children often walked as much as three or four miles and then waited in line an hour or two for the daily drinking water. In the dry season the distance was often further because the regular well became saline. There was seldom electricity, frequently no road of any sort to the outside world, and no communication except by foot.

[The peasant] was beset by insects, by rats that could literally make a hamlet uninhabitable and become fierce enough to attack humans (in one province alone, some five million rats were killed in a two-month, U.S.-sponsored drive in 1962), by floods and by droughts. He was seared by the sun and whipped by the rain, and his bare feet became calloused, unfeeling boards. The beauty of his women was destroyed by their mid-twenties, and by the mid-thirties they were hags, wracked by years of merciless burden, and often by disease.

And forever there were the flies, chiltering the stinking fish at the village market, swarming the open sores in the skin of his infant son, harassing his sleep. To survive his mind became numb, reconciled forever to submission and pain without end.[6]

Then strangers appeared in the night. They brought no gifts, no money, no food. Sometimes they asked for food, paying if they could. They sat by the fire, they talked, they listened, and because they had once been of these hamlets themselves, they soon did not seem strange. They brought sympathy, understanding, and compassion. They brought what no one had ever brought before: genuine interest in the peasant's welfare. They brought a solution to pernicious poverty, the National Liberation Front which would seize the country from foreign hands to give them a land of peace and freedom—and sufficient land for the crops to feed often hungry mouths. They preached more. They carried a materialistic bible with thousands of appealing verses. These agit-prop agents did not hurry to convert the listener. At first they settled for passive acceptance. Their continued interest and honeyed words of promise often produced the desired effect, and that was to arouse hope and, with it, new-found dignity. The peasant now had something to fight for.[7] Now he would lend his children to the Viet Cong, the younger as messengers, the older as fighters. Now he would donate to the cause, now he would pay taxes, now he would supply food and sanctuary and guides who would help guerrillas transit twenty-five miles of tortuous terrain in five hours of night marches. The agent recruited the female as well. He organized the guerrilla version of a Fem-Lib movement. He stressed the ghastly lot of women during the French colonial and the Diem regimes. The PRP pledged itself to " . . . total liberation of women in every respect . . . for economic equality, political equality, cultural equality, social equality . . . and equality in the family."[8]

Having aroused the peasant, the Viet Cong kept him aroused: "struggle meetings," "denunciation meetings," "ceremonial meetings," "people's conventions"; dozens of front organizations, each tailored to a specific target; newspapers, leaflets, theatrical troupes, cultural teams, radio, motion pictures—an altogether-well-organized, massive propaganda effort almost constantly misunderstood and underrated by South Vietnamese and American officials. The American-Diem military effort helped to sustain the propaganda effort. Each bomb dropped, each machine-gun bullet fired, each gallon of defoliant, was worth a thousand persuasive words.

Probably not one Viet Cong agent in a thousand could read English, yet each knew the truth long-before written by Lawrence of Arabia: " . . . A province would be won when we had taught the civilians in it to die for our ideal of freedom. The presence of the enemy was secondary. Final victory seemed certain, if the war lasted long enough for us to work it out."[9]

The prevailing political atmosphere in Saigon could hardly have engendered a national will so necessary to combating Communist influence in the countryside. Diem's continued failure to allow urgently needed economic, agrarian, and social reforms and to decentralize political control meant an apathetic peasantry who remained peculiarly prone to propaganda and blandishments offered by NLF and PRP cadres.[10]

So long as peasants remained apathetic or hostile, the military effort against the Viet Cong could not succeed—no matter how expansive it became. Unfortunately, this unpalatable truth, emphasized repeatedly since 1945 and preached by vigorous, intelligent, and experienced voices, did not wash against the American military priesthood who were well on their way to the fateful formula for disaster that combined arrogance of ignorance with arrogance of power.

Kennedy's decision to go along at least in part with the Staley and Taylor-Rostow recommendations tipped an expansion that by early 1962 reached impressive proportions. The Vietnamese task force already existed. The Pentagon soon opened an Office on Counter-Insurgency and Special Activities, headed by Major General V. H. Krulak, a marine officer who enjoyed direct access to the Joint Chiefs of Staff and also to McNamara. The State Department set up a "counter-insurgency course" to train civil officials; the armed forces began similar specialized training. In Saigon, Ambassador Nolting headed the Country Team of civil and military officials, and he also headed the Country Task Force, which, in theory, functioned " . . . as an extension of the Vietnam Task Force in Washington." In reality, General Paul Harkins, who arrived in March 1962 as head of MACV (formerly MAAG), almost at once became the dominant figure, which meant, among other things, that the military effort continued to receive priority over the civil effort. By early 1962, the United States was funding a hefty increase in South Vietnam's armed forces and it was also financing what it hoped would prove to be a widespread "strategic hamlet" program. American army and marine helicopters began ferrying Vietnamese troops to and from "combat areas." By spring, some six thousand Americans were serving in Vietnam; a significant portion of field advisers and helicopter crews were being shot at; some military advisers were beginning to shoot back, as were armed helicopter crews. Special Forces teams working with the CIA were active in the central highlands and in the North, trying to woo heterogeneous Montagnards to fight on the government's side.

In the South, in the Mekong Delta area, the infusion of weapons and material sparked a great series of "offensives," of "search-and-destroy" operations, of regimental and division sweeps supported by T-28 and B-26 aircraft strafing and bombing (too often on speculation) and burning out "enemy" complexes with napalm. Communiqués sounded like those issued by the French in the late 1940s. According to one source, enemy battle deaths were running between four and five hundred a month, with another thousand men being wounded or taken prisoner. Mobility offered by helicopters allowed ARVN forces to catch numerous units off guard and posed a tactical challenge not immediately met by the Viet Cong. Captured NLF and PRP documents showed Communist consternation, as did increased terrorist tactics including kidnapings and assassinations. In some areas, the Viet Cong forcibly recruited guerrilla replacements and kept them in line by threatening reprisals against their families; they kept families in line by threatening to punish the sons. Wilfred Burchett, the peripatetic Australian Communist reporter in Hanoi at the time, later wrote that the Viet Cong were on the point of yielding the Mekong Delta and withdrawing to the mountains.[11]

All this was heady stuff that impressed a good many American officials. Secretary of Defense Robert McNamara returned from Vietnam, in May 1962, and stated: " . . . Every quantitative measurement we have shows we're winning this war." General Maxwell Taylor returned from a second trip to Saigon impressed by "a great national movement" that would destroy the Viet Cong. In January 1963—the American presence in Vietnam had increased to nearly ten thousand—President Kennedy, in his State of the Union message, said: " . . . The spearhead of aggression has been blunted in South Vietnam."[12]

These and other glossy statements were unduly optimistic. Tactical gains amounted to little more than a gossamer sheen woven by temporary technological superiority. Despite intensification of fighting, the problem remained essentially a guerrilla suppression problem and for this the Vietnamese army and a large proportion of American advisers proved singularly ill-prepared, not only showing themselves unable either to adjust tactically or to exploit tactical gains by a forceful and effective civil-affairs program. Not understanding basic tenets of guerrilla warfare, Vietnamese and American senior officers converted fatalities into "victories." This was a great mistake: Dead bodies do not mean destroyed infrastructure. Dead bodies, particularly those of innocent peasants, mean a strengthening, not a weakening, of the insurgent cause. The NLF and PRP were down, but scarcely out. At the time retreat was being discussed, an NLF delegation headed by Nguyen Van Hieu, secretary-general of the NLF Central Committee, was touring Eastern Europe to introduce the NLF to the world. At the same time, southern cadres who had been living in the North took to what was to become famous as the Ho Chi Minh Trail to infiltrate back to the South. About thirty-seven hundred had arrived in 1961, according to Douglas Pike, who suggested that in 1962 another fifty-eight hundred arrived.[13] More would come the next year.

As 1962 turned to autumn, the Viet Cong began to display a new and disturbing aggressiveness. If they were not yet actively picking fights with ARVN troops, they were not avoiding them either. And they were continuing to strike Civil Guard and Self-Defense Corps outposts, both to supply themselves with new American arms and to prove their power to the peasants. Such was their success that to American advisers the outposts became known as Viet Cong PXs.[14]

Nor was ARVN showing well. As the Viet Cong recovered and began to shoot back, Diem's army seemed reluctant to fight. The battle of Ap Bac, in January 1963, exposed the awkward truth.[15] A task force of more than three South Vietnamese battalions, lifted in part by helicopters and armored personnel carriers, failed to destroy a Viet Cong battalion though having had it surrounded and greatly outgunned. ARVN's failure underlined the futility of trying to fight a guerrilla war with a conventional army that lacked both will and know-how. The U. S. Army's training program had denied it necessary flexibility. Armored personnel carriers and artillery had sharply decreased cross-country mobility. Confined to roads, ARVN units, just like French units formerly, remained vulnerable to ambush. Units lifted by helicopter could not long sustain themselves in the field without logistic support they had been taught to expect. ARVN staff work remained haphazard, particularly in vital intelligence sections. Operations remained uncoordinated. Diem refused to establish a supreme commander and general staff, instead running what virtually amounted to a war-lord arrangement. This meant spotty operations with slow response to hit-and-run guerrilla tactics. Intelligence, the vital ingredient in counterguerrilla warfare, was missing to a disastrous degree, the inevitable result of governmental failure to identify with peasants. Lacking intelligence on which to base small, selective, surprise raids, army units resorted to "sweeps," which often damaged and destroyed crops and hamlets but generally failed to kill or capture significant numbers of enemy. Troop looting and torture of villagers to obtain information nullified any psychological gain from show of force. If ARVN did clear an area of enemy, failure to occupy, consolidate, and protect villagers soon brought back the Viet Cong. U. S. Army advisers, with few exceptions and almost none at senior levels, could not be persuaded to adopt a proper counterinsurgency strategy: viable search-and-hold operations with concomitant political and military pressure on Diem to force his government to initiate a genuine strategic-hamlet program.

Over-all failure only sapped ARVN of remaining will and made its ranks more prone to enemy propaganda—the *binh van* (proselyting) program. Although the Viet Cong sought to induce desertions whenever possible, they also relied on internal disintegration, on the process the French called *pourrissement*. This was generally a private deal between the NLF and the low-level village official in which the latter escaped death in return for neutralizing government programs:

> This could be done by a slowdown, by snarling the program in red tape, or by outright falsification of reports to higher headquarters. For instance, a strategic-hamlet chief could go through the motions of creating a village security apparatus that only appeared to have succeeded in separating the guerrillas from the villagers. Vietnamese Information Service posters and leaflets arriving from Saigon could be distributed only superficially, in areas where district officials would be likely to notice them, and the rest destroyed. A military patrol leader could lead his patrol noisily down a well-travelled path and after an hour return to the hamlet, never having made a serious effort to determine whether guerrillas were in the area but with his superiors being none the wiser. The effect was to place a premium on mediocrity in low-level administration at a time when excellence was vital . . . many ARVN military operations were ruined by Vietnamese military or civil servants gratuitously passing on information to NLF agents or persons they presumed to be in contact with the NLF, simply in an effort to ingratiate themselves with the NLF—as a sort of life insurance policy.[16]

The CIA and Special Forces found lucrative operational possibilities in the central highlands, where more than a hundred thousand Montagnards had fled their villages, the result of NLF failure to capture their loyalty.[17] American teams began recruiting and training Montagnard units to return to the hills to fight the Viet Cong.[18] Initial successes here also proved illusory: The Montagnards, while willing in some instances to fight as mercenaries in American pay, refused to transfer loyalty to the Diem government; to the South Vietnamese, they were known as *moi*, or savages, treated similarly, and responded predictably. So long as Americans remained, the effort prospered; with their departure, it failed.

By end of 1962, the highly touted "strategic hamlet" program, which aimed to fortify eleven thousand, or two thirds, of the country's hamlets by 1963, had also bogged down. In theory, this was an excellent idea. Its genesis traces not to Eugene Staley but to the head of the British Advisory Mission to Viet-Nam, Robert Thompson, who arrived in Saigon in autumn of 1961.[19] A veteran of Orde Wingate's follies in Burma in World War II and of the later Malayan Emergency, Thompson had been instrumental in relocating Chinese villages in order to cut insurgents from local sources of intelligence, supply, and recruits, as well as protecting villagers from insurgent infiltration and attacks. (See Chapter 46.) The idea was not original. As Gallieni and Lyautey realized, protection is an essential part of pacification. Area clearance had been used subsequently in emergencies, for example by General Weyler in Cuba, by the American army in the Philippines, by Kitchener in the Boer War, more recently by the French in Indochina and Algeria, and by the British in Malaya and Kenya. The present concept called for the army to clear and hold an area while the government helped villagers fortify hamlets into defensive complexes defended with militia, civil guards, and police, with regular troops on call. The Diem government refused Thompson's original suggestion because brother Nhu did not like it. When Staley favored it, which spelled American financing, Nhu swung around and made it his own project—something quite different from what Thompson or Roger Hilsman had in mind.

Though valid enough, the concept, at best, was no panacea, which Thompson would have been the first to point out. Like most pacification measures, it called for a patient, methodical, and selective approach best illustrated by Lyautey's phrase *tache d'huile*. It had several drawbacks. The Mekong Delta, for example, was rich enough to feed guerrillas, fortified hamlets or no. The concept demanded efficient administration, and particularly effective internal and external security arrangements. When it worked, it worked well, and might have proved the key to solving the pacification problem but for two major defects. The first was a failure to integrate the strategic-hamlet program into a single, over-all strategy evolved by Hilsman and others and discussed above. Thompson and Hilsman wanted the program to start in the heavily populated Mekong Delta and work slowly out from there. Instead, under Nhu's aegis, strategic hamlets sprang up like rice shoots. The government could not possibly provide enough civic action and security teams necessary to revamp hamlets and to organize and train peasant militia, nor did police exist in sufficient quantity to ferret out Viet Cong agents and sympathizers from within defended complexes. Once again, massive American aid, dollar and material, filtered through venal fingers to lose intended impact. In most areas, the program mired in ooze of bureaucratic corruption and ineptitude.

This was bad enough in its own right. But, as it was happening, the enemy was admitting the threat and, once again, was adjusting tactics. NLF leadership judged the threat of such proportions that it began subordinating the political struggle to the armed struggle and made the strategic-hamlet program a priority tactical target—at a time when ARVN and local militias were particularly vulnerable. Many of the hastily constructed complexes lacked adequate fortifications and remained physically vulnerable to Viet Cong propaganda, infiltration, and attacks. Rudimentary communications and regular army inefficiency slowed reaction time and thus lowered promised protection. Battery-operated transmitter-receiver radios to provide village-to-garrison communications proved of slight value since " . . . calls for help were so rarely answered [by ARVN], or answered so slowly as to be useless."[20]

A second major defect centered on Nhu's ulterior motives. As with the previously unsuccessful *agrovilles* and "fighting hamlets," Nhu saw fortified hamlets as a convenient form of population control, with neighbor reporting on neighbor.[21] In places, they became little more than concentration camps full of unwilling guests. These were peasants who until the government-enforced move had been listening to a siren song, his deception the greater because his ears had never before heard music. Then, suddenly, he was scooped up, placed in a strategic hamlet—and found the same miserable life of old, the same arrogant and corrupt officials, the same squeeze, the same sicknesses. A song became a nightmare and a program went to pot.

Here was the real failing, not alone of the strategic-hamlet program but of the entire counterinsurgency effort. The Diem government and its foreign advisers may not have known it, but they were fighting essentially an idea, and fortifications, in the long run, are invalid against ideas. As Hilsman had discerned, the only valid weapon against an idea is a better idea—and Ngo Dinh Diem's abortive doctrine of Personalism, which the Eisenhower and Kennedy administrations kept trying to insist was democracy, did not fill the bill. The Diem government may have given peasants barbed wire and advisers and even a civil-guard unit, but failure to provide vigorous counterideas—to give the peasant something to fight for—left hamlets and villages as vulnerable as ever to vigorous NLF and PRP propaganda.

Far from protecting the peasant, the strategic-hamlet program frequently alienated him. Despite strenuous efforts of some American field advisers and a good many Vietnamese officers and officials, this unhealthy situation continued into 1963. Whether the situation could have been retrieved then is debatable; if Diem could have brought himself to initiate legitimate reforms, it is possible that he still could have claimed the upper hand.

This was not to be. Kennedy's kid-glove treatment of the Diem hierarchy had backfired. Diem and his circle of intimate advisers grew increasingly difficult to deal with. At times, Diem held himself practically inaccessible; on other occasions, he granted audiences and then subjected ranking callers such as Nolting or Harkins to hours-long monologues. To most observers, he appeared firmly under the thumb of brother Nhu and Mme. Nhu, and, to some observers, the former was as mad as the latter was corrupt and ambitious.

What was the official American reaction? It was as if Diem and his failures did not exist. In March 1963, the Secretary of State, Dean Rusk, stated that the war was " . . . turning an important corner . . . Government forces clearly have the initiative in most areas of the country." In April,

> . . . he discerned a "steady movement toward a constitutional system resting upon popular consent," declared that "the 'strategic hamlet' program is producing excellent results," added that "morale in the countryside has begun to rise," assured his listeners that "to the Vietnamese peasant" the Viet Cong "look less and less like winners" and concluded, "The Vietnamese are on their way to success. . . . "[22]

Roger Hilsman later reported an April meeting in Honolulu between Harkins and McNamara:

> . . . General Harkins gave us all the facts and figures—the number of strategic hamlets established, number of Viet Cong killed, operations initiated by government forces, and so on. He could not, of course, he said, give any guarantee, but he thought he could say that by Christmas it would be all over. The Secretary of Defense [McNamara] was elated. He reminded me that I had attended one of the very first of these meetings, when it had all looked so black—and that had been only a year and a half ago.[23]

In May, when the NLF was collecting taxes in forty-one of South Vietnam's forty-four provinces, Harkins told Saigon reporters that the war would be won " . . . within a year." A month later—American troops in Vietnam now numbered over fifteen thousand—Ambassador Nolting told reporters: " . . . South Viet-Nam is on its way to victory over communist guerrillas."[24] To gain that victory, the administration had progressively raised its commitment from six hundred to fifteen thousand troops; as an adviser had warned Dean Acheson in 1950: " . . . These things have a way of snowballing."

The brilliance of official statements suddenly dimmed in the flare of Buddhist revolts. The Buddhist problem had been building for a long time. Like the peasant problem, it was essentially political, although it held religious overtones. South Vietnam is overwhelmingly Buddhist, with some eleven million persons carrying the appellation. Like all great religious movements, Buddhism had splintered into many variations, and perhaps four million could be called orthodox Buddhists.[25] The disillusionment of this majority bloc began when Diem installed northern, Catholic refugees in the more important and lucrative administrative posts and otherwise favored the minority (1.5 million) Catholic population. Buddhist grumblings grew increasingly severe in 1961. Instead of righting wrongs and admitting Buddhist leadership into his government, Diem, as usual, relied on repression. Open rebellion broke out in May in Hué when government troops, attempting to disperse a Buddhist crowd, opened fire and killed nine Buddhists. Although the Diem government blamed this on Communist agitators, it gave in to some Buddhist demands. During negotiations a Buddhist fanatic, following an ancient sacrificial custom, burned himself to death in a public ceremony in Saigon, an act photographed by Malcolm Browne and one that helped turn world opinion sharply against the Diem regime.[26] Subsequent immolations kept the issue alive and brought continuing demands from the Kennedy administration for a settlement. Instead, Nhu, prodded by his wife (who heartlessly described the suicides as "barbecues"), persuaded Diem to declare martial law followed by police raids of Buddhist pagodas throughout South Vietnam—his police supplemented by Vietnamese Special Forces, a unit organized with CIA aid and one supposedly dedicated to counterguerrilla warfare.

With these acts, Diem and Nhu signed the death warrant of their government and, as it turned out, themselves. The raids brought thousands of protesting students into Saigon and Hué streets, where their arrest by army troops caused additional thousands of vociferous protests. Meanwhile, the NLF was shifting emphasis to the armed struggle. This was partly at the instigation of its own leaders and of the PRP, partly at Hanoi's instigation. In April 1963 in Hanoi, the secretary-general of the Lao Dong, Le Duan, " . . . made the case for a violent versus a peaceful path to power [in the South]."[27] Hanoi also sent south a particularly skillful leader, Tran Nam Trung (an alias), who became secretary-general of the PRP, which held responsibility for the armed struggle. The NLF continued to step up guerrilla operations—the armed struggle was about to command the political struggle. The situation was far from simple. Dissident groups existed in the NLF and also in Hanoi. Moscow did not want the war escalated, but Peking did. Apparently, moderates in both South and North still controlled the situation—in any event, the NLF and Hanoi now released peace proposals sufficiently concrete to cause General de Gaulle to ask for neutralization of the area.

President Kennedy also dispatched a new ambassador, Henry Cabot Lodge, who was instructed to maintain a " . . . posture of silent disapproval" vis-à-vis the Diem government. Kennedy further suspended $12 million of monthly aid and, as a particular snub to Nhu, Lodge arranged for recall of the CIA chief, John Richardson, who was overtly sympathetic to the regime. The American Government's new firmness began jelling an incipient army revolt that had been brewing for over a year and now joined hands, albeit obliquely, with a more recently formed generals' plot.

743

Although the Kennedy administration would willingly have continued to support Diem in return for sincere political and economic reforms, Diem's continued intransigence and particularly the anti-American raillery indulged in by Nhu and his vicious wife finally wore Kennedy's patience thin. In a famous speech of early October 1963, he told a television audience that " . . . a change of policy and perhaps personnel" was required in the Saigon government.

Rightly or wrongly, the generals plotting a coup regarded the President's words as a green light, and they seem to have been further encouraged by some American officials, both in Washington and Saigon, who had been made aware of their plans:

> . . . On October 10th, the American go-between informed [General Duang Van] Minh that the United States would not stand in the way of a coup if it took place, and that if it was successful and if a new regime could improve military morale and effectiveness, could obtain popular support, and could deal on a practical basis with the American government, it would receive aid.[28]

Plots and counterplots developed during the next three weeks. The coup began in earnest on the first day of November. Diem activists such as Colonel Tung, who commanded the dreaded Special Forces, lost their lives on the first day; Diem and Nhu refused Ambassador Lodge's offer of sanctuary and flight and, on the following day, were arrested and summarily executed by army officers.

The coup might have solved many problems, particularly had the American administration followed with a firm policy vigorously pursued. Unfortunately, less than three weeks after Diem and Nhu met their deaths, President Kennedy was assassinated.

CHAPTER FIFTY-NINE

1. Zagoria, 112–16. See also, Pike, 136 ff.
2. Zagoria, 116–17.
3. Lacouture, 59–60.
4. Pike, 55.
5. Ibid., 85 ff.
6. Mecklin, 75–6. See also, Pike, 109–10 for a contrasting description. Other personal observations, my own included, not to mention sociological statistics, favor Mecklin's report.
7. Tanham, *War Without Guns*, 13 ff. See also, ibid., 20: Dr. Tanham interviewed a guerrilla prisoner in Thailand. The man said he had become dissatisfied with his government in June 1959. Pressed as to why the date was so specific, he answered: " . . . A man told me I was unhappy with certain things and I suddenly realized he was right."
8. Pike, 174.
9. Lawrence, "Guerrilla Warfare."
10. Tanham, *War Without Guns*, spells out many of these. See also, Pike, 60:

Diem's land-reform program lasted only " . . . 3 years and aided only about 10 per cent of the landless."

11. Burchett.
12. Schlesinger, *The Bitter Heritage* . . . , 24–5.
13. Pike, 324.
14. Mecklin, 97.
15. Hilsman, 447–50. See also, Halberstam, *The Making of a Quagmire*, 147, 150, 157.
16. Pike, 257–8.
17. Ibid., 205.
18. Mecklin, 68: In 1963, Special Forces took over the program and eventually trained 20,000 troops with varying success. See also, Pike.
19. Robert Thompson, *Defeating Communist Insurgency*. See also, Clutterbuck, *The Long Long War*; Mecklin; Tanham, *War Without Guns*.
20. Mecklin, 67. See also, Tanham, *War Without Guns*.
21. Pike, 64 ff. See also, Halberstam, *The Making of a Quagmire*; Warnke.
22. Schlesinger, *The Bitter Heritage*, 25.
23. Hilsman, 466–7.
24. Schlesinger, *The Bitter Heritage*, 25.
25. Shaplen, *The Lost Revolution*, 192.
26. *The Times* (London), January 29, 1971:

> . . . The ancient custom which Thich Quang Duc [the 73-year-old monk who burned himself to death] revived takes its origin in a Mahayana Buddhist text written in India in the first century A.D. Called the Saddharma-pundarika-sutra, it tells the story of Bhais-hayjaraja, who ate incense, drank oils, and bathed in essences for 12 years before setting fire to himself as an offering to Buddha.
>
> This text was translated into Chinese (about 223 A.D.) and the cult first became established in China and Vietnam in the fifth century A.D. In the next 500 years there are records of at least 25 Buddhists (including two nuns and one layman) ceremonially burning themselves. The fanatics commonly dieted before igniting themselves, to make their bodies more combustible. Others made more modest offerings by cutting off and burning fingers or hands.

See also, Lacouture, whose authority is M. Folliozat, a specialist in the tradition of Indian Buddhism:

> . . . One may see in these acts primarily an affirmation of eminent dignity and purification. By burning his arm—which is the most traditional gesture—or his body, the initiate, who is "free" or "awakened," freely disposes of what he has come to know to be simple appearance. No longer attached to things, he heroically demonstrates that he understands real values, a deeper order, and in this fashion condemns the attitude of those who persecute his co-religionists.
>
> F. adds that such cremations could also be gestures of protest, condemnation, or vengeance; he states, too, that these acts constitute exploits of an extraordinary psychosomatic technique which, it seems, reduces the sufferings caused by the sacrifice. . . .

27. Zagoria, 108.
28. Shaplen, *The Lost Revolution*, 203–4.

CHAPTER 60

WHY DID JOHN KENNEDY fail in Vietnam?

The reasons are several and complex. Taken together, they do not compliment the man's historical image, nor do they present a comforting picture of American officialdom, military or civil, and the decision-making process. Taken together, they emphasize the theme of this book—the arrogance of ignorance—and they must be analyzed, if only briefly, for us to understand subsequent events in Vietnam, the continuing and ever expanding rift in American political, diplomatic, and military circles, the resultant widening and in many ways dangerous schism between government and people, and the precarious moral position in which the United States finds itself vis-à-vis the world today.

Although Kennedy had interested himself in Indochina since 1951, his was a politician's interest, in his case a well-meaning, liberal desire to put matters right, but scarcely a profound understanding of basic issues. Kennedy never recovered sufficiently from initial ignorance to give Indochina the priority attention it required. The situation demanded a dynamic, imaginative, courageous, and even incautious policy on Kennedy's part. Instead, he remained wedded to the inherited ambition: *stop communism*. This presupposed that communism is a physical thing like a tank or a division of troops or a bullet, and not an abstract idea so theoretically appealing as to have survived elaborate corruptions placed upon it by a dozen pinchpenny dictators. Stopping communism was an ambition that disallowed occasional short-term "defeat" in the process of winning long-term "victory." Hindering communism while proving the virtues and strengths of democracy is a policy that demands a planned course of conduct based on a realistic recognition of "strategic conveniences" as opposed to "strategic necessities," and one that accepts temporary setbacks in the process of insuring healthy survival with potential growth.

Kennedy's tense political situation—". . . The margin of voices that proclaimed him President was so thin as to be almost an accident of counting"[1]—dissuaded him from disowning his inheritance. Instead, he bowed to forces of fear, both Republican and Democratic—and, almost to the end, remained prisoner to the Diem regime and to those officials who favored a predominantly military approach to a political problem.

Two other bonds held him in thrall. One was Vietnam's relatively low priority in international affairs. Kennedy no sooner entered the White House than, like Truman and Eisenhower before him, he faced a host of major international and domestic problems. "Each day the crises multiply," was his plaintive cry to his countrymen soon after he took office. "I must inform the Congress that . . . in each of the principal areas of crisis—the tide of events has been running out and time has not been our friend."[2]

Kennedy assumed office during the Laotian blow-up, with Vietnam a secondary problem. Before he could come to grips with Vietnam, he was involved in the Berlin crisis, with resultant political strains at home. Then the moratorium on nuclear testing, the Bay of Pigs fiasco, the missile challenge, the 1962 Congressional elections, the quarrel with Great Britain over Skybolt, the De Gaulle crisis, the civil-rights battle, the confrontation with the Soviet Union over Cuba—one followed the other, a political TV serial, a house of troubles with the Vietnam issue now and again popping in like an unwanted relative. Not until the Buddhist revolts in spring of 1963 did Vietnam become an Administration "crisis area." Until late 1963, only three American news media—Associated Press, United Press International, and the New York Times—maintained full-time staff correspondents in Vietnam.[3]

A second bond strengthened the first. Kennedy, essentially, was a positive person. He entered office as a young and healthy man with a sincere belief in himself and his philosophy of government. This was one of the most appealing things about the man: his belief in America and America's greatness. He had not yet defined the meaning of or need for humility. He had not yet defined sufficiently the word "force" to realize that, in addition to virtues, it contains defects; that it is a word of nuance and limit; indeed, that use of force is engendered by fear, a subtle truth that explains, among other things, the remarkable success of judo and karate.

Kennedy's refusal to disown his inheritance of an impractical ambition was in part the result of the tense political situation—its genesis was the fall of Chiang Kai-shek—but it also resulted in part from Kennedy's insistence on playing a crusader role. At a time when polarized communism was defrosting, Kennedy embraced the monolithic theory which threatened the engulfment of the "free" world.[4]

Kennedy was full of himself and his country, and insisted on having that confidence justified. He wanted to believe reports of responsible officials who, when it came to insurgency warfare, were as enthusiastic, confident . . . and ignorant as he himself—and for some time, for too long, he believed them.

Kennedy welcomed dissent no more than most of us. Despite severe and persevering contradictions offered by the historical record and presented by talented, courageous, and knowledgeable civil and military experts, historians, and correspondents—a cumulative body of intelligent opinion derived from historical and contemporary experience—Kennedy refused what President Eisenhower had refused before him: to force a political settlement to what was in essence a political, not a military, problem.[5]

By allowing the military mastiff to overshadow the political cat, Kennedy erred egregiously, thus insuring the frequently pernicious and often unchallenged pre-eminence of the Pentagon in determining national security policy. It was partly his own fault in that he had appointed a man of limited stature as Secretary of State. A more effective stance would have been difficult to achieve in any case, but, as Roger Hilsman has pointed out, Dean Rusk " . . . regarded Vietnam as essentially a military problem even though a number of his colleagues in the State Department disagreed."[6] To worsen matters, Kennedy appointed Walt Whitman Rostow, an unmitigated hawk, as his national security adviser, which turned out to be a disaster of the first order.

Neither did McNamara or Taylor serve the President well. Not understanding the complexities of insurgency warfare himself, he could not know that they had escaped the conventional mind of Taylor and the computer mind of McNamara, both of whom often accepted false reports from the field, quantitative reports presenting a dangerously inaccurate picture. Perpetrators of these reports probably intended no deception at first. Alike untrained in insurgency warfare, military and civil advisers and observers, with some splendid exceptions, misread field developments to report extravagant tactical gains that so excited Washington officialdom in 1962. This is understandable if scarcely commendable. Top officials, military and civil, were putting careers on the line. Vanity was at work and so was ambition, but over these rode an appalling ignorance that produced an unhealthy, indeed fatal, arrogance that would admit of no error. When the bloom wore off, these people refused to accept that the tactical flower had died, and when mourners turned up for the funeral, they were brusquely advised there was no funeral.

Although several factors combine to explain this unfortunate fact, it was due primarily to American military ascendancy in Vietnam affairs since 1954 and concomitant insistence on seeking a military solution to an essentially political problem. Once the military began to rule the American presence, arrogance of ignorance asserted itself to begin eliminating rational thought. And when rational thought disappears, error multiplies finally to explode into catastrophe—which is what happened to the U.S. effort in Vietnam.

To understand this is to understand something of the American military profile at the time. Most of our military leaders did not grasp the concept of limited war. Thanks to Korea (and to MacArthur's inept strategy), the generals privately agreed that a limited ground war in Asia must be avoided in the future, that the requirement demanded an all-or-nothing strategy. They failed to agree on which arm was to accomplish the inane concept of "massive retaliation" strategy, with the result that the armed forces became more divisive than ever, with each grabbing for a disproportionate piece of the budgetary pie (a morbid condition that continues today).

Kennedy did not take kindly to either the military strategy or the military plant that he inherited. He did not wish to rely entirely on massive retaliation, which he feared would bring a nuclear war, and he did not trust so-called "tactical" nuclear weapons.[7] Prompted by Maxwell Taylor, who had argued against air force predominancy in a controversial book, *The Uncertain Trumpet,*[8] Kennedy returned to a conventional-force strategy, in short: " . . . a limited Communist conventional action . . . could best be deterred by a capacity to respond effectively in kind."[9] At this stage of the cold war, however, the Communists were no longer interested in waging costly conventional actions such as that in Korea. Kennedy now realized that the U.S. military was " . . . wholly unprepared to fight—or even to train others to fight—a war against local guerrillas."[10] To repair this tactical ignorance, he directed the Department of Defense to a priority effort.

Enter Special Forces—the Green Berets—who belonged to the army, a small unit operating under such a cloak of secrecy that, in the mid-

1950s, it very nearly secreted itself out of existence.[11]

Special Forces was and is a valid operational concept. Without going into detail, it attempted to amalgamate the best features of SOE/OSS World War II guerrilla operations to come up with teams based on the Jedburgh and OG prototypes (see Chapter 25). These teams varied in size, but each consisted of specialists trained to infiltrate into a target area and there contact and organize indigenous guerrilla forces either known, or believed by intelligence, to exist. In the mid-fifties, the U.S.S.R. and its satellites formed the major targets, but another Special Forces unit, based on Okinawa, was undoubtedly casting covetous eyes on China's hinterland. Despite some favorable publicity, Special Forces remained small and relatively unimportant until 1961.[12]

Special Forces skyrocketed to fame when President Kennedy recognized its elite status, authorized its unofficial emblem, the green beret, and increased its numbers and scope of responsibility. In effect, Kennedy made Special Forces what it was never intended to be and what it had not trained for, a counterinsurgency force.

The United States possessed still another agency which, perhaps unconstitutionally, had concerned itself with guerrilla warfare. This was the CIA, concurrently operating in Laos, clandestinely arming, supporting, and transporting pro-Western Laotian units to meet Pathet Lao guerrilla incursions supported by North Vietnam. In spring of 1961, by presidential authority, the CIA began infiltrating South Vietnamese forces into southeastern Laos " . . . to locate and attack Communist bases and lines of infiltration." The agency also began infiltrating agents into North Vietnam, where they were to form " . . . networks of resistance, covert bases and teams for light harassment inside North Vietnam." Judging from results and from later events, these operations were not very successful, though better than other efforts.

Nor was the CIA successful in the political field. The conflict between intelligence collection and analysis and executive operations had already emerged in the agency. The CIA in Laos and Vietnam was in the policy-making business to an alarming degree, its recommendations based on reports written by its chief, John Richardson, who insisted to one reporter that Diem's villainous brother, Nhu, " . . . was a great nationalist."[13]

At the beginning of the Kennedy administration, then, the country possessed precious little guerrilla expertise. The armed forces were operating in a state of flux, each more concerned with trying to maintain a state of readiness necessary to carry out conventional missions than in probing unconventional depths of insurgency warfare. A military correspondent in 1961 was asked to cover NATO Operation Wintershield, in Bavaria, not MAAG activities in Vietnam, and was ticked off by the air force for writing critically of its concentration on strategic bombers at the expense of tactical air support.[14] Insurgency and guerrilla warfare were not subjects of general military discussion. The *Marine Corps Gazette* scooped its competitors by devoting its January 1962 issue to guerrilla warfare: President Kennedy was so moved that he wrote the editor a personal letter of congratulation and directed the Pentagon to pay special attention to what he would soon tell the graduating class at West Point:

> ...This is another type of war, new in its intensity, ancient in its origins—war by guerrillas, subversives, insurgents, assassins; war by ambush instead of by combat; by infiltration, instead of aggression, seeking victory by eroding and exhausting the enemy instead of engaging him. ... It requires in those situations where we must counter it . . . a whole new kind of strategy, a wholly different kind of force, and therefore a new and wholly different kind of military training."[15]

But, in spring of 1962, when the first American helicopter units were flying in South Vietnam, Kennedy nevertheless entertained the Shah-in-Shah of Iran by taking him to Camp Lejeune, North Carolina, where hordes of marines performed a conventional amphibious landing. And in spring of 1962, a military correspondent could ask the chief of staff of Fleet Marine Force, Atlantic, what the immense command—some forty thousand ground and air troops—was doing about counterinsurgency, and could hear in reply: "What is it?"[16]

Kennedy had yet to learn that a presidential directive cannot work miracles. He failed to respect the soldier's fondness for tradition. It had taken a century to remove the soldier from the horse, once the rifle claimed the battlefield. A piece of paper could not overnight reorient armed forces that had grown up on gasoline, especially when most senior commanders agreed with Army chief of staff General George Decker that " . . . any good soldier can handle guerrillas." Convinced that the challenge was primarily military, commanders of all services, including twenty-two American army generals in Saigon,[17] began trying to convert an unorthodox area of operations into an orthodox theater of war. Not understanding the new rules, they could not tactically adapt. Whatever the President said about guerrilla warfare, these officers, in general, secretly believed that military professionalism would prove more than a match in any battle with "irregulars." Although, in time, some of the younger advisers would realize this error, the bulk remained convinced that professionalism—by which they meant adherence to Western military doctrines—would *win the war.* They had never heard of Major Callwell's writings on small wars, so they would never have pondered his sage advice to regard the native as the professional, the newcomer as the amateur (see Chapter 12). They had never studied Gallieni's and Lyautey's pacification campaigns (see Chapter 13). They had never heard of General Gwynn and so did not realize that, in countering an insurgency, the military was fulfilling a police role and had to apply *minimum*, not maximum, force; nor would they have known of his warning that a lull in guerrilla action is usually a danger sign, not a "victory" (see Chapter 23).

Some of their own people tried to educate them—with no success. As early as 1950, a regular marine officer, an Annapolis graduate, wrote a series of articles on guerrilla warfare in the *Marine Corps Gazette*. This was Colonel Samuel B. Griffith, who had served in Nicaragua, had personally observed Mao Tse-tung's tactics in China and was the first to translate his writings into English, and had served with great distinction as a Raider commander in World War II. Griffith stressed that " . . . modern arms and techniques have greatly increased the capabilities of partisans":

> . . . Ten thousand partisans organized into a number of columns can easily tie up 10, 20, or 30 times their own number of regular troops. Radio makes possible concerted partisan effort in widely separated areas. It also insures close strategic and tactical coordination between conventional and partisan forces and provides a means for the uninterrupted flow of information.

The partisan can be defeated, the author went on, but not by conventional military operations:

> . . . Anti-partisan operations embrace political, economic, and psychological measures, as well as those of a military nature. Indeed, the latter are of the least significance. The basis of partisan operations is in the people, or at least in a proportion of them. It becomes the first task then to win away important segments of this support, a task which requires correct policies in the three fields named. These policies will also make it possible to recruit one's own partisans, who should constitute the major part of the anti-partisan forces. Partisans must be beaten at their own game. This means that mobile columns must be the primary military agency. These columns should be equipped with the lightest weapons consonant with delivery of maximum fire effect . . . [they] cannot be dependent upon supply trains; supply, replacement, and evacuation must be carried out by aircraft so that the columns need not be tied to a base. Equipment must be transportable by light aircraft and helicopters in order that an entire column may be moved from place to place within its operating area with the greatest possible rapidity. Two or three anti-partisan "flying columns" of several

hundred men each would thus, even if operating in an area of one hundred miles square, never be out of mutually supporting distance. . . . Too much centralization of control over operations of anti-partisan columns must be avoided. . . . Operational rigidity can result only in disaster.[18]

Lacking suitable background, the American command did not realize that Western-style warfare is quantitative and that insurgency warfare is qualitative. To fight the latter successfully is frequently to reverse normal standards of measurement, just as trick mirrors in an amusement park make a fat person thin and a thin person fat. From the beginning, the American command erred by trying to use maximum, not minimum, force, and by designating the guerrilla the primary target rather than the population that supported him. Dead guerrillas became "victories"—enough "victories" would "win" the war. They did not understand that an insurgency is not "won"—except that it fades into relative quiescence. Unlike the Western battlefield, a rising body count in an insurgency is a danger sign. So is the necessity for "surprise" encounters, no matter how successfully fought. Progress is not made in an insurgency situation until local peasants are protected sufficiently and have sufficient reason to support government forces and supply necessary information on which to base operations. The oft-expressed American desire to persuade the Viet Cong "to stand and fight," a desire inherited from the French, was another pathetic fallacy. These were professional guerrillas who would not stand and fight—except on their own terms.

The Americans also failed to understand that qualitative warfare calls for careful target selection—that "saturation" of a battle area contains a number of built-in booby traps in an insurgency situation. The more units involved, the more-attenuated the lines of communication, thus the more targets available to the enemy. Rusk, Rostow, and the JCS could bleat their combined heart out about arms and supply from the North—the grim fact remained that the Viet Cong was deriving the bulk of its arms and supply from ARVN, exactly as Mao Tse-tung had done from the armies of Chiang Kai-shek. Worse than this, saturation of a battle area invariably damaged the peasants' crops and villages, frequently killing innocent people, thereby alienating the very persons the government needed to "win."

Our military commanders could not understand this. When General Harkins " . . . was asked about the political consequences when villages were hit with napalm, he replied that it 'really puts the fear of God into the Viet Cong.' 'And that,' he said, 'is what counts.' "[19]

*   *   *

753

A large part of the American failure in South Vietnam derived from ignorance of respective forces. A long time ago, Sun Tzu advised military commanders: " . . . Know the enemy and know yourself; in a hundred battles you will never be in peril. When you are ignorant of the enemy but know yourself, your chances of winning or losing are equal. If ignorant both of your enemy and of yourself, you are certain in every battle to be in peril."[20]

Prompted by Diem and Nhu, who, like Chiang Kai-shek, regarded guerrillas as "Communist bandits," American commanders in Saigon in large part oversimplified the enemy and particularly his goals. They would not accept that he was waging revolutionary warfare as defined by Mao and modified by Ho Chi Minh and Vo Nguyen Giap. Our senior officers refused to differentiate between the "political struggle" and the "armed struggle" or realize the importance of the former and its determinant influence on the course of war. They accepted militarily "quiet" areas as "won" areas, where, often, the reverse was true and they were politically "active" areas calling for the greatest concentration of government counteractivity. Such was their arrogance, such their ignorance, that they refused to respect adverse reports filed by subordinates from the field—reports that frequently contradicted information being fed to Washington.

Conversely, they found it difficult, if not impossible, to understand the temperament and mentality of the ARVN troops they were advising. They did not understand the evolutionary requirement of making a military silk purse out of a native sow's ear. They would not admit that expensive American-trained ARVN was avoiding contact with the VC, not seeking it—that the Civil Guard and Self-Defense Corps, which were running on slim budgets, were taking the bulk of casualties in defending static positions against VC night assaults. They failed to realize that the edifice had to be scrapped and rebuilt, with will a cornerstone, if a viable army was to result. As corollary to this failure, they did not understand that defectors gained by the government's Open Arms (Chieu Hoi) program did not necessarily mean loyal government supporters—that, in a larger sense, diminishing NLF strength did not mean added Diem strength.

With a few splendid exceptions, American advisers did not understand very much. They came with confidence instead of caution; they taught before they learned. From Nolting on down, too many of them resembled Alden Pyle—Graham Greene's Quiet American, " . . . who was impregnably armored by his good intentions and his ignorance."[21] The insurgencies of our time, not to mention those of history, might never have happened. The lessons they furnished weren't so much lost— they were never learned. To accomplish the military goal in Vietnam, to "win the war," to achieve "victory," the American military command sought to repair doctrinal deficiencies with machines. It relied on technology as opposed to motivation, on helicopters and jeeps and trucks and armored personnel carriers, aircraft and ships as opposed to men. It did precisely what the American military command in China had done nearly twenty years earlier. It attempted to remedy political, social, and economic deficiencies with metal.

The advisers were not at first discouraged because the new technology brought illusory success. The South Vietnamese Government estimated that the Viet Cong began the year with about sixteen thousand hard-core guerrillas. They estimated that in 1962 they had killed about twenty thousand "guerrillas" (I use quotation marks because we shall never know how many innocents were included in the figure). Yet VC strength, they estimated, had increased to twenty thousand! " . . . At the same time," Roger Hilsman later wrote, "captured documents, interrogation of prisoners, and other intelligence indicated that *at the most* only three to four thousand infiltrators had come down the Ho Chi Minh trail."[22] The other replacements came from hamlets and villages, and if some arrived under duress, a great many others came freely.

Despite ARVN "victories," the Viet Cong retained control of major areas. In summer of 1962, this writer flew several missions with U. S. Marine Corps helicopter squadrons operating out of Soc Trang, south of Saigon, the mission being to haul ARVN units to this or that threatened area. Fuel for these machines came from Saigon by tank truck, the Saigon trucker paying the Viet Cong a "toll" in order to pass to Soc Trang. This meant that at any moment the Viet Cong could prevent marine helicopters from flying. This rarely if ever happened—should it not have occurred to MACV that the effort could scarcely have been hurting the Viet Cong if the choppers were allowed to keep flying?

The fallacy of the new approach was already becoming evident. Initial Viet Cong fright soon turned to bewilderment; analysis followed to produce countertactics. Night operations increased, since helicopters at first did not fly at night. Assassinations and kidnapings greatly increased, the reasons being to enforce discipline, demonstrate determination, and gain recruits. By spring of 1962, the Viet Cong were beginning to fight back, and, by autumn, were not only pursuing active guerrilla tactics but were standing against ARVN units.[23] Once again, Viet Cong countertactics were immensely aided by intelligence derived from peasant networks that, while on the defensive, were scarcely defunct. Marines at Soc Trang and American field units elsewhere were living, to use Bernard Fall's term, in a fishbowl, their every movement, their take-off and landing, their resupply, noted and reported by Viet Cong agents.

The new technology did nothing to repair the existing gap between Vietnamese army units and peasants; indeed, helicopter delivery widened the intelligence gap by flying troops *over* villages and thus eliminating personal contact with the peasants—perhaps a good thing in the case of rapacious army units. The new vehicles also proved expensive. Helicopters and armored personnel carriers require large workshop and storage complexes, installations that in Vietnam demanded ground troops to provide security and nonetheless remained vulnerable to guerrilla attack, as did their lines of communication to major supply centers. Troops so assigned inevitably assumed a static role, to the guerrilla's benefit. Armor plate and motors did not erase poorly conceived plans. American and Vietnamese planners were trying to strike the enemy all over the place. All too often, these were random strikes, because the commands lacked proper intelligence on which to base specific and profitable operations. Where good intelligence existed, Viet Cong intelligence frequently countered it. Helicopters and APCs are noisy, and a black-pajama-clad Viet Cong did not take long to ditch his weapon and either commence work in the field or hide along the reeded bank of a nearby canal. By summer of 1962, frustrated American airmen had begun developing new tactics, for example "eagle flights," whereby helicopters landed a unit in a suspect area. If contact resulted, other, lingering helicopters immediately brought in reinforcements. The poverty of this tactic is too obvious for comment.

When the Viet Cong recovered from surprise and started to shoot, helicopter crews shot back.[24] At first, this was primitive; a crew member firing from the cargo doorway. Then Vietnamese planes, T-28s, sometimes piloted by American advisers, began strafing missions prior to helicopter landings. In late 1962,

> . . . the armed helicopters arrived, with four mounted machine guns and sixteen rocket pods; they were to escort the unarmed helicopters into battle and were not to fire until fired on. . . . By mid-1963 the armed helicopters were often serving as fighter planes, carrying out strafing missions.[25]

The net result was an increase in quantitative tactics—or escalation of the tactical effort.

CIA and Special Forces operations in the central highlands produced two results. One was a diminution of effort on part of the Vietnamese when left to their own resources. Once American teams moved on, Montagnard projects wilted and died to create tribal disillusionment and thus fertile ground for Viet Cong propaganda. The other was an extension of the war by building military outposts such as that at Pleiku, outposts that had to be defended, supplied—and finally evacuated.

At the same time, the civil effort burst into fresh bloom. This concentrated on the expensive strategic-hamlet program, which, as we have seen, was rapidly becoming dangerous in that false reports were endeavoring to prove it a success. Not only were the hamlets host to the sea of troubles already discussed, but they in no way answered the root problem of land reform. The reader will perhaps remember that highly restrictive land-distribution laws had made about 20 per cent of total ricelands available for peasant purchase. By the end of 1962, only about 25–30 per cent of the available land had been transferred to peasant hands. The former big landowners, rich Vietnamese, French *colons,* and the Catholic Church remained principal owners, with members of Diem's family and government claiming huge chunks of sequestered lands. Despite Diem's promises to American officials, nothing had changed. John Mecklin later wrote of " . . . at least one area where we found tax collectors attached to military units. The idea was that this was a convenient way to collect back taxes for absentee landlords in hamlets where government authority had totally collapsed, often several years later."[26]

The fallacy of the American approach did not escape certain observers. A small press corps almost unanimously contradicted optimistic statements of various American officials. Official statements emanating from Saigon and Washington, they wrote, scarcely reflected true feelings of American advisers in the field. The war admittedly had picked up speed, but, to what ultimate purpose, was not clear. Certainly by the turn of the year, it was obvious that the South Vietnamese army was not doing its share, the result of manacled command and poor morale, and it was obvious that the strategic-hamlet program had bogged down. Some disillusioned American field advisers had learned the difference between right and wrong, and were increasingly passing their observations to perceptive journalists. Roger Hilsman later noted that " . . . every faction was so passionately convinced of the rightness of its cause that leaking to the press became a patriotic act."[27] As befits a democratic system, a number of these journalists avoided the subjective thinking that crowned the Saigon mission and attempted to report the situation objectively.[28] Their accounts of what was happening conflicted at almost every point with what Saigon *wanted* to be happening. The official reaction was attempted news management and suppression in the totalitarian tradition—thus, a State Department directive of February 1962 that virtually ordered reportage favorable to the regime while denying " . . . newsmen access to whole segments of U.S. operations."[29] American reporters reacted predictably, and a feud of massive proportions developed. Contradiction crowned contradiction until a veritable communications breakdown developed—with awesome results in the United States.

Some evidence exists that President Kennedy was already worried about the Pandora's box of power he had opened. Faced with a pessimistic report from Hilsman's office in December 1962, he sent Hilsman and Michael Forrestal (son of the former Secretary of Defense) on still another "fact-finding" mission. The two emissaries found Harkins and Nolting " . . . strongly and quite genuinely optimistic," despite the battle at Ap Bac (which Harkins insisted was a "victory"). As for the strategic-hamlet program, the British expert Robert Thompson, though admitting certain shortcomings, was now " . . . the most optimistic" of all. Their report to the President began: " . . . The war in South Vietnam is clearly going better than it was a year ago." After a review of facts, the report continued:

> . . . Our overall judgment, in sum, is that we are probably winning, but certainly more slowly than we had hoped. At the rate it is now going, the war will probably last longer than we would like, cost more in terms of both lives and money than we had anticipated, and prolong the period in which a sudden and dramatic event could upset the gains already made.

The report went on to object to a lack of an over-all plan, to an inadequate police system, and to a predominance of "search-and-destroy" and "elaborate, set-piece" tactics; it also questioned the " . . . increasing use of air power." A top-secret "eyes only" annex, after listing other serious failures, went on in damning words:

> . . . The real trouble, however, is that the rather large U.S. effort in South Vietnam is managed by a multitude of independent U.S. agencies and people with little or no overall direction. No one man is in charge. What coordination there is results mainly from the sort of treaty arrangements that we arrived at in the country team meetings. . . . The result is that the U.S. effort is fragmented and duplicative. . . . What is needed ideally is to give authority to a single strong executive, a man perhaps with a military background but who understands that this war is essentially a struggle to build a nation out of the chaos of revolution. . . . [30]

How much credence the President attached to this report is not known, but Hilsman's promotion to Assistant Secretary of State for Far Eastern Affairs seemed to lend it at least presidential grace. In spring of 1963, Lieutenant Colonel John Vann, a senior field adviser, returned to Washington to report his dissent with ARVN performance, a bit of healthy heterodoxy that probably reached White House ears. In April, John Mecklin personally reported to the President the unsavory relationship between officialdom and press in Saigon. William Truehart, Nolting's deputy, was beginning to express grave doubts about the Diem regime. In September, Rufus Phillips, who headed the $20-million

Rural Affairs program in Vietnam, told President Kennedy that, despite Phillips' own earlier optimism, the program was failing. When Henry Cabot Lodge arrived in Saigon as the new ambassador, William Flippen, deputy chief of AID, who had been in South Vietnam for six years, " . . . delivered a bitter attack on our previous policy. Flippen added that the American military had been consistently wrong in its reports and interpretations ever since he arrived in Vietnam, and stated flatly that the war was being lost."[31]

Such dissidents formed a minority. Nolting, Richardson, and Harkins refused to admit that the American effort had turned sour. By spring of 1963, these people resembled company directors surrounded by charts and statistical reports showing favorable production and sales at a time when, unknown to them, the factory was shutting down. Their obdurate attitude found reflection in visiting officials, some of whom should have known better. At one point, Major General V. H. Krulak, an incisive little man jocularly known to his Marine Corps associates as "the Brute," arrived in Saigon as McNamara's counterinsurgency expert. At a time when the strategic-hamlet program was bursting at the seams, Krulak, although aware of Vann's strong feelings on this and other matters, reported favorably to McNamara. Later, when Rufus Phillips flew to Washington to acquaint Kennedy with disaster, he " . . . was immediately and bitterly challenged by Krulak, who doubted his veracity and his competence . . . "[32]—a curious stand, considering Krulak's lack of background in guerrilla warfare.

The conflict between Saigon and the field—between wishes and facts—had already produced a chilling corollary: extreme intolerance, on the part of both the Saigon regime and the American mission, of journalists who questioned the validity of allied performance. In March 1962, Mme. Nhu had begun persuading President Diem to expel three troublemakers, the veteran news correspondents Homer Bigart of the *New York Times,* François Sully of *Newsweek,* and James Robinson of NBC, each of whom was increasingly harassed by the Saigon government, as were other correspondents who, in Joseph Buttinger's words, were " . . . accused of being part of an international Communist-inspired conspiracy to slander the regime."

> . . . The U.S. mission was anything but forceful in defending these correspondents against abuse and ill-treatment, and almost apologetic in explaining that these men were merely trying to live up to the American concept of a free press. Ambassador Frederick E. Nolting, Jr., and General Paul Harkins in particular were incensed by the American newsmen's attacks on the regime. . . . They, as well as their superiors in Washington, spoke repeatedly of the "slanted" or even "irresponsible" press reporting out of Saigon,

convinced not only that the correspondents who criticized the regime did harm to U.S.-South Vietnamese relations, but also that they were wrong.[33]

Nolting and Harkins took it upon themselves to deny the democratic right of free speech, and it is to John Kennedy's shame that, while publicly calling for journalistic freedom,[34] he tried to muzzle the outspoken Halberstam by suggesting to his publisher, Arthur Hays Sulzberger, " . . . that he might give Halberstam a vacation to remove him from Vietnam."[35] Sulzberger refused, and Halberstam, along with Malcolm Browne, went on to win a Pulitzer prize. Another dissident, Charles Mohr of *Time*, who reported pessimistically on the deteriorating situation, found his copy suppressed by senior editors, and resigned in disgust.[36] Reporters who wrote favorable accounts, among them Marguerite Higgins, Joseph Alsop, and Richard Tregaskis, received comforting little pats for their part in what was rapidly becoming the great deception. The Administration was running scared.

The double standard of reporting continued into 1963. As each new allied effort flared and wilted, MACV continued to insist that the war was being won; the press, in general, continued to insist that it was being lost. If conditions were somewhat dicey in the Mekong Delta, briefing officers said, it was because " . . . the guerrillas had been pushed south by successful operations in northern areas."[37] If conditions were somewhat dicey in the delta, reporters wrote, it was because the strategic-hamlet program was failing—the inevitable result of a despot-ridden regime whose venality and corruption penetrated the entire command system of ARVN. (The reader should take note that almost every disclosure made by American reporters earlier and at this time was confirmed, and then some, by discoveries made after Diem's death!)

The eye-opening Buddhist revolts favored the reporters, however. Throughout summer of 1963, some of the truths they had been writing began emerging in official reports. National Security Council meetings grew more tense and acrimonious as the civil-versus-military battle mounted in Administration circles. In September, the President sent out still another civil-military fact-finding team, consisting of Krulak, the Pentagon's expert on insurgency warfare, and J. S. Mendenhall, a veteran diplomat with extensive service in Vietnam. In due time, they returned to Washington and a meeting of the National Security Council. Krulak reported enthusiastically on the situation, Mendenhall unfavorably. So diametrically opposed were the reports that President Kennedy dryly commented, " . . . Were you gentlemen in the same country?"[38] The President was probably not impressed, either, with General Harkins, who stated in October: " . . . I can safely say the end of the war is in sight."[39]

760

The end of the war, though not as Harkins meant it, might have been in sight had President Kennedy lived. In September 1963, one of his most trusted advisers, Robert McNamara, theretofore an optimist, returned from Saigon to report a *volte-face* that brought Kennedy up short. On previous inspection tours, McNamara had been sold a bill of goods by Harkins and Nolting that bore but slight resemblance to facts. Henry Cabot Lodge had replaced Nolting and was dissatisfied with what he found, apparently, pressing his views with considerable vigor on McNamara. McNamara back in Washington " . . . reportedly told Kennedy that the military had been wrong, that the war was not going well and that the official version of military events was inaccurate."[40] McNamara and Taylor nonetheless continued to insist on a military approach, reporting

> . . . their judgment that the major part of the United States military task can be completed by the end of 1965. . . . They reported that by the end of this year [1963] the U.S. program for training Vietnamese should have progressed to the point that one thousand U.S. military personnel assigned to South Vietnam can be withdrawn.[41]

Despite this optimism, misplaced as usual, the situation continued to deteriorate with such rapidity that, shortly after McNamara's return, Kennedy decided to dump Diem or at least not stand in the way of those who wished him dumped.

A former presidential aide, Kenneth O'Donnell, disclosed in 1970 that Kennedy, for some time, had been entertaining private personal doubts as to the American role in Vietnam. In late 1962, Senator Mike Mansfield had urged that the President stop escalating the American effort and withdraw all American forces from what was a civil war.

> . . . A continued steady increase of American military advisers in South Vietnam, the senator argued, would lead to sending still more forces to beef up those that were there, and soon the Americans would be dominating the combat in a civil war that was not our war . . .

When Mansfield continued to press the argument, Kennedy called him to the White House in spring of 1963, a private meeting witnessed by O'Donnell:

> . . . The President told Mansfield that he had been having serious second thoughts about Mansfield's argument and that he now agreed with the senator's thinking on the need for a complete military withdrawal from Vietnam.

761

"But I can't do it until 1965—after I'm re-elected," Kennedy told Mansfield.

President Kennedy felt, and Mansfield agreed with him, that if he announced a total withdrawal of American military personnel from Vietnam before the 1964 election, there would be a wild conservative outcry against returning him to the Presidency for a second term.

After Mansfield left the office, the President told me that he had made up his mind that after his re-election he would take the risk of unpopularity and make a complete withdrawal of American forces from Vietnam. "In 1965, I'll be damned everywhere as a Communist appeaser. But I don't care. If I tried to pull out completely now, we would have another Joe McCarthy red scare on our hands, but I can do it after I'm re-elected. So we had better make damned sure that I *am* re-elected."[42]

What the President allegedly thought is not what the President told the public. Neither doubts nor maturity embossed his statement given at a news conference in September 1963: " . . . we have a very simple policy in that area. In some ways I think the Vietnamese people and ourselves agree: we want the war to be won, the Communists to be contained, and the Americans to go home. That is our policy. . . . "[43]

As we said earlier, that was no policy, that was an ambition. What would have happened had the President lived and been re-elected is futile to speculate. We know that, until his death, he continued publicly to support the American commitment to Vietnam. His successor, Lyndon Johnson, chose to expand it.

CHAPTER SIXTY

1. White, *The Making of the President 1960*, 349.
2. Kennedy, *Public Papers of* . . . , I, 22–3.
3. Mecklin, 122. Robert Shaplen also covered the area for *The New Yorker* magazine.
4. Zagoria, 26:

   . . . During the decade in which the triangular relationship [among Moscow, Peking, and Hanoi] replaced the bipolar, the United States was slow to appreciate its own role in the process. Top American officials recognized the existence of the Sino-Soviet dispute only belatedly, then were extremely cautious about acknowledging it, and were always at a loss to know whether or how to exacerbate it.

5. Ellsberg: " . . . In early 1952, writing to the President to argue against sending combat units to Vietnam or otherwise deepening our involvement, J. K. Galbraith spoke of his fears that the bright hopes of the New Frontier would be sunk in the rice paddies of Southeast Asia." See also, Hilsman, 423: Chester Bowles argued for extending the area of neutrality beyond Laos to include Vietnam, Burma, Thailand, and Malaya; although Kennedy took no action, he seemed to favor a neutral Southeast Asia as a long-term goal.

6. Hilsman, 421.
7. Sorensen, 625–6:

> ... some of these "small" weapons carried a punch five times more powerful than the bomb that destroyed Hiroshima. Those ready for use in Europe alone had a combined explosive strength more than ten thousand times as great as those used to end the Second World War. If that was tactical, what was strategic?

8. Maxwell Taylor, *The Uncertain Trumpet.*
9. Sorensen, 626.
10. Ibid., 651.
11. The near disaster caused a change of public-relations heart, and in 1956 this writer was given an open-arms welcome as a military correspondent by the Special Forces unit headquartered in Bad Tölz, Bavaria.
12. In 1956, after a period in field and garrison at Bad Tölz, I wrote a favorable article for *Army* magazine. Alas! the secrecy cloak had not lifted to mini-size: My relatively short article was returned with fifty-five security violations noted, one of which was a recommendation to give Special Forces units on-the-job training in Vietnam. My article was not published. In 1961, as special correspondent for *Army* magazine, I revisited the scene of my earlier crime, was again welcomed and again impressed. Whether I was less perceptive or whether army security precautions had relaxed, my article was finally cleared and published, and it even elicited a congratulatory letter from the chief of the army's Information Section upon its inclusion in a volume on special warfare. See also, Sorensen, 632: Special Forces consisted of " ... only eighteen hundred men ... preparing for a wholly different kind of action in a general war in Eastern Europe. Their equipment was outmoded and insufficient, unchanged since the Second World War."
13. Halberstam, *The Making of a Quagmire*, 223.
14. I was the correspondent. Scene: U. S. Air Force Public Information Office, Pentagon. Serious Major Sunderman tapping copy of offensive article in *Army* magazine: " ... I must inform you, Mr. Asprey, that you have ruined General LeMay's afternoon."
15. Hilsman, 411.
16. Again, I was the correspondent. This brings to mind Admiral Ernest King's lament in early 1942: "I don't know what the hell this 'logistics' is that [General] Marshall is always talking about, but I want some of it." Griffith, *The Battle for Guadalcanal*, 30.
17. Hilsman, 455.
18. Griffith, "Guerrilla."
19. Hilsman, 442. See also, Shaplen, private letter to the author: Harkins' attitude at times approached the incredible. In 1962, the highly respected and experienced *New Yorker* correspondent Robert Shaplen brought a CBS television documentary to Saigon. Called *The End of an Empire*, it was a photographic record of the Viet Minh fighting at Dien Bien Phu—"by far the most graphic picture of its kind ever filmed." Harkins refused to let it be shown to either American advisers or South Vietnamese officers because it would "frighten" them to see how well the Viet Minh had fought!
20. Griffith, *Sun Tzu ...* , 84.
21. Graham Greene, 214.
22. Hilsman, 450–1. See also, Pike; Halberstam, *The Making of a Quagmire;* Bushell.
23. Author's personal observation. See also, Mecklin; Halberstam, *The Making of a Quagmire.*
24. Mecklin, 66: By the end of 1962 American combat deaths numbered 21; in 1963, 97 were killed.
25. Halberstam, *The Making of a Quagmire*, 81. See also, Harvey.

26. Mecklin, 86.
27. Hilsman, 499.
28. More subjective reporting, e.g., by Halberstam and Browne, came later—induced in part, it should be added, by the hopeless corruption and inefficiency of the Diem regime, in part by obtuse and obdurate behavior of American civil and military officials.
29. Mecklin, 115. See also, Salinger, 323.
30. Hilsman, 453, 462, 464–6.
31. Halberstam, 249.
32. Ibid., 254. See also, Hilsman.
33. Buttinger, II, 989. See also, Mecklin.
34. Kennedy, *Public Papers of . . .* , I, 304.
35. Salinger, 325. See also, Halberstam, 268.
36. Halberstam, 269 ff.
37. Ibid., 172.
38. Schlesinger, *A Thousand Days*, 993.
39. Schlesinger, *The Bitter Heritage*, 25.
40. Halberstam, 258. See also, Hilsman, 509: McNamara " . . . came back doubting the statistics he loved so well—or at least recognizing that unquantifiable political factors might be more important than he had been willing to believe before"; Kahin and Lewis.
41. Hilsman, 509.
42. O'Donnell.
43. Hilsman, 506.

CHAPTER 61

Enter President Lyndon Johnson • Duong Van Minh's provisional government • Political anarchy in the South • Revolutionary pressures • Nguyen Khanh takes over • McNamara's report (I) • Operation Plan 34A • Intelligence experts dissent • JCS hawks • Nguyen Khanh's reforms • McNamara's report (II) • Renewed VC offensives • The situation deteriorates • The Lodge plan: "carrot and stick" • Johnson backs the hawks • CIA rebuttal • Seaborn's mission to Hanoi • Hanoi hawks • Taylor relieves Lodge: the military situation • The new Saigon team • The Tonkin Gulf incident • William Bundy's Congressional resolution

NOTHING in President Johnson's background presaged a healthy change of policy in Vietnam. So far as that dismal situation went, he assumed office with one foot in a trap, albeit a trap he had helped set. Like John Kennedy, Johnson embraced a number of simplistic tenets. Unlike Kennedy, he was unable to question and perhaps outgrow them. He was wedded to the grand ambition: *stop communism.* He accepted the "aggression from the North" theory, and if the monolithic-Communist-conspiracy theme had developed a major crack, Peking conveniently replaced Moscow as master villain. The new President regarded South Vietnam as a military rather than a political problem; drawing on Prometheus and Robert Frost, he " . . . held with those who favored fire" for its solution.

Johnson faced a presidential election within a year, and that, rather than personal doubts, at first checked his use of overt force. As Kennedy had done in 1961, Johnson ordered a program greatly enlarged from the earlier civilian effort, but he also embraced force to compel the North to stop the war.

* * *

President Diem's demise had opened the way for a reform government that, properly pressured by the American Government, could possibly have retrieved the situation in South Vietnam. Instead, a provisional government showed itself weak and divided. Headed by a cardboard premier, it consisted of twelve generals who chopped off as many pro-Diem heads as possible—and then sat still, content to collect eggs from the American golden goose while their country went down the drain. In a situation that demanded firm and vigorous domestic policy carried out by trustworthy, trained, and confident officials, Duong Van Minh and his fellow generals proved themselves incapable of rule, indeed even of trusting one another.

Here was a power vacuum that a determined effort on the part of American advisers might have filled. But lack of viable American policy dictated inaction at a crucial time. As Robert Shaplen put it:

> . . . we dealt repeatedly in tired shibboleths, in continued bland expressions of optimism; and in consequence our policy, if indeed we had one, was obscured in a welter of words that unfortunately soon became involved in a Presidential political campaign. The admission must be made that we had no more of a post-coup plan than the Vietnamese had.[1]

With government fragmented by Diem's death and daily challenged by the Viet Cong, the situation soon grew calamitous. In the cities, political parties proliferated—sixty-two of them within a month and a half of the coup! The factious bodies in no way influenced the junta government into framing and passing reform legislation. A Council of Notables, which was supposed to draft a new constitution (but never did), included " . . . no representatives of the peasantry or of the labor movement."[2]

Although the junta removed some important pro-Diem officials, a number of them survived in office, as did thousands of lesser bureaucrats imbued with mandarin philosophy. Part of the reason was necessity: Trained officials remained in short supply. But part was political: Each junta member held ties to the old regime, his power resting, in part, on cliques and cabals within the framework of Diem's government, including the army. Power had merely shifted from one house of rule to another, with no seeming intention to improve the peasant's lot, no seeming recognition that here was a political revolution being overwhelmed by demands for a social revolution.

In autumn of 1963, the politically organized NLF-PRP was on hand to exploit the very real desire in the South for social revolution in cities and countryside. Within a month after the junta had assumed power, Viet Cong guerrillas opened carefully planned offensives throughout

South Vietnam. By December, guerrillas had ARVN on the run; once again, a cloud of jeopardy covered the land.

The failure of Minh's junta government promoted increasing intrigue that resulted in a bloodless military coup in late January 1964—General Nguyen Khanh now replaced Duong Van Minh.

Shortly after taking office, President Johnson conferred with Ambassador Lodge and with CIA Chief John McCone. Johnson later described Lodge as "optimistic" (as opposed to McCone):

> . . . I told Lodge that I had not been happy with what I had read about our Mission's operations in Vietnam earlier in the year. There had been too much internal dissension. I wanted him to develop a strong team; I wanted them to work together; and I wanted the Ambassador to be the sole boss. I assured him of full support in Washington. . . . [3]

We still don't know the exact relationship of that period. We do know that a stronger man than Lodge was needed to halt the internecine warfare being fought between not only American civil and military missions, but between sections within each. We also know that McCone's pessimism was justified. In December 1963, President Johnson sent Secretary of Defense Robert McNamara to Saigon for a two-day visit. McNamara reported that " . . . the situation is very disturbing. Current trends, unless reversed in the next 2–3 months, will lead to neutralization at best and more likely to a Communist-controlled state"; the new Saigon government was " . . . the greatest source of concern. It is indecisive and drifting." The "second major weakness," McNamara reported, was the Country Team, or *ad hoc* civil-military U.S. committee that was supposed to co-ordinate the American effort:

> . . . It lacks leadership, has been poorly informed, and is not working to a common plan. . . . [Ambassador] Lodge has virtually no official contact with Harkins. Lodge sends in reports with major military implications without showing them to Harkins, and does not show Harkins important incoming traffic. My impression is that Lodge simply does not know how to conduct a co-ordinated administration.

McNamara told the President that the situation has " . . . been deteriorating in the countryside since July to a far greater extent than we realize because of our undue dependence on distorted Vietnamese reporting." Infiltration of men and equipment from the North also played a part: " . . . The best guess is that 1000–1500 Viet Cong cadres entered

South Vietnam from Laos in the first nine months of 1963." In order to co-ordinate the American effort, McNamara wanted major operational changes, better U.S. staff personnel to improve reporting, improved pacification measures, and covert action—sabotage and psychological warfare operations—against North Vietnam.[4]

Johnson was sufficiently impressed to order significant changes in reporting methods from the field including direct " . . . detailed weekly reports from Ambassador Lodge which pulled no punches in describing problems as well as progress."[5] He also authorized additional American personnel, both civil and military, for the Saigon missions, as well as covert operations in the North. The latter effort, known as Operation Plan 34A, called for a variety of actions ranging from U-2 flights to commando-type raids designed " . . . to result in substantial destruction, economic loss and harassment"—what the Pentagon called "destructive undertakings." Two other covert operations complemented Plan 34A. One was an air effort directed by the CIA in Laos, where a force of twenty-five to forty T-28 fighter-bombers interdicted Pathet Lao operations. The other consisted of U. S. Navy destroyer operations in the Gulf of Tonkin. Code-named DeSoto patrols, they were mainly designed as a show of force, but " . . . the destroyers collected the kind of intelligence on North Vietnamese warning radars and coastal defenses that would be useful to 34A raiding parties."[6]

Along with other Administration officials, McNamara was apparently convinced from radio intercepts " . . . that Hanoi controlled and directed the Vietcong." McNamara recommended Plan 34A to the President in the hope that " . . . progressively escalating pressure from the clandestine attacks might eventually force Hanoi to order the Vietcong guerrillas to halt their insurrections." The plan went into effect in February 1964. Two important bodies remained unimpressed with the covert effort. The first was the intelligence community in general, which held that raids would not affect NLF operations in the South. Taylor and the JCS argued that "a much higher level of activity" was necessary, meaning raids into Laos, aerial bombing of the North, and committing American troops in sufficient numbers to meet the combat challenge in the South, including any specific response from the North such as invasion in the Korean style.[7] In large part, this parroted JCS thinking on Laos in 1961 and also bore direct resemblance to the Taylor-Rostow plan of late 1961. Walt Rostow, once again in the State Department, continued to press his "aggression from the North" thesis, urging punitive action against Hanoi. Ho Chi Minh, he informed Dean Rusk, " . . . has an industrial complex to protect: he is no longer a guerrilla fighter with nothing to lose."[8]

As with earlier plans, the new JCS plan glossed over the danger of escalating local insurgency into thermonuclear war, but whatever the danger, " . . . The Joint Chiefs of Staff consider that the strategic importance of Vietnam and of Southeast Asia warrants preparations" for the recommended escalation.[9]

In Saigon, meanwhile, General Nguyen Khanh was trying to rule through a mélange of vice-premiers, a Cabinet, and an enlarged Military Revolutionary Council. His top officials consisted mainly of Dai Viet nationalists, his government, in general, excluding other important nationalist groups and parties.

In March 1964, presumably prodded by American advisers, Khanh announced a Program of Action that included ambitious and bold political, social, economic, and military reforms. In place of Nhu's defunct strategic-hamlet program, Khanh substituted a concept called New Rural Life Hamlets. Theoretically a reversion to Lyautey's *tache d'huile* concept of pacification, Khanh's plan called for clearing, consolidating, and defending specific rural areas. Unlike former programs, however, the new effort bowed to NLF success in mobilizing from the inside. Integral to it were Advance People's Action Groups:

> . . . Directed by Vietnamese after being organized and trained by the United States Central Intelligence Agency, they were, specifically, guerrilla outfits of six men each who, dressed in black pajamas, like those worn by the Vietcong, surreptitiously entered a Vietcong-controlled hamlet, usually at night, engaged in direct armed counterinsurgency action against the Communists; and followed this up, once the Vietcong were dispersed, by staying on the scene and helping the people harvest their rice and repair whatever damage had been done.[10]

By going after what one counterinsurgency expert, Richard Clutterbuck, aptly terms "the man with the knife," the groups were attacking the fundamental fear that allowed Communist agitation/propaganda agents to organize the infrastructure essential to guerrilla operations. Once covert groups had removed Viet Cong agents, political and social action would consolidate the gain, new areas would be cleared and held . . . and so on until South Vietnam lived free of Viet Cong. To aid the process, Khanh wanted the Civil Guard brought up to strength, some eighty thousand, and joined to the regular army; the Self-Defense Corps would also be brought up to its authorized strength, seventy-two thousand. Specific land reforms would win over peasant groups, while "national mobilization" would eliminate inequities in conscription laws.[11]

To some American observers, Khanh appeared determined to lead South Vietnam out of chaos created by Diem and subsequent junta governments. Secretary of Defense McNamara

... found many reasons for encouragement in the performance of the Khanh government to date [March 1964]. Although its top layer is thin, it is highly responsive to U.S. advice, and with a good grasp of the basic elements of rooting out the Viet Cong.

McNamara advised Johnson to instruct appropriate government agencies:

... To make it clear that we are prepared to furnish assistance and support to South Vietnam for as long as it takes to bring the insurgency under control. ... To make it clear that we fully support the Khanh government and are opposed to further coups. .... [12]

The United States, already contributing directly $500 million a year to South Vietnam, now added another $50 million a year.

Alas, the new strong man could not lift the weight of government. Not only did he fail to fuse dissident political and religious elements into a governing whole, but he also fell victim to a self-made legacy of quarreling, jealous, and ambitious generals, not to mention veteran nationalist politicians. In protecting his flanks of power, he slowed and ultimately doomed forward movement. In contrast, the NLF-PRP became increasingly aggressive, passing in 1964, so Hanoi claimed

... to the tactic of conducting an uninterrupted offensive against the enemy. ... Efforts to kill Americans have developed with great vigor and on a large scale in all regions, and particularly in Saigon proper. [13]

Black-clad agit-prop teams proclaimed Khanh another American lackey in the Diem tradition, and made capital propaganda out of his attempts to cut losses by abandoning weak and isolated strategic hamlets as Viet Cong attacks continued. ARVN remained the VC's major supply depot, contributing an average one thousand weapons per month. [14]

The South Vietnamese army seemed no more able to halt the rot than previously. McNamara and Taylor reported upon their return from Saigon in March 1964 that " ... the situation has unquestionably been growing worse." About 40 per cent of the countryside was " ... under Viet Cong control or predominant influence." Civil and military morale was low, ARVN and para-military desertion rates high, draft-dodging extensive. The report recommended contingency plans capable of putting " ... new and significant pressures upon North Vietnam" by limited ARVN incursions into Laos and Cambodia and "retaliatory bombing strikes" of the North by South Vietnamese and American planes. [15]

President Johnson accepted the bulk of McNamara's recommendations, agreeing with him that it was too early to take overt military action against the North,[16] particularly since "... we expect a showdown," as he cabled Lodge, "between the Chinese and Soviet Communist parties soon and action against the North will be more practicable after than before a showdown."[17]

Johnson's other immediate concern was increasing indigenous sentiment in Saigon for a neutralist settlement in form of a coalition government with the NLF, a solution that he and his advisers deemed tantamount to Communist victory, in view of Khanh's fragile government. Lodge was to knock "... the idea of neutralization wherever it rears its ugly head."[18]

Various courses of action were discussed at a high-level strategy meeting of American officials in late April in Saigon. In general, two schools of thought were at work: a go-slow and a go-fast. The major check on go-fast escalation, aside from American and international public opinion, was lack of adequate information "... concerning the nature and magnitude" of infiltration from the North. Its appeal, however, to the bulk of the President's top advisers, was only too obvious. The JCS had already approved a plan submitted by Commander-in-Chief, Pacific (CINCPAC) Admiral Harry Felt:

> ... It tabulated how many planes and what bomb tonnages would be required for each phase of the strikes, listed the targets in North Vietnam with damage to be achieved, and programed the necessary positioning of air forces for the raids. A follow-up operation plan ... calculated the possible reactions of China and North Vietnam and the American ground forces that might be necessary to meet them.[19]

William Bundy, who headed Intelligence Security Affairs—a sort of private State Department in the Department of Defense—was also preparing a sixteen-point "scenario" for escalation. Bundy and Rusk had questioned a tacit assumption that the insurgency's continuing success hinged on aid from the North. Rusk sent a former *New York Times* correspondent, William Jorden, to Saigon to assemble available data. What became known as the Jorden Report apparently convinced Rusk and Bundy that sufficient infiltration existed to justify attacks against the North—sufficient, at least, to justify such attacks to the American public. In late May, Bundy drafted a resolution for Congress that would free the President's military hand.[20]

In May, Pathet Lao offensives in Laos heated up that situation and caused the Administration to commit American navy and air force planes to low-level reconnaissance flights. Although this crisis blew over, continuing deterioration in South Vietnam did nothing to dampen hawk enthusiasm. At another high-level meeting in June, Ambassador Lodge, theretofore moderate, began arguing for bombing the North, believing that " . . . most support for the VC [Viet Cong in South Vietnam] would fade as soon as some 'counterterrorism measures' were begun against the D.R.V. [North Vietnam]." In discussing the necessity for a Congressional resolution to free the President's hand prior to escalating military action, McNamara noted that it might be necessary " . . . to deploy as many as seven [U.S.] divisions," while Rusk

> . . . noted that some of the military requirements might involve the calling up of reserves, always a touchy Congressional issue. He also stated that public opinion on our Southeast Asia policy was badly divided in the United States at the moment and that, therefore, the President needed an affirmation of support.

According to William Bundy's memorandum:

> . . . General Taylor noted that there was a danger of reasoning ourselves into inaction. From a military point of view, he said the U.S. could function in Southeast Asia about as well as anywhere in the world except Cuba.

Although the assembled notables advised President Johnson to delay overt action in order to gain time " . . . to refine our plans and estimates,"

> . . . Mr. [William] Bundy emphasized the need for an "urgent" public relations campaign at home to "get at the basic doubts of the value of Southeast Asia and the importance of our stake there."[21]

At a subsequent JCS meeting, enemy reaction to escalation was discussed. Admiral Felt asked for the option to use nuclear weapons, " . . . as had been assumed under various plans":

> . . . Secretary McNamara then went on to say that the possibility of major ground action also led to a serious question of having to use nuclear weapons at some point. Admiral Felt responded emphatically that there was no possible way to hold off the Communists on the ground without the use of tactical nuclear weapons.[22]

During this crucial period, President Johnson continued to follow a wait-and-see policy, but one that held aggressive overtones. He permitted

American aircraft to engage in combat operations in Laos; he evidently authorized official leaks to emphasize the Administration's determination " . . . to support its allies and uphold its treaty commitments in Southeast Asia"; he authorized military preparations for troop movements to the area. But doubt apparently entered his mind, at least to the extent that he formally asked the CIA: " . . . Would the rest of Southeast Asia necessarily fall if Laos and South Viet-Nam came under North Vietnamese control?" Neil Sheehan, who studied these particular highly classified documents, later wrote that the CIA replied on June 9:

> . . . With the possible exception of Cambodia, it is likely that no nation in the area would quickly succumb to Communism as a result of the fall of Laos and South Vietnam. Furthermore, a continuation of the spread of Communism in the area would not be inexorable, and any spread which did occur would take time— time in which the total situation might change in any number of ways unfavorable to the Communist cause.
>
> . . . The C.I.A. analysis conceded that the loss of South Vietnam and Laos "would be profoundly damaging to the U.S. position in the Far East" and would raise the prestige of China "as a leader of world Communism" at the expense of a more moderate Soviet Union. But the analysis argued that so long as the United States could retain its island bases, such as those in Okinawa, Guam, the Philippines and Japan, it could wield enough military power in Asia to deter China and North Vietnam from overt military aggression against Southeast Asia in general.[23]

The CIA analysis said, in effect, that South Vietnam was a strategic convenience, *not* a strategic necessity. If ever a green light flashed for a President and his advisers to accept facts, re-examine objectives, reform priorities, and realign effort—to change from a collision course to a crafty and intelligent course designed to attain national aims at a reasonable cost—it was in June 1964. We don't know Johnson's reaction to this reply. Judging by subsequent events, he was unimpressed; at least, he appears not to have questioned sharply those spurious and dangerous postulates pleaded by those around him. Instead he sent a Canadian official, Blair Seaborn, on a secret mission to Hanoi to warn Premier Pham Van Dong that, if he he did not stop supporting the Viet Cong, the action would escalate.[24] The premier's alleged humble acceptance of the warning was at decided odds with his and others' hawkish belief that it was only a matter of time until the Saigon government collapsed.

Hoping to forestall more overt action, at least until after the presidential election, Johnson continued to approve massive doses of American aid to the South. In June, he recalled Ambassador Lodge, who had never quite made "the team" and now wanted to campaign for the Republican presidential nomination. He replaced Lodge with a powerful "team": General Maxwell Taylor as ambassador and U. Alexis Johnson, a hawkish career diplomat, as deputy ambassador—appointments that confirmed priority of the military over the political role. General William Westmoreland already had replaced General Harkins; Admiral Ulysses S. Grant Sharp would soon replace Admiral Harry Felt as CINCPAC. A corps of American military and civil specialists descended on Saigon to help Khanh revive his moribund Program of Action.

The influx of American advisers did not serve Khanh well. At Taylor's insistence, South Vietnamese officials directly controlled materials provided by American aid, which resulted in two major disasters: First, relatively little reached the essential target, the peasants, whose cooperation was vital to neutralizing VC operations; and second, in siphoning off and selling American arms, equipment, and material to make personal fortunes, GVN officials and ARVN officers (frequently the same) furnished the enemy with more equipment than was arriving from Hanoi. The Americans found themselves enmeshed in corruption and intrigue that made most thrillers read like nursery stories. Lacking linguistic ability, not to mention an understanding of insurgency warfare, they floundered while attempting to repair inadequate performance by quantitative methods: American agencies quickly proliferated into numerous bureaucratic empires staffed by highly paid civil servants who, like war lords of old, too often fought each other instead of the common enemy. To add to Taylor's problems, as the internal situation worsened during summer of 1964—at this time the NLF-PRP correctly claimed to control much of South Vietnam—Khanh sought to save his neck by carrying the war into North Vietnam, a "March North" propaganda campaign squelched only with difficulty by Taylor.

Covert operations involving " . . . trained sabotage teams, electronic intelligence-gathering equipment, C-123 transports for the airdrops and fast PT boats for the coastal raids" mounted in scope and intensity. At the end of July, one of MACV's South Vietnamese naval commando teams raided two North Vietnamese islands. Two days later, enemy patrol boats searching the area attacked a DeSoto patrol destroyer, USS *Maddox*. Her guns and American carrier planes knocked out three of the boats, and *Maddox* sailed South. The next day, President Johnson ordered *Maddox* and another destroyer back north along with air cover.[25] On August 1 and 2, T-28 planes bombed North Vietnamese villages on the Laotian border; and on the night of August 3, MACV launched two more covert attacks by South Vietnamese-manned PT boats. On the following night, North Vietnamese patrol boats allegedly attacked the two American patrol destroyers.[26] Washington reacted promptly. Planes from two U.S. aircraft carriers struck DRV naval installations along a hundred miles of coast. President Johnson ordered previously alerted aircraft squadrons to South Vietnam, as called for in JCS strike plans; he also alerted army and marine ground forces for deployment against North Vietnamese or Chinese reaction to the raids. In announcing these momentous events that night on television, the President assured his audience, " . . . we still seek no wider war."

This might have been so, but Johnson nonetheless wanted authority to wage wider war if necessary. Bundy's resolution was now dusted off, altered slightly, and introduced into Congress.[27] In secret and hastily held Congressional hearings, Robert McNamara threw up a verbal dust screen to inquisitive senators. To Senator Wayne Morse, who had learned of the August 3 raids and suggested that McNamara was aware of them and that the American navy had been involved, he replied:

> . . . First, our Navy played absolutely no part in, was not associated with, was not aware of, any South Vietnamese actions, if there were any. . . .
> I did not have knowledge at the time of the attack on the island. There is no connection between this patrol and any action by South Vietnam.[28]

Partly on the basis of this and presumably other false, distorted, and incomplete testimony from top American officials, an alarmed and emotional Congress passed the Southeast Asia Resolution (commonly known as the Tonkin Gulf Resolution), which authorized the President " . . . to take all necessary steps, including the use of armed force, to assist any member or protocol state of the Southeast Asia Collective Defense Treaty requesting assistance in defense of its freedom." Although some critics, including two senators, dissented on the grounds that DRV attacks were shrouded in mystery and that the resolution partially abrogated Congressional responsibility for placing the nation in war, the bulk of American people seemed to accept it with equanimity and trust—even with pride.

CHAPTER SIXTY-ONE

1. Shaplen, *The Lost Revolution*, 214.
2. Ibid., 224–5. See also, Pike; Carver; Lansdale, "Viet Nam: Do We Understand Revolution?"
3. Johnson, *The Vantage Point . . .* , 44.
4. Sheehan, Smith, Kenworthy, and Butterfield, 271–4. See also, Johnson, *The Vantage Point . . .*
5. Johnson, *The Vantage Point . . .* , 64.
6. Sheehan et al., 240.
7. Ibid., 274–7.

8. Ibid., 241.
9. Ibid., 277.
10. Shaplen, *The Road from War,* 38.
11. Shaplen, *The Lost Revolution,* 238–9.
12. Sheehan, et al., 277–83.
13. Lacouture, 177–8.
14. Ibid., 185:

    ... Between January 1 and October 1, 1964, the Viet Cong took
    nine thousand arms from government troops, that is an average of
    eight hundred per month between January and July, and close to
    fifteen hundred per month between July and October.

15. Sheehan et al., 278–83.
16. Johnson, *The Vantage Point...,* 66–7. See also, ibid., 119: Chief of CIA
    John McCone, according to Johnson, also wished to escalate the action, be-
    lieving that McNamara's measures were " ... too little, too late."
17. Sheehan et al., 285–6. See also, Johnson, *The Vantage Point...,* 66–7, whose
    stated reason later became the necessity to avoid massive Communist inter-
    vention.
18. Sheehan et al., 285–6.
19. Ibid., 247.
20. Ibid., 286.
21. Ibid., 250–2.
22. *The Sunday Times* (London), June 27, 1971.
23. Sheehan et al., 254.
24. Ibid., 256.
25. Ibid., 259. See also, Johnson, *The Vantage Point...; Public Papers of...
    (1963–64).*
26. Sheehan et al., 305. A number of qualified observers, including a senior ma-
    rine intelligence officer, have informed me that it is doubtful if the North
    Vietnamese attacks ever occurred. Confidential information in the author's
    files. See also, Corson, 63: The chief sonarman of the *Maddox* reportedly
    stated " ... that the North Vietnamese PT boats used harassing movements,
    but they did not fire shells or torpedoes;" *International Herald Tribune,* July
    12, 1993:" ... Admiral Stockdale [a U.S. Navy pilot] witnessed what hap-
    pened that day [August 4, 1964, in the Tonkin Gulf] and reported to his
    superiors that there was *no* attack on a U.S. vessel and no sign of enemy
    boats." [My italics]
27. Sheehan et al., 264. See also, Johnson, *The Vantage Point...; Public Papers
    of... (1963–64);* William P. Bundy.
28. Sheehan et al., 265–6.

CHAPTER 62

General Taylor reports from Saigon • William Bundy's program of escalation • Admiral Sharp's recommendations • Taylor's operational plans • Pentagon voices • Johnson: " . . . we still seek no wider war" • September meeting in the White House • Enemy estimate of the situation • Douglas Pike's analysis • Edward Lansdale's analysis • The Bien Hoa attack • John McNaughton's adjusted aims • "Fast full squeeze" and "hot-blood actions" • Rostow on power • George Ball's doubts • Taylor's pessimism • The intelligence panel dissents • Khanh's dictatorship • Dissent in Saigon • Tran Van Minh takes over

ADMINISTRATION HAWKS had won the day. Shortly after American planes had bombed North Vietnam, United Nations Secretary-General U Thant proposed a meeting between Ho Chi Minh and U.S. envoys. Ho Chi Minh accepted, Lyndon Johnson did not.[1] Ambassador Taylor, when secretly queried in Saigon as to the advisability of an international conference, replied:

> . . . Rush to conference table would serve to confirm to Chicoms [Chinese Communists] that U.S. retaliation for destroyer attacks was transient phenomenon and that firm Chicom response in form of commitment to defend NVN [North Vietnam] has given U.S. "paper tiger" second thoughts. . . . [2]

Taylor would shortly report to McNamara and the JCS that the Khanh government, " . . . beset by inexperienced ministers who are jealous and suspicious of each other . . . has a 50/50 chance of lasting out the year." Since there was "no one in sight to replace Khanh," we must "do everything possible to bolster the Khanh government." The American Government must " . . . be prepared to implement contingency plans against North Vietnam with optimum readiness by January 1, 1965."[3]

At the same time, William Bundy, now working in the State Department, where he had replaced Roger Hilsman as Assistant Secretary of State for Far Eastern Affairs, was drawing up an action memorandum calling for

> ... a combination of military pressures and some form of communication under which Hanoi (and Peiping) eventually accept the idea of getting out. Negotiation without continued pressure, indeed without continued military action, will not achieve our objectives in the foreseeable future.

Bundy and John McNaughton in the Pentagon agreed with Taylor that the United States must not consent to an international conference on Vietnam, at least until North Vietnam was "hurting" from retaliatory pressures.[4] Bundy's program called for "military silence" for the rest of August, then for "limited pressures," both covert and overt, until the new year, then "more serious pressures" such as interdicting " . . . infiltration routes and facilities" leading up to bombing oil depots, bridges, and railroads and mining Haiphong harbor.[5] Admiral Sharp in Honolulu sharply rejected this gradual program:

> ... Further demonstration of restraint alone could easily be interpreted as period of second thoughts about Pierce Arrow [U.S. bombing attacks] and events leading thereto as well as sign of weakness and lack of resolve. . . . A conference to include Vietnam, before we have overcome the insurgency, would lose U.S. our allies in Southeast Asia and represent a defeat for the United States.

Sharp next got to the nub of his and the Saigon mission's desires:

> ... [W]e must recognize that immediate action is required to protect our present heavy investment in RVN [South Vietnam] ... a successful attack against Bien Hoa, Tan Son Nhut, Da Nang ... would be a serious psychological defeat for U.S. MACV reports that [sic] inability of GVN to provide requisite degree of security and therefore we must rely on U.S. troops. . . . consideration should [also] be given to creating a U.S. base in RVN [to] provide one more indication of our intent to remain in S.E. Asia until our objectives are achieved. . . . Such a base should be accessible by air and sea, possessed of well developed facilities and installations, and located in an area from which U.S. operations could be launched effectively. Da Nang meets these criteria. . . . [6]

Sharp's recommendations introduced a sinister note into the proceedings. The general Administration view at this time, at least as out-

lined in a joint State and Defense departments publication, did not call
for committing American combat troops:

> ... The military problem facing the armed forces of South Viet
> Nam at this time is not primarily one of manpower. Basically it is
> a problem of acquiring training, equipment, skills, and organiza-
> tion suited to combating the type of aggression that menaces their
> country. ... U.S. combat units would face several obvious disad-
> vantages in a guerrilla war situation of this type in which knowl-
> edge of terrain, language, and local customs is especially important.
> In addition, their introduction would provide ammunition for
> Communist propaganda which falsely proclaims that the United
> States is conducting a "white man's war" against Asians.[7]

Although Taylor ostensibly remained cool to massive U.S. troop deployment, he nonetheless developed two operational plans which ultimately would bring this about. The first was a go-slow plan—U-2
overflights of North Vietnam, resumption of 34A coastal raids and destroyer patrols, and air and ground strikes against infiltration routes in
Laos—which the United States would implement in return for Khanh's
promise " ... to stabilize his government and make some progress in
cleaning up his operational backyard." This, Plan A, called for a specific
"precautionary military readiness": " ... Hawk [anti-aircraft] units to
Da Nang and Saigon, landing a Marine force at Da Nang for defense
of the airfield and beefing up MACV's support base." Course B, a go-
fast plan, would ask

> ... virtually nothing from the Khanh Government, primarily be-
> cause it is assumed that little can be expected from it. It avoids the
> consequence of the sudden collapse of the Khanh Government and
> gets underway with minimum delay the punitive actions against
> Hanoi. Thus, it lessens the chance of an interruption of the pro-
> gram by an international demand for negotiation by presenting a
> fait accompli to international critics.

Taylor added,

> ... it increases the likelihood of U.S. involvement in ground action
> since Khanh will have almost no available ground forces which
> can be released from pacification employment to mobile resistance
> of DRV attacks.

Taylor recommended adopting Course A, " ... while maintaining
readiness to shift to Course of Action B." The JCS preferred Taylor's
Course B: " ... an accelerated program of action with respect to the

DRV is essential to prevent a complete collapse of the U.S. position in Southeast Asia."[8]

All this contrasted starkly with President Johnson's " . . . we still seek no wider war" theme, which he was laboring against his Republican opponent, Senator Barry Goldwater, who was calling for all-out air strikes against North Vietnam. In late August, Johnson told a crowd at an outdoor barbecue in Texas:

> . . . I have had advice to load our planes with bombs and to drop them on certain areas that I think would enlarge the war and escalate the war, and result in our committing a good many American boys to fighting a war that I think ought to be fought by the boys of Asia to help protect their own land.[9]

While Johnson was soothing Texas constituents, one of his top officials, John McNaughton in the Pentagon, was writing still another operational memorandum designed " . . . to reverse the present downward trend. Failing that, the alternative objective is to emerge from the situation with as good an image as possible in U.S., allied and enemy eyes." McNaughton's proposals included a significant enlargement of " . . . the U.S. military role in the pacification program . . . e.g., large numbers of U.S. special forces, divisions of regular combat troops, U.S. air, etc., to 'interlard' with or to take over functions of geographical areas from the South Vietnamese armed forces" as well as for actions against North Vietnam that would cause the enemy to react in such a way as to give the American Government initiative to escalate the action at will. At best, McNaughton suggested, this program would cause Hanoi to call off its support, thus allowing pacification of the South. It might result in either "explicit settlement" or "tacit settlement": " . . . If worst comes and South Vietnam disintegrates or their behavior becomes abominable, to 'disown' South Vietnam, hopefully leaving the image of 'a patient who died despite the extraordinary efforts of a good doctor.' "[10]

Administration officials thrashed out various points of view at the White House in early September, finally agreeing that air attacks against North Vietnam would have to be employed, but on a go-slow, "low-risk" basis, since Khanh's government was too weak to withstand probable enemy reaction to rapid escalation by American forces. Undoubtedly with the rapidly approaching election in mind, Johnson agreed to this course, but approved various covert actions along with a significant increase in expenditures inside South Vietnam.[11]

Hanoi did not react passively to the continuing American counteroffensive. In mid-September, North Vietnamese patrol boats attacked DeSoto patrol destroyers, an action that President Johnson let slide. Administration nerves again jangled in October, when Communist China exploded a nuclear pile. Also in October, Saigon observers reported an increase in infiltration, including a GVN claim that ARVN had captured four North Vietnamese soldiers in South Vietnam. American intelligence analysts did not seem overly worried about action from the North. A Special National Intelligence Estimate (SNIE) of early October read in part:

> ... While they [Hanoi and Peking] will seek to exploit and encourage the deteriorating situation in Saigon, they probably will avoid actions that would in their view unduly increase the chances of a major U.S. response against North Vietnam (DRV) or Communist China. If despite Communist efforts, the U.S. attacks continued, Hanoi's leaders would have to ask themselves whether it was not better to suspend their support of Viet Cong military action rather than suffer the destruction of their major military facilities and the industrial sector of their economy. ... [12]

This estimate fell considerably wide of the mark, as did American insistence that the fulcrum of insurgency lay in Hanoi. The NLF-PRP had by no means decided on a specific course of action during these momentous months. Ever since major American intervention in 1962— the beginning of what the NLF called Special War—the enemy had been debating how to win the war. As Douglas Pike has pointed out, this was a major doctrinal problem that occupied enemy minds during 1963 and 1964.

Three options existed:

> ... the military ending, or third stage; the social ending, or General Uprising; and the political-infiltration and takeover ending, or the negotiated settlement. All three were doctrinally acceptable ...

In 1964 the NLF was defending the "dominant doctrine of the General Uprising" while

> ... the regular cadres from the North held for increased militarization of the effort, a calculated military challenge to the ARVN, and greater emphasis on military assaults, including assaults on exclusively American military installations in Vietnam. For a time, as the debate raged, the armed struggle took on a schizoid character: NLF activities for a few weeks would be predominantly military, then switch to political approaches, and then back to military actions. ... In the end the Northerners won the NLF debate, and military activities increased in scope, tempo, and nature. [13]

Though allowing that the fulcrum of insurgency lay in the South, the Johnson administration continued to believe that its *raison d'être* came from the North. They could not understand the true situation as explained, for example, by Edward Lansdale. After discussing favored Administration options, he wrote: " . . . The anomaly in these reactions is that each falls short of understanding that the Communists have let loose a revolutionary idea in Viet Nam and that it will not die by being ignored, bombed or smothered by us. Ideas do not die in such ways." He then called for essentially a political approach, which would

> . . . oppose the Communist idea with a better idea and to do so on the battleground itself, in a way that would permit the people, who are the main feature of that battleground, to make their own choice. A political base would be established. The first step would be to state political goals, founded on principles cherished by free men, which the Vietnamese share; the second would be an aggressive commitment of organizations and resources to start the Vietnamese moving realistically toward those political goals. In essence, this is revolutionary warfare, the spirit of the British Magna Carta, the French "Liberté, Egalité, Fraternité" and our own Declaration of Independence.

South Vietnam had to have a "cause," and the American effort primarily had to go

> . . . on helping the Vietnamese leadership create the conditions which will encourage the discovery and most rapid possible development of a patriotic cause so genuine that the Vietnamese willingly will pledge to it "their lives, their fortunes, their sacred honor.

After suggesting a number of ways in which this could be done, Lansdale warned that the most urgent function is " . . . to *protect* and *help* the people":

> . . . When the military opens fire at long range, whether by infantry weapons, artillery or air strike, on a reported Viet Cong concentration in a hamlet or village full of civilians, the Vietnamese officers who give those orders and the American advisers who let them "get away with it" are helping defeat the cause of freedom. The civilian hatred of the military resulting from such actions is a powerful motive for joining the Viet Cong.[14]

On November 1, the Viet Cong launched a surprise mortar attack against Bien Hoa, the American airbase outside of Saigon, killing four airmen and destroying a number of B-57 aircraft. Although Lyndon Johnson was elected President two days later by a large majority, he did not use the Bien Hoa attack as an excuse to escalate the war— despite urgings by the JCS for extensive reprisal action. The Pentagon Papers reveal beyond question that ranking officials of the Department of Defense, the JCS, the State Department, and the American mission in Saigon intended to escalate the war;[15] it was a matter of when and how, as it had been for some months. From the standpoint of the American public, the record is one of dissembling, if not outright fraud. Thus, a draft paper dated November 5, prepared on Johnson's instruction by an interagency working group under William Bundy,[16] reads in part:

> . . . Congress must be consulted before any major action, perhaps only by notification if we do a reprisal against another Bien Hoa, but preferably by careful talks with key leaders . . . Query if it should be combined with other topics (budget?) to lessen the heat.
> We probably do not need additional Congressional authority [to that granted in the Tonkin Gulf Resolution], even if we decide on very strong action. A session of this rump Congress might well be the scene of a messy Republican effort.
> We are on the verge of intelligence agreement that infiltration has in fact mounted, and Saigon is urging that we surface this by the end of the week or early next week. Query how loud we want to make this sound. Actually Grose in the Times had the new estimate on Monday; so the splash and sense of hot new news may be less. We should decide this today if possible. . . . In general, we all feel the problem of proving North Vietnamese participation is less than in the past, but we should have the Jorden Report updated for use as necessary. . . . [17]

Apparently as a result of this thinking, the State Department sent another representative, Chester Cooper, to Saigon to report on infiltration, meanwhile stressing the fact of mounting efforts from Hanoi by means of "leaks."[18]

McNamara's assistant secretary, John McNaughton, was also drafting a paper that adjusted Administration aims in South Vietnam. The task now became, according to McNaughton and presumably McNamara:

> . . . (a) To protect U.S. reputation as a countersubversion guarantor.
> (b) To avoid domino effect especially in Southeast Asia.
> (c) To keep South Vietnamese territory from Red hands.
> (d) To emerge from crisis without unacceptable taint from methods.

Although admitting that the real problem of South Vietnam lay in the South, McNaughton noted that " . . . action against North Vietnam is to some extent a substitute for strengthening the government in South Vietnam. . . . " McNaughton offered a three-option plan. Option A called for continuing the present course of action: In essence, go-slow, low-risk operations against the North with reprisals when necessary. Option B called for " . . . fast full squeeze . . . with pressure actions to be continued at a fairly rapid pace and without interruption until we achieve our central present objectives." Option C called for

> . . . progressive squeeze-and-talk. Present policies plus an orchestration of communications with Hanoi and a crescendo of additional military moves against infiltration targets . . . [and] other targets in North Vietnam . . . designed to give the U.S. the option at any point to proceed or not. . . .

In his opinion, reaction from the North was not a vital worry:

> . . . The DRV and China will probably not invade South Vietnam, Laos or Burma, nor is it likely that they will conduct air strikes on these countries. The USSR will almost certainly confine herself to political actions. If the DRV or China strike or invade South Vietnam, U.S. forces will be sufficient to handle the problem.

McNaughton showed considerable concern for the effects of escalation on South Vietnam:

> . . . Military action against the DRV could be counterproductive in South Vietnam because (1) the VC could step up its activities, (2) the South Vietnamese could panic, (3) they could resent our striking their "brothers," and (4) they could tire of waiting for results.

However, McNaughton continued,

> . . . Should South Vietnam disintegrate completely beneath us, we should try to hold it together long enough to permit us to try to evacuate our forces and to convince the world to accept the uniqueness (and congenital impossibility) of the South Vietnamese case.[19]

Apparently, neither Department of Defense nor State Department senior officials seriously considered holding the line with Option A. William Bundy and McNaughton were said to favor Option C. The JCS, however, preferred Option B—" . . . fast full squeeze," with what the Pentagon called "hot-blood actions"—"... with something like Option C as a fall-back alternative."[20]

Still another voice sounded a cry for escalation. In mid-November, Walt Rostow wrote McNamara his feeling that the American Government must clearly "signal" Hanoi its intentions, including escalation if desired. Rostow was "... convinced that we should not go forward into the next stage without a U.S. ground force commitment of some kind." A few days later, he expanded his thinking in a memorandum to Secretary of State Rusk. Convinced that Hanoi wished to avoid destruction of its industrial plant (as postulated in the October SNIE), Rostow wrote:

> ... Our most basic problem is, therefore, how to persuade them that a continuation of their present policy will risk major destruction in North Viet Nam; that a preemptive move on the ground as a prelude to negotiation will be met by U.S. strength on the ground; and that Communist China will not be a sanctuary if it assists North Viet Nam in counterescalation.

Calling for retaliation against the North "... for continued violation of the 1954–1962 [Geneva] Accords" and "... the introduction of some ground forces in South Viet Nam and, possibly, in the Laos corridor," Rostow wanted to go further:

> ... Perhaps most important of all, the introduction into the Pacific Theater of massive forces to deal with any escalatory response, including forces evidently aimed at China as well as North Viet Nam, should the Chinese Communists enter the game. I am increasingly confident that we can do this in ways which would be understood—and not dangerously misinterpreted—in Hanoi and Peiping.

But deployment of forces and "... even bombing operations in the north" would not form a "decisive signal." The situation called for "... that kind of Presidential commitment and staying power" familiar to the Berlin and Cuba crises. In Rostow's mind, the danger existed that Hanoi would either "... pretend to call off the war in South Viet Nam, without actually doing so," or would "... revive it again when the pressure is off." American troops in South Vietnam, as well as an American naval blockade, were essential to prevent this and to force Hanoi to stop supporting the NLF and the PRP. In summing up, Rostow wrote:

> ... Considering these observations as a whole, I suspect what I am really saying is that our assets, as I see them, are sufficient to

see this thing through if we enter the exercise with adequate determination to succeed. I know well the anxieties and complications on our side of the line. But there may be a tendency to underestimate both the anxieties and complications on the other side and also to underestimate that limited but real margin of influence on the outcome which flows from the simple fact that at this stage of history we are the greatest power in the world—if we behave like it.

"The greatest power in the world," according to Rostow, could bring limited Utopia to " . . . the Asian community," provided that it acted swiftly and surely. Among other deeds, he called for:

> . . . immediate direct communication to Hanoi to give them a chance to back down before faced with our actions, including a clear statement of the limits of our objectives but our absolute commitment to them.

Should this fail, as was likely, physical actions were in order.[21]

In late November, a select committee of the National Security Council (NSC) met to discuss the working group's draft proposals. Present at this meeting of ranking Administration officials was Under Secretary of State George Ball, who challenged basic Administration postulates, a brave act, considering the prevailing temper of his associates. According to William Bundy's memorandum of this meeting,

> . . . Mr. Ball "indicated doubt" that bombing the North in any fashion would improve the situation in South Vietnam and "argued against" a judgment that a Vietcong victory in South Vietnam would have a falling-domino effect on the rest of Asia.[22]

As Neil Sheehan later wrote,

> . . . While the working-group sessions had been in progress, the [Pentagon] study discloses, Mr. Ball had been writing a quite different policy paper "suggesting a U.S. diplomatic strategy in the event of an imminent GVN collapse."
> In it, he advocated working through the U.K. . . . who would in turn seek cooperation from the U.S.S.R., in arranging an international conference . . . which would work out a compromise political settlement for South Vietnam. . . .

Although Ball alone stood for this particular approach, other dissent emerged during the meeting. Secretary of State Rusk said

. . . that while he favored bombing North Vietnam, he did not accept an analysis by Mr. McNaughton and William Bundy that if the bombing failed to save South Vietnam "we would obtain international credit for trying."

"In his view," the [Pentagon] analyst writes, "the harder we tried and then failed, the worse our situation would be."

McGeorge Bundy [the President's special assistant for national security affairs] demurred to some extent, the account goes on, but Mr. Ball "expressed strong agreement with the last Rusk point."

General Wheeler [who had replaced Maxwell Taylor as chairman of the JCS], reflecting the viewpoint of the Joint Chiefs, argued that the hard, fast bombing campaign of Option B actually entailed "less risk of a major conflict before achieving success," in words of the study, than the gradually rising air strikes of Option C.[23]

The meeting ended with no decision as to which option would be recommended to the President. On the following day, Ambassador Taylor joined the select group of officials to report on the Vietnam situation. His words could not have been more gloomy. A new civilian government in Saigon was proving no more effective than the former military government, either in the capital or in the provinces. The Viet Cong everywhere had advanced and were threatening to cut the country in half. Despite heavy casualties produced by an increasingly stronger professionally competent ARVN (!), the Viet Cong not only were making good their losses but were adopting new and improved tactics:

The ability of the Viet-Cong continuously to rebuild their units and to make good their losses is one of the mysteries of this guerrilla war. . . . [We find] no plausible explanation of the continued strength of the Viet-Cong if our data on Viet-Cong losses are even approximately correct. Not only do the Viet-Cong units have the recuperative powers of the phoenix, but they have an amazing ability to maintain morale. Only in rare cases have we found evidences of bad morale among Viet-Cong prisoners or recorded in captured Viet-Cong documents.

One reason for continued Viet Cong growth, Taylor continued, was increasing infiltration from the North. Although the real problem lay in the South, where effective government had to be established in order to run an effective counterinsurgency, pressure also had to be brought on the North by a combination of methods already discussed. Not only could escalating American military operations cause Hanoi to back off from the war, but they could also be used to gain the South Vietnamese Government's promise to promise more effective government. Taylor added ominously, however, " . . . In any case, we should be prepared for emergency military action against the North if only to shore up a collapsing situation." For the moment, he favored carrying on with Option A; once Saigon leaders promised to reform, he favored the first actions in Option C.[24]

One more voice remained to be heard from, however. Bundy's working group included an "intelligence panel" composed of representatives from CIA, the State Department's Bureau of Intelligence and Research, and the Pentagon's Defense Intelligence Agency. This panel faulted the prevailing desire for air strikes against the North. It did not believe the chances were great of " . . . breaking the will of Hanoi"; it suggested that such strikes would cause a much wider war; and it did not attach much weight to Walt Rostow's thesis, embraced by a good many top military officers, that Hanoi would back down in order to preserve its industrial base:

> . . . We have many indications that the Hanoi leadership is acutely and nervously aware of the extent to which North Vietnam's transportation system and industrial plant is vulnerable to attack. On the other hand, North Vietnam's economy is overwhelmingly agricultural and, to a large extent, decentralized in a myriad of more or less economically self-sufficient villages. Interdiction of imports and extensive destruction of transportation facilities and industrial plants would cripple D.R.V. industry. These actions would also seriously restrict D.R.V. military capabilities, and would degrade, though to a lesser extent, Hanoi's capabilities to support guerrilla warfare in South Vietnam and Laos. We do not believe that such actions would have a crucial effect on the daily lives of the overwhelming majority of the North Vietnam population. We do not believe that attacks on industrial targets would so greatly exacerbate current economic difficulties as to create unmanageable control problems. It is reasonable to infer that the D.R.V. leaders have a psychological investment in the work of reconstruction they have accomplished over the last decade. Nevertheless, they would probably be willing to suffer some damage to the country in the course of a test of wills with the U.S. over the course of events in South Vietnam.[25]

No one seems to have respected the intelligence panel's doubts, which (correctly) refuted official thinking, particularly Rostow's optimistic thesis. Ignoring professional opinion, the principals agreed on a course of action more or less as outlined by Taylor. For the moment, the go-slow school prevailed, and William Bundy's intention " . . . to publicize the evidence of increased DRV infiltration" at the earliest feasible date was shelved. The plan presented to the President in early December, in essence, called for a two-pronged course of action: Phase I—go-slow, low-risk until the South Vietnamese Government swung around to making a real war effort; then Phase II—increasing air strikes against the North while concentrating on the pacification program in the South. The President seems to have accepted the plan, at least sufficiently to brief Prime Minister Wilson on its operational aspects and send various emissaries off to inform other allies of its salient points.[26]

The Tonkin Gulf action served South Vietnam's Nguyen Khanh well. In mid-August, he submitted a constitutional charter " . . . that gave him virtually complete powers"; the Military Revolutionary Council approved it and elected him President of South Vietnam.[27] The new charter immediately brought protests from such important elements as students and Buddhists. Instead of trying to placate them, Khanh chose imperial aloofness. Dissenters responded with mass demonstrations against the government. Catholic groups spilled out to fight them. Viet Cong infiltrators effectively fanned rampant hatreds. Riots in Saigon spread to Hué and Da Nang. Khanh refused to accept dissident demands, summoned the Military Revolutionary Council, and resigned as president! He was reinstalled as prime minister in a caretaker government headed by himself and Generals Minh and Khiem—a deceptively simple solution for a most complex problem.[28]

The new government brought a shaky end to demonstrations by promising a better constitution than the one framed by Khanh. The new constitution would be written by a new High National Council; as soon as possible, government would return to civilian hands.

The dust had not settled when a group of disgruntled generals attempted another coup. This failed, in part because some younger and powerful officers remained loyal to Khanh, notably the head of the Vietnamese air force, Air Commodore Nguyen Cao Ky, a former pilot in the French air force, and an ambitious young man whose slick mustache, purple scarf, and Captain Midnight flight suit would soon become prominent on the Vietnamese scene.

Civil government succeeded no better than military government. The new premier, a sixty-year-old former schoolteacher and mayor of Saigon, Tran Van Huong, quickly fell prey to now-familiar dissident elements. Although he received American backing, his hands were tied, in part by General Khanh, who retained real power in the form of ARVN. Beset by various demonstrations in cities and by military reverses in the countryside, the new government soon foundered. The High National Council splintered into opposing cliques, and, in December, the young generals "purged" it in favor of an Armed Forces Council. This was not to Ambassador Taylor's liking. On Christmas Eve, he assembled a group of errant officers, including General Nguyen Van

Thieu and Air Commodore Nguyen Cao Ky. " . . . Do all of you understand English?" the ambassador asked. When the officers indicated that they did, the ambassador-general lowered the boom:

> . . . I told you all clearly at General Westmoreland's dinner we Americans were tired of coups. Apparently I wasted my words.. . .
> I made it clear that all the military plans which I know you would like to carry out are dependent on governmental stability. Now you have made a real mess. We cannot carry you forever if you do things like this.[29]

Taylor could not understand the mess, let alone straighten it out. He now backed Huong, who backed down. General Khanh next launched a virulent anti-Taylor, anti-American campaign, at a time when the American Government was attempting to preserve South Vietnam's identity by spending $1.5 million per day. Although Taylor advised Huong to defy the purge, the premier instead reached a shaky compromise with the young generals. Khanh allied himself briefly with the Buddhist cause, the Buddhists opened their own anti-American campaign, the young generals ousted the Huong government—and Khanh again was in power.

But not for long. His new government, headed by Premier Phan Huy Quat, proved no more stable than its predecessors. Plots and counterplots swirled through the capital.[30] On February 19, 1965, an attempted military coup succumbed to counterforces. But Taylor notwithstanding, the young generals had had enough of Khanh. They now deposed him as army commander in chief in favor of General Tran (Little Minh) Van Minh.

CHAPTER SIXTY-TWO

1. Zagoria, 44–5.
2. Sheehan et al., 346.
3. Ibid., 291–4.
4. Ibid., 295.
5. Ibid., 294–8.
6. Ibid., 298–300.
7. Department of State Publication 7724.
8. Sheehan et al., 349–55.
9. Ibid., 311.
10. Ibid., 355–7.
11. Johnson, *The Vantage Point* . . . , 120–1. See also, Sheehan et al., 357–60.
12. Sheehan et al., 419–20.
13. Pike, 105–8. Pike does not emphasize that these were NLF or Viet Cong attacks. Although he asserts that militarizing the effort in late 1964 " . . . included ordering thousands of NorthVietnamese regular army soldiers to the South," he cites no evidence for this statement. Administration officials subsequently claimed that regular North Vietnamese army (PAVN) units ap-

peared in the South in late 1964, but these contradictory and confusing claims tend to validate contrary assertions that regular PAVN units did not appear in appreciable numbers until after mid-1965 and then mainly in the central highlands and the North.

14. Lansdale, "Viet Nam: Do We Understand Revolution?"
15. Sheehan et al., 322. See also, Johnson, *The Vantage Point* . . . , 121.
16. Sheehan et al., 363–4.
17. Ibid.
18. Ibid., 338. See also, Cooper.
19. Sheehan et al., 365–8.
20. Ibid., 368–70.
21. Ibid., 418–23.
22. Ibid., 325–6.
23. Ibid.
24. Ibid., 370–3.
25. Ibid., 331–2.
26. Johnson, *The Vantage Point* . . . , 128.
27. Shaplen, *The Lost Revolution*, 270–1.
28. Ibid., 275–7. See also, Carver. This article by a CIA official examines political compatibilities in the South where, the author stresses, a social revolution was occurring, as distinct from a northern-imposed insurgency.
29. Sheehan et al., 379–81.
30. Shaplen, *The Lost Revolution*, 283 ff., for a splendid account of this political maelstrom.

CHAPTER 63

THE INTERNECINE WAR in Saigon scarcely benefited the real war. Each crisis and each coup expended untold amounts of energy that could better have been used in the countryside. Even optimum government would have made the outcome "a near-run thing." Inept government resulted in continuing VC gains of such importance as to decide Hanoi and the NLF-PRP to launch the third, or all-out offensive, phase of the insurgency.

Fresh VC offensives caused something akin to panic among American officials in Saigon and Washington. By end of December 1964, the Saigon trinity—Taylor, Alexis Johnson, and Westmoreland—apparently despaired of rigging a stable South Vietnamese government and notified Washington that the air campaign should start " . . . under any conceivable alliance short of complete abandonment of South Vietnam."[1] In early January, Johnson received a report from Taylor that concluded, " . . . we are presently on a losing track and must risk a change. . . . To take no positive action now is to accept defeat in the fairly near future."[2]

This attitude gained currency among Administration officials in January. Both William Bundy and McNaughton openly favored air strikes and the possibility of committing "limited" numbers of American ground troops to South Vietnam. Secret preparations for more overt action continued during the month, as pessimistic reports continued to roll in. In late January, McGeorge Bundy sent a memorandum to the President stating that he and McNamara were " . . . pretty well convinced that our current policy can lead only to disastrous defeat." President Johnson later wrote:

> . . . Bundy and McNamara saw two alternatives: either to "use our military power in the Far East and to force a change of Communist policy" or to "deploy all our resources along a track of negotiation, aimed at salvaging what little can be preserved with no major addition to our present military risks." They said that they were inclined to favor the first alternative—use of more military power—but they believed that both courses should be studied carefully and that alternative programs should be developed and argued out in my presence. . . . The January 27 memo concluded by pointing out that Dean Rusk did not agree with the McNamara-Bundy assessment. . . . "What he [Rusk] does say," the memo stated, "is that the consequences of both escalation and withdrawal are so bad that we simply must find a way of making our present policy work. This would be good if it was [sic] possible. Bob [McNamara] and I do not think it is."

President Johnson responded by asking " . . . Rusk to instruct his experts once again to consider all possible ways for finding a peaceful solution." In addition, he sent McGeorge Bundy and a team of experts to Saigon to make still another report.[3]

In early February, Viet Cong guerrillas attacked two American camps in the central highlands, Pleiku and Camp Holloway, killing nine and wounding a hundred and forty American troops. While helicopter-borne troops pursued and killed a substantial number of guerrillas, American naval aircraft and South Vietnamese bombers carried out an attack on North Vietnamese barracks and staging areas at Dong Hoi, some forty miles north of the 17th parallel. The President also ordered American dependents withdrawn from South Vietnam. A few days later, Viet Cong guerrillas struck again, attacking both American and South Vietnamese installations on the central coast. U.S. naval jet fighter-bombers and bombers responded by striking North Vietnamese "installations." Political confusion in Saigon largely negated morale benefits derived from this new and tough line. While South Vietnamese politicians continued to behave as if no national crisis threatened, Viet Cong attacks continued in the central highlands. Johnson earlier had authorized Westmoreland to commit combat aircraft in support of ARVN. Now, to prevent the enemy from slicing off the northern provinces, Westmoreland released U. S. Air Force F-100 fighter-bombers and B-57 light jet bombers to bomb and strafe alleged VC concentrations in support of South Vietnamese troops.

McGeorge Bundy and his team of experts were in Saigon when the VC attacked Pleiku. On his way back to Washington, he wrote a memorandum for the President that began,

> . . . The situation in Vietnam is deteriorating, and without new U.S. action defeat appears inevitable—probably not in a matter of weeks or perhaps even months, but within the next year or so. There is still time to turn around, but not much. . .

. . . Arguing that a negotiated withdrawal of American forces would mean " . . . surrender on the installment plan," Bundy instead proposed a policy of " . . . graduated and continuing reprisal" against North Vietnam. He also pointed to specific courses of action in the South, " . . . such as helping to strengthen the Vietnamese political structure and improving pacification," and concluded:

> . . . There is one grave weakness in our posture in Vietnam which is within our own power to fix—and that is widespread belief that we do not have the will and force and patience and determination to take the necessary action and stay the course.
>
> This is the overriding reason for our present recommendation of a policy of sustained reprisal. Once such a policy is put in force, we shall be able to speak in Vietnam on many topics and in many ways, with growing force and effectiveness.
>
> One final word. At its very best the struggle in Vietnam will be long. It seems to us important that this fundamental fact be made clear and our understanding of it be made clear to our own people and to the people of Vietnam. Too often in the past we have conveyed the impression that we expect an early solution when those who live with this war know that no early solution is possible. It is our own belief that the people of the United States have the necessary will to accept and to execute a policy that rests upon the reality that there is no short cut to success in South Vietnam.[4]

An annex, apparently written by John McNaughton, recommended sustained reprisal against North Vietnam:

> . . . We cannot assert that a policy of sustained reprisal will succeed in changing the course of the contest in Vietnam. . . . What we can say is that even if it fails, the policy will be worth it. At a

minimum it will damp down the charge that we did not do all that we could have done, and this charge will be important in many countries, including our own. Beyond that, a reprisal policy... will set a higher price for the future upon all adventures of guerrilla warfare, and it should therefore somewhat increase our ability to deter such adventures. We must recognize, however, that that ability will be gravely weakened if there is failure for any reason in Vietnam.[5]

Other Administration hawks, particularly Rostow and members of the JCS, did not adopt such a pessimistic attitude. This school held that strategic bombing of the North would "win" the war. What it could not ignore was that strategic bombing of the North could well lead to a nuclear war. Primarily for this reason, President Johnson adopted the lesser course of action, "...a policy of sustained reprisal" against North Vietnam.[6]

The Administration's justification for escalation rested fundamentally on the aggression-from-the-North theme. The State Department now added a diplomatic exclamation point to military plans by publishing a fourteen-thousand-word treatise called "Aggression from the North—The Record of North Viet-Nam's Campaign to Conquer South Vietnam." This White Paper, which William Bundy had called for in his "escalation scenario" of May, made it clear that the Johnson administration held North Vietnam fully responsible for fomenting, directing, and supporting the VC insurgency in the South.

In early March 1965, U.S. and South Vietnamese planes struck a North Vietnamese ammunition depot and naval base. A few days later, an American marine expeditionary force of two reinforced battalions— some thirty-five hundred troops—landed at Da Nang to defend the airfield against VC reprisal attacks. At a news conference at his Texas ranch in late March, the President repeated a pledge he had made a year before:

...For ten years, under three Presidents, this Nation has been determined to help a brave people to resist aggression and terror. It is and it will remain the policy of the United States to furnish assistance to support South Viet-Nam for as long as is required to bring Communist aggression and terrorism under control.

A few days later, he repeated this sentiment in a formal presidential statement. The American public may not have known it, but their country had gone to war.[7]

*   *   *

795

VIETNAM
1964–1965
• Towns and Cities

American air strikes against the North, what became known as Operation Rolling Thunder, coupled with American marines landing in Da Nang, bolstered GVN and ARVN morale, particularly at top echelons, but did little to improve existing deficiencies in either government or armed forces. Nor, as Robert Shaplen pointed out, did it imbue ARVN with the offensive attitude so heavily desired by American military advisers. Improved morale at top levels soon gave way to renewed political turbulence and crises that continued to inhibit beneficial governmental action in the countryside, where the bulk of South Vietnam's peasants—that is to say, the bulk of the South Vietnamese people—did not share Saigon's enthusiasm for a widening war. American actions alarmed many peasants who, contrary to what most people in the United States believed, had yet to be touched by insurgency. In numerous areas of the South, the war still resembled a distant cloud of locusts, and escalation seemed a threatening wind that moved this cloud uncomfortably closer. When it exploded to release phosphorus and napalm bombs, streams of machine-gun bullets, high-explosive artillery shells, and nausea-producing gases, all of which too often failed to distinguish between Viet Cong and innocent folks, it also unleashed a counterstorm of world opinion that included many vociferous voices in the United States.

By spring of 1965, the Johnson administration's escalation policy had failed on two counts: North Vietnam seemed singularly unimpressed either by American air strikes or by grim warnings that they would continue. And, despite an expenditure of millions, the landing of several thousand troops, and the presence of over twenty-five thousand advisers, the American Government seemed as far from accomplishing the necessary task of establishing viable government in South Vietnam as it ever had.

As one result, President Johnson faced a situation familiar in embryo to Presidents Eisenhower and Kennedy. Reduced to simplest terms, it called for the American Government to demand that the Saigon government produce or else stand (or fall) alone. It was not an easy ultimatum but it was the one action, short of arbitrarily terminating aid and withdrawing, that might have fused dissident elements sufficiently to fight a counterinsurgency.

Where Eisenhower and Kennedy failed, so did Johnson. Instead of demanding an about-face from the Saigon government, instead of confining the war to the South and treating it for what it was, a politically motivated civil conflict, the President attempted to convert it to an international ideological conflict that had to be resolved by American arms with or without the tacit co-operation of either the South Vietnamese or American people.

Throughout March, air strikes mounted in intensity. Although President Johnson authorized use of napalm early in the campaign, he confined air strikes to south of the 19th parallel, which infuriated service chiefs as well as Ambassador Taylor in Saigon. Pressures mounted during March for a sustained bombing program north of the 19th parallel. Also in March, the JCS and General Westmoreland began calling for SEATO ground forces (which would have to be predominantly American) both to hold coastal enclaves and to patrol northern and northwestern border areas. Westmoreland wanted about seventy thousand troops by June " . . . and indicated that more troops might be required thereafter if the bombing [of the North] failed to achieve results." The JCS recommended sending in three divisions, two American and one Korean, " . . . for offensive combat operations against the guerrillas." Ambassador Taylor argued against the requests, " . . . because he felt the South Vietnamese might resent the presence of so many foreign troops—upwards of 100,000 men—and also because he believed there was still no military necessity for them."[8] McNamara tended to support the requests, but his deputy, John McNaughton, wanted them integrated into a specific course of action.[9] CIA chief John McCone held still other ideas. In line with Walt Rostow's thesis, McCone believed that " . . . forcing submission of the VC can only be brought about by a decision in Hanoi." A decision in Hanoi, in turn, could only result from a massive air campaign that would impose "unacceptable damage" and threaten the DRV's "vital interests":

> . . . We must hit them harder, more frequently, and inflict greater damage. Instead of avoiding the MIG's, we must go in and take them out. A bridge here and there will not do the job. We must strike their airfields, their petroleum resources, power stations and their military compounds. This, in my opinion, must be done promptly and with minimum restraint. . . . [10]

President Johnson met with his top advisers at the White House in early April. Although VC guerrillas had just blown up the American embassy in Saigon, the President declined to take drastic overt action (other than asking Congress for a million dollars in order to build a new one), but instead set the stage further. Among other decisions, he authorized two more marine battalions and one marine air squadron for the Da Nang enclave, and a further eighteen to twenty thousand support troops for South Vietnam. More important, he authorized marines to change from defensive to offensive operations in the Da Nang area.

In early April, in what became known as his Baltimore speech, the President set forth the Administration's position in Southeast Asia. Like Kennedy before him, he was Prometheus on the podium. He left no doubt as to the villains: " . . . The first reality is that North Viet-Nam has attacked the independent nation of South Viet-Nam. Its object is total conquest." Hanoi, however, was not acting unilaterally: " . . . Over this war—and all Asia—is another reality: the deepening shadow of Communist China. The rulers in Hanoi are urged on by Peiping. . . . The contest in Viet-Nam is part of a wider pattern of aggressive purposes." As for American presence in South Vietnam:

> . . . We are there because we have a promise to keep. Since 1954 every American President has offered support to the people of South Viet-Nam . . . over many years, we have made a national pledge to help South Viet-Nam defend its independence. . . . To dishonor that pledge . . . would be an unforgivable wrong. We are also there to strengthen world order. . . . Let no one think for a moment that retreat from Viet-Nam would bring an end to conflict. The battle would be renewed in one country and then another. The central lesson of our time is that the appetite of aggression is never satisfied. To withdraw from one battlefield means only to prepare for the next. We must say in Southeast Asia—as we did in Europe—in the words of the Bible: "Hitherto shalt thou come, but no further."

What did the United States wish to accomplish?

> . . . Our objective is the independence of South Viet-Nam and its freedom from attack. We want nothing for ourselves—only that the people of South Viet-Nam be allowed to guide their own country in their own way. We will do everything necessary to reach that objective, and we will do only what is absolutely necessary.

Having applied the stick, the President offered the carrot that General de Gaulle had recommended to President Kennedy four years earlier. The United States had been and remained ready " . . . for unconditional discussions" in order to bring an end to the fighting. If fighting stopped, he would ask Congress to fund a billion-dollar investment program in Southeast Asia that would bring a new and better life to the peoples of Southeast Asia, including those of North Vietnam.[11]

If President Johnson expected his words to propel Ho Chi Minh to the conference table, he was quickly disappointed. Although, at one time, the United States might have influenced the Communist leader to conciliatory action, since 1950 the U.S.A. had emerged as archenemy in northern eyes. That did not mean that they stood ready to rush army divisions to the South. Thanks to Pentagon and State Department fulminations, we tend to forget that Hanoi's investment in the southern

rebellion was still minimal. Hanoi had contributed by training Southerners who had come North and who returned to work up the insurgency. During 1964, Hanoi began infiltrating *northern* cadres, at the
most probably twenty-five hundred. These people joined an extremely
viable organization that was Communist-dominated in part by means
of the PRP, but one that was largely self-supporting. For years, the NLF
had controlled large areas of the South; it collected taxes, sold war
bonds, extorted money, captured arms, ammunition, medical supplies,
and other material from ARVN—all this to a remarkable degree, described in detail by Douglas Pike who estimated that the 1964 NLF
budget was $75 million with Hanoi contributing about 20 per cent, a
minimum investment that kept the pot of rebellion not only boiling but
daily growing more savory.[12]

In this respect, Johnson and his coterie of hawks were aiming at
the wrong target. Not only was the NLF-PRP carrying on the war, but
Hanoi would have had its hands full in persuading the southern organization to stop fighting. Put another way: successful negotiations with
the NLF-PRP could have stopped the war. At this point, Hanoi was
still conforming to standard Communist revolutionary doctrine as defined by Moscow and Peking, whose leaders believed that a rebellion
had to come from within although it could be helped from without.
Hanoi's help remained contingent on satisfactory progress of the southern insurgency. This is the essence of protracted revolutionary warfare;
it is a political axiom derived from a tactical tenet: If an insurgency
fails, back off, wait, and try again. This is very important to understand,
for it means that the fulcrum of insurgency is interior, not exterior.

By spring of 1965, Hanoi's commitment to the southern insurgency
was remarkably slight and for good reason. Years of toil had produced
a formidable southern guerrilla force that from some five thousand in
1959 numbered in early 1965 an estimated fifty-five to eighty thousand—"perhaps the toughest, most experienced guerrilla fighters to be
found anywhere on earth."[13] In view of this growth, Hanoi would have
been foolish to interrupt local dynamics, the more so because the insurgency continued to expand. The 1964 decision to concentrate on a
military solution did not mean seriously involving North Vietnam's
fourteen regular infantry divisions (though this army might have been
tempted into overt invasion had the American military acted wisely). It
was to be a southern-based military solution, as it had to be if only
some twenty-five hundred Northerners came South in all of 1964.[14]

In 1965, Hanoi infiltrated an estimated eleven thousand Northerners, but this figure must be qualified: Considering NLF-PRP strength, it
was neither impressive nor was it necessarily accurate. Dean Rusk told
the Senate Foreign Relations Committee in April 1965 that the 325th
North Vietnamese division had moved across the border " . . . as a di-

vision" between November 1964 and January 1965[15]—a presence repeatedly referred to by Lyndon Johnson in his memoirs as justification for subsequent attacks against the North.[16] But Rusk and Johnson apparently were not using William Bundy's intelligence sources. Bundy later stated,

> " . . . we know that one North Vietnamese regiment entered South Vietnam by December 1964, and we know that several other regiments entered in the spring of 1965. . . . Hanoi, as we suspected then and later proved, had taken major steps to raise the level of the war before the bombing began."[17]

Enter Westmoreland, who told an interviewer that " . . . in 1965 he [the enemy] began to move regular North Vietnamese Army units into Vietnam through Laos."[18]—but Rusk said that the enemy began to do this in 1964! Now enter McNamara, who, in the same month that Rusk testified before the Senate committee, revealed that

> . . . it was not until the end of March [1965]—four weeks after the systematic bombing of North Vietnam was initiated and three weeks after the Marines had landed—that intelligence confirmed the presence of North Vietnamese troops in South Vietnam. Moreover, McNamara indicated, the unit was only one battalion of 400 to 500 men from the North Vietnamese Army's 325th Division. Tacitly it was noted that the 325th Division was still in North Vietnam.[19]

By August 1965, according to General Wheeler, chairman of the Joint Chiefs of Staff, approximately fourteen hundred North Vietnamese troops were serving in the South (as opposed to seventy-five thousand American troops); by year's end, North Vietnamese troops numbered fourteen thousand, U.S. troops two hundred thousand![20]

American reinforcements which followed the President's reassuring speech once again seemed to breathe new life into the Saigon government and ARVN. After blunting the Viet Cong's winter offensives, ARVN had moved against the enemy in the Mekong Delta area, the central coastal areas, and the North; government troops had killed impressive numbers of guerrillas and had opened major roads in several areas.

In April, another three thousand American marines reached the Da Nang area to build the commitment to some eight thousand men supported by artillery, armor, aircraft, and naval gunfire. Marine patrols were now fanning out from Da Nang, the first steps in contesting Viet

Cong control of that area. McNamara and the JCS subsequently persuaded President Johnson to enlarge the ground role by committing an American airborne brigade to the Bien Hoa-Vung Tau areas, outside of Saigon, " . . . to secure vital U.S. installations."[21] Despite these reinforcements, the situation in South Vietnam remained fragile in the extreme. As usual when ARVN forces made substantial gains, they failed to exploit them by consolidating operational areas. Instead, they withdrew to defensive positions.

If the Viet Cong had failed to divide South Vietnam, it did not mean that they were defeated. In the best guerrilla tradition they withdrew to the hills to fortify villages, lick wounds, and reorganize units with replacements and supply obtained locally and from the North. Fresh American efforts again had caused them to think twice about the war. An ominous portent of their thinking emerged in a CIA report of late April, which identified a regiment of the North Vietnamese army [PAVN] in the province of Kontum.[22]

Most American principals now agreed that bombing the North was not going to bring "victory" (but nevertheless most wanted it intensified). At a high-level meeting in Honolulu, John McNaughton noted general agreement that the decision would be gained in the South: " . . . The current lull in Vietcong activity was merely the quiet before a storm. The victory strategy was to 'break the will of the D.R.V./VC by denying them victory.' "[23] Members of the JCS, Westmoreland, and other hawks continued to argue for aggressive tactics to bring the war home to the enemy. They accordingly asked for more troops from the United States and other countries. Ambassador Taylor, according to the Pentagon study, " . . . protested the 'hasty and ill-conceived' proposals for the deployment of more forces with which he was being flooded" and called for " . . . a clarification of our purposes and objectives."[24] The Honolulu conference ended in a clear victory for the Pentagon, which recommended a 100 per cent increase in American troop strength, raising the total from about forty thousand to over eighty thousand; in addition, another seventeen battalions, eleven American and six South Korean, could be deployed at a later stage.[25]

The President was still hopeful that extraneous action would force the North to call off the war. In May, he proposed a bombing halt of the North to coincide with Buddha's birthday. A paragraph in a message sent to Ambassador Taylor offers an interesting insight into presidential thinking at this stage:

> . . . You should understand that my purpose in this plan is to begin to clear a path either toward restoration of peace or toward increased military action, depending upon the reaction of the Communists. We have amply demonstrated our determination and our

commitment in the last two months, and I now wish to gain some flexibility.[26]

Three days later, the President suspended air strikes, a four-day halt that brought no response from Moscow, Hanoi, or Peiping (formerly Peking). Although he resumed Operation Rolling Thunder, he refused to authorize strikes in the vicinity of Hanoi. His obdurate attitude infuriated the JCS, just as his cryptic statement that " . . . a military victory is impossible" alarmed one of the more bellicose of his civil advisers, Walt Rostow. Rostow informed Rusk in late May that there was no reason the U.S.A. could not win a clear victory in South Vietnam. In Rostow's mind, Hanoi, which in February had hoped to obtain victory through political collapse and subsequent coalition government in Saigon, was now

> . . . staring at quite clear-cut defeat, with the rising U.S. strength and GVN morale in the South and rising costs in the North. That readjustment in prospects is painful; and they won't in my view, accept its consequences unless they are convinced time has ceased to be their friend, despite the full use of their assets on the ground in South Viet-Nam, in political warfare around the world, and in diplomacy.[27]

While Rostow was writing this remarkable prognosis, the situation in South Vietnam was deteriorating at an alarming pace. In late May, VC guerrillas ambushed an ARVN battalion to open an action that " . . . completely decimated" two ARVN battalions. In June, two VC regiments attacked an ARVN outpost and then ambushed reinforcements. Around Da Nang, U. S. Marine Corps patrols were encountering increasing numbers of enemy, and in April and May suffered about two hundred casualties. Johnson's decision to widen the bombing effort in the North by way of reprisal brought still another ominous reaction, when Britain's Prime Minister Harold Wilson "dissociated" his country from it.[28]

In Saigon, the political situation remained as confused and torn as ever. Renewed fighting between Buddhist and Catholic factions led to the generals' ousting Premier Quat in early June. In place of civil government appeared a National Leadership Committee headed by forty-two-year-old General Nguyen Van Thieu. The ten-man committee included most of the familiar military faces, among them thirty-five-year-old Nguyen Cao Ky, the airman who now became premier. Although Ky imposed a number of dictatorial measures including summary trial and execution of terrorists, black marketeers, speculators, and corrupt officials, government remained weak and ineffective.[29]

With a Viet Cong offensive obviously developing, General Westmoreland reported to the JCS, via CINCPAC, on June 7:

> . . . In pressing their campaign, the Viet-Cong are capable of mounting regimental-size operations in all four ARVN corps areas, and at least battalion-sized attack in virtually all provinces. . . .
>
> ARVN forces on the other hand are already experiencing difficulty in coping with this increased VC capability. Desertion rates are inordinately high. Battle losses have been higher than expected; in fact, four ARVN battalions have been rendered ineffective by VC action in the I and II Corps zones.

Force ratios on which earlier estimates had been made were thus upset, Westmoreland continued. His solution was to become a MACV theme song:

> . . . I see no course of action open to us except to reinforce our efforts in SVN with additional U.S. or third country forces as rapidly as is practical during the critical weeks ahead.

Westmoreland now requested a whopping increase in outside troop strength, to a total of forty-four battalions. Admiral Sharp (CINCPAC) endorsed the request with approval and noted: " . . . We will lose by staying in enclaves defending coastal areas." The JCS were not antagonistic to the request but wanted to know " . . . where Westmoreland intended to put this force in Vietnam." Westmoreland's reply, according to a Pentagon analyst,

> . . . was extremely important, for in it [he] spelled out the concept of keeping U.S. forces away from the people. The search and destroy strategy for U.S. and third country forces which continues to this day [1967–68] and the primary focus of RVNAF (ARVN) on pacification both stem from that concept. In addition, Westmoreland made a big pitch in this cable for a free hand to maneuver the troops around inside the country.[30]

Westmoreland's request aroused considerable controversy inside the government. At the same time, however, Johnson's decision to allow American troops to indulge in combat operations had slowly leaked to the public, segments of which were already uneasy by a supplementary appropriation of $700 million authorized by Congress in early May " . . . for military needs in Viet-Nam." Mounting intensity of fighting due to the Viet Cong's monsoonal offensive now caused some critical questioning of Administration policy. In mid-June, Senator J. W. Fulbright addressed his fellow senators:

... It is clear to all reasonable Americans that a complete military victory in Viet-Nam, though theoretically attainable, can in fact be attained only at a cost far exceeding the requirements of our interest and our honor. It is equally clear that the unconditional withdrawal of American support from South Viet-Nam would have disastrous consequences. ... Our policy therefore has been—and should remain—one of determination to end the war at the earliest possible time by a negotiated settlement involving major concessions by both sides.

In view of the then-current Viet Cong offensive and advantages derived by them from the monsoonal season, Fulbright warned of American setbacks:

... As the ground war expands and as American involvement and American casualties increase, there will be mounting pressure for expansion of the war.

Indeed, such pressures already existed, and the President must continue to ignore them in favor of "restraint and patience":

... we must persuade the Communists that Saigon cannot be crushed and that the United States will not be driven from South Viet-Nam by force; second, we must continue to offer the Communists a reasonable and attractive alternative to military victory.[31]

Fulbright's tolerance was shared neither by the JCS nor by Westmoreland, whose hand was steadily being reinforced by the deteriorating political and military situation in South Vietnam. In May, President Johnson had authorized Westmoreland " ... to use his forces in combat support if it became necessary to assist a Vietnamese unit in serious trouble." In June, the President authorized him to use his forces "independently" of South Vietnamese forces. At the end of June, Westmoreland committed an airborne brigade to a search-and-destroy operation in conjunction with an ARVN battalion and an Australian battalion northwest of Saigon. Meanwhile, General Wheeler, chairman of the JCS, asked Westmoreland " ... if the 44 battalions were enough to convince the enemy forces that they could not win." According to the Pentagon study, Westmoreland replied

... that there was no evidence the VC/DRV would alter their plans regardless of what the U.S. did in the next six months.
The 44-battalion force should, however, establish a favorable balance of power by the end of the year. If the U.S. was to seize

the initiative from the enemy, then further forces would be required into 1966 and beyond.[32]

A few days later, the JCS approved a planned deployment of nearly two hundred thousand American troops in South Vietnam. In mid-July, influenced by a new report from McNamara, President Johnson authorized this build-up and also gave Westmoreland authority to commit American troops to combat at his discretion.[33]

Although these measures remained secret, at least for the moment, they caused considerable consternation within the Administration. On July 1, Under Secretary of State George Ball submitted a lengthy memorandum to President Johnson:

> . . . The South Vietnamese are losing the war to the Viet Cong. No one can assure you that we can beat the Viet Cong or even force them to the conference table on our terms, no matter how many hundred thousand *white, foreign* (U.S.) troops we deploy.
>
> No one has demonstrated that a white ground force of whatever size can win a guerrilla war—which is at the same time a civil war between Asians—in jungle terrain in the midst of a population that refuses cooperation to the white forces (and the South Vietnamese) and thus provides a great intelligence advantage to the other side.

The President, Ball stated, had one question to decide:

> . . . Should we limit our liabilities in South Vietnam and try to find a way out with minimal long-term costs?
>
> The alternative—no matter what we may wish it to be—is almost certainly a protracted war involving an open-ended commitment of U.S. forces, mounting U.S. casualties, no assurance of a satisfactory solution, and a serious danger of escalation at the end of the road.

The President, Ball believed, had to decide on the answer now:

> . . . So long as our forces are restricted to advising and assisting the South Vietnamese, the struggle will remain a civil war between Asian peoples. Once we deploy substantial numbers of troops in combat it will become a war between the U.S. and a large part of the population of South Vietnam, organized and directed from North Vietnam and backed by the resources of both Moscow and Peiping. . . . Once we suffer large casualties, we will have started a well-nigh irreversible process. Our involvement will be so great that we cannot—without national humiliation—stop short of achieving our complete objectives. *Of the two possibilities I think*

humiliation would be more likely than the achievement of our objectives—even after we have paid terrible costs.

Ball did not recommend a unilateral withdrawal from South Vietnam. Instead, he proposed a total troop commitment of seventy-two thousand men to support restricted combat operations; he also agreed to the present bombing program. Simultaneously, he called for a diplomatic offensive by unilateral approach to Hanoi, the general idea being that Johnson could pressure the Saigon government and Ho to bring the NLF to the conference table to hammer out " . . . a multi-national agreement guaranteed by the U.S., the Soviet Union and possibly other parties, and providing for an international mechanism to supervise its execution."[34]

Ball next examined short-term costs of a compromise solution. Astute diplomacy could hold these to a minimum. The United States had good allies in Southeast Asia and would continue to support them. If South Vietnam fell to Communist control, Burma, Cambodia, and Indonesia would probably enter the Eastern orbit—but they were scarcely in the Western orbit at this time. Other nations could be expected to hold, with proper backing from the U.S.A. As for Thailand: " . . . Providing we are willing to make the effort, Thailand can be a foundation of rock and not a bed of sand in which to base our political/military commitment to Southeast Asia." As for U.S. world-wide credibility: With the possible exception of West Germany,

> . . . [our NATO allies] will be inclined to regard a compromise solution in South Vietnam more as new evidence of American maturity and judgment than of American loss of face. . . . On balance, I believe we would more seriously undermine the effectiveness of our world leadership by continuing the war and deepening our involvement than by pursuing a carefully plotted course toward a compromise solution. In spite of the number of powers that have—in response to our pleading—given verbal support from feeling of loyalty and dependence, we cannot ignore the fact that the war is vastly unpopular and that our role in it is perceptively eroding the respect and confidence with which other nations regard us. We have not persuaded either our friends or allies that our further involvement is essential to the defense of freedom in the cold war. . . .[35]

Neither Johnson nor the majority of his advisers was to be swayed by this memorandum, which, although a bail-out course that need never have been necessary had proper measures originally been taken, was at the time a bold, imaginative, and courageous policy that had been needed since 1954. Ball further dissented from Administration thinking during a late-July session with Johnson. At Camp Aspen a few days later, Johnson also found his close adviser Clark Clifford " . . . in a reflective and pessimistic mood":

> " . . . I don't believe we can win in South Vietnam," he said. "If we send in 100,000 more men, the North Vietnamese will meet us. If North Vietnam runs out of men, the Chinese will send in volunteers. Russia and China don't intend for us to win the war."
>
> He urged that in the coming months we quietly probe possibilities with other countries for some way to get out honorably. "I can't see anything but catastrophe for my country," he said.

Senator Mike Mansfield, who had dissented from Johnson's February decision to begin bombing North Vietnam, also expressed " . . . serious doubt and opposition" to the present course.[36]

Refined and properly applied, this dissentient thinking, echoed variously by influential citizens throughout the country, might have led to a solution that would have given Lyndon Johnson that place in American history he so obtrusively desired. Instead, he rejected compromise in favor of a "win" strategy. At a press conference in late July he said:

> . . . The lesson of history dictated that the U.S. commit its strength to resist aggression in South Vietnam. . . . I have asked the commanding general, General Westmoreland, what more he needs to meet this mounting aggression. He has told me. We will meet his needs.

Having declared a collision course with disaster, the President still thought it was necessary to deceive the American public. A reporter asked,

> . . . Mr. President, does the fact that you are sending additional forces to Vietnam imply any change in the existing policy of relying mainly on the South Vietnamese to carry out offensive operations and using American forces to guard American installations and to act as an emergency back-up?

At a time when an American airborne brigade had already sharply engaged the Viet Cong in a search-and-destroy mission, at a time when marines were seeking out Viet Cong and were planning a major search-and-clear operation, at a time when McNamara, Westmoreland, and the JCS were flexing military muscles to "come to grips" with the enemy[37]—at this time, the President of the United States replied:

> . . . It does not imply any change in policy whatever. It does not imply change of objective.[38]

808

1. Sheehan et al., 337.
2. Johnson, *The Vantage Point* . . . , 122.
3. Ibid., 122–3.
4. Ibid., 126–7. See also, Sheehan et al., 423.
5. Sheehan et al., 423–7.
6. Johnson, *The Vantage Point* . . . , 128–9. See also, Sharp.
7. Johnson, *Public Papers of* . . . , 1965, Book I, 300.
8. Sheehan et al., 399.
9. Ibid., 438.
10. Ibid., 440–1.
11. Johnson, *Public Papers of* . . . , 1965, Book I, 394–7. See also, ibid., Johnson's statement to the press, "Tragedy, Disappointment, and Progress" in Vietnam, April 17, 1965.
12. Pike, 304. See also, O'Neill.
13. Pike, 238–9. See also, ibid., 232–52, for excellent detail on Viet Cong organization and tactics.
14. Ibid.
15. Corson, 63–4.
16. Johnson, *The Vantage Point* . . . , see, for example, 121–2, 232.
17. William P. Bundy.
18. *U.S. News and World Report,* November 28, 1966.
19. Corson, 64–5.
20. Ibid., 65.
21. Sheehan et al., 402–3.
22. Ibid., 409: Statements of Administration officials aside, this would appear to be the first major PAVN unit in the South.
23. Ibid., 407. See also, Johnson, *The Vantage Point* . . .
24. Sheehan et al., 406–7, 443–6.
25. Ibid., 408.
26. Ibid., 446–7.
27. Ibid., 448. See also, Gilpatric, whose recital of American strengths and weaknesses was tempered only by the possibility that the American people would not want to fight a prolonged war.
28. Sheehan, 448–9.
29. Shaplen, *The Lost Revolution,* 345–6.
30. Sheehan, 409–10, 413. See also, Johnson, *The Vantage Point* . . .
31. Raskin and Fall, 205–10, for full text of Senator Fulbright's speech.
32. Sheehan et al., 413–14.
33. Johnson, *The Vantage Point* . . . , 153. See also, ibid., 145–6. McNamara, according to Johnson, reported a seriously deteriorating situation that could be met with one of three courses of action: cut losses and withdraw under the best conditions that could be arranged; continue at present level; expand promptly and substantially. McNamara recommended the third course.

> . . . With the force that he and the others were proposing, McNamara was convinced that the South Vietnamese and allied armies could reverse the downward trend and move to the offensive. He said that the military commanders planned to locate, engage, and destroy the North Vietnamese and Viet Cong main-force units. At the same time, they believed we should press our anti-infiltration campaign by hitting enemy supply lines by air and on the sea. We would also carry the air war more intensively into Viet Cong base

areas in the South. . . . [Ibid., *Public Papers of . . .* , 1965, Book I, "The President's News Conference of July 13, 1965"]

34. Sheehan et al, 449–54.
35. Ibid.
36. Johnson, *The Vantage Point . . .* , 148.
37. Sheehan et al., 457–8.
38. Johnson, *Public Papers of . . .* , 1965, Book II, 795–801.

CHAPTER 64

The fighting escalates • Viet Cong setbacks • American and ARVN gains • The air war • Westmoreland's strategy • Search-and-destroy tactics • The American build-up • Westmoreland's four wars • The "other war" • American arms and equipment • Army operations in the central highlands • Westmoreland's "spoiling" tactics • Operation Crazy Horse • Marine operations in I Corps area • Walt's pacification program • PAVN crosses the DMZ: Operation Hastings, Operation Prairie • Operations in III Corps area • The air war escalates • The naval war • The "other war": the Honolulu Conference • Ky's Revolutionary Development program • Elections in the South • The Manila Conference • General allied optimism

AMERICAN INFUSION OF STRENGTH again steadied the fibril-lating heart of South Vietnam's government and army. If the Viet Cong nowhere accomplished its major objective of permanently dividing the country in vicious fighting during summer and autumn of 1965, its battalions and regiments, increasingly reinforced by PAVN units from the North, cut road and rail communications, attacked ARVN outposts almost at will, ambushed ARVN forces sent to relieve beleaguered garrisons, and continued a campaign of sabotage and terror against South Vietnamese and American installations and personnel. But ARVN units, in some cases supported by American forces, also generally fought hard, and new American units showed every willing-ness to fight,[1] even if hamstrung by MACV's overly cautious and utterly impracticable *Rules of Engagement*, " . . . specifically the one that pre-cluded a U.S. soldier firing his weapon if not fired upon."[2] " . . . In guerrilla-controlled areas," a marine lieutenant later wrote, one could not fire "at unarmed Vietnamese *unless they were running*."[3] Thus hin-dered, American marines based at Da Nang mounted Operation Starlight in August, a sweeping operation designed to evict Viet Cong from Chu Lai Peninsula. In a several-day action, marines recorded fifty killed and one hundred and fifty wounded, but claimed over five hundred Viet Cong deaths. Meanwhile, the American army's 1st Cavalry (Airmobile) Division set up shop at An Khe, in the central highlands—a base from which units would attempt to screen the neighboring Cambodian border while clearing enemy from the immediate area. When North Vietnamese units, an estimated two regiments, attacked a Special Forces camp at Plei Me, near the Cambodian border, the American garrison held out and then mounted a counterattack, which led to bloody fighting in the Chu Phong and Ia Drang area. The Americans recorded two hundred and forty killed and four hundred and seventy wounded, but claimed over fifteen hundred enemy deaths.[4]

Simultaneously, air strikes against the North rose impressively. During the summer, the purpose of Operation Rolling Thunder had changed from breaking Hanoi's will to " . . . cutting the flow of men and supplies from the North to the South."[5] In addition to striking barracks, ammunition depots, and staging points, pilots at their own discretion attacked vehicles, locomotives, and barges. Sorties increased from nine hundred a week in July to fifteen hundred a week in December; by end of 1965, fifty-five thousand sorties had been flown and thirty-three thousand tons of bombs dropped.

As troops continued to arrive in South Vietnam, General Westmoreland and his chief of operations Brigadier General William DePuy increasingly implemented an attrition strategy—a dependence on superior American military manpower, firepower, and mobility to wear down and finally force the enemy from the war. This was the World War I syndrome, a meaningless and costly concept challenged by a host of thinking military professionals for the last five decades. Lieutenant General Dave Palmer, for example, taught his students when he was an instructor at West Point: " . . . attrition is not a strategy, but the absence of any strategy, and . . . the commander who resorts to it admits his failure to conceive an alternate strategy."[6] Precedents for Westmoreland's choice already had appeared during the Eisenhower and Kennedy administrations, which had adopted increasingly quantitative approaches for fighting this insurgency but had managed to retain limited objectives. The Johnson administration enlarged the concept to embrace an all-out "win" strategy. America's armed forces implemented this strategy by relying on quantitative, or search-and-destroy, tactics: find the enemy—fix him—kill him. By the end of 1965, Westmoreland's strategy and tactics had yielded results deemed favorable by military leaders. Westmoreland had received about one hundred and fifty thousand of a promised two hundred thousand troops. New units were arriving daily, as were tons of equipment and supply. Energetic com-

VIETNAM
1965 - 1966
• Towns and Cities
⚓ U.S. Naval Forces

Red R.

Black R.

TONKIN

Hanoi

South
China
Sea

N

LAOS

DMZ   Ben Hai R.
Khe Sanh Dong Ha   17°N
QUANG
TRI   Phu Bai
Da Nang

THAILAND

HO CHI MINH TRAIL

Chu Lai
QUANG NGAI
BINH DINH
Route 19   Pleiku   Duc Pho
Ia Drang Valley   An Khe   Qui
Plei Me   Nhon
CAMBODIA   CENTRAL HIGHLANDS   TF 77

ZONE C
Iron   ZONE D
Triangle   BINH THUAN   Cam Ranh Bay
Saigon

Mekong Delta

miles
0   100   200

M.E.P.

manders were slowly sorting out initial supply snags while simultaneously pushing the enemy on several fronts. American commands were working around the clock. American planes were striking enemy units in North and South. American patrols were seeking contacts and fighting when possible. A pervasive air of aggression was pushing aside the stale air of defeatism. That winter in South Vietnam even the most cynical observer had to admit that the Americans were obviously determined to impose their will on the enemy.

The man chosen to command the American military effort in Vietnam, General William Childs Westmoreland, seemed ideally fitted for the task. A South Carolinian and West Pointer (1936), he had served as an artillery commander in World War II in Africa and Europe, and had commanded an airborne regiment in Korea. Promoted to brigadier general at thirty-eight years, he had served subsequently as secretary of the general staff, commanding general of the 101st Airborne Division, and superintendent of West Point, adding a star for each new billet. Now fifty-one years old, he stood nearly six feet tall, a rugged, fit man of one hundred and eighty pounds, a devout Episcopalian who frowned on swearing, smoking, and hard drinking, and who was said to keep a Bible on his desk and to read it.[7]

General Westmoreland soon found himself fighting four distinct, though intimately related, shooting wars: the "original" guerrilla, or counterinsurgency, war that challenged the NLF-VC organized in regular and paramilitary units throughout the country; the quasi-conventional ground war in the central highlands and south of the Demilitarized Zone (DMZ) that was fought against VC and regular units of the North Vietnamese army (PAVN); the naval war; and the air war. Each of these efforts bred certain political, economic, and psychological problems, which, taken together, influenced what some called "the other war," the contest to win people's "hearts and minds"—what a few persons accurately called "the only war."[8]

To fight the shooting wars, General Westmoreland disposed of a force so impressive as to bring to mind the prophet Jeremiah's description of the ancient army that would irrupt into Judah: " . . . his chariots shall be as a whirlwind: his horses are swifter than eagles. . . . Their quiver is as an open sepulchre. . . . " From the standpoint of technology, the world had never seen a more sophisticated armed host than that committed by the Americans in South Vietnam. Literally no expense had been spared in equipping and training these infantry and airborne and marine divisions and air units and naval armadas before committing them to combat.

In addition to standard arms and equipment, troops received rapid-firing Armalite rifles, at first the controversial M-16, later the improved M-14 which fired a lighter, 7.62-mm. round. Each squad carried flame throwers, light machine guns, and grenade launchers; in addition to fragmentation and smoke grenades, troops were equipped with a variety of nauseous gases and rocket launchers. Platoons and companies carried such organic support weapons as 60- and 81-mm. mortars and 90- and 106-mm. recoilless rifles. Supporting artillery units carried 4.2-inch mortars and 105-mm., 155-mm., and eight-inch howitzers. More effective artillery shells appeared, for example the 105-mm. "Beehive," which, upon detonation, released eight thousand steel "fléchettes"—tiny darts to tear through whatever body got in the way. Small-unit communications were vastly improved, as were tropical clothing, boots, ancillary equipment, field rations. Combat troops also received such sophisticated identity aids as electronic sensory devices, or "man sniffers," infrared night-sighting equipment, short-range ground radars. A galaxy of specialist units—medical, engineer, communications—supported ground operations; where necessary, commanders could count on heavy artillery, armor, and, along the coast and inland waterways, naval-gunfire support.[9]

Commanders also relied on armored personnel carriers and on large numbers of helicopters for improved mobility. The U. S. Marine Corps, a pioneer in helicopter "vertical assault" tactics, brought its own "chopper" squadrons as integral components of its air wings. The U. S. Army, which employed helicopter companies organic to the ground division, went so far as to build two divisions around this machine. Each "airmobile" division consisted of approximately sixteen thousand troops equipped with 434 aircraft, mostly helicopters, and sixteen hundred land vehicles (compared to a normal army division's one hundred organic aircraft and over three thousand vehicles).

A vast flotilla escorted troop-carrying helicopters into action. Conventional aircraft often "prepared" the "target": F-100, F-104, F-105, F-4C, and F-5 planes, to name a few, not only bombed and machine-gunned but also carried a varied and highly destructive kit that included conventional high-explosive bombs, delayed-action bombs, white-phosphorus bombs, napalm, and rockets. Some of these were tailored for the tactical situation, for example "daisy-cutters"—bombs fitted with a delayed fuse so as to detonate in water and destroy by concussion any Viet Cong hiding there—and CBUs, or Cluster Bomb Units, which contained thousands of small metal balls released on impact and scattered lethally by compressed air. Huey gunships—helicopters armed with 7.62-mm. machine guns, rockets, and grenades—usually accompanied troop-carrying helicopters (also armed with machine guns) to furnish immediate fire support in case of enemy fire during approach and landing or in later retrieval operations. Ground commanders also were supported by specially fitted aircraft, old and slow-flying Douglas DC-3s and C-47s, for night defense. These relics, known as Puff the Magic Dragon and Smokey the Bear, circled for hours, dropping magnesium flares and pouring in thousands of rounds from three electrically operated rapid-fire machine guns, each capable of firing six thousand rounds per minute.

Helicopters also played an immensely important support role. Small, fast machines that land most anywhere whipped commanders around extended battle areas to give a tactical cohesion unfamiliar since Napoleonic warfare—or so it was claimed. Larger machines landed reinforcements and supply to hard-pressed units, and evacuated the wounded. Medical evacuation (MedEvac) techniques became so polished that the American army claimed a "save" ratio of eighty-two out of a hundred men wounded (as opposed to seventy-one out of a hundred in World War II); the Marine Corps pointed out that no wounded man was " . . . more than 30 minutes . . . from a fully staffed and equipped hospital."[10]

The quasi-conventional ground war at first centered north of Saigon, specifically in the central highlands of II Corps area and the northern coastal provinces of I Corps area. Having foiled the enemy's 1965 plan to cut South Vietnam in half, Westmoreland turned to the twofold task of preventing the enemy from resuming the offensive, then eventually isolating and destroying him in detail while energetically pacifying areas reclaimed from enemy control. To accomplish the first task, Westmoreland depended primarily on a wide variety of search-and-destroy missions, or what he called "spoiling" tactics, that is, blocking and enveloping actions designed to keep the enemy off-balance and thus "spoil" his plans.

Operations in the central highlands were carried out by the 1st Cavalry (Airborne) Division, based at Camp Radcliffe, a huge complex protected by a ten-mile-long barrier beneath Hong Kong mountain. This division "fed" a variety of permanent and temporary fortified bases in the surrounding area. These, in turn, supported numerous operations ranging from small patrols to task-force "sweeps" but including special missions by other units, for example Civilian Irregular Defense Groups (CIDG) composed of Special Forces teams and friendly Montagnard tribesmen.

In winter and spring of 1966, the division was carrying out a threefold mission: countering enemy operations in the central highlands; interdicting border areas where six or seven PAVN regiments were believed to be hovering across the line, in Cambodia; protecting communications from Pleiku along Highway 19 to the sea.

Division operations almost always utilized helicopters. The American army believed that extreme mobility offered by these machines was the key to fighting successful counterinsurgency warfare. Early in the division's operations, William DePuy, now a major general commanding the division, told Frank Harvey: "... the VC needs ten days to transfer three battalions. We manage five battalions in a day."[11]

Standard operating procedure in the highlands called for extensive patrolling designed to find the enemy, then fix him and destroy him. Based on information derived from such as aerial observation, Special Forces units, and friendly local peasants, preliminary action generally fell to a special Reconnaissance Squadron so organized as to first locate and then, circumstances permitting, engage the enemy.

Exploitation assumed a number of forms. One was an ambush patrol, usually carried out by special teams infiltrated into the target area by helicopters using appropriate deceptive techniques. Another was the combat patrol, which sought out and engaged the enemy. If action developed favorably, division could escalate it to a major operation, thanks to mobility offered by helicopters and to fire support supplied by base artillery, helicopters, and tactical (and even strategic) aircraft. If a fire fight developed adversely, the local commander could usually evacuate his patrol, including wounded and dead, by helicopter under cover of supporting fire.

These actions were generally very confused, and co-ordinating them into a meaningful whole taxed the ability of competent senior commanders. The flamboyant American military correspondent, S. L. A. Marshall, described one such operation, known first as Crazy Horse, later as the battle of Vinh Thanh Valley, in detail. The action began when a CIDG patrol surprised an enemy patrol and killed five PAVN soldiers, including a lieutenant. Captured documents indicated that PAVN had moved 120-mm. mortars into the area and was probably going to attack the CIDG base camp in battalion strength (as had been rumored by local villagers). The division commander, Major General Jack Norton, turned the problem over to First Brigade, which was tactically responsible for the area. Although strapped for troops, its commander, Colonel John Hennessey, committed a company-strength patrol into an area "fed" by Landing Zone (LZ) Savoy and, beyond that, by LZ Hereford. When the patrol encountered substantial resistance—it was ambushed and mauled—another company joined the action. Suspecting a lucrative target, Norton enlarged the operation to brigade strength.

According to Marshall, who monitored the action, its purpose was twofold: "... to purge the mountain country beyond LZ Hereford of Communist forces and to make it so costly to them that they would be loath ever again to attempt using it as a sanctuary."

Subsequent patrols did not encounter many enemy units, at least not on favorable terms. Although captured enemy documents soon confirmed that the Americans were fighting elements of five battalions from two PAVN regiments, as well as local Viet Cong units, none of the patrols captured prisoners or attracted defectors, who could have offered precise enemy locations, strength, and intentions. As one result, operations continued on a hit-and-miss basis. Patrols sometimes "found" the enemy, too often by virtue of stumbling into ambushes, but their troop back-up rarely succeeded in "fixing" and "destroying" him. Although the "kill" ratio at times was favorable, it was never decisive. At home in the terrain, the enemy seemed to have little difficulty in breaking off an action at will and in evading pursuit. Within two weeks, the operation bogged down.

This was only one of dozens of such operations. Task forces ranging from reinforced companies and battalions to brigades and even divisions tramped through the highlands and border country to the west in almost constant pursuit of the elusive enemy. So successful did MACV deem search-and-destroy tactics that over sixty operations a month were mounted in South Vietnam in the first six months of 1966, an effort that, according to MACV, yielded a "kill" figure of over sixteen thousand PAVN/VC troops.[12]

An equally impressive effort simultaneously was occurring in the more heavily populated I Corps areas on the coast. Here the build-up of III Marine Amphibious Force had been rapid and efficient. Commanded by Major General (soon to be Lieutenant General) Lewis Walt, the force soon numbered nearly sixty thousand troops, including air units.

We have already discussed the marines' early and, in some ways, successful clearing of Chu Lai Peninsula. Before that area could be pacified—that is, the Viet Cong infrastructure rooted out and replaced by government authority—Walt had been forced to expand his command area: In just over a year, it would grow from eight square miles to eighteen hundred-plus square miles, mostly under Viet Cong control. His mission also had altered: In addition to defending airfields at Da Nang, Chu Lai, and Phu Bai, he was supposed to destroy PAVN and main-force Viet Cong units in the area and root out VC infrastructure, as part of an extensive pacification program.[13]

Tactical operations at first remained at small-unit level and consisted primarily in patrol and ambush work essential to command security. By summer of 1966, marine units had carried out thousands of patrols, while helicopters and marine fixed-wing aircraft had flown thousands of sorties, an activity that resulted in several thousand confirmed enemy dead[14]—though how many were enemy and how many were peasants is a moot question.

For some time, marines relied on search-and-destroy tactics favored by the American army. Two reasons explained the choice. One was command ignorance. General Walt later explained that, when he assumed command in Vietnam, he did not understand the nature of the war.[15] Senior marine commanders echoed Walt's confusion (with some exceptions) and attempted to fight the war with conventional methods. The second fact was I Corps area, which had been under VC control for a long time. I Corps area comprised five provinces (about ten thousand square miles) and over 3 million people, 90 per cent of whom lived in the narrow coastal strip. Although the South Vietnamese Government exercised some control in the cities, the countryside, in general, belonged to the Viet Cong. Marine units sent to outlying areas such as Duc Pho, in Quang Ngai province, lived in a sea of hostility provoked both by regional resentments of Saigon government and by fear of the Viet Cong. A marine who had served in Duc Pho later told Jonathan Schell

> . . . that for the first month they had been unable to travel five hundred yards beyond their camp without running into heavy enemy fire. After receiving reinforcements, they had moved out farther but had still been unable to penetrate many areas.[16]

An important result of this tactical impasse was lack of intelligence on which to base operations—a complaint common to all allied commands in Vietnam, and one generally met by random destruction of "suspected" VC hideouts. Schell, who was appalled at the amount of destruction in Quang Ngai province, explained its etiology:

> . . . The villages had been destroyed in many ways and in a great variety of circumstances—at first by our Marines and later by our Army. In accordance with the local policy of the 3rd Marine Amphibious Force, a village could be bombed immediately and without the issuing of any warning to the villagers if American or other friendly troops or aircraft had received fire from within it. This fire might consist of a few sniper shots or of a heavy attack by the enemy. Whatever the provocation from the village, the volume of firepower brought to bear in response was so great that in almost every case the village was completely destroyed. A village could also be destroyed if intelligence reports indicated that the villagers had been supporting the Vietcong by offering them food and labor, but in such a case the official 3rd Marine Amphibious Force rules of engagement required that our Psychological Warfare Office send a plane to warn the villagers, either by dropping leaflets or by making an airborne announcement . . . There was no official ruling on when troops on the ground were permitted to burn a village, but, generally speaking, this occurred most often after fire had been received from the village, or when the province chief had given a

specific order in advance for its destruction. In some cases, the villagers had been removed from an area in a big-scale operation and then the area had been systematically destroyed. . . . [17]

Such tactics did not endear the allied cause to local populations. So long as peasants remained hostile or apathetic, marines were not going to obtain information on enemy locations and movements, which they needed in order to fight successfully. In a relatively short time, they set about obtaining this information by introducing civic programs designed to win over local people. These varied considerably in effectiveness. Some of them proved outstanding. One enterprising commander instituted the Golden Fleece program, wherein marines guaranteed four villages a secure rice harvest in return for information on local Viet Cong. Other programs seemed to prosper, but progress remained slow, owing both to interruptions caused by enemy attacks and to widespread xenophobia and peasant apathy, perhaps the inevitable result of this particular civil war. A second method was more efficacious. Beginning with villages south of Da Nang, marines provided medical services and began assisting in various construction projects. This necessitated working with I Corps commander Lieutenant General Nguyen Chanh Thi, a suspicious Buddhist nationalist who shortly would be involved in a minor civil war with the Saigon government. Walt nonetheless persuaded Thi to co-operate in establishing a joint area-pacification council of civil and military members, under whose aegis the pacification program slowly spread to a nine-village area. Not content with creeping progress, Walt borrowed a page from the old Nicaraguan campaign and persuaded Thi to go along in establishing a Combined Action Group—an integrated company of marines and Popular Forces (local militia) designed to provide village security. First tried at Phu Bai, the experiment worked almost at once. Robert Shaplen, who visited the village in early 1966, observed marines and militia working together and even learning each other's language:

> . . . As a result of these joint patrols, the Vietcong network in four villages around Phu Bai has been measurably damaged, though the Communists still slip in eight or ten armed agents at a time to collect food and taxes from the population and nothing as advanced as a Census/Grievance and Aspiration unit can yet function safely. Road traffic in this area has picked up noticeably, and hamlet markets now attract buyers and sellers from as far off as two kilometers, which may not sound like much but is a lot compared with what the safe-travel radius was six months ago. [18]

Such was the impact of Combined Action Groups that Walt extended the program as rapidly as possible, his goal being seventy-five groups by year's end.

Two events interrupted the burgeoning pacification program. In March 1966, Buddhist riots in Hué, which involved Thi and brought an eyeball-to-eyeball confrontation between ARVN and Walt's marines, seriously set matters back. By the time this crisis ended, intelligence was reporting indications of a planned North Vietnamese attack through the DMZ. This was the so-called "neutral strip," established by the Geneva Accords, at the 17th parallel. It ran almost sixty miles inland to the Laotian border and extended three miles on either side of the parallel. Although Hanoi had used it for infiltration purposes (as undoubtedly had the South for covert purposes), the bulk of their troops and supply were reaching the South either by means of the Ho Chi Minh Trail through Laos and Cambodia, or by the sea route.

U.S./ARVN counteroperations in the central highlands and to the south were probably beginning to make the long land route less attractive, as were air and naval interdiction operations. A political factor also entered. The Viet Cong had controlled large parts of I Corps area for years; the Buddhist riots in Hué—in effect a civil war—must have further enhanced the area in the eyes of the North. All these factors have been discussed in still another brilliant *New Yorker* article by Robert Shaplen, whose book *The Road from War* is essential to an understanding of these crucial years.

In spring of 1966, at least four PAVN divisions were known to be immediately north of the DMZ. Intelligence reports increasingly confirmed that PAVN units were crossing the line and busily " . . . preparing the battlefield" for subsequent operations. Communist movement began in late May, when vanguard units of Division 324B crossed the DMZ into the rugged terrain of northern Quang Tri province. This was a "regular" army division, some ten to twelve thousand troops well armed and equipped, though perhaps not so well fed. Soldiers carried

Chinese copies of Soviet weapons, the AK-47 assault rifle with fifty to a hundred rounds of 7.62-mm. ammunition, RPD light machine guns, SKS carbines, RPG-2 rocket launchers, and grenades. Shaplen later wrote:

> . . . Each man's supplies further consisted of two khaki, green, or purple uniforms, a canteen, a canvas bag, a raincoat, a pair of rubber sandals, a pair of boots, a hammock, a blanket, a mosquito net, some halazone water-purification tablets, some quinine tablets, some vitamin pills, a small can of chicken or shrimp, a kilogram and a half of salt, and seven kilograms of rice. According to information obtained later from prisoners and from captured documents, food, especially rice, was in very short supply, and several of the battalions had to be pressed into service as transport units, going back and forth a number of times to bring more rice down from North Vietnam before crossing the Ben Hai River for good.[19]

General Westmoreland in Saigon had been keeping a close eye on the situation, as had General Walt in Da Nang, and had worked out contingency plans that involved both Marine Corps and ARVN units. In July, a small marine reconnaissance team reported enemy presence in strength, reports confirmed by ARVN units who had taken some prisoners in the same area. Operation Hastings now began. It called for "spoiling" operations by a marine force of seven battalions plus artillery units—Task Force Delta, some eight thousand troops, commanded by Brigadier General Lowell English. While Delta operated well to the northwest, an ARVN force of five infantry and airborne battalions—about three thousand men—moved into the eastern and southcentral zones.

English hoped to surprise the enemy by landing two battalions by helicopter at either end of a valley about a mile south of the DMZ and northeast of a prominent terrain feature known as the Rockpile. The enemy reacted instantly, furiously, and effectively. He first prevented a juncture of the two battalions; by the time they joined fighting was so intense that English broke it off in favor of a new attack from the south, a withdrawal that provoked more severe fighting. English meanwhile committed other battalions to block the southern portion of the area. For several days, marines fought a series of hot actions ranging from squad to battalion strength while a small reconnaissance team occupied the Rockpile to call in air, artillery, and naval gunfire on nearby PAVN columns. ARVN units to the south and east also, on occasion, engaged enemy units, and claimed several hundred enemy lives.

Operation Hastings ended in early August with a general backing off of PAVN regiments. Pointing to enemy losses—nearly nine thousand confirmed killed and several thousand wounded—Marine Corps spokesmen claimed a "victory" of major proportions. In some respects, however, it was a Pyrrhic victory: The marines lost over two hundred killed and several hundred wounded. If PAVN division 324B had been knocked out, it was temporary, and three other divisions remained in the immediate area. Finally, as General Walt later noted, the enemy accomplished two major objectives: " . . . they had slowed the pacification of the I Corps area by forcing me to commit men into the largely barren north, and they had made many headlines in the United States about escalation and American casualties."[20]

Operation Hastings gave way to Operation Prairie. Increasingly bloody contacts soon confirmed that Division 324B, despite its pummeling, was still active in the DMZ, where it was fortifying the area in the vicinity of the Rockpile. In frustrating this plan, the marines fought another series of bloody actions, in some cases using tanks. The description of the fighting at the time in various papers and magazines reminded more than one marine veteran of both World War II and Korean actions, particularly the assault and capture of Hills 400 and 484, which dominated the enemy's main line of resistance in the DMZ and forced him once again to withdraw to the North. Operation Prairie terminated in early October. The marines claimed over twelve hundred "counted" dead, with another sixteen hundred "probable," at a cost of about two hundred marine lives. The area would remain a hot spot; further action would center on Khe Sanh, not many miles to the south.[21]

While army and marine units fought in the central highlands and coastal areas, Westmoreland continued to build up forces and to undertake operations in III Corps area, which included Saigon, and in IV Corps area, the Mekong Delta, which was almost completely a guerrilla challenge.

The enemy was strong in both these corps areas. In III Corps area, Zones C and D and the Iron Triangle had been Viet Minh centers of resistance and were extremely well fortified and organized. Early in 1966, a combined ARVN-U.S. force had swept part of Zone D in Binh Duong province to capture over six thousand enemy documents and large amounts of supply and munitions. Probing efforts continued during the year and consisted both of search-and-destroy and more permanent, clear-and-hold operations such as those undertaken by an Australian task force southeast of Saigon and very well described in a book by an Australian soldier and scholar, Robert O'Neill, *Vietnam Task*.

Throughout 1966, allied troops, including Australians, a few New Zealanders, and the vanguard of a Korean division, continued to arrive in South Vietnam. Once sufficient numbers were on hand, the American command directed a series of giant "sweeps" through sanctuary zones. Toward the end of 1966 and in early 1967, such operations as Attleboro, Cedar Falls, and Junction City uncovered and destroyed miles of tunnel defenses, underground hospitals, and supply depots.

Simultaneously, other troops were fighting other wars.

The air war consisted of two parts. One was the out-country war already familiar to us—the strategic bombing of North Vietnam and tactical interdiction of supply routes leading to and running through Laos and Cambodia. Rolling Thunder utilized both B-52 bombers (carrying 500- and 750-pound bombs) flying from Thailand and Guam, and a host of air force, navy, and marine planes flying from immediate land and carrier bases. In spring of 1966, President Johnson yielded to pleas of military advisers and authorized strikes against oil-storage depots, including those around Hanoi and Haiphong. In December, Johnson authorized strikes against the theretofore prohibited inner ring of Hanoi. In 1966, pilots flew 138,000 missions to drop 128,000 tons of bombs on targets in the North. In February 1967, B-52 flights would increase from sixty to eight hundred monthly (including missions over South Vietnam).[22]

Air force, navy, and marine planes, including giant B-52 bombers, also carried on an in-country aerial war consisting of conventional strategic bombing of alleged VC base areas and defensive complexes, tactical interdiction of supply routes along borders and inside South Vietnam, and tactical and logistic support of ground units. During 1966, air force pilots alone " . . . flew more than 70,000 attack sorties in South Vietnam." During the first three days of Operation Attleboro, air force planes delivered three hundred thousand pounds of rations, ammunition, and other supplies to the ground forces.

The air war also involved a host of special missions including around-the-clock rescue of downed airmen. High-flying planes bombarded Vietnam with millions of Chieu Hoi (Open Arms) amnesty leaflets, which exhorted the enemy to surrender (and prosper thereby)—according to the air force, these leaflets brought in over nineteen thousand "ralliers" by end of 1966.[23] RB-57s, RB-66s, " . . . supersonic RF-101 Voodoos and double-sonic RF-4C Phantoms" patrolled the skies on thousands of reconnaissance missions, each utilizing highly sophisticated techniques to photograph targets that ranged from the immediate ground battle scene to enemy lines of communication and suspected enemy concentration areas. During 1966, air force technicians processed four million feet of film a month, while aerial reconnaissance furnished " . . . 85 per cent of all immediate intelligence data in Southeast Asia."[24] Still another aerial effort involved chemical defoliation, the theory being to deprive the enemy of natural cover as well as of food in his base areas. This mission fell to the Ranch Hand Squadron, whose motto, according to correspondent Frank Harvey was: "Only You Can Prevent Forests." The squadron's motivation was noteworthy for its brevity: " . . . Dresser showed me around the squadron rooms. It was a spartan place. The familiar sign, FUCK COMMUNISM, which was painted horizontally in stripes of red, white and blue, was tacked to one wall." Ranch Hand pilots performed the hazardous duty of spraying chemical defoliants from a hundred fifty feet at a slow speed over generally enemy-infested areas. An eleven thousand-pound pay load, which cost five thousand dollars, took four minutes to spread and killed everything green over three hundred acres.[25]

The American navy was also fighting two wars: an out-country effort, which attempted to intercept coastal junks bringing arms and supply from North to South, and the in-country effort, which involved coastal and inland-waterway patrols to intercept supplies intended for the Viet Cong. The out-country naval war included a support role for American marines and ARVN units in I Corps area, a role later expanded southward to include operations in the Mekong Delta.

Both efforts quickly escalated to majestic proportions. The out-country interdiction task fell to Task Force 77, an armada of five aircraft carriers, four hundred aircraft, about twenty-five support ships, and over thirty thousand men operating from "Yankee Station," in Tonkin Gulf. A pamphlet issued by Seventh Fleet described the mission in precise enough terms. Besides aerial bombardment (planes were soon flying thousands and even tens of thousands of missions), TF 77's surface arm—" . . . the guided missile cruisers, frigates and destroyers— are prowling the Vietnamese coast, foiling attempts to infiltrate by sea and pumping tons of ordnance into shore battery positions and coastal supply routes."[26] Interdiction of coastal operations north of the DMZ became the task of destroyers charged with Operation Sea Dragon, which, in its first six months, destroyed or damaged more than one thousand barges and junks that were allegedly carrying supplies South. Still another armada, of radar picket escorts and smaller craft, both navy and coast guard, carried out Operation Market Time, below the DMZ, in an effort to disrupt infiltration of supplies along the thousand miles of coastline. Naval-gunfire support hinged on another armada, of heavy and light cruisers, guided-missile destroyers and frigates, destroyers, destroyer escorts, and radar-picket escorts. This combined might could send eight-inch 55-caliber shells, each weighing over 250 pounds, some fifteen miles, or six-inch, five-inch, or three-inch shells to a lesser range.[27] This effort would soon be garnished with a battleship, USS *New Jersey,* removed from mothballs and reconditioned at a cost of $40 million.

The in-country, or riverine, warfare also quickly grew. Fought mainly in the Mekong Delta, it introduced a host of specially adapted craft ranging from PGM patrol gunboats to PBR river patrol boats and " . . . unsinkable styrofoam and fiber-glass swimmer support boats, Swift Boats, patrol air cushion vehicles (capable of traveling over 65 knots, combat loaded, over land or water), and an impressive list of modified amphibious craft, including monitors and armored troop carriers, sampans and junks." These operated either on their own or in conjunction with American and ARVN troop units. Sea-air-land, or SEAL, teams extended the offensive aspect of river patrol operations inland, and the Navy-Army Mobile Riverine Force, an amphibious strike force of two army battalions, eventually began to penetrate fortified Viet Cong areas.[28]

There remained the final war, the "other war," the war for people's "hearts and minds," the real war. This had also gained impetus in mid-1965 when, reappointed as American ambassador, Henry Cabot Lodge brought with him as principal assistant a counterinsurgency expert, veteran of the earlier Philippine and French Indochina campaigns, Edward Lansdale. Lansdale had always advocated grass-roots pacification as the key to revolutionary warfare. As opposed to centralized direction of the program from Saigon down to hamlet level, Lansdale wanted to begin at hamlet level and work outward and upward—a decentralized, horizontal concept practiced with such telling effect by the National Liberation Front.

Like previous regimes, the Thieu-Ky government opposed such an approach, since it would force Saigon to yield partial control not only of provinces and of pacification cadres but of immensely valuable supplies daily arriving from the United States and daily adding to personal fortunes of South Vietnamese officials. In addition to Vietnamese bureaucracy, Lansdale also found himself at odds with a vast number of American agencies, a proliferation of bureaucracy, civil and military, so ably described by Robert Shaplen.[29]

The end result was a sluggish pacification program. Thanks mainly to Lansdale, the Johnson administration was not allowed to forget this vital failure, and pressure continued on the Thieu-Ky government to take necessary action.

In February 1966, President Johnson met with South Vietnamese leaders in Honolulu, where Ky impressed the President by his determination to build " . . . a really democratic government, one which is put into office by the people themselves and which has the confidence of the people." The pacification program, Ky promised, would go ahead full steam. Unaware that Ky's speech had been written by his American advisers,[30] the grateful President responded by promising full support, albeit with an expectation of rapid results. By the next meeting between the South Vietnamese and Americans, he wanted " . . . coonskins nailed to the wall."[31]

Thieu and Ky already had established a Ministry of Revolutionary Development, headed by Major General Nguyen Duc Thang, whose principal assistant was Major Nguyen Be. Thang and Be had recognized for some time the inadequacy of the principal pacification instrument, the forty-man People's Action Team, which was neither large enough nor sufficiently motivated to eliminate hamlet deficiencies. A new fifty-nine-man Revolutionary Development Group, trained at Be's special center, was to carry out a new program which emulated existing Communist doctrines. Its over-all objective was two-fold: to pacify the hamlet and to help build a better life for its people. Once a hamlet was militarily secure, government forces would concentrate on rooting out VC infrastructure while simultaneously helping the people to build a viable "community of responsibility."

The new program faced a number of difficulties, which we shall discuss later. Buddhist riots in spring of 1966 added to manifold problems, and the RD program failed to make significant headway during the summer. An effective pacification program depended, as always, on an effective government, and here some progress seemingly did appear. At American urging, in September 1966, the junta held elections for a constituent assembly that would write a new constitution. Although polls opened in only 55 per cent of the country, American officials applauded a turnout of " . . . 81 per cent of over 5 million registered voters, in spite of Vietcong intimidation and terrorism."[32] In general, American observers commented favorably on electoral procedures. If the mechanism appeared clumsy and in places questionable, no one could deny that the elections introduced the "democratic idea" to the South Vietnamese.

And few denied that definite progress was being recorded in general. The enthusiasm of both governments was plain at a conference in Manila in October 1966, which produced " . . . specific plans for the postwar and long-term civil development of Viet Nam." A Joint Development Group, " . . . an organization composed of a private American company . . . and a group of Vietnamese professionals," was charged with " . . . the task of postwar planning, of creating a design and a strategy for the transition from a wartime to a peacetime footing, and of making an objective assessment of the prospects of South Viet Nam's economy in the years ahead."[33]

As the year ended, a new optimism seemed to have emerged in South Vietnam, and with some justification. ARVN forces totaled 285,000, with another 284,000 Regional and Popular troops, plus about 130,000 police and some thirty thousand Revolutionary Development cadres. The infusion of American strength was daily freeing

ARVN units for pacification duties. Although the Viet Cong continued to control over half of the countryside, American counteraction, with out doubt, had blunted their offensive plans. American troops numbering 350,000 were in South Vietnam, and more were on the way—though not as many as Westmoreland and the JCS would have liked. The ground, naval, and air wars continued to escalate. More than ever, the U.S.A. seemed determined to win the war.

CHAPTER SIXTY-FOUR

1. Leftwich.
2. Hackworth, 466.
3. Caputo, 74.
4. Hackworth, 484.
5. Sheehan et al., 468.
6. Rice, 103.
7. Ibid.
8. See Mulligan for a description of enemy forces in detail. See also, Shaplen, *The Lost Revolution;* Pike; Marshall; O'Neill; *U.S. News and World Report,* November 28, 1966, for General Westmoreland's description of the war as he saw it.
9. West. See also, Mulligan; Duncan.
10. U.S. Air Force. See also, Harvey; Asprey, "Tactics."
11. Harvey, 117. See also, Hackworth, 562, for a professional appraisal of DePuy's strategy and tactics.
12. O'Ballance, "Strategy in Viet Nam." See also, Duncanson, "The Vitality of the Viet Cong."
13. Walt, *Strange War, Strange Strategy.* See also, Stolfi, for a detailed description of this transition period.
14. U.S. Marine Corps, "III Marine Amphibious Force . . . " See also, West.
15. New York *Times,* November 18, 1970. See also, Walt.
16. Schell, 16.
17. Ibid., 14–15, who points out that printed warnings often failed in purpose because villagers were illiterate. We have pointed out that a similar situation existed in the Rif rebellion (Chapter 22).
18. Shaplen, *The Road from War,* 44–5. See also, Mulligan; Corson; Stanford; Evans; Stolfi.
19. Shaplen, *The Road from War,* 97.
20. Walt, *Strange War, Strange Strategy,* 141.
21. Shaplen, *The Road from War,* 118.
22. Sheehan et al., 480. See also, U.S. Air Force; Fall, "Viet Nam in the Balance": According to Fall, who quoted McNamara, the 1966 "bombing plan" called for expending 638,000 tons of "aerial munitions"—thirty-eight thousand tons *more* than dropped in the Pacific theater in *all* of World War II.
23. Harvey, 69. See also, U.S. Air Force.
24. U.S. Air Force.
25. Harvey, 69.
26. U.S. Seventh Fleet, "Task Force 77."
27. U.S. Seventh Fleet, "Cruisers and Destroyers in Vietnam." See also, U.S. Navy.
28. U.S. Navy.
29. Shaplen, *The Road from War,* 27–30. See also, Corson.
30. Karnow, 431.

31. Johnson, *The Vantage Point* . . . , 243–4.
32. Thompson, *No Exit from Vietnam,* 102. See also, Shaplen, *The Road from War,* 83, who questions the 81 per cent figure as optimistic; Tran Van Dinh, who offers interesting background on electoral problems.
33. Lilienthal.

CHAPTER 65

Blurs on the operational canvas • Failure of Operation Rolling Thunder (I) • Increasing cost of aerial warfare • Shortcomings of attrition strategy and search-and-destroy tactics • The refugee problem • Manpower facts • The numbers game • Russian and Chinese aid to the North • The ground war • Increasing American costs (I) • The logistics picture • The Jurassic dinosaur

A NUMBER OF BLURS marred the operational canvas in Vietnam. One was the failure of Operation Rolling Thunder—bombing North Vietnam—to accomplish its objectives (already being variously changed by Administration officials). The theory advocated by the JCS and such presidential advisers as Walt Rostow was to hurt the North sufficiently to cause Hanoi to call off the war in the South. Top-level intelligence reports at end of 1965 confirmed that bombing had indeed " . . . reduced industrial performance," but: " . . . the primary rural nature of the area permits continued functioning of the subsistence economy." Moreover, reports agreed, Hanoi seemed as determined as ever to support the war in the South. Although a greatly expanded bombing effort in 1966 reportedly destroyed 70 per cent of North Vietnam's original oil storage capacity,[1] it soon became clear that the enemy could get by on fuel dispensed in drums. According to a CIA estimate, the total bombing effort " . . . accomplished little more than in 1965."[2] In 1966, American planes encountered " . . . the most sophisticated and concentrated air defense network ever faced in any war."[3] Although American fliers shot down thirty-six MIGs and otherwise carried out bombing and interdiction missions, the effort cost another 147 American aircraft—a total of 318 crews and machines lost. Direct operational costs rose from $460 million in 1965 to $1.2 billion in 1966.[4]

Rolling Thunder also continued to reap heavy criticism within and without the Administration. Reports of heavy civilian casualties raised an uproar in the world press, the more so since Harrison Salisbury of the *New York Times* was reporting directly from Hanoi at the time. Although the Johnson administration denied the accusation, top-secret CIA estimates put the casualty figure in North Vietnam at thirty-six thousand for 1965 and 1966; of this figure, about 80 per cent were civilians.[5] The new effort may also have caused Hanoi to back off from talks that some hoped would lead to negotiation. According to John Hightower, AP diplomatic correspondent in Washington, the Soviet Union and European satellites brought considerable pressure on North Vietnam at the Bulgarian Party Congress in November 1966 to open the way for a peace conference. Negotiations by Polish intermediaries were allegedly proceeding favorably when the bombing of Hanoi's outskirts caused Hanoi to break off proceedings. President Johnson later made light of this effort in his memoirs; Mr. Hightower, however, suggested that Johnson realized the bombing was a major blunder and that this was the major reason for the later, four-month halt in bombing Hanoi as well as for a secret peace initiative (admitted, in part, by Johnson).[6]

A second blur centered on the ground war and Westmoreland's choice of attrition strategy and search-and-destroy tactics. The problem faced by allied forces was essentially pacification that demanded a qualitative and selective approach. The tactical task was to clear an area of Viet Cong so that civil teams could move in to build a viable and secure community. The military tactic thus required was clear-and-hold. The first task was to free an area from main-force guerrilla control. This called for fragmenting, dispersing, and destroying main-force units.

But that was only the beginning. Having cleared an area, military units had to "hold" it—that is, they had to provide area security while helping police forces to root out the all-important Viet Cong infrastructure, while, simultaneously, other specialized government forces undertook area rehabilitation and established viable government. Military strength was insufficient to clear and hold *all* enemy-infested, or even challenged, areas simultaneously. This meant that priority areas of operation had to be established, along with "economy of force" areas, which received only limited military pressure. Some challenged areas would perforce have had to be ignored until later in the pacification process. The real target was the peasant, not the guerrilla, and the only way the peasant's support could be gained was by establishing secure and viable local-area government—a slow and difficult task amply demonstrated throughout history.

American strategy and tactics did not respect this essential requirement. Large "sweeps" through an area, though uncovering supply dumps and killing a few enemy, essentially answered nothing. Neither did search-and-destroy tactics respect the essential military task. On rare occasions, enemy concentrations, such as those in certain areas of the

DMZ, could be countered by conventional-warfare methods. As a rule, such methods inflicted grievous damage on people whose co-operation was necessary if the over-all mission was to be accomplished. Instead of clearing and holding small areas as first essential steps in winning peasant support, marine and army units pushed out in all directions in huge, awkward attempts to "kill" the enemy. The results were several, and each contained the seeds of important failure.

The first was to widen the war. Up to spring of 1965, fighting in South Vietnam had remained selective, on the whole. Douglas Pike, an official and careful observer and analyst, later wrote:

> Thousands of Vietnamese villagers lived through the entire 1960–1965 period without being involved in, and hardly ever being inconvenienced by, either the NLF's armed struggle or the GVN's military operations. Although subjected to great NLF organizational and political attention, the average rural Vietnamese was seldom if ever a direct victim of its violence program. . . . The result was that he did not perceive the situation in Vietnam as a "war" in the same way that Americans regard the Vietnam "war." Thus the frequently stated observation that the Vietnamese peasant "has known nothing but war for twenty years," although technically accurate, is also misleading . . . [7]

Escalation inevitably changed this low-key situation. By July 1965, over four hundred thousand refugees had fled South Vietnam's countryside. The bulk of these unfortunates either ended in ghastly shantytowns around larger cities or in hastily constructed and very primitive camps. Their potential importance was tremendous. Roger Hilsman testified before the Senate in late 1965:

> . . . The refugees are, in my judgment, a key [to an effective counterguerrilla program]. . . . What I am suggesting is that the refugee program should not be just to feed, house, and care for these people, but to train them for the job of making their villages guerrilla proof when they return—to train them as village defenders, as school teachers, medical technicians, agricultural advisers and so on. If an imaginative, positive effort is made, in sum, the refugees can become the vanguard of a peaceful revolution in the Vietnamese countryside sponsored by the free world—which is the only way that the bloody, Communist revolution can be circumvented.

Wesley Fishel, who was originally involved in Ngo Dinh Diem's government as head of the Michigan State University team (see Chapter 50), warned the same Senate committee:

832

> ...If this refugee problem is badly handled, these people...
> could further intensify the political instability of South Vietnam
> and create even greater problems for the Government than it now
> faces.
>
> If this situation is treated with some intelligence, then these
> 600,000 refugees of the moment could become a major asset to
> the Vietnamese Government. ... If these people are handled well
> the Saigon government is going to secure the manifest loyalty
> which it needs. ...

The refugees were not being well handled. AID officials had estimated
a hundred thousand refugees in 1965 and was unprepared to cope with
a larger number. GVN's 1965 budget called for 370 million piasters for
refugees; as of July just less than 25 million piasters had been spent.
The committee concluded that the refugee program

> ...reflected the absence of an overall strategic concept and pro-
> gram which fully integrates the political, economic, and social as-
> pects of the Vietnamese conflict with the needed military effort.[8]

The second result of promiscuous search-and-destroy tactics was
frequent damage to either person or property or both of peasants who
remained and whose strength was necessary to effectively counter the
insurgency. The third result was frequently to tire the troops with
"Yorkish" operations that produced no real benefits:

> The noble Duke of York,
> He had ten thousand men,
> He marched them up to the top of the hill,
> and he marched them down again.

The fourth result was to flood the country with foreign troops. The fifth
result was to increase the troop commitment and eventually relieve
ARVN of combat duties, which, in turn, called for a larger American
military investment that merely compounded incipient failures.

By end of 1966, then, it was becoming clear that American troops
had undertaken a task for which they were neither organized nor
trained, a task that they did not understand—indeed, a task that could
only have been accomplished by the South Vietnamese themselves. It is
a great pity that the innate ineptness of Westmoreland's strategy and
tactics was not more obvious. Unfortunately, the "indicators," or criteria selected by the military, to judge progress in Vietnam seemed reasonable to many Americans, who at first trusted their government and
armed forces. But, as any number of experts had earlier pointed out
and as Bernard Fall once again emphasized in 1966, MACV and the

JCS continued to judge progress by such military measurements as troop increases, expended ammunition, enemy dead, structures destroyed, rice confiscated, and weapons captured—conventional criteria meaningless in a counterinsurgency.[9] " . . . Our mission was not to win terrain or seize positions," Lieutenant Philip Caputo later wrote,

> but simply to kill. . . . Victory was a high body-count, defeat a low kill-ratio, war a matter of arithmetic. The pressure on unit commanders to produce enemy corpses was routine, and they in turn committed it to their troops. This led to such practices as counting civilians as Viet Cong. 'If it's dead and Vietnamese, it's VC,' was a rule of thumb in the bush.[10]

The military's chief criterion was "kill" figures; as James Reston wrote, " . . . death became the official measure of success." Commanders had to succeed in order to satisfy their superiors which, as David Hackworth noted, soon made "everyone a bounty hunter and a liar," with concomitant injury to the traditional and healthy concept of military honor.[11]

Pointing to an alleged forty to fifty thousand enemy dead a year and many more wounded and deserters, MACV, the JCS, and Administration hawks argued that enemy morale would have to crumble. There was nothing new about the argument. It was the old World War I syndrome. In Vietnam a half century later, the enemy did not seem to have much difficulty in keeping units up to strength or in bringing in fresh units from the North. Despite an estimated sixty thousand battle deaths, local VC recruitment continued at thirty-five hundred a month. By mid-1966, VC-PAVN forces in the South had increased within a year from 110,000 to 270,000, the bulk of which came from the South.[12] Four PAVN divisions were deployed north of the DMZ, nine more divisions farther north, and the Chinese army north of there. Soviet aid, already half a billion dollars in 1965, substantially increased in 1966 and included " . . . ground-to-air missiles, 'complex antiaircraft guns with radar guidance systems, and antiaircraft automatic guns of 'large caliber,' " along with some fighter aircraft. Later in the year, the Soviet Union agreed to contribute another $800 million worth of aid. Hanoi was successfully playing off Moscow against Peking, which was also supplying arms and equipment and very probably stood ready to supply "volunteers" if necessary.[13]

A more subtle difficulty also existed. This was the fallacy inherent in the numbers game. Owing in large part to Robert McNamara's influence in the Pentagon, American military analysts had become slaves to statistical studies. Testifying before the Senate Foreign Relations Committee in February 1966, Maxwell Taylor stated:

... Since history has shown that the government forces success-fully opposing a guerrilla insurgency in the past have required a much greater preponderance of strength, ten to one or twelve to one for example, it was quite clear the Vietnamese could not raise forces fast enough to keep pace with the growing threat of the Viet Cong in time. It was this sobering conclusion that led to the de-cision to introduce American ground forces with their unique mo-bility and massive fire power to compensate for the deficiency in Vietnamese strength. With such forces available, it was felt that the ratios of required strength cited above would lose much of their validity.[14]

Taylor was misquoting history. As Major General Richard Clutterbuck, the British counterinsurgency expert, pointed out in 1966, the 12:1 or 10:1 soldier versus guerrilla ratio is virtually meaningless, since the guerrilla's strength derives from the people, and his numbers must in-clude not only those persons sympathetic to his aims but those too frightened or too apathetic to contest those aims. Successful Roman commanders in Spain had realized this before the birth of Christ. In 1775, General Gage had warned that American rebels would not be easily subdued (see Chapter 5):

... Since other colonies would undoubtedly come to the aid of the north, " ... he urged that the Ministry estimate the number of men and the sums of money needed, and then double their figures."

When another realist, William Tecumseh Sherman, was asked how many men he would need to pacify the Cumberland area during the Civil War, he replied: "Two hundred thousand" (see Chapter 9).

American bombing and interdiction of supply routes in the North and Laos and in South Vietnam were only partially successful in inter-rupting the flow of supply south. Planes could bomb and strafe roads and railroads and warehouses and vehicles, but thousands of peasants repaired roads and bridges, and trucks continued to travel at night, as did hundreds of thousands of bicyclists carrying " ... 100-pound loads for long distances," children easily carrying " ... their own weight."[15]

The Viet Cong also received supply from sampans sailing from the North, from peasants sympathetic to the rebel cause, from corrupt South Vietnamese officials, and, not least, from attacks on government outposts, hamlets and villages. Such was the extent of local support and participation that Dennis Duncanson termed Vietnam a *symbiotic in-surgency:* " ... one, that is, in which, for the great bulk of its resources, the revolutionary movement draws its requirements from the supplies of its adversaries"[16]

Thus it was all the more necessary to use Lyautey's qualitative tactics, a slow, methodical approach in order to win peasant alliance rather than Westmoreland's search-and-destroy tactics defined by one senior American commander in Vietnam as " . . . Grab 'em by the balls and the hearts and minds will follow."[17] Too often this was warfare at its most violent and stupid, and those who ordered it and condoned its excesses were placing themselves in a dangerous legal and moral position.[18] The inane order issued to Marine Corps units not to fire on unarmed Vietnamese *unless they were running* " . . . left us bewildered and uneasy," Lieutenant Caputo later wrote. " . . . What if we shot a Vietnamese who turned out to have a legitimate reason for running? Would that be a justifiable act of war or grounds for court-martial?"[19]

The choice of search-and-destroy tactics was perhaps inevitable, considering the tactical "shape" of American units—and this introduces still another blur. Despite emphasis placed on counterinsurgency warfare since 1961, U.S. divisions, regiments, and battalions were neither organized nor properly trained to wage irregular warfare. Colonel David Hackworth later wrote of the dangerously inadequate individual and small-unit training at Fort Benning where, instead of running around in meaningless regimental and division exercises, the soldier should have learned " . . . the stuff that keeps you alive."[20] Westmoreland's quantitative approach was necessarily expensive in manpower and resources. In 1965, the U.S. officer death rate in Vietnam rose above the 5 per cent rate of World War II and Korea. By spring of 1966, U.S. casualties totaled four thousand killed and twenty-one thousand wounded, cumulative totals that would rise sharply by year's end. Also upsetting, of 240,000 U.S. troops in South Vietnam, " . . . only 50,000 at most were actual combat troops"—and those suffered the bulk of casualties.[21] Westmoreland perforce developed an insatiable appetite for troops, only a relatively small percentage of whom could undertake combat/pacification tasks. Added to this was a personnel policy that limited a tour of duty to one year: thus, those who fought the enemy did so for only twelve months before returning to the United States—in the case of draftees, for discharge.[22] But, such was the American military's administrative requirement, that roughly three months were spent coming, three months going. And such was the peculiar nature of the war that a man needed the other six months to learn how to fight it. If he survived enemy mines and booby traps and ambushes and pungi stakes and jungle rot and malaria—if he lived and remained intact in body and mind—he was just becoming valuable when he went home.

An enormous logistics requirement adversely affected the situation in several ways. In the opening months, indeed well into 1966, combat troops were forced to subsist mainly on C-rations, a poor diet at best but a criminal diet in a tropical jungle-mountain environment. Army fatigues and Marine dungarees were too hot for jungle warfare (for which the troops were untrained in virtually every respect, particularly in countering mines and booby traps, which accounted for a large proportion of casualties); boots and field shoes soon fell to pieces and were only slowly replaced with light canvas jungle boots. Units lacked such necessaries as preservative oil and cleaning patches for weapons that needed cleaning several times a day. Search-and-destroy tactics in a hostile environment utilized an expenditure of ammunition that is difficult to comprehend. The official explanation for abrogation of what older soldiers know as "fire discipline" is to the effect that, lacking sufficient numbers to fight the war, American forces had to compensate by increased mobility and firepower. Lieutenant Caputo described a marine action, Operation Blast Out, in August 1965: " . . . Three thousand Marines and ARVN soldiers, supported by tanks, artillery, planes, and the six-inch guns of a U.S. Navy cruiser, managed to kill two dozen Viet Cong in three days. . . . "[23] In describing one marine patrol action in mid-1966, Captain Francis J. West wrote:

> . . . Less than two minutes after reception of the message, the guns were firing. So swift was the reaction that the message alerting the patrol of an impending fire mission reached the patrol via the relay station after the shells had fallen. The battery fired 1,188 pounds of high explosives to discourage the trackers. It did.
>
> Twenty minutes later, from task force headquarters came the order to blanket the entire target area. At higher headquarters, the thinking was that, if the North Vietnamese had organized a pursuit, they must have returned to their base camp and been in the process of digging out. The battery fired another area saturation mission, dropping 10,692 pounds of high explosives in the stream bed, base camp, and hill complex.[24]

This was theater policy and far too often it amounted to promiscuous firing that accomplished very little, often damaged a great deal—and was very expensive.

Quasi-conventional operations were equally expensive. To field what amounted to nearly a marine division during Operation Hastings required a supply effort that suggested a World War II amphibious landing. To give the 1st Cavalry (Airmobile) Division helicopter mobility meant supplying five hundred tons of material a day.[25] Such was the appetite of conventionally organized American units that a division required a logistics "tail" of over forty thousand troops.

Another factor inexorably exacerbated the supply problem. With exception of a few elite units, American armed forces had grown used to comfort, and even elite units expected amenities provided by no other armed forces in the world or in history. This disturbing trend began after World War II and stemmed in part from a national pride of an affluent society buttressed by swollen defense budgets. By the time of Korea, it had grown sufficiently for one commander, General Mark Clark, to complain. Shortly after assuming command in Korea, he later wrote,

> . . . I felt strongly that we would have to pull in our belts, cut off some fat. We have always wanted the best of everything for our men. . . . In Korea that search for the best went so far as to make ice cream an item of regular distribution to front-line units. . . . But the amenities in the American Army will have to be the first casualty in any big war with communism.[26]

By the end of 1966, the amenities in South Vietnam had increased, particularly in the rear echelons, and they added heavily to the logistics requirement.

The logistics burden otherwise adversely influenced the tactical situation. As General Matthew Ridgway's 1954 report had emphasized, the theater of war was not compatible with the support requirement of conventional forces. Base development, as Ridgway forecast, proved an enormous task. Westmoreland himself later wrote that, lacking " . . . a fully developed logistic base" to support combat units rushed into South Vietnam, he had to use " . . . backed-up ships as floating warehouses."[27] What he did not point out was the large number of combat troops initially tied up in base-construction tasks during this crucial period. But conventional organization also meant undue reliance on mechanical transport and on supporting weapons that tended to "tie" small units to centralized operations and also consumed "combat troops" in administrative and support duties. Each new installation produced a new security requirement, both to protect the installation and to provide security for convoys carrying material to combat units, and this, in turn, demanded more troops. As base camps grew in size, so did guerrilla attacks against them—which meant providing even more troops for static security duty, less for field operations. At one base camp, one third of an airborne brigade was tied up in guard duty, at a time when some infantry companies were fighting at 50 per cent of combat strength.[28]

A second result was more indirect but equally invidious. To supply the insatiable hunger of a few combat divisions, base supply areas developed and rapidly expanded. Each held thousands of troops who could not but influence local economies—too often, adversely. A heavy expenditure of piasters contributed to an already ugly inflation. A black market invariably sprang up, one not alone fed by millions of dollars' worth of PX and commissary supplies but often by combat equipment and arms—significant quantities of each ultimately ending in Viet Cong hands. Bored garrison soldiers also constituted a problem: bars, dance halls, whorehouses, each multiplied to exacerbate already difficult community relations, particularly between American and ARVN soldiers. Large numbers of Vietnamese employees—around a hundred thousand, many in servile occupations—inside American bases not only upset local economies but insured that Americans continued to live inside a fish bowl.

All these factors combined to produce a highly unsatisfactory military profile. By the end of 1966, Westmoreland's military plant, which should have been lean and fit, resembled the Jurassic dinosaur, which became weaker as it grew larger.

CHAPTER SIXTY-FIVE

1. Sheehan et al., 480.
2. Ibid., 523. See also, ibid., 462, 469, 494, 502–9, 518, 522.
3. U.S. Air Force.
4. Sheehan et al., 523.
5. Ibid., 513–15, 523.
6. Zagoria, 60. See also, Johnson, *The Vantage Point* . . . ; Brandon, who discusses this in detail.
7. Pike, 372–3.
8. U.S. Senate, *Refugee Problems in South Vietnam.*
9. Fall, "Viet Nam in the Balance."
10. Caputo, xviii. See also, Hackworth, 667–8.
11. Hackworth, 572.
12. Fall, "Viet Nam in the Balance."
13. Parry. See also, Zagoria.
14. Fulbright, *The Vietnam Hearings.*
15. Rogers.
16. Duncanson, "The Vitality of the Viet Cong."
17. Corson, 68.
18. Telford Taylor for an interesting study of this difficult and controversial subject.
19. Caputo, 74.
20. Hackworth, 454–5.
21. Fall, "Viet Nam in the Balance."
22. Barclay.
23. Caputo, 203.
24. West.
25. Weller.
26. Mark W. Clark, 190.
27. *U.S. News and World Report,* November 28, 1966.
28. Hackworth, 556.

CHAPTER 66

More blurs on the canvas • American tactical problems • Operation Gibraltar • Ia Drang—the enemy learns • Operation Attleboro • Marshall and Hackworth's mission • Operation of Paul Revere IV • Operation Crazy Horse • Colonels Henry Emerson and John Hayes define the tactical challenge • U. S. Marine Corps operations • Captain Miller's observations • The intelligence failure • Mines and booby traps • VC intelligence network • Captain Jim Cooper's discovery • The pacification failure • Continued South Vietnamese governmental abuses • ARVN's failure • Dissent in the U.S.A. • The Vietnam hearings • The thoughts of James Gavin and George Kennan • The secret thoughts of Robert McNamara • Escalation pressures • The hawks win again

FOUR OTHER BLURS had appeared on the allied operational canvas by end of 1966. One was the difficulty of American combat units in adapting to the tactical challenge; one the proclivity of MACV in announcing fictitious "victories" to the world; one the continued inept performance of South Vietnam's government and army; and one the influence of these on American opinion, both official and public.

American combat units faced severe tactical problems in South Vietnam, most of which resulted from trying to impose Western tactical doctrines on an insurgency environment. Contemporary accounts of fighting in 1965 and 1966 leave little to be desired regarding individual and unit bravery. Young officers, non-commissioned officers, soldiers, marines, sailors, and airmen generally fought hard and sometimes gave more than they got. But were they fighting wisely?

Operation Gibraltar, the seizure of An Khe from the Viet Cong by units of the 101st Airborne Division, was broadcast by Westmoreland

840

as a "great victory." More accurately, one officer participant termed it "a blundering success"; another stated that "the VC saved [our] day by walking away."[1] One helicopter assault landed " . . . dead in the middle of the 95th [Viet Cong] Battalion's training base and was shot to ribbons." "Friendly" American fire killed thirteen and wounded twelve of our own troops.[2]

The highly touted "victory" at Ia Drang had more holes than a Swiss cheese. In addition to heavy casualties from "friendly" fire, " . . . inadequate [air] lift and piecemeal commitment," one battalion landed " . . . virtually at the enemy's front door," and thus was "incredibly outnumbered."[3] Wounded officers from this battalion later spoke of " . . . annihilation, almost to the man of . . . units as big as company size." These unpalatable facts of what Westmoreland called "an unprecedented victory" were not announced to the American Congress or to the public.[4] The enemy's heavy losses at Ia Drang were cited by MACV as proof of the validity of an attrition strategy. In truth, as noted by a prescient American army-officer-turned-civil-adviser, the legendary John Paul Vann, whose short life is so well told by Neil Sheehan's *A Bright and Shining Lie,* they were suffered by the enemy in order " . . . to figure out how to beat the Americans' incredible firepower and amazing mobility." Although badly hurt, they learned " . . . to hug the 'belt' of their enemy," as David Hackworth later wrote,

> . . . to come in as close as they could in order to neutralize the killing power of our artillery and air support. At Ia Drang, the North Vietnamese *learned how to fight us* . . . even if the battle was an unprecedented victory for the Americans in our war of attrition, it was an equally unprecedented victory for our enemy in their protracted guerrilla war.[5]

Neither did such giant search-and-destroy sweeps through sanctuary zones like Operation Attleboro live up to MACV's claims of success. David Hackworth, who earlier had made his mark as a battalion commander and at this time was escorting the well-known military journalist S. L. A. Marshall on an official fact-finding tour, later revealed that their in-depth study of Attleboro confirmed that " . . . the same lethal mistakes" on the battlefield were "being made again and again . . . ":

> the operation (which claimed 155 U.S. lives and another 741 wounded in action) was just another case of dancing to the tune, a tune written years before during the Indochina war. The tactics the NVA and Main Force VC employed were right out of [Bernard Fall's] *Street Without Joy. . . .*

Detailed interrogation of officers, NCOs and men who carried out this operation

> . . . revealed that the VC initiated or controlled almost every action. (During Attleboro, they sucked U.S. units into well-prepared killing zones . . . and then ate the Americans up at eyeball-to-eyeball range. All our men could do was try their damnedest to extricate their dead and wounded and themselves, and get some distance so they could hammer the enemy with our unbeatable firepower.) And yet, when I asked the company and battalion commanders who'd participated in Attleboro whether they'd read Bernard Fall's basic primer on the war, few could answer in the affirmative.[6]

Marshall and Hackworth's detailed examination of Operation Paul Revere IV along the Cambodian border, a "classic encounter," as a briefing team told Robert McNamara and Generals Wheeler and Westmoreland,

> . . . revealed that there was almost *no correlation* between the official Army report . . . and what actually happened on the ground. . . . If Paul Revere IV were viewed as it had to be, from the perspective of the war of insurgency that it was, then we did *not* win and we were *not* brilliant. In fact, we were stupid, lethally so. . . . The enemy sucked the American units into well dug-in killing zones along the Cambodian border, killing more than 140 and wounding more than 560 of our men on terrain that favored them completely (once they'd accomplished their mission, they could scoot right across the border to regroup).

Hackworth for the first time

> . . . realized that probably no one at the very top had any idea that the reports were wrong. . . . These reports . . . made it all the way back to Washington unchallenged. And there they became the basis of critical decisions made on the war.[7]

Subsequent operations showed little tactical adaptation or invention. We looked briefly at Operation Crazy Horse and its negative results in Chapter 64. Did anyone at corps or division or brigade level consider the possibility of accomplishing the mission by beating the enemy at his own game? The CIDG had made a good start by bushwhacking an enemy patrol—a prosperous tactic that should have impressed senior commanders. Marshall does not suggest alternate plans. No mention is made of carrying on as usual while setting a trap for the enemy lurking up in the mountains.

Estimate of enemy intentions is relatively simple: He is going to attack the CIDG camp—a small and minor installation—or he is going to shell Camp Radcliff with mortars, or he is going to do nothing until more reinforcements reach him by means of routes shown on the captured map. To accomplish either of the first two objectives, he would have to bring forward his units and thus subject them to ambush. What would have been the result had not one ambush team of the type described by Marshall (which is larger than necessary) but a score or forty or eighty such teams spotted the few routes of approach? What would have happened had similar teams staked out ingress routes?

Put another way, why hurry to ferret out the enemy on other than your own terms? The war was not going to end the next day. Senior commanders knew enough of the area to know their ignorance concerning enemy strength and locations. Intelligence had furnished some reasonable indications of enemy presence in strength. By this time, senior commanders knew that the enemy rarely acted impulsively—that he prepared the battlefield, in this case his mountain base. Lacking patience to prepare a reception for the enemy, did no one want to find out more before committing a company? What was the matter with using the CIDG force, which operated extremely well in the mountains? Lacking this force, where were the small guerrilla teams that were needed to work the area? Why an orthodox approach, when, from beginning to end, the units would be operating in the blind? Marshall's only explanation is unsettling in the extreme:

> ...So it became agreed, as it was later done, an inspiration of which nothing better can be said than that it seemed to look good at the time. At the top level of the cavalry division there was still no firm belief that the hills so close to home base were loaded with big game.[8]

Almost nothing of the subsequent operation suggests even normal tactical savvy. PAVN repeatedly used both ambushes and envelopment with telling effect. American units twice walked *through* areas holding sizable numbers of enemy, hidden, weapons zeroed in, patiently waiting for a propitious moment to strike. The American soldiers paid for their carelessness.[9]

A few commanders learned, most did not. Lieutenant Colonel Henry Emerson, commanding a battalion in the 101st Airborne Division, soon learned the rewards to be gained from small-unit tactics, for example by infiltrating a company into the bush during darkness and from there having seven-man patrols fanned out to comb the land.

> ...At the end of each day, these small teams became ambush patrols spread out all over the battle area. Besides regularly draw-

843

ing blood, continuity allowed us to interdict the enemy's ingress-egress routes—in essence, to take the battlefield away from our foe.... Slowly the men began to understand a little more about their enemy and to respond in kind. Slowly they began to develop patience, that VC strong point.[10]

Another paratrooper battalion commander formed

... an all-volunteer, Raider-like unit ... [which] gave the battalion a long range reconnaissance and ambush element that would operate independently, as well as the flexibility of a handy fourth maneuver element.[11]

Colonel John Hayes tossed the book out the window in commanding Delta Force which, in Hackworth's opinion,

... pound for pound and weighed against its cost, was the most effective fighting force in Vietnam [in late 1966].... Delta Force was infinitely successful with its tactics, doctrine, and a basic philosophy at odds with the Army's regular units."[12]

Marines up north also found the tactical going extremely difficult, be it in fighting guerrilla warfare south of the DMZ or in fighting larger, quasi-guerrilla operations in and around the DMZ. Part of the problem was normal: that of adapting to a new tactical environment made the more difficult by insufficient training for counterinsurgency warfare and by inadequate logistic support. "... The Marines in I Corps lived hard," Lieutenant Philip Caputo, who landed at Da Nang early in the war, later wrote. "... Dirt, filth and mosquitoes filled our hooches at night. Our one cooked meal seemed always to be rice and beans. C-rations constituted the other two meals."[13] Caputo graphically described his first search-and-destroy mission, his platoon being part of a two-company force:

... Lemmon's men moved out first. A machine-gunner sprayed the jungle on the far side of the field. This was called "reconnaissance by fire," a fancy term for what amounted to shooting at bushes to see if they shot back.... It took us all morning to cover the three miles between the [helicopter] landing zone and the village. Four hours to walk three miles, and the company had not once run into significant enemy resistance. It was the land that resisted us, the land, the jungle, and the sun.[14]

844

An experienced veteran of these early days, Captain John Miller, later offered a remarkably candid analysis of small-unit actions and problems encountered by the newcomers. Miller found the climate to be hostile:

> . . . The constant heavy rains of the wet monsoon can swell rifle stocks to the point where the trigger cannot be depressed completely and where disassembly and assembly are out of the question. Rust and corrosion of metal surfaces are, of course, accompanying side effects.

Marines had to learn how to keep as dry as possible and avoid omnipresent evils such as immersion foot (from wet socks) and flu/pneumonia (from generally wet surroundings). Terrain, too, posed immense problems:

> . . . The unit leader must constantly fight the recurring problem of canalization. Both the thickly wooded highlands and the open paddy areas tend to force his unit—be it squad or company—into a column, vulnerable to directional mines, ambushes, and similar evils. His choices are limited. If he departs from a jungle trail, he must cut his own—and pay the price in terms of slow movement plus wear and tear on his trailbreakers. If he leaves the paddy dikes, he can count on the same slow pace in moving through the muck and (sometimes) high water and high grass. In deciding, he must constantly weigh the requirements of his mission against his vulnerability, adopting whatever dispersion and security measures he can effect.[15]

Miller also commented feelingly about "the load" as did another marine officer, Captain Francis J. West, who described a patrol with the 9th Marines:

> . . . The Marines wore helmets and flak jackets. Each rifleman carried 150 rounds of ammunition and 2 or more hand grenades. The men of the two machine gun crews were draped with belts of linked cartridges totalling 1,200 rounds. The two 3.5-inch rocket launcher teams carried five high explosive and five white phosphorus rockets. Four grenadiers carried 28 40mm shells apiece for their stubby M79s. Sergeant Cunningham had given six LAAWs [a 66-mm. one-shot disposable rocket launcher for use against tanks] to some riflemen to provide additional area target capability. . . .
>   The platoon moved out at 1100. There was no breeze and no shade. The temperature was 102 degrees. Within five minutes, every Marine was soaked in sweat. . . . [16]

Although the patrol acquitted itself well, the weight problem continued to bother unit commanders.

One of the most difficult problems faced was enemy use of booby traps and mines. Whether planted passively or electrically detonated by guerrillas, they extracted a heavy toll, not alone from the initial explosion but often in subsequent pursuit actions that involved enemy-prepared terrain and ambush. Discussing small-unit operations in spring of 1966, Captain West pointed out that of ten marines killed and fifty-eight wounded in one company in five weeks, " . . . two men were hit by small arms fire, one by a grenade. Mines inflicted all the other casualties."[17] As one senior intelligence officer pointed out to this writer, the peasant *invariably* knew the location of booby traps and mines but for one or more reasons, usually fear of the VC, would not warn the intended victims, thereby further eliciting American fury.

These and other substantial problems usually stemmed, at least in part, from a supreme problem: lack of intelligence. Marine patrols, more often than not, were operating in the dark, trying to guess enemy locations while keeping oriented with unsatisfactory, 1:50,000 maps. Captain John G. Miller noted that:

> . . . target acquisition is one of the rifleman's biggest problems. The presence of civilians on the battlefield requires each Marine to exercise the finest degree of judgment in applying any number of local rules of engagement. This situation sometimes puts Marines in the unhappy position of having to "lead with their chins" in order to make contact with the enemy.[18]

Leading with their chins was exactly what the enemy wanted marines to do. The enemy reacted in one of several ways. Sometimes they slipped away, usually leading the marine unit a merry chase before so doing. Sometimes they fought and, though suffering themselves, usually inflicted relatively high casualties on the marine units involved; but, more important than that from the enemy standpoint, he usually arranged the firefight so that peasants tasted marine wrath.

What allied forces in Vietnam refused to recognize, at least for some time, was what Callwell had pointed out nearly a hundred years earlier: In a guerrilla situation, the guerrilla is the professional, the newcomer the amateur. A veteran marine intelligence officer later wrote of a VC intelligence officer, " . . . a wizened little man wearing black pajamas and tire-tread sandals":

> . . . Ai No U does not have aerial observers; no infra-red, no SLAR, no TV; no digital data "real time" readout computerized equipment. But he is successful. This confounds Americans. The

result is a communist psychological operation by accident; more effective than if by design. How does he do it?

Ai No U relies upon two things: (1) the People's Military Intelligence Concept, and (2) the American Military penchant for the SOP [standard operating procedure], a commander's tactical signature.

American tactical predictability frequently contributed to enemy successes. Fragmentary reports (frequently from VC sympathizers) too often tipped the American commander's hand and allowed a VC unit to disperse. The ensuing operation, while accomplishing no concrete result, often further antagonized the peasants, strengthening VC control over them.[19]

The key remained the peasant. Despite the aggression-from-the-North theme, constantly hammered home by senior American officials and officers, the real enemy was indigenous to the area; as Viet Minh, he had fought the French; as Viet Cong, he was fighting ARVN and the Americans. He had lived in this area for a long time; he had devoted his every effort to his task. He held a detailed knowledge of most operational areas, knowledge gleaned from personal reconnaissance, often over the years and sometimes even decades, and from information supplied either by guerrillas or local peasants. He also profited from an adaptive ability noted by one experienced marine officer: " . . . His techniques and tactics are not exotic innovations; his strength lies only in the ability to apply fundamentals and to adjust his tactics to those of his opponent."[20]

This was precisely the challenge faced by marines. They were fighting to clear an area infested by gophers: For too long, their answer was to rip up terrain in an attempt, vain of course, to kill the gophers rather than to make that terrain sufficiently unpleasant for the gophers to go away. Some commanders twigged the essential problem and tried to do something about it. In mid-1966, one company commander, Captain Jim Cooper, saw the futility of operating from an isolated combat outpost on top of a hill. Cooper moved his people into a hamlet of about three hundred fifty peasants, one of several in a village complex of some six thousand population, set up proper security, increased patrols and ambushes, and slowly integrated a theretofore isolated Popular Forces unit into hamlet life: " . . . The hamlet chief moved from the ARVN fort back into his own home. . . . Cooperation followed friendship. The hamlet chief showed the Marines the favorite ambush and hiding places of the Viet Cong." Cooper was on to the real secret of fighting an insurgency. But, despite his impressive success, he learned by a cunning maneuver that VC sympathizers and informers continued to live *in the hamlet*, while VC units shifted operations elsewhere. Converting the village to the government's side would have taken a major effort and much patience and time.

> ... Less than a month after their arrival, the Marines did leave to go on an operation. They left the marks of their influence behind in the village and especially in the hamlet. The Vietnamese had reopened two schools and a pagoda. They were washing. Their medical ills had been treated. A Vietnamese public health nurse and two school teachers had come to the village. The hamlet and village chiefs had returned. The Popular Forces were acting more like disciplined troops.
> What would happen in the future, Cooper was not about to guess. ... [21]

What happened to that particular village, we are not told. What frequently happened both in I Corps area and elsewhere was a return of the VC the moment allied troops departed.[22] Once again, the situation cried for clear-and-hold tactics followed by a viable pacification or rehabilitation campaign. General Walt and his marines finally came to understand this, at least in part, and were on the right track with Combined Action Groups. In time, marines might have overcome the language obstacle and even innate corruption of most Saigon and I Corps area officials, who did not want viable government in the villages and sabotaged the American effort at almost every turn.[23] But marines lacked time and, so long as Giap sucked marine units into quasi-conventional warfare, they lacked men. The marine pacification effort was never more than a drop in the bucket. In 1966, the Viet Cong controlled about three quarters of I Corps area, either outright or through parallel hierarchies. By mid-1966, of 169 villages within the marine area, only thirty-seven were regarded as 80 per cent or more pacified; less than half of the area's nine hundred thousand people lived therein.[24]

Prime Minister Ky's highly touted Revolutionary Development program, so fervently embraced by President Johnson, suffered from two perhaps irreconcilable difficulties. The first was a definition of terms. The democracy that the Johnson administration wanted in South Vietnam was an ambition, not a feasible goal; the assumption that this was a form of government also wanted by Thieu and Ky and the special interests they represented was false. As the *enfant terrible* of the Marine Corps, Lieutenant Colonel William R. Corson, put it:

> ... we call it democracy—they call it obedience. [The] Honolulu [Conference of February 1966] left unanswered the questions

"What is pacification?" and "What are we really trying to do?" The generalized and idealized statements about a "better world," "hearts and minds," and such are not, and were not then, operational. You can't sell a product if you can't define it.[25]

The situation in South Vietnam did not fit the picture being reported by Lodge and Westmoreland, whose claims of significant pacification progress were frequently broadcast to the nation by its President, despite his being informed to the contrary by Robert McNamara (among others). While Johnson promised Thieu and Ky the moon and a piece of cheese at the Manila conference in October 1966, *all* governmental abuses so far discussed continued in force. No matter who was elected to the constituent assembly or what type of constitution would result, neither Thieu nor Ky nor the ruling junta of generals intended to liberalize government, much less institute a representative government that would appeal to either peasants or dissident sects or Buddhist or minorities or classes or professions—that would appeal to those complex elements constituting the political invention of South Vietnam. The generals stood as far removed from peasant aspirations as their American counterparts. A preponderance of northern Catholics occupied major posts both in Saigon and the countryside. The peasants were as badly off as formerly, and in some cases worse. Land reform was a dead issue: Landlords continued to accompany troops to claim back taxes from peasants, and to invoke heavy, usually illegal rents.[26] Friction continued, not only with increasingly militant Buddhists, but with other dissident southern groups such as remnant Cao Dai and Hoa Hao. GVN failure to live up to promises made to the Montagnards also cost heavily: More than two thirds of the two hundred fifty-man Montagnard garrison at Plei Me had defected the day prior to the Viet Cong attack, and some Montagnards had subsequently gone over to the enemy.[27]

Government failure meant that old abuses continued. The administration's chief hatchet man, General Nguyen Ngoc Loan, used the most violent methods to eliminate political opponents. Jails remained jammed with political prisoners; favored sons remained exempt from military duty; bribery and corruption claimed almost every transaction. At virtually each level of government, officials extracted "squeeze." Peasants bringing vegetables and fish to market paid squeeze to the police for protection; people buying and selling commodities paid squeeze for necessary licenses; students wanting scholarships to the U.S.A. paid for them; sick people wanting treatment on American hospital ships paid for it; peasants and refugees wanting food and clothes supplied by American funds paid for them.

This would have been bad enough under normal circumstances, but, considering South Vietnamese needs, it proved catastrophic. A dangerous political climate suppressed intelligent opposition and discouraged worthy Vietnamese who had fled abroad from returning at a crucial time. As one example, of the country's eight hundred doctors, five hundred served the army, a hundred fifty served private patients, and a hundred fifty treated fifteen million people;[28] yet, over seven hundred Vietnamese doctors were in Paris and refused to return![29]

Continuing VC gains in the countryside and the infusion of American troops exacerbated the situation. Rampant inflation developed, as did an enormous black market—an economically confused situation ably exploited by VC resident agents and infiltrators in two ways: by buying or stealing military needs from American stockpiles (while MACV and the JCS continued to worry about enemy supply lines from the North), and by agitation and propaganda among the hundreds of thousands of refugees generated from search-and-destroy tactics.

Governmental failure inevitably influenced ARVN, which contained nearly as many organizational and operational flaws as previously. The advisory system, in which so much hope had been placed, had already backfired—just as it had in the case of Chiang Kai-shek's Kuomintang army. A good many American army advisers were ill-equipped for the task and proved ineffective and, in some cases, dishonest and dangerous. The turbulent military situation, language deficiencies, and a one-year tour of duty combined to thwart the hard work of a good many capable and courageous Americans. Try as they would, they could not overturn a ruling mandarin philosophy and get ARVN units into the boondocks and keep them there. ARVN increased in 1965 from 493,000 to 640,000, but it counted ninety-three thousand desertions for the year.

Continued government and ARVN failures explained the second difficulty of the Revolutionary Development program, which was operational. Few GVN officials and ARVN officers shared Major Be's expressed idealism (see Chapter 64). Although ARVN units became increasingly available to provide hamlet security (as American soldiers and marines took over virtually the entire combat role), they proved, in general, as unsatisfactory in pacification as in combat. One American adviser, Dwight Owen—a highly motivated and sincere young man who left a postgraduate course to serve in Vietnam, where he would shortly die—wrote of this period:

> ... At present the ARVN has little or no responsibility or responsiveness to the people of Vietnam. They fight but do not build. ... Garrisons in towns and villages are notoriously inactive in CA [civic action] work. Often this is because they lack initiative and spirit. ... Good pay, promotions, decent quarters, good rations, leave, and many other benefits most armies enjoy are lacking in

many respects in the Vietnamese army. This undercuts morale and thus troop effectiveness. . . . [30]

ARVN soldiers from corps commanders to privates received squeeze to the extent that peasants saw little difference between friends and enemies. Ky's Revolutionary Development program soon brought to mind Ngo Dinh Nhu's earlier efforts to control the peasant population rather than win it to the government's side (see Chapter 59). William Corson, who was intimately involved in the pacification effort in I Corps area, later wrote:

> . . . The 30,000 members of the Armed Combat Youth (ACY) are a bargain-basement mob of thugs who counterterrorize the Vietnamese people while promoting "democracy" GVN style. The ACY units—or as they are being renamed, the Revolutionary Development Peoples' Groups (RDPG)—are organized to promote Nguyen Cao Ky's "strength through joy" approach to individual liberty. Through this borrowed Hitlerian concept Ky is attempting to build up an absolute form of political control that makes Nazi Germany look like Thomas More's "Utopia." . . . The fear generated by the presence of the ACY in a hamlet is exceeded only by presence of one of the "elite" ARVN units such as the Rangers, Airborne, or Vietnamese Marines.[31]

Nor did the American-directed reorganization result in streamlined operations that were needed. Province advisers at all levels found themselves enmeshed in bureaucratic and military corruption that sometimes defied imagination. Some of these advisers were conscientious, hard-working, and brave persons. Others were not. Most did not speak the language and had to rely on interpreters. Most knew little of customs of the people they were trying to help, and their aid estimates frequently lacked practicality or proper priority. Most were also endowed with the desire to do the job themselves. In the same letter quoted above, Dwight Owen wrote:

> . . . Our pacification effort is not making significant headway. The first major problem is a lack of realistic appraisal by U.S. officials of what is needed. Plans have been grandiose and have not considered the realities of the situation—too much and too fast. We have not allowed pacification cadre adequate time in hamlets by assigning them a quota of so many hamlets a year, which allows them about 2–3 months per hamlet. The plans have lacked follow-through. After the cadre leave, the job is considered finished, when, in reality, it is only beginning. . . .

Agency infighting frequently ruled an American camp, and agencies often collided with the military, both ARVN and American. A British adviser on counterinsurgency, Robert Thompson, later told a seminar audience, " . . . when I added up the intelligence organizations which were operating in Saigon in 1966 against the Vietcong, there were seventeen, both American and South Vietnamese, and none of them were talking to each other!"[32]

What possibly could have been a viable pacification program became just another in a long series of flaccid, money-wasting efforts—a development incessantly harped on by NLF-PRP-Hanoi propaganda which exhorted South Vietnamese peasants to fight against U.S. imperialists and their Saigon lackeys.[33] If Hanoi ever displayed nervousness, it was over the allied pacification effort. In a major speech delivered in January 1967, Vo Nguyen Giap returned to the subject with the reluctant persistence of Raskolnikov returning to his evil deeds in Dostoyevsky's *Crime and Punishment*. And well he might: Pacification was the key to combat in the South, a fact repeatedly proved by history, ancient and modern, a fact never understood by American military planners who refused to fight a complex war of nuance and subtlety in preference to a good old black-and-white shooting match, a fact never understood by Johnson or his hawkish advisers who refused to formulate objectives consonant to fact in preference to wild ambition that demanded an undefinable and thus unrealizable nothing called "victory."

By early 1966, a good many doubts had risen in public and private minds within the United States as to the wisdom of American actions in Vietnam. Taken together, they began to suggest that the Johnson administration had bought a gold brick made the more fraudulent by size and weight. In February 1965, the *New York Times* had published a petition, "An Open Letter to President Johnson," signed by over four hundred New England academics, including sixty-six from the Massachusetts Institute of Technology and sixty-two from Harvard. In this " . . . careful, cautious and even generous letter," the signatories pointed to the deteriorating position in Vietnam and called for a negotiated peace: " . . . If we are not to widen the war beyond all conscience, as reasonable men we must negotiate while there is still time."[34] A letter to Dean Rusk, signed by nearly seven hundred academics, appeared in the *Times* in May—a strong rebuttal to a speech in April by Rusk, who had attacked academic critics of the war. A distinguished scholar, Professor Hans Morgenthau, a political scientist and government consultant, next questioned the Johnson administration's policy in Vietnam in a televised debate with McGeorge Bundy in June 1965 in which Bundy came out second best. Morgenthau followed this effort with a lengthy article, "Vietnam: Shadow and Substance," in the *New York Review of Books* in September 1965. After defining the nature of foreign policy and national prestige, Morgenthau explained " . . . the realities of power and the American misunderstanding of those realities." The prestige of France, he went on, was never lower than during its wars in Indochina and Algeria; only after it liquidated those enterprises did its prestige rise " . . . to heights it had not attained since the beginning of the Second World War." Moving to the moral plane, Morgenthau wrote that victory in a guerrilla war can be achieved only by genocide. " . . . We have tortured and killed prisoners; we have embarked on a scorched-earth policy." Morgenthau warned that this indiscriminate killing would get worse as our armed forces became brutalized, that this was our dirtiest war, and there was no end and no justice in sight. The reader worried about national prestige, he concluded, should reflect on " . . . the kind of country America will become when it emerges from so senseless, hopeless, brutal and brutalizing a war."[35] In late October 1965, over 650 professors removed the velvet glove in another letter to President Johnson, published in the *Times,* which forcefully told the President to " . . . stop the bloodshed in Vietnam."[36] In February 1966, the *New York Review of Books* published an article, "Call to the American Conscience," which was sponsored by a score of notable authors who invited readers to " . . . a read-in for peace in Vietnam" to be held at Manhattan's Town Hall. In this same month, the *Times* published an "Open Letter on Vietnam" in which nearly thirteen hundred academics voiced their protest and warning: " . . . U.S. bombs, napalm, and chemical warfare are making a desert of the country. The only peace that can be achieved in this way is the peace of the grave. We recoil in horror."[37] Such was the continuing flow of petitions and articles that a contemporary historian, David Schalk, has recently concluded that in 1966 Lyndon Johnson had become to the dissenting academics and other members of the antiwar movement, " . . . a subject of antipathy, mockery, savage satire and devastating caricature."[38]

Nor were the academics and other conscience-stricken Americans standing alone. In February 1966, *Harper's Magazine* published a letter-article from a retired soldier with a fine World War II combat record and a lengthy postwar record of distinguished public and private service. This was General James Gavin, who now challenged the logic of escalation. What became unfairly known as a demand for "enclave strategy" was an intelligent attempt to reassess a complex situation, and fit limited resources to realistic goals.

Gavin's article was published shortly before the Senate Foreign Relations Committee, whose chairman was William Fulbright, opened what became the famous Vietnam hearings. These televised sessions left little doubt that the situation was not as black-and-white as the Johnson administration proclaimed. The Administration's position was presented by Dean Rusk and Maxwell Taylor, each of whom reaffirmed the domino theory and aggression-from-the-North-under-Peking-aegis thesis (and each of whom was pretty well worked over in question periods).

As devil's advocates, the Senate called on General Gavin and Ambassador George Kennan. Gavin warned the Foreign Relations Committee and the listening American public of dangers inherent in further expanding the war, particularly since no tactical need existed. As he had already written in *Harper's Magazine:*

> ... Today we have sufficient forces in South Vietnam to hold several enclaves on the coast, where sea and air power can be made fully effective. By enclaves I suggest Camranh Bay, Danang, and similar areas where American bases are being established. However, we are stretching these resources beyond reason in our endeavours to secure the entire country of South Vietnam from the Viet Cong penetration. This situation, of course, is caused by the growing Viet Cong strength.

To expand the American presence and the war would create new problems, for example Chinese intervention or a new war in Korea. Instead, the United States should pursue a strategy compatible to the area's importance and to the tactical challenge: " ... if we should maintain enclaves on the coast, desist in our bombing attacks in North Vietnam, and seek to find a solution through the United Nations or a conference in Geneva, we could very likely do with the forces now available. . . . "

Frederick the Great, in speaking of his foray from Silesia against the Austrians, noted that " ... this plan was simple, proportionate to the possibility of execution, and adapted to circumstances; there was therefore every reason to hope it would succeed." The same could be said of the Gavin plan, but such was the power of the hawks that it became perverted into a strategy of defeat and would not soon have the chance to prove itself. Such was the Administration's outcry against the "enclave theory," that few persons paid attention to what possibly was Gavin's most important point. As Mao Tse-tung had suggested some years before, Gavin believed that warfare had radically changed:

> ... Since the advent of the Space Age, there has been a revolution in the nature of war and global conflict. The confrontation in Vietnam is the first test of our understanding of such change, or our lack of it. The measures that we now take in Southeast Asia must stem from sagacity and thoughtfulness, and an awareness of the nature of strategy in this rapidly shrinking world.[39]

Ambassador Kennan already had challenged the wisdom of American commitment to South Vietnam.[40] Once again, he contradicted Administration hawks who proclaimed that South Vietnam was of vital strategic interest to the United States:

> . . . if we were not already involved as we are today in Vietnam, I would know of no reason why we should wish to become so involved, and I could think of several reasons why we should wish not to. Vietnam is not a region of major military, industrial importance. It is difficult to believe that any decisive developments of the world situation would be determined in normal circumstances by what happens on that territory.

After expatiating on this statement, which must have shaken thoughtful senators, Kennan suggested that, since we had become militarily involved, we could not hastily abandon our posture. But that was no reason to enlarge the posture. The political situation in the South permitted no easy solution; American military might could not overcome such factors as enemy space and manpower, and an attempt to subdue the North by invasion would probably draw China into the fray. As it was, the war was severely damaging American relations with the U.S.S.R. and Japan. Kennan wanted the American presence liquidated as soon as possible:

> . . . In matters such as this, it is not, in my experience, what you do that is mainly decisive. It is how you do it, and I would submit that there is more respect to be won in the opinion of this world by a resolute and courageous liquidation of unsound positions than by the most stubborn pursuit of extravagant or unpromising objectives.

As for the "obligation" maintained by Johnson and his advisers, Kennan, sounding like a diplomatic Socrates, continued:

> . . . I would like to know what that commitment really consists of, and how and when it was incurred.
>
> What seems to be involved here is an obligation on our part not only to defend the frontiers of a certain political entity against outside attack, but to assure the internal security of its government in circumstances where that government is unable to assure that security by its own means.
>
> Now, any such obligation is one that goes obviously considerably further in its implications than the normal obligations of a military alliance. If we did not incur such an obligation in any formal way, then I think we should not be inventing it for ourselves and assuring ourselves that we are bound by it today. But if we

did incur it, then I do fail to understand how it was possible to enter into any such commitment otherwise than through the constitutional processes which were meant to come into play when even commitments of lesser import than this were undertaken.

Although Kennan felt the deepest personal sympathy for the South Vietnamese and repugnance toward the Viet Cong, he nonetheless maintained that

> . . . our country should not be asked, and should not ask of itself, to shoulder the main burden of determining the political realities in any other country, and particularly not in one remote from our shores, from our culture, and from the experience of our people. This is not only not our business, but I don't think we can do it successfully.[41]

Three months later, another hard-charging soldier spoke up. This was David Shoup, a retired four-star Marine Corps general, winner of the Medal of Honor at Tarawa, former commandant of the Marine Corps, member of the Joint Chiefs of Staff, and unofficial military adviser to President Kennedy. Speaking in Los Angeles in May 1966, Shoup denied South Vietnam's strategic importance:

> . . . The Administration, he said, has never realistically assessed whether the United States' own self-interest is at stake in Southeast Asia. The Administration has never presented a timetable proving that there would be "irreparable effects upon this nation at the end of five, ten, fifteen, fifty years" if South Vietnam were overrun by the Communist Vietcong guerrillas.

Pointing to drastic changes in the world Communist order, Shoup declared that Administration reasons for American intervention in South Vietnam " . . . are too shallow and narrow for students, as well as other citizens. Especially so, when you realize that what is happening, no matter how carefully and slowly the military escalation has progressed, may be projecting us toward world catastrophe." In case any one missed the point, General Shoup stated: " . . . I don't think the whole of Southeast Asia, as related to the present and future safety and freedom of the people of this country, is worth the life or limb of a single American."[42]

So it was that in 1966, influenced by Morgenthau, Gavin, Kennan, Shoup, and myriad other voices, large numbers of America's educators were becoming opponents of Johnson's war. Although Lyndon Johnson publicly treated these and other dissentient voices with insouciance tinged with contempt, members of his own inner circle continued to express certain doubts that could not altogether be ignored. These were occasioned mainly by the increasing expense of the war as fought by Westmoreland and the JCS.

No sooner had Johnson authorized committing nearly two hundred thousand troops by the end of 1965 than Westmoreland, in July of that year, informed McNamara that these would suffice only to stop the enemy offensive by the end of the year. In order to resume the offensive in priority areas and to continue the pacification program, Westmoreland requested another 112,000 troops for the first half of 1966; he also warned McNamara that he would need even more troops to defeat the enemy by the end of 1967. A few months later he asked for another 154,000 bodies.

After considerable soul-searching, McNamara agreed: If a bombing pause failed to produce a satisfactory reaction from Hanoi, he recommended a troop increase to seventy-four battalions, or about 400,000 men, by the end of 1966, but warned that at least two hundred thousand additional troops would perhaps be needed in 1967! McNamara concluded his memorandum to the President in somber but ambivalent words that bring to mind the western-front syndrome of World War I:

> . . . We should be aware that deployments of the kind I have recommended will not guarantee success. U.S. killed-in-action can be expected to reach 1000 a month, and the odds are even that we will be faced in early 1967 with a "no-decision" at an even higher level. My over-all evaluation, nevertheless, is that the best chance of achieving our stated objective lies in a [bombing] pause followed, if it fails, by the deployments mentioned above.[43]

McNamara's recommendation for a bombing halt touched off an intra-Administration quarrel that would continue to the end of Johnson's administration. Johnson later wrote that he viewed McNamara's proposal to halt the bombing with a "deep skepticism" shared by McGeorge Bundy, Dean Rusk, and Ambassador Lodge, not to mention military chiefs and advisers. Pertinent factors slowly brought some of these persons around. In private discussions, McNamara went so far, according to the President, as to question " . . . assurance of military success in Vietnam," stating that " . . . we had to find a diplomatic solution":

> . . . I asked him whether he meant that there was no guarantee of success no matter what we did militarily. "That's right," he answered. "We have been too optimistic. One chance in three, or two in three, is my estimate."[44]

857

McNamara also pointed out that if the pause failed to move Hanoi to the conference table, " . . . it would at least [demonstrate] our genuine desire for a peaceful settlement and thereby temper the criticism we were getting at home and abroad."[45] International diplomatic activity, particularly from the U.S.S.R. and Hungary, also seemed to promise negotiations if the bombing halted. In the end, according to the President, McGeorge Bundy and Rusk joined McNamara and George Ball in urging the halt. Against JCS advice, the President stopped the bombings in late December. When Hanoi showed no inclination to come to the conference table—critics of the Administration pointed to Johnson's intractable conference position as one reason—the President ordered bombing resumed at the end of January.

The hawks were now definitely in the ascendancy. In February 1966, the *New York Times Magazine* published an article, "The Case for Escalation," by veteran military analyst Hanson Baldwin. Arguing that the domino theory was valid, Baldwin seemed willing to accept war with China if that was necessary to defeat North Vietnam; meanwhile, he called for declaration of a national emergency and a greatly expanded war.[46]

The next round started with the Buddhist revolts in March 1966, which precipitated a new crisis and forced the Thieu-Ky government to use ARVN units to recapture the cities of Hué and Da Nang. Again the Washington administration split on the issue. Pessimists argued that Ky could never form an effective government, which meant that he could not maintain a viable pacification program; optimists pointed out that he commanded enough loyalty, at least in the army, to settle the issue and that, as a bonus, the government and Buddhists agreed to elections for a constituent assembly to draw up a new constitution. Although the crisis occasioned another fierce argument within the Administration (with Under Secretary of State Ball once again calling for disengagement), President Johnson sided with those who favored pursuing the current program, escalating as necessary. With the appointment of Walt Rostow as presidential assistant (replacing McGeorge Bundy as presidential adviser on national security in deed if not in word), the hawks won a major round, and the American commitment continued to increase.

The doubts that had already formed in Secretary of Defense Robert McNamara's mind now began to develop dramatically. In August of 1966, the Secretary received an unpleasant, if not entirely unexpected, surprise: a report from forty-seven of the nation's top scientists whom he had secretly mobilized to study the effects of Operation Rolling Thunder and to consider alternate means of stopping enemy infiltration from the North. Their report stated that not only had the twin objectives of Rolling Thunder—to reduce infiltration and to force Hanoi to call off the insurgency—failed (a conclusion previously reached by CIA reports), but that an expanded bombing program would probably fail to accomplish either objective. Instead, the group recommended building a sophisticated barrier across the southern border of the DMZ and curling on the Laotian panhandle—all together some forty to sixty miles—this to comprise new and secret mines and sensors that would locate infiltrators, who would then be destroyed by patrolling troops and supporting arms. The system would cost perhaps a billion dollars to build and about $800 million a year to operate.[47]

McNamara was still digesting the morbid contents of the scientists' findings when he received another unpleasant surprise: a new request from General Westmoreland to provide a total 570,000 troops in South Vietnam by end of 1967. A few weeks later, the JCS, which approved Westmoreland's newest request (favorably endorsed by Admiral Sharp), " ... urged what the Pentagon study calls 'full-blown' mobilization of 688,500 Army, Navy, Air Force and Marine reservists to help provide more troops for Vietnam and also to build up the armed forces around the world."[48]—a move pressed on the American public by Hanson Baldwin in the October *Reader's Digest*.[49]

The Westmoreland-Sharp-JCS-Baldwin thinking was not to McNamara's liking. In October, he again flew to Saigon (where an attempt was made on his life). Upon his return to Washington, he reported in detail to President Johnson that, although

> ... We have done somewhat better militarily than I anticipated
> ... my concern continues ... in other respects. This is because I
> see no reasonable way to bring the war to an end soon. Enemy
> morale has not broken—he apparently has adjusted to our stop-
> ping his drive for military victory and has adopted a strategy of
> keeping us busy and waiting us out (a strategy of attriting our
> national will). He knows that we have not been, and he believes
> we probably will not be, able to translate our military successes
> into the "end products"—broken enemy morale and political
> achievements by the GVN.

The September elections in South Vietnam were healthy enough, he opined, but the South Vietnamese Government had not come to terms with the real problem:

> ... Pacification is a bad disappointment ... [and] has if anything
> gone backward. As compared with two, or four, years ago, enemy
> full-time regional forces and part-time guerrilla forces are larger;
> attacks, terrorism and sabotage have increased in scope and inten-
> sity; more railroads are closed and highways cut; the rice crop
> expected to come to market is smaller; we control little, if any,

more of the population; the VC political infrastructure thrives in most of the country, continuing to give the enemy his enormous intelligence advantage; full security exists nowhere (not even behind the U.S. Marines' lines and in Saigon); in the countryside, the enemy almost completely controls the night.[50]

In McNamara's opinion, the United States had to " . . . continue to press the enemy militarily" and also to make "demonstrable" progress in pacification, but

> . . . we must add a new ingredient forced on us by the facts. Specifically, we must improve our position by getting ourselves into a military posture that we credibly would maintain indefinitely—a posture that makes trying to "wait us out" less attractive.

McNamara called for " . . . a five-pronged course of action": contrary to Westmoreland's, Sharp's and JCS desires, he wished to limit troop increases to seventy thousand which, in the current round, would give a total of 470,000—enough, he believed, to neutralize enemy operations and get on with pacification; to save troops, and thus avoid mobilizing reserves, and to find an effective substitute for expensive and relatively useless bombing of the North, he recommended building an electronic barrier across the DMZ as suggested by the earlier-mentioned scientists' report; he called for stabilizing Operation Rolling Thunder: eighty-four thousand attack sorties had failed to attain stated objectives. We were then flying twelve thousand attack sorties per month (at an operational cost of $250 million per month), which was sufficient to " . . . continue the pressure and would remain available as a bargaining counter to get talks started (or to trade off in talks)." Moreover,

> . . . At the proper time . . . I believe we should consider terminating bombing in all of North Vietnam, or at least in the Northeast zones, for an indefinite period in connection with covert moves toward peace. Pursue a vigorous pacification program—if necessary, reorganize. Press for negotiations.

He did not believe that either military action or negotiations offered more than a "mere possibility" of ending the war. As opposed to Westmoreland and the JCS, McNamara believed that

> . . . The solution lies in girding, openly, for a longer war and in taking actions immediately which will in 12 to 18 months give clear evidence that the continuing costs and risks to the American people are acceptably limited, that the formula for success has been found, and that the end of the war is merely a matter of time. All

of my recommendations will contribute to this strategy, but the one most difficult to implement is perhaps the most important one—enlivening the pacification program. The odds are less than even for this task, if only because we have failed consistently since 1961 to make a dent in the problem. But, because the 1967 trend of pacification will, I believe, be the main talisman of ultimate U.S. success or failure in Vietnam, extraordinary imagination and effort should go into changing the stripes of that problem.

President Thieu and Prime Minister Ky are thinking along similar lines. . . . They expressed agreement with us that the key to success is pacification and that so far pacification has failed. They agree that we need clarification of GVN and U.S. roles and that the bulk of the ARVN should be shifted to pacification. Ky will, between January and July 1967, shift all ARVN infantry divisions to that role. . . . Thieu and Ky see this as part of a two-year (1967–68) schedule, in which offensive operations against enemy main force units are continued, carried on primarily by the U.S. and other Free-World forces. At the end of the two-year period, they believe the enemy may be willing to negotiate or to retreat from his current course of action.

Neither Westmoreland nor the JCS agreed with McNamara's conclusions. The JCS vigorously dissented from stabilizing the air campaign against the North, calling instead for a radical expansion of the effort along with an increase in targets and additional naval action.[51] Other hawks agreed, and President Johnson was inclined to agree with the hawks.

McNamara did persuade Johnson to limit troop increases, but only for a short time. In November, McNamara, obviously with presidential assent, informed the JCS that Westmoreland could have 469,000 troops at his disposal by mid-1968.[52]

CHAPTER SIXTY-SIX

1. Hackworth, 468–9, 474.
2. Ibid.
3. Ibid., 486.
4. Ibid., 487.
5. Ibid., 488–9.
6. Ibid., 559–60.
7. Ibid., 569–70.
8. Marshall, 42. See also, Hackworth, 545 ff., 568–71, 582–6, for a professional appraisal of this veteran military correspondent.
9. Marshall, 43 ff.
10. Hackworth, 513.
11. Ibid., 485.
12. Ibid., 572.
13. Caputo, 65.
14. Ibid., 86–7.

15. Miller.
16. West.
17. Ibid. See also, O'Neill.
18. Miller.
19. Grier.
20. Rogers. See also, Mack, "Ambuscade."
21. West.
22. O'Neill, 137–58, who writes feelingly on the subject.
23. Clement. See also, Corson.
24. U.S. Marine Corps, "III MAF . . . "
25. Corson, 59.
26. Fall, "Viet Nam in the Balance."
27. Corson, 91.
28. U.S. Senate, *Refugee Problems in South Vietnam.*
29. Corson, 273.
30. Dwight Owen, private letter in the author's files.
31. Corson, 91.
32. Royal United Service Institution Seminar.
33. Vo Nguyen Giap, "The Strategic Role . . . " See also, Snepp, 11–12: CIA personnel alone numbered 600. See also, ibid., *Big Victory, Great Task.*
34. Schalk, 118–19.
35. Ibid., 53–4.
36. Ibid., 120.
37. Ibid., 121.
38. Ibid.
39. Gavin, "A Soldier's Doubts." See also, Fulbright, *The Vietnam Hearings.*
40. Raskin and Fall. See, for example, Kennan's testimony before the House Committee on Foreign Affairs, May 1965, 15–31.
41. Fulbright, *The Vietnam Hearings.*
42. Deakin.
43. Sheehan et al., 487–9.
44. Johnson, *The Vantage Point . . . ,* 234–6.
45. Ibid., 234.
46. Baldwin, "The Case for Escalation."
47. Sheehan et al., 483–5, 502–9.
48. Ibid., 48.
49. Baldwin, "To End the War in Vietnam, Mobilize!"
50. Sheehan et al., 542–51. See also, Giap, "The Strategic Role . . . "
51. Sheehan et al., 552–3.
52. Ibid., 520–1.

CHAPTER 67

The war continues • President Johnson's optimism • The February bombing halt • Operation Cedar Falls • Fighting in the highlands • The marine war • New tactical techniques • Khe Sanh defended • Air and naval wars • Ambassador Bunker and pacification • South Vietnam's political progress • Allied profits for the year • "... Light at the end of a tunnel"

IN HIS STATE OF THE UNION MESSAGE in early January 1967, President Johnson once again justified American presence in Vietnam in the strongest possible terms. Once again he spoke of specific "commitments" and the evil that would follow should the United States fail to uphold them. He promised no easy way out of what he called this "limited war":

> ... I wish I could report to you that the conflict is almost over. This I cannot do. We face more cost, more loss, and more agony. For the end is not yet. I cannot promise you that it will come this year—or come next year. Our adversary still believes, I think, to-night, that he can go on fighting longer than we can, and longer than we and our allies will be prepared to stand up and resist.

The answer to that was to continue Westmoreland's attrition strategy:

> ... Our men in that area—there are nearly 500,000 now—have borne well "the burden and the heat of the day." Their efforts have deprived the Communist enemy of the victory that he sought and that he expected a year ago. We have steadily frustrated his main forces. General Westmoreland reports that the enemy can no longer succeed on the battlefield.
> So I must say to you that our pressure must be sustained— and will be sustained—until he realizes that the war he started is costing him more than he can ever gain.[1]

863

His speech made it clear that he was committed to a hawk strategy and did not want to change.

The President continued to place great faith in the bombing of the North. He approved none of McNamara's "stabilizing" suggestions made the previous autumn and, indeed, drastically raised the number of authorized B-52 missions, to take effect in late February. Although international pressures caused him to halt bombing the North for a few days in February, he ignored the British prime minister's plea to hold off until the Soviet premier could discuss negotiations with Hanoi. How much this was due to his own belief and how much to the work of hawks is anyone's guess. The President made his attitude clear in two documents, however. In a secret letter of early February to Ho Chi Minh, his moral indignation at Hanoi's transgression is apparent—it is all he can do to swallow it and offer to stop bombing the North if Hanoi would stop infiltration into the South. Ho replied, in effect, that the U.S.A. had no right to bomb the North in the first place and that discussions between the two countries could occur only when bombing and other unjustified acts of war ceased.[2]

Not only was bombing the North morally and legally justified in the President's mind, but, contrary to reports from the nation's top intelligence analysts, he insisted that the bombings were producing very real effects. Although Johnson emphasized in his memoirs that he did not expect bombing of the North to win the war, the record strongly suggests that he regarded air power as his chief punitive weapon and could not understand why Hanoi did not submit in order to call off the punishment. In any event, the air war, both North and South, escalated to frantic proportions in 1967.

The President did not exercise such active control over the ground war in the South as he did over bombing of the North. He nonetheless vigorously supported Westmoreland. By year's end, South Vietnam's armed forces climbed to over seven hundred thousand (at least on paper); American troop strength approached half a million with 525,000 authorized; Korea supplied forty-five thousand troops; Australia, six thousand; Thailand, twenty-five hundred, with the promise to furnish a division; New Zealand, a few hundred. Direct operational costs for the year zoomed to over $25 billion. By October 1967,

> . . . 40 percent of our combat-ready divisions, half of our tactical air-power, and at least a third of our naval strength . . . were waging full-throated war on the Southeast Asian peninsula.[3]

One analyst aptly called it more of the same.

In January, Operation Cedar Falls—an allied force spearheaded by the American army's 1st Division—began to sweep through a B-52-bomb-plastered Iron Triangle, northwest of Saigon. In this traditional Viet Cong defense complex, troops discovered an "underground city" and seized half a million enemy documents and enough rice to feed "...an estimated 13,000 soldiers for one year."[4] More sweeps followed to push the enemy from the Iron Triangle and from Zones C and D and keep him on the defensive while bringing alleged stability to surrounding provinces. An active and tactically profitable year in vital III Corps area: by December, U.S.-ARVN-allied forces claimed 22,500 enemy dead; more important, Viet Cong main-force units had retreated north to Cambodian border areas. Summarizing the war at year's end, *Newsweek* magazine quoted Lieutenant General Frederick Weyand, commanding U.S. forces in III Corps area: "...The three enemy divisions that used to ring Saigon are now 80 and 90 miles away from the capital, where their targets are outside the key areas. ...The enemy can't suck me out of the populated areas now by attacking an outpost. We now have the strength to respond to such attacks and still maintain control of the population."[5]

Farther south, in IV Corps area, U.S.-ARVN forces also reported significant gains and claimed to be destroying one thousand Viet Cong guerrillas per month. Where once enemy units had proved elusive, contacts now were frequent: "...The units we fight now will break and run," says one general. "Two years ago you couldn't pry them out."[6] Particularly productive in this corps area were riverine warfare operations conducted by U. S. Navy personnel often in conjunction with American and Vietnamese ground units.

Similarly, large-scale "spoiling" operations in II Corps area, both along the coast and in the central highlands, were said to be keeping the enemy temporarily off balance. These sophisticated operations differed only in quantity and location from ones earlier discussed. American army operations continued in the two coastal provinces throughout summer and autumn. The correspondent Jonathan Schell found operations virtually unchanged from previous months. American army units continued to sweep hostile areas and to call in air and artillery strikes on suspect villages. Each operation strongly resembled the others; each depended on the quantitative approach that had now become the hallmark of American tactics.[7]

In October, enemy forces again became active in the northwest. To prevent them from seizing the provincial capital of Kontum, Westmoreland broke off coastal operations to fight a number of fierce actions in the vicinity of Dak To. Then, in mid-November, in III Corps area, in the south, two enemy regiments attacked an allied outpost at Loc Ninh, a town only nine miles from the Cambodian border, a fierce action that claimed 926 confirmed North Vietnamese dead, with another two or three thousand wounded. Another attack, against Dak To, was beaten back with five hundred Communist dead claimed; week-long fighting cost 177 American dead and 761 wounded, and 279 ARVN dead.[8] In early December, the enemy again attacked the base camp at Dak To, a vicious five-day battle that again resulted in heavy Communist casualties: 1,599 confirmed dead at a cost of 150 U.S. paratrooper lives and 250 wounded. Another attack, a week later, at Bo Duc was also beaten off.

In the North, in I Corps area, Walt's marines had been kept busy fighting three wars: one against main-force Viet Cong and PAVN units in and around the DMZ, one against VC units south of the DMZ, and finally, the "other war," that which involved protecting hamlets and villages while trying to win peasants to the government's side.

Marines fought the first war from a series of strong points designed to prevent infiltration south by PAVN units crossing the DMZ or entering from Laos. The effort involved screening enemy movements and harassing or disrupting them by ground action and/or artillery, air, and naval fire when possible. Although major fire fights continued to exact heavy enemy casualties, the enemy seemed no less strong, and as the year wore on, he began employing " . . . sophisticated Russian howitzers, artillery, mortars and rockets"—the result of increasing Soviet aid.[9] Action flared variously in the area, in general the marines reacting rather than acting. One marine strong point was at Khe Sanh, a scrubby, isolated combat base with airstrip, originally the home of a CIDG—some two hundred Vietnamese irregulars and Special Forces advisers.[10] A few miles from the Laotian border, the base was held by a reinforced company. As with other combat bases, Khe Sanh filled a dual role: Patrols constantly issued forth to observe and sometimes interdict enemy movement, and to respond, along with base supporting weapons, to calls from neighboring Combined Action units.

In April 1967, a marine patrol from Khe Sanh had set up an observation post on Hill 861, part of a nearby triangular terrain feature. Unknown to marines, elements of two PAVN regiments had been moving to these hills, presumably in preparation for an attack on Khe Sanh itself. When enemy attacked the marine patrol on Hill 861, a fire fight of major proportions developed, to culminate in a marine counteroffensive: violent assault and capture of Hills 861, 881 North, and 881 South, actions that reminded older marines of World War II operations. The twelve-day battle ended in a marine "victory" in that the PAVN regiments retired, having lost, according to marine figures, nine hundred lives with two or three that number wounded. Marine casualties numbered 138 dead and 397 wounded.[11]

An even more frustrating war continued against VC units south of the DMZ. Although marines fought this war with grim determination, they possessed neither tactics nor strength essential to clear and hold areas that, long since, had been dominated by VC cadres. Every time a quasi-conventional action developed in the DMZ area, the effort to the south suffered. In early spring of 1967, VC units were sufficiently strong to open a general offensive, shelling Hué and Da Nang and even over-running Quang Tri, while other units struck at pacification teams throughout the provinces.

VC gains led to important reorganization of the area. Marine units, now some seventy-five thousand strong, concentrated in the three northern provinces. South of them, a new army unit moved in, the Americal Division, whose four brigades were reinforced with a fifth, airmobile brigade. ARVN troops were increased to some thirty thousand, and units began fighting in conjunction with American troops. In June, Lieutenant General Robert Cushman, U. S. Marine Corps, replaced General Walt in command of III MAF, whose operational area had grown to over two thousand square miles in I Corps area (which comprised five provinces and some three million people and was commanded by Lieutenant General Huong Xuan Lam). In addition to troops listed above, the area held a Korean brigade, CIDG units, eighteen thousand American sailors, and seven thousand American airmen, not to mention countless civil and military advisers.

That summer and autumn, fast and furious actions continued to be fought throughout the long coastal area and in the north. In summer, marine and ARVN units began Operation Beau Charger, designed to root out VC forces in and south of the DMZ prior to making it a "free fire zone"—a complicated and costly task that, among other things, meant relocating some thirteen thousand civilians, to add to refugee hordes already crowding Da Nang and Hué.[12] In autumn, as engineers began surveying terrain as the first step in constructing McNamara's "fence" across the southern boundary of the DMZ, marine units fought frequent savage actions in defending strong points such as Cam Lo and Con Thien—"spoiling" operations that bore heavy price tags: In September alone, marine casualties totaled over twenty-two hundred.[13]

The scope of fighting, not only in I Corps area but throughout South Vietnam, is difficult to comprehend. By August 1967, marine units had mounted over three hundred thousand patrols—over 1,200 a day since early 1967—set 114,000 ambushes, and fought over two hundred battalion-size or larger actions. Marine fixed-wing aircraft had flown 128,000 missions; marine helicopters registered a total of 859,000 flights. At year's end, the claimed kill figure for I Corps area would reach thirty-eight thousand.[14]

Pacification also showed impressive gains. Of 219 villages (with a population exceeding 1.2 million) in the marine area, forty-three (with a population of five hundred thousand) were declared 80 per cent or more pacified by late autumn. ARVN units had been working in the area for over a year, and Combined Action Platoons now numbered seventy and were to expand to 114. Navy doctors attached to marine units had treated over two million Vietnamese, dentists over a hundred thousand. Marines had distributed over four million pounds of food, had helped build or rebuild a hundred schools and a hundred other buildings such as churches and dispensaries; they had dug over a hundred wells, built forty-nine bridges, and serviced four hundred miles of roads.[15] Pacification techniques were improving, as witness this account of an operation called County Fair:

> . . . A Marine unit in cooperation with Vietnamese units surrounds a hamlet or village usually before dawn and cordons it off to prevent anyone from leaving. After the people are assembled, Vietnamese officials with Marine support begin a series of actions to gain their confidence. A census is taken. A field dispensary is set up and medical attention given to those who need it. Sometimes a dentist accompanies the party. Meals are cooked and served. Lectures and movies are presented. A Marine band may play for an hour or so. Much of this activity takes place under canvas which probably accounts for the name County Fair. A careful house-to-house search is aimed at VC guerrillas and VC political personnel who may be part of the local cadre. . . . The County Fair technique has had excellent results and is now a routine type operation, although each one varies in its specifics.[16]

The marines also improved techniques in an attempt to repair intelligence deficiencies. A long-overdue step involved recruiting scouts from enemy defectors, the Kit Carson Scout Program, variations of which had proved so successful in Malaya and Kenya (see Chapters 46 and 52), indeed in the Philippines at the turn of the century (see Chapter 11). Marine intelligence officers recruited these people from Viet Cong and North Vietnamese who had surrendered under the Chieu Hoi program. After training, they were normally assigned in pairs to an infantry battalion deployed in search-and-destroy missions. The former enemy soldiers proved invaluable in detecting ambush sites and booby traps, and also in acting as interpreters. When possible, they were employed in areas where they were familiar with the terrain, people, and their former units. Marines initially procured fifty per division, later a hundred; the program was so successful that the army adopted it.

A complementary solution involved developing a unit's own scouts in the form of small, long-range patrols that came to be known as Sting Ray operations, similar to those practiced by a few enlightened army

VIETNAM 1967
• Towns and Cities
Zones C & D
▲ Iron Triangle

| 0 | 50 | 100 | 150 | 200 miles |

M.E.P.

units in the central highlands and the Mekong Delta. Such a patrol consisted of a few highly trained men equipped to find the enemy, then call in friendly air, artillery, or naval gunfire by radio. A patrol infiltrated either on foot or by helicopter operated normally for five days, gathering intelligence and employing disruptive tactics by establishing appropriate ambushes. If a fire fight developed unfavorably, a patrol sought to extricate itself either by guerrilla tactics of fading into the terrain, or by helicopter call-in; one enterprising marine lieutenant, when greatly outnumbered, ordered his men to don gas masks, then saturated the area with tear gas, which held off the enemy until helicopters arrived.

This same officer, who led patrols over a period of several months, obtained a final kill ratio of 226 confirmed VC dead to the loss of a few wounded marines, a figure he believed would have been five times greater had an assault company, controlling its own helicopter transport, been instantly available to exploit numerous chances for severely punishing observed enemy units.[17] Still another tactic involved two-man sniper teams that were especially trained to stake out a position and wait for opportunity. The 1st Marine Division claimed that, in eight months, its ninety snipers recorded over four hundred fifty confirmed kills against four marine dead. Called "13-cent killers," because of the price of a rifle cartridge, the tactic was carried out by some five hundred army and marine snipers during the year.[18]

Despite improved tactics and techniques, as autumn gave way to early winter, army and marine commanders continued to dance to the enemy's tune. As earlier noted, coastal pacification operations now yielded to meeting new enemy threats around Kontum. In the north, the Khe Sanh area had remained relatively quiet through summer and autumn, but, in October, enemy activity again increased. In November, General Cushman opened Operation Scotland and, by mid-December, had bolstered the small garrison with two reinforced battalions. At year's end, patrols were confirming heavy enemy build-up in western Quang Tri province in general and around Khe Sanh in particular.

Air and naval wars, both in- and out-country, also escalated, with thousands of sorties flown to drop thousands of tons of bombs and napalm and expend thousands of rockets and millions of rounds of ammunition. Naval-marine amphibious groups conducted twenty-three battalion-force landings along the South Vietnamese coast in 1967, which allegedly " . . . kept the enemy off balance, disrupted his logistical support, and denied him profitable coastal areas."[19] From June 1966 to July 1967, the Coastal Surveillance Force " . . . boarded or inspected over 500,000 watercraft" in an attempt to interrupt VC supply lines.[20] In-country naval operations in the Mekong Delta also expanded to involve water-borne search-and-destroy operations in conjunction with American army and ARVN units. Provisional reconnaissance units also appeared in the delta country; these were small groups of former VC guerrillas who had changed sides and were employed mostly as night raiders sent to attack VC camps and strongholds. Where camps could not be attacked, American planes attempted to uncover them and deprive them of food: During 1967, Ranch Hand planes " . . . dumped more than four million gallons of herbicide and defoliation chemicals on South Vietnam . . . four times the annual herbicide productive capacity of *all* American chemical companies."[21]

Simultaneously, the "other war" grew in size and complexity. In spring of 1967, the new American ambassador to South Vietnam, Ellsworth Bunker, once again reorganized the pacification program, at least from the American standpoint. Called now Civil Operations and Revolutionary Development Support (CORDS), it was headed by a deputy ambassador, former presidential aide Robert Komer, who administered it under MACV's jurisdiction with large amounts of funds going directly to the South Vietnamese government. The general idea was to coordinate military aspects, particularly security, which had always been a weak point, with civil aspects. During 1967, the Revolutionary Development program grew to some fifty-five thousand cadres, including nearly five hundred Revolutionary Development Teams. Their work was measured by Komer's people, using an elaborate computerized system called Hamlet Evaluation System (HES). Data furnished by U.S. advisers, who monthly reported on eighteen criteria, went into computers, which then graded villages anywhere from totally secure ("A") to VC-controlled ("V"). By year's end, Komer claimed that two thirds of the population lived under government control—" . . . only one South Vietnamese in six now lives under VC control."[22]

Administration voices also emphasized substantial political progress in South Vietnam. At Guam, in March, Thieu and Ky had unveiled their new constitution, a document heralded by President Johnson as slightly more important than the Magna Carta, particularly since he secretly exacted a pledge from the two Vietnamese not to break up the fragile South Vietnamese Government by reason of personal vendettas. Spring elections followed in about eight hundred villages and four thousand hamlets. An autumn presidential election placed Thieu in power, with Ky as vice-president; voters also elected a sixty-man senate and a 137-man house of representatives.

The Administration's line was clear: By continuing to pursue a winning strategy, the President was going to give the American people a well-deserved victory in South Vietnam. In various speeches around the United States, Lieutenant General Walt assured audiences that we were "winning" (at least in I Corps) and that it would be folly to stop now: " . . . wise or unwise, we have committed ourselves in Vietnam; weakness, vacillation, irresolution here at home are being paid for on the battlefields of Vietnam with the lives and blood of our fighting men."[23] MACV spokesmen in Saigon continued to report positive gains during the summer. In October, General Westmoreland told newsmen that " . . . the enemy is in the worst posture he has been in since the war started." Prior to leaving for Washington, in November, Westmoreland told newsmen that he was " . . . more encouraged than at any time since I arrived here."[24] Ambassador Bunker and Robert Komer, Bunker's pacification chief, reflected Westmoreland's optimism; indeed, according to *Time*, " . . . all three brimmed with confidence." At a White House meeting, Bunker told the President, " . . . It's going to be all right, Mr. President. Just let's keep on, keep on."[25] At President Johnson's request, Westmoreland addressed a joint session of Congress, which learned " . . . that the war was being won militarily. He outlined 'indicators' of progress and stated that a limited withdrawal of American combat forces might be undertaken beginning late in 1968."[26] As the year closed, President Johnson said, " . . . General Abrams tells me that the ARVN is as good as the Korean Army was in 1954."[27] At the turn of the year, Secretary of State Rusk spoke optimistically of " . . . a clear . . . turn of events on the ground."

Although the President wrote in his memoirs that the tactical situation was very crucial at this time, and that he had warned of "kamikaze tactics" to come, the record does not show that he disapproved of Westmoreland's strategy or was in any mind to heed warning voices. Shortly before the new year, he stated that the Communists " . . . can't point to one single victory" in Vietnam. His State of the Union address in January 1968 implied satisfactory progress, with more to come. General Westmoreland's annual report, delivered on January 27, included the following paragraph:

> . . . Interdiction of the enemy's logistics train in Laos and NVN [North Vietnam] by our indispensable air efforts has imposed significant difficulties on him. In many areas the enemy has been driven away from the population centers; in others he has been compelled to disperse and evade contact, thus nullifying much of his potential. The year ended with the enemy increasingly resorting to desperation tactics in attempting to achieve military/psychological victory; and he has experienced only failure in these attempts.[28]

CHAPTER SIXTY-SEVEN

1. Johnson, *Public Papers of . . .*, 1967, Book I, 12.
2. The letters are published in *Survival,* June 1967.
3. Hoopes, 57.
4. Johnson, *The Vantage Point . . .*, 258.
5. *Newsweek,* January 1, 1968.
6. Ibid.
7. Schell, 35 ff.
8. *Reuters,* Saigon, November 16, 1967. See also, Shaplen, *The Road from War,* for details of these actions.
9. Shaplen, "Viet-Nam: Crisis of Indecision."
10. Walt, "Khe Sanh—The Battle That Had to Be Won."
11. U.S. Marine Corps, "The Battle for Hills 861 and 881." See also, Corson, 72, who cites 155 dead and 425 wounded.
12. Corson, 69.
13. *Time,* October 6, 1967.
14. *Newsweek,* January 1, 1968.

15. U.S. Marine Corps, "III MAF Force . . . " See also, Wagner.
16. McCutcheon. See also, Walt, *Strange War, Strange Strategy.*
17. Private information in the author's files. See also, Asprey, "Guerrilla Warfare"; ibid., "Tactics"; West.
18. *Time,* October 27, 1967.
19. Department of the Navy.
20. U.S. Navy.
21. Corson, 76.
22. *Newsweek,* January 1, 1968. See also, Snepp, 12.
23. Walt, "Our Purpose in Vietnam." See also, ibid., "Are We Winning the War in Vietnam?"
24. *Time,* November 17, 1967.
25. Ibid., November 24, 1967.
26. Kissinger, "The Viet Nam Negotiations." See also, Johnson, *The Vantage Point . . . ,* 376: Westmoreland told the President that his "central purpose" over the next two years was to transfer additional responsibility to the South Vietnamese. Westmoreland, the President wrote, " . . . was convinced that within that time—that is, by the end of 1969—we could safely begin withdrawing American forces."
27. Corson, 103.
28. Sheehan et al., 593.

CHAPTER 68

More blurs on the canvas • Allied losses • Failure of Operation Rolling Thunder (II) • The numbers game • Westmoreland wants more troops (III) • John McNaughton: "... A feeling is widely and strongly held that 'the Establishment' is out of its mind." • McNamara's new policy paper • The President's middle course • Increasing American costs (II) • MACV headquarters: "Disneyland East" • Senior commanders' life-style • The fallacy of attrition warfare • The other war • Have we killed all the enemy? • Failure of the Revolutionary Development program • Komer's "indicators" • South Vietnam's government corruption • Failure of land reform • Electoral restrictions and irregularities • Increasing opposition to the war at home and abroad • Press and TV coverage The experts dissent • The Clifford mission • Johnson's San Antonio offer • Thwackum and Square

As WESTMORELAND'S OPERATIONAL CANVAS expanded in 1967, the blurs that had appeared in 1966 grew more prominent. Physical losses and financial cost sharply increased. During 1967, nine thousand Americans were killed in Vietnam and over sixty thousand were wounded, to make cumulative totals of about sixteen thousand dead and one hundred thousand wounded since 1961.[1] Other allies lost fifteen hundred killed. South Vietnamese deaths were reported at sixty thousand, of which ten thousand were ARVN deaths. Steadily improving anti-aircraft defenses in the North exacted increasing toll of aircraft. In December, an official American spokesman put cumulative U.S. losses at 1,822 planes and 1,416 helicopters.[2]

The air offensive was proving no more effective than in 1966, despite official claims to the contrary. Testifying before a Senate subcommittee in August 1967, Robert McNamara pointed out that North Vietnam had the capacity to import fourteen thousand tons of supply per day, but was importing only fifty-eight hundred tons. North Vietnam and Viet Cong forces in the South, he told senators, required under one hundred tons of supply per day from the North.[3] American air power was not preventing this small amount from reaching the enemy, nor would it do so. Townsend Hoopes later wrote that, by October 1967, " . . . the cold, unhypothetical fact remained that the flow of men and supplies from North Vietnam to South Vietnam had definitely increased in absolute terms."[4]

Almost incessant bombing, far from breaking Hanoi's will, was cementing its intransigence and was drawing increasing criticism, from critics within and without the United States. As in previous years, it continued to frustrate well-intentioned efforts by intermediaries to bring both sides to a conference table. Prime Minister Wilson of Great Britain was particularly offended by Johnson's attitude in February during behind-the-scenes negotiations. Wilson ascribed the hard-line attitude to "mentally confused" hawks and later wrote, undoubtedly with Rostow in mind, " . . . The more I saw of certain White House advisers, the more I thought Rasputin was a much maligned man."[5]

Despite official claims that enemy units could not win a major tactical victory in the South and could not maintain main-force units close to cities, the Viet Cong seemed more active than ever, while PAVN forces continued to call the play in the highlands and in the North. MACV's claims of some eighty thousand enemy dead and three or four times that number wounded in 1967 seemed irrelevant in that the enemy apparently had ample human resources and ammunition, not to mention open supply lines from both China and the U.S.S.R. and to the South. VC terrorists murdered 3,820 people, double the count for 1966; nearly six thousand Southerners were kidnaped as part of a determined effort to display continuing strength in and control of specific areas. If enemy morale suffered, as captured soldiers attested and as MACV claimed while pointing to twenty-five thousand deserters, it did not show in determined fighting, whether in defense or attack. Confusion as usual obfuscated MACV figures. This headquarters had stated in 1966 that 280,000 enemy were fighting in South Vietnam; in 1967, the figure had risen to 378,000, a dramatic increase scarcely in keeping with official claims of enemy casualties and one weakly explained in Saigon as owing to a new method of calculating enemy strength.

The new figures brought further dissension among President Johnson's close circle of advisers and officials. To regain the "tactical initiative," Westmoreland requested more troops: a "minimum essential force" of about one hundred thousand; an "optimum force" of about two hundred thousand, which would have meant a total of some 670,000 Americans in South Vietnam. The JCS passed this request on, with favorable endorsement, to McNamara. The JCS in turn proposed

> ... the mobilization of the reserves, a major new troop commit-
> ment in the South, an extension of the war into the VC/NVA sanc-
> tuaries (Laos, Cambodia and possibly North Vietnam), the mining
> of North Vietnamese ports and a solid commitment in manpower
> and resources to a military victory. The recommendation not un-
> surprisingly touched off a searching reappraisal of the course of
> U.S. strategy in the war.[6]

In late April, Westmoreland returned to the United States to argue his case before the President. According to notes made by John McNaughton, Lyndon Johnson was not pleased at future prospects:

> ... When asked about the influence of increased infiltration upon
> his operations the general [Westmoreland] replied that as he saw
> it "this war is action and counteraction. Anytime we take an action
> we expect a reaction." The President replied: "When we add di-
> visions can't the enemy add divisions? If so, where does it all end?"

Westmoreland explained that, with the minimum increase he requested, the war could continue for three years; with the maximum increase, for two years. General Earle G. Wheeler, the hawkish chairman of the Joint Chiefs of Staff warned that American troops would possibly have to invade Cambodia, Laos, and North Vietnam; he also pointed out that the air effort had nearly run out of targets and would have to be extended to port areas.[7]

Almost no ranking civilian official agreed with the proposed new and aggressive strategy. Townsend Hoopes, who had been promoted to Under Secretary of the Air Force, argued that, despite American bombing, Hanoi, " ... in absolute terms," was sending more, not fewer, men and materials to the South. He himself had concluded " ... that the Administration's Vietnam policy had become a quietly spreading disaster from which vital U.S. interests could be retrieved only if the policy were reversed or drastically altered."[8] William Bundy argued strongly against extending ground operations to North Vietnam, " ... asserting that the odds were 75 to 25 that it would provoke Chinese Communist intervention."[9] He also warned that an attack on northern ports could bring Soviet counteraction, a position supported by CIA reports. A call-up of reserves, in Bundy's opinion, was to be avoided for domestic political reasons. Walt Rostow, theretofore as hawkish as the generals, did not agree with mining North Vietnamese harbors or bombing ports; in his opinion, this would make Hanoi more dependent on China and would increase United States tensions with the Soviet Union and China.[10] Instead, he wanted to concentrate the air effort " . . . on the 'bottom of the funnel,' the lines of communication and infiltration routes in southern North Vietnam and through Laos. . . . "[11] Dr. Alain Enthoven, Assistant Secretary of Defense for Systems Analysis, held that the requested troop increases would not produce proportionate enemy casualties:

> . . . On the most optimistic basis, 200,000 more Americans would raise [the enemy's] weekly losses to about 3,700, or about 400 a week more than they could stand. In theory we'd wipe them out in 10 years.[12]

John McNaughton, slated to become Secretary of the Navy, was equally firm. Hoopes described him at this time as

> . . . physically exhausted and deeply disenchanted with the Administration's Vietnam policy . . . [he was] appalled by the catastrophic loss of proportion that had overtaken the U.S. military effort in Vietnam. "We seem to be proceeding," he said to me in barbed tones, after returning from a particular White House session, "on the assumption that the way to eradicate Viet Cong is to destroy all the village structures, defoliate all the jungles, and then cover the entire surface of South Vietnam with asphalt."[13]

McNaughton wanted the air war shifted to lines of communication south of the 20th parallel, a definite cutback, designed primarily to save American pilots and planes; any significant troop increase was merely " . . . more of the same" and would resolve nothing. In early May, McNaughton advised McNamara (belatedly)

> . . . that the "philosophy" of the war should be fought out now so everyone will not be proceeding on their own major premises, and getting us in deeper and deeper; at the very least, the President should give General Westmoreland his limit (as President Truman did to General MacArthur). That is, if General Westmoreland is to get 550,000 men, he should be told, "That will be all, and we mean it."

McNaughton, who was to die shortly in an air crash, continued:

> . . . A feeling is widely and strongly held that "the Establishment" is out of its mind. The feeling is that we are trying to impose some U.S. image on distant peoples we cannot understand (any more than we can the younger generation here at home), and we are carrying the thing to absurd lengths.

Related to this feeling is the increased polarization that is taking place in the United States with seeds of the worst split in our people in more than a century.[14]

On the basis of these and other arguments, Robert McNamara submitted a major policy paper to President Johnson which recommended a scaling down of the air effort and very limited troop increases.[15] Even more important, he recommended that the ambitions enunciated by President Kennedy and carried on by President Johnson in National Security Action Memorandum 288 be changed to reasonable political goals. He attempted first to quiet unreasonable fears by abolishing the domino theory he himself had once embraced. He went on in words made the more intelligent, bold, and courageous in that they reflected his own reversal of thought at a time when the President was embracing force more than fact:

> ... The time has come for us to eliminate the ambiguities from our minimum objectives—our commitments—in Vietnam. Specifically, two principles must be articulated, and policies and actions brought in line with them: (1) Our commitment is only to see that the people of South Vietnam are permitted to determine their own future. (2) This commitment ceases if the country ceases to help itself.
>
> It follows that no matter how much we might *hope* for some things, our *commitment* is *not:*
> —to expel from South Vietnam regroupees [Viet Cong], who are South Vietnamese (though we do not like them),
> —to ensure that a particular person or group remains in power, nor that the power runs to every corner of the land (though we prefer certain types and we hope their writ will run throughout South Vietnam),
> —to guarantee that the self-chosen government is non-Communist (though we believe and strongly hope it will be), and
> —to insist that the independent South Vietnam remain separate from North Vietnam (though in the short-run, we would prefer it that way). (Nor do we have an obligation to pour in effort out of proportion to the effort contributed by the people of South Vietnam or in the face of coups, corruption, apathy or other indications of Saigon failure to co-operate effectively with us.) We *are* committed to stopping or offsetting the effect of North Vietnam's application of force in the South, which denies the people of the South the ability to determine their own future. Even here, however, the line is hard to draw. Propaganda and political advice by Hanoi (or by Washington) is presumably not barred; nor is economic aid or economic advisors. Less clear is the rule to apply to military advisors and war matériel supplied to the contesting factions.

The importance of nailing down and understanding the implications of our limited objectives cannot be overemphasized. It relates intimately to strategy against the North, to troop requirements and missions in the South, to handling of the Saigon government, to settlement terms, and to US domestic and international opinion as to the justification and the success of our efforts on behalf of Vietnam.[16]

McNamara, in effect, was recommending a dramatic shift to viable policy; he was recognizing (after a long hiatus) that South Vietnam was a "strategic convenience" and should be treated as such. If it could be held with a limited effort, fine; but its retention was not worth a world war and was not worth a deepening schism inside the U.S.A. If the South Vietnamese could not come to terms with themselves, the country would be "lost" and could be "lost" without undue damage to American interests in Southeast Asia (which had never "owned" it, to start with). McNamara recognized that he was asking the President to adopt a difficult course of action, which would be sharply criticized and possibly would cause a government crisis in South Vietnam: " . . . Not least will be the alleged impact on the reputation of the United States and of its President. Nevertheless, the difficulties of this strategy are fewer and smaller than the difficulties of any other approach."[17]

President Johnson did not agree with Secretary McNamara, and this document probably marks the beginning of McNamara's decline and fall from presidential grace. Indeed, the Secretary allegedly offered to resign at this time. His own doubts were reflected the following month, when he commissioned what since has become known as the Pentagon report—a highly secret attempt to explain how and why the United States became and remained involved in South Vietnam.

Neither did the President altogether agree with hawks who refuted McNamara's conclusions and recommendations with practiced fervor and ability similar to those of Viet Cong agit-prop agents. Although he refused to alter what he liked to call Administration policy, he did not authorize troop increases requested by Westmoreland, Sharp, and the JCS. Instead, he sent McNamara to Saigon to work out still another compromise with Westmoreland. Early in August, he announced an increase of fifty-five thousand troops, to bring total American commitment to 525,000. He did, however, authorize expanding the air war to include targets in Hanoi and in the China buffer zone.[18]

The war was also costing more and more money. Direct war expenditures totaled $24–27 billion in 1967 and billions more in indirect costs. Part of the expense was due to the technology of war as Amer-

879

icans fought it. Airplanes, helicopters, APCs, self-propelled artillery, tanks, vast naval armadas, all cost a great deal of money to manufacture, maintain and replace if destroyed. Part of the expense stemmed from the vast logistics effort which tied up some 80 per cent of the armed forces in supporting about 20 per cent of combat troops. This shameful situation started in Saigon or rather in the U. S. Army and MACV headquarters (the latter known to the field troops as "Disneyland East"), each of which was "incredibly plush," the home of hordes of rear-echelon commandos (known to the field troops as "rear-echelon motherfuckers"), all wearing pressed jungle fatigues and new canvas boots, all drawing the same combat pay as the guys getting wounded and killed.[19] It continued in Field Force or Corps headquarters. David Hackworth described Lieutenant General Julian Ewell's generals' mess as

> ... the most lavish I'd ever seen ... he had a very large general staff, all of whom, when I arrived, were in the middle of their cocktail hour, mingling with martinis in perfectly starched jungle fatigues and camouflage scarves, a million miles away from the war of the grunt, which ran along unabated just beyond the berm of Long Binh's base camp.[20]

It was the prodigal life-style familiar to senior allied and German command headquarters on the western front in World War I. It carried to other base camps such as that at Di An where Hackworth

> ... was assigned to share an air-conditioned bungalow (complete with a bar in the corner of the living room and a full-time Viet maid who kept shoes polished, clothes washed and pressed, and beds made with perfectly starched white sheets ... [The assistant division commander] emerged from his room each morning wearing pajamas and a dressing gown ...[21]

Senior officers and important visitors at the 1st Air Cavalry headquarters, An Khe, lived in Hilton-standard suites:

> ... throughout each evening's three course, five-star quality gourmet meal (presented on fine china embossed with the Cav insignia and served by black waiters in white starched jackets ... [with] after-dinner cigars, liqueurs, coffee and conversation ...[22]

Finally, a large portion of the logistics burden stemmed from Westmoreland's quantitative strategy whereby commanders defended vast ammunition expenditures on grounds of saving lives. At Dak To in November a *single* B-52 raid dropped one hundred and fifty thousand pounds of bombs,[23] " . . . a million-dollar strike . . . responsible for some [estimated] two hundred enemy casualties."[24] Put another way: The official claim of 1,644 enemy killed depended in part " . . . on 2096 air strikes (about one and a half air strikes per enemy dead), and the expenditure of 151,000 rounds of artillery (92 rounds per enemy dead) . . . "[25] Thus the battle of Dak To in which 344 American soldiers were killed (twenty by "friendly" aerial bombing) and 1,441 wounded,[26] scarcely a satisfactory ratio so long as Ho Chi Minh was willing to lose ten of his men for one of the enemy. Jonathan Schell summed up a search-and-destroy operation up north, not a particularly big one, in which an armored brigade in two weeks destroyed an estimated 65 per cent of the houses of perhaps seventeen thousand natives in the Chu Lai area:

> . . . On August 28th, when Operation Benton came to a close, Task Force Oregon announced that the troops taking part in it had killed, and counted the bodies of, three hundred and ninety-seven of the enemy, and that forty-seven American soldiers had been killed. Into an area of ten by twenty kilometres they had dropped 282 tons of "general-purpose" bombs and 116 tons of napalm; fired 1,005 rockets (not counting rockets fired from helicopters), 132,820 rounds of 20-mm. explosive strafing shells, and 119,350 7.62-mm. rounds of machine-gun fire from Spooky flights; and fired 8,488 artillery rounds. By the end of the operation, the Civil Affairs office had supervised the evacuation of six hundred and forty of the area's seventeen thousand people, to the vicinity of government camps.[27]

During the twelve-day battle for Hills 861 and 881, in the marine area, gunners fired over eighteen thousand artillery rounds,[28] tactical aircraft dropped 1,375 tons of bombs, and B-52 aircraft dropped 1,750 tons of bombs.[29] Small-unit commanders relied on supporting artillery and aircraft fire as probably no commanders in history. The "mad minute" became standard operating procedure in many units. In the Vietnam version of this World War I tactic, at first light the unit fired every available weapon for at least sixty seconds, the theory being to disrupt an attack *in case* the enemy had infiltrated "close in" during the night. If on occasion it scored a major hit, this was rare enough. Had the U.S. forces been fighting the war correctly, the tactic would not have been necessary except on singular occasion. American supporting arms, particularly from warships and B-52 bombers, responded to later Communist attacks of Con Thien with what Westmoreland called the heaviest concentration of firepower " . . . on any single piece of real estate in the history of warfare."[30]

Most accounts of army and marine operations in this period stress use of supporting weapons employed by commanders to rectify tactical disadvantages caused by inadequate intelligence. Spoiling tactics were scarcely the precise operations implied by MACV; for the most part, they were "encounter" battles often initiated and almost always broken off by the enemy when he wished. Valiant as was the American effort to hold defensive outposts or "capture" prominences, it didn't really solve anything. It proved once again that an enemy was hard put to stand against either a determined defense backed by co-ordinated supporting fires (the major tactical lesson of the 1905 Russo–Japanese War and of World War I) or against a determined offense also backed by co-ordinated supporting fires (the major tactical lesson of World War II)—but in South Vietnam damage inflicted on the enemy was scarcely decisive, particularly when that enemy held ample reserves and reasonably secure lines of communication.

These actions continued to demonstrate the fallacy of American attrition strategy. So long as American commanders lacked good intelligence (that could only come from the locals), they would have to fight in the most expensive possible way. Trumpeted to the world as American "victories," encounter battles, in view of cost in human lives and suffering and in material versus tactical results did little more than illustrate the truth of an ancient axiom: " . . . from no victory shall the ass's kick be missing." Or, as Captain Roeder had put it while watching Napoleon's army invade Russia: " . . . Every victory is a loss to us."

It was so unnecessary. History repeatedly had shown its basic fallacy. Why did American commanders, faced with unpalatable facts, keep insisting that this was the way to "win" the war? Why had no attention been paid to the prognoses of such professionals as Matthew Ridgway, Roger Hilsman, and James Gavin? The crime is compounded by the fact that a few commanders, realizing the error of doctrinaire ways, successfully revised their thinking to fashion valid small-unit tactics and, in the case of such as Colonel Henry Emerson, to reach tactical parity with the professional guerrilla. Early in 1967, David Hackworth discovered that General Willard Pearson, commanding an airborne brigade at Phan Rang, had developed what he called " . . . "semiguerrilla" tactics—stealth, deception, and surprise, units infiltrating the battlefield at night and without the use of choppers or accompanying H&I [harassing and interdicting fire]." These economy of force tactics resulted in outambushing the enemy with commensurate rewards: in one instance a fifteen-man ambush team " . . . killed nineteen NVA, took one prisoner and eighteen weapons for no casualties of their own"; in another instance they gained a " . . . very high weapon-to-body count ratio (143 weapons . . . to 149 enemy dead) . . . [plus] seventy-six prisoners."[31]

Claimed enemy casualties were increasingly dubious. Marine commanders would have been hard put to explain the discrepancy between a claim of 28,455 "confirmed enemy dead" and 3,952 weapons captured. American army claims were rendered suspect not alone by various factors discussed in earlier chapters, but by tactical surprises such as that at Bo Duc in early December. The previous month, at Loc Ninh, Major General John Hays' 1st Infantry Division claimed to have inflicted almost 50 per cent casualties on the two regiments of the 9th VC Division, with Hays predicting " . . . that it would be three to six months before the 9th VC Division . . . would be able to fight in force again."[32] One of the "decimated" regiments attacked at Bo Duc less than a month later. Granting that enemy casualties were heavy, the enemy nonetheless initiated the actions that caused the casualties—and for good reason. His attacks in the central highlands caused Westmoreland to divert units from pacification operations in the coastal provinces. His continued presence in and around the DMZ, his attacks at Khe Sanh and Con Thien, his continued probes in the general area—all slowed marine pacification efforts by causing General Cushman to commit battalions and resources needed for pacification duties, and by adding to a refugee flow that, in late 1967, numbered some five hundred thousand in I Corps area alone.

Thus we return to the other war. Despite the barrage of statistics fired by MACV and III MAF at all visitors, pacification was not going well anywhere. The marines in I Corps area erred in several respects. As elsewhere in South Vietnam, search-and-destroy tactics continued to antagonize people who had to be won over. Marines were operating in a vast sea of fear that could easily turn to hatred, and frequent fire fights, no matter how carefully conducted, could not but exacerbate the situation—moving bullets are promiscuous. Marine bands could play, and marines could distribute food and clothing, and doctors could help villagers, but these advantages paled when one, two, or more villagers were killed in a fire fight or by bombs, rockets, naval shells, or napalm. Marines attempted to prevent this in two ways: either to evacuate villages or to help them to protect themselves. In 1967, nearly three hundred thousand of half a million refugees were living in hastily constructed camps, sometimes in appalling conditions. Far from being rehabilitated and trained for the day when they could return to their hamlets, they were fortunate to survive, considering the rapacious officialdom that surrounded them. Since numerous Viet Cong agents accompanied refugee groups, the camps presented a bewildering security problem, as did 176 villages that were under 80 per cent pacified.

In attempting to protect villages, marines erred by trying to do the job themselves: Marines could hold "county fairs" until doomsday, but,

883

unless carried to fruition, they were not only meaningless but dangerous, in that they brought forward either friendly or potentially friendly villagers who were subsequently exposed to VC wrath. Nothing was new about the county-fair technique; Lyautey used almost an identical procedure, but Lyautey was smart enough to back it with reasonably honest administration that improved tribal life, at least initially. Moving in government development teams too often subjected villagers to rents and various forms of squeeze that soon neutralized attendant advantages. As far as the psychological approach went, the Viet Cong did it better: Few Vietnamese peasants would prefer to hear a marine band in preference to Vietnamese acting out dramas and operas in their own tongue and their own cultural traditions. Although marines made better progress in pacification than either the American army or ARVN, their program left considerable to be desired, and, in view of South Vietnamese civil and military corruption, it is doubtful if it would ever have succeeded. One of the most tragic cameos to come from I Corps area is this, related by a senior marine intelligence officer:

> ... one day [in 1966] the commanding general remarked to me, "We've been doing well lately. Don't you think we are now really eliminating the enemy? Haven't we just about killed them all?" Looking out the window, I thought of the hundreds of thousands of peasants living on that vast rice plain; of the patient and thorough way in which a highly-motivated enemy for decades had been organizing that society at all levels. I answered only, "No, sir. We haven't killed all the enemy."[33]

The pacification effort elsewhere in South Vietnam caused the largest blur to occur on Westmoreland's operational canvas. The reader may remember that one reason for an extensive American build-up was to replace ARVN combat units with American units, so that ARVN could reorganize while undertaking the major task of protecting the pacification program. This program worried the enemy more than any other action, because, where it worked, it seriously challenged his presence. Unfortunately, it did not work in many places. Although the Revolutionary Development program had expanded drastically during 1967 under Robert Komer's aegis, the performance of ARVN units assigned to protect the teams proved disappointing, and VC terrorism increased substantially in some areas during the year. Increased South Vietnamese control of funds and materials added to already widespread corruption to further hinder the program's effectiveness. Despite widespread failures noted and reported by a host of observers, Komer continued to claim substantial progress based on "indicators" that, like those used by the American military, were not always pertinent to a counterinsurgency situation. A particularly hostile critic of Komer, William Corson, later wrote concerning one of CORDS's projects:

> ... When the General Accounting Office (GAO) reviewed AID/ CORDS stewardship of the funds for War Relief and Support [about $70–75 million annually], it was not misled by Komer's reports. Under Komer, progress is indicated by the amount of money pushed into the hands of the GVN. However, the GAO noted that in the October 1967 report only one out of ten "scheduled" houses had been rebuilt, one out of eight "New Life" hamlets constructed, one out of nine public-health sanitation facilities erected, and more than half of the refugees had received *no* assistance. Senator Edward Kennedy, in commenting on the GAO report, said that the findings "show that the refugee program and the medical program in South Vietnam are a scandal." ... [34]

Komer also claimed substantial progress in regaining control of hamlets, his indicator here being the Hamlet Evaluation Estimate program. But William Lederer noted that " ... the evaluation of the conditions in approximately 13,000 hamlets is made by U. S. Army officers who are advisers to Vietnamese district chiefs. They send in Hamlet Evaluations monthly. I estimate that 99 percent of the U. S. Army advisers have neither language facility nor the knowledge of Vietnamese culture to know what is happening in their own district." Lederer continued:

> ... I have seen samples of the Hamlet Evaluation Estimates sent to headquarters by U. S. Army advisers. These estimates are fraudulent, or, to be charitable, they are distorted with errors. Under the present system they can be no other way. It is not only that the U. S. advisers and their interpreters are intellectually and culturally unable to make accurate estimates, but the taint of dishonesty has swept through the entire United States government reporting system in Vietnam. This pollution sinks down from the top. In Washington, Walt Rostow (who advises President Johnson) suggests—sometimes even insists—that his colleagues deemphasize unfavorable facts. Occasionally when his assistants refuse to alter facts Rostow goes into tantrums. Once he threw a water pitcher at a colonel who showed that Rostow's figures were biased. Unwillingness to face unwelcome facts has spread throughout the government, and it has of course reached Saigon and down to the Army advisers in remote South Vietnamese districts.[35]

A RAND analyst, Konrad Kellen, included the pacification program as one of eleven American fallacies,

... aside from the fact that Pacification is impossible because our Pacification aims and methods are unacceptable to the people in the Vietnamese countryside, there is another aspect to this which makes Pacification a doubly impossible aim: the choice of Americans entrusted with it. ... One need only to have met a member of AID and Army representatives to know that all these men, despite their great goodwill, and ample knowledge of local detail, can never do anything but confuse and antagonize any foreign population, and disorganize, if not destroy, its social fabric. And there are no other men to do the job, which cannot be done in the first place.[36]

The people who should have taken on the pacification task, the South Vietnamese, could not accomplish it owing to government inefficiency, pervasive corruption, and lack of individual will or even desire. Horrified U. S. senators learned that only half of an estimated four million refugees received the fourteen ounces of rice and five cents a day that the South Vietnamese Government was supposed to be providing—at U.S. expense. The same report alleged that numerous refugees never received a $42 resettlement allowance and a six-month rice supply.[37] One American official, John Vann, senior adviser in IV Corps area, " ... managed to have 75 GVN officials removed for corruption, only to find all of them reinstated within six months in equal or better jobs."[38] William Lederer was informed by one knowledgeable Vietnamese that the black market in South Vietnam involved about $10 *billion* a year, all American goods and moneys, an incredible situation that " ... could not exist without American collusion." He described a visit to a black-market warehouse in Saigon:

> ... The place looked like a U. S. Army Ordnance Depot. Everything seemed to be painted brown and to smell of either oil or fresh paint. Ordnance equipment was arranged in orderly lines, and neatly printed price tags hung from everything. Automatic rifles were $250. A 105 mm mortar ... was priced at $400. ... There were about a thousand American rifles of different kinds standing neatly in racks. M16s cost $80. On one side of the loft were uniforms of all services. ...

So much American military transport had been stolen, that " ... the American military has been renting its own stolen jeeps from black-market operators at $250 a month. The same double indignity and multiple cost applies to U.S. government trucks." Lederer pointed out that, in three years, South Vietnam's gold reserves increased from $130 to $450 million (all at American expense) and that, according to Swiss and Chinese informants, approximately $18 *billion* " ... has been sent to foreign banks by private Vietnamese individuals since 1956. Not so long ago, Madame Nhu, through a silent partner, purchased outright the second largest bank in Paris, for cash."[39]

The same blatant corruption pervaded the pacification program. Land reform remained a bad joke. As two congressmen, John Moss and Ogden Reid, informed Secretary of State Dean Rusk in December 1967, " . . . Land distribution in South Vietnam has been at a virtual standstill since 1962." Their letter continued:

> . . . Of 2.47 million acres acquired by the Government of Vietnam only 667,000 acres have been distributed to 128,000 families since 1954, including 51,800 acres to 12,000 families in 1967.
> Of 566,000 acres of choice rice land acquired by the government in 1958 from French owners, 240,000 have been rented to small farmers, but no actual distribution was made until October 1966, eight years after the land was expropriated. . . . [40]

Landlords frequently violated rent-control laws. Although limited by law to paying 25 per cent of the principal crop as maximum rent, " . . . four out of five peasants pay a land rent equal to more than fifty per cent of the crop because there is no valid attempt to enforce the provisions of the land-rent law."[41]

Aid programs similarly suffered: Almost without exception, South Vietnamese officials and ARVN officers sold food and material to hamlets and villages, a shocking corruption freely admitted by American personnel in the field and in Saigon.[42] The political progress applauded by MACV and embassy spokesmen was in many ways meaningless. Townsend Hoopes later wrote that American efforts to produce a South Vietnamese constitution and elections had resulted only in continuing military rule.[43]

Thus despite escalation, despite increasing costs in lives and money, despite official optimism, the U.S.A. and South Vietnam were no closer to "winning" the war than ever and, in some respects, were even farther from this ambition. President Johnson's expressed determination to persevere unto "victory" was also in jeopardy. *Ramparts,* an outspoken, militant anti-Vietnam periodical, reached a U.S. circulation of three hundred thousand in 1967.[44] Increasingly influential and strident voices were questioning not only the conduct but the very *raison d'être* of the war. In February 1967, Noam Chomsky's explosive essay, "The Responsibility of Intellectuals," appeared in the *New York Review of Books* and thereafter was widely circulated—one of the " . . . key documents in the intellectual resistance to the Vietnam War,"[45] in that it called for the nation's intellectuals, who passively opposed American participation in the war, to become *engagé*—in David Schalk's term—and even *embrigadé* or counterlegal if necessary " . . . to speak the truth and to expose lies."[46] In this watershed essay, Chomsky blasted such "establishment intellectuals" as Arthur Schlesinger, Jr., Walt W. Rostow, McGeorge Bundy, and Henry Kissinger

> ... for their abandonment of the critical role that should fall to them because of their privileged status. These academics who had entered politics displayed a kind of "hypocritical moralism" that hid American imperialism with pieties and masked and apologized for aggression, especially American aggression in Vietnam.[47]

Other influential voices added to the fire of protest, a debate characterized in British Prime Minister Harold Wilson's words by " ... great passion, great feeling, and great emotion." In early 1967, Walter Lippmann challenged the desire of such Congressional hawks as Mendel Rivers " ... to flatten Hanoi if necessary and let world opinion go fly a kite." If the United States adopted genocide as a national policy, Lippmann wrote, it would find itself dangerously isolated. It would not only earn the suspicion and hatred of neutrals but even of allies: " ... We would come to be regarded as the most dangerous nation in the world, and the great powers of the world would align themselves accordingly to contain us." The President, Lippmann went on, found himself confronted

> ... with the agonizing fact that limited war has not worked because *limited war can be effective only for limited objectives.* The reason why the President is confronted with the demand for unlimited war is that he has escalated his objectives in Vietnam to an unlimited degree.[48]

In April anywhere from a quarter of a million to a million antiwar demonstrators in New York marched from Central Park to the United Nations Plaza—the "spring demonstration" that horrified the White House and Congress. In June, a petition called "Individuals Against the Crime of Silence," holding that the war was immoral and illegal, stated that " ... the conscience of America is not dead."[49] More and more American citizens believed that Lyndon Johnson had lost control of the situation—that the praying mantis of earlier portraits had become a preying menace to common sense. Businessmen were speaking up and so were some congressmen. Capable journalists were continuing to report adversely, their copy often reflecting dissident views of American civil and military officials, particularly at lower levels, with official policy. TV coverage of battle areas increasingly brought home the agony of war in all forms. What some American officials called distorted camera coverage in reality emphasized the stupidity of search-and-destroy tactics and, at the same time, questioned optimistic claims of military spokesmen. Embarrassed Administration officials continued to blame press and television correspondents for twisting news, an accusation frequently implied by President Johnson and one that scarcely modified the growing antagonism between press and government. Although a few correspondents did allow personal emotion to overcome objective reporting, a great many did not, and the Administration erred grievously in attempting to cast doubt on the veracity of many courageous and intelligent observers whose analyses often contained constructive criticism.

In October, still another anti-war petition signed by such well-known dissenters as the Jesuit priest Philip Berrigan, Noam Chomsky, Herbert Marcuse, Edgar Snow, and Dr. Benjamin Spock appeared in the *New Republic* and the *New York Review of Books,* the petitioners asserting that the war was unconstitutional and illegal and that American troops were indulging in "crimes against humanity."[50] The famous march on the Pentagon followed to further embarrass the Administration.

Interested and experienced observers such as Generals Gavin, Ridgway, and Shoup added to the criticism, as did portions of the business world—thenceforth, the BEM (Business Executives Move for Peace in Vietnam), whose military board included one of the United States' few genuine guerrilla-warfare experts, Brigadier General Sam Griffith, would become increasingly influential and, through its publication, *Washington Watch,* hostile to Administration policy. Other new voices were heard: In mid-November, General Lauris Norstad, former NATO chief and subsequently a top business executive, told a Los Angeles audience that Washington should seriously consider such moves as an unconditional halt of bombing and unilateral cease-fire in South Vietnam if these would move Hanoi to the conference table.[51]

Writing in the *New York Times,* John Kenneth Galbraith pointed to a shifting tide of feeling within the United States and within Congress:

> ... I next assume that public opinion in the United States has turned very strongly against the war—and especially against those who hope to bring it to a military solution. The public opinion polls show it. So do the altered stands of political and other leaders ...

The Administration's credibility, Galbraith continued, was rapidly approaching ground zero:

> ... The consequence of this ghastly sequence of promise and disappointment is that now nearly everything that is said in defense

of the war is suspect. This, in turn, nullifies the natural advantage of the Administration in access to press and television. There isn't much advantage in being able to get your side before the people if they no longer believe what you say or do not listen.

Since " . . . it is now a war that we cannot win, should not wish to win, and which our people do not support," it was essential for the Administration to change objectives and reverse present policy.[52]

Senator Eugene McCarthy was equally critical: In his best-selling book *The Limits of Power,* the senator from Minnesota called for a fundamental change in general foreign policy and as swift an exodus as possible from Vietnam.[53] At year's end, Senator Fulbright told constituents that national pride, not national security, is the reason that Americans are fighting in Vietnam. Experts added persuasive testimony: Douglas Pike, in his quasi-official work *The Viet Cong,* identified the real enemy; George Tanham, in his quasi-official work *War Without Guns,* pointed to errors in American aid programs. Foreign experts also contributed: Richard Clutterbuck's *The Long Long War* and Robert Thompson's *Defeating Communist Insurgency* threw considerable, if not always pertinent, light on the Vietnamese challenge as seen by two veterans of the Malayan emergency. The British strategist Alastair Buchan, in the January 1968 issue of *Encounter,* warned that Vietnam was the greatest tragedy that had befallen the U.S.A. since the Civil War. By diminishing American influence, it was giving superb diplomatic advantage to its adversaries while destroying the confidence of its own people in their vision of law and order and international justice. In December, a group of scholars and former Administration officials and officers that included General Ridgway and Roger Hilsman produced a short analysis, the "Bermuda Statement," which urged the Administration to de-escalate the war and start giving it back to the South Vietnamese Government. All this and more caused American citizens to begin questioning the fact of war, and this particularly applied to campuses, to students and teachers, and if emotion sometimes colored the questioning process, it was usually genuine emotion expressed by youngsters who eventually would probably wind up in Vietnam fighting a war for which, more and more, they saw less and less reason.

Johnson and the majority of his advisers either ignored what they regarded as minority voices or, when these spoke too powerfully to be ignored, brushed them aside with considerable petulance that too often questioned the dissenter's loyalty to his country.

Dissent was not to disappear. In late summer, Johnson had sent one of his closest advisers, Clark Clifford, and Maxwell Taylor on a tour of Southeast Asia, an informal attempt to persuade concerned countries to increase troop support of the war. The dominoes that had played

such a major role in shaping the American commitment seemed unusually inert. Thailand, South Korea, Australia, and New Zealand
showed no interest in increasing minimal contributions (which, in the
case of Korea and Thailand, were subsidized by the United States);
the Philippines government asked President Johnson to avoid sending
the team to Manila, for political reasons! The experience deeply impressed Clifford: " . . . It was strikingly apparent to me that the other
troop-contributing countries no longer shared our degree of concern
about the war in South Viet Nam." In his later words:

> . . . I returned home puzzled, troubled, concerned. Was it possible
> that our assessment of the danger to the stability of Southeast Asia
> and the Western Pacific was exaggerated? Was it possible that
> those nations which were neighbors of Viet Nam had a clearer
> perception of the tides of world events in 1967 than we? Was it
> possible that we were continuing to be guided by judgments that
> might once have had validity but were now obsolete? In short,
> although I still counted myself a staunch supporter of our policies,
> there were nagging, not-to-be-suppressed doubts in my mind.

What portion of these doubts brushed against President Johnson is
problematical, but, in late September, at San Antonio, he did offer to
halt bombing in the North if Hanoi wished to negotiate (an offer already made privately to Hanoi by Henry Kissinger, acting as presidential agent). Although Clifford and other advisers found this a step in
the right direction, their optimism was brief:

> . . . As I listened to the official discussion in Washington, my feel-
> ings turned from disappointment to dismay. I found it was being
> quietly asserted that, in return for a bombing cessation in the
> North, the North Vietnamese must stop sending men and matériel
> into South Viet Nam. On the surface, this might have seemed a
> fair exchange. To me, it was an unfortunate interpretation that—
> intentionally or not—rendered the San Antonio formula virtually
> meaningless. The North Vietnamese had more than 100,000 men
> in the South. It was totally unrealistic to expect them to abandon
> their men by not replacing casualties, and by failing to provide
> them with clothing, food, munitions and other supplies. We could
> never expect them to accept an offer to negotiate on those condi-
> tions.[54]

Thus, bombing continued and so did the ground war. In late September, General Westmoreland asked Washington to speed the arrival
of promised troops. Worried by reports of a general enemy build-up,
Johnson agreed. Once again, McNamara tried to prevent further escalation and in early November sent the President another general analysis

of the war. Rejecting increased military actions because of the risks they entailed in widening the war, he wanted Johnson to halt bombing in the North by end of the year, to stabilize operations in the South with no increase in American troop strength, and to reshape the southern effort in order to give the South Vietnamese a larger share of responsibility in fighting the war.

This precipitated a new Administration row. Johnson later wrote that, after careful consideration of the views of various advisers, he decided against the proposal in view of an increasing enemy build-up. The record contradicts the carefully drawn self-portrait of studied calm presented in his memoirs. If his public utterances are to be believed, he ended the year as firmly convinced of a pending American victory as at year's beginning. In discussing the President's performance at one point, the British Prime Minister evoked the image of the czar's court. That was wrong: In 1967, Johnson did not sound so much like Czar Nicholas as he did George III, who, during the American Revolution, forever demanded "total submission" of American colonists.

But even George III could not match Johnson's ideological motivation. The President spoke and wrote at this time and later as if he were St. George bent on destroying the dragon of communism. Whether writing to Senator Jackson to explain resumption of bombing the North, or addressing the Tennessee legislature and announcing "a new team" for South Vietnam, or in introducing David Lilienthal and Robert Komer to discuss their optimistic appraisal of the situation in South Vietnam, or in lengthy news conferences where star performers such as Robert McNamara or William Westmoreland or Ellsworth Bunker confirmed his expressed optimism, or at Guam or Canberra or Cam Ranh Bay—whenever and wherever possible, in discussing the war, the President sounded like Thwackum and Square discussing Tom Jones' frequent aberrations. And if he identified Ho's intransigence without understanding it, he nonetheless made it clear to any who would listen that the transgressor would be punished—no matter the time, no matter the effort, no matter the cost.

CHAPTER SIXTY-EIGHT

1. Institute for Strategic Studies, "The United States," *Strategic Survey, 1967.*
2. Reuters, December 15, 1967. See also, Hoopes: From February 1965 to December 1967, the United States lost, from all causes, in Vietnam some 3,000 aircraft (including helicopters), at a cost of $2.9 billion.
3. Hoopes, 87.
4. Ibid., 81.
5. Wilson.
6. Sheehan et al., 528. See also, Johnson, *The Vantage Point . . .* , 259; Hoopes.
7. Sheehan et al., 567–8. See also, Johnson, *The Vantage Point . . .* : According to Johnson, Westmoreland

... pointed out that heavy infiltration and continuing recruitment in the South were making up for battle casualties, but he was hopeful that the 'crossover' point—when losses exceeded the ability to replace those losses—might be reached reasonably soon.

8. Hoopes, 92.
9. Sheehan et al., 530–1.
10. Ibid., 533.
11. Ibid., 573–7.
12. Ibid., 531.
13. Hoopes, 51.
14. Sheehan et al., 534–5.
15. Ibid., 577–85. See also, Johnson, *The Vantage Point* . . .
16. Sheehan et al., 583–4.
17. Ibid., 585.
18. Johnson, *The Vantage Point* . . . , 369:

> . . . I rejected the suggestion that we use air power to close the port of Haiphong and knock out part of the dike system in the Red River delta. I felt that there was too grave a risk of Communist Chinese or even Soviet involvement if those measures were carried out, and I wished to avoid the heavy civilian casualties that would accompany destruction of the dikes.

19. Hackworth, 552.
20. Ibid., 708.
21. Ibid., 556–7.
22. Ibid., 555.
23. *Time*, November 17, 1967. See also, Sheehan et al., 525.
24. Hackworth, 542.
25. Ibid., 610. See also, Atkinson, 240–53.
26. Ibid.
27. Schell, 178–9.
28. U.S. Marine Corps, "The Battle for Hills 861 and 881."
29. Shaplen, *The Road from War*, 138.
30. *Time*, October 6, 1967. Perhaps the general forgot about Hiroshima and Nagasaki?
31. Hackworth, 566.
32. *Time*, December 8, 1967.
33. Private information in the author's files.
34. Corson, 216 ff., who offers numerous illustrations of gross incompetence, maladministration, and corruption—all bad enough in their own right as damaging American aid programs—but damage *always* compounded by a high percentage of missing items and supplies ending up in the enemy camp.
35. Lederer, *Our Own Worst Enemy*, 160–2.
36. Kellen.
37. *Time*, October 20, 1967.
38. Kellen.
39. Lederer, *Our Own Worst Enemy*, 97–8, 132, 164–5.
40. Corson, 127.
41. Ibid., 129.
42. Lederer, *Our Own Worst Enemy*, 137 ff.
43. Hoopes, 72–3.
44. Schalk, 9.
45. Ibid., 57.
46. Ibid., 142–3.
47. Ibid., 143.
48. *Newsweek*, January 16, 1967.

49. Schalk, 122.
50. Ibid., 123.
51. *Time,* November 17, 1967.
52. Galbraith, 25–32.
53. McCarthy, 187 ff.
54. Clifford.

CHAPTER 69

The Pueblo fiasco • The Tet offensive • Enemy aims and accomplishments • Defeat or victory? • The Johnson-Westmoreland stand • General Wheeler's report • MACV objectives • Westmoreland demands more troops (IV) • Hawks versus doves • Dean Acheson: ". . . With all due respect, Mr. President, the Joint Chiefs of Staff don't know what they're talking about." • The Clifford Group • Action in the North • The other war • Dissension within America • Johnson's compromise • Westmoreland is relieved • Johnson steps down • Paris peace talks • Saigon's intransigence • The second Tet offensive • Operation Phoenix: pros and cons • Westmoreland's swan song • Creighton Abrams takes command • The 1968 price tag

THE CONFIDENT if not ebullient pose maintained by the Johnson administration was transmitted to Congress and the American people by the President in his annual State of the Union message in mid-January 1968. In this major speech, the President listed what he regarded as major gains in South Vietnam. Although he noted that " . . . the enemy continues to pour men and material across frontiers and into battle, despite his continuous heavy losses," he left little doubt that the situation was under control: " . . . Our patience and our perseverance will match our power. Aggression will never prevail."[1]

The President later wrote, in his memoirs: " . . . Looking back on early 1968, I am convinced I made a mistake by not saying more about Vietnam in my State of the Union report. . . . I did not go into details concerning the build-up of enemy forces or warn of the early major combat I believed was in the offing. . . . "[2]

This would have been well-advised. The first of a series of military disasters had already struck by the time General Westmoreland's comforting report reached the White House in early 1968 (see Chapter 67).

In late January, patrol boats of the North Korean navy attacked and captured an American ship, the USS *Pueblo*. Although the *Pueblo* carried highly sensitive and top-secret electronic gear, with which she was intercepting North Korean communications, she was sailing in international waters, her mission common to both American and Soviet ships. As her captain, Lloyd Bucher, later made clear in his book, neither officers nor crew were fully trained in destruction procedures, and her armament was virtually non-existent; Bucher's messages to higher authorities elicited no response—no planes, nothing.[3]

The Western world was still stunned with this act of piracy and seeming American impotence to contest it, when tragedy reverted sharply to Vietnam. Despite official optimism, MACV and the marines had been worried about a continuing enemy build-up in the South. Since the turn of the year, the enemy had repeatedly struck positions in III and I Corps areas, attacks beaten off only with fighting described by Westmoreland as " . . . the most intense of the entire war."[4] In the first two weeks of 1968, VC units had shelled forty-nine district and provisional capitals, attacking eight of them and twice occupying two within thirty miles of Saigon—activity suspiciously at odds with General Weyand's comfortable claims of superiority made less than a month before (see Chapter 67). During those two weeks, MACV claimed to have killed five thousand enemy, and Westmoreland announced that " . . . the Communists seem to have run temporarily out of steam."[5]

Westmoreland nonetheless was carefully watching Khe Sanh, where the enemy was daily building up attacking forces. The presumed importance of Khe Sanh can be gathered from later official statements. General Walt regarded the place " . . . as the crucial anchor of our defenses along the demilitarized zone."[6] General Wheeler would shortly stress its strategic and tactical importance as the Western anchor of the American defensive line. " . . . To lose it," Wheeler said, "would allow a deep Communist penetration into South Vietnam."[7] General Cushman, probably with Dien Bien Phu in mind, allegedly was not happy about tying up several marine combat battalions in a static defense of a position vulnerable to long-range enemy artillery fire, tactically dominated by heights, some of them enemy-held, and at the fog-shrouded end of a twenty-seven-mile supply line that guerrilla interdiction made dependent solely on air delivery. In any event, Westmoreland expected a major attack against the garrison either before or after the Tet holiday, and, at his instigation, Cushman continued to build up the garrison while other units moved north to bolster defenses in the DMZ area. By month's end, the Khe Sanh garrison comprised four marine infantry battalions, one marine artillery battalion, one ARVN ranger battalion, U. S. Air Force and Seabee detachments. Armament included 105-mm. howitzers, 90-mm.-gun tanks, and 106-mm. recoilless rifles. During the final twelve days of January, the garrison fired thirteen thousand artillery and mortar rounds and was supported by nearly four thousand tactical air missions and 288 B-52 bomber missions.[8] Meanwhile, Westmoreland was said to have moved over half of his combat battalions north.

This was not, however, the tragedy referred to, though it would play a significant part. At the end of January, with allied eyes anxiously watching Khe Sanh, the enemy opened what soon became famous to the world as the Tet offensive—so named because it began during the Tet, or lunar new year, holidays, when a truce had been established and large numbers of South Vietnamese soldiers were on leave. For some days prior to January 31, Viet Cong and North Vietnamese commando squads had infiltrated areas around allied bases and in principal cities and towns, where they were hidden by VC sympathizers. Simultaneously, battalion-size units had worked into the surrounding countryside. Numbering between fifty and sixty thousand, the attack force consisted predominantly of Viet Cong units reinforced by about six thousand PAVN soldiers. Early in the morning of January 31, the commandos attacked key targets in cities and towns while their fellows attacked from without. In addition to Saigon and Hué, the enemy struck thirty principal towns and seventy district towns. The targets included human beings: Special squads sought out and executed military and police officers, civil officials, and their families. In Saigon, a VC commando unit (whose ranks included Vietnamese working for the U.S. government) penetrated American embassy grounds while other units captured the radio station and attacked Joint General Staff Headquarters (where Westmoreland was), near the airport, and naval headquarters near the Saigon River. Extensive damage included some 125 planes and helicopters fully or partially destroyed.

In most places, heavy fighting lasted a week or two. As perhaps foreseen by the enemy, ARVN and American counterattacks caused tremendous damage; in Hué, where the enemy held out almost to the end of February, allied counterattacks destroyed perhaps half the city and inevitably added to civilian casualties. About four thousand American and South Vietnamese troops lost their lives, and some twelve thousand were wounded. Thousands of civilians were killed or wounded and thousands more made homeless. Continuing rocket and mortar attacks from surrounding countryside added to general carnage. But the enemy did not escape unscathed; according to government figures, thirty-six thousand Communists were killed by February 18, a figure that probably included large numbers of non-Communists.[9]

The psychological effect could not have been greater. Many readers will remember the force of surprise and shock that hammered America—the futility that one felt upon seeing blood-spattered bodies, friendly and enemy, in the American embassy compound, or the famous black-and-white photograph of General Loan about to shoot a mana- cled VC officer through the head, or the statement made by an unwit- ting American army major to the Australian correspondent Peter Arnett as the two looked over the smoking ruins of Ben Tre: " . . . The city had to be destroyed in order to save it." The sum formed an overdraft on the meager balance of credibility maintained by the Johnson admin- istration, " . . . seriously damaging," as an Institute of Strategic Studies bulletin later noted, "the reputation of those analysts who had con- cluded that the ability of the enemy to organize military action on a national or regional scale had been eliminated during 1967."[10] The Tet attacks brought home to the American people that, despite official op- timism, the war was likely to continue *ad nauseam.* As surely foreseen by Hanoi, they added a particularly volatile fuel to the already blazing row within top echelons of the Johnson administration. Perhaps the main accomplishment of the Tet offensive, from the enemy standpoint, was to finally polarize existent but theretofore divergent opposition to Administration policy in Vietnam.

Johnson, the JCS, Sharp, Westmoreland, and other hawks at once adopted a simplistic stand on the attacks. At a news conference in early February, the President told correspondents:

> . . . We have known for several months, now, that the Commu- nists planned a massive winter-spring offensive. We have detailed information on Ho Chi Minh's order governing that offensive. Part of it is called a general uprising.
>
> We know the object was to overthrow the constitutional gov- ernment in Saigon and to create a situation in which we and the Vietnamese would be willing to accept the Communist-dominated coalition government.
>
> Another part of that offensive was planned as a massive attack across the frontiers of South Vietnam by North Vietnamese units. We have already seen the general uprising.

After emphasizing maximum enemy and minimum American casualties, the President announced that " . . . the biggest fact is that the stated purposes of the general uprising have failed." However, he warned,

> . . . we may at this very moment be on the eve of a major enemy offensive in the area of Khe Sanh and generally around the De- militarized Zone.

The enemy's second objective, Johnson explained, was to attain a psy- chological victory, and he was trying to prevent that from being achieved. In this lengthy conference, he implied that nothing of the situation was surprising and that matters were firmly under control; as for further deployment of U.S. troops: " . . . There is not anything in any of the developments that would justify the press in leaving the impression that any great new overall moves are going to be made that would involve substantial movements in that direction."[11]

The salve of this business-as-usual approach comforted almost no one, and the President probably would have been wiser to share some of his apprehensions with the American people. If his later writings are to be believed, these must have been considerable:

> . . . This is not to imply that Tet was not a shock, in one degree or another, to all of us. We knew that a show of strength was coming; it was more massive than we had anticipated. We knew that the Communists were aiming at a number of population centers; we did not expect them to attack as many as they did. We knew that the North Vietnamese and the Viet Cong were trying to achieve better co-ordination of their country-wide moves; we did not believe they would be able to carry out the level of co-ordination they demonstrated. We expected a large force to attack; it was larger than we had estimated. Finally, it was difficult to believe that the Communists would so profane their own people's sacred holiday.[12]

In Saigon, Westmoreland went Johnson one better. The American commander's ebullience reminds one of Lord Cornwallis insisting that the battle of Guilford Courthouse (see Chapter 6) was a "victory"—a victory, perhaps, responded the *Annual Register*'s scribe, but a victory " . . . productive of all the consequences of defeat." In reviewing dispatches of the time, one would suppose that the American general had himself planned the Tet offensive. On February 2, he told newsmen that there was evidence to suggest that the enemy " . . . is about to run out of steam."[13] Westmoreland interpreted the attacks as designed to drive American troops from Khe Sanh, which was the enemy's real objective: The Communist attacks, he told newsmen, were prelude to a "go-for-broke" attack on Khe Sanh and the two northern provinces.[14] This plan would fail, as had the rest of the enemy plan—by February 6, Westmoreland believed that enemy losses, which he put at 21,330 dead, " . . . may measurably shorten the war."[15] Westmoreland, in short, viewed the attacks as a desperate move of a dying enemy: He went so far as to tell a disbelieving André Beaufre " . . . that he compared this decision [of Giap's] with that of Hitler on the eve of the Ardennes offensive in the autumn of 1944, that is to say a decision of despair by an enemy at his wit's end."[16]

* * *

The plot now thickens, the record suggesting something like the following. Early in the Tet offensive the President asked Westmoreland how he could help him—a reasonable and sympathetic request. On February 3, Wheeler allegedly cabled Westmoreland: " . . . The President asks me if there is any reinforcement or help that we can give you." On February 8, having received no reply [!] from Westmoreland, Wheeler cabled:

> . . . Query: Do you need reinforcement? Our capabilities are limited. We can provide 82d Airborne Division and about one-half a Marine Corps division, both loaded with Vietnam veterans. However, if you consider reinforcements imperative, you should not be bound by earlier agreements [i.e., a troop limit of 525,000]. United States Government is not prepared to accept defeat in Vietnam. In summary, if you need more troops, ask for them.

Westmoreland immediately requested the units named by Wheeler and also asked " . . . that the President authorize an amphibious assault by the marines into North Vietnam as a diversionary move." A day later, he outlined his need for additional troops to contain the enemy's "major campaign" in the north and " . . . to go on the offensive as soon as his attack is spent," to otherwise carry out previous campaign plans, to bolster a weakened ARVN, and " . . . to take advantage of the enemy's weakened posture by taking the offensive against him."[17] According to the President, Westmoreland

> . . . saw the situation as one of heightened risk but of great opportunity as well.
> "I do not see how the enemy can long sustain the heavy losses which his new strategy is enabling us to inflict on him," he reported. "Therefore, adequate reinforcements should permit me not only to contain his I Corps offensive but also to capitalize on his losses by seizing the initiative in other areas." He believed that exploiting the opportunity "could materially shorten the war."[18]

When Westmoreland requested early delivery of troops, the JCS pointed out that such a deployment would compromise the strategic reserve and should be deferred—a tactic allegedly designed to cause Johnson to call up the reserves, a major step in full-scale mobilization, which had so long been desired by the JCS. According to Johnson, debate centered on sending Westmoreland six maneuver battalions, or about ten thousand men, and all agreed to do this while holding off on the subject of a reserve call-up. The JCS also requested presidential authority to bomb closer to the centers of Hanoi and Haiphong—a request opposed by McNamara and by Paul Warnke, who had replaced John McNaughton, and one finally turned down by the President.

Johnson now sent Wheeler to Saigon, from where he reported that "... the current situation in Vietnam is still developing and fraught with opportunities as well as dangers." The enemy offensive had hurt ARVN more psychologically than physically. Nonetheless, two to three months were needed to recover equipment losses; three to six months to regain pre-Tet strength. The worst damage occurred to the Rural Development Program; in many areas, the VC now openly controlled the countryside. In order to put things right, Westmoreland wanted a "... 3 division-15 tactical fighter squadron force"—a whopping levy of over two hundred thousand more troops to be deployed by end of 1968.[19] Responsible commanders, Wheeler reported, regarded 1968 as "the pivotal year" and warned that, without the troop increase, "... we might have to give up territory, probably the two northernmost provinces of South Vietnam...." The troop increase requested by Westmoreland and the JCS placed the President in an extremely awkward position. Hawk that he was, he was also politician, and he was naturally upset at the national furor generated by the Tet offensive. In his later words,

> ... I did not expect the enemy effort to have the impact on American thinking that it achieved. I was not surprised that elements of the press, the academic community, and the Congress reacted as they did. I was surprised and disappointed that the enemy's efforts produced such a dismal effect on various people inside government and others outside whom I had always regarded as staunch and unflappable. Hanoi must have been delighted; it was exactly the reaction they sought.[20]

It was also a reaction justified in large part by specific facts. Hanson Baldwin, parroting the official line, may have concluded in an article in the March *Reader's Digest* that "... the enemy can no longer find security in his South Vietnamese sanctuaries,"[21] but the enemy seemed to be doing pretty well without security. Astute advisers also questioned Westmoreland and the JCS's interpretation of the attacks as a desperation move on the part of the NLF-PRP-VC and Hanoi. Costly though the attacks proved to the enemy, the NLF still disposed of over sixty thousand hard-core guerrillas, augmented by twice that many active supporters and by some sixty thousand more PAVN troops, with impressive reserves untouched in North Vietnam (not to mention China, which, as James Reston once noted, was down to her last 700 million men). Advisers such as Clark Clifford questioned the magic number of 205,000, where perhaps a half million to a million men would be required. Advisers such as Philip Habib pointed to divided opinions in the Saigon mission as to the wisdom of sending *any* large reinforcement as opposed to insisting on the South Vietnamese doing the job.[22] Subordinate but influential voices added to the general protest. Townsend Hoopes later wrote:

> ... In the Pentagon, the Tet offensive performed the curious service of fully revealing the doubters and dissenters to each other, as in a lightning flash. Nitze suddenly spoke out on "the unsoundness of continuing to reinforce weakness," and wrote a paper that argued that our policy in Vietnam had to be placed in the context of other U.S. commitments in the world. Warnke thought Tet showed that our military strategy was "foolish to the point of insanity." Alain Enthoven ... confided that, "I fell off the boat when the troop level reached 170,000" ... and other influential civilians expressed their strong belief that the Administration's Vietnam policy was at a dead end.
>
> One thing was clear to us all: The Tet offensive was the eloquent counterpoint to the effusive optimism of November. It showed conclusively that the U.S. did not in fact control the situation. ... [23]

Johnson was so insulated by Rostow from dissident opinions that it is doubtful if these attitudes reached him. Nonetheless, he remained keenly aware of the national mood, and he was also brought abruptly to heel by a senior adviser, Dean Acheson. Acheson had no love for Johnson and did not eagerly accept his summons to the White House in late February. Townsend Hoopes later described the meeting:

> ... When the President asked him his opinion of the current situation in Vietnam, Acheson replied he wasn't sure he had a useful view because he was finding it impossible, on the basis of occasional official briefings given him, to discover what was really happening. He had lost faith in the objectivity of the briefers: "With all due respect, Mr. President, the Joint Chiefs of Staff don't know what they're talking about." The President said that was a shocking statement. Acheson replied that, if such it was, then perhaps the President ought to be shocked.[24]

The sum of these factors persuaded the President to two important moves. He asked Acheson to make an independent study, drawing on expert testimony at subordinate levels of government; and he ordered his new Secretary of Defense, Clark Clifford, to convene his most responsible officials to study the Westmoreland-JCS request, indeed to appraise fully the situation in Vietnam.

Sixty-two years old, Clark Clifford had recently replaced the disillusioned McNamara. A well-known Washington attorney, a close friend of the President and loyal supporter of Johnson's Vietnam policy, he had served for years as a confidential adviser. The previous summer, as we have related, he had undertaken a presidential mission to persuade Asian countries to increase troop support in Vietnam, an unsuccessful effort that caused him to entertain certain doubts concerning the war.

What became known as the Clifford Group included Secretary of State Dean Rusk, Secretary of the Treasury Henry Fowler, Under Secretary of State Nicholas Katzenbach, Deputy Secretary of Defense Paul Nitze, General Wheeler, CIA director Richard Helms, presidential assistants Walt Rostow and Maxwell Taylor, and numerous other ranking officials. Subsequent meetings predictably accentuated the current rift between hawks and doves. General Maxwell Taylor presented the prevailing JCS view in a memorandum both to the group and directly to President Johnson:

> ... We should consider changing the objective which we have been pursuing consistently since 1954 [!] only for the most cogent reasons. There is clearly nothing to recommend trying to do more than we are now doing at such great cost. To undertake to do less is to accept needlessly a serious defeat for which we would pay dearly in terms of our worldwide position of leadership, of the political stability of Southeast Asia and of the credibility of our pledges to friends and allies.[25]

Doves did not agree. Prompted by CIA reports, most civilian members of the group apparently argued that any substantial increase of American forces could be easily offset by North Vietnamese troops. Dr. Alain Enthoven typified the realistic pessimism of the doves:

> ... While we have raised the price to NVN [North Vietnam] of aggression and support of the VC [Viet Cong], it shows no lack of capability or will to match each new U.S. escalation. Our strategy of "attrition" has not worked. Adding 206,000 more U.S. men to a force of 525,000, gaining only 27 additional maneuver battalions and 270 tactical fighters at an added cost to the U.S. of $10-billion per year raises the question of who is making it costly for whom.
> ... We know that despite a massive influx of 500,000 U.S. troops, 1.2 million tons of bombs a year, 400,000 attack sorties per year, 200,000 enemy K.I.A. [killed in action] in three years, 20,000 U.S. K.I.A., etc., our control of the countryside and the defense of the urban areas is now essentially at pre-August 1965 levels. We have achieved stalemate at a high commitment. A new strategy must be sought.[26]

Enthoven and other experts argued that Westmoreland should call off search-and-destroy attrition strategy in favor of protecting population centers while the South Vietnamese Government and armed forces developed effective capability—which was more or less what General James Gavin had recommended in 1965.

Nothing better illustrates the abject poverty of Administration thinking than Clifford's later account of these high-level meetings:

> . . . In the colloquial style of those meetings, here are some of the principal issues raised and some of the answers as I understood them:
>
> "Will 200,000 more men do the job?" I found no assurance that they would.
>
> "If not, how many more might be needed—and when?" There was no way of knowing.
>
> "What would be involved in committing 200,000 more men to Viet Nam?" A reserve call-up of approximately 280,000, an increased draft call and an extension of tours of duty of most men then in service.
>
> "Can the enemy respond with a build-up of his own?" He could and he probably would.
>
> "What are the estimated costs of the latest requests?" First calculations were on the order of $2 billion for the remaining four months of that fiscal year, and an increase of $10 to $12 billion for the year beginning July 1, 1968.
>
> "What will be the impact on the economy?" So great that we would face the possibility of credit restrictions, a tax increase and even wage and price controls. The balance of payments would be worsened by at least half a billion dollars a year.
>
> "Can bombing stop the war?" Never by itself. It was inflicting heavy personnel and matériel losses, but bombing by itself would not stop the war.
>
> "Will stepping up the bombing decrease American casualties?" Very little, if at all. Our casualties were due to the intensity of the ground fighting in the South. We had already dropped a heavier tonnage of bombs than in all the theaters of World War II. During 1967, an estimated 90,000 North Vietnamese had infiltrated into South Viet Nam. In the opening weeks of 1968, infiltrators were coming in at three to four times the rate of a year earlier, despite the ferocity and intensity of our campaign of aerial interdiction.
>
> "How long must we keep on sending our men and carrying the main burden of combat?" The South Vietnamese were doing better, but they were not ready yet to replace our troops and we did not know when they would be.

When Clifford asked for a military plan, he was told that no plan for victory existed " . . . in the historic American sense" due to presidential limitations that prohibited invading North Vietnam, pursuing into Laos and Cambodia, and mining Haiphong Harbor. Clifford now asked:

... "Given these circumstances, how can we win?" We would, I was told, continue to evidence our superiority over the enemy; we would continue to attack in the belief that he would reach the stage where he would find it inadvisable to go on with the war. He could not afford the attrition we were inflicting on him. And we were improving our posture all the time.

I then asked, "What is the best estimate as to how long this course of action will take? Six months? One year? Two years?" There was no agreement on an answer. Not only was there no agreement, I could find no one willing to express any confidence in his guesses. . . .

A disturbed man now asked a disturbed question:

... "Does anyone see any diminution in the will of the enemy after four years of our having been there, after enormous casualties and after massive destruction from our bombing?"

The answer was that there appeared to be no diminution in the will of the enemy. . . .

The total experience was salutary if dismal. It had reinforced Clifford's earlier doubts:

... I was convinced that the military course we were pursuing was not only endless, but hopeless. A further substantial increase in American forces could only increase the devastation and the Americanization of the war, and thus leave us even further from our goal of a peace that would permit the people of South Viet Nam to fashion their own political and economic institutions. Henceforth, I was also convinced, our primary goal should be to level off our involvement, and to work toward gradual disengagement.[27]

The Clifford report attempted to resolve the contretemps by compromise. Although Clifford later wrote that he favored a reversal of strategy, the hawks proved sufficiently strong to prevent this recommendation. The final document did not question present strategy except by indirection, in that it recommended limiting troop reinforcement to a maximum twenty-two thousand. It did not recommend a new peace initiative or a proposed cutback in the bombing of the North.[28]

Clifford's group paid considerable attention to the air question. The JCS submitted three general plans for consideration: an increase in bombing, including expansion of targets around Hanoi and Haiphong to include railroad equipment in the Chinese buffer zone and the dike system that supported the North's agriculture, and mining Haiphong Harbor; a shift in bombing away from the Hanoi-Haiphong area in favor of striking roads and supply trails in the southern part of North

Vietnam, including the Laotian Panhandle; an interdiction campaign in the South " . . . designed to substitute tactical airpower for a large portion of the search-and-destroy operations currently conducted by ground forces, thus permitting the ground troops to concentrate on a perimeter defense of the heavily populated areas." Wheeler, Taylor, and Rostow wanted the first course of action; other principals held for the second and third.

Since the report left matters largely as they were, it pleased no one. One of the President's objections to the document centered on its negative approach to negotiations. The CIA had reported to the Clifford group that if the United States were to call off bombing of the North, " . . . Hanoi would probably respond to an offer to negotiate, although the intelligence agency warned that the North Vietnamese would not modify their terms for a final settlement or stop fighting in the South."[29] In discussing the possibility of renewed negotiations, Secretary of State Dean Rusk suggested a bombing halt in the North during the rainy season except in battle zone areas. His suggestion continued the argument already being waged within Administration circles, one that would intensify during the rest of March.

The Clifford report kicked off what proved to be an exciting, exasperating, and crucial month in American affairs. The military situation was by no means as favorable in Vietnam as Westmoreland was reporting. Although enemy attacks had been beaten back, enemy units surrounding towns and cities continued to strike and interdict road communications while rebuilding bases in the countryside. At Khe Sanh the marine-ARVN garrison continued to withstand severe buffeting while the greatest aerial bombing effort in history pounded the besiegers. The situation worried Westmoreland to the extent that he considered using "a few small tactical nuclear weapons" or possibly chemical agents.[30]

Westmoreland's preoccupation with Khe Sanh did not lessen the real and devastating importance of the other war. In contrast to claims advanced by MACV and Washington, Robert Shaplen offered an eyewitness account of the scene:

> . . . Since the Tet attack, the Communists have maintained their countrywide harassment of cities, airfields, and various Allied installations, primarily with rocket and mortar fire. They have made occasional fresh ground assaults against about a dozen cities, mostly in the Delta, and particularly on March 3rd and 4th, when it seemed that a second wave of the offensive might be beginning. They have recruited as many as thirty thousand new troops, ranging in age from fifteen to forty. Most of the recruiting has been

done in the Delta, where the Communists moved in to fill the vacuum in the countryside following the withdrawal of American and government troops to positions of defense around the cities and the towns. Hanoi has continued to infiltrate troops both to reinforce the North Vietnamese forces now totalling a hundred and twelve thousand men in South Vietnam (five more North Vietnamese divisions are said to be alerted to move south) and to build up the main-force Vietcong units that suffered the heaviest losses during Tet. . . .

The attacks had not only badly hurt ARVN and halted the pacification program, but had further splintered the Saigon government, widening the dangerous rift between Thieu and Ky. Once the emergency had passed, a sense of shock set in. Shaplen noted

> . . . a continuing erosion of morale and a growing sense of foreboding. Vietnamese I have known for many years are as frank as they are sad these days in their prognoses; they sound more and more like men who know they are suffering from an incurable malady.[31]

Pessimism so prevalent in Saigon found ample voice throughout the United States. At the end of February 1968, George Kennan told a Newark audience that we " . . . have pushed stubbornly and heedlessly ahead, like men in a dream, seemingly insensitive to outside opinion, seemingly unable to arrive at any realistic assessment of the effects of [our] acts."[32] Large numbers of influential Americans, including leading business executives, agreed. Throughout the country, campus demonstrations, draft-card burnings, and civic protestations were becoming the order of the day. Norman Mailer's incendiary *Armies of the Night* further heated already hot tempers. Congress was becoming increasingly rebellious. The Senate Foreign Relations Committee opened televised hearings on the Foreign Aid Bill and called Dean Rusk before it. Almost at once, the hearings became a debate on Vietnam. For almost two days, a beleaguered Rusk fielded generally hostile questions with what many persons believed were less than candid answers—altogether a performance that further fueled nationwide fires of dissent.

The pressure was telling on the President. The veteran British correspondent Henry Brandon later wrote:

> . . . Anyone who had the opportunity of seeing President Johnson around March 11, 1968, in person and in private, was taken aback by the near-exhaustion that had overcome him. He was a man in torment as I had never seen one before. His face was ashen, his eyes sunken, his skin flabby, and yet, underneath, his expression was taut.[33]

The President was to find little relief ahead. Almost no one agreed with anyone else. Ambassador Bunker, although a hawk who agreed with the necessity of supplying Westmoreland with more troops, wanted a limit of seven battalions, since he felt that more men would dissuade the South Vietnamese from putting their own army right. Rusk and Clifford pointed to a practical difficulty: The United States could not supply an additional half million men with weapons and at the same time furnish modern arms to an expanding ARVN. Civilian dissension was also increasing: Paul Nitze, Clifford's deputy, allegedly asked to be excused from appearing before the Senate committee to defend Administration policy in Vietnam. Then came Eugene McCarthy's near victory in the New Hampshire primary elections—McCarthy was a dove and outspoken critic of Johnson's Vietnam policy. A few days later the President received another unpleasant surprise in the form of Dean Acheson, who had been conferring with numerous officials on the Vietnam question. At a private luncheon,

> . . . Acheson told the President he was being led down a garden path by the JCS, that what Westmoreland was attempting in Vietnam was simply not possible—without the application of totally unlimited resources "and maybe five years." He told the President that his recent speeches were quite unrealistic and believed by no one, either at home or abroad. He added the judgment that the country was no longer supporting the war. . . .[34]

The following day, the President's real political nemesis, Robert Kennedy, announced his candidacy for the Democratic nomination.

It was all too much for tired old Johnson. After a final show of truculence, he accepted facts and acted accordingly. In late March, he announced Westmoreland's imminent relief. He also convened a senior advisory group of prominent civil and military officials, past and present, including Dean Acheson, George Ball, Arthur Dean, Henry Cabot Lodge, McGeorge Bundy, and Matthew Ridgway. Meeting for two days in late March, this group, known as the Wise Men, heard a special briefing delivered by an interdepartmental executive team that included the army's Major General William DePuy, the State Department's Philip Habib, and CIA's George Carver. Although opinions differed in detail, only three of fourteen members agreed with Administration policy; seven, including former hawk McGeorge Bundy, argued for a basic change; four expressed grave doubts. Johnson's reaction to this new dissension, particularly on the part of McGeorge Bundy, brings to mind Mrs. Western's furious words to her brother, the squire: " . . . Thou art one of those wise men whose nonsensical principles have undone the nation; by weakening the hands of our Government at home, and by discouraging our friends, and encouraging our enemies abroad." Johnson was allegedly so upset that he insisted on hearing the same briefing, which he later said contained information that he had been receiving all along.[35]

Johnson now decided to send only a token troop reinforcement to South Vietnam, although he did ask Congress for an additional $4 billion defense appropriation. He also announced that the American Government would concentrate on building up ARVN (a task begun thirteen years earlier!) so that it could relieve American forces of major combat tasks. Finally and more important, he summarily halted bombing of North Vietnam beyond the 20th parallel. At the same time, he asked Hanoi to begin talks that would lead to peace, and he attempted to underline his sincerity by withdrawing from coming presidential elections.

In this dramatic speech, President Johnson offered to meet the enemy "anywhere." When Hanoi responded favorably, American officials rejected one place after another, to settle finally on Paris, where peace talks opened officially on May 13. Meanwhile renewed fighting in Vietnam flared in the background like an ancient omen of evil, and while American and North Vietnamese delegations argued about protocol—who would sit where—many thousands of human beings bled and died. Once again, ARVN and allied forces pushed from beleaguered cities and towns to try to reclaim the countryside from the VC or at least open communications between cities. Once again, MACV announced "successful" offensives with such improbable code names as "Complete Victory"; once again, MACV stressed enormous enemy losses: fifteen thousand dead at Khe Sanh alone; seventy-one thousand dead since Tet began. And once again, in early May, the enemy launched another, a second Tet offensive, that undeniably hurt the South, psychologically, by again demonstrating a strength he wasn't supposed to have, physically, by causing more casualties and destruction. The total carnage was ghastly: The two offensives resulted " . . . in 13,000 civilians killed, 27,000 wounded, 170,000 homes destroyed or damaged; and created 1,000,000 refugees with property damage estimated at $173,500,000."[36] American and allied casualties shot upward and would continue to rise.

Westmoreland, about to leave for the United States, claimed that the offensives had hurt the enemy worse than he admitted. He pointed to some impressive facts: Nowhere had the enemy succeeded in realizing military objectives. Having failed to take Khe Sanh, in early April he had lifted the siege and stolen away—at a cost of an estimated ten to fifteen thousand dead (an action we shall discuss later). Elsewhere he was neutralized by American "spoiling" tactics, which were effectively keeping him off balance. Although damage done by the Tet offensives was great, the Saigon government and country had survived. Meanwhile, pacification operations slowly revived, as did Operation Phoenix, a long-overdue effort to identify, infiltrate, and destroy Communist political networks in the south.[37]

The Phoenix program, which has been condemned as an "instrument of civilian terror," is still a subject of considerable controversy among historians. It was basically a CIA concept, in theory an excellent one in that it was designed to eliminate the Viet Cong infrastructure (including "the man with the knife") that infested villages to hold back or even prevent the pacification process. This was the job of CIA-supported Provisional Reconnaissance Units (PRUs),[38] altogether about 4,500 South Vietnamese "advised" by several hundred Americans who infiltrated target villages to smoke out the VC infrastructure, be it "the man with the knife," be it the men, women, and youths who secretly supplied the VC with food and information. In 1968, over thirteen thousand persons were handed over to the authorities, thousands more were interrogated and released. Frequent assassinations of suspected VC were carried out, although the defenders of the program insist that these were "killings" resulting from shootouts with security forces. During the next few years

> . . . the program assertedly accounted for about seventeen thousand members of the Viet Cong infrastructure who had been amnestied, twenty thousand who had been killed, and twenty-eight thousand who had been captured and, in the majority of cases, sentenced to imprisonment.[39]

Critics of the program point to its promiscuous, corrupt, and cruel character, not to mention its general ineffectiveness.

> . . . Despite all the intelligence effort devoted to the program, only about two percent of those claimed as having been eliminated from the infrastructure had been specifically targeted: The names and whereabouts of the vast majority of its personnel were not known. Indeed, nine out of ten of those killed, many of them in the course of military operations, were killed anonymously, and only later identified—or misidentified—as members of the infrastructure.[40]

Such was the corruption in the South Vietnamese security forces that one critic claimed that "70 percent of the Vietcong suspects captured bought back their freedom."[41] As had happened in earlier fighting, such was the pressure to kill that any civilian victim of a shootout was automatically listed as a VC. Village officials

> . . . also rounded up innocent peasants in order to inflate police blotters, then spared those who could pay them off, and they fre-

910

quently tortured villagers on no more evidence than the accusation of jealous neighbors.[42]

Undoubtedly to his surprise, the writer of those words, Stanley Karnow, years later heard top officials confirm the damage done to the Communists by Phoenix. "We never feared a division of troops," a veteran VC leader told him, "but the infiltration of a couple of guys in our ranks created tremendous difficulties for us." A senior officer complained of "the loss of thousands of our cadres"; another called it "extremely destructive"; still another said that it "wiped out many of our bases" in South Vietnam, forcing army and Viet Cong troops to take sanctuary in Cambodia.[43]

This perhaps is true but it is also true that in many areas VC operations continued. Had the program been a part of a genuine pacification program from the beginning, there might well have been a more satisfactory result. By the time it got going, the VC had won a large and dedicated following that it was impossible to eradicate:

> . . . at the village level the infrastructure was highly decentralized and could operate autonomously, regardless of what happened to cadres of the vertically organized command structure.[44]

General Creighton Abrams, Westmoreland's deputy who for over a year had been trying to reshape ARVN also reported considerable progress. Asked by the President to compare the South Vietnamese effort with the earlier Korean effort, Abrams replied, "I would say the Vietnamese are doing as well, if not better, than the Koreans."[45] In April, General Westmoreland personally reported to the President that "militarily, we have never been in a better relative position in South Vietnam."[46]

Westmoreland continued to display the optimism so admired by the President. Shortly before his return to the United States to take up the post of army chief of staff—surely the most extraordinary appointment since King James I knighted a piece of beef—he launched into a vigorous defense of his generalship. Dismissing enclave strategy as "defeatist," and "oil-spot" strategy as impractical in view of a limited number of troops [!], Westmoreland told reporters:

> Our strategy in Viet Nam is most definitely not a search-and-destroy strategy, and it is unfortunate that it has been so characterized by some. Search and destroy is merely an abbreviated version of a time-honored infantry mission: "Find, fix, fight and destroy the enemy." It is not a strategy or a tactic; it is a mission. . . .

911

The general repeated what he had told the President: "The allies are in the strongest relative military position in Viet Nam today that we have yet achieved."[47]

At this point, a good many Americans refused to take Westmoreland or his pronouncements seriously. Not only Westmoreland but Pentagon "spokesmen" had become a supreme embarrassment to the Democratic Party and its leading candidate Hubert Humphrey. Unable to dissociate himself from Vietnam policy, Humphrey attempted to chart a cunning course that elevated Vietnam tactical issues to world strategic issues, where he could say more without almost automatically being contradicted by unpalatable fact. The leading Republican contender, Richard Nixon, on the other hand, blasted American policy in Vietnam and spoke mysteriously of a "new plan" to end the American involvement and regain American "superiority" in strategic matters.

While political debate claimed the American scene in summer and autumn of 1968, fighting continued sporadically in Vietnam, with Saigon frequently under rocket bombardment and VC/PAVN troops showing little hesitation in attacking where and when they wished. Although the enemy was hurting and infiltration from the North had slowed, it nonetheless continued at an estimated ten thousand men per month, a figure that allegedly, on occasion, approached thirty thousand.[48] In the country, some hope appeared in a fundamental tactical change reportedly made by Westmoreland's successor, fifty-three-year-old Creighton Abrams, a West Pointer (1936) and World War II tank commander. As later reported in *Time*:

> ... Abrams has found that forays by sub-battalion-size units—companies, platoons, even squads—can be mounted more quickly, more often and in more places [than battalion and brigade actions]. Such surprise sweeps also achieve better results. Thus the general's sting-ray tactics, designed to interdict the movement of North Vietnamese units and supplies, involve the same number of men but hundreds and sometimes thousands more of what Abrams prefers to call "initiatives" rather than "offensives." As Abrams explained it ... " ... all our operations have been designed to get into the enemy's system. Once you start working in the system that he requires to prepare his offensive operations, you can cause him to postpone his operations or to reduce their intensity or length."[49]

This was a diluted version of Sting Ray tactics, which the Marine Corps and a few army units had been using for over two years in an overdue effort to respect Roger Hilsman's dictum of fighting guerrillas with guerrillas—a qualitative approach calling for small, highly trained patrols experienced in guerrilla tactics, as opposed to a quantitative approach, yet one that still tied units to artillery protection. Unfortunately, what Abrams ordered and what army and marine unit commanders did were frequently two different things. So wedded were some commanders to search-and-destroy tactics that they sabotaged the new directives in favor of the old.[50] Elsewhere, the tactical environment defeated them. In early July, Abrams abandoned the Khe Sanh position (a sensible move that nonetheless further bewildered an already bewildered American public, who, thanks to Westmoreland and Walt, regarded it as of Verdun-like importance). But other fire bases remained, and so did the problem of keeping open communications.

Nor did Hanoi appear in any hurry to sit down at the Paris conference table and hammer out the longed-for peace. In retaliation for Hanoi's refusal to admit the Saigon government to the talks, as well as to stop fighting in the South, Johnson authorized resumption of limited bombing in the North:

> ... I said [to Abrams] that we had reached the crucial stage of both military and diplomatic operations. We would never achieve the kind of peace we wanted unless the enemy was kept on the run, unless he realized he could never win on the field of battle. I instructed Abrams to use his resources and manpower in a maximum effort to achieve that goal and to inspire the South Vietnamese army to do the same.[51]

Matters were still at a standstill when the two presidents met in Honolulu in mid-July. Prior to the meeting, Secretary of Defense Clifford flew in from Saigon. The Secretary was

> ... oppressed by the pervasive Americanization of the war: we were still giving the military instructions, still doing most of the fighting, still providing all the matériel, still paying most of the bills. Worst of all, I concluded that the South Vietnamese leaders seemed content to have it that way.[52]

Johnson described President Thieu as " ... more confident than I had ever seen him." Thieu spoke of the splendid job of reorganizing ARVN and privately told Johnson that the United States would be able to start withdrawing forces in mid-1969, perhaps sooner.[53]

Johnson's honeymoon with Thieu was short-lived. In October, the North Vietnamese delegation in Paris quietly signaled that they would admit Saigon to the talks in return for a bombing halt. Johnson and his advisers, including the JCS, went along with this. Thieu refused to send a delegation, and was persuaded to do so only with considerable difficulty and delay—an attitude that reinforced Clifford's belief that " ... the goal of the Saigon government and the goal of the United States were no longer one and the same, if indeed they ever had been. . . . "[54] Johnson later wrote, " . . . It was one of those rare occasions, in my years of dealing with them, that I felt Thieu, Ky, and their advisers had let me down. More important, I felt that their action put in peril everything both governments had worked so long and sacrificed so much to achieve. . . . "[55] The President scarcely veiled his annoyance in a major speech at the end of October, when he announced a total bombing halt of the North and implied that South Vietnam would henceforth take over a larger share of the fighting.[56]

As American voters went to the polls to elect Richard Nixon the thirty-seventh President of the nation, American and North Vietnamese officials in Paris continued to argue over the shape of the conference table, a momentous issue still unsettled by year's end.

Whatever the results in Paris, the United States would not rejoice. At the end of 1968, a tally offered by a responsible organization read as follows:

> From 1961 to 1967, 16,022 American troops had been killed in action in Vietnam. 14,592 more were killed during 1968. When deaths from accident and disease were added, 35,724 Americans had lost their lives in Vietnam since 1961. Communist casualties were far greater still: the United States claimed over 191,000 of the enemy killed during 1968 alone. In all, the war had caused more than half a million deaths in South Vietnam within eight years. Even the high Communist casualties had cost the United States dearly. Allied forces used conventional munitions in Vietnam during 1968 at a rate of nearly $14 million a day. The value of equipment destroyed was hardly less remarkable. Since 1961, combat action had claimed 919 American aircraft and 10 helicopters over North Vietnam, together with 327 aircraft and 972 helicopters over South Vietnam, 1,247 aircraft and 1,293 helicopters had been destroyed on the ground or in accidents. The cost of this attrition of aircraft alone was at least $4,800 million [$4.8 billion]. Figures for the complete cost of the war to the United States were incalculable, but $27,000 million [$27 billion] was a reasonable estimate for 1968.[57]

These figures, which are conservative, represented only part of the price paid. The direct result of escalation and attrition strategy, they did not include the cost of a nation torn, with no visible means of immediately repairing the damage, and at a peculiar historical time of particular stress from within and without. The human and material costs, however, emphasized the poverty of a strategy founded on ignorance and executed in arrogance, a strategy whose failure drove a

President from the White House—a defeated man, " . . . unwept, un-honored and unsung."

CHAPTER SIXTY-NINE

1. Johnson, *Public Papers of* . . . , 1968, Book I, 25.
2. Johnson, *The Vantage Point* . . . , 380. Johnson here characteristically attempted to shift blame to the press corps: " . . . I relied instead on the 'background' briefings that my advisers and I, as well as the State and Defense departments, had provided members of the press corps for many weeks. In those briefings we had stressed that heavy action could be expected soon." See also, Westmoreland, 321: " . . . In retrospect, I believe that I and officials in Washington should have tried to do more to alert the American public to the coming of a major offensive. . . . "
3. Bucher. See also, Gallery. Although the North Koreans released the crew eleven months later, they kept the ship and her secrets.
4. *Time,* January 19, 1968.
5. Ibid., January 26, 1968.
6. Walt, "The Nature of the War in Vietnam."
7. UPI, Washington, February 5, 1968.
8. U.S. Marine Corps, "Khe Sanh Wrap-Up."
9. Shaplen, *The Road from War,* 192, 212–13. See also, Karnow, 523–66, for a comprehensive account of this action.
10. Institute for Strategic Studies, "The United States," *Strategic Survey,* 1968.
11. Johnson, *Public Papers of* . . . , 1968, Book I, 155–8.
12. Johnson, *The Vantage Point* . . . , 384. See also, Schandler, 74–91, for a concise analysis of the action and its public effect.
13. AP, UPI, Saigon, February 2, 1968.
14. UPI, Saigon, February 2, 1968.
15. UPI, Saigon, February 6, 1968. See also, Westmoreland, 332, who claims 37,000 enemy killed.
16. Beaufre.
17. Kalb and Abel, 209–10. See also, Sheehan et al., 594–5.
18. Johnson, *The Vantage Point* . . . , 386.
19. Sheehan et al., 615–21. See also, Hoopes; Shaplen, *The Road from War,* 192–3: "American officials estimate that the whole [pacification] program, which was just beginning to make some small headway, has lost three or four months, and maybe more."
20. Johnson, *The Vantage Point* . . . , 384.
21. Baldwin, "The Foes Is Hurting."
22. Johnson, *The Vantage Point* . . . , 389.
23. Hoopes, 145–6.
24. Ibid., 204–5. See also, Brandon.
25. Sheehan et al., 600. See also, Johnson, *The Vantage Point* . . . ; Hoopes.
26. Sheehan et al., 600–1.
27. Clifford.
28. Sheehan et al., 601–3. See also, Hoopes, 176.
29. Sheehan et al., 599.
30. Westmoreland, 338. See also, Schandler, 90.
31. Shaplen, *The Road from War,* 210–11, 208.
32. Kellen.
33. Brandon. See also, Heren.
34. Hoopes, 205.
35. Ibid. See also, Ridgway, "Indochina: Disengaging"; Brandon, 133:

To Acheson's surprise, his views were shared by more among those present than he had expected. The one who mattered most, because he too had been a strong supporter of the war, was McGeorge Bundy. He summed up for those supporting Acheson's views and admitted, in self-flagellating mood, that "for the first time in my life I find myself agreeing on this issue with George Ball."

36. Personal letter from General Walt to the author.
37. Institute for Strategic Studies, "The United States," *Strategic Survey,* 1968. See also, Colby, 168–9, 231–4, 267–86.
38. Colby, 234.
39. Rice, 108. See also, Blaufarb, 246–8; Colby, 234, 266–76; Lewy.
40. Rice, 108. See also, Lewy.
41. Hackworth, 736.
42. Karnow, 602.
43. Ibid.
44. Rice, 108
45. Johnson, *The Vantage Point* . . . , 417.
46. Johnson, *Public Papers of* . . . , 1968, Book I, 499.
47. *Time,* May 10, 1968.
48. Ibid., June 21, 1968.
49. Ibid., June 6, 1969.
50. Jenkins.
51. Johnson, *The Vantage Point* . . . , 523.
52. Clifford. See also, Johnson, *The Vantage Point* . . . , 511, who did not find Clifford so pessimistic.
53. Johnson, *The Vantage Point* . . . , 512.
54. Clifford. See also, Kissinger, "The Viet Nam Negotiations," which questions the advisability of American insistence on Saigon's participation in the first place.
55. Johnson, *The Vantage Point* . . . , 524.
56. Johnson, *Public Papers of* . . . , 1968, Book I, 1099 ff.
57. Institute for Strategic Studies, "The United States," *Strategic Survey,* 1968.

CHAPTER 70

The summing up (1): the Bible and the Sword • *Not "reason good enough"* • *Communists and dominoes* • *Inside South Vietnam* • *Economics* • *Government versus press: America—the communications failure*

LYNDON JOHNSON FAILED in Vietnam for many of the same reasons that John Kennedy failed (see Chapter 60). The key to failure lay in substituting ambition for policy. *Stop communism* appealed to Johnson, a man of " . . . little background and much uncertainty in foreign affairs" (in the words of one subordinate),[1] even more than it had appealed to Kennedy. A Texas Baptist, Johnson had been raised in shadows of GOOD and EVIL. He was a great believer in the Bible and the Sword, and while he quoted one, he wielded the other. When neither faith nor force served him well, he was lost.

Johnson's downfall began before he was elected President. Like other worthy but myopic Americans, he accepted the "strong man" thesis that resulted in the American government's prostrating itself before the pudgy form of Ngo Dinh Diem. As a southern Democrat, Johnson wore scars from the Republican excoriation that followed the loss of Nationalist China to Mao's Communists. In spring of 1954, following the Geneva Conference, he said, " . . . American foreign policy has never in all its history suffered such a stunning reversal. . . . We stand in clear danger of being left naked and alone in a hostile world."[2] He did not believe that his party could survive another such loss, and when Diem—whom he had called the Winston Churchill of Southeast Asia—failed him, he turned to force.

The President early displayed his line of thought in a National Security Action Memorandum which he approved shortly after assuming office and which read in part:

> . . . It remains the central objective of the United States in South Vietnam to assist the people and Government of that country to

win their contest against the externally directed and supported communist conspiracy. The test of all U.S. decisions and actions in this area should be the effectiveness of their contribution to this purpose.[3]

Johnson greatly expanded this relatively mild statement in his famous Baltimore speech of April 1965 (see Chapter 63), where he repeated misplaced ambition emphasized by misdirected appeal, neither to change during the next three years. His eloquence not only failed to propel Ho Chi Minh to the conference table, but it prompted a rather negative reaction both in the United States and throughout the world. This should have warned Johnson and his advisers. In his peroration, he had asked the American people: " . . . Have we, each of us, all done all we can do? Have we done enough?" The true leader leads by example. Had Johnson asked himself this question, he would have had to reply no. In his crusading zeal, the President was forgetting wise Demades' admonition to the assembly " . . . to have a care lest in guarding heaven they should lose earth." Like an emperor of old, he was crying, "Justice must be done, even if the world should perish."[4] The President should have respected the dissident opinions of those who attempted to warn him of Demades' words. Critics with such credentials as George Kennan, Matthew Ridgway, James Gavin, and David Shoup should not have been lightly dismissed. Sufficiently disturbing currents were at work at the beginning of Johnson's administration to call for the most penetrating examination of policy. The President might have asked himself, as for example Edward Lansdale, an expert on Vietnam, later asked *himself*, " . . . What is it exactly, that we seek in Viet Nam? . . . We have to answer the question *fully*. . . . Without a sound answer, the seemingly endless war in Viet Nam becomes just that—seemingly endless. Alternatively, it may be headed for an end that could be dishonorable, with profound consequences."[5] He could have listened to intelligent and courageous officers such as General Matthew Ridgway, who in 1967 warned:

> . . . A war without goals would be most dangerous of all, and nearly as dangerous would be a war with only some vaguely stated aim, such as "victory" or "freedom from aggression" or "the right of the people to choose their own government." Generalities like these make admirable slogans, but authorities today must be hardheaded and specific in naming exactly what goal we are trying to reach and exactly what price we are willing to pay for reaching it. Otherwise, we may find that, in spite of ourselves, the whole conduct of the war will be left in the hands of men who see only victory as the proper objective and who have never had to define

that word in terms plain enough to be understood by all the world's people.

Ridgway continued in words strengthened by simplicity:

> . . . A limited war is not merely a small war that has not yet grown to full size. It is a war in which the objectives are specifically limited in the light of our national interest and our current capabilities. A war that is "open-ended"—that has no clearly delineated geographical, political and military goals beyond "victory"—is a war that may escalate itself indefinitely, as wars will, with one success requiring still another to insure the first one. . . . [6]

Had Johnson pursued this question of specific goals, had he demanded that civil and military advisers answer it fully, had he taken counsel not so much of fears as of unpalatable facts, he would not have weakened his position, as he did, by basing it on arguable premises. To pursue the strategy foisted by his military and civil advisers, demanded "exquisite reason," but, unlike Sir Andrew, the President lacked even "reason good enough." At a time when he and his advisers should have been questioning, they were accepting. Townsend Hoopes, who became Deputy Assistant Secretary of Defense for International Security Affairs in January 1965, discerned no " . . . central guiding philosophy" in American foreign policy, only hit-and-miss efforts motivated by the belief of Johnson and his principal advisers in a monolithic Communist threat, despite both Russia's traditional disinterest in Southeast Asia and her current quarrel with China (indisputably the most significant international development since Tito's defection and Chiang Kai-shek's fall). Dean Rusk, McGeorge Bundy, Robert McNamara, Walt Rostow, Maxwell Taylor, William Westmoreland, members of the JCS—each spoke frequently and feelingly of "Communist aggression," while never fully defining the term or fitting the facts to the precise situation in Vietnam. Hoopes later wrote that " . . . to the President's men in early 1965, there seemed no logical stopping point between isolationism and globalism." Perhaps even more dangerous, he found these men supremely confident of militarily stopping the North Vietnamese and, with that, all "wars of national liberation."[7]

The President and his advisers grossly erred in trying to make a complex problem so simple. Unduly influenced by American economic and military power, frightened by the bogeyman of international communism, they accepted shibboleths bequeathed by Eisenhower and Kennedy and polished them with perfervid rhetoric made the more specious by crusade-like appeal. With one or two exceptions, they were yesterday's men living in tomorrow's world—like great-power exponents of another century, they tried to stop the clock of history and succeeded only in producing cacophonous chimes. Listen to Lyndon Johnson writing on the September 1964 White House meeting:

> ... As one gloomy opinion followed another, I suddenly asked whether anyone at the table doubted that Vietnam was "worth all this effort." Ambassador Taylor answered quickly that "we could not afford to let Hanoi win in the interests of our overall position in Asia and in the world." General Wheeler strongly supported the Ambassador's view. It was the unanimous view of the Chiefs of Staff, he said, that if we lost South Vietnam we would lose Southeast Asia—not all at once, and not overnight, but eventually. One country after another on the periphery would give way and look to Communist China as the rising power of the area, he said. John McCone agreed. So did Secretary Rusk, with considerable emphasis.[8]

Johnson failed to add that a great many experts, including top CIA analysts, did not agree with these views.

During the next two years, opposing voices, many of them expressing experience and study of decades, made it clear that the issues at stake were anything but black-and-white. With one or two exceptions, presidential advisers refused to listen. Maxwell Taylor and William Bundy continued to stress but in slight disguise the monolithic-Communist thesis that produced the domino theory: If one falls, all fall. Johnson and most of his advisers persisted in this belief despite demonstrable facts: that a good many insurgencies of two decades stood remote from communism; that insurgency in South Vietnam could not have lasted a month without peasant support; that by threatening Hanoi's existence, American arms had nearly brought rapprochement between China and Soviet Russia, they had brought an internal political development inside China whose full effects might well threaten America's best interests, and they had brought the Soviet presence into an area in which, historically, Russia had displayed little interest.[9] The President and his advisers could have heard these facts from a score of highly qualified and eminently patriotic observers at home and abroad. C. P. Fitzgerald, for example, a distinguished scholar who lived in China for twenty-five years, demolished the domino theory (as others had done earlier): His article in *The Nation,* June 28, 1965, "The Fallacy of the Dominoes," should have been required Administration reading. Fitzgerald pointed out that since if one falls, all fall, then it follows that if one stands, all stand. But this was patently false at a time when Indonesia was in more danger of being taken over by Communists—their own—than Vietnam. He denied the validity of regional protective pacts, for clearly stated historical reasons; in short, he said here was an immensely complicated political situation with deep historical roots:

> ... All these ancient claims and quarrels are more important, more real and more urgent to the peoples of South-East Asia than the conflict of communism backed by China and anti-communism backed by the United States. That contest is seen essentially as the quarrel of two great outsiders, to be used for promoting national ambitions or thwarting those of traditional foes, but in itself extraneous to the countries themselves. The Asians may well be wrong to take such an attitude, but the West is also much deluded when it thinks of these states as being without personalities of their own, willing to enlist on one side or the other in a global conflict, obedient to the behests of Washington or Peking.

The real appeal in these countries, evidence suggests, is nationalism, and this is one reason why the presence of Western armed forces, which provide an anti-nationalist target, is so dangerous. The challenge calls for a much more subtle approach and for extremely limited objectives: " ... it must be remembered that this area is the region adjacent to China, in which its influence through the centuries has always been present, sometimes powerful and active, at other times dormant, but by the mere facts of geography, never extinct."[10]

Not a word do we find of such heretical notions either in official statements of the day or in the Pentagon papers. Were similar opinions reported by American diplomats throughout the area? Were such opinions debated in high councils? Perhaps someday we shall know the answers. Some argument must have existed, though Johnson's memoirs are lacking substance in this respect. In the January 1967 issue of *Foreign Affairs,* we find McGeorge Bundy carefully disclaiming the theretofore sacrosanct domino theory, but, by then, Bundy had left the government;[11] we also find indirect confirmation in later disillusionment expressed by Clark Clifford and Townsend Hoopes. In 1965, however, and for the next two years, any government official daring to question the cornerstone of Administration policy would have been tagged a "nervous Nellie" and relegated to limbo.

The President's top civil and military officials equally could insist on Hanoi's dominant role in the war as proclaimed in the 1965 White Paper.[12] But this did not wash with a good many American and foreign observers and experts, who were aware of the early minimum role played by Hanoi, particularly in troop and supply categories. If a "constant stream" of trained men and supplies was flowing from North to South, a veritable flood of such had already flowed from West to East.[13] Similarly, Communist China's participation in the conflict had been minimal, despite menacing growls from Peking. The partnership between Ho and Mao implied by the President did not exist. Writing in 1967, Donald Zagoria pointed out that

> ... any careful study of Chinese foreign policy during the past fifteen years would have to conclude that although China is a revolutionary power opposing the present status quo, it does not aim to bring about change by its own military force.
>   ... [It is] one of the key messages in Lin Piao's article [September 3, 1965] and one of the basic principles of "liberation wars"—that Communist revolutionaries throughout the world must make their revolutions on their own. Far from giving any notice of any intention to intervene aggressively in Vietnam or in other "people's wars," Lin Piao was rationalizing Peking's unwillingness to intervene directly and massively in such wars. He was reiterating what is essentially a "do-it-yourself" model of revolution for foreign Communists.[14]

In 1965, Ho was walking a tightrope between Chinese and Soviet camps, and President Johnson's attempts to stress the Chinese threat while not mentioning the theretofore prominent villain, the Soviet Union, did not impress intelligent auditors.

The President's "national pledge" was equally specious: " ... We are there because we have a promise to keep." What promise? When? President Eisenhower said that the United States would supply limited aid to South Vietnam, providing Diem carried out essential reforms. Here was a reasonable proposition. Nothing was new about it. It was the beginning of a temporary alliance with presumed attendant advantages to each party. Such alliances crowd the pages of history, and such have been commented on through the ages as, for example, by Spinoza, who, as Leopold Ranke noted,

> ... starts from the principle that states permanently subsist in a state of nature with respect to one another, and does not hesitate to assert that a treaty has force only so long as the causes of it— fear of injury or hope of gain—exist; that no ruler is to be reproached with faithlessness for breaking an alliance he had formerly concluded, as soon as any of the causes which determined him to it should have ceased, since that condition is equal for both parties.

This is little more than common sense. Yet, in less than a decade, Eisenhower's casual alliance became promoted, mostly by American military voices, into a "promise" and now into "a national pledge to help South Viet-Nam defend its independence." Listen to Maxwell Taylor, writing in 1967:

> ... If we are convinced, as I am, that the stake is important, that we are honor-bound to obtain for the people in South Vietnam the right to freedom, then every dollar and every man we have committed in my opinion is justified.[15]

By right to freedom, Taylor undoubtedly included rule by Diem and Nhu and Thieu and Ky and whatever other national war lords would appear in the future—neither Taylor nor any of the other ancient citizens who surrounded the President, with the possible exception of Clifford, realized that Administration ambitions for South Vietnam bore almost no resemblance to the relatively simple goal of the Saigon government, which was to maintain and enlarge its own power structure while yielding minimum freedoms to its peoples. And if the U.S.A. was honor bound to intervene in South Vietnam, then why not in Rhodesia, South Africa, Greece, most of the South American and all the Iron Curtain countries, indeed in any country whose government did not conform to American system or desire?

Attempting to put the record in proper perspective, in 1967 Senator Eugene McCarthy wrote:

> ... It is said that we fight to ensure the credibility of our commitments, to show the world that we honor our treaty obligations. This is the rationale of our politico-military prestige. Yet we have already demonstrated our reliability in Korea and in the protection of Taiwan as well as in Europe.
>
> It is said that we must carry on the war in Vietnam in order to preserve and defend our national honor. Our national honor is not at stake, and should not so readily be offered. In every other great war of the century, we have had the support of what is generally accepted as the decent opinion of mankind. We do not have that today. We cannot, of course, depend only on this opinion to prove our honor; it may not be sound. But always in the past we have not only had this support, but we have used it as a kind of justification for our action.[16]

As for the unforgivable wrong of abandoning " ... this small and brave nation to its enemies, and to the terror that must follow," the President again was indulging in fiction. The homogeneous national picture that he implied did not exist. Viet Cong cadres had controlled large areas of South Vietnam since 1954; in 1965, the enemy controlled probably 90 per cent of the countryside. In 1965, as in 1955, Saigon rule was remote in some areas, ruthless in other areas. A large percentage of peasants did not care who ruled so long as they could till crops and get a fair shake in the market place. The peasants' main concern was not democracy but survival with dignity, and the splendid rhetoric that burbled from Washington and Saigon officialdom was virtually meaningless to bent bodies laboring in rice paddies and on rubber plantations. No one had shown peasants that democracy was worth fighting for, because no one had shown them democracy. As Johnson spoke, the gulf between the Saigon government, the sects, and the peasants was as wide as ever, growing wider.[17]

People who would have been eliminated by a Communist takeover constituted, for the most part, a rapacious ruling minority whose greed and intransigence were keeping the nation, such as it was, in its turbulent, impotent condition. And here was Johnson, like Kennedy and Eisenhower before him, compounding the damage by unfounded fears and loose rhetoric. Once again, Johnson was saying that the West could not survive without this geographical neutrino, this whirling nothing of a country. So many Americans had insisted that a dubious political entity called South Vietnam was an indispensable ally in the war against communism, that South Vietnamese Catholics, Buddhists, mandarins, generals, landowners, merchants, intellectuals, and students began to believe it—so indispensable, that, on occasion, South Vietnamese government leaders such as Khanh could indulge the most virulent language and defiant behavior to the country that was keeping them alive. About this time, a Vietnamese political observer told Robert Shaplen: " . . . In a way, after all the pent-up years under the French and under Diem, we are like children letting off steam. Maybe there will have to be yet another half-dozen coups before we settle down—even though we know we can't afford them."[18] He was wrong. South Vietnam could afford them—as long as the United States insisted on bestowing unqualified support on a rump government whose totalitarian characteristics contradicted a heritage held sacred by thoughtful American citizens. In spring of 1965, a firm threat to abandon South Vietnam was perhaps the only action that could have produced the social-political cohesion necessary to make a nation. The Vietnamese politicians may not have admitted it, but they were in a classic "backs-to-the-wall" position. President Johnson's "solution," his Baltimore speech, removed the wall.

No one could fault the President's assertion of great stakes in play in the international power game. But if retreat from Vietnam would not bring an end to conflict, neither would "victory" in Vietnam. The President was trying to produce a black-and-white center-ring act from a multicolored sideshow. Neither Moscow nor Peking particularly wanted the war to escalate: Moscow did not want to upset its détente with Washington; Peking did not want a strong American military presence on the Asian mainland. However, once the United States made a major commitment in South Vietnam, Moscow and Peking rolled with the punch and moved to exploit the situation. No matter how big, powerful, and rich the U.S.A., no nation could be everywhere at once. While

President Johnson was talking to the world, Chinese money and Chinese technicians were on their way to Tanzania to begin construction of a sixteen-hundred-mile railroad into the interior of Africa; Soviet money and Soviet technicians were working in Cairo's defense ministry; satellite money and satellite technicians were scouring underdeveloped parts of the world for investment and prestige purposes. While American priority effort went to a strategically unimportant country, the Soviet Union and China reinforced their presence in Africa and the Middle East—indeed anywhere that dangerous insurgencies were brewing—to the detriment of the West and with the knowledge that the U.S.A. could not launch a maximum countereffort.

The President's stated objective of "independence" for South Vietnam also rang hollow. Whether the United States or South Vietnam liked it or not, the tragic rump would remain economically and militarily dependent on the United States, just as had Cuba and the Philippines for so many decades, just as Taiwan and Korea were doing.

In trying to justify the American action, the President resembled a boy whistling his way past a cemetery on a dark night. The most cursory reader of American newspapers, magazines, and books knew that the President's stated resolution was not shared by an increasingly influential portion of the nation, including legislators who were beginning to hold second thoughts about the Tonkin Gulf Resolution. Leaving aside domestic and major international problems that were crying for enormous expenditures of expertise and money, nothing in the American character suggested the qualities of patience that Lyndon Johnson claimed in pursuing his ambitions. His statements presupposed a national interest and stamina that did not exist—and for several reasons. The first was a failure in communications that we have already discussed with regard to the Kennedy era. Speaking in 1954 as a senator, Johnson had said: " . . . We will insist upon clear explanations of the policies in which we are asked to cooperate. We will insist that we and the American people be treated as adults, that we have the facts without sugar coating."[19] When, during the Kennedy administration, the press attempted to give the facts, a good many senior American officials bridled and a minor war developed. Kennedy's press representative, Pierre Salinger, warned of the coming storm in 1963, and Vice-President Johnson must have been aware of the dangerous situation. As President he foolishly exacerbated it, and relations between press and officialdom continued to deteriorate. In an article in *Foreign Affairs* in July 1966, veteran correspondent James Reston again warned of a communications breakdown. Far from heeding him, Johnson increasingly scorned the press (which he criticized throughout his memoirs).

As one result, a good many senior officials in Saigon and Washington continued to dissemble; some reporters continued to distort. So complex was the Vietnamese scene that even highly talented correspondents had their hands full in communicating its complex turbulence to the American public. With a few splendid exceptions, not many, publishers unfortunately did not present the war in depth. A British expert on counterinsurgency, Major General Richard Clutterbuck, after visiting South Vietnam, accused three journalist friends

> ... of reporting only what occurred above 12,000 feet. If you put cloud over the world at 12,000 feet, the only things that stick up are rugged and spectacular, and that is what gets reported. They agreed that that was what they did, and said that if they reported anything below 12,000 feet, it would not get into their papers anyway; no one would read it if it did, and they would lose their jobs. We had to leave it at that, and so the real blame falls on the public.[20]

While newspaper publishers, TV-station owners, and public admittedly were culpable, the statement is not altogether true. Reporting in depth (by far the most accurate and intelligent coverage came from Robert Shaplen of *The New Yorker*) was well received by impressive segments of the public, who became aware that the situation scarcely resembled the black-and-white situation described in presidential platitudes.

But for every informed American citizen and even vaguely informed American citizen, dozens existed who had only the foggiest notion of what was going on in Vietnam. Even had it wished to, the Administration could not have alleviated national ignorance by a well-conceived and well-executed educational program because it had already decided that the issues were black and white, and that it was a question of imposing American military will on Hanoi—and damn any American citizen who didn't agree.

The communications problem, which resulted in continuing national ignorance (thus frustration and resentment), gave rise to an even more serious condition. Johnson had embarked on a crusade that the American public did not understand but at first supported, though by no means eagerly, because it trusted its national leaders and its military and civilian officials and because it shared, at least in part, their arrogance of ignorance. But not very long after the Tonkin Gulf Resolution, a tradition began quietly to assert itself. As Bill Moyers, Johnson's press man, later pointed out, the American democratic concept embraces not only a tradition of dissent, but also of consent:

> ... Our system assumes a sense of participation by the people in the making of critical national decisions. When that sense of involvement is absent, when the public feels excluded from the judg-

ments that are made in its name, a policy is doomed from inception, no matter how theoretically valid it may be.

Translating this to Vietnam, Moyers continued:

> ...War is clearly one of those questions on which a government—a democratic government—dare not act without evidence of genuine support. In this case, that support was not deliberately withheld—it simply was not sought. And it was not sought because few if any officials anticipated the war would ever reach the proportions that would require a declaration.[21]

Rather than leveling with the American people, Johnson and his advisers continued in the hope that they could clean up matters—that they could "win"—before the American public realized quite what had happened. That this hope was doomed by a false military strategy did not at first occur except to a very few advisers, and these Johnson ignored and later banished. When truth began leaking out, when casualties and expenses rose out of all proportion to gained results, impressive portions of the American public rebelled.

Parts of the United States were already rebelling at the time of Johnson's Baltimore speech in the spring of 1965. Although Communist leaders in South and North Vietnam were provincial and often naïve, they sensed currents at work in the United States that suggested France of an earlier day. These leaders had experienced protracted warfare, many had been fighting since 1943 and even earlier (some since 1932), and from 1946 onward, they had witnessed the pressures of protracted guerrilla warfare at work on Western countries. In their minds, protracted warfare had gained one victory. It could now gain another. An American president could proclaim that his nation would not be defeated or would not grow tired—but Communists had only to read American newspapers and magazines to realize that this was proclamation without solid national support. Throughout his memoirs, the President repeatedly stressed Hanoi's unwillingness to negotiate a peace in these crucial years. Never once, apparently, did it occur to him to ask himself why; never once does he suggest that, being human, he was fallible and his basic precepts could have been fallacious.

CHAPTER SEVENTY

1. Hoopes, 2.
2. *New York Times,* May 7, 1954, quoted in Eden, *Towards Peace in Indo-China,* 7.
3. Johnson, *The Vantage Point . . . ,* 45.
4. *Fiat justitia, pereat mundus.*
5. Lansdale, "Viet Nam—Still the Search for Goals." This article demon-

strates only a few contradictions that occur when ambition is substituted for policy.

6. Ridgway, *The Korean War*, 232, 245.
7. Hoopes, 1, 16.
8. Johnson, *The Vantage Point . . .* , 120.
9. Zagoria, *Vietnam Triangle . . .* , 27 ff.
10. Quoted in *Survival*, September 1965. See also, C.P. Fitzgerald; Zagoria, "Who Fears the Domino Theory?"; Harries, "Should the U.S. Withdraw from Asia?" for a dissenting opinion; Reischauer, an acknowledged expert on the Far East and Asia, whose telling arguments as to the minimal importance of a Communist "victory" in Vietnam were validated by that very "victory"; Soedjatmoko; Harris; Salisbury, "Image and Reality in Indochina," which discusses distorted viewpoints of both sides.
11. McGeorge Bundy.
12. See, for example, Taylor, *Responsibility and Response*, 26: " . . . as early as 1961 when I headed a mission to Vietnam . . . the mission called attention to the fact that the real source of the guerrilla strength in South Vietnam was not in South Vietnam but in North Vietnam. It was perfectly clear that the direction, the supplies, the reinforcements, and the leadership came from the North. . . . "
13. Morrock, "Revolution and Intervention in Vietnam," in Horowitz, *Containment and Revolution*, 244–5. Hans Morgenthau commented: " . . . Let it be said right away that the (State Department) white paper is a dismal failure. The discrepancy between its assertions and the factual evidence adduced to support them borders on the grotesque." See also, U.S. Department of Defense, "Working Paper on the North Vietnamese Role in the War in South Vietnam," which asserts, rather than proves, Hanoi's dominant role from the beginning; Tanham and Duncanson:

   . . . In reality, the Marxist-Leninists of the East not only take pride in winning power with a minimum contribution from their own side, but have found from experience that this is a more reliable road to victory. Besides concealing the directing hand, it leaves the door open to repudiation of unsuccessful insurgencies. . . .

   Lacouture, 182, cites Pentagon advice " . . . that the deliveries from the North were . . . on the order of fifteen to twenty per cent [of Viet Cong needs]."
14. Zagoria, *Vietnam Triangle . . .* , 79. See also, H.L. Duncan.
15. Maxwell Taylor, *Responsibility and Response*, 37.
16. McCarthy, 190–1.
17. Duncanson, *Government and Revolution in Vietnam*.
18. Shaplen, *The Road from War*, 7.
19. Deakin.
20. Royal United Service Institution Seminar: Brigadier Kenneth Hunt of the Institute for Strategic Studies also complained of a press deficiency:

   . . . The most dispiriting thing is to go to a Press conference in Saigon. It is not merely because the quality of the briefing is kindergarten, that it comes out in a dead-pan American style. The quality of the questions asked by reporters is also often poor and amateurish. That is reflected in what comes back and is printed.

21. Moyers.

CHAPTER 71

The summing up (II): use of air power • The Douhet theory • Strategic bombing in World War II • The paradox of nuclear stalemate • Lessons of the Korean War • American expectations in North Vietnam • Historical factors • Harrison Salisbury reports from the North • Bombs and international diplomacy

THE PRESIDENT'S DECISION to carry the war to the North undoubtedly came as an unpleasant surprise to Hanoi. But this decision could not change the axis of war, which remained in the South. Moreover, the intention to alter enemy will by use of aerial bombardment introduced several factors that seem to have escaped official cognizance.

The use of air power produces both moral and material results, and the tally means one thing to the user, another to the receiver. On advice of his military chiefs, Johnson was embracing a modified Douhet theory of aerial bombing when he agreed to send American planes over North Vietnam. This theory emerged in 1921, when Giulio Douhet, an Italian air officer, wrote a small book, *The Command of the Air.*

Douhet correctly foresaw the importance of the new arm:

> . . . By virtue of this new weapon . . . the battlefield will be limited only by the boundaries of the nations at war, and all of their citizens will become combatants since all of them will be exposed to the aerial offensives of the enemy. There will be no distinction any longer between soldiers and civilians . . . All of this must inevitably effect a profound change in the form of future wars. . . .

Air power, Douhet prophesied, would prove omnipotent as it already had in World War I despite " . . . anti-aircraft guns, and reconnaissance and pursuit planes." Douhet made no claim to selectivity or subtlety:

. . . The complete destruction of the objective has moral and material effects, the repercussions of which may be tremendous. To give us some idea of the extent of these repercussions, we need only envisage what would go on among the civilian population of congested cities once the enemy announced that he would bomb such centers relentlessly, making no distinction between military and non-military objectives.

In Douhet's mind, as in Foch's before him, the moral was as important as the physical:

. . . We should always keep in mind that aerial offensives can be directed not only against objectives of least physical resistance, but against those of least moral resistance as well. For instance, an infantry regiment in a shattered trench may still be capable of some resistance even after losing two-thirds of its effectives; but when the working personnel of a factory sees one of its machine shops destroyed, even with a minimum loss of life, it quickly breaks up and the plant ceases to function.[1]

Professional airmen in the West such as Billy Mitchell in the United States and Hugh Trenchard in England, who were attempting to build air forces and were obstructed at every turn by army and navy traditionalists, embraced Douhet's theory as another argument in favor of the new arm. In the late twenties, Mitchell sacrificed his career by demonstrating that bombs could sink a battleship; as we have seen, the British claimed strategic-tactical successes in Iraq and in northwestern frontier provinces in India, as did U. S. Marines in Nicaragua (see Chapter 23). Goering's Luftwaffe experimented with the theory during the Spanish civil war, at one point eliminating the town of Guernica; at another, testing results of carpet bombing.

Variations appeared early in World War II. Older readers will remember horrendous pictures of Stuka dive bombers preparing cities such as Rotterdam for paratroop invasion and later attacking refugee columns in France in order to cause panic and impede military movement. The Battle of Britain raised the psychological level of the theory, but the Luftwaffe failed to bring England to its knees. When skillful and determined RAF opposition produced heavy German losses in aircraft and pilots, which could not easily be replaced, Hitler terminated the campaign.

The theory did not die with this failure. RAF and American strategic air bombings attempted to destroy Hitler's industrial plant and thereby force Germany from the war. RAF saturation bombings culminating in the destruction of Dresden attempted to break the German people's will; American fire bombings of Tokyo and the final destruction of Hiroshima and Nagasaki by atomic bombs did play a major role in breaking Japanese will to continue war.

Thus the Douhet theory: At its nicest, strategic bombing; at its ugliest, genocide. And this is why the theory is fallacious: first, the more bombs dropped, the lower the morale—but not necessarily a significant lessening of will to resist. This is a challenge situation familiar to psychology. Challenge, discipline, and incentive all play major roles; resistance is never easily analyzed. These factors help to explain why medieval fortresses held out against overwhelming odds, why, in World War I, neither side would yield on the western front, why men in battle, for example American marines on Guadalcanal in those black days of late 1942, tolerated weeks of bombing and shelling by Japanese aircraft and ships without losing their will to fight. Civilians of London, Berlin, Tokyo, and numerous other cities reacted similarly. Aerial bombings subverted civil will to resist only by killing the holders of that will. Conventional strategic bombing did not kill enough holders of that will fast enough; atomic bombing did.

The advent of the atomic bomb seemed to fructify Douhet's theory, but only as long as one side held a monopoly. Even then, moral aspects outweighed the practical: Premeditated genocide is not an acceptable clause in the Western code of civilization, as the Germans discovered. And not only the Germans. At the height of allied bombing in World War II, the American air force general Carl ("Tooey") Spaatz caviled at the RAF's saturation bombing program. The American people's reaction to the atomic bombings of Hiroshima and Nagasaki was also disturbed, and if those of us who were training for the invasion of Japan proper were pleased with the war's sudden termination, this did not erase a feeling of guilt, however nebulous, in the national conscience. As General Matthew Ridgway wrote in 1956, when discussing the use of strategic air power: " . . . to my mind, such mass destruction is repugnant to the ideals of a Christian nation. It is incompatible with the basic aim of the free world in war, which is to win a just and enduring peace".[2]

Once the Soviet Union broke atomic monopoly, the atomic bomb's omnipotence evaporated in an air of retribution. The paradox of nuclear stalemate—of destructive impotence—resulted. Both moral and practical aspects prevented American use of atomic bombs in Korea and in North Vietnam. At the height of the bombing of North Vietnam, in October 1967, Robert McNamara laid the issue on the line in a top-secret memorandum to President Johnson:

> . . . It is clear that, to bomb the North sufficiently to make a radical impact upon Hanoi's political, economic and social structure, would require an effort which we could make but which would

931

not be stomached either by our own people or by world opinion; and it would involve a serious risk of drawing us into open war with China.[3]

Material results of strategic bombing are something else again. Strategic-bombing proponents have frequently overstated their case, which is usual with minority arguments. World War II offered excellent examples of bombing's strength and weaknesses. Any interested reader can find myriad statistics in the postwar *Strategic Bombing Survey*, whose directors included George Ball, John Galbraith, and Paul Nitze. The survey cited impressive accomplishments of allied air forces, giving fliers their due and then some; but it also established that workers did not flee an area when first bombs fell, as Douhet and later strategic-bombing proponents had it. Bombing, although interrupting production, rarely halted it, at least until the very end, when allied ground forces already had invaded Germany. Permanent damage was not nearly so great as current estimates had suggested, and in some areas production even increased, while in others reserve stocks and emergency measures provided short-term compensation for havoc wrought. Bombing raids in July and August 1943 on Hamburg killed some sixty to a hundred thousand people and destroyed 55–60 per cent of the city, including three hundred thousand homes. Yet

> ... Hamburg as an economic unit was not destroyed. It never fully recovered from the bombing but in five months it had regained 80 per cent of its former productivity, despite the fact that great areas of the city lay, and still lie, in dust and rubble. As in the case of industrial plants where it was found much easier to destroy the buildings than the machines within, so also it is much easier to destroy the physical structures of a city than to wipe out its economic life.

Saturation bombings, what the RAF called "area raids," also provided startling "kill" figures. The Strategic Bombing Survey estimated that bombs eliminated 3.6 million homes, or approximately 20 per cent of Germany's total dwelling space; bombs killed about three hundred thousand people and injured some 780,000. Although " ... bombing appreciably affected the German will to resist," bombs did not crumble that will:

> ... War production is the critical measuring rod of the effects of lowered morale in the German war effort. Allied bombing widely and seriously depressed German civilian morale, but depressed and discouraged workers were not necessarily unproductive workers.

As has been seen, armaments production continued to mount till mid-1944.

Strategic bombing also received a setback from a cost-analysis standpoint. It proved very expensive in both lives and cost of bombers and bombs. The establishment required to operate a peak twenty-eight thousand combat planes numbered 1.335 million men. Nearly eighty thousand American and eighty thousand British airmen were lost in action, while eighteen thousand American and twenty-two thousand British planes were lost or damaged beyond repair. Up to VE-day, the American air effort in Europe alone cost over $43 billion! A final factor emerged after the war: Industrial complexes that had been damaged and destroyed, not to mention surrounding urban areas, had to be rebuilt, with the victors, primarily the U.S.A., picking up the tab.[4]

Strategic-tactical bombing and interdiction also proved chimerical. Lavish claims advanced by proponents of air power were often matched by lavish failures. Few, if any, interested persons disputed tactical advantages derived from command of the air. We have glanced at these in the 1920s and 1930s. But, as Gwynn pointed out in 1934, air power was not a tactical panacea and could not apply in all places at all times. In World War II, tactical air power proved a tremendous boon to allied armies, not only in clearing skies of enemy aircraft but in close air support, a fine art developed particularly by U. S. Marines. But such accomplishments did not obliterate shortcomings: Tactical air power did not "win" ground battles, any more than strategic air power "won" the war. Writing years later, General Matthew Ridgway recalled that limitations of air power " . . . were never better illustrated than in World War II, when the Germans were able to maintain some twenty-six divisions south of the Alps in Italy, using a few mountain passes to keep them supplied for two years, regardless of uncontested Allied air supremacy."[5]

The Korean War added to lessons already learned (but either ignored or forgotten by proponents of aerial warfare). Air Force, Navy and Marine aircraft controlled the skies, destroying every industrial target in North Korea, flying thousands of tactical missions, interdicting enemy communications and supporting allied ground troops—but air power did not prevent ammunition, food, and replacements from reaching the enemy's front-line units. "For the Air Force," General James Gavin wrote,

> . . . Korea had been a disillusioning and frustrating experience. Air Force leaders had assumed that air superiority, air surveillance and air attacks would smash the North Korean drive and demolish the North Korean military establishment. They had trumpeted this

point of view both to the public and to the President. When the bombing failed to halt the North Korean war effort they developed the myth of the Yalu sanctuary. If only they could bomb Red Chinese Manchuria, which lay beyond the Yalu River, they said, everything would turn out all right. Thus the Air Force was able to avoid, at least in public, confronting the evidence that in Korea both strategically and tactically air power had failed. Unfortunately from their frustration sprang a readiness to answer any challenge to American power with threats of total nuclear war.[6]

In those momentous months of 1964 and 1965, Johnson and his advisers displayed massive historical ignorance of air power. Johnson himself had fallen victim to a powerful civil-military lobby that preached virtues of air power without mentioning its severe limitations. Ignorant of the true nature of the war in Vietnam, frustrated at lack of progress in "winning" it, and frightened by recent and substantial reverses, Johnson proved particularly prone to panaceas.

Judging from later events, he probably also believed that he could control the action, that he needn't place all military eggs in one basket. In his mind, he could turn air power on and off like a water tap, and if this did not succeed, he could follow with ground and sea power, a rationale enthusiastically preached by the JCS and some top civil advisers. This fallacious reasoning is of interest, first because as bombing began and failed it changed; second because the Nixon administration would bring it back to life. Maxwell Taylor early wrote:

> . . . by February, 1965, it had become perfectly apparent that we must strike at this external base [North Vietnam] and do so for three reasons . . . to let the people of South Vietnam feel that for the first time, after eleven years of bitter warfare, they were striking back against the source of all their troubles [!] . . . to utilize our superiority in the air to strike military targets which, if destroyed, would have the effect of restraining or making more difficult the infiltration of men and supplies from North Vietnam into South Vietnam . . . to remind the leadership in Hanoi, the men who were directing this war in the South, that little by little through the progressive, restrained application of force by bombing, they would pay an ever-increasing price for a continuation of their aggression in the South. In other words, we were following the basic military principle applicable to all wars—that the objective of military action is the will of the enemy—in the conviction that, by the use of our air power, we could operate on that will and eventually create in the minds of the leadership of Hanoi a picture of the inevitability of defeat and the realization of the prohibitive cost of continued aggression. . . . [7]

Some hawks went even further. Admiral Sharp would inform a *Reader's Digest* audience in 1969 that the secret to "winning" the war in Vietnam was relatively simple: " . . . All that we had to do to win was to use our existing air power—properly."[8] Sharp, as well as members of the JCS and other hawks, argued from the beginning for the Pentagon's Option B: " . . . fast full squeeze" with "hot-blood actions" (see Chapters 62 and 63). He and his "colleagues in the field" wanted " . . . to bring the economy of North Vietnam to a halt," naturally by bombing. Parroting Rostow's earlier thesis, Sharp argued that " . . . the primary purpose of the air campaign against North Vietnam should have been to disrupt the enemy's economy and thus destroy his ability to wage war." Sharp wanted " . . . a sustained, maximum-effort attack on all of the enemy's war-supporting industries, transportation facilities, military complexes, petroleum-storage depots . . . "; he wanted Haiphong Harbor mined and the port closed. Although he understood that " . . . the Joint Chiefs of Staff supported my position 100 percent," most of his requests were denied by Secretary of Defense McNamara, who " . . . arbitrarily and consistently discarded the advice of his military advisers."

About all the reader can say is thank God he did, for Sharp goes on:

> . . . It may well be that our civilian leadership believed that to use our military tools properly, to eliminate the enemy's ability to make war would have been to risk a nuclear confrontation with the Soviet Union. Personally, I believe the risk was minimal; in any case, a nation which is not willing to take calculated risks to achieve its objectives should never go to war in the first place. Further, I believe that once a political decision is made to commit American troops to battle, we are morally obliged to use our military power in such a way as to end the fighting as quickly as possible.[9]

If Taylor and other advisers did not go as far as Rostow, Sharp, and the JCS, they nonetheless erred, not only in estimating strategic effects of air power but also in estimating tactical effects of air power in guerrilla warfare. It is a great pity that these influential experts had never studied such recent insurgencies as those in Indonesia, the Philippines, Malaya, Cyprus, and French Indochina, where interdiction air raids played about as effective a role in the ground action as Drake's naval raids on the Spanish Main played in England's war against Spain. In the same work quoted above, Taylor pointed to

> . . . the inability of the enemy to maintain and keep in action an indefinite number of men supported only by a clandestine logistic system. Their logistic problem increases if we continue to conduct

air attacks against their lines of supply. It grows if, by the use of our mobile offensive capability, our heli-borne forces keep attacking the main forces of the Vietcong, requiring them to defend themselves, to consume ammunition and supplies, and to suffer heavy casualties. Under such pressures, they probably cannot maintain much larger forces than they have now.[10]

Taylor was seeing the enemy in Taylor's terms, failing to realize that PAVN had not attained Western military sophistication and that its logistic demands were not to be compared with American demands. Tactical bombing against conventional armies brings meager rewards—against quasi-guerrilla armies, it brings virtually no rewards. American intelligence estimated that the *entire* Viet Cong needed twelve tons of outside supply per day[11] (versus five hundred tons daily needed to support operations by the 1st Cavalry [Airmobile] Division alone!) to carry on. How are you going to interdict effectively such a meager supply requirement?

President Johnson's decision in 1965, then, ignored two primary lessons concerning air power. The first was that chances were virtually nil of bending Hanoi's will to the extent of bringing a cringing North Vietnamese government to the conference table. Unless, it should be added, atomic bombs were employed—but this was unacceptable from both moral and practical viewpoints, and the President knew this.

The second was that aerial interdiction could impede but not stop passage of men and supplies from North to South. Neither could it noticeably halt production in North Vietnam, because the industrial complex essential to furnishing targets to bombers did not exist. To halt cottage production meant eliminating cottages, a lengthy, repugnant, and expensive task, as we learned in the strategic-bombing effort against Japan in World War II. To stop arms and equipment from entering North Vietnam meant risking war by interdicting Chinese and Soviet supply lines, and since the Administration wished to avoid war with either nation, this meant that supply lines would remain open.

These lessons proved valid. Almost everything that history either had suggested or confirmed about aerial bombing was demonstrated in North Vietnam and along the Ho Chi Minh Trail by end of 1967. The first outstanding fact was expense in American lives and machines. Although North Vietnam possessed neither an air force nor early-warning systems, the Soviets and Chinese vied in supplying anti-aircraft guns and missiles. Soviet SAM missile sites soon appeared around priority objectives. As early as 1966, American pilots were reporting that North Vietnam bridges were protected by " . . . an awesome curtain of exploding steel,"[12] words similar to those used by American pilots flying over Dien Bien Phu in 1954. Hundreds of aircraft were shot down;

those pilots and crews not killed were to languish in ghastly North Vietnamese prison camps.

The second fact was operational cost compared to results obtained. It is difficult even for a student of warfare to comprehend the vastness of the American air effort. By end of 1967, American airplanes—air force, navy, and marine—had dropped more bombs on Vietnam than the allied total expended on Germany in World War II. We must add to this hundreds of thousands of rockets and machine-gun bullets and tons of napalm. Initial operational costs shot upward and continued to rise, not a matter of millions of dollars, but of billions, which did not include more billions of indirect cost.

The third fact was international opprobrium wrought by bombings. In Ramsey Clark's words,

> ... Few people in Asia, Africa or Latin America can identify sympathetically with well-fed representatives of a rich society journeying ten thousand miles to pilot multimillion dollar B-52s and drop death and destruction on underfed Indochinese in miserable villages or along jungle trails.[13]

In early 1966, George Kennan warned the Senate Foreign Relations Committee that strategic bombing would jeopardize American relationships with Japan and other nations:

> ... Our motives are widely misinterpreted, and the spectacle ... of Americans inflicting grievous injury on the lives of a poor and helpless people, and particularly a people of different race and color, no matter how warranted by military necessity or by the excesses of the adversary our operations may seem to us to be or may genuinely be, produces reactions among millions of people throughout the world profoundly detrimental to the image we would like them to hold of this country.[14]

International voices soon confirmed the validity of this warning. In Charles de Gaulle's words, " ... We find it totally detestable that a small country should be bombed by a very big one." Arthur Schlesinger concluded that bombings have brought

> ... the rise of a new form of anti-Americanism, emotional rather than ideological, leading toward a serious estrangement between Europe and America. ... When we began to bomb the oil deposits, James Reston wrote, "There is now not a single major nation in the world that supports Mr. Johnson's latest adventure in Hanoi and Haiphong. ... "[15]

Other difficulties were unique to Vietnam. Townsend Hoopes, who was Assistant Secretary of the Air Force in 1967, later listed " . . . four adverse and intractable factors" when it came to bombing effectiveness in the North: the relatively small supply needs of the North, both for its own purposes and to pursue war in the South; the North's ability to keep going under heavy bombardment; poor weather from late September to early May (" . . . visual bombing attacks were possible on the average of only five days per month, and were frequently precluded for from two to three weeks at a time"); this meant not only diminution of attacks, but inaccurate bombing (" . . . in bad weather the bombs fell, on the average, between 1,500 and 1,800 feet from the target center"). Due to the military policy of "massive retaliation" during the Eisenhower era, " . . . bombing accuracies had improved hardly at all in the period between Korea and Vietnam."[16]

What was the net accomplishment?

Very little, except once again to disprove the Douhet theory and confirm Sir Robert Thompson's later suggestion that " . . . the bombing of the North was probably the greatest of the strategic errors of the war."[17] In fairness to Douhet, and as any number of American air force officers and other hawks have repeatedly stated, the American effort was selective (in theory, anyway) and not a saturation-bombing program. At President Johnson's insistence, planes bombed and strafed "military" targets only. Major targets at first consisted of forward supply depots and installations and of "choke points," for example key bridges or railroad yards or warehouses and oil depots. As these were neutralized or destroyed, air intelligence officers furnished secondary targets, usually smaller depots and railheads. Planes flying "armed reconnaissance" also fired on targets of opportunity, such as convoys and trains, repair parties, occasional troop units; if nothing else, planes dropped bomb loads on roads and rail lines.

As bombs and bullets killed more bridges and culverts and roads, then exploded on factories and refineries, then crept around and into Hanoi and killed and wounded thousands of civilians, and as General Curtis LeMay spoke of bombing the North Vietnamese back to the stone age—the moral and material fallacies were becoming more apparent. Harrison Salisbury, veteran correspondent of the *New York Times*, visited Hanoi in December 1966 and January 1967. He found the city in a state of defense, with thousands of individual concrete shelters " . . . spaced three or four feet apart along every boulevard and street in the city, round dark cavities with concrete lids." Rather than shocked and frightened, the people struck him as determined:

938

... I seldom talked with any North Vietnamese without some reference coming into the conversation of the people's preparedness to fight ten, fifteen, even twenty years in order to achieve victory. . . . I began to realize that this was a national psychology. It might have been inspired by the regime, but it certainly was entirely natural. And, I believed, it suited the North Vietnamese temperament. . . .

The regime had little trouble in exploiting this feeling into strength. Mr. Salisbury was shown what could hardly have been a staged scene: the wreck of the Vandien truck park, on the outskirts of Hanoi,

> . . . listed as one of the major targets of our December 13 [1966] attack. It was not a formidable target when I viewed it from Route Nationale No. 1—just a half-dozen loading sheds, blasted by American bombs. But in attacking these the bombers had wrecked what was called the Polish Friendship School, probably half a mile distant on the other side of the highway. . . . I could accept the bombing of the school as an accident. But I was not surprised to find that the North Vietnamese thought it was deliberate. . . .

The "major" target, incidentally, contained twelve or fourteen broken-down buses and trucks. As Salisbury rhetorically asked: " . . . For this kind of target was it worth jeopardizing $2 million dollar planes and the precious lives of American pilots?"[18]

The North Vietnamese Government constantly exploited, from the propaganda standpoint, other bombing mistakes, such as destruction of Namdinh village in an attempt to neutralize its rail yards. Even without mistakes, the government would have had little difficulty in exploiting the people's hatred. Fixed installations were few in North Vietnam; they had been built by personal sacrifice, and the people could hardly refrain from hating that which destroyed them. The government went so far as to arm factory workers and some citizens in Hanoi with ordinary rifles, which they fired at attacking planes. A Communist diplomat in Hanoi told Salisbury: " . . . I think something like this happened in England . . . in the days when the German Air Force attacked the British. As a Communist I have been interested to see the ideological propaganda gradually being replaced by national patriotic appeal. Maybe you remember something like this in the Soviet Union during the critical days of the German attack."[19]

Not only did Hanoi's will survive bombing, but substantial material gains failed to result. As expert and experienced voices soon pointed out, interdiction was not materially influencing the flow of men and supply to the South. A bomb can hit a train or a truck only with difficulty; it can rarely hit a coolie pushing a loaded bicycle along a narrow jungle trail. A bomb can interdict a bridge, which a mass labor force can either repair, replace, or bypass in a night. A bomb can interdict roads and slow traffic. But, as the French learned, mass labor can repair roads quickly; supply will get through and so will small guerrilla forces marching at night or under jungle cover to evade eyes flying overhead.

If air strategists such as Taylor, LeMay, Sharp, and Wheeler had studied Harrison Salisbury's report, they might have had second thoughts. Salisbury personally saw what past experience and present photographic reconnaissance already had demonstrated: that bombs had closed neither roads nor railroads to traffic:

> . . . We had certainly destroyed sections of the railroad time and again. I could see bridges that had been blasted beyond repair. I bumped over stretches of highway that had been relaid several times. Yet traffic was moving. It was moving in very large quantities. And this, I quickly learned, was not just because a Christmas truce was on. . . . Never, so far as I could learn, had it been seriously impeded. Difficulties, yes. Barriers, no.[20]

Even by the time of Mr. Salisbury's visit, the maximum effect of American bombing had been achieved, and it was little enough. It had not stopped Chinese and Soviet supplies from entering Vietnam, and it had slowed, but in no instance stopped, those supplies from going south. Escalation of the air war and a change of emphasis from North to South and then back again resulted in few substantial accomplishments, with almost no effect on the war in the South. The greatest accomplishment of the air war in the North lay in the reconnaissance field. On occasion, infrared radar cameras spotted troop build-ups such as that north of the Demilitarized Zone in the spring of 1967, and resulted in profitable bombing operations—isolated instances that did not alter the program's destructive failure.

Like a medicine that failed to cure a disease, bombing of the North resulted in unpleasant side effects. Selective bombing did not prevent civil casualties, which Hanoi from the beginning exploited internationally. North Vietnam had no air force and at first only primitive air defenses to counter American planes, and to some, the United States appeared as an aggressive bully, a posture exploited by Communist propaganda everywhere. Another side effect concerned Hanoi's relations with Moscow and Peking. In late 1964 and early 1965, the U.S.S.R. cautiously favored another Geneva conference, a notion rejected by Peking, which was posing as friendly protector to Hanoi. In February 1965, Soviet Russia's Premier Kosygin made an important bid to replace Chinese influence in the North Vietnamese capital. He led a strong delegation to Hanoi, where he found some support for settlement by negotiation—despite American air attacks, which Washington hastily explained were taken in "retaliation" for an NLF attack against Pleiku. The situation was later analyzed by a particularly astute observer, Professor Donald Zagoria:

> ... It thus appears that as of early 1965, Moscow was anxious to bring about negotiations, Peking was trying to forestall them, and the Hanoi leadership was somewhere in the middle—ready to listen to American proposals, but internally divided on whether to continue applying military pressure on the south or to negotiate.

The March bombings, followed by a massive commitment of American troops, placed Hanoi moderates in an impossible position and thus altered the diplomacy of the U.S.S.R. As Zagoria wrote, " ... Hanoi's position began to harden and the Russians became increasingly sensitive to Chinese criticism that they were anxious to make a deal with the United States to end the war on terms disadvantageous to Hanoi." The Soviet Union, in other words, had to react to the new set of rules imposed by the American government, and so did China. Where, formerly, aid to Hanoi was spasmodic and never particularly generous, now it became a token in the Sino-Soviet conflict—to Hanoi's profit. And along with that, Moscow ditched any hope for a negotiated settlement, or, as Zagoria wrote, " ... the Russians moved to the diplomatic sidelines, letting initiatives pass to North Vietnam and the NLF.[21]

But that was only one facet of this complicated situation. By spring of 1965, the rift between Peking and Moscow had grown very wide. Officials in both capitals displayed a loquacious virulence that has few parallels in historical non-shooting situations. American diplomacy had played almost no part in developing this rift. So far as the West was concerned, it came as a bonus from the historical process; it was the greatest boon to the West since Tito's defection, in 1947, and was far more momentous, and it should have been carefully nurtured and exploited by American diplomacy. As we have seen, the Kennedy administration seemed surprisingly unaware of the developing rift. The Johnson administration seemed almost bewildered by it. Far from appreciating its importance, Johnson continued with the one policy that could have led to rapprochement between the two titans. Khrushchev's departure from the Soviet Government, coupled with the March bombings, touched off a political quarrel in Peking, where influential members of the army argued for a common front with the U.S.S.R. to resist American aggression. The quarrel exploded into civil war, which Mao Tse-tung won only with the greatest difficulty.

All this was bad enough, but whatever the attitude of the Soviet Union and China, Hanoi could not have remained complacent in response. Whether Ho Chi Minh and his advisers wanted the North to participate more actively in the South is not known. We do know that, at the time (and later), the Hanoi power group contained hawks and doves, just as did the NLF in the South. This was only natural: The war in the South had created definite stresses in the North, and there were those who wished to terminate it and those who wished to escalate it and those who wished to pursue a middle course. By reducing and even eliminating these intraparty stresses, American bombings gave Hanoi hawks virtually a free hand to escalate the action further.

CHAPTER SEVENTY-ONE

1. Douhet, 14, 22, 24.
2. Ridgway, *Soldier* . . . , 275.
3. Sheehan et al., 542–51.
4. U.S. Government, *The United States Strategic Bombing Survey* . . .
5. Ridgway, *The Korean War*, 244.
6. Gavin, *Crisis Now*, 43.
7. Maxwell Taylor, *Responsibility and Response*, 26–8.
8. Sharp.
9. Ibid. See also, Johnson, *The Vantage Point* . . .
10. Maxwell Taylor, *Responsibility and Response*, 36.
11. Browne. See also, McNamara's analysis in Sheehan et al., 550–1, 577–85; Hoopes; Weller.
12. Harvey, 141.
13. Ramsey Clark.
14. Fulbright, *The Vietnam Hearings*.
15. Schlesinger, *The Bitter Heritage* . . . , 56.
16. Hoopes, 77–8.
17. Royal United Service Institution Seminar.
18. Salisbury, *Behind the Lines—Hanoi*, 43, 144, 68. See also, Schoenbrunn, "Journey to North Vietnam"; ibid., *Vietnam*.
19. Salisbury, *Behind the Lines—Hanoi*, 147.
20. Ibid., 87–8.
21. Zagoria, *Vietnam Triangle* . . . , 45–9.

CHAPTER 72

The summing up (III): the war on the ground • Westmoreland's strategy • Westmoreland, Walt, and the enemy • The helicopter • Khe Sanh • The tactical challenge • American frustration and atrocities • Failure of the school solution • The Australian success story • Colonel David Hackworth's extraordinary achievement • The pacification fiasco • American tactics: mobility without purpose and purpose without mobility

THE STRATEGY CHOSEN to fight the war in South Vietnam was another major reason for President Johnson's failure. It was not altogether his fault: President Kennedy had yielded to military control in Vietnam, and Johnson also supposed he could trust the knowledge and judgment of such responsible military advisers as the Joint Chiefs of Staff, theater commanders, and special advisers such as Maxwell Taylor.

This was a mistake.

A long time ago, Clausewitz noted that " . . . the most important single judgment a political or military leader can make is to forecast correctly the nature of war upon which the nation is to embark. On this everything else depends." Johnson's military advisers failed to forecast correctly the nature of this war; Johnson held neither knowledge nor experience to question their judgment, and he lacked inclination to consult those who could have helped him. Once he had erred, first by bombing the North, second by committing a large number of conventional American troop units, he compounded error by permitting further escalation. It would have taken a much more intelligent and courageous man to withstand surrounding pressures and do otherwise. He did otherwise only when a greater pressure—American public opinion—forced him to it.

* * *

The United States armed forces were relatively well organized for either nuclear or non-nuclear war when they were committed in strength to Vietnam, in spring of 1965. They were neither well organized, properly equipped, nor adequately trained to cope with insurgency warfare.

We have already discussed Westmoreland's attrition strategy—a dependence on superior U.S. military manpower, firepower, and mobility to wear down and finally force the enemy from the war. This was a quantitative, as opposed to a qualitative, or selective, strategy: an open-ended strategy in a challenge that called for task-force strategy. If so many men and machines could not "win," its proponents argued, more men and machines could "win." Considering size and weight of the American military machine, commanders probably felt much as Roman commanders had felt when setting out to subdue recalcitrant Iberian tribes, or as Napoleon's generals felt two thousand years later when leading armies into Spain. Our own command confidence was as misplaced. It is a great pity that our officers and officials had not analyzed these and other irregular campaigns, that they had not heeded warnings such as that delivered by Jomini in 1838:

> ... All the gold of Mexico could not have procured reliable information for the French [in Spain]; what was given was but a lure to make them fall more readily into snares.
>
> No army, however disciplined, can contend successfully against such a system applied to a great nation, unless it be strong enough to hold all the essential points of the country, cover its communications, and at the same time furnish an active force sufficient to beat the enemy wherever he may present himself. If this enemy has a regular army of respectable size to be a nucleus around which to rally the people, what force will be sufficient to be superior everywhere, and to assure the safety of the long lines of communication against numerous bodies?
>
> The Peninsular War should be carefully studied, to learn all the obstacles which a general and his brave troops may encounter in the occupation or conquest of a country whose people are all in arms. ... [1]

American command ignorance was not justified in Vietnam. The Viet Cong repeatedly had demonstrated that they could fight and fight well.

Hanoi's failure to panic when American bombs started dropping in the North was surely significant, as was Vo Nguyen Giap's statement, in June 1965, that the Viet Cong would fight " ... only to the point that the enemy could be brought to the conference table and there defeated"—which was the position of the Viet Minh vis-à-vis France in 1954. The Viet Cong offensive in summer of 1965 added weight to

Giap's words, as did the first appearance in strength of North Vietnamese (PAVN) regiments. When the American build-up blunted the enemy effort—essentially a VC effort—still another cautionary voice sounded from the enemy camp. This was Mao's top general, Lin Piao, who, in September 1965, wrote a lengthy and somewhat ambiguous article on liberation wars. If some persons interpreted his words as warning to Hanoi not to expect active Chinese involvement in Vietnam, he nonetheless made it clear that Hanoi held the option of changing strategy and fighting a protracted war.

Such was the initial success of American arms in the South that this thought seemingly did not intrude itself into American strategic thinking. The military bias of American strategy effectively shielded the political bias of enemy strategy. Westmoreland and other military leaders, and civilians as well, could not but see the war in conventional terms despite its guerrilla trappings. They consistently underestimated the enemy's military potential. Westmoreland believed that the enemy was unimaginative and inflexible. In November 1966, he was asked: "What are the chances of the Viet Cong main-force units reverting to strictly guerrilla warfare?" He made this incredible reply:

> . . . Of course, if the enemy did this, he would be going contrary
> to his doctrine. He has rigidly followed Mao Tse-tung's three-phase
> doctrine for Communist insurgency warfare. Under this doctrine,
> phase one provides the political structure, phase two the guerrilla
> force, and phase three large, conventional-type formations that can
> fight open warfare. If he moved back to phase two, it would be
> admitting defeat. And I think this would be hard on the morale of
> the leadership and the troops.[2]

Westmoreland's words suggest that he had never studied either Mao Tse-tung's writings (see Chapter 21) or Giap's campaigns against the French (see Chapters 37–41 and 47–48). His confusion was matched only by the first marine commander in Vietnam, Lieutenant General Lewis Walt, who, according to the *New York Times,* told newsmen in Washington, in November 1970,

> . . . that when we went to Vietnam in the summer of 1965, he did
> not understand that this was primarily a guerrilla war. Like many
> officers who were over-optimistic in the early years of the war, he
> thought in terms of World War II and the Korean War, when the
> enemy was easy to identify.
>
> To illustrate what he termed his naiveté, he said he had once
> interviewed a man in a Vietnamese village who claimed to be the
> village chief and who gave him an optimistic report. Later he felt
> a tug at his pocket and found that a village woman had slipped a

note into his pocket warning him that he had been talking to the regional chief of the Vietcong.[3]

Walt further expressed his confusion in his book *Strange War, Strange Strategy,* and explained it in these extraordinary words:

> . . . Before our involvement in Vietnam we knew practically nothing of its people. As late as 1958 there was no history of them printed in the English language. There are only two or three today, none widely read.[4]

If the reader will turn to my bibliography, which does not include extensive intelligence studies of Indochina available to the author in the early 1950s (and surely to General Walt), he will note that the general errs. As for Walt's stigmatization in his book of Giap as an inept commander, this is a matter of criteria. One thinks of Foch walking in his garden at critical times in World War I and asking himself, "De quoi s'agit-il?"—What is the problem? It appears that Giap held a rather more fundamental grasp of the problem than either Walt, Westmoreland, the JCS, or those amateur strategists in the White House.

Having committed the military crime of underrating the opponent, our military leaders fell victim to tactical panaceas occasioned by technology. Early ground actions caused a good many commanders, not all, to believe that they had found the key to fighting insurgency warfare. The key was the helicopter, which furnished mobility essential to locating the enemy and bringing superior firepower to bear on him. So impressed was Secretary of Defense Robert McNamara with early operations of the 1st Cavalry (Airmobile) Division, that he said the helicopter marked " . . . the beginning of a new era in land warfare."

But dissident voices also spoke. As early as February 1966, Sir Robert Thompson, a veteran counterinsurgency campaigner, complained of American misuse of helicopters in general, pointing out that they should primarily support clear-and-hold operations rather than chase " . . . Viet Cong guerrilla units around the jungle." Thompson astutely observed that extensive availability of helicopters " . . . has exaggerated two great weaknesses of the American character in counterinsurgency—impatience and aggressiveness."[5]

Other shortcomings in American tactics soon appeared. Increased mobility proved expensive. The army's airmobile concept, while sacrificing armor, armored personnel carriers, and firepower heavier than the 105-mm. howitzer, nevertheless demanded hefty logistic support— " . . . as much as 500 tons per day if the entire division is in combat"— and could be met by air transport delivery only at virtually prohibitive cost.[6] Thus land communications, in this case from the coast to An Khe, had to be kept open—a supporting operation that neither broke up guerrilla units nor brought relief to peasants, yet furnished targets to guerrillas. The security requirement of the base camp, a huge area essential to house and feed the helicopters, also proved onerous, as did security requirements of outlying bases, permanent or temporary. If a hundred thousand troops were needed to maintain twenty thousand combat troops, then fifteen thousand combat troops were needed to produce five thousand troops actively pursuing the enemy.

Neither did the initial impact of the helicopter last long. Guerrillas heard and recognized helicopters, which meant that the user often forfeited tactical surprise. Although commanders developed decoy techniques and low-level approaches, the deception nonetheless alerted the enemy that something was up. More often than not, he slipped away before the machines landed, or he fired on machines and then slipped away, or he engaged landing parties and then slipped away. Sometimes American soldiers and marines killed, wounded, or captured him, but he also shot down a great many helicopters, ambushed a great number of ground units, and killed a great many soldiers and marines.

The increase in command communications offered by the helicopter also proved a mixed blessing. Properly exploited, it helped bring a new cohesion to the battlefield. But, as one disgruntled colonel told me, " . . . In a tactical environment where the company and battalion commanders should rule, the command helicopter often brought the brigade or division commander to the small unit tactical scene before either the company or battalion commander could arrive—the net result was to dissipate further the lower level commander's already tenuous operational control."

At the same time, American units wasted time, effort, and money in blindly pursuing the enemy. Noise limitation combined with excellent enemy intelligence caused a veteran if disillusioned marine combat officer to claim that " . . . less than two percent of all U.S. offensive operations produce any contact whatsoever with the Viet-Cong."[7]

Neither did blocking operations prosper. Units along Cambodian and Laotian borders expended great effort in blocking Viet Cong lines of communication only to find, as commanders had discovered throughout history, that they expended the bulk of their strength in static defense duties while the enemy made end runs around them. The United States could not furnish enough troops to seal off borders, and strength in one area meant weakness in another. If defense concentrated on a particular zone, the Viet Cong, unburdened by maintenance of large barrack areas and supply depots, ceased operations in favor of striking elsewhere.

Blocking actions in the north, in I Corps area, proved no more decisive. Lacking intelligence, marines blundered into costly fire fights in and south of the DMZ, where they defended strong points such as Khe Sanh only at considerable effort and cost. General Walt subsequently called the siege of Khe Sanh the most important battle in the war.[8] As he explained to a *Reader's Digest* audience, but for the "holding" action at Khe Sanh, two North Vietnamese divisions would have been able to attack Hué during the Tet offensive.

Walt's claim seems meaningless to this writer. At the time of the Khe Sanh build-up, no one in the American or South Vietnamese camp, with the possible exception of some newspaper correspondents, dreamed of a massive Tet offensive against cities and towns. This offensive did not depend on PAVN troops, whether in the Khe Sanh area or elsewhere: The enemy used only a few thousand of an available sixty thousand PAVN troops *already* in South Vietnam. What neither Walt nor Westmoreland nor their planners nor other hawks seemed to appreciate was Giap's momentum tactics: If a battle prospered, pursue it no matter the cost; if a battle did not prosper, take your losses and get out. (Giap had learned this the hard way while fighting the French.) Had the Tet offensive succeeded (assuming that Giap was calling the signals), had the South Vietnamese people risen, Giap had no less than four divisions immediately north of the DMZ that he could, and probably would have committed, along with a substantial troop reserve in South Vietnam. During the fighting at Khe Sanh, marines discovered a secret road *south* of Khe Sanh, which the enemy was using to infiltrate men from Laos.

Khe Sanh was one more American effort in a chimerical series to create a battle of Dien Bien Phu, one that American firepower would "win." Khe Sanh was neither "blocking" nor "holding." It was a tactical excrescence and was recognized as such three months after the American "victory"; in July, marines evacuated the place, which, according to a marine division commander, Major General Ray Davis, was " . . . a yoke around my neck." Despite heavy enemy casualties, Giap continued to hold the initiative in and around the DMZ and tie down thousands of marines and ARVN troops needed for counterinsurgency operations.[9]

Westmoreland's "spoiling" and "blocking" tactics may have unbalanced the enemy on occasion, but they did not gain the Americans the initiative. Even worse, as quantitative tactics, they contained the seeds of their own destruction. They called for combat troops that Westmoreland did not have and could not have so long as the American military machine yielded one combat soldier per ten soldiers. They produced maximum friendly casualties for results obtained. They proved incredibly expensive in supporting arms, and in the end they proved unacceptable to the American people, whose support was necessary if the war was to continue to escalate.

Why did Westmoreland use "spoiling" tactics, and why did the JCS condone them? The first reason was ignorance both of irregular and counterinsurgency warfare. Prior to departing for Vietnam to serve as Harkins' deputy, Westmoreland called on General Douglas MacArthur for paternal advice:

> ...Do not overlook the possibility, he [MacArthur] concluded, that in order to defeat the guerrilla, you may have to resort to a scorched earth policy. He also urged me to make sure I always had plenty of artillery, for the Oriental, he said, "greatly fears artillery."[10]

So armed, Westmoreland implemented an attrition strategy and search-and-destroy tactics that defied historical precedent. One has to search no farther than Marshal Lyautey's *tache d'huile* concept, which employed clear-and-hold tactics. Whether moving against an active or a potential enemy, the commander's strength limited his ambition. He had to move slowly, forcing himself to build a "show-piece" community of such dimensions as to attract loyalty and support of people on the spot and the attention of peoples yet to be pacified. Successful application of the concept called for a slow and methodical approach—the will to resist encroachment into "asleep" areas until means became available to clear and hold them. Then came adequate protection of the inhabitants, the issuing of identification cards, the digging out of the VC, "the man with the knife," be it by normal police methods or, those failing, by more radical Phoenix-like measures. It was slow-slow-slow, but when an area was pacified in the true meaning of the word, when the peasant enjoyed fair land distribution, fair rents, fair crop prices, adequate protection—then and only then did the word pass to make other areas receptive, a slow, often painful but ultimately rewarding process. The reader may ask, what of the enemy forces? The answer is that our all-too-few successful pacification gains nearly drove them crazy. It was the one thing that truly frightened them and in every case they reacted violently. Had the pacification process developed in a qualitative, orderly, and intelligent manner, the enemy probably would have attacked in force and been flattened by unquestionably superior firepower.

Westmoreland's refusal to accept this basic precept was shared by most of his military contemporaries—the inevitable result of "molding" American officers to staff and command norms as if they were some kind of human dough. It was an attempt to solve an unconventional tactical situation with conventional weapons and tactics, an attempt to make ordinary war out of extraordinary war. The Joint Chiefs of Staff,

Westmoreland, and various planning staffs did not and possibly could not understand that this was a war to be fought for the people rather than against a physical enemy. No matter that information was available to prove this a thousand times over—one had only to read Douglas Pike's *Viet Cong*—our people would not accept it. Little was new about the situation, either politically or tactically. Throughout history, aggressors and defenders have been faced with extraordinary political and military challenges. Those who responded wisely, those who adapted to meet the task at hand are the great captains; the others rest in Valhalla, or, hopefully, in Limbo, where they bore only their fellows with tales of battles almost but not quite won.

Having gotten priorities wrong, Westmoreland and his fellows in the Pentagon failed to realize that a quantitative effort in the highlands and the North was counterproductive. Conventional firepower possessed little validity or effectiveness in an insurgency situation. Conventional weapons "killed" without question—but they killed quantitatively. "Free fire zones" were but an admission of tactical poverty. The tactical problem was one of identifying and neutralizing enemy and reversing the political orientation of a peasantry motivated by terror, if not conviction, to anti-Western attitudes. When weapons killed the innocent, they contributed positively to the insurgent cause. And when weapons were used in such abundance as they were used in Vietnam in 1965–68, they killed many innocents.

The problem of enemy identification constantly plagued American commanders. Lacking an enemy actually firing a weapon or attempting to hide same, the American soldier was forced to identify on the basis of observation (a patrol, for example, sighting an enemy unit) and interrogation. His best intelligence source remained the peasant, but, in addition to usual hazards of obtaining military intelligence from civilians and of obtaining exact information from Orientals, the linguistic block asserted itself in nearly all cases, as did fear, distrust, and general xenophobia.

The collection process is difficult enough under the most favorable circumstances. In South Vietnam, the American soldier's distrust of the native complicated it. His superiors could speak loud and long about "hearts and minds," and President Johnson could continue to praise those "true democrats," Thieu and Ky, but the words didn't mean very much. Excepting a few isolated instances, Americans did not readily identify with South Vietnamese, toward whom they generally displayed contempt, sometimes genial, sometimes not—at worst reflected in such tactical savagery as that occurring at My Lai.

The young soldier, like his superiors totally untrained in the psychology of insurgency warfare, could not be blamed for this attitude. It was more an exuberance of confidence than of innate arrogance, more a blind belief in the American way of life. The monthly pay of an American private exceeded that of senior South Vietnamese officials and army officers. The young American raised in a technological society could not be expected, without a great deal of training which he did not receive, to respect Vietnamese peasants, the more so since he could not communicate with them. Despite the claims of many American servicemen to a Christian ethos, the bulk of them regarded peasants as gooks or slope-heads; they were human beings, yes, they should be fed and protected where possible, yes—but they were an inferior race.

This probably did not surprise the peasant, who had suffered decades of humiliation from the French and from ruling Vietnamese mandarins and army. It added, however, to a fundamental xenophobia that further widened the gulf to damage greatly the intelligence-collection process with the concomitant result of repeated tactical failures and ever-mounting casualties.

In time, and not a very long time, the young soldier began to feel that anyone not in American uniform was against him. As jungle environment told, as fevers appeared, as sores opened and festered, as men fell victim to mines and booby traps, as units walked into ambush, tired and nervous men grew more tired and more nervous and, if fired upon, sometimes did not hesitate to invoke the available total wrath of the American equivalent of Zeus. Commanders who were enjoined to kill as many enemy as possible at cost of the fewest American lives, too often failed to delimit the target before committing the vast armory at their disposal. When such fury failed to evoke expected results, tempers flared further and sometimes innocent people suffered as a result. Early denunciations of ARVN cruelty to villagers horrified many Americans. Yet, as the war continued, American forces sometimes indulged in the fatal error of promiscuous brutality. One disillusioned marine combat officer, Lieutenant Colonel Corson, charged that " . . . search-and-destroy tactics against VC-controlled areas have degenerated into savagery. The terrorism of the enemy has been equally matched by our own."[11] Corson's indignant cry was dismissed by hawks as that of a malcontent. Unfortunately, his words soon gained currency when My Lai became a part both of the American vocabulary and American shame.[12]

The shame of My Lai was not singular. American marines were not long in the field when they began to answer VC atrocities in kind. "We paid the enemy back, sometimes with interest . . . ," Philip Caputo wrote of those early days. "Some line companies did not even bother taking prisoners; they simply killed every VC they saw, and a number of Vietnamese who were only suspects."[13] As David Hackworth later put it, " . . . It really was a wonder there were not more My Lais."[14]

The reader may well ask: Was there a way around this difficulty, a

951

solution? The answer is yes, and it is not an answer of hindsight since in part it was demonstrated with favorable results.

The first solution would have been to choose civil and military commanders who understood insurgency warfare and were mentally and morally equipped to report realities, not dreams, to Washington. This would have dictated two complete turn-arounds in American policy. It would have demanded a supreme commander, a single director of civil and military operations—a temporary dictator, if you will, but a qualified one that would have been jammed down Ngo Dinh Diem's unwilling patrician throat. It would also have demanded a clear-and-hold pacification strategy, a qualitative approach demanding more time and far less physical and financial investment as onus was slowly but methodically transferred to local, indigenous authority.

On the tactical level, a primary solution would have been to utilize native talent. Robert Shaplen has pointed out to the writer that, whereas Americans find the Vietnamese language difficult to learn, the Vietnamese learn English fairly well and quickly, if properly taught.[15] A viable teaching program did not develop, and as one result, most ARVN soldiers did not speak English, which made it even more difficult to integrate them into American units. Moreover, thanks to early American army influence, most ARVN soldiers were not counterguerrilla-oriented and did not often respect the peasant or identify with him.

One answer was the Kit Carson scout program, which, in general, worked very well. The surprising fact, in view of the historical precedent of such programs, is that it took so long to initiate and remained so limited.

The army and marines were also on the right track with long-range reconnaissance patrols, probably the most successful tactic employed by either service in Vietnam. It remained to go a step further and cut the umbilical cord to artillery and air support—in other words, to fight guerrillas with guerrillas, as Roger Hilsman, among others, had recommended years earlier, and as a few outstanding field-grade and company-grade army and marine officers were doing. To have fought guerrillas with guerrillas would have dictated an entirely different tactical approach. American military doctrine does not accept decentralized tactical control. Reluctance of senior commanders, from Pentagon to battalion level, to turn this war over to small-unit commanders was a major tactical deficiency that neither time nor experience repaired. The Australians did not so err. Having analyzed the tactical problem in their area of operations, they " . . . concentrated solely on jungle warfare at a ten-thousand-acre tropical rain forest training ground." Eschewing battalion- and company-size tactics, they " . . . used squads to make a contact, and brought in reinforcing elements to do the killing; they planned in the belief that a platoon on the battlefield could do anything 'including get out' . . . the Australians understood the war better than our guys ever would."[16]

Young American soldiers, both officers and non-coms, often resented the doctrinaire approach, especially in such a variegated combat environment. Young, active, bright, confident, and often imaginative, they respected without fearing the enemy. My friend Lieutenant X, cited in a previous chapter, like dozens of others, proved time and again that he and his men were as capable of sneaking through and fighting in the boondocks as the Viet Cong. Had such men been encouraged to perfect appropriate tactics, the war could have been fought with minimum expenditure to gain maximum results. So impressed was Lieutenant Colonel Hackworth with the Australian doctrine that, when commanding a battalion, he sent three platoon leaders to train with them, even though he had been refused official permission to do so—"selective insubordination," he called it, in this case to save lives.[17]

Hackworth later commanded a battalion, composed mostly of recent draftees, in the Mekong Delta where he faced a main-force VC regiment. Employing a great deal of effort and ingenuity, he managed to convert the battalion into a genuine counterinsurgency force, with each of four rifle companies intensely trained in one operational specialty, be it day and night, long- and short-range ambush; be it day and night small-unit patrols; be it sniper teams operating from helicopters or equipped with starlight scopes, flying at night in choppers to fire tracers on VC groups so that following gunships could work them over; be it inserting two-man sniper teams by night into "enemy" country to wait-wait-wait, then WHAM! By means of an intelligent admixture of " . . . surprise, deception, mobility, imagination, and familiarity with the terrain," he attained the vital shock action and flexibility necessary to " . . . out-guerrilla the guerrilla." The result? An early success that resulted in 143 dead VC at a cost of eight lightly wounded American soldiers. Then 120 hard-core VC dead versus four lightly wounded American soldiers. In a few months, over 2,500 VC dead in return for twenty-five American lives. Here was counterinsurgency warfare as it should have been fought from the beginning. Here is what history, what Hilsman and Gavin and Griffith had recommended. Higher echelons duly honored Hackworth's achievement, as well they should since it belonged in the *Guinness Book of Records* and since he had been wounded four times in achieving it. He was awarded more medals. " . . . And yet no one tried to copy us. . . . Even General Abrams said that all his battalions should fight like 4/39, but no effort was made to make sure they did. . . . So in the end, yet again, there were no lessons learned, and the same mistakes were allowed to be made, day after day after day."[18]

Higher echelons of the American military had no intention of departing from traditional command and staff doctrines. The inevitable result was reliance on what the military calls "the school solution." Secondary operations such as Sting Ray patrols were tolerated but not particularly encouraged. The writer attempted to discuss the success of small, long-range patrols with a senior marine officer only to be told, " . . . Oh, we have dozens such patrols—one's the same as the other." Had other patrols scored the tactical success of the ones the writer was attempting to discuss, half of General Walt's tactical problems would have been solved. But as Frederick the Great sagely pointed out, " . . . The jackass who experienced twenty of [Prince] Eugene's campaigns was none the better tactician for it."

Small-unit tactics, no matter how well conducted, would have been wasted without the other essential: a strong political base from which they could be launched and which could be expanded as they succeeded—in effect, Lyautey's *tache d'huile* concept. Nothing better illustrated the disparity in thought in top military and civil echelons than this requirement. Despite MACV's authority, it did not command a unified effort. The Saigon government and ARVN remained outside its administrative and operational control, as did such allied units as the Koreans. This meant a variety of pacification efforts, each with its own administrative complex. But MACV also faced internal problems. U. S. Army commanders did not see the pacification task in the same light as Foreign Service officers in CORDS. The U. S. Air Force, U. S. Navy and U. S. Marine Corps, which reported directly to CINCPAC, generally did not agree with the army concept. So far apart were the U. S. Army and U. S. Marine Corps on the pacification issue, that the situation became reminiscent of nineteenth-century warfare, when commanders, separated and out of touch, waged the type of campaign each deemed best.

MACV held for occupation of "liberated" areas by ARVN units working in conjunction with the Saigon government's Revolutionary Development program—an inadequate solution (as discussed earlier) in that ARVN units furnished neither adequate military security nor economic sustenance to peasants, with whom they did not seem able to identify. The marines approached the problem differently, and made some substantial progress. William Lederer pointed out that, during 1967, the number of villages under NLF-PLP control increased " . . . except in one small area where the United States Marine Corps combined action platoons (CAP) are operating." In his opinion, it was " . . . the only successful American project of any kind whatsoever in Vietnam."[19] A British counterinsurgency expert, Richard Clutterbuck, reported that the marine effort represented one of " . . . two grains of encouragement" in Vietnam in 1968. Clutterbuck was impressed be-

cause the CAP tackled the basic village problem of VC intimidation—
in his effective phrase, " . . . the man with the knife":

> . . . The normal popular force [militia] in Vietnam now does not
> live in the village at night, but outside. In the village at night the
> man with a knife can get in. If 15 Marines and 35 Popular Forces
> live inside the village at night, you get somewhere, and you can
> also patrol the village street at night.

At the time of Clutterbuck's visit, eighty CAPs had been formed, and
in 80 per cent of the concerned villages " . . . the hamlet chief can sleep,
whereas he can only do so in 20 per cent of the villages in the rest of
Vietnam." Although CAPs suffered high casualties, " . . . they are only
50 per cent of the casualties of the normal infantry or marine battalions
being flown around by helicopter on large scale operations."[20] Clutterbuck did not add that casualties would radically lower as village complexes were consolidated, policed, and redeveloped.

What went wrong with CAP?

A number of things. By mid-1968, the program included nearly two
thousand Americans and twenty-seven hundred Vietnamese militia
working in a hundred different hamlets. These figures are not impressive: I Corps area comprised five provinces, with a total 2.7 million
population. The prototype program could only expand if additional
combat personnel were made available. These would have had to come
from one of two sources: from operational units, which would have
meant adopting a defensive posture, in other words severely limiting or
even ending search-and-destroy or "spoiling" tactics; or from fresh units
sent from the United States.

But Westmoreland (later Abrams), MACV, and the JCS held no
intention of abandoning large-scale actions. Another British observer,
Brigadier K. Hunt of The Institute for Strategic Studies, was also favorably impressed with the CAP program, but " . . . when I went down
to MACV and referred to this, they said that I had been fixed by the
Marines, been brain-washed! They did not agree and said that in any
case it would be too expensive."[21] MACV refused to accept early successes and went out of its way to sabotage the program by forcing Walt
to commit increasing numbers of combat units to the DMZ fighting.
To emphasize displeasure, Westmoreland created a new command in
the north under an army general, which exacerbated already tense command relations between the two services.[22]

But even MACV's intransigent attitude was not the major stumbling
block to a viable pacification program. Walt and Westmoreland could
have committed a hundred thousand American troops to the effort and

still drawn a blank—so long as the South Vietnamese Government failed to govern properly.

By end of 1968, then, American tactics continued to provide mobility without purpose and purpose without mobility. They continued to expend American lives and dollars for minimum combat results while destroying the vital ingredient of counterinsurgency warfare: peasant co-operation. In trying to win the shooting war, American military strategy was contributing to the loss of the real war. How to reverse the situation or at least to salvage some semblance of national self-respect from it was perhaps the chief problem inherited by Richard Milhous Nixon.

CHAPTER SEVENTY-TWO

1. Jomini, 32.
2. *U.S. News and World Report, November 28, 1956.*
3. *New York Times,* Washington, November 18, 1970.
4. Walt, *Strange War, Strange Strategy,* 92.
5. Robert Thompson, "Feet on the Ground."
6. Weller.
7. Corson, 147.
8. Walt, "Khe Sanh—The Battle That Had to Be Won."
9. UPI, Saigon, July 5, 1968. See also, Hackworth, 610–11. Neither did Mc-Namara's fence solve anything. Fences, walls—barriers of all kinds—had been tried from the dawn of history, and most had been found wanting in even favorable terrain. The difficult terrain of the DMZ, ground hotly contested and often controlled by VC and PAVN units, ground interdicted by long-range artillery, made such a project initially impractical. Neither was sensor technology so advanced as scientists claimed. Finally, the enemy had never infiltrated through the DMZ to the extent reported, but rather through Laos by the Ho Chi Minh trail, which it continued to use. See O'Ballance, "The Ho Chi Minh Trail." In the event, McNamara's folly was quietly dropped—after an expenditure of several million dollars.
10. Westmoreland, 40.
11. Corson, 68.
12. Hersh, "My Lai 4."
13. Caputo, 178.
14. Hackworth, 694.
15. Private letter to the author.
16. Hackworth, 494–5.
17. Ibid., 498.
18. Ibid., 700–4.
19. Lederer, *Our Own Worst Enemy,* 158, 186.
20. Royal United Service Institution Seminar. See also, Mulligan.
21. Royal United Service Institution Seminar.
22. Saipan all over again! See Vandegrift and Asprey, 259–64.

CHAPTER 73

Richard Nixon's promise • His position on Vietnam • Enter Henry Kissinger • His plan for disengagement • General Creighton Abrams' tactics • Cambodian sanctuaries • Le petit prince Norodom Sihanouk and Cambodian neutrality • The Bowles mission • President Nixon's decision to bomb enemy sanctuaries in Cambodia • Operation Menu

As THE KOREAN WAR had influenced 1952 presidential elections, the Vietnam War produced heated debate throughout 1967 up to the November elections of 1968.[1] Richard Nixon not only secretly criticized President Johnson's Vietnam policy, but implied that he had a secret plan to win the war. As he told prospective voters in New Hampshire early in the year:

> . . . I pledge to you the new leadership will end the war and win the peace in the Pacific. . . . I do not suggest withdrawal from Vietnam. I am saying to you that it is possible if we mobilize our economic and political and diplomatic leadership it can be ended. The failure in Vietnam is not the failure of our fighting men in Vietnam but the failure of our leadership in Washington, D.C., to back them up.[2]

In his inaugural address, he spoke of moving from " . . . an era of confrontation to an era of negotiation." In March 1969, he would tell his cabinet that " . . . I expect the war to be over in a year."[3] (So Nixon, and Kissinger along with him, joined the ranks that from the beginning had underestimated Hanoi's resilience and determination.) If Nixon supporters imagined that he was going to pull an Eisenhower—visit Vietnam and bring about a cease-fire (a dramatic effort with disappointing results in the case of Korea)—they were soon disappointed. Nixon was a man of covert compromise, and in his mind Vietnam called for a particularly careful political approach which in essence was to be

M.E.P.

based on gunboat diplomacy, in this case massive aerial bombing, and, when this failed, enlarged ground action.

Nixon entered office a prisoner of three major forces: his own fears of communism, which he had repeatedly emphasized by provocative and even bellicose statements and actions in refuting the idea of negotiation as a proper basis for ending the Vietnam War; a hawkish military strategy (he had " ... favored the use of American bombers to rescue the French at Dien Bien Phu and asserted that 'tactical atomic explosives are now conventional and will be used against the target of any aggressive forces' ");[4] the South Vietnamese Government, which he had helped to build. From 1962 onward, he consistently pushed for escalation of the war in Vietnam in order to prevent Chinese hordes from overrunning all of Asia. In 1966, he told an American Legion audience:

> . . . In the event that Vietnam is either lost at the conference table or on the battlefield, it will mean that the Pacific will become a Red Sea, that Communist China will become the dominant power in that area of the world, and that World War Three will be inevitable.[5]

Although he began to backtrack in 1968, he could not summarily cut the bonds of these forces, and he never did. At some point after his election, he told one of his keepers, H. R. Haldeman, that his strategy rested on military threat:

> . . . I call it the Madman Theory, Bob. I want the North Vietnamese to believe I've reached the point where I might do *anything* to stop the war. We'll just slip the word to them that "for God's sake, you know Nixon is obsessed about Communism. We can't restrain him when he's angry—and he has his hand on the nuclear button"—and Ho Chi Minh himself will be in Paris in two days begging for peace.[6]

Shortly after taking office, Nixon relieved negotiator William Averell Harriman in favor of Henry Cabot Lodge, whom he instructed to avoid private negotiations at the Paris talks. At the same time, he permitted General Creighton Abrams, Westmoreland's successor in South Vietnam, to continue attrition strategy by keeping pressure on the enemy. So far, this was "more of the same," but the new President also made an appointment that surprised a good many persons: he named Henry Kissinger to the influential post of presidential adviser on national security affairs.

Kissinger's appointment would have raised eyebrows under normal circumstances. Forty-five years old, he had come to America in 1938, a German-Jewish refugee who studied at Harvard and subsequently became a professor of government there. Within the Establishment he was well known as a theoretician and writer on national strategy and limited war—indeed, about the only Republican with such a background. One of his early outpourings called for replacing John Foster Dulles' insane doctrine of "massive [nuclear] retaliation" with "limited nuclear war," an equally insane doctrine preached by, among other military futurists, Herman Kahn, and later watered down by Kissinger to the more sensible limited conventional war.[7] Kissinger had advised three administrations on international affairs; he had for some time been involved in behind-the-scenes diplomacy concerning Vietnam during which he had made several fact-finding trips to that country,[8] and he had served a "... short, unhappy stint in McGeorge Bundy's National Security Council" before returning to Harvard and to Governor Nelson Rockefeller's political fiefdom.[9]

Kissinger considered himself brilliant, witty, and charming, and some agreed with that assessment. Others considered him overly pedantic, short-tempered, arrogant, and rude, an intellectual opportunist who wanted power and more power. He also considered himself a man of honor—to my knowledge he never defined the term—who was intent on saving America and the world from the evils of communism. Some of his judgments did show a certain prescient brilliance, for example in 1968 he declared that Richard Nixon was "unfit to be President"—"the most dangerous" of the candidates.[10] Events quickly altered those harsh judgments. According to Nixon, Kissinger shortly before the 1968 presidential election was using his contacts with the Democrats "... to uncover foreign policy information that he passed on to help Nixon's campaign."[11]

From the hawk standpoint, Kissinger initially appeared to be a disappointing selection. He was not a military man nor did he necessarily embrace force as a proper solution to political problems. He was willing to listen to those who favored a military solution, but he did not suffer fools gladly, and he had an annoying habit of producing facts and figures that weighed heavily against those cited by various hawks. The latter's fears were greatly increased when the January 1969 issue of *Foreign Affairs* carried his work, "The Viet Nam Negotiations," as its lead article. After briefly reviewing the situation in South Vietnam, Kissinger discounted American attrition strategy, which "... failed to reduce the guerrillas and was in difficulty even with respect to the North Vietnamese main forces." A predominant military influence "... caused our military operations to have little relationship to our declared political objectives. Progress in establishing a political base was excruciatingly slow; our diplomacy and our strategy were conducted in isolation from each other." This explained, among other things, the failure of the pacification program. The Tet offensive, which militarily Kissinger judged an American "victory," was "... a political defeat in the countryside for Saigon and the United States." This action

> ... marked the watershed of the American effort. . . . Denied the very large additional forces requested, the military command in Viet Nam felt obliged to begin a gradual change from its peripheral strategy to one concentrating on the protection of the populated area. This made inevitable an eventual commitment to a political

solution and marked the beginning of the quest for a negotiated settlement.

Kissinger went on to review earlier, behind-the-scenes negotiations, and emphasized the difficulties that had to be overcome before meaningful talks could occur. A variety of factors were at work in each of the interested countries, and these combined in a dozen ways to affect internal and external relationships, thereby limiting each country's freedom of maneuver. At best, Kissinger believed, the United States could expect " . . . prolonged negotiations progressing through a series of apparent stalemates."[12]

The newly elected President was not familiar with this article, so the story goes, when he tapped its author for the new and responsible job of national security adviser. His choice implied tacit acceptance of Kissinger's somewhat vague and convoluted thinking. Kissinger's appointment, however, spelled no immediate or drastic action, at least in connection with the Vietnam War. Kissinger's main effort in the early days seemed to concentrate on reorganizing, with the help of able assistant Morton Halperin, the National Security Council in such a way as to effectively seal off the Departments of State and Defense from the President's office.[13] This was done by setting up a number of powerful committees, each chaired by Kissinger, who in a short time held more titles than ever dreamed of by Poo-Bah. (Halperin would soon be accused of trying to thwart the monster he had helped to create. After having had his telephone tapped and suffering other indignities, he resigned as did other top assistants including Roger Morris, who later described the National Security Council as " . . . a seizure of power unprecedented in modern American foreign policy.")[14]

So armed, Kissinger turned to the major problem of carrying out Nixon's "plan," which apparently existed only in embryo. As for Kissinger's article, several of its points had been raised over a year earlier by a proven authority on Indochina, Robert Shaplen, also writing in *Foreign Affairs*.[15] Instead of a specific program, Kissinger offered general guidelines. The disparate factors he had discussed that existed in Hanoi, Saigon, and Washington exerted themselves on the new Administration just as they did on Saigon and Hanoi governments. Top American officials, civil and military, were still divided into hawks and doves. Three months after Nixon assumed office, *Newsweek* reported that a canvass of the Pentagon, the State Department, the American embassy in Saigon, and the American team in Paris made it clear

> . . . that none of these governmental "satrapies" could agree on the facts of the Vietnam conflict, much less on what conclusions to draw from those facts. As a result, at the first full-dress National

Security Council meeting devoted to Vietnam, the participants were asked to consider no fewer than nine possible courses of action to end the war—four military and five political.[16]

Shortly after Abrams relieved Westmoreland, American tactics had begun to alter. Although Abrams was a World War II tank commander wedded to conventional Western military thinking, he apparently entertained some doubts about Westmoreland's attrition strategy with emphasis on large-unit search-and-destroy operations. As stated earlier, he converted in part to Sting Ray tactics—smaller patrols instead of battalion and brigade actions essential to successful prosecution of this type of war.

Three factors lessened the beneficial effects derived from this tactical modification. The first was that Abrams did not seem to understand the nature of this war any more than had Westmoreland. He insisted on gaining a military solution by keeping "maximum pressure," so-called "pile-on" tactics, against an enemy willing to fight back. In time, perhaps, Abrams' tactical adaptation might have produced sufficiently important results to bring a change from the quantitative to the qualitative, with emphasis on political aspects of the war. But now the second factor emerged: Abrams' changes, minor enough, encountered doctrinal hostility from *within the U. S. Army* whose senior commanders were lukewarm to *any* tactical changes, the more so because they still did not and perhaps never would comprehend the nature of this war, much less its tactical challenges. Related to this was a third factor: each arm attempting to outdo the other in staking its claim as the arm most suitable for fighting counterinsurgency warfare and, in the process, frequently operating in such a way as to reduce or totally neutralize beneficial effects of civil pacification programs.

Lack of progress had of course to be justified. In addition to a claimed insufficiency of troops; a temporary lid on the bombing of the North; American civilian, press, and television hostility, the favorite scapegoat was enemy sanctuary in Cambodia with alleged vast amounts of arms and equipment from China reaching the Communists through the port of Sihanoukville. Never mind that it had been obvious from the beginning that the guerrillas would rely on this sanctuary just as had the Viet Minh in the war against the French. As American clear-and-destroy operations multiplied, Viet Cong and PAVN units, when caught short or when tired or when needing resupply, merely slipped across the border into the mountains and forests of northeast neutral Cambodia, which in time housed a complex that supported an estimated forty thousand troops.[17] It was natural enough for MACV and ARVN to want

962

to invade the sanctuaries and thereby, as it was believed, eliminate the potential threat of a massive attack on Saigon only twenty-five to thirty miles from the border.

The difficulty was that Cambodia, a French protectorate-cum-colony since 1864, had gained independence with its neutrality guaranteed by the 1954 Geneva Agreements. For some years its ruler, Prince Norodom Sihanouk—a flamboyant, irascible, anti-American playboy—was willing to ignore the restricted VC and PAVN intrusions, just as his forefathers had accepted the existence of bandits in the mountainous southwest, the pirates that infested the rivers, and the Khmer Loeu hill tribes in the northeast mountains.[18] Such was Sihanouk's erratic but dictatorial rule that his political base in Phnom Penh was far from firm. Although he was a virtual god to the feudal peasantry (a very important fact consistently overlooked by American planners), he had to rule through a variety of fiefdoms controlled by various powerful war lords. He had no army to speak of, he feared the traditional Vietnamese enemy, and he wanted desperately to keep Cambodia out of the war. A major complication had been solved after the Geneva Agreements when several thousand Cambodian Communists went into voluntary exile in North Vietnam (where they were trained in insurgency warfare). The few Communists who remained—Sihanouk named them les Khmers Rouges—poised no immediate challenge to an essentially conservative peasantry, nor did a nationalist guerrilla group, the Khmer Serai, cause great concern. Sihanouk's main purpose was not to rock his very vulnerable ship of state, as reflected in his refusal to join John Foster Dulles' cardboard alliance called SEATO, thus raising American ire another degree (see Chapter 49).[19] Not-so-subtle American attempts to change this policy resulted in increasing estrangement marked by Sihanouk's concomitant move toward Russia and China, a move paralleled by the CIA's support of Sihanouk's rival, Son Ngoc Thanh, and by a disruption campaign as stupid as it was vicious designed to woo the urban elite and the officer corps from supporting Sihanouk, an effort so threatening that an enraged Sihanouk broke diplomatic relations with the United States in 1965 and subsequently permitted the VC and later PAVN units to take sanctuary in the east and to allow China to ship arms to the port of Sihanoukville from where they eventually reached Viet Cong and PAVN units.

Details of the sanctuary area were vague. Covert American and South Vietnamese intelligence-collection operations inside Cambodia—Programs Salem House and Daniel Boone—carried out by CIA and Special Forces' recruited Civilian Irregular Defense Groups (CIDG) had met with only limited success: " . . . in 1,835 missions over four years they captured twenty-four prisoners."[20] MACV nonetheless reported and aerial reconnaissance partially confirmed the alleged existence of fifteen enemy bases in the border area. To his credit, President Johnson refused to subvert international law by condoning overt retaliation. He did not share the State Department's aversion to Sihanouk—"Everything I hear about the Prince suggests that we ought to get on well with him," he told his staff in 1966[21]—and he did not believe that America could violate Cambodia's sovereignty with impunity.

That a severe threat both to South Vietnam and potentially to Cambodia existed was beyond doubt. Taken with Sihanouk's fear of massive retaliation against the sanctuaries by the Americans, it caused him to seek rapprochement with the Johnson government. In late 1967 he told a journalist, Stanley Karnow, that

> ... he would grant the U.S. the right of "hot pursuit" against the North Vietnamese and Vietcong in Cambodia—so long as no Cambodians were harmed. ... Plainly trying to prevent Cambodia from becoming a battlefield, Sihanouk said: "We are a country caught between the hammer and the anvil, a country that would very much like to remain the last haven of peace in Southeast Asia."[22]

An official mission headed by Chester Bowles, U.S. ambassador to India, soon arrived in Phnom Penh. Exactly what was or was not agreed to is not clear. William Shawcross writes that the State Department subsequently edited and excised official records (which has happened before and after). Nixon later wrote that Sihanouk requested American retaliation " . . . either with 'hot pursuit' on the ground or by bombing the sanctuaries."[23] The somewhat cloudy record does not substantiate Nixon's statement, and neither Bowles nor mission members agreed with it:

> ... The State Department notes that by the end of the visit the Bowles party believed that "there seemed little doubt that on the Cambodian side fears of 'hot pursuit' [by American and South Vietnamese forces] had been allayed." The Americans, for their part, stressed that a catastrophic widening of the war had been averted and that the Bowles mission had succeeded in overcoming many of the problems which had embittered United States-Cambodian relations.[24]

Shawcross later wrote that Sihanouk told Bowles that " . . . he was ready to restore relations with Washington if only the Americans would recognize the inviolability of Cambodia's existing borders."[25] There is a serious contradiction in the record here, but President Johnson's refusal to violate the border other than with small covert raids suggests that this was no black-and-white affair, at least in the international

964

tribunal. Sihanouk is a very quixotic little man, and indeed may have said different things to different people. In the end it did not matter what he said since Nixon and Kissinger summarily judged that " . . . the concerned territory . . . was no longer Cambodian in any practical sense."[26]

President Nixon was perfectly willing to resume relations with Cambodia on a quid pro quo basis that he and Kissinger hoped would wean Sihanouk from neutrality. The sanctuary problem seemed to offer a good beginning. How could the United States best "quarantine" Cambodia was an early question Nixon put to the JCS. The reply came from Saigon where MACV had steadily invoked the Cambodian sanctuary as the reason for the continuing failure of American and ARVN strategy and tactics, and in so doing had created a mythical picture of an enemy Pentagon in the middle of the Cambodian jungle. In early February, General Creighton Abrams informed the JCS that " . . . recent information gives us hard intelligence on COSVN Hq [North Vietnam's Central Office for South Vietnam] facilities in Base Area 353."[27] Abrams predicted

> . . . a large-scale enemy offensive around Saigon in the near future. An attack on COSVN, he argued, "will have an immediate effect on the offensive and will also have its effect on future military offensives which COSVN may desire to undertake."[28]

Abrams recommended " . . . a short-duration, concentrated B-52 attack of up to sixty sorties. . . . There is little likelihood of involving Cambodian nationals if the target boxes are placed carefully."[29] This fitted nicely with Nixon's question, and when the North Vietnamese launched a new offensive in February, which Nixon interpreted as a test of his determination and which in three weeks cost over a thousand American lives and far more South Vietnamese lives, he approved Abrams' recommended bombing program—providing it was carried out in total secrecy. Operation Menu began with Breakfast on March 18. Each B-52, flying from Guam, carried thirty tons of bombs which were dropped on a " . . . box . . . about a half mile wide by two miles long": " . . . forty-eight of such boxes were stamped upon neutral Cambodia by the express order of the President."[30] Breakfast was succeeded by Lunch, Snack, Dinner, and Dessert—in fourteen months, 3,630 B-52 raids were carried out against a neutral country.[31]

Nixon and Kissinger's aerial offensive was unique in several respects. Elaborate precautions were taken to maintain secrecy. Congressional authority was not sought. According to Nixon and Kissinger, only a few of the people's representatives were informed. They included Senators Richard Russell and John Stennis of the Senate Armed Services

Committee: " . . . both men," Nixon wrote, "thought that the bombing was the right decision, and both said they would back me up in the event that it became public."[32] Neither the Secretary nor the Chief of Staff of the Air Force was told. Defense Secretary Melvin Laird and Secretary of State William Rogers were informed and they argued against it; Laird at least wanted it to be made public but Kissinger and Nixon refused to consider this. A week after the Breakfast bombing began, the *New York Times* reported that Abrams had requested air strikes against the Cambodian sanctuaries. The White House issued a "qualified denial."[33] Ironically, when the *Times* and other papers broke the story in April and May no one, including members of pertinent Congressional committees, paid attention except Nixon and Kissinger, who in their fury at the leak had a number of assistants, officials, and journalists wiretapped by the FBI.[34] Other than that blip, secrecy and deniability were achieved by a system of dual reporting so involved that " . . . the bombing was not merely concealed; the official, *secret* records showed that it never happened."[35] Indeed it was not until 1973 that the scam was exposed by a conscience-stricken radar officer who blew the whistle to his senator. In a subsequent series of Senate hearings, the principals either disclaimed knowledge or responsibility or both, or swore that Sihanouk had sanctioned the raids. General Brent Scowcroft, one of Kissinger's principal aides, stated that " . . . the falsification was done on direct White House orders."[36] The investigation possibly would have gone deeper except that America was tired of the war and for some time Watergate had replaced it as the country's chief interest.

What did the bombings achieve? They certainly killed some of the enemy and eliminated some rude enemy installations. Although General Abrams and Ambassador Ellsworth Bunker, according to Melvin Laird, were convinced that " . . . Menu has been one of the most telling operations of the war,"[37] there is considerable evidence that the multimillion-dollar operation did not live up to tactical expectations— bombings rarely do especially if you are bombing forest and jungle. Roger Morris, also a principal Kissinger aide, later wrote that " . . . according to the best CIA and Pentagon intelligence fourteen months [and over 100,000 tons of bombs] later . . . [it had] no appreciable effect on enemy capabilities in enemy areas."[38] A special stand-by infantry team was told prior to the first bombing that " . . . if there was anybody still alive out there they would be so stunned that all [we would] have to do [was] walk over and lead him by the arm to the helicopter." The team duly moved in immediately after the strikes and was slaughtered by enemy fire. A second team refused to go in—its members, when threatened with arrest, were legally advised that " . . . you can't be arrested for refusing to violate the neutrality of Cambodia."[39]

Enemy units dispersed by Operation Menu merely moved farther west to set up new camps. Bringing the war closer to the Cambodian people complicated Sihanouk's position even more—and perhaps that was the Administration's intention. There remains the question of civilian casualties inflicted by the bombings. Nixon and Kissinger later insisted that the target areas were free of Cambodian civilians.[40] That does not appear to be accurate:

> ... Classified documents published later were to disclose that Abrams and other top officers, knowing the targeted areas to be populated by civilians, had secretly conceded that "some Cambodian casualties would be sustained in the operation."[41]

According to William Shawcross:

> ... The Joint Chiefs themselves informed the administration as early as April 1969 that many of the sanctuary areas were populated by Cambodians who might be endangered by bombing raids.[42]

Base Area 353, for example, was believed to have had " ... a total population of approximately 1,640 Cambodians, of whom the Joint Chiefs reckoned 1,000 to be peasants."[43] One should keep in mind that the peasants had neither warning nor air raid shelters. There is no doubt that many of them, as harbinger of the future, were killed and wounded—no one knows how many.

CHAPTER SEVENTY-THREE

1. U.S. Congress, "The Candidates' Views." See also, White, *The Making of the President 1968.*
2. U.S. Congress, "The Candidates' Views."
3. Nixon, *Memoirs,* 390.
4. Shawcross, 76.
5. Reichley, 106.
6. Haldeman, 83.
7. Shawcross, 75. See also, Morris, 53.
8. Kissinger, *The White House Years,* 232–5.
9. Shawcross, 75. See also, Reichley, 114.
10. Shawcross, 79. See also, Karnow, 584–5; Fallaci, 37: In 1972, Oriana Fallaci, an exceedingly perceptive Italian journalist, asked Kissinger:

    > O.F.: Power is always alluring. Dr. Kissinger, to what degree does power fascinate you? . . .
    > H.K.: . . . You see, when you have power in your hands and have held it for a long period of time, you end up thinking of it as something that's due you . . . what interests me is what you can do with power. Believe me, you can do wonderful things.

11. Shawcross, 79.
12. Kissinger, *The White House Years*, 234 ff.
13. Mollenhoff, 156 ff. See also, Morris, 47 ff., 78–83.
14. Karnow, 587. See also, Haldeman, 100–3, for the etiology and subsequent developments of the FBI wiretaps " . . . inspired by Henry's rage and ordered by Nixon"; Morris, 154–63, on wiretaps.
15. Shaplen, "Viet-Nam: Crisis of Indecision."
16. *Newsweek,* April 7, 1969.
17. Nixon, *Memoirs,* 381.
18. Shawcross, 37. See also, Sihanouk.
19. Sihanouk, 75 ff. See also, Colby, 149–50, who mistakenly dates the rupture from 1959.
20. Shawcross, 65. See also, Kiernan, 385.
21. Shawcross, 66.
22. Karnow, 590.
23. Nixon, *Memoirs,* 382.
24. Shawcross, 70–1.
25. Ibid., 71, 94.
26. Kissinger, *The White House Years,* 240, 246.
27. Shawcross, 19.
28. Ibid., 20. See also, Nixon, *Memoirs,* 380.
29. Shawcross, 20. See also, Kissinger, *The White House Years,* 242–3.
30. Shawcross, 23.
31. Ibid., 27. See also, Nixon, *Memoirs,* 383–5.
32. Nixon, *Memoirs,* 382. See also, Kissinger, *The White House Years,* 253; Karnow, 592 ff.
33. Shawcross, 33.
34. Nixon, *Memoirs,* 389–90. See also, Kissinger, *The White House Years,* 252–3; United States Senate, *Role of Dr. Henry A. Kissinger in the Wiretapping of Certain Government Officials and Newsmen;* Note 14 above.
35. Shawcross, 31.
36. Ibid., 95. See also, ibid., 287–91, for a detailed discussion of Nixon and Kissinger's responsibility for the bombing campaign, despite their subsequent attempts to deny it.
37. Kissinger, *The White House Years,* 249.
38. Morris, 156.
39. Shawcross, 25.
40. Kissinger, *The White House Years,* 240 fn. General Abrams, according to Kissinger, assured Nixon in February " . . . that *the target* was at least a kilometer distant from any known Cambodian hamlets . . . " (my italics). The trouble is, there was no *target,* there were *targets,* each of which was a "box" a half mile wide by two miles long; See also, ibid., 250, 252, 254.
41. Karnow, 591.
42. Shawcross, 28.
43. Ibid.

CHAPTER 74

The war escalates • Lieutenant Colonel Herbert's charges • Operation Dewey Canyon • Operation Hamburger Hill • ARVN's failure at Ben Het • President Nixon reverses course • Dissent on the home front • The hawks and the Hellespont • Soedjatmoko speaks out • Stalemate in Paris • Kissinger's secret talks with Hanoi • Saigon obstructionism • The President's new plan • First troop withdrawals • The Midway meeting • The Clifford Plan (I)

OPERATION *MENU* had not long been under way when it became obvious that the overt American military operations under Abrams' command differed not in kind but only in degree. All the wars previously discussed—air, naval, and ground—continued to escalate. As search-and-destroy operations blossomed anew throughout South Vietnam, so did the attendant evils earlier discussed. A heavily decorated army officer, Lieutenant Colonel Anthony Herbert, later testified that in mid-February 1969 he witnessed a battle with the Viet Cong near Cuu Loi:

> . . . after the fire fight, I walked up on these [civilian] detainees—there were about 15 of them—and they were in the custody of an ARVN unit and an American lieutenant.
>
> There were four dead already, and when I walked up, they had a knife at the throat of a woman. Her baby—there were several kids in the bunch—her baby was screaming and grabbing at her leg, and her other child . . . was being suffocated by an ARVN who was pushing its face into the sand with his foot.
>
> I ordered them to stop, but with me just standing there looking, they proceeded to slit the woman's throat. I asked the lieutenant what the hell was going on and then I ordered him to get his tail out of the area and take his ARVN with him. They left and I sent one of my sergeants with the detainees to the L.Z. [landing

969

zone]. I told him to get them out and back so they could be processed.

Well, it wasn't long after he left that I heard firing in the direction he'd taken them. He came running back, yelling, mad as hell. He told me the American lieutenant and the ARVNs had jumped him, overpowered him and killed all the detainees. I followed him back and found the bodies. All of them. The children, too.

Herbert subsequently witnessed torture of prisoners by American military intelligence personnel. His insistent reports of these criminal activities won him only opprobrium of his seniors, Lieutenant Colonel J. Ross Franklin and Major General John Barnes, and he was shortly relieved of his command and sent to military limbo.[1]

Other evils appeared. Despite intense security, Viet Cong guerrillas continued to penetrate American base areas such as that at Cu Chi where special raiding teams, covered by rocket and small-arms fire, destroyed nine and severely damaged three Chinook helicopters in a brief night action, an estimated $16-million loss described by MACV as "light material damage."[2] In warding off a Tet attack on the big American base at Long Binh, American aircraft were forced to level the village of Bien Hoa, a frantic action that resulted in heavy enemy casualties and was, once again, claimed by MACV as a "victory." Contrarily, a captured enemy document noted that the spring offensive

> . . . was a significant tactical and a great strategic victory . . . we killed more Americans than we did in the 1968 spring offensive. [It] upset Nixon's plan, because U.S. forces were heavily hit. . . . The antiwar movement in the U.S. flared up again strongly demanding the withdrawal of U.S. troops.[3]

Matters did not greatly improve in I Corps Area where American marines seem to have learned few lessons. In February, the 3rd Marine Division in conjunction with ARVN units had kicked off Operation Dewey Canyon, an immense sweep of tortuous terrain running west to the Laotian border. Although few enemy contacts resulted, marine spokesmen called the operation one of " . . . the most successful of the war" and insisted on the importance of captured weapons and matériel (some 450 tons) to justify 121 dead marines, several hundred wounded, and units exhausted. Marines followed this with sweeping operations around Khe Sanh while air and naval units continued to pound enemy positions in and around the DMZ, a gigantic effort that included USS *New Jersey* firing one-ton shells on suspected bunker positions.

In late May, paratroopers of the 101st Airborne Division, while carrying out a months-long sweep of A Shau Valley south of the marine area of operations, "surprised" an enemy force dug in on Ap Bia Hill.

The mission of the paratroopers, in the words of a company commander participant, Captain Bob Harkins, was " . . . to find and destroy NVA [North Vietnamese Army] units and supply bases . . . to insure that a recurrence of the previous [1968] 'Tet' did not happen."[4] The 101st at this time was so dispersed that it was impossible to mass what forces were available. In view of this and of the enemy's estimated strength, the local commander might have decided to isolate the hill complex and eliminate or at least badly hurt the dug-in enemy by a mixture of air strikes and artillery fire. Instead, presumably never having studied Napoleon's treatise on mountain warfare, much less the expensive lessons learned by the U. S. Army in northern Italy in World War II, he chose to make that most difficult maneuver, an uphill attack—an effort approved by the division commander, and one that would soon resemble lead soldiers storming a red-hot stove. For several days, well-disciplined and very brave paratroopers fought up what became famous as Hamburger Hill. It was "captured" at a cost of eighty-four dead and 480 wounded against an estimated six hundred enemy dead. It was evacuated a few days later. When North Vietnamese troops again occupied it, the division commanding general announced " . . . that if ordered to take the hill again, 'I am prepared to commit everything that it takes, up to the entire division, to do the job.' "[5]

While paratroopers were bleeding and dying on Hamburger Hill, Giap as usual was preparing another unpleasant surprise for allied forces. This time he chose the old battle areas around Dak To and Ben Het, the latter defended primarily by ARVN units. In May, South Vietnamese patrols had attempted to upset Giap's plans, but the newly reorganized army that American advisers were boasting about did not hold together. By early June, the South Vietnamese were dug in at Ben Het. By mid-June, PAVN units had cut the strong point from the American garrison at Dak To, besieged it for a month, and disappeared, having taken an estimated three thousand casualties mainly from massive doses of napalm and bombs dropped by American aircraft. Despite the fact that an ARVN relief force thinned by 20 to 30 per cent desertion, reached the besieged garrison several days *after* the enemy had departed, MACV touted the relief as a "great victory," certain proof that Vietnamization was working. Colonel David Hackworth, who investigated the action, concluded that " . . . whatever the hype, the truth was that ARVN had failed dismally in its first real test."[6]

The Administration had already suggested that matters were not going to improve radically overnight. In early March, the President defended his policy, blaming it on the enemy:

> . . . we had no other choice but to try to blunt the offensive. Had General Abrams not responded in this way, we would have suf-

fered far more casualties than we have suffered, and we have suffered more than, of course, any of us would have liked to have seen.[7]

In view of the current offensive, the President said, " . . . there is no prospect for a reduction of American forces in the foreseeable future." In mid-March, Secretary of Defense Melvin Laird warned that the United States could not reduce troop commitment until North Vietnam withdrew its troops; according to military commanders in South Vietnam, another two years would be required to bring the situation "in hand."[8]

The Administration's "more of the same" attitude unleashed increasingly vocal and hostile voices in the United States. In late March, a protesting congressman placed the names of 31,379 American dead in the *Congressional Record*. In early April, Henry Niles, chairman of the increasingly influential BEM (Business Executives Move for Peace in Vietnam), complained that " . . . over 2,000 Americans have been killed since President Nixon took office. . . . The honeymoon is over. We want peace."[9] A *New York Times* dispatch from Saigon of May 22 stated that U.S. commanders in Vietnam

> . . . are still under orders to pursue the enemy relentlessly, using every tactic and weapon at their command, to deny the North Vietnamese and Vietcong troops any strategic advantage as a result of the halt in bombing. The United States commanders in the field have followed the order to the letter, and have dramatically stepped-up the number of offensive operations initiated by the allies.[10]

Edward Kennedy reminded fellow senators that Nixon had not ordered or intended to order any reduction of military activity in Vietnam; he continued:

> . . . President Nixon has told us, without question, that we seek no military victory, that we seek only peace. How then can we justify sending our boys against a hill a dozen times or more, until soldiers themselves question the madness of the action? The assault on "Hamburger Hill" is only symptomatic of a mentality and a policy that requires immediate attention.[11]

A month earlier in the April issue of *The Atlantic*, a former marine commandant, General David Shoup, warned the public of a new and

972

dangerous American militarism, "a poisonous weed" that would have to be exterminated.[12]

Shoup's article caused a major furor in Administration circles as did continued press criticism of military actions in Vietnam. Assistant Commandant of the Marine Corps General Lewis Walt charged that "... news coverage of the war, assessment of the caliber of the South Vietnamese army and allegations of corruption in the Saigon government" were "inadequate or misleading." Chief of Naval Operations Admiral Moorer "... complained of the reporting on American military morale and the 'so-called existence of an evil military-industrial complex.'" The *Washington Post* noted: "... Criticism of press and television has joined ABM [anti-ballistic missile] boosterism as a predictable ingredient in top Defense Department speeches."[13]

Military hawks were fighting a losing battle. In taking on the national press, they were going to prove as effective as Xerxes when he tried to punish the Hellespont for destroying his bridge.* Like the Hellespont, the nation's press was too big, powerful, and insensitive, particularly when intelligent and politically influential observers around the world were pointing out fallacies that had underlain American policy in Vietnam. One of the most intelligent voices belonged to the Indonesian ambassador in Washington, Soedjatmoko, who told a Honolulu audience on the same day that President Nixon addressed the nation,

> ... the future of the South-east Asian region will not be determined solely by the outcome of that war.... Firstly, the population of Vietnam, or even of the whole of erstwhile Indo-China together, constitutes less than one-third of the total population of South-east Asia. On the other hand, Indonesia's population alone accounts for almost half of that total. In keeping the Vietnam war in its proper proportions, it is important to realize that if Indonesia had become a Communist country, any military gains in the Vietnam war would have been nullified.

The domino theory, still popular in American administration circles, was fallacious because it did not respect regional facts:

> ... It is, therefore, not the political color of a regime that counts in the end, but its capacity for nation-building and development. More important than the question whether a country will turn towards Communism—however important that may be to the

---

* Herodotus, 369: "... [Xerxes] straightway gave orders that the Hellespont should receive three hundred lashes, and that a pair of fetters should be cast into it. Nay, I have even heard it said, that he bade the branders take their irons and therewith brand the Hellespont."

country concerned—is the question whether in doing so it will become a satellite of outside forces or not. For underlying my whole argument is the conviction that in the present world situation no outside power can for long force any South-east Asian country to do its bidding. The South-east Asian nations do not constitute lifeless entities that automatically fall one way or the other, depending on which way their neighbor falls. History does not operate that way. What matters is the will, the political will, the determination of a nation to preserve its own identity. Out of our own national experience, we in Indonesia more than ever believe that this is the crucial element in the equation. Without such a will and determination, the infusion of external power will fail to make much difference. The domino theory, therefore, is to us rather a gross over-simplification of the nature of the historical processes that go on in the area. It obscures and distorts rather than illuminates our understanding and offers no guide-lines for realistic policy.

So long as China pursued its present policy, the ambassador continued, the primary threat to South-east Asian nations "is one of internal subversion and insurgency." But:

> ... It is not primarily a nation's military capability that will determine its capacity to overcome these threats to internal security, but rather the cohesion of its political system, the viability and the effectiveness of its government in dealing with the problems of poverty, social inequalities and injustices, in bringing about economic development and in continually expanding its base for popular participation. Here again it is not only factors of economic growth, but beyond that the elements of will and determination that are decisive, as well as the people's loyalty to the government and faith in its purposes.[14]

At some point in this spring of 1969, President Nixon decided to temper overt hawkish desire for military victory with an attempt to win a negotiated settlement (but meanwhile continuing to impress the enemy with his determination by such as Operation Menu and continued furious bombing of Laos. His decision did not make the deed. Although some observers drew comfort from the limited action of the 1969 Tet offensive, the action nonetheless showed an unhealthy enemy strength, as did expensive encounter actions in the DMZ and particularly along the Cambodian border which continued to take a high toll of American lives. Enemy intransigence also showed in Paris, and was complemented by President Thieu's lukewarm attitude in Saigon until virtually an impasse had been reached. Mounting criticism at home alarmed Administration officials while Nixon's continued silence infuriated critics.

Finally in a speech in early April, the President hinted that secret talks were taking place with Hanoi:

> ...we think we are on the right track but we are not going to raise false hopes. We are not going to tell you what is going on in private talks. What we are going to do is our job and then, a few months from now, I think you will look back and say what we did was right.[15]

Meanwhile, he told his audience, he wanted time. As for Administration intentions, Secretary of State William Rogers informed a Senate committee two days later, " . . . We're prepared, if the other side is prepared, to have a [troop] withdrawal over a very short period of time."

The other three sides—the Saigon government, the Communists in the South, and the Hanoi government—did not seem in a hurry to begin productive talks. About the last action desired by the Thieu regime was an American withdrawal. As it had attempted to sabotage every major American effort toward de-escalating the war in the previous three years, so now it obfuscated major issues with dreary dilatory procedures that tried American officials nearly as much as the NLF and Hanoi's mouthings of all or nothing. Writing from Paris in early May, Stewart Alsop concluded that the Communists "presently have no intention whatever" of agreeing to mutual withdrawal: " . . . to believe that the Communists have any interest in a reasonable settlement it is necessary, like the Red Queen, to 'believe six impossible things before breakfast.' "[16]

Nixon was in a position where he had to believe *more* than six impossible things before breakfast, and he chose to make the best of a difficult situation. Administration spokesmen pointed to indications of a possible breakthrough: The enemy was sitting at a table in Paris along with Saigon government representatives. That government had tabled a six-point peace proposal; Hanoi had countered with a four-point plan. In May, the NLF proposed a ten-point plan. If all this seemed relatively meaningless, particularly to the combat soldier in Vietnam, the Nixon administration accepted it as necessary window-dressing to Kissinger's secret talks, disappointing as they had been.

Just how far the Administration had moved from the previous public bellicose attitude became apparent in mid-May when the President appeared on television to make a major policy speech " . . . on our most difficult and urgent problem."[17] Nixon had temporarily concluded that the get-tough approach was a failure. Nor did Hanoi buy Kissinger's secret approach: " . . . They insisted that political and military issues were inseparable, that American troops must be withdrawn unilaterally, and that Thieu must be deposed as a precondition to serious talks." An effort to involve Russia in the negotiations had proved useless.[18] The political stalemate, coupled with increasing domestic opposition, now decided the Administration that some American forces must be withdrawn and that the war must become Vietnamized, that is "... that we could train, equip, and inspire the South Vietnamese to fill the gaps left by departing American forces... it was largely on the basis of Laird's enthusiastic advocacy that we undertook the policy of Vietnamization."[19]

Bits and pieces of the new strategy appeared in the President's speech. He defended the American presence in Vietnam as necessary to accomplish the American objective, which he now defined as "... the opportunity for the South Vietnamese people to determine their own political future without outside interference." This and other bromides ("... we seek no bases ... we insist on no military ties") were to be expected. But he also "... ruled out attempting to impose a purely military solution on the battlefield," committed the Administration (and, by implication, the Thieu-Ky government) to negotiation, formal or informal, and offered a one-year plan for mutual troop withdrawals under international supervision. Once a final cease-fire was negotiated, national elections could be held.[20]

Although *Time* magazine greeted the plan as a sort of political Sermon on the Mount, its importance did not lie in the relatively vague proposals to the enemy, or even in Nixon's expressed willingness to negotiate theretofore *verboten* points such as the Saigon-NLF relationship and an interim provisional government. Its importance lay in Nixon's determination to proceed with negotiations, a not-so-hidden message that the Administration had no intention of maintaining the status quo; thenceforth the South Vietnamese would begin to share the combat burden and would search for a satisfactory internal political solution. Prior to the speech, Administration officials leaked the existence of a plan for unilateral withdrawal of American troops.

Thieu's government reacted quickly and sharply. Thieu at once rejected any talk of coalition government and in so doing emphasized his respect for democratic procedures by banning distribution of American magazines that covered the speech. But the Administration refused to budge. At Midway Island where Thieu and Ky met with Nixon in early June, they learned not only that Washington intended to push for elections in South Vietnam, but that it intended to emphasize its desire for negotiated settlement by slowly withdrawing American combat support. The Administration, Nixon announced, was unilaterally withdrawing twenty-five thousand troops to evidence pacific intentions: "... We have opened wide the door to peace," Nixon announced back in Washington in words sounding as if Billy Graham had written them, "and now we invite the leaders of North Vietnam to walk with us."[21]

The message was intended for both North and South Vietnam. Although Thieu at Midway had promised the usual reforms (including still another land-distribution program) and spoken optimistically of ARVN's increasing ability to take over the military load, the Nixon administration emphasized its intentions when Secretary of Defense Laird suggested that further withdrawals would be considered come August.

The President's action did not silence important critics at home. Writing in the July 1969 issue of *Foreign Affairs,* Clark Clifford, former secretary of defense in the Johnson administration, called for a complete reappraisal of American policy in Vietnam. Pointing to profound, and from the Western standpoint favorable, political changes in Southeast Asia and in Asia generally, Clifford argued that South Vietnam could stand increasingly on its own feet and should be left with minimum American logistic and air support. Clifford wanted a hundred thousand American soldiers withdrawn by end of 1969, the remainder by end of 1970.[22] Stung by this and other attacks, Nixon suggested further imminent troop withdrawals. Although White House aides nervously suggested that the President had not committed himself, Nixon privately spoke of a desire to virtually end American military participation by the last day of 1970.

CHAPTER SEVENTY-FOUR

1. Wooten.
2. *The Times* (London), February 26, 1969.
3. Shawcross, 609.
4. Private letter to the author, September 26, 1991.
5. *Time,* June 27, 1969. Hamburger Hill almost instantly became the most hotly criticized operation of the Vietnam War, and it played a vital role in bringing what one experienced combat commander later described as "such large scale madness" to an end. It remains a controversial issue. Twenty years after the slaughter, the on-the-spot (in a helicopter) brigade commander, Colonel Joe Conmy, described the battle as a "success" which " . . . probably saved thousands of American and Vietnamese lives." Conmy blamed the subsequent criticism of "politicians and members of the press" for the public outcry. (*International Herald Tribune,* June 3–4, 1989, citing Conmy's letter to the *Washington Post.*) I asked Colonel David Hackworth to comment on Conmy's revisionist remarks and received the following reply:

   > . . . Hamburger Hill was a classic example of how not to fight in Vietnam. Conmy's remarks reinforce my long-held conclusion that few American senior officers who commanded there understood the nature of that war. . . . The seizing of a jungle mountain-top like Ap Bia [Hamburger Hill] was total madness. Such a misuse of our combat forces would be like charging into entrenched German machine guns with mounted cavalry. . . . Had I been the theater commander I would at once have arrested and court-martialed [Melvin] Zais [commanding 101st Airborne] and Conmy on grounds of criminal negligence." [Private letter to the author, September 7, 1991.]

Conmy's assertion that the hill *per se* was a tactical necessity is refuted by the company commander (now Colonel Robert Harkins) quoted in my text: " . . . The Hill was worthless. What made it important was the fact that there were 'bad guys' *on the* Hill. Once again our mission was to find and destroy NVA units. We had done exactly that. It was never our intent to hold the Hill." (Private letter to the author, September 26, 1991.) This returns us to the question, Why try to take the hill against such adverse tactical odds, particularly when units could have been drawn back to let air and artillery fire neutralize it? The reader will probably not be surprised to learn that General Westmoreland later condoned the attacks as " . . . a feature of American tactics throughout the war. Aggressive tactics may produce sharp initial losses, but they save lives in the long run, for in a protracted battle, as in a protracted war, casualties inevitably accumulate." (Westmoreland, 152.) But this would seem to contradict his earlier statement: " . . . To have left the North Vietnamese undisturbed on the mountain [sic] would have been to jeopardize our control of the valley and accept a renewed threat to the coastal cities." (Ibid., 151.) Surely the threat was renewed when the enemy again occupied the hill?

6. Hackworth, 712–13.
7. *Nixon, Public Papers of the President 1969*, Vol. 1, 211.
8. *The Times* (London), Washington, March 19, 1969.
9. Ibid., April 9, 1969.
10. *Washington Watch,* May 26, 1969.
11. Ibid.
12. Shoup and Donovan.
13. *Washington Watch,* June 23, 1969.
14. Soedjatmoko.
15. *Newsweek,* April 7, 1969.
16. Ibid., May 5, 1969.
17. Nixon, *Public Papers of the President 1969,* Vol. 1, 369 ff.
18. Ibid., 390–1.
19. Ibid., 392.
20. Ibid., 369 ff.
21. Ibid., 443, 451. See also, Nixon, *Memoirs, 393.*
22. Clifford.

CHAPTER 75

*The Hanoi scene • Emergence of the PRG • Combat action drops
• General Wheeler's stand • The doves reply • Dissent increases •
Nixon's decision • Kissinger's secret talks in Paris • The Nixon
Doctrine • Administration problems • CIA and Special Forces •
Averell Harriman out, Henry Cabot Lodge in • CIA operations in Laos
• Ho Chi Minh's death • Nixon strikes again • Further troop
withdrawals • Progress in South Vietnam • The President and the
silent majority • The Thompson report • Blurs on the canvas*

WE DO NOT KNOW the exact effect of President Nixon's June
1969 overtures in Hanoi or in enemy ranks in the South.
They could not have been unwelcome, however. Considerable friction
existed in party ranks both in Hanoi and in the South prior to the 1968
Tet offensive. While hawks such as Truong Chinh, Vo Nguyen Giap,
and probably Le Duan continued to demand total victory in the South,
more moderate voices including those of Ho Chi Minh and Premier
Pham Van Dong could point to devastating losses, morale problems
occasioned by heavy casualties and supply shortages, severe economic
difficulties in part brought on by floods, and suggest that some form of
negotiated settlement was in order, particularly if it would result in an
American exodus which would leave the North free to undermine the
Thieu-Ky government and eventually take over the South.

Dissident factions apparently compromised in June when the National Liberation Front (NLF) announced creation of a new "Provisional Revolutionary Government of the Republic of South Vietnam,"
the PRG, which was quickly recognized as a legitimate government by
the Soviet Union and twelve other nations. The announcement created
a brief flurry of interest, which subsided when the North Vietnamese
delegation in Paris failed to follow with specific proposals. That something was astir, however, became apparent in early July when the enemy

suddenly broke off a major attack against an ARVN post, Ben Het. Action elsewhere faded and American killed-in-action figures dropped to the lowest in 1969, one hundred fifty a week. Three North Vietnamese regiments reportedly withdrew north across the DMZ while intelligence also reported a significant drop in infiltration via the Ho Chi Minh trail. Although spasmodic guerrilla attacks continued, the action further slowed until in late July American fatalities numbered under a hundred a week.

The over-all trend set off an explosive if secret debate in Washington. Pentagon and State Department hawks argued that enemy disengagement was meaningless. General Wheeler, chairman of the JCS, announced in Saigon at the end of a brief inspection tour that the recent lull did not appear to be politically significant; he disputed reports that PAVN regiments had withdrawn north and seemed to imply that American military de-escalation was not justified.[1] Wheeler praised the continued development of ARVN—the U. S. Army had been "developing" ARVN since 1954, the current project costing over $6 *billion*—and said that allied forces " . . . are well prepared for any new military initiatives the enemy may attempt." He also said in words undoubtedly intended for presidential ears " . . . that the [South] Vietnamese could not take over the full war effort by the end of 1970."[2] In a secret briefing of the Senate Armed Services Committee at month's end, he allegedly said that " . . . the Nixon plan to de-Americanize the war had been dropped. He inferred a more aggressive strategy was needed to win the war."[3]

Doves retorted that the lull was politically significant just as it had been after President Johnson halted the bombing. The military had erred then, the argument ran, by keeping up military pressure after Hanoi had withdrawn three PAVN divisions north of the DMZ. This time, doves insisted, Hanoi must be given a chance to show true intentions, particularly since it apparently had forsaken military conquest and reverted to political struggle as suggested by the creation of the new Provisional Revolutionary Government (PRG) in the South.[4]

Nixon had already decided to wind down the shooting war. Hanoi's reactions aside, he was in serious political trouble. Early in July, the figure of American dead in South Vietnam had gone over the thirty-seven-thousand mark. Official figures admitted loss of 5,666 aircraft including nearly 2,900 helicopters—a total financial loss of above $3 billion.[5] These and other unpalatable facts and figures were being spewed to the nation not only by the daily press but by a powerful underground press that in 1969 amounted to almost five hundred newspapers with a circulation approaching five million.[6] The American people, not only students and other "troublemakers," were slowly realizing that an era of militarism was bankrupting the United States both spiritually and financially. More than two thirds of federal expenditure since World War II—over $1 *trillion*—had gone to armaments and armed forces. Vietnam expenditures for fiscal year 1968–69 would come to $30 billion.[7] The 1970 defense budget topped $80 billion. Military leaders were clamoring for new weapons systems, new bombers, strategic missiles, tanks, aircraft. While poverty claimed large areas of the United States, while the population was outgrowing schools and social services, while American cities were coming apart at the seams, the Vietnam war would take $28 billion in *direct* costs in the new fiscal year. As David Calleo of the Washington Center of Foreign Policy Research put it:

> ... It is not isolationism that is reviving in the United States but humanism. Prodded by the prolonged agony of Vietnam many Americans now perceive grotesque distortions in their Government's values. The United States, they believe, is sacrificing the quality of its national life to the demands of a military empire.[8]

Widespread dissent continued to show itself, not only in draft-card burning and student demonstrations, but in the intellectual fabric of America and increasingly in Congress. In that summer of 1969, Nixon in many ways was facing an incipient rebellion, and it is a great argument for the worth of democracy that, though he favored force, public opinion was pushing him toward disengagement.

Nixon in mid-July wrote to Ho Chi Minh to offer negotiation or military escalation, the choice to be made by the first of November at the latest. This led to a secret meeting between Kissinger and Xuan Thuy in Paris, the first of a three-year series. In late July, Nixon sent orders to Abrams not only to cut down offensive missions but to begin withdrawing American units from combat positions as rapidly as ARVN units could replace them. Nixon now undertook a tour of Asia to spread a new gospel that became known as the Nixon Doctrine: America would thenceforth offer economic and limited military aid to those nations willing to supply the manpower necessary to defend themselves.[9] Although the United States would honor its commitments in Southeast Asia, the President explained to leaders in Djakarta, Saigon, and Bangkok, it would thenceforth emphasize economic rather than military action. The time had come, Nixon proclaimed, to end a war and build a peace.

If Nixon hoped to quiet American critics by such oratory, he was quickly disappointed. A series of shocks now befell the Administration and particularly the armed forces. In late July, a Congressional subcommittee, in a report on the *Pueblo* disaster (see Chapter 69), rapped the military soundly on the knuckles:

> ... The inquiry reveals the existence of a vast and complex military structure capable of acquiring almost infinite amounts of information but with a demonstrated inability ... to relay this information in a timely and comprehensible fashion to those charged with the responsibility for making decisions.[10]

Further adverse publicity spilled over the U. S. Navy a month later when it announced that the USS *New Jersey,* the battleship that had been refitted for service in Vietnam waters at a cost of $40 million, was being mothballed after eighteen months' service. In early August, a scandal broke in Saigon with the arrest of one Huynh Van Trong and some fifty associates. Trong was special assistant and confidant on political affairs to President Thieu. He was charged with running an espionage ring for North Vietnam. The American public was still digesting this upsetting development when MACV announced the arrest of eight Special Forces soldiers including the Green Beret commander in South Vietnam, Colonel Robert Rheault, for murdering a Vietnamese civilian. The victim, who allegedly worked for both CIA and Special Forces, was said to have been "doubled" by the Communists. When that was discovered, CIA ordered him "terminated with extreme prejudice"—a death sentence allegedly carried out by Special Forces.

The case caused tremendous speculation, mostly critical, concerning American policy. NBC, for example, reported that Special Forces had committed over three hundred political assassinations in South Vietnam including those of senior Vietnamese officials. It also caused problems in the Phoenix program, the joint American-South Vietnamese effort that had been trying to root out VC infrastructure in liberated areas. The covert part of this program involved assassination of enemy agents. Nearly five hundred American "advisers" now wondered if they were to be tried for murder. CIA's refusal to produce witnesses for the prosecution of Rheault and his fellows caused the army to drop the case.[11] Instead of airing policy CIA claimed executive privilege and Nixon allowed the altogether dubious claim. This did not repair damage done to the prestige of Special Forces nor did it quiet critics who objected to CIA's terminating people with or without "extreme prejudice." To a good many intelligent Americans the terminology belonged to SMERSH and James Bond, not to a democracy that claimed to embrace the principle of trial by jury.

More was to come. An article by two American scientists in the August issue of *Scientific Research* condemned the defoliation program in South Vietnam and directly challenged U. S. Army claims that herbicides caused only minimal damage. Pointing to established decreases in rice and rubber production caused in part by killing plants and trees, the scientist-authors claimed that herbicides were causing long-term ecological damage, as was B-52 bombing. They pointed out that in 1968 American bombs had created 2.6 million craters " . . . with currently incalculable consequences for the countryside."[12]

Still more criticism broke over the Administration when President Thieu replaced his civilian prime minister, the rather gentle Tran Van Huong, with General Tran Thien Khiem, who was generally considered a hawk. Administration critics bluntly accused Saigon of pursuing a militaristic policy at a time when the United States was trying to negotiate a peace. In late September, Averell Harriman, whom Nixon had relieved as envoy at the Paris peace talks in favor of Henry Cabot Lodge, stated that the United States must ignore Saigon and forge an agreement with North Vietnam and with the National Liberation Front in the South. The Nixon administration was acting " . . . as though it is some sort of a satellite of the Saigon government . . . the personal interests of President Thieu and Vice President Cao Ky should not be allowed to become the premises of American policy."[13] Also in late September, Senator Mike Mansfield returned from a tour of Asia to state that " . . . the American involvement in Laos had grown to such an extent that it could lead to another Vietnam war." Citing Nixon's new Asian doctrine, he added that " . . . present tendencies in Laos were running directly counter to what should be expected."[14] Mansfield's remarks brought correspondents to the Laotian scene like bees to honey. In late October, the *New York Times* reported details of the private war being run by CIA in Laos. Once again critics had a field day and not a few Americans agreed with Senator Stuart Symington, a one-time hawk who now expressed worry about extensive American commitments in light of a worsening domestic situation: " . . . We spend $44 for every child's education up to college age, but in Vietnam we spend $21,600 in ammunition alone to kill one enemy soldier."[15]

President Nixon did not accept this and additional criticism passively, and his temper was improved by a few streaks of light in otherwise somber skies. Some were transitory. Ho Chi Minh's death in early September brought hopeful prophecies from some Hanoi-watchers of a power struggle that would probably end in a peace party gaining dominance. It did nothing of the sort. Pham Van Dong, who headed the new government, publicly admitted to severe problems but showed himself equally unwilling to respect Nixon's "ultimatum."[16]

Nixon sent two specific signals to the new government. One was a three-day halt of B-52 raids in South Vietnam. When this evoked no response, the raids were resumed. In mid-September, he announced that he was withdrawing at least another thirty-five thousand American troops before the end of 1969, an occasion used to place the onus again on North Vietnam with an appeal to begin "meaningful negotiations." Nixon also canceled draft calls for November and December and dismissed General Lewis B. Hershey, octogenarian head of the draft board and subject of extreme criticism, particularly from students objecting to the draft's bias.

The President also continued his partial-withdrawal policy in South Vietnam, and here he scored a major gain. By late September, most American combat units had been withdrawn from the Mekong Delta area. To the surprise of all but genuine counterinsurgency experts, pacification now proceeded much more rapidly than it had when the military was tearing up the countryside with search-and-destroy missions. Village elections were being held throughout the delta. Assassinations by VC terrorists continued, but the Phoenix program at last seemed to be taking hold. Although military hawks argued that such progress was the result of attrition strategy, other observers insisted that the key lay in withdrawing American combat units. Nixon accepted the arguments of the latter group and MACV turned toward a strategy not dissimilar to that recommended by General James Gavin in 1965—an enclave strategy derided by hawks at the time. If nothing else, however, casualties dropped significantly despite warnings of military experts that they would rise.

Nixon was walking a political tightrope during this autumn and early winter of 1969. Faced with increasing dissent including a nationwide moratorium kicked off by 250,000 anti-war demonstrators in Washington, his major pitch continued to be a plea for time. In late September, he pointed to some hopeful facts, for example that North Vietnamese infiltration into the South was down two thirds from the previous year; American casualties had decreased by a third; combat remained at a minimum level. If the American people formed a popular front behind his peace proposals, the President predicted, the Vietnam war would end the next year.[17]

In early November, the President made another major policy speech, in which he dramatically appealed to "the great silent majority of Americans" to let him continue fighting and negotiating as he thought best. He would not accept defeat, he told his audience; he would not withdraw all of America's military forces from South Vietnam until Vietnamization was a fact.[18] The silent majority, without really having much to go on except innate hope and presidential rhetoric, vocally responded overwhelmingly in favor of its President as did some members of Congress. Another majority continued to stage increasingly large anti-war rallies and university sit-ins while newspapers and television continued to criticize the Administration.

Nixon's confidence grew, however, as good news kept arriving from the war-torn country. The Saigon government announced that in October over five thousand Viet Cong rallied to the government's side to make a total of nearly forty thousand defectors for the year. Lieutenant

General Julian Ewell, commanding III Corps area north of Saigon, told reporters that " . . . the Vietcong were rapidly becoming non-existent, the North Vietnamese were being forced to write off certain units to be withdrawn." The general claimed that 97 per cent of the rural population in his area was " . . . under nominal government control"; 82 per cent of the remaining sixty-one thousand enemy, he continued, were North Vietnamese. The British correspondent Fred Emery, who reported the above, wrote in a dispatch the following day that VC defectors had climbed to twenty-six thousand this year, that Regional and Popular Forces recruitment had doubled, and that a million peasants had joined the People's Self-Defense Forces. High percentages of Mekong Delta villages and hamlets had elected their own officials:

> . . . None of these figures, it is true, supports the contention that people have been swung behind the government. . . . Yet there is little doubt that many people are living freer from direct harassment than they can perhaps remember.[19]

A month later, *Time* correspondent Mark Clark reported from Saigon that although " . . . statements of optimism are far more muted than in the halcyon days that preceded *Tet* in 1968, there is an unmistakable air of confidence." The Thieu regime, Clark reported, " . . . is a going concern. While Thieu is not a popular hero, he heads a government that is stable."[20] A similar report was made to the President in late December by a British counterinsurgency expert, Sir Robert Thompson, whom Nixon sent to Vietnam to "reassess" the situation. Nixon later wrote that in October Thompson was " . . . clearly not in favor of escalation.. . . His estimate was that, continuing the current U.S. policy and assuming South Vietnamese confidence that we would not pull out, victory could be won within two years." Something of Thompson's naïve geopolitical astuteness may be adduced from his reply to Nixon's question " . . . whether he thought it was important for us to see it through." Thompson replied, " . . . Absolutely. In my opinion the future of Western civilization is at stake in the way you handle yourselves in Vietnam."[21]

The corpus of Thompson's subsequent report based on a five-week tour remained secret, but in articles, interviews, and private conversations, he displayed enthusiasm made the more impressive by contrast to the critical and pessimistic tone of his book *No Exit from Vietnam* published in March 1969. Interviewed in London, Thompson optimistically discussed pacification progress and the increasingly stable performance of the South Vietnamese Government and concluded:

> . . . The war in South Vietnam can therefore be won, in the sense that a just peace can be obtained, whether negotiated or not, and

that the South Vietnamese people will be in a position to determine their own future without any interference or compulsion from the North. This after all is the limit of the American aim, and has been very clearly laid down by the President, particularly at the Paris peace talks.[22]

In a major speech in mid-December, Nixon announced that he was withdrawing another fifty thousand American troops, mostly combat units, before April 1970.[23] Two months later, President Thieu emphasized his claim of controlling 93 per cent of the South Vietnamese countryside by staging a 475-mile bicycle race whose seventy-three contestants pedaled the course without VC opposition.

As with optimistic pictures previously drawn by Saigon and Washington administrations, a few blurs marred this canvas. The first was the Administration's negotiating position. Nixon's injured tones in discussing Hanoi's intransigence bore little semblance of reality. Whatever his hopes, he had few reasons to expect Hanoi to negotiate an unfavorable peace after fighting a war that had destroyed much of North Vietnam and, by the American administration's own figures, taken the lives of 450,000 enemy soldiers, not to mention those of thousands of civilians, within the previous six years. The President could resume bombing of the North but, short of people, little remained to bomb. According to one National Security Council official, Kissinger set up a special group to " . . . examine new military options, including . . . possible one-time use of a nuclear device"—the "savage blow" that Kissinger believed would knock North Vietnam out of the war. Fortunately, Melvin Laird learned of the goings-on and told Nixon that bombing people out of existence—Giulio Douhet's strategic-genocide theory—would not be permitted either by American or world civil opinion.[24]

What Nixon and his advisers and a good many American citizens failed to realize was that Hanoi could not be further hurt. It had suffered—but it had survived. Peking continued to vie with Moscow to supply essential needs and, in Moscow's case, to guarantee general postwar rehabilitation. American bombing had long since given the North Vietnamese people a genuine stake in the war. They would continue to exist on a subsistence level—a disciplined people is as essential to protracted war as flexibility in strategy and tactics. Whatever methods had been chosen to fight the war so far, Hanoi never forgot the requirements of protracted war. As Colonel Bouquet had instructed in 1766 and Charles Callwell had repeated in 1899, the "savages" were the professionals in their own environment.

Other factors entered. Hanoi was on the brink of winning a tremendous psychological victory by chasing American forces from the scene. Decades before, Lyautey had protested regarding the Spanish withdrawal in Morocco: " . . . My God! An army retreats when it must but it does not announce the fact to the enemy in advance." Nixon was forced to make this very announcement which increased the influence of Hanoi hawks; negotiations or no, they saw themselves on the verge of obtaining a major objective. Why hurry to negotiate when continuing criticism of the war both in the United States and throughout the world would force Nixon's hand further and further? In mid-November, the scandal of the My Lai killings had broken and though the full effect of the shock on the American people had not yet been wrought, cacophonous voices were already shrilling the shameful facts. Senator Fulbright, a long-time critic of the war, publicly criticized growing presidential power to involve the United States in such areas as South Vietnam where " . . . the United States has no vital security interest."[25] Fulbright kept up his attack in December, stating that Nixon's Vietnamization policy meant " . . . a continuing war of stalemate and attrition." Other legislators reacted adversely to reports of a secret war in Laos, and in mid-December the Senate voted to bar American combat troops from Laos and Thailand.[26] Dissension, in short, now ruled Washington councils as it ruled the nation—all to Hanoi's benefit.

What about the optimistic situation in the South Vietnamese countryside? Here again the Administration exhibited considerable naïveté by treating a lull in guerrilla activity as if it were a major victory—precisely what Sir Charles Gwynn had warned against thirty-five years earlier (see Chapter 23). American commanders would have been wise to have respected the Spartan admonition to Philip of Macedon: "If you imagine that your victory has made you greater than you were, measure your shadow." If parts of South Vietnam were being cleared of enemy, large numbers of enemy remained. In early November, the respected Washington correspondent of *The Times* (London), Louis Heren, reported that of PAVN's 430,000 troops about 130,000 were in the South or in border sanctuaries. He placed VC strength at sixty thousand trained guerrillas, ninety thousand in political cadres, and perhaps fifty thousand in local irregular forces.[27] Fred Emery reported from Saigon in mid-November that the enemy was launching sporadic attacks and that terrorist incidents have "barely gone down at all."

> . . . It is precisely because, whatever the military lull, they can inflict retribution on this scale, discriminately and indiscriminately, that pacification is shown to be rarely the same thing as security. And the difference is vital.[28]

In a later dispatch that quoted General Ewell's optimistic reports concerning eleven provinces north of Saigon, Emery also noted that the

American general envisaged "a war around here somewhere for the next 50 to 150 years."[29] President Nixon in his mid-December speech also noted "one disturbing new development," which was a substantial increase in infiltration—some eight thousand men a month from the North.[30]

Sir Robert Thompson's expressed optimism also glossed over some disturbing facts. Thompson had been enthusiastic before—in 1963 for example—and had been wrong. Whatever the total content of his report to the President, he had to admit to grave deficiencies in the scene that he had surveyed as paid consultant to the Nixon administration. Thompson had always deemed a constable force necessary for defeating an insurgency and maintaining the peace. At a London seminar in early 1969, he had pointed to the South Vietnamese failure to build a viable rural police force, and this had not been repaired. Another deficiency to which he privately admitted was a lopsided economic position by which a country of 17.5 million people with an estimated GNP of $2.5 billion (in large part U.S. subsidized) was supporting an armed force over one million strong (including 472,500 regular troops).[31] This condition could scarcely improve under what Thompson called "a long-haul, low-cost strategy" (with South Vietnam increasingly assuming the military burden) that would be necessary for at least three to five years " . . . before Hanoi is compelled to give up her purpose and to negotiate a real settlement."[32]

Thompson shared *Time* magazine's enthusiasm concerning the Saigon government and publicly spoke admiringly of Thieu, whom he considered a real politician. Thieu might have been a real politician—whatever that meant—but he already had proved himself a strong man in the worst totalitarian tradition: as someone disparagingly remarked, "The brown Sahib has replaced the white Sahib." Thieu's officials censored newspapers as frequently as his secret police arrested political dissidents. Magazines disavowing any of his acts such as *Time* and *Newsweek*, were suppressed; he filled jails with political prisoners (Communists, yes, but also non-Communists); his secret police arrested and held opponents without charge. Some of his legislation was as oppressive as that dreamed up by the Diem-Nhu regime. General Duong Van Minh, leader of the revolt against Diem, returned from a four-year exile in Thailand and almost immediately denounced the minority basis of Thieu's government stating, according to Fred Emery, that " . . . the Government has cut itself off from the people, and he adds that this cannot be."[33]

So long as this government remained authoritarian, so long as Thieu's political base rested on army and secret police and force, so long as a gulf existed between mandarin bureaucracy and peasants, the

Viet Cong would continue to operate. In the enemy's mind, American presence or no, the Saigon government would eventually fall. So the problem for Hanoi and the PRG was what it had always been: helping the process along with flexible tactics of revolutionary warfare.

Incredibly, neither Nixon nor his advisers yet seemed to understand that they were grappling with a political problem. Kissinger already had sounded the key word: *honor*. The Administration was embracing Comines' dictum, "He who has success has honor," while overlooking Talleyrand's remark, "Honor in our age of corruption has been invented in order to make vanity do the work of virtue." Nixon failed to see that victory could come only from within a country whose government was attuned to the demands of its peoples. Failing to see this, he made the fatal error of yielding to bellicose civil and military advisers who forever believed that the threat was external and who, if they had had their way, would have enlarged the action to nuclear-warfare proportions.

CHAPTER SEVENTY-FIVE

1. *The Times* (London), July 20, 1969.
2. Ibid.
3. *Washington Watch,* August 7, 1969.
4. Shaplen, *The Road from War,* 293 ff.
5. *The Times* (London), July 25, 1969.
6. Schalk, 9.
7. Kissinger, *The White House Years,* 235.
8. *The Times* (London), July 29, 1969.
9. Nixon, *Memoirs, 395.*
10. *The Times* (London), July 28, 1969.
11. Mollenhoff, 73.
12. *The Sunday Telegraph* (London), August 10, 1969.
13. *The Times* (London), September 18, 1969.
14. Ibid., September 21, 1969. See also, Grant.
15. *The Sunday Times* (London), November 2, 1969.
16. Nixon, *Memoirs,* 401–2.
17. Nixon, *Public Papers of the President 1969,* Vol. 1, 752. See also, *The Sunday Times* (London), November 5, 1969.
18. Nixon, *Public Papers of the President 1969,* Vol. 1, 901–9. See also, Hackworth, 667.
19. *The Times* (London), November 24, 25, 1969.
20. *Time,* December 26, 1969. See also, Blaufarb, 267.
21. Nixon, *Memoirs,* 404–5.
22. Robert Thompson, "On the Way to Victory."
23. Nixon, *Public Papers of the President 1969,* Vol. 1, 1025–28.
24. Reichley, 118.
25. *The Times* (London), November 13, 1969.
26. Ibid., December 15, 1969.
27. Ibid., November 3, 1969.
28. Ibid., November 11, 1969.

29. Ibid., November 24, 1969.
30. Nixon, *Public Papers of the President 1969*, Vol. 1, 1027.
31. Royal United Services Institution Seminar, 1969.
32. *Time*, December 26, 1969.
33. *The Times* (London), November 14, 1969.

CHAPTER 76

Confused U.S. objectives • *Congressional opposition mounts* • *Involvement in Laos* • *President Thieu's stand* • *President Nixon's dilemma* • *The Cambodian invasion* • *Disappointing results* • *Dissent on the home front* • *Clark Clifford's new plan (II)*

CONGRESSIONAL DISAPPROVAL of the President's course in Vietnam continued into 1970. In mid-February, the President submitted a foreign-policy report to Congress that contained no specific statement of international objectives—" . . . a disappointment to those who looked for an ordered definition, as opposed to a declamation, of American interests."[1] A staff study in the same month published by the Senate Foreign Relations Committee concluded that " . . . the assumptions on which American policy [in Vietnam] are based are ambiguous, confusing, and contradictory." Nixon's policy depended on three factors, the study suggested: progressive Vietnamization, the stability of the Saigon government, and lack of enemy interference, each "uncertain" of success: " . . . Dilemmas thus seem to lie ahead in Vietnam, as they have throughout our involvement in this war that appears to be not only far from won but far from over."[2] Individual senators in public hearings bluntly made clear their hostility. Charles Goodell spoke of "illusions" entertained by the Administration and concluded, " . . . We have not Vietnamized the war: we have cosmetized it." Senator Fulbright cogently asked, " . . . In what exact ways have we advanced toward peace? The war, as we know, is still going on. Replacements are still being sent to Vietnam; we are still suffering about 750 casualties a week; and the war is still costing the American people about $70 millions a day." Senators Harold Hughes and Thomas Eagleton proposed a resolution calling on the Saigon government for immediate reforms; in lieu thereof, " . . . the President of the United States should declare officially that our commitment to the present Government of South Vietnam is ended."[3]

Adding to legislative dissatisfaction was the increasingly serious situation in Laos. The 1962 Geneva Agreements confirmed the neutrality of an independent Laos governed by Souvanna Phouma's coalition government. The Soviet Union terminated its supply flights to North Vietnamese army [PAVN] units and to Pathet Lao guerrillas; CIA halted its supply flights to Meo tribesmen guerrillas, and Special Forces withdrew its training teams. When Hanoi did not remove its PAVN units, an estimated seven thousand troops working with the Pathet Lao, CIA and Special Forces recommenced their operations, organizing, training, and supplying Meo tribesmen, who thenceforth fought a formidable guerrilla war against the Pathet Lao-North Vietnamese army.[4] In 1969, the Nixon administration upped the ante by authorizing an all-out bombing campaign that included napalm and phosphorus bombs and centered on and north of the contested Plain of Jars. Such was its intensity that in 1970 few villages remained, their inhabitants having been forced underground. " . . . We never saw the sun," one refugee reported; another stated, " . . . There wasn't a night that we went to sleep that we thought we'd live to see the morning."[5] In January 1970, Hanoi further fueled the situation by suddenly reinforcing its already substantial forces north of the Plain of Jars where Pathet Lao guerrillas were being held in uneasy check, not so much by the Royal Laotian Army, which despite years of American training and the expenditure of millions of dollars, remained " . . . hardly fit to face the enemy,"[6] as by some thirty-six thousand CIA-sponsored Meo guerrillas.[7] The expected enemy offensive opened in mid-February and soon cleared the high ground leading to the plain. After considerable dithering, the White House authorized a small B-52 strike that became known and tripped off Congressional and public accusations of further escalation. Nixon's refusal to deny or confirm alleged American involvement drew strong criticism from Senator George McGovern, who, like most of his brethren, knew of neither the secret Operation Menu bombings of Cambodia nor the simultaneous bombing campaign in Laos. Requesting that the Senate debate the subject *in camera,* McGovern condemned the notion of a secret war:

> . . . It is absolutely incredible that a great nation such as ours could be waging a major military operation in a foreign country without the knowledge of either citizens or its Congress. But that is the fact.[8]

Although Nixon assured Congress that no American ground forces would be sent to Laos, he did not explain the presence of those already there—estimated from one to five thousand—nor did he offer details of the aerial bombing. Secretary of State Rogers scarcely mollified worried congressmen by stating that " . . . the possibility of using American ground forces in Laos could not be ruled out, although there were no plans to do so at present."⁹

Meanwhile the Communist offensive gathered steam and in late March had reached the Long Thieng area, the last stop before the capital of Vientiane. But now the Laotian army, stiffened by "volunteers" from Thailand and by the Meo guerrillas, opened what turned out to be a successful counteroffensive. By end of March, the situation had stabilized and would remain so for the rest of the year.

The incipient American exodus suffered another setback when President Thieu reverted to the hackneyed tack of the domino theory: if the United States withdrew from the Asian mainland, the Chinese would take over Laos, Cambodia, Malaysia, and Indonesia. South Vietnam, Thieu stated, was the key to the entire area: " . . . We have to contain the rush of the Communists right here—not in the U.S., not at Midway or Hawaii or in mid-ocean, but right here on the Asian mainland." Thieu insisted that " . . . there was no fixed timetable for the withdrawal of American troops. The South Vietnamese forces must be given sufficient and adequate means to fight the Communists." Thieu had every reason for maintaining a state of emergency. It was his principal justification for running one of the most repressive and corrupt governments in the world. The American military, both MACV and the JCS, agreed in part with Thieu. Louis Heren wrote that " . . . the [American] Army is resisting further cuts [in South Vietnam]. General William Westmoreland, the Chief of Staff, is reported to be pressing for a six-month delay ostensibly because the rate of 'Vietnamization' is too fast for safety and comfort."¹⁰

In spring of 1970, Nixon was caught between two powerful forces: public opinion at home, military opinion at home and abroad. If for no other than domestic political reasons, he had to continue winding down the war in Vietnam. At the same time, MACV and the Pentagon were pointing to forty thousand Communist troops active in Cambodia and to renewed enemy activity in South Vietnam, and were violently arguing against further troop withdrawals. In trying to satisfy everybody, Nixon satisfied no one. He further erred by reintroducing the bogey of atomic warfare, which alarmed and enraged other countries, friendly, neutral, and enemy. In late April, the President told the nation that he had based his troop-withdrawal program on three criteria. Two had been met. Training and equipping South Vietnamese forces had "substantially exceeded our expectations"; and there had been "extensive progress" in pacification (including a new land-reform bill that, in theory, would provide over three million acres for distribution.¹¹ No progress, however, had been made on the negotiating front. Nonetheless he was planning to withdraw another 150,000 American troops by spring of 1971, more if progress was made in negotiations:

... I again remind the leaders of North Vietnam that, while we are taking these risks for peace, they jeopardize the security of our remaining forces in Vietnam by increased military action in Vietnam, in Cambodia, or in Laos.... If I conclude that increased enemy action jeopardizes our remaining forces ... I shall not hesitate to take strong and effective measures.[12]

"... It is not too much to say," James Reston noted, "that he will use any weapon at his command, repeat *any* weapon, to avoid the destruction of his remaining soldiers."[13]

Extensive B-52 bombings had not greatly damaged enemy sanctuary areas, but they had driven the enemy considerably deeper into Cambodia, where they had begun clashing with village authorities and Cambodian army troops.[14] Taken with CIA support of Prince Norodom Sihanouk's rival, Son Ngoc Thanh, whose nationalist-guerrilla group, the Khmer Serai, was located in South Vietnam, and of an American-sponsored disruption effort that was moving the urban elite and the officer corps in Phnom Penh away from Sihanouk, the bombings had helped to destabilize Sihanouk's rule at a particularly critical time. In August 1969, Sihanouk had formed a new rightist government with General Lon Nol as prime minister. Lon Nol, an alleged anti-Communist, was as corrupt as another of Sihanouk's rivals, his cousin Prince Sisowith Sirik Matak, indeed as Sihanouk himself. Lon Nol as defense minister had run a lucrative business with the Communist enemy by taking large bribes to permit the passage north of Chinese arms sent to Sihanoukville. But the increasing penetration of the enemy westward had caused Lon Nol to challenge the Communist presence and to persuade Sihanouk to protest to Hanoi. Sihanouk himself seemed to be tilting toward the West by forming a regional balance of power that he hoped would preserve Cambodian independence, but at the same time he was preserving his ties to Moscow and Peking in the hope that they could moderate if not eliminate the North Vietnamese and Viet Cong presence in Cambodia.[15]

Sihanouk made his big mistake in January 1970 by taking himself off to a fat farm on the French Riviera. He was not long departed when Lon Nol and Prince Sirik Matak decided to oust him, a move heartily favored by Son Ngoc Thanh across the border in South Vietnam. We shall probably never know the extent of American involvement in the coup. Nixon and Kissinger claim innocence, but their historical recall is not always to be taken seriously, and there is also damaging evidence later provided by Roger Morris, one of Kissinger's senior analysts: "... It was clear in the White House that the CIA station in Phnom

Penh knew the plotters well, probably knew their plans, and did nothing to alert Sihanouk. They informed Washington well in advance of the coup. . . ."[16] Lon Nol had been a strong-man favorite of the Administration for some time, and recently had added to his luster by closing the port of Sihanoukville to Communist arms shipments and by demanding that Hanoi withdraw its troops from the country.[17] A CIA analyst in Saigon later wrote that in early 1970 the CIA was encouraging both Son Ngoc Thanh and Lon Nol to replace Sihanouk. MACV and the CIA believed that if Lon Nol replaced the prince, " . . . he would welcome the United States with open arms and we would accomplish everything"[18]—such as being invited to invade Cambodia and start a second war in Southeast Asia.

Sihanouk did not gracefully accept defeat. Three days after the coup, he conferred with China's foreign minister Chou En-lai and Hanoi's premier Pham Van Dong in Peiping, where he was persuaded to accept leadership of the Khmer Rouge guerrillas, Cambodia's native Communists. After establishing a provisional government-in-exile, he appealed to his countrymen " . . . to engage in guerrilla warfare in the jungles against our enemies," an appeal immediately embraced by the North Vietnamese, who thenceforth would join the Khmer Rouge in waging war against Lon Nol's Cambodian army.[19] A large force of Cambodian Communists who had fled their country in 1954 and who had been trained in guerrilla warfare by the North Vietnamese now marched down the Ho Chi Minh trail into Cambodia, where they would attempt to take command of the guerrilla movement.

If Lon Nol and his officials scoffed at Sihanouk's words, peasants in the countryside listened to them. Riots broke out in towns and villages which the army put down, often brutally. An alarmed Lon Nol, to divert attention, now turned the army loose on the nearly half-million Vietnamese who had remained in Cambodia after the Geneva Accords, insisting that they were all Viet Cong who must be eliminated—and many of them were. Within weeks, the warp and woof of Cambodian society were unraveling in Lon Nol's dangerously ineffective hands.[20]

Whether American-inspired or not, the coup seemed a heaven-sent opportunity to Nixon, Kissinger, the JCS, the bellicose Admiral John S. McCain, Jr., in Honolulu, and Abrams and his MACV planners, and the Thieu government in Saigon. With Nixon's overt approval, Administration hawks at once demanded substantial support for the new ruler. Secretary of Defense Melvin Laird, while in Saigon in February, authorized MACV to give logistical support to South Vietnamese units which were crossing the border into Cambodia to attack enemy supply dumps. In April, responding to North Vietnamese gains in Cambodia and to Lon Nol's request for arms, the President secretly authorized MACV to send him several planeloads of captured Soviet-made AK-47 rifles (the first step in a futile two-year expenditure of $1.7 billion) to arm the burgeoning Cambodian army's seventy thousand volunteers— an order that, leaked to the *New York Times* William Beecher, caused another Congressional confrontation.

That was only the beginning. The JCS and MACV had long been wanting to strike enemy sanctuaries across the border. Planners now dusted off previous contingency plans that soon covered Washington desks. Nixon and Kissinger were fascinated by the prospect of a blue-plate special: COSVN captured, sanctuaries cleansed and closed; the security of U.S. forces assured; Vietnamization to continue its allegedly remarkable progress. Enthusiastic planning continued into April while ARVN troops probed the border areas and more American-supplied arms arrived in Phnom Penh for the army that was being built over-night. Son Ngoc Thanh and his Khmer Serai guerrillas were moved to Cambodia along with other U.S.-trained Khmer units.

There were some problems. In one White House briefing, William Safire pointed out that the proposed invasion did not square with the Nixon Doctrine of keeping American soldiers out of Asian battles. Kis-singer explosively told him, " . . . We wrote the goddamn doctrine, we can change it."[21] Other important voices disagreed with Nixon, Kissin-ger, and the hawks. One of the most frightening, indeed tragic, aspects of the Vietnamese, Cambodian, and Laotian wars was the abject refusal of its American parents to even listen to, much less respect, dissentient opinions of well-qualified professionals. Six days after Prince Sihanouk had been deposed, the veteran diplomat and chargé d'affaires in the American embassy in Phnom Penh, Lloyd Rives, warned about the dan-gers of escalation. Marshall Green, a senior diplomat who represented the State Department in the Washington Special Action Group, a high-powered committee chaired by Henry Kissinger, agreed with Rives and recommended to Kissinger and Rogers that

> . . . the United States should try to work through the French and the Algerians to find a diplomatic solution to Cambodia's new problems. . . . Green believed that the only hope for Cambodia lay in continuing Sihanouk's policies if not actually helping to restore Sihanouk himself. Green pointed out the paradox that "without massive U.S. support the Government of Cambodia cannot rebuild its position . . . but U.S. support could restrict its neutrality, which is its greatest resource." He argued, moreover, that Congress would see aid to Lon Nol as widening the war and might therefore impose further restrictions on aid to Vietnam. Helping Cambodia could hinder Vietnamization. This is exactly what happened.[22]

By being essentially correct and having the courage to say so, Green earned Administration ire and great harm to his career.

Secretary of State Rogers and Secretary of Defense Laird strongly opposed any move into Cambodia until the international political dust raised by the coup had settled.[23] Each subsequently remained strongly against deploying American troops inside Cambodia. The Nixon-Kissinger answer to this dissent was to eliminate them from the planning process by means of Kissinger's office dealing directly with the JCS and by Nixon and Kissinger using a secret back-channel to deal directly with Abrams and Bunker in Saigon, at the same time pressuring Rogers and Laird to condone the operation. Rogers never did come around. Laird caved in but only because he believed that an ARVN invasion *without* American troops would not push Communist troops farther westward to lessen the threat to Saigon while Vietnamization continued. As for the great Communist central control headquarters, COSVN, Laird accurately told Nixon that " . . . COSVN in that sense did not exist and had never existed."[24]

Nixon decided to employ American troops only at the last minute. Appropriate Congressional committees were not informed, although Administration favorite Senator John Stennis, who had been made privy to Operation Menu, was easily won over when briefed by Kissinger, a touching scene as described by the briefer lacking only darkies, mint juleps, banjoes, and magnolia blossoms.[25] Lon Nol was not informed— he learned of the invasion only after it had begun. Kissinger cut most of his staff out of the planning. When the invasion was announced, three important aides resigned in disgust.[26]

Operation Toan Thang (aka Operation Rock Crusher) kicked off on April 29.[27] American artillery prepositioned in South Vietnam, opened preparatory fire while South Vietnamese fighter-bomber aircraft softened the target area. Three ARVN armored columns—some twelve thousand men with perhaps fifty American advisers—then invaded a border area known as Parrot's Beak. American helicopters including gunships supported the operation as did various logistic and medical-evacuation teams.

Shortly after Vietnamese columns began clanking into Parrot's Beak, a combined task force commenced Operation Prometheus north of the Beak. After preparatory air and artillery fire, some five thousand American troops pushed into an area called Fish Hook, which contained two of Operation Menu's target areas and, according to Abrams, was where COSVN was still functioning—despite the twenty-nine thousand tons of bombs dropped there over the past year.[28] This two-pronged

VIETNAM 1970
• Towns and Cities
← A.R.V.N.-U.S. invasions

0   100   200 miles

M.E.P

operation included three South Vietnamese paratroop battalions landed by American helicopters and was designed to close a trap around the enemy. Military spokesmen described the total operation as a "quick-strike" pincers movement converging on COSVN.

The offensive came as a surprise to nearly everyone (except the enemy). President Nixon appeared on television to justify his deeds by pointing out that " . . . the United States had 'scrupulously respected' Cambodia's neutrality for the last five years and had not moved against the sanctuaries," a patent lie " . . . repeated by Kissinger in his background briefings to the press."[29] Nixon went on to explain, somewhat ingeniously, that the invasion was not an invasion. The Cambodian operation was intended to eliminate " . . . the headquarters for the entire communist military operation in South Vietnam. This key control center has been occupied by the North Vietnamese and Viet Cong for years in blatant violation of Cambodia's neutrality." The present limited action, the President explained, was indispensable for the continuing success of the withdrawal program, for ending the war, and for keeping U.S. casualties to absolute minimum.[30] But there was something more, the President insisted, and that was the threat from " . . . the forces of totalitarianism and anarchy . . . [to the] free nations and free institutions throughout the world . . . [if] the world's most powerful nation, the United States of America, acts like a pitiful, helpless giant. . . . "[31]

This was vintage Nixon, but the wine was sour. Senator Edmund Muskie of Maine responded that " . . . this speech confirms a judgment that I've been reluctant to make: the President has decided to seek a military method of ending the war rather than a negotiated settlement." Senator Walter Mondale of Minnesota held that " . . . this is not only a tragic escalation, which will broaden the war and increase American casualties, but is outright admission of the failure of Vietnamization." Other critical voices joined the dissentient chorus, but they were not to down the high-flying President, who at the Pentagon the next day caused several nervous breakdowns by blithely ordering plans made to "take out" *all* the sanctuaries.[32]

Military operations meanwhile proceeded smoothly enough. Major General Ely Roberts, commanding 1st Cavalry (Airmobile) Division, told correspondents, " . . . We think we have them in the bag. In a day or two we shall reach inside the bag and see what we have. We can't be sure."[33] On the fifth day of operations, MACV claimed a total 1,094 enemy killed and 242 captured at a cost of eight American dead and thirty-two wounded. Allied troops also reported capturing large caches of rice and weapons.[34] So far, so good. But not very good. As in the fairy tale, Roberts' bag had grown increasingly lighter—with grim results: he reached inside to find almost no enemy. Had he done so, had enormous "kills" and captures been confirmed, had COSVN headquarters been overrun, had prominent VC and North Vietnamese officers surrendered and been hauled in tumbrels through Saigon streets—had any of this happened, Nixon might have got away with the invasion of Cambodia.

But nothing like this did happen. How could it? How could responsible military officers and civilian officials ever have dreamed of anything like this happening? Had they not by now discovered the basic elements of guerrilla warfare? Did they really believe the nonsense spoon-fed to (in some cases unsuspecting and gullible) correspondents? Did they really believe that " . . . the operational area [to quote one correspondent] which includes the Viet Cong's base areas 352 and 353, 'contains the headquarters of the Central Office for South Vietnam [COSVN], the headquarters of the South Vietnam Liberation Army . . .' . . . a command complex said to be the nerve center for the enemy war effort in the southern half of South Vietnam?" Did they really believe that there in the Cambodian jungles they were going to find the North Vietnamese version of the Pentagon and Fort Meyers? Did they believe that Viet Cong and North Vietnamese forces were going to stand quietly by to await a pitched battle in circumstances overwhelmingly favorable to enemy firepower? Did they believe that in an ARVN and a Saigon government known to be penetrated with Communist agents this operation would surprise the enemy?

Despite MACV's eulogistic communiqués, correspondents soon began to express doubts that made them unpopular with the American command. James Merba of the *New York Times,* for example, pointed out that, as opposed to Administration claims of an immense Communist build-up in South Vietnam, enemy activity according to American intelligence officers had been quite normal. Michael Hornsby of *The Times* (London) reported that observers were questioning the discrepancy between large numbers of enemy killed and captured versus the small number of weapons found on the battlefield—were dead civilians being mistaken for dead enemy? Five days after the beginning of the operation, military leaders were backtracking. Reports to Washington from the Fish Hook area were "not encouraging"; in Washington Ian McDonald of *The Times* (London) wrote that " . . . military commanders now hint that the enemy might have had advance word of the operation."[35]

By this time, President Nixon was undoubtedly sorry that he had ever heard of either the American army or Cambodia. A significant portion of Congress and the nation, on the other hand, was sorry that it had ever heard of Nixon. Nixon later claimed that his subsequent briefing of bipartisan Congressional leadership drew unanimous applause.[36] If so, the euphoria did not last long. Not having taken either the nation's legislators or its citizens into his confidence, the President reaped Congressional and popular wrath. Senator William Fulbright called the operation " . . . a major expansion of the war . . . If you accept the premises on which our justification and objectives have been based, this is consistent with our war policy. It is not consistent with any plan for ending the war."[37] Senator Mike Mansfield complained that " . . . we are sinking deeper into the morass. The feeling of gloom in the Senate is so thick that you could cut it with a knife."[38] Neither was morale exactly high in the White House, where Nixon ordered more wiretaps placed on officials and journalists. State Department officials who had not been advised of the invasion joined the chorus of disapproval, pointing out that Lon Nol's bellicose stand, taken without an adequate army at his disposal, had brought many of his troubles on himself, just as had Nixon who had "isolated himself from his State Department and depended almost entirely on military advice and White House staff work." The invasion of Cambodia caused several officials

1000

to resign while three hundred others in the State Department signed memoranda of protest.[39] Senators from both parties quickly moved " . . . to introduce legislation barring the use of funds to support American troops in Cambodia for any reason."[40]

Lon Nol also proved embarrassing. President Nixon reportedly had not taken the head of state into his confidence, but Lon Nol rolled easily with the punches and at once used the rationale of the Nixon Doctrine by requesting " . . . arms for 250,000 men, for helicopters, and equipment for a national army of some four hundred battalions."[41] Forever tied to the South Vietnam syndrome—arms and more arms for an army incapable of using them properly—White House and Pentagon would enable Lon Nol's army to number a theoretical 220,000 within a year.

Nixon also faced growing public hostility. By spring of 1970, the government's overdraft on credibility was considerable, and though large numbers of Americans still listened to their President and in general wanted to believe what he told them, a mean cynicism was pervading the country, particularly when it came to Pentagon and MACV communiqués. Some hostility was not so vague. A number of Harvard professors, Kissinger's former colleagues, called on him in Washington, " . . . a group of people," as their leader explained to Kissinger, "who have completely lost confidence in the ability of the White House to conduct our foreign policy, and we have come to tell you so. We are no longer at your disposal as personal advisers. . . . " After pointing out that

> . . . the invasion could be used by anyone else in the world as a precedent for invading another country in order, for example, to clear out terrorists . . . [Professor Thomas] Schelling told him: "As we see it, there are two possibilities. Either, one, the President didn't understand when he went into Cambodia that he was invading another country; or, two, he did understand. We just don't know which one is scarier.[42]

The National Student Association called for Nixon's impeachment. Violent demonstrations that included the theretofore "moderate middle" of both students and faculties erupted on nearly eight hundred campuses. Student protests in Ohio and Mississippi so alarmed authorities that police and national guardsmen shot twenty-seven and killed four students at Kent State and Jackson State universities—we shall not tolerate dissent.

We will not tolerate dissent—but dissent swirled around the Administration like smoke from an angry jinni's lamp and it did not fail to

1001

engulf an uncomfortable President who had ingeniously de-escalated war by invasion and who now was in trouble, his White House heavily guarded during a demonstration of seventy-five to one hundred thousand irate citizens, his capital invaded by thousands of angry students, his Congress lobbied by lawyers, educators, doctors, corporate executives. Such was Congressional hostility—increased by the Kent State killings—that Nixon promised Congressional leaders of both parties that all American forces would be pulled out of Cambodia within six weeks and that troop withdrawals from South Vietnam would proceed as planned. Meanwhile, Nixon not only wanted but had to have a "victory."

Victory was nowhere in sight. The invasion was not going at all the way the generals had promised. COSVN was not to be found. In searching for it, MACV had launched new incursions into Cambodia; one report estimated that fifty thousand troops were now involved. As invasion became non-invasion, so now non-victory became victory. Military communiqués described in glowing terms the capture of such enemy complexes as "the city" (a group of huts twenty miles west of the Fish Hook area). Two weeks after the operation had begun, MACV claimed 3,740 dead and 1,041 captured along with over three thousand tons of ammunition with but relatively minor American and South Vietnamese casualties.[43]

These figures disguised neither over-all failure of allied action in the South nor an unpleasant political complication. Nixon, like Napoleon after the conquest of Vitebsk, might have asked, "Do you think I have come all this way just to conquer these huts?" Despite continuing exultant press releases, Communist prisoners seemed in short supply. After some three weeks of operations, the Pentagon explained that COSVN " . . . had moved back into Cambodia beyond the 21-mile limit set up for U.S. ground operations."[44] That however, did not mean the end of the operation. Vice-President Ky had stated that ARVN troops would remain in Cambodia after the American withdrawal scheduled for the end of June. How long would they remain? For " . . . several months at the least . . . until the Cambodians were strong enough to defend themselves against North Vietnamese and Viet Cong."[45] Ky's statement further depressed Administration officials—as well it might considering Indochinese historical enmities.

Adding to Nixon's woes was a *Life* magazine article by Clark Clifford, President Johnson's disaffected secretary of defense, a onetime hawk who had become a powerful critic of the war. Clifford accused Nixon of contradicting stated policy with positive action—of widening the war to American and world detriment. After denying validity of the domino theory and pointing to the lack of contributing allies in Southeast Asia, he accused the President of holding a "curious obsession" about Asia in general and Indochina in particular. To consider South Vietnam a strategic necessity—an area where the future of the world would be decided—made no sense: " . . . The war in Vietnam is a local war arising out of the particular political conditions existing in southeast Asia. I consider it a delusion to suggest that it is part of a worldwide program of common aggression." As to the war's nature:

> . . . our problem in Vietnam is due not only to our inability to attain the military goals, despite our great effort, but to the fact that the struggle is basically a political one. The enemy continues to symbolize the forces of nationalism. The regime which we support is a narrowly based military dictatorship.

The Cambodian venture, Clifford went on, was meaningless militarily. The enemy would stay beyond our reach no matter how long troops remained in the area. Once troops were withdrawn, the enemy would return to old haunts. Despite this inevitable result, " . . . a determined effort will be made to portray the entire adventure as a success, even though no major engagements will have taken place and the number of enemy casualties will be woefully small." More than ever a political settlement was needed to end the war. Clifford offered a three-point program that called for total disengagement from combat by end of 1970 and total withdrawal by end of 1971.[46]

CHAPTER SEVENTY-SIX

1. International Institute for Strategic Studies, *Strategic Survey 1970,* "The Super-Powers."
2. Louis Heren, *The Times* (London), Washington, D.C., February 2, 1970.
3. Ian McDonald, *The Times* (London), Washington, D.C., February 3, 1970.
4. Colby, 191–5.
5. Isaacs, 162.
6. Ibid., 163.
7. Colby, 198. See also, Isaacs, 164–9.
8. Louis Heren, *The Times* (London), Washington, D.C., March 3, 1970. See also, Paul, for an analysis of the reason for (and fallacy of) American official silence; Kissinger, *The White House Years,* 450–7.
9. Louis Heren, *The Times* (London), Washington, D.C., March 17, 1970.
10. *The Times* (London), Washington, D.C., March 9, 1970.
11. *Time,* April 6, 1970.
12. *The Times* (London), April 22, 1970.
13. James Reston, *The Times* (London), New York, April 21, 1970.
14. Shawcross, 163.
15. Kissinger, *The White House Years,* 460.
16. Morris, 173.
17. Shawcross, 115 ff. See also, Snepp, 19–20. Although CIA had constantly insisted that the bulk of Communist supplies arrived via the Ho Chi Minh trail, captured Communist records later divulged that " . . . nearly 80 percent of the materiel" came from North Vietnam through the port of Sihanoukville.

18. Shawcross, 115. See also, Kiernan, 300–2.
19. Shawcross, 126. See also, Kiernan, 297–300.
20. Shawcross, 131–2. See also, Kiernan, 303.
21. Karnow, 609.
22. Shawcross, 129.
23. Nixon, *Memoirs,* 447.
24. Morris, 175.
25. Kissinger, *The White House Years,* 496.
26. Nixon, *Memoirs,* 451. See also, Morris, 174.
27. More precisely, Complete Victory 42 and 43, following forty-one earlier Complete Victory operations begun after the 1968 Tet offensive.
28. Shawcross, 140.
29. Ibid., 146.
30. Reuters, Washington, D.C., May 1, 1970.
31. Nixon, *Memoirs,* 452.
32. Ibid., 453–4. See also, Westmoreland, 388.
33. *The Times* (London), May 1, 1970.
34. Sihanouk, 174–5. The South Vietnamese Communist NLF had refused to arm the Khmer Rouge until after Sihanouk's departure and only when it was obvious that the frontier areas would be invaded and the caches of arms captured. Weapons were then freely supplied to the Khmer Rouge and to the "guerrilla Sihanoukists."
35. Ian McDonald, *The Times* (London), Washington, D.C., May 3, 1970.
36. Nixon, *Memoirs,* 451.
37. Ian McDonald, *The Times* (London), Washington, D.C., May 1, 1970.
38. *Time,* May 11, 1970.
39. John Franklin Campbell.
40. Ian McDonald, *The Times* (London), Washington, D.C., April 30, 1970.
41. Shawcross, 130–2. See also, Fred Emery, *The Times* (London), Phnom Penh, April 30, 1970.
42. Shawcross, 156. See also, Kissinger, *The White House Years,* 514, for an injured account of this meeting.
43. *The Sunday Telegraph* (London), May 10, 1970.
44. *The Times* (London), Washington, D.C., May 21, 1970.
45. Michael Hornsby, *The Times* (London), Saigon, May 12, 1970.
46. Clifford.

CHAPTER 77

The Cambodian invasion backfires • *ARVN in Cambodia* • *Congress rebels* • *The Administration's reply* • *Nixon's dominoes* • *PAVN's new threat* • *The Cambodian sinkhole* • *Administration reverses* • *Paris: peace plan versus peace plan* • *The leaked CIA report* • *Pacification in South Vietnam: fact versus fiction?* • *Enemy offensive moves*

ALTHOUGH THE American public was not to know, the invasion of Cambodia had upset negotiations outside of and Vietnamization within South Vietnam. A special CIA estimate " . . . showed that United States interests in Indochina had been seriously compromised" by the invasion. A top-level Pentagon report stated that " . . . these operations have not substantially reduced NVA [North Vietnamese Army] capabilities in Cambodia. . . . Captured supplies can be reconstituted in about seventy-five days with opening of additional supply routes through Laos and in Cambodia." A secret State Department analysis " . . . concluded that the invasion had caused 'a traumatic reaction in the world at large' and a blow to American prestige."[1] In short, influenced by his coteries of hawks, by the JCS and MACV, Nixon had made the fundamental error of awakening what Lyautey would have considered, relatively speaking, an "asleep" area.

The Nixon administration remained seemingly oblivious to such classified reports or to other outspoken criticism. At the end of May, the President told the nation that " . . . the Cambodian intervention was the most successful operation of a long and difficult war."[2] His statement found few believers. Twist and wiggle in his wormlike style, Nixon could not evade the fact that he had enlarged the war without accomplishing the stated mission of eliminating the enemy's operational headquarters in Cambodia. MACV spokesmen could jabber on about captured weapons and rice stocks but could not deny that since 1932 the Vietnamese had proved they could go without either and still fight. Hanoi-watchers could discern crisis in the North and point to a burgeoning manpower shortage but could not deny that Moscow and Peking were continuing to supply the enemy and that fresh troops continued to enter South Vietnam. American diplomats in Moscow warned Washington in June that the drain on North Vietnam in Cambodia and Laos was again turning Hanoi toward China; to counter that, Moscow agreed to furnish more weapons and matériel to North Vietnam, thus continuing the vicious circle of great-power escalation of the war.

So it was that enemy strength in the South remained basically unaltered: about a hundred thousand North Vietnamese either in the border areas or in South Vietnam and perhaps a hundred thousand "regular" Viet Cong supported by sixty thousand provincial guerrillas and a civilian network of supporters and sympathizers. The real challenge remained in South Vietnam, where the highly touted ARVN was scarcely showing professional brilliance in the Cambodian operations and was otherwise beset with the cancer of command corruption that was gradually killing the body politic. Colonel David Hackworth, an experienced ARVN adviser, told one journalist that " . . . Vietnamization is a word which must be a product of Madison Avenue. It's a public-relations dream. I haven't seen an improvement in ARVN. . . . Perhaps from a cosmetic viewpoint they look a little better in that they wear their helmets and keep their equipment on."[3] Hackworth's blunt words were reinforced by the normal ARVN desertion rate of eight thousand a month rising to twelve thousand a month.[4] One American adviser watched his ARVN battalion, 525 strong, melt to two hundred combat effectives within thirty days, not from enemy action but from desertion.[5] " . . . Raping, looting and burning" were the orders of the day in claimed retaliation for Lon Nol's recent bloodbath of resident Vietnamese in Cambodia.[6] Hackworth, who accompanied ARVN paratroopers in the invasion, was appalled by the

> . . . wholesale destruction of Cambodian towns and villages . . . and the looting was almost unimaginable. As the days passed, whenever I looked into the sky, I saw furniture, motorcycles, and luxury automobiles (Mercedes, Peugeots, Citroëns) flying along, suspended from Vietnamese Air Force (VNAF) choppers bound for some senior ARVN or VNAF officer's home, garage, or other stash point.

For many ARVN soldiers it was their first combat experience and it didn't wash well. " . . . In all, Cambodia was mines and booby traps, snipers and small hit-and-run attacks on our units, which pretty well eroded whatever fighting spirit our ARVN charges had had." Most

ARVN units moved like glue. One supporting American rocket battalion plastered enemy forces reported by ARVN units " . . . with more than ten thousand rounds"—more than a million dollars' worth of ammunition to kill seven enemy.[7]

As always, inept military strategy had created more problems than it solved. Having supported Lon Nol's regime without being requested to do so, Nixon could not leave the country open to enemy vengeance. The Administration now veered to supporting a continued ARVN presence in Cambodia and even requested Congress to extend the deadline for American troop withdrawal. Congress was having none of it. Not only did a Senate vote defeat the amendment but a week later the Cooper-Church amendment was passed, which demanded that Nixon recall at once all American troops in Cambodia, and which prohibited the Administration from using funds to support U.S. operations in that country—" . . . the first restrictive vote ever cast on a President in war time," Nixon later fumed, ignoring the fact that the country was not officially at war.[8]

The Administration and MACV now ignored the nation's law. American planes were already overflying "limits" stated by Nixon and were attacking Communist supply routes in western Cambodia. As with Operation Menu, the bombing reports were falsified and there was almost no "bomb damage assessment"[9]—God alone knows how many more Cambodian civilians were blown up. MACV quietly assured the Saigon government of continued support of its troops in Cambodia. When the last American troops headed for South Vietnam in late June, " . . . leaving behind a lingering form of tear gas, blown bridges and damaged roads in an effort to slow communist reoccupation of the area," thirty thousand ARVN troops remained behind. The Administration publicly continued to insist that it had gained an impressive victory while privately admitting that the enemy controlled one third of Cambodia, moved freely in another third, and was expected to reoccupy its old border sanctuaries within a few months.[10]

President Nixon completed the last act of a play within a play by appointing a new ambassador to the Paris peace talks, seventy-three-year-old David Bruce, and by again making a public appeal to Hanoi: " . . . We are prepared, by negotiation, to bring out all of our forces and have no forces at all in South Vietnam if the enemy . . . will withdraw theirs." The American government attached only two conditions, the President continued. The South Vietnamese must remain free to determine their own future, and the United States would not impose a coalition government. What if the people chose a Communist government? Nixon would accept their judgment since he was sure that this would not happen—no Communist government had ever been freely

1007

elected.* However, he would not hand over South Vietnam to the Communists. The domino theory, the President insisted, was still valid:

> ... Now I know there are those that say, "Well, the domino theory is obsolete." They haven't talked to the dominoes. They should talk to the Thais, Malaysians, to Singapore, to Indonesia, to the Philippines, to the Japanese, and the rest.
>
> And if the United States leaves Vietnam in a way that we are humiliated or defeated, not simply speaking in what are called jingoistic terms but in very practical terms, this will be immensely discouraging to the 300 million people from Japan clear round to Thailand and in free Asia.
>
> And even more important, it will be ominously encouraging to the leaders of Communist China and the Soviet Union who are supporting the North Vietnamese. It will encourage them in their expansionist policies in other areas.[11]

So the presidential voice sounded on that final day of June 1970. It might have been Eisenhower in 1956, Kennedy in 1962, Johnson in 1966. The record was the same. After ten years, nearly forty thousand American lives and over $100 billion the United States was returning to square one.

More of the same followed. In early July, the American chief of the Vietnamization program in the Mekong Delta, John Paul Vann, personally reported to President Nixon that the enemy effort had been reduced to " ... dispersed and dispirited units of five North Vietnamese regiments." Citing the NLF's latest directive, Vann's report spoke of waning enemy confidence. This in part was brought on by the fallout of the Tet offensive—VC losses that led to increased taxes and enforced recruitment in VC-occupied areas, and by a South Vietnamese land reform program under which nearly one million hectares of land would be redistributed to peasant tenant farmers.[12] The NLF now admitted the possibility of a cease-fire, in which case " ... only continuing guerrilla warfare can achieve our purpose in the ensuing complicated situation. ... Strike now at only a few objectives over a wide area. Where necessary and so directed, local cells will go into retirement and await opportunity and orders."[13]

Several developments tempered Vann's expressed optimism. One was increasing enemy activity inside South Vietnam. MACV already had reported that in the last two weeks of May, 221 Americans had been killed in South Vietnam compared to 138 in Cambodia.[14] Two

---

*The President evidently forgot the Chilean elections.

weeks after Vann had submitted his report, an American military spokesman warned of a pending Communist offensive in the central highlands. Five thousand ARVN troops and some fifteen hundred American marines pushed west from Da Nang in a search-and-destroy mission designed to disrupt the enemy build-up. While that was occurring, enemy units attacked an American airborne division base camp eleven miles from the Laotian border, killing at least thirty-two Americans, wounding 148 and forcing evacuation of the area.[15] The action continued to build until in mid-August MACV launched one of the heaviest air interdiction efforts of the war: nearly a hundred B-52 bombers struck North Vietnamese supply and staging areas on both sides of the Laotian border.[16] In early September, enemy reinforcements were coming down the Ho Chi Minh trail while local cadres were reoccupying old border bases in Cambodia.

Cambodia itself was proving a sinkhole. The $7.9 million in arms hastily authorized in May did not go very far; the Nixon administration slated $25 million for military aid in fiscal year 1970–71 but that figure quickly shot to $75 million. In early September, twenty-one South Vietnamese battalions supported by 25 per cent of South Vietnamese air strikes (all paid for by the United States government) were operating in Cambodia,[17] while in Washington the Senior Review Group, chaired by Kissinger, in effect ended Cambodia's "neutrality": the subsequent JCS plan would soon result in a greatly enlarged U.S. advisory team in Phnom Penh, its task to convert the Cambodian army into a conventional force some 220,000 strong plus a paramilitary force of 143,000[18]—precisely what had happened in South Vietnam in the formative early sixties. Throughout summer of 1970, Lloyd Rives in the American embassy in Phnom Penh had warned of Lon Nol's " . . . 'over-grandiose dreams,' and in one cable begged for help to bring Nol 'out of the clouds of his planning.' "[19] In August, the CIA station chief in Phnom Penh reported " . . . the inability of the [Nol] government to communicate at all with the people . . . [and] he believed 'the initial enthusiasm generated by the overthrow of Norodom Sihanouk has dissipated to a large extent.' "[20] Owing to the fighting in the countryside, refugees in Phnom Penh had increased from six hundred thousand to two–three million; rubber production was at a standstill; rice production was diminishing. " . . . By the end of 1970 the government . . . [would be] spending five times its revenue and earning nothing abroad."[21] Corruption controlled the government. The austerity program was a joke—millions of dollars' worth of luxury goods were flowing into Phnom Penh. Corrupt army commanders were receiving pay for soldiers who existed only on paper. The sale of weapons and ammunition to the enemy was commonplace. Some commanders sold rations provided for the troops; hungry soldiers stole from villagers, who soon leaned toward the enemy. These deficiencies would not be repaired in the fighting ahead. They would only increase until ended by defeat.[22] It was the China-Vietnam syndrome apparently unfamiliar to Nixon and his cohorts.

As had been the case in China and Vietnam, the U. S. government was in large part footing the bill. Despite not-so-subtle hints from American officials, SEATO and other Asian nations proved reluctant to help erect a new Cambodian bulwark against communism. These were the "dominoes" referred to by President Nixon, the ones who stood in fear and trembling of the Communist threat: Domino Australia sent a little civil aid, dominoes New Zealand and Korea sent some medicines, domino Thailand refused Lon Nol's request to send troops. In late July, domino Cambodia " . . . rejected the idea of Cambodian membership in SEATO. Reiterating his government's policy of neutrality, Lon Nol said Cambodia had no intention of taking arms against her enemies if they withdrew from Cambodian territory."[23]

The Nixon administration was faring no better on either the Saigon or the home front. Fighting in Cambodia had returned Vietnam to national and international front pages and little escaped notice. In early July, the story broke of appalling conditions in South Vietnamese prisons—the inhuman "tiger cages." This led to a rash of survey stories mostly critical of Thieu's dictatorship. In America, a Congressional committee investigating the My Lai massacre concluded that:

> . . . all details of the killing were covered up at the divisional level. There was, the investigation states in a report released tonight, "a concerted effort among military and State Department officers to suppress all evidence of the allegation and its investigation."
>
> It said that senior officers in both the Americal Division and the State Department were guilty of casting "a blanket of silence" over the massacres.[24]

Then came the Scranton report on the extent of unrest in American colleges and universities: " . . . The divisions splitting American society [were] 'as deep as any since the Civil War . . . nothing is more important than an end to the war' in Vietnam."[25]

In Paris, meanwhile, the Communist delegation put forward a new, eight-point peace plan, which David Bruce dismissed as new wine in old bottles. Kissinger's secret negotiations in Paris had come to naught: in late September he broke off still another fruitless meeting and refused to reschedule a new one. In early October, with midterm elections less than a month away, President Nixon offered what he fondly described as a "peace offensive." Addressing the nation on television, the President announced that his new initiative had been made possible by the remarkable success of the Vietnamization policy of the past eighteen months, and that it had won the concurrence of the South Vietnam, Laos, and Cambodia governments. As for his plan, vintner Nixon was offering old wine in old bottles. Like the magician who promised to produce an elephant and came up with a mouse, his proposals were a diluted version of Henry Kissinger's 1969 plan that itself remarkably resembled a plan presented by Robert Shaplen in 1967. Nixon now called for a cease-fire in place to be "effectively supervised" by international observers (a qualification realistically dismissed by Shaplen), a new international conference, negotiated troop withdrawals, and immediate release of all prisoners of war.

The Communist delegation in Paris shortly and sharply rejected a cease-fire in place, as Shaplen had warned they would if inhibited by international supervision. Thieu in Saigon made it known that he violently disagreed with Nixon: he did not want a cease-fire; he would not accept neutrality; he wanted the Communists to leave his country and American troops to remain; and he would not release forty thousand Communist prisoners. To some observers in the United States the proposal seemed so politically inspired as to deserve contempt. As James Reston put it,

> . . . All governments operate on two levels—the moral and the political—but seldom in recent history has any administration matched the Nixon Administration's spectacular combination of priggish moralizing and political expediency. One day it sounds like Billy Graham and the next it acts like Machiavelli.[26]

Considering election results, Nixon failed to derive much political profit from his diplomatic ploy. Too many factors were operating against him. The momentous issue of Vietnam had been steadily tearing Americans from normal loyalty to the executive. We saw the beginning of this process in the early sixties when pro and anti sides steadily leaked classified information to suit their purposes (see Chapter 60). A certain amount of official leakage has always been a part of American government—a case can be made for it as integral to the system of checks and balances. But major leakages of what are called "state secrets" were now developing. In May, the CIA had circulated a top-secret report on South Vietnam that contained devastating information of Communist infiltration of the South Vietnamese government. Concerned U.S. officials took it upon themselves to inform the *New York Times* of this document. In mid-October, the *Times* carried the story written by veteran reporter Neil Sheehan. According to the CIA report, shortly after the 1968 Tet offensive the Communists

... decided to shift their long-range strategy from intense military activity to political erosion. They stepped up their infiltration of secret agents into various branches of the South Vietnamese government.

Most of the agents were natives of the southern part of divided Vietnam, and they were infiltrated into the armed forces, the police force and the South Vietnamese intelligence organizations whose task it was to eradicate the Vietcong and their North Vietnamese allies.

The Communists, the report continued, had infiltrated over thirty thousand agents into the South Vietnamese Government " . . . in an apparatus that has been virtually impossible to destroy." Some twenty thousand of the agents operated in ARVN. According to the report,

> . . . the enemy network could not exist without the tacit complicity whether from fear, sympathy or apathy, of the majority of South Vietnamese soldiers and policemen and [the report] says that such feelings provide evidence that the Saigon government could not command the deep loyalty of the men on whom it depends to defend itself.

With virtually unlimited intelligence at its disposal, the enemy would have little trouble in surviving military pressures to emerge (and presumably take over control) once the United States had withdrawn its troops.[27]

White House officials downplayed the importance of the report. It was "overly pessimistic," they claimed, and plainly contrary to present progress. President Thieu insisted that 98 per cent of South Vietnam's population was under government control, and if this figure contradicted an official U.S. estimate of 75 per cent, no one could deny that progress was being made in pacification. American troops were daily withdrawing from actual combat; U.S. deaths were down to about forty a week. Over-all troop withdrawal was proceeding on schedule. Forty thousand more troops were to leave by year's end. By spring of 1971, all combat troops would be gone, leaving some 270,000 "support" troops in the area. President Thieu, Administration spokesmen emphasized, was actively widening his political base in preparation for presidential elections scheduled for autumn of 1971. Thieu's seat would be challenged by General Duong Van Minh, who reportedly would campaign on a "peace" ticket—if that wasn't democracy, what was?

A pretty picture, but more blurs. Ninety-eight per cent of the population under government control? Seventy-five per cent? This was fine except some qualified observers suggested that " . . . the indices upon which such assessments are based . . . [are] largely meaningless."[28] Until villages were properly policed, no one would know the depth of relationship between peasants and enemy who still controlled large areas of South Vietnam. So long as guerrilla units continued to strike virtually at will without peasants warning government authorities, government did not either command peasant support or control peasants. And what of White House silence following Sir Robert Thompson's *second* visit to Vietnam in the autumn? What of *New York Times* reports " . . . asserting that Sir Robert had reported on the continuing failure of the South Vietnamese to uproot the Viet Cong's underground political structure?"[29]

. The Administration's definition of combat forces was also suspect. American aircraft were interdicting Communist supply lines in Cambodia and were also furnishing close air support to Cambodian forces. Although South Vietnam was building an air force, it had a long way to go. As of November, its helicopter fleet counted two hundred and fifty machines compared to some four thousand American machines in the area, and Secretary of the Air Force Robert Seamans admitted that U. S. Air Force units would have to remain in Indochina for years.[30] Plans to remove *all* combat forces also changed. Two combat divisions, the 101st Airborne and the 1st Cavalry (Airmobile), would remain to provide security for bases such as Da Nang and Cam Ranh Bay.

Nor did the Administration confine MACV entirely to a defensive posture. American deaths may have been reduced but they did not cease—forty deaths a week is over two thousand a year. Installations suffered guerrilla attacks and patrols suffered casualties. The enemy shot down an American reconnaissance plane in North Vietnam and in late November the President authorized bombing strikes—"protective reaction"—to resume south of the 19th parallel. MACV at the same time launched a helicopter raid on an alleged prisoner-of-war camp near Hanoi. Ostensibly designed to free American prisoners, it also demonstrated American ability to penetrate North Vietnamese defenses. It failed on the first count and in so doing symbolized the over-all intelligence failure of American arms: no prisoners were in the camp. As for psychological effect, Hanoi already knew that American arms were capable of invading the North, just as its leaders knew that American atomic bombs could eliminate Hanoi. That wasn't the crux of the matter. Hanoi also knew that what happened subsequently might well end civilization.

The threat of renewed bombing of the North, obviously an attempt to influence intractable North Vietnamese negotiators in Paris, brought general outcry from around the world. In defending it, indeed in threatening to resume it in earnest, Defense Secretary Laird cited what he insisted was an "understanding" with the North when President Johnson stopped the bombing in late 1968. Hanoi predictably denied that any "understanding" existed. Laird should have read Kissinger's analysis of these negotiations in his celebrated *Foreign Affairs* article and respected the devastating effect of morbid linguistic behavior induced by the two countries' inability to identify with each other.

A more valid reason for threatening to resume bombing was embarrassing. American intelligence was reporting indications of a build-up from the North that scarcely jibed either with Hanoi's alleged state of exhaustion or Administration claims of "victory" in Cambodia. An Institute for Strategic Studies analysis of the Cambodian incursion concluded:

> ... The immediate effect was to reduce pressure on American forces in Vietnam and thus to ease the course of American withdrawal and "Vietnamization." But the North Vietnamese had not been crippled. Other supply routes, based not only on expanding the "Ho Chi-minh trail" but also on the Mekong and Sekong rivers, were developed with some speed to replace that through [the port of] Kompong Som [Sihanoukville]. At the same time, military efforts in both southern Laos and eastern Cambodia were stepped up.

The same analysis pointed out that in South Vietnam

> ... the leadership in Hanoi had openly reverted to a policy of "protracted struggle" by guerrilla forces and organized activity by major Viet Cong and North Vietnamese units was increasingly restricted to the sparsely populated fringes of the country.[31]

In mid-December, a Brazilian journalist reported from Hanoi that the North Vietnamese were preparing " ... a new and perhaps decisive round of fighting on the ground." He continued:

> ... There is every evidence to the visitor here that, for all the reports out of Washington and Saigon and even Moscow that the Viet Cong are exhausted and the North Vietnamese over-extended, preparations are under way for another push.[32]

As the year drew to a close, the enemy was fighting hard in Laos and Cambodia and remained uncomfortably evident in South Vietnam, as witness the shelling of Saigon. His negotiators in Paris showed little inclination to negotiate. In mid-December, Hanoi radio predicted "more complex" and "more violent" fighting throughout Indochina in 1971.

CHAPTER SEVENTY-SEVEN

1. Shawcross, 173.
2. Louis Heren, *The Times* (London), Washington, D.C., June 4, 1970.
3. *Newsweek,* July 5, 1971.
4. Frances Fitzgerald, 418.
5. Hackworth, 732–3.
6. Shawcross, 151.
7. Hackworth, 732–4.
8. Nixon, *Memoirs,* 467–8.
9. Shawcross, 214.
10. Louis Heren, *The Times* (London), Washington, D.C., June 29, 1970.
11. Ibid.
12. Blaufarb, 266–7.
13. Richard Hughes, *The Sunday Times* (London), Hong Kong, July 5, 1970.
14. Louis Heren, *The Times* (London), Washington, D.C., June 2, 1970. Vann would be killed in a helicopter crash in the central highlands in June 1972.
15. *The Times* (London), AP and Reuters, Saigon, July 23, 1970.
16. *The Times* (London), and AP, August 17, 1970.
17. Shawcross, 179.
18. Ibid., 194.
19. Ibid., 182.
20. Ibid., 183.
21. Ibid. 220.
22. Ibid., 221, 313 ff.
23. *The Times* (London), Bangkok, July 23, 1970.
24. Ian McDonald, *The Times* (London), Washington, D.C., July 14, 1970.
25. Karnow, 25–6.
26. James Reston, *The Times* (London), October 15, 1970.
27. Neil Sheehan, *The Times* (London), October 19, 1972.
28. Michael Hornsby, *The Times* (London), Saigon, October 26, 1970.
29. Fred Emery, *The Times* (London), Washington, D.C., January 17, 1971.
30. *The Times* (London) and AP, Saigon, November 5, 1970.
31. International Institute for Strategic Studies, *Strategic Survey 1970,* "Eastern Asia."
32. Henry Brandon, *The Sunday Times* (London), Washington, D.C., December 13, 1970.

CHAPTER 78

The Nixon administration's new strategy • Hanoi's position • The war in Cambodia • Opposition at home • ARVN invades Laos: "the golden opportunity" • Battlefield alchemy: disaster • Reasons why • Picking up the pieces • Flies in the Nixon ointment • The Calley case • Captain Daniels writes the President

IN EARLY 1971, two voices sounded words as prophetic as those uttered by Shakespeare's witches dancing around another devil's brew. One belonged to Secretary of Defense Melvin Laird, who announced that the U.S. combat role in South Vietnam would end within twelve months. More time would be needed, however, for the South Vietnamese " . . . to replace American air support, logistics and administration." By May, American strength in Vietnam would be reduced to 285,000 men.[1] Laird's brave words complemented Nixon's effort to close a political coffin before it claimed what rapidly was becoming an executive corpse. Militarily his statement was as flaccid as the rest of the Nixon Doctrine. Primarily a political ploy designed to ease anti-Administration pressures within the United States, it also was intended to allow the Administration certain strategic and tactical flexibility within South Vietnam and Cambodia. By tying American troop withdrawals to the progress of Vietnamization, it enabled the Administration to plead that overt military action against the enemy within South Vietnam, Cambodia, Laos, and North Vietnam was necessary to save American lives. It also established the notion of a large and expensive residual force remaining in South Vietnam (for the next hundred years). Politically it was cheap, militarily it was unsatisfactory, diplomatically it was meaningless.

The other voice emanating from the devil's brew belonged to Prime Minister Pham Van Dong, who announced from Hanoi that " . . . the Vietnamese people would insist on unconditional withdrawal by the Americans and that this point was not negotiable."[2] The prime minister's intransigence was reflected in Paris, from where Ambassador David Bruce continued to report no progress in peace talks, and also in Laos, Cambodia, and South Vietnam, where guerrillas and PAVN units continued to fight brisk if isolated actions. Le Duan, first secretary of Hanoi's Communist Party, emphasized this stand by announcing that the North's " . . . strategic guideline is to fight a protracted war, gaining strength as one fights." " . . . To engage in military struggle under unfavorable circumstances," he said, echoing Sun Tzu, "is a serious mistake."

Le Duan's words seemed to some Western observers to be an admission of defeat and in a sense they were. But they scarcely were tantamount to capitulation. They instead marked a shift in strategy, one predicated primarily on the realization that American public opinion was forcing American disengagement from the war. Where two years earlier Hanoi was ignoring internal damage in favor of prosecuting the war in the South, it now turned to repairing this damage as part of growing strong internally in order to carry on protracted warfare. A visiting Canadian journalist, Michael Maclear, found that the government had pulled all stops in the North. Not only were conscription-age men and women assigned to labor brigades, but the government was even offering such incentives as cash bonuses and home-building loans to further its program of repairing war damage and rebuilding the economy.[3] This shift in strategy represented a victory of sorts for the moderate factions in the Politburo—as we shall see, it was all too transitory.[4]

Internal stress did not mean an end to combat operations in the South. Despite U.S.-ARVN attacks of the previous spring, the Communist position in Cambodia remained strong, in part owing to increased aid from China. Sihanouk later wrote that by March 1971 seventy of the country's one hundred administrative districts had been "liberated" by the guerrillas and that 751 of 1,129 villages were in guerrilla hands. By September, guerrillas would claim control of four fifths of the country, which held five million of Cambodia's seven million population.[5] Supplies continued to flow south via the Ho Chi Minh trail in defiance of American air interdiction (at this point American planes had dropped more bombs on Indochina than it had on both the European and Pacific theaters during World War II).[6] In November, Communist units had occupied a strategic pass in Cambodia to cut Highway 4, the single road connection between the capital of Phnom Penh and Kompong Som (Sihanoukville), Cambodia's single deepwater port (see map on page 998). The capital soon suffered a fuel shortage. Convoys carrying fuel from South Vietnam on the Mekong River fell victim to guerrilla ambushes. In early January, a combined Cambodian-ARVN task force heavily supported by American planes moved to reopen the highway. When ground

M.E.P.

attacks bogged down, American helicopter gunships joined the action. Although Cambodian troops captured the target pass, Viet Cong suicide squads a few days later struck Phnom Penh's airport, virtually eliminating the fledgling Cambodian air force, and shelled the capital to send morale plunging. MACV responded with massive airlifts of barbed wire, sandbags, and more arms and ammunition to Phnom Penh. Simultaneously in Laos, PAVN units knocked out a series of Meo guerrilla outposts in the important Bolovens Plateau area—outposts secretly organized and supported by the CIA.

The new action caused a furor in Congress. Opposition members including Republicans interpreted it as a violation of the Cooper-Church amendment, which prohibited the Administration from using funds for U.S. operations in Cambodia. The Administration justified the action as necessary to protect American troops as well as, in Melvin Laird's words, " . . . to supplement the efforts and the armed forces of our friends and allies who are determined to resist aggression."[7] Secretary of State Rogers repeated this theme to an angry Senate Foreign

Relations Committee and to a bewildered but restive American public. The Administration, he said, was prepared to use air power in Indochina " . . . to the fullest possible extent necessary."[8]

The powerful fumes of Congressional and public dissent had not yet dissipated when reports of another Nixon surprise began to reach American newsrooms. Despite a blackout imposed by MACV and the White House, the American public learned that some twenty thousand South Vietnamese soldiers, the elite of ARVN, were moving toward southern Laos. This task force, backed by an impressive armored task force of some ten thousand American troops, was said to be occupying once-familiar terrain in northwestern reaches of South Vietnam. A second ARVN task force was reportedly moving into eastern Cambodia. In early February, an uneasy world learned that South Vietnam had invaded the panhandle of southern Laos. American planes and artillery had prepared the way; American helicopters supported the action; American armor backed the effort but remained in South Vietnam.

ARVN Operation Lam Son 719 and U.S. Operation Dewey Canyon II were designed to sever the Ho Chi Minh trail leading to Cambodia— a "golden opportunity," according to advocates including Abrams and the JCS, to eliminate enemy supply lines and thereby shorten the war.[9] Vice-President Nguyen Cao Ky told correspondents in Saigon that ARVN forces would probably remain in Laos until the end of the dry season in May and would probably repeat the operation the next year. It might be necessary, he said, to bomb North Vietnam in the process. Nixon blithely announced in Washington that the operation was "consistent with international law." It was as well that attorney Nixon did not have to debate the legal issue. Congressional opponents such as Senator Mike Mansfield deplored the action as a "deepening of the tragedy." The Royal Laotian Government condemned it, as did UN Secretary-General U Thant "in strong terms."[10]

As in the case of the invasion of Cambodia the previous spring, front-line communiqués (issued from back-line headquarters) told of slight resistance with impressive captures of food and ammunition. According to General Hoang Xuan Lam, ARVN commander of the invasion, whose headquarters at Quang Tri, despite incredibly inefficient communications, were unbelievably located fifty miles from the Tchepone target area, " . . . the southward flow of North Vietnamese men and supplies down the Ho Chi Minh trail . . . has been completely halted." The general claimed that his forces were deployed along Highway 9 fifteen to twenty miles inside Laos and that 750 North Vietnamese had been killed at a cost of forty to fifty ARVN troops.[11] Abrams informed Washington that " . . . I am confident that the task that was initially laid out will be done."[12]

Ugly rumors were already creeping into newsrooms, however. *Time* magazine noted that in the first five days of combat, twenty-nine thousand troops supported by " . . . 493 gunship attacks, 216 air cavalry missions, and 4,025 separate lifts of troops and supplies . . . destroyed two trucks, exploded one ammunition storage area and found one 57-mm. recoilless rifle, the mount for a mortar and a few dozen 105-mm. artillery shells."[13] Although MACV announced the loss of twelve helicopters, journalist Michael Hornsby suggested that as many as fifty had been damaged or destroyed. If this was true, it followed that enemy resistance must be more than sporadic. Sure enough two days later President Nixon repeated a report from General Abrams that although ARVN was fighting in "a superior way," it had "run into heavy resistance."

Abrams' words precluded battlefield alchemy. In the harsh crucible of tactical reality, the "golden opportunity" was turning into base disaster: Operation Lam Son 719 was coming apart at the seams. Communist forces had fallen back only to snake around clanking ARVN armor columns to strike vulnerable lines of communication—a tactic as old as war. Once ARVN units occupied various positions, usually in battalion strength, VC and PAVN units joined to launch "suicide" attacks, exactly as they had done at Dien Bien Phu, Ia Drang, and elsewhere. As at Dien Bien Phu, they now sprang a tactical surprise in the form of tanks, old Russian PT-76s whose presence had gone undetected by American fliers (but was undoubtedly known to local peasants).

Washington attempted to break the truth as painlessly as possible. On February 22, the South Vietnamese Government, which earlier had spoken of minimum enemy forces in the area, changed its tune. President Thieu said the invasion was to prevent a North Vietnamese invasion of South Vietnam's five northern provinces. While Secretary of Defense Laird insisted that ARVN units were " . . . achieving their objective of major disruption of enemy supply routes," the enemy not only had shifted to western arteries beyond ARVN's reach but was overrunning ARVN positions in the vicinity of Highway 9. By February 25, the battle so wished for by MACV and ARVN was on. For ten days, ARVN seemed to be holding its own and then some. On March 7, Saigon proudly announced the capture of Tchepone, a major Communist staging and supply area. Vice-President Ky, never at a loss for the dramatic, told correspondents that his government was looking for a "Dien Bien Phu in reverse." General Lam claimed that his forces had cut "the main portion" of the Ho Chi Minh trail: the enemy was taking casualties twenty times heavier than his own and had lost about six thousand killed and hundreds more wounded by air strikes as well as 112,000 tons of ammunition, 245 vehicles including seventy-four tanks, and thirteen hundred tons of food.[14] In a dramatic Pentagon press conference,

Laird and Lieutenant General John Vogt, Jr., proudly displayed a piece of enemy pipeline used to bring gasoline from the North—but failed to mention that it had been captured weeks earlier by a commando raid.

ARVN losses were also heavy. In the week ending March 4, they reportedly amounted to 898 killed and over two thousand wounded. American deaths numbered sixty-nine. *Time* magazine stated that "... in three weeks, no less than five ARVN battalions had, for all practical purposes, been knocked out of action."[15] Journalist Derek Wilson reported fourteen helicopters shot down in one day; an American pilot had told him that "... we're being knocked off like flies."[16]

ARVN still seemed to claim the upper hand as further units slogged into battered Tchepone, twenty-five miles inside Laos. President Nixon continued to insist that the operation was a success. The fighting proved, according to General Abrams, that ARVN could "hack it" against top PAVN units.

Abrams apparently did not know that President Thieu had placed a casualty cap of three thousand on the operation.[17] Suddenly on March 11, General Lam began pulling units out of Tchepone only days after they had occupied it. And now ARVN units began yielding artillery fire bases one after the other, often destroying guns and vehicles to prevent capture by the enemy, before being evacuated by helicopters—or killed. American efforts to save ARVN units reached frantic proportions. One day's operations cost thirty-seven out of forty helicopters engaged.[18] By March 21, only four thousand ARVN soldiers remained in Laos. The day after television viewers around the world had watched desperate South Vietnamese soldiers clinging to helicopter skids in order to save themselves, Secretary of Defense Laird admitted that "withdrawal" was under way but that it was according to plan.[19] Three days later, ARVN had left Laos. A week later, enemy trucks were driving down the Ho Chi Minh trail.

Administration spokesmen now began singing new tunes. Lam Son 719 had not been designed only to cut enemy supply lines. Lam Son 719 had been designed to mass enemy troops and make them vulnerable to American air power. The world learned that over eleven thousand enemy soldiers had died and ten PAVN battalions had been annihilated by an operation that also relieved enemy pressure on Cambodia. The new paint was peeling before it dried. The cost of Lam Son 719 was tremendous. The Saigon government admitted to five thousand ARVN casualties (some observers thought ten thousand more likely) plus seventy American lives, thousands of ARVN deserters, morale shattered, perhaps 140 helicopters, thirty tanks, and scores of armored personnel carriers and artillery pieces lost.

What happened? Overconfidence played a major part. The earlier invasion of Cambodia, which had not provided an accurate test of ARVN's tactical effectiveness, had misled military commanders and experts whose optimism too often stemmed from second-hand observation and biased, often dishonest readiness reports. Sir Robert Thompson, Nixon's counterinsurgency guru, had given ARVN high marks and had agreed with Abrams that 70 percent of South Vietnam's army " . . . is on a fighting par with U.S. troops." Shortly after the debacle, Thompson in a report to Kissinger " . . . praised its military success and stated that the major factor in the war was now the question of South Vietnamese psychology and confidence."[20] Abrams, Thompson, and a good many others were continuing to confuse quality with quantity and were again ignoring General Gwynn's teaching that a lull in guerrilla warfare did not necessarily mean enemy impotence. ARVN found a flexibly organized and determined enemy willing to yield a branch or two of the Ho Chi Minh trail until the tactical position became clear. They found an enemy which had secretly brought down tanks and SAM missiles; an enemy that reinforced itself during battle with units from the DMZ; an enemy that skillfully employed guerrilla tactics to bewilder, slow, and isolate ARVN columns and outposts until they were ready for assault.

Divided command also came into play. ARVN and MACV together seem to have underestimated enemy strength—scarcely a new failing. Kissinger later wrote that on February 23, Westmoreland " . . . did not think that the forces assigned to the Laos operation were adequate; he himself [at an earlier point] had considered that four American divisions would be needed to seize and hold Tchepone; the South Vietnamese had allotted less than two to the operation."[21] But as army chief of staff, Westmoreland sat on the JCS and, according to Kissinger, had endorsed the plan " . . . together with the other Joint Chiefs of Staff."[22] Abrams allegedly urged Thieu to send in more forces than proposed, but Thieu refused. Thanks largely to U. S. Army indoctrination, ARVN commanders held almost mystical belief in the efficacy of air and artillery power, and this undoubtedly influenced Thieu's decision. Yet many Vietnamese air controllers could not speak English[23]—this after more than a decade and billions of dollars spent in trying to make ARVN a viable force. Once opposition developed, Abrams is said to have again urged Thieu to commit more troops but probably for domestic political reasons he refused and instead terminated the action.

Although Nixon and his aides attempted to present a satisfactory picture—Nixon later blamed MACV for providing inadequate air cover but insisted that the operation was a "success" with " . . . most of the military purposes achieved"²⁴—the invasion itself let alone its obvious failure brought heavy criticism from within the United States.

Concurrent with its confused and contradictory course came a variety of other ills resulting from the American presence in Indochina. Despite reduction of American forces in the area and a claim that direct military expenditures in Indochina had decreased to $16 billion for the current fiscal year, over-all defense spending was to rise to $76 billion for fiscal year 1971–72. Even before the operation began, the American army reaped widespread opprobrium by dropping charges against Major General Samuel Koster for attempting to cover up the My Lai massacre. Koster was reduced in rank, given a letter of censure, and allowed to retire, the first of a series of mild punishments awarded for major dereliction of duty.²⁵ The operation was only just under way when a heart attack felled the Cambodian Prime Minister, Lon Nol, to confuse further that already confused situation. Then the story of bribery and corruption in American military clubs and post exchanges in South Vietnam (and elsewhere) broke; it would involve a brigadier general and the Sergeant Major of the Army, the most prestigious enlisted rank in the army.²⁶ ARVN's most able general, Do Cao Tri, was killed in a helicopter crash. On February 22, Lieutenant William Calley began a recital to a military court of his shocking actions at My Lai. A few days later, the army decided to court-martial his brigade commander, Colonel Oran K. Henderson. While fighting in Laos increased, four VC guerrillas blew up 75 per cent of Cambodia's oil refinery system. The American people next learned that so zealous was its army as to keep card files on 25 million American citizens. Sounding more like a police-state official than an American public servant, Assistant Secretary of Defense Robert Froehlke stated that

> . . . surveillance designed to cope with civil violence that might eventually require the use of army troops would continue. To protect people and property in an area of civil disturbance with the greatest effectiveness, he said, "military commanders must know all that can be learnt about that area and its inhabitants."²⁷

Army agents might better have been employed studying their own establishment. While PX scandals mounted, the General Accounting Office accused American defense contractors of making wildly excessive profits. The public was also forcefully reminded that some soldiers in Vietnam, in addition to insubordination including refusal, on occasion, to fight and to drug addiction, had picked up the quaint habit of "fragging": eliminating overzealous officers with a hand grenade, in a word, murder. Writing of an army he had once considered " . . . the best Army the United States ever put into the field," Colonel Robert Heinl, a retired marine turned journalist, concluded in May 1971 that the " . . . United States armed forces, wrenched by seemingly insurmountable problems within and without, appear to have reached their lowest point in this century in morals, discipline and battleworthiness." After citing numerous incidents within and without Vietnam, Heinl quoted General Matthew Ridgway, former chief of staff of the army: " . . . Not before in my lifetime . . . has the Army's public image fallen to such low esteem."[28] While army undercover agents continued to cover public gatherings in the United States and record covertly the words of American citizens, a military court at the end of March found William Calley guilty of callously murdering South Vietnamese civilians and sentenced him to life imprisonment.

The verdict set off still another internal domestic row. People had heard Calley describe the massacre at My Lai, yet some held that the young lieutenant was no more guilty than others. Bowing to pressures, President Nixon called the court to task and mitigated Calley's sentence to twenty years, later using the occasion to castigate further Congressional, media, and anti-war opponents.[29] Captain Aubrey Daniels, the twenty-nine-year-old army officer who had prosecuted, now wrote an open letter to his commander in chief. After expressing shock and dismay at the reaction of many people to the sentence, Daniels suggested that " . . . the war in Vietnam has brutalized us more than I care to believe" and that it must therefore cease. He continued:

> . . . But how much more appalling it is to see so many of the political leaders of the nation who have failed to see the moral issue or, having seen it, to compromise it for political motive in the face of apparent public displeasure with the verdict.

Mouse Daniels then took lion Nixon to task:

> . . . In view of your previous statements concerning this matter, I have been particularly shocked and dismayed at your decision to intervene in these proceedings in the midst of the public clamor. Your decision can only have been prompted by the response of a vocal segment of our population, who while no doubt acting in good faith, cannot be aware of the evidence which resulted in Lieutenant Calley's conviction.

Not only had the President " . . . damaged the military judicial system . . . [and] subjected a judicial system of this country to the criticism that it is subject to political influence," but

... the image of Lieutenant Calley, a man convicted of the premeditated murder of at least 21 unarmed and unresisting people, as a national hero, has been enhanced.

He concluded:

... I would expect the President of the United States, a man whom I believed should and would provide the moral leadership for this nation, would stand fully behind the law of this land on a moral issue which is so clear and about which there can be no compromise.

For this nation to condone the acts of Lieutenant Calley is to make us no better than our enemies.

CHAPTER SEVENTY-EIGHT

1. Patrick Brogan, *The Times* (London), Paris, January 6, 1971.
2. Ibid.
3. Michael Maclear, *The Times* (London), January 19, 1971. See also, Shaplen, "We Have Always Survived," for developments in Hanoi after Ho's death.
4. Snepp, 21
5. Sihanouk, 180.
6. Frances Fitzgerald, 417.
7. *Time*, February 8, 1971.
8. *The Times* (London), Washington, D.C., January 29, 1971.
9. The operation was named after a Vietnamese victory over China in the seventeenth century, a belated attempt to profit psychologically as the North had been doing all along. Dewey Canyon was a misspelled code name.
10. *The Times* (London), New York, February 8, 1971.
11. Michael Hornsby, *The Times* (London), Quang Tri, February 15, 1971. See also, Davidson, 644–59, for an excellent analytical account of the battle.
12. Kissinger, *The White House Years*, 1004.
13. *Time*, February 15, 1971.
14. Derek Wilson, *The Times* (London), Khe Sanh, March 8, 1971.
15. *Time*, March 8, 1971.
16. *The Times* (London), Khe Sanh, March 8, 1971.
17. Kissinger, *The White House Years*, 1004. See also, ibid., 1008: " ... As early as March 8 Abrams informed me that South Vietnamese commanders, having occupied the Tchepone area, considered their mission accomplished and were eager to retreat."
18. *Time*, March 15, 1971.
19. *The Times* (London), Washington, D.C., March 22, 1971. See also, Hackworth, 768.
20. Nixon, *Memoirs*, 499.
21. Kissinger, *The White House Years*, 1005.
22. Ibid.
23. Ibid., 1003.
24. Nixon, *Memoirs*, 428.
25. Hersh, "Coverup."
26. *The Times* (London), Washington, D.C., March 3, 1971. See also, Mollenhoff, 39–44; Shaplen, "We Have Always Survived":

... a conservative estimate is that fifteen thousand Americans, in uniform or out, have been involved in this process of corruption. These Americans have encouraged the black-marketing of all sorts of goods, have encouraged pilferage for payoffs, have raked huge profits from the smuggling of drugs and other goods, from the illicit trade in dollars, from the operation of night clubs, from the importation of American call girls and so on. . . .

27. Ian McDonald, *The Times* (London), Washington, D.C., March 2, 1971.
28. Heinl, "The Armed Forces: "Are they 'near collapse'?"
29. Nixon, *Memoirs*, 499–500.

CHAPTER 79

To TRY TO bolster waning popularity, President Nixon in early April 1971 announced another large troop withdrawal and began to hint at a new diplomatic offensive which by restoring "the common purpose" would create "a new national unity." The words sounded somewhat forlorn in view of massive anti-war demonstrations including those by Vietnam veterans, some in wheelchairs, who flung their medals onto the White House lawn, and in less than a month their sentiments would be mocked by police batons cracking American citizens' skulls during a "May Day" demonstration in Washington. Nor was the President's posture strengthened by events in Saigon, where Vice-President Ky, openly breaking with President Thieu, not only called for a political solution based on coexistence with North Vietnam but also questioned Thieu's integrity and compared the country to a "sinking ship." In the polemics that followed, he stated what all critics had been saying for years: " . . . There is no social justice [in South Vietnam] right now."[1]

Military news was no better. A benumbed American public learned that large numbers of American troops in South Vietnam were using hard drugs in addition to widespread use of marijuana.[2] In mid-June, the nation began reading extracts from theretofore top-secret documents delivered to public media by a former analyst and RAND employee, Daniel Ellsberg. The first depressing revelations of extreme official dissembling published in what soon became famous as *The Pentagon Papers* were still rebounding when the General Accounting Office suggested that nearly two billion dollars budgeted for South Vietnam pacification programs from 1968 to 1970 could not be accounted for and listed ominously, among the problems, "misappropriation of funds."[3]

Worse was to come. Fury at the inane conduct of the war by supposedly professional generals had slowly been building in such able and immensely brave and qualified subordinates as Colonel David Hackworth. Hackworth had been trying for years to educate his seniors in order to save men's lives, generally without success. His own major tactical achievements, his increasingly critical articles in professional military journals, his not-so-subtle scorn for the rear-area commandos—all had combined to annoy army brass and deprive him of a well-earned brigade command. The illegal invasion of Cambodia had infuriated him; President Nixon's intervention in the Calley case sickened him. In an interview with ABC television in late June 1971, this battle-scarred combat leader, hero to many senior and junior officers, hard-bitten NCOs, and young soldiers in the field, was broadcast nationwide in America. A few of his answers told the American people the story of the incredibly inept military and civil performance in Vietnam.

On training:

" . . . in the main the training for Vietnam from the standpoint of the individual soldier, the young officer, and even the battalion, brigade, and division staff officers and senior commanders has been totally inadequate. . . . " As one result of poor training, Hackworth believed " . . . that our casualties were at least thirty percent higher . . . or even higher than that"; further, according to an official Pentagon classified study, 15 to 20 per cent of the casualties were the result of friendly fire—"one man shooting another man; friendly artillery firing on a friendly element; friendly helicopters firing on a friendly unit; tac[tical] air striking a friendly unit. . . ."

On American generals:

" . . . the average general that came to Vietnam did not have a good concept, good appreciation of the nature of guerrilla warfare. In most cases because of their lack of reading in depth about guerrilla warfare, they were not prepared for the war and they had to fall back on Korea and World War II." Without question this brought more casualties: " . . . one of the most classic examples is

Hamburger Hill. Here was a hill that had to be taken. Hundreds and hundreds of casualties occurred taking this hill. . . . [The Americans] had the hill for a few days and pulled off. So what was the reason for taking the hill? Why not stand back if the enemy is on it and bomb, but why use infantry to take the hill?"

Did senior commanders learn from mistakes and make appropriate changes?

" . . . I don't think so. I don't think that the top level ever developed a realistic strategic plan nor did they ever have tactics to support that strategic plan." Take, for example, the invasion of Laos: " . . . Conventional thinking put us in that operation rather than training a light, mobile guerrilla force . . . [to operate] in there like guerrillas." Echoing Roger Hilsman nearly ten years earlier, Hackworth wanted to fight guerrillas with guerrillas—small numbers " . . . well trained, highly motivated."

Asked if the silence of those officers who disagreed with MACV strategy and tactics was not in part responsible, Colonel Hackworth replied, " . . . That is right, and that is why perhaps we who have not been vocal should be charged for just criminal neglect."[4]

Not surprisingly, the President's popularity continued to decline and he was in serious political trouble. His Administration had recorded a fiscal-year deficit of over $23 billion, the second largest since World War II and one estimated to increase in the current fiscal year. The balance of trade also measured an unhealthy deficit, which meant, among other things, that the dollar's value stood in jeopardy. No less an authority than former chief presidential economic adviser Gardner Ackley warned

. . . that failure to act to stem inflation and unemployment "can threaten the stability of the social and political order." He said that inflation and unemployment were exaggerating the poverty problem to the point where current policies could provoke outright revolution.[5]

Although the Administration gained some hope from Henry Kissinger's secret mission to Peking (Beijing) followed by Nixon's state visit in February 1972, little encouraging news arrived from Indochina. As American, Thai, and Australian troop units continued to depart, President Thieu left no doubt that he headed a military dictatorship, a fact shortly emphasized when he alone ran for election. This was primarily the work of CIA, which spent "millions of dollars" in cowing and neutralizing Thieu's opposition in pursuing its policy of strengthening his government "at all costs." A senior CIA official in Saigon later wrote, ". . . By October 1972 . . . we had bought, bribed and sold so many South Vietnamese military and political figures that our spies and collaborators inside the government were mere extensions of ourselves."[6] Prime Minister Lon Nol in neighboring Cambodia added to the authoritarian air in mid-October by declaring a state of emergency and appointing ". . . a new government to rule by 'ordinance' rather than by constitutional law. He said that he no longer would 'play the game of democracy and freedom' since it stood in the way of victory."[7] Less than a month later, Field Marshal Thanom Kittikachorn overthrew Thailand's parliamentary government in favor of rule by revolutionary council.

Political issues seemed more clearly if unhappily settled than military issues. In Paris, the enemy had proposed in July a new seven-point peace plan unacceptable to either Washington or Saigon. As fighting receded inside South Vietnam, it continued to mount in Laos where the American government was spending hundreds of millions of dollars in fighting a clandestine war. In Cambodia, about thirty thousand PAVN troops supplemented by perhaps fifteen to twenty thousand Cambodian Communists, the Khmer Rouge, claimed control of about half the country. Morale in the Cambodian army continued to sink owing to confused communications (Lon Nol, as had Ngo Dinh Diem, insisted on commanding the army from Phnom Penh), corrupt and poorly trained officers (David Hackworth later wrote of the futility of trying to train "the playboy lackadaisical Cambodian officer" who had no intention of going to battle),[8] and political differences so pronounced between senior commanders that some who secretly sided with Sihanouk constantly sold arms and ammunition to the Khmer Rouge and PAVN units.[9] In October, an army task force relieved a besieged town north of Phnom Penh only to be cut to ribbons, two battalions decimated "by casualties and wholesale desertions," with huge losses of tanks, armored vehicles, artillery, machine guns, and rifles (all recently supplied by the American army).[10] As 1971 drew to a close, guerrillas were bombarding the capital, Phnom Penh, a threat that caused Saigon to send some twenty-four thousand troops across the border to bolster ARVN units already in Cambodia.

The situation in South Vietnam remained in flux. In September, a combined ARVN-U.S. task force hastily moved north against enemy activity in the demilitarized zone. Some two hundred American helicopters lifted thousands of ARVN troops to Quang Tri province where three brigades backed by about two thousand American troops began a giant "sweep" of the area. Enemy forces inside Cambodia continued to contest the border area. In the Mekong Delta, about forty thousand VC continued active. In mid-October, VC guerrillas slipped into an

American base eight miles from Saigon to blow up two helicopter gunships and damage three others.[11] Frank Snepp, the senior CIA analyst in Saigon, later wrote:

> . . . The tone and content of the reporting [from Saigon] was becoming increasingly ominous, and several colleagues and I concluded that a major North Vietnamese offensive was in the offing. Our over-cautious superiors at the CIA [in America], however, were not so sure and decided to check our conclusions with Kissinger . . . [who, preoccupied with negotiations] could not imagine the North Vietnamese might be preparing to revert to their old bad habits. . . . Our superiors therefore dutifully blocked, qualified or modified any analyses that tended to suggest they were.[12]

In early 1972, " . . . President Thieu and his staff drew up an assessment predicting a massive North Vietnamese drive across the demilitarized zone into the northernmost provinces of the country."[13]

The turbulent situation again brought dangerous Congressional antagonism. In late October, the Senate Foreign Relations Committee approved an amendment that limited " . . . all spending in Indochina to the single goal of withdrawing American troops."[14] The Administration loftily replied that it would continue operations necessary to protect American forces. A few days later, waves of B-52 bombers supplemented by naval gunfire worked over enemy positions in the demilitarized zone. About the same time, Secretary of Defense Laird announced that American troops might still be fighting long after the bulk of American forces had been withdrawn. He told reporters in Saigon that he found the progress of Vietnamization " . . . most encouraging . . . that Saigon's position was militarily strong and the main problem facing South Vietnam was economic. It was one of strengthening and stabilizing the economy so that the country could support its armed forces."[15] A few days later, President Nixon announced that another forty-five thousand troops would be withdrawn " . . . and proclaimed the end of the U.S. offensive role in the war." Further withdrawals " . . . would be determined by the level of enemy infiltration and combat activity, the success of Vietnamization, progress in securing release of American prisoners in North Vietnam and obtaining an Indochina cease-fire." If no progress resulted from the Paris talks, " . . . it will be necessary to maintain a residual force" of American troops in the country, he said.[16] Ten days later he told newsmen, " . . . Air power, of course, will continue to be used. We will continue to use it in support of the South Vietnamese until there is a negotiated settlement or, looking further down the road, until the South Vietnamese have developed the capability to handle the situation themselves." If the enemy increased infiltration,

". . . we will have to not only continue our air strikes, we will have to step them up."[17] No progress had resulted from the Paris talks, one reason probably being that General John Lavelle, commanding the U. S. Air Force in Vietnam, had taken it upon himself to open a secret air offensive against the North—in defiance of orders.[18]

Kissinger meanwhile had virtually eliminated Rogers and Laird from the policy-making process, and it is a matter of wonder why these two most important Cabinet members could be so dangerously spineless in publicly supporting the Administration when so many of their roles and responsibilities had been usurped by Kissinger's National Security Council. The villain in Laird's case was the JCS-NSC liaison office, an office that Laird had wanted eliminated since 1969, and with good reason:

> . . . According to J. Fred Buzhardt, the Pentagon's General Counsel . . . the Chairman [of the JCS] would actually send Kissinger the drafts of memoranda he was writing to Laird so that Kissinger could revise them, if he wished, to his own advantage.[19]

The love-match between Kissinger and the JCS received a major setback when Kissinger disagreed on such important topics as the strategic arms limitation negotiations. The JCS now installed a navy yeoman clerk in the liaison office to spy on Kissinger and " . . . to try to obtain any NSC documents that might interest the Chiefs and that Kissinger's staff might not provide." This was Yeoman Radford, who later testified to the Senate Armed Services Committee " . . . that he was ordered to obtain anything of interest to the Chiefs [JCS]—talk of troop cuts, agreements between the White House and Thieu, meetings with Swank [U.S. ambassador in Phnom Penh], assurances to Lon Nol . . ." Radford accompanied Kissinger's principal assistant, Colonel Alexander Haig, on several trips to Saigon and Phnom Penh, merrily photographing any documents of interest including those in Haig's briefcase. His greatest coup, however, came when he accompanied Kissinger to Pakistan, from where the latter departed for China and secret talks with Chou En-lai:

> . . . Radford rummaged through the burn bags in the plane and through Kissinger's briefcase. He read as much as he could of the transcript of Kissinger's meeting with Chou En-lai . . . [and] he obtained about 150 documents on the trip.[20]

The saga was exposed in December 1971 when columnist Jack Anderson " . . . published an account of an NSC meeting on the Indo-Pakistan war in which Kissinger had stressed that United States policy was to pretend neutralism but actually to 'tilt' towards Pakistan." The ensuing explosion in the White House caused one of Nixon's principal keepers, John Ehrlichman, to order a covert and highly illegal bunch of hoodlums—the so-called "plumbers"—to find the leak. Admiral Robert Welander, who headed the liaison office, now informed Haig what Radford had been doing. To Kissinger's fury, Radford and Welander were transferred "in silence."[21]

Beset by internal and external disorder in the extreme, the President could only play for time in the hope that overtures to Peking (Beijing) and Moscow would come to fruition. With the approach of an election year, he could not renege on repeated promises to withdraw the bulk of American troops from South Vietnam. Neither could he risk collapse of Thieu's government. He instead chose a middle course, that of using the American presence, particularly American air and naval power, to buttress ARVN until Vietnamization reached the point where Hanoi would see the light and come to the peace table willing to work a deal. To help Hanoi make up its mind, American planes made over a thousand raids on North Vietnam during December 26–30, 1971. No matter that neither Russia nor China contested the raids, no matter severe air interdiction in all areas, the enemy continued operations in Laos and Cambodia while MACV reported intense preparations for what appeared to be another Tet offensive.

Nixon put a brave face on failure to bring the enemy around. His insistence on the favorable progress of Vietnamization brought dissembling echoes from Administration officials, for example Melvin Laird testifying before the House Appropriations Committee in late February 1972 that

> ... the other side had been forced to switch from main-force to low-level guerrilla activity because of the "buildup of the South Vietnamese forces" and could not "conduct a large-scale military operation for a substantial period of time" because "they do not have the logistic support" or the "personnel."[22]

Five weeks later, Giap opened the spring offensive earlier predicted by CIA analysts in Saigon and ignored by Kissinger. Giap's effort involved elements of ten enemy divisions, some 150,000 troops whose armament, mainly from Soviet Russia's arsenals, included tanks, anti-aircraft and anti-tank heat-seeking missiles, MIG-21 aircraft and radar-guided antiaircraft guns.[23] In the North, two divisions spilled through the DMZ to fragment a newly formed ARVN division and chase it from Quang Tri, a task aided by poor weather which largely prevented interference from American aircraft. Units of two more divisions pushed in eastward from the Ho Chi Minh trail toward Hué while a fifth division remained north of the DMZ in close reserve. In the central highlands, elements of three PAVN divisions, already in control of the northern portion of II Corps area, began to push on Kontum. Another three divisions moved into III Corps area from Cambodia, besieging An Loc and controlling large areas north and west of Saigon.

The most serious threat existed in the northern part of the country. To defend Hué, President Thieu moved in his best units while Washington rushed naval and air support to the area. Abrams, who up to now had been boasting about ARVN's capabilities, cabled that " . . . it is quite possible that the South Vietnamese have lost their will to fight, or hang together, and that the whole thing may be lost." Nixon was appalled. "How can this have happened?" he asked Kissinger. "The South Vietnamese seem to go in cycles," Kissinger suggested. "They're very good for about a month, and now they're caving in on schedule."[24] Adding to Nixon's confusion was army chief of staff General Westmoreland's belief that the [enemy] drive would fade " . . . 'in a matter of days because the staying power of the enemy is not great.' " (The battle lasted well into June.)[25]

Whatever the prognosis, Nixon was determined that the new offensive would not succeed. If only sixty-nine thousand American ground troops remained in South Vietnam when Giap's drive started, he still held peripheral strengths. Within five weeks of the beginning of the offensive the U. S. Seventh Fleet was maintaining a task force in the Gulf of Tonkin that included six carriers, five cruisers, and forty destroyers, in all manned by forty-one thousand men. While air armadas including B-52 bombers struck enemy units throughout South Vietnam, MACV hastened to repair Thieu's material losses and to assure him and the world of continuing American support. Nixon's response at first seemed to produce a conciliatory diplomatic result but when this came to nothing, Nixon decided on the risky but dramatic move of mining North Vietnam's ports and increasing air strikes on North Vietnamese targets in accordance with Kissinger's suggested "November Option" of 1969, the "brutal blow" not then implemented because of political reasons.[26] This was now necessary, Nixon told the American people, to protect remaining American troops in Vietnam. As for total withdrawal of those troops, that would be to admit "an American defeat," which would " . . . encourage aggression all over the world." Sounding not unlike Lyndon Johnson at Baltimore seven years earlier, the President pointed to Hanoi's intransigence, which could only be surmounted by " . . . decisive military action to end the war." At the same time, he offered a new peace plan: total withdrawal of U.S. forces within four months in return for an internationally supervised cease-fire, return of American prisoners of war, and a political settlement negotiated by the Vietnamese themselves.

This was the sort of dramatic move favored by the Nixon-Kissinger psyche. As with past military escalations, notably the Cambodian and Laotian excursions, it brought national and international opprobrium marked by massive demonstrations and a host of new militant protesters inspired in part by publication of Frances Fitzgerald's Pulitzer prize-winning best-seller, *Fire in the Lake: The Vietnamese and the Americans in Vietnam*. The old curmudgeon I. F. Stone suitably epitaphed the new bombing in the North: " . . . air power had not given us victory" but "only prolonged the agony before defeat."[27] Neither did the effort produce a real political effect. Hanoi already had girded itself for resumption of bombing. Its Paris delegation claimed decided military advantages and spurned the President's latest proposals.

About all the escalation accomplished was to cheer a morose Saigon government. Gone was the earlier bravado. As reported by *Time* magazine:

> . . . Saigon's 492,000-man regular army is suffering from more than battered morale. There are fewer than 150,000 Communist soldiers committed to the invasion; nonetheless they have not only tied up all of ARVN's reserve strength but have also knocked out an ever-growing list of South Vietnamese units—one full infantry division, a third of another division, five infantry regiments, six armored regiments, three artillery battalions, nine ranger battalions, two airborne brigades and three battalions of marines, Saigon's best troops. The South Vietnamese have admitted to heavy casualties: 4,610 dead and 14,093 wounded. U.S. military men hope that, with unstinting American air support and Nixon's morale-boosting moves, ARVN can hold up at least through May, when monsoon rains are expected to dampen the action in the southern two-thirds of the country.[28]

To many observers it was a repeat of Chiang Kai-shek and China. Like General Lon Nol in Cambodia and Field Marshal Thanom Kittikachorn in Thailand, General Thieu now threw off the light cloak of Western-inspired democracy to declare martial law and ask the national assembly for emergency powers. Simultaneously, his new commander in the field, Lieutenant General Ngo Quang Truong, started probing attacks toward Quang Tri.

Having focused allied eyes on Quang Tri and Hué, Giap in late May opened a new offensive against An Loc, a furious action that again isolated the town's six thousand defenders. When a relief force stalled some miles south of the town on Highway 13, a helicopter lift brought in two regiments to reinforce the battered garrison. As battle slowed and partial lull claimed various areas, the American bombing effort intensified with thousands of tons of television- and laser-guided "smart" bombs dropping on North Vietnam, complemented by thousands of sorties that hammered enemy forces around Hué, Kontum, and An Loc.

Although ranking American officers claimed enormous damage to the enemy, it remained painfully clear that if ARVN was holding, it was only because of American air and naval power (over two hundred B-52 bombers were engaged by end of May). Giap's offensives had caused the Saigon command to strip the vital Mekong Delta of troops. The pacification effort there virtually ceased. VC cadres appeared as the government yielded control throughout the vast area. By end of June, the offensives had generated over one and a half million refugees and had cost ARVN over seventy thousand casualties. Thieu's secret police had arrested thousands of "suspected Viet Cong sympathizers" and would continue to arrest some fourteen thousand a month. Thieu continued to invoke emergency measures and in September, like Diem before him, abolished hamlet elections to return South Vietnamese government to the feudal days.

Still, his government had held together and in September an ARVN task force finally reoccupied Quang Tri, a city of rubble evacuated by the enemy, who continued to hover nearby. Similarly, key cities and towns in center and south felt the hot breath of enemy troops which controlled perhaps 50 per cent of South Vietnam and operated almost without opposition in Laos and Cambodia. Giap had taken heavy casualties but had achieved his primary goal of disrupting the highly vaunted Vietnamization and pacification of the South.

He had achieved a great deal more by causing a new surge in America's antiwar movement. In October, no less a person than the world-famous historian, Henry Steele Commager, fired a major salvo with his essay in *The New York Review of Books*, "The Defeat of America":

> . . . Using the documents then available, a close examination of the long and gradual escalation of the war demonstrated the tremendous difficulty in finding any coherent logic or rational objective behind our involvement in Vietnam, beyond some vague "honor" that in any case we have forfeited. For Commager there was a "demented" quality to the American military effort in Vietnam; by 1972 with Nixon's trip to China and the thaw between Washington and Beijing, the original goal, if goal it was, of containing China had obviously been abandoned.
>
> Commager reviewed evidence and arguments from eight years of governmental deception . . . [to show that] we Americans had blithely come to accept a double standard: German reprisals in World War II were seen as war crimes punishable by death, "but when we wipe out defenseless villages with 'incontinent ordinance', or engage in massacres as brutal as that at Lidice, these are mistakes or aberrations that do not mar our record of benevolence."

President Nixon, like his predecessor, was determined not to go down in history as presiding over the first American defeat, but Commager believed it was too late. America had unalterably been defeated, "not, to be sure, on the field of battle, but in the eyes of history." We have the power to destroy Vietnam and call it victory, but such insensate destruction would be madness, not victory. This is a war we cannot win and "a war we must lose if we are to survive morally." Commager contended that true patriots throughout this awful episode in American history had been the war resisters.[29]

CHAPTER SEVENTY-NINE

1. Derek Wilson, *The Times* (London), Saigon, May 2, 16, 1971.
2. Frances Fitzgerald, 423: "... In the spring of 1971 the U.S. command [in Vietnam] itself estimated that 10 percent of the troops in Vietnam were taking heroin, and that 5 percent were addicts."
3. *The Times* (London), Washington, D.C., July 11, 1971.
4. Hackworth, 776–7.
5. Harlow Unger, *The Sunday Times* (London), August 1, 1971.
6. Snepp, 14–15, 19 ff.: Most of the millions of dollars was "... pocketed by members of the Thieu regime."
7. *Time,* October 21, 1972. See also, Shawcross, 229.
8. Hackworth, 747.
9. Shawcross, 202.
10. Ibid., 203.
11. *The Times* (London), Saigon, October 13, 1971.
12. Snepp, 21.
13. Ibid., 22.
14. *The Times* (London), Washington, D.C., October 20, 1971.
15. Derek Wilson, *The Times* (London), Saigon, November 7, 1971.
16. Ian McDonald, *The Times* (London), Washington, D.C., November 12, 1971.
17. *Time,* November 22, 1971.
18. Ibid., June 26, 1972. Lavelle's action by disrupting peace talks may well have prolonged the war; at the very least it lent credence to enemy charges of American dissembling. Lavelle's punishment was retirement as a three-star general with a pension of $2,250 a month.
19. Shawcross, 205.
20. Ibid., 205–6.
21. Ibid., 206–7.
22. Stone, "Why Nixon Won His Moscow Gamble." See also, Kissinger, *The White House Years,* 1099–1100. Abrams had been warning of an "imminent enemy offensive" since early January 1972.
23. Shaplen, "Letter from Vietnam." As usual, Mr. Shaplen offers an excellent and detailed account of this action.
24. Nixon, *Memoirs,* 598.
25. Karnow, 642.
26. Woodward and Bernstein, 189. See also, Morris, 163–4.
27. Schalk, 154.
28. *Time,* May 22, 1972.
29. Schalk, 157.

CHAPTER 80

HANOI'S POLITICAL and military position was not as favorable in autumn of 1972 as it would have the world believe. Giap's offensives, which had begun to stall in July, had cost him dearly in men and matériel. The blockade of northern ports together with massive aerial interdiction of road and railroad transport and bombing of troop units had slowed supply to bring serious ammunition and other shortages. Hanoi had been especially alarmed by Nixon's summit meeting with Soviet Premier Leonid Brezhnev in Moscow in late May and by Russia's cooling attitude and Nixon's incipient rapproachement with China. Poll ratings in the United States clearly favored Nixon's re-election, which would mean continuing military and economic support to Saigon. The anti-war movement in America, comforting as it was to Hanoi, had noticeably weakened—the student protest sharply diminished when Nixon announced that no more draftees would go to Vietnam unless they volunteered. Hanoi could no longer win a military victory—but a political victory was still possible.

After a summer of intense diplomatic activity in which Kissinger persuaded the enemy to accept a cease-fire without prior approval of President Nguyen Van Thieu, Le Duc Tho met secretly with Kissinger in Paris in late September to present a new ten-point peace plan. When this was rejected, he followed with still another plan in October which, according to Nixon, " . . . met almost all our major requirements." That those "requirements" had been watered down so as to mean virtually nothing did not upset Nixon, who later claimed that the new plan " . . . amounted to a complete capitulation by the enemy. They were accepting a settlement on our terms"[1] (along with a promise of hefty economic aid to the North).[2]

Nixon responded to the new offer by reducing the bombing of the North while authorizing " . . . a massive airlift of military equipment and supplies" to Saigon, which would not be possible once the agreement was signed. Negotiations with the North continued throughout October, the chief stumbling block being the Thieu government in Saigon, which understandably would not accept the provision that North Vietnamese troops would remain in South Vietnam—nor was Thieu swayed by Kissinger's absurd argument " . . . that the Communist forces, already weakened by battle and deprived of reinforcements, would eventually wither away."[3] More to the point, Nixon informed Thieu that " . . . you have my complete assurance that if Hanoi fails to abide by the terms of this agreement it is my intention to take swift and retaliatory action."[4] Having good reason to believe that Nixon could not live up to a commitment that would keep American forces in Vietnam, Thieu did not buy this either, remaining so truculent as to be threatened with a cutoff of U.S. aid and a separate agreement between Washington and Hanoi with the South left out in the cold.[5]

Continued stalemate was driving Nixon frantic. His temper worsened considerably in October when the Nobel committee in Stockholm, instead of awarding him its peace prize, shared the prize with Kissinger and Le Duc Tho—which elicited Oriana Fallaci's succinct comment,

". . . Poor Nobel. Poor peace."[6] Kissinger's concept of "honor" allowed him to accept.[7] Le Duc Tho declined, notifying the committee that ". . . peace has not yet been established in Vietnam. In these circumstances it is impossible for me to accept."[8]

As Nixon had blamed Congress, the press, television, the American people, and even Kissinger's diplomacy for his failure to end the war, so now he struck out at the JCS, which was ordered in December to launch another massive B-52 bombing of the Hanoi area and to reseed the mines in Haiphong harbor, what James Reston called "war by tantrum," and what Senator Mike Mansfield termed a "stone-age tactic." Hanoi's signal for renewed negotiations was scarcely a capitulation brought on by the sacrosanct B-52 bombing, as Nixon later claimed. ". . . Its terms differed only very slightly from those that Hanoi had offered three months before," noted one observer,[9] and its attitude had probably been altered by a promise of over $4 billion in U.S. reconstruction aid.[10]

Negotiations resulted in an "Agreement on Ending the War and Restoring the Peace in Vietnam," signed by the principals in late January 1973. President Thieu, who had been shut out of the talks, was only slightly mollified by a second promise from Nixon: " . . . You have my assurance that we will respond with full force should the settlement be violated by North Vietnam."[11]

The cease-fire promised by the "Agreement on Ending the War . . . " was never to materialize. Nixon and Kissinger's "peace with honor" was as thin a piece of paper as ever was signed. Nowhere did the Paris agreement treat the basic problem of " . . . who would rule postwar South Vietnam."[12] Once the shooting stopped, Thieu's government was supposed to work with the Communist PRG to establish a Council of National Reconciliation and Concord that, by *unanimous* consent, would decide on the shape of the future South Vietnamese Government and arrange the requisite elections for it.[13]

This body was never formed because the shooting never stopped. The highly touted cease-fire was a sham. In theory, it was to be carried out with the help of two teams, one composed of members from the opposing sides, one of Hungarians, Poles, Indonesians, and Canadians. Since team decisions had to be unanimous, they were rarely made or, if made, were ineffective. Prior to the agreement being signed, both sides rushed to build up their forces and armament, which in the case of South Vietnam was accomplished by an enormous airlift of U.S. weapons and ammunition.

" . . . According to field statistics, more than 6,600 South Vietnamese soldiers were killed in the first three months of the truce"[14]—and that was only the beginning. To help cover Thieu's military vulnerability, Nixon ordered U.S. planes to open a prolonged B-52 and tactical aircraft bombing and strafing campaign that would probably still be going on had an enraged Congress not killed it a few months later. Owing to the agreement's muddled language, heavy fighting would continue in South Vietnam; owing to a vital omission of language, the agreement did not state a specific deadline for the withdrawal of foreign troops from either Cambodia or Laos. The senior CIA analyst in Saigon at the time summed it up well:

> ... In sum, then, the peace of Paris was no peace at all. It imposed no limitation, or obligation on either side that could not be nullified through the unanimity principle, and apart from withdrawal of U.S. forces, all major provisions were subject to reinterpretation and further debate.[15]

In short, even the most dim-witted observer had to recognize that the Paris agreement would not end the war in Indochina.

The cease-fire in theory left President Thieu in control of " ... roughly 75 percent of South Vietnam's territory and about 85 percent of its population."[16] Thanks to an overflowing cornucopia of American aid, his army numbered over a million men equipped with a variety of modern weapons, including 175-mm. guns and M-60 tanks, supported by the fourth largest air force in the world, which included modern fighters, gunships, and helicopters, and even by a small navy.[17]

Its endemic weaknesses were several, however. Thieu's national government along with numerous local governments were penetrated by Communist agents who reported virtually all secret plans and developments to Hanoi. Thanks to the professional ministrations of MACV over the years, the armed forces had never learned how to fight either an insurgency or a conventional war on their own. They had become almost totally dependent on American advisers, American artillery, and American air support. Despite years of expensive, even lavish, training, the officer corps lacked talent and motivation, largely the result of promotion by favoritism and purchase. The army, like the government, was corrupt from the highest-ranking general to the lowest-ranking private; payrolls were padded, rations diverted, arms and ammunition sold to the enemy—precisely as had been the case with Chiang Kai-shek's Nationalist army some years earlier.[18] That aside, in the early months of 1973, it was making substantial territorial gains (so much for the cease-fire) against a partially fragmented enemy, which in part explains why its fragile condition was not yet apparent to the outside world. But in large part continued deception was the work of the new American ambassador, a Thieu-fanatic named Graham Martin, and the Defense Attaché's Office (formerly MACV) whose $30-million-a-year budget maintained " . . . 400 civilian employees, 50 American military officers, and 2,500 American civilian contract workers," a combination that by means of biased reports often succeeded in preventing the ugly truth from reaching concerned policy makers in Washington.[19]

More apparent was Thieu's continued authoritarian rule. Instead of trying to develop a broader political base in order to support future travails, his government continued to jail thousands of dissidents of a dozen varieties. Opposition, however, continued to mount. Millions of refugees had no jobs, inflation soared, army desertions increased owing in part to pay problems brought on by a treasury drained by vast military expenditures and all-pervasive corruption.

The enemy also had problems. The 1972 offensive, although resulting in psychological and territorial gains, had been expensive. The economic condition in the North was " . . . in dreadful shape—poorer than any country in Asia," with future prospects bleak owing to greatly reduced support from Russia and China.[20] Serious disagreements existed in the top-level leadership, PAVN and the VC suffered from high desertion rates, there was a serious manpower shortage, relations with the Khmer Rouge insurgents were worsening—" . . . the Cambodians are even denying food to their Vietnamese allies and could not be trusted with any important combat assignment in our offensive."[21] In 1811, the French Marshal Bessières, who had just taken over an army command in Spain, ended his appreciation with these words:

> . . . Everyone allows that we are too widely scattered. We occupy too much territory, we used up our resources without profit and without necessity: we are clinging on to dreams.

In early 1973, a prominent North Vietnamese general described PAVN's condition:

> . . . We had not been able to make up our losses. We were short of manpower as well as food and ammunition, and coping with the enemy was very difficult.[22]

Party leaders eventually decided on a compromise policy of "no war, no peace,"

> . . . a careful balancing act that would enable them to husband resources at home while slowly building toward military parity in the south, behind the "shield" of the Paris agreement.[23]

1042

Hanoi still owned precious assets (not least of which was strategic and tactical flexibility). The cease-fire confirmed Communist holdings in the South, both along the western border mountain country and some isolated areas in the Mekong Delta. Thirty thousand PAVN troops remained in Cambodia where, according to Prince Sihanouk, Khmer Rouge guerrilla units were commanded by PAVN officers. " . . . In Laos, PAVN field units, numbering perhaps 50,000, were stationed along the Ho Chi Minh trail, besides garrisoning the central Plain of Jars and several frontier districts." Combat troops in South Vietnam were beefed up after the cease-fire from an estimated forty thousand to 170,000 supported by some six hundred medium and light tanks and heavy artillery, not to mention the People's Liberation Armed Forces (PLAF) sixty thousand strong. While ARVN forces were wearing themselves out with search-and-destroy operations in the Mekong Delta and along the Cambodian border, the Communists were building twelve airfields, " . . . ten of them defended by surface-to-air missiles (SAM), and several all-weather roads were under construction in northern South Vietnam and along the Lao-Vietnam border."[24] While lying low tactically—commanders were instructed to " . . . attack only when they were clearly superior to Thieu's troops"[25]—the army simultaneously embarked " . . . on a huge logistical program designed to create a springboard for an eventual offensive of vast proportions." This included building an all-weather highway from Quang Tri province down to the Mekong Delta, a three-thousand-mile oil pipeline from Quang Tri to their headquarters seventy-five miles northwest of Saigon, which in time housed " . . . a modern radio grid . . . that enabled them to communicate directly with Hanoi and with their field units." As Stanley Karnow presciently concluded:

> . . . That the Communists could undertake such a stupendous enterprise testified to the failure of American bombings to destroy the equipment and fuel that they had amassed in North Vietnam over the preceding years.[26]

The amazing resilience of the guerrilla enemy showed itself in spring of 1973 when VC units began hitting isolated ARVN outposts and supply dumps. Taken with intelligence reports of Communist construction projects in the South, renewed VC activity brought a veiled threat from the White House of renewed American intervention in South Vietnam, a quaint notion that died in mid-August with the termination of the B-52 bombing campaign in Cambodia. Sir Robert Thompson allegedly had advised Thieu that Nixon would find a way around the Congressional bombing ban.[27] Hoping to impress the American people with his determination and capabilities, Thieu resumed offensive operations and did make some impressive gains. But any hope of renewed B-52 bombings were dashed by Nixon's increasing involvement in the filth and cover-up of the Watergate scandal.[28]

ARVN's stepped-up operations caused General Giap to demand increased PAVN attacks. Owing to North Vietnam's lack of allies, faltering economy and disagreement among senior Communist leaders (some of whom wanted priority given to rebuilding the North's economy), these were restricted to raids against isolated ARVN outposts and fuel and supply dumps, but escalation became so serious that in late October the American president, despite his increasingly perilous political position, warned North Vietnam " . . . against the resumption of major war and reminded it of past 'miscalculations' about American responses."[29] Those words died with the passage in early November of the War Powers Act (over Nixon's veto), which further restricted the executive's war-making powers.

By year's end, it was apparent that North Vietnam, although unable to mount a "general offensive," had radically improved its position in the South. It was just as apparent that Thieu's position had weakened owing to skyrocketing inflation, decreasing American interest in the country and thus a falling off of economic and military aid, increasingly corrupt civil and military officials, and greatly lowered army morale.

For the first time in many years, relative quiet reigned in Laos, the people and soil of which had been the recipients of over two million tons of bombs—" . . . two-thirds of a ton of bombs for every single man, woman, and child in Laos"—dropped by U.S. aircraft, "three-quarters of that after Nixon's inauguration."[30] A cease-fire had gone into effect in late February under the terms of a peace agreement that provided for " . . . the withdrawal of all foreign troops within ninety days, and the formation of a coalition government within thirty days. The Communist Pathet Lao controlled about 75 percent of the country but most of the people lived in the government-held portion."[31] Although a coalition government had not been achieved by year's end, the Communists were in the stronger position in that they completely controlled the border areas where the Ho Chi Minh trail had been converted into practically a superhighway " . . . dotted with truck rest and service areas, oil tanks, machine shops . . . all protected by hilltop antiaircraft emplacements."[32]

Matters were not so quiescent in Cambodia, which was rapidly being torn to pieces. Already in 1972, the Communist Khmer Rouge was moving toward what it termed the "Democratic Revolution." In some areas, peasants " . . . were henceforth forbidden to wear the traditional multicolored sarong; all were now required to wear the plain black shirt and trousers normally worn by peasants at work, which later became the uniform of Democratic Kampuchea."[33] Early in 1973, the Khmer Rouge " . . . began an intensified campaign to drive the Vietnamese from the country, in combination with a new purge of Sihanoukists and other dissident 'Third Force' cadres."[34] In February, the Khmer Rouge opened a new military offensive at once answered by an American B-52 bombing campaign, the planes flying over sixty missions a day,[35] from bases in Thailand and secretly orchestrated in part from the American embassy in Phnom Penh—an effort that would cost $7 billion before Cambodia's fall.[36] Owing in part to a lack of up-to-date large-scale maps, bombing inaccuracies caused thousands of civilian casualties even though killing sixteen thousand Khmer Rouge guerrillas (according to Seventh Air Force).[37] In destroying some Khmer Rouge units, it also brought a flow of recruits to the Communists and caused a good many moderate party members to move to the hard-line right and away from any co-operation with the North Vietnamese: " . . . The 'Democratic Revolution' was both a product of, and a capitalization upon, the U.S. aerial war . . . the bombing sowed a whirlwind which the CPK [Communist Party Kampuchea] Centre was ready to reap."[38] William Shawcross concluded that the campaign would " . . . destroy the old Cambodia forever."[39] Bombing or no, by April some fifteen thousand Khmer Rouge guerrillas had almost surrounded Phnom Penh, which probably would have fallen but for the B-52 strikes; Khmer Rouge command problems that prevented co-ordinated attacks; supply problems, in particular a shortage of ammunition occasioned by increasingly difficult relations with PAVN and VC troops; and the onset of the rainy season.

There seemed but one possibility of saving Cambodia and this was by a plan of the French ambassador in Peking (Beijing) for China to arrange a cease-fire and return Prince Norodom Sihanouk as ruler, a plan endorsed by American ambassadors in Saigon and Phnom Penh. Unfortunately, Henry Kissinger, who had refused to see Sihanouk on several occasions, felt that withdrawal of U.S. backing for the Lon Nol regime would be seen in Peking and other foreign capitals

> . . . as a sign of American weakness. . . . "I don't want to hear about Laos-type compromise," he told John Dean, the U.S. ambassador in Phnom Penh . . . "Your job is to strengthen the military position so we can negotiate from strength."[40]

As one result of this myopic policy, American military advisers had assumed virtually full control of American policy, to the fury of most embassy civilian officials. Incredibly, this policy included the import of enough weapons and supply to equip four conventional Cambodian divisions. Through summer and autumn of 1973, ships and planes brought in thousands of tons of arms: " . . . 105- and 155-mm. artillery; over a hundred armored personnel carriers; more heavy river craft; 81-mm. mortars; grenade launchers; recoilless rifles; 45,000 more M-16 rifles . . . equipment for the headquarters and the combat support elements of four divisions"[41]—most of which existed only on paper.

Contrarily, the Khmer Rouge numbered about sixty thousand well-disciplined and motivated men who again sprang into action when the rainy season ended in November. At year's end, Phnom Penh was holding out—the Communists controlled an estimated " . . . 70 percent of the country and 50 percent of the population."[42]

The situation did not essentially alter until late in 1974. Laos was the first to go under. The Communist hand was greatly strengthened by the emergence of a coalition government. That was soon destroyed by the Pathet Lao, which in early December abolished the monarchy in favor of the People's Democratic Republic. Prince Souvanna Phouma's illness was used as a pretext to replace him with his half brother, Prince Souvanouvong, veteran leader of the Pathet Lao guerrillas. Souvanouvong became president of the new government and immediately established diplomatic relations with Hanoi.

Cambodia held out a trifle longer. In November, Kissinger, having realized that he had made a major diplomatic blunder, appeared in Peking to ask for Chinese mediation, a fruitless attempt since he refused to abandon the Lon Nol regime and work for Sihanouk's restoration.[43] In late December 1974, Khmer Rouge guerrillas, aided by Chinese-supplied water mines and heavy artillery, launched a new offensive that soon cut Phnom Penh from its Mekong River supply line. The situation was similar to that in China in its last months of agony. Government forces held the capital and important cities and towns; Communist forces controlled the countryside and the major roads and waterways. Despite heavy fighting and horrendous casualties, isolated government garrisons fell one after the other while Khmer Rouge forces closed in on the capital. The end came in mid-April with the fall of Phnom Penh. The Khmer Rouge insurgents moved in quickly, executed all government officials it could find, and forcibly evacuated all residents to the countryside—the opening moves in what would become one of the ugliest bloodbaths in history.

South Vietnam came last. There the Communists continued their ambitious road and base program while keeping ARVN off balance by guerrilla hit-and-run raids. ARVN counterattacks slowed, the inevitable result of tying up too many troops in defense of fixed positions—the same error earlier made by American troops—and of the cutback in artillery and air firepower. That cutback was necessitated in part by the reduction of American military aid, in part by ARVN quartermasters knowing neither what type and quantities of ammunition they possessed nor where the stuff was located. Maintenance problems also increased with reduced American support, but there was still no sign of the major Communist offensive so feared by Thieu. Although PAVN troops scored significant gains in the central highlands, the Iron Triangle north of Saigon, and in the Mekong Delta, Thieu derived some comfort from President Gerald Ford, who succeeded the disgraced Nixon in August and who shortly after assured Thieu of "continued support."[44] Bolstered by military and economic grants of millions of dollars from Washington to answer the inflated needs supplied by the American embassy in Saigon, Thieu's government, though increasingly shaky, seemed as if it might survive. But Communist gains had whetted Communist appetites for more territory. In December, Communist forces from Cambodia struck in the Mekong Delta to disrupt the all-important rice harvest. Simultaneously, PAVN and VC units moved into Phuoc Long province, which bordered Cambodia only seventy-five miles north of Saigon. In early January 1975, the provincial capital of Phuoc Binh fell to the enemy, a severe blow to South Vietnamese military and civil morale and a portent of things to come.

Such was the continued Communist pressure that, once an entire ARVN division had disintegrated in the central highlands, Thieu in mid-March ordered the evacuation of the central and northern provinces, which he called the " . . . unproductive areas of the country."[45] By month's end, the enemy claimed thirteen of South Vietnam's forty-four provinces. Four of ARVN's thirteen divisions no longer existed and millions of dollars' worth of arms, aircraft, munitions, and equipment were in enemy hands. ARVN's strategy was Chiang Kai-shek's strategy: defend cities and towns. Giap's strategy was Mao Tse-tung's strategy: cut communications with cities and towns to force retreat or annihilation (and sometimes both).

The Ford administration was beside itself. The army's chief of staff, General Frederick Weyand, was sent to Saigon from where he reported that the capital could be held with more American military aid. Ford asked Congress for one billion dollars and Congress said no. With the capital almost surrounded and with his own divisions dispersed, Thieu resigned and the Americans and some South Vietnamese—some sixty thousand in all—were evacuated by helicopter to waiting U.S. ships. It was left to General Duong Van Minh to negotiate a settlement with the Viet Cong, whose leaders refused to negotiate. On the last day of April 1975, Van Minh unconditionally surrendered to end the war in Vietnam.

*   *   *

The division of Vietnam formally ended in July 1976 with the emergence of the Socialist Republic of Vietnam governed by Premier Pham Van Dong. Although armed resistance to the government was minimal, the administrative task of converting the South to the mysterious ways of Communist government was immense and was far from accomplished by year's end. Laos also faced severe difficulties owing in part to an exodus of government officials and businessmen necessary to revive a shattered economy, in part to continued resistance by royalist troops in the South. Cambodia, now renamed Kampuchea and governed by Khmer Rouge leader Pol Pot, was in the throes of a massive bloodbath brought on by the Khmer Rouge's genocidal campaign to eliminate the urban intelligentsia and re-educate the masses while turning the country back to the stone age, an incredible travesty of civilization graphically told by William Shawcross, among others.[46]

Although the emergent countries formed a new power structure in the region, it was anything but the monolithic empire that a host of U.S. conservatives feared would sweep through Thailand and down the Malaysian Peninsula to turn all of Southeast Asia into a Communist camp. Instead, centuries-old fears and hatreds began to assert themselves almost immediately. If the Khmer Rouge government was giving top priority to conducting massive genocide, its army still found time to clash with Thailand's security forces in trying to halt the flow of Kampuchean refugees from leaving the country, and with Vietnamese troops which continued to occupy areas along the eastern border. Continuing clashes reportedly escalated in 1977 " . . . into heavy fighting involving between 10,000 and 20,000 men . . . using heavy artillery and tanks."[47] On the last day of the year the Phnom Penh government charged Vietnam with "large-scale unwarranted aggression," broke off diplomatic relations, and refused to enter into negotiations to settle the border problem even though its one ally, China, along with other neighboring countries had urged it to do so.[48] Heavy fighting continued in January. Apparently believing that it had taught its bumptious neighbor a salutary lesson, Hanoi pulled out its troops and in early February proposed to settle matters by creating a three-mile-deep internationally policed cordon sanitaire on either side of the line. Rejecting this sensible proposal, Pol Pot continued to fight.

The lines were now clearly drawn: Kampuchea, client state of a China intent on preserving its influence in the area and only too happy to supply Kampuchea with arms and equipment, including tanks and artillery; Vietnam, client state of a Soviet Union intent on further expanding its influence in Southeast Asia and only too happy to supply massive military and economic aid to Vietnam; Laos, perhaps unwilling host to fifty thousand Vietnamese troops, but clearly in the Soviet-

Vietnam sphere of influence; the ASEAN nations (Indonesia, Malaysia, Philippines, Singapore, and Brunei) terrified of Chinese, Soviet Union, and Vietnamese aspirations, wringing their hands and wailing like banshees; the United States, finally appalled at having opened this Pandora's box of evil winds, a disconsolate spectator seemingly content to mutter platitudes about those evil Khmer Rouge savages.

The situation could only escalate. Vietnam signed a treaty of friendship with the Soviet Union and sent more forces south. China increased its troop strength along the China-Vietnam border, and began edging diplomatically toward its American enemy. In late December 1978, a Vietnam army about 120,000 strong stormed into Kampuchea. After a few disastrous stands against the intruders, Khmer Rouge forces wisely retreated into the interior in order to fight a guerrilla war. In less than two weeks, the Vietnamese owned Phnom Penh, and Kampuchea had a new government, the People's Republic of Kampuchea headed by a Pol Pot defector, Heng Samrin, who presided over a People's Revolutionary Council. By early summer, the invaders, now about two hundred thousand strong, controlled most of the country, having pushed an estimated thirty thousand surviving Khmer Rouge guerrillas into the northwest corner where they were given limited sanctuary in Thailand and supplied with weapons and equipment from China.[49]

The fallout from the Vietnamese blitzkrieg was intense. China could not accept the Vietnamese presence in Kampuchea, which by extension threatened to replace Peking's (Beijing's) traditional influence by that of the Soviet Union. In early 1979, in order to "punish" Vietnam, a Chinese army perhaps one hundred thousand strong crossed the border, pushed back local troops, seized a provincial capital, and in less than a month returned to Chinese soil, a seemingly pointless operation that cost the army an estimated twenty thousand casualties while failing to discourage Vietnamese operations in Kampuchea.[50] Hanoi, however, having captured a blood-soaked wasteland, was already discovering that it needed increased economic aid from the Soviet Union. Moscow gladly accommodated but in return claimed increased naval facilities at Cam Ranh Bay and Da Nang. In November 1979, the United Nations General Assembly passed a resolution " . . . calling for the immediate and total withdrawal of Vietnamese forces from Kampuchea,"[51] but this produced no more efficacious results than various regional attempts to contain the spreading fire.

Hanoi meanwhile was consolidating its position in Kampuchea, a task that in spring of 1980 caused its forces to make brief incursions into Thailand both to force refugee camps to be moved inland from the border areas and to discourage Thailand from giving further aid to the Khmer Rouge. The Vietnamese action caused an instant international outcry and brought large shipments of weapons, including tanks, anti-tank missile systems, aircraft, and helicopters from the United States to the Thai army.[52]

The diplomatic and military stalemate carried over into 1981. In an effort to improve its international reputation, Khmer Rouge leaders had replaced Pol Pot with Khieu Samphan, at least titularly. Khmer Rouge forces, thanks to China's largesse, had by now regrouped and numbered an estimated thirty to thirty-five thousand. In addition, the Khmer People's National Liberation Front (KPNLF), headed by Son Sann, a former prime minister in the old Sihanouk government, fielded perhaps five thousand guerrillas; Prince Norodom Sihanouk, the former quixotic ruler of Cambodia who in 1975 had enthusiastically endorsed the Khmer Rouge cause, was putting together what would become the non-communist Sihanouk National Army (ANS) with the aid of Chinese arms and equipment.[53] Grave differences abounded in the insurgent camps, however. Son Sann refused to work with the despised Khmer Rouge, nor would he serve under Sihanouk. The Khmer Rouge had dedicated itself to drive the Vietnamese and the puppet PRK government out of the country, a stance endorsed by its patron, China. Contrarily, Son Sann and Sihanouk favored a negotiated settlement that would keep the Khmer Rouge from returning to power. Despite these and other differences, the three groups in 1982 formed the Coalition Government of Democratic Kampuchea (CGDK) with Sihanouk as president, Khieu Samphan as vice-president and Son Sann as prime minister.

The war meanwhile had settled into a give-and-take affair with one side then the other gaining the upper hand. Vietnamese and PRK forces generally took the offensive during the dry season (November to May) but were unable to claim any outstanding victories. The rebel forces continued to grow. In 1984, the Khmer Rouge army counted an estimated forty thousand troops maintained by frequent large shipments of arms and equipment that arrived in Thailand by boat from China. Sihanouk's ANS numbered about ten thousand and Son Sann's force had also increased. Co-ordinated operations might have brought better results, but these were not to be. Each group occupied its separate enclaves and fought its own war, the Khmer Rouge being by far the most active.

The military stalemate radically altered in early 1985 when a series of large-scale attacks by twenty to twenty-five thousand Vietnamese and PRK troops, supported by heavy artillery, tanks and aircraft, methodically eliminated the guerrilla camps inside the Kampuchean border, forcing the insurgents to disperse and retreat into Thailand. Although they eventually regrouped, they were unable to resume normal operations for a considerable period.

1050

The guerrillas nevertheless slowly recovered and, despite large numbers of enemy troops deployed along the border, resumed often effective hit-and-run raids that underlined the indisputable fact that an expensive stalemate existed. The Vietnamese Government in particular had made a serious error in embarking on a course of imperialistic expansion before putting its economic house in order. Unable to manage its own economy, it had been suddenly faced with having to manage Kampuchea's affairs, in essence of having to oversee and fund a rebuilding of the country. Russia at first was willing to make the heavy financial investment which seemed to be justified by the potential strategic return. Already in 1982, Vietnam was receiving from the Soviet Union about $3 million a day—$1.1 billion a year—and Kampuchea additional enormous sums, expenditures that continued for the next several years. In 1986, however, Mikhail Gorbachev made the Kremlin take a hard look at the Southeast Asia investment. The look hardened in 1987 when it was evident that the Soviet Union was on the verge of a financial crisis and, as one result, was almost desperately seeking rapprochement with Washington and Peking (Beijing). Since a major obstacle to this tack was the war in Kampuchea, the Kremlin now began to pressure Hanoi to withdraw its forces from Kampuchea as a first step in ending what had become an unwanted war.

Hanoi did not fail to grasp the significance of this development. For some time it had realized the cost of rampant imperialism. An empty treasury taken with a moribund economy had made survival almost totally dependent on the Soviet Union. If the Soviet goose dried up, Hanoi would find it difficult to keep alive, let alone sustain the Kampuchean venture. In 1987, the government announced that it was withdrawing twenty thousand troops from Kampuchea, a propitiatory move directed toward the U.S. and China in the hope of eventually attracting sufficient investment to compensate for waning Soviet patronage. In 1988, Hanoi removed another fifty thousand troops along with the Vietnamese senior command headquarters.[54] The economic situation was now so serious that in November, Hanoi decided to give priority to reshaping the economy, which could be done only by a 50 per cent cut in military spending in 1990.[55] In September 1989, the last forces were withdrawn (although some units may have returned in response to increased Khmer Rouge operations).

The message had become clear to the PRK government in Phnom Penh with the first departure of Vietnamese troops: the weight of the war would soon fall on its militarily weak shoulders. The same faults that had bedeviled Lon Nol's army—corrupt and unqualified commanders; inept tactics; communication and supply failures; low morale—made it doubtful if the government could survive a sustained Khmer Rouge offensive, a fear shared by a good many other governments. As one result, Hun Sen, who had replaced Heng Samrin, changed political direction by tilting toward a capitalist economy while murmuring soft words to the United States and China, indeed to the world, in the hope of gaining the political and financial support necessary if it came to peace negotiations with his opponents.[56]

Thailand too was tiring of the border war. Chatichai Chunhavan, who became prime minister in August 1988, wanted Indochina to change "from a battlefield to a marketplace," a goal he emphasized by a new political flexibility that included the unprecedented act of inviting Hun Sen to Bangkok, to the consternation of Thailand's ASEAN partners.[57] This promising initiative was abruptly canceled in early 1991 by a military coup and Chunhavan's fall from power, but at least it emphasized the need for direct talks with the principal parties.

Exploratory talks already had occurred in late 1987 and these led to a generally fruitless series of conferences and formal meetings. Hopes were high for a breakthrough at the Paris conference in July and August 1989, but once again stalemate resulted.

So it was that the hurdles leading to a negotiated peace were high, the runners slow and awkward. As one expert put it, " . . . Clearly, the best outcome for Cambodia would be a comprehensive political settlement that demilitarized the internal struggle, neutralized Cambodia as an arena for superpower and regional rivalry, and gave the Khmer people an opportunity for free and fair elections."[58] If few could fault this, the few included the three groups of the CGDK and the incumbent PRK. As president of the CGDK, Prince Sihanouk proposed a quadripartite formula that basically called for dissolving the CGDK and PRK in favor of sharing power on a four-party basis under United Nations supervision until elections could be arranged.[59] Prime Minister Hun Sen of the PRK, on the other hand, wanted a " . . . ceasefire in place and a continuation of the political status quo—the PRK regime—until general elections" that would be organized by a "steering committee" and held under United Nations supervision.[60] Neither proposal was accepted but each was getting warm.

The impasse was broken by two unlikely sources, a United States congressman from New York, Stephen J. Solarz, whose basic plan formed the foundation for a subsequent diplomatic initiative by Australia's foreign minister. As worked out, the plan essentially turned the problem over to the United Nations, which would arrange and police a cease-fire, install an interim government, demobilize and disarm the opposing forces, repatriate nearly four hundred thousand refugees, and, finally, organize and monitor a general election to take place in spring of 1993. Although this plan circumvented a number of earlier objections, it was faulted because of the very high cost (an estimated $2 billion) of UN participation and because there was no surety that the

UN was capable of running the government in the interim phase. It would probably not have been accepted by Prime Minister Hun Sen had Hanoi not put on the pressure and kept it on—in return for limited rapprochement with and a promise of economic aid from the United States if all went well.

All of course did not go well. The peace accords were signed in October 1991 after months of furious squabbling between the four factions and various concerned governments. The first troops—a contingent of about two hundred men—of the UN peacekeeping force arrived in early November, but owing to budgetary and other problems the build-up to ten thousand peacekeepers vital to the peace process was delayed until December. In mid-November, Prince Norodom Sihanouk returned to a warm welcome in the capital and took charge of a "national reconciliation council" (Supreme National Council) that would run the coalition government until elections were held in 1993.

It was scarcely a pacific atmosphere. Shortly after Sihanouk's return, the Khmer Rouge accused him of collusion with Hun Sen in an attempt to limit Khieu Samphan's influence in the new government. Khieu Samphan's arrival in Phnom Penh created new problems in that he was attacked, beaten, and nearly lynched by a furious mob which prompted him to flee only eight hours after he arrived.[61] Only upon Khieu Samphan's return did the Supreme National Council hold its first inaugural meeting, which seems to have been an exercise in futility. By February, Khmer Rouge agents were busily destabilizing Hun Sen's already wobbly government while its guerrillas were grabbing as much government land as possible in the central and northwestern provinces. In February, fighting broke out between government forces and the Khmer Rouge,[62] and had increased in intensity by late March.[63]

Although the arrival of the main body of the UN peacekeepers bolstered general morale, it did not rub off on the Khmer Rouge, which predictably displayed an openly obstructive policy, refusing to allow UN monitors into their areas and rejecting the second phase of the plan, which called for each group to demobilize 70 per cent of its strength.[64]

Khmer Rouge destructive tactics carried into autumn as UN strength rose above twenty thousand. A three-month boycott of the Council was broken only by a threat of UN sanctions, but few believed that renewed talks would lead to partial demobilization as called for by the Accords. By end of October, the Khmer Rouge was again boycotting Council meetings. In the following months, Pol Pot and Khieu Samphan did everything possible to sabotage the peace plan. Roads were mined, trains and bridges blown up, "traitors" shot, UN voter-registration teams fired on, UN personnel seized and held prisoners, UN teams kept from operating in Khmer Rouge–controlled areas. Also contributing to the mayhem were President Hun Sen's security forces doing all they could to intimidate supporters of Prince Norodom Ranariddh's royalist party, Funcinpec, several members of which were assassinated during the pre-election campaign.

All to no avail. Thanks to the determination and courage of the 22,000-man UN command, UNTAC, headed by veteran Japanese diplomat Yasushi Akashi, with its military arm commanded by the no-nonsense Australian Lieutenant General John Sanderson, and thanks to the overwhelming desire of the Cambodian people for peace, an amazing 4.6 million or 90 percent of eligible voters went to the polls in spring of 1993.[65]

Despite militant Khmer Rouge threats that continued to the last minute, the polls opened on schedule on May 23 and closed five days later, a "free and fair" election, according to UN observers (and a surprisingly peaceful one after all the Khmer Rouge bluster). The winner was Prince Norodom Ranariddh, the forty-nine-year-old son of Prince Norodom Sihanouk, the seventy-year-old former king, who returned to Cambodia from exile in China. Ranariddh's royalist party, Funcinpec, won a surprising 46 percent of the vote and fifty-eight seats in the new constituent assembly; Hun Sen's ruling CPP won 38 percent of the vote and fifty-one seats. Although the royalist party lacked the necessary majority to form a new government, Ranariddh managed to convene the constituent assembly, whose 120 members set about writing the new constitution that was called for in the 1991 peace accords.

When it had become apparent that Funcipec was winning the election, furious CPP leaders cried foul and demanded a new election in several provinces. Despite or perhaps because of the old Prince Norodom Sihanouk's somewhat convoluted ministrations as head of state, a new civil war loomed for several tense weeks as Hun Sen, refusing to accept election results, refused to leave office. If Sihanouk contributed to the confusion, he also in part resolved it by arbitrarily dissolving the government and proclaiming himself " . . . chief of state, prime minister and supreme commander of the Cambodian armed forces, reserves and police."[66] Although this declaration precipitated another series of crises, a kind of peace was reached by Sihanouk who appointed his son and Hun Sen "co-prime ministers," a power-sharing arrangement that disallowed the Khmer Rouge (which had boycotted the elections) any say in government.

Khmer Rouge guerrillas now began attacking army outposts. Simultaneously, however, Khieu Samphan (with Pol Pot looking over his shoulder) offered to merge his ten thousand guerrillas with the new national army and to yield control of his domains (about 20 percent of Cambodia) in return for a place in that government. This deal might have gone through in one form or another but for the adamant refusal of Western nations, in particular the United States, which threatened to cancel an $880 million aid program if the government accepted Samphan's proposal. Since the government was broke (civil and military wages being months in arrears), it had little choice but to back down. Intensified Khmer Rouge attacks followed, but in August the new army responded in strength to force the guerrillas from recently seized army outposts.

The next surprise came in September when Norodom Sihanouk and his son arbitrarily decreed that Cambodia was a constitutional monarchy with Sihanouk as king. Sihanouk at once appointed his son first prime minister and Hun Sen second prime minister, a coalition government approved in October by the new parliament, along with a new constitution. By this time, however, Sihanouk was in Beijing undergoing treatment for cancer and not expected to return to Cambodia until spring of 1994.

Although departure of most of the UN command during November passed without undue incident (excepting the theft of millions of dollars worth of its vehicles and other equipment),[67] the government must surmount a great many hurdles if it is to survive. Prince Ranariddh has continued trying to persuade Khmer Rouge leaders to break up their private army and yield control of their operational areas to the government. Sihanouk recently changed his tune, which is not unusual, and announced that selected Khmer Rouge officials would be given governmental posts if the Khmer Rouge surrendered,[68] an offer soon retracted owing to the objection of Prince Ranariddh.[69]

Despite its still significant strength, the Khmer Rouge should not be able to topple the government, providing that the latter's present strength (December 1993) is maintained, and it is possible that in time Khieu Samphan (but not Pol Pot) will be allowed a place in government. Considering the government's disparate elements, however, not to mention the widespread corruption that infests its ranks, the road ahead will be rocky, particularly if King Sihanouk should die. Sihanouk and his son nonetheless seem to be generally optimistic as regards the future. For the sake of the long-suffering Cambodian people, we must hope that this guarded optimism is not misplaced.

CHAPTER EIGHTY

1. Nixon, *Memoirs*, 691–2.
2. Shawcross, 261.
3. Nixon, *Memoirs*, 699. See also, Snepp, 78.
4. Nixon, *Memoirs*, 718. See also, Snepp, 88: " ... It [the President's statement to Thieu] was the opening flourish in Washington's postwar commitment to South Vietnam, one on which the U.S. Congress would never be consulted."
5. Snepp, 29.
6. Fallaci, 30. See also, Haldeman, 84.
7. Kissinger, *Years of Upheaval*, 369.

8. Isaacs, 142.
9. Ibid., 61.
10. Snepp, 51.
11. Karnow, 658. See also, Shawcross, 260.
12. Snepp, 48.
13. Ibid., 48–9. My italics.
14. Isaacs, 84.
15. Snepp, 50.
16. Karnow, 657.
17. Isaacs, 49. The Vietnamese had more planes than pilots; according to a later U.S. Air Force study, the force of over 3,000 combat aircraft was " . . . completely beyond their ability to maintain."
18. Snepp, 103, who quotes from an official GAO report for the two years following the so-called cease-fire:

   . . . over $200 million of materiél had been lost or squandered by the South Vietnamese during the same period. . . . Large amounts of equipment, it said, had been stolen or sold illegally to the Communists. Among the items listed as "missing" or "unaccounted for": 143 small warships valued at $37 million; $2 million worth of ammunition, declared unusable because of poor storage; and $10 million in small arms which had simply disappeared from supply depots. . . . The Pentagon and the Defense Attaché's Office [in Saigon], in an effort to reconcile the separate balance sheets, simply wrote off $44 million in military aid. . . . The American taxpayer, in short, was asked to subsidize Saigon's corruption, and the Vietnamese foot soldier was obliged to die for it.

19. Ibid., 78, 99–101.
20. International Institute for Strategic Studies, *Strategic Survey 1973*, 73.
21. Ibid.
22. Karnow, 659.
23. Snepp, 55.
24. International Institute for Strategic Studies, *Strategic Survey 1973*, 70. See also, Snepp, 55–6.
25. Karnow, 659.
26. Ibid., 659–60.
27. Snepp, 91.
28. Woodward and Bernstein, 54 ff.
29. International Institute for Strategic Studies, *Strategic Survey 1973*, 73.
30. Isaacs, 161. " . . . This was approximately the tonnage dropped by U.S. air forces in all of World War II in both the European and Pacific Theaters of war."
31. International Institute for Strategic Studies, *Strategic Survey 1973*, 74. See also, Isaacs, 175–89.
32. Karnow, 663.
33. Kiernan, 338.
34. Ibid., 357.
35. Snepp, 51.
36. Shawcross, 350.
37. Kiernan, 390.
38. Ibid., 391.
39. Shawcross, 264, 271–2, 275–6.
40. Snepp, 97.
41. Shawcross, 313.
42. International Institute for Strategic Studies, *Strategic Survey 1973*, 74.
43. Snepp, 123.
44. Ibid., 113–14.

45. Ibid., 185.
46. Shawcross, 389.
47. The International Institute for Strategic Studies, *Strategic Survey 1977,* 84.
48. Ibid., 84–5. See also, Shawcross, 385 ff.
49. International Institute for Strategic Studies, *Strategic Survey 1979,* 57.
50. Ibid., 58.
51. Ibid. *1980–81,* 100.
52. Ibid., 99.
53. Shawcross, 378–80.
54. International Institute for Strategic Studies, *Strategic Survey 1988–89,* 114.
55. Ibid., 116.
56. Richburg, 118.
57. Ibid., 119.
58. Solarz, 99.
59. Ibid., 104.
60. Ibid.
61. *International Herald Tribune,* November 28, 1991.
62. *Newsweek,* February 10, 1992.
63. *International Herald Tribune,* March 27, 1992. See also, *The Independent* (U.K.), March 31, 1992.
64. *International Herald Tribune,* June 13–14, 1992. See also, *Newsweek,* June 29, 1992.
65. *International Herald Tribune,* April 17–18, November 15, 1993.
66. Ibid., June 9, 1993.
67. Ibid., September 3, 1993.
68. Ibid., November 23, 1993.
69. Ibid., December 2, 1993.

PART FOUR

THEN UNTIL NOW:
A SURVEY

Anyone is a criminal who promotes an avoid-
able war; and so is he who does not promote
an inevitable civil war.

JOSÉ MARTÍ—HERO OF THE 1895 CUBAN REVOLUTION

CHAPTER 81

The Latin American problem: poverty, guerrillas, and drug barons • Venezuela's short insurgency • The Guatemala experience • Raúl Sendic's Tupamoros of Uruguay

> It is the time of the furnaces, and it is only necessary to see the glow.[1]
>
> JOSÉ MARTI

ALTHOUGH THE twenty countries of Central and South America differ greatly in size, population and natural resources, their peoples share a great many things in common, not least of which is a growing desire to participate in the community of democratic nations. They also share a tragic history of foreign rule that decimated their peoples and reduced their resources. That was followed by economic exploitation by foreign interests whose governments did not hesitate to intervene militarily when necessary to preserve the political, economic, and social status quo of a small, wealthy elite controlling a repressive police and army. This explains in part many decades of authoritarian government, mostly by the military, with concomitant political assassinations, civil rights abuses, and some of the most inefficient, corrupt, and ruthless dictators in the history of the world, an unpleasant state of affairs difficult to contravene owing both to the highly passionate Latin American temperament which frequently militates against political stability, and in most of the countries to the slow growth of a stabilizing middle class with members intent on pursuing a career of public service. As a young Argentinian diplomat recently explained to me, suitably qualified persons such as university graduates regard politics more "as an opportunity to improve one's financial and social standing . . . rather than a chance to serve one's people."

This general middle class non-involvement in, indeed scorn of politics helps to explain the slow progress of today's reformist governments

in reversing a disastrous legacy: a tradition of corruption at all levels of government (including police and military); antiquated and wasteful farming production and distribution; massive child labor—at least " . . . 30 million children aged ten to fourteen" at work today, of whom perhaps fifteen million are working and often living in the streets;[2] rabbit-warren slums with no running water, no electricity, no toilets— " . . . an estimated 100 million people without adequate drinking water";[3] vast numbers of unemployed in the cities and countryside; landowning elites sufficiently rich and powerful to torpedo land distribution and other vital programs; an appalling shortage of elementary schools and qualified teachers, thus high rates of illiteracy; poor and in some cases no medical and social services (with noteworthy exceptions such as Uruguay), thus the inevitable rampant endemic diseases (including the present cholera epidemic, the first in a century); finally, the result in large part of Roman Catholic teachings to illiterate peasants, ever-mounting birthrates in countries where over half the population is living below the poverty line and which have a high percentage of the population under fifteen years of age—despite the death of nearly one million children " . . . under five years of age every year."[4] Should the reader think this is alarmist writing, I refer him or her to country-by-country statistics presented in the elegant 1991 edition of the *Encyclopaedia Britannica,* which, together with the indispensable *Annual Register and Record of World Events, Keesing's Contemporary Archives, Keesing's Record of World Events, Facts on File,* and the impressive publications of the prestigious International Institute for Strategic Studies, I have relied on heavily for this survey.

Adding to the burden of contemporary reformist governments is an understandable tradition of insurrections attempted and sometimes carried out by guerrilla warfare. Initially sporadic, these efforts were greatly encouraged by the successful Russian Revolution—during the last seven decades, scores of guerrilla bands and organizations have sprung into existence. Nurtured by Marxian seeds planted in the fertile ground of human hopelessness, watered by repression instead of weakened by reform, cultivated by Russian gold and Western greed, fertilized by Fidel Castro's seizure of Cuba in 1959, these rural guerrilla and urban guerrilla terrorist movements, by challenging established governments, have brought nightmares of violence to countries around the world.

It did not take long for the shock waves of the Cuban revolution to roll over Latin America. The fallout was intense. All the ingredients necessary for revolution were abundantly on hand in Latin America when Fidel Castro became Cuba's ruler and chief guru of guerrilla wars of liberation designed to turn Latin America into one gigantic Communist camp.

Most of the insurgencies that followed were not co-ordinated. They occurred at different times and places under different conditions and in a number of forms. At first, the emphasis was on Maoist-Castro rural strategy: " . . . In the underdeveloped Americas," Che Guevara wrote, "the countryside must be the basic formula for the armed struggle."[5] Guevara's failure in fomenting a rural guerrilla war in Bolivia (see Chapter 57) and the failure of other rural uprisings in Guatemala, Colombia, Peru, Venezuela, and Chile brought an insurgency turnaway from Mao Tse-tung back to basic Marxist-Leninist urban guerrilla warfare. " . . . Today the epicenter of the war must be in the great urban zones," the Spanish anarchist Abraham Guillén insisted.[6] "The urban guerrilla's reasons for existence," wrote Carlos Marighela, "the basic condition in which he acts and survives, is to shoot."[7]

A wave of urban insurgencies fueled by the New Left revolutionary thinking propounded by Herbert Marcuse, Guillén, Marighela, Régis Debray, and other radical commentators now swept over the hemisphere and indeed the world, its hallmark violence: robbery, extortion, kidnaping, assassination, airplane hijackings, mass murder by indiscriminate bombing. Techniques and goals varied. Headlines beginning in the late 1960s were claimed for a decade by groups consisting of social dropouts who practiced random terrorist acts with only nebulous goals such as a demand for world revolution: the Black Panthers, the Weathermen, and the Symbionese Liberation Army in the United States, the Japanese Red Army, the Red Army Faction (Baader-Meinhof) in West Germany, the Angry Brigade in Great Britain, the Red Brigades in Italy, Middle Eastern groups that splintered from the Palestine Liberation Organization such as the Popular Front for the Liberation of Palestine-General Command and Abu Nidal's terrorists based in and supported by Libya—to name only a few. Leroy Eldridge Cleaver, Angela Davis, Patty Hearst, Ulrike Meinhof, Andreas Baader, Daniel Cohn-Bendit, and others became the darlings of the militant radicals, but not for long. Society in general soon came to regard them as very dangerous criminals to be dealt with by law enforcement agencies, as indeed they were. After flourishing in the late 1960s and early 1970s, their activities slowed and frequently stopped as many of their leaders were imprisoned or killed, some by members of the same organization. A few remain active today, seemingly more interested in practicing terror for terror's sake than in bringing about world revolution.

This was only one category of urban guerrilla terrorist groups. The other category consisted of groups with specific goals, particularly those operating in conjunction with rural guerrilla movements, which lasted somewhat longer. Failure to build a secure political base—the *bête noir* of urban guerrilla groups—eventually caught up with the majority of them. If they made life hell for many citizens, if they toppled some governments, if they drastically damaged economies, they nevertheless often forced political, social, and economic reforms necessary if their countries were to enter the democratic mainstream to provide some hope for the millions of their peoples.

Generally they did not in the end prosper. Generally they either dried up or converted to legitimate political parties or remained a small, often fragmented force in being responsible for an occasional bank robbery or kidnaping or assassination—a challenge to security forces but not a major threat to government. There are exceptions: today they remain a serious threat to the governments of Colombia and Peru.

Now comes the irony. When most Latin American governments were gaining on the guerrillas, when some reforms were starting to take hold, when some guerrilla supporters and sympathizers were tiring of seemingly endless internecine warfare with its daily ration of bombs and corpses, a new element emerged to enlarge political, economic, social, and security problems a thousandfold. That element was drugs, at first to feed the huge North American market, where the same factors that fueled guerrilla movements in Latin America—unemployment, poverty, illiteracy, and disease—combined to provide one of the most lucrative markets for any product in world history.

Rather than recognize the problem at home and treat it as the crisis it is, rather than take emergency action (and damn the cost) to begin eliminating the desire and need for drugs, the American government in large part shifted the blame to the drug-producing and drug-trafficking countries, mainly to Peru, Colombia, Bolivia, and Panama, with tentacles all over the place. The school solution to the problem as seen in the Reagan and Bush administrations was to eliminate drug production. The U. S. Drug Enforcement Administration (DEA), which had nearly secreted itself out of existence, suddenly became a household word. Millions of dollars were given over to suppression programs. Teams of experts were sent to target countries; ships patrolled the seas, airplanes combed the skies—and they are doing so today.

The rise of the drug barons was a boon to Latin American guerrillas, who had been finding it not so easy to carry on, what with funds from extortion, robberies, and kidnapings shrinking, what with Castro's quasi-defection from their cause in 1983, what with increasingly effective government countermeasures and reduced popular support, what with Mikhail Gorbachev's turnaway from exported revolution followed by a bankrupt and crumbling Soviet Union. But by 1989, some guerrilla leaders had long since found a two-way bonanza, first in selling Mafia-style "protection" to peasant coca growers, second in selling services to drug barons, anything from murdering political opponents to protecting roads and hidden airstrips and processing and refining areas from government forces in return for heaps of hard cash, their perverted rationale presumably being that they were serving the revolutionary cause by contributing significantly to the decline of capitalist and Western society (and so they were—and are).

So it was that at an already difficult time a new and disturbing factor entered into the age-old challenge of fighting insurgency warfare. It will probably not be the last, and in time it will probably be countered if concerned governments and guerrilla movements will come to their senses, and if Western societies will open crash programs to get their children off the streets and back into schools and jobs. As will be seen in the following survey, in several Latin American countries guerrilla warfare is still alive and well or at least nascent; in other countries where it has been suppressed often at a great cost to political, economic, and social structures, the threat of renewed guerrilla outbreaks remains—this in proportion to the strength and achievements of reformist governments.

One of the early and certainly one of the most curious insurgencies inspired by Fidel Castro's seizure of Cuba in 1959 sprang up in Venezuela. In spring of 1960, a group of young militants in Caracas formed the Movement of the Revolutionary Left (MIR) under Cuban auspices. In addition to money received from extortion, the group embarked on a profitable series of robberies, kidnapings, and hijackings of ships and planes. Cuba supplied most of its arms, trained recruits in Cuban camps, and supplied veteran guerrilla "advisers" who fought in MIR ranks. In its formative years, the MIR insurgency was largely confined to terrorist acts in the cities but in 1962, the insurgency was joined by members of the Venezuelan Communist Party (PCV), which founded another guerrilla group, the Armed Forces of National Liberation (FALN), also Cuban-inspired since at this time Castro was intent on exporting revolution to Latin America and had hit upon Venezuela as a pilot model.

Castro's model did not turn out too well. Although MIR grew steadily in the 1960s, in particular attracting students to its banner, internal dissension was already weakening its effort. The villain was MIR excesses, which upset life in the cities to lose the movement much of its popular support. With public blessing, President Romulo Betancourt authorized a counterinsurgency campaign that severely blunted MIR operations. First to desert the movement was its founder. He was followed in the mid-1960s by a large number of rank-and file who believed that it was futile to continue armed violence. By 1970, the movement was moribund although a few splinter groups carried on guerrilla operations in one form or another. The MIR itself recovered politically and in the mid-1970s won representation in the national assembly. It remained radically left but did not return to guerrilla operations. The defection of Cuba from the goal of a Communist Latin America, the demise of Communist Russia, and the end of insurgencies in Nicargua and El Salvador damaged its political importance, but it remains a potential force in the turbulence of Venezuelan politics.

The FALN did not fare so well. A number of its members soon began to resent Communist Party emphasis on urban instead of guerrilla war. The break came in 1966 when its leader, Douglas Bravo, a former Politburo member, acted without PCV authority and was expelled from the party, taking most of the FALN guerrillas with him. Bravo's two major lieutenants did not share his faith in a rural strategy and a major rift soon developed. As with the MIR, other members grew disillusioned with the armed struggle and left the group. Once Castro's darling, Bravo grew increasingly distant from the Cuban leader, and by the end of the decade embraced a Maoist strategy while openly criticizing Castro in his widely disseminated writings. Around 1970, the FALN dissolved into a number of splinter groups which in one form or another carried on the struggle until the late 1970s, when it vanished from the scene.[8]

A third group appeared in 1969 with the fall of the MIR. That was the Red Flag Party (PBR) led by Gabriel Puerta Aponte and consisting of about a hundred guerrillas from the MIR. Never large, the PBR funded itself by bank robberies and ransoms derived from kidnaping wealthy Venezuelan ranchers; it was also supported by Cuba and by sympathetic South American revolutionary movements. It suffered a severe setback with Puerta's arrest in 1981 followed by a successful police operation two years later that netted thirteen of its "international terrorists." Factionalism also damaged its operations and public appeal. It is still alive, a member of Venezuela's leftist political group, and is believed to be working with the Colombian ELN in protecting the drug routes from Colombia into Venezuela, from where the cocaine is shipped to foreign markets.[9]

Drug trafficking in Venezuela has grown to the extent that in 1992 President Andrés Pérez ordered "all-out war" on the traffickers, a particularly courageous move considering his own precarious position as survivor of two recent military coup attempts. Unfortunately, his "war" dissolved into political scandal in spring of 1993 when he was forced from office to stand trial, along with several political associates, on charges of massive corruption. After months of political turbulence, including several bombings, December elections installed seventy-seven-year-old Rafael Caldera Rodríguez as the new conservative president. Considering the close election results, the meager election turnout (reportedly less than 10 percent of the eligible voters), and the weak state of the economy, the chances are that the PBR not only will survive but, in view of the power of the international drug barons, may even prosper.

Guatemala's insurrectionary problems go back nearly fifty years. Continued governmental failure to give the people a fair shake spurred the growth of liberal and Marxist movements until in 1944 a general strike toppled a weak interim government to place organized labor in a dominant political position. This social revolution, inherited by Guatemala's first popularly elected president, philosophy professor Juan José Arévalo Bermejo, brought a new labor code and some land reforms, but it was hindered by internecine quarrels and coup attempts, during which Guatemalan Communists captured the labor movement and helped to elect the leftist politician Jacobo Arbenz Guzmán to the presidency in 1951.

A need for land reform had long been obvious. The major villain was the United Fruit Company, a United States company which had kept numerous Guatemalan dictators in its pocket. In 1953, United Fruit owned 42 percent of Guatemala's land yet was growing bananas on only 139,000 of its three million acres.[10] This lopsided situation was threatened by an agrarian reform law that authorized the Arbenz government to expropriate 225,000 acres of uncultivated land for distribution to landless peasants.

The United Fruit Company is a very powerful organization with a lot of important friends. In 1953, these included John Foster Dulles, Eisenhower's Secretary of State; Allen Dulles, chief of CIA; retired army General Walter Bedell Smith, Under Secretary of State; Henry Cabot Lodge, U.S. ambassador to the United Nations; and John Moors Cabot, Assistant Secretary of State for Inter-American Affairs. In 1953, United Fruit spent a great deal of money in hiring public relations firms to circulate a total message to the effect that " . . . Guatemala was ruled by Communists bent on conquering Central America and seizing the Panama Canal."[11] The company's influential friends and a fair portion of an uninformed electorate readily accepted this warning. According to Eisenhower, John Moors Cabot convinced him that Guatemala was " . . . openly playing the Communist game,"[12] an assertion substantially reinforced by the new ambassador to Guatemala, John Peurifoy.[13]

Arbenz in reality was playing the reform game. Edward Rice, a retired senior American diplomat has recently pointed out that no Communists held cabinet-level or army command posts, and of fifty-one deputies in Arbenz's ruling coalition four were Communists. That there was a Communist influence at working levels and in labor unions was true enough. That was perfectly legitimate (and certainly understandable), and it was also true that Guatemala had consistently supported

1068

the United States on major cold war issues in the United Nations.[14]

This was the situation when Eisenhower authorized the CIA to open a covert campaign designed to overthrow Arbenz. It began with a misinformation campaign that put the Guatemalan government " . . . in a false light abroad and [created] fear and uncertainty within."[15] After bribing a suitable numer of Guatemalan army officers, the CIA sent in a force of Guatemalan dissident exiles and mercenaries commanded by dissident Carlos Castillo Armas with a small air cover provided by CIA. Castillo's "Liberation Army" invaded in June 1954 and probably would have failed in its mission had President Eisenhower not authorized additional air power.[16] Although there was no popular rising against the Arbenz government and no army mutiny, neither was there army support for Arbenz, who resigned and took refuge in Mexico. He was eventually replaced by Castillo. Backed by the Eisenhower administration, this "farseeing and able statesman" (in Eisenhower's words)[17] canceled all reform programs (and returned the expropriated land to the United Fruit Company). He was assassinated three years later. His replacement, General Miguel Ydígoras Fuentes, provided the CIA with secret training areas for the Cuban invasion, an unpopular move that precipitated an uprising of army officers in 1960, put down with CIA help. Some surviving officers fled to the hills, where they organized diverse guerrilla bands and called for a national revolution. The Guatemalan army put a stop to this—the bands were soon decimated, most of their leaders killed.

Guatemala was ruled by military government for the next nearly twenty-five disastrous years. All attempts at reform either failed or were so watered down as to be meaningless. Shrinking world markets and rampant inflation fueled in large part by inept administration and massive corruption increased general dissatisfaction until at times virtual civil war existed. Guerrilla terrorist murders of two U.S. military advisers and the U.S. ambassador in 1968 and of the German ambassador in 1970 were answered in kind by security forces. Violence escalated. Suspected dissidents, those who had earlier supported liberal presidents—students, trade unionists, doctors, lawyers, teachers—were hunted down by death squads composed of urban guerrilla terrorists of the right condoned and often encouraged by the security forces. Simultaneously, massive counterinsurgency campaigns cleansed the countryside to the extent that one official study put the number of children who had lost one or both parents at 110,000.[18] Such was the carnage that in 1977, President Carter cut off military aid to the government.[19]

That solved nothing. General Romeo Lucas García, who became president in 1978, at once turned loose paramilitary bands to wipe out " . . . the social democratic parties and the left-leaning labor and peasant organizations that had been allowed to emerge in the mid-1970s."[20]

It was not a good time for freedom. " . . . Literally hundreds of non-violent opposition leaders were murdered and many more were sent into exile."[21] By 1982, the killings totaled perhaps thirteen thousand.[22] That scarcely squelched the guerrilla opposition, " . . . which for the first time in history succeeded in mobilizing important sectors of the Indian community, which comprises over half of the total population. . . . As repression grew in the countryside, so did guerrilla strength and renewed activity."[23]

Fraudulent elections held in 1982 in an attempt to persuade Washington to renew military aid led to another coup that installed a born-again Christian, General Efraín Rios Montt, in the presidency. Montt managed to restrain the more violent activities of the death squads while launching a counterinsurgency offensive designed to bring the countryside under government control. In six months, this effort resulted in an estimated five thousand Indian deaths, some 250,000 Indians displaced from their villages, thirty thousand refugees who fled into Mexico, and fifty thousand villagers press-ganged into civil patrols whose mission was to kill any surviving dissidents.[24] Despite this abominable record, Rios persuaded President Ronald Reagan to lift the arms embargo and resume selling arms to the Guatemalan Government, albeit in limited quantities. As Christopher Dickey has pointed out, there seems little doubt that Rios' strong-arm methods coerced a great many villagers, at least temporarily, into passive acceptance of the regime.[25]

Leaving aside his failure to repair an ailing economy, Rios got into political trouble by yielding to the dictates of his California Protestant evangelists over those of his predominantly Catholic generals.[26] Ousted by a military coup in late 1983, he was replaced by his defense minister, who soon turned the government to shambles. In 1985, when thousands of peasants were dying from malnutrition and when Guatemala City was rocked by massive riots, the militarists finally bowed to regional and international protests and allowed an election.

The election was won by a political moderate member of the Christian Democratic Party, Marco Vinicio Cerezo, who had escaped three assassination attempts by death squads. Vinicio's efforts to demilitarize "a thoroughly militarized country" and to consolidate " . . . a democratic process in a country with almost no real civilian institutions"[27] were from the beginning hamstrung by military overseers working hand in hand with the country's economic elite.[28] The new president, who inherited the worst depression in half a century, instituted an austerity program that met with only partial success. Though officially proscribed, death squads continued their violence in the cities, where their activities were increasingly challenged by urban guerrilla terrorists until killings and counterkillings became the order of the day. Renewal of military aid by the Reagan administration, inspired in part by the growing insurgency in El Salvador and the CIA effort to topple the Sandinista government in Nicaragua, enabled the thirty-thousand man army to expand counterguerrilla operations. Various guerrilla bands responded by forming the Guatemalan National Revolution Unity (URNG) of perhaps a total of two thousand hard-core guerrillas. Some hope for an eventual compromise peace appeared in August 1987 when Guatemala joined with other Central American countries in signing the regional Arias peace plan that called for Central America to solve its own problems without the help of external powers.

This could not take place overnight. Vinicio's increasingly inept and corrupt government survived but could not tame military extremists, who continued political assassinations, kidnapings, and torture while remaining immune from prosecution.[29] In December 1989, a general officer told a graduating class of the army's elite counterinsurgency corps to " . . . forget all humanitarian principles and become war machines . . . because from now on, they will be called Masters of War and Messengers of Death."[30] Anyone suspected of being a leftist rebel was fair game for arrest and often execution; peasant villages suspected of aiding leftist rebels were wiped out.[31]

Vinicio's humiliating defeat in the November 1990 elections brought some important and hopeful changes to this ugly state of affairs. The new president, Jorge Serrano Elias, a right-wing Protestant evangelist, promised to end the thirty-year-old civil war that had cost an estimated 120,000 deaths and resulted in what he called "a culture of death." After surviving an assassination attempt shortly after taking office, Serrano started well by having government officials and military officers meet with guerrilla heads of the URNG (which unfortunately came to nothing). He also gained kudos by replacing the military head of the national police force with a civilian who fired three thousand policemen within ten months. Members of the armed forces "for the first time" were " . . . charged with violations of human rights."[32]

Unfortunately these reforms were more cosmetic than real. Serrano's reign ended in spring of 1993 when, beset by critics for failing to end the thirty-two-year-old insurgency, by a deteriorating economy, and by one of the worst human rights records in the world, he summarily dissolved congress and the supreme court—an *autogolpe,* or one-man coup, that at once caused the U.S. government to suspend a $30 million aid program. This action, taken with massive civil protests, caused military chiefs to back away from the self-proclaimed dictator, whose regime lasted only a week before a bloodless military counter-coup forced him into hurried exile. Within days, the Guatemalan congress elected a new president, a human rights activist, Ramon León Carpio.

Although Guatemala's fragile democracy had seemingly survived, Leon's new government has had its hands full in trying to right the country's many wrongs. Several thousand kids still roaming the streets are systematically beaten, tortured, and murdered by the police despite widespread international protests that culminated in sharp reductions of aid from several countries.[33]

Nor is the guerrilla situation comfortable. According to Michael Radu and Vladimir Tismaneanu, at least three major groups continue to operate. The Rebel Armed Forces (FAR), born circa 1960, almost eliminated in 1968 but responsible for the ambassadorial killings of that year and 1970, revived in 1978 and are today operationally active though with perhaps only two hundred hard-core members; the Guerrilla Army of the Poor (EGP), born circa 1972, was about two thousand strong a decade later but subsequently declined sharply; the Revolutionary Organization of the People in Arms (ORPA), born circa 1982, is estimated at about a thousand strong today and is operationally very active—"... in many ways its approach to revolutionary violence is similar to the Peruvian Sendero Luminoso."[34]

The comparatively small numbers of guerrillas should not be misinterpreted, because these groups are supported by thousands of sympathizers. But neither should the trappings of unity claimed by the UNRG be taken too seriously. Their essential weakness remains their failure to unite in one revolutionary ideology, be it Marxist-Leninist, Maoist, or a combination of the two with a touch of Castroism to lend it a social democratic flavor. Their individual and combined threat to the government is nevertheless very real and has recently increased owing to heavy drug trafficking across the northern part of the country. Since 1990, U. S. DEA agents allegedly have been working closely with the Guatemalan military to interdict this trade and its guerrilla support. The Catch-22 here is that this means U.S. financial support of the Guatemalan military, which is still violating human rights on a large scale while preventing necessary political and economic reforms from being carried out.[35]

One thing is certain: The guerrillas are not going to be either pacified or eliminated until proper reforms are instituted and respected, that is until the Guatemalan people are given decent housing, decent food, decent land plots, decent jobs, and decent health services. Although Guatemala is potentially the richest country in Central America, it also has "... the most extreme disparities between wealth and poverty ... [with] religious and racial tensions ... acute and growing."[36] The task of turning this around remains. Over a decade ago, a very astute journalist, Alan Riding, concluded, "No matter what fantasies are projected by idealism or ambition, in the end it is sheer underdevelopment—political, religious and cultural, as well as economic—that determines the limits of hope."[37]

Some three years after Castro's takeover of Cuba, a nationalist revolutionary organization called the National Liberation Movement (MLN) appeared in the sprawling capital of Montevideo, home to perhaps 50 per cent of tiny Uruguay's three million people. This group was known as the Tupamoros—the name deriving from an Inca prince who led a revolt against Spanish rule in the late eighteenth century—was led by Raúl Sendic, a young union organizer of sugarcane field workers, who had recently been released from prison.[38] Sendic and his fellows wished to set up a socialist state devoid of foreign economic and political entanglements, which they blamed for Uruguay's severe economic problems.

The insurgents faced a peculiar problem in that the sparsely populated countryside bereft of mountain or jungle sanctuaries did not offer a suitable *loco* for rural guerrilla warfare.[39] They perforce turned to the teeming capital and to urban guerrilla warfare with stress on terrorism as spelled out in the writings of Régis Debray, Abraham Guillén, and Brazilian Communist Carlos Marighella (whose rather pedestrian work, *The Minimanual of Urban Guerrilla Warfare*, was soon to become the bible of guerrilla terrorists everywhere).

Sendic's Tupamoros did not rush into action. Perhaps twenty in number, they recruited selectively from the professions, schools, universities, women's rights organizations, trade unions, the local Communist Party, the Roman Catholic clergy, and even from the military. By 1965, " . . . there were five hundred fully committed guerrillas, with more than five thousand people sympathetic to the movements."[40]

The movement came out of the closet in 1968 by publicly announcing its aim of bringing down the government. One of its first acts was to steal a loan company's books which revealed illegal currency speculations by several government officials.[41] The movement also gained favorable publicity and more adherents by stealing milk and food trucks and distributing the contents to the pitiful children of Montevideo's squalid barrios.

As its cellular organization in large part protected its activists and as intelligence, finance, and numbers improved, tactics expanded to robbing stores and warehouses for supplies (including chemicals with which to make bombs). Banks and post offices were robbed for money; intimidation of important persons and business executives extorted more money. Prominent citizens, foreign executives, and diplomats were kidnaped, often brutally (the British ambassador Geoffrey Jackson was held for eight months), both for political blackmail (release of guerrilla prisoners, improved factory conditions, publicity for the cause), and for ransom ($250,000 was paid for the Brazilian consul's release).[42] Foreign firms were sabotaged in the hope of making them leave the country and thus further damaging the economy; raids on police stations and army posts yielded weapons, ammunition—and publicity. Murder was a final tactic, the victims being policemen, government officials, politicians, and anyone else who opposed the insurgency (including a U.S. CIA police adviser who was kidnaped and killed in 1970, an act which did considerable harm to the guerrilla cause).[43]

There were setbacks. Equipped increasingly with modern technology and instructed by U.S. advisers, the police were gradually getting their act together and the military, theretofore quiescent, was also coming to life. In 1970, Raúl Sendic and eight hard-line Tupamoros were arrested and imprisoned.[44] Fueled in part by general dissatisfaction with the shrinking economy, the government's harsh austerity program and runaway inflation, the movement nonetheless continued to grow, perhaps to as many as 1,500 to three thousand members in 1971 when Tupamoros gangs carried off daring jailbreaks to free about one hundred fifty of their fellows (including Sendic). They seemed also to have won substantial sympathy if not support. A poll in 1971 showed that " . . . 59 percent of the Uruguayan public thought of them as an organization motivated by social justice and human motives."[45] That was perhaps true but at the time the average citizen did not know very much about the Tupamoros (one result of excessive secrecy and effective cellular security measures), much less about what the movement hoped to achieve. Toppling the government was one thing, building a new government was another. What did the Tupamoros intend? No one seemed to know. Robberies and kidnapings and killings went on. Those tactics had brought a rightist backlash and with it increasing activity of rightist death squads that included the police and military and which were turning Montevideo into a nightmare of counterkidnapings, torture, and murder.

Arrogance now caught up with the Tupamoros. In 1971, an attempt to spread the revolution to the countryside failed. A sharp decline in public sympathy already had occurred, owing in part to the kidnaping of the British ambassador, a Catholic, and his prolonged imprisonment, during which he displayed tremendous fortitude when exposed to journalists, and to the murder of the U.S. police adviser, Don Mitrione, a Catholic with nine children. This reversal showed in the national elections in which the left-wing coalition suffered defeat. In 1972, the Tupamoros made a major mistake by killing an army officer, which brought down the wrath of the traditionally non-political military.[46] A military coup the following year was followed by an army crackdown in which some three hundred Tupamoros were killed and three to five thousand jailed.

During the subsequent ten years of military dictatorship, thousands of political "suspects" were arrested and often tortured before being imprisoned or killed. The bloodbath, which had drawn the ire of the civilized world, fortunately was interrupted in 1985 by the election of a civilian government headed by the Colorado Party's candidate. President Júlio María Sanguinetti reinstituted democratic rule, amnestied all police and military personnel guilty of human rights violations from 1973 to 1985, pardoned Raúl Sendic (who died four years later from " . . . the effects of his torture while a prisoner,"[47] released many political prisoners (despite severe opposition), and allowed the Tupamoros to re-emerge as a legitimate political party. In 1989, the Colorado Party lost to the Blanco Party candidate, Luis Alberto Lacalle Herrera, an opponent of the blanket amnesty law, who subsequently has tried to revitalize the economy by privatization and other measures while respecting the legacy of democratic rule. Although the left-wing Broad Front coalition party came third in the presidential elections, it did carry Montevideo and thus remains a force to be reckoned with.

Just how long the new democracy will survive is a moot question, although to date, December 1993, President Luis Alberto Lacalle seems to have kept the army and most former guerrilla groups under control. If the latter, as members of the leftist *Frente Amplio* (FA) or Broad Front political party, have so far behaved, not all of them have rejected armed revolution as a means to secure still overdue reforms. For the moment, however, FA leadership seems to be upholding the democratic principle while frantically preparing for the scheduled November 1994 elections, which they hope will remove the traditional Blanco and Colorado ruling parties from power.

CHAPTER EIGHTY-ONE

1. Lavan, 44.
2. *Newsweek,* October 19, 1992.
3. Ibid.
4. Ibid.
5. Halperin, 8.
6. Ibid., 10.
7. Ibid.
8. Radu and Tismaneanu, 361–3. In preparing this survey, I have frequently relied on this scholarly and detailed compilation of guerrilla movements and their operations in Latin America.
9. Ibid., 365–8.
10. Rice, 39.
11. Ibid., 41.
12. Eisenhower, *Mandate for Change,* 422.
13. Ibid. Peurifoy informed Eisenhower and Dulles, " . . . It seemed to me that the man [Arbenz] thought like a Communist and talked like a Communist, and if not actually one, would do until one came along." See also, ibid., 423: In October 1954, Peurifoy testified before a U.S. Congressional committee

that " . . . the Arbenz government beyond any question was controlled and dominated by Communists. These Communists were directed from Moscow."

14. Rice, 42.
15. Ibid., 43.
16. Eisenhower, *Mandate for Change*, 426.
17. Ibid.
18. Rice, 49.
19. International Institute for Strategic Studies, *Strategic Survey 1982–83*, 126.
20. Riding, 653. See also, The International Institute for Strategic Studies, *Strategic Survey 1980–81*, 24.
21. Riding, 653.
22. International Institute for Strategic Studies, *Strategic Survey 1982–83*, 126.
23. Riding, 653.
24. Ibid. See also, International Institute for Strategic Studies, *Strategic Survey 1982–83*, 126–7; *Newsweek*, August 31, 1992.
25. Dickey, 685.
26. Ibid., 686.
27. International Institute for Strategic Studies, *Strategic Survey 1985–86*, 197.
28. Best, 99–117.
29. International Institute for Strategic Studies, *Strategic Survey 1989–90*, 185. See also, ibid., *1990–91*, 121–2.
30. Moss, 431.
31. Ibid. See also, *Newsweek*, August 31, 1992, "Subtle Clues in Shallow Graves."
32. *The Annual Register of World Events 1991*, 77.
33. *The Independent* (U.K.), March 31, 1992.
34. Radu and Tismaneanu, 235–68.
35. Moss, 453.
36. International Institute for Strategic Studies, *Strategic Survey 1990–91*, 122.
37. Riding, 643.
38. Goode, 72–3. See also, Radu and Tismaneanu, 348.
39. Rice, 58.
40. Goode, 76.
41. Ibid., 77.
42. Clutterbuck, *Living With Terrorism*, 36–7. See also, Jackson.
43. Halperin, 143.
44. *The Annual Register of World Events, 1971*.
45. Goode, 79.
46. International Institute for Strategic Studies, *Strategic Survey 1972*, 65.
47. *The Annual Register of World Events 1989*, 74.

CHAPTER 82

The Somoza dictatorship • Birth of the Sandinista Liberation Front Nicaragua (FSLN) • FSLN revolutionary aims • Stringent government suppression of civil liberties • FSLN guerrillas open fire • Government excesses • Somoza's fall • The FSLN Communist regime • The CIA and the Contras • Daniel Ortega's Sandinistas • CIA excesses • Contra reverses • Irangate • The stalemate war • 1990 elections won by Violeta Barrios de Chamorro • The reconstruction task • Revolt of the recontras *and* revueltos *• The hostage crisis • The secret arms cache • Continuing rebel threat*

THE MURDER of Nicaragua's famed guerrilla leader Augusto César Sandino in 1934 (see Chapter 23) was the work of Anastasio Somoza García, chief of the Nicaraguan National Guard and a favorite of U. S. Secretary of State Henry Stimson. In 1936, Somoza overthrew the civilian president to become president in an unopposed election, the beginning of a dictatorship that lasted until his assassination in 1956. The dictatorship was continued by his elder son, who died in 1963, and, after a brief interim government, by his brother, Anastasio Somoza Debayle, a 1946 West Point graduate who ruled until 1979. The Somoza dictatorship, supported by a series of American administrations on behalf of private commercial interests, formed one of the most corrupt and cruel regimes in the world. Somoza's personal fortune was estimated at $500 million;[1] he owned " . . . one fourth of Nicaragua's cultivatable land, 130 businesses and industries, vast quantities of rental property and, with officers of the 7,000 strong National Guard, monopolized gambling and prostitution."[2] Thanks to the elder Somoza much of Nicaragua's land was converted to such export crops as cotton and coffee, thus reducing growing areas for traditional staple crops essential to feed a rapidly growing population. The inevitable result was widespread hunger and malnourishment that brought a shockingly high infant mortality rate. The sudden demise of the Somoza regime surprised a great many Americans—the only surprise to observers of the area was why it had not come earlier.

In 1961, a small group of radical students founded an insurgent political party called the National Liberation Front (FLN), which under the aegis of three Marxist Nicaraguans soon was renamed the Sandinista Liberation Front (FSLN) in honor of non-Marxist César Sandino. The aim of the FSLN was to topple the Somoza government by an armed guerrilla group, the Sandinistas.[3] It was not a coherent movement, it lacked funds and direction, and its operations were repeatedly broken by the National Guard, whose officers had been trained in counterinsurgency warfare by the U. S. Army—by 1967 twenty-five American military advisers were stationed in Nicaragua teaching the Guard how to use the flow of weapons and equipment provided by Washington.[4] A distinguished diplomat named Edward Rice tells us that after ten difficult years the FSLN " . . . had no more than a score of men in the mountains undergoing military training and a handful of members in the cities."[5] Michael Radu and Vladimir Tismaneanu recently concluded that " . . . by 1970 the FSLN practically ceased to exist."[6] The movement probably would have collapsed but for continued governmental excesses.

The watershed occurred when a major earthquake in 1972 left some six thousand dead and over three hundred thousand without shelter. Instead of doing their job, National Guard soldiers often deserted their posts to join in widespread looting. American soldiers were flown in to restore order but could not prevent National Guard officers and civilian politicians from stealing quantities of medicines and relief supplies— " . . . about half of the $32 million supplied by the United States for reconstruction was never accounted for."[7] This rapacious behavior resulted not only in numerous peasant recruits for the Sandinista guerrillas but also considerable sympathy from other political parties including the important middle-class liberal party, the Democratic Union of Liberation (UDEL) founded by Pedro Joaquín Chamorro, scion of an old liberal family and publisher of Managua's leading newspaper *La Prensa* (The Press).

Dissidence grew in 1974 when Somoza pushed through a new constitution, declared opposition parties illegal, abolished freedom of the press, threw the protesting Chamorro in jail, and was elected president. Shortly after he was sworn in, a small group of Sandinista guerrilla terrorists burst into the mansion of a wealthy businessman to seize and hold hostage a number of prominent dinner guests. They were released unharmed when Somoza paid a large ransom, freed fourteen political prisoners, published a Sandinista proclamation, and flew the rebels out of the country (cheered by crowds on their way to the airport).[8]

Somoza responded to this guerrilla derring-do by a ruthless counterinsurgency campaign in the countryside that would last for over three years. Among the victims was Carlos Fonseca Amador, one of the three founders of the FSLN (and a national hero today), whose death strengthened the hand of the single surviving founder, Tomás Borge, an adherent of the Cuban style of Marxism. The FSLN at this time was split into three factions: one small faction which proposed a dogmatic, class-centered approach . . . limited to isolated urban terrorist activities;[9] the Maoists, who wanted to wage guerrilla warfare designed " . . . to drain Somoza's resources in a long term but elusive military campaign," but " . . . never really established a popular line of support among the peasants";[10] and finally Borge's Terceristas, the largest faction, which held for immediate action, be it terrorism in the cities or guerrilla warfare in the countryside or both.[11] The Terceristas " . . . played a major role" in bringing the FSLN to power while openly advocating socialism and popular democracy and establishing " . . . extensive alliances and coalitions with groups on all sides of the political spectrum," a lesson learned from Castro's revolution.[12] The Terceristas gained an important ally, Costa Rica, whose government " . . . permitted the formation, arming and training on its soil of a Sandinista invasion force."[13] Other Sandinista recruits received military training in Cuba, which also supplied some arms.[14] In autumn of 1977, FSLN guerrillas attacked National Guard garrisons in five cities. Although the attacks were repulsed, they brought a show of support from prominent religious and professional leaders who demanded Somoza's removal.[15]

Somoza erred fatally in early 1978 by having the newspaper publisher Pedro Chamorro murdered. Chamorro's funeral drew thousands of mourners and was followed by widespread riots, a three-week general strike and the conversion of more prominent Nicaraguans to the revolutionary movement. The government suffered another serious setback in the autumn when a group of Terceristas led by Éden Pastora and wearing National Guard uniforms stormed the National Palace to seize fifteen hundred hostages including the country's legislators. Somoza was forced to pay another hefty ransom, release sixty prisoners (including Borge), publish FSLN decrees, and fly the escapees to Cuba. Fresh guerrilla attacks sparked off major insurrections in several cities and brought on a new round of bloodletting by National Guard forces—with an estimated three thousand rebels and sympathizers killed.[16] In spring of 1979, Pastora, now famous as Commander Zero, struck again, this time leading one thousand five hundred guerrillas from his Costa Rica base into Nicaragua, a final offensive that attracted thousands of local sympathizers to his banner. This time the National Guard lost. A panic-stricken Somoza fled the country in July (and was assassinated in Paraguay in 1980).

The Pyrrhic victory cost perhaps fifty thousand dead. An interim government headed by the FSLN looked on a ruined economy and about half a million homeless people. This tragic situation was soon worsened when it became increasingly obvious that the FSLN was not only infested with corruption but was determined to turn Nicaragua into a Communist state along Cuban lines complete with secret police, neighborhood surveillance, press censorship, and suppression of opposition political parties, anti-Sandinista religious groups, labor unions, and private business groups.[17] What had approached a heterogeneous insurgency now fragmented as UDEL and other political groups began turning their backs on the new government.[18]

Washington had watched these developments with a wary eye. Although President Carter had stopped military aid to Somoza after Chamorro's murder, he also treated the dictator with considerable moderation, a feckless stance that tended to bring Nicaraguan moderates into the radical camp. Where Carter liberals had been inclined to play both sides while hoping for a new and better day for Nicaragua, Reagan conservatives proclaimed the FSLN a major threat to democracy (as if the Somoza government had been a bastion thereof) and invoked the old shibboleth of falling dominoes which would result in a communist Central and South America, a charge which gained certain currency in the United States in view of the FSLN's support of an insurgency in neighboring El Salvador, as well as state visits to Managua by PLO leader Yasser Arafat and Fidel Castro, and by " . . . a trade and aid agreement with Soviet Russia."[19]

Fired by such hawks as Secretary of State Alexander Haig and his subordinate Thomas Enders and using Nicaraguan aid to the Salvadoran insurgents as justification, President Reagan in 1981 suspended all aid to the Nicaraguan Government, the first step in an attempt to topple the Sandinista regime. U.S. fleet units were to prepare to position off Central American coasts; the ubiquitous CIA was to begin destabilizing an already floundering economy and was to organize, train, and support a guerrilla force of counterrevolutionaries that would eventually fight under the flag of the Nicaraguan Democratic Force (FDN).

The Contras, as they were soon termed, were a rather unattractive, in some ways forlorn mixture of disaffected liberals, National Guard fugitives, polyglot mercenaries, and peasant *campesinos*—in all an estimated five thousand men being trained in camps spotted along Honduras border areas, an effort for which another $19 million was allocated to the CIA in 1982.

In Costa Rica, the disaffected hero of the revolution, Éden Pastora, headed the exiled Revolutionary Democratic Alliance (ARDE), which included other prominent Sandinista dropouts and which, once its demands for political reforms were spurned by the Sandinistas, would field its own guerrilla force. But Pastora would have nothing to do with FDN resistance training in Honduras because its military high command " . . . was mainly composed of former officers of Somoza's National Guard."[20]

For this and other reasons, Contra operations were initially disappointing although they did draw the support of some disaffected Miskito Indians who had been forcibly evicted from their homelands by the Sandinistas.[21] Early spring offensives met determined resistance from government forces. Inside Nicaragua, there was little evidence of popular support for the Contras and all attempts to seize a town and make it the capital of a liberated area (in the Mao-Guevara-Castro tradition) were bloodily repulsed.

Rumors of repeated Contra atrocities during raids inside Nicaragua were circulating in Washington, and these were suddenly polarized by *Newsweek* magazine's explosive revelation of America's newest "secret war." Suddenly, the American public became aware that U.S. aid to Honduras had tripled to $33 million in 1982 with another $13 million spent on building three air strips capable of handling large U.S. troop carriers; that U.S. military advisers were working with the Honduran army, which in July had participated in joint maneuvers with U.S. forces.[22] Was Reagan intent on merely interdicting Nicaraguan arms supply to El Salvador guerrillas—or was Reagan intent on building an army with which to invade Nicaragua? Suspicious U.S. lawmakers in December 1982 publicly approved the Boland Amendment (secretly passed four months earlier), which barred " . . . the Reagan administration from supporting military operations aimed at overthrowing the Sandinista government."[23] In an attempt to sway a hostile Congress, President Reagan in July 1983 announced with considerable fanfare that a bipartisan commission headed by Henry Kissinger would review U.S. strategy and policies in Central America, a brave effort since in a good many minds there did not seem to be a strategy that, as one expert put it, " . . . links a clear statement of national interests with a sober sense of national capabilities."[24] Also in July, two U.S. Navy carrier battle groups positioned off the Central American coast as prelude to combined ground maneuvers with the Honduran army—by year's end more than four thousand U.S. troops were still in Honduras where they would continue to participate in exercises with the Honduran military.[25] In late 1983, the on-again-off-again U. S. Congress yielded to presidential plea and authorized the CIA to spend another $24 million in military and non-military aid to the Contras, who now claimed perhaps ten thousand fighters,[26] but whose fresh offensives in the northern Nicaragua border area in 1983 had met with no more success than earlier efforts.

The Kissinger report released in January 1984 was a non-event recommending as it did supplementary aid to the tune of $400 million for fiscal year 1984–85 and a whopping $8 billion in aid for the next five years. Such a proposal had to be stillborn not alone because of the grotesque sums involved and because a large portion of those sums would merely enrich corrupt politicians and generals without bringing a change for the better, but also because, as a consultant to the Kissinger Commission later wrote, " . . . even this recommended level of assistance would hardly secure the Commission's goal of 'strong and free economies' in Central America."[27]

By early 1984, Contra funds were running out and the Reagan administration again turned to Congress. But now the story broke of the CIA's participation in mining Nicaraguan ports, a blatant act of war, followed by the Administration's refusal to accept jurisdiction of the International Court of Justice in a suit brought by Nicaragua.[28] This unacceptable act provoked a Congressional blanket shut-off of any "covert" aid to the Contras, a decision that hardened when the American public learned of other CIA excesses such as instructing Contra teams in how to assassinate Nicaraguan leaders.

Although the U. S. government prevented the Sandinista regime from securing large loans from such as the World Bank and the International Monetary Fund, it was subsidized by Russia (which by 1989 would have furnished some $3 billion in aid) and by Cuba (whose aid was sharply curtailed after the U.S. invasion of Grenada in October 1983), both countries sending weapons and large numbers of military advisers, and also by Communist-bloc countries in Eastern Europe and by Iran, France, and Libya. A general election in late 1984 although boycotted by some liberal parties was won by Daniel Ortega Saavedra with over 60 per cent of the vote. International observers judged the election to be fair but the Reagan administration called it a sham and greeted Ortega's inauguration by imposing a trade embargo to stifle further the Nicaraguan economy.

Contra reverses combined with a slowdown of military aid meanwhile had brought a return to small-unit guerrilla warfare, mostly in the northern and eastern regions where the Contras won some support from the Miskito Indians. Renewal of $27 million worth of "nonmilitary" aid to the Contras in August 1985[29] greatly improved their transport and communication capabilities, but that did not change the slow pace of and only minor gains from operations inside Nicaragua.[30]

But more help was on its way. In 1985, the Reagan administration was tacitly supporting Iraq in its prolonged war against Iran. Reagan now authorized his national security adviser, Robert McFarlane, to arrange for the secret sale of arms to Iran in an attempt to persuade the Iranian government to use its assumed influence on Shiite Hezbollah terrorists who were holding American hostages in Lebanon. This altogether fanciful scheme soon grew like the national debt—it was the perfect way to end-run Congress in order to get funds to the Contras. The scheme was for international weapon traffickers—those persons who rate just below drug traffickers on the sleaze scale—to secretly supply Israel with arms purchased from U.S. arsenals. Israel would then sell them to Iran through middlemen at vast profit. Not only would Iran gratefully arrange for the release of the hostages, so the argument went, *but* a share of the profits apparently to be determined by the weapon traffickers would be transferred to secret offshore Contra bank accounts for additional arms purchases by the traffickers using shell corporations in Switzerland, Portugal, Panama, and other countries. This Machiavellian operation—CIA director William Casey allegedly called it "the ultimate covert operation"[31]—was in the hands of McFarlane and his successor Vice-Admiral John Poindexter, who turned it over to one of his staffers, the young and zealous Lieutenant Colonel Oliver North, an Annapolis graduate and Marine Corps officer who undoubtedly saw silver leaves turning to silver stars. A further secret initiative, apparently the result of North's fecund if somewhat twisted mind, involved obtaining voluntary donations for the Contras from private supporters in the United States and abroad, the latter donors including the king of Saudi Arabia, the sultan of Brunei and the Taiwanese government, a matter of many millions of dollars deposited in secret bank accounts controlled by the arms traffickers.

Several things were wrong with this mickeymouse operation. Supplying the Contras with money to buy arms placed the national security adviser and certain co-operating officials in covert sections of CIA and the Departments of State and Defense in direct contravention of the Boland Amendment despite the Administration's later invocation of "executive privilege" (which constitutionally does not exist); a joint Congressional investigating committee concluded that " . . . the common ingredients of the Iran and Contra policies were secrecy, deception and disdain for law."[32] It violated the U. S. government's own embargo on arms sales to Iran. It made a mockery of the U. S. government's formal pledge to other Western nations that ransom would not be paid to guerrilla terrorist kidnapers. In the case of Saudi Arabia, Brunei, and Taiwan, it committed the Reagan administration to quid pro quo future favors; more directly, it lent itself to blackmail—according to Oliver North, one of the middlemen had to be paid $4.5 million to shut him up once he was cut out of the operation.[33] It contradicted U. S. Department of State and Department of Defense policies not to mention common sense: there was no assurance that the Iranian government controlled the Hezbollah guerrilla terrorists, which indeed it did not—during negotiations two *more* hostages were seized. Adding insult to injury, the bulk of the large profits accruing from supplying arms to a potentially dangerous enemy went to a group of amoral arms-trafficking mercenaries whose secret contracts called for open-end profits with no questions asked.[34] Of the estimated $12 million of illicit profits made from the arms sales, one authority believes that only $4 million reached the Contras, the rest going to various middlemen and their cohorts; the same authority believes that the Contras received some $30 million from Saudi Arabia and less than $4 million from private U.S. sources.[35] Finally, what could not possibly have been kept secret was not kept secret. In October 1986, Sandinista forces shot down a CIA aircraft that was flying a resupply mission to Contra forces in Nicaragua. Revelation of the arms sales followed. The subsequent Irangate (aka Iranamok, Iranagua) scandal summarily ended Poindexter and North's cowboy nonsense but it also severely damaged the Administration's international prestige and ripped further the already tattered fabric of the American people's belief in their government.[36] Subsequent investigations, arrests, trials, sentences, and retrials that finally freed the miscreants cost millions of dollars in addition to raising serious questions in many citizens' minds as to the impartiality of American justice and the seemingly unlimited power of the executive branch of government to make a mockery of the law. The fiasco widened in December 1993 when President George Bush saw fit to pardon two former senior CIA officials, former Secretary of Defense Caspar Weinberger and former Attorney General Edwin Meese. Fortunately for the record Special Prosecutor Lawrence Walsh persevered with his extensive Contra-Iran investigations, a detailed report of which was published in early 1994 to leave little doubt as to presidential culpability in this scandalous deceit. Still unsettled is the question of George Bush's denial of the operation while serving as Vice-President, which could lead to serious charges.

Although the Contras received $100 million in U.S. aid in 1986 and were said to number fifteen thousand, they remained a " . . . largely cross border raiding party,"[38] and nowhere succeeded in holding a town or even a village. By year's end, they numbered only about a thousand active combatants. Operations nonetheless continued and even expanded. One observer claimed that by spring of 1987, there had been 372 rebel attacks in more than two thirds of the country and that the guerrillas were increasing attacks on electric power grids, bridges, communications facilities, fuel depots, and roads.[39]

This was no mean achievement since Ortega's army numbered over sixty thousand with another fifty thousand in the reserves and local militias. Units were increasingly well equipped with Soviet-supplied weapons including assault helicopters and gunships, tanks, armored vehicles, and heavy artillery, not to mention an estimated thirty-five hundred Cuban advisers, many of them veterans of guerrilla warfare in Angola and elsewhere. Ortega's problem was the Vietnam syndrome; in short, the Sandinistas were trying to fight a counterinsurgency with quantitative rather than qualitative tactics, for example, by relocating 160,000 villagers in 1987 without providing adequate facilities or compensation. Both sides practiced atrocities, but in so doing a large army makes more enemies than a small guerrilla force. Terrain more often than not favored the guerrilla, particularly in areas where César Sandino's guerrillas had led U. S. Marines a merry chase over half a century earlier.

Here was a war that no one was winning, a war that was impoverishing hundreds of thousands of Nicaraguans while driving the Ortega government into bankruptcy. The war had also caused a political crisis in the United States, where the Reagan administration was determined to topple the Sandinistas by military force and where Administration opponents believed negotiations to be the answer, a stance shared by many other governments, which further believed that the solution lay in purely regional negotiations by the Contadora Group (Mexico, Colombia, Panama, and Venezuela) backed by the Contadora Support Group (Peru, Argentina, Brazil, and Uruguay) and by more active support of the Organization of American States (OAS) and the United Nations—even though this combined effort had not made much visible progress in the past.[40]

Ortega's Marxist government responded to internal and external pressures in 1987 by coming up with a new constitution generally " . . . acknowledged to contain most of the principles of representative democracy" and by promising national elections in 1990.[41] This was followed by a renewed Central American peace initiative that in August led to the signing of Esquipulas II (the revised Arias Plan first presented the previous February by Costa Rica's President Oscar Arias) by Costa Rica, El Salvador, Guatemala, Honduras, and Nicaragua. This was a bold and imaginative initiative that " . . . attempted to bring peace and stability to the region by taking the initiative away from all of the external actors—the U.S., the USSR, Cuba and the Contadora Group and Contadora Support Group countries."[42] A provision of this agreement called for a ninety-day cease-fire to commence in April 1988.

Although a hoped-for extension of the cease-fire did not materialize—the fault largely of the Contras—the spark had gone out of the war. As peace appeared to be possible, the already divisive command of the Contras split, with authority seemingly left to the hard-liners. But Contra fortunes further deteriorated when the U. S. Congress again shut off military aid. On the Sandinista side, the economy continued to plunge until inflation was totally out of control (33,000 per cent).[43] Ortega's austerity programs, never popular, were leading to increasing unrest and stringent demands by four opposition parties, which recently had formed the National Opposition Union (UNO). Such were the pressures exacerbated by a serious earthquake, by Soviet aid drying up, by the U.S. blockade, and by the eclipse of Cuban influence that in 1990 Ortega honored a constitutional commitment to hold internationally supervised elections, which nearly all observers expected the FSLN to win. Instead, Violeta Barrios de Chamorro (widow of the murdered publisher), the UNO coalition party's candidate openly backed and financed by Washington, emerged as the victor. A 90 per cent voter turnout gave UNO 55 per cent of the vote against 41 per cent for the Sandinistas.[44] To almost everyone's surprise, the Sandinistas turned over the government to the new administration (with the dangerous proviso that the Sandinistas retained control of army and police) and swore allegiance to Chamorro and to the constitution.

As in 1979, victory was somewhat Pyrrhic. The economy was in shambles. A good many Contras did not take kindly to the cease-fire and subsequent turning in of their weapons by an estimated twenty thousand members; nor were they pleased when Chamorro kept certain Sandinista leaders in office. Vital economic reforms were also contested both by right-wing parties and by FSLN-dominated labor unions, which led a series of major strikes and a threatened insurgency in summer of 1990, an ugly situation resolved only by army and police. Despite considerable financial aid from the United States and other international sources—over $500 million in 1991—the economy continued to decline, largely the result of a weak and corrupt reformist government unable to overcome obstructionist tactics from left and right extremist parties.

As of this writing, December 1993, the poverty level is estimated to stand at 70 percent, illiteracy at 50 percent.[45] Unemployment is an estimated 60 percent;[46] social, medical, and educational services remain meager: Nicaragua is now judged to be the second poorest country in the hemisphere (after Haiti).[47]

Promises of land grants and financial assistance to Contra and Sandinista veterans who turned in their arms have not been kept. In 1991 bands of armed Contras known as *recontros* appeared in northwestern Nicaragua to demand both what had been promised them as well as the dismissal of Sandinista senior army and police officials who, they believed, were responsible for their plight.[48] Government failure to act on their behalf was followed by the outbreak of sporadic guerrilla warfare in the countryside by some three thousand Contra and Sandinista veterans—the *revueltos*. According to one source, in the first half of 1993 there were over eighty-five skirmishes with more than one hundred dead.[49] In July a rebel force of about 150 former Sandinista soldiers invaded a town in the north to rob banks and raid police stations before being rounded up by a sizable army force. The following month a group of disgruntled Contras seized thirty-seven government officials as hostages to their demands for land; pro-Sandinistas in Managua responded by seizing some fifty members of the rightist National Opposition Union, including the country's vice-president, a crisis thankfully resolved without bloodshed.[50]

An even more disturbing event embarrassed Chamorro's beleaguered government prior to the hostage crisis. In late May an explosion in a Managua automotive repair shop revealed an enormous secret cache not only of guerrilla arms, including surface-to-air missiles, but a horde of documents that connected the arms to the supposedly disarmed FMLN guerrilla organization in El Salvador, besides suggesting that the holding could be traced to a group of international guerrilla terrorists that included the Spanish Basque ETA. Over three hundred passports, many of them blank, from twenty-one countries, were seized along with the names of company executives and 150 prominent Latin American families who were to be kidnaped for ransom.[51] Although Chamorro's defense minister, General Humberto Ortega, disclaimed any knowledge of the exposed arsenal, skeptics found this difficult to believe, particularly when FMLN informants in El Salvador pinpointed several more secret caches in Managua. Particularly skeptical was the U.S. Senate which cut off $90 million in aid pending further investigation of an alleged Sandinista connection with international guerrilla terrorists.[52]

In partial palliation Violeta Chamorro announced in October that army commander Ortega would be replaced in 1994. Such is her loose control of government that this does not mean he will go—nor would his departure necessarily mean the end of what appears to be a seriously burgeoning rebel guerrilla movement.

CHAPTER EIGHTY-TWO

1. International Institute for Strategic Studies, *Strategic Survey 1979*, 80.
2. Rice, 31. See also, International Institute for Strategic Studies, *Strategic Survey 1979*, 108–9.
3. Radu and Tismaneanu, 292–3.
4. Rice, 32.
5. Ibid., 34.
6. Radu and Tismaneanu, 299.
7. Rice, 34. See also, International Institute for Strategic Studies, *Strategic Survey 1979*, 109.
8. Rice, 35.
9. Radu and Tismaneanu, 299.
10. Ibid.
11. International Institute for Strategic Studies, *Strategic Survey 1979*, 109. See also, Rice, 35.
12. Radu and Tismaneanu, 299–300.
13. Rice, 35.

14. International Institute for Strategic Studies, *Strategic Survey 1979,* 112.
15. Ibid., 109.
16. Ibid., 110.
17. Dickey, 671.
18. Riding, 650–2.
19. International Institute for Strategic Studies, *Strategic Survey 1980–81,* 24.
20. International Institute for Strategic Studies, *Strategic Survey 1983–84,* 116–17. See also, Riding, 649–50; Dickey, 672.
21. Dickey, 668 ff.
22. Riding, 673.
23. Ibid., 649.
24. Treverton, 128–38.
25. International Institute for Strategic Studies, *Strategic Survey 1983–84,* 116–17.
26. Purcell, 119. See also, North, 234.
27. Treverton, 135.
28. International Institute for Strategic Studies, *Strategic Survey 1984–85,* 32.
29. Purcell, 119.
30. International Institute for Strategic Studies, *Strategic Survey 1985–86,* 202–3.
31. North, 13.
32. International Institute for Strategic Studies, *Strategic Survey 1987–88,* 74.
33. North, 281.
34. Ibid., 21.
35. Purcell, 119. See also, North, 265: Owing to an administrative error, North tells us, the sultan of Brunei's hefty donation was placed in the wrong secret Swiss bank account and was apparently not used; International Institute for Strategic Studies, *Strategic Survey 1986–87,* 76–9.
36. International Institute for Strategic Studies, *Strategic Survey 1986–87,* 76–9.
37. *Newsweek,* November 2, 1992.
38. Shultz, 363.
39. Purcell, 122.
40. Treverton, 128–38. See also, Purcell, 110–11, for the alleged defects of the proposed Contadora treaty.
41. Best, 101.
42. Moss, 421. See also, ibid., 427–8, for details of the plan; Purcell, 111–13.
43. International Institute for Strategic Studies, *Strategic Survey 1989–90,* 186.
44. Ibid., 1990–91, 123.
45. *International Herald Tribune,* June 2, 1993.
46. *Newsweek,* August 2, 1993.
47. *International Herald Tribune,* June 2, 1993.
48. Ibid., August 3–4, 1991.
49. *Newsweek,* August 2, 1993.
50. *The Independent* (U.K.), August 22, 24, 26, 1993.
51. *International Herald Tribune,* July 15, 1993.
52. Ibid. August 20, 1993.

CHAPTER 83

Birth of the Brazilian insurgency • Early terrorist guerrilla successes • Carlos Marighela's death • Guerrilla reverses and final failure of the insurgency • Birth of the Argentinian insurgency • Montoneros terrorist guerrilla aims • Early guerrilla successes • "The dirty war" • Final guerrilla defeat • The Chilean scene: Allende and Pinochet • Soviet Russia and Cuba end aid to the insurgents • Pinochet's electoral defeat

BRAZILIAN INSURGENTS ALSO chose urban guerrilla warfare in attempting to overthrow a military dictatorship and establish a Marxist-Leninist form of government similar to that in Fidel Castro's Cuba. The nucleus of three guerrilla groups that emerged in the late 1960s came from a split in the Brazilian Communist Party (PCB) which, guided by Moscow, was pursuing a reformist as opposed to a militant policy.

First to rebel was a long-time member of the PCB Politburo and a veteran revolutionary, Carlos Marighela, who together with a few other dissidents broke away in 1967 to establish the National Liberation Action (ALN) in São Paulo. About the same time, another group of dissidents in the state of Rio Grande do Sul left the PCB to form the October 8 Revolutionary Movement (MR-8)—named for the date that Che Guevara was captured in Bolivia. Still other disillusioned members of the PCB broke away to form the Revolutionary Brazilian Communist Party (PCBR). Finally, a group of retired left-wing army officers emerged in the Revolutionary People's Vanguard (VPR) whose leader was Carlos Lamarca.[1]

The common denominator of these groups was revolutionary violence as propounded by Carlos Marighela in *The Minimanual of Urban Guerrilla Warfare*. In 1968, the ALN opened a guerrilla terrorist campaign of robberies, kidnapings, and assassinations which the MR-8 and PCBR groups quickly emulated. After such successes as the 1969 kidnaping of a U.S. ambassador (released in exchange for fifteen political prisoners and publication of a guerrilla manifesto), it ran into serious trouble despite an impressive growth in members. A police ambush in 1969 eliminated its most aggressive leader, Carlos Marighela, as his group was carrying out a bank robbery. In 1970, the group kidnaped the German and Swiss ambassadors (released in exchange for forty and seventy prisoners respectively),[2] but Marighela's successor and several other leaders were killed. By 1972, the ALN was no longer a cohesive force although about fifty guerrilla terrorists remained active.[3]

MR-8 was considerably smaller than the ALN—perhaps less than a hundred members and about the same number of sympathizers—and it too soon came on hard times. Like the ALN, it confined itself to urban guerrilla terrorism and at times successfully worked with ALN guerrillas in robbing banks and in kidnapings. It suffered from slack security, however, and in 1969 was all but knocked out by the arrests of a large number of its members. It revived in the early 1980s as an adjunct to the PCB but its operations allegedly were hamstrung by PCB ortho-doxy.[4]

The PCBR was the best survivor. Backed by Cuba, it enjoyed significant growth, but like the other groups it never did establish a solid base of operations (a major difficulty faced by most urban guerrilla terrorist organizations). After dimming out in the late 1970s, it revived in the 1980s and continues active today.[5]

The VPR suffered the ALN's fate when its leader Carlos Lamarca was killed in a shootout in 1971 from which the organization never recovered.[6]

The reason for the over-all failure of the Brazilian insurgent movement is twofold. First was the error in striking out against the establishment without being able to win the average citizen's support—the same error made by the Tupamoros in Uruguay. Government excesses, particularly the highly publicized accusations of torture, won the guerrillas some sympathy, but such were guerrilla excesses that in the end the average citizen was not sorry to see them go. Second was their failure to take the revolution to the countryside, to establish what Régis Debray called a *foco*—a secure base from which to expand revolution by converting Marshal Lyautey's *tache d'huile* concept to revolutionary goals. Marighela recognized this failure. As Michael Radu wrote:

> . . . Early in 1969 . . . he tried to work out a coherent interpretation of the relation between the urban and rural guerrilla, considering that the success of each type of strategy depended on the effectiveness of the other . . . [but] "The whole urban struggle, whether on the guerrilla or mass-movement front, must always be seen as tactical struggle . . . the decisive struggle will be in the rural area."[7]

It followed that guerrilla terrorism was an integral part of guerrilla warfare, "an arm the revolutionary can never relinquish."[8]

So the urbanists came and went, leaving the usual carnage of corpses and unrequited hopes for a more just social order behind them. Dreary military government followed dreary military government with corruption endemic at all levels. But then in 1990 along came a charismatic provincial governor named Fernando Collor de Mello, who in the first direct elections in twenty-nine years was overwhelmingly elected president on a reform ticket with a promise to end corruption and reduce a whopping inflation.

He started well enough by introducing an ambitious program designed to bring inflation under control, reduce public spending, and spur economic growth. Alas, the program was stillborn. He did not revitalize the economy nor did he do much about inflation, nor did he satisfactorily tackle such glaring social evils exemplified in a federal police report in Brasília which stated that

> ... a total 4,611 children and adolescents had, it was estimated, been killed over the last three years and thousands more raped, abused, and sold into prostitution. Military personnel were reliably reported to have been implicated in the killings.[9]

What Collor did do was to turn his back on his promises and open his pocket to a massive corruption scheme amounting to an alleged $300 million, of which he is believed to have received a very satisfactory chunk. And for which, after months of roiling Brazilian politics, he was impeached, removed from office, and subsequently indicted on several charges before finally resigning in disgrace.

To everyone's relief, the army showed no inclination to take over government. In winning the day at least temporarily, Brazilian democracy can be congratulated—but only if it begins to eliminate the massive social inequities that inspired Marighella and his guerrillas to stop talking and start shooting.

Unusual violence erupted in Argentina with the assassination in 1970 of a former president of the country. This was the work of the Montoneros Perónista Movement (MPM), an urban guerrilla terrorist group whose leader was a professional terrorist, twenty-two-year-old Mario Firmenich. The following year, the Montoneros and another guerrilla group, the People's Revolutionary Army (ERP), threw down the urban guerrilla gauntlet by a series of robberies and kidnapings that soon turned to indiscriminate murders answered in kind by security forces and private murder squads to begin a terrifying decade still referred to in Buenos Aires as "the dirty war."[10]

The Montoneros, so named in an attempt " . . . to identify with the Andean pastoral hill-rebels in the nineteenth century,"[11] derived from the left-wing faction of the earlier Perónist regime. Their aim was to achieve revolution by violence, not alone in Argentina but throughout Latin America. Kidnapings in 1971 soon became big business conducted under the guise of humanitarian good works such as feeding and clothing the poor. Enormous ransoms were paid by international companies for the return of their executives; other companies paid huge ransoms for "protection" Mafia-style.[12] Guerrilla activities were temporarily dampened in 1973 with the return to power of the former exiled president, Juan Domingo Perón, who soon outlawed the ERP. Perón's death a year later brought his widow, Isabel Perón, to power. Although the Montoneros, who claimed a large union membership, helped her to be elected, she soon turned on them, a mistake in that her weak and vacillating government could not cope with this now-powerful movement:[13] some five thousand hard-core guerrillas; fifteen thousand active sympathizers;[14] several million dollars in funds; and close connections with Cuba and with several Latin American revolutionary movements and, eventually, with the PLO, the Spanish Socialist Party (PSOE), the Spanish Communist Party (PCE), Sweden's Social Democrats, and with several African revolutionary movements.[15]

The ERP evolved from Trotskyite extreme left-wingers of the Perónist regime. The movement was led initially by Mario Roberto Santucho, who in 1972 was forced into exile.[16] Led by Enrique Haroldo Gorriarán Marle, the ERP accumulated a war chest estimated at $30 million by spring of 1974, mostly from ransoms of kidnaped victims, a figure that may have tripled in 1975 when an Argentinian company allegedly paid $60 million for the release of three executives.[17] Despite the ban imposed by Perón, the ERP grew to perhaps three thousand active members and several thousand supporters. In 1975, it attempted to open a rural insurgency in Tucumán province, a two-year effort finally suppressed by security forces. Meanwhile, the ERP had attracted guerrilla refugees from failed insurgencies in Uruguay, Bolivia, and Chile. It now put up $5 million to form remnant rebel movements in those countries into an international revolutionary junta which would spread war to the countryside,[18] and in addition would send hit teams to assassinate Latin American diplomats in European embassies.[19]

In the next two years, urban guerrilla warfare turned many parts of the beautiful city of Buenos Aires into a murderous hell of terrorists waging all-out war with rightist death squads, police, and army. " . . . Right there," an Argentinian friend told me some years later, "right there I watched my best friend jumped by three men and thrown into a car—we never saw him again."

Failure of security forces to best ERP terrorists brought a military coup in 1976 and a repression that claimed an estimated ten thousand lives of guerrillas and "suspects"—or too often innocent civilians who failed to get out of the way of war. Brutal as it was, the counterinsurgency campaign spelled an end to organized guerrilla insurgency—at least to the present day.

Since its foundation in 1922, the Communist Party of Chile (PCCh) played an integral role in the political turbulence that long has characterized this elongated coastal nation of over twelve million people. After a good many ups and downs, the leftist heyday arrived in 1970 when the Popular Unity coalition candidate Salvador Allende Gossens was elected president in what most observers deemed to be a fair election. Trouble was: Allende was a dedicated Marxist Socialist (a founding member of the Chilean Socialist Party) burdened with an opposition-controlled congress. Although he nationalized a large number of companies and reduced unemployment, he failed to control inflation nor did he implement other promised reforms. His problems ended in 1973, courtesy of a military coup strongly supported if not planned by the CIA, during which he was killed. General Augusto Pinochet Ugarte was installed as dictator, a position he retained until 1989.

The Pinochet dictatorship proscribed the Communist and Socialist parties. Luis Corvalán, secretary-general of the PCCh, was jailed along with thousands of his fellows and eventually exiled. Largely owing to his efforts, the PCCh revived and in 1980 officially adopted a policy of violence to carry out its revolutionary strategy.

This decision was warmly greeted by members of the Movement of the Revolutionary Left (MIR), which had come to life in 1965 under the leadership of Dr. Miguel Enríquez, " . . . a fervent admirer of Fidel Castro and a supporter of the Cuban strategy of subversion in Latin America."[20] Violence was a basic tenet of this large revolutionary group, " . . . one of the main instigators of the unrest and antidemocratic actions that led to the military counter-reaction in 1973."[21] Enríquez was killed by a police raid in 1974. His replacement, Arturo Villavella, a Marxist fanatic, was captured in the same year, exiled after three years in jail, returned to Chile, and was killed in 1983. He was replaced by a left-wing extremist, the nephew of Salvador Allende, Andrés Pascal Allende, whose continuing commitment to terrorism alienated most of the more moderate political parties. The MIR never fully recovered from Pinochet's crackdown and has been limited to isolated guerrilla terrorist actions in the major cities, sometimes in conjunction with the FPMR.

Both the PCCh (FPMR) and MIR were generously supported by voluntary (and involuntary) contributions and by foreign sympathizers, notably Soviet Russia and Cuba. In 1986, Chilean security forces stumbled on an incredible find, a PCCh guerrilla camp disguised as a coastal fishing village and featuring a small airstrip, advanced communications, underground classrooms and an armory of over three thousand rifles, Soviet-made rocket launchers, American-made anti-tank weapons, two tons of TNT, and quantities of plastic explosives.[22]

MIR probably would have continued to re-establish itself but for improved counterinsurgency operations, along with Pinochet's defeat in the 1989 elections and, most important, the demise of the Soviet Union, the near bankruptcy of Cuba, and the end of insurgencies in Nicaragua and El Salvador.

CHAPTER EIGHTY-THREE

1. Radu and Tismaneanu, 115–27.
2. Halperin, 14.
3. Radu and Tismaneanu, 118. See also, Halperin, 8–9.
4. Radu and Tismaneanu, 123.
5. Ibid., 124.
6. Ibid., 127.
7. Ibid., 117.
8. Ibid.
9. *Annual Register of World Events 1991,* 70.
10. Clutterbuck, *Living with Terrorism,* 44–50, for details of the kidnapings.
11. Radu and Tismaneanu, 95.
12. Clutterbuck, *Living with Terrorism,* 45.
13. Pimlott, 125–7.
14. Radu and Tismaneanu, 94. See also, Halperin, 9.
15. Radu and Tismaneanu, 99.
16. Ibid., 102.
17. Halperin, 17.
18. Clutterbuck, *Living with Terrorism,* 45.
19. Laqueur, *Terrorism,* 187.
20. Radu and Tismaneanu, 140.
21. Ibid.
22. Ibid., 136.

CHAPTER 84

The background of revolution in El Salvador • The National Coalition Party (PCN) in power • José Napoleón Duarte's opposition party, the Democratic Nationalist Organization (ORDEN) • War with Honduras • Rise of the Communist guerrilla movement, the Farabundo Martí Popular Forces of Liberation (FPL) • The shooting starts • Guerrilla techniques and tactics • Formation of the Farabundo Martí National Liberation Front (FMLN) • Guerrilla setbacks and disunity • Duarte's new government • Rise of Roberto d'Aubuisson Arrieta's ultra-right party, the National Republican Alliance (ARENA) • ORDEN's right-wing death squads • U.S. military and economic aid to Duarte's junta • Soviet, Cuban and other external aid to the insurgents • Military stalemate • Insurgents lose external aid • The Arias peace plan • The United Nations peace offensive • The war ends • The United Nations peacekeeping force • The cost • Continuing government repression • The UN Truth Commission • President Cristiani objects • The secret FMLN arms cache in Nicaragua • The death squads strike again • Incriminating U.S. intelligence files • The last chapter is not yet written

. . . El Salvador is at war because it is one of the sickest societies in Latin America. Its archaic social structure remains basically colonial. Despite some efforts at change, a tiny urban elite and dominating cast of army officers essentially rule, but do not effectively govern, an illiterate, disease-ridden and frustrated majority of peasants and urban slum-dwellers. Order is often imposed by violence; there is not now, nor has there ever been, a just legal system. The rebels, in short, have had ample cause to lead a revolution.

JAMES LeMOYNE, 1989[1]

As WITH other Latin American countries, tiny El Salvador's five million people look back on a long history of rebellion, first from Spanish rule, then from the rule of poverty and hopelessness imposed by a small elite which owned 60 percent of the arable land and which controlled what was virtually a private army. Protest movements occasionally sprung up during the nineteenth and early twentieth centuries only to be suppressed by a harsh succession of authoritarian, usually military, governments, but not until 1932 did extreme violence begin to become a way of life.

In 1932, the secretary-general of the small Communist Party (PCES), Augustín Farabundo Martí, led a peasant insurrection put down by the summary execution of ten thousand people—the *matanza* (slaughter) never to be forgotten by the little people. More military governments followed, the dust settling in 1961 when a coup put Lieutenant Colonel Adalberto Rivera of the National Conciliation Party (PCN) in power. Rivera's six-year rule was repressive enough but he did improve the country's economy and increase its export trade. Rivera's administration saw the rise of the opposing Christian Democratic Party (PDC) whose candidate, José Napoleón Duarte, was elected mayor of the capital, San Salvador. Rivera attempted to counter the PDC and a growing Communist opposition by forming the Democratic Nationalist Organization (ORDEN)—" . . . a large, secretive paramilitary organization"[2] whose death squads ruthlessly attempted to eliminate *any* opposition.

Rivera's successor, Colonel Fidel Sánchez Hernández, ran into economic difficulties brought on by the fall of cotton and coffee prices and by the outbreak of a brief war with Honduras in mid-1969, a senseless dispute provoked by Salvador accusing Honduras of a genocidal policy toward some three hundred thousand mostly illegal immigrant Salvadoran workers in Honduras.[3] After several thousand lives were lost and a great deal of money spent, the shooting ended in a precarious truce.

At this time, the secretary-general of El Salvador's Communist Party, Salvador Cayetano Carpio, tried to persuade the party to open a Maoist-style protracted revolution, an effort that caused his expulsion from the party. Undeterred, Cayetano Carpio and a small band of guerrillas, after training in Cuba, Vietnam, and elsewhere, returned to El Salvador to establish the country's first guerrilla organization, the Farabundo Martí Popular Forces of Liberation (FPL), which commenced a series of guerrilla terrorist actions in San Salvador and soon grew in numbers and operation to form a formidable threat to the government.

In 1972, a patently fraudulent election, in which the coalition party's candidate, José Napoleón Duarte, made an unsuccessful challenge, placed Colonel Arturo Molino of the PCN in office. A postelection coup attempt by Duarte having failed, he was arrested and exiled to Venezuela.

Molina's regime was a disaster as was that of his PCN successor, General Carlos Humberto Romero, president from 1977 to 1979. Instead of trying to come to terms with rising opposition, the ruling junta was determined to eliminate it. Growing excesses committed by police, soldiers, and death squads of off-duty right-wing policemen and soldiers—in 1975, a dozen protesting students were shot to death—caused even Roman Catholic priests to defy superiors and become political activists, in some instances joining Cayetano Carpio's and other burgeoning guerrilla movements whose members, actively operating in cities and the countryside, were frequently at odds with each other as had happened in Nicaragua.[4]

The PCES, pressed by the Soviet Union, meanwhile had reversed course and in 1979 accepted armed struggle as the only means to achieve its revolutionary ends—as Carpio had insisted all along. At Fidel Castro's urging, its secretary-general, Schafik Jorge Handal, now turned to the task of uniting all revolutionary groups into one central organization.

At this time, five major guerrilla groups were operating in El Salvador: the PCES with some two thousand members, some of them guerrilla fighters soon to be formed into the Armed Forces of Liberation (FAL); Cayetano Carpio's FPL, which was allied with the Popular Revolutionary Block (BPR), a mass organization with perhaps fifty to eighty thousand members; Joaquín Villalobos' People's Revolutionary Army (ERP), a splinter group from the PCES which had grown to some two thousand guerrilla fighters; Fernan Cienfuegos' Armed Forces of National Resistance (FARN), a splinter group from the ERP which claimed one hundred thousand supporters; and Robert Roca's (probably an alias) Revolutionary Party of Central American Workers (PRTC) with only a few hundred activist, mostly urban, guerrilla terrorists.[5]

Disparate as were these groups, they shared a great many things in common. Semantics aside, their basic goal was to impose a Communist government on El Salvador along the lines of Castro's Cuba, although at least one leader, ERP's Villalobos, saw victory in El Salvador as a springboard to a Communist Central America.[6] All agreed that the only way to make the revolution succeed was by violence, be it in the cities or in the countryside.

To finance their operations, the groups depended initially on the traditional means of bank robberies and kidnapings for ransom, but such are the expenses of revolution that all groups were soon beholden to foreign countries which either donated or sold them arms and equipment: the Soviet bloc, Libya, the PLO, the Basque ETA, Cuba, Angola, Ethiopia, various Latin American revolutionary movements, and radical movements including those within the United States.

Marked similarities also showed in propaganda techniques, recruitment (middle-class intellectuals, students, workers, peasants), indoctrination (tough and merciless), organization, intelligence collection, use of front groups, security, training at home and abroad, the intransigent doctrinaire stance of leaders and lieutenants, and the preference of group leaders to conduct operations from Managua, capital of Nicaragua.

But grave differences existed in other spheres owing to capricious leaders, conflicting ideologies, incompatible strategy and tactics, cohesiveness, varying degrees of morale, discipline, security, and, most of all, operational effectiveness. Although a single revolutionary party, the Farabundo Martí National Liberation Front (FMLN) appeared in 1980, its guerrilla components were not going to change their ways even though urged to do so by moderates of the political front, the Democratic Revolutionary Front (FDR). Had they done so, there might well have been a coalition or even a Communist government in El Salvador today.

When Romero's government fell to a military coup by a short-lived junta of younger reformist officers, José Napoleón Duarte returned from exile to merge his Christian Democrats (PDC) with a new ruling junta dominated by senior generals, the majority of whom held no interest in promulgating what the PDC ostensibly championed—social and economic reforms, elimination of human rights abuses, negotiations with rebel leaders. The day after Duarte joined the PDC to the junta, seven PDC leaders left the party, declaring that a " . . . program of reform with repression runs contrary to the fundamentals of the Christian Democrats."[7] Although Duarte pushed through a land reform bill that initially " . . . redistributed about 20 percent of El Salvador's arable land," owing to right-wing obstructionism " . . . it had little of the sweeping social and political effect for which it was designed."[8] That did not deter the Carter administration, upset by the Sandinista victory in Nicaragua, from sending a team of U.S. military advisers to El Salvador and from preparing to resume "nonlethal" military aid which it had suspended in 1977.[9]

Violence occasioned by military, police, ORDEN, and guerrilla excesses was now routine. In early 1980, a right-wing death squad murdered powerful critic Archbishop Oscar Arnulfo Romero while he was saying mass. In June, soldiers stormed the National University, a left-wing stronghold, killed at least fifty students, and permanently closed the institution. Later in the year, six opposition party leaders were kidnaped and murdered and four Roman Catholic nuns, U.S. citizens, were murdered by right-wing goons (which caused a brief suspension of U.S. aid). Leftist terrorists countered with kidnapings and civil demonstrations, which led to more killings. By year's end, the fighting in cities and countryside would claim nine thousand lives in what was becoming all-out civil war,[10] recognized as such by the Carter administration which in October sent more U.S. military advisers.

Recruits meanwhile flocked to guerrilla banners, but the new umbrella revolutionary party, the FMLN, could not hold off the erosion of separatism. There was no central guerrilla command. The major guerrilla forces continued to run their own wars, some striking in the cities, some in rural areas, some in both, and they were also divided on the subject of protracted war versus negotiated peace.[11] Throughout 1980, these groups variously ambushed rural army units, raided garrisons to steal weapons and ammunition, and blew up roads and bridges both to disrupt army communications and to prevent export crops from getting to market. During this period, Nicaragua's Sandinistas were believed to be smuggling Russian- and Cuban-supplied arms to Salvadoran rebels via Honduras, though not in the quantities claimed by either San Salvador or Washington.

Early in 1981, the guerrillas opened a "final offensive" in the north and called for a general strike to bring down the government, a move correctly condemned by Cayetano Carpio as premature. This Salvadoran version of the Vietnam Tet offensive failed. The army sent guerrilla forces reeling, no major strike developed, and the insurgents, at that time particularly powerful in the cities, lost many of their urban bases and were forced to retreat to mountainous areas for temporary sanctuary. It is interesting to note that " . . . the United States sent no arms to El Salvador between 1977 and 1981; the San Salvador military thus defeated the guerrilla offensive of January 1981 *without* significant US assistance."[12]

The growing guerrilla threat taken with Romero and the PDC's fall from power had brought a hardening of the right that swung landowners and business executives to the support of Major Roberto d'Aubuisson Arrieta's ultra-right party, the National Republican Alliance

(ARENA). In early 1981, the lame-duck Carter administration authorized $5 million worth of military equipment to the junta.[13] The new Reagan administration, apparently having learned nothing from Vietnam and convinced that it could eliminate what it called the Cuban-Russian-inspired insurgency within a few months, chose to attempt to settle a social revolution by military power as opposed to seeking a political solution through regional diplomacy. Duarte's junta was given a total fifty-four U.S. military advisers who were to reorganize, train, and equip the Salvadoran military forces: $25 million worth of military aid was granted to supply modern weapons including a squadron of A-37 fighter planes; simultaneously, fifteen hundred officers and men were being trained at United States camps, a figure that would rise to nine thousand by 1983 and would result in doubling the size of an already inflated officer corps and more atrocities such as the massacre by the new Atlactl Battalion of a reported eight hundred people including forty-two children in a remote village.[14]

The refurbished Salvadoran army, largely trained in conventional warfare by U.S. advisers, more and more resembled the laggard South Vietnam ARVN of the sixties and seventies, including impossibly corrupt commanders, low morale, a rising desertion rate, and severe repressive measures against anyone suspected of aiding the insurgents. So blatant were human rights abuses that the U. S. Congress passed a law under which President Reagan had to certify that the Salvadoran government was making satisfactory progress in eliminating human rights abuses before military aid was provided. Reagan's grudging compliance was academic, his favorable pronouncements virtually meaningless; in late 1983, he ended certification by vetoing a bill that called for its continuation.

In 1982, the ultra-rightist Roberto d'Aubuisson was elected president of a constituent assembly whose members belonged predominantly to the right wing. At Washington's insistence, a conservative lawyer, Alvaro Magaña, was appointed interim president of the country while the assembly prepared a new constitution. During this period, Washington's hopes for a quick military victory were dashed by the continuing poor performance of the Salvadoran army. The guerrillas, on the other hand, had recovered in large part from the humiliating defeat of their 1981 "final offensive." In early 1982, a successful raid by an eight-man ERP guerrilla team trained in Cuba knocked out most of the fledgling air force (including several U.S.-supplied helicopters) at Ilopango Air Base. Attacks on isolated army garrisons increased to the extent that in 1983 " . . . the guerrillas could make credible claims that most of their weapons, including even mortars and artillery pieces, came from the United States by way of captured government troops."[15] Once emerged from mountain sanctuaries, the insurgents had begun carrying the revolutionary message to rural peasant areas, which increasingly fell under their control as they continued to ambush and attack government troops and to sabotage the infrastructure by blowing up roads, bridges and power lines, and burning cotton, coffee and sugar crops and factories. Simultaneously, the FMLN infiltrated San Salvador and other cities, where urban guerrilla terrorists functioned as the guerrilla equivalent of ORDEN's feared death squads. Yet such was the lack of the Communist political appeal that in many areas the guerrillas were suffered rather than enjoyed. In 1983, it was evident that a military stalemate existed, with some observers giving the edge to the insurgents.[16]

Insurgent morale suffered a major setback when Fidel Castro, as one result of the successful U.S. invasion of Grenada in October 1983, prudently announced that his client countries could not count on military assistance from Cuba in case they were attacked by the United States. Equally upsetting were the 1984 spring elections which brought a moderate Christian Democrat government led by José Napoleón Duarte to power and with that another hefty increase in U.S. military aid. A major split also occurred in guerrilla ranks. Salvador Cayetano Carpio, leader of the large FPL guerrilla force, had always insisted on a policy of "protracted war." When his second-in-command and former mistress, Mélida Anaya (Commandante Ana María), followed Cuban and Nicaraguan wishes in opting for a more conciliatory negotiating policy, Cayetano Carpio had her murdered and soon after committed suicide. The cause was further damaged when one of Cayetano Carpio's urban groups killed a U.S. naval officer, as well as by the highly publicized murder of thirty captured soldiers by his guerrillas.[17]

These and other guerrilla aberrations hindered but did not halt operations. One experienced observer noted that at year's end, " . . . the Salvadoran army allowed the most modern U.S. designed garrison in the nation to be overrun by a guerrilla force that it had not even known was in the area. Two days later, in the first hours of 1984, the rebels blew up the largest, and supposedly the most heavily guarded bridge in the country."[18]

More mobile tactics introduced by an army now numbering forty-two thousand equipped with helicopters and gunships seemed to favor government chances, but it soon became apparent that the army could not divorce itself from U.S.-imposed conventional strategy and tactics.[19] Although the guerrillas suffered heavy casualties, including those from aerial bombing attacks which also produced counterproductive civilian casualties, these were replaced and guerrilla strength remained at an estimated nine to eleven thousand.[20] Search-and-destroy missions inside guerrilla country in the northern and eastern areas accomplished little more than to cause the enemy to regroup in small units, which carried the war to the central and western areas and to the cities in the form of guerrilla terrorist attacks. To the government's consternation, the guerrillas retained sufficient mobility to mass their forces for large-scale attacks on military garrisons and other key targets. Since government forces failed to hold guerrilla areas, the guerrillas continued to be supported by large numbers of peasants who, often under duress, furnished money, food, and information.

Rebel tactics changed considerably in 1985. ERP leader Joaquín Villalobos despite opposition from subordinates ordered his guerrillas to plant large numbers of antipersonnel mines within rebel-controlled areas, a promiscuous tactic believed to have accounted for 70 per cent of army casualties (807 dead and 1,885 wounded from July 1984 to June 1985) and also civilian casualties, which of course cost the guerrillas some support.[21] Although the guerrillas continued on occasion to attack in strength, they relied increasingly on urban terrorism: an attack in June killed four U. S. Marines and some civilians; local mayors were kidnaped and some were killed; President Duarte's daughter was kidnaped and released in return for freeing a number of important prisoners. Government forces and secret death squads answered this offensive with the usual repressive measures—and the war went on.

Duarte was in trouble. His attempts at reform had been stymied in almost every direction by rightist opposition. Meetings with guerrilla leaders led to nothing. Inflation and unemployment stood at over 50 per cent; labor unrest continued to grow. This unsatisfactory situation continued into 1986 and 1987 with only slight changes, although a further increase in the size of the military forces and an additional $111.5 million in U.S. military aid allowed some pressure to be put on the insurgents. Hope for peace briefly revived in 1987 with the announcement of a regional peace plan worked out by Costa Rica's President Arias, but its eminently sensible provisions brought an immediate backlash from the right that was marked by significant gains of d'Aubuisson's ARENA party in the legislative and municipal elections in early 1988, as well as by a sharp increase in violence caused by renewed death squad murders and guerrilla car-bombings in the cities and greatly increased insurgent activity in the countryside.

The rebels also were in trouble. Soviet Premier Mikhail Gorbachev's diplomatic initiative designed to win great-power backing for a new Russia boded ill for further Soviet-Cuban support, already reduced to a trickle; nor did the Sandinistas seem any longer overly enthusiastic in fomenting Central American rebellions. Neither was their position inside El Salvador all that favorable. The top command remained split as to whether to continue protracted war or to join peace negotiations; almost no rational leader believed that a general uprising was possible or even that the insurgents could win a general election. This left a negotiated peace that was anathema to hard-liners convinced that such would sound the death knell for the revolution. There remained but one course. Documents captured by the army in 1988 revealed " . . . the most rigid, arid Marxist analysis imaginable and outline[d] a strategy of revolutionary war based on sabotage, terrorism, military attack and negotiation [as a tactic to win power]."[22] That was precisely the form of warfare that the Salvadoran army was least able to fight. As a later report " . . . by four senior U.S. Army officers notes: 'despite ESAF's [Salvadoran armed forces] improved battlefield skills, failure to develop a proper framework for counterinsurgency operations led to a deadlock. . . . As of April 1988, a tough, resourceful opponent remains in the field . . . showing no inclination to give up.' "[23]

This strategy was confirmed during the two months prior to the 1989 elections. With the victory of Alfredo Cristiani, a businessman and the ARENA candidate, the government swung further to the right although Cristiani himself headed a group of "moderates" within this ultra-right party. Cristiani's early measures, which included steep price increases in public transport and electricity, the return of banks to private ownership, unpopular modifications in the land reform program, and increased arrest of left-wing political activists, were guaranteed to insure continued violence. But Cristiani also named " . . . a national commission for contacts with the FMLN" that he hoped would lead to peace talks.[24]

After a summer of murder, preliminary talks between government and FMLN representatives in Mexico and Costa Rica produced little more than an airing of previous intransigent stands before being broken off during another violent orgy of fighting that led to intensive bombing of the poorer portions of San Salvador occupied by FMLN units, declaration of a state of siege, new anti-terror laws, mass arrests, and more death squad murders including the shocking killing of six Jesuit priests. By year's end, the fighting had claimed 401 guerrilla, 476 military, and over two thousand civilian lives and of course thousands more wounded and homeless.[25]

The standoff continued into 1990 but, as had happened earlier in Nicaragua, internal and external pressures weighed heavily on both sides. President Cristiani was in a very uncomfortable position. It was all too clear that his armed forces had acted impetuously and stupidly in the recent fighting, to the extent that some heretofore sympathetic members of the U. S. Congress now considered motions to curtail or even withdraw military aid. This antagonism softened somewhat when a colonel and eight soldiers were charged with murder for killing the Jesuit priests and when Cristiani fired his chief of the air force. At the end of January, he was received in the White House where President Bush reiterated his complete support although stressing the necessity of military and other reforms vital to any renewal of negotiations and indeed to continuing U.S. aid. All this, however, did not lessen the fact of a seemingly determined enemy bent on destroying a wavering state.

But this enemy was in an even more precarious position than Cristiani's government. Guerrilla units had suffered heavy casualties in the recent fighting, losses no longer easily replaced. The Soviet Union's disintegration taken with the newly elected Chamorro government in Nicaragua spelled a virtual end to external arms support (which the government would continue to receive). Recent security force round-ups had severely damaged urban guerrilla terrorist movements and had sent sympathetic left-wingers scurrying for cover and even escape from the country. Even the most intransigent FMLN leaders could not deny the movement's increasing isolation with concomitant loss of resources and morale.

These various factors combined to open the door to a new United Nations peace initiative in 1990. The UN had long been concerned with the war and with the various regional and U.S. initiatives that one after another had come to nothing. Backed now by Russia and the U.S., in April it brought Salvadoran Government and FMLN representatives to Geneva where each side agreed to accept further negotiations under UN auspices. The UN's goal was a cease-fire in September but that was not achieved owing to the old conundrum—which came first, the chicken-and-egg: the refusal of the military to accept reforms including a major reduction in size and the refusal of the FMLN to accept a cease-fire and give up its arms before those reforms were accomplished. The U. S. Congress showed its displeasure with the military's intransigence by voting to halve the current $85 million in military aid,[26] but the FMLN also earned displeasure by conducting a series of co-ordinated attacks against military targets (for the first time using surface-to-air missiles supplied by Nicaragua). Undeterred and strongly backed by other isthmus countries as well as by the U.S., Mexico, Venezuela, Colombia and Spain, the UN continued its paternal efforts. Legislative elections in March 1991 cost the ARENA party its majority and were taken as an encouraging sign of political moderation necessary if peace was ever to be achieved. Negotiations continued during summer of 1991 with each side moderating its demands and agreement reached on a number of sweeping constitutional and institutional (particularly military and po-lice) reforms that had been major stumbling blocks in past talks. As had been the case in Vietnam, a great deal of fighting accompanied the negotiations, inspired in large part by the FMLN wanting to control more territory as chances for a cease-fire improved.

Nonetheless, negotiations proceeded with one issue settled here, another there. Although the year ended with no agreement, only two weeks later the last hurdles were overcome and a peace settlement signed. Under its terms the Cristiani government agreed to a series of human rights reforms including a purge of those members of the army and police forces who had involved themselves with the infamous death squads. The FMLN guerrillas, on their part, agreed to turn in all their arms and to form a legitimate political party. The agreement also included a very welcome cease-fire on the first day of February 1993 that was followed by the arrival of a United Nations peace-keeping force (ONUSAL) and pledges by Western nations to help rebuild the country.

Thus the end of a twelve-year guerrilla war that cost at least seventy-five thousand killed, perhaps a million refugees, billions of dollars in property damage and a shattered economy.

Well, not quite.

In September 1992 ONUSAL officials and those of the human rights group Americas Watch said that ". . . the end of the war has reduced human rights violations but that summary executions, arbitrary arrests and cruel treatment of police suspects continue."[27] As increasing evidence pointed to continuing army and police complicity in human rights violations, suspicious UN officials sponsored a three-member Truth Commission, which ". . . found the state and military responsible for most of the atrocities of El Salvador's civil war," and which recommended, among other things, "the dismissal of the nation's supreme court and the immediate dismissal of forty officers accused of human rights abuses."[28]

President Alfredo Cristiani, who had singularly failed to carry out the purge of the military and police agreed to in the peace terms, was still not to be moved. The report, in his words, did not fulfill "the desires of the majority of Salvadorans." Sounding like the leading members of the U.S. Republican Party after the fall of Vietnam, he went on: "That desire is to forgive and forget the painful past that has caused us so much suffering."[29]

The UN effort received another major setback in May, this time from the Farabundo Martí Liberation Front (FMLN). Only days after FMLN leaders told UN Secretary General Butros Butros-Ghali that all guerrilla arms had been destroyed or turned in, an accidental explosion in the Nicaraguan capital of Managua revealed an enormous arsenal of diverse FMLN weapons, probably hidden with the connivance of Nicaraguan Sandinista leaders. Butros' protests to the FMLN caused voluntary informants to pinpoint fifteen more arsenals in Managua, after which embarrassed FMLN leader Schafik Jorge Handal insisted that *now* all arms had been destroyed.[30]

Cristiani's subsequent attempts to dampen criticism by announcing the relief of his defense minister General René Emilio Ponce—the person said to have ordered the murder in 1989 of six Jesuit priests—failed to satisfy disgruntled liberal critics while infuriating extreme rightists. In November rightist death squads assassinated two prominent FMLN party leaders, killings at once denounced by Cristiani, who promised "serious investigations."[31]

The Cristiani government, facing elections in March 1994, suffered another blow in November when the U.S. government released twelve thousand heretofore secret documents that both confirmed and enlarged the unpalatable facts of Salvadoran death squad activities from the early 1980s onward, activities known to but overlooked by both the Reagan and Bush administrations. They also confirmed the participation of some of Cristiani's current political colleagues, including officeholders, in these activities.[32]

As of this writing, December 1993, the U.S. Congress is pressing the Clinton administration to force the release of still more pertinent documents that undoubtedly will greatly embarrass the Cristiani government (not to mention Messrs. Reagan and Bush), but just may cause it to get serious about implementing promised reforms before the March elections. Sadly enough, a great deal more violence will undoubtedly occur. As Jorge Castañeda has pointed out in his informative book *Utopia Unarmed*, El Salvador is one of the Latin American countries where a last chapter is yet to be written.[33]

CHAPTER EIGHTY-FOUR

1. LeMoyne, 106–7.
2. *Encyclopaedia Britannica*, 1991, Vol. 15, 694.
3. International Institute for Strategic Studies, *Strategic Survey 1968*, 55 ff.
4. Rice, 106. See also, Thomas Anderson; LeMoyne.
5. Radu and Tismaneanu, 187–8, 189, 194, 205, 220–1, 228–9.
6. Ibid., 219.
7. Bonner, xvi.
8. Dickey, 680.
9. Bonner, xv.
10. International Institute for Strategic Studies, *Strategic Survey 1980–81*, 22–7.
11. Riding, 645–6.
12. Treverton, 137.
13. International Institute for Strategic Studies, *Strategic Survey 1980–81*, 24.
14. *Newsweek*, November 2, 1992.
15. Dickey, 677.
16. Gleijeses, 1060–61.
17. Dickey, 681–2.
18. Ibid., 683.
19. Shultz, 362.
20. International Institute for Strategic Studies, *Strategic Survey 1984–85*, 198.
21. Ibid, *Strategic Survey 1985–86*, 198. See also, Radu and Tismaneanu, 214.
22. LeMoyne, 116.
23. Shultz, 362.
24. International Institute for Strategic Studies, *Strategic Survey 1989–90*, 190.
25. Ibid., 191.
26. *International Herald Tribune*, June 26, 1991.
27. *The Independent* (U.K.), September 3, 1992.
28. *International Herald Tribune*, March 20, 1993.

29. Ibid., March 20, 1993.
30. *Newsweek,* July 26, 1993. See also, *International Herald Tribune,* November 9, 1993.
31. *International Herald Tribune,* November 9, 1993.
32. Ibid., November 10, 1993.
33. Castañeda.

CHAPTER 85

Spread of Communist insurgency in Colombia • Divergent terrorist guerrilla groups • Varying guerrilla fortunes • The drug equation • Government counterinsurgency measures • The guerrillas strike back • The government declares war on the drug-guerrilla alliance • Cartel king Pablo Escobar Gaviría's imprisonment and escape • Escobar's death • Continuing guerrilla activity • Security forces and human rights abuses • Turbulent Peruvian politics • Emergence of terrorist guerrilla groups in the 1960s • Governmental disasters • Rise of Abimael Guzmán Reynoso's terrorist guerrilla party, Sendero Luminoso (SL), or Shining Path • The guerrilla alliance with the cocaine cartels • Guzmán's gains • Peru's economic decline • The refugee problem • Enter President Alberto Fujimori • Fujimori cleans the government's house • Guzmán goes to jail • Guzmán's about-face • The SL's decline • Remaining guerrilla strength • The task ahead

SPURRED BY economic dissatisfaction and the stunning success of Fidel Castro's revolution, a flurry of guerrilla groups emerged in Colombia in the 1960s. The first group, the National Liberation Army (ELN), was formed by dissident young members of the Colombian Communist Party (PCC) in 1964. Operating primarily in rural northeastern Colombia and financed by robberies, kidnapings, voluntary contributions, extortions and " . . . continual and substantial report from Cuba,"[1] it grew to a few hundred active guerrillas by the late 1960s.

A second group, the Revolutionary Armed Forces of Colombia (FARC), appeared in 1966 as the militant branch of the PCC. Initially it was a rural movement of a few hundred peasants led by a thirty-six-year-old peasant activist Pedro Antonio María (aka Manuel Marulanda Vélez). Based mainly in the south and funded similarly as the ELN, it

1108

continued to grow during the 1960s though failing to establish Régis Debray's concept of a revolutionary *foco*, that is a liberated area secure from the intrusion of security forces. A third guerrilla group, the People's Liberation Army (EPL), was formed in 1967 as the militant arm of a splinter Communist Party, the Communist Party of Colombia-Marxist-Leninist (PCC-ML), which pledged fealty to Chinese communism and was supported in part by China. It remained small, perhaps 250 guerrillas, and enjoyed only limited success in its Maoist-inspired insurgency in the provinces north-northwest of Medellín. A fourth group, the 19 of April Movement (M-19) appeared in southern Colombia only in 1974.[2] Aided by the now-standard means of financing— robberies, kidnapings, voluntary contributions, extortion, aid from Cuba, and, increasingly, payments from drug traffickers—M-19 grew rapidly to number perhaps five thousand members within a few years.

These divergent groups might have operated for years without gaining undue prominence and strength had it not been for the multibillion-dollar traffic in a drug called cocaine. Cocaine has been around for a long time—in the 1890s it was openly sold by Parke Davis in the United States and it has always been a suspected ingredient of Coca-Cola[3]— but it only started to become big business when markets expanded in Western nations beginning in the late 1960s and 1970s (a residue of the Vietnam War in the case of the United States). Cocaine comes from the humble coca leaf, of which tons are grown and processed into coca paste in remote areas of Peru, Bolivia, and Colombia for refining into cocaine and marketing by two Colombian cartels, the Cali cartel some 150 miles southwest of Bogotá and the Medellín cartel about the same distance to the northwest. As demand in the United States increased, so did cultivation. In 1981, Colombian peasants produced twenty-five hundred tons; in 1985 about eighteen thousand tons. In 1985, " . . . the street value of cocaine exported from Colombia to the U.S.A. was estimated to be $80 billion a year."[4]

This pernicious industry affected Colombian guerrilla groups in several ways. During the 1970s, guerrilla leaders homed in on peasant coca growers and in Mafia style demanded 10 per cent of crop sales " . . . in exchange for 'protection' from the police and military."[5] For the FARC, this eventually brought in about $40 million a year. Another vast sum came from the cartels, which hired guerrillas to protect refinery operations from army and police raids. It was primarily drug money that enabled M-19 to grow so rapidly and expand northward, setting up guerrilla terrorist groups in the principal cities. These groups soon sold their services to the drug barons in the form of hit operations against dangerous opponents in government, the judiciary, police, and army.

It was not all easy going for the guerrillas. The Colombian police and army contained a great many well-trained men loyal to the government. As these organizations received advisers and improved equipment such as helicopters, mainly from the United States, their operations improved. By 1979, ten of the ELN's top leaders had been killed. If in the same year M-19 guerrillas made headlines by tunneling into a Bogotá armory to seize nearly six thousand weapons,[6] an ensuing army operation captured an estimated hundred of its members. In 1984, a raid on a cocaine-refining complex netted the government nearly fourteen tons of cocaine (street value $1.2 billion).[7] Another challenge came from disgruntled policemen and soldiers who formed death squads which mercilessly eliminated anyone even suspected of left-wing affiliations (a campaign all too familiar to other Latin American governments which reaped international opprobrium and in some cases either a decrease or a cutoff in aid as a result). The groups also suffered from internal dissension and from failure to establish secure liberated areas essential for a successful rural insurgency.

In spring of 1984, these and other factors resulted in President Belisario Betancur Cuartas' government bringing about a truce with M-19, EPL, and FARC (the diehard ELN refused to deal). It soon broke down and violence increased. In 1985, cartel leaders had the minister of justice murdered. Betancur declared a state of siege—detention of terrorists without bail, trial by military courts, even possible extradition to the United States for trial.[8] A few months later, M-19 terrorists stormed the Palace of Justice in Bogotá, undoubtedly upon order of the cartels. The ensuing shoot-out cost about a hundred lives including those of the president of the Supreme Court, several of his justices, and all of the terrorists, among whom were a number of important leaders.

This was the mess inherited by the new president, Virgilio Barco Vargas, in 1986. At first the guerrillas, urban and rural, had things their own way, as did the drug barons. The ELN had been hurt but it was still strong and rich enough to carry out several urban and rural operations culminating in 1986 when it opened a campaign to drive foreign oil companies out of northeastern Colombia, mainly by sabotage and raids on installations. In time this would total $50 million in damages and seriously threaten oil production in Colombia and Venezuela.[9] M-19 was also hurt but still managed to establish and maintain contacts with revolutionary groups in Peru, Ecuador, Venezuela, El Salvador, Guatemala, Nicaragua, and Panama.

The guerrilla operations that were designed to turn Latin America into a socialist paradise were increasingly taking a backseat to the drug war. In early 1987, a massive police operation pulled in over seventy important drug cartel members, their arrogance frighteningly demonstrated by one who declared that " . . . his supporters would kill a judge

1110

a week in Colombia or the USA until he was released."[10] In late 1988, Alan Riding reported from Bogotá:

> ... So far this year, 3,000 people have died in the political violence in this country of 31 million, including almost 800 soldiers and policemen and 700 guerrillas. More than 300 have been kidnapped by leftists or criminals, while one of the country's six loosely allied rebel groups has bombed a pipeline carrying the country's oil exports on at least sixty occasions this year.

But Riding also wrote that:

> ... with the country exhausted by violence, the front line of the war has become the battle for peace, with the main leftist guerrilla groups and the government blaming each other for continuation of the conflict.[11]

Only in 1989 did the government agree to open talks with M-19 and other guerrilla groups. Although these led to the temporary breakup of M-19, they scarcely stemmed the omnipresent killings (for some years one murder every three hours in Medellín) that led up to the 1990 presidential elections.

By now the guerrillas were no longer the major security threat to the country. The drug traffickers were. Aided by massive assistance from the United States, President Barco opened war. The cartels responded predictably. Another wave of terrible violence covered the stricken country. Cartel thugs, many of them guerrillas, killed judges and local officials, journalists were taken hostage, newspaper offices burned, a commercial aircraft blown up with 107 killed. Three anti-cartel presidential candidates were murdered. Nevertheless, the anti-cartel candidate of the Liberal Party, César Gaviría Trujillo, was elected president, a clear mandate to continue the war.

At first it seemed as if the government was gaining the upper hand. In early 1991, the joint leader of the Medellín cartel, Jorge Luis Ochoa, surrendered. Two months later, the Maoist guerrilla group (EPL) converted into a legal political party. But in February, a blast in the center of Medellín City killed twenty-two and injured 135 persons, apparently in retaliation for Jorge Luis Ochoa's surrender. In the same month, as protest to the opening of the new Constituent Assembly, FARC and ELN guerrillas struck a variety of targets to produce a new round of heavy fighting. But a congressional decision in May to repeal the law that permitted extradition of drug traffickers (primarily to the United States) brought the unexpected surrender of the Medellín cartel leader,

Pablo Escobar Gaviría. A terrorist amnesty law in the summer was said to prove effective and new anti-terrorist laws passed that autumn seemed to presage at least a partial solution of the cartel problem.

This hope died shortly after birth. Escobar's imprisonment only enhanced the Cali cartel's operations, which, despite new laws and millions of dollars of aid from the United States, not only continued to flourish but to expand to new large markets in Europe.

This was bad enough, but then came the horrible truth that Escobar had jobbed his own arrest. Escobar's "prison" (which he helped to design) included a luxury complex, " . . . the work of a professional interior designer for a rich bachelor."[12] According to British journalist Tim Ross, Escobar's new home included a richly furnished salon with bar, TV, Jacuzzi, waterbed (soon familiar to imported whores), and an office full of the latest communications technology (supplemented by fifty carrier pigeons) necessary to run his international drug empire as if he were sitting in Medellín. When life palled, he could retreat to a nest of luxury cabins secluded in the woods.[13] Guards were a joke. He was surrounded by his own security force (Ross who supplemented his article by detailed photographs speculated that fears of assassination may have prompted Escobar's surrender). This was the secure prison cosmeticized by barbed-wire fences, searchlights, and even a minefield to reassure the public that Enemy Number One was safely out of harm's way.

The blowup came when the government, stung by publicized allegations of Escobar's luxurious life- and business-style while a guest of the nation, announced that he would be transferred to another prison. In July 1992, the prisoner, who may have undergone plastic surgery to disguise himself, escaped along with seven "guards" after a shoot-out with the army. Although his escape made little difference to the drug traffic, which the Cali cartel had largely taken over, his capture at once became a point of honor with the greatly embarrassed Gaviría government. After months of concentrated police work by a special unit, aided by a CIA intelligence team, the quarry was run to ground in early December—not surprising in view of a $5 million price on his head—and was killed in a police shootout.[14]

This was something of a Pyrrhic victory. Despite President César Gaviría's assurances in July 1993 that the Cali cartel would soon be broken up, and despite a warrant that has been issued for the arrest of the Cali boss, Miguel Rodríguez Orejuela, the Cali organization continues to prosper.[15] As of this writing, December 1993, there are disturbing rumors of a possible deal being made between the government and the cartel whereby the latter would be dissolved in return for its bosses retaining their billions of dollars and being accepted as legitimate businessmen.

Nor do the two major guerrilla organizations, ELN and FARC,

seem to be on the point of surrender, as Gaviría also suggested was the case.[16] In 1992 oil lines were blown up over sixty times, which cost the state oil company millions of dollars; twenty more such attacks had occurred by mid-1993.[17] As of December 1993 guerrillas still control large areas in the countryside and are active in the cities. In going after them, Colombia's security forces, along with the infamous death squads, have reaped considerable, apparently justified opprobrium from diverse human rights groups, which claim that far more opponents of the Gaviría regime have been eliminated than either guerrillas or members of the drug cartels.[18] Should Gaviría ever succeed in eliminating major drug trafficking—no easy task—his next job will be to return his country to the democratic processes that he claims to embrace.

The Republic of Peru is the third largest and one of the most backward countries in South America and, from the standpoint of guerrilla warfare, by far the most perverse. It also has one of the most turbulent political records in Latin America, which helps to explain the problems of its twelve-year-old attempt to fashion a democratic government.

A major insurgency against a military dictatorship occurred in 1961 with the emergence of the Revolutionary Front of the Left (FIR). This Trotskyite group after mobilizing an estimated three hundred thousand peasants in the Cuzco area nearly four hundred miles southeast of Lima began seizing the enormous haciendas and distributing their hundreds of thousands of acres of land to the Indian peasants. The movement was broken by the army in 1962 and its leader, Hugo Blanco, was imprisoned. But now a splinter group from the Peruvian Communist Party (PCP) organized the more militant National Liberation Army (ELN), while still another splinter group of young rebels created the Movement of the Revolutionary Left (MIR), both movements being Castro-inspired and -funded, and both eliminated in 1965 as serious threats with the arrest of one leader and the death of the other.

In 1963, another military dictatorship gave way to the election of Fernando Belaúnde Terry as president. During the next five years, Belaúnde pushed through important reforms that included expropriation and distribution to landless Indians of half a million acres of farmland, a major factor in ELN and MIR's failure to bring off a successful rural insurgency.

Belaúnde was forced from office in 1968 by a leftist military junta led by Juan Velasco Alvarado, a self-styled "revolutionary nationalist."[19] For seven years, the Velasco government pushed Peru back to an economic stone age by expropriating foreign (mainly U.S.) companies, breaking up vast haciendas, and, inevitably, forcing large sums of gold and foreign capital from the country. Heavy military expenditures did

1113

improve the combat potential of the army but only to fight conventional, *not* counterinsurgency warfare.

In 1975, still another coup, led by General Francisco Morales Bermúdez, resulted in a new constitution and, in 1980, the return of Belaúnde to the presidency. Belaúnde inherited an economic disaster, the dimensions of which can be judged from inflation rising to 3,240 per cent in five years. As if that weren't sufficient, he also inherited a new insurgency.

The threat was twofold. It came first from a Maoist group that had splintered from the PCP in 1964 and after many twists and turns finally consolidated itself as the Sendero Luminoso, or Shining Path (SL). Based primarily at the University of San Cristóbal in Ayacucho about two hundred miles southeast of Lima, the movement's leader was Abimael Guzmán Reynoso (aka Chairman Gonzalo), a messianic professor of philosophy who had built a disciplined cult of young disciples into a militant guerrilla movement. Guzmán's revolutionary goal was to replace capitalist rule by the ancient agricultural system of the Incas, a "pure" socialism that had appealed to Mao and Castro and would in time be emulated by Pol Pot in Cambodia (Kampuchea).[20]

The second threat came from a small Socialist splinter group of mostly university radicals and surviving members of the MIR. The Túpac Amaru Revolutionary Movement (MRTA) emerged as an urban guerrilla terrorist group in 1982 when it commenced a prolonged bombing campaign against international companies and foreign banks, probably in collusion with if not control of the SL, the idea being to drive pernicious foreign influence and capital out of the country.[21]

SL members amounted to perhaps two to three thousand in 1983, of which about half were Indians speaking only the Quechura language. Training was rudimentary. The guerrillas lacked weapons, depending for the most part on those bought or stolen from the army or taken from wounded or dead policemen and soldiers, and on dynamite stolen from the numerous mines in the area. Guzmán's attempt to establish liberated areas proved to be an expensive failure—in 1983 security forces claimed three thousand guerrilla casualties including a thousand dead.[22] Although this hurt the SL, it in no way terminated their operations, which soon expanded into the cities. Kidnapings and assassinations brought reprisals both by security forces and allied death squads. Human rights abuses rose as did Guzmán's own allies, inflation, and unemployment.[23]

And always those damn guerrillas. And coca.

The situation was this: Peru grows over 60 per cent of the world's supply of coca leaf, which is processed into coca paste and smuggled to drug cartels in Colombia and Mexico where it is refined to the white cocaine vicariously sold on North American (and increasingly European) streets. Long a staple commodity, coca's legal production is fixed at an annual eighteen million kilograms but " . . . illegal production is estimated to be in excess of fifty million kilograms."[24] According to one authority, James Anderson, " . . . the arable land devoted to growing coca" in the Tingo María area " . . . increased from 4,800 acres in 1970 to over 40,000 by the mid-1980s, the legal [cultivated] limit for the entire country."[25] By 1987, sixty-two thousand acres were reportedly under cultivation in the Upper Huállaga Valley alone.[26] When the government, pushed by the United States, attempted to wean peasants from coca cultivation in favor of other crops, it was met by blanket hostility, understandable in that *each* local resident in the producing areas was paid around $400 a month, virtually a fortune.[27] Nor was the government entirely enthusiastic about the program. Anderson estimates that in 1986 illegal exportation of cocaine amounted to $4 billion, of which " . . . some $1 billion found its way into the Peruvian economy."[28] Even worse, drug barons had bought a good many public servants including judges, administrators, mayors, police, and army personnel at all levels—in 1985, security forces smashed a huge drug smuggling operation run by personnel in the Peruvian Ministry of the Interior,[29] and this was probably just the tip of the iceberg. Either corrupt or intimidated judges have released an estimated 85 percent of guerrillas or guerrilla suspects seized by the military.

Add to this the guerrilla factor. Guzmán, a fanatic revolutionary who believes in the violent destruction of representative government in order to bring about world revolution, was welcomed by both coca-growing peasants and coca-paste-exporting drug barons. Despite the Belaúnde government's claim of guerrilla suppression, by 1984 the SL had expanded into the Tingo María area some 220 miles northeast of Lima on the "cocaine highway" to Colombia. Its presence there was no accident. In 1984, the coca trade was threatened by the U.S.-sponsored " . . . largest crop substitution program in South America."[30] SL guerrillas attacked the main camp near Tingo María, killed the local employees, and with them the program. On the one hand, SL guerrillas "protected" peasant growers and processors from thieves, for which they received a satisfactory "contribution"; on the other hand, they "protected" the processors and shippers from police and army intrusions in return for an alleged $500 million a year. This enabled Guzmán to fund his ever-expanding organization that cost a great deal of money to run and also to equip his guerrillas with more-modern weapons. The more cocaine paste exported the better in Guzmán's mind—for nothing could have been of greater assistance in toppling what he considered to be the already decadent Western society than hard drugs.

Belaúnde was replaced in the 1985 elections by the populist party APRA's candidate, Alan García Pérez, whose radical economic and financial policies eventually cost Peru international funding without drastically improving the over-all situation. As with Belaúnde so with García—Peru isolated from the international finance community, a stagnant economy, an 8,000 per cent inflation, massive unemployment, murders around the clock, corrupt and intimidated judges, a feckless and corrupt military, general strikes, more than two hundred thousand peasant refugees living in shantytown squalor, elected officials resigning for fear of the guerrillas, and all the while the SL growing stronger and expanding operations. Although security forces claimed some six thousand guerrilla causalties in 1987, the movement was still estimated to number ten thousand,[31] and had established liberated areas in the Andes Valley northwest of Ayacucho, key provinces that the SL would control in 1989 when, according to one report, half of the nation was " . . . living in emergency zones in which the army is given wide powers to combat the guerrillas."[32]

This was the scenario inherited by Alberto Fujimori, the son of immigrant Japanese parents who unexpectedly won the 1990 presidential election on a reformist ticket. Backed by a comfortable majority, Fujimori turned to the Peruvian equivalent of cleansing the Augean stables. Amazingly, he made considerable progress. He reduced human rights violations by the police, military, and death squads, he engineered an austerity budget that brought inflation under control, he resumed payments to the World Bank and thus regained eligibility for further loans, he stirred a reluctant army into organizing armed peasant patrols to defend villages against the SL guerrillas, and he supported a radical "new town" project. By means of government assistance, displaced migrants to the cities were given 90 square meter plots in theretofore "waste" areas on which to build their own brick houses and develop and run their own communities—the *pueblos jóvenes,* settlements of about five thousand people.[33]

He did none of this gracefully. Not being a politician, Fujimori did not hide his contempt for opposition congressmen; nor for corrupt judges, whom he called "jackals"; nor for a supine Roman Catholic Church hierarchy, which he called "medieval and recalcitrant"; nor for President Bush's anti-drug campaign, which he correctly criticized for being aimed more at the growers than at the users in the United States.[34] In running what was basically a one-man show, he continued to have both popular and military backing. But there was a price tag. To maintain popular backing, he had to secure a better way of life for his people. To retain military backing, he had to coddle the armed forces not only by overlooking a good many abuses but by allowing the military to rule its own house in the hope of persuading far too many reluctant officers to move determinedly against Abimael Guzmán's ever-expanding and richer SL.

Guzmán's SL gained far more than it lost in the first two years of Fujimori's presidency. It had forged more links in the "iron belt" around Lima. Recruiting was brisk in refugee-crammed shantytowns; assassinations and killings rose as more officials were intimidated or bought off. Operations in coca-growing areas were more profitable than ever, too often unimpeded by army units most of whose officers were either in Guzmán or the traffickers' pay or both. By now, Guzmán had expanded his propaganda effort to the major cities of the Western world, where agents, operating under a "Sun-Peru" logo, sold " . . . books, leaflets and posters" depicting the SL as saviors of Peru who would ultimately achieve world revolution—an invidious campaign which Fujimori was unable to stop despite urgent appeals to foreign government heads.[35]

But already a tiny cloud had appeared on Guzmán's horizon. Early in Fujimori's presidency, he had concentrated his meager anti-terrorist resources on the single task of capturing Guzmán. A newly formed special unit almost succeeded in doing that in spring of 1990 and in January 1991, the quarry escaping only by minutes.[36]

Fujimori meanwhile was chafing under congressional restraints while SL guerrillas were closing in on Lima. Feeling himself hamstrung by an opposition Congress and by a corrupt judiciary, he startled the world in April 1992 by carrying off an *autogolpe*—a one-man coup (backed by police and military). Congress was dissolved overnight, political opponents arrested, civil liberties suspended, journalists detained, and heavy censorship imposed on the capital.[37] Reaction from abroad was instant and harsh. President Bush suspended aid; Spain and Japan made threatening noises to do so; the OAS spoke of imposing sanctions. Within Peru, 71 per cent of the people approved his dissolving Congress and 89 per cent approved his plan to reorganize the judiciary.[38]

Guzmán's SL reacted by opening a guerrilla terrorist campaign against the middle class. In late July, SL terrorists exploded a car bomb—six hundred kilograms of dynamite—in a prosperous Lima suburb killing over twenty people and wounding some 150. A series of indiscriminate car bombings and assassinations followed as some experts believed the SL was moving in for the kill.

And indeed it was. In mid-September, the president's counterterrorist task force raided a house in a quiet Lima suburb. Within minutes, the work of years paid off. Arrested were Guzmán and three key subordinates who were completing plans for an enormous October offensive. Other documents soon led to the arrest of two hundred more members of the movement.[39]

Guzmán's arrest brought a new wave of optimism to the jaded Peruvian people, most of whom blamed him personally for an estimated twenty-three thousand deaths and $20 billion of property destruction in the last twelve years. Without question, the SL movement experienced violent shock waves at the loss of its leader. More shock waves followed in October 1993 when in a televised broadcast from jail Chairman Gonzalo stated his desire for a peace settlement and " . . . praised the political and economic policies of Fujimori." This startling about-face was apparently engineered by Fujimori's behind-the-scenes intelligence guru, Valdimiro Montesinos, who was said to have "broken" Guzmán to the extent that he followed his broadcast by issuing brief communiqués in praise of the government (in return for additional prison comforts).[40]

Qualified observers point to a loss of three thousand SL militants and cadres since Guzmán's arrest; to a leadership crisis brought on by 80 percent of the 1992 Central Committee being in jail or dead;[41] to a considerable increase in SL desertions; and to the cautious return of natives to abandoned villages around Ayacucho, once Guzmán's private fiefdom, and of farmers and ranchers to estates north of Lima, an area no longer considered a "red zone." Peruvian experts claimed in late 1993 that the SL has lost " . . . about fifty percent of its firepower, of its capacity to carry out major operations."[42]

Perhaps so, but this does not necessarily prove that Guzmán's defection is decisive. SL leaders insist that he has been tortured and drugged—indeed, he was reportedly cut from nearly all human contact, placed under a restricted food diet and deprived of books, magazines, television, or radio—all to make him amenable to the alleged psychological ministrations of Montesinos.[43] There are probably still between fifteen and twenty thousand guerrillas operating from a number of military "regions," each with its own command and staff organization to control a "principal force" along with militia forces maintained in zones and villages. These organizations are backed by a cleverly constructed series of "support bases" and are funded from an estimated $20 to $100 million annual income derived from the drug cartels but also from extortion, bank robberies, and "revolutionary taxes" collected from the people.[44]

SL guerrilla terrorists remained uncomfortably active in 1993, as witnessed by urban and countryside offensives in May, August, September, and October that killed over one hundred civilians and wounded several hundred more.[45] Only half as many people died from political violence in the year following Guzmán's arrest as in the previous year, but the figure still reached over sixteen hundred. Taken with guerrilla losses, the tally for the thirteen-year-old war is now twenty-seven thousand dead and $23 billion of property destruction.

Although Fujimori has improved police and army morale and, with that, counterinsurgency effectiveness, the army's senior commanders remain divided as to the best counterinsurgency strategy. The "French

1118

school" insists on a strictly military-dominated administration in contested areas, the method employed by the French army in Algeria, a war the French ultimately lost (see Chapters 54, 55). The "British school" holds for a counterinsurgency campaign conducted by military-police-civil committees which first must ensure that villages are protected in order to obtain intelligence necessary to identify and eliminate the SL support organiztion,[46] the successful strategy employed in Malaya (see Chapter 46). Although Fujimori is said to prefer the latter strategy—he reportedly plans to appoint civil governors in the contested areas—he is not going to reform the army overnight, particularly when its senior commanders remain prone to corruption by the drug cartels. I am informed that he is currently under pressure by some senior generals to choose the French school's approach, and it would appear from the series of attacks on remote villages in 1993 that these villages are not being adequately protected. One must hope that, being an intelligent man, Fujimori sees the inherent fallacy in this approach and is strong enough to insist on that of the proven British school.

Even if the movement should be neutralized eventually, there remains the immense problem of eliminating the coca growers, processors, and traffickers. Then there is the even more immense task of bringing about a more equitable society by at least narrowing the gulf between the haves and have-nots (the basic reason for all guerrilla wars)—and when all that is accomplished, there is the vital matter of resuming democratic government.

CHAPTER EIGHTY-FIVE

1. Radu and Tismaneanu, 160.
2. Ibid., 156, 149, 162, 168.
3. *Newsweek*, November 16, 1992.
4. Clutterbuck, *Terrorism and Guerrilla Warfare*, 90–2.
5. Ibid., 92.
6. Radu and Tismaneanu, 171.
7. Clutterbuck, *Terrorism and Guerrilla Warfare*, 93.
8. Ibid., 94.
9. Ibid., 121.
10. Ibid., 95.
11. Alan Riding, *International Herald Tribune*, December 17–18, 1988.
12. Tim Ross, *The Sunday Times* (London), August 9, 1992.
13. Ibid.
14. *Newsweek*, December 13, 1993.
15. *The Independent* (U.K.), July 28, 1993.
16. Ibid.
17. Ibid.
18. See, for example, *The Independent* (U.K.), July 26, 1993.
19. International Institute for Strategic Studies, *Strategic Survey 1970*, 62.
20. Clutterbuck, *Terrorism and Guerrilla Warfare*, 115–20, for a more detailed exposition.
21. Radu and Tismaneanu, 339–43.

22. Ibid., 325.
23. Ibid.
24. James Anderson, 46.
25. Ibid.
26. *International Herald Tribune,* December 19, 1991.
27. James Anderson, 46.
28. Ibid.
29. Ibid.
30. Ibid., 47.
31. Radu and Tismaneanu, 325.
32. *International Herald Tribune,* June 13, 1989.
33. *Newsweek,* April 20, 1992. See also, Clutterbuck, "Peru: How to Defeat SL?"
34. Ibid.
35. *International Herald Tribune,* December 19, 1991.
36. *Newsweek,* September 28, 1992.
37. *The Independent* (U.K.), April 8, 1992.
38. *Newsweek,* April 20, 1992.
39. Ibid., September 28, 1992.
40. *International Herald Tribune,* October 23–24, November 30, 1993.
41. Ibid., November 30, 1993.
42. Ibid.
43. Ibid.
44. Clutterbuck, "Peru: How to Defeat SL?"
45. *International Herald Tribune,* May 18, October 23–24, 1933. See also, *The Independent* (U.K.), August 21, 1993.
46. Clutterbuck, "Peru: How to Defeat SL?"

CHAPTER 86

Ireland divided by treaty • Rise and fall of the Irish Republican Army (IRA) • The "Protestant Ascendancy" in Ulster • IRA survival • Failure of political, social, and economic reforms in Ulster • The 1969 riots: Catholics versus Protestants • The British army takes over • The IRA splinters: Officials versus Provincials • Internment of IRA members and "suspected" members • Violence escalates • Bloody Friday • Loyalist Protestant death squads • British army operations • IRA setbacks • Failure of political solutions to the conflict • IRA and Loyalist Protestant excesses • 1993: Violence continues • Tentative peace discussions • The Hume-Adams talks • Britain's secret talks with the IRA • The Major-Reynolds peace plan • The situation in December 1933

> ... out of this national liberation struggle a
> new Ireland will emerge, upright and free ...
> this then is our aim, an independent, united
> democratic Irish Republic. For this we shall
> fight until the [British] invader is driven from
> our soil and victory is ours.
>
> Irish Republican Army (IRA) proclamation,
December 11, 1956[1]

OUR CHAPTER 17 left an Ireland ravaged by war, first against the British, which resulted in the partition treaty of 1921; then between rebel guerrillas of the Irish Republican Army (IRA), who wanted to abrogate it, and the legitimate government of the Irish Free State, which was equally determined to uphold it. The treaty was scarcely ideal in that it created a sore spot by forming six of the north-

NORTHERN IRELAND (ULSTER)

Londonderry
LONDONDERRY · ANTRIM
Loch Neagh · Antrim
T Y R O N E
Omagh
Belfast
Loch Erne
D O W N
Downpatrick
Armagh
Enniskillen
A R M A G H
FERMANAGH
E I R E
Irish Sea
0   20 miles
N

ern counties into the Protestant-dominated separate government of Northern Ireland (Ulster), which had its own parliament but remained part of the United Kingdom.

The IRA at this time numbered about a hundred thousand members but was scarcely a cohesive organization, being split into pro- and anti-treaty factions, the latter wanting to resume war against England. In 1922, dissident IRA guerrillas kidnaped a member of the Dail (Senate), which brought down governmental wrath—in two months, twelve thousand IRA militants were in jail and seventy-seven were executed by firing squad.[2] By spring of 1923, the IRA irregulars were defeated "politically and militarily," but a few extremists kept the movement alive. Patrick Bishop and Eammon Mallie in their excellent book *The Provisional IRA* wrote that by end of the 1920s the organization " . . . had been reduced to a dedicated rump of conspirators, bound together by a sense of betrayal, in the service of an invisible republic"[3]—and by a belief that extreme violence was the sole method to drive the British out of Northern Ireland.

Thanks to strong government measures, the IRA decline continued, nor did its fortunes improve when the Free State evolved into the independent Republic of Ireland in 1937. During World War II, Eamon de Valera's government locked up four hundred of its members. In 1947, its strength was estimated at two hundred active members. The following year it concluded an alliance with the Sinn Fein (Republican)

Party before deciding " . . . to launch a guerrilla war against the British troops occupying Northern Ireland."[4]

The next four years were devoted to obtaining weapons, mostly from raids on police stations and military camps, but also from sympathizers in the Irish Republic, including some civil officials and military personnel. By late 1965, units were being recruited and trained in the North, an effort complemented by armed teams crossing the border to carry out sabotage missions mainly in the South Armagh border area. It soon became clear that the projected operations were overly ambitious. The Protestant-dominated North—the six counties which contain one third of Ireland's population and in which the Catholics are in a minority one third—was controlled by a Unionist parliament at Stormont Castle outside Belfast. Over the years, the Royal Ulster Constabulary (RUC) had become an efficient police force backed by a twenty-five-thousand-man anti-Republican auxiliary called the Ulster Special Constabulary—the "B" Specials, which later would be replaced by the Ulster Defense Regiment (UDR).[5] After IRA teams began blowing up bridges, railroads, power stations and other facilities in the border areas, Stormont passed an internment law which enabled the RUC to sweep up hundreds of Ulster Republicans. Even without the support of Catholics North and South, the campaign lasted into 1962, when a discouraged IRA headquarters in Dublin publicly terminated it.

IRA failure brought a change in strategy engineered by a new Marxist chief of staff, Cathal Goulding. Influenced by the Campaign for Nuclear Disarmament in Britain and the civil rights movement in America, Goulding hoped to bring Catholics and Protestants in Ulster together in a civil rights campaign, the first step in melding the workers in North and South into a revolutionary force that would bring about a united Communist Ireland.[6]

Considering IRA factionalism and general inactivity outside Dublin, this grand design would probably not have got off the ground but for two factors. One was the patently unfair treatment of Catholics by the "Protestant Ascendancy" government of Northern Ireland. Stormont was controlled by Protestant Unionists including such extremists as the Reverend Ian Paisley and William Craig, who had no intention of allowing Catholics to have a place in the sun. Little or no attempt had been made to bring them into a predominantly Protestant society. Catholic children attended Catholic schools, Protestant children Protestant schools. Far too many Catholics lived in segregated, generally poor areas of cities and towns; they got the crumbs from the civil jobs table, their education was often sparse with limited access to university places; they were discriminated against in housing, unemployment ran high, resentment deep. Admittedly their status was slowly improving by the 1960s, and probably a large majority and certainly most of the growing middle class were opposed to violence. In 1965, large numbers of Catholics and Protestants had welcomed the Ulster prime minister's efforts to eliminate discrimination, efforts ruthlessly blocked by Ian Paisley and his fellow extremists.[7]

The other factor stemmed from the blocking of Prime Minister Terence O'Neill's attempted reforms. This was a Catholic non-violent civil rights campaign for reform, which in 1967 emerged as the Northern Ireland Civil Rights Association (NICRA).[8] Violence had entered the previous year when a march by Catholic protesters was physically disrupted by the Ulster Volunteer Force (UVF), an illegal right-wing Protestant paramilitary group in Belfast. Infiltration of the civil rights movement by left-wing trade unionists and Communists soon exacerbated matters as did the formation of the republican Catholic Nationalist Party and an insurgent People's Democracy, a group of far left student militants whose member Bernadette Devlin won passing headline fame.[9] In 1968, civil rights marchers were being routinely harassed by Protestant mobs, which on occasion also attacked Catholic shops and homes. It was a pivotal year, for had the RUC not made " . . . the fatal error of failing to protect the right to demonstrate," as counterinsurgency expert Richard Clutterbuck pointed out, the IRA would have had no grounds to assert its traditional role in protecting the trod-upon Catholics.[10] That the campaign largely succeeded showed in November when the Stormont government belatedly announced a program that met most of the demands of the movement and in 1969 even transcended them by passing housing and electoral reforms and by establishing a Ministry of Community Relations " . . . responsible for ensuring equality of opportunity in all fields,"[11] reforms fought tooth and nail by right-wing Unionists, who were further infuriated by the Westminster-inspired decision to disarm the RUC in an attempt to convert it from a paramilitary to a regular police force, thus in theory making it less resented by the Catholic population, but in fact turning the subsequent response role to IRA attacks over to the army in direct contradiction to valid counterinsurgency strategy.

In this period of increasing violence, the IRA played a minimal role. The movement was already split, Dublin headquarters still nonsectarian, still demanding caution, Ulster members definitely sectarian and increasingly militant but not yet in a position to open effective fire. In 1969, active members in Belfast counted less than sixty; inactive members probably numbered about forty with about three hundred to five hundred mostly middle-aged sympathizers. In Londonderry, probably no more than ten persons " . . . regarded themselves as members."[12] Nevertheless, some of them already had infiltrated the NICRA leadership and inevitably grew more involved as violence increased.

The British army also had played a minimal role. But now Protestant sabotage of key installations had caused Westminster to order garrison soldiers to protect electric power plants and water reservoirs. Their pacific role ended in July. Unemployed youths in Bogside, Londonderry's Catholic area, reacted to a commemorative march of ultra-Unionists celebrating the unsuccessful siege of Londonderry by the Catholic Stuart, James II, in 1689 by hurling bricks and petrol bombs, then burning cars and looting shops, a riot broken up by RUC police using water cannon and tear gas. A subsequent three-day riot resulted in heavy fighting between the rioters, the RUC, Paisleyite mobs, and eventually the "B" Specials, a donnybrook brought under control only by the arrival of a British army battalion, but with a large number of wounded and several million pounds' worth of property damage.[13] A simultaneous five-day riot in West Belfast was finally suppressed by British troops, the toll being seven killed, 750 wounded, and fifteen hundred Catholic and three hundred Protestant families forced to abandon their homes.[14]

A major result of these riots was to splinter the IRA, its militant members forming the Provisional IRA (named in commemoration of the Provisional Government proclaimed in Dublin in 1916). The new organization at once gained money, arms, and training facilities through the connivance of certain Irish Republic politicians, including two government ministers, civil officials, and army and customs officers, who apparently feared the Communist objectives of the Official IRA while sympathizing, at least in part, with the insurgent aims of the Provisional IRA, chiefly that of eliminating the British presence in Northern Ireland.[15] The Provisionals' Army Council in Dublin was headed by Chief of Staff Sean MacStiofain with Rory O'Brady's non-Marxist Provisional Sinn Fein Party (opposed to the Marxist Sinn Fein) as its political front. Traditional IRA aims, " . . . to beat the Protestants to their knees, drive out the British and reunify Ireland," were to be carried out by a three-phase program of violence, first in defending Catholic areas against Protestant, RUC, and British army incursions; second in eye-for-an-eye retaliation if an IRA member was killed; finally in an all-out offensive against the British "occupation" of Ulster.[16]

At this point, the British army was not the villain of the scene in most Catholic eyes; indeed the soldiers had been welcomed in Londonderry and Belfast as protectors against the RUC and Protestant extremist groups during the 1969 riots. This attitude began to change in 1970 when increasingly severe IRA-instigated riots brought on army house-to-house searches by often overzealous troops along with overly harsh military strictures such as "anyone seen with a petrol bomb was liable to be shot dead."[17] Riot control is never an easy task, even with trained troops. With untrained troops, excesses are almost impossible to avoid, particularly when a tired, uncertain, and often frightened young soldier is unduly provoked by having to dodge a petrol bomb or a brick or by being cursed, spat upon, or shot at. The rule of self-preservation can often surmount the wording of a regulation. But provocation works both ways. Stormont's announcement that any rioter arrested would be given a six-month mandatory jail sentence brought swift reaction as did overenthusiastic employment by security forces of nausea-producing CS gas followed by swinging nightsticks. Both IRA factions, the Officials and the Provisionals, were swamped with recruits, mostly young Catholic males looking for a supposedly adventurous escape from all-too-familiar poverty and unemployment. As early as 1970, the theretofore small Belfast Provisional IRA, now called the Belfast Brigade, had built fourteen operational units and divided the city into three combat "battalion" areas from which they carried out 153 bombings of shops and factories by year's end.[18] Weapons were still in short supply, as was money, but dynamite and gelignite were easily stolen from quarries and turned into bombs, and empty milk bottles filled with petrol and fitted with a jury-rigged fuse produced formidable results. The explosions frightened and intimidated people, cost jobs when stores and factories were blown up, and, perhaps most important, brought an increased army presence in the form of patrols, vigorous house searches, and time-consuming vehicle checkpoints to upset the daily life of the average citizen—and of course headlines to keep the movement in the public eye. Army house-to-house searches discovered pistols, rifles, automatic weapons, shotguns, home-made bombs, and explosives. Driblets of arms were arriving from sympathetic Irish Americans and would soon increase as the result of an IRA propaganda campaign carried out by American sympathizers who formed the Northern Aid Committee (NAC). This was fertile ground. There are about twenty-two million Irish Americans, the result of the embittered emigrations of the last century. NAC soon boasted a hundred chapters across the U.S., which raised about $600,000 a year for the cause.[19] In Belfast, IRA guerrillas robbed banks and post offices for money to buy more arms, and as the movement grew in strength, it resorted to extortion Mafia-style and even opened legitimate businesses.

Insurgency breeds its own escalatory dynamics. The flow of recruits to the IRA was matched by the flow of recruits to right-wing paramilitary groups. Excesses on one side produced excesses on the other side. The situation could only deteriorate further unless someone changed the rules. Brigadier Frank Kitson, an innovative veteran of several counterinsurgencies (see Chapter 52), arrived in Belfast in September 1970 as commanding officer of a British brigade. It was at once evident to him that the rules had to be changed, his plan being to defuse the situation by persuading moderate Catholic and Protestant elements to support the government. Once isolated and properly combated, Kitson argued, the extremists would slowly run out of steam and eventually the authorities would restore peace and order while the Stormont government came to its senses and legislated further necessary reforms.[20]

This very sensible plan of "deescalation and attrition," in effect the *raison d'être* for the army's presence, fell victim to overwhelming circumstances. British army tactics, higher command intransigence, RUC and "B" Special operations, and right-wing guerrilla terrorist acts already had turned a majority of Catholics against the government and its security forces to make them either sympathizers with, supporters of, or participants in IRA operations.

As matters stood, violence could only escalate. In early 1971, the Official IRA in Belfast had grown to perhaps twelve companies and in January defied Dublin policy by opening its own armed offensive marked by selective as opposed to indiscriminate assassinations, an effective tactic that intimidated some judges, most jury members, and not a few potential defectors from the cause. Simultaneously, the Provisionals, who were receiving more and more arms from the United States, turned to attacks on army posts and RUC stations, killing where possible, and to indiscriminate bombing of pubs, a nasty business answered by the government bringing in more troops and by increasingly severe army countermeasures. In December 1970, there were six thousand British troops in Ulster; a year later, over fourteen thousand.[21] By mid-July 1971, ten British soldiers had been killed. The Provisional IRA in Londonderry meanwhile had remained relatively quiescent until two Catholic youths were shot and killed by soldiers in July to bring a fresh flow of volunteers to take up arms.

To try to dampen the violence, Prime Minister Brian Faulkner's government introduced Eamon de Valera's old weapon of internment— detention without trial of anyone suspected of IRA activities. In Belfast darkness, army and police teams swept into Catholic ghetto areas, an ill-planned operation that snatched up about fifty low-level IRA members; a similar raid in Londonderry fared better by picking up most of the active Provisionals.[22] The haul was meager compared to the public relations disaster.[23] Within thirty-six hours of the raids, seventeen people had been killed, hundreds of houses set on fire, extended attacks opened on soldiers and police, and an all-out bombing campaign ordered by Dublin headquarters.[24] Official and Provisional IRA units were again inundated with young volunteers all too eager to start shooting; most of the remaining Catholic moderates swung to support of the IRA; the Roman Catholic Church publicly condemned the new law; the Catholic Social Democratic and Labor Party (SDLP) opened a major campaign of civil disobedience—by year's end, twenty-two thousand Catholic households were refusing to pay municipal rent, which in some cases brought on a collapse of local government.[25]

This dismal picture darkened in 1972 with a steady increase in bombings and killings. In late January, a march in Londonderry turned into a riot quelled in part by British paratroopers at a cost of thirteen Catholic lives. What at once was termed Bloody Sunday added to the "climate of sympathy" created by internment and sustained by punitive counterinsurgency tactics, chiefly overaggressive street patrols, hot pursuit into Catholic areas, and often overzealous, and generally ineffectual house-to-house searches by British soldiers, as many as twenty-five hundred in one month.[26] Although patrols and house searches from time to time uncovered small caches of arms, they rarely caught important IRA members. Children were posted to report on intruders and housewives warned of intrusive patrols by banging garbage lids together thus giving IRA guerrillas time to evade patrols or, in some instances, to set up ambushes.

Stormont's failure to get its act together and implement additional reforms brought about Brian Faulkner's resignation. In March, Prime Minister Edward Heath's Conservative government prorogued the Stormont parliament, its responsibilities taken over by a Secretary of State for Northern Ireland, William Whitelaw. This in effect made the British army responsible for law and order, a questionable but perhaps unavoidable move that relegated the RUC to the sidelines in a situation where police should always play the predominant role, *supported* by the army when necessary. On the other hand, the abrupt end of fifty years of Stormont rule exercised a propitiatory effect on Catholic public opinion, which saw in it the seeds of constitutional reform, and it marked the beginning of IRA decline that increased as Whitelaw worked to bring all political parties together in order to fashion a politically viable Northern Ireland.

IRA operations were already slowing. A major change in British army policy was lowering military visibility, thus reducing friction with the civil population. British army intelligence was improving, mainly the work of Brigadier Frank Kitson who, as in Kenya and Cyprus, insisted on the value of low-level intelligence and covertly inserted his soldier agents into Catholic areas to obtain information that, once properly evaluated, collated and distributed, led to the arrest and imprisonment of often important IRA members by the RUC Special Branch. A series of senseless IRA bombings had caused a good many Catholics to question their support of the organization. Incipient challenge of IRA rule began growing in Catholic areas only to be countered by the invidious practice of "kneecapping": the victim was shot through the back of the knee, often to be crippled for life. Young ladies who fraternized with British soldiers were routinely tarred and feathered; people who were not easily intimidated were shot dead. Reappearance of Protestant death squads formed by members of the Ulster Defense Association

(UDA) was met by IRA indiscriminate killings of Protestants, which solved nothing but added to an increasing war-weariness. By spring of 1972, Catholic housewives were circulating petitions that called for peace. In May, the Official IRA, reverting to its original doctrine, called a cease-fire against the security forces and condemned the brutal violence of the Provisionals, terming them " . . . little more than racketeers."[27] Stung by this criticism, the Provisionals declared a cease-fire in June and attended an official conference in London, which came to nothing owing to impossible IRA demands, an egregious error that suggests the Provisionals were now fighting for fighting's sake rather than for achievement of political aims.

Then came Bloody Friday in late July, an insensate one-day IRA car-bombing campaign in Belfast which killed nine and wounded 130 citizens, mostly women and children. In response to public protest, the army was reinforced to a total twenty-one thousand troops and with the RUC, its members once again carrying arms, stormed theretofore no-go Catholic enclaves in Belfast and Londonderry. This coup markedly reduced IRA intimidation in these areas, which in time resulted in an increased flow of intelligence. Intimidation of juries was also checked when Westminster suspended trial by jury of arrested guerrilla terrorists and suspects in favor of one-judge verdicts—the highly controversial but very effective Diplock courts. By October and November, "leading members of the IRA were being arrested at the rate of one a day,"[28] and contributions from the United States had sharply lowered.[29] IRA excesses also brought a change of heart in Dublin, whose government declared the IRA to be illegal and jailed a large number of its members including Chief of Staff Sean MacStiofain. Minister Whitelaw meanwhile had been courting both the strongly Catholic SDLF and Brian Faulkner's Unionist Party in trying to win support for a concessionary compromise that among other things would guarantee Catholic politicians a place in government.

Though somewhat improved, the situation was still dicey from the security forces' standpoint. As if police and army did not have enough on their hands, a new element of sectarian killings emerged in 1972, the result not so much of conflicting religious and political ideologies as of gang warfare. In financing operations, both the IRA and Protestant guerrilla and paramilitary groups had built up lucrative incomes derived from robbery and extortion, in the case of the IRA an estimated £1 million in 1972.

The IRA had now to recognize that Britain had no intention of relinquishing its governmental responsibilities. Any doubts of IRA leaders on this score were soon banished by the arrival in Belfast in early 1973 of a hard-charging commander in chief of British forces, Lieutenant General Frank King. Following Kitson's line, King concentrated more on low-level intelligence collection by covert surveillance on which to base overt action by small, mobile units that replaced large foot patrols. Improved intelligence brought a significant increase in the identity, arrest, and conviction of guerrilla terrorists. Sixteen Provisionals were picked up in June in Belfast, among them the Belfast Brigade's commanding officer, young Gerry Adams. One report stated that "in Belfast a Provisional unit was forced to suspend operations due to lack of arms"; in Londonderry the Provisionals were reduced from three "brigades" to about fifty gunmen, "most of whom operated as nomadic terrorist groups with a loose military structure." The Provisional IRA now had to depend on Active Service Units (ASUs) consisting in theory of five to eight men "but often nothing more than a single gunman."[30] King also emphasized individual training and community relation activities, which considerably alleviated the sting of the unpopular house-to-house searches.

The results were dramatic. In 1972, 467 people were killed in Northern Ireland: 103 British soldiers, 17 police, 26 UDR soldiers, and 321 civilians. In 1973, 250 people were killed: 58 British soldiers, 13 police, 8 UDR soldiers, and 121 civilians. The situation further improved in 1974 (a total 215 dead) when a policy change placed emphasis on "police primacy" in all operations. Although the numbers killed in 1975 and 1976 increased to 247 and 297 respectively, the bulk of these were civilian deaths attributed in large part to IRA operations being challenged by various Protestant paramilitary groups.[31] Guerrilla terrorist tactics practiced by the Ulster Defense Association (UDA), the UVF and a new group called the Ulster Freedom Fighters (UFF) for some time had been as much of a challenge to security forces as to the IRA. It was now apparent that the UVF and UFF operated more for bloodthirsty revenge and monetary gain than for political reasons— indeed the RUC estimated that over 75 per cent of their members were criminals.[32] From 1977 to late 1992, death totals ranged from a low of 54 to a high of 113, the majority resulting from sectarian shootings. (Deaths from automobile accidents during this same period ranged from a low of 173 to a high of 355.)

The IRA was to be further hurt. In March, the Irish Republic navy intercepted a cargo ship carrying five tons of arms intended for the IRA, the first shipment of a total $5 million worth of arms supplied by Libya's Muammar al-Qaddafi. Minister Whitelaw's political maneuverings had in large part weaned SDLP support from the IRA and with that Irish-American contributions dropped from $600,000 to an estimated $160,000 a year.[33] Provisional IRA operations in the border area of South Armagh caused the Dublin government to increase the number of Irish Republic soldiers assigned to border duties. Increased cooperation with the RUC and British forces followed, though scarcely to the desired degree, as did the arrest in Dublin of the IRA Chief of Staff Seamus Twomey.

This combined initiative brought some unfortunate spinoffs. One was increased IRA recruitment of ten- to sixteen-year-olds, who found violence more fun than school and soon became able enough assassins, bombers, and arsonists.[34] Another was the shift of the major guerrilla effort to the South Armagh countryside, which, in view of a three-hundred-mile-long border and limited number of army and police brought an awkward challenge; despite the most strenuous efforts, the security forces never entirely blocked the supply of smuggled arms from Eire to the North. Still another was an extension of operations to England proper where the first car bombs were detonated in March to cause one dead and 180 wounded.[35] Older readers will remember the savage Birmingham pub bombings and the activities of the notorious Balcombe Street gang, which planted bombs in some private clubs and one exclusive school to kill six people and earn each perpetrator over thirty years in jail. Then came the Guildford pub bombings that killed five and wounded 54 civilians. Those efforts were complemented by similar bombings in Ulster. In addition to bombs detonated in parked cars, the "proxy bomb attack" appeared: a private car was stopped, loaded with a bomb and the driver " . . . forced to drive to a specific target" for detonation.[36] Fire bombings also increased with the development of an incendiary device the size of a cigarette package.

Headlines generated by these acts could not disguise IRA setbacks. Owing to the British Government's initiative, a proposal for power sharing by Ulster Protestants, Ulster Catholics, and the British Government had emerged along with various proposals for constitutional and electoral reforms necessary for such a system to work. After several months of severe political turbulence, an agreement of sorts resulted in the election of a new Ulster parliament and a cabinet consisting of six Protestant and five Catholic members serving under Prime Minister Brian Faulkner, thus in theory bringing together for the first time " . . . Catholic and Protestant leaders in an effort at conciliation and reconstruction."[37] This optimistic development was followed by a British incentive to establish a Council of Ireland designed to improve relations between Eire and Ulster. This plan backfired because a large Protestant majority regarded it as " . . . the prelude to a sell-out to Southern papists," a massive indignation shown at the polls in early 1974 when eleven of the twelve members elected to represent Northern Ireland at Westminster actively opposed the agreement.[38] Owing to this backlash, incited principally by Ian Paisley and other extremists and exemplified by a ten-day strike that brought virtual paralysis to Ulster, and by massive car bombings in Dublin and Monaghan that in one evening killed thirty-six and wounded over two hundred persons, the attempt to produce "conciliation and reconstruction" had failed by spring of 1974. Brian Faulkner resigned and the Ulster parliament and cabinet collapsed to leave government again in the hands of Westminster.[39]

Despite these setbacks, Wilson's new minister for Ulster, Merlyn Rees, pressed on with power sharing in local government (by 1977, Catholics would sit on all but three of twenty-six local councils), and he also persuaded the army to lessen the number of the despised house searches. In addition, he offered to phase out internment and gradually release detainees provided the IRA co-operated by ending violence.* This policy coerced the IRA to co-operate and in December 1974 its leaders agreed to a brief cease-fire that in 1975 was expanded in return for the release of all the remaining IRA detainees, though not to the particular pleasure of the security forces.[40]

If not yet moribund, the entire IRA apparatus was in trouble. The Official IRA suffered a major blow in late 1974 when a Trotskyite splinter group formed the Irish Republican Socialist Party (IRSP), which in time fielded the guerrilla Irish National Liberation Army (INLA). This led to war among the Official IRA, the IRSP, and the Provisional IRA, which, when they weren't killing each other, were killing and being killed by Protestant members of the UVF and UDA.[41] In 1974, 215 people were killed in Northern Ireland. In 1975, the year of the cease-fire, 247 persons were killed and over a thousand were charged with shootings, bombings, robberies, and other terrorist-related crimes.[42] Catholic sympathy with the IRA was at an all-time low, not only in Northern Ireland but in Eire and the U.S. Ordinary citizens seemed equally disgusted with the atrocities perpetrated by Protestant groups: 60 per cent of those arrested were thugs, many with criminal records.[43] Continued violence in 1976 brought the emergence of the Women's Peace Movement with huge marches that included Protestant women in Belfast and Dublin (a noteworthy effort that unfortunately had faded from the scene by 1980).

By the end of the cease-fire, the British army had fine-tuned its technical skills, particularly in the collection of intelligence, although a great deal remained to be done in improving RUC collation and analysis techniques and in strengthening the all-important RUC Special Branch, whose members were operating without vital technology such as computers. The RUC gained much sharper teeth in 1976, however, with the passage of the Emergency Powers Act. IRA suspects could now be held for seven days before being charged. Harsh, often brutal, interrogations

---

* This was not altogether altruistic. Public opinion had forced the government to categorize interned IRA members as "political prisoners" with concomitant privileges. Once released, they could be rearrested if they returned to their old ways—this time as common criminals with few if any perquisites.

so increased the flow of intelligence that " . . . between 1976 and 1979 about three thousand people were charged with terrorist offenses, most of them on the basis of confessions obtained under interrogation."[44] But relations between the RUC and the army remained strained, with each wanting operational control over the other, a conflict that greatly hampered the intelligence process described by one commentator as being in 1979 " . . . still an uncoordinated mess."[45] What was needed was a completely co-ordinated security effort commanded by one person as had been the case with previous successful British counterinsurgencies. A succession of army commanders had asked for the right of direct communication with the Irish Republic army as well as the right of "hot pursuit" of terrorists using Eire as a sanctuary, requests predictably denied on constitutional grounds.

The Provisional IRA was also changing. Its leaders were now younger members who were putting greater emphasis on training and on co-ordinated operations. There was also increased emphasis on gaining political control " . . . with an Armalite [rifle] in one hand and a ballot box in the other."[46] Provisional IRA leaders were in contact with West German, Libyan, Iranian, and Spanish Basque guerrilla terrorists, the latter advising them to stop killing low-level soldiers and concentrate on " . . . judges, generals and top ministers." Although these organizations supplied some arms, the bulk still came from the U.S., as did perhaps $150,000 a year in cash, but the IRA's main income derived from armed robbery, extortion, and racketeering, which continued to bring in $1 million or $2 million a year or more.[47]

It soon appeared that the new leaders had profited but little from past errors in trying to build a popular power base without offering the Catholic public a coherent political philosophy which included a statement of realistic aims. Not only were the Provisionals fighting the Official IRA, the INLA, the RUC, Protestant paramilitary groups, and the British army, but increasingly they had been forced to use intimidation to retain support inside the Catholic areas. It seemed almost as if they went out of their way to increase their isolation by courting general condemnation. In 1976, an IRA hit team murdered the British ambassador to Eire.[48] In 1977, IRA guerrilla terrorists carried out a fire-bombing campaign against tourist hotels in twenty Northern Ireland towns, of course putting a lot of their own people out of work. In early 1977, an ASU team murdered the British ambassador to The Hague. A month later, the Conservative Party spokesman for Northern Ireland, Airey Neave, was blown up in London in his booby-trapped car. Later in the year, a commando team murdered Lord Louis Mountbatten of World War II fame to reap further opprobrium (another team killed a British officer and seventeen soldiers the same day). Two years later, a team detonated a bomb in a pub frequented by soldiers and their Irish girlfriends—sixteen killed, sixty-six wounded. In 1982, bombs were exploded in London parks—eight killed, fifty-three wounded. In 1983, car bombs were exploded behind Harrods department store in London—eight killed. In the same year, thirty-eight hard-core terrorists escaped from a maximum security prison (five years later, ten escapees were still at large).[49]

Criticism of these tactics was somewhat muted in Ireland when IRA prisoners went on a hunger strike that in one form or another lasted from 1981 to 1983. The death of ten IRA prisoners from starvation brought a tremendous outpouring of sympathy from the Catholic populations of both Eire and Ulster. As one result, the Sinn Fein Party grew considerably in membership. Gerry Adams, now out of prison and head of the Provisional IRA's Army Council, for some time had been steering the movement in a political direction by again fronting it with Sinn Fein. In 1982, Sinn Fein won five of seventy-eight seats in the short-lived Ulster National Assembly. In the 1983 general elections, it won 13.4 per cent of the vote and Adams was elected a member of parliament for West Belfast.[50]

This did not spell real prosperity for the cause. By 1984, IRA guerrilla activists were reduced to an estimated 250 diehards, but this was an experienced, highly disciplined, and ideologically devout group supported by a large number of sympathizers. Nor did the figure presumably include "sleeper" agents who had infiltrated Irish communities in England to lie dormant until called upon to launch new terrorist campaigns such as those of 1991–92. On the other hand, intelligence collection was momentarily improved by the recruitment of highly placed IRA and republican officials—supergrasses—who informed on their fellows in return for a new life abroad, a project only partially successful since appeals courts began overturning convictions based on testimony of the supergrass informers, most of whom were dangerous criminals with but slight credentials of probity. Not only were a large number of prisoners convicted on supergrass testimony released by appeals courts, but some of the supergrasses in turn were tried for and convicted of murder.[51] Continued IRA guerrilla terrorist operations eventually told on Sinn Fein, which lost considerable ground in the 1986 elections, a development that only brought more violent attacks by the Provisionals.

Meanwhile, the political situation had radically changed. In late 1981, the Westminster and Dublin governments had established the Anglo-Irish Inter-Governmental Council (AIIC), designed to improve relations between the two countries and to find a political solution to the Northern Ireland problem. Progress was slow but in November 1985, Prime Ministers Margaret Thatcher and Garret FitzGerald signed an Anglo-Irish agreement which " . . . affirmed that any change in the status of Northern Ireland would only come about with the consent of the majority of the people of Northern Ireland" (that is, the Protestants). The agreement promised regularly scheduled conferences between Dublin and Stormont to deal with " . . . political matters, with security and related matters, with legal matters (including the administration of justice), and with the promotion of cross-border cooperation."[52] The first conference was followed by another in early 1986 and included discussion on improved cross-border co-operation. Meanwhile, the Republic of Ireland signed the European Convention on the Suppression of Terrorism and the U. S. Government approved an assistance package of $250 million in support of the Anglo-Irish agreement.[53]

The agreement was immediately attacked by both Catholics and Protestants in Northern Ireland, the former infuriated by Dublin's seeming recognition of England's continued presence in Ulster, the Protestants by the introduction of the Irish Republic in the affairs of Ulster. Massive demonstrations of both sects, boycotting of the National Assembly, civil disobedience campaigns—all combined to topple the fragile Northern Ireland Assembly, which was dissolved in spring of 1986. Once again direct rule was invoked and anarchy threatened. New Protestant guerrilla terrorist groups appeared. Armed robberies rose to 724 for the year with sixty-one recorded deaths and 1,450 wounded.[54]

It was all-out war once more. In spring of 1987, a major IRA attack on a police station in County Armagh was frustrated with eight IRA members shot, " . . . the worst loss suffered by the IRA since the 1920s," Gerry Adams reportedly complained.[55] In reprisal, the IRA planned a large bombing, which in the event misfired to kill eleven and wound sixty-one innocent civilians in Enniskillen.[56] Anglo-Irish conferences seemed to produce more words than action. Arms continued to reach the IRA, including a new plastic explosive, Semtex, reportedly " . . . almost invisible to security scanners."[57] Security forces in Armagh routinely stumbled on arms and explosive dumps. The French navy intercepted a ship carrying 150 tons of arms including Soviet-built SAM-7 missiles and rocket launchers intended for the IRA. The RUC gained another five hundred men to put it above thirteen thousand and units of Britain's crack counterterrorist organization, the Special Air Service Regiment (SAS), were reportedly deployed to the provinces.

In early 1988, a SAS team shot three IRA terrorists to death in Gibraltar. The IRA retaliated with a series of attacks on security forces in Ulster and British garrisons in Germany, a campaign continued into 1989 and 1990. In 1991, the IRA opened another offensive in England with a mortar attack on Number 10 Downing Street, which caused some property damage but no fatalities and was followed by a bomb exploded in Victoria Station—one killed, forty wounded.[58]

The almost hopeless scenario was challenged by a new Secretary of

State for Northern Ireland, Peter Brooke, who for over a year had been leading a political offensive involving all major political parties in Ulster. All-party talks in the spring were quickly sabotaged by right-wing Unionist leaders Paisley and Molyneaux and were soon terminated. Following Prime Minister John Major's intervention, the talks resumed in March only to be suspended until after the British general election. The Provisional IRA celebrated Major's re-election by exploding a large bomb in London's financial district—three killed, over ninety wounded, £1.5 billion worth of structural damage to buildings.[59] All-party talks resumed in May, but were stymied by Unionist refusal to allow the Dublin government to participate. In an effort to curb sectarian violence, Westminster declared the Ulster Defense Association (UDA) to be illegal. Members of the largest Protestant paramilitary group in Ulster can now be summarily imprisoned for up to ten years.[60] In August, an Ulsterman won the sad distinction of becoming the three thousandth fatality of the insurgency.[61] In September, all-party talks resumed only to be boycotted by Ian Paisley's party. Also in September, the Provisionals exploded an enormous bomb, which destroyed the forensic science laboratory outside of Belfast; miraculously, no one was killed but property damage was estimated at £20 million and essential police work seriously delayed. Guerrilla terrorists closed out the year with a series of bombings in Manchester and London.

This violent scenario but slightly changed in 1993. Commencing in April, Britain's Prime Minister John Major and Northern Ireland Secretary of State Sir Patrick Mayhew tried unsuccessfully to revive the suspended peace talks. The political spectrum broadened in July when the Irish Republic's Prime Minister Albert Reynolds talked about asking President Bill Clinton to intervene if the talks were not resumed.[62] At work here was the intransigent stance of Protestant Ulster diehards who refused to negotiate unless the Irish Republic canceled its constitutional claim to the sovereignty of Ulster, a demand that as of December 1993 has prevented the talks from resuming.

Although British officials claimed that the Provisional IRA guerrilla terrorists were hurting, the latter continued to carry out terrorist operations in the cities and countryside, and in waging virutally open warfare with Loyalist paramilitary groups (now considered by many army and police officials to be a more serious threat than the IRA). In truth, the violence potential of both sides is enormous, as witness the recent security-force seizure of a three-thousand-pound IRA bomb; or the finding of an immense IRA bomb under Bournemouth pier in England that would have taken hundreds of holiday-makers' lives; or the IRA September bombing of a Belfast supermarket to cause £1 million damage; or the intercepted shipment from Poland of two hundred assault rifles, two tons of explosives, and thousands of rounds of ammunition intended for Protestant guerrilla terrorists in Northern Ireland; or the random Protestant killings of five Catholics in eight days in September; or the Halloween massacre by a UFF Protestant terrorist of seven people in a bar in November.

Is there an end in sight for what some regard as a twenty-three year-old, others as a three-hundred-year-old, insurgency? Last year the answer would have been no, and there are still a great many people on both sides who foresee an endless war. In 1993, however, there have been some positive signs that the concerned governments are facing up to an increasing groundswell of public demand for an end to the senseless killing.

The IRA can claim credit for part of the initiative by having secretly approached the British government in February 1993 with a peace feeler. Subsequent talks apparently hinged on the IRA's willingness to abandon violence, but the content of the talks is murky owing to conflicting statements by Sinn Fein chief Gerry Adams and British government spokesmen, the latter greatly embarrassed when the world learned in the following November of the secret meetings. The substance is probably similar to that of more open talks begun by John Hume, leader of the SDLP's 650,000 Catholics, and Gerry Adams last spring, the idea apparently being to persuade IRA militants to lay down their arms in return for an official position at the negotiating table. Hume subsequently briefed Prime Minister Major and Prime Minister Reynolds on these discussions, the latter greeting the peace effort as a first step toward a "just and lasting solution" to the war. Major was sufficiently impressed to appeal to Adams to renounce terror " . . . and join the dialogue on the way ahead,"[63] and to want to keep the talks going.[64] Both Dublin and London governments seemed to be showing new flexibility, Major stating that "some cherished positions will have to be modified" in the "quest for peace,"[65] and Reynolds allegedly suggesting that the Irish Republic would consider altering its constitutional claims to sovereignty of Northern Ireland.[66] According to one report, in early December IRA spokesmen said " . . . they were, and remain, interested in a cease-fire leading to substantive talks."[67]

Despite the recent conciliatory words flowing from Dublin, a meeting between the prime ministers in early December merely emphasized the dichotomy in official thinking.[68] But then came the bombshell, when at a subsequent meeting Major and Reynolds put on the table a specific peace plan that, inter alia, offered self-determination to Northern Ireland and a position at the peace table for the IRA after it had carried out a no-nonsense cease-fire for three months.

All well and good, but the momentum will not be easy to maintain. Reverend Ian Paisley predictably greeted the Major-Reynolds plan with accusations that the British were betraying Ulster Protestants. Protestant moderates of the Ulster Unionists party, which is larger than Paisley's, are however showing an interest in these events, motivated in part by an increasing war weariness displayed by both Catholic and Protestant civic groups. But the Paisleyites and other extremist groups are well organized, financially strong, totally obdurate, and utterly ruthless. The same may be said of the militant IRA guerrilla terrorists, and there is certainly no guarantee that Gerry Adams, even if so inclined, could bring them to heel.

The rising Ulster middle class, though tired of the brutal and senseless killings and costly, disruptive bombings, is still neither sufficiently aroused nor organized to assert the political clout necessary to change things. Unlike many other insurgencies, this one is relatively easy to accept—anything from 54 to 113 deaths a year are not very many in a shooting war (in 1992 there were 800 gang-related homicides in Los Angeles). The U.K. and Irish Republic governments have not overly exerted themselves in pursuit of peace in the past, but again, an increasing war weariness in both countries, as well as an annual cost of $3 to $5 billion to Britain, appears to have shaken off their lethargy.

As 1993 closes, then, the hope for an eventual peace is brighter than it has been for a quarter of a century. Virtually everything hinges on the IRA's acceptance or rejection of the Anglo-Irish proposal. The debate in IRA circles will be acrimonious, but there must be many militants who realize that the odds in the long run are against them, particularly as police intelligence techniques improve and as security forces increasingly win the cooperation of a general public sickened by the shameful and revolting violence of what more often than not is gang warfare with religious overtones.

CHAPTER EIGHTY-SIX

1. Bishop and Mallie, 26.
2. Ibid., 21.
3. Ibid., 22.
4. Ibid., 23.
5. Bruce, 2–7.
6. Bishop and Mallie, 33–5. See also, Clutterbuck, *Guerrillas and Terrorists,* 64–5; International Institute for Strategic Studies, *Strategic Survey 1988–89,* 100.
7. Clutterbuck, *Guerrillas and Terrorists,* 65.
8. Goode, 129–30.
9. Institute for the Study of Conflict, *Conflict Studies Number 36,* June 1973, 2.
10. Clutterbuck, *Guerrillas and Terrorists,* 66.
11. Institute for the Study of Conflict, *Conflict Studies Number 36,* June 2, 1973 See also, ibid., *Conflict Studies Number 50,* October 1974, 27.
12. Bishop and Mallie, 73, 108.
13. Ibid., 68. See also, Bell, 364.
14. Bishop and Mallie, 83, 88.
15. Joe Jackson.

16. Bishop and Mallie, 106–7. See also, Clutterbuck, *Guerrillas and Terrorists,* 67.
17. Bishop and Mallie, 116.
18. Ibid., 109–10, 120–7.
19. Ibid., 235. See also, Institute for the Study of Conflict, *Conflict Studies Number 36,* June 1973, 18, which estimates that the NAC raised £1 million between 1969 and 1973.
20. Hamill, 41–2.
21. International Institute for Strategic Studies, *Strategic Survey 1971,* 68.
22. Bishop and Mallie, 144–5.
23. Clutterbuck, *Guerrillas and Terrorists,* 69. See also, International Institute for Strategic Studies, *Strategic Survey 1971,* 69–70.
24. Bishop and Mallie, 145: There had been 157 IRA bombings in 1970, a figure that rose to over a thousand by end of 1971.
25. International Institute for Strategic Studies, *Strategic Survey 1971,* 69.
26. Bishop and Mallie, 159.
27. Institute for the Study of Conflict, *Conflict Studies Number 50,* October 1974, 10.
28. Ibid., *Conflict Studies Number 36,* June 1973, 7. See also, Goode, 133–4.
29. Clutterbuck, *Guerrillas and Terrorists,* 70.
30. Institute for the Study of Conflict, *Conflict Studies Number 50,* October 1974, 7.
31. Clutterbuck, Private letter to the author. See also, Hamill, 143.
32. Institute for the Study of Conflict, *Conflict Studies Number 50,* October 1974, 11. See also, *Conflict Studies Number 36,* June 1973, 8.
33. Bishop and Mallie, 241.
34. Goode, 135.
35. Bishop and Mallie, 198–9.
36. Institute for the Study of Conflict, *Conflict Studies Number 50,* October 1974, 9.
37. Ibid., 2.
38. Ibid., *Conflict Studies Number 108,* June 1979, 4.
39. *Irish Times,* May 12, 1974, and May 17, 1990. See also, *NOW in Ireland,* May 1990; Raymond Murray, 108–21.
40. Clutterbuck, *Guerrillas and Terrorists,* 72.
41. Bishop and Mallie, 221.
42. Ibid., 255.
43. Clutterbuck, *Guerrillas and Terrorists,* 74. See also, Institute for the Study of Conflict, *Conflict Studies Number 108,* June 1979, 19.
44. Bishop and Mallie, 255.
45. Hamill, 242.
46. Ibid., 228.
47. Ibid., 235, 239. See also, Clutterbuck, *Terrorism and Guerrilla Warfare,* 160.
48. Goode, 137.
49. *Keesing's Record of World Events,* Vol. 34, 1988. December 1988, 36,238.
50. Bishop and Mallie, 305–7.
51. *Keesing's Record of World Events,* Vol. 31, 1985. October 1985, 33,939.
52. Ibid., Vol. 36, 1990. December 1990, 34,070.
53. Ibid., Vol. 37, 1991. April 1991, 34, 315–18.
54. Ibid., May 1991, 35,156.
55. Ibid., Vol. 34, 1988, October 1988, 36,327.
56. Ibid.
57. Ibid., 36,238.
58. *The Independent* (U.K.), April 11, 1992.
59. *Keesing's Record of World Events,* Vol. 38, 1992. April 1992, 38,869.
60. *The Independent* (U.K.), August 11, 1992.
61. Ibid., August 28, 1992.

62. *The Independent* (U.K.), July 4, 1993.
63. *New York Times,* November 23, 1993.
64. *International Herald Tribune,* December 1, 1993.
65. *New York Times,* November 23, 1993.
66. *International Herald Tribune,* December 2, 1993.
67. Ibid., December 2, 1993.
68. Ibid., December 4–5, 1993.

CHAPTER 87

The Basque legacy • *Rise of the ETA* • *The "armed struggle"* • *Government countermeasures* • *The ETA splits: ETA-PM versus ETA-M* • *Franco's death* • *ETA refusal of government's amnesty and limited autonomy offer* • *Increased violence* • *The French connection* • *ETA setbacks* • *The drug factor* • *Continuing ETA guerrilla attacks* • *The situation in late 1993*

TUCKED AWAY in the coastal mountain country of northwest Spain are four provinces which, taken with three French provinces on the other side of the Pyrenees, comprise an ancient ethnic community whose language bears no relation to other European tongues. This is Basque country, home of some of the finest cooking in Europe and home also of a long-standing insurgency carried out by the ETA and other guerrilla terrorist groups dedicated to winning total independence for the province from Spain. Although that goal is not shared by a large proportion of the region's 2.3 million inhabitants, of whom 65 per cent are native Basques,[1] there seems little doubt that the majority do want greater autonomy than the Madrid government to date has granted. There also seems little doubt that the majority do not accept ETA's doctrine of guerrilla terrorist violence to accomplish the stated goal although some are certainly in sympathy with the goal and apparently are willing to overlook ETA excesses in trying to accomplish it.

The Basques stem from the seventh century if not earlier. They have always occupied a unique position on the Iberian Peninsula, their semi-autonomous position guarded by mountains and sea and by a series of provincial *fueros,* or special local statutes such as that authorizing them to maintain their own customs posts. This began to change in the nineteenth century, owing to the encroachment of political centralization and the industrial age, during which most of the *fueros* were abolished. Adept as always, the coastal Basques soon established important in-

THE BASQUE
PROVINCES

dustrial centers, but by attracting foreign capital and workers from the poorer Spanish provinces, these began to dilute the homogeneous quality of Basque life. These changes led to a rise of nationalism and in 1895 to the founding of the Basque Nationalist Party (PNV) by Sabino de Arana, who, as Edward Moxon-Browne tells us,

> . . . gave shape to the course of Basque nationalism by baptizing the new state Euzkadi, designing its flag, and working to encourage the dissemination of the Basque language. Arana laid the foundation of the Basque nationalist ideology which, among other things, comprised a dedication to the Catholic religion, the espousal of non-violent methods to achieve political goals, the belief that all Basques should be united across the Pyrenees, and the assertion that language should be the defining characteristic of the Basque race. With a few modifications, and with a flexible view on the appropriate political structures to underpin these goals, those principles have remained the core of PNV orthodoxy up to the present time.[2]

Matters might have remained thus had it not been for the Spanish civil war (1936–39) and the dictatorship of Generalissimo Francisco Franco (1939–75). Franco loathed the coastal Basques, who fought as Republicans in the civil war. He not only banned the language, he banned its teaching and he ordered the burning of Basque books. Repression is not easily accepted by an intelligent people. In the early

1142

1950s, a group of young nationalists splintered from the PNV to form the Euzkadi ta Azkatasuna (ETA—Basque Nation and Liberty), " . . . a simple nationalist movement with Basque independence as its sole objective."[3] The ETA did not advocate armed struggle but nevertheless it was treated as a subversive movement, and in the early 1960s its leaders went underground, moving to France, Belgium, Algeria, Ireland, and Venezuela.[4] Continued police repression brought a militant *cambio de sentido*, a change of mind, in 1966, at least to thirteen of the forty-five members who attended the movement's Fifth Assembly and who opted for violence—the "armed struggle"—to achieve their aim of turning the provinces into a Communist country. A series of bank robberies, attacks on military and police posts, and the murder of a provincial Basque police chief in 1968 were met with emergency decrees that enabled Franco's police to disarm the armed struggle by locking up hundreds of Basque dissidents (including several Roman Catholic priests), many of them receiving long prison sentences handed down by *military* courts in the best fascist tradition, a highly controversial affair that culminated in the 1970 Burgos trials in which six militants were sentenced to death for the murder of the Basque police chief.[*5] These hotly criticized trials, which attracted world attention, probably more than any single factor insured the growth of the movement—hundreds of young Basques flocked to revolutionary banners to continue a campaign of robberies, bombings, kidnapings (both for ransom and an improvement of working conditions), and killings. The government, encouraged by pro-Franco demonstrations such as a turnout of five hundred thousand in Madrid, evoked further emergency decrees including the right of the police " . . . to detain arrested persons for up to six months without trial."[6] In 1972, four ETA guerrilla terrorists struck on the unlikely but imaginative plan of kidnaping Franco, who would be exchanged for 150 ETA prisoners.[7] Once this proved infeasible, they killed Franco's new prime minister and presumed successor, Admiral Carrera Blanco, in late 1973 by tunneling under a street, packing the tunnel with high explosive and blowing admiral, bodyguard, chauffeur, and car over a five-story building, an incredibly bizarre operation well told by Peter Janke.[8] A few months later, the ETA's Sixth Assembly, attended by only thirty-six members, split into two factions, the ETA-PM (political-military), which stuck to the original goal of achieving Basque autonomy by building a powerful political base but also by using violence when necessary, and the ETA-M (military) whose proclaimed objective " . . . was the establishment of a Basque socialist state by armed action."[9]

---

* Such was the domestic and foreign outcry that Franco commuted the sentences to thirty years.

Unlike many guerrilla terrorist organizations, ETA-M believed in selective killing, " . . . symbolic attacks cumulatively expressing a coherent message to the public and the government," as Moxon-Browne elegantly put it.[10] Of an estimated 240 victims of ETA-M between 1968 and 1980, two thirds were soldiers or police, the Guardia Civil " . . . accounting for one third of all fatalities and a quarter of all those wounded. National and local policemen accounted for 23 percent of the fatalities. . . . "[11] Other victims included the governors of Madrid and of the Basque province of Guipuzcoa, leading opposition figures, mayors of several Basque towns, and, inevitably, a considerable number of luckless bystanders. The ETA was not fighting alone. In 1975, five terrorists belonging to ETA-M and to the Revolutionary Anti-Fascist and Patriotic Front (FRAP) were found guilty of murdering police officers and were executed by firing squad, an event that caused widespread international protest.[12]

Two major events now affected the ETA's campaign of violence. One was Franco's death in 1975, the other the establishment of a parliamentary democracy under the popular King Juan Carlos and the election by the people of a *Cortes,* or parliament. These major changes greatly improved PNV chances for gaining increased autonomy and undoubtedly would have resulted in further gains but for ETA intransigence. The *Etarras,* as ETA members were called, would have nothing to do with the new government, in their eyes a "pseudo democracy" that did not alter the status of the "real powers . . . the military, the financial oligarchy, the Church."[13] That the ETA did not stand alone was made clear in 1978 by the hostile reception in Basque country of the new constitution. Although this document, endorsed by a majority of Spaniards, effectively ended Franco-style fascism in favor of democratic government, 63 per cent of Basque voters rejected it on grounds that it failed to restore traditional Basque rights and did not grant sufficient autonomy to the provinces. Two more militant parties, the Euzkadika Eskerra (EE) and the Herri Batasuna (HB), the latter the political front for ETA-M, surfaced to advocate " . . . the compulsory teaching of Basque in schools, the withdrawal of Spanish troops from Basque soil and various measures against 'capitalism.' "[14] As a sign of the times, each party won significant representation in Basque parliamentary elections held in 1980 at the height of ETA-inspired violence.

So violence it was, and violence it would remain. The targets were selective but diffuse, members of the Guardia Civil and the National Police being favorites. Token bombings were carried out at resort towns along the Mediterranean coast in unsuccessful efforts to disrupt the financially all-important tourist trade. Prominent persons were kidnaped and held for ransom. Army officers and soldiers stationed in Basque country were killed and also became targets in other places such as Madrid, where in 1986 an ETA-M "Spanish Commando" began to operate. A provincial military governor was killed as were a few business executives.

The government had tried to ward this off. As opposed to Franco's rigid policy of centralized government, the new government in principle had agreed on limited autonomy not only for the Basque provinces but also for Catalonia, Galicia, and Andalucia. Under the provisions of the 1978 constitution, the Basques and Catalans were to obtain full autonomy in 1980, including, in the case of the Basques and only after acrimonious argument, a favorable tax situation and an all-Basque police force as guaranteed in the 1979 Statute of Guernica.[15] The government, however, refused to withdraw the generally detested Guardia Civil.

When the ETA refused to accept this conciliatory policy, the government replied in kind. The year 1980 brought new anti-terrorist laws. Suspected terrorists could be jailed for ten days; security forces had the right to search houses without a warrant, intercept mail, and tap telephones. Tougher laws followed in 1981 and still tougher laws two years later when specially trained Guardia Civil police were assigned to the Basque provinces and given what amounted to combat pay.[16] With the advent of Felipe Gonzalez's socialist (PSOE) government in 1984, ETA sanctuary in France also was further compromised.

France was in a difficult position vis-à-vis Spain. Neither the French Government nor large numbers of the French people had been sympathetic to the Franco regime; nor was the "new democracy" at once accepted as genuine. The three French Basque provinces contained a large number of sympathizers with the ETA and its demand for an all-Basque independent state. The French Government prided itself on upholding the nation's traditional acceptance of political refugees.[17] Although ETA excesses had caused the French to ban the ETA organization in 1972, these factors not only resulted in an open tolerance of ETA activities on French soil but also in a refusal to extradite Spanish Basque ETA-suspects, who were termed "political refugees," to Spanish custody. According to one report, in 1980 two hundred Spanish guerrilla terrorists were based in the French border provinces. Covert efforts by Spanish intelligence to penetrate the Basque network were resented by France while French intransigence angered Madrid. A further complication arose when some Basque industrialists, tired of paying extortion to ETA militants, began to support a rightist paramilitary organization, the Anti-Terrorist Liberation Group (GAL), which concentrated on murdering suspected ETA members operating in France.

The new socialist government in Spain began to change the French attitude. Although François Mitterrand's socialist government still refused to extradite ETA suspects to Spain, it did begin to get them out of harm's way by deporting them to such countries as Uruguay and

Venezuela. Madrid in time also offered new terms to ETA-M members, including a policy of "social reintegration" by which terrorists in Spain and abroad could gain amnesty in return for " . . . renouncing all future acts of violence."[18] The offer was followed by a brief slowdown in ETA operations while Spanish government officials secretly met with a leader of the "nationalist ETA" (as opposed to the Marxist ETA in France) in Algeria, talks broken off when this man was killed in February. ETA kidnapings, bombings, and killings began again in March.

The ETA-M suffered a major setback some months later when a French court ruled in favor of sending four Spanish ETA members suspected of "criminal" as opposed to political activities back to Spain, an act that brought an immediate ETA offensive against the French presence in Spain. ETA-M tactics also sharply altered with the introduction of the car bomb (as had been the case with the IRA in Northern Ireland) and the advent of regional commando groups such as the Barcelona Commando, the Madrid Commando, the Itinerant Commando, which often acted, sometimes unwisely, on their own initiatives. Even loyal ETA sympathizers found it difficult to accept a car bomb explosion in Madrid " . . . in which five civil guards were killed and a further eight people injured."[19]

Despite persistent ETA operations, it was increasingly clear in 1986 that the security forces were slowly winning the battle. In April, ETA-M's military chief was arrested in France and deported to Gabon. Other ETA-M guerrilla terrorists received heavy sentences in French courts: some were deported to far away lands, others handed over to Spanish authorities without formal extradition proceedings. One French raid in Hendaye swept up six ETA activists, an arsenal of weapons, about a million French francs, and " . . . plans for attacks in Madrid and Barcelona."[20] Security forces continued to score in 1987, breaking up several ETA-M commando groups in Basque country and badly hurting the Spanish Commando by the arrest of its members and seizure of arms, explosives, and papers.

These setbacks understandably brought dissension in ETA ranks, the Marxist element in France holding out for prolonged war, the nationalist element in Algeria favoring negotiations with Madrid. In July 1987, government officials again met secretly with ETA-M leaders in Algeria, talks designed according to government sources only " . . . to bring an end to violence and not negotiation on the Basque region's political future."[21] French co-operation was also increasing as a result of guerrilla activities of a French Basque organization called Imparretarrak (Those of the North). In pursuing members of this organization, French police uncovered a Spanish ETA-M supply dump and arrested a man " . . . believed to have been ETA's supreme commander for the past two years, directing the activities of its commandos."[22] A Franco-

Spanish operation in October resulted in the arrest of over a hundred ETA suspects. In November, Spanish police claimed to have " . . . dismantled almost the entire infrastructure in Guipuzcoa [province]" and in December French police picked up another senior leader.

The ETA-M fought back hard, if not wisely. In June, the Barcelona Commando exploded a car bomb underneath a supermarket, killing twenty-one citizens, wounding thirty, and bringing out five hundred thousand Catalans of all political persuasions in a protest march. Continued killings of Guardia Civil and other policemen culminated in December when an ETA-M commando exploded a car bomb outside a police barracks, killing four Guardia Civil plus two women and five children to bring public indignation to a boil in Basque country as well as in the rest of Spain.[23]

This sordid pattern continued throughout 1988, which brought two new complications. One was French anger at the criminal activities of the Spanish rightist group, GAL, a quarrel duly settled with the socialist Mitterand government. The other was the wholesale importation of cocaine, one ton of which was seized by police in the Basque border town of Irun, the beginning of a massive problem that eventually would move the ETA to second place on the villain list. While violence dominated the mainland, talks continued with ETA-M in Algeria. Hopes for a settlement rose in early 1989 when ETA-M announced a cease-fire, but these were soon dashed by the extravagance of ETA-M demands and fighting began again in March.

So it was one step forward, two steps backward. Violent excesses continued to capture headlines. A Madrid court sentenced *each* of four ETA members to 2,232 years of imprisonment for having blown up a police bus three years earlier.[24] An ETA commando kidnapped a Pamplona industrialist, held him for eighty-four days, and released him for a ransom believed to have been close to $3 million.[25] Early in 1990, the Basque parliament passed a resolution " . . . proclaiming the right of the Basque people to self-determination and to decide fully and democratically on its political, economic, social and cultural status." Self-determination, however, " . . . could only come about gradually and democratically and with due regard to 'historical context.' "[26] The ETA responded by mailing five parcel bombs. Security forces arrested the leader of ETA-M's Itinerant Commando, who rather unwisely was carrying over six hundred pounds of explosive in his car, which was intended to blow up the colorful Sevilla *feria*—one of the most revered fairs in Spain. That arrest led to seventeen more in France—and the *feria* was saved. ETA-M next declared war on the World's Fair and Olympics scheduled for 1992 in Spain, a declaration emphasized by exploding a car bomb near Barcelona, killing six policemen and wounding eight.[27]

1991 brought more of the same: a car bomb exploded outside a Guardia Civil barracks, leaving nine dead including four children. ETA teams bombed Spanish diplomatic and commercial buildings in Rome, Milan, Bologna, Munich, Düsseldorf; in August, for the third year running, bomb threats against the Spanish rail system disrupted travel plans of over two hundred thousand people.[28]

These were desperate acts of desperate men. Arrests throughout the year continued to fragment the ETA organization. But the hard-core movement was not ready to die, nor was it entirely isolated. ETA deaths in prison or from shootouts invariably brought protests in the form of demonstrations or even strikes in the Basque country. To those within the movement who believed that " . . . the armed struggle was lost, was senseless and was damaging the Basque Nationalist left, and that ETA must face up to defeat," the hard-core leadership replied that " . . . the armed struggle remained the decisive factor in the process of attrition against the 'political enemy,' " a proclamation followed by the arrest of thirty ETA suspects, which in turn was followed by a bomb exploding under an army bus in Madrid to kill four soldiers and a bystander and wound seven passers-by.[29] More arrests of senior leaders occurred in spring and summer.[30]

Expo-92 in Sevilla and the World Olympics at Barcelona opened and closed without visible interference—a psychological disaster for what was left of ETA.

The organization was undoubtedly hurting, but was scarcely moribund. In June 1993 ETA guerrilla terrorists exploded two car bombs in Madrid that killed six senior military officers and wounded twenty-five civilians,[31] an action that caused a shocked minister of the interior to realize that the ETA could still murder "when and where they want."[32] In July guerrillas kidnaped a Basque industrialist (eventually released for a reported ransom payment of $4 million). In August four bombs were exploded in Barcelona, wounding five innocents; the following month ETA gunmen killed a Spanish army general.

These and other acts have turned public opinion in the Basque country sharply against the ETA. Elections in June 1993 returned only two members of the ETA political front, the Herri Batasuna, to the national parliament. In September thousands of demonstrating *vascos* identified themselves as ETA opponents by wearing blue lapel ribbons.

This is not to suggest that ETA will die overnight. There is still a stong nationalist movement in the Basque provinces, and the ETA militants, although sharply reduced in number, still have numerous sympathizers and a good deal of money. Presumably they will require both if they are to survive as an organized threat to the state.

CHAPTER EIGHTY-SEVEN

1. Moxon-Browne, 1.
2. Ibid., 2.
3. Ibid.
4. Janke, 7.
5. *Keesing's Contemporary Archives,* Vol. 18, 1971. January 1971, 24,405–8, for an interesting digest of these events including the Burgos trials.
6. Ibid., 24,406.
7. Janke, 2.
8. Ibid., 2–3.
9. Ibid., 6.
10. Moxon-Browne, 6.
11. Ibid., 7.
12. *Keesing's Contemporary Archives,* Vol. 21, 1975. November 1975, 27,463. See also, *The Times* (London), September 5, 1975; International Institute for Strategic Studies, *Strategic Survey Autumn 1975,* 72–4.
13. Moxon-Browne, 5.
14. Ibid., 4.
15. *Keesing's Contemporary Archives,* Vol. 26, 1980, April 1980, 30,181.
16. Ibid., Vol. 30, 1984. August 1984, 32,802.
17. Ibid., Vol. 19, 1983. May 1973, 25,907.
18. *Keesing's Record of World Events,* Vol. 32, 1986. February 1986, 34,182.
19. Ibid., December 1986, 34,825.
20. Ibid.
21. Ibid., Vol. 34, 1988. April 1988, 35,851.
22. Ibid.
23. Ibid., 35,852.
24. Ibid., Vol. 35, 1989. November 1989, 37,050.
25. Ibid., Volume 36, 1990. February 1990, 37,263.
26. Ibid.
27. Ibid., April 1990, 37,330, 37,387.
28. Ibid., Vol. 37, 1991. August 1991, 38,300, 38,356, 38,402. See also, *International Herald Tribune,* August 10–11, 1991.
29. *Keesing's Record of World Events,* Vol. 38, 1992. February 1992, 38,783.
30. *The Independent* (U.K.), March 30, 1992.
31. *International Herald Tribune,* June 26, 1993.
32. *Daily Telegraph* (U.K.), June 22, 1993.

CHAPTER 88

> . . . life for life, eye for eye, tooth for tooth, hand for hand, foot for foot, burning for burning.
>
> EXODUS 21:23–5

WE LEFT PALESTINE ON the verge of being partitioned between Jews and Arabs (see Chapter 45), the details to be worked out by a special United Nations committee. The committee's solution was reluctantly adopted by the Jewish Agency (the executive body of the international Zionist organization) once the British Government made it clear that it intended to yield the mandate and withdraw its troops in the near future. The resolution was passed by UN General Assembly vote, by no means unanimous, in late 1947. The Arab League responded by ordering attacks against Jewish settlements not only in Palestine but throughout the Middle East.

The partition was immensely complicated and rather unrealistic, thus a fitting supplement to the Balfour Declaration of 1922, which set the scene for the interminable guerrilla wars prior to World War II. As Sydney Bayley wrote of the 1947 partition in his excellent book, *Four Arab Israel Wars and the Peace Process:*

> ... the Jewish state was to comprise 56 percent of the area of Palestine and would have a Jewish population of 449,000 and an Arab population (including Bedouin) of 510,000. The Arab state would comprise 43 percent of the area, with an Arab population (including Bedouin) of 747,000 and about 10,000 Jews. The international enclave [the city of Jerusalem together with Bethlehem] would total about 68 square miles and have about 100,000 Jews and 100,000 Arabs. A Palestine Commission of five members [from Bolivia, Czechoslovakia, Denmark, and the Philippines] was given responsibility for implementing the partition plan, under the guidance of the Security Council.[1]

It is doubtful that a more powerful time-bomb has ever been constructed. Not unnaturally the Palestinian Arabs and other Arab states—Egypt, Iraq, Lebanon, Saudi Arabia, Syria, Transjordan, and Yemen—regarded the plan as an attempt to settle a Western-created problem at their expense, and they rejected it as "illegal and unjust."[2] While the Arab League recruited and trained an Arab Liberation Army, Palestinian and Egyptian guerrillas began attacking Jewish motor convoys and isolated Jewish settlements busy turning desert sands into profitable farming communities. Jewish Haganah (Defense Organization) counterattacks of Arab villages followed. In this opening exchange, the Jews had the upper hand. Neither the Arab Liberation Army nor local Arab militias in Palestine were well-trained or well-organized forces. The Haganah and its Palmach assault units, on the other hand, had been fighting Arabs and the British for nearly three decades. World War II saw the birth of two guerrilla terrorist groups, the Irgun Tsvai Leumi (Etzel)—the National Military Organization—and the Lokhammei Kherut Israel (Lehi)—Fighters for the Freedom of Israel—better known as the old Stern Gang (see Chapter 45), which now conducted independent operations against the Arabs. Isolated Jewish settlements had long since been providing their own protection in much the same way pioneers in nineteenth-century America had protected their settlements against Indians. When a kibbutz was violated, retaliation by Haganah and guerrilla units was swift and harsh. Perhaps inevitably, this led to pre-emptive strikes against Arab targets, the ar-

THE ISRAEL SCENE

LEGEND
Occupied Territories
Israeli Security Zone

0   50 miles

gument being that these were "defensive"[3]—a semantic perversion historically known as "preventive war" and practiced by, among other aggressors, Frederick the Great and Eric Ludendorff. Some of the strikes were unnecessarily harsh, for example that by Israeli guerrillas who in 1948 put one village to the torch after killing 250 Arabs, half of them women and children.[4] Arab guerrillas at once retaliated by ambushing a convoy and killing seventy-seven Jews, but it was the village massacre that captured headlines and led not only to international opprobrium but also to the Arabs leaving their villages in increasing numbers, the beginning of what grew to be an unmanageable and enormously tragic refugee problem.[5]

Unable to stem escalating violence the UN Palestine Commission, supported by the Jewish Agency, asked for an international military force to intervene, but nothing came of this largely because of U.S. resistance,[6] nor was the dispirited British army scheduled for departure about to help. The British mandate ended in May 1948, whereupon David Ben-Gurion declared that the Provisional Government of Israel had come into being. It was a stormy birth at once contested by Arab League armies invading from Egypt, Lebanon, Syria, and Jordan. UN special envoy Count Folke Bernadotte of Sweden somehow managed to arrange a cease-fire policed by a force of UN observers, but guerrilla forces refused to accept it and when fighting resumed in July, the Israeli army soon gained the upper hand. Bernadotte's repeated efforts to achieve a compromise settlement by granting Israel western Galilee and the Arabs the Negev led to his assassination by Israeli guerrilla terrorists in September 1948. Despite the pleas of UN envoy Ralph Bunche, who had replaced Bernadotte, Israeli forces continued to push into Galilee and the Negev, routing the Arab Liberation Army and even briefly pushing into Egypt before year's end.

Bowing to U.S. demands, Israel pulled back from Egypt early in 1949 and accepted a cease-fire that left it with more land than it had been granted by the partition. It had been quite a year: over half a million Arabs had fled their Palestinian villages; an estimated one hundred thousand Jewish immigrants had arrived in Palestine and many more were to come.[7] The Arab League was in disarray. In January, what was now the Government of Israel signed an armistice with Egypt; similar agreements followed with Lebanon and Syria, and in spring of 1949 Israel was admitted to the United Nations. Under UN auspices, Armistice Demarcation Lines supervised by UN personnel were established. In July 1949, Ralph Bunche informed the Security Council that fighting had ended in Palestine.[8]

This happy event was not long lasting. As Israel consolidated its territorial gains, as Israeli citizens "made the desert bloom," as the young nation grew in confidence and manpower—over half a million immigrants, many of them from Arab countries, received with open arms between 1949 and 1956—the Arab states festered in disunity, refusing to recognize Israel's place in the sun yet unable to challenge it by other than pinprick raids by guerrillas, the *fedayeen,* answered rapidly and roughly by an increasingly mobile Israeli army equipped with modern U.S. weapons to defend its vulnerable borders with Egypt, Jordan, Syria, and Lebanon. The refugee problem, roughly one million Arabs jammed into camps in Jordan, Lebanon, Syria, and the Gaza Strip, went unheeded. Israel did not want them back, indeed David Ben-Gurion washed his hands of any responsibility for their plight; the Arab states did not want them, and those who managed to escape the camps and settle in those states were shabbily treated.[9] Each side was too busy feeding hatred to allow humanitarianism to interfere. For Arabs, it was a matter of revenge; for Israelis, preservation. Border raids increased; Egyptian suicide teams were sanctioned by Egypt's Gamal Abdul-Nasser; Israeli retaliation followed; armistice agreements bent and broke; Jordan grew antagonistic and seized the West Bank;* superpowers entered the fray; Russia replaced U.S. influence in Egypt; the U.S. continued to support Israel; wanting to isolate Israel economically, Gamal Abdul-Nasser closed the Suez Canal to Israeli use and blockaded the Gulf of Aqaba; Nasser nationalized the Canal; to retrieve it, Britain and France supported by Israel launched a surprise attack during which Israeli troops seized the Sinai Peninsula and passed into Egypt—an ill-planned, ill-executed, and very costly fiasco that terminated in November 1956, the UN sending in a six-thousand-man force to police up the mess while the principals withdrew their troops. Though pressed by the U.S., Israel refused to yield either the Gaza Strip or the western coast of the Gulf of Aqaba. In 1958, Egypt and Syria formed the United Arab Republic; Moslems in Christian-dominated Lebanon started a civil war; Iraq and Jordan formed a union that lasted for six months, ending with King Faisal's murder . . . and so it went. As Julian Becker put it: " . . . Manifestly the desire for Arab unity was the chief cause of Arab disunity."[10]

Nearly a decade passed before the next decisive development in the Arab-Israeli conflict, not that there was a lack of regional crises during this period. Although Egypt stopped sending guerrilla teams into Israel, partly owing to UN observation posts along the border, such attacks continued from Jordan, Syria, and Lebanon. Some of these were made by Syrian guerrillas recruited from Palestinian refugee camps in Leba-

---

* The West Bank of the Jordan River is inaptly named. The area containing the biblical lands of Judaea and Samaria and such cities as Jerusalem, Nablus, Jericho, and Bethlehem measures nearly eighty miles north to south and thirty miles east to west, thus amounting to a considerable portion of Palestine. Its western border is only about nine miles from the sea at its nearest point.

non, some by factions of Ahmed Shuqairi's Palestine Liberation Organization (PLO), a new movement formed by six Palestinian groups at Egyptian President Nasser's instigation, its goal the "liberation" of Palestine.[11] The principal group, the Movement for the Liberation of Palestine, or al-Fatah, was organized in 1957 by, among others, twenty-six-year-old Yasser Arafat, a Palestinian refugee and an officer in the 1956 war. Al-Fatah guerrillas first went into action in 1964, small raids that publicized the group and won financial support from the Arab world.

As Israel again moved toward war with its neighbors—this time the *casus belli* was a dispute over Israeli use of water from the Jordan river—the PLO became increasingly active but was temporarily eclipsed by Israel's overwhelming military victory in June 1967—the famous six-day war which left Israel in possession of the Sinai Peninsula, Gaza, the West Bank of the Jordan, and the Golan Heights, a land area three times the size of Israel.[12]

But victory is an illusory word. The new lands included "a million hostile Arabs," in the words of one realistic Israeli politician.[13] Israel's victory and subsequent harsh military occupation of the West Bank and Gaza guaranteed implacable hatred that could not but result in another war.[14] In an attempt to forestall this, the UN in November 1967 passed Resolution 242, which called for " . . . Withdrawal of Israeli armed forces from 'territories occupied in the recent conflict . . . [and] a just settlement of the refugee problem,' " the latter exacerbated by the addition of another three hundred thousand refugees to a total 1.5 million.[15]

As superpower positions polarized, the U.S. supporting Israel, the Soviet Union supporting Egypt and Syria, it was apparent to the Palestinians that an impasse had developed. In their minds, their only recourse was guerrilla warfare, and it was not long before PLO guerrillas of the Palestine Liberation Army (PLA) were striking Israeli positions from Jordan and Lebanon with Israeli forces retaliating in kind.

The PLO was gaining in strength, drawing on the immense pool of young refugees and a horde of youthful volunteers from Arab countries for its guerrilla recruits and on rich Arab states such as Saudi Arabia, Libya, and Kuwait for money to buy arms. Shuqairi's death late in 1967 was followed by the young Yasser Arafat's ascendancy.[16] In early 1969, Arafat was elected chairman of the PLO's executive committee. Of the organization's several guerrilla groups, Arafat's al-Fatah with about seven to nine thousand guerrillas was the most important and also the least militant. More recently formed groups included Dr. George Habash's Popular Front for the Liberation of Palestine (PFLP), a Marxist guerrilla terrorist group of about five hundred members formed in 1968; and two splinter groups from the PFLP, Ahmed Jibril's Popular Front for the Liberation of Palestine—General Command (PFLP-GC), and Naif Hawatmeh's Popular Democratic Front for the Liberation of Palestine (PDFLP).[17] In addition to these groups was a large Syrian Ba'ath guerrilla organization founded in 1968 and called Vanguards of the Popular Liberation War, its military arm being al-Saiqa (Thunderbolt), led by Zuhayr Muhsin.[18] Of these organizations, Arafat's Fatah, Hawatmeh's PDFLP, and Muhsin's Saiqa ". . . wanted political negotiation and territory for Palestinian self-determination wherever it could be won."[19] The remaining groups, refusing these notions in favor of an all-out "armed struggle" to annihilate Israel, formed the Rejection Front, itself of fragile lasting power.[20] Indeed, had it not been for the intense factionalism that led to countless quarrels between the Arab guerrilla groups, it is doubtful that Israel could have survived.

By 1969, several thousand Saiqa and PLO guerrillas were based in southern Lebanon where they infiltrated refugee camps that held some one hundred thousand Palestinians and ". . . were turning the camps into centers for guerrilla training and indoctrination."[21] Arafat's major guerrilla force in Jordan had expanded sufficiently to control large areas of the kingdom and there was talk that he was planning a coup against King Hussein.

In 1969, guerrillas based in Lebanon and Jordan carried out an estimated thirty-nine hundred guerrilla actions against Israel and in 1970 were averaging about five hundred a month including raids from Lebanon as far into Israel as Haifa.[22] Israel did not take this lying down, and most observers give the army high marks for its counterguerrilla tactics. When an El Al plane was hijacked, Israel responded by an airborne commando raid on the Beirut airport that destroyed thirteen planes belonging to Arab countries. Ground forces were authorized to make "hot pursuits" into Lebanon and Jordan and also to make preemptive strikes against suspected guerrilla concentrations.

George Habash's PFLP terrorists made world headlines in May 1970 by blowing up the pipeline that carried Saudi Arabian oil to Mediterranean ports.[23] Later in the year, PFLP terrorists hijacked four Western commercial aircraft and held passengers and crew hostage until the release of some imprisoned guerrillas. After releasing the hostages, they blew up the planes. That action, coupled with increasing encroachments by the PLO in Jordan and two attempts by PFLP terrorists to assassinate Hussein, led to what the PLO would remember as Black September: its forceful eviction by the Jordanian army after heavy fighting which cost the guerrillas perhaps three thousand dead before the groups retreated dispiritedly into Syria and southern Lebanon.[24] Guerrilla terrorists of the PFLP and of a new group, the Black September Organization operating out of Syria, now began claiming headlines by such operations as the murder of nine Israeli athletes at the Olympic Games in Munich

1156

in September 1972 (after previously carrying out a series of assassinations in Europe).

What few people seemed to realize was that the PLO could not exist without Palestinian refugees.[25] It was all very well to have forced those people from their lands, but surely it was incumbent on the responsible parties—Britain, the U.S., Israel, Egypt—to find them a new homeland and in conjunction with their oil-rich fellow Arabs—Saudi Arabia, Libya, Iraq, Kuwait, Yemen—to give them the money necessary to build new livelihoods. It was not as if the Israelis had been given or had taken the world—"... in 1984," wrote one commentator, "the size of the Jewish State is less than a quarter of 1 percent of Arab territory, and the Arabs have some two dozen states."[26] There is almost no mention of this collective responsibility. In 1972, King Hussein did come up with a plan to build a federated United Arab Kingdom with Jordan, a plan immediately denounced by Israel, Egypt, and Syria,[27] and soon forgotten. Yet almost everyone in a responsible position stressed again and again that there could never be a suitable peace between Israel and the Arab world until the "Palestinian question" was satisfactorily resolved.

Various attempts to bring about Israeli evacuation of the vast Sinai Peninsula having failed, in 1973 Egyptian and Syrian armies opened a surprise invasion of Israel which caught its army off guard. Although the October war ended favorably for Israel, it also deepened Arab hostility and for the first time opened Arab eyes to the value of oil as a weapon against the West. We should take note that the war could not have been fought without massive U.S.-Soviet military aid to the belligerents; indeed it very nearly provoked a clash between the two superpowers.

The war left the Palestinian refugee problem unsolved. It was, however, becoming better recognized thanks in part to headlines engendered by PLO terrorist attacks abroad. In 1974, the UN General Assembly, ignoring Israel and U.S. protests, listened to Yasser Arafat talk about Middle East problems, an impressive performance that helped win the PLO an observer's role in the United Nations, full membership in the Arab League, and general recognition that the Palestinian refugees must be provided with a homeland.

In mid-1977, Prime Minister Menachem Begin (whose Irgun guerrilla terrorists had helped to force Britain from Palestine) visited America's new President, Jimmy Carter, who

> ... made it clear that there was no hope for a settlement in the Middle East without a homeland for the Palestinians. ... Carter stressed that the establishment of Jewish settlements in the occu-

pied territories was a serious obstacle to peace, but Begin insisted that there was no way of stopping Jews from settling in biblical Israel. . . . Begin ruled out any contact with the PLO and said that Israel would never agree to a Palestinian homeland or entity."[28]

Carter's determined attempts to break the deadlock, notably by sending veteran negotiator and now Secretary of State Cyrus Vance to the troubled area, finally brought an unprecedented meeting between President Sadat of Egypt and Prime Minister Begin under the auspices of President Carter. This resulted in Israel and Egypt signing the Camp David accords and subsequently a formal peace treaty in 1977. Under its terms, Israel agreed to a phased withdrawal from the entire Sinai Peninsula. The treaty also affirmed " . . . the legitimate rights of the Palestinian people and their just requirements." Although the Israel Knesset, or parliament, approved the accords, Israeli right-wingers vigorously opposed them. President Sadat for his part won only open censure from the Arab world and Egypt was expelled from the Arab League. As for "the legitimate rights of the Palestinian people," no action was taken and little more was heard for the next few years.

An important casualty of the Middle East deadlock was Lebanon, whose once-prosperous facade had been shattered by continual political turbulence compounded by the presence of Zuhai Mohsen's Syrian-backed Saiqa guerrillas and the influx of PLO guerrillas evicted from Jordan. Early in 1975, a new civil war broke out between Christians and Moslems, the left-wing Druze groups of the latter being supported by Palestinian guerrillas. By early 1976, the almost defunct Lebanese army and the Maronite Christians, whose main military strength rested in Pierre Gemayel's Phalange militia, were on the verge of defeat by Arafat's PLO guerrillas and socialist Kamal Jumblatt's Druze militia (themselves in conflict with the Rejection Front of splinter guerrilla groups). Not wanting this to happen, Syria's Hafez Assad sent in an armor division to support the Maronites and Israel began supplying them with weapons. Owing largely to the leadership of Gemayel's son Bashir, the war ended in October in the Maronites' favor, a hollow victory in view of the casualties—at least forty thousand killed, one hundred thousand wounded and half a million people displaced from their homes.[29] Syrian armies remained in northern Lebanon and in the Bekáa Valley "as a peacekeeping force" and most of the PLO bases in Beirut and in northern and southern Lebanon remained intact, their presence formally accepted by the Lebanese Government.[30]

This was anathema to Bashir Gemayel, who, supported by the slippery Phalange patriarch Camille Chamoun, eventually persuaded Israel to guarantee " . . . the safety of the Lebanese Christian community."[31] Begin did not encourage Gemayel's bellicose intentions of ejecting the Syrians from Lebanon. Gemayel's desire for a confrontation with Syrian troops in the Bekáa Valley probably would have been frustrated by Begin's government had it not been for the PLO presence in southern Lebanon, the supportive presence of Secretary of State Alexander Haig in Washington, and the hawkish presence of Ariel Sharon, the Minister of Defense in Begin's cabinet.

Ironically, Yasser Arafat's presence in southern Lebanon resulted from the mass of refugees caused by Israel's victories over the Arab states. Arafat's guerrillas had easily infiltrated the refugee camps eventually to build "a state-within-a-state," gathering the support of Shiite Moslems in the countryside and Sunni Moslems in the cities: " . . . the PLO had become by 1976 the sole instrument of rule in the western sector of Lebanon stretching from Beirut to the Israeli border,"[32] from where PLO guerrillas stole into Galilee and elsewhere. Israeli troops retaliated by striking PLO camps in Lebanon—in early 1978, twenty-five thousand Israeli troops pushed across the border and, aided by Major Sa'ad Haddad's expanding Christian militia, burned dozens of Palestinian villages and left some seven hundred dead before withdrawing.[33]

In 1981, Menachem Begin was taking an even stronger line against the PLO enemy. With the exception of a surprise air raid that knocked out Saddam Hussein's nuclear reactor plant in Iraq and the abrupt annexation of the Golan Heights later that year (actions that infuriated his U.S. ally), Begin's main thrust was against the PLO. A host of raids by land and sea accompanied by heavy aerial bombing raids of PLO camps in Beirut and southern Lebanon brought prolonged PLO artillery shelling of the Galilee settlements, a duel interrupted by a cease-fire in July. But Begin and his closest advisers had decided that the PLO had to leave southern Lebanon if Israel's northern flank was ever to be secure, the plan being to clear the area of enemy and establish a twenty-five-mile-deep security zone north of the border. But now a secret plan was hatched by central players Ariel Sharon, Foreign Minister Yitzhak Shamir, and a few military hawks, who intended not only to drive Arafat's PLO and Assad's Syrians out of Lebanon but to install Bashir Gemayel as president. This fitted in nicely with Alexander Haig's current vendetta against Syria although the extent of his encouragement to Sharon (against Reagan's wishes) has not yet been fully revealed; that it was considerable is suggested by his quarrel with Reagan and subsequent removal from office.

The Machiavellian details of Sharon's double-dealing and the subsequent mainly conventional and very cruel war that began on June 6, 1982, by Israeli forces pushing into Lebanon are not pertinent to this survey. It is enough to say that Israeli soldiers and fliers won an overwhelming victory against both Syrian and PLO armies.[34] Arafat was forced into asylum in Tripoli and an estimated eight thousand of his followers were dispersed in various Arab states.[35] This was a solid enough gain for Israel but it was tempered by the majority of three hundred thousand Palestinian refugees, including several thousand guerrillas, remaining in their squalid Lebanon camps; by a large Syrian army based in the Bekáa Valley, from where it controlled over half the country; by a strong Druze militia holed up in the Shouf Mountains, where Bashir Gemayel's Phalange militia suffered a serious defeat in attempting to evict them; by the precarious position of Bashir Gemayel's new government; by his assassination in September; and by the opprobrium heaped on Israel from Cairo, Washington, and other capitals for invading Lebanon and then carrying out a prolonged and bloody occupation.

Suddenly aware that Sharon's war had placed him in a vulnerable position, Menachem Begin decided that both Israeli and Syrian troops must vacate the country, leaving the Lebanese responsible for policing the border security zone. Here Israel-manned surveillance posts would be supported by Major Sa'ad Haddad's Christian militia of fifteen hundred to two thousand troops. Washington agreed with the plan, a "simple and logical" solution in Secretary of State George Shultz's words, but one that depended on Christian Maronite control of the country.

Amin Gemayel, who had replaced his brother as president, did not control the country. The steps taken by the Reagan administration to gain him control did not sufficiently respect either the intense religious and political factionalism in Lebanon or the political acumen of Syria's Hafez Assad generously supported by an extremely anti-Israel Soviet Union.

The basis of the plan was a multinational armed force to keep the peace while Gemayel relied on U.S. economic and military aid to build a strong army. Meanwhile, Arafat's remaining forces in Lebanon would be given sanctuary in Iraq and Jordan. A Lebanese-Israeli-PLO treaty would further isolate Syria. The Reagan administration had made the supreme error of underestimating Assad. Increasing aid to the Moslem Druze militia, he reinforced his army in Lebanon to a total twelve hundred tanks, increased his Soviet military advisers to five thousand, and surrounded Damascus with batteries of SAM-5 ground-to-air missiles.[36]

What of the PLO? There was no doubting that it had suffered " . . . the worst blow in its eighteen-year existence."[37] It had lost heavily in numbers—estimates vary from one to five thousand—and it also had lost its corporate "homeland." Its various groups were widely dispersed. Arafat and about a thousand guerrillas finally ended up in Tunisia. Leaders of small terrorist groups found refuge in Damascus but their fighters had to go as far as South Yemen and Algeria. An estimated two thousand guerrillas remained secretly in Beirut while others joined the three to four thousand guerrillas still in the Bekáa Valley and in north Lebanon.

Yasser Arafat remained chairman of the PLO and, after beating off a rebellion in his own Fatah Party, was soon touring the Arab states, pulling the strands together.[38] If the PLO had been weakened, it certainly was not moribund, and such countries as Saudi Arabia and Libya continued to contribute generous amounts of money. Arafat's task was daunting, not only organizationally and logistically but politically. The big question was, what next? Some within the organization wanted to intensify " . . . the armed struggle for the total liberation of Palestine." Others realized that Israel was there to stay and believed that the solution lay in an independent state comprising the West Bank and Gaza.[39] Some Arab countries agreed with this, others did not. In September 1982, President Reagan, borrowing from King Hussein's 1972 proposal, called for an end of Israeli settlements in the occupied territories, refused the notion of converting these lands into an independent Palestinian state, and concluded: " . . . it is the firm view of the United States that self-government by the Palestinians of the West Bank and Gaza in association with Jordan offers the best chance for a durable, just and lasting peace." Considering that the PLO still refused to recognize Israel's existence, that Israel refused to negotiate with the PLO, that Jordan did not recognize Israel, that any thought of Jordan mixing into PLO affairs was anathema to Syria and the PLO splinter groups in Damascus, neither Reagan's nor any other plan was to be even debated, much less accepted. Israel rejected the plan outright. Although Arafat did not directly reject it, he effectively neutered it by insisting on " . . . the national rights of the Palestinian people 'under the leadership of the PLO, its sole legitimate representative' and demanded the setting up of 'an independent Palestinian state with Jerusalem as its capital.' "[40]

In mid-September, Israeli troops in the shattered city of Beirut joined with Amin Gemayel's Phalangist militia in storming PLO refugee camps in West Beirut which were believed to be harboring militant guerrillas, a two-day operation that turned into a sickening slaughter of an estimated three thousand Palestinians.[41] World-wide condemnation of the action was shared within Israel by protest marches of up to four hundred thousand people and by the emergence of a Peace Now movement. It also brought harsh words from President Reagan and it cost Israel a great many former friends including some important Jewish figures.[42]

The unhappy occupation continued throughout 1983. In September, Prime Minister Begin resigned, reportedly distraught by the occupying army's high casualty rate, but such was the power of the military that occupation continued into 1984. In April, the government announced that its forces would stay in Lebanon until the South Lebanese Army

(SLA)—formerly the Christian militia commanded by Major Sa'ad Haddad (and after his assassination by Antonio Lahad)—was ready to replace them.[43] This decision was tempered later in the year when a Jordan-PLO initiative based on UN Resolution 242 called for Israel to respect " . . . the principle of territory in exchange for peace" and withdraw from the West Bank and Gaza.[44] Wiser heads now recognized that the political priority had to shift southward (where it had always been despite Sharon's costly frolic into Beirut) and a three-stage withdrawal from Lebanon commenced in early 1985. Owing to guerrilla interdiction, this was a slow and painful operation completed only in June.

Such was the perpetual turmoil in the Middle East that one crisis was scarcely over before another began. While members of the major factions continued to kill each other in Lebanon and while the Jordan-PLO initiative was making tentative approaches to Israel's new "national unity" Labor government headed by Shimon Peres, the world's attention shifted to the Iran-Iraq war which ended only in 1987. By then, Hussein and Arafat's attempt to bring Israel into peace negotiations had come to naught. Also by then, the long-suffering Palestinian refugees living under Israeli rule in the occupied territories had had enough.

In 1987, rumbles of civil revolt heard for years turned to thunder. When an Israel taxi driven by a Jew crashed into and killed four Palestinian laborers, the storm boke. The ensuing Arab uprising, or *intifada,* in the West Bank, Gaza, and the Golan Heights was carried out on the one hand by youths hurling stones and petrol bombs, on the other by passive resistance in the form of general strikes, resignations of Arab officials and policemen, refusal of Arabs to pay taxes and boycott of Israeli-owned shops and Israeli-made goods.

The Israeli government moved fast and hard to quell the uprising. Prime Minister Yitzhak Shamir's "iron fist policy" was spelled out by Minister of Defense Yitzhak Rabin as giving priority to "might, power and beatings."[45] This resulted in several hundred Palestinian deaths, seven to eight thousand wounded and twenty-two thousand imprisoned in 1988.[46] It also resulted in massive official protests by the U. S. and U. K. governments, the European parliament, the UN Security Council, and not least by the general Israeli public. As the rebellion spread in 1989, Israeli security forces began firing plastic bullets in carrying out an official policy of "shoot-to-wound,"[47] to achieve Rabin's announced goal of "hurting them . . . leaving scars."[48] By year's end, the number of Arab deaths from military action had risen to six hundred plus 150 caused by Arab vigilantes killing suspected Arab collaborators. Jewish deaths numbered forty. Although some schools reopened in the West Bank, the intifada was becoming a way of life: " . . . The government, army and the public had settled into an attitude of acceptance of the level of violence and a pattern of attrition was established."[49]

The intifada apparently caught the PLO by surprise, although Arafat hastened to support it politically and financially. Arafat's authority, however, was seriously challenged by Palestinian members of Hamas, a growing militant Islamic resistance movement which advocated " . . . an Islamic state in all of Palestine (including Israel) and rejected the PLO's giving growing reliance on political struggle and a compromise solution."[50] The gulf between Arafat's PLO and other guerrilla terrorist groups widened visibly in late 1988 when, in presenting a peace plan to the UN, he " . . . condemned terrorism in all its forms," later telling journalists, " . . . I repeat for the record that we totally and absolutely renounce all forms of terrorism."[51] Secretary of State Shultz took the next important step in agreeing to open talks with the PLO, though without recognizing it as a Palestinian state. Shultz's successor, James Baker, openly criticized the Israeli Government for continuing its policy of armed struggle. Shamir shrugged off his words, the PLO committed itself to more not less violence, the Islamic Hamas gained in strength and influence, and the intifada intensified.

Once again, the "Palestinian problem" was shunted aside by war, this time brought on by Saddam Hussein's invasion of Kuwait in August 1990 and the ensuing Gulf War. That crisis resolved (at least in part), the intifada regained center stage as the Israeli government expanded its settlement program, which, according to an official U.S. report, had established " . . . over 200,000 Israeli settlers . . . in some 200 settlements in the occupied territories" and was growing as much as 10 per cent annually.[52] Hoping to halt the program, the Bush administration delayed approval of $10 billion in promised loan guarantees to Israel, but at the same time pushed ahead on bringing Israelis and Palestinians to the negotiating table, no mean feat that was accomplished in Madrid in late 1991. More talks ensued, intransigence prevailed, intifada violence reached a new high as Israel's relations with Washington reached a new low, the Bush administration holding firm in refusing to release the loan guarantees until the settlement program was halted.

In February 1992, Prime Minister Shamir publicly reneged on Israel's commitment to the Camp David Accords.[53] Seemingly nothing could alter conservative Likud intransigence, that is until mid-1992 when, *mirabile dictu*, the conservative government gave way to Yitzhak Rabin's center-left coalition. The new government held out the olive branch to Washington by canceling future settlement building. In mid-August, Rabin opened peace negotiations with Syria, going so far as to offer Hafez Assad a portion of the Golan Heights in return for a peace treaty between the two governments—tacit acceptance of the "land for peace" formula originally set forth in UN Resolution 242.[54] At peace talks in Washington in late August, Israeli Foreign Minister Shimon Peres did not offer much more than some form of Arab autonomy in the occupied territories, but he subsequently stated that he wanted a political settlement, a goal that he realized could be achieved only by pursuing the "land for peace" formula.

Negotiations came to an abrupt halt in December 1992 when the Israeli government summarily expelled 415 Palestinian Islamic fundamentalists—suspected Hamas guerrilla terrorists—from the West Bank. Because no other country offered sanctuary, the unfortunates, some of whom were *not* guerrilla terrorists, were consigned to a bleak hillside in Israeli-occupied Lebanon, there to spend a cold winter in tents with neither adequate food nor medical care—a TV spectacular that, although blackening the Israeli image, failed to change the government's stance until spring of 1993. Indeed, the government in March again moved firmly when, in an attempt to end Palestinian guerrilla attacks inside Israel, it closed the borders of the West Bank and the Gaza Strip, thus preventing over 100,000 Arabs of the 1.8 million in these territories, from keeping their jobs in Israel.[55]

These events, taken with frequent riots and killings in the occupied territories, did not encourage a resumption of peace talks, and it was only by a superhuman diplomatic effort that Secretary of State Warren Christopher brought delegations from the concerned parties—Israel, Syria, Jordan, Lebanon, and the Palestinians—together in Washington for the ninth round of talks. This time a new and important face appeared at the table, that of Faisal Husseini, the leader of the Palestinian team, who heretofore at Israeli insistence had not been permitted to attend the talks. For this slight plus, however, there was a very large minus, and that was the absence of the well-known scruffy face of the all-time guerrilla survivor, Yasser Arafat, a political pariah in the eyes of Washington and Israel. The ninth round of what Clyde Haberman aptly termed "the stutter-start negotiations" ended three weeks later with the usual whimper, the all-important question of Palestinian self-rule in the occupied territories no closer to a solution than ever.[56]

The tenth round of talks that resumed in mid-June, again without the presence of Yasser Arafat, ended "with such gloom there was not even talk of a date to talk again."[57]

Matters might well have remained in limbo had it not been for fourteen rounds of secret talks in an isolated Norwegian farmhouse that had begun in May. A month earlier the doughty political columnist Flora Lewis had called attention to Yasser Arafat's appeal to end the violence and hold elections in the occupied territories. More important, he "accepted that the first stage of negotiations be linked to 'self-government,' without reference to the later goal of statehood."[58] This became the basis for the ultra-secret talks between Yasser Arafat and

1164

Israeli Foreign Minister Shimon Peres under the aegis of the Norwegian government.

Without revealing the existence of the talks, Peres in late June ". . . joined the growing number of Israeli politicians . . . urging that the Israeli-occupied Gaza Strip be turned over to Palestinians 'as soon as possible' and that the Israeli army retreat from most of the area."[59] Concurrent with this development, certain Israeli cabinet ministers realized that the bête-noire of the Washington negotiations was the absence of Yasser Arafat and, contrary to Washington's policy, that the time had come for direct talks with the PLO—a feeling that gained weight during a summer of heavy fighting and the increasing threat from Islamic guerrilla terrorists in the West Bank and Gaza, not to mention a dangerous stalemate with Syria over the Golan Heights and Syrian support of guerrilla terrorists in Lebanon.

Although Prime Minister Yitzhak Rabin still refused to recognize either Yasser Arafat or the PLO, that decision was forced on him in late August when the story broke of Shimon Peres' secret negotiations having produced " . . . a radical new peace formula under which Palestinians hope independence would be tested first in the Gaza Strip and in the West Bank town of Jericho."[60]

This was the concept, an *Arab* concept, that won almost instant approval by the members of the eleventh round of peace talks then taking place in Washington. Within a week the logjam of years had been broken: Israel and the PLO formally recognized each other; the U.S. recognized the PLO; Yatzik Rabin and Yasser Arafat not only signed the agreement at a special White House ceremony but *publicly shook hands.*

The ratified agreement called for a withdrawal of Israel troops by December 13, 1993, from the Gaza Strip and the town of Jericho, security to be taken over by Palestinian police. An interim Palestinian government is to be replaced by election of a Palestine Council in spring of 1994. It was anticipated that the agreement would pave the way for separate agreements between Israel and Jordan (accomplished), and between Israel and Syria-Lebanon (not accomplished), and would lead eventually to Israel's turning over all of the West Bank to Palestinian rule.

The agreement was at once denounced by powerful factions both in Israel and the PLO. The Israeli right-wing Likud Party pronounced it a betrayal of Israel's interests as did the 100,000 or so Jewish settlers in Gaza and the West Bank. The Israeli army grumpily announced that it had not been consulted and pointed to security dangers that would accrue from an Israeli troop-police evacuation. Yasser Arafat faced an incipient rebellion in the PLO, whose governing council nevertheless approved the agreement.

Scarcely a day has passed since ratification without a crisis developing in the occupied territories, all to the delight of the gloom-and-doom factions on each side. As fighting intensified between Jewish settlers and Palestinian Arabs in late November and early December, Prime Minister Rabin warned of a possible delay in troop evacuation, much against the wishes of Yasser Arafat. Sure enough, the day arrived—and the troops remained. The world must hope that this is only a temporary setback now that the way has at last been opened for peace.

CHAPTER EIGHTY-EIGHT

1. Bayley, 1.
2. Ibid., 4.
3. Ibid., 3.
4. Goode, 90–1.
5. Bayley, 12–13.
6. Ibid., 8.
7. Ibid., 44.
8. Ibid., 66–70.
9. Becker, 2.
10. Ibid., 37.
11. Bayley, 187.
12. Ibid., 240.
13. Ibid.
14. Cobban, 36–9.
15. Bayley, 270–1, 243. See also, Clutterbuck, *Guerrillas and Terrorists*, 79.
16. Cobban, 21–35, is excellent on the origin and growth of Arafat's al-Fatah and the PLO.
17. Becker, 73, for biographical details of the various leaders.
18. Ibid., 72–3.
19. Ibid., 82.
20. Cobban, 15.
21. Goode, 102.
22. Ibid., 101.
23. International Institute for Strategic Studies, *Strategic Survey 1970*, 45.
24. Cobban, 49–52. See also, Becker, 75–6.
25. Cobban, 7–8, 38–42.
26. Becker, 30.
27. Bayley, 293.
28. Ibid., 351.
29. Becker, 136.
30. Cobban, 81.
31. Schiff and Ya'ari, 29.
32. Ibid., 79.
33. Cobban, 94–5.
34. Becker, 205–7.
35. Cobban, 3.
36. Schiff and Ya'ari, 295.
37. International Institute for Strategic Studies, *Strategic Survey 1982–83*, 75.
38. Cobban, 4–5.
39. International Institute for Strategic Studies, *Strategic Survey 1982–83*, 77.
40. Ibid., 78.
41. Cobban, 129–30.

42. International Institute for Strategic Studies, *Strategic Survey 1982–83,* 71–2, 75–7.
43. *Keesing's Record of World Events* Vol. 31, 1985. February 1985, 33,438.
44. Ibid., March 1985, 33,494.
45. Ibid., Vol. 34, 1988. April 1988, 35,859.
46. International Institute for Strategic Studies, *Strategic Survey 1988–89,* 157–8.
47. *Keesing's Record of World Events* Vol. 35, 1989. December 1987–December 1988, 36,436.
48. International Institute for Strategic Studies, *Strategic Survey 1988–89,* 159.
49. *The Annual Register and Record of World Events 1989,* 197–8.
50. International Institute for Strategic Studies, *Strategic Survey 1988–89,* 159.
51. *Keesing's Record of World Events,* Vol. 35, 1989. December 1987–December 1988, 36,438.
52. Ibid., Vol. 37, 1991. April 1991, 38,168.
53. *International Herald Tribune,* February 8–9, 1992.
54. *Newsweek,* March 2, 1992.
55. *International Herald Tribune,* April 12, 1993.
56. Ibid., June 8, 1993.
57. *The Independent* (U.K.), July 6, 1993.
58. *International Herald Tribune,* April 16, 1993.
59. Ibid., June 29, 1993.
60. *The Independent* (U.K.), August 29, 30, 31, 1993.

CHAPTER 89

Emperor Haile Selassie of Ethiopia toppled • The Dergue's Marxist-oriented urban and rural guerrilla opposition • The Eritrean challenge • War in Ogaden province • Soviet and Cuban military presence • Guerrilla reverses • The massive refugee problem • Lieutenant Colonel Mengistu Haile Mariam's regime • Widespread famine • Guerrilla gains • Mengistu's fall • 1993: Independent Eritrea • The divided Sudan: Moslem versus Christian • Guerrilla warfare in Equatoria • The 1972 Addis Ababa accord • Colonel Mohammed al-Numiery's rule • John Garang's guerrilla army • 1990 Sudan: "a human rights disaster" • Lieutenant General Hassan al-Bashir's Islamic government • Pope John Paul II protests • Starvation • Bashir's Islamic fundamentalist state • Anarchy in the South

IN 1941, ETHIOPIAN GUERRILLAS supported by British troops delivered the first defeat to the Axis powers in World War II by forcing the Italian invaders to retreat from their country. Emperor Haile Selassie thereupon returned from exile to resume rule of this vast land (some 472,000 square miles) that held forty-six million people of diverse ethnic, tribal, and religious beliefs. Although preaching a policy of modernization, the emperor failed to introduce vital political and economic reforms; nor did his autocratic command of the army insure undivided loyalty. In 1974, he was deposed by a military coup after forty-four years of rule. He was replaced by a military dictatorship carried out by the Provisional Military Administrative Council, or Dergue, one of whose leaders was a Marxist lieutenant colonel, Mengistu Haile Mariam.

The new government, like that of Mohammed Daud in Afghanistan, lorded over what essentially was an impoverished agrarian society, a tribal nation, one of the poorest in the world, life expectancy forty years, high illiteracy, a host of killing endemic diseases, few schools, hospitals, or clinics. To put this right, the Dergue socialist government nationalized industries and banks, implemented a radical land reform program—and jailed or executed any members of the former regime who stood in its way.

The new government faced several threats to its existence. One came from urban middle-class members of the largest ethnic group, the Amharas, who formed the Ethiopian People's Revolutionary Party (EPRP), a Marxist group whose guerrilla terrorists began eliminating important government and trade union officials, army officers, and police to bring on the harshest possible countermeasures in the form of thousands of arrests and large-scale executions to the extent that the movement was largely neutralized by 1978.[1]

Another threat came from the enormous semidesert province of Ogaden, home to some two million Somali-speaking traditionally unruly nomads, in the form of a large guerrilla group called the Western Somali Liberation Front (WSLF) supported by Somalia. In 1977, the WSLF went to war against the government, the vanguard of an invasion by the Soviet-trained Somali army. The invaders made good progress initially but then bogged down and in 1978 were forced from the country by Ethiopian troops supported by a large Cuban contingent. This was only a victory of sorts in that it left a simmering insurgency that would challenge Ethiopian-Cuban forces for many years.

Other threats were not so easily neutralized coming as they did from a number of insurgent guerrilla groups: the Eritreans and Tigreans in the north, the Afars in the east, the Harrars in the southeast, and the Oromos (Gallas) in the south, all wanting independence for their provinces.

The coastal province of Eritrea with its six-hundred-mile coastline on the Red Sea had been a problem since 1952. A former Italian colony, it was forced into federation with Ethiopia by the United Nations in order to provide Ethiopia with access to the sea. Subsequently a trouble spot, Haile Selassie sought to solve the problem by abrogating the treaty and making Eritrea an Ethiopian province,[2] an act that brought on a full-scale guerrilla insurgency. The major guerrilla group was Ahmed Mohammed Nasser's Eritrean Liberation Front (ELF), which was supported financially by Somalia, Libya, Iraq, and South Yemen.[3] The ELF fought government forces from 1960 on, eventually becoming a " . . . well-armed, well-trained, well-disciplined and highly motivated" force some twenty-two thousand strong.[4] Two other guerrilla groups emerged in time: Ramadan Mohammed Nour's Marxist Eritrean People's Liberation Front (EPLF), which split from the ELF in 1971 and numbered about twelve thousand; and Oosman Saleh Sabbe's ELF-Popular Liberation Forces (ELF-PLF), about two thousand strong. In 1977, these forces controlled most of the province, and had it not been for intense internecine squabbling, they might well have claimed the entire province. Once the Somalis were expelled from Ogaden province, however, army reinforcements arrived in the north and the guerrilla offensive was temporarily checked. Another insurgency sprang up in the neighboring province of Tigre, where guerrillas of the People's Liberation Front (PLF) were in control of most of the province. A third challenge came from the Oromo Liberation Front (OLF), which was also fighting for independence. More fighting took place in the northwest province of Begemder, where Ethiopian refugees in the Sudan formed a guerrilla group that enjoyed only limited success. But in the east, Afar guerrillas systematically cut road and rail lines connecting Addis Ababa with the Djibouti outlet to the sea.

To counter these insurgencies and fight the war in Ogaden, the Dergue maintained an army of about three hundred thousand (including militias). This force had received $400 million worth of U.S. military aid since 1953 and was being trained by a three-hundred-man U.S. military advisory group. Washington continued to support the government for the first two and a half years of Dergue rule, a nebulous relationship that noticeably cooled as Mengistu clawed his way up the leadership rostrum, his way cleared by his executing scores of former comrades and others accused of "counterrevolutionary crimes." Mengistu became chairman of the Dergue in 1977 and announced that henceforth only socialist countries would supply weapons to Ethiopia. The U.S. canceled its aid program and soon withdrew its advisers. Soviet arms and Cuban soldiers were now arriving in quantity. By early 1978, an estimated one thousand Soviet and two thousand Cuban military advisers were working with the greatly expanded Ethiopian army.[5] During 1978, the army received " . . . some 600 tanks and over 90 combat aircraft, including twenty of the sophisticated MiG-23s."[6] There were now an estimated fifteen thousand Cuban troops in the country. In late 1978, Mengistu was received in the Kremlin, where he signed a twenty-year treaty of friendship. At year's end, Ethiopian and Cuban forces were more than holding their own in the continuing guerrilla war in Ogaden. Eritrean guerrillas had been forced to disperse to bases in Sudan; the ELF had been particularly hard hit, leaving the EPLF " . . . as the main force for Eritrean independence."[7] In the east, both the Tigrean and Afar guerrilla groups were badly damaged and in the west the guerrillas were almost out of business.[8] A "red terror" campaign against the urban EPRP killed an estimated twenty-five hundred insurgents with tens of thousands arrested and sentenced to "political reeducation"[9] to virtually end the movement.

The new government nonetheless continued to face massive problems as famine swept the land and as revitalized guerrilla groups in Eritrea and Tigre continued to fight. By 1984, more than six million people were believed to be starving and at least half a million close to death.[10] A massive program that resettled six hundred thousand northerners to the south had to be halted because of widespread protests that sent thousands more refugees into Somalia and Sudan. Once the rains came and harvests improved, Mengistu renewed the program. He also introduced a new constitution, which was accepted by 81 per cent of the vote. Under its terms, Ethiopia became the Popular Democratic Republic theoretically run by an 835-member parliament, the Shengo. The republic came into being in late 1987 with Mengistu as president assisted by a cabinet of twenty members, seventeen of whom came from the old Dergue.[11]

The new government had no sooner taken office than another famine struck that would affect up to five million people. Both the army and guerrilla groups would as in the past obstruct relief efforts by holding up food convoys when it suited their political purposes. By February 1989, the TPLF occupied all of Tigre province and the EPLF held all of western Eritrea. Together with the perilous state of the economy and the famine crisis, these gains brought on an unsuccessful coup attempt by fourteen senior military officers including five major generals.[12] The Shengo now voted unanimously to start peace talks with the EPLF in London and the TPLF in Rome, something the somewhat apprehensive

Soviet Union had been pressing Mengistu to do for some time.

Heavy fighting meanwhile continued in both provinces. In early 1990, EPLF forces seized the vital port of Massawa and had encircled the Second Army of about one hundred thousand men holding the Eritrean capital Asmara.[13] Mengistu earlier had been forced to pull his best units out of Eritrea to counter the TPLF's advance on Addis Ababa, a combined effort with several smaller guerrilla groups fighting under an umbrella organization, the Eritrean People's Democratic Revolutionary Front (EPDRF). In a radio broadcast in March, Mengistu admitted the failure of his socialist regime and announced a number of liberal reforms of more capitalist than socialist thrust. His old socialist party was now renamed the Ethiopian Democratic Unity Party (led by Secretary-General Mengistu and an eleven-man Politburo), in which opposition groups were welcome to participate.[14] The guerrilla groups scorned his proposals, rightly identifying them as a play for time. Nor did Mengistu's chief patron, the Soviet Union, seem impressed, suggesting coldly that he lay " . . . particular emphasis on promoting talks on peace and national reconciliation."[15] Apparently unimpressed with this paternal advice, Mengistu in June refused a cease-fire offer by the EPDRF in return for the establishment of a broad-based transitional government. He next called for general mobilization in order to win the war.[16]

Peace talks between the government and EPLF in Washington in early 1991 brought a renewed offer of autonomy for Eritrea similar to the one sabotaged by Haile Selassie in 1960—an offer countered by the EPLF with a demand for a referendum on Eritrean independence.[17] While EPLF guerrillas continued to fight in the northwest, OLF units were fighting west of Addis Ababa and EPDRF forces, moving in from the northwest, were only thirty miles from the capital in late March.[18]

The end was drawing near. On April 19, in a three-hour broadcast Mengistu offered to resign " . . . if that will preserve the unity of the country," but in the same speech he attacked " . . . tribal secessionists . . . mercenaries and traitors."[19] Two days later, he presented the Shengo with a resolution to set up a " . . . peace forum with all opposition parties and unity forces" in order to form a transitional government.[20] In early May, he was making frantic peace moves, which went generally unheeded. Then on May 21, he suddenly disappeared (reportedly to be given asylum in Zimbabwe).

A week later, EPDRF guerrillas moved into Addis Ababa against almost no opposition, its leader Meles Zenawi announcing " . . . that a transitional government would be formed in consultation with other groups, pending elections"; EPLF leaders who set up a provisional government in Eritrea promised to co-operate with the EPDRF administration in Addis Ababa.[21]

In July, acting head of state Meles Zenawi called a conference of hundreds of delegates from twenty-five political parties, to whom he presented a transitional charter of government that was to remain in force until a future general election. The provisional government of Eritrea announced that a referendum on independence would be held in 1993.

In April 1993 over 99 percent of the Eritrean electorate voted for separation from Ethiopia in a UN-declared "free and fair" election, the first step toward a promised democracy for the new state.

> The [Sudanese] rebels will be crushed by the end
> of the year.
>
> Premier Mohammed Ahmed Mahgoub,
> November 1965[23]

The Republic of the Sudan was born in 1956. A former British possession, Sudan is the largest country in Africa, nearly a million square miles complete with mountain ranges, timbered hills, grassy plains, swamps, rain forests, and deserts. Home of the Mahdi, of Ombdurman and General Gordon's ill-fated stand at Khartoum, home also to the famous White Nile and Blue Nile, whose histories are so wonderfully told by Alan Moorehead, home also to 572 tribes speaking 114 languages, all of which spell intense poverty, ignorance, and misery.[24]

Under British control, the country for all practical purposes was divided into the larger Arab Moslem North of about 7.5 million people and the Negro Christian-Animist South of 2.75 million, of whom 250,000 were Christian converts. The North continued to grow, the South to lie dormant. Arabic became the official language, which closed most civil servant jobs to blacks—the Southerners were given exactly six of eight hundred positions made vacant by the British exodus in 1954.[25] Political differences abounded in the new government. One important northern party wanted an independent unified Sudan, another an alliance if not union with Egypt. The southern party wanted autonomy for the South in a federated union. Militarily, the North also dominated the South. The Sudan Defense Force was officered by northerners. The older Equatoria, or Southern Corps, was staffed by twenty-four northern officers with only nine junior southern officers, and a similar imbalance existed in the police and civil administration.[26]

The trouble started in August 1955, when a southern infantry company ordered to the North mutinied. More mutinies followed, all put down in a few weeks with some of the leaders executed and the Southern Corps disbanded, many of its soldiers slipping off into the bush with their weapons. The uneasy relationship continued after independence, southern resentment growing as northern politicians and army officers moved swiftly to autocratic rule. Such were the constant crackdowns on southern political aspirations that in 1966 their political leaders fled to Uganda, Kenya, and Ethiopia, where they established the Sudan African National Union (SANU).

Up to this point, the fugitive members of the disbanded Southern Corps had been relatively quiescent, stealing food from luckless natives while evading government forces, supplementing their meager number of rifles with " . . . bows and arrows, spears and machetes."[27] In 1968, however, these disparate groups merged into the Land Freedom Army (LFA), which soon was renamed Anya-Nya (Snake Poison).[28] Working from base camps in frontier areas, the guerrillas attacked police and army posts, gradually growing in strength as northern repression caused southern dissidents to join their ranks. By 1965, they would number perhaps five thousand but would still lack weapons.

The North meanwhile had plunged into a sort of controlled anarchy, with premiers resigning, coalition governments coming and going, riots, strikes, corruption, inflation—the usual fate of any country governed by the few for the profit of the few. In the South, SANU, never united, splintered into various groups. The gulf between North and South remained as wide as ever, the southerners demanding self-government, the northerners refusing to consider more than regional reforms. In remote southern areas, the guerrillas struck where possible, then retreated into jungle or mountain camps to leave frustrated soldiers burning villages and killing indiscriminately as famine and disease covered the land. In other areas, guerrillas controlled the countryside, imposing taxes, even setting up their own administrations. But there was neither military nor political unity. Guerrilla leaders ruled their fiefs and political leaders squabbled as parties formed and dissolved. In 1969, there were three governments in the South with one in exile. The guerrilla movement lacked any co-ordination and often deteriorated into savage tribal wars.

The semianarchic picture North and South changed in 1969 when thirty-eight-year-old Colonel Mohammed al-Numiery led a successful coup against the Khartoum government, set up a revolutionary council to govern the new Democratic Republic of Sudan, and dissolved all political parties to rule as military dictator of a socialist government suppressing all "liberation movements," including Yasser Arafat's Palestine Liberation Organization.[29]

Shortly after Numiery had taken over the government, the guerrilla movement began to achieve cohesion. That was the work of Joseph Lagu, an army lieutenant who defected to the Anya-Nya and eventually commanded the Eastern Equatoria region. In August 1971, Lagu formed the Southern Sudan Liberation Movement (SSLM), but in December a government drive by some fourteen thousand troops and six thousand police chased the guerrillas into Uganda. In March 1972, both sides agreed to a cease-fire and subsequently signed a treaty, the Addis Ababa accord, that in theory guaranteed the South's autonomy and offered generous concessions to the guerrilla insurgents, many of whom were absorbed into the regular forces.

After several years of relative quiet on the shooting front, increased friction between Moslem settlers and indigenous southerners caused Numiery (recently elected to a third six-year term by a 99.6 per cent vote)[30] to renege on the Addis Ababa agreement by dividing the South into its former three separate regions, which the Southerners interpreted as an abrogation of autonomy. Tempers were already short owing to the government's international exploitation of southern oil fields that resulted in the presence of numerous foreigners intruding into what the Southerners regarded as their own land. Khartoum's recent failure to ameliorate serious food shortages—by 1983 the Numiery government was awash in a sea of domestic and foreign relations crises—was also a bone of contention as was Numiery's mutual defense agreement with Egypt, regarded by many as prelude to political-military integration with Cairo and thus a further strengthening of Moslem power. Hostility increased in October 1983 when Numiery announced that " . . . the penal code had been revised in order to link it 'organically and spiritually' with Islamic law (sharia)."[31]

A revitalized guerrilla movement now emerged to fight what was regarded as injustices, the Sudanese People's Liberation Front (SPLF) and its militant guerrilla wing, the Sudanese People's Liberation Army (SPLA), led by John Garang. The guerrilla aim was to overthrow Numiery's government and install a "people's democratic government."[32] In early 1983, veterans of the old Anya-Nya group re-formed into Anya-Nya II (allegedly controlled by the SPLF) and began attacking police and army posts, operations subsequently expanded to sabotage of railroads and bridges and kidnapings of foreign oil company employees.[33] In December, the army reported that in breaking a guerrilla siege of a town it had killed 480 guerrillas.

Real trouble had begun in February 1983, as it had in 1955, with a mutiny by a southern army unit which refused to be transferred to the North. Fighting soon flared between southern and northern army units. In May, a southern battalion mutinied and in the ensuing battle seventy-eight soldiers were reportedly killed.[34] Sporadic fighting continued as guerrilla strength grew. In spring of 1984, Numiery declared a state of emergency and moved additional troops to the South to fight a new civil war.

It was more a tragic war than an interesting one, at least from the guerrilla standpoint. It was expensive, costing an estimated $1 million a day (30 per cent of the budget) when the country faced a $12 billion external debt.[35] It was a war interrupted by turbulent political change and meaningless cease-fires. In 1985, a military coup deposed Numiery to put government in the hands of a Transitional Military Council. Colonel John Garang's SPLA declared a brief cease-fire, which led to nothing. Elections in 1986 resulted in a coalition government headed by Prime Minister Sadeq el-Mahdi, but peace talks with Garang soon broke down and the war continued, a war of protest but also a war of bloodthirsty tribal feuds fought against a background of almost unimaginable human suffering occasioned by widespread famine and the subhuman behavior of both guerrilla and government forces. As in Ethiopia, both sides used food as a weapon, often holding up and even seizing urgently needed food supplies in order to score politically with one or another tribe.

Garang's SPLA, armed now with surface-to-air missiles, scored a series of notable victories in 1987 to leave government forces in shaky control of southern provincial capitals and little else. Further government reverses in 1988 produced a crisis in Khartoum, political intervention by the United States, and a demand from Sudanese army leaders that the government make peace.[36] As sieges and countersieges of towns and cities continued and as rapacious soldiers and guerrillas ravaged the countryside, the flow of refugees, many of whom were near starvation, jammed camps within and without the country. Conditions in North and South worsened; repression increased. By 1990, according to Africa Watch, Sudan was "a human rights disaster"—civil war and famine had taken more than five hundred thousand lives " . . . while thousands of women and children in the south had been sold into slavery."[37]

There seemed to be no end to this Dantesque nightmare. In June 1989, the government was deposed by a coup and replaced by Lieutenant General Hassan al-Bashir's fundamentalist Islamic military dictatorship. Not surprisingly, peace talks between government and southern leaders broke down at year's end—as the specter of another far more violent famine hovered over the land.

Disaster struck in early 1990 when an estimated eight million Sudanese (roughly one third of the population) were facing starvation. Far from co-operating with relief efforts, the Bashir government downplayed the severity of the famine while continuing to consolidate its power by torturing and executing hundreds and probably thousands of political, military, and religious opponents, real or imagined. In the midst of this chaos, Bashir definitively tipped his political hand by supporting Iraq in the Gulf War and by establishing a National Islamic Front that called for a *jihad* or holy war against the West.

Trouble meanwhile had broken out in John Garang's guerrilla army, whose leaders had split over whether the revolutionary goal was that of "a united, secular Sudan" (Garang's belief) or that of "an independent black state" (the dissident Nasir group's belief).[38] The schism and subsequent severe fighting between the two factions caused postponement of further peace talks. It also allowed government forces to open a large offensive in February 1992 that succeeded in overrunning a number of towns formerly held by the SPLA.

Peace talks that finally began in late May did not halt the fighting. By October, government forces had regained control of a dozen towns, while Garang's increasingly hard-pressed guerrillas were tied up in besieging the provincial capital of Juba.[39] Elsewhere in the South, Bashir's troops were continuing a campaign of civil murders that some observers compared with the Serbian "ethnic cleansing" of Bosnia-Herzegovina. The pogrom worsened during the winter to the extent that Pope John Paul II publicly scolded the Sudanese leader, Lieutenant General Omar Hassan al-Bashir, " . . . who called allegations of human-rights abuses 'grotesque fabrication,' " this at a time when according to a United Nations' estimate, " . . . 800,000 Sudanese faced imminent starvation,"[40] in part owing to brutal factional fighting in the South.

This unhappy situation continued into spring of 1993, the fate of Sudan's nearly eight million non-Moslem peoples growing more hopeless as Bashir and the Islamic National Front continued to try to convert the country to a strict fundamentalist Moslem state. This activity was supported by Iran, which has helped Bashir turn his country into the world's major terrorist-training center as well as into an international pariah. Bashir's government is not only at odds with its neighbors, dangerously so in the case of Egypt, but also with the U.S. government, which in August 1993 placed Sudan on its list of terrorist nations (Iran, Iraq, Syria, Libya, Cuba, and North Korea), for both supporting and at times harboring Abu Nidal's guerrilla terrorist organization, the Lebanese Hezbollah, and the Palestinian Islamic Hamas group.[41]

Fighting in the South meanwhile intensified to the extent that the United Nations has had increasingly to suspend its relief operations.[42] There is no sign of a letup in this guerrilla war. In June peace talks between Garang's SPLA and the government came to nothing. With the advent of the dry season in September, government forces opened a new offensive against SPLA guerrilla units. That, taken with increasing food shortages, can mean only more massive starvation in the months ahead.

CHAPTER EIGHTY-NINE

1. International Institute for Strategic Studies, *Strategic Survey 1977*, 24.
2. Makinda, 13.
3. International Institute for Strategic Studies, *Strategic Survey 1974*, 87.
4. Ibid. *1977*, 22.
5. Ibid., 20.
6. Ibid., *1978*, 94.
7. Ibid., 97.
8. Ibid., *1979*, 97.
9. Ibid.
10. Ibid., *1984–85*, 100.
11. Ibid., *1987–88*, 188.
12. *Keesing's Record of World Events*, Vol. 36, 1990. January 1990, 37,173.
13. Ibid., February 1990, 37,239. See also, International Institute for Strategic Studies, *Strategic Survey 1990–91*, 230.
14. *Keesing's Record of World Events*, Vol. 36, 1990. March 1990, 37,310.
15. Ibid., April 1990, 37,368.
16. Ibid., Vol. 37, Supplement February 1991, 38,053.
17. Ibid., 37,996.
18. Ibid., March 1991, 38,089.
19. Ibid., 38,137.
20. Ibid.
21. Ibid., News Digest for May 1991, 38,174.
22. Ibid., July 1991, 38,322.
23. O'Ballance, *The Soviet War in the Sudan: 1955–1972*, 79.
24. Ibid., 18.
25. Ibid., 37.
26. Ibid., 40.
27. Ibid., 57–8.
28. Ibid., 59.
29. Ibid., 105.
30. *Keesing's Contemporary Archives*, Vol. 39, 1983. July 1983, 32,292.
31. Ibid., Vol. 30, 1984. July 1984, 33,009. See also, International Institute for Strategic Studies, *Strategic Survey 1985–86*, 182–3.
32. *Keesing's Contemporary Archives*, Vol. 30, 1984. July 1984, 33,010.
33. Ibid.
34. Ibid., Vol. 29, 1983. July 1983, 32,293.
35. International Institute for Strategic Studies, *Strategic Survey 1986–87*, 183–4.
36. Ibid., *1988–89*, 184–5.
37. *Keesing's Record of World Events*, Vol. 36, 1990. April 1990, 37,367.
38. Ibid., Vol. 37, 1991. September 1991, 38,426.
39. *Newsweek*, October 5, 1992.
40. *Newsweek*, February 22, 1993.
41. *International Herald Tribune*, August 20, 1993. See also, *The Independent* (U.K.), August 19, 1993.
42. *Newsweek*, July 19, 1993.

CHAPTER 90

The Western (Spanish) Sahara partitioned between Mauritania and Morocco • Decision contested by the Popular Front for the Liberation of the Sequiet el-Hamra and Rio de Oro (Polisario) guerrillas • Algerian-Libyan backed Polisarios force Mauritania from the war • Polisario's continued successes • Reagan government backs Morocco • The "Hassan Wall" • Polisario's setbacks • The United Nations proposed referendum • Morocco agrees but refuses scheduled elections • The Western Sahara in limbo

AT FIRST GLANCE, the future of the Spanish Sahara, subsequently known as the Western Sahara, did not seem of much importance—something over 102,000 square miles of desert detritus providing a forlorn existence for some sixty thousand Saharan Arabs, a few thousand foreign settlers, and as many Spanish legionnaires. Bowing to a United Nations resolution passed in 1973, Spain agreed to yield its control until a future plebiscite decided whether the area should become independent or be ruled by Spain or Morocco. Not trusting a vote, King Hassan II of Morocco pre-empted matters by sending 350,000 of his people into the area in 1975—the famous "Green March" that briefly claimed world headlines. This dramatic gesture was intended to bolster the king's popularity at home, insure the security of his southern flank, and, not least, give him possession of the rich Bu Craa phosphate mines, which, taken with his own extensive phosphate holdings, would give him a near world monopoly.[1]

Spanish forces peremptorily stopped the Moroccan march a few miles inside the country, but a subsequent private agreement with Spain gave Morocco control of the larger northern sector that included Bu Craa, and Mauritania control of the southern portion. This agreement pleased neither the local Saharans nor Morocco's immediate neighbor, Algeria, which wanted an independent Western Sahara that eventually

THE MAGHREB

LEGEND
Road
Railroad
Original wall
Final wall

0   100 miles

would fall into Algeria's sphere of influence. Toward this end, the Algerian government had backed a guerrilla movement, the Popular Front for the Liberation of the Sequiet el-Hamra and Rio de Oro (Polisario), which in 1973 began attacking Spanish desert garrisons. In 1976, an emboldened Polisario headquarters in Algeria claimed the Western Sahara as the Sahara Arab Democratic Republic (SADR).

This was no ragtag guerrilla army. One authority wrote that it consisted " . . . of about 10,000 guerrillas armed with recoilless rifles, Soviet-made heavy mortars, and SAM-7 missiles mounted on Land Rovers . . . highly mobile, well organized and well trained troops with a close knowledge of the terrain."[2]

The ensuing war was a disaster for Mauritania. Polisario guerrillas almost at once struck its long and vulnerable railroad that carried vital iron ore exports to the sea. In a futile effort to protect the line, the small Mauritanian army expanded tenfold and was soon devouring 65 per cent of the national budget.[3] A beaten and financially stricken Mauritania left the war in 1979—and left the Western Sahara to Morocco.

Owing to Libyan Colonel Qaddafi's largesse buttressed by Syria and Iraq, Polisario guerrillas received so many arms and so much equipment, including armored vehicles and even tanks, that they began tilting toward conventional tactics. In 1979, Polisario smelled victory. Thirty-five states, mostly African, had recognized the SADR, the Office of African Unity in Addis Ababa supported it, and the United Nations General Assembly passed a resolution in its favor. By 1981, Moroccan forces were increasingly on the defensive, but in that year the new Reagan administration in the United States provided the first shipments to King Hassan of $400 million worth of arms including combat aircraft and helicopters. In 1982, a military stalemate had developed, a typical insurgency situation with regular forces holding about 10 per cent of the territory including cities and towns, the insurgent forces the rest. But also in 1982, the Moroccan army had stumbled on what proved to be the winning formula.

Earlier in this book, we commented on the general uselessness of walled barriers as a valid counterinsurgency weapon, for example the Morice Line used by the French in Algeria (see Chapter 55) or the multimillion-dollar fiasco built by the Americans in Vietnam (see Chapter 66). Conditions were uniquely different in the Western Sahara, however. Here there were fixed flanks, one being the Moroccan border guarded by static defenses, the other the sea. In 1982, with ample sand, rocks, and labor on hand, Moroccan army engineers built a four-hundred-mile-long wall to protect the northwestern part of the area that included the Bu Craa phosphate mines. The ten- to twelve-foot-high wall, holding sensors and radars that detected enemy presence several miles away, was defended by units from the eighty-thousand-man Moroccan army now based in Western Sahara.

The results were dramatic in the best tradition of Marshal Lyautey's *tache d'huile* concept (see Chapter 13). Not only did the Polisario fail to breach the line but the land behind the line became alive. The Bu Craa mine reopened, investment poured in, general prosperity followed.[4] Following *tache d'huile* tactics, a second line followed in late 1983 to enlarge the protected area. Moroccan fortunes rose even further in 1983 when King Hassan startled the diplomatic world by opening a dialogue with Colonel Qaddafi. A resultant agreement called for Qaddafi to halt arms shipments to the Polisarios if Hassan gave him a free hand for his foray into Chad in support of Goukouni Queddeï's Forces Armées Populaires, which was again challenging Hessène Habré's shaky regime.

Diplomacy was all very well but the secret of Hassan's success was the expanding fortified lines—a third one in spring of 1984, a fourth in October, a fifth in 1985. The net external result of what became known as the "Hassan Wall" was to slowly push the guerrillas back into Algeria despite their frantic attempts to blast through using mortars, rockets, and even tanks. The net internal result was $2 billion worth of foreign investments in the protected area.[5]

Hassan's position had improved so much in 1986 that he abrogated the treaty with Qaddafi (who that spring had been temporarily *hors de combat* as a result of a major U.S. air strike) and " . . . stated his willingness to abide by a unilateral ceasefire and accept a UN-sponsored plebiscite."[6] Despite repeated Polisario attacks, Moroccan army control of Western Sahara continued to expand. In 1988, Hassan restored diplomatic relations with Algeria, itself in a state of severe economic decline, and in June joined the four other Maghreb leaders in their first meeting for a quarter of a century (the prelude to the founding of the Arab Maghreb Union in 1989). Along with SADR leaders, he also agreed to a United Nations plan which called for " . . . a vote by residents of the former Spanish colony either to set up an independent state or to become part of Morocco."[7] In early 1989, King Hassan received Polisario leaders for "discussions" of the peace plan.

Following a year of on-again-off-again fighting, Polisario offered a unilateral cease-fire provided that Morocco agreed to an early referendum. That did not begin to materialize until spring of 1991, when United Nations officials came up with a plan: once a large number of Western Sahara refugees had been repatriated (estimated cost $34 million), Morocco would withdraw two thirds of its armed forces; a carefully supervised registration of voters, based on a 1974 Spanish census, would follow and voting would take place in January 1992.[8]

What happened next to this $200 million project?

A great deal. The 1974 Spanish census listed seventy-four thousand eligible Saharans but the Polisario claimed that the figure had risen to two hundred thousand. Hassan for his part sent in tens of thousands of troops and settlers who he claimed were eligible voters.[9] Despite the confusion, UN officials were about to get preparations under way in early August 1991 when Moroccan forces broke a relatively peaceful two-year lull by aerial bombing and strafing of a Polisario base.[10] Hassan defended the action on grounds that Polisario guerrillas were infiltrating Western Sahara in order to sabotage the elections. Moroccan soldiers simultaneously began "cleaning-up operations" in the area between the protective wall and the border. Then, in late August, King Hassan, having apparently concluded that Morocco would not win the plebiscite, disputed the UN's approved list of seventy-four thousand "eligible" voters while rejecting 120,000 names deemed eligible by Morocco.[11]

Further clashes aside, a formal UN cease-fire came into effect in September as UN preparations for the election continued. More trouble followed, including a threat by Moroccan forces to fire on UN monitors. January 1992 came and went as Hassan pulled one delaying tactic after another.

Direct talks between Morocco and the Polisario guerrillas in July 1993 proved humiliating to the latter when Moroccan delegates refused even to discuss the referendum.[12]

As of this writing, December 1993, and after the expenditure of millions of dollars, the UN-engineered referendum has still not taken place—the fault in large part of Morocco's obdurate King Hassan, in part of members of the UN Security Council for letting him get away with it.

CHAPTER NINETY

1. International Institute for Strategic Studies, *Strategic Survey 1975*, 45–6.
2. Ibid., *1979*, 95.
3. Ibid., 93.
4. Ibid., *1983–84*, 108.
5. Ibid., *1988–89*, 193.
6. Ibid., *1986–87*, 184.
7. *New York Times*, December 28, 1988.
8. *Keesing's Record of World Events*, Vol. 37, 1991. April 1991, 38,169.
9. *New York Times*, December 28, 1988.
10. *Daily Telegraph* (U.K.), August 8, 1991.
11. *Keesing's Record of World Events*, Vol. 37, 1991. August 1991, 38,410.
12. *The Independent* (U.K.), July 23, 1993.

CHAPTER 91

Portuguese colonial rule in Africa • Origin of the African National Council • Colonial rule challenged in the 1950s • The Angolan black uprising • Guerrilla shortcomings • Rise of Jonas Savimbi's National Union for Complete Independence of Angola (UNITA) • The Liberation Front of Mozambique (FRELIMO) • Hard-pressed Portugal grants independence to its colonies • War between Agostinho Neto's Popular Movement for the Liberation of Angola (MPLA), Helden Roberto's Popular Union of Angola (UPA—later FNLA), and Savimbi's UNITA • The Soviet-Cuban presence in Angola • Rise of black nationalism in South West Africa (renamed Namibia in 1968) • Sam Nujoma's South West African People's Organization (SWAPO) opens guerrilla campaign • Civil war in Angola • Pretoria and Washington's military and financial aid to UNITA • Namibia wins independence • Angolan peace agreement signed in 1991 • Savimbi loses 1992 elections and renews the war • Mozambique's war against Rhodesia and the Republic of South Africa • Rhodesia becomes Marxist Zimbabwe • Mozambique's political changes • Effects of widespread famine

OF A GREAT many execrable colonial governments, those of the Portuguese in Africa must stand near the top of the list. Beginning in 1505, the Portuguese presence was purely exploitive in the worst sense. Two and a half centuries of social crimes were compounded in the 1950s by a claim that Angola and Mozambique were " . . . overseas provinces . . . an integral part of the Portuguese state."[1]

These provinces-to-be were peopled largely by African natives, the *indigenes,* ruled by the *non-indigines,* a polyglot mixture of *mestizos* or half-castes, *assimilados* or "civilized" Africans, and preponderantly by Portuguese nationals. The widely separated colonies had one thing in

The map includes labels: CABINDA, ZAIRE, Dar es Salaam, Luanda, TANZANIA, ANGOLA, Lobito, Benguela, ZAMBIA (N. RHODESIA), Lusaka, MALAWI, CALUEQUE DAM, Harare, ZIMBABWE (S. RHODESIA), Beira, MOZAMBIQUE, Windhoek, NAMIBIA (S. W. AFRICA), BOTSWANA, Gaborone, Pretoria, Johannesburg, Maputo (Lourenço Marques), SWAZILAND, Durban, SOUTH AFRICA, LESOTHO, Cape Town, Port Elizabeth, Atlantic Ocean, Indian Ocean, THE PORTUGUESE LEGACY

LEGEND
········· Road
++++ Railroad
----- Oil line

0   500 miles

common: the miserable state of their African native populations owing to penurious white governments unwilling to support even basic social services. Such was the lack of schools, for example, that by 1961 barely 1 per cent of the natives had reached "civilized"-African status.[2]

Colonal rule in Africa had for long been challenged by spasmodic, usually disorganized, black uprisings put down sooner or later by government forces, often with immense losses of native lives. The first major political challenge to white rule came in 1912 with the emergence of the African National Congress (ANC) " . . . aimed at eliminating all color bars and obtaining black representation in [the South African] parliament."[3] Spreading the political gospel by protest marches and strikes, the party managed to survive and indeed to spawn other opposition groups before World War II. Its flowering came after the war when South Africa's dominant National Party pledged itself to apartheid and white supremacy. In 1952, ANC membership counted one hundred thousand and was rapidly growing. Simultaneously, colonial rule elsewhere was challenged by the emergence of nationalist, usually tribal-based leftist parties, in the case of Angola and Mozambique Eduardo Mondlane's Liberation Front of Mozambique (FRELIMO), Helden Roberto's Popular Union of Angola (UPA) and Agostinho Neto's Popular Movement for the Liberation of Angola (MPLA).

Real trouble started in Angola in 1961 when an estimated six thousand UPA guerrillas from northeastern Angola massacred several hundred whites and several thousand *mestizos* and *assimilados*, a revolt supported by the Soviet Union and carried into the next year (when the UPA became the Liberation Front of Angola or FNLA). In 1963, the FNLA's rival, the MPLA, joined the action.

The rebels had several advantages. They were recognized politically by the Organization of African Unity and a number of members of the United Nations General Assembly were sympathetic to their cause. Neighboring countries, themselves in throes of self-determination, provided convenient sanctuary for the FRELIMO and the MPLA in Zambia and Tazmania, the FNLA in Zaire. The Soviet Union, China, Cuba, North Korea, and eventually the United States offered economic and military support, a decidedly mixed blessing that began the insidious process of removing revolt from a local and regional to a superpower plane with concomitant damage to social infrastructures—we are still paying the price today.

The rebels also suffered disadvantages. As with guerrilla groups in Ethiopia, Sudan, and some Latin American states, the African guerrillas lacked a valid aim other than to throw out the foreigners and gain a self-ruled independence with which they were in no way prepared to cope. They also lacked weapons—in the early stages, there were more machetes and spears than rifles—and they faced a determined foe: a few thousand Portuguese troops in 1961 grew to 130,000 (including blacks) in 1964 armed with modern weapons and supported by tanks, artillery, aircraft, and helicopters. Nor did the guerrilla groups claim undivided tribal loyalties. Recruitment of blacks into the army rose significantly with the abolition of the hated indigenes–non-indigines classification system.[4]

In relatively short order, counterinsurgency programs were resettling tribes in protected villages and providing long-overdue social services. Security forces in Angola had regained control of most of the northeast by late 1961, the guerrillas having suffered heavy casualties while being pressed back into Zaire. Neither did MPLA operations particularly prosper, its estimated five to seven thousand guerrillas being forced to utilize Zambian bases with operations confined largely to eastern border districts. The guerrillas nonetheless survived and in 1966 were joined by Jonas Savimbi's recently founded National Union for Complete Independence of Angola (UNITA), a splinter group from the FNLA of which Savimbi had been secretary-general. UNITA's few hundred guerrillas operated in central and eastern Angola where in time they would establish a viable political base among the large Ovimbunda tribes which accounted for 40 per cent of the total population.[5]

FRELIMO guerrillas in Mozambique, who had opened fire in 1964, also experienced mixed fortunes owing to the immensity of the country (some 308,000 square miles, home to nineteen major tribes, hundreds of subtribes, and seventeen languages plus dialects) and to several pro-Portuguese tribes including the Macuas, which made up about 40 per cent of the population. The guerrillas operated mainly in the north, usually conducting hit-and-run raids against military and police posts while trying to win over the diverse tribes. In 1969, FRELIMO leader Eduardo Mondlane was assassinated and was replaced by a diehard Marxist, Samora Machel. Aided by arms from Russia and China, Machel branched out and by late 1973 was fighting in the south and east.[6]

His was an uphill battle. The Portuguese command had removed the most exposed tribes into defended villages and in 1972 opened a massive civil program that included construction of schools, medical clinics, roads, and railroads. Captured guerrillas were given the choice of joining the government's forces or returning to their guerrilla unit, and a reported 90 per cent chose government. But it was all too little and too late. The war had become almost prohibitively expensive to Portugal. By 1974, the military forces had suffered an estimated eleven thousand dead and thirty thousand wounded.[7] More and more veterans lacking arms, legs, eyes, and minds filled Portugal's streets. The country's defense budget had risen as its international standing dropped. In 1974, a coup by disaffected left-wing army officers ousted the government and attempted to find a political solution to the insurgencies. Following six months of political turmoil, a replacement government finally decided to leave the war. Mozambique was given its independence under FRELIMO rule in 1975. Angola gained independence in late 1975 but only after a vicious civil war fought more on conventional than guerrilla lines, on the one side Agostinho Neto's MPLA, backed by Soviet Russia and supported by three thousand recently arrived Cuban ground troops and probably by guerrillas from the Southwest People's Organization (SWAPO) of Namibia; on the other side Helden Roberto's FMLA and Jonas Savimbi's UNITA, supported by South African ground troops. The war ended (briefly) with Neto's victory in 1976. Under communist MPLA rule the country became the People's Republic of Angola.

Aided by fifteen thousand Cuban troops and large shipments of arms from the Soviet Union, the indirect result of South African troops intervening in Angola in October 1975, Agostinho Neto moved rapidly to consolidate his victory. Large-scale military operations in 1976 forced FNLA and UNITA guerrillas to leave their strongholds and take to the bush to fight guerrilla warfare. South African troops, which had moved into Angola initially to protect a large hydroelectric project earlier undertaken with Portugal, and which in subsequent fighting had penetrated up to two hundred miles inside Angola, were withdrawn to South Africa's neighboring colony of South West Africa (Namibia) early in 1976. In February, the Organization of African Unity recognized Neto's government and general international recognition followed.

Neto's problems were scarcely over. Jonas Savimbi, the forty-one-year-old leader of UNITA, now claimed to command anywhere from two to ten thousand guerrillas who were fighting in central and south eastern Angola. Among other accomplishments, this effort prevented the government from opening the all-important Benguela railroad that runs over twelve hundred miles from the port of Lobito to Zambia and Zaire. In late 1976, Savimbi claimed to control four provinces and to have killed fifteen hundred Cubans and more than two thousand MPLA troops.[8] A new guerrilla group based in Zaire, the Front for the Liberation of the Enclave of Cabinda (FLEC), announced that it had killed three hundred Cuban soldiers who were protecting the oil fields (from which Angola derived 90 per cent of its income).[9] So effective was this guerrilla resistance that Fidel Castro, instead of beginning to withdraw his soldiers as he had stated, committed more troops—by summer twenty thousand Cuban troops were in the country.[10]

The situation could only escalate. From Neto's standpoint, the key factor was the strong military support from Russia and the presence of Cuban troops. The key factor from the opposition's standpoint was South Africa's determination to topple the communist MPLA regime in Luanda in order to prevent the Soviet-Cuban virus from spilling over the twelve-hundred-mile-long border into Namibia, and by projection into South Africa itself. Missing from the equation was U.S. support for the insurgents. After a brief period of U.S. aid and despite fervent pleas by President Ford and Secretary of State Kissinger, the latter wanting to send U.S. troops to Angola, Congress voted overwhelmingly in 1976 " . . . to refuse funds for arms in support of the 'pro-Western' liberation movements in Angola."[11]

South West Africa (renamed Namibia in 1968) had been a problem area for some time. Two thirds the size of the Republic of South Africa, its 318,000 square miles held an estimated 1.3 million people, mostly unenfranchised tribal blacks.[12] It had fallen under Germany's control in 1884, an unhappy experience demonstrated by a major native rebellion which, lasting into 1908, was broken by the army at an estimated cost of fifty-four thousand native lives. Thenceforth the country was administered in typical colonial fashion, its peoples exploited to Pretoria's profit while remaining impoverished and uneducated. In 1920, the League of Nations mandated the area to South Africa but in 1946 the

United Nations rejected Pretoria's claim to incorporate it into the Union of South Africa. The spreading wave of nationalism soon engulfed the unenfranchised blacks. Thanks largely to the African National Congress, the first black resistance organization in South West Africa was formed in 1958 and in 1960 became the South West African People's Organization (SWAPO), aimed at achieving independence from South Africa. Led by Sam Nujoma, this was a rural group of several hundred guerrillas, some of whom had been trained in Eastern-bloc countries.[13] In 1964, the UN ended South Africa's mandate. Two years later, the Pretoria government refused an order from the UN to withdraw from the country. Meanwhile, SWAPO guerrillas, having achieved little by relatively peaceful means, converted to the Marxist armed struggle. A guerrilla insurgency rapidly developed. In its formative stages, SWAPO's military wing, the People's Liberation Army of Namibia (PLAN), established bases in Zambia and Angola from where they infiltrated into Namibia to attack outposts of the South African Defense Force (SADF) along with police stations, from which they derived arms and ammunition.

When civil war broke out in Angola in 1975, South Africa allied itself with Jonas Savimbi's UNITA guerrilla group, which at that time was receiving U.S. military aid. SADF units from Namibia and from a large garrison that was guarding a hydroelectric project about twenty miles north of the border now began raids, some in conjunction with UNITA guerrillas, that penetrated as far as two hundred miles inside Angola, the pretext being "hot pursuit" of SWAPO guerrillas, whose forays into Namibia had become frequent and increasingly difficult to counter.

The civil war in Angola soon reached stalemate: the FNLA in general control of the north, the MPLA in control of the north-central, and UNITA generally dominant in the central-southeast. Buttressed by Cuban troops, MPLA forces contested FNLA and UNITA by frequent search-and-destroy missions that led to heavy but scarcely decisive fighting during 1976–83. By 1981, a reported ninety-five thousand South African troops (including Namibian levies) were in Namibia, units were frequently fighting in Angola, and South African planes were actively supporting Savimbi's guerrillas and bombing suspected SWAPO camps.

South African control of Namibia, however, was being increasingly challenged by African and Western nations, to the extent that in 1978 the UN General Assembly passed Resolution 435, which called for an independent Namibia, something Pretoria refused to consider so long as Cuban troops remained in Angola.

Up to 1982, peace talks had come to nothing. But with Angolan government forces generally on the defensive, the economy shattered, and with South Africa's heavy expenditure of men and money and increasing political isolation, both sides had good reason to reach a peaceful settlement. Hopes for this rose in 1984 when U.S. mediators persuaded the two governments to agree to a cease-fire to be followed by South Africa withdrawing its troops. Initial enthusiasm soon waned as accusations of cheating thundered back and forth. Nor did the cease-fire cover UNITA, whose guerrillas continued to harass MPLA troops while SWAPO guerrillas continued to fight their war against South Africa. In protest Pretoria slowed, then stopped the withdrawal of its troops, which were still twenty-five miles inside Angola in early 1985 and did not finally leave the country until April. Subsequent government offensives against Savimbi's stronghold in southeastern Angola brought renewed support from the SADF, which also continued "hot pursuit" of SWAPO guerrillas inside Angola.[14]

The war escalated in 1986 in part owing to the U. S. Congress lifting the ban on supplying arms to one side or the other in southern Africa's numerous conflicts. The Reagan administration had long wanted to topple the Luanda government, which after Agostinho Neto's death was headed by José Eduardo dos Santos, and now began reinforcing Savimbi's UNITA with $30 million worth of ground-to-air and anti-tank weapons, thus allying itself with South Africa to the discomfiture of many Congressional and other liberals. As the U. S. State Department had warned Reagan, this returned the war to superpower level. Soviet Russia responded by sending more fighter-bomber planes, tanks, armored personnel carriers, helicopters, advanced radar equipment, ground-to-air missile batteries and additional Cuban troops—a total fifty thousand in 1988. Despite this largesse, government offensives met no better success than formerly thanks in part to continuing U.S. military aid to UNITA of about $15 million a year and to SADF operations including air strikes and heavy artillery support of UNITA guerrillas.[15]

The costly stalemate might have continued but for the rise of Mikhail Gorbachev. Not only was the war in Angola costing the Soviet Union over $1 billion a year, it was seriously impeding his diplomatic initiatives in the West. As in 1985, both Luanda and Pretoria also had good reason to end the war. It had shattered Angola's economy and had made the government's survival almost totally dependent on the Soviet Union and the presence of Cuban troops. It was costing Pretoria millions a year in direct expenses, $80 million a year in subsidies to UNITA, millions more in grants to Namibia and, perhaps worse, was instrumental in keeping South Africa an international pariah.

In our day, and perhaps earlier, it almost seems that political settlement of an insurgency depends on mutual exhaustion of opposing sides. After months of U.S.-sponsored negotiations, Angola, Cuba, and South Africa agreed on a cease-fire in August 1988. Later in the year, the three countries called for Cuban troops to leave Angola and for South African troops to withdraw from Angola and Namibia; a cease-fire between the SADF and SWAPO was to begin in spring of 1989 to be followed by elections for a constituent assembly, the first step toward promised independence, in November. Meanwhile SADF forces would be restricted to barracks and SWAPO forces to their Angolan camps, this arrangement to be enforced by a UN contingent of seventy-five hundred troops.[16]

Owing to UN delay in deploying its peacekeeping force (reduced to forty-five hundred to save money),[17] the agreement came into force two months late and then only after considerable bloodshed.[18] After further serious clashes cooled by UN mediation, SWAPO leader Sam Nujoma returned to his homeland amidst much fanfare in September. In November, 670,000 Namibians—90 per cent of those eligible to vote[19]—elected a constituent assembly, 41 of its 72 seats going to SWAPO. Since SWAPO needed a two-thirds majority to implement its own constitution, Nujoma had to write one acceptable to all parties. That was done and in March 1990, Nujoma was sworn in as independent Namibia's first president.

Matters did not similarly prosper in Angola, in part because of the Bush administration's decision to continue supplying Jonas Savimbi's UNITA with arms while refusing to recognize José Eduardo dos Santos' MPLA until Dos Santos agreed to enter into direct talks with Savimbi. Supported by Washington, Savimbi in early 1989 refused Dos Santos' offer of a general amnesty. In June, both sides finally agreed to a cease-fire but fighting soon broke out, and in September Savimbi backed off from signing the agreement. Owing in part to further supplies of arms by the Soviets to MPLA and by the U.S. to UNITA, the fight-talk-fight syndrome ran its costly course during 1990 and into spring of 1991 when both sides signed a peace agreement brokered by the U.S., Portugal, and Russia. The accord called for MPLA and UNITA forces to meld into a single national army while the parties prepared for UN-monitored multiparty general elections.

The national army was never formed. Elections were held in September 1992 following more than two years of frantic political maneuvering during which UNITA forces, an estimated thirty-five thousand regular and auxiliary guerrilla fighters, remained intact in southeastern Angola. Although Jonas Savimbi seemed confident of victory, he suffered from a poor press that resulted from his own autocratic manner, and from well-founded charges that he had murdered opponents within the UNITA leadership and had condoned if not encouraged barbaric UNITA excesses that accounted for thousands of civilian deaths. Perhaps his greatest weakness was his failure to organize a strong political base. José Eduardo dos Santos by contrast enjoyed good press relations despite the known corruption of his government. Aware of Russia's decline and his own precarious economy, he adroitly abandoned his Communist stance and began moving toward the capitalist West, even changing the country's name to the comfortable-sounding Republic of Angola. An election in which 90 per cent of nearly five million voters participated and which was deemed fair by some eight hundred UN observers gave Dos Santos 49.6 per cent of the vote to about 40 per cent for Savimbi. Because Dos Santos did not receive over 50 per cent of the vote, a runoff was necessary. Savimbi, however, shouted fraud and reopened the shooting war only a few weeks after the election. Although both sides agreed to new talks, this came to nothing and the violent civil war continued into 1993 with Savimbi and the UNITA guerrillas getting the worst of it, although finally recapturing their traditional stronghold of Huambo in the central highlands (after two months of fighting that cost an estimated ten thousand dead).[20]

A new round of UN-sponsored talks between the MPLA and UNITA in April failed when the Dos Santos government accepted and Savimbi refused to accept a UN-brokered peace plan. Savimbi faced further isolation when President Clinton reversed traditional U.S. policy by recognizing the Dos Santos government in Luanda.

Fighting once again escalated. In July the United Nations reported that "more than one thousand people are dying every day from war and its consequent starvation";[21] "that 100,000 people have been killed in fighting since October [1992 when Savimbi refused to accept election results] and two million more are in danger of starvation."[22] A cease-fire offer from Savimbi in August went largely unheeded, not surprisingly, since his troops had hurled some three thousand shells into the besieged city of Kinto in the two previous days.[23] That the almost constant fighting was telling on UNITA forces was suggested by a still stronger offer from Savimbi in September, prompted, according to observers, by a desire to prevent a UN-embargo on supplies, especially oil, to the rebel organization.

It is possible that Savimbi will be forced back to the negotiating table. The Luanda government has gained some important allies. U.S. spy satellites are feeding intelligence to the MPLA army;[24] Britain has lifted its arms embargo on Luanda;[25] South Africa is reportedly permitting a private force of five hundred veteran guerrilla fighters to bolster MPLA forces.[26]

In November the Angolan government stated that two thousand people a day were being killed in what nearly all experts consider to be a stalemate war.[27] As of this writing, December 1993, the war continues—to the cost of millions of long-suffering blacks who must deserve something better.

*   *   *

As Portugal's hasty withdrawal from Angola plunged southwest Africa into prolonged war, its departure from Mozambique brought profound conflicts with the Republic of South Africa and Rhodesia, not unnaturally since President Samora Machel declared Mozambique to be a Leninist-Marxist state dedicated to improving the livelihood of the masses. Machel certainly had his hands full. Almost the size of Namibia, this oddly elongated, potentially rich country supported about 13.5 million people, mostly Bantu-speaking blacks practicing Islamic, Christian, and animist religions. Portuguese colonists had not been kind to the country. Few schools or hospitals existed; illiteracy and illness were widespread; life expectancy was forty-five years. The country was virtually bankrupt, food was short in many towns, and famine was looming in the central and northern regions. The guerrilla war had damaged an already inadequate infrastructure. Roads and railroads needed extensive repairs, port facilities at the capital Lourenço Marques (soon to become Maputo) and Beira needed overhaul and expansion, the economy was at a standstill—and the people necessary to start the country running again for the most part had fled. Although China delivered some military aid, it soon pulled out of the area, leaving it to Russia, which supplied mostly small arms, and to Cuba which furnished numerous military instructors.

To worsen matters, Machel had a very determined enemy on the other side of his eight-hundred-mile-long western border. That was Rhodesia, whose white government headed by Ian Smith was being threatened by a black nationalist insurgency. The trouble had started when Rhodesia was still a British colony. In 1957, the black nationalist Joshua Nkomo had founded the Rhodesian African National Congress. Three years later, he joined with four other nationalists—the Reverend Malabaningi Sithole, Robert Mugabe, and Herbert Chitipo—in forming the National Democratic Party, a militant group that wanted an independent Rhodesia with one-man, one-vote government.[28] In 1961, Great Britain implemented a new constitution for the colony that suggested the possibility of future majority rule, albeit very gradually. That was not to the liking of the ruling white minority—220,000 out of well over four million. Angry (and frightened) whites now formed the conservative Rhodesian Front Party, which, determined to remain in power, cracked down hard on the black nationalist movement.

Had the black National Democratic Party remained intact, it possibly could have brought about desired reforms—liberal world opinion was certainly on its side. Instead, it split into two parties, Joshua Nkomo's Zimbabwe African People's Union (ZAPU) and Malabaningi Sithole's Zimbabwe African National Union (ZANU). In 1964, Great Britain granted independence to Northern Rhodesia, which became Zambia, and to Nyasaland, which became Malawi. Also in 1964, Ian Smith's government in Southern Rhodesia outlawed both the ZANU and the ZAPU, whose members fled to Zambia. To Smith's demand for independence, the British government replied that the whites would have to bring blacks into the governing process. In 1965, a furious Smith backed by a majority of whites declared a unilateral independence. That made Rhodesia a political pariah second only to the Republic of South Africa and brought it heavy political and economic sanctions levied by Britain and later the United Nations to increase further its isolation.

ZANU recruits meanwhile were being trained and armed by Russian and Cuban instructors in Zambia and Eastern-bloc countries. Small guerrilla groups now began to infiltrate into Rhodesia, where for the next four years they were effectively neutralized by a small but efficient army buttressed by Rhodesian police and some two thousand paramilitary South African police. Tactical failure only increased the friction between ZANU and ZAPU leaders. In 1969, Sithole and his lieutenants, deciding to wage a rural war in the Maoist style, formed the Zimbabwe African National Liberation Army (ZANLA), whose recruits were trained by Chinese instructors in Tanzanian camps. Posted to camps in northern Mozambique (with FRELIMO blessing), they began infiltrating into northeastern Rhodesia. Rhodesian security forces responded with large-scale raids into Mozambique, a campaign so successful that according to one authority there were only a hundred ZANLA guerrillas still fighting in 1974.[29] The war slowed the following year when the South African Government attempted to negotiate a peace—without success. When fighting resumed in 1976, the Rhodesian Government faced two guerrilla threats, one from ZANU, led now by Robert Mugabe, in the east, the other from Joshua Nkomo's ZAPU based in Zambia. The two organizations meanwhile had formed a Patriotic Front—more a truce than a party—to fight a guerrilla war with forces greatly strengthened by thousands of recruits trained in Tanzania, Zambia, and Angola and armed with modern Russian and Chinese weapons. ZANLA guerrillas continued to be based in northern Mozambique, from where they were to open a "front" along the eight-hundred-mile border. ZAPU's military arm, ZIPRA, which counted eight to ten thousand guerrillas, was based in Zambia, from where it would open "fronts" in both east and west.

This then was the situation in spring of 1976 when Samora Machel, using Rhodesian army raids into Mozambique as pretext, closed the border to Rhodesia, a desperate act since it was possible that it would cause Rhodesia to invade Mozambique and since it deprived financially strapped Mozambique of millions of dollars a year in customs, port dues, and railway charges formerly incurred by landlocked Rhodesia. In partial palliation, Machel signed a twenty-year Treaty of Friendship with the Soviet Union and with the help of Russian, Cuban, and North Korean military advisers began converting his FRELIMO force into a conventionally organized army. He also sent FRELIMO guerrilla units to work with Rhodesian guerrillas based in Mozambique.

The ensuing war was hideous in the extreme. As ZANLA and ZIPRA guerrillas attempted to block Rhodesian communications by cutting road and rail networks, a process accompanied by kidnaping or killing any whites or blacks who refused to support them, Rhodesian security forces replied in kind by making large-scale attacks against camps in Zambia and Mozambique, claiming (probably accurately) to have killed hundreds of guerrillas. As part of this counterinsurgency effort, the Rhodesian army in 1977 sponsored the Mozambican National Resistance, or RENAMO, group led by Afonso Dblakama. This polyglot guerrilla force was composed of former white settlers, Portuguese soldiers, army deserters, juvenile delinquents, renegades from FRELIMO, and other dissentient blacks, just the sort of mixture that spells unbridled brutality—which henceforth was the case. By 1978, Rhodesian security forces numbered some 115,000 including eight thousand regular and thirty-five thousand reserve policemen.[30] Despite an all-out counterinsurgency campaign, the guerrillas appeared to be on top and they probably would have toppled the government had there been a unified insurgent political and military command. There was nothing remotely resembling this. As it was, a transitional government, which the Smith regime had had to accept in early 1978, a prelude to majority rule, was not accepted by Mugabe and Nkomo's Patriotic Front whose own internal rivalries led to serious armed clashes between ZANLA and ZIPRA guerrillas in 1979. By then, however, a new constitution had been approved and the first one-man, one-vote elections held for a multiparty house of assembly. The elections, in which 63 per cent of an estimated two million electorate had voted, were won by the Rhodesian African National Congress, whose internal branch was led by Bishop Abel Muzorewa who was now prime minister of what had become Zimbabwe/Rhodesia.[31] In 1980, a second election was won by the Patriotic Front and the former colony became the nation of Zimbabwe with Robert Mugabe, a dedicated Marxist, its first president.

Although the insurgent victory in Rhodesia eased Samora Machel's military position, it did not alter his deteriorating economic situation. The war had cost Mozambique dearly. Incessant raids had not only taken thousands of civilian lives, they had created hundreds of thousands of civilian refugees. Thousands of farms had been abandoned and many of those that survived had fallen victim to inept management of Russian and Cuban "experts" who had also run the meager industrial plant into the ground. The Soviet Union had not proved to be the hoped-for generous patron; indeed Machel's fervent Marxist rhetoric had noticeably softened as he started edging toward the West. The conversion was encouraged by drought and famine that from 1982 to 1984 displaced and killed hundreds of thousands, a period in which the Soviet Union's limited aid contrasted sharply with generous Western and United Nations relief efforts. But now Machel faced another problem in the form of a guerrilla campaign designed to end his regime.

This was the work of the RENAMO group operating from bases in South Africa's Transvaal. With the fall of the Smith regime in Rhodesia, RENAMO had been adopted by the South African Government and army; other important donors were former Portuguese colonial landowners, Oman, Brazil, Saudi Arabia, and right-wing organizations in Germany and the United States (reportedly the American Heritage Foundation in Washington, where RENAMO was said also to maintain a lobbying organization).[32]

After infiltrating Mozambique, RENAMO guerrillas, operating in units of up to a hundred men, employed tactics similar to those used by Salvadoran guerrillas, that is striking communication lines, blowing up bridges, burning farms, slaughtering livestock, blocking wells, demolishing schools and health clinics, all to force the people to leave the land to seek refuge in overburdened camps,[33] tactics that in time would drive five million subsistence farmers from the land. Despite the best efforts of the army, theoretically inspired by Machel's strident call for a revival of "people's war,"[34] the guerrillas prospered, partly because of the immensity of the land and mounting RENAMO strength, estimated at eight to ten thousand by late 1983 when its guerrillas " . . . had succeeded in removing large areas of Mozambique . . . from any vestige of government control."[35] So overstrained were Mozambique's inadequate defenses that in this same period South African commandos successfully carried out air and ground strikes against suspected African National Congress offices in the capital, Maputo.[36]

Faced with this new threat and trying to cope with a widespread famine, looking at a moribund economic and agrarian future, increasingly removed from Russian aid, Machel now approached his South African enemy. Pretoria was also having difficulties as a result of the worst drought in memory, the heavy costs of the war in Angola, and the widespread sabotage of vital installations by ANC and FRELIMO guerrillas. The result was the Nkomadi Accord of 1984, a non-aggression pact hammered out with the help of U.S. mediators. In brief, Pretoria would cease support of RENAMO in return for Mozambique closing down African National Congress offices in Maputo. The accord also called for committees to be set up to provide various joint economic development ventures in Mozambique. Hailed by President P. W. Botha as having " . . . set a new course in the history of South Africa,"[37] the accord was more a victory for Pretoria than for Mozambique. Theretofore none of the Front Line States (Angola, Botswana, Mozambique, Tanzania, Zambia, Zimbabwe) had recognized apartheid government by opening diplomatic relations with Pretoria. Machel's decision to do so was resented not alone by these governments but also by powerful factions in the FRELIMO party. Even worse, although he dutifully set about expelling ANC officials and guerrillas, he could not expel all of them. Pretoria on the other hand made a big show of cutting its links with RENAMO, but not until a large supply drop had been made to its units inside Mozambique and not before another fifteen hundred to two thousand trained and equipped guerrillas had slipped into Mozambique.[38] It then transpired that elements in South Africa's army refused to accept the agreement and continued to supply RENAMO forces. The result was an *increase* in RENAMO operations during the rest of 1984—and a rapid deterioration in Mozambique-South African relations. These worsened as RENAMO attacks increased in 1985 and as ANC sabotage revived in South Africa. Such was the growing threat from RENAMO that Mozambican and Zimbabwean paratroops attacked what was believed to be its headquarters in the western mountains. Here sufficient evidence of South Africa's continued support of the insurgents was found to elicit an admission of guilt from Pretoria. In palliation, South Africa's public loans to and private investment in Mozambique increased in 1985. Machel's temper was further softened by $2 million worth of military equipment from Pretoria, a million dollars of U.S. aid,[39] by the U.S. and eleven other countries imposing economic sanctions on South Africa,[40] and by his being cordially received at the White House by President Reagan.

The war continued into 1986 as the government tried to counter RENAMO's increasing gains. In part it was a case of poacher turned gamekeeper. RENAMO guerrillas were officially called "armed bandits" and all stops were pulled to eradicate them. As the FRELIMO had taught the Portuguese army, this was difficult if not impossible. An amnesty offer brought no dramatic result. Machel might well have gone under but for reinforcement by the vanguard of twelve thousand soldiers from Zimbabwe and three thousand from Tanzania deployed to assist Mozambican forces in guarding the vital 180-mile road, railroad, and pipeline corridor that stretched from the Rhodesian border to the Mozambique port of Beira. In September, Machel, supported by Zimbabwe and Tanzania, forced Malawi to expel all RENAMO forces with the result that ten thousand enemy guerrillas debouched into the northern province of Zambezia, " . . . capturing, and for the first time holding, major bridges and several towns."[41] At this crucial point, Machel was killed in an air crash believed by some observers to have been arranged by pro-RENAMO elements in the South African army.[42] Machel was replaced by Joaquim Chissano, who, supported financially by Western nations and the Front Line States, pledged himself to pursue victory over RENAMO while continuing to build a socialist state, a task aided by additional troops from Zimbabwe who helped to clear the Zambezia valley of RENAMO guerrillas. As is so often the case in counterinsurgency warfare, this resembled putting a finger on a drop of mercury—in short order, fugitive guerrilla units reassembled in central Mozambique where, presumably supplied from South Africa, they continued offensive operations, in July killing over four hundred civilians including women and children in one attack, and in October hitting a truck convoy to kill over three hundred people and wound hundreds more,[43] all in the most bestial way such as reportedly boiling children in front of their parents—the ghastly story is told in William Finnegan's *A Complicated War*. RENAMO also declared war on Zimbabwe and began "hot pursuits" across the border, actions that drove thousands more civilians into perilously overcrowded refugee camps.[44]

The hideous situation gradually altered in 1988 owing in part to the world-shaking change in Soviet policies evoked by Mikhail Gorbachev, but also in part to President Joaquim Chissano's realization that government forces could not defeat the guerrillas, that his country was rapidly approaching bankruptcy, and that all indications pointed to the prospect of an appalling famine. Using the occasion of a FRELIMO congress in July, Chissano presented a twelve-point peace plan and announced that the government would enter into "indirect" negotiations with RENAMO providing that the group would "renounce violence and agree to abide by the Constitution."[45] Congressional delegates next learned, undoubtedly to their astonishment, that the base of the FRELIMO party was to be expanded, thenceforth to include " . . . private property owners and members of the business community" as well as members of all religious faiths.[46] In fact, Chissano, like Mikhail Gorbachev, was admitting socialist defeat as shown by a new constitution " . . . which provided for a multiparty system, direct elections and a free-market economy."[47]

Predictions of a horrible famine proved all too accurate. In 1990, nearly two million Mozambicans were approaching starvation, and severe fighting had forced another quarter million to leave their lands.[48] Nevertheless, direct talks were held in Rome in July, August, and September. Owing to RENAMO delaying tactics—it needed time to form a political party—progress was slow, but in November when the new constitution was introduced the government recognized RENAMO's status as a political party. In March 1992, at the ninth round of peace talks, an electoral system was agreed on. The two sides edged closer to agreement during the eleventh round of peace talks in July, during which progress was made concerning the composition of a future army.[49]

CHAPTER NINETY-ONE

1. Pimlott, 80.
2. Ibid.
3. *Encyclopaedia Britannica*, 1986, Vol. 1, 135.
4. Pimlott, 83.
5. International Institute for Strategic Studies, *Strategic Survey 1975*, 9.
6. Pimlott, 85.
7. Ibid.
8. *Newsweek*, November 1, 1976.
9. International Institute for Strategic Studies, *Strategic Survey 1976*, 45. See also, ibid., *1988–89*, 147.
10. *Keesing's Contemporary Archives*, Vol. 22, 1976. May, 1976, 78,072.
11. International Institute for Strategic Studies, *Strategic Survey 1975*, 2.
12. *Encyclopaedia Britannica 1991*, Vol. 8, 494.
13. Pimlott, 13.
14. International Institute for Strategic Studies, *Strategic Survey 1985–86*, 186–9.
15. Ibid., *1987–88*, 194. See also, ibid., *1988–89*, 197; *International Herald Tribune*, June 27, 1989.
16. International Institute for Strategic Studies, *Strategic Survey 1989–90*, 75. See also, *New York Times*, December 22, 1988; *International Herald Tribune*, June 7, 1989.
17. *International Herald Tribune*, December 22, 1988.
18. *USA Today*, International Edition, April 5, 1989.
19. *Encyclopaedia Britannica 1991*, Vol. 11, 46.
20. *New York Times*, March 7, 1993.
21. *The Independent* (U.K.), July 9, 1993.
22. Ibid., July 23, 1993.
23. Ibid., August 13, 1993.
24. Ibid., August 30, 1993.
25. Ibid., August 10, 1993.
26. *Newsweek*, October 25, 1993.
27. *International Herald Tribune*, November 10, 1993.
28. Pimlott, 88.
29. Ibid., 92.
30. *Keesing's Contemporary Archives*, Vol. 24, 1978. April 28, 1978, 28,948.
31. Ibid., Vol. 25, 1979. August 10, 1979, 29,757, 29,759.
32. *Keesing's Record of World Events*, Vol. 34, 1988. February 1988, 35,686.
33. Ibid., 35,685.
34. International Institute for Strategic Studies, *Strategic Survey 1982–83*, 108.
35. Jaster, 258. See also, International Institute for Strategic Studies, *Strategic Survey 1984–85*, 107.
36. Jaster, 259.
37. International Institute for Strategic Studies, *Strategic Survey 1984–85*, 107.
38. Jaster, 260.
39. Ibid., 262.
40. International Institute for Strategic Studies, *Strategic Survey 1985–86*, 185.
41. Ibid., *1986–87*, 190.

42. Ibid., *Adelphi Papers Number 227, 1987–88,* 18: *Pravda* openly charged South Africa with the crime.
43. Ibid., *Strategic Survey 1987–88,* 197. See also, Finnegan.
44. *Keesing's Record of World Events,* Vol. 34, 1988. January 1988, 35,628: One camp administrator reported that by the end of October, there were over 22,000 refugees in a camp built for 10,000 and that 1,000 were arriving every month. See also, ibid., August 1988, 36,084: The United Nations reported in July that there were already 570,000 Mozambican refugees in Malawi with 20,000–40,000 arriving every month.
45. Ibid., Vol. 35, 1989. July 1989, 36,804. See also, *International Herald Tribune,* October 10, 1989.
46. Ibid.
47. *Keesing's Record of World Events,* Vol. 37, 1991. February 1991 Supplement, 38,044.
48. Ibid., January 1991, 37,945–6.
49. *Newsweek,* July 27, 1992.

CHAPTER 92

Afghanistan old and new • Political disunity • Prime Minister Mohammed Daud's rise and fall • The Soviets install Nur Mohammed Taraki's Marxist government • The jihad (holy war) declared by mujaheddin guerrillas • Collapse of the Afghan army • The Soviet army versus the guerrillas • Soviet military deficiencies • Mujaheddin disunity • Pakistan's role • U.S. military aid to the mujaheddin • Military stalemate • The Mohammed Najibullah regime • Mikhail Gorbachev pulls out • The war continues: Gulbuddin Hakmatyar versus Ahmed Shah Massoud • The drug factor • United Nations attempts to end the fighting fail • The war continues

> Oh Gods! From the venom of the Cobra, the teeth of the Tiger, and the vengeance of the Afghan—deliver us.
>
> OLD HINDU SAYING[1]

AFGHANISTAN'S PRESENT TROUBLES began in 1839 when Great Britain, intent on preventing Russian expansion southwards, invaded the land, the first of three wars that did much to increase a traditional xenophobia in what became known as "the hermit's kingdom,"[2] an undisciplined group of tribal fiefdoms squeezed between British India and czarist Russia.

The country remained under British hegemony until 1919, when it won full independence, to be governed in theory by young King Mohammed Zahir but in fact by the king's ultraconservative Pashtun uncles. It did not begin to come of age until a non-violent political revolution ushered in Mohammed Daud as Prime Minister Lieutenant General Daud Khan, who intended to rule *sans* the royal uncles. A cousin of the king, Daud was a latter-day Kemal Ataturk determined

1201

to lead his country into the modern world by an extensive program of economic development—an extremely ambitious if highly laudable goal.

His task was complicated not only by a politically fragmented nation, but also by quarrelsome, aggressive neighbors: in the north a seven-hundred-mile border with the former Soviet Central Asian republics marked for hundreds of miles by the Amu Darya River (the Oxus River of antiquity crossed and recrossed by Alexander the Great in his pursuit of Bactrian guerrillas—(see Chapter 1); in the west and southwest, Islamic Iran; in the east, Pakistan; and in the south, Pakistan's desert pendant Baluchistan. Afghanistan's backbone, the formidable Hindu Kush mountain range, stretches 450 miles from southwest to northeast, the stern parent of wildly undisciplined fertile valleys sloping to river-cut plains and deserts that are home to nearly 90 per cent of an estimated fifteen million people who are as diverse as their landscape. Of the several ethnic and religious groups, the Pashtuns, the traditional rulers, are the largest with about seven million spread into fiercely independent tribes and clans " . . . varying in size from a thousand to a million."[3] Pashtun cohesion is further obstructed by Afghanistan's arbitrarily drawn border with Pakistan, the Durand Line imposed by Britain that cut a number of Pashtun tribes in half, part of them living in Afghanistan, part in the Northwest Frontier province of Pakistan. Farsi and Turkic are the two principal languages but numerous other tongues vie with each other and with a feast of dialects often foreign to a neighboring tribe. The country people are poor but proud. Illiteracy is high, serious illnesses and epidemics abound, only 20 per cent of the drinking water is safe, life expectancy is low.

So it was that Mohammed Daud set himself a Herculean task. Ironically, his rise to power occurred in 1953 at the height of the cold war between Soviet Russia and the West. Fearful of Soviet expansion southward as imperial Britain had been before him, U. S. Secretary of State John Foster Dulles knocked together a "northern tier" defensive coalition, the Central Treaty Organization (CENTO) of Pakistan, Iran, Turkey, and Iraq, an unlikely alliance of capricious rulers if ever there was one. The alliance did not include Afghanistan and Daud's request for arms was turned down: Washington was afraid that Afghanistan wanted to invade pet-of-the-moment Pakistan or at least prevent Pakistan from merging the Northwest Frontier province, home to a large number of Pashtuns, with the rest of the country.[4] Daud in reality wanted an efficient army in order to control his country's diverse tribes. Washington's limited amount of economic aid only partially ameliorated the resentment felt in Kabul.

While U.S. diplomacy vis-à-vis Afghanistan stumbled, Soviet diplomacy soared. Where the U.S. spent a few million dollars on educational

AFGHANISTAN

and engineering projects, the Soviet Union spent over $200 million to modernize the army and build new roads.

Daud's ambitious reforms continued as he attempted to follow a foreign policy of non-alignment even though tilting toward Moscow. By 1959, he had largely eliminated the traditional veil and the *purdah,* or seclusion of upper-class women from public view.[5] But in relying on the new and young educated elite to carry out his reforms, he overlooked the importance of the diverse ethnic and tribal elements that formed the real if splintered power of the land. As progress faltered and criticism increased, his regime grew more oppressive. Instead of respecting traditional rule by joining it to government rule he ignored it and since traditional rule governed about 90 per cent of the land, that meant that he was making the cardinal error of failing to establish a political base necessary to support his reformist program.[6] Here was the basic reason for his ultimate failure, indeed for the fragmented non-government of today's Afghanistan.

As if there weren't sufficient problems at home, Daud challenged Pakistan over the Northwest Frontier province. Continued friction there led to Iraq's summary closing of the border, which shut off Afghanistan's trade routes to the east, ended his policy of non-alignment, cut off most U.S. aid, and committed him to the Soviet sphere of influence. In 1963, controlled anarchy became uncontrollable and Daud resigned. Government returned to King Mohammed Zahir. A new constitution did little to quiet political turbulence that brought five prime ministers between 1965 and 1972 and also brought into existence in 1965 the People's Democratic Party of Afghanistan (PDPA) with its two opposing factions, the very radical Khalq (Peoples) Party and the more moderate pro-Moscow Parcham (Banner) Party, the latter supporting Daud. In 1973, Daud regained power in a bloodless coup, abolished the monarchy, wrote a new constitution, and made tentative peace with Pakistan. Again he failed to establish a strong political base, relying instead on opportunistic sycophants to run an ineffectual but repressive government. In 1978, following a violent period of assassinations, anti-government demonstrations and wholesale arrests, pro-Soviet extremists within the two factions of the PDPA brought off another coup that cost Daud his life and established the pro-Soviet Democratic Republic of Afghanistan.

The central government of Afghanistan was now in the hands of a revolutionary council formed by members of the Marxist-Leninist PDPA headed by Nur Mohammed Taraki, a power group so extreme that even the Kremlin advised modification of its policies.[7] The PDPA soon split as Taraki, a member of the Khalq faction, consolidated his position by dismissing such opposition leaders of the Parcham faction as Deputy Prime Minister Babrak Karmal (sent to Prague as ambassador). Taraki's intensified reform program, which included a highly controversial land distribution scheme, alienated more tribal leaders and mullahs (Islamic priests) as it filtered down to the countryside; a major literacy campaign that included teaching women how to read and write drew instant condemnation from conservative males.[8]

The first armed revolt by guerrilla *mujaheddin* (holy warriors) occurred in the central provinces in late summer of 1978 and soon spread to other parts of the country, the start of a declared *jihad,* or holy war. Guerrilla terrorists were soon exploding bombs in the cities and in early 1979 they murdered the U.S. ambassador in Kabul. In March, guerrilla riots in Herat were suppressed by troops but only after the deaths of perhaps five thousand people. The split in the PDPA widened. Deputy Prime Minister Hafizullah Amin, who replaced Taraki as prime minister, ordered a bloodbath in which thousands of political opponents were jailed or executed. Meanwhile, the Afghan army was folding under guerrilla onslaught. In September, Taraki, supported by the Soviet Union, tried to oust Amin and was murdered.

Russia's stake in Afghanistan had grown considerably and for good reason. Soviet hegemony would mean exclusive access to the rich underdeveloped northern gas fields and in time to undeveloped copper, chrome, iron, and bauxite deposits. It would also move Russia five hundred miles toward the warm waters of the Arabian Sea and its prosperous parent, the Indian Ocean, whose waters lapped the major oil-producing nations of the world. Beyond Afghanistan lay Pakistan's desert province, Baluchistan, with its two-hundred-mile coastline and three ports and with many of its sixty tribes not overly fond of Pakistan rule.[9] By late 1978, thousands of young officers had been trained in the Soviet Union and the Kremlin had supplied an estimated $3.5 billion in economic and military aid, the latter including tanks, jet fighters, and helicopter gunships:[10] additional military aid was promised under the terms of a twenty-year Treaty of Friendship signed that year.

Now, in 1979, as four to five thousand Soviet military advisers were in Afghanistan, as the Afghan army continued to disintegrate, and as Amin continued his repressive police actions (more than a thousand mullahs had been killed during his regime),[11] the Kremlin was faced with an either/or situation: either to continue supporting a client state with the hope of eventually profiting from its investment or to abandon it and thereby lose face at a crucial time in the cold war.

Probably without realizing the innate if unco-ordinated strength of the mujaheddin jihad, the Kremlin chose not so much to support the client state as to rule it. Amin was no longer acceptable. His radical reforms and vicious purges had alienated far too many important Afghans and were held to be partly responsible for what appeared to be a losing counterinsurgency campaign. A coup arranged by Moscow brought Amin's murder and replacement in late 1979 by Babrak Karmal. Using the patently flimsy pretext that Karmal had invoked the Treaty of Friendship to call for help, the Kremlin sent in an expeditionary force and the war was on.

By the time the dust cleared, several thousand Soviet military advisers in Kabul had been joined by five thousand airborne troops complete with armored vehicles, tanks, and artillery. Simultaneously, the vanguard of a fifty-thousand-man army moved in from the north. Once Karmal's government was secure, Soviet forces occupied the major cities, towns, and airfields in order to offer the Afghan army safe garrisons from which to fight the mujaheddin.[12] Karmal meanwhile attempted to gain popular support by releasing thousands of prisoners and promising extensive reforms—words ignored by thousands of key officials who either fled the country or joined the mujaheddin.

We should keep in mind that the Soviet high command was about as familiar with the realities of counterinsurgency warfare as the U.S. command had been in Vietnam. Among its many mistakes was that of underestimating the fighting capabilities of what it derisively termed "counterrevolutionary bandits." Few preparations had been made, linguistically or otherwise, to use the indigenous population as a source of intelligence. That probably explains why troops from the Central Asian republics were used to occupy the northeastern provinces and were then hastily replaced when they struck up too strong a kinship with the locals. Still another error was to suppose that the Afghan army, already reduced from ninety thousand to about thirty thousand by casualties and sickness but mainly by desertion (in some cases of entire brigades), could wage a successful counterinsurgency. Its increasingly dismal performance perforce turned the Soviets themselves to the task, where they at once erred by deploying large airborne and armor formations in mountain country with troops neither tactically nor technically trained for that type of warfare.[13] Repeated failures eventually brought tactical modifications and a change " . . . to combined operations involving motorized infantry, tanks and helicopter gunships."[14]

Who were the enemy?

The mujaheddin comprised several hundred groups of variously armed guerrilla fighters generally isolated from each other not only by rugged terrain but by important tribal differences—one thinks in passing of T. E. Lawrence and the Arab tribes (see Chapter 16). What happened in one province or even part of a province did not often affect events elsewhere. This isolation taken with generally inadequate arms in the opening phase of the insurgency should have made those groups easy game for the hunters, but such was not the case.

The guerrilla groups came in different sizes and colors. Seven of the main organizations were headquartered in Peshawar, a town about forty miles inside Pakistan that marks the western end of the Khyber Pass. Dominant among these was the Hezb-i Islami, an Islamic fundamentalist group headed by a Pashtun, Gulbuddin Hakmatyar, an Islamic extremist who repeatedly clashed with leaders of more moderate fundamentalist beliefs such as the Hanafi sect of Sunni Islam, but who managed to garner an estimated 70 per cent of the arms and money received from foreign sources.[15] Other major groups based inside Afghanistan fought independently of the Pakistan-based groups. Some were large such as Ahmed Shah Massoud's rival coalition, the Islamic Jihad Council, which controlled the Panjshir Valley area; some were small such as the Hazaryat guerrillas in central Afghanistan. Together the mujaheddin numbered about ninety thousand. Had one leader harnessed this vast potential, the security forces would have been overwhelmed. As it was, the Soviets were able to fight a tough protracted war with a relatively small number of men.

What were the mujaheddin fighting for? Principally to remove the PDPA communist regime and with it the Soviet army before returning to their own way of life. What was to replace the regime? Most of the mujaheddin did not know or care. Certain of their leaders did care but only in a power-grabbing sense as opposed to establishing a legitimate civil government capable of homogenizing a dispersed, illiterate, and fiercely independent population. This was the essential weakness of the insurgents. No one had anything positive to offer politically.

Despite disunity and lack of arms, the guerrillas more than held their own in 1980, even challenging government control of such important cities as Kandahar and Herat. Additional weapons were acquired from dead and wounded soldiers, from deserters and in time from China and Egypt (using U.S. and Saudi Arabian money to buy them). Millions of dollars also came from extensive cultivation of the opium poppy, which was refined into heroin for sale in the U.S. and Europe.[16]

In early 1981, the Kabul government insisted " . . . 'the main band of rebels' had been destroyed, and that it only remained to mop up the small groups which had survived,"[17] a matter of six months—this at a time when the Afghan army had been reduced to thirty thousand men and Russian construction teams were working overtime to build a road and rail bridge across the Amu Darya River in the hope of clearing seriously clogged supply lines. Although counterinsurgency tactics had improved by decentralization of command authority—the motorized rifle battalion was now the basic maneuver unit—and by increased use of helicopter gunships, Soviet military analysts had begun complaining about the efficacy of guerrilla sniper fire, frequent ambushes of convoys, guerrilla-made forest fires and avalanches, the blowing up of bridges and mining of roads, and infiltration from Pakistan where " . . . a solid barrier has been set up against the bandits, but [insurgents] keep coming through."[18] Co-ordinated ground-helicopter assaults such as those in the Panjshir Valley north of Kabul often yielded short-term gains, but these were costly: Russian casualties rose from an estimated fifteen to seventeen hundred in 1979 to a total five thousand by end of 1981.[19] They were also expensive in money and they solved very little, since there were not sufficient troops to hold the seized areas, but by destroying everything in sight they did force many locals to join refugee camps in the cities and thus increase already serious food and power shortages. To compensate for tactical failures, Soviet commanders introduced a scorched-earth policy carried out both by ground troops burning villages and crops and slaughtering livestock, and by indiscriminate bombing of cities, towns, and villages in order to create more refugees and to deprive guerrillas of food and information—a deliberate attempt to make "terror reign."[20]

The picture did not radically change in 1983, although Soviet casualties rose to about ten thousand with large numbers down from typhoid fever, dysentery, and pneumonia.[21] Soviet troop strength rose to an estimated 105,000 and the Afghan army to perhaps thirty-five thousand but the government was no closer to victory. The stalemate continued throughout 1984, the sixth year of the increasingly expensive Soviet occupation, with all sides hardening their positions. Since 1982, the United Nations envoy Diego Cordovez had been trying to start talks between the Kabul government and Pakistan and Iran but with no success, nor would Kabul negotiate directly with the mujaheddin. Guerrilla bombings and assassinations continued in the cities, particularly in Kabul, and some mujaheddin groups received ground-to-air missiles, ground-to-ground rockets, anti-tank weapons and radio equipment. Mujaheddin leaders continued to squabble in Peshawar, but some commanders inside Afghanistan began to co-ordinate local military actions, with considerably improved results. Continued guerrilla offensives caused the Kremlin to up the manpower ante to 115,000. Although Soviet forces received improved equipment, sick-lists remained long and individual morale lower, with the troops frequently using drugs. Casualties also rose. Total Soviet losses from 1979 were " . . . estimated at 20–25,000 (roughly one-third of them killed)"; total financial cost to the Kremlin was reportedly $12 billion.[22] Food and fuel shortages increased in cities and towns and so did serious epidemics, with little or no medicines for the ill. Afghan army morale was low; the conscription age was now sixteen. Karmal had won some favor by adopting a pro-Islamic stance, by softening and even discarding some of the more stringent Amin reforms, by releasing some political prisoners, and by extending the franchise, but his increasingly fragmented regime was believed to control just over 20 per cent of the population.[23]

In 1985, the first year in which Western journalists were legally allowed to enter Afghanistan, the war seemed to tilt in the government's favor as security forces gained control of most cities and towns and began pushing guerrillas back to the mountains. Karmal established a Ministry of Islamic Affairs, announced elections for local assemblies, and convened large meetings of tribal, religious, and political elders as well as of frontier tribesmen, in an effort to win their support in the crucial Pakistan border areas. In addition to adding non-party persons both to the Council of Ministers and the Revolutionary Council, he made other conciliatory moves designed to win over businessmen, mullahs, and intelligentsia. Behind this facade of Islamic democracy, Sovietization proceeded apace. The teaching of the Russian language was now compulsory from an early age and thousands of youngsters were sent to Central Asian provinces for ten years of schooling.[24] On the military side, the policy of terror against villages suspected of guerrilla sympathies was changed to a policy of coercion, which in many areas resulted in the formation of local militias that guarded villages and gave information on guerrilla movements and location to the Khad, the Afghanistan secret police. An amnesty program brought in a large number of defectors, including one group of a thousand guerrillas which was organized into a local defense militia.[25]

Despite some of the biggest Soviet/Afghanistan drives of the war, the killing of large numbers of mujaheddin, and the capture of guerrilla arms dumps, the fighting was scarcely decisive. More weapons were flowing into mujaheddin camps—the U.S. reportedly supplied $250 million worth in 1985—and nowhere did the resistance seem broken. In truth, both sides were tiring of the war but now the mujaheddin gained a new and totally expected ally in the form of Russia's Mikhail Gorbachev. To the outspoken Gorbachev, who was staring encroaching national bankruptcy in the face, the Afghan insurgency was a "bleeding wound." It had cost thirty-five thousand Soviet casualties (including fifteen thousand dead) to date; it was costing $15 million a day; it was standing in the way of detente with the West, China, and the Arab states; and it was bringing increasing domestic dissatisfaction in Russia.[26]

As a first step in extricating Russia from the war, Gorbachev selected Dr. Mohammed Najibullah, chief of the secret police, to head a program of "national reconciliation." That was a somewhat odd choice in that, as head of Khad, Najibullah personally had been responsible for many thousands of deaths from torture of political prisoners. Nevertheless, he replaced Karmal as head of the PDPA and ruler of the country and offered a six-month cease-fire during which the government would organize a "coalition of national unity," write a new constitution, and oversee the election of a national assembly. Gorbachev himself promised the phased withdrawal of six Soviet regiments to begin in 1987 and to continue providing the mujaheddin joined the cease-fire and co-operated with the policy of national reconciliation.[27]

The mujaheddin were not interested. They had largely recovered from tactical setbacks in 1985 and were again in front militarily, having received some $500 million worth of arms in 1986, about half of which were furnished by the U.S., including ground-to-air Stinger missiles.[28] Nor were they interested in "national reconciliation" or even in a new constitution which made Islam the official religion. Despite the political window-dressing, it was all too obvious that Najibullah was running a Soviet-dominated dictatorship. When the Soviet regiments, some seven thousand troops, began to depart in 1987, it was also obvious that Russia was tiring of the war. Mujaheddin military successes continued to mount as the flow of foreign arms increased—over $600 million worth from the U.S. and many more millions from China and Saudi

Arabia in 1987. Increasingly, the Soviet forces and what remained of the Afghan army were on the defensive in the cities and countryside, to the extent that in early 1988 Gorbachev no longer tied Soviet troop withdrawal to perpetuation of the PDPA regime in Kabul, stating that " . . . Soviet troops would leave the country in less than ten months, beginning on 15 May provided that there was no interference from Pakistan and the U.S."[29] Confirmed by the UN-sponsored Geneva Accords, which Gorbachev signed in April, the withdrawal began on schedule and was completed in mid-February.[30]

Most Western experts predicted that the Najibullah regime would fall and be replaced by a mujaheddin government.[31] Nothing of the sort happened. The Kremlin continued to supply Najibullah with arms (including long-range Scud missiles), food, and fuel brought in by air—" . . . nearly $2 billion in military equipment by mid-October."[32] To general surprise, the hard core of the Afghan army, perhaps ten thousand veterans, more than held its own in the battle for the cities. Conversely, the increasingly fragmented mujaheddin fought either spasmodically or not at all. This was owing first to the nature of the beast, second to a massive failure brought on by U.S./Pakistan interference. In late 1988, the U.S. and Pakistan decided to form an Afghan Interim Government (AIG), which would replace the Kabul regime. To hasten this event, an offensive commanded by Pakistan's Inter-Service Intelligence organization was opened against government garrisons at Jallalabad and Khost, battles fought much more along conventional than guerrilla lines and as a result ending in stalemate with a large loss of guerrilla lives.[33] Meanwhile, members of the AIG were elected but these came from the Sunni Party alliance in Peshawar and excluded field commanders, the eight Shiite guerrilla groups based in Iran and most moderates, thereby insuring continued diversity and strife. This spilled over to other governments, with Iran and the Soviet Union holding for a coalition government in Kabul, Pakistan and Saudi Arabia pushing for an extreme fundamentalist government controlled by Hekmatyar's Hezb-i Islami.

The political and military impasse continued into 1989, but each side was hurting. In February, Najibullah declared a state of emergency and in May offered the Pakistan-based mujaheddin, addressed now as "brothers" not "bandits," a series of important concessions including an invitation to join the government in return for a cease-fire. The coalition was in greater disarray than ever. A ten-week siege of Islamabad had been defeated, the guerrillas again suffering heavy casualties.[34] In July, a faction of Hekmatyar's Hezb-i Islami ambushed and killed thirty mujaheddin including several of Ahmed Shah Massoud's commanders, an act that caused AIG President Mojadiddi to call Hekmatyar a "criminal" and a "terrorist,"[35] and cost the Hezb-i Islami, already suspected of selling Stinger missiles to Iran, U.S. support. Hekmatyar in turn accused Massoud of the crime and broke with the AIG. Massoud responded by attacking Hekmatyar's strongholds in Afghanistan. A second siege of Islamabad in November also failed, again with heavy casualties.

Najibullah had scant cause to rejoice. The PDPA was as divided as the mujaheddin. In March 1990, dissident army and air force officers led an unsuccessful attack on the presidential palace.[36] Najibullah not only survived but such was the tepid performance of the enemy that in spring of 1990 he called an end to the emergency and presented still another peace plan at once rejected by the mujaheddin.[37]

Subsequent events bear a curious resemblance to those that finally brought an end to the stubborn civil war in El Salvador. The United Nations had been trying to bring about a peace since 1982 with little progress until the signing of the Geneva Accords in 1988. In late 1989, a small UN force was created " . . . to monitor the withdrawal of foreign troops from Afghanistan as well as other aspects of the Geneva Accords of 1988."[38] In 1991, after a major mujaheddin offensive had captured the garrison city of Khost, UN Secretary-General Perez de Cuellar announced a peace plan based in part on proposals by the exiled Afghanistan King Zahir Shah. Its basic points were a cease-fire, an end to external influence, including the supply of arms to either side, and a UN-supervised election. Although Najibullah, who had lost considerable Soviet support after the fall of Gorbachev, accepted the plan, the hard-core mujaheddin—Hekmatyar's Hezb-i Islami and the AIG—refused to consider it: " . . . if Najibullah is there, there can be no cease-fire."[39] Hekmatyar's stance sparked off another round of internecine war, but the moderate groups representing an estimated 90 per cent of all mujaheddin agreed to consider the plan. Subsequent talks between the Iran-based groups, four of the seven AIG Pakistan groups and Pakistan and Iran representatives came to nothing. The picture changed radically in September with a U.S.-Soviet decision to end all weapon deliveries to the opposing sides. After more fighting and more talking, the mujaheddin majority met with Soviet Union officials in November. The battered Soviets, their own empire crumbling around them, agreed to end support for the Najibullah regime, which would be replaced by an interim government until elections could be held. That demarche was followed by further UN action which resulted in Najibullah's resignation and the establishment of an interim government in Kabul despite hard-core fundamentalist rejection of the resolution.[40] In theory the fifteen-year-old war, which had taken an estimated 1.5 million lives and had torn over five million Afghans from their homes, was over.

Well—not quite. The interim council, composed of representatives from the ten major guerrilla groups and headed by President Burhanuddin Rabbini, the non-Pashtun leader of the Jamait-i Islami group of fighters, was not universally applauded. While it was being organized, Hekmatyar's Pashtun guerrillas and Massoud's non-Pashtun guerrillas were securing control of their respective areas. Najibullah's fall from power in mid-April sent these groups racing to Kabul, Hekmatyar's troops moving in from south and east, Massoud's men from the north, a victory march on Massoud's part joined by scores of local government militia forces before he reached Kabul.[41] Prior to their arrival, Najibullah had attempted to escape the country but was intercepted by Major General Abdul Rashid Dostam, the non-Pashtun Uzbek leader of a strong government militia that had defected to the new government. When Hekmatyar and Massoud's forces reached Kabul in late April, a series of bloody battles followed. Massoud supported by Dostam forced the Hezb-i Islami fighters from the city to the southern hills. Reinforced by tanks and artillery brought up from his rear area base, Hekmatyar opened an artillery attack on the capital, killing seventy-three people and wounding nearly four hundred.[42] In late May, the two leaders signed a peace agreement but it was soon vitiated when the government not only refused to disband Dostam's force but incorporated it into the army.

The sides were now drawn for what has become a second civil war, this time Moslem Afghans fighting Moslem Afghans. The key players are Hekmatyar, supported by some powerful Pashtun leaders and reportedly by some Pakistani and Saudi Arabian officials; and Massoud, supported by most Shiite and other non-Pashtun leaders. Each side has ample stocks of weapons and ammunition, courtesy of Russia, the U.S., China, and Saudi Arabia. The result is stalemate, neither force being able to militarily defeat the other. The war has turned Kabul into virtually a ghost town, with no hospitals, no medicines, no electricity, no telephones, intermittent water supply, severe food shortages, embassies deserted, thousands of houses and shops buried in rubble. Various guerrilla factions are constantly at each other's throats, stealing and murdering. Hekmatyar's artillery shells and rockets fall on the city with maddening frequency. By late August, over two thousand people had been killed: " . . . more citizens of Kabul have died since the mujaheddin took power than during fourteen years of civil war."[43]

As a final crime, heroin production and distribution in the eastern border areas has grown so that it is now " . . . beyond the control of all the regionally interested governments, not only of Kabul and Islamabad, but also of Teheran and Moscow."[44]

Unfortunately, the anarchic situation continued in the following months as regional guerrilla leaders lorded it over independent fiefdoms such as the enclaves belonging to Sayer Jaffer Naderi and Rashid Dostum in the north. Despite almost constant fighting in and around Kabul, all attempts to bring about meaningful peace negotiations have failed.

As of this writing, December 1993, the war goes on—and with it the probable dissolution of Afghanistan as we have known it.

CHAPTER NINETY-TWO

1. Fletcher, 7.
2. Ibid., 1.
3. Ibid., 2, 5, 289 ff.
4. Ibid., 266–8.
5. Ibid., 272–3.
6. Rubin, 153 ff.
7. Ibid., 152.
8. Urban, 28.
9. Riencourt, 423–4.
10. International Institute for Strategic Studies, *Strategic Survey 1979,* 53.
11. Ibid, *1985–86,* 131.
12. Ibid., *1980–81,* 64. See also, Urban, 51–3.
13. Hart, 61.
14. International Institute for Strategic Studies, *Strategic Survey,* 64. See also, Urban, 66–8.
15. Schultheis.
16. Urban, 56–8, 77–8.
17. International Institute for Strategic Studies, *Strategic Survey 1981–82,* 93.
18. Hart, 63. See also, International Institute for Strategic Studies, *Adelphi Papers Number 259,* Summer 1991, 46–7; Urban, 98–9.
19. Ibid., *Strategic Survey 1981–82,* 94.
20. Malhuret, 428.
21. International Institute for Strategic Studies, *Strategic Survey 1982–83,* 87. See also, Urban, 128.
22. Ibid., *1984–85,* 73.
23. Ibid.
24. Ibid., *1985–86,* 131–3.
25. Ibid., 137.
26. Ibid., *Adelphi Papers Number 259,* 47.
27. Ibid., *Strategic Survey 1986–87,* 135.
28. Ibid, 138.
29. Ibid., *1987–88,* 137.
30. *USA Today,* International Edition, February 1, 16, 1989.
31. Ibid., February 15, 16, 1989.
32. Rubin, 162.
33. See, for example, *International Herald Tribune,* May 6–7, 1989.
34. Rubin, 156–9, for what went wrong.
35. Ibid., 159–60.
36. *Keesing's Record of World Events,* Vol. 36, 1990. March 1990, 37,314–5.
37. Ibid., May 1990, 37,453.
38. Ibid., March 1990, 37,355.
39. Ibid., Vol. 37, May 1991, 38,194.
40. *International Herald Tribune,* March 20, April 11–12, 1992.
41. *The Independent* (U.K.), April 15, 1992. See also, *International Herald Tribune,* April 24, 1992.
42. *Newsweek,* May 18, 1992.
43. *The Independent* (U.K.), August 28, 1992.
44. International Institute for Strategic Studies, *Strategic Survey 1989–90,* 163–4.

SELECTED BIBLIOGRAPHY

Abel, E. See Kalb, M.L.

Abernathy, M. Glenn, Dilys Hill, and Phil Williams, eds. *The Carter Years: The President and Policy Making*. London: Francis Pinter, 1984.

Acheson, Dean. *Present at the Creation: My Years in The State Department*. New York: W.W. Norton, 1969.

Adcock, F.E. *The Roman Art of War Under the Republic*. Cambridge, Mass.: Harvard University Press, 1940.

Alastos, Doros. *Cyprus Guerrilla: Grivas, Makarios and the British*. London: William Heinemann, 1960.

Alba, Victor. *The Mexicans: The Making of a Nation*. New York: Frederick A. Praeger, 1967.

Alden, J.R. *The American Revolution, 1775–1783*. New York: Harper and Brothers, 1954.

————. *A History of the American Revolution: Britain and the Loss of the Thirteen Colonies*. London: MacDonald, 1969.

————. *The South in the Revolution, 1763–1789*. Baton Rouge, La.: State University Press, 1957.

Aldington, R. *Lawrence of Arabia: A Biographical Enquiry*. London: Collins, 1955.

Alleg, Henri. *The Question*. London: John Calder, 1958.

Alsop, S., and T. Braden. *Sub Rosa: The OSS and American Espionage*. New York: Reynal and Hitchcock, 1946.

Altamira, Rafael. *A History of Spain*. New York: D. Van Nostrand, 1949.

Amery, Julian. *Sons of the Eagle: A Study in Guerrilla Warfare*. London: Macmillan, 1948.

Anders, W. *An Army in Exile*. London: Macmillan, 1949.

Anderson, James. *Sendoro Luminoso: A New Revolutionary Model?* London: Institute for the Study of Terrorism, 1987.

Anderson, Thomas P. *Politics in Central America: Guatemala, El Salvador, Honduras, and Nicaragua*. New York: Frederick A. Praeger, 1982.

The Annual Register of World Events. London: Longman, 1975–91.

Anon. *An Historical Account of the Expedition Against the Ohio Indians in the Year MDCCLXIV Under the Command of Henry Bouquet, Esq*. London: n.p., 1766.

Appian, *Appian's Roman History*, Vol. 1 of 4 vols., tr. Horace White. London: William Heinemann, 1964.

Armbrister, Trevor. *A Matter of Accountability: The True Story of the Pueblo Affair*. London: Barrie and Jenkins, 1970.

Armstrong, J.A., ed. *Soviet Partisans in World War II*. Madison, Wis.: University of Wisconsin Press, 1964.

Armstrong, J.A., and K. DeWitt. "Organization and Control of the [Soviet] Partisan Movement." In Armstrong, op. cit.

1214

Aron, Robert. *De Gaulle Before Paris: The Liberation of France June–August 1944,* tr. H. Hare. London: Putnam, 1962.

Arrian, *Anabasis Alexandri,* Vol. 1 of 2 vols., tr. P.A. Brunt. London: William Heinemann, 1929.

Arthur, George. *Life of Lord Kitchener,* Vol. 1 of 2 vols. London: Macmillan, 1920.

Asprey, Robert B. "The Peninsular War" and "Wellington at Waterloo," *Army Quarterly,* Vols. 77–78, April and July, 1959.

―――. "Waller of Samar," *Marine Corps Gazette,* May and June, 1961.

―――. "Special Forces: Europe," *Army,* January, 1962.

―――. "Small Wars—1925–1962," *Leatherneck,* 1962.

―――. "Guerrilla Warfare," *Encyclopaedia Britannica,* 1969.

―――. "Jungle Warfare," *Encyclopaedia Britannica,* 1969.

―――. "Tactics," *Encyclopaedia Britannica,* 1971.

―――. *War in the Shadows: The Guerrilla in History,* 2 vols. Garden City, N.Y.: Doubleday, 1975.

―――. *Frederick the Great: The Magnificent Enigma.* New York: Ticknor and Fields, 1986.

―――. "Guerrilla Warfare," *Encyclopaedia Britannica,* 1991.

Atkin, Ronald. *Revolution: Mexico 1910–1920.* New York: John Day, 1969.

Atkinson, Rick. *The Long Gray Line.* London: Collins, 1990.

Azan, Paul, ed. *Par l'Epée et par la Charrue: Écrits et Discours de Bugeaud.* Paris: Presses Universitaires de France, 1948.

Badian, E. "Alexander the Great and the Unity of Mankind." *Historia,* Vol. 7, pp. 425–44. Wiesbaden: Franz Steiner Verlag, 1952.

Baker, Carlos. *Hemingway: The Writer as Artist.* Princeton, N.J.: Princeton University Press, 1967.

Baldwin, Hanson. "The Case for Escalation," *New York Times Magazine,* February 27, 1966.

―――. "The Foe is Hurting." *Reader's Digest,* March 1968.

―――. "To End the War in Vietnam, Mobilize!" *Reader's Digest,* October 1966.

Ball, George W. *The Past Has Another Problem: Memoirs.* New York: W.W. Norton, 1982.

Barclay, C.N. "The Western Soldier Versus the Communist Insurgent," *Military Review,* February 1969.

Barea, A. *The Track,* tr. Ilsa Barea. London: Faber and Faber, 1943.

Barker, Dudley. *Grivas: Portrait of a Terrorist.* London: Cresset Press, 1959.

Barnett, Donald L., and Katari Njama. *Mau Mau from Within: Autobiography and Analysis of Kenya's Peasant Revolt.* New York: Monthly Review Press, 1966.

Barrett, David D. *Dixie Mission: The United States Army Observer Group in Yenan, 1944.* Berkeley, Calif.: University of California Press, 1970.

Bass, Robert D. *Swamp Fox: The Life and Campaigns of General Francis Marion.* London: Alvin Redman, 1959.

Batista, Fulgencio. *Cuba Betrayed.* New York: Vantage Press, 1962.

Bayley, Sydney D. *Four Arab-Israeli Wars and the Peace Process.* London: The Macmillan Press, 1990.

Beaufre, André. "Prospects for the New General," *The Sunday Times* (London), March 24, 1968.

Becker, Julian. *The PLO: The Rise and Fall of the Palestine Liberation Organization.* London: Weidenfeld and Nicolson, 1984.

Beckett, J.C. *The Making of Modern Ireland 1603–1923.* London: Faber and Faber, 1966.

Beeler, John. *Warfare in England, 1066–1189.* Ithaca, N.Y.: Cornell University Press, 1966.

―――. *Warfare in Feudal Europe, 730–1200.* Ithaca, N.Y.: Cornell University Press, 1971.

Behr, Edward. *The Algerian Problem.* London: Hodder and Stoughton, 1961.

Bell, J. Bowyer. *The Secret Army: The IRA 1916–1979*. Dublin: The Academy Press, 1979.

Bennett, Richard. *The Black and Tans*. London: Hulton, 1959.

Bennoune, Mahfoud. *The Making of Contemporary Algeria 1830–1987*. New York: Cambridge University Press, 1988.

Berman, Larry. *Lyndon Johnson's War: The Road to Stalemate in Vietnam*. New York: W.W. Norton, 1989.

————. *Planning a Tragedy. The Americanization of the War in Vietnam*. New York: W.W. Norton, 1983.

Bernard, Stéphane. *The Franco-Moroccan Conflict, 1943–1956*. New Haven, Conn.: Yale University Press, 1968.

Bernstein, Carl. See Woodward, Bob.

Bertrand, L., and C. Petrie. *The History of Spain*. London: Eyre and Spottiswoode, 1934.

Best, Edward. "An Alternative American Policy for Nicaragua." *Survival* March/April 1987. International Institute for Strategic Studies.

Besterman, Theodore. *Voltaire*. London: Longmans, Green, 1969.

Béthouart, Hilaire. "Combat Helicopters in Algeria." In Greene, T.N., ed., op. cit.

Bianchi, A. See Seers, D.

Bigelow, John. *Principles of Strategy*. Philadelphia: J.B. Lippincott, 1894.

Billias, George A., ed. *George Washington's Opponents*. New York: William Morrow, 1969.

Bird, M.J. *The Secret Battalion*. London: Muller, 1965.

Bishop, Patrick, and Eamonn Mallie, *The Provisional IRA*. London: William Heinemann, 1987.

Black, Eugene R. *Alternative in Southeast Asia*. London: Pall Mall Press, 1969.

Blair, C.N.M. *Guerrilla Warfare*. London: Public Records Office WO 231/80.

Blanch, Leslie. *The Sabres of Paradise*. London: John Murray, 1960.

Blaufarb, Douglas E. *Counterinsurgency Era: U.S. Doctrine and Performance. 1950 to the Present*. New York: The Free Press, 1977.

Bleicher, Hugo. *Colonel Henri's Story*, ed. Ian Colvin. London: William Kimber, 1954.

Blow, Rex. "With the Filipino Guerrillas." *Australian Army Journal*, 1966.

Bohannan, C.T.R. See Valeriano, N.D.

Bohlen, C.E. *The Transformation of American Foreign Policy*. New York: W.W. Norton, 1969.

Bonner, Raymond. *Weakness and Deceit: U.S. Policy and El Salvador*. New York: Times Books, 1984.

Boswell, James. *The Journal of a Tour to Corsica; and Memoirs of Pascal Paoli*, with an Introduction by Morchard Bishop. ed. London: Williams and Norgate, 1951.

Bouchier, E.S. *Spain Under the Roman Empire*. Oxford: Blackwell, 1914.

Boyle, Andrew. *Trenchard*. London: Collins, 1962.

Brandon, Henry. *Anatomy of Error: The Secret History of the Vietnam War*. London: André Deutsch, 1970.

Brett-James, Antony. *Wellington at War 1794–1815*. London: Macmillan, 1961.

Bridgland, Fred. *Jonas Savimbi: A Key to Africa*. Edinburgh: Mainstream Publishing, 1986.

Brown, Malcolm, and Julie Cave. *A Touch of Genius*. London: J.M. Dent, 1988.

Browne, Malcolm. "Why South Viet Nam's Army Won't Fight." *True* magazine, October 1967.

Bruce, Steve, "Northern Ireland: Reappraising Loyalist Values." *Conflict Studies Number 249*, March 1992. Institute for the Study of Conflict.

Brzezinski, Zbigniew. *Power and Principle: Memoirs of the National Security Adviser (1977–1981)*. New York: Farrar, Straus and Giroux, 1983.

Bucher, Lloyd M. *Bucher: My Story*. Garden City, N.Y.: Doubleday, 1970.

Bullitt, W.C. "A Report to the American People on China." *Life,* October 13, 1947.

1216

Bundy, McGeorge. "The End of Either/Or." *Foreign Affairs,* June 1967.

Bundy, William P., "The Path to Vietnam." *Survival,* October 1967. International Institute of Strategic Studies.

Burchett, W.G. *Vietnam: Inside Story of the Guerrilla War.* New York: International Publishers, 1965.

Burn, A.R. *Alexander the Great.* New York: Macmillan, 1947.

———. *Persia and the Greeks.* London: Edward Arnold, 1962.

Burne, A.H. *The Agincourt War.* London: Eyre and Spottiswoode, 1956.

———. *The Crecy War.* London: Eyre and Spottiswoode, 1955.

Burton, Sandra. "Aquino's Philippines: The Center Holds." *Foreign Affairs, America and the World, 1986.*

Bury, J.B. *A History of the Eastern Roman Empire.* London: Macmillan, 1912.

———. *A History of Greece: To the Death of Alexander the Great.* London: Macmillan, 1959.

———. *History of the Later Roman Empire,* 2 vols. London: Macmillan, 1923.

Bushell, A.H. "Insurgency and the Numbers Game," *Army Quarterly,* April 1967.

Butler, J.R.M. *History of the Second World War, Grand Strategy,* Vol. 2. London: Her Majesty's Stationery Office, 1957.

Butterfield, Fox. See Sheehan, Neil.

Buttinger, Joseph. *Vietnam: A Dragon Embattled,* Vol. 1 of 2 vols. New York: Frederick A. Praeger, 1967.

Byford-Jones, W. *Grivas and the Story of EOKA.* London: Robert Hale, 1959.

Cabezas, Omar. *Fire from the Mountain: The Making of a Sandinista.* New York: Crown, 1985.

Caesar, Julius. *Commentaries on the Gallic War.* 2 vols, tr. T. Rice Holmes. London: Macmillan, 1908.

Caird, L.H. *The History of Corsica.* London: Unwin, 1899.

Callinan, Bernard. *Independent Company.* London: William Heinemann, 1953.

Callwell, C.E. *Small Wars: Their Principles and Practice.* London: Her Majesty's Stationery Office, 1899.

———. *The Armed Strength of Roumania.* London: Her Majesty's Stationery Office, 1888.

———. *Hints on Reconnaissances in Little Known Countries.* London: Her Majesty's Stationery Office, 1890.

———. *Handbook of the Armies of the Minor Balkan States.* London: Her Majesty's Stationery Office, 1891.

———. *Handbook of the Turkish Army.* London: Her Majesty's Stationery Office, 1892.

Calvert, Michael. *Prisoners of Hope.* London: Jonathan Cape, 1952.

Calvert, Peter. *The Mexican Revolution, 1910–1914: The Diplomacy of Anglo-American Conflict.* London: Cambridge University Press, 1968.

Cameron, James. *The African Revolution.* New York: Random House, 1961.

Campbell, Arthur. *Jungle Green.* London: Allen and Unwin, 1953.

Campbell, John Franklin. " 'What Is to Be Done?' Gigantism in Washington." *Foreign Affairs,* October 1970.

Cannon, Lou. *President Reagan: The Role of a Lifetime.* New York: Simon and Schuster, 1991.

Cannon, M.H. *The War in the Pacific—Leyte: Return to the Philippines.* Washington, D.C.: U.S. Government Printing Office, 1954.

Capps, Walter. *The Vietnam Reader.* New York: Routledge, 1991.

Caputo, Philip. *A Rumor of War.* New York: Holt, Rinehart and Winston, 1977.

Carr, E.H. *Karl Marx: A Study in Fanaticism.* London: J.M. Dent and Sons, 1934.

———. *Studies in Revolution.* London: Macmillan, 1950.

Carr, Raymond. "Spain and Portugal—1793 to c. 1840." *The New Cambridge Modern History,* Vol. 9 of 12 vols. London: Cambridge University Press, 1965.

Carter, James. *Keeping Faith: Memoirs of a President.* New York: Bantam Books, 1982.

Carver, George A., Jr. "The Real Revolution in South Viet Nam." *Foreign Affairs,* April 1965.

Casella, Alessandro. "The Militant Mood." *Far Eastern Review,* May 16, 1968.

Castanáneda, Jorge 6. *Utopia Unarmed: The Latin America Left After the Cold War.* New York: Alfred A. Knopf, 1993.

Caulaincourt, Duke of Vicenza. *Memoirs,* 3 vols., ed. Jean Hanoteau, tr. Hamish Miles. London: Cassell, 1950.

Cave, Julie. See Brown, Malcolm.

Chanda, Navan. *Brother Enemy: The War After the War.* New York: Collier Books, 1986.

Chapelle, Dickey. "How Castro Won." In Greene, T.N., ed., op. cit.

Chapman, Leonard. "Remarks." U.S. Marine Corps release, n.d.

Charters, David A. *The British Army and Jewish Insurgency in Palestine 1945–1947.* London: Macmillan, 1989.

Charles, First Marquis Cornwallis. *Correspondence,* Vol. 1 of 3 vols., ed. Charles Ross. London: John Murray, 1859.

Chauvet, P. See Deschamps, H.

Cheetham, Sir Nicolas. *A History of Mexico.* London: Rupert Hart-Davis, 1970.

Cheshire, H.T. "The Great Tartar Invasion of Europe." *The Slavonic Review,* Vol. 5. London, 1926.

Chester, Edmund A. *A Sergeant Named Batista.* New York: Henry Holt, 1954.

Chorley, K.C. *Armies and the Art of Revolution.* London: Faber and Faber, 1943.

Christiansen, Eric. *The Origins of Military Power in Spain—1800–1854.* London: Oxford University Press, 1967.

Churchill, Peter. *Of Their Own Choice.* London: Hodder and Stoughton, 1952.

Churchill, Randolph S. *Winston S. Churchill,* Vol. 1 of 2 vols. London: William Heinemann, 1966.

Churchill, Winston S. *Marlborough:—His Life and Times,* Vol. 1 of 2 vols. London: G.C. Harrap, 1933.

———. *The World Crisis,* Vol. 5. London: Thornton Butterworth, 1929.

Clark, Mark W. *From the Danube to the Yalu.* New York: Harper and Brothers, 1954.

Clark, Ramsey. "On Violence, Peace and the Rule of Law." *Foreign Affairs,* October 1970.

Clark, R.W. *The Birth of a Bomb.* London: Phoenix House, 1961.

Clarke, H.B. *Modern Spain 1815–1898.* London: Cambridge University Press, 1906.

Clausewitz, Carl von. *The Campaign of 1812 in Russia.* London: John Murray, 1843.

———. *On War,* Vol. 2 of 3 vols., tr. J.J. Graham. London: Routledge and Kegan Paul, 1968.

Clement, David A. "Le May: Study in Counter-Insurgency." *Marine Corps Gazette,* July 1967.

Clery, C.F. *Minor Tactics.* London: Kegan Paul, Trench, 1887.

Clifford, Clark M. "A Viet Nam Reappraisal: The Personal History of One Man's View and How It Evolved," *Foreign Affairs,* July 1969.

———. *Counselor to the President: A Memoir.* New York: Random House, 1991.

Clinton, Sir Henry. See Willcox, William B.

Clutterbuck, Richard L. *The Long Long War—Counter-Insurgency in Malaya and Vietnam.* New York: Frederick A. Praeger, 1966.

———. "Peru: How to Defeat SL?" *Army Quarterly and Defense Journal,* October 1992.

———. *International Crisis and Conflict.* London: Macmillan, 1993.

———. *Guerrillas and Terrorists.* Athens, Ohio: Ohio University Press, 1980.

———. *Living With Terrorism.* New Rochelle, N.Y.: Arlington House, 1975.

———. *Conflict and Violence in Singapore and Malaysia 1945–1983.* Singapore: Graham Brash (PTE), 1984.

————. *Protest and the Urban Guerrilla*. New York: Abelard-Schuman, 1974.

————. *Kidnap, Hijack and Extortion*. London: Macmillan, 1987.

————. *Terrorism and Guerrilla Warfare*. London and New York: Routledge, 1990.

————. *International Crisis and Conflict*. London: Macmillan, 1993.

Cobban, Helena. *The Palestinian Liberation Organisation: People, Power and Politics*. Cambridge, U.K.: Cambridge University Press, 1989.

Cohan, Leon. "Intelligence and Viet-Nam." *Marine Corps Gazette*, February 1966.

Cole, D.H., and E.C. Priestley. *An Outline of British Military History, 1660–1936*. London: Sifton Praed, 1936.

Collier, Ellen C. See Library of Congress.

Colonial Office (Corfield, F.D.). *Historical Survey of the Origin and Growth of Mau Mau*. London: Her Majesty's Stationery Office, 1960. (Command Paper 1030.)

Commager, Henry Steele. "A Limit to Presidential Power?" *The New Republic*. Quoted in International Institute for Strategic Studies, *Survival*, July 1968.

————. See Morison, S.E.

Coogan, Tim P. *Michael Collins*. London: Hutchinson, 1990.

Cookridge, E.H. *Inside SOE: The Story of Special Operations in Western Europe 1940–45*. London: Arthur Barker, 1966.

Cooper, Chester L. *The Lost Crusade: The Full Story of U.S. Involvement in Vietnam from Roosevelt to Nixon*. London: MacGibbon and Kee, 1970.

Corfield, F.D. See Colonial Office.

Cornwallis, First Marquis. See Charles.

Corson, William R. *The Betrayal*. New York: W.W. Norton, 1968.

Costigan, G. "The Anglo-Irish Conflict, 1919–1922." *University Review*, Dublin, Spring 1968.

Cowell, Alan. *Wars of Power and Freedom from Zaire to South Africa*. New York: Simon and Schuster, 1992.

Crosthwaite, Charles. *The Pacification of Burma*. London: Edward Arnold, 1912.

Cumberland, Charles C. *Mexico: The Struggle for Modernity*. New York: Oxford University Press, 1968.

Dallin, Alexander. *German Rule in Russia, 1941–1945*. London: Macmillan and Co., 1957.

————, R. Mavrogordato, and W. Moll. "Partisan Psychological Warfare and Popular Attitudes." In Armstrong, op. cit.

Dalton, H. *The Fateful Years*. London: Muller, 1957.

Davidson, Basil. *Partisan Picture*. London: Bedford Books, 1946.

————. *Africa in Modern History. The Search for a New Society*. London: Allen Lane, 1978.

————, Lionel Cliffe, and B. H. Selassie, eds. *Behind the War in Eritrea*. London: Spokesman, 1980.

Davidson, Phillip B. *Vietnam at War: The History: 1946–1975*. London: Sidgwick and Jackson, 1988.

Davies, Edmund F. *Illyrian Venture: The Story of the British Military Mission to Enemy-Occupied Albania 1943–1944*. London: Bodley Head, 1952.

Davis, Leonard. *Revolutionary Struggle in the Philippines*. London: Macmillan Press, 1989.

Deakin, F.W.D. *The Embattled Mountain*. London: Oxford University Press, 1971.

Deakin, James. "Big Brass Lambs." *Esquire*, December 1967.

Dean, John W. III. *Blind Ambition: The White House Years*. New York: Simon and Schuster, 1975.

De Beer, Gavin. *Alps and Elephants: Hannibal's March*. London: Geoffrey Bles, 1955.

————. *The Struggle for Power in the Mediterranean*. London: Thames and Hudson, 1969.

Debray, Régis. *Revolution in the Revolution?—Armed Struggle and Political Strug-*

gle in Latin America. New York: Monthly Review Press, 1967.

de Gaulle, Charles. *Memoirs of Hope,* Volume 1 of 2 vols., tr. Terence Kilmartin. London: Weidenfeld and Nicolson, 1970.

———. *The War Memoirs of Charles de Gaulle,* Vol. 3, *Salvation 1944–1946,* tr. R. Howar. New York: Simon and Schuster, 1960.

Deschamps, H., and P. Chauvet. *Gallieni Pacificateur.* Paris: Presses Universitaires de France, 1949.

Devillers, Philippe, and Jean Lacouture. *End of a War: Indochina, 1954.* New York: Frederick A. Praeger, 1969.

Devine, Alex. *Montenegro in History, Politics and War.* London: T. Fisher Unwin, 1918.

DeWitt, K. See Armstrong, J.A.

DeWitt, K., and W. Moll. "The Bryansk Area." In Armstrong, op. cit.

Dickey, Christopher. "Central America: From Quagmire to Cauldron?" *Foreign Affairs, America and the World, 1983.*

Dictionary of National Biography 1922–30. London: Oxford University Press, 1937.

Dodge, T.A. *Hannibal,* vol. 1 of 2 vols. Boston: Houghton Mifflin, 1891.

Donovan, James A. *Militarism, U.S.A.* New York: Charles Scribner's Sons, 1970.

Donovan, James A. See Shoup, David M.

Douhet, Giulio. *The Command of the Air,* tr. D. Ferrari. London: Faber and Faber, 1943.

Dowas, Frederick. *The Killing Zone: My Life in the Vietnam War.* New York: W.W. Norton, 1978.

Draper, Theodore. *Castroism: Theory and Practice.* London: Pall Mall Press, 1965.

———. *Castro's Revolution: Myths and Realities.* London: Thames and Hudson, 1962.

Duncan, Donald. *The New Legions.* New York: Random House, 1967.

Duncan, H.L. "Does China Want War?" *Army Quarterly,* July 1967.

Duncanson, Dennis J. *Government and Revolution in Vietnam.* London: Oxford University Press, 1968.

———. "The Vitality of the Viet Cong." *Encounter,* December 1966.

———. See Tanham, George K.

Durrell, Lawrence. *Bitter Lemons.* London: Faber and Faber, 1959.

Earle, E.E., ed. *Makers of Modern Strategy.* Princeton, N.J.: Princeton University Press, 1941.

Eden, Anthony. *The Memoirs of Anthony Eden: Full Circle.* Boston: Houghton Mifflin, 1960.

———. *Towards Peace in Indo-China.* London: Oxford University Press, 1966.

Éditions G.P. *La Merveilleuse Histoire de l'Armée Française.* Paris, 1947.

Edmonds, James E. "Jomini and Clausewitz." *Army Quarterly,* April 1951.

Ehrlich, Blake. *The French Resistance.* London: Chapman and Hall, 1966.

Eisenhower, Dwight D. *Mandate for Change 1953–1956.* London: William Heinemann, 1963.

———. *Waging Peace 1956–1961.* London: William Heinemann, 1966.

Eldridge, F. *Wrath in Burma.* New York: Doubleday, 1946.

Ellsberg, Daniel. *Escalating in a Quagmire.* Boston: Center for International Studies, MIT, 1970.

Encyclopaedia Britannica, 33 vols. Chicago: Encyclopaedia Britannica, 1991.

Enthoven, Alain C., and K. Wayne Smith. *How Much Is Enough?* New York: Harper and Row, 1971.

Evans, D.L. "Civil Affairs in Vietnam," *Marine Corps Gazette,* March 1968.

Fagg, J.E. *Latin America: A General History.* London: Macmillan, 1969.

Falk, Pamela S. "Cuba in Africa." *Foreign Affairs,* Summer 1987.

Fall, Bernard. *Hell in a Very Small Place: The Siege of Dien Bien Phu.* London: Pall Mall Press, 1967.

————. *Street Without Joy.* London: Pall Mall Press, 1963.

————. *The Two Viet-Nams: A Political and Military Analysis.* London: Pall Mall Press, 1963.

————. "Viet Nam in the Balance." *Foreign Affairs,* October 1966.

Fallaci, Oriana. *Interview with History,* tr. John Shepley. New York: Liveright, 1976.

Falls, Cyril. *A Hundred Years of War.* London: Gerald Duckworth, 1953.

————. See MacMunn, G.

Fellowes-Gordon, Ian. *Amiable Assassins: The Story of the Kachin Guerrillas of North Burma.* London: Robert Hale, 1957.

Fergusson, Bernard. *Beyond the Chindwin.* London: Collins, 1962.

————. *Trumpet in the Hall.* London: Collins, 1970.

————. *The Wild Green Earth.* London: Collins, 1946.

Finnegan, William. *A Complicated War. The Harrowing of Mozambique.* Berkeley, Calif.: University of California Press, 1993.

Fischer, Louis. *The Story of Indonesia.* New York: Harper and Row, 1959.

Fisher, H.A.L. *Europe: Ancient and Medieval.* London: Eyre and Spottiswoode, 1938.

Fitzgerald, Frances. *Fire in the Lake.* London: Macmillan, 1972.

Fitzgibbon, Constantine. *Out of the Lion's Paw.* London: MacDonald, 1970.

Fletcher, Arnold. *Afghanistan Highway of Conquest.* Ithaca, N.Y.: Cornell University Press, 1965.

Foley, Charles. *Island in Revolt.* London: Longmans, Green, 1962.

————, and W.I. Scobie. *The Struggle for Cyprus.* Stanford, Calif.: Hoover Institution Press, 1975.

Foot, M.R.D. *SOE in France.* London: Her Majesty's Stationery Office, 1966.

————. *Resistance: An Analysis of European Resistance to Nazism 1940–1945.* London: Eyre Methuen, 1976.

Ford, Gerald R. *A Time to Heal: The Autobiography of Gerald R. Ford.* London: W.H. Allen, 1979.

Fortescue, John. *Wellington.* London: Ernest Benn, 1925.

Fox, Guy. See Scigliano, Robert.

Fox, Robin Lane. *Alexander the Great.* London: Allen Lane, 1973.

Franke, Wolfgang. "The Taiping Rebellion." In Franz Schurmann, op. cit.

Frédéric II, *Oeuvres (Histoire de Mon Temps),* Vol. 2 of 30 vols., ed. J.D.E. Preuss. Berlin: Decker, 1846.

————. *Oeuvres (Militaires),* Vols. 28 and 30 of 30 vols., ed. J.D.E Preuss. Berlin: Decker, 1856.

Frizzell, Donaldson D. See Thompson, W. Scott.

Fulbright, J. William. "In Thrall to Fear." *The New Yorker,* January 8, 1972.

————, ed. *The Vietnam Hearings.* New York: Vintage Books, 1966.

Fuller, J.F.C. *British Light Infantry in the Eighteenth Century.* London: Hutchinson, 1925.

————. *The Conduct of War, 1789–1961.* New Brunswick, N.J.: Rutgers University Press, 1961.

————. *The Decisive Battles of the Western World,* Vols. 1 and 2 of 3 vols. London: Eyre and Spottiswoode, 1956.

————. *The Generalship of Alexander the Great.* London: Eyre and Spottiswoode, 1958.

Furneaux, Rupert. *Abdel Krim: Emir of the Rif.* London: Secker and Warburg, 1967.

Galay, N. "The Partisan Forces." In Liddell Hart, B., ed., *The Soviet Army,* op. cit.

Galbraith, John K. *How to Get Out of Vietnam.* New York: Signet, 1967.

Gallery, Daniel V. *The Pueblo Incident.* Garden City, N.Y.: Doubleday, 1970.

Gallieni, General. *La Pacification de Madagascar (Opérations d'Octobre 1896 à Mars 1899).* Paris: Librairie Militaire R. Chapelot, 1900.

García, Mauro. *Documents on the Japanese Occupation of the Philippines.* Manila: Philippines Historical Association, 1965.

Gardner, Brian. *German East.* London: Cassell, 1963.

Garnett, David, ed. *The Letters of T.E. Lawrence,* London: Jonathan Cape, 1927.

Garthoff, R.L. *Soviet Military Doctrine.* Glencoe, Ill.: The Free Press, 1953.

Gavin, James. *Crisis Now.* New York: Random House, 1968.

———. "A Soldier's Doubts." *Harper's Magazine,* February 1966.

Gaxotte, Pierre. *Frederick the Great.* London: G. Bell and Sons, 1941.

Gettleman, Marvin E., ed. *Viet-Nam: History, Documents, and Opinions on a Major World Crisis.* New York: Fawcett, 1965.

Gheusi, P.B. *Gallieni et Madagascar.* Paris: Éditions du Petit Parisien, n.d.

Giap, Vo Nguyen. *Big Victory, Great Task.* New York: Frederick A. Praeger, 1968.

———. *People's War, People's Army.* New York: Frederick A. Praeger, 1967.

———. "The Strategic Role of the Self-Defense Militia Force in the Great Anti-U.S. National Salvation Struggle of our People." Foreign Broadcast Information Service, April 1967.

Gilbert, Felix. "Machiavelli: The Renaissance of the Art of War." In Earle, op cit.

Gillespie, Joan. *Algeria: Rebellion and Revolution.* London: Ernest Benn, 1960.

Gilpatric, Roswell W. "Vietnam and World War III." *New York Times,* May 30, 1965.

Giraldus Cambrensis. *The Autobiography of Giraldus Cambrensis,* ed. and tr. H.E. Butler. London: Jonathan Cape, 1937.

Giskes, H.L. *London Calling North Pole.* London: Arthur Barker, 1966.

Gleijeses, Piero. "The Case for Power Sharing in El Salvador." *Foreign Affairs,* Summer, 1983.

Goldenberg, Boris. *The Cuban Revolution and Latin America.* London: Allen and Unwin, 1965.

Goode, Stephen. *Guerrilla Warfare and Terrorism.* New York: F. Watts, 1977.

Goodhart, Philip. See Henderson, Ian.

Goodrich, L.C. *A Short History of the Chinese People.* London: Allen and Unwin, 1969.

Gordon, C.D. *The Age of Attila.* Ann Arbor, Mich.: University of Michigan Press, 1960.

Gowers, Andrew, and Tony Walker. *Behind the Myth: Yasser Arafat and the Palestinian Revolution.* London: W.H. Allen, 1990.

Grant, Zalin. "What Are We Doing in Thailand?" *The New Republic,* May 24, 1969.

———. *Facing the Phoenix: The CIA and the Political Defeat of the United States in Vietnam.* New York: W.W. Norton, 1991.

Graves, Robert. *Lawrence and the Arabs.* London: Jonathan Cape, 1927.

Greene, Graham. *The Quiet American.* London: William Heinemann, 1955.

Greene, T.N., ed. *The Guerrilla and How to Fight Him.* New York: Frederick A. Praeger, 1962.

Grier, S.L. "Black Pajama Intelligence." *Marine Corps Gazette,* April 1967.

Griffith, Samuel B. *The Battle for Guadalcanal.* Philadelphia: J.B. Lippincott, 1963.

———. *The Chinese People's Liberation Army.* New York: McGraw-Hill, 1967.

———. "Guerrilla." *Marine Corps Gazette,* August 1950.

———. *Sun Tzu: The Art of War.* London: Oxford University Press, 1963.

———. *In Defense of the Publick Liberty.* London: Jonathan Cape, 1977.

Grivas, George. *General Grivas on Guerrilla Warfare,* tr. A.S. Pallis. New York: Frederick A. Praeger, 1965.

———. *The Memoirs of General Grivas,* ed. Charles Foley. New York: Frederick A. Praeger, 1964.

Grossman, David, "Guests Can Be Shown the Door." *New York Times Magazine,* December 13, 1992.

———. *Sleeping on a Wire: Conversations with Palestinians in April,* tr. Haim Watzman. New York: Farrar, Straus and Giroux, 1992.

Groves, Leslie. *Now It Can Be Told.* London: André Deutsch, 1963.

Guedalla, Philip. *Wellington.* New York: Harper and Brothers, 1931.

Guevara, Ernesto Che. *Bolivian Diary,* tr. Carlos Hansen and Andrew Sinclair. London: Jonathan Cape, 1968.

————. *Che Guevara on Guerrilla Warfare,* ed. Harries-Clichy Peterson. New York: Frederick A. Praeger, 1961.

————. *Che Guevara Speaks: Selected Speeches and Writings,* ed. George Lavan. New York: Grove Press, 1967.

————. *Reminiscences of the Cuban Revolutionary War,* tr. V. Ortiz. New York: Grove Press, 1963.

Gurtov, Melvin. *The First Vietnam Crisis: Chinese Communist Strategy and United States Involvement 1953–1954.* New York: Columbia University Press, 1967.

Hackworth, David. *About Face.* New York: Simon and Schuster, 1989.

Haig, Alexander. *Caveat.* New York: Macmillan, 1983.

Halberstam, David. *The Making of a Quagmire.* New York: Random House, 1965.

————. *The Best and the Brightest.* New York: Random House, 1972.

Haldeman, H.R., with Joseph DiMona. *The Ends of Power.* New York: Times Books, 1978.

Hall, D.G.E. "Thailand (History)." *Encyclopaedia Britannica,* Vol. 21. 1968.

Halperin, Ernst. *Terrorism in Latin America.* Beverly Hills, Calif.: Sage Publications, 1976.

Hamill, Desmond. *Pig in the Middle: The Army in Northern Ireland 1969–1984.* London: Methuen, 1985.

Hammer, Ellen J. "Genesis of the First Indochina War: 1946–1950." In Gettleman, op. cit.

————. *The Struggle for Indochina 1940–1955.* Stanford, Calif.: Stanford University Press, 1966.

Hammond, J.W. "Combat Journal." *Marine Corps Gazette,* July and August 1968.

Hargreaves, Reginald. *Beyond the Rubicon.* New York: New American Library, 1966.

Harries, Owen. "Should the U.S. Withdraw from Asia?" *Foreign Affairs,* October 1968.

Harrison, H.D. *The Soul of Yugoslavia.* London: Hodder and Stoughton, 1941.

Harrison, John A. *China Since 1800.* New York: Harcourt, Brace and World, 1967.

Harrison, J.P. *The Endless War: Fifty Years of Struggle in Vietnam.* New York: The Free Press, 1982.

Hart, Douglas M., "Low Intensity Conflict in Afghanistan: The Soviet View." *Survival,* March/April 1982. International Institute for Strategic Studies.

Hart, Robert. *These from the Land of Sinim: Essays on the Chinese Question.* London: Chapman and Hall, 1903.

Harvey, Frank. *Air War: Vietnam.* New York: Bantam Books, 1967.

Haukelid, Knut. *Skis Against the Atom.* London: William Kimber, 1954.

Hayes-McCoy, G.A. *Irish Battles.* London: Longmans, Green, 1969.

Heelis, J.E. "Triumph in Malaysia." *Marine Corps Gazette,* January 1967.

Heilbrunn, Otto. "Counter-Insurgency Intelligence." *Marine Corps Gazette,* September 1966.

————. "Counter-Insurgency Tactics: A Question of Priorities." *Army Quarterly,* January 1967.

————. *Warfare in the Enemy's Rear.* New York: Frederick A. Praeger, 1963.

Heinl, Robert D. *Soldiers of the Sea.* Annapolis, Md.: U.S. Naval Institute, 1962.

————. "The Armed Forces: Are They 'Near Collapse'?" Detroit *Sunday News,* May 23, 1971.

Hemingway, Ernest. *For Whom the Bell Tolls.* London: Penguin Books, 1955.

Hemphill, Marie de Kiewiet. "The British Sphere 1884–94." In Oliver and Mathew, eds., op cit.

Henderson, G.F.R. *Stonewall Jackson and the American Civil War.* London: Longmans, Green, 1961.

Henderson, Ian, with Philip Goodhart. *The Hunt for Kimathi.* London: Hamish Hamilton, 1958.

Henderson, William. "South Vietnam Finds Itself." *Foreign Affairs,* January 1957.

Henisart, Paul. *Wolves in the City. The Death of French Algeria.* London: Rupert Hart-Davis, 1970.

Heren, Louis. *No Hail, No Farewell.* London: Weidenfeld and Nicolson, 1971.

Herodotus. *The History of Herodotus,* Vol. 1 of 2 vols., ed. A.J. Grant, tr. George Rawlinson. London: John Murray, 1897.

Herr, Michael. *Dispatches.* New York: Alfred A. Knopf, 1978.

Herring, George C. *America's Longest War: The United States and Vietnam, 1950–1975.* New York: John Wiley and Sons, 1979.

———. "America and Vietnam: The Unending War." *Foreign Affairs,* Winter 1991/92.

Herring, H.A. *A History of Latin America.* London: Jonathan Cape, 1955.

Hersh, Seymour M. "Coverup." *The New Yorker,* January 22 and January 29, 1972.

———. "My Lai 4." *Harper's Magazine,* May 1970.

———. *The Price of Power: Kissinger in the Nixon White House.* New York: Summit Books, 1983.

Heymann, Frederick G. *John Ziska and the Hussite Revolution.* Princeton, N.J.: Princeton University Press, 1955.

Hiebert, Murray. "Pessimism for Peace." *Far Eastern Economic Review,* May 30, 1991.

Higgins, Marguerite. *Our Vietnam Nightmare.* New York: Harper and Row, 1965.

Hilsman, Roger. *To Move a Nation: The Politics of Foreign Policy in the Administration of John F. Kennedy.* Garden City, N.Y.: Doubleday, 1967.

Ho Chi Minh. *Prison Diary,* tr. Aileen Palmer. Hanoi: Foreign Languages Publishing House, 1962.

———. *Ho Chi Minh on Revolution. Selected Writings 1920–1966,* tr. Bernard Fall. New York: Frederick A. Praeger, 1967.

———. *Ho Chi Minh: Selected Articles and Speeches, 1920–1967,* ed. Jack Woddis. London: Lawrence and Wishart, 1969.

Ho Kan-chih. "Rise of the Working Class Movement." In Schurmann, op. cit.

Hodges, D.C., ed. *Philosophy of the Urban Guerrilla: The Revolutionary Writings of Abraham Guillén.* New York: William Morrow, 1973.

Hodgkin, Thomas. *Vietnam: The Revolutionary Path.* London: Macmillan, 1981.

Holt, Edgar. *Protest in Arms: The Irish Troubles 1916–1923.* London: Putnam, 1960.

Hoopes, Townsend. *The Limits of Intervention.* New York: McKay, 1969.

Hoover Institution on War, Revolution, and Peace. *France During the German Occupation, 1940–1944,* 3 vols., tr. P.W. Whitcomb, Stanford, Calif.: Stanford University Press, 1957.

Hordern, Charles. *Military Operations East Africa 1914–1916,* Vol. 1. London: Her Majesty's Stationery Office, 1941.

Horne, Alistair. *A Savage War of Peace: Algeria 1954–1962.* London: Macmillan, 1977.

Horowitz, David. *Containment and Revolution.* Boston: Beacon Press, 1967.

Hosmer, S.T. (Chairman). *Counterinsurgency: A Symposium—April 16–20, 1962.* Santa Monica, Calif.: RAND Corporation, 1963.

Howard, Michael. "Jomini and the Classical Tradition in Military Thought." *Studies in War and Peace.* London: Maurice Temple Smith, 1970.

Howard-Johnston, James. "Studies in the Organization of the Byzantine Army in the Tenth and Eleventh Centuries," Ph.D. thesis. Oxford: 1971.

Howe, Sonia E. *Lyautey of Morocco.* London: Hodder and Stoughton, 1931.

Hoyt, Robert S. *Europe in the Middle Ages.* New York: Harcourt, Brace and Company, 1957.

————. *Life and Thought in the Early Middle Ages.* Minneapolis: University of Minnesota Press, 1967.

Htin Aung, Maung. *A History of Burma.* New York: Columbia University Press, 1967.

————. *The Stricken Peacock: Anglo-Burmese Relations 1752–1948.* The Hague: Martinus Nijhoff, 1965.

Huberman, Leo, and Paul Sweezy. *Cuba: Anatomy of a Revolution.* London: Routledge and Kegan Paul, 1960.

Hughes, Richard. "After Ho, Watch for Giap and a Tougher Line in Hanoi." *The Sunday Times* (London), September 7, 1969.

Hull, Cordell. *Memoirs.* New York: Macmillan, 1948.

Ibarruri, Dolores. *They Shall Not Pass.* London: Lawrence and Wishart, 1966.

Insor, D. Thailand. *A Political, Social and Economic Analysis.* London: Allen and Unwin, 1963.

Institute for the Study of Conflict. "Ulster: Politics and Terrorism." *Conflict Studies No. 36.* London: June 1973.

————. Janke, Peter. "Ulster: Consensus and Coercion." *Conflict Studies No. 50.* London: October 1974.

————. "Ulster: A Decade of Violence." *Conflict Studies No. 108.* London: June, 1979.

————. "Spanish Separatism: ETA's Threat to Basque Democracy." *Conflict Studies No. 123:* London: October 1980.

International Institute for Strategic Studies. *Strategic Survey, 1968–92.*

————. *Survival, 1975–92.*

————. "The Lessons of the Soviet/Afghan War." Adelphi Paper 259, Summer 1991.

Isaacs, Arnold R. *Without Honor. Defeat in Vietnam and Cambodia.* Baltimore: Johns Hopkins University Press, 1983.

Isaacs, Harold. *The Tragedy of the Chinese Revolution.* Stanford, Calif.: Stanford University Press, 1962.

Isaacson, Walter. *Kissinger: A Biography.* New York: Simon and Schuster, 1992.

Ivanov, Miroslav. *The Assassination of Heydrich,* tr. Patrick O'Brian. London: Hart-Davis, MacGibbon, 1974.

Izady, Mehrdad R. *The Kurds: A Concise Handbook.* London: Crane Russak, 1992.

Jackson, Geoffrey. *People's Prison.* London: Faber and Faber, 1973.

Jackson, Joe, "Lawyers, Guns and Money," *Magill Monthly Magazine* (Eire), May 1980.

Jacoby, A. See White, T.H.

James, Daniel. *Che Guevara: A Biography.* London: Allen and Unwin, 1970.

————, ed. *The Complete Bolivian Diaries of Ché Guevara: And Other Captured Documents.* London: Allen and Unwin, 1968.

Janke, Peter. See Institute for the Study of Conflict.

Jaster, Robert S. "The Security Outlook in Mozambique." *Survival,* November/December 1985. International Institute for Strategic Studies.

Jenkins, Brian. "The Unchangeable War," RAND Corporation, n.d.

Johnson, Lyndon B. *Public Papers of the President,* 10 vols. Washington, D.C.: U.S. Government Printing Office, 1965–70.

————. *The Vantage Point: Perspectives of the Presidency.* New York: Holt, Rinehart and Winston, 1971.

Jolly, R. See Seers, D.

Jomini, Baron de. *The Art of War.* Philadelphia: J.B. Lippincott, 1862.

Jules, Roy. *The Battle of Dienbienphu,* tr. Robert Baldich. London: Faber and Faber, 1965.

Jumper, Roy, and M.W. Normand. "Vietnam: The Historical Background." In Gettleman, op. cit.

Just, Ward. *To What End. Report from Vietnam.* Boston: Houghton Mifflin, 1968.

————. *Military Men.* New York: Alfred A. Knopf, 1971.

Kahin, George M. *Nationalism and Revolution in Indonesia.* Ithaca, N.Y.: Cornell University Press, 1952.

————, and John W. Lewis. *The United States in Vietnam: An Analysis in Depth of America's Involvement in Vietnam.* New York: The Dial Press, 1967.

Kahn, Herman. "If Negotiations Fail." *Foreign Affairs,* July 1968.

Kalb, M.L., and E. Abel. *Roots of Involvement: The U.S. in Asia 1784–1971.* New York: W.W. Norton, 1971.

Karnow, Stanley. *Vietnam: A History.* London: Century Publishing, 1983.

————. *In Our Image.* New York: Random House, 1989.

Keesing's Contemporary Archives, 1970–1987.

Keesing's Record of World Events, 1988–present.

Kellen, Konrad. "Fourth Round or Peace in Vietnam?" RAND Corporation, 1968.

Kendall, P. *The Story of Land Warfare.* London: Hamish Hamilton, 1957.

Kennan, George F. *American Diplomacy, 1900–1950.* London: Secker and Warburg, 1952.

————. *The Decision to Intervene.* London: Faber and Faber, 1958.

————. *Memoirs.* London: Hutchinson, 1968.

————. *Russia Leaves the War.* London: Faber and Faber, 1956.

See also x.

Kennedy, John F. *The Strategy of Peace.* New York: Harper and Brothers, 1960.

————. *Public Papers of John F. Kennedy,* Vol. 1 of 2 vols. Washington, D.C.: U.S. Government Printing Office, 1962.

Kenworthy, E. W. See Sheehan, Neil.

Kenyatta, Jomo. *Facing Mount Kenya: The Tribal Life of the Gikuyu.* London: Secker and Warburg, 1938.

Kiernan, Ben. *How Pol Pot Came to Power: A History of Communism in Kampuchea, 1930–1975.* London: Verso, 1985.

Kirby, S.W. *The War Against Japan: The Loss of Singapore.* London: HMSO, 1957.

Kirkpatrick, F.A. *The Spanish Conquistadores.* London: Adam and Charles Black, 1934.

Kissinger, Henry. *Nuclear Weapons and Foreign Policy.* London: Oxford University Press, 1957.

————. *The White House Years.* London: Weidenfeld and Nicolson and Michael Joseph, 1979.

————. *Years of Upheaval.* London: Weidenfeld and Nicolson, 1982.

Kitson, Frank. *Gangs and Counter-Gangs.* London: Barrie and Rockliff, 1960.

————. *Low-Intensity Operations.* London: Faber and Faber, 1971.

————. *Bunch of Five.* London: Faber and Faber, 1977.

Knightly, P., and C. Simpson. *The Secret Lives of Lawrence of Arabia.* London: Nelson, 1969.

Kochan, Lionel. *Russia in Revolution 1890–1918.* London: Weidenfeld and Nicolson, 1966.

Koestler, Arthur. *Promise and Fulfilment: Palestine, 1917–1949.* London: Macmillan, 1949.

Kohl, J., and J. Lift. *Urban Guerrilla Warfare in Latin America.* Cambridge, Mass.: MIT. Press, 1974.

Kovic, Ron. *Born on the Fourth of July.* New York: McGraw-Hill, 1976.

Krausnick, H. *Anatomy of the SS State.* London: Collins, 1968.

Krepinevich, Andrew F., Jr. *The Army and Vietnam.* Baltimore, Md.: Johns Hopkins University Press, 1986.

Kriegel, Richard. "Revolutionary Development." *Marine Corps Gazette,* March 1967.

Krulak, V.H. "Address to Western Newspaper Industrial Relations Bureau . . . ," U.S. Marine Corps release, n.d.

Kun, Ernst, and Joseph Kun. "North Vietnam's Doctrine." *Survival,* February 1965. International Institute for Strategic Studies.

Laber, Jeri, and Barnett Rubin. *A Nation is Dying: Afghanistan Under the Soviets.* Chicago: Northwestern University Press, 1988.

Lacouture, Jean. *Vietnam: Between Two Truces,* tr. K. Kellen and J. Carmichael. London: Secker and Warburg, 1966.

———. *Ho Chi Minh,* tr. Peter Wiles. London: Allen Lane/The Penguin Press, 1968.

Lacroix, Paul. *Military and Religious Life in the Middle Ages and the Renaissance.* London: Bickers and Son, c. 1874.

Lafeber, Walter. *Inevitable Revolution: The United States in Central America.* New York: W.W. Norton, 1983.

Laffan, R.G.D. *Select Documents of European History,* Vol. 1 of 2 vols. London: Methuen, 1930.

Lancaster, Donald. *The Emancipation of French Indochina.* London: Oxford University Press, 1961.

Lansdale, Edward G. "Viet Nam: Do We Understand Revolution?" *Foreign Affairs,* October 1964.

———. "Viet Nam: Still the Search for Goals." *Foreign Affairs,* October 1968.

Lapp, Ralph E. *Arms Beyond Doubt: The Tyranny of Weapons Technology.* Chicago: Cowles Book Company, 1970.

Laqueur, Walter. *The Guerrilla Reader: A Historical Anthology.* New York: The New American Library, 1977.

———. *Terrorism.* Boston: Little, Brown, 1977.

Larteguy, Jean. *The Centurions,* tr. Xan Fielding. London: Hutchinson, 1961.

Lavan, George. See Guevara, Ernesto Che.

Lawrence, T.E. "Guerrilla Warfare." *Encyclopaedia Britannica,* Vol. 10. 1957.

———. *Revolt in the Desert.* London: Jonathan Cape, 1927.

———. *Seven Pillars of Wisdom.* London: Jonathan Cape, 1973.

Leakey, L.S.B. "Colonial Administration from the Native Point of View." *Comparative Methods of Colonial Administration.* London: Chatham House, 1930.

———. *Defeating Mau Mau.* London: Methuen, 1954.

———. *Kenya: Contrasts and Problems.* London: Methuen, 1936.

———. *Mau Mau and the Kikuyu.* London: Methuen, 1952.

———. *White Africa.* London: Hodder and Stoughton, 1937.

Lederer, William. *Our Own Worst Enemy.* New York: W.W. Norton, 1968.

———. *The Ugly American.* New York: W.W. Norton, 1958.

Lees, Michael. *The Rape of Serbia: The British Role in Tito's Grab for Power 1943–1944.* New York: Harcourt Brace Jovanovich, 1991.

Leftwich, William G. "Decision at Duc Co." *Marine Corps Gazette,* February 1967.

Le Moyne, James. "El Salvador's Forgotten War." *Foreign Affairs,* Summer 1989.

Lenin, V.I. *Selected Works,* Vol. 3 of 3 vols. Moscow: Foreign Languages Publishing House, c. 1961.

Leonard, R.A. *A Short Guide to Clausewitz on War.* London: Weidenfeld and Nicolson, 1967.

Leopold, Richard. *The Growth of American Foreign Policy.* New York: Alfred A. Knopf, 1965.

Lettow-Vorbeck, General von. *My Reminiscences of East Africa.* London: Hurst and Blackett, 1920.

Lewis, John W. See Kahin, George M.

Lewy, Guenter. *America in Vietnam.* New York: Oxford University Press, 1978.

Li, D.J. *The Ageless Chinese.* New York: Charles Scribner's Sons, 1965.

Library of Congress, Congressional Research Service. "Instances of Use of United States Armed Forces Abroad, 1798–1989," ed. Ellen C. Collier. Washington, D.C.: Congressional Research Service, 1989.

———. *U.S. Low-Intensity Conflicts 1899–1990.* Washington D.C.: U.S. Government Printing Office, 1990.

Liddell Hart, B.H. *The Decisive Wars of History: A Study in Strategy*. London: G. Bell and Sons, 1929.

————. *T.E. Lawrence*. London: Jonathan Cape, 1934.

————, ed. *The Soviet Army*. London: Weidenfeld and Nicolson, 1956.

Lift, J. See Kohl, J.

Lilienthal, David E. "Postwar Development in Viet Nam." *Foreign Affairs*, January 1969.

Lippmann, Walter. *The Cold War: A Study in U.S. Foreign Policy, 1947*. New York: Harper and Brothers, 1947.

Lloyd, E.M. *A Review of the History of Infantry*. London: Longmans, Green, 1908.

————. "The Third Coalition." *The Cambridge Modern History*, Vol. 9 of 13 vols. London: Cambridge University Press, 1904.

Lohbeck, Don. *Patrick J. Hurley*. Chicago: Henry Regnery, 1956.

Longford, Elizabeth. *Wellington: The Years of the Sword*. London: Weidenfeld and Nicolson, 1969.

Lorch, Netanel. *The Edge of the Sword: Israel's War of Independence, 1947–1949*. New York: G.P. Putnam's Sons, 1961.

Lowenthal, Richard. "Russia and China: Controlled Conflict." *Foreign Affairs*, April 1971.

Luce, Siméon. *Histoire de Bertrand du Guesclin et de Son Époque*. Paris: Librairie Hachette, 1867.

Lyautey, H. "Du Rôle Social de l'Officier" and "Du Rôle Colonial de l'Armée." *Revue des Deux Mondes* (1891 and 1900).

————. *Lettres du Sud de Madagascar (1900–1902)*. Paris: Librairie Armand Colin, 1935.

————. *Lettres du Tonkin*, 2 vols. Paris: Éditions Nationales, 1928.

————. *Lettres du Tonkin et de Madagascar (1894–1899)*. Paris: Librairie Armand Colin, 1933.

Lyautey, Pierre. *Lyautey L'Africain: Textes et Lettres du Maréchal Lyautey Présentés par Pierre Lyautey*, 4 vols. Paris: Librairie Plon, 1953.

MacDonald, J.R.M. "The Terror." *The Cambridge Modern History*, Vol. 8 of 13 vols. London: Cambridge University Press, 1904.

Mack, R.E. "Ambuscade." *Marine Corps Gazette*, April 1967.

————. "Minbotrap." *Marine Corps Gazette*, July 1967.

Mackenzie, A.M. *Robert Bruce King of Scots*. London: Oliver and Boyd, 1934.

Mackesy, Piers. *The War for America 1775–1783*. London: Longmans, Green, 1964.

Maclean, Fitzroy. *Disputed Barricade*. London: Jonathan Cape, 1957.

————. *Eastern Approaches*. London: Jonathan Cape, 1949.

Maclear, Michael. *The Ten Thousand Day War. Vietnam: 1945–1975*. New York: St. Martin's Press, 1981.

MacMunn, G., and C. Falls. *Military Operations: Egypt and Palestine*, Vols. 1 and 2. London: Her Majesty's Stationery Office, 1928, 1930.

Madariaga, Salvador de. *The Fall of the Spanish American Empire*. London: Hollis and Carter, 1947.

Mahan, A.T. *The Influence of Sea Power upon the French Revolution and Empire 1783–1812*, 2 vols. London: Sampson, Low, Marston, 1892.

————. *The Influence of Sea Power upon History 1660–1783*. London: Sampson, Low, Marston, 1900.

————. *Sea Power in Its Relations to the War of 1812*. London: John Murray, 1829.

Mahon, Lord. *The Life of Belisarius*. London: John Murray, 1829.

Mailer, Norman. *Armies of the Night: History as a Novel. The Novel as History*. New York: New American Library, 1968.

Makinda, Samuel, "Shifting Alliances in the Horn of Africa." *Survival*, January/February 1985. International Institute for Strategic Studies.

Malaya, Department of Information. *Communist Banditry in Malaya*. Kuala Lumpur: Department of Information, n.d.

Malhuret, Claude. "Report from Afghanistan." *Foreign Affairs,* Winter 1983–1984.

Mallie, Eamonn. See Bishop, Patrick.

Mao Tse-tung. *On Guerrilla Warfare,* tr. and with an Introduction by Samuel B. Griffith. New York: Frederick A. Praeger, 1962.

———. *Selected Works,* Vol. 1. Peking: Foreign Languages Press, 1964.

———. *Basic Tactics,* tr. and with an Introduction by Stuart R. Schram. New York: Frederick A. Praeger, 1966.

Marcum, John A. "Angola." *Survival,* January/February 1988. International Institute for Strategic Studies.

Marighela, Carlos. *For the Liberation of Brazil.* London: Penguin, 1971.

———. *The Minimanual of Urban Guerrilla Warfare.* San Francisco: People's Press, 1970.

Markham, Felix. *Napoleon.* London: Weidenfeld and Nicolson, 1963.

Marlowe, John. *The Seat of Pilate: An Account of the Palestine Mandate.* London: Cresset Press, 1959.

Marshal, Bruce. *The White Rabbit.* London: Evans Brothers, 1964.

Marshal, S.L.A. *Battles in the Monsoon.* New York: William Morrow, 1967.

Martin, David. *The Web of Disinformation: Churchill's Yugoslav Blunder.* New York: Harcourt Brace, 1990.

Masaryk, G.T. *The Spirit of Russia,* Vol. 1 of 2 vols. London: Allen and Unwin, 1919.

Mathew, Gervase. See Oliver, Roland.

Matthews, Herbert L. *Castro: A Political Biography.* New York: Simon and Schuster, 1969.

———. *Revolution in Cuba.* New York: Charles Scribner's Sons, 1975.

———. *The Cuban Story.* New York: George Braziller, 1961.

Matthews, Tanya. *Algerian ABC.* London: Geoffrey Chapman, 1961.

Mavrogordato, R., and E. Ziemke. "The Polotsk Lowland." In Armstrong, op. cit.

May, E.S. *A Retrospect on the South African War.* London: Sampson, Low, Marston, 1901.

Mazour, A.G. *Russia: Tsarist and Communist.* New York: D. Van Nostrand, 1962.

McBeth, John. "Electronic Warfare." *Far Eastern Economic Review,* May 23, 1991.

McCarthy, Eugene. *The Limits of Power.* New York: Dell, 1967.

McCuen, John J. *The Art of Counter-Revolutionary War.* London: Faber and Faber, 1966.

McLaren, Moray. *Corsica Boswell.* London: Secker and Warburg, 1966.

McCutcheon, Keith B. "Air Support for III MAF." *Marine Corps Gazette,* August 1967.

McGaffin, William, and Erwin Knoll. *Scandal in the Pentagon: A Challenge to Democracy.* Greenwich, Conn.: Fawcett, 1969.

Mecklin, John. *Mission in Torment.* Garden City, N.Y.: Doubleday, 1965.

Meinertzhagen, R. *Kenya During 1902–1906.* London: Oliver and Boyd, 1957.

Menenger, Charles. *Northern Ireland: The Troubles.* London: Hamlyn, 1985.

Mijatovich, Chedo. *Servia of the Servians.* London: Putnam and Sons, 1911.

Miksche, F.O. *Secret Forces: The Technique of Underground Movements.* London: Faber and Faber, 1950.

Millar, George. *Horned Pigeon.* London: William Heinemann, 1946.

———. *Maquis.* London: William Heinemann, 1945.

Miller, John G. "From a Company Commander's Notebook." *Marine Corps Gazette,* August 1966.

Miller, Judith. "Terrorism around the Mediterranean." *Adelphi Paper No. 230,* Spring 1988. International Institute for Strategic Studies.

Mills, C. Wright. *Castro's Cuba.* London: Secker and Warburg, 1960.

Mitchell, Philip. *African Afterthoughts.* London: Hutchinson, 1954.

Moll, W. See DeWitt, K.

Mollenhoff, Clark R. *The Man Who Pardoned Nixon*. London: St. James Press, 1976.

———. *Game Plan for Disaster: An Ombudsman's Report on the Nixon Years*. New York: W.W. Norton, 1976.

Mommsen, Theodor. *The History of Rome*, Vols. 2 and 3, tr. W.P. Dickson. London: Macmillan and Co., 1906.

Montross, Lynn. *U.S. Marine Operations in Korea 1950–53*, Vol. 3 of 3 vols. Washington, D.C.: U.S. Government Printing Office, 1957.

Moorehead, Alan. *The Russian Revolution*. New York: Harper and Brothers, 1958.

Morison, S.E. *Leyte: June 1944–January 1945*, Vol. 12 of 15 vols. London: Oxford University Press, 1958.

———. *The Oxford History of the United States 1783–1917*.

———, and H.S. Commager. *The Growth of the American Republic*, Vol. 2 of 2 vols. New York: Oxford University Press, 1962.

———, and M. Obregón. *The Caribbean as Columbus Saw It*. Boston: Little, Brown, 1964.

Morris, J.E. *The Welsh Wars of Edward I*. London: Oxford University Press, 1901.

Morris, Roger. *Uncertain Greatness. Henry Kissinger and American Foreign Policy*. New York: Harper and Row, 1977.

Morrock, Richard, "Revolution and Intervention in Vietnam." In Horowitz, op. cit.

Mosley, Leonard. *Duel for Kilimanjaro*. London: Weidenfeld and Nicolson, 1963.

Moss, Ambler H., Jr. "Peace in Central America." *Survival*, September/October, 1990. International Institute for Strategic Studies.

Mountbatten, Vice-Admiral the Earl. *Report to the Combined Chiefs of Staff by the Supreme Allied Commander South-East Asia, 1943–1945*. London: Her Majesty's Stationery Office, 1951.

Moxon-Browne, Edward. "Spain and the ETA. The Bid for Basque Autonomy." *Conflict Studies No. 201*, 1987. Institute for the Study of Conflict.

Moyers, Bill D. "One Thing We Learned." *Foreign Affairs*, July 1968.

Mulligan, Hugh A. *No Place to Die*. New York: William Morrow, 1967.

Munro, D.C. See Strayer, J.R.

Munslow, B. *Mozambique: The Revolution and Its Origins*. London and New York: Longmans, 1983.

Murphy, John F. *State Support of International Terrorism*. London: Mansell, 1989.

Murray, M. *Hunted: A Coastwatcher's Story*. London: Angus and Robertson, 1967.

Murray, Raymond. *Special Air Service in Ireland, 1969–89*. London: Mercier Press, 1990.

Murtha, John P. "Combat Intelligence in Vietnam." *Marine Corps Gazette*, January 1968.

Myers, E.C.W. *Greek Entanglement*. London: Rupert Hart-Davis, 1955.

Myrdal, Gunnar. *Asian Drama: An Inquiry into the Poverty of Nations*, 3 vols. London: Allen Lane/The Penguin Press, 1968.

Nasution, Abdul Haris. *Fundamentals of Guerrilla Warfare*. New York: Frederick A. Praeger, 1965.

Navarre, Henri. *Agonie de l'Indochine*. Paris: Librairie Plon, 1956.

Neave, Airey. *Saturday at MI-9*. London: Hodder and Stoughton, 1969.

Neustadt, Richard E., and Ernest R. May. *Thinking in Time: The Uses of History for Decision-Makers*. New York: The Free Press, 1986.

Newman, Robert P. *Owen Lattimore and the "Loss" of China*. Berkeley, Calif.: University of California Press, 1992.

Nixon, Richard M. "Asia After Viet Nam," *Foreign Affairs*, October 1967.

———. *Public Papers of the President*. Washington, D.C.: U.S. Government Printing Office, 6 vols., 1971–75.

———. *The Memoirs of Richard Nixon*. London: Sidgwick and Jackson, 1978.

Njama, K. See Barnett, Donald L.

Nolff, M. See Seers, D.

Norman, M.W. See Jumper, Roy.

Nuechterlein, Donald E. *Thailand and the Struggle for Southeast Asia*. Ithaca, N.Y.: Cornell University Press, 1965.

Nutting, Anthony. *Lawrence of Arabia*. London: Hollis and Carter, 1961.

O'Ballance, Edgar. *The Soviet War in the Sudan: 1955–1972*. London: Faber and Faber, 1977.

——. *The Kurdish Revolt 1961–1970*. London: Faber and Faber, 1973.

——. *The Algerian Insurrection 1954–1962*. London: Faber and Faber, 1967.

——. *The Greek Civil War, 1944–1949*. London: Faber and Faber, 1966.

——. *The Red Army*. London: Faber and Faber, 1964.

Oberdorfer, Don. *Tet!* New York: Doubleday, 1971.

Obregón, M. See Morison, S.E.

O'Donnell, Kenneth. "LBJ and the Kennedys." *Life*, August 7, 1970.

Ogburn, Charlton. *The Marauders*. New York: Harper and Brothers, 1959.

O'Hea, Patrick. *Reminiscences of the Mexican Revolution*. Mexico City: Editorial Fournier, 1966.

Olcott, C.S. *William McKinley*, Vol. 2 of 2 vols. New York: Houghton Mifflin, 1916.

Oldenbourg, Zoé. *Catherine the Great*. London: William Heinemann, 1965.

Oliver, Roland, and Gervase Mathew, eds. *History of East Africa*, Vol. 1 of 3 vols. London: Oxford University Press, 1963.

Oman, C.W.C. *A History of the Art of War in the Middle Ages*, Vol. 1 of 2 vols. London: Methuen, 1924.

——. *A History of the Peninsular War*, 7 vols. London: Oxford University Press, 1902.

O'Neill, Robert J. *Vietnam Task*. Melbourne: Cassell Australia, 1968.

Otway-Ruthven, A.J. *A History of Medieval Ireland*. London: Ernest Benn, 1968.

Paget, Julian. *Counter-Insurgency Campaigning*. London: Faber and Faber, 1967.

Palmer, Dave R. *Summons of the Trumpet: A History of the Vietnam War from a Military Man's Standpoint*. New York: Ballantine Books, 1978.

Palmer, Dave Scott, ed. *Shining Path of Peace*. London: Hurst and Co., 1992.

Palmier, Leslie. *Indonesia and the Dutch*. London: Oxford University Press, 1962.

Pares, Bernard. *A History of Russia*. New York: Alfred A. Knopf, 1933.

Paret, Peter. *Yorck and the Era of Prussian Reform*. Princeton, N.J.: Princeton University Press, 1966.

——. *French Revolutionary Warfare from Indochina to Algeria: The Analysis of a Political and Military Doctrine*. London: Pall Mall Press, 1964.

——, and John Shy. *Guerrillas in the 1960s*. London: Pall Mall Press, 1962.

Parker, H.M.D. *The Roman Legions*. Cambridge, U.K.: W. Heffer and Sons, 1958.

Parry, Albert. "Soviet Aid to Vietnam." *The Reporter*, January 12, 1967.

Paul, Elliott. *Life and Death of a Spanish Town*. London: Peter Davies, 1939.

Paul, Roland A. "Laos: Anatomy of an American Involvement." *Foreign Affairs*, April 1971.

Payne, Robert. *The Civil War in Spain*. London: Secker and Warburg, 1962.

——. *Lawrence of Arabia: A Triumph*. New York: Pyramid Books, 1963.

——. *Mao Tse-tung*. London: Abelard-Shuman, 1967.

Pearson, C.H. *History of England During the Early and Middle Ages*. London: Bell and Daldy, 1867.

Perlez, Jane. "A New Chance for a Fractured Land." *New York Times Magazine*, September 22, 1991.

Perroy, E. *The Hundred Years War*, tr. W.B. Wells. London: Eyre and Spottiswoode, 1951.

Petrie, C. See Bertrand, L.

Pflaum, Irving. *Tragic Island: How Communism Came to Cuba*. Englewood Cliffs, N.J.: Prentice-Hall, 1961.

Phillips, Ruby Hart. *Cuba: Island of Paradise*. New York: McDowell, Obolensky, 1959.

Pike, Douglas. *Viet Cong: The Organization and Techniques of the National Liberation Front of South Vietnam*. Cambridge, Mass.: MIT Press, 1967.

Pimlot, John, ed. *Guerrilla Warfare*. New York. The Military Press, 1985.

Piquet-Wicks, Eric. *Four in the Shadows*. London: Jarrolds, 1957.

Pisor, Robert. *The End of the Line: The Siege of Khe Sanh*. New York: W.W. Norton, 1982.

Platonov, S.F. *History of Russia*, tr. E. Aronsberg. London: Macmillan, 1925.

Plutarch. *Lives*, Vol. 3 of 5 vols., tr. A.H. Clough. London: Macmillan, 1902.

Pokrovsky, M.N. *Brief History of Russia*, 2 vols., tr. D.S. Mirsky. London: Martin Lawrence, 1933.

Polo, Marco. *The Travels of Marco Polo*, tr. Ronald Latham. Harmondsworth, Middlesex, U.K.: Penguin Books, 1958.

Polybius. *The Histories*, Vol. 2 of 6 vols., tr. W.R. Paton. London: William Heinemann, 1922.

Ponteil, Félix. *L'Eveil des Nationalités et le Mouvement Libéral*. Paris: Presses Universitaires de France, 1968.

Poole, A.L., ed. *Medieval England*, Vol. 1 of 2 vols. London: Oxford University Press, 1958.

Pratt, Fletcher. *Ordeal by Fire*. London: Bodley Head, 1950.

Prescott, William H. *The History of the Conquest of Mexico*. Chicago: University of Chicago Press, 1966.

Preston, R.A. *Men in Arms*. London: Thames and Hudson, 1962.

Priestley, E.C. See Cole, D.H.

Proxmire, William. *Report from the Wasteland: America's Military-Industrial Complex*. New York: Frederick A. Praeger, 1970.

Purcell, Susan K. "The Choice in Central America." *Foreign Affairs,* Fall 1987.

Pushkin, A.S. *The Captain's Daughter*. Moscow: Progress Publishers, 1954.

Pye, Lucien W. *Guerrilla Communism and Malaya: Its Social and Political Meaning*. Princeton, N.J.: Princeton University Press, 1956.

Radu, Michael, and Vladimir Tismaneanu. *Latin American Revolutionaries*. London: Pergamon-Brassey's, 1990.

Rankin, Hugh F. "Charles Lord Cornwallis: Study in Frustration." In Billias, op. cit.

Rapoport, Anatol, ed. *Clausewitz on War*. London: Penguin Books, 1968.

Raskin, Marcus G., and Bernard B. Fall. *The Viet-Nam Reader: Articles and Documents on American Foreign Policy and the Viet-Nam Crisis*. New York: Random House, 1967.

Ray, J.K. *Transfer of Power in Indonesia 1942–1949*. Bombay: P.C. Manaktala and Sons, 1967.

Reagan, Ronald. *An American Life*. New York: Simon and Schuster, 1990.

Reeves, Richard. *A Ford, Not a Lincoln: The Decline of American Political Leadership*. London: Hutchinson, 1976.

Reichley, James A. *Conversations in an Age of Change*. Washington, D.C.: The Brookings Institution, 1981.

Reischauer, Edwin O. *Beyond Vietnam*. New York: Alfred A. Knopf, 1967.

Rice, Edward E. *Wars of the Third Kind: Conflict in Undeveloped Countries*. Berkeley, Calif.: University of California Press, 1988.

Richburg, Keith. "Back to Vietnam." *Foreign Affairs,* Fall 1991.

Ridgway, Matthew B. "Indochina: Disengaging." *Foreign Affairs,* July 1971.

———. *Soldier: The Memoirs of Matthew B. Ridgway*. New York: Harper and Brothers, 1956.

———. *The Korean War*. Garden City, N.Y.: Doubleday, 1967.

Riding, Alan. "The Central American Quagmire." *Foreign Affairs, America and the World,* 1982.

Riencourt, Amaury de. "India and Pakistan in the Shadow of Afghanistan." *Foreign Affairs*, Winter 1982–1983.

Rings, Werner. *Life with the Enemy: Collaboration and Resistance in Hitler's Europe 1939–1945*, tr. J. Maxwell Brownjohn. London: Weidenfeld and Nicolson, 1979.

Roberts, Adam, ed. *The Strategy of Civilian Defense*. London: Faber and Faber, 1967.

———. "Lessons of Geneva 1954." *The Times* (London), April 23, 1968.

Roberts, Chalmers M. "The Day We Didn't Go to War." *The Reporter*, September 14, 1954.

Robinson, Linda. "The End of El Salvador's War." *Survival*, September/October 1991. International Institute for Strategic Studies.

Robinson, R.E.R. "Reflections of a Company Commander in Malaya." *Army Quarterly*, October 1950.

Roeder, Franz. *The Ordeal of Captain Roeder*, tr. and ed. Helen Roeder. London: Methuen, 1960.

Rolo, Charles J. *Wingate's Raiders*. London: G.C. Harrap, 1944.

Romanus, C.F., and R. Sunderland. *The China-Burma-India Theater: Stilwell's Problems*. Washington, D.C.: U.S. Government Printing Office, 1956.

Rose, J.H. "The Second Coalition." *The Cambridge Modern History*, Vol. 8 of 13 vols. London: Cambridge University Press, 1904.

Ross, Stanley K. *Francisco I. Madero: Apostle of Mexican Democracy*. New York: Columbia University Press, 1955.

Rostow, W.W. *The United States in the World Arena*. New York: Harper and Brothers, 1960.

Rovere, Richard H. *The Eisenhower Years*. New York: Farrar, Straus and Cudahy, 1956.

Roy, Jules. *The Battle of Dien Bien Phu*. New York: Carrol and Graf, 1984.

Royal United Services Institution Seminar. *Lessons from the Vietnam War*. London: RUSI, 1969.

Ruark, Robert. *Something of Value*. London: Hamish Hamilton, 1955.

Rubin, Barnett R. "The Fragmentation of Afghanistan." *Foreign Affairs*, Winter, 1989–1990.

——— see Laber, Jeri.

Salinger, Pierre. *With Kennedy*. Garden City, N.Y.: Doubleday, 1966.

Salisbury, Harrison E. *Behind the Lines: Hanoi*. New York: Harper and Row, 1967.

Sansom, Robert L. *The Economics of Insurgency in the Mekong Delta of Vietnam*. Cambridge, Mass.: MIT Press, 1970.

Schalk, David. *War and the Ivory Tower*. New York: Oxford University Press, 1991.

Schandler, Herbert Y. *The Unmaking of a President: Lyndon Johnson and Vietnam*. Princeton, N.J.: Princeton University Press, 1977.

Schell, Jonathan. *The Military Half*. New York: Alfred A. Knopf, 1968.

———. *The Time of Illusion*. New York: Alfred A. Knopf, 1975.

Schell, Orville. See Schurmann, Franz.

Schevill, F. *History of the Balkan Peninsula*. New York: Harcourt Brace, 1922.

Schiff, Ze'ev, and E. Ya'ari. *Israel's Lebanon War*, ed. and tr. Ina Friedman. London: George Allen and Unwin, 1985.

Schlesinger, A.M. *Political and Social History of the United States*. New York: Macmillan, 1926.

Schlesinger, Arthur M., Jr. *The Bitter Heritage: Vietnam and American Democracy 1941–1966*. Boston: Houghton Mifflin, 1967.

———. *A Thousand Days*. Boston: Houghton Mifflin, 1965.

Schoenbrun, David. "Journey to North Vietnam." *The Saturday Evening Post*, March 1968.

Schram, Stuart R. *Mao Tse-tung*. New York: Simon and Schuster, 1967.

Schulten, A. "The Romans in Spain." *The Cambridge Ancient History*, Chapter 10 of Vol. 8. London and Cambridge, U.K.: The University Press, 1930.

Schultheis, Rob. "In Afghanistan, Peace Must Wait." *New York Times Magazine*, December 29, 1991.

Schurmann, F.L. *Russia Since 1917*. New York: Alfred A. Knopf, 1957.

Schurmann, Franz, and Orville Schell, eds. *China Readings 1 (Imperial China: The Eighteenth and Nineteenth Centuries)*. New York: Penguin Books, 1967.

―――. *China Readings 2 (Republican China: Nationalism, War, and the Rise of Communism, 1911–49)*. New York: Penguin Books, 1968.

Scigliano, Robert. *South Vietnam: Nation Under Stress*. Boston: Houghton Mifflin, 1964.

―――, and Guy Fox. *Technical Assistance in Vietnam: The Michigan State University Experience*. New York: Frederick A. Praeger, 1965.

Scobie, W.I. See Foley, Charles.

Scullard, H.H. *Scipio Africanus, Soldier and Politician*. London: Thames and Hudson, 1970.

Seers, D. et al. *Cuba: The Economic and Social Revolution*. Chapel Hill, N.C.: University of North Carolina Press, 1964.

Ségur, Philippe-Paul de. *Napoleon's Russian Campaign*, tr. J.D. Townsend. London: Michael Joseph, 1958.

Servan-Schreiber, Jean-Jacques. *Lieutenant in Algeria*, tr. Ronald Matthews. London: Hutchinson, 1958.

Seton-Watson, Hugh. *The Decline of Imperial Russia, 1815–1914*. London: Methuen, 1952.

―――. *The East European Revolution*. London: Methuen, 1956.

Shaplen, Robert M. "Letter from Vietnam." *The New Yorker*, May 13, 1972.

―――. *The Lost Revolution*. New York: Harper and Row, 1966.

―――. *The Road from War*. New York: Harper and Row, 1970.

―――. "Viet-Nam: Crisis of Indecision." *Foreign Affairs*, October 1967.

―――. "We Have Always Survived." *The New Yorker*, April 15, 1972.

Sharp, U.S. Grant. "We Could Have Won in Vietnam Long Ago." *Reader's Digest*, May 1969.

Shawcross, William. *Sideshow: Kissinger, Nixon and the Destruction of Cambodia*. London: Andre Deutsch, 1979.

Sheean, Vincent. *Personal History*. New York: Doubleday, Doran, 1936.

Sheehan, Neil. *A Bright Shining Lie: John Paul Vann and America in Vietnam*. New York: Random House, 1988.

―――. "Annals of War, An American Soldier in Vietnam." *The New Yorker*, June 27, 1988.

―――― et al. *The Pentagon Papers*. New York: Bantam Books, 1971.

Sherwood, Robert E. *Roosevelt and Hopkins*. New York: Harper and Brothers, 1948.

Shoup, David M., and James A. Donovan. "The New American Militarism." *The Atlantic*, April 1969.

Shoup, Lawrence H. *The Carter Presidency and Beyond: Power and Politics in the 1980s*. Palo Alto, Calif.: Ramparts Press, 1977.

Shultz, Richard H., Jr. "Low Intensity Conflict: Future Challenges and Lessons from the Reagan Years." *Survival*, July/August 1989. International Institute for Strategic Studies.

Sidey, Hugh. *John F. Kennedy, President*. New York: Atheneum, 1963.

Sihanouk, Norodom, as related to Wilfred Burchett. *My War with the CIA: Cambodia's Fight for Survival*. London: Penguin Books, 1973.

Skeen, Sir Andrew. *Passing It On: Short Talks on Tribal Fighting on the North-West Frontier of India*. London: Gale and Polden, 1932.

Skidmore, Thomas E., and Peter H. Smith. *Modern Latin America*. New York: Oxford University Press, 1984.

Skobeleff, General. *Siege and Assault of Denghil-Tépé,* tr. J.J. Leverson. London: Her Majesty's Stationery Office, 1881.

Skodvin, Magne. "Norwegian Non-Violent Resistance During the German Occupation." In Adam Roberts, op. cit.

Slane, P.M. "Tactical Problems in Kenya." *Army Quarterly,* 1954.

Slessor, Sir John. *The Central Blue.* London: Cassell, 1956.

Slim, William R. *Defeat into Victory.* London: Cassell, 1956.

Slimming, John. *Malaysia: Death of a Democracy.* London: John Murray, 1969.

Smith, Earl E.T. *The Fourth Floor: An Account of the Castro Communist Revolution.* New York: Random House, 1962.

Smith, Hedrick. See Sheehan, Neil.

Smith, R.B. *An International History of the Vietnam War,* 2 vols. London: Macmillan, 1987.

Smith, R. Harris. *OSS: The Secret History of America's First Central Intelligence Agency.* London: University of California Press, 1972.

Smyth, John. *Percival and the Tragedy of Singapore.* London: MacDonald, 1971.

Snepp, Frank. *Decent Interval: An Insider's Account of Saigon's Indecent End Told by the CIA's Chief Strategy Analyst in Vietnam.* New York: Random House, 1977.

Snow, Edgar. *The Other Side of the River: Red China Today.* New York: Random House, 1961.

———. *Random Notes on China 1936–1945.* Cambridge, Mass.: Harvard University Press, 1957.

———. *Red Star over China.* New York: Random House, 1938.

Soedjatmoko. "South-East Asia and Security." *Survival,* October 1969. International Institute for Strategic Studies.

Solarz, Stephen J. "Cambodia and the International Community." *Foreign Affairs,* Spring 1990.

Sorensen, Theodore C. *Kennedy.* New York: Harper and Row, 1965.

Special Operations Research Office (American University). *Casebook on Insurgency and Revolutionary Warfare.* Washington, D.C.: American University, 1962.

Spencer-Chapman, F. *The Jungle Is Neutral.* London: Chatto and Windus, 1949.

Standing, Percy Cross. *Guerrilla Leaders of the World: From Charette to Delvet.* London: Stanley Paul, 1912.

Stanford, R.K. "Bamboo Brigades." *Marine Corps Gazette,* March 1966.

Stenton, F.M. *Anglo-Saxon England.* London: Oxford University Press, 1943.

Stephens, Robert. *Cyprus: A Place of Arms.* London: Pall Mall Press, 1966.

Stilwell, Joseph W. *The Stilwell Papers,* ed. T.H. White. New York: William Sloane, 1948.

Stolfi, Russel H. *U.S. Marine Corps Civic Action Efforts in Vietnam—March 1965–March 1966.* Washington, D.C.: U.S. Marine Corps, 1968.

Stone, I.F. "Why Nixon Won His Moscow Gamble." *The New York Review of Books,* June 15, 1972.

Strauss, Lewis. *Men and Decisions.* New York: Doubleday, 1962.

Strayer, J.R., and D.C. Munro. *Middle Ages, 395–1500.* New York: Appleton-Century, 1942.

Strong, Simon. *Shining Path: The World's Most Deadly Revolutionary Force.* London: HarperCollins, 1992.

Stschepkin, E. "Russia Under Alexander I, and the Invasion of 1812." In *The Cambridge Modern History,* Vol. 9 of 13 vols. London: Cambridge University Press, 1904.

Sukhanov, N.N. *The Russian Revolution, 1917,* ed. and trans. Joel Carmichael. London: Oxford University Press, 1955.

Sulzberger, C.L. *The Test: De Gaulle and Algeria.* London: Rupert Hart-Davis, 1962.

Summers, Harry G., Jr. *On Strategy: A Critical Analysis of the Vietnam War.* Novato, Calif.: Presidio Press, 1982.

Sunderland, R. See Romanus, C.F.

Sutherland, C.H.V. *The Romans in Spain.* London: Methuen, 1939.

Sweet-Escott, Bickham. *Baker Street Irregular.* London: Methuen, 1965.

Sykes, Christopher. *Orde Wingate.* London: Collins, 1959.

————. *Cross Roads to Israel.* Bloomington, Ind.: Indiana University Press, 1975.

Szulc, Tad. *The Illusion of Peace: Foreign Policy in the Nixon Years.* New York: Viking Press, 1978.

Taber, Robert. *M-26: Biography of a Revolution.* New York: Lyle Stuart, 1961.

————. *The War of the Flea.* London: Paladin, 1970.

Talbott, John. *The War Without a Name. France in Algeria, 1954–1962.* London: Faber and Faber, 1981.

Tanham, George K. *Communist Revolutionary Warfare: From the Vietminh to the Viet Cong,* rev. ed. New York: Frederick A. Praeger, 1967.

————. *Trial in Thailand.* New York: Crane, Russak, 1974.

————. *War Without Guns.* New York: Frederick A. Praeger, 1966.

————, and Dennis J. Duncanson. "Some Dilemmas of Counterinsurgency." *Foreign Affairs,* October 1969.

Tannenbaum, Frank. "The United States and Latin America," *Political Science Quarterly,* June 1961.

Tarlé, Eugène. *Napoleon's Invasion of Russia, 1812,* tr. G.M. London: Allen and Unwin, 1942.

Tarleton, Banastre. *A History of the Campaigns of 1780 and 1781, in the Southern Provinces of North America.* London: T. Cadell, 1787.

Tarn, W.W. *Alexander the Great and the Unity of Mankind,* Vol. 1 of 2 vols. London: Oxford University Press, 1933.

Taruc, Luis. *He Who Rides the Tiger.* New York: Frederick A. Praeger, 1967.

Taylor, Alistair M. *Indonesian Independence and the United Nations.* London: Stevens and Sons, 1960.

Taylor, L.A. *The Tragedy of an Army: La Vendée in 1793.* London: Hutchinson, 1913.

Taylor, Maxwell. *Responsibility and Response.* New York: Harper and Row, 1967.

————. *The Uncertain Trumpet.* New York: Harper and Brothers, 1960.

Taylor, Telford. *Nuremberg and Vietnam: An American Tragedy.* New York: Quadrangle Books, 1970.

Tee, W.S. "Solutions in Counter-Insurgency Operations." *Army Quarterly,* October 1967.

Temperley, H.W.V. *History of Servia.* London: G. Bell and Sons, 1917.

Thayer, Charles W. *Guerrilla.* New York: Harper and Row, 1965.

Thayer, George. *The War Business.* London: Weidenfeld and Nicolson, 1969.

Thomas, Hugh. *Cuba or The Pursuit of Freedom.* New York: Harper and Row, 1971.

————. *The Spanish Civil War.* New York: Harper and Brothers, 1961.

Thompson, Robert. *Defeating Communist Insurgency: The Lessons of Malaya and Vietnam.* New York: Frederick A. Praeger, 1966.

————. "Feet on the Ground." *Statist,* February 4, 1966.

————. "My Plan for Peace in Vietnam." *Reader's Digest,* March 1970.

————. *No Exit from Vietnam.* London: Chatto and Windus, 1969.

————. "On the Way to Victory." *The Sunday Times* (London), December 21, 1969.

————. *Revolutionary War in World Strategy 1945–1969.* London: Secker and Warburg, 1970.

Thompson, Virginia. *French Indo-China.* London: Allen and Unwin, 1937.

Thompson, W. Scott, and Donaldson D. Frizzell, eds. *The Lessons of Vietnam.* London: Macdonald and Jane's, 1977.

Thucydides. *History of the Peloponnesian War,* Vol. 2 of 4 vols., tr. Charles F. Smith. Cambridge, Mass.: Harvard University Press, 1953.

Tillion, Germaine. *Algeria: The Realities.* London: Eyre and Spottiswoode, 1958.

Tinker, Hugh. *South Asia: A Short History*. London: Macmillan, 1989.

Tismaneanu, Vladimir. See Radu, Michael.

Tolstoy, Leo. *War and Peace*, tr. Constance Garrett. London: William Heinemann, 1971.

Toy, Sidney. *A History of Fortifications*. London: William Heinemann, 1955.

Trager, Frank. *Why Viet Nam?* New York: Frederick A. Praeger, 1966.

Tran Van Dinh. "Elections in Vietnam." *The New Republic,* July 2, 1966.

Trevelyan, George. *George the Third and Charles Fox,* 2 vols. London: Longmans, Green, 1914.

Treverton, Gregory F. "U.S. strategy in Central America." *Survival,* March/April 1986. International Institute for Strategic Studies.

Trinquier, Roger. *Modern Warfare: A French View of Counter-Insurgency*. New York: Frederick A. Praeger, 1964.

Truman, Harry S. *Year of Decision 1945*. London: Hodder and Stoughton, 1955.

———. *Years of Trial and Hope*. Garden City, N.Y.: Doubleday, 1956.

Tse-tung. See Mao Tse-tung.

Tsiang Ting-fu. "The English and the Opium Trade." In Schurmann, op. cit.

Tuchman, Barbara W. *Stilwell and the American Experience in China—1913–45.* New York: Macmillan, 1971

U.S. Air Force. "The U.S. Air Force in Southeast Asia." Washington, D.C.: Headquarters, U.S. Air Force, 1967.

U.S. Congress. "The Candidates' Views." *Congressional Quarterly,* May 3, 1968.

U.S. Department of the Army. *German Antiguerrilla Operations in the Balkans (1941–1944)*. Washington, D.C.: U.S. Government Printing Office, 1954.

U.S. Department of Defense. "Working Paper on the North Vietnamese Role in the War in South Vietnam." Washington, D.C.: 1968.

U.S. Department of the Navy. "Riverine Warfare." Washington, D.C.: U.S. Government Printing Office, 1967.

———. "Chinfonote 5721." Washington, D.C.: U.S. Navy, March 28, 1968.

U.S. Department of State. *Viet Nam: The Struggle for Freedom*. Publication 7724 (Department of Defense, Gen.-8). Washington, D.C. U.S. Government Printing Office, 1964.

———. *United States Relations with China—With Special Reference to the Period 1944–1949*. Washington, D.C.: U.S. Government Printing Office, 1949. Subsequently published as *The China White Paper—August 1949,* Stanford, Calif.: 2 vols. Stanford University Press, 1967.

U.S. Government. *The United States Strategic Bombing Survey—Over-all Report*. Washington, D.C.: U.S. Government Printing Office, 1945.

U.S. Marine Corps. "III Marine Amphibious Force—The Mission—And How It Is Fulfilled." Washington, D.C.: Headquarters, U.S. Marine Corps, October 1967.

———. "The Battle for Hills 861 and 881." N.p., n.d.

———. "Khe Sanh Wrap-Up." N.p., n.d.

U.S. Senate. *Refugee Problems in South Vietnam*. Washington, D.C.: U.S. Government Printing Office, 1966.

———. *Role of Dr. Henry A. Kissinger in the Wiretapping of Certain Government Officials and Newsmen*. Washington, D.C.: U.S. Government Printing Office, 1974.

———. *Hearings Before the Committee on the Philippines of the United States Senate in Relation to the Philippine Islands,* 2 vols. Washington, D.C.: U.S. Government Printing Office, 1902.

U.S. Senate Committee on Foreign Relations. *Background Information Relating to Southeast Asia and Vietnam*. Washington, D.C.: U.S. Government Printing Office, 1967.

———. *United States-Vietnam Relations 1945–1967,* 12 vols. Washington, D.C.: U.S. Government Printing Office, 1971.

1237

U.S. Senate Republican Policy Committee. *The War in Vietnam.* Washington, D.C.: Public Affairs Press, 1967.
U.S. Seventh Fleet. "Cruisers and Destroyers in Vietnam." N.p., n.d.
——. "Task Force 77." N.p., n.d.
Urban, Mark. *War in Afghanistan.* London: The Macmillan Press, 1988.
Uris, Leon. *Exodus.* London: Allen Wingate, 1959.
Urrutia Lleó, Manuel. *Fidel Castro and Company, Inc.: Communist Tyranny in Cuba.* New York: Frederick A. Praeger, 1964.
Usborne, C.V. *The Conquest of Morocco.* London: Stanley Paul, 1936.
Utley, Freda. *Last Chance in China.* Indianapolis: Bobbs-Merrill, 1947.
Vagts, Alfred. *Defense and Diplomacy: The Soldier and the Conduct of Foreign Relations.* New York: Kings Crown Press, 1956.
Valeriano, N.D. and C.T.R. Bohannan. *Counter-Guerrilla Operations: The Philippine Experience.* New York: Frederick A. Praeger, 1962.
Vance, Cyrus. *Hard Choices: Critical Year in American Foreign Policy.* New York: Simon and Schuster, 1983.
Vandegrift, A.A., and R.B. Asprey. *Once a Marine.* New York: W.W. Norton, 1964.
Vandenbosch, A., and M.B. Vandenbosch. *Australia Faces Southeast Asia: The Emergence of a Foreign Policy.* Lexington, Ky.: University of Kentucky Press, 1967.
Vandenbosch, M.B. See Vandenbosch, A.
Vernadsky, George. *A History of Russia.* New Haven, Conn.: Yale University Press, 1945.
Vidal-Naquet, Pierre. *Torture: Cancer of Democracy.* Harmondsworth, Middlesex, U.K.: Penguin Books, 1963.
Vlekke, B.H.M. *Nusantara: A History of Indonesia.* The Hague: W. van Hoeve, 1959.
Volckmann, R.W. *We Remained.* New York: W.W. Norton, 1954.
Wagner, David H. "A Handful of Marines." *Marine Corps Gazette,* March 1968.
Waley, Arthur. *The Book of Songs.* London: Allen and Unwin, 1937.
Walker, Lannon. "Our Foreign Affairs Machinery: Time for an Overhaul." *Foreign Affairs,* January 1969.
Walker, Walter. "How Borneo Was Won." *The Round Table,* January 1969.
Wallace-Hadrill, J.M. *The Barbarian West, 400–1000.* London: Hutchinson, 1952.
Walsh, W.B. *Russia and the Soviet Union.* Ann Arbor, Mich.: University of Michigan Press, 1958.
Walt, L.W. "Are We Winning the War in Vietnam?" Washington, D.C.: Headquarters, U.S. Marine Corps, n.d.
——. "Khe Sanh: The Battle That Had to Be Won." *Reader's Digest,* August 1970.
——. "The Nature of the War in Vietnam." Washington, D.C.: Headquarters, U.S. Marine Corps, n.d.
——. *Strange War, Strange Strategy.* New York: Funk and Wagnalls, 1970.
Ward, Christopher. *The War of the Revolution,* Vol. 2 of 2 vols., ed. J.R. Alden. New York: Macmillan, 1952.
Warnke, Paul, and Leslie Gelb. "Security or Confrontation." *Foreign Policy,* Winter 1970–71.
Watteville, H. de. *Lord Kitchener.* London: Blackie and Son, 1939.
Webb, James. *Fields of Fire.* Englewood Cliffs, N.J.: Prentice-Hall, 1978.
Webster, Graham. *The Roman Imperial Army of the First and Second Centuries A.D.* London: Adam and Charles Black, 1969.
Wedemeyer, A.C. *Wedemeyer Reports.* New York: Henry Holt, 1958.
Wehl, David. *The Birth of Indonesia.* London: Allen and Unwin, 1948.
Weigley, R.F. *History of the United States Army.* New York: Macmillan, 1967.
——. *The American Way of War: A History of United States Military Strategy and Policy.* New York: Macmillan, 1973.

Weinberg, G.L. "The Yelna-Dorogobuzh Area of Smolensk Oblast." In Armstrong, op. cit.

Weinberger, Caspar. *Fighting for Peace.* New York: Warner Books, 1991.

Weller, Jac. "The U.S. Army in Vietnam: A Survey of Aims, Operations, and Weapons, Particularly of Small Infantry Units." *Army Quarterly,* October 1967.

Welles, Sumner. *The Time for Decision.* New York: Harper and Brothers, 1944.

West, Francis J. "Small Unit Action in Vietnam." Washington, D.C.: Headquarters, U.S. Marine Corps, 1967.

West, Rebecca. *Black Lamb and Grey Falcon,* Vol. 1 of 2 vols. London: Macmillan, 1942.

Westmoreland, W.C. *A Soldier Reports.* New York: Da Capo Press, 1989.

White, Lynn, Jr. *Medieval Technology and Social Change.* London: Oxford University Press, 1962.

White, T.H. *The Making of the President 1960.* New York: Atheneum, 1961.

————. *The Making of the President 1968.* New York: Atheneum, 1969.

————, and A. Jacoby. *Thunder Out of China.* New York: William Sloane, 1946.

————. See Stilwell, Joseph W.

Wickwire, Franklin, and Mary Wickwire. *Cornwallis: The American Adventure.* Boston: Houghton Mifflin, 1969.

Wickwire, Mary. See Wickwire, Franklin.

Wighton, Charles. *Heydrich: Hitler's Most Evil Henchman.* London: Odhams Press, 1962.

Wilcken, U. *Alexander the Great,* tr. G.C. Richards. London: Chatto and Windus, 1932.

Willcox, William B., ed. *The American Rebellion: Sir Henry Clinton's Narrative of His Campaigns, 1775–1782, with an Appendix of Original Documents.* New Haven, Conn.: Yale University Press, 1954.

————. *Portrait of a General: Sir Henry Clinton in the War of Independence.* New York: Alfred A. Knopf, 1962.

————. "Sir Henry Clinton: Paralysis of Command." In Billias, op. cit.

Williams, Phil. See Abernathy, W. Glenn.

Williamson, R.E. "A Briefing for Combined Action." *Marine Corps Gazette,* March 1968.

Wilson, Harold. "The Night LBJ Wrecked Our Secret Manoeuvres for Peace." *The Sunday Times* (London), May 16, 1971.

Wingate, Ronald. *Wingate of the Sudan.* London: John Murray, 1935.

Winstedt, R.O. "Malaysia (History)." *Encyclopaedia Britannica,* Vol. 14. 1968.

Wolfert, Ira. *American Guerrilla in the Philippines.* New York: Avon Books, 1945.

Wolff, Leon. *Little Brown Brother.* Garden City, N.Y.: Doubleday, 1961.

Womack, John. *Zapata and the Mexican Revolution.* London: Thames and Hudson, 1968.

Wood, Bryce. *The Making of the Good Neighbor Policy.* New York: Columbia University Press, 1961.

Woodhouse, C.M. *Apple of Discord.* London: Hutchinson, 1948.

————. *The Story of Modern Greece.* London: Faber and Faber, 1968.

Woodhouse, J.M. "Some Personal Observations on the Employment of Special Forces in Malaya." *Army Quarterly,* April 1955.

————. *The Struggle for Greece 1941–1949.* London: Hart-Davis, MacGibbon, 1979.

Woodruff, Philip. *The Men Who Ruled India: The Guardians,* Vol. 2 of 2 vols. London: Jonathan Cape, 1954.

Woodward, Bob, and Carl Bernstein. *The Final Days.* New York: Simon and Schuster, 1976.

Woolman, David. *Rebels in the Rif.* Stanford, Calif.: Stanford University Press, 1969.

Wooten, James T. "How a Supersoldier Was Fired from His Command." *New York Times Magazine,* September 5, 1971.

Wren, C.S. "A Sunday with Westmoreland." *Look,* October 18, 1966.

Wright, G.N. *Life and Campaigns of Arthur, Duke of Wellington,* 4 vols. London: Fisher and Son, 1841.

X (Kennan, George F.). "The Sources of Soviet Conduct." *Foreign Affairs,* July 1947.

Zaffiri, Samuel. *Hamburger Hill, May 11–20, 1969.* Novato, Calif.: Presidio Press, 1988.

Zagoria, Donald S. *Vietnam Triangle: Moscow, Peking, Hanoi.* New York, Pegasus, 1967.

———. "Who Fears the Domino Theory?" *New York Times Magazine,* April 21, 1968.

Ziemke, E. "Composition and Morale of the Partisan Movement." In Armstrong, op. cit.

———. See Mavrogordato, R.

Zinn, Howard. *Vietnam: The Logic of Withdrawal.* Boston: Beacon Press, 1967.

Zorza, Victor. "Vietnam: Long or Short War." *The Guardian* (U.K.), February 15, 1968.

INDEX

Note: "Postwar" refers to post–World War II. Acronyms are spelled out in text.

Bragg, Gen. Braxton, 105–6
Brandon, Henry, 907
Bravo, Douglas, 1067
Brazil, 1085; insurgency, 1089–90
Breasted, Prof., 4
Brest-Litovsk, treaty of, 219
Bretons, 46–7
Brezhnev, Prem. Leonid, 1039
Briand, Aristide, 273
Briggs, Gen. Sir Henry, 568–9; Briggs Plan, Malaya, 568
British Commandos, 313
British East Africa, see Kenya
British East India Company, 232
Brittany, 46–7, 74–6
Brooke, Gen. Sir Alan, 425, 427
Brossolette, Pierre, 316
Browne, Malcolm, 760
Browne, Lt. Col. Thomas, 69
Brozovich, Josip, see Tito, Marshal Josip (Broz)
Bruce, David, 1007, 1010, 1027
Bruce, Robert, 44–6
Brunei, sultan of, 1083
Brussels Conference (1874), 110
Buchan, Alistair, 890
Bucher, Capt. Lloyd, 896
Buck, Pearl, 230
Bu Craa mines, Western Sahara, 1179, 1181
BUDC, Philippines, 529
Buell, Gen. Don C., 105
Buford, Col., 64
Bugeaud, Gen., 97–100, 111, 658
Bulgaria, 27, 30, 32; World War II, 338, invaded by Germany, 297
Buller, Gen. Sir Redvers, 143–4
Bunche, Ralph, 1153
Bundoola, 102
Bundy, McGeorge, 74, 787, 793–4, 852, 857–8, 888, 908, 919, 921, 960
Bundy, William, 771–2, 778, 783, 788, 793–5, 801, 876, 920; preparation of Congressional resolution, Tonkin Gulf, 771; escalation "scenario," 771
Bunker, Amb. Ellsworth, 870–2, 892, 908, 966, 995
Burchett, Wilfred, 737
Burgoyne, Gen. John, 60–1
Burguete, Gen. Ricardo, 269–70
Burma, 102–3; map, 420; British conquest (1820–1825), 102, 140,

second war (1852), 140, pacification of Upper Burma (1885–1890), 140–3; British administration (1890–1941), 415–6; World War II: British retreat, 414–5, Burma rifle regiments, 419, anti-British attitude, 415, Allied ground operations, 421, 433–4, Allied/Burmese guerrilla operations, 417–8, 425–7, 431–5; see also Slim, Gen. Sir William; Stilwell, Gen. Joseph; Wingate, Maj. Gen. Orde
Burma Road, 396, 415–6
Burmese National Army, 435–6
Burn, Prof. A.R., 4
Bury, Prof. J.B., 4
Bush, Pres. George, 1065, 1084, 1103, 1106, 1116–7, 1163
Bussaco, battle of, 80
Butros-Ghali, Butros, 1105
Buttinger, Joseph, 151–2, 595, 615, 759
Buzhardt, J. Fred, 1032
Byrnes, James, 483
Byzantine Empire, 29–34; map, 31

Cabot, John Moors, 1068
Caesar, Julius, 9–11, 20, 58
Cairo Conference, 431
Cajeme, 163
Caldera Rodríguez, Pres. Rafael, 1067
Calenzana, battle of, 53
Cali drug cartel, Colombia, 1109, 1112
Calleo, David, 981
Calley, Lt. William, 1023–5
Callinan, Maj. Bernard, 373
Callwell, Gen. Charles E., 76, 137–40, 150, 282, 751, 846, 986
Calvert, Michael, 425–7
Cambodia (Kampuchea), ix, 395, 397, 582, 596, 816, 865, 911, 1114; map, 478; fall of Sihanouk, 994–5; U.S. bombing of, 876, 962–7, 974, 992, 1018; Geneva Agreements, 963; Viet Minh guerrilla attacks, 582; Lon Nol government: 994–5, 1030; peasant repression, 995; army, 1030; U.S. support, 995–6, 1045–6; Lon Nol's fall, 1046; PAVN/VC sanctuary, 902–4, 962–4, 993–4, 1030; U.S./South Vietnam invasion of, 996–1003, 1019; guerrilla war, 1017–8, 1049–55: Khmer Rouge, 963, 1043–6; Khmer Serai, 963,

Debray, Régis, 700, 712–3, 1073, 1090, 1109
Decembrist uprising (1825), 202
Decius, Emp., 24–5
Decker, Gen. George, 751
Decoux, V. Adm. Jean, 396–8
De Gaulle, Gen. Charles, 310, 315, 318–19, 474, 483, 659, 662–3, 675–8, 726, 793, 937
Delamare, Lord, 628–9
De Lanessan, 151
De la O, 164
De la Rey, 145
De Lattre de Tassigny, Gen. Jean, 500–6, 508–9; "De Lattre Line," 502, 513, 577, 582
Delauvrier, Paul, 675, 677
Delestraint, Gen., 316
Delta Force, 844
Demilitarized Zone (DMZ), *see* United States: Vietnam
Democratic Army, Greek Communist, 519–21
Democratic Republic of Afghanistan, 1204
Denikin, Gen., 213, 217, 220–2
Denktash, Pres. Ruaf, 655
Denmark, World War II: occupied by Germany, 296, resistance, 303
De Puy, Gen. W.E., 812, 817, 908
Deraa, 186
De Rivera, Gen. Primo, 270–2
De Saxe, Marshal, 184, 186
De Soto patrols, 768
De Tham ("Tiger of Yen Tre"), 392
De Valera, Eamon, 193–4, 1122, 1127
Deventer, Gen. van, 174, 177–8
Devillers, Philippe, 477, 607, 615
Devlin, Bernadette, 1124
Dewavrin, Maj. André (Col. Passy), 311, 316
De Wet, Christian, 145–6
Dewey, Commodore George, 114, 120, 123, 126
Dewey, Thomas E., 462
DeWitt, K., 329
Diálogo Cívico, Cuba, 699
Diaz, Porfirio, 162–4, 166
Dickey, Christopher, 1030
Diem, Pres. Ngo Dinh, 392, 482, 595, 597–8, 600, 604, 616, 622–3, 719–20, 727–8, 732, 741, 747, 754, 759, 766, 922–3, 952; army, 600; background, 597–8; censorship, 757;

759–60; centralized rule, 606–8; dictatorship, 605–10, 727–8; opposition to, 599, 601, 606–9, 618–20; fall of and death, 742–4
Dien Bien Phu, battle of, 582–5, 587–9, 591–2, 896, 948, 958
Dighenis, *see* Grivas, Gen. George
Dinaussauts, 502
Diocletian, Emp., 25
Dixie Mission, China, 446–7
Dodge, Col. T.A., 7
Domino theory, 462, 578, 589, 621, 727, 858, 890–1, 920, 973, 993, 1008, 1080
Dong, Pham Van, 395, 773, 979, 983, 1016–7, 1048
Dong Khu, 497–8
Dong Minh Hoi (Vietnam Revolutionary League), 402
Donovan, William J., 299–300
DOPs, Algeria, 670
Dos Santos, José Eduardo, 1190–2
Dostam, Maj. Gen. Abdul Rashid, 1212
Douglas, William, 44
Douhet, Giulio, 929–32, 938, 986
Douro River, battle of, 80
Draper, Theodore, 686
DR party, Cuba, 699
Druze militia, 1158
Druze Moslems, 1158, 1160
DRV, Vietnam, 403, 475, 575, 586; Geneva Conference, 584–6, 615–6
Duarte, José Napoleón, 1095–8, 1100–2
Ducasse, Col., 670
Du Guesclin, Bertrand, 46–7
Dulles, Allen, 601, 699, 710, 1068
Dulles, John Foster, 577, 582, 585, 587, 589–90, 592, 594–7, 601, 610–11, 617, 959, 1068, 1202
Duncanson, Dennis, 835
Dunkerque, 296
Durand Line, 1202
Durban, 143
Durbrow, Elbridge, 718, 731
Dutch East India Company, 55
Dzerjinsky, Feliks Edmundovich, 212–213

Eagleton, Sen. Thomas, 911
EAM/ELAS, Greek Communist organization, 515–8, 524–5
Early, Gen., 107

1249

Ebro River, 14, 77
Eden, Anthony, 313, 399, 516, 590, 648, 652
EDL, Colombia, 809–11
Edmonds, Sir James E., 93–4
Edson, Col. (Red Mike), 288
Edward I, king of England, 39–44
EE, Spain, 1144
Ehrlichman, John, 1033
Einsatzgruppen, 324, 326
"Einstein letter," 301
Eisenhower, Pres. Dwight D., 577, 582–3, 587, 589–92, 701, 704, 709–10, 719, 748, 919, 922, 1068–9; Geneva Conference, 594–6; Cuba, 692; South Vietnam, 599, 601–2; Diem, 599, 601–2, "row-of-dominoes," 590; French Indochina, 577, intervention in Vietnam, 589–92, 726, Ridgeway report, 592
Elgin, Lord, 236
Eliot, Sir Charles, 628–9
Elizabeth I, queen of England, 51
Ellsberg, Daniel, 1028
ELF, Eritrea, 1170–1
ELN, Colombia, 1102, 1110–2
ELN, Peru, 1113
El Salvador, 1096–1106; map, 1062; repressive governments, 1096 ff.; growth of guerrilla movements, 1096–8; guerrilla insurgency, 1097 ff.; guerrilla tactics, 1100–2; counterinsurgency tactics, 1100–1; atrocities, 1099, 1101–3; cease-fire and peace, 1104–6
El Sordo, 292
Ély, Paul, 587, 589, 592
Élysée Agreements, 486
Emergency Regulations Act, 565
Emerson, Lt. Col. Henry, 843–4, 882
Emery, Fred, 985, 987
Emporiae (Ampurias), 13
ENA, Algeria, 659
enclave theory, 853–4
Encounter magazine, 890
Encyclopaedia Britannica, 1063
Enders, Thomas, 1080
Engels, Friedrich, 467
England: maps, 39, 57, 65, 73, 146, 177, 187, 401, 406, 420, 626, 655, 1122; Afghan War (1837–1842), 137; American Revolution, 63–70; Egypt, 180; Arab revolt, World War I, 179–91; Africa: First Boer War

(1881), 137; Second Boer War (1899–1902), 140, 143–8; Burma: conquest of (1820–1825), 102, 140, second war (1852), 140, pacification of Upper Burma (1885–1890), 140–3, 236; World War II, *see* England: World War II; Wales, pacification of, 39–43; Scotland, pacification of, 43–6; Corsica, 54; China, 232–3, 236–7; Vietnam, 403, 803, postwar occupation, 471–2; RAF, 473; refuses Allied intervention, Dien Bien Phu, 590; Afghanistan, 1201–2; Greece, 515–8, 520; Indonesia, 543–6; Malaya: prewar, 408–9; World War II, *see* Malaya; postwar, 563–74; Mexico, 161, 166–7; Kenya, 624–42; India: 72–4, 280, 284–5; Indian Mutiny (1857), 137; German East Africa, 172–4, 176–8; Palestine, *see* Lawrence, Col. T.E.; Ireland, 92–101, 1121–4; Ulster, 1121–38; Mesopotamia, 277–80; Cyprus, 643–55; Portugal, 76–83; Spain, 76–83; Russia, 209–10, 215–6, 219–22; World War II: SOE operations, 299, 300, 305, 307–8; 310–4, 316–9, 342–8, 352–3, 359–63, 390–1, 750; Malaya: 407–12; defense of, 405–7; Spencer-Chapman, 408–13; France, 310–9; Yugoslavia, 342–7, 351–4; Norway, 299, 308; Greece: defense of, 357; guerrilla resistance, 359–63; Albania, 365–6; Burma: retreat from, 414–5; Allied ground operations, 421, 433–4; long-range penetration, 425–7, 436–8; SOE operations, 300, 415, 417, 435; Allied/Burmese guerrilla operations, 417–8, 433–6; Slim's achievements, 418–21, 430–1, 435–6; Wingate's folly, 423–7, 431–2; Ethiopia, 423–4
English, Brig. Gen. Lowell, 822
English East India Company, 408
Enosis, Cyprus, 643–5, 652, 654
Enríquez, Dr. Miguel, 1093
Enthoven, Dr. Alain, 877, 903
EOKA, Cypriot guerrillas, 646–53
EPLF, Ethiopia, 1170–2
EPRF, Eritrea, 1172
EPRP, Ethiopia, 1169
Eremenko, Stepan, 88
Eritrea, 1170–2

France (*continued*)
  political situation, 482, 485–8;
  (1950–1953): the military situation,
  497, 502, 508–9, French defects,
  497–8; the political situation, 499–
  500, 503–6; strategic errors, 508–9,
  512, 514; political failure, 509–10;
  tactics, 473, 475, 477, 480–1, 508–
  9, 512, 514; continuing political
  failure, 575; (1953): the military
  situation, 576; Navarre's mission,
  575; strategy, 577; tactics, 577;
  increased U.S. aid, 577–8, 582; the
  "Navarre Plan," 582; fortified
  airheads, 582; Dien Bien Phu, 582–
  5, battle of, 587–9, casualties, 592;
  Navarre on policy, 585; French
  withdrawal, 585; World War II:
  map, 311; German invasion and
  occupation, 296; guerrilla resistance,
  303, 305, 310–19, Communist
  element, 314; postwar: 470–1;
  Communist threat, 471
Francis, Ahmed, 663
Francis, Amb. David, 215
Franco-Bahamonde, Gen. Francisco,
  265, 270–1, 289, 892, 1142–5
Frank, Gov. Gen. Hans, 306
Franke, Prof. Wolfgang, 233
Franklin, Lt. Col. J. Ross, 970
Franks, 27, 32–3, 36
Fredericksburg, battle of, 110
Frederick the Great, king of Prussia,
  guerrilla opposition, 50, 56, 58, 854
Frederick William, elector of
  Brandenburg, guerrilla opposition,
  51–3; map, 52
Frederick William III, king of Prussia,
  88
Freeman's Journal, 193
Freikorps, French and Prussian
  irregulars, 53
FRELIMO, Mozambique, 1185–7,
  1194–8
French, Gen. Sir John, 143, 145–6
French and Indian War, 56–64; map, 57
French *maquis,* 308, 315–9
French Revolution, 74
French Union, 486
Fridigern, 27–8
Friedman-Yellin, David, 555
Froehlke, Fred, 1023
Frunze, Gen. Mikhail V., 321
FSLN, Nicaragua, 1078–80, 1096

Fuchs, Klaus, 464
Fujimori, Pres. Alberto, 1116–9
Fukien province, 247, 250
Fulbright, Sen. William J., 804–5, 853,
  890, 987, 991, 1000
Fuller, Maj. Gen. J.F.C., 4, 105
Funston, Gen. Frederick, 130–1, 535
Furneaux, Rupert, 269

Gage, Gen. Thomas, 59–60, 835
Gaillard government, 673–4
GAL, Basque insurgency, 1145, 1147
Galba, Servius, 18
Galbraith, John Kenneth, 889–90, 932
Galilee, 1153, 1159
Gallieni, Gen. Joseph, 136, 152–3,
  156, 392, 752
Gambiez, Gen., 678
GAMO, 510
Gandhi, Mahatma, 284
Gapon, Georgi, 205–6
Garang, John, 1175–7
García, Calixto, 116
García Pérez, Alan, 1115–6
Gardner, Arthur, 692, 701, 704
Gatacre, Sir William, 143
Gates, Gen. Horatio, 66–8
Gaul, 7, 13, 58
Gauss, Clarence, 442
Gavin, Gen. James, on Dien Bien Phu,
  720; Laos, 720; Vietnam, 853–4,
  856, 882, 889, 904, 918, 953
Gaviría Trujillo, César, 1111–3
Gaza Strip, 1154–5, 1161–2, 1164–5
Gazelle Force, 418
GCMA, 502–3, 512, 583, 585
Gégêne torture, 670
Gemayel, Amin, 1160–1
Gemayel, Bashir, 1158–60
Gemayel, Pierre, 1158
Geneva Accords, Soviet Union/
  Afghanistan, 1210–1
Geneva Conference, 584, 590, 594–6,
  610
Genghis Khan, 36–7
Genocide: French in Algeria (1830–
  1844), 99; Germans in Russia
  (World War II), 324–6; Nazi
  Germany, 326; Douhet's concept of
  aerial warfare, 931
Gent, Sir Edward, 565
George III, king of Greece, 356
Georgia, 63–4, 108
Germain, Lord George, 64

1252

German East Africa: map, 177; Lettow-Vorbeck's guerrilla war, 172–8
German *Ostarbeiter* program, 326
German *Untermensch* philosophy, 324–5
Germany, 469, 930, 932; East Africa, *see* German East Africa; Spanish Civil War, 290–1; World War II: air offensive against England, 296–7; Albania, 365–8, 297; Bulgaria, 297; Denmark, 296; France, 296, 310–9; Greece, 297, 356–63; Holland, 296; Hungary, 297; North Africa, 297; Norway, 296; Romania, 297; Soviet Union: 297, 321–36, map, 333; Yugoslavia, 297, 338–54; division of, 338; forces committed, 348; war crimes, 342–3; casualties, 347–8
Gestapo, 315, 324
Gettysburg, battle of, 110
Giap, Gen. Vo Nguyen, 395, 402, 476, 489, 664, 848, 948; guerrilla strategy, 489–90, 497, 501, 508–9, 511, 577–8, 852; tactics, 489–90, 501, 508–9, 511; battles, 497–8, 500–1, 511, 577–8; Dien Bien Phu, 583–5, 588, 592; invasion of Cambodia, 582; Minister of Defense, 620; on revolutionary warfare, 489, 754
Giau, Tran Van, 395, 472, 490
Gideon Force, 424
Gilpatric, Roswell, 725
Giraldus Cambrensis (Gerald de Barri), 40–1
Giraud, Gen., 310, 313
Girona, Gen., 265
Godoy, Manuel de, 77
"God-Worshipers," China, 234
Goebbels, Joseph, 324, 331
Goering, Hermann, 324–5, 930
Golan Heights, 1155, 1159, 1163, 1165
Goldwater, Sen. Barry, 780
Gómez, Pres. José Miguel, 116, 689
Gómez, Maximo, 116
González, Abraham, 163, 167
González, Pr. Min. Felipe, 1145
González, Manuel, 162
González, Gen. Pablo, 170
Goodell, Sen. Charles, 991
Good Neighbor Policy, U.S., 691

Gorbachev, Mikhail, 1065, 1102, 1190, 1198, 1209–10
Gordon, Prof. C.D., 28
Gordon, Gen. Charles George, 137
Gosselin, Capt., 152
Goulding, Cathal, 1123
Goths, 4–5, 27–30
Goya, Francisco, 197
GPRA, Algeria, 675, 677
Gracchus, Tiberius, 17
Gracey, Maj. Gen. Douglas, 403, 472–3
Graham, Col. J.J., 94
"Grand Companies," Brittany, 46
Granma, Cuba, 699–700
Grant, Gen. Ulysses S., 105–7
Grau San Martín, Dr. Ramón, 691–2
Graves, Maj. Gen. W.S., 215
Greater East Asia Co-Prosperity Sphere, Japan, 370, 390, 398, 400
Great Northern War, 50
Great Wall concept: China, 36, 229, 447; Algeria, 98
Greece: maps, 367, 524; World War II: invaded by Italy, 297; German occupation, 356–63; background, 356–8; Communist guerrillas, 357–63; German withdrawal, 363; postwar: British occupation, 518, 520; reconstruction task, 515–7, 525; Communist insurgency: aims, 515, 517; training in Albania and Yugoslavia, 515, 519–20; guerrilla tactics, 516–7; successes, 517–9, 521; setbacks, 519–22, errors, 519–20, 523–5; government counterinsurgency: 518, 520–2, U.S. support, 520–2; army successes, 521, 523; shortcomings, 518–9; cease-fire, 523; casualties, 523; analysis, 523–5
Greek Cypriotes, 643–5, 647–9, 651–2, 654–5
"Greek fire," 32
Green, Marshal, 996–7
Greene, Gen. Nathanael, 69–70
Green Gang, 241
Grenada, 1082, 1101
Grey, David, 42
Griffith, Arthur, 193–4
Griffith, Brig. Gen. Samuel B., 438, 752, 889, 953; on partisan warfare, 752–3
Grivas, Gen. George (Dighenis), 518,

Helms, Richard, 903
Hemingway, Ernest, 290, 292–4
Henderson, G.F.R., 107–8
Henderson, Ian, 638
Henderson, Col. Oran K., 1023
Henderson Field, Guadalcanal, 372
Hennessy, Col. John, 817
Henriques, Robert, 136
Henty, G.A., 99
Hephaistion, 6–7
Heraclius, 34
Herbert, Lt. Col. Anthony, 969–70
Heren, Louis, 987, 993
Herodotus, 3–4
Hershey, Gen. Lewis B., 984
Herzen, Alexander, 203
Herzl, Theodor, 551
Heydrich, Reinhard, 305
Heyduks, 339–40
Hezb-i Islami guerrillas, Afghanistan,
    1206, 1210–2
Hidalgo, Miguel, 161
Hieu, Nguyen Van, 732, 737
Higgins, Marguerite, 760
Hightower, John, 831
Hilsman, Prof. Roger, 721, 723, 725–
    6, 742, 748, 755, 757–8, 778, 832,
    882, 912, 952–3; Forrestal-Hilsman
    report, 758; on guerrilla warfare,
    740
Himalaya Mountains, 25, 279
Himmler, Heinrich, 324, 326–7
Hinde, Maj. Gen. W.R.N., 636–7
Hindu Kush, 4, 280
Hindus, 284
Hindus, Marathas, 72
Hinh, Gen. Nguyen Van, 599–60
Hiong Nu tribe, 24–5
Hiroshima, 930–1
Hiss, Alger, 464
Hitler, Adolf, 252, 293, 296, 316,
    324–5, 331, 338–9, 356, 552, 930
Hoa Binh, 508–9
Hoa Hao, South Vietnam sect, 395,
    472, 600–1, 619, 849
Hoar, Sen. George F., 133
Hoche, Gen. Lazare, 75–6, 83n.
Ho Chi Minh, 475–6, 484–7, 489–90,
    492–3, 496, 575, 582, 595, 597,
    599, 611, 711, 754, 768, 777, 821,
    864, 898, 918, 922, 959, 979; in
    World War II, 300, 402–3;
    education, 393; early Communist

activities, 393–6; writings, 400, 467;
    agrarian reforms, 616; postwar:
    474–5; offers French a cease-fire and
    negotiation, 582; DRV proclaimed,
    403; dependence on China and
    Soviet Union, 616; negotiations with
    French, 475–6; insistence on general
    election, 610, 616; NLF, 615;
    priorities, 617; PRP, 615; South
    Vietnam insurgency, 599, 615;
    strategy, 489; Three Year Plan, 617;
    Viet Minh, 615 ff.; death, 983
Ho Chi Minh Trail, see North
    Vietnam
Hofer, Andreas, 84–5
Hogard, Col., 665
Hohenfriedburg, battle of, 53
Holland, 72, 543; invaded by
    Germany (1940), 296; postwar, see
    Indonesia
Holland, Lord, 54
Homonoia, concept of, 7
Honan province, 246
Honduras, 288–9, 1080–1, 1085,
    1096, 1099
Honey, P.J., 607
Hong Kong, 120, 123, 128–9
Honolulu Conference (South Vietnam/
    U.S.), 826, 848
Hoopes, Townsend, 875–7, 887, 902,
    919, 921, 938
Hoover, Pres. Herbert, 690
Hopei province, 252, 260
Hornsby, Michael, 1000, 1020
Hottentots, 173
Hovas, 102, 153
Howard-Johnston, James, see
    Johnston, James Howard-
Howe, William, Lord, 59
Hoxha, Enver, 364–7, 519
Hoyt, Prof. R. S., 28
Huang, Hsing, 238
Hudson, Capt., 342, 344
Huerra, Gen., 166–8
Hughes, Sen. Harold, 911
HUK, Philippine Communist guerrillas,
    378, 384, 528–37, 540–1; see also
    Philippines
Hull, Cordell, 483
Hume, John, 1137
"Hump" (Himalaya Mountains), 415,
    422, 440–1
Humphrey, V.-Pres. Hubert, 601, 912

Resolution 242, 1155; PLO guerrilla attacks, 1155–6; October War, 1157; invasion and occupation of Lebanon, 1158–62; the *intifada,* 1163 ff.; Islamic guerrilla terrorists, 1165; Israeli/PLO peace agreement, 1164–6

Istiq-lal party, Morocco, 658

Istrians, 9

Italy, 30, 338; intervention in Russian Revolution, 209–10, 215–22; Spanish Civil War, 290; World War II: invasion of Greece, 297, 357; North African disaster, 297; internal resistance, 303, 307–8; Yugoslavia, 344; Albania, 363–5; postwar: 470; Communist threat, 471

Jabotinsky, Vladimir, 554

Jackson, Amb. Geoffrey, 1073

Jackson, Sen. Henry, 892

Jackson, Gen. Thomas J. "Stonewall," 107–8

Jagdkommando, 328

Jamait-i Islamic guerrillas, Afghanistan, 1212

James, Daniel, 710, 713, 715

Jameson's raid, 143

Janissaries, 340

Janke, Peter, 1143

JANL, Yugoslavia, 344

Japan, 464, 1117; intervention in Russian Revolution, 209–10, 215–22; invasion of Manchuria and China, 240, 252–61; attacks U.S., 261; World War II: China, 438–40: gains, 439–40; 1944 offensive, 442–4; 1942 strategic defensive, 445; Okamura's policy, 445; invasion and occupation of: Guadalcanal, 371–2; Timor, 374; counterguerrilla operations, 374–7; Philippines, 378; counterguerrilla operations, 379–87; occupation policy, 380–2, 385; Indonesia, 543–4; occupation policy, 389–90; Thailand, 390–1; Vietnam, 399–400; Malaya, 405–13; counterguerrilla operations, 412–13; Burma, 414–37; use of quasi-guerrilla tactics, 418–19; mobility in jungle, 418; occupation policy, 435; use of Burmese Fifth Column, 416–7

Japanese Red Army, 1064

Java, 36, 373, 389, 544–9

Jaxartes River, 6

Jesup, Maj. Gen. Thomas, 103

Jewish Agency, 552–4, 556–9, 561, 1150, 1153

Jewish Brigade Group, 553

"Jewish Resistance Movement," 556

Jibril, Ahmed, 1155

Joffe, Adolf, 240–1

John of Brittany, 46

John Paul II, Pope, 1177

Johnson, Pres. Lyndon B., xi, 589, 720, 762, 777, 793–4, 800–1, 849, 852–3, 856–7, 861, 863–4, 871–2, 875–6, 878–9, 887–8, 890–2, 895, 898, 903, 906, 908–9, 911, 913–5, 929, 931, 936–8, 941, 943; background, 765, 917; aim, 765; policy, 765; ambitions/goals, 917–8; reports to Kennedy on Southeast Asia, 720; escalation of war, 768–70, 771–5; questions domino theory, 773; McNamara's report, 767–8, Operation Plan 34–A, 768–9; Baltimore speech, 798–9, 918, 924, 927; Cambodia, 964; Honolulu Conference, 826–7; critique of the Administration, 917–27

Johnson, U. Alexis, 774, 792

Johnston, Gen. Albert, 105

Johnston, James Howard-, 33, 35n.

Jomini, Henri, Baron de, 90, 94–6, 113; on guerrilla war, 94–6, 944

Jonnart, Gov. Gen., 154, 156

Jordan, 1151–7

Jorden, William, 771

Joseph, Chief (U.S.), 113

Joseph Bonaparte (King Joseph of Spain), 77, 81–2

Jouhaud, Edmond, 678

Juan Carlos, king of Spain, 1144

Juárez, Benito, 161–2

Judd, Walter, 585; biased report on Indochina, 588–9

Jumblatt, Kamal, 1158

Junot, Gen. Andoche, 77–8

Junta of Unity, Cuba, 708

Justinian, Emp., 29–30; map, 31

Kabul, 280, 1202, 1204–5, 1207

Kabylie, 100

Kachin guerrillas, 417–8, 432–5

Kafi, Ali, 682

Kahin, Prof. George, 544, 615

Kahn, Herman, 959

Makhno, Nestor, 221
Makron Teichos, see Long Wall
Malaya, 36; maps, 406, 570;
  background, 408–9; World War II:
  Japanese invasion and occupation,
  405–8; failure of British defenses,
  405–7; limited SOE operations, 408,
  412; Communist resistance, 409–13;
  postwar: political hiatus, 563; Chin
  Peng's Communist guerrillas, 563–5;
  Communist aims and strategy, 564–
  5; Communist tactics, 566–7;
  counterinsurgency strategy: 566–71;
  command organization, 560, 570;
  decentralized tactics, 567–8, 572;
  final success, 573; counterinsurgency
  lessons, 572–3; casualties, 573
Malayan Communist Party, 409, 563–
  6, 572
Mallie, Eammon, 1122
Malolos, 127
Malraux, André, 290
Manchu dynasty, 231, 236, 238, 241,
  243, 245, 457–63
Manchuria, 235, 250, 260, 439, 449
Mandalay, 141, 427, 435
Mandalay-Myitkyina railroad, 427
Mangin, Gen. Charles "Butcher," 156
Manifest Destiny, 124
Manila, 123–5, 127
Manila Bay, 120; battle of, 123
Manila Conference, 827
Mansfield, Sen. Mike, xi, 599, 601,
  808, 983, 1000, 1019, 1040; Diem,
  599; Vietnam, 761
Manzikert, battle of, 34
Mao Tse-tung (Mao Zedong), 227,
  243, 245–61, 395, 422, 438, 440,
  445, 453, 459, 465, 474, 524–5,
  550, 660, 664, 676, 700, 711, 754,
  854, 922, 945, 1064, 1114;
  background, 245–7; prewar
  Communist activities, 247–51;
  retreat to Shensi, 250–1; war against
  Nationalists, 252–8; war against
  Japan, 259–61, 438, 445–8, 451,
  453–7; writings on revolutionary
  warfare, 253–9; postwar battles
  against Nationalists, 457–60;
  military victory, 463–4
Marabout (holy man), 96
Maracanda (ancient Samarkand), 6
Marathas, 72, 74
Marceau, Gen., 76

Marcellus, Cladius, 17
Marco Polo, 37–8
Marcos, Pres. Ferdinand, 537–8, 541
Marcos, Imelda, 538, 541
Marcuse, Herbert, 889, 1064
María Luisa, queen of Spain, 76
Marighela, Carlos, 1064, 1073, 1089–
  91
Marine Corps Gazette, 751–2
Maring (Comintern agent), 240
Marion, Francis "Swamp Fox," 67–8
Marlborough, duke of, 50
Marmont, Marshal Auguste de, 97
Maronite Christians, Lebanon, 1158
Marshall, Bruce, 314
Marshall, Gen. George C., 447–8,
  459–60, 462, 483
Marshall, S.L.A., 817, 841–3
Marshall Plan, 549, 841–2
Martí, Augustín, Farabundo, 1096
Martí, José, 116, 692, 696, 1059,
  1061
Martin, David, 352
Martin, Amb. Graham, 1042
Martín Díaz, Juan, 78
Martinet, Gen. Jean, 49
Martínez de Campos, Arsenio, 116,
  118
Marx, Karl, 200–1, 203, 467, 699
Masouri, Nur, 538, 541
Massegetae, 6
Masséna, Marshal André, 80–1
Massive retalilation doctrine, U.S.,
  585, 749
Massoud, Ahmed Shah, 1112, 1206,
  1210
Massu, Maj. Gen. Jacques, 669–70,
  677
Masters, John, 136
Matak, Prince Sisowith Sirik, 994
Matanza, El Salvador, 1096
Matthews, Herbert, 701–3
Mau Mau rebellion, *see* Kenya
Maurice, Emp., 30, 32–4, 138
Maurice of Nassau, 50
Mauritania, 1179–81; war with
  Polisario guerrillas, 1180–1
Maximilian, Archduke Ferdinand,
  161–2
Mayer, Col., 53
Mayhew, Sir Patrick, 1136
May Tenth movement, China, 240
Mazour, A.G., 204
Mecca, 101, 181, 183

Mountbatten, Adm. Lord Louis, 430, 432, 435–6, 448, 543–4, 1133
Moxon-Browne, Edward, 1142, 1144
Moyers, Bill, 926–7
Mozambique, 1185–7, 1193–9; map, 1185; guerrilla warfare under Portuguese rule, 1185–7; Machel's government, 1193: guerrilla war with Rhodesia and South Africa, 1194–7; shifts allegiance to the West, 1198–9
MPL, Philippines, 530–1
MPLA, Angola, 1185–7, 1191–2
MPM, Argentina, 1091–2
MR–8, Brazil, 1089–90
MRLA, Malaya, 567, 569, 571
MRTA, Peru, 1114
MTLD, Algeria, 659–60, 662, 668
Mugabe, Robert, 1193–5
Muhsin, Zuhayr, 1156, 1158
Mujaheddin guerrillas, Afghanistan, 1204–11
Mukden, siege of, 463
Murat, Gen., 77
Muraviev, Col., 214
Mus, Paul, 399
Muskie, Sen. Edmund, 999
Mussolini, Benito, 293, 297
Muzorewa, Bishop Abel, 1195
Myers, Gen. Samuel, 622
Myitkyina, 446
My Lai massacre, *see* South Vietnam
Myrdal, Gunnar, 578–9

Naderi, Sayer Jaffer, 1212
Naegelen, Marcel Edmond, 660
Nagasaki, 931
Nairobi, 173
Najibullah, Dr. Mohammed, 1209–12
Nanking, 235–6, 238, 242, 253, 259
Nantes, 314; battle of, 74
Napier, "Fagin," 136
Napoleon, Emp. (Napoleon Bonaparte), 54, 76, 80–92, 339, 882
Napoleon III, Emp., 161–2
Napoleonic wars, 113
Naranjo, Jr., Francisco, 165
Narses, Gen., 29–30
Nasser, Ahmed Mohammed, 663, 1170
Nasser, Gamal Abdul-, 1154–5
Nasution, Gen. Abdul Haris, 549
National Broadcasting Company (NBC), 759

National Defense Council, Greece, 518, 521, 523
National Democratic Front, Philippines, 538–40
National Democratic Party, Rhodesia, 1193
National Front, Indonesia, 546
National Islamic Front, Sudan, 1177
National Liberation Committee of Vietnam, 403
National Security Council, U.S., *see* United States
Nation magazine, 920
NATO, 673, 678
Naulin, Gen., 274
Navarre, Gen. Henri-Eugène, 514, 575–7, 582–5, 587–8, 592; Navarre Plan, 582, 589
Neave, Airey, 313, 1133
Nedić, Gen., 338, 341, 343
Negev desert, 1153
Nelson, Donald, 445–6
Nenita operations, Philippines, 533
Neo-Destour Party, Tunisia, 658
Neri, 164
Nero, Claudius, 14
Neto, Agostinho, 1185, 1187–8, 1190
New Delhi, 429, 433
New Guinea, World War II, 371, 373, 389
New Republic magazine, 889
Newsweek magazine, 759, 865, 961–2, 988, 1081
New Yorker magazine, 821, 926
New York Review of Books, 853, 887, 889
New York Times, 701–3, 771, 831, 852–3, 938–9, 945–6, 966, 972, 983, 996, 1000, 1011, 1013
New York Times Magazine, 858
Nez Percé Indians, North America, 113
Nhu, Mme. (Tran Le Yuan), 605, 727, 743–4, 759, 791, 887
Nhu, Ngo Dinh, 605, 607, 727, 739, 741, 743–4, 750, 754, 923
Nicaragua, 1085–6, 1094, 1099, 1104; map, 1062; Somoza dictatorship, 1077–9, guerrilla opposition, 1077–9, Communist Sandinista Liberation Front (FSLN), 1078–80: successes, 1078–9, factions, 1079, overthrow of government, 1079; condition of country, 1080; Sandinista

1263

Nicaragua (*continued*)
government, 1080; U.S. (CIA) destabilization program, 1080: support of Contra and ARDE guerrilla groups, 1080–1; cost, 1081; Contragate, 1082–4; national elections, 1085–6; Ortega government, 1082, 1085–6, counterguerrilla campaign, 1084–5; Chamorro government, 1086–7; guerrilla revival, 1086–7, *recontras*, 1086–7, *revueltos*, 1086–7
Nicholas I, Czar, 100, 202
Nicholas II, Czar, 204, 206, 208
Nidal, Abu, 1064, 1177
Nien Fi rebellion, 235
Nihilists, 203
Nikephoros Phokas, Emp., 33
Niles, Henry, 972
19 of April Movement (M–19), Colombia, 1109–11
Nitze, Paul, 903, 908, 932
Nixon, Pres. Richard M., ix, xi, 589–90, 699, 912, 934, 956–61, 965–7, 979–81, 983–9, 991–1003, 1005, 1007–8, 1010–1, 1013, 1016, 1019, 1022, 1024–5, 1027–9, 1031, 1033–4, 1037, 1039–41, 1043–4; basis of strategy, 958–9; visit to China, 1029; visit to Soviet Union, 1039; Cambodia, ix, 965–7, 994–1003; Nixon Doctrine, 981, 996, 1016
Nkomadi Accord, Mozambique, 1196
Nkomo, Joshua, 1193–5
NKVD, 321–2, 332
NLF, Vietnam, 615, 619–20, 728, 731–4, 736–7, 739–43
Nogales, 167
Nolting, Amb. Frederick E., 719, 727, 736, 741–2, 758–61
Non-injury oath, 595
Normans, 36
Norstad, Gen. Lauris, 889
North, Lt. Col. Oliver, 1083–4
Northern Aid Committee, U.S., 1126
Northern Ireland, *see* Ulster
Northern Ireland Civil Rights Association, 1124
Northern Katchin Levies, Burma, 443–4
North Vietnam: maps, 796, 813, 869, 958, 998, 1018; army (PAVN): 816–18, 821–2, strength, 834, 936, logistics, 835, 875, 936, 1038–9, 1042, casualties, 834, 1039,

desertion, 1042, strategy and tactics, 843, 859, 927, 1042–3, infiltration of the South, 767–8, 781, 800, 907, Cambodian sanctuary, 962–3, 965, 993–4, 1016–7, 1043, Laos sanctuary, 1019–22, 1043, use of Ho Chi Minh trail, 700, 755, 800–1, 936, 979, 1017, 1019, 1021–2, 1043–4; offensives in the South, 817–8, 821–3, 834, 840–2, 864–70, 875, 901, 912, 945, 971, 979–80, 987, 1006, 1030–1, Tet offensive, 897–8, 1972 spring offensives, 1033–6; economy, 830, 1042; manpower, 800, 1042; U.S. bombing, 774–5, 830–1, 929, 939–42, reaction, 797, 830–1, 944, 986; civilian casualties, 830–1; hawks and doves, 979; dissident leaders, 979–80, 1042, 1044; peace negotiations, 777, 909, 986, 1016–7; reunification, 1046–8; *see also* Socialist Republic of Vietnam
Norton, Maj. Gen. Jack, 817
Norway, World War II: invaded by Germany, 296; destruction of heavy water, 302, guerrilla resistance, 303, 308
Nour Ramadan Mohammed, 1170
Novara, battle of, 92
NPA, Philippines, 537–40
Nuclear weapons, *see* Atomic bomb
Nueva Segovia, 287
Nujoma, Sam, 1191
Numiery, Mohammed al-, 1174–6
Nuremberg trials, 306

OAS, Algeria, 678–9
OAS, America, 707, 1085, 1117
OAU, Africa, 1186
O'Ballance, Maj. Edgar, 516, 523, 668, 678
O'Brady, Rory, 1125
Obregón, Álvaro, 167–8, 170
Ochoa, Jorge Luis, 1111
October Manifesto of 1905, Russia, 207
October War, Arab/Israel, 1157
O'Daniel, Gen. J.W., 600, 611-2; on Dien Bien Phu, 587
O'Donnell, Kenneth, 761–2
Ogdai, Khan, 37–8
Ohio River, 106
Okamura, Gen., 445

1264

Provisional Reconnaissance Units, 910
Provisional Revolutionary Government of South Vietnam, 979–80
Provisional Sinn Fein Party, Ireland, 112
PRP, Vietnam, 615, 731–2, 736–7, 741, 743
Prussia, 90, 114; map, 52; army, 51–3; *levée en masse,* 90; militarism, 113–4
Psaros, Col., 357, 362
PSP, Cuba, 692, 695
Pueblo, battle of, 161
Puerta Aponte, Gabriel, 1067
"Punic faith," 22

Qaddafi, Muammar al-, 1130, 1181–2
Quadrillage, 480, 663, 672
Quat, Premier Phan Huy, 790, 803
Quebec, 59; Conference, 429–30
Quezon, Pres., 534
Quirino government, Philippines, 536

Rabat, 155
Rabbini, Pres. Burhanuddin, 1211–2
Rabigh, 181–2
Rabin, Yitzhak, 1162–3, 1165–6
Radcliffe Constitution, Cyprus, 651
Radetzky, Fld. Marshal, 92
Radford, Adm. Arthur, 589–90, 592, 622
Radford, Yeoman, 1032–3
Radio Rebelde, Cuba, 708–9
Radu, Michael, 1072, 1078, 1090–1
Raisuli, Ahmed el-, 264, 266, 269, 271
Ramgarh, 422, 433
Ramos, Pres. Fidel Váldez, 540–1
Ramparts magazine, 887
Ranke, Leopold, 922
"Rape of Nanking," 259
Rasputin, Grigori, 208
Rattisage, 480, 509, 663, 672
Rawdon, Lord, 70
Raziel, David, 554
Razzia, *see* Scorched-earth policy
Reader's Digest magazine, 859, 901, 948
Reagan, Pres. Ronald, xi, 1070, 1080–3, 1065, 1070, 1085, 1089, 1106, 1159–61, 1181, 1190, 1197
Red Army, China, 249, 258–9
Red Army, Soviet Union, 321 ff.
Red Army Faction (Baader-Meinhof gang), 1064

Red Brigades, 1064
Red Guards, 209, 214, 217
Redmond, John, 101
Red River, 473, 497, 509, 583
Red Sea, 180
Red Terror, 213–4, 222
Rees, Merlyn, 1132
Regroupement program, Algeria, 674–5
Reid, Ogdan, 887
Reinhardt, Amb. G. Frederick, 602
Remarque, Erich Maria, vi
RENAMO, Mozambique, 1195–8
Rendulic, Col. Gen., 350
Rennes fortress, 46
Reno, Maj., 112–3
Renville Agreement, Indonesia, 547–8
Réserve Générale, Algeria, 672
Reston, James, 834, 901, 925, 937, 994, 1011, 1040
Revers, Gen., 482, 497
Revisionist Party, Palestine Jews, 544
Reynolds, Pr. Min. Albert, 1136–7
Rheault, Col. Robert, 982
Rhodesia, 1193–6
Rhodesian African National Congress, 1193, 1195
Rhodesian Front Party, 1193
Rice, Edward, 1068, 1078
"Rice-bowl Christians, 236
Richardson, Cliff, 379
Richardson, John, 743, 750, 759
Ridgway, Gen. Matthew B., 591–2, 724, 727, 838, 882, 889–90, 908, 918–9, 931, 933, 1029; Dien Bien Phu, warning to Pres. Eisenhower, 591–2; Indochina, 591–2
Riding, Alan, 1072, 1111
Rif rebellion, Spanish Morocco, 263–75; map, 268; historical background, 263–6; guerrilla war, 266–75
Ríos Mott, Gen. Efraín, 1070
Rivera, Lt. Col. Adalberto, 1096
Rivera, Gen. Primo de, 123
Rivero, Aqüero, 709
Rivers, Mendel, 888
Rives, Lloyd, 906, 1009
Rizal, Dr. José, 122–3
Roberto, Helden, 1185
Roberts, Chalmers, 589
Roberts, Maj. Gen. Ely, 999
Roberts, Fld. Marshal Lord, 144–5, 147–8
Robertson, Walter S., 621

781, 800, 875, 962, new tactics, 787, high morale, 787, fresh offensives, 782–3, 792–3, 803–4, administration, 800, strength, 800, 834, 848, 901, 1006, infiltration of refugees, 803–4, logistics, 835, 875, 936, tactics, 845–6, continuing gains, 850, propaganda, 852, retreat, 865, capabilities, 944, peace talks, 975, alleged desertions, 984–5, Viet Minh cadres, 606, 612–3, 617–8, guerrilla terrorist tactics, 618–9, 755; Washington lobby, 623; strategic-hamlet program, 722, 736, 739–41, 758, 760, failure, 739–42, 756–7, abandoned, 769; Chieu Hoi (defector) program, 754; policy, 559–60, 610–3, 615–6; provisional government, 767, political disunity, 766–7; Khanh government (1964–February 1965): 767, 769–71, 774, 778–80, 789–90, Program of Action, 769, New Rural Life Hamlets, 769, Advanced People's Action Groups, 769, 827, deterioration of government and army, 777, anti-American display, 790, dictatorship, 789, fall of, 790; Thieu-Ky government (1965–1974): 803, 826–8, 840, pacification program, 826–8, elections, 827, 859, 871, Revolutionary Development Groups, 827, 871, failure of, 848–51, 858–60, corruption, 849–50, 886–7; repressive government, 849–50, 988–9, 993, 1010, Montagnard defection, 849, Guam Conference, 871, new constitution, 871, civilian casualties, 875, 897, 909, VC/PAVN Tet offensives, 897–900, 909, 948, psychological effect of, 906–7, Phoenix program, 910–1, Honolulu meeting, 913, quarrel with U.S., 913–4, overall casualties, 914, effect of U.S. bombings, 941–2, Midway Island conference, 976–7, disclosure of Communist espionage ring in government, 982, Communist infiltration of government, 1011–2, invasion of Cambodia, 996–1000, 1002, continued ARVN presence in Cambodia, 1007, invasion of Laos, 1019–22, failure of, 1020–2, casualties, 1021, Thieu/Ky quarrel,

1027, elections, 1029–30, Thieu declares martial law, 1035, cease-fire, 1040, PAVN/VC gains, 1042, unconditional surrender to North Vietnam, 1047

Southwest Africa (Namibia), 1188–91; background, 1188; insurgency, 1188–91; UN intervention; 1190–1, given independence, 1191

Souvanouvong, Prince, 1046

Soviet Union, 454, 919–20, 922, 924–5, 931, 1065, 1094, 1104; maps, 216, 333; following World War I: consolidation of the revolution, 213–24, Red Terror, 213–4, Allied intervention, 215–6, 218–22, Red Army, 217–8, 220, NEP, 223–4, Comintern, 223–4, in Chinese Revolution, 240–3, in Chinese civil war, 249–50, 252, aid to Spanish Nationalists, 291–4; World War II: 321–37, German invasion, 297, 321–2, German occupation policy, 324–6; guerrilla resistance, 303, 321–3, 325–7, 331–2, 334–6, German countertactics, 327–30; postwar: Poland, 306–7, Manchuria, 458, China, 458, 578, recognition of DRV, 486, aid to, 616, Geneva Conference, 594–6, aid to North Vietnam, 616, 834, 875, 936, 992, 1006, reduces aid, 1042, 1048–9, 1051; aid to: Nicaraguan insurgency, 1079, 1082, Chilean insurgency, 1094, El Salvador insurgency, 1097–8, Egypt and Arab countries, 1154, 1157, Ethiopia, 1171, Angola, 1186, 1190–1, Mozambique, 1193, 1195–6, Afghanistan government, 1202–3, 1205–10

Spaatz, Gen. Carl, 931

Spain, 72, 103; maps, 13, 79, 117, 268, 1142; Roman invasion and occupation, 13–21; Celtiberians, 13–4, 17–8, 78; French invasion and occupation, 76–83, "the Spanish Ulcer," 84–5; Spanish-American War, 111, 688; Cuban insurrection, 115, 116–20; the Tercios, 265, 269, 271, 289; Philippines, 123, 125–6; Morocco, see Rif rebellion; Civil War, 74, 289–94, 930, 1142, Communist element, 291 ff., guerrilla warfare, 291–4; Spanish

1271

948–50, 955, 993, 1022;
background, 814; replaces Harkins,
774; attrition strategy, 812; 816–26,
863–4; failure of strategy and
tactics, 832–4; critique of, 836–9,
840–8, 879–83, 943–56
Weyand, Lt. Gen. Frederick, 865, 896,
1047
Weyler, Gen., 116, 118–19
Wheeler, Gen. Earle G., 724, 787,
801, 805, 842, 876, 896, 900–1,
903, 920, 940, 980
White, Maj. Gen. George, 141–2
White, T.H., 421–2
Whitelaw, William, 1128–9
White Terror, China, 242–3, 248
White Terror, Russia, 208
Wickwire, Franklin and Mary, 71n.
Wildman, U.S. Consul, 123–4
Williams, Maj. Gen. Samuel, 611
Wilson, Pr. Min. Harold, 789, 803,
875, 888
Wilson, Amb. Henry Lane, 166–7
Wilson, Pres. Woodrow, 159, 166–9,
213, 239
Wingate, Maj. Gen. Orde, 423–7,
429–33, 512, 553, 583
Wingate, Sir Reginald, 182
Wise Men, 908
Wolfe, Gen. James, 89
Wolfert, Ira, 379
Women's Peace Movement, Ulster,
1132
Woodhouse, C.M., 358–9, 361–3
Woolman, David, 269, 271, 273
World Bank, 541, 1082

Yalta Conference, 449–51, 458, 461,
472
Yamashita, Gen., 386
Yangtze River, 235, 260, 447; Valley,
238, 242
Yaqui uprising, 162–3

Ydígoras Fuentes, Gen. Miguel, 1069
Yellow River, 251
Yelui Chutsai, 37
Yenan, 252, 445–6, 460
Yen Bai, 393, 512
Yenbo, 182–3, 186
Yeo-Thomas, Cmdr., 316
Yishuv, 552, 558
Yoke Force, 422, 434
Yorktown, battle of, 70
Yüan-chang, Chu, 231
Yüan Shih-k'ai, 238–9
Yucatán, 163
Yudenich, Gen., 221
Yugoslavia, x; map, 347; German
invasion and occupation of, 338–9
ff.; guerrilla resistance, 338–54,
Chetnik guerrillas, 341–5; Partisan
guerrillas, 341–8; SOE mission to
Tito's Partisans, 342–8; analysis of
guerrilla effectiveness, 348–54;
postwar: supports Greek Communist
insurgents, 517, 519–20, breaks with
Soviet Union, 578

Zabegern, 30
Zacharias, R. Adm. Ellis, 450
Zagoria, Prof. Donald S., 615, 732,
922, 941
Zahir, King Mohammed of
Afghanistan, 1201, 1204, 1211
Zakhariadis, Nikos, 517, 522–3, 525
ZANU, Zimbabwe, 1193–4
Zariaspa, 6
Zayas, Pres. Alfredo, 689
Zeid, Prince, 180–2
Zeller, André, 678
Zervas, Col., 357, 360
Zoco el Telata, 266
Zog, king of Albania, 363
Zones excentrigues, 582
Zouaves, 157
Zubatov, Col., 205
Zulu war, 137